CALENDAR

OF

TATE PAPERS,

DOMESTIC SERIES,

JAMES I.

1611—1618.

CALENDAR

OF

STATE PAPERS,

DOMESTIC SERIES,

OF THE REIGN OF

JAMES I.

1611—1618,

PRESERVED IN THE

STATE PAPER DEPARTMENT

OF

HER MAJESTY'S PUBLIC RECORD OFFICE.

EDITED BY

MARY ANNE EVERETT GREEN,

Author of "The Lives of the Princesses of England," &c.

UNDER THE DIRECTION OF THE MASTER OF THE ROLLS, AND WITH THE SANCTION OF HER MAJESTY'S SECRETARY OF STATE FOR THE HOME DEPARTMENT.

LONDON:

LONGMAN, BROWN, GREEN, LONGMANS, & ROBERTS.

1858.

CONTENTS OF THIS VOLUME.

	Page
Calendar, James I, 1611—1618	1
General Index	615
Errata	709

DOMESTIC PAPERS.

JAMES I.

Vol. LXI.—January, February, 1611.

1611.
Jan. 2. 1. Valuation of a diamond chain [given by the King to Lady Elizabeth,] delivered by Sir Wm. Herrick and Sir John Spilman, at command of Lord Harrington.

Jan. 3. Paris. 2. Hen. Lord Clifford to Salisbury. Will take his advice, and remain in Paris till March. Incloses a letter for his wife, and will be glad to hear of her return to London. Rejoices at the improvement in his Lordship's health.

Jan. 7. Carlisle. 3. Sir Wm. Cranston to the Earl of Dunbar. He and Sir Wm. Seaton have held a meeting at Carlisle for redress of complaints. Some persons are desirous to obtain his Lordship's place. Wishes for a seat in the Council of the North.

Jan. 8. Carlisle. 4. Sir Wm. Cranston and Sir Wilfrid Lawson to the Earls of Cumberland and Dunbar. They have met and heard complaints from the inhabitants of either country, a few of which are referred to their Lordships.

Jan. 9. Bindon. 5. Visct. Bindon to the Earl of Salisbury. The Irish mariner, about whom he lately wrote, may have been trusted with great secrets. Influence of the papists in the western parts. Imprudence of questioning them, save on good proofs.

Jan. 9. Westminster. 6. Instructions by the King to the Master and Council of the Court of Wards and Liveries, for careful custody of Wards, &c. Printed.

Jan. 10. 7. Estimate of the subsidies, &c. payable before Midsummer, and their inequality to the assignations thereof already made.

Jan. 10. 8. Notes of Commissions for treaties with Germany, France, and Holland, and of honours conferred on foreigners, since April 5, 1610.

VOL. LXI.

1611.

Jan. 10. 9. Declaration by His Majesty of his intention to dissolve the present Parliament, so that the members need not attend on the day appointed for meeting.

Jan. 11. Grant to Thos. Cockayne of the office of keeper of the game on the river near Royston and Thetford, cos. Norfolk and Suffolk, for life. [*Grant Bk.*, *p.* 68.]

Jan. 12. 10. Rich. Parry, Bishop of St. Asaph, to Salisbury. Miserable state of his diocese, for lack of a learned resident ministry. Intreats that the vicarage of Henllan may not be reannexed to its rectory. Efforts are made and bribes offered to procure many annexations. Llanywllyn was made a lay fee the year before. Latin.

Jan. 13. Leaver. 11. Sir Ralph Ashton to the Same. Being a Receiver for the Duchy of Lancaster, cannot come up before Hilary Term to answer a debt of 380*l.* to His Majesty, as security for John Crompton, deceased.

Jan. 13. Paris. 12. Hen. Lord Clifford to the Same. Has heard from Lord Cranborne, and will correspond with him during their mutual absence from England.

Jan. 13. Eton. 13. Sir Hen. Savile to Sir Dud. Carleton. Terms upon which Eton College is willing to assign the lease of a house to Carleton. Is sorry for his exclusion from the library at Venice. Thinks it is contrary to the foundation charter.

Jan. 14. Londesborough. 14. Fras. Earl of Cumberland to Salisbury. Will take means for the settling of his estate, as desired.

Jan. 14. [Guildhall.] 15. Report of the Common Council of London, reciting His Majesty's letter, dated Dec. 28, 1610, to Sir Wm. Craven, Mayor, and others, for Lionel, son of Rich. Wright, to have the reversion, after his father, of the office of common packer to the City, and stating their compliance therewith.

Jan. 17. St. John's. 16. Sir Simon Weston to Salisbury. Wishes him to require Mr. Unton, who pretends to have a patent to be bailiff of the hundred of Pirehill, co. Stafford, to collect certain moneys, for doing which he receives 100 marks per annum.

Jan. 17. King's College, Cambridge. 17. Dr. Fogg Newton, Vice Chancellor of Cambridge, to the Same. Will hold a meeting of the heads of colleges to discuss the admission of Scottishmen. Thanks for his Lordship's protection of the privileges of the University against encroachments of the town. The prisoner required shall be sent, though there is no precedent for so doing, and it is a breach of privilege.

Jan. 17? 18. Note of the answer of the heads of colleges, Cambridge, that, by their Statutes, Scottish students cannot be admitted to that University; with remarks thereon [by Salisbury].

VOL. LXI.

1611.

Jan. 17. 19. Note of manors, &c. wherein are no copyholds, not included in the Queen's jointure, nor in the assignment to the Prince and Duke of York, nor assigned to the contractors for purchase of lands.

Jan. 19. London. 20. Justice Yelverton to Salisbury. Solicits his favour for his nephew, Capt. Yelverton, formerly on service in Ireland.

Jan. 19. 21. Warrant for payment of 1,600*l.* monthly, instead of 1,500*l.*, to Henry Prince of Wales, for charges of his household.

Jan. 19. Entry of the above. [*Warrant Book*, II., *p.* 189.]

Jan. 19. Warrant for payment of extraordinary charges to the Cofferer of the Household, for the diet of Marshal de la Verdine, to be sent Ambassador from the King of France. [*Ibid.*, *p.* 190.]

Jan. 21. 22. Edw. Reynoldes to Jas. Bagg. Will deduct 30*l.* claimed by him as due from Reynoldes's late brother, from a debt of 105*l.* due from Bagg to Reynoldes. With note of Bagg's compliance with the proposal.

Jan. 21. 23. The Attorney General to Dud. Norton. Wishes certain papers to be shown to Lord Salisbury. *Incloses,*

23. I. *Memoranda by Adam King of the characters, &c. of such Jesuits, seminaries, &c. as he was acquainted with at Rome,* 1589–1595. *Curious particulars of the mode in which priests are conveyed into England. Details of King's travels abroad in* 1604. *His conversations at Seville with Father Cresswell, and at Cologne with Father Baldwin. Their hints relative to the Gunpowder Plot. Interviews between Winter and Baldwin, &c. Will try to recall more, but his memory is impaired by long imprisonment.*

Jan. 21. 24. Copy of the above letter and inclosure.

Jan. 21. Commission to Sir Edw. Phelips, Master of the Rolls, Sir Pet. Warburton, Sir Dav. Williams, and others, to hear causes in Chancery. [*Grant Bk.*, *p.* 66.]

Jan. 22. 25. Sir Robt. Johnson to Salisbury. Reminds him of his former projects for advancing the King's profits on forests. Incloses another project, which he thinks good. His book to the King is composed of the contents of letters written to Salisbury. Wants occupation. *Incloses,*

25. I. *Considerations by Sir Robt. Johnson of four plans for increasing the King's revenue, of which he prefers the fourth, viz., to improve the fee-farm rents of Crown lands, on all renewals of leases.*

Jan. 22. Warrant to pay to the Earl of Dunbar, Keeper of the Privy Purse, 400*l.*, to be employed as the King shall direct. [*Warrt. Bk.*, II., *p.* 189.]

VOL. LXI.

1611.

Jan. 23. Berwick. 26. Sir Wm. Bowyer and Geo. Nicholson to the Earl of Dunbar. Statement of abatements in the charges at Berwick. *Inclose*,

26. I. *Note of the diminishment, by decease and otherwise, of His Majesty's charge at Berwick, from the time of Lord Dunbar's appointment, Sept.* 8, 1607, *to Christmas*, 1610. *Jan.* 23, 1611. *Berwick. Two papers.*

Jan. 23. Berwick. 27. Sir Wm. Bowyer to the Same. Inquires if certain allowances made by his orders, for relief of some soldiers, may continue. Is ready to come up to London, if needful. Dangerous condition of Berwick Bridge.

Jan. 23. Berwick. 28. Geo. Nicholson to the Same. His payments have been regulated by Bowyer's muster books. If abatement is to be made of the charge in Berwick, begs his Lordship will make it himself. Asserts his own integrity in the service.

Jan. 23. Berwick. 29. The Same to the Same. Sends up his year's accounts; begs directions about payments for his Lordship's building, on which John Gospoole, the Dutch carver, is set to work.

[Jan.] 30. Observations and queries on the above letters.

Jan. 24. Warrant to pay to Sir Thos. Parry, Chancellor of the Duchy of Lancaster, 300*l.*, for diet, lodging, and other necessaries, for the Lady Arabella Stuart and five of her servants, during the seven months of her continuance with him. [*Warrt. Bk.*, II., *p.* 190.]

Jan. 25. Malton. 31. Sir Wm. Eure to Salisbury. Sir David Fowlies' imputations against him are because he refuses his claim upon some land pretended to be purchased of his late father. Lord Eure has sustained many wrongs from Knaggs, Fowlies' keeper.

Jan. 25. Ash. 32. Wm. Glover to the Same. Has surveyed his Lordship's manor of Snettisham. Was thwarted in the survey of Barton-Bendish by Sir Robt. Rich, who has land there.

Jan. 26. 33. Sir Walter Cope to Sir Dud. Carleton. Joy at Lord Cranborne's amendment and promised return. Parliament is dissolved, and no supplies given. The Lord Treasurer uses all his wits to abate expenses. Purchases of old paintings, at a reasonable rate, would be acceptable to the Prince or the Lord Treasurer.

Jan. 26. Warrant to pay to Wm. Wich 40*l.*, for furnishing the King with ducks and other fowl for his recreation. [*Warrt. Bk.*, II., *p.* 190.]

Jan. 28. Ludlow Castle. 34. Sir Rich. Lewkenor to Salisbury. His proceedings in the cause referred to him for settlement, between the poor tenants of Aberfraw and Wm. Owen and Owen Wood.

Jan. 28. Paris. 35. Hen. Lord Clifford to [the Same]. Will obey his instructions in not crossing the Alps. Is careful of his health. Thanks for the offer of a bill of exchange, which he will need ere long.

VOL. LXI.

1611.

Jan. 28. Tavistock. 36. Wm. Earl of Bath to Salisbury. Thanks for his favours, especially for his having been allowed absence from Parliament.

Jan. 30. 37. Estimate by Thos. Wilson and others, of the expense of bringing water in pipes of earth from the springs to the dell at Hatfield.

Jan. 30. Rome. 38. Sir Robt. Basset to the Earl of Northampton. Sorrow for past offences. Desires to return to England, on account of recent measures against him, but cannot without His Majesty's pardon, and protection against his creditors.

Jan. 39. List of new year's gifts bestowed by the King. Anno 8.

Jan. 40. Statement of the losses and inconveniences of billetting horses in the pastures at Holdenby.

Jan. ? 41. Note of all Grants made to the Earl of Dunbar which passed the Great Seal.

Jan. ? Lease to John Eldred and Wm. Whitmore, of lands, tenements, &c., cos. York and Wilts, and in the Isle of Wight, value 88*l.* 14*s.* per ann., as part of the grant of 2,000*l.* per ann. to Eldred and other contractors. Latin. [*Sign Manual, vol.* I., *Nos.* 66, 67.]

Feb. 1. 42. Robt. Twist to Salisbury. Desires an audience that he may prove himself honest to the State.

Feb. 1. Westminster. 43. Edw. Reynoldes to [Fras. Mills, Clerk of the Privy Seal]. Reforms in the Privy Seal Office projected. Mills' prospects of promotion, and private affairs.

Feb. 1. Warrant to pay 8,000*l.* each to the Earl of Montgomery, Visct. Fenton, Visct. Haddington, and Lord Hay, and 2,000*l.* to Sir Roger Aston. [*Warrt. Bk.*, II., *p.* 191.]

Feb. 2. 44. Sir Hen. Montague, Recorder of London, to Salisbury. Things prepared for a mass, bags of money, and letters directed to foreign parts, were found in Lockey's house, near Aldersgate Street.

Feb. 2. 45. Re-assurance from Sir Geo. Rivers, of Chawford, Kent, and Thos. Bridges, of Westminster, to Rich. Earl of Dorset, of the boroughs of East Grinstead and Seaford, and of the hundred of Hartfield, and other lands, co. Sussex.

Feb. 2. Warrant to pay 30*l.* per ann., with arrears, to Ellis Rothwell, page of the bedchamber, for washing the King's sheets. [*Warrt. Bk.*, II., *p.* 191.]

Feb. 3? 46. Petition of Sir Ant. Ashley to Salisbury, to be present at the hearing of his cause in the Star Chamber, on charges maliciously preferred against him by Sir Jas. Creichton.

Feb. 3. 47. Thos. Phelippes to the Same. Remonstrates against Sir Ant. Ashley's business being transferred to the Star Chamber. Accuses him of protecting sundry Papists conspiring against the King.

1611. Vol. LXI.

Feb. 4. [Whitehall.] 48. [Lord Salisbury ?] to Jas. Necton, Deputy Surveyor of Middlesex. Warrant to survey and estimate a parcel of void ground near the King's store-house for fish, in Westminster.

Feb. 4. Warrant to pay arrears due to Eric Stanson, servant to the Princes, for his wages. [*Warrt. Bk.*, II., *p.* 191.]

Feb. 4. Berwick. 49. Thos. Swinhoe to Salisbury. Was appointed Captain of Norham by the late Earl of Dunbar, by whose demise his authority ceases. The people of Norham and Holy Island are disorderly; desires that some one may be authorized to supply the place, &c.

Feb. 5. Britain's Burse. 50. Thos. Wilson to the Same. The value of the 20,000 vines sent to his Lordship by Mdme. de la Boderie, is 50*l.* sterling, &c., and there are 10,000 more coming. Asks instructions about the pipes for drainage.

Feb. 5. Tuesday. 51. Robt. Hopton to the Same. Is brother to the widow of Sir Geo. Morton, who has left a large family. Prays that the wardship of Sir George's heir may not be granted away, but that his creditors may be relieved from the estate during the minority.

Feb. 5. Compton. 52. Sir Rich. Verney, Edw. Boughton, and Wm. Barnes to the Same. Detail their proceedings in the business of Killingworth. *Inclose*,

52. i. *Certificate of the allowances made by Sir Robt. Dudley to Fras. Phipps, for keeping the chace and park of Killingworth. Signed by Alice Lady Dudley and Sir Thos. Leigh.*

52. ii. *Sir Thos. Leigh to Sir Rich. Verney, Edw. Boughton, and Wm. Barnes. Particulars of the appointment of Fras. Phipps as keeper of the chace and park of Killingworth, and of his allowances. Jan. 2, Stanley.*

Feb. ? 53. Petition of Fras. Phipps to Salisbury. Prays to be established in the place of keeper of Killingworth Chace, and asks an abatement in the rent, according to the increase in the number of the deer.

[Feb.] Warrant to Sir Rich. Verney and others to make an abatement in the rent payable by Fras. Phipps for the park and chace of Killingworth, according to the increase in the number of deer. [*Docquet.*]

[Feb.] Warrant for allowance of timber for repairing the barns, stables, &c. at Killingworth. [*Docquet.*]

Feb. [5 ?] 54. Dr. Hen. Atkins to Salisbury. Has relapsed into his former illness; should it prove fatal, recommends his son to his favour.

Feb. 5. Berwick. 55. Geo. Nicholson to the Same. Requests directions on sundry points relating to Berwick, the governorship being void by the decease of the Earl of Dunbar. Thinks another governor unnecessary, as the garrison gradually decreases by death.

VOL. LXI.

1611.

Feb. 5. Berwick. 56. Sir Wm. Bowyer, Geo. Nicholson, and Wm. Josey to Salisbury. Report their proceedings for the safe keeping of the late Earl of Dunbar's goods, &c.

Feb. 5. Berwick. 57. Sir Wm. Bowyer to the Same. Will write to him frequently, which he could not properly do whilst under the Earl of Dunbar. There are many sheep and cattle belonging to the Earl, not mentioned in a former letter.

Feb. 6. Berwick. 58. The Same to the Same. Certifies, at request of the Mayor, &c. of Berwick, to the great anxiety of the late Earl of Dunbar about the rebuilding of Berwick Bridge. Insecure condition of the present bridge. Has received His Majesty's commission to deliver all things belonging to the late Earl, to the Chancellor of Scotland, Lord Wm. Howard, and Lord Burly, of Scotland.

Feb. 6. 59. Sir Walter Chute to the Same. Solicits an appointment as one of the ten who are to serve His Majesty with especial diligence, at a pension of 200*l.* per annum.

Feb. 7. Edinburgh. 60. John Stewart Earl of Mar to the Same. Regret for the death of the Earl of Dunbar and Lord Kinloss. Fears they will live to see all their old friends die. As the King has lost faithful servants, those who remain must serve him the better.

Feb. 7. Sarum. 61. Hen. Cotton, Bishop of Salisbury, to the Same. The petition of the citizens of Sarum, now renewed, to obtain a Corporation, will be prejudicial to the liberties of the Cathedral. Requests his Lordship's protection therein.

Feb. 7. Special Commission to the Earl of Salisbury, Master of the Court of Wards and Liveries, and the Council of the same court. Business not named. [*Grant Bk., p.* 68.]

Feb. 7. Commission to the Lord Chancellor, Earl of Salisbury, and others, to sell or let to farm certain Crown lands. [*Ibid., p.* 68.]

Feb. 7. 62. Certificate respecting copyhold manors of inheritance in Auditor Fulwer's office.

Feb. ? 63. List of Commissioners nominated to treat with copyholders.

Feb. ? 64. List of Commissioners to treat with copyhold tenants of the duchy [of Lancaster], in counties specified.

Feb. ? 65. Particulars of the Commission to treat with copyholders.

Feb. ? 66. Considerations on the proposition to fine copyholders at a certain number of years' rent.

Feb. ? 67. Analytical digest of the nature of lands comprehended in the Act of Parliament for confirmation of copyholds, &c., and of the compositions already made by certain tenants of Wakefield and Lancashire.

1611. Vol. LXI.

Feb. ? 68. Petition of Thos. Fortescue to Salisbury. Has served his Lordship and others as deputy in the Office of Alienations, for 20 years. Prays permission to nominate a person in his place.

Feb. 8. 69. The Same to the Same. Having received no reply to his petition, begs to know whether his kinsman, Mr. Knaplock, may act as his deputy in the Office of Alienations.

Feb. 8. Edinburgh. 70. Earl of Dunfermline to the Same. Grief at the Earl of Dunbar's unexpected decease. Will go to Berwick, as commanded, to inventory his goods. The burden of Scotch affairs will now weigh heavily on himself.

Feb. 8. Edinburgh. 71. The Same to the Same. Has fulfilled the King's orders that none of the Earl of Dunbar's goods in Scotland should be meddled with until his further pleasure be known. Recommends Mr. Herbert, who has been deprived by the Earl's death of a good master.

Feb. 9. 72. Earl of Northumberland to the Same. Requests a warrant to the Attorney General for delivery of his opinion relative to a bond lying in the Exchequer for his [Northumberland's] nonappearance.

Feb. 9. Newcastle. 73. Sir Geo. Selby to the Same. Has fulfilled his orders relative to an inventory of the goods of the late Earl of Dunbar. *Incloses,*

73. i. *Inventory of cattle belonging to the late Earl of Dunbar, within Riddesdale and Kidland.*

Feb. 9. Londesborough. 74. Earl of Cumberland to the Same. Great regret for the decease of the Earl of Dunbar. Has taken effective measures for the preservation of good order on the Borders.

Feb. 9. 75. Charges of the works, &c. on sundry of the King's houses, in January last.

Feb. 9. Warrant to pay 2,000*l.* imprest to the Treasurer of the Chamber for defraying the expenses of that office, which has fallen into great arrear. [*Warrt. Bk.*, II., *p.* 193.]

Feb. 9. Warrant for payment of 4,978*l.* 12*s.* 7½*d.*, residue of rent due to Henry Prince of Wales, 721*l.* 7*s.* 6*d.* surplusage for his apparel, and the sums due for his robes on his creation as Prince of Wales. [*Ibid*, *p.* 192.]

Feb. 9. Warrant to pay to Sir Art. Throgmorton and other tenants of Pauler's Pury, 50*l.*, for ground conveyed to the King for enlarging Grafton Park, co. Northampton. [*Ibid.*, *p.* 192.]

Feb. 9. Warrant to pay 12*d.* per diem to Deodatus Bynion, keeper of the garden at Royston. [*Ibid.*, *p.* 192.]

VOL. LXI.

1611.

Feb. [10 ?] Berwick. 76. Sir Wm. Bowyer to Salisbury. Lord Wm. Howard has arrived. Lord Burly came, but refuses to stay, and the Chancellor of Scotland talks of putting another into the Commission in his place. Dares not deliver the Earl of Dunbar's goods to any but the three persons named by the King. Caution against granting any request of the townspeople for the governor's house, &c.

Feb. 10. 77. Sir Hen. Balfour to the Same. Was made ill by the death of the Earl of Dunbar. Is displeased with a man who abused the Council for depriving him of a reward which he expected for service to the late Queen. Would have killed him, but he was an Englishman, and the King dislikes frays between the nations. Solicits a pension payment of his debts, having served the King 15 years.

Feb. 10. 78. Robt. Anstruther to the Same. Asks favour in his suit to the King. The King of Denmark will give his Lordship thanks for any patronage shown him.

Feb. 10. Warrant to pay 6*d.* per diem to Wm. Tuckey, for keeping pheasants and partridges for the King, at Hounslow Heath. [*Warrt. Bk.*, II., *p.* 196.]

Feb. 10. Warrant to pay to Wm. Court, 199*l.* 11*s.* 8*d.*, for surrender of the moiety of a lease of Denton coal mines, co. Northumberland. [*Ibid.*, *p.* 193.]

Feb. 11. Warwick. 79. Sir Rich. Verney, Wm. Barnes, and Edw. Boughton to Salisbury. Beg permission to resign their lease of Killingworth, because they would be held responsible for repair of the castle, for which it contains no covenant.

Feb. 12. Wingfield House. 80. Sir Rowland Lytton to Sir Dud. Carleton. The French Marshal [de la Verdine] is gone, the Parliament dissolved, and the King departed to Royston. News of the day. Projected successions to bishoprics and law offices, &c.

Feb. 12. 81. Account of John Suckling, Receiver of Fines for Alienations, for the past year.

Feb. 14. 82. Sir Robt. Cross to Salisbury. Urges a former petition for recompence of his services in the late and the present reign. If he may not be relieved, begs leave to quit the country, and hide his poverty abroad.

Feb. 14. Augusta. 83. Visct. Cranborne to Sir Dud. Carleton. Thanks for favours. Has a favourable journey towards Holland. French.

Feb. 15. Berwick. 84. Sir Wm. Bowyer to Salisbury. Thanks for kindness. Has delivered the [Earl of Dunbar's] things to the Earl of Dunfermline and Lord Wm. Howard, who have now re-delivered to him the charge of them.

Feb. 15. 85. Petition of Robt. Swinglehurst, John Proctor, and other tenants of Slaidburn, co. York, to Salisbury, to be allowed to make composition for their tenures, which are called in question as not belonging to the Duchy [of Lancaster]. With order thereon.

VOL. LXI.

1611.

Feb. 15. 86. Names of such lords and ladies as have not yet discharged the first payment of the subsidy of 7 Jac. 1.

Feb. 15. 87. Copy of the above.

Feb. 17. Royston. 88. Sir Thos. Lake to Salisbury. Returns letters concerning Count Emden. Hears nothing of the Swedish gentleman. Sends a draft letter to the King of Denmark for revision. Bills for pensions despatched. The King disapproves of the Spanish lady's supping with the two priests before their execution. He favours the inhabitants of Waltham Forest, who petition for exemption from purveyance.

Feb.? 89. The Same to the Same. His Majesty has despatched the bill, and commends his Lordship's industry in recovering money from one whom he termed a bankrupt.

Feb. 17. 90. Earl of Northumberland to the Same. Has required his accounts from the auditor. Requests release of 80*l.* illegally stopped. Sir Wm. Selby has been nibbling at some of his property.

Feb. 18. 91. Examinations of Simon Houghton, Keeper of Newgate, Abraham Reynolds, Margery White, and Christiana Damme, relative to the visits and presents of the Spanish Ambassador and Spanish ladies to the prisoners in Newgate, especially to Roberts the priest.

Feb. 18. Warrant to pay to Sir John Parker, Captain of Pendennis Fort, Cornwall, 296*l.* 4*s.*, for repairs of the fortifications. Also 40*l.* to Gilbert Thacker, for the use of Robt. Briscoe, for his interest in lands in Dacre and Bleck Hall, co. Cumberland. [*Warrt.Bk.*, II., *p.* 193.]

Feb. 19. Royston. 92. Sir Thos. Lake to Salisbury. His Majesty commands exemplary punishment on the keepers of the prison where the supper took place. Extravagant petition [of Mr. Bruncard] presented to the King by Sir Robt. Carr. A letter is sent to the justices of assize for amending the highways.

Feb. 20. Newmarket. 93. The Same to the Same. Letters to be conveyed to the Bishop Almoner. Mr. Bruncard's petition is countermanded; it was, that the powder and munitions supplied to divers forts and castles in the Queen's time, and unaccounted for, should be given to him. A long stay has taken place in passing grants of recusants' lands, &c., because of projected alterations in the grants. A draft proviso sent for revision.

Feb. 20. 94. Thos. Dewhurst to the Same. Begs to be permitted to sue for 5*l.* or 6*l.* per ann., which he has lost by an exchange of lands with the King.

Feb. 20. 95. Particulars of the guild and chantry lands, co. Northampton, taken for the purpose of letting them in fee farm.

Feb. 20. Licence to John Minshon, of the sole printing of the "Glosson Etimologicon," or dictionary etymological of 12 languages, for 21 years. [*Grant Bk.*, *p.* 73.]

Vol. LXI.

1611.

Feb. ? 96. Statement of the value of the Crown lands assigned to the King, Queen, Prince, and Duke of York.

Feb. 20. 97. Book of valuation of all the manors, lands, &c. in the late annexation of lands to the Crown, from which some are to be chosen for sale which are no part of the lands assigned to the Queen, the Prince, and Duke of York. Classed according to counties.

Feb. 20. Warrant to pay 4,677*l.* 6*s.* 8*d.* to Lady Carey, and others of the Royal Household, on whom His Majesty has lately bestowed pensions, as enumerated. [*Warrt. Bk.*, II., *p.* 194.]

Feb. 20. Warrant to pay to John de Olive, 3,200*l.* due to him from the King. [*Ibid.*, *p.* 194.]

Feb. 20. Warrant to pay to Thos. Boteler, 3,400*l.* due to him from the King. [*Ibid.*, *p.* 194.]

Feb. 21. Warrant to pay to Peter Van Lore, Merchant, of London, 6,000*l.* due to him from the King. [*Ibid.*, *p.* 195.]

Feb. 22. Newmarket. 98. Sir Thos. Lake to Salisbury. The Spanish Ambassador is to be expostulated with for his priest's visiting popish prisoners. Sends letters concerning Gunderrot to the King of Denmark. Nothing is heard of the Swedish gentleman, nor of Sir Rob. Stewart. Answer to be made to the Duke of Saxony. Sir Robt. Carey is chided for thinking 16 horses necessary for the Duke of York.

Feb. 22. Newmarket. 99. The Same to the Same. The King is resolved that the keeper of Newgate shall be severely punished for allowing reverence to priests, masses in prison, &c. Two prohibitions granted by Lord Chief Justice [Coke] in two cases of the Church, show his perverse spirit, and unless he can assign good reasons for them, the King will dismiss him and no longer be vexed with him. The gentleman of Sweden has just arrived.

Feb. 22. 100. Estimate of moneys due from collectors of subsidies and fifteenths.

Feb. 22. 101. Rate of the improvement of the manors of Fryerning and More Hall, co. Essex, purchased by Nich. Wadham, deceased.

Feb. 23. Gatehouse. 102. Jas. Conway, prisoner, to Jas. Primrose. Ill-usage inflicted on him by the keeper of the Gatehouse, because of letters which he wrote to the Lord Treasurer and the late Lord Kinloss. *Annexed is*,

> 102. I. *Statement of Thos. Newton, John Buckley, and Jas. Cambell, recusants in the Gatehouse, of the cruelties of their keeper. They beg to be liberated, exiled, or sent to a more humane keeper.*

Feb. 23. Warrant for payment of 23*l.* 4*s.* to Edw. Lord Denny, for bridges newly erected near Waltham. [*Warrt. Bk.*, II., *p.* 195.]

1611. Vol. LXI.

Feb. 24. Newmarket. 103. Sir Thos. Lake to Salisbury. Sir Geo. Chaworth saw the Spanish lady. The King has been writing to Salisbury, to the Queen, the Spanish Ambassador, &c. Instructions in a case pending before the Judge of the Admiralty. The King would have the Spanish Ambassador's house watched to see who goes to mass, but not openly so as to attract his notice.

Feb. 24. Peterly. 104. Sir Robt. Dormer to the Same. Requests particulars of the manor of Great Missenden, co. Bucks, which he wishes to purchase.

Feb. 24. Warrant to pay 182*l.* 3*s.* 8*d.* to Wm. Purvey, for enlarging Cheshunt Park, and 50*l.* to Thos. Dewhurst, for lands surrendered by him for that purpose. [*Warrt. Bk.*, II., *p.* 197.]

Feb. 24. Warrant to pay 800*l.* to Rob. Jossy, to be employed under His Majesty's direction. [*Ibid.*, *p.* 195.]

Feb. 24. Paris. 105. Hen. Lord Clifford to Salisbury. Sends a few lines by Mr. Calvert, at his request.

Feb. 25. Newmarket. 106. Sir Thos. Lake to the Same. His Majesty requests the Lord Treasurer and Lord Admiral's opinion on [Sir Robt. Stewart's] petition enclosed, for leave to fell two trees out of every hundred in the King's woods. *Incloses*,

106. I. *Petition of Sir Robt. Stewart to the King for a grant of two trees out of every* 100 *of decayed or fuel trees, not timber, in the King's manors, his former grant of tops and lops not sufficing to pay his creditors.*

Feb. 25. Newmarket. 107. The Same to the Same. The King has chosen the Bishop of London to be Archbishop of Canterbury, as being an able man, and recommended by the late Earl of Dunbar, whose memory is dear to His Majesty. Oath to be administered to the Bishop that he neither has given nor will give any bribe for this preferment. *Annexed is*,

107. I. *Copy of the above oath, with certificate of its having been taken by the Bishop of London, Feb.* 27.

Feb. 25. 108. Sir Thos. Shirley to the Same. Thanks that no process is issued against him out of Mr. Osborne's office. Requests stay of certain bonds issued against him and his sureties by Sir Hen. Fanshaw. *Annexed is*,

108. I. *List of those who were bound with Sir Thos. Shirley, sen., for payment of his debts to the late Queen.*

Feb. 25. Kingston-upon-Hull. 109. Mayor, &c. of Hull to the Same. Thank for favour towards their decayed corporation. Request confirmation of their charter. Beg his acceptance of five fothers of lead from the town.

Feb. 25. Warrant to pay to Wm. Greenwell and Thos. Stiles, 1,507*l.* 2*s.* 5*d.*, for cordage for the navy. [*Warrt. Bk., I., p.* 105.]

Feb. 26. Newmarket. 110. Sir Thos. Lake to Salisbury. Sir Rich. Wigmore has been suitor to His Majesty for some benefit of recusants by allotment of counties. The King inquires if any counties remain unallotted, and his Lordship's opinion on the grant.

Feb. 26. Temple. 111. W. Crashaw to the Same. Beseeches him to read the enclosed. Requests that he may have one of each of the popish books newly taken.

VOL. LXI.

1611.

Feb. 26. Paris. 112. Wm. Lord Roos to Salisbury. Professions of service. Proposes to take the Low Countries in his way to England. Hopes still to meet with Lord Cranborne on his travels.

Feb. 26. 113. Sir Wm. Slingsby to the Same. Requests that Sir Edw. Zouch and others may not obtain a patent of the newly invented furnaces for making glass with sea coal, as it would infringe on the original patent to himself and others, the inventors, which he desires a printed declaration to enforce.

Feb ? 114. Jean Carre to the Lord Secretary. Has established glass-houses in Sussex and London at his own great cost, and to the benefit of the kingdom, relying on a promise that he should have the advantage thereof. Hears that another is likely to have the privilege of making glass, and entreats it may be prevented. French.

Feb. 27. Newmarket. 115. Sir Thos. Lake to the Same. Lord Chief Justice Coke, in a conversation with the King, denied any knowledge of the two prohibitions [*see Feb.* 22], but confessed it in private to others. Inquiries are to be made thereon. Mr. Bruncard has been again at Court with his petition formed anew, but the King will not refer it, ordering him to proceed in the case by common law.

Feb. 27. Newmarket. 116. The Same to the Same. Sir Thos. Bartlett used unseemly and desperate language in preferring petitions to the King for protection and relief. He is sent to the Council to receive admonition. The King would grant him protection rather than be haunted with him again.

Feb. 27. 117. Morgan Colman to the Same. On his project for economical reforms in the management of His Majesty's Household.

Feb. 28. 118. Sir Thos. Shirley to the Same. Reasons why Sir Hen. Fanshaw has awarded process against him and his friends. Requires a warrant from his Lordship to stay the same, &c.

Feb. 28. 119. Sir Jas. Cromer and Wm. Boys, Surveyor General of Kent, to the Same. Certificate of decays in the manor of Milton.

Feb. ? 120. Sir Thos. Mewtas to the Same. His estate brought low by expenses of his lost limb. Begs the King's aid to buy an Exchequer pension of 1,000 marks per ann., which is to be sold for 2,500*l.*, to support the rank lately conferred on him.

Feb. 121. Receipts by various persons of copies of the book relating to Wards and Liveries, to be proclaimed in the market places of various towns. Two papers.

Feb.? 122. Receipts, principally by stewards and bailiffs of manors, for letters from the Lord Treasurer, relative to the state of the King's manors in divers counties.

Feb. ? 123. [Earl of Salisbury] to Dr. Langton [President of Magdalen College, Oxford]. Requests that a youth recommended by Sir Noel de Caron may be elected a demy of the College. *Annexed is,*

123. I. *Sir Noel de Caron to Salisbury. In favour of the youth above named, one of the many children of the Minister of Cheins. South Lambeth, Feb.* 28, 1611.

1611.

VOL. LXII. MARCH, 1611.

March 1. 1. Book of the manors remaining unsold after the choice of the last contractors.

March 2. 2. Comparison between the first payment in London of the third subsidy of 3 Jac. I. and the first payment of the subsidy 7 Jac. I.

March 3. Blisworth. 3. Inhabitants of Blisworth to ——. Remonstrate against the appointment of Mr. Lewis as teacher of their school, because his proctorship will often cause him to be absent. Recommend Samuel Preston, who is well accustomed to tuition. *Inclose,*

3. I. *Edw. Saunders and others, to —— in favour of Sam. Preston as teacher of Blisworth Free School.*

March 4. Newcastle. 4. Mayor, &c. of Newcastle-on-Tyne to Salisbury. Recommend that the survey directed of His Majesty's coal mines, in Durham and Northumberland, should not be required before Michaelmas, the weather not permitting it to be completed by Easter.

March 4. Berwick. 5. Sir Wm. Bowyer to the Same. Private suggestions respecting the building of the bridge at Berwick. *Incloses,*

5. I. *Estimate for making a stone bridge over the Tweed at Berwick,* 5,440*l.* 10*s.* 4*d.*; *the length to be* 140 *yards.*

March [4 ?] Westminster. Grant to Wm. Whiting, of Canterbury, of pardon for a supposed rape. [*Sign Man., vol.* I., *No.* 61.]

March 4. Warrant to pay 185*l.* 15*s.* 8*d.* to Hen. Seckford, administrator of Sir Hen. Seckford, deceased, Master of the Toils, for surplusage due on his account. [*Warrt. Bk.*, II., *p.* 79.]

March 5. Grant to Sir Geo. Carew and Francis, his son, of the office of Prothonotary of Chancery, and of making letters patent of pardon and outlawry, and all writs of supplicavit and supersedeas. [*Grant Bk.*, *p.* 67.]

[March 5.] Grant to Sir Walter Cope of the office of Public Registrar for general commerce. [*Ibid.*, *p.* 68.]

March 5. Newcastle. 6. Mayor of Newcastle and Wm. Jackson to Salisbury. They have taken bonds of five tenants of His Majesty's coal mines at Denton, Northumberland, for payment of 900*l.*

March 5. Kew. 7. Lord Harrington to the Same. As his son shows symptoms of measles, suggests that Lady Elizabeth be removed to Whitehall.

March 6. 8. Names of the assessors of subsidies for the City of London.

March 7. 9. Alice Collingwood to Lady Arabella Seymour. Solicits relief in her necessity, being detained from her lawful husband, through whom she has rights of great value.

March 7. 10. Charges of works, &c. on sundry of His Majesty's houses in February.

VOL. LXII.

1611.

March 8. 11. Account of the Crown manors, &c., valued at 6,996*l.* 1*s.* 5*d.*, last returned by the contractors, with particulars of the survey of a portion thereof.

March 9. 12. Book of manors and lands in the late annexation, in which are no copyholds above the rent of 20*s.* per ann.

March 9. 13. Copy of the above, with index and final digest omitted.

March 9? 14. Book of manors, parks, woods, &c., delivered in by the contractors, as part of their grant of lands, value 2,000*l.* per ann., but which are not to be passed to them.

March 11. Grant to Sir Thos. Monson of the office of keeper of the armoury in the galleries near the Tiltyard, Greenwich, for life. [*Grant Bk., p.* 74.]

March 11. Berwick. 15. Sir Wm. Bowyer and the Mayor of Berwick to Salisbury. Thanks that by his favour their hopes of the building of the bridge have not been put an end to by Lord Dunbar's death. Have sent Mr. Burrell, the surveyor, and two aldermen, to attend the Privy Council thereon.

March. Berwick. 16. Abstract [drawn up by Sir Thos. Lake for Salisbury] of the correspondence relating to Berwick Bridge.

March 11. Berwick. 17. Geo. Nicholson to Salisbury. Part of Berwick Bridge has fallen in so much in the night as to prevent horses passing. With a sketch of the bridge, showing the part fallen in.

March 11. Berwick. 18. Mayor of Berwick, Hugh Grigson, and Mich. Sanderson to the Same. That very night, since the departure of Mr. Burrell and three other Commissioners, two arches of the old wooden bridge have given way.

March 11. Berwick. 19. Sir Wm. Bowyer and the Mayor of Berwick to the Same. To the same effect.

March? 20. Statement [by Mr. Burrell and the other Commissioners] of the nature and situation of the proposed bridge at Berwick, of the materials requisite, of such as are already provided, and of moneys expended upon it, &c.

March 12. St. James's. 21. Walsingham Gresley to Hugh Lee, Consul at Lisbon. His master will not consent to be paid with paper, but desires a power to sell Lee's lands in discharge of the debt. If this be done, his master will try to obtain Lee's consulship.

March 12. Westminster. Grant to Robt. Baxter, of Carleton, co. York, of pardon for coining. Latin. [*Sign Man., vol.* I., *No.* 62.]

March 13. Westminster. Grant to Hen. Bridges, of Avening, co. Gloucester, of pardon for piracy. Latin. [*Ibid., No.* 63.]

March 13. Westminster. Grant to Fras. Galbraith, serjeant of the pantry, of pension of 40*l.* per ann. for life. [*Ibid., No.* 64.]

1611. Vol. LXII.

March 13? 22. List of Protections Royal passed since March 25, 1603.

March 13. 23. Accounts of the Calamine and battery works, from Feb. 10, 1611, with an inventory of their stock, goods, debts, &c., as delivered to Sir John Bourchier.

March 13. 24. Copy of part of the above, with other memoranda on the same subject.

March 13. Warrant for payment of necessary sums for the charges of Lady Arabella Seymour, committed to the custody of the Bishop of Durham. [*Warrt. Bk.*, II., *p.* 196.]

March 13. Madrid. 25. Wm. Lord Roos to [Salisbury]. Will obey his wishes in returning early from Spain, instead of remaining there a year, as he had intended. Thanks his Lordship for not crediting the rumours of his having turned Romanist. Hopes he shall never so disgrace his parentage. Will have nothing to do with traitors or fugitives in his travels.

March 13. Paris. 26. Lord Clifford to the Same. Acknowledges favours. Was invited by the young King [of France] to see him exercise. Admires his fencing. The King gave him two books of his Latin exercises.

March 14. 27. Lady Arabella Seymour to the Council. Is so weak that it would occasion her death to be removed any further. Asks delay to recover her strength, which she could do the sooner if not continually molested.

March 15. 28. Sir Geo. Gifford to Salisbury. Has served 39 years without reward. Is in difficulties. Requests favour, as his Lordship's wife's kinsman, to obtain 2,000*l.* worth of goods forfeited for not paying customs.

March 15. 29. Sir Edw. Cooke to the Same. Solicits the loan of 2,000*l.*, on security of his manor of Chadwell, Essex.

March 16. Highgate. 30. Bishop of Durham to the Council. Has received Lady Arabella Seymour at Lambeth Ferry, and conveyed her to Highgate. Describes her weak and ailing condition. She will not consent to proceed at once on her journey.

March 16. Ludlow Castle. 31. Lord Eure and others to Salisbury. The claim of the late Deputy Sheriff of Carmarthenshire for allowance for removing a force at Whitland in that county is unjust, the force being not removed by him but by the next sheriff.

March 16. Magdalen Coll., Oxford. 32. Wm. Langton, President of Magdalen College, Oxford, to the Same. Will forward his Lordship's recommendation of Nich. Halswell for a fellowship.

March 16. 33. Estimate of the charges of works intended to be done at Somerset House.

March 16. 34. Charges of reparations at Somerset House, from May 1609 to February 1610.

VOL. LXII.

1611.

March 16. 35. Petition of Fras. Carter, Keeper of Guildford Park under John Murray, to Salisbury, for a lease of the Castle garden in St. Mary's parish, Guildford. With reference and certificate thereon.

March 18. 36. Book of the manors in the entail in cos. Kent, Surrey, Sussex, Oxford, Leicester, Lincoln, Nottingham, and York.

March 18. Grant to Sir Hen. Wotton of leave to fill the second vacancy among the six clerks. [*Grant Bk.*, *p.* 81.]

March 19. Warrant to pay 388*l.* 2*s.* 7*d.* to certain artificers, for making a barge for the Duke of York, and for other works for the Queen, Prince, and Lady Elizabeth. [*Warrt. Bk.*, II., *p.* 198.]

March 19. Warrant to pay to Wm. Gudourons, His Majesty's Serjeant Surgeon, 500 marks for his house adjoining Somerset House, bought for improving the gallery there. [*Ibid.*, *p.* 197.]

March 19. Warrant to pay to Thos. Tilney, executor of Edm. Tilney, late Master of the Revels, 120*l.* 14*s.* 4*d.*, for surplus due on his account. [*Ibid.*, *p.* 197.]

March 19. Berwick. 37. Geo. Nicholson to Salisbury. Has not made up his last year's account for the pay of the garrison, &c., because of the late Lord [Dunbar]'s affairs. Desires an order to Mr. Scudamore for the half-year's pay, and directions for future proceedings.

March 20. 38. Sir Vincent Skinner to the Same. Begs his influence with the Chancellor of the Duchy that his son-in-law, Rob. Middleton, may take his place as Receiver in Lincolnshire, and asks favour in reference to the payment of his own debt.

March 20. Warrant to pay to Phil. Henslow and Edw. Allen, Masters of the Game at Paris Garden, 42*l.* 10*s.*, and 12*d.* per diem, in future, for keeping two white bears and a young lion. [*Warrt. Bk.*, II., *p.* 198.]

March 21. Barnet. 39. Bishop of Durham to Salisbury. Arrival of Lady Arabella at Barnet. Sends his own servant because the Postmaster refused to despatch an express. *Incloses*,

39. I. *Bp. of Durham to the Council. After six days' stay at Highgate, Lady Arabella travelled thither, but was very ill on the journey. Thanks for their sending Sir Jas. Croft to relieve him. Lady Arabella's extreme reluctance to proceed on her journey compelled the use of the means prescribed, which were employed with all decency and respect. March* 21, *Barnet.*

March 21. Warrant for cessation of payment for certain stages of posts, maintained in time of war, but not now necessary. [*Warrt. Bk.*, II., *p.* 200.]

March 22. Kew. 40. Sir Art. Gorges to Salisbury. Thanks for his favour concerning his patent for commerce. Requests permission to have the office for it in Britain's Burse.

VOL. LXII.

1611.

March 22. Westminster. Grant to Edw. Blencarne, of London, of pardon, for having formerly refused to take the Oath of Allegiance, which he has now taken. Latin. [*Sign Man.*, *vol.* I., *No.* 65.]

March 22. Grant to Sir John Eyres of 500*l.* as a gift. [*Warrt. Bk.*, II., *p.* 198.]

March 22. Warrant to pay 250*l.* per month to Sir David Fowlies for the household expenses of the Duke of York, 200*l.* per quarter to Sir Rob. Carey for provisions for his person, and 100*l.* per annum to the same for his privy purse expenses. [*Ibid.*, *p.* 199.]

March 22. Grant to Sir Sigismund and Hen. Zinzan of 100*l.*, as a free gift. [*Ibid.*, *p.* 200.]

March 23. Commission to the Earls of Salisbury, Nottingham, and others, to survey and inventory the jewels in the Tower. [*Grant Bk.*, *p.* 69.]

[March 23.] 41. Account for apparellings and riding charges in hunting journeys for the King's servants, Anno 8.

March 24. 42. Account of the farm of the duty on silk for the past year.

March 25. Ceremonial of creating Sir Rob. Carr Visct. Rochester. [*Dom. Corresp.*, *Nov.* 4, 1613.]

March 25. Westminster. Confirmation to Rich. Earl of Dorset of a grant of the manor of Salisbury Court, together with Salisbury House, alias Sackville Place, alias Dorset House, and divers messuages in St. Bride's and St. Dunstan's, on his compounding for defective titles. Latin. [*Sign Man.*, *vol. I.*, *No.* 68.]

March 26. Brussels. 43. Wm. Lord Roos to Salisbury. Note of courtesy and affection.

March 27. London. 44. Sir John Bennet to Sir Dud. Carleton. Displeasure of the patriots at the late dissolution of Parliament. Sir Robt. Carr has been created Baron of Winwick, a lordship of his in Northamptonshire, and Visct. Rochester. Several Lords of Scotland, spiritual and temporal, are at Court, to arrange the affairs of that kingdom, which were wholly managed by the late Earl of Dunbar, for whom, though he is buried in Scotland, the King has appointed a funeral at Westminster. Private affairs.

March 27. 45. Sir Thos. Denis to Salisbury. His Lordship's niece, the Lady Marchioness [of Northampton], is desirous to buy Dyley Woods.

March 27. Westminster. Grant in reversion to Reade Wildgoose, of a Poor Knight's room at Windsor. [*Sign. Man.*, *vol. I.*, *No.* 69.]

March 28. Westminster. Grant to Roger Wyvell of purchase of the manor of Osgodby, and other lands, in Cayton, co. York, as part payment of 50,000*l.* due to John Eldred and other contractors. [*Ibid*, *No.* 70.]

VOL. LXII.

1611.

March 28. 46. Deputation by John and Chas. Young, of Chichester, to Jeremy Spracklin, of London, of the power to search all vessels sailing from certain ports, for ordnance unlawfully exported, according to a patent granted to the late Sam. Thomas, of St. Peter's parish, Tower, and since conveyed to John and Chas. Young, granting them the moiety of certain forfeitures incurred by unlawful export of ordnance.

March 29. Warrant for payments to be made to John Williams and others, for making gold and silver plate, &c. [*Warrt. Bk.*, III., *p.* 1.]

March 30. 47. Petition of Rob. Kay, merchant, to the Council, for mitigation of their decree against him, to forbear his trade, as being to the prejudice of the clothiers of York and Hull, and for stay of further suit in the Star Chamber, as he is ready to submit to their Lordships' order.

March 31. East Barnet. 48. Sir Jas. Croft to Salisbury. Lady Arabella dressed herself as well as her extreme weakness would permit, and showed readiness to remove, but could not, because nothing was prepared for her at Mr. Conyer's house. She has had a violent attack in the head.

March. 49. Bill of Wm. Walker, keeper of the fowl at St. James's, for extraordinary charges in keeping birds and beasts.

March. 50. Monthly charges of the houses at Richmond and St. James's since June 1, 1610. Total 2,946*l.* 16*s.* 4½*d.*

March? 51. Charges for services for the Queen in the Great Wardrobe for the year 1610.

March. 52. Account of fees on certain grants and warrants for the month of March.

March. 53. Sir Wm. Bowyer to Salisbury. Berwick Bridge is strongly mended. Suggests the fittest way of keeping up the wooden bridge, if a stone bridge cannot be obtained. Asks directions as to the quarterly pay of the garrison, &c.

March. 54. Alex. Earl Home to the Same. Deplores the decease of the Earl of Dunbar, his patron. Throws himself on his Lordship's protection for the future.

March? [King's Bench.] 55. Hen. Wyndham to the Lord Treasurer. Reminds him that Jones and Salter's Patent of the Customs expires at Christmas next. Will be faithful if employed in the service [about the Customs].

March? 56. Reasons to induce the Lord Treasurer to grant the Plumbers' petition, that in their charter of corporation, they may have extension of their licence to travel 100 miles from London, to certain places named, which are beyond that distance. [*Charter granted April* 12, 1611.]

March? 57. List of the servants above stairs of the Prince.

1611. Vol. LXII.

March? 58. Warrant to Thos. Lord Knyvet and Edm. Doubleday, to pay to the said Lord Knyvet or his heirs, 2,000*l.* as the King's gift, from the profits of the Mint. [*See April* 28 *infra.*]

March? 59. Bill, answer, and proofs, in the case of the Attorney General against Sir Wm. Pope respecting certain closes, &c. in Whichwood Forest, co. Oxon.

March? 60. Draft of the proofs in the above case.

March? 61. Particulars of Sir Wm. Pope's lands in Whichwood Forest.

March? 62. Petition of Wm. Wich, a tenant of the manor of Crowland, co. Lincoln, to Salisbury, for extension of time for payment of a balance of 47*l.*, the composition money for which he has contracted, and for a letter to the other tenants urging their more speedy payments to him.

Vol. LXIII. April, May, 1611.

April 1. 1. Justices, &c. of Hertfordshire to Salisbury. On assurance that the treaty for composition [for tenures] is to put an end to all purveyance, they have chosen eight persons to attend about it. *Annexed is,*

1. I. *Names of the above-mentioned eight gentlemen of Hertfordshire.*

April 1. 2. Petition of Wm. Beecher to the Council, that the cause between him and Mrs. Babington may be heard on the first day of their Lordships' sitting. With order thereon. Prefixed is an order in the Exchequer for hearing the above cause, dated Jan 30, 1611.

April. 1. 3. Note of money due for victualling His Majesty's ships, in harbour, and in the narrow seas, for the last half year.

April 2. East Barnet. 4. Sir Jas. Croft to the Council. Lady Arabella was removed from Barnet to East Barnet, Mr. Conyer's house, yesterday, but was extremely ill on the journey.

April 3. Londesborough. 5. Earl of Cumberland to Salisbury. Thanks for his advice in settling his estate, and his affection to his son, now his Lordship's son-in-law, whose course is to be regulated by him. Supposes nothing can be resolved relative to his patent for cloths, till the place where the Merchant Adventurers shall trade to is fixed.

April 3. 6. Sir Wm. Bowyer to the Same. The report that he was rejoiced at the death of the Earl of Dunbar is most false. Has many enemies on the Borders who invent ill of him; rejoices that the Earl of Dunbar's daughter is likely to be matched as her father wished.

April 3. Carlisle. 7. Jos. Pennington, Sir Wm. Hutton, and Hen. Fetherston to the Same. Have surveyed the citadel at Carlisle. 220*l.* would be needed for repairs to fit it for use as the common gaol.

Vol. LXIII.

1611.

April 4. Royston. 8. Sir Thos. Lake to Salisbury. The King has signed the bills, but desired to know what reasons there were for a paymaster for Berwick, as he had ordered the discharge of the garrison.

April 4. Royston. 9. The Same to the Same. The King and Council of Scotland have been considering the Scottish affairs, which are at a stay by the death of the Earl of Dunbar. The King thinks of revoking the lieutenancy granted to the Earls of Dunbar and Cumberland, and of governing by commission, as before. Lord Cumberland to be compensated by the lieutenancy of some county.

April 5. 10. Charges of the works and reparations done on His Majesty's houses in March.

April 5. Warrant to pay 326*l.* 10*s.* 6*d.* to Lady Carey, wife of Sir Robt. Carey, who lately had the tuition of Charles Duke of York. [*Warrt. Bk.*, III., *p.* 2.]

April 5. Warrant to pay 50*l.* to John Norton, for books for the King's use. [*Ibid.*, *p.* 4.]

April 5. Warrant to pay 137*l.* 18*s.* 2*d.* to Robt. Treswell, for repair of the house and inclosures of Ditton Park. [*Ibid*, *p.* 3.]

April 5. Warrant to pay 30*l.* to John Wood, for training cormorants for fishing. [*Ibid.*, *p.* 3.]

April 5. Warrant to pay an annuity of 200*l.* to Chas. Paget, out of the Exchequer, the lands from which he formerly received it being settled on the Prince. [*Ibid.*, *p.* 3.]

April 5. Warrant to the Lord Treasurer and Chancellor of the Exchequer to nominate a fit person as Paymaster of the Garrison at Berwick, and to assign funds for the payments, those of the Receiver of Yorkshire being no longer sufficient, on account of the sale of lands. [*Ibid.*, *p.* 5.]

April 6. 11. Chas. Anthony to Edw. Anthony. Will perform the business of his lease with Mr. Eldred, so as to save him the trouble of coming up to London, if possible.

April 6. Royston. 12. Sir Thos. Lake to Salisbury. The King sees no reason for keeping the garrison of Berwick a quarter longer in pay. He wishes to know at once whether the former Border Commission be in force, and who should be employed as Commissioners, that he may match them on the Scottish side. Sir Wilfrid Lawson, Sir Wm. Selby, Sir Hen. Wodrington, and Lord Wm. Howard have been named. The Dutch ship detained in Scotland is to be restored, at request of Sir Noel Caron.

April 6. Royston. 13. The Same to the Same. The names of the Border Commissioners may await His Majesty's return. The masses at the foreign Ambassadors' houses are to be considered. The King wishes to bestow 40*l.* or 50*l.* on Andrew Melvin, at his departure.

Vol. LXIII.

1611.

April 7. Royston. 14. Lake to Salisbury. The King has received a letter from the Spanish Ambassador, which surprises him, as it is not usual for Princes to deliver up offenders. The Council and Judge of Admiralty are to be consulted thereon. The Ambassador in France is to be written to, to forward the removal of Mr. Casaubon's family and library into England. The Lord Chancellor of Scotland has permission to pass over his pension to Sir John Brook and Sir John Burlacy, who have bought it.

April 8. Royston. 15. The Same to the Same. The Chancellor of Scotland will do as his Lordship wishes about Berwick. Mr. Pickering objected to as Commissioner for the Borders. The Lords of Scotland are going away.

[April] 8. 16. Lord Admiral Nottingham to [the Same ?]. Concerning the transportation of Sir John Digby into Spain. Capt. Wood should still continue in Scotland, to keep the pirates in awe.

April 8. Royston. 17. Sir Geo. Bruce to the Same. In consideration of his long services in manufacturing white salt, the King recommends to the Commissioners for Suits his petition to furnish Boston, Lynn, and Hull with salt. Prays his Lordship's furtherance of his suit, in memory of his love to his late brother, Lord Kinloss.

April 9. King's Bench. 18. Rob. Booth to the Same. Has ventured to translate [Jean de] Barclay's book into English, because, though it admits the Pope's spiritual jurisdiction, it gives weighty reasons against his temporal power. The King and several Bishops approve his translation. Writes from a place where his own credulity and the credulity of a lawyer have plunged him.

April 9. 19. Names of persons who sent presents at the Archbishop of Canterbury's confirmation.

April 10. Royston. 20. Sir Thos. Lake to Salisbury. Forwards the Privy Seal for 60*l*. for Andrew Melvin. Submits to his Lordship a letter on causes ecclesiastical written to the Lord Deputy of Ireland, at request of the Bishop of the Isles and Bishop of Raphoe. Sir Stephen Le Sieur is with the King.

April 10. Royston. 21. The Same to the Same. Sir Jas. Murray has delivered the two letters from the Elector of Brandenburg. His Lordship is to consider whether the Ambassador in Holland [Sir Ralph Winwood] may be spared for the journey [to Cleves].

April ? 22. Morgan Colman to the Same. His project has rendered him hateful to all the household, and brings him jeers and derisions below stairs. Prays that it may be examined, as it will reduce the King's household expenses 20,000*l*. below those of last year.

April 10. 23. The Same to the Same. The opinion of some that his project will not hold does not discourage him. Is certain that he can reduce the King's household expenditure to 58,000*l*. per ann., and his bounty to be increased.

Vol. LXIII.

1611.

April ? **24. Morgan Colman to Salisbury.** His well-intended service heaps disgrace upon him. Although a settled course is resolved upon for the household, his service will profit, if examined into, and he may be saved banishment from Court.

April 10. Richmond. 25. Fras. Tunstall and Adam Middleham to the Same. The tenants of Middleham and Richmond, Yorkshire, refuse to pay to Sir Thos. Metcalfe the composition ordered.

April 10. Warrant to pay to Thos. Lord Knyvet and Edm. Doubleday, Wardens of the Mint, 120*l.*, for providing gold for coining angels used in curing the king's evil. [*Warrt. Bk.*, III., *p.* 4.]

April 11. Trinity Coll., Cambridge. 26. John Fortho to Salisbury. Andrew Bendloss the younger, of Burnthall, Essex, a learned Papist, on his death bed deliriously spoke sundry extravagant words, as that he had killed the King, a meritorious deed, &c.

April 11. Grant to Andrew Melvin of 60*l.* as a gift. [*Warrt. Bk.*, III., *p.* 5.]

April ? 27. Notes of the persons to whom recusants' estates in different counties have been granted. Indorsed [by Salisbury] "Melvin, Merry."

April 12. Royston. 28. Lake to Salisbury. Sends back the Prince of Anhalt's letters. The King was in hopes that the Londoners had assented to his wishes. The bearer, Simpson, servant of the Earl of Dunbar, to be appointed Messenger to the Council of Scotland. Suit of the discharged posts to be employed as messengers.

April 12. Royston. 29. The Same to the Same. The reluctance of the shires to compound shows the King that the Lower House has taken away all respect for him out of the people. An escheat to be granted to Patrick Ramsay, brother of Lord Haddington.

April 12. Royston. 30. The Same to the Same. Sir Oliver Lambert complains to the King that the reversion of the Marshal's place in Ireland has been granted away from him, and solicits in compensation that the Lord Deputy be made a Viscount of that kingdom, and himself and the present Marshal, Sir Rich. Wingfield, Barons, &c.

April 12. Berwick. 31. Geo. Nicholson to the Same. Has received commands to continue Paymaster till Midsummer; will then close and bring up his accounts. *Incloses,*

31. i. *Estimate of the pay of Berwick for* 1610, *and till Midsummer* 1611. *April* 12, *Berwick.*

April 12. Westminster. Constitution of the office of Surveyor of all Ships, in order to estimate the increase or decrease of the navy, and grant thereof, with survivorship, to John Grent and Thos. Aylesbury. [*Sign Man.*, *vol.* I., *No.* 71.]

April 13. Royston. Proclamation for the British undertakers of the escheated lands in Ulster, to repair into Ireland, before the beginning of May next. Printed. [*Procl. Coll.*, *No.* 16.]

Vol. LXIII.

1611.

April 13. Brussels. 32. Tobie Matthew to [Salisbury]. The three years of his banishment have seemed very long. Has acted with great loyalty abroad in not making ostentation of his conversion, nor receiving pensions from foreign Princes, nor complaining of persecution at home. Has always spoken honourably of His Majesty. Begs that if his Lordship is convinced of the integrity of his recent conduct, he will allow him to return, as his health and fortunes decay by his absence.

April 15. 33. Geo. Lord Carew to the Same. Her Majesty is satisfied with the progress of certain works. She dines that day with Sir Wm. Cornwallis.

April 15. Hackney. 34. Sir Fulk Greville to the Same. Thanks for continuance of favour.

April 17. 35. Sir Art. Mainwaring to Mr. Griffith. Signifies his lord's allowance that Mr. Bendbo and Mr. Pinches should become suitors for writing Commissions of Appeal, &c.

[April 17.] 36. Reasons on behalf of the petition of John Bendbo and Wm. Pinches, suitors to His Majesty for the writing of Commissions of Appeal in Chancery, after the death of Fras. Kindesley.

April ? 37. Petition of Wm. Longe, Clerk in Chancery, to Salisbury. His grant in reversion of the sealing of all Commissions of Appeal has been stayed on misinformation, and the place granted to Mr. Benbo and Mr. Pinches. Prays that his own grant may pass the Privy Seal.

April 17. Barnet. 38. Sir Jas. Croft to the Council. Asks further instructions for Lady Arabella's journey to Durham. She is somewhat better and lightsomer, but has not yet walked the length of her chamber, and is full of fears about going so far off as Durham.

April 19. Compton. 39. Sir Rich. Verney, Edw. Boughton, and Wm. Barnes to Salisbury. Entreat to be discharged of their tenancy of Sir Rob. Dudley's lands.

April 20. Charing Cross. 40. Sir Wm. Lane to the Same. Requests a commission to inquire into the lands of Wm. Copley, the benefit of whose recusancy has been granted to him.

April 22. Ripton. 41. Oliver Lord St. John to Sir Dud. Carleton. Thanks for favours conferred on his son, Rowland St. John, at Venice.

April 22. Berwick-upon-Tweed. 42. Mayor of Berwick to Salisbury. Thanks for his favouring their bridge. Will use the utmost care and diligence about it. *Incloses*,

42. I. *Estimate for making a stone bridge over the Tweed at Berwick, in length* 280 *yards*,—8,426*l*. 8*s*. 4*d*.

April 23. Londesborough. 43. Earl of Cumberland to the Same. Is satisfied with the change in the Commission for the Government of the Borders, if it may be understood not to proceed from dissatisfaction with his conduct. His services therein have been laborious. Approves of the four Commissioners appointed.

VOL. LXIII.

1611.

April 23. 44. Petition of the 100 soldiers at Berwick to Salisbury, against the reduction intended in their pay. *Inclose,*

44. I. *Statement of the names, ages, and families of the* 100 *soldiers at Berwick. April* 23. [*See May* 25.]

April 23. Gloucester. 45. Mayor, &c. of Gloucester to Salisbury. Pray his influence that they may purchase from Sir Wm. Cooke the fines and amerciaments within the hundred of Dudstone and King's-Barton now granted to him, from which the city formerly paid its fee-farm rent to the Crown. [*See May* 2.]

April 24. Ludlow Castle. 46. Lord Eure and Sir Rich. Lewkenor to the Same. Have been advertised by the Receivers for North and South Wales that they can no longer pay the diet money or Judges' fees as usual, which is a great detriment to the Council. They are also put to great charges in defence of their jurisdiction. Pray that certain vexatious suits may be stayed by injunction, and that payment of their moneys may be made elsewhere. *Inclose,*

46. I. *Thos. Trafford, Receiver of North Wales, to Lord Eure. The revenues within his charge being now assessed to the Prince, all payments for diet, &c. for the Council of the Marches are to be made out of the Exchequer at Westminster. April* 15, *Wrexham.* [*See May* 13.]

April 24. Serjeants' Inn. 47. Sir Nich. Bacon to Salisbury. Is prevented waiting on him by a fit of the gout. Thanks for favours.

April 24. Paris. 48. Hen. Lord Clifford to the Same. Likes Paris, though it be somewhat noisome in summer; pleasant walks in the Tuilleries.

April 26. 49. Petition of Emma, wife of Wm. Melsham, to the Same. That Roger Mousdale be made to pay a debt he owes her of 60*l.* With order thereon dismissing the petition.

April 27. Berwick. 50. Sir Wm. Bowyer to the Same. The hundred soldiers at Berwick are too old to enter other service, or to be removed to Ireland, as proposed. Recommends that the reduction of expense be made by discharging those who remain absent without leave, or are guilty of other faults, instead of diminishing the pay, &c.. Also desires for himself a grant of land in Ireland, if he may not have Rob. Atwood's pension, as promised him by the Earl of Dunbar.

[April 27.] 51. Abstract of the above letter [drawn up by Sir Thos. Lake for Salisbury].

April 28. Warrant to pay to Thos. Lord Knyvet 2,000*l.* from the Exchequer, for good and faithful service to His Majesty, the profits of the Mint being decayed, and not sufficing therefor. [*Warrt. Bk.*, III., *p.* 6.]

April 28. 52. Draft of the above warrant.

1611. Vol. LXIII.

April 30. Lambeth. 53. Archbp. of Canterbury, Bp. of Winchester, and others, Commissioners for Causes Ecclesiastical, to Rich. Bratie and Walter Salter, Messengers of the King's Chamber. Instructions to search for and seize Papists, Jesuits, and Seminary Priests, popish books, relics, &c.

April 30. Berwick. 54. Geo. Nicholson to Salisbury. Explanations of his proceedings and those of Capt. Bowyer, relative to the reduction of charge for the soldiers at Berwick. The soldiers distrust Bowyer, and have secretly petitioned him (Nicholson) to obtain their pay, with their freedom. *Incloses,*

54. i. *Geo. Nicholson to Capt. Bowyer. Begs Bowyer to transmit his own reply to Lord Salisbury at once. Will write himself in a few days. April 27, Berwick.*

54. ii. *Petition of the 100 soldiers to Nicholson, to request Lord Salisbury that if their pay be reduced, they may be freed from further servitude.*

54. iii. *Nicholson's project for lessening the charge of the garrison at Berwick by repressing sundry offices, &c. April 30, Berwick.*

April 30. 55. Charge of repairs, &c. at Richmond House, and for the new library, gallery, &c. at St. James's, since the first of June 1610. Indorsed [by Salisbury] "Charges of the Prince's Works."

April 30. 56. Petition of John Sewell of Grafton Regis, co. Northampton, to Salisbury, that the contractors for leases may allow him a lease of certain lands in Grafton for 50 years, as agreed, instead of for 30, to which they wish to reduce it. With reference to the contractors.

April 30. Warrant to pay to Geo. Baker, 698*l.* 12*s.* for making gold and silver spangles for the coats of the guard, royal footmen, messengers, &c. [*Warrt. Bk.*, III., *p.* 8.]

April 30. Warrant to pay to John Vachell, 100*l.* arrears of a pension granted him by the late Queen out of Sir Thos. Tresham's fines due for recusancy, from Christmas 1602 to June 1605, when Sir Thomas died. [*Ibid.*, *p.* 6.]

April 30. Warrant to pay to Wm. Broderick, 130*l.* 19*s.* 4*d.* for embroidering 248 red coats with roses and crowns imperial, for the King, Queen, and Prince's servants. [*Warrt. Bk.*, III., *p.* 8.]

April 30. Warrant to pay to Thos. Elston, Clerk of the Cheque of the Guard, 17*l.* 2*s.*, for embroidering 76 red coats for the grooms and pages of the King, Queen, and Prince's Chambers, &c. [*Ibid.*, *p.* 6.]

April 30. Warrant to pay to the Same various sums for red cloth, &c., for liveries of the guard and others of the Household. [*Ibid.*, *p.* 7.]

VOL. LXIII.

1611.

April. Tower. 57. Sir Thos. Bartlett to Salisbury. Renews his conformity and submission, and desires favour.

April. 58. Memorandum of the King's debts, which are put off to a future time, but not assigned to any certain payment.

April. 59. Copy of the above, with an addition to June 24.

April. 60. Sir Hen. Hobart, Attorney General, to Salisbury. Has persuaded Sheriff Barkham to withdraw his refusal to continue the loan, and to influence others to the same effect.

April? 61. Project for bringing money to the King by conferring the title of Vidom (vice Dominus), anciently used in England, on two gentlemen of every shire, with the privilege of sitting in the House of Commons, and of freedom from arrest.

April? 62. Notes to prove that the Knights of the Bath are not higher in dignity than Knights Bachelors.

April? 63. Distinctions in rank, privileges, &c. between Barons by Writ, Barons by Patent, and Barons by Tenure, properly called Bannerets or Baronets, but by ancient custom termed Baron.

April? 64. Project for erecting the new dignity of Baronets, between Barons and Knights.

April? 65. Memorandum relative to the service to be required from and precedency granted to Baronets.

April? 66. Form of warrant for the creation of a Baronet.

May 1. Warrant for delivery of stuff for the installation of Charles Duke of York as Knight of the Garter at Windsor. [*Docquet.*]

May 1. Warrant for delivery of stuff to the Earl of Arundel and Visct. Rochester as Knights and Companions of the Garter, for their liveries. [*Docquet.*]

May 2. Londesborough. 67. Earl of Cumberland to Salisbury. Congratulates himself on their late mutual alliance. Has daily experience of his Lordship's care of his son, of himself, &c.

May 2. 68. Sir Wm. Cooke to the Same. Asks his advice about assigning to the Mayor and Aldermen of Gloucester his grant of fines and amerciaments in Dudstone and King's-Barton. They oppose his collection of the fines. [*See April* 23.]

May? 69. Reasons why the Burgesses of Gloucester should not have the issues, fines, &c. of Dudstone and King's-Barton added to their charter; and why they should be added to Sir Wm. Cooke's lease.

Vol. LXIII.

1611.

May 3. Letter to the Lord Treasurer to give orders to the Officers of the Woods at Stowe, Shotover, &c., near Oxford, to deliver certain timber to Sir Thos. Bodley for enlarging the public library at Oxford, which timber was to have been employed for making the Thames navigable to Oxford, but that work does not proceed. [*Docquet.*]

May 3. Grant to Andrew Zinzan, alias Alexander the younger, one of the King's Riders, of pension of 51*l.* per ann. [*Docquet.*]

May 3. Grant to Sir Jas. Fullerton of the office of Surveyor General of all the honors, castles, lands, &c. of the Duke of York, during good behaviour, not to be executed during the Duke's minority, unless he have warrant under the Exchequer Seal. [*Docquet.*]

May 3. Grant to Thos. Huntly of an almsroom in Ely Cathedral. [*Docquet.*]

May 3. Grant to Alex. Redich of redemption of certain manors and lands not named, which he conveyed to the late Queen Elizabeth. [*Docquet.*]

May 3. Grant to Thos. Crafford, on surrender of Chas. Johnson, of the captaincy of the green bulwark of Arch-cliff, Dover, and of the black bulwark on Dover Pier, for life. [*Docquet.*]

May 3. Greenwich. 70. Visct. Fenton to Salisbury. The King will be at Whitehall at 2 o'clock on the morrow, about the matter of the Mint. The letter to the King of Denmark to be despatched.

May [4] 71. The Same to the Same. The King will be at Whitehall at 1 o'clock, instead of 2. The parties are to be there in time, as the King is "unpleasand when he must attend the cumming of uthers."

May 4. 72. Sir Julius Cæsar to the Woodward of Northamptonshire. Order to deliver timber from the forest of Whittlewood, for repair of His Majesty's house at Holdenby.

May 4. Brussels. 73. Wm. Lord Roos to [Salisbury]. Has received honours from the Archduke and Infanta, which he thinks were accorded because of his relationship to his Lordship. Hopes to be in England in a month.

May 4. 74. Examination of Dr. Wm. Bishop, of Brailes, Warwickshire. Particulars of his residence in Rome and France. Professes to oppose the Jesuits, but will not take the oath of allegiance, as Blackwell and others have done, because he wishes to uphold the credit of the secular priests at Rome, and get the English college there out of the hands of the Jesuits.

May 4. Warrant to pay to Rob. Treswell 81*l.* 13*s.* 4*d.*, for repair of the lodge in Pauncill Walk, forest of Barnwood, co. Bucks. [*Warrt. Bk.*, III., *p.* 9.]

May. Docquet of the above. [*Docquet, May* 3.]

VOL. LXIII.

1611.

May 6. 75. Earl of Northumberland to Salisbury. Desires renewal of his lease of a certain corn rent from towns in Tynemouthshire.

May 7. London. 76. Robt. Lord Lisle, Sir Fras. Bacon, and others of the Company of Wireworkers, to the Same. Ask preference as purchasers of the King's wood, to be sold in the Forest of Dean, for the use of their works at Tintern and Whitbrook.

May? 77. Wm. Stallenge to [Salisbury]. Asks warrant for payment of his account for the Irish soldiers, and allowance for going to Gravesend. Has nine pounds of silk spun from the cods. Requests instructions concerning the mulberry garden. Wishes to sell his annuity of 3*s*. 4*d*. per diem. A demand is made on him for impost on pilchards laden at Dartmouth, which he has already paid.

May 7. Warrant to pay to Wm. Stallenge, 258*l*. 2*s*. 5*d*. disbursed by him for mulberry leaves, sweetwood, &c., for His Majesty's silkworms; also 120*l*. per ann. for the same purpose. [*Warrt. Bk.*, III., *p.* 9.]

May 7. Docquet of the above. [*Docquet.*]

May 7. 78. Charges of works, &c. at sundry of His Majesty's houses in April.

May 7. Warrant to pay 100 marks to the Earl of Pembroke, for repair of the old church at Portsmouth, used as a storehouse for ordnance and munition. [*Warrt. Bk.*, III., *p.* 9.]

May 7. Docquet of the above. [*Docquet.*]

May 7. Lease to Humph. Tufton of the King's two parts of the manors of Rickling and Quendon, Essex, and of the King's third part of a messuage, called Sempringham Hed House, parish of St. Sepulchre, London, forfeited by the recusancy of Jas. Wilford. Also two parts of the reversion of the manor and rectory of Lenham, and other lands, co. Kent, on the death of Thomas, father of Jas. Wilford, with certain reservations. [*Docquet.*]

May 7. Grant to Fras. Gould, in reversion after Edm. Masters, of the office of keeper of the King's game near Oatlands. [*Docquet.*]

May 7. Warrant to deliver stuff to the footmen, &c. of the Queen, the Duke of York, and Lady Elizabeth, for their liveries. [*Docquet.*]

May 7. Presentation of Ant. Lapthorne to the rectory of Minchinhampton, co. Gloucester, in the King's hands by the minority of Lord Windsor. [*Docquet.*]

May 7. Grant of pardon to Wm. Bate, indicted twenty years since for practising invocation of spirits for finding treasure, the evidence being found weak, &c. [*Docquet.*]

May 7. Licence to Sir Geo. Chowne, of Oxhenhoath, Kent, to travel. [*Docquet.*]

May 7. Licence to Rich. and Winnifred Bannister to go to Spain. [*Docquet.*]

VOL. LXIII.

1611.

May 7. Grant to John Welford of the benefit of the recusancy of Edw. Lyngen, of Sutton, co. Hereford. [*Docquet.*]

May 7. Grant to seven poor prisoners, long imprisoned, of pardon for certain felonies. [*Docquet.*]

May 7. Warrant for allowance to be made to the farmers of the tonnage and impost of sweet wines, out of the new impost on Spanish wines, on a specified consideration. [*Docquet.*]

May 7. Grant to Thos. Goodridge of an almsroom in the hospital of Ewelme, co. Oxford. [*Docquet.*]

May 7. Grant to Robt. Bridges, on surrender of Robt. Gosnold, of the captaincy of St. Andrew's Castle, co. Hants. [*Docquet.*]

May 7. Grant to Rich. Bingley, on surrender of Sir John Trevor, of the surveyorship of the King's ships. [*Docquet.*]

May 8. Week, Hampshire. 79. Edw. Lord Beauchamp to Salisbury. Begs to understand the ground on which his Lordship has sent complaints of him to his father, and to be allowed to exculpate himself.

May 8. London. 80. Visct. Cranborne to Sir Dud. Carleton. Hopes he will not impute his silence to negligence. There has been a duel between two Scotchmen, Buchanan and Pringle, in which the former fell.

May 8. 81. Note of jewels of the secret jewel house in the Tower remaining with the Queen.

May 10. Grant of new foundation to the Hospital of the Virgin Mary in Newcastle-upon-Tyne. [*Docquet.*]

May 10. Grant to Hen. Browne of a Poor Knight's room at Windsor. [*Docquet.*]

May 10. Grant to Chas. Chambers, Groom of the Queen's Chamber, and Geo. Chambers, his brother, of protection for six months. [*Docquet.*]

May 10. Presentation of Thos. Ashall to the rectory of Edgmond, diocese of Coventry and Lichfield. [*Docquet.*]

May 12. Whitsunday. 82. Sir Hen. Savile to Salisbury. An old gentlewoman having died, the benefit of a lease devolves to Edw. Tredway, a ward committed to his custody by the Earl of Salisbury. Asks directions thereon.

May 13. Greenwich. 83. Sir Rob. Stewart to the Same. Begs him to consider his necessities, which are pressing. His creditors have obliged him to fly to the Court at Greenwich for sanctuary from imprisonment. His debts are a round sum, but he hopes the King will pay them, as he has neither liberty nor means to search out new suits.

VOL. LXIII.

1611.

May 13. Warrant for payment of certain sums out of the Exchequer to the Cofferer of the Household and the Justices of Sessions in North Wales, for diet of the President and Council of Wales, the Receivers General of counties being no longer able to discharge their usual payments, on account of the sale of lands. [*Warrt. Bk.*, III., *p.* 10.]

May. Docquet of the above. [*Docquet, May* 16.]

May 14? Greenwich, Tuesday. 84. Sir Roger Aston to Salisbury. The King will not despatch the ship which brought the deer, before he knows what Salisbury gave for the last that came. Wishes Sir Thos. Lake to send word, that the ship may be despatched.

May 16. Warrant to pay to Sir Wm. Lane, 160*l.* per ann., out of moneys arising from the recusancy of Wm. Copley, of Gatton, co. Surrey; also 50*l.* for his expenses in prosecuting the same. [*Warrt. Bk.*, III., *p.* 11.]

May 16. Docquet of the above.

May 16. Warrant to pay to John Terry 200*l.* for two garters given by the King to the Earls of Arundel and Rochester, now chosen Knights of the Garter. [*Warrt. Bk.*, III., *p.* 16.]

May 16. Docquet of the above.

May 16. Warrant to pay 161*l.* 19*s.* 2*d.* to Thos. Woodward, Mercer, for stuffs for the Queen. [*Warrt. Bk.*, III., *p.* 19.]

May 16. Docquet of the above.

May 16. Grant to Simon Harvey of pension of 200*l.* per ann., on surrender of a like pension by Sir John Hume. [*Docquet.*]

May 16. Royal Assent for Dr. John King, elected Bishop of London. [*Docquet.*]

May 16. Warrant for payment of 200*l.*, to Sir Gerard Harvey and Geo. Blondell, in consideration of their present payment of 2,000*l.* into the Court of Wards and Liveries, not due before March 20 ensuing. [*Docquet.*]

May 16. Commission for Rich. St. George, alias Norroy King-at-Arms for the North beyond Trent, to visit all the parts of that province belonging to his office, for reform of abuses appertaining to arms. [*Docquet.*]

May 16. Grant to Arch. Armstrong of pension of 2*s.* per diem during pleasure. [*Docquet.*]

May 16. Instalment of 2,682*l.* 12*s.* 2*d.*, the first fruits of the Archbishopric of Canterbury, for Geo. Abbot, late Bp. of London, now elected Archbishop, to be paid in four years, the tenths being deducted. [*Docquet.*]

VOL. LXIII.

1611.

May 16. Grant to Edw. Stubb, of Buxton, co. Norfolk, of the remainder, now vested in the Crown, of certain manors, rectories, and tithes, in Buxton, &c., co. Norfolk, of which he is tenant in tail. [*Docquet.*]

May 16. Licence to Thos. Mildmay, of Moulsham, co. Essex, to travel for three years. [*Docquet.*]

May 16. Grant to Hen. Lord Herbert, Hen. Poole, and Geo. Huntley, of coppices in the Forest of Dean, co. Gloucester, with leave to cut them down for charcoal for making iron, &c. [*Docquet.*]

May 16. Grant to Sir Thos. Tracy of the benefit of the recusancy of Katherine Reade, co. Gloucester. [*Docquet.*]

May 16. Grant to Case Surley of the benefit of the recusancy of Elizabeth Blackwell. [*Docquet.*]

May 17. 85. Estimate by Inigo Jones and others of the charge of piling, planking, and brickwork for the three islands (aits) at Richmond.

May 17. Westminster. Proclamation that merchandise conveyed between England and Scotland shall pass through Berwick or some known port, and there pay duty, according to the Statute of 22 Edw. IV. Printed. [*Proc. Bk., p.* 240.]

May 17. Basswell Park. 86. Edw. Mar. Knight [a pseudonym] to Salisbury. Commends the secrecy and fidelity of the bearer, who will acquaint his Lordship with what has been done in the matter required. Indorsed "Brought to my Lord Chamberlain by a woman, and sent to my Lord, Sept. 3rd."

May 18. Sandal Hall. 87. Will. Whor. [a pseudonym] to the Same. Of the same tenor as the preceding, and similarly indorsed. [*These two letters are in the same handwriting.*]

May 18. Hatfield. 88. John Dackombe to the Same. The cottagers of Hatfield have agreed to the improvement of Hatfield Wood, and the Commissioners will that day stake out his Lordship's ground; wherefore he postpones an engagement to attend Justice Walmsley about Bermondsey. *Incloses,*

88. I. *Report to Salisbury of the exact state of the building at Hatfield. May* 17.

May 18. Greenwich. Proclamation against melting or conveying out of the King's dominions gold or silver coin. Printed. [*Proc. Coll., No.* 17.]

May 19. Cowdry. 89. Ant. Visct. Montague to Salisbury. Thanks for many past favours; submits to his Lordship's pleasure in reference to the course taken for his estate.

May 20. 90. Jas. Lord Hay to the Same. The King has resolved to present to M. de Vitry, with his own hand, a ring worth 1,000 French crowns.

Vol. LXIII.

1611.

May 21. Winestead. 91. Sir Chris. Hildyard to Salisbury. Prays to be discharged of the remainder of a debt claimed from him for a sum falsely alleged to have been received by Sir Chris. Hildyard, his uncle, when High Sheriff of Yorkshire, from the goods of certain recusants.

May 21. Warrant for payment of 8,000*l.*, by instalments, to the Mayor, Bailiffs, and Burgesses of Berwick, for building a stone bridge there. [*Warrt. Bk.*, III., *p.* 12.]

May 21. Docquet of the above. [*Docquet.*]

May 21. Grant to John Rowdon of an annuity of 50*l.*, on payment of 250*l.* to Sir Jas. Sempill and Sir Jas. Creichton, in part compensation for their relinquishment to the King of a rent of 200*l.* per ann., payable by the O'Ferrols and other freeholders of Annally, Ireland. [*Docquet.*]

May 21. Similar grants to Thos. Pemble and Robt. Hassard of annuities of 50*l.*, and to Wm. Snelling of 100*l.*, on like considerations. [*Docquet.*]

May 21. Licence to John Pory to travel for three years. [*Docquet.*]

May 21. Patent to Rich. Dike, Matthias Fowler, Hum. Phipps, and John Dade, for the sole making of gold and silver thread, commonly called Venice gold and silver. [*Docquet.*]

May 21. Letter to the Bishop of Winchester, Visitor of St. John's College, Oxford, for Dr. Laud to be President of the said College. [*Docquet.*]

May 21. Grant to Sir John Brook of an annuity of 200*l.* for life, at the nomination of the Earl of Dunfermline, Chancellor of Scotland, on surrender of an annuity of 400*l.* heretofore granted to the Earl. The other 200*l.* to be granted to Lady Burlacy. [*Docquet. See May* 23.]

May 23. Lease to Sir John Stafford, Gentleman Pensioner, of tenements, gardens, &c., parcel of the old palace of Westminster. [*Docquet.*]

May 23. Grant, with survivorship, to Hum. May, Groom of the Bedchamber, and Jane, his wife, of pension of 16*s.* per diem. [*Docquet.*]

May 23. Grant to Lewis Macklock, of pardon for burglary, committed 16 years since, in the house of Robt. Bradshaw, Leicestershire. [*Docquet.*]

May 23. Grant to Thos. Brugg and his heirs of the King's reversion of lands and tenements in East Ham and West Ham, co. Essex, and of a messuage in Candlewick Street, near Eastcheap, London, improperly conveyed to the Crown by Wymond Brugg, brother of Thos. Brugg. [*Docquet.*]

May 23. Remission to John Blount of part of the punishments imposed on him by the Star Chamber, for counterfeiting a letter and forging a bond. [*Docquet.*]

VOL. LXIII.

1611.

May 23. Grant to Lady Burlacy of an annuity of 333*l.* 6*s.* 8*d.* on surrender of two several annuities granted to the Earl of Dunfermline and Sir Alex. Hay. [*Docquet. See May* 21.]

May 23. Grant to Edm. Haworth of two messuages and lands in Nether Darwen, co. Lancaster, lately belonging to Giles Haworth, attainted for murder. [*Docquet.*]

May 23. Grant, with survivorship, to Fras. Poulton and Edw. Hobson, on surrender by Wm. Duck, sen. and jun., of the keeping of the King's game about Hampton Court, Hounslow Heath, and places adjacent. [*Docquet.*]

May 23. Patent to Dr. Dan. Selme and Hen. Briggs, of their invention for refining lead and extracting silver therefrom, and for draining lead ores and mines, paying to the King 100*l.* per annum. [*Docquet.*]

May 24. Bishop's Auckland. 92. Bishop of Durham to Salisbury. The 300*l.* appointed from the tenths for Berwick shall be ready, and also his half-year's pay of 44*l.*, though he could have wished moneys to be left in his hands towards Lady Arabella's charges. States the payments he has already made from his diocese. Desires the passing in form of a warrant dormant granted him by the King, for venison in all His Majesty's parks. *Incloses,*

92. I. *Memoranda of the occasion of the payment of a pension of 880l. to Berwick by the Bishops of Durham, with reasons why the same should now cease.*

May 25. Berwick. 93. Geo. Nicholson to the Same. General complaints about the reduction of the pay at Berwick. The 400*l.* assigned to him from the customers at Newcastle, and the 300*l.* from the Bishop of Durham, are not yet paid.

May 25. Greenwich. 94. Sir Robt. Stewart to the Same. Solicits his favour in the cause of the poor men of the hospital of Bedford, to be heard before the Lord Chief Baron.

May 25. Warrant to the Lord Treasurer to discharge the garrison or band of 100 at Berwick, and reduce them to half-pay, from Midsummer ensuing; Sir Wm. Bowyer, their captain, and other officers, to be provided for at pleasure. Also to supply the place of the Commissary of Musters. [*Warrt. Bk.*, III., *p.* 12.]

May 25. Docquet of the above. [*Docquet.*]

May 25. 95. Authority from the Mayor of Canterbury to Wm. Reade, to receive 500 French crowns, which M. de Vitry promised to pay for damage done by fire to the postmaster's stables at Canterbury, hired by him for his horses.

VOL. LXIII.

1611.

May 27. York. 96. Sir Chas. Hales and Sir Wm. Gee to Salisbury. Send up by the Pursuivant, as required, Alex. Blair, a Scotch prisoner.

May 27. 97. Bond of Edm. Porter and Edm. Page, alias Wheller, both of Mickleton, co. Gloucester, under penalty of 20*l.*, to pay 11*l.* to Thos. Freeman, of Duncote, Worcestershire.

May 27. Grant to Wm. Ramsay of 600*l.* as a gift, to be paid from forfeitures in the Exchequer. [*Warrt. Bk.*, III., *p.* 11.]

May. Docquet of the above. [*Docquet, May* 28.]

May 27. Warrant to pay to the Earl of Mar 15,000*l.* purchase money, to be paid into the Exchequer by Wm. Lord Cavendish for His Majesty's manors of Hundon and Chipley, co. Suffolk, surrendered by the Earl of Mar. [*Warrt. Bk.*, III., *p.* 14.]

May 27. Warrant to pay to Sir John Spilman 5,781*l.* 17*s.* 5½*d.*, for jewels and work done for the King, from Feb. 29, 1608, until Jan. 1, 1610. [*Ibid.*, *p.* 14.]

May 27. Docquet of the above.

May 27. Warrants for payment of wages and allowances to Jas. Rotherford, Thos. Duckworth, and Wm. Shortis, grooms of the Lady Elizabeth. [*Docquet.*]

May 27. Grant of conveyance to Lord Cavendish and his heirs, on payment of 15,000*l.*, of the manor of Hundon, the manor or abbey of Chipley, and Culverdon Grove, co. Suffolk, heretofore granted to the Earl of Mar and his heirs, with licence to keep two yearly fairs, &c. [*Docquet.*]

May 27. Grant to Lord Cavendish and his heirs of authority to enter the manors above mentioned, by virtue of Letters Patent and fine. [*Docquet.*]

May 27. Warrant for delivery of one or more tallies to Lord Cavendish, on payment by him of 15,000*l.* in consideration of the surrender of the manors aforesaid by the Earl of Mar. [*Docquet.*]

May 27. Warrant dormant to pay to Thos. Sibson, master of the Lady Elizabeth's barge, 20 marks per ann. for wages. [*Docquet.*]

May 27. Grant to Rich. Widmer, on surrender of Rich. Trestean, of the office of Serjeant-at-Arms. [*Docquet.*]

May 28. Londesborough. 98. Earl of Cumberland to Salisbury. On complaints made by Lord Burleigh's tenants of the manor of Ross, about the sewers in Holderness, will endeavour to have them rectified the first opportunity. Imperfect.

VOL. LXIII.

1611.

May 28. Londesborough. 99. Earl of Cumberland to Salisbury. Murder of an Englishman by Scottish Borderers. Has written to the Chancellor of Scotland for their apprehension. *Incloses,*

99. I. *Sir Wm. Fenwick to the Earl of Cumberland. An inroad of 70 armed Scots, Elliotts, Armstrongs, and others, attacked Lionel Robson's house in Leaplish, and shot him and several others."* *May 26, Bellingham in Teviotdale. Incloses,*

99. II. *Lists of the slain and wounded, and of divers offenders in the above attack.*

May 28. Grant, with survivorship, to Thos. Morrison and Christ. Wyvill, of the office of Reader of the Law Lecture in the University of Cambridge, on surrender of Dr. Cowell. [*Docquet.*]

May 28. Grant to Lord Sheffield of an annuity of 1,000*l.* per annum, for 13 years, on surrender of a like annuity for 10 years. [*Docquet.*]

May 28. Warrant to Lord Carew, Master of the Ordnance, for delivery of ordnance to Sir Thos. Waller, Captain of Dover Castle, and other captains of castles and bulwarks belonging to the Cinque Ports. [*Docquet.*]

May 29. Calais. 100. M. de la Barre to the Mayor of Canterbury. The Sieur de Vitry will not break his engagement to pay 2,000 crowns for the postmaster's stable, burnt at Canterbury, although the King says he need not pay it. French.

May 28. 101. Advertisements respecting Berwick, powder spent, munition sold, men in pay dead, men entered contrary to the establishment, &c.

May 30. Berwick. 102. Sir Wm. Bowyer to Salisbury. Discontent of the garrison of Berwick at their discharge. Their ill speeches of him, &c. They threaten to come to town to remonstrate. Understands his Lordship is angry with him. Requests protection against the threatened revenge of some of the garrison. Deprecates his displeasure, and apologizes for his long letters, which he fears have offended.

May 30. Berwick. 103. Mayor, &c. of Berwick to the Same. Promise divers privileges to the discharged soldiers, to enable them to provide for themselves. Thanks that the Mayor of Berwick is appointed to govern the town, as in the boroughs of England.

May 30. Warrant to pay to John Murray, Keeper of the Privy Purse, 500*l.*, to be disbursed according to His Majesty's direction. [*Warrt. Bk.*, III., *p.* 14.]

May. Docquet of the above. [*Docquet, May* 31.]

May 30. 104. Thos. Bellott to Salisbury. Solicits employment, &c.

VOL. LXIII.

1611.

May 31. 105. Petition of the inhabitants of Fotheringay, co. Northampton to Salisbury, against Thos. Lindsell, who greatly neglected the office of schoolmaster there, and appointed Barth. Elam in his place, but again intruded himself. Pray that Elam may be confirmed in the place. With reference and replies thereon.

May 31. Whitehall. Proclamation that the oath of allegiance be administered according to the laws. Printed. [*Proc. Coll., No.* 18.]

May 31. 106. Warrant for certain payments to Lord Carew, Vice Chamberlain to the Queen, for his expenses to and from Ireland, whither he is about to be sent by the King.

May 31. Grant to John Bassett of pardon for manslaughter of Sam. Beswick, in consideration of 60*l.* paid by Bassett to the widow of the deceased. [*Docquet.*]

May 31. Grant to Robt. Grayne of the office of Keeper of the King's House at Royston. [*Docquet.*]

May 31. Grant to Wm. Sanders of an almsroom in St. Stephen's, Westminster. [*Docquet.*]

May 31. Licence to Sir Robt. Wroth to enclose Benhold Wood, in Bradfield, and 300 acres of land, in Finchingfield, Shalford, and Great Bradfield, co. Essex, to join them to the Great Park there, and use them as a free park, with liberty of park and warren. [*Docquet.*]

May. 107. C. Bucke to the Same. Requests letters in his behalf to the Deputy Lieutenants of Herefordshire, to admit him Muster Master in that county.

May ? 108. Elizabeth Lady Southwell to Salisbury. Begs him to stand godfather to her daughter.

May ? 109. Lodowick Briskett to the Same. Is reduced to great distress, and disappointed of the help he expected from Lord Rochester. His calamity in his unfortunate employment abroad was a forerunner of those at home. Has had an interview with the King at Hampton Court.

May. 110. Monthly account of the fees of the Clerks of the Signet.

May ? 111. Edw. Reynoldes' memorial to the Court [of Common Pleas ?] as to the disposal of a bequest of his late wife, Catherine, to the poor kindred of John Mills, her first husband.

May ? 112. Computation of the decrease in expense of the establishment at Berwick now to be made, as compared with that made in Sept. 1607.

May ? 113. Account of the stipend allowed to the dissolved garrison at Berwick.

May ? 114. Memoranda relating to Berwick. The palace to be delivered to lodge the garrison in. A victualler robbed, and a house set on fire. Clarke and Boothe discontented.

VOL. LXIV. JUNE, 1611.

1611

June 1. Berwick. 1. Geo. Nicholson to Salisbury. Grief of the soldiers on hearing the letters read for the reduction of their pay. Implores, on their behalf, that they may have 5*d.* per day. Also that two put into the hundred by the Earl of Dunbar may be allowed to stand, for his sake.

June 2. Londesborough. 2. Earl of Cumberland to the Same. Five Northumberland men have been with him, who say they were the parties wronged by the Elliots and Armstrongs. Divers of the Grahams banished to Ireland have returned into Scotland. The officers of the Countess Dowager (of Cumberland) have done great spoil in the woods of Whinfield, &c.

June 4. 3. Sir Wm. Monson to the Same. Gives an account of certain gentlemen, associates of Wm. Seymour, and of a young gentleman and a gentlewoman who passed Blackwall in boats, and were taken on board a French bark, and sailed for Calais. Has sent to pursue them. Indorsed "Sir Wm. Monson certifying what he found by examination of certain watermen concerning the Lady Arabella and Wm. Seymour's escape."

June 4. Greenwich. Proclamation concerning the Lady Arabella and Wm. Seymour, forbidding any person to harbour or assist them. Printed. [*Proc. Bk.*, *p.* 244.]

June 4. Grant to the Lord Treasurer of the lands lately belonging to Chas. Brook. [*Docquet.*]

June 4. Discharge to the Mayor and Corporation of York of 200*l.* due to Queen Elizabeth for subsidies; also of 50*l.* due for one fifteenth granted last Parliament. [*Docquet.*]

June 4. Grant to Sir Rich. Molyneux of the office of Butler in the county palatine of Lancaster, for life, upon surrender of a former patent during pleasure. [*Docquet.*]

June 4. Grant to Rich. Rice of the benefit of the recusancy of Geo. Throgmorton, Elizabeth Fitzhughes of Walcall, and John Ashfield of Hethropp. [*Docquet.*]

June 4. Warrant for Lord Hay to have process for collecting 1,500*l.* of debts due to the Crown, to complete his first grant of 10,000*l.* [*Docquet.*]

June 4. Commission for the Archbp. of Canterbury, the Lord Treasurer, and others, to determine certain causes of dilapidations between the Bishop of Ely, and Alice, widow of Martin Heton, late Bishop there. [*Docquet.*]

June 4. Grant to Hen. Chapman, of Sussex, of pardon for murder. [*Docquet.*]

June 5. 4. Earl of Nottingham to Salisbury. The wind being east and by south and south-east four days past, the fugitives [Lady Arabella and Wm. Seymour] cannot be past the Downs or Margate. Thinks it would be best to take little notice of their escape.

Vol. LXIV.

1611.

June 5. 5. Sir Wm. Waad, Lieutenant of the Tower, to Salisbury. Lady Arabella came to Blackwall in man's disguise, took boat, and went on board a French vessel below Lee, with several attendants.

June 5. 6. Visct. Fenton to the Same. Returns the proclamation. A post to be directed to Calais with all speed, and letters to be written to France for arrest of the fugitives.

June 5. Greenwich. 7. The Same to the Same. The King has heard that the Earl of Hertford is dead; if not, he is to be sent for. Mr. Rodney's movements to be examined into. The French Ambassador to be requested to learn who they were that dealt for the boat in which the Lady [Arabella] and her husband are gone, &c.

June 5. 8. Fras. Seymour to his Grandmother the Countess of Hertford. It is uncertain what has become of the fugitives; they will be utterly undone. Is confined to his lodging on suspicion of aiding them, but is as innocent as a child born yesterday.

June 5. Greenwich. 9. Visct. Haddington to Salisbury. Requests fulfilment of a promise made to Hodgson, Lieutenant of Berwick, by the late Earl of Dunbar, that he should have 5*s.* per diem for his services, &c.

June 5. Richmond, Wednesday. 10. Adam Newton to the Same. The Spanish Ambassador waits on the Prince that afternoon. The King hopes the fugitives have left no tail behind. Asks any new intelligence of them. Requests delay in a payment due from Sir Hen. Carey for land bought of His Majesty, as the Prince is bargaining with him for Berkhampstead.

June 5. Cambridge. 11. Vice Chancellor, &c. of Cambridge to Salisbury, their Chancellor. Thanks for his submitting to them the draft of the new charter solicited by the town of Cambridge. The enlargement of privileges sued for by the town is incompatible with their privileges. Wish to renew the University charter at the same time with that of the town.

June 6? 12. Sir Theodore de Mayerne to [Sir Thos.] Windebank. Is hindered from completing his business by the ill health of the Treasurer. Asks what ceremonies there are on taking the oath. Hopes there will be no expense thereon, his patent having cost enough already.

June 7. Greenwich, Friday. 13. Visct. Fenton to the Same. The King desires Sir Thos. Lake to bring the oath that Mons. Mayerne or Turquet should make, and he will rectify it, &c.

June 7. 14. Thos. Lord Arundel to the Same. Has been unable to obtain the twenty marks of land assigned to him in lieu of 460*l.* paid to Sir Walter Cope, the chantry lands being in the hands of contractors; begs to have the land elsewhere or his money returned.

June 7. 15. Charges of works, &c. at sundry of His Majesty's houses in May.

June 7. Bugden. 16. Wm. Barlow, Bishop of Lincoln, to Salisbury. Recommends the petition of Thos. Stirrop, his tenant of the parsonage of Bardney, Lincolnshire. It concerns God's right, and the Bishop's, great portion of the tithe being withheld.

1611. Vol. LXIV.

June 7. Grant to the Company of Vintners of a new charter enlarging their liberties. [*Docquet.*]

June 7. Grant to the Earl of Southampton of an annuity of 2,000*l.* out of the customs on sweet wines. [*Docquet.*]

June 7. Demise to Wm. Earl of Pembroke of the manor, town, and castle of St. Briavell's, Forest of Dean. [*Docquet.*]

June 8. Berwick. 17. Geo. Nicholson to Salisbury. The old soldiers intended to send a deputation to London, but Sir Wm. Bowyer persuaded them to petition instead. Desires that Sir Ralph Gray and Sir Wm. Selby may be present at the muster and discharge at Midsummer, and have power to take the oaths of all there.

June 8. 18. Geo. Marshall to the Same. For leave to make over to Sir Wm. Bowyer his surety bonds for 800*l.*, given by the King in behalf of Sir Robt. Stewart.

June 8? 19. Petition of the founders of brass ordnance to the Same. For a warrant necessary to confirm the increase of allowance for casting brass ordnance, granted them by Lord Carew. *Inclose,*

19. I. *Petition of the Same to Lord Carew, for increase of allowance on account of the increased price of provisions. With his reference to the officers of ordnance, and their recommendation thereof. June* 8.

June 8. Westminster. 20. Warrant to draw out a grant of augmentation of arms and supporters to Robt. Carr, Visct. Rochester.

June. Docquet of the above. [*Docquet, June* 7.]

June 8. Grant to Edw. Forsett of the manor of Tyburn, co. Middlesex. [*Docquet.*]

June 8. Grant to Fras. Burges, on surrender of Thos. Hamilton, of pension of 20*l.* per ann. [*Docquet.*]

June 8. Warrant for the Lord Treasurer to appoint Commissioners to survey the arms, munition, &c. in the Tower, or any other place appertaining to the office of Master of the Armoury, lately in custody of Sir Hen. Lee, deceased, and to deliver the inventory to Sir Thos. Monson, now Master of the Armoury. [*See Docquet.*]

June 8. Letter to the President of the Council at York, requiring him to admit Sir Wm. Bamburgh and Sir John Bourchier to be of the Council there. [*Docquet.*]

June 8. Grant of new foundation to the Hospital of St. Mary Magdalen, Newcastle-on-Tyne. [*Docquet.*]

June 9. 21. Lady Eliz. Lumley to Salisbury. Her brother [Lord Darcy] has sent his Lordship from Italy a marble table, with a head of Ferdinando, late Duke of Tuscany.

VOL. LXIV.

1611.

June 9. Fleet [Prison]. 22. Thos. Felton to Salisbury. Fears his Lordship is displeased with his accusations against Hen. Spiller. If he desire it, will forbear them for ever, though much wronged by Spiller, ever since he had charge of the dangerous service against recusants. Will relinquish all other recompence for confirmation of that granted him by the late Queen. Begs his freedom, his debt being paid out of his allowance.

[June 9.] Sunday. 23. Earl of Northampton to the King. Abstract of discoveries relative to the Lady Arabella's escape. Lady Shrewsbury was the only contriver of her "bedlam opposition" to the King, and her purse the only instrument of her escape, she having given Lady Arabella 850*l.* for some things which she had, belonging to the Queen of Scots. Much mystery in it, being confined to persons that will rather die than discover one another. All except needful preparations left till it was seen how she would be received by foreign powers. Probabilities that Lady Shrewsbury will deny all complicity. Lady Arabella dares not clear her by oath, though she clears all foreign Princes. Discreet reply of Visct. Rochester to Lady Arabella, &c.

June 10. Greenwich. Monday. 24. Visct. Fenton to Salisbury. The King desires his attention to the despatch of Lord Carew to Ireland, to the affair of the baronets, and to the order for settling the Household.

June 10. 25. Thos. Phelippes to the Same. Thanks for former composition of his debt. Beseeches leave to petition his Lordship in reference to his accounts. Thinks they ought to be discharged by Sir Sam. Saltonstall, who now holds his office, though his own patent still stands in force.

June 10. Grant to Hen. Mainwaring, on surrender of Robt. Gosnold, of the reversion, after Wm. Christmas, of the office of Captain of St. Andrew's Castle, co. Hants. [*Docquet.*]

June 10. Grant to Thos. Eldred and Wm. Whitmore, of certain manors, lands, and rents, of the value of 354*l.* 6*s.* 10¾*d.* per ann. [*Docquet.*]

June 10. Grant to Chris. Fletcher and Thos. Gosnoll, on payment of 60*l.* by the Earl and Countess of Derby, of the King's remainder of the manor of Blagdon, co. Somerset, expectant after an estate tail. [*Docquet, June* 10 *and June* 15.]

June 10. Letter to the Vice Chancellor and Heads of Colleges, Cambridge, to admit Leonard Mawe, Fellow of Peter House, to be Doctor in Divinity, dispensing with the Statutes by virtue of the King's prerogative, although he has not taken his degree of Bachelor. [*Docquet.*]

June 10. Warrant to the Earl of Worcester to admit John Rowell, one of the King's coachmen, to attend the Lady Elizabeth. [*Docquet.*]

June 10. Letter to the Same to order that the allowance of liveries for certain horses and nags and for the feeding of horses for the use of the Duke of York and his servants be entered in the office of the Avery. [*Docquet.*]

1611. Vol. LXIV.

June 10. Warrant for delivery of stuff, for their coats and livery, to the footmen of the King, Queen, Lady Elizabeth, and the Duke of York, and to the grooms of their litters and coaches. [*Docquet.*]

June 11. 26. Sir Wm. Waad to Salisbury. Sends Reeves' declaration. Lady [Arabella] wishes Lady Chaworth to be with her. There is a report that Mr. Seymour landed at Ipswich, and took shipping again the next day, &c.

June 12. 27. Gervase Lord Clifton to the King. Has bestowed his daughter in marriage according to His Majesty's command. Prays that it may not be to his destruction, in consequence of the fraudulent proceedings of the Duke [of Lenox] and Lord Aubigny, which are detailed.

June 12? 28. "Statement for the Lord Treasurer" of the unjust conduct of [Gervase] Lord Clifton towards the Duke [of Lenox], in getting the Duke's lands into his hands, on occasion of the marriage of the Duke's brother, Lord Aubigny, with Catherine, daughter of Lord Clifton.

June 12. Lupton. 29. Sir Edw. Seymour to Salisbury. Solicits a grant of the wardship of his son-in-law, Mr. Parker. Thanks for his Lordship's deeming him worthy to be ranked in the order of baronets, intended for none but the well-deserving, &c.

June 12. Berwick. 30. Sir Wm. Bowyer to the Same. Has heard of the escape of the Lady Arabella. Caused John Bright to be examined, he having been asked to receive on board his ship some suspicious persons, and take them to Calais. Also respecting Nicholson, and the pay and discharge of the garrison, slanders against himself, &c. *Incloses,*

30. I. *Examination of John Bright, Master of the Thomas, of Lynn. Descriptions of three men and two women, in two wherries, who hailed him while at anchor in the road of Lee, and offered him any money to take them to Calais. On his refusal, they asked him to direct them to a French ship, on board of which they went. June 12, Berwick.*

June 12. Berwick. 31. Mayor, &c. of Berwick to the Same. Have offered their services to Sir Wm. Bowyer for his protection, but it appeared there was no cause for him to fear, as the soldiers were very peaceable and downcast.

June 12. Warrant to pay to Jacob Harderet, jeweller, 926*l.*, for a chain for the Lady Elizabeth. [*Warrt. Bk.*, III., *p.* 27.]

June 12. Docquet of the above.

June 12. Grant to the city of Lincoln of foundation of an hospital, to be called "The Hospital of Jesus Christ," founded by Rich. Smith, doctor of physic. [*Docquet.*]

VOL. LXIV.

1611.

June 12. Grant to Visct. Rochester of the office of Keeper of Westminster Palace for life. [*Docquet.*]

June 12. Grant to Chas. Chambers of the goods and chattels of Margaret Langford, recusant, co. Derby, and demise to him of the King's two parts in the manor of Langford, at a reserved rent. [*Docquet.*]

June 12. Presentation of Wm. Murray to the rectory of the parish church of Lanivet, Cornwall. [*Docquet.*]

June 12. Confirmation to the Lord Treasurer and Chancellor of the Exchequer of a contract between them and certain contractors for cords of wood and tons of timber. [*Docquet.*]

June. 12. Grant to Sir Wm. Cornwallis of the forfeited recognizance of 500*l.*, acknowledged by Sir Phil. Stanhope, Geo. Wakelyn, and Robt. Steynton, for the personal appearance of Sir Philip at the ensuing Assizes at Derby, and for his keeping the peace towards Walter Ferrers. [*Docquet.*]

June 12. Grant to Thos. Garland, Yeoman of the Stirrup, of 967*l.* 10*s.* old debts due to the Crown. [*Docquet.*]

June 12. Grant in reversion to Thos. Juett of a Gunner's place in the Tower. [*Docquet*]

June 12. Paris. 32. Hen. Lord Clifford to Salisbury. Recommends the bearer [Mr. Puckering ?], who has been his associate at the Academy, as a fit person for the dignity of a baronet.

June 13. Fleet Prison. 33. Sir Jas. Croft to the Same. Solicits his enlargement, being wholly innocent of the escape of Lady Arabella. Trusts he may not lose the King's favour and the reward of 36 years' service.

June 13. 34. Order of the Court of Exchequer that on account of the villainous extortions of Rich. Heaton, in pursuing His Majesty's subjects as recusants who were not, and unjustly obtaining money from them for his own use, the gaoler of the Fleet do no more permit him to go abroad, but keep him close prisoner.

June 14. 35. Thos. Bilson, Bishop of Winchester, to the King. Illegal methods pursued in the election of Dr. Laud as President of St. John's College, Oxford.

June ? 36. The King to the Bishop of Winchester. Asks whether the illegality in Dr. Laud's election proceeded from faction or misconstruction of the Statutes. The counsel on both parties are to be re-heard for a final decision.

June 14. Clitheroe. 37. Sir Rich. Molyneux and Sir Ralph Ashton to Salisbury. Unwillingness of the tenants of Clitheroe, Lancashire, to compound for their copyhold estates. Juries are ordered to make a strict survey thereof, by which means it is expected they will soon desire composition.

June 15. 38. Sir Thos. Shirley to the Same. Requests further stay of process against him, for his debt to the Crown.

VOL. LXIV.

1611.

June 15. 39. Note of gifts to the servants of the Archbp. of Canterbury by Drs. Thompson and Buckeridge, Bps. of Gloucester and Rochester, at their consecration, June 1, and by the Countess of Shrewsbury, June 15.

June 15. Grant to John Persall of the benefit of the recusancy of John Draycot, co. Stafford. [*Docquet.*]

June 15. Grant to Theodore de Mayerne, Physician in Ordinary, of pension of 400*l.* [*Docquet.*]

June 15. Grant to Margaret Elburgh de Boetzler, wife of the above, of annuity of 200*l.* after his decease. [*Docquet.*]

June 15. Holyrood House. 40. Earl of Dunfermline to Salisbury. Thanks for intelligence of the escape and re-capture of Lady Arabella. Complains of the postmaster's delay in conveyance of packets; they have been six days in passing, although three or four might suffice.

June 16. 41. Sir John Bourchier to the Same. Complains of a fraud by Churchill in a sale to him of the manor of the Rock, which is indebted to the King for 1,000*l.* Offers to pay the debt by degrees, if he may retain the land.

June 16. Westminster. 42. E. Reynoldes to Fras. Mills. Private affairs. Glad that Sir Thos. Clerk joins with them in their motion to Mr. Allington for reformation [in the Privy Seal Office].

June 16. Whitehall. 43. Sir Julius Cæsar to the Clerk of the Pipe [Sir Art. Mainwaring]. To rectify a defective grant to John Eldred and Wm. Whitmore, of Shute Grange, Brixton, Isle of Wight. [*See* 1611, *Nov.* 26.] *Annexed is*,

43. I. *Particulars of Shute Grange above alluded to, with order from the Earl of Salisbury and other Commissioners for a lease of it to be made to Thos. Loviband, of Gatcomb, Isle of Wight, in reversion after Wm. and Geo. Jackman, as part of the* 2,000*l. granted to Eldred and other contractors.*

June 17. London. 44. Sir Thos. Dutton to Salisbury. Begs favour for his offence in killing his foe in self-defence. If he has offended General Cecil, the loss of the King's favour, and of his company in the States, has punished him.

June 17. Grant to the Earl of Northampton, in fee simple, of a parcel of waste ground in Greenwich, and of the moiety of a ditch adjacent to his mansion about Whitehall. [*Docquet.*]

June 17. Grant to Ant. Knyvet of certain silver ore which came out of Scotland, as a free gift. [*Docquet.*]

June 17. Order to spare the game for three years in the Forest of Lyfield Park and Beamont. [*Docquet.*]

VOL. LXIV.

1611.

June 17. Grant to Sir Wm. Button of the reversion of two farms called Gate and Glossoms, co. Sussex, escheated by attainder of Thos. Abington, but concealed. [*Docquet.*]

June 17. Licence to Thos. Sutton to erect an hospital in the Charter House, East Smithfield, to be called "The Hospital of King James, &c." [*Docquet.*]

June 17. Letter to the Contractors for Leases to pass to Sir Wm. Godolphin certain lands called Crabes Cattle, co. Norfolk. [*Docquet.*]

June 17. Grant to Sir Edw. Greville of the benefit of the recusancy of Thomasine Greville, of Zeazencott, co. Gloucester, Frances Witchcombe, of Bucklebury, co. Berks, and Sir Richard and Dame Dorothy White. [*Docquet.*]

June 17. Letter to Queen's College, Cambridge, for Dr. Meriton to be chosen Master instead of Dr. [Humphrey] Tyndall, deceased. [*Docquet.*]

June ? 45. Petition of John Errington, of Bewfront, Northumberland, to Salisbury. Prays protection against Sir John Fenwick, who has forcibly dispossessed him of a lead mine in Fallowfield, on pretence that it belongs to the King. With order thereon by Baron Altham.

June 18. 46. Petition of the Same to the Same, to be reinstated in possession of the lead mine above mentioned, discovered on his freehold at Fallowfield in Northumberland. With order thereon.

June 18. Warrant to the Officers of the Exchequer to pay 100*l.* per ann. to Sir Rich. Lewkenor, Chief Justice of Chester, and 20*l.* per ann. to him and Sir Hen. Townshend, his associate, for their diet, and for holding the Great Sessions at Chester; the Receiver of Chester being no longer able to pay the same, by reason of the grant of the Earldom and County Palatine of Chester to the Prince of Wales, and the sale of lands there. [*Warrt. Bk.*, III., *p.* 16.]

June. Docquet of the above. [*Docquet, June* 17.]

June 18. Warrant for payment of certain sums to Lord Carew and others for repairs of Castle Cornet, Guernsey, and St. Andrews, Southsea, and Hurst Castles, co. Hants; two lodges in Waltham Forest, and the fences of Finchley Walk in Chute Forest. [*Warrt. Bk.*, III., *p.* 15.]

June. Docquet of the above. [*Docquet, June* 17.]

June? 47. Petition of Rich. Withers, the Queen's Yeoman of the Bows and Keeper of the Forest of Dowles, to Salisbury. To order Mr. Norden to proceed with the repair of the Lodge of Dowles, as he has done with that of Chute.

June 18. Warrant for payment of 200*l.* to Dr. Theodore Mayerne for charges in removing himself and family out of France. [*Warrt. Bk.*, III., *p.* 15.]

June. Docquet of the above. [*Docquet, June* 17.]

1611. Vol. LXIV.

June 18. Grant to Sir Rich. Hussey and his heirs, of a remainder of lands and tenements, co. Montgomery, fraudulently conveyed to the King and his heirs by Robt. Lloyd and his wife, with purpose to prevent Godfrey Lewis from disposing of the same, &c. [*Docquet.*]

June 18. Letter to Sir Ralph Gray and Sir Wm. Selby, directing them to repair to Berwick, and, with Sir Wm. Bowyer and Geo. Nicholson, to assemble the garrison, and communicate to them that they are discharged by the King, with a grant of half their wages. [*Docquet.*]

June 18. Grant to Wm. and Elizabeth Snelling of pension of 60*l.* per ann., in consideration of 300*l.* paid to Lord Aubigny. [*Docquet, June* 18 *and* 19.]

June 18. Grant to John Hendley of pension of 100*l.* per ann., in consideration of 500*l.* paid to Lord Aubigny. [*Docquet.*]

June 18. Like grant to Hen. Lide of pension of 20*l.* per ann., in consideration of 100*l.* paid to Lord Aubigny. [*Docquet.*]

June 18. Grant to Nich. Webling and his heirs, of the King's third part in certain lands and tenements in Barking, co. Essex, and a messuage called Falstolfes in Southwark, demised to them by Wessell Webling, stranger denizen, one third of which is by law due to the King. [*Docquet.*]

June 18. Grant to Dr. Wm. Goodwin of the deanery of Christchurch, Oxford. [*Docquet.*]

June 19. Lease to Sir Thos. Waller, in reversion after Ann Lady Waller, of the prisage and butlerage of all wines, except those within the Principality of Wales, Duchy of Cornwall, and Earldom of Chester, and those imported by aliens. [*Docquet.*]

June 19. Grant to Arch. Armstrong of a pension of 2*s.* per diem for life. [*Docquet.*]

June 20. 48. Sir John Spilman to Salisbury. Solicits payment of money due to him two years past from the King. Has long paid interest for the pearls that were the Queen's last new year's gift [from the King].

June 20. 49. Thos. Lloyd to the Same. Requests the loan of 100*l.* to enable him to take his doctor's degree.

June 20. Somerset House. 50. Declaration of the Queen's Council that the fines of the tenants of her manor of Pulham, co. Norfolk, shall be considered certain, in gratitude for which they present Her Majesty with 100*l.* Indorsed with note of enrolment thereof.

June 20. Warrant, &c. for payment of 100*l.* and other allowances to Robt. Treswell, Surveyor of Woods on this side Trent, to be expended in enclosing and fencing coppices about the Forest of Dean, co. Gloucester. [*Warrt. Bk.*, III., *p.* 16.]

VOL. LXIV.

1611.

June. Docquet of the preceding warrant. [*Docquet, June* 17.]

June 20. Writ of restitution of temporalities for Dr. Buckeridge, Bishop of Rochester. [*Docquet.*]

June 20. Writ of restitution of temporalities for Dr. Thompson, Bishop of Gloucester. [*Docquet.*]

June 20. Grant to Gamaliel Purefey, Thos. Carlton, and Nath. Johnson, of pardon for life and goods, and for life only to Peter Marston and Wm. Rogers, for killing Peter Manzer, in Derby. [*Docquet.*]

June 20. Grant to Edw. Barnett of pardon for life only, for stealing money in the house of Edw. Hereford, of Bristol. [*Docquet.*]

June 20. Grant to the Mayor and Burgesses of Barnstaple of incorporation and confirmation of privileges. [*Docquet.*]

June 20. Grant to Ferdinando Heyborne of pension of 100 marks per ann. for life. [*Docquet.*]

June 20. Letter to the Justices of Assize of the Western Circuit to determine a controversy between a certain town and its neighbours. [*Docquet.*]

June 20. Warrant dormant to deliver to Wm. Darrent, Yeoman of the Harriers, 3*l*. 16*s*. per ann., for his livery. [*Docquet, June* 20 *and July* 10.]

June 20. Orleans. 51. Grey Bruges Lord Chandos to Salisbury. Thanks for giving his name to his son, who lived not long to enjoy it.

June 21. Savoy. 52. Geo. Lord Carew to the Same. Recommends the bearer, Sir Robt. Jacob, His Majesty's Solicitor in Ireland, in his reasonable suits.

June 21. Warrant for payment of 650*l*. to Jas. Bovey, Serjeant of the Cellar, sent into France to make provision of wines. [*Warrt. Bk.*, III., *p.* 20.]

June. Docquet of the above. [*Docquet, June* 20.]

June 22. Grant to Jas. Bovey and Abm. Jacob of 2*s*. 6*d*., payable to the King as composition money for every butt or pipe of sweet wine brought into London, Bristol, or Southampton, in consideration of 40 butts of sweet wine, which they are yearly to deliver, free of expense, to the King's household. [*Docquet.*]

June 22. Grant to Sir Geo. Speke and his heirs, of the hundreds of Abdick and Bulstone, co. Somerset, at nomination of John Eldred and other contractors. [*Docquet.*]

June 22. Grant to Hen. Harward of pardon for clipping and diminishing English coin at Poole. [*Docquet.*]

VOL. LXIV.

1611.

June 22. 53. Thos. Lord De la Warr to Salisbury. Is weak from sickness, but would not have returned so suddenly if the winds had favoured his voyage for the West Indies, at his departure from Virginia. That country is in a most hopeful state. Will proceed in the business, if it is to be prosecuted.

June 24. London. 54. Dorothy Lady Cope to Carleton. Thanks for an excellent pot of mithridate, alias treacle. Lady Bodley and Lady Russell are dead. Lady Arabella escaped from her abode with the Bishop of York, and Mr. Beauchamp [Wm. Seymour] from the Tower. She was re-taken at sea near Calais, and is prisoner in the Tower, as is Lady Shrewsbury. Mr. Pory going to Ireland with Lord Carew. Sends a list of the baronets, who weighed 1,000*l.* a piece.

June 25. 55. Sir Ralph Gray and Sir Wm. Selby to Salisbury. Have executed the commission to declare the reducement of the garrison at Berwick, and have assured the men that their misfortune was not occasioned by Bowyer or Nicholson. They bore it very well.

June 26. Littleton, Wednesday. 56. Earl of Hertford to the Same. Sends for the Council's correction a draft of a letter to his disobedient unfortunate grandchild, Wm. Seymour, &c.

June 26. Richmond. 57. Visct. Fenton to the Same. The King has given permission for the enlargement of Alex. Blair, on condition of his quitting the kingdom. *Incloses,*

57. I. *Petition of Alex. Blair, Scottish prisoner in the Gatehouse, to Visct. Fenton, to intercede with His Majesty for his discharge.*

June 26. Tower. 58. Thos. Lord Grey to Salisbury. Begs to be allowed to walk under the Ordnance House, and in one of Mr. Pidgeon's gardens; Lord Northumberland, Sir Walter Raleigh, and Lord Cobham having a similar privilege. His health is failing, and his only sister is ill, and likely to die.

June 26. Warrant to pay to Visct. Rochester 8,000*l.* still remaining due to him from sums bestowed on him by His Majesty. [*Warrt. Bk.*, III., *p.* 20.]

June 26. Warrant for payment of 193*l.* 4*s.* 6*d.* arrears, and of 400*l.* imprest, to the Earl of Worcester, Master of the Horse, for providing horses, geldings, &c. for the use of the Queen, the Duke of York, and the Lady Elizabeth; and also discharge of 400*l.* formerly advanced on imprest for the same service. [*Ibid.*, *p.* 17.]

June. Docquet of the above. [*Docquet, June* 27.]

June 26. Warrant to pay 66*l.* 10*s.* 4*d.* to John Norden, surveyor, for repairing decays in the lodges of Braden Forest, co. Wilts. [*Warrt. Bk.*, III., *p.* 17.]

June. Docquet of the above. [*Docquet, June* 28.]

June 26. Warrant to pay to Hen. Reynolds 131*l.* 18*s.* 4*d.*, for fees and other charges at the late installation of Charles Duke of York [as Knight of the Garter]. [*Warrt. Bk.*, III., *p.* 17.]

June. Docquet of the above. [*Docquet, June* 27.]

VOL. LXIV.

1611.

June 27. Hadham. 59. Sir Art. Capell to Salisbury. Thanks for the wardship of Art. Pulter. Sends a buck as a token of good will.

June 27. Warrant to pay to Thos. Bedingfield, Master, and Edm. Monday, Yeoman of the Tents, 33*l.* 6*s.* 8*d.* per ann., being half of 100 marks formerly divided between the Masters of the Tent and of the Toils for providing a room to put them in, and also 33*l.* 6*s.* 8*d.* towards their charges in building the room. [*Warrt. Bk.*, III., *p.* 18.]

June. Docquet of the above. [*Docquet, June* 28.]

June 27. Warrant to pay to Thos. Jones, Master of the Toils, 600*l.* in two sums, and 50*l.* yearly for eight years. [*Warrt. Bk.*, III., *p.* 18.]

June 27. Docquet of the above. [*Docquet, June* 17 *and* 27.]

June 27. Warrant appointing an officer in the Court of Exchequer to receive the bonds and recognizances of Baronets for payment of the sums imposed on them by their patent of creation, in order to their cancelling when the sums are paid. [*Warrt. Bk.*, III., *p.* 19.]

June 27. Docquet of the above.

June 27. Commission of Lieutenancy for cos. Cumberland, Northumberland, and Westmoreland, for the Earl of Cumberland. [*Docquet.*]

June 27. Warrant to the Earl of Shrewsbury, Justice of Oyer and Terminer beyond Trent, to order all keepers of parks, &c. within his charge to deliver to Sir Jas. Fullerton, surveyor of the Duke of York's lands in the north, such venison as he shall desire, not exceeding a brace of bucks from each. [*Docquet.*]

June 27. Letter to the President and Fellows of Magdalen College, Oxford, for Tim. Holland, a poor scholar in their house, to be elected to a scholarship. [*Docquet.*]

June 27. Grant to Geo. Grimsditch of pension of 100*l.* per ann. for life, in consideration of his surrender of part of the customs and subsidies payable in the port of Dublin. [*Docquet.*]

June 27. Lease to Fras. Phelips and Rich. Moore, and their heirs, of certain rectory and chantry lands, value 53*l.* 3*s.* per ann. [*Docquet.*]

June 27. Grant to Art. Mills, Groom of the Privy Chamber, of the benefit of the recusancy of Lady Isabel Thorold, widow, co. Lincoln; Merill Wicklift, of Wicklift, co. York; Ant. Rooper, of Eltham, co. Kent; Cordwall Bradbury, of Pickenham, co. Norfolk; and Mary Gerard, of St. Clement Danes, co. Middlesex. [*Docquet.*]

June 27. Grant to Sir John Tufton and his heirs of the site of the Hospital of St. Bartholomew of Playden, and of the manor of Playdon, near Rye, co. Sussex. [*Docquet.*]

June 29. 60. Lease from Thos. Elliot to Robt. Haning, both of London, of a messuage on St. Mary Hill, parish of St. Mary-at-Hill, London.

Vol. LXIV.

1611.

June 29. 61. Survey of His Majesty's ships, pinnaces, and gallies, taken by the principal officers of the Navy, by command of the Lord High Admiral.

June ? 62. Petition of Sir John Thornborough to Salisbury, that the arrears of his fees as Constable of Scarborough Castle may be paid, and an order given for their payment half-yearly, and also for repayment of 6,000*l.* advanced by him in the late reign for levying soldiers for Ireland.

June 29. Warrant to pay to Sir John Thornborough, Keeper of Scarborough, 128*l.*, for arrears of his fee for eight years, at 16*l.* per ann., &c. [*Warrt. Bk.*, III., *p.* 20.]

June. Docquet of the above. [*Docquet, June* 27.]

June 30. Richmond. 63. Charge of digging and levelling the ground of the friars, the works about the aits, &c., at Richmond, since Nov. 1, 1610.

June ? 64. Sketch of the ground plot of the friars at Richmond, &c.

June 30. Eton. 65. Sir Hen. Savile to Carleton. Instructions for the purchase of Palladius' works and other books. Is better of his sickness: 200 baronets made. The Savoyan Ambassadors are over for the Princess's marriage.

June 30 ? 66. Particulars of the committal to prison of the Wardens of the Tailors' Company, New Sarum, for patronising morris dancers on the Sunday; including a letter to them from the Mayor against Sabbath profanation. Also of their appearance before him to answer the non-fulfilment of his orders, and of their committal, and admission to bail, June 28.

June 30. Warrant to pay to Sir Jas. Fullerton for the privy purse of the Duke of York 200*l.* per ann., and any further sums which the Lord Treasurer may think fit. [*Warrt. Bk.*, III., *p.* 22.]

June 30. Docquet of the above.

June 30. Grant to Sir John Graham, Gentleman of the Privy Chamber, of 220*l.*, as a gift, from casualties in the Exchequer. [*Warrt. Bk.*, III., *p.* 22.]

June 30. Docquet of the above.

June 30. Grant to Sir Noel Caron, Levinus Munck, and Simeon Ruytnick, in fee simple, of two tenements, with gardens, &c., in Austin Friars, London, in trust for the Dutch Church. [*Docquet.*]

June 30. Warrant for payment of certain allowances to Sir Roger Wilbraham, Sir Jas. Ley, Sir Ant. St. Leger, Sir Jas. Fullerton, the Clerks of the Council, and other persons employed in their attendance, touching the service of the plantation. [*Docquet.*]

June 30. Re-grant to the Earl of Suffolk of the moiety of all seizures of Venice gold and silver, the same as by a former Privy Seal passed in the fifth year of the King. [*Docquet.*]

Vol. LXIV.

1611.

[June 30.] 67. Note that it is the King's pleasure to grant to Visct. Montague pardon of certain fines for recusancy, on the payment of 6,000*l.* at fixed terms, and that the Oath of Allegiance should not be again tendered to him.

June 30. Grant to Lord Montague of pardon for refusing to take the Oath of Allegiance, for offences of recusancy, for harbouring Seminary Priests, and for sending his children beyond seas, &c. [*Docquet.*]

June 30. Letter to Magdalen College, Oxford, for Nich. Halswell to be chosen fellow, provided it be not to the prejudice of Mich. Oldsworth, who was formerly recommended. [*Docquet.*]

June 30. Warrant to the Council to cause the charges of apprehending and bringing up Lady Arabella Stuart and her company to be defrayed out of such gold as may have been found upon her or in her company, at the time of her escape. [*Docquet.*]

June 30. Grant of incorporation to the merchants trading to France, with provisoes of saving to the vintners, and of revocation, if desirable. [*Docquet.*]

June. 68. G. Gerard to Salisbury. Solicits to succeed Mr. Harman in his place, if he be deprived of it.

June. Paris. 69. Hen. Lord Clifford to the Same. Is anxious about his father's payment of his debts, and settlement of his estates; begs his Lordship to urge it on him once again.

June. 70. Pat. Cumming to the King. Offers a project for increasing the revenue of Scotland to 100,000*l.* a year, which he has submitted to the judgment of the Lord Treasurer.

June. 71. Survey and inventory of all the armour, munition, &c. in the armouries of the Tower, Greenwich, and Woolwich; late in charge and custody of Sir Hen. Lee, deceased, and now of Sir Thos. Monson, Master of the Armoury.

June. 72. Copy of the above.

June. 73. Charge of day wages, provisions, and materials for the works at Somerset House, for the month of June.

[June.] 74. Accounts of moneys paid into the Hanaper, in Hilary, Easter, and Trinity Terms last.

Vol. LXV. July, August, 1611.

July 1. Greenwich. 1. Sir Robt. Stewart to Salisbury. Prays a letter to the Chancellor of Denmark, for his more speedy despatch through Denmark, and to the King of Sweden.

Vol. LXV.

1611.

July 1. 2. Sir Geo. Buck to Dud. Norton. Sends documents relating to allowances for a house, &c. for the revels. Begs that a Privy Seal for the same may be speedily obtained. *Incloses,*

2. i. *Earl of Salisbury and Sir Julius Cæsar to the Auditors of the Prest, to allow* 30*l. per ann. to Sir Geo. Buck, Master of the Revels, in lieu of the house and lodgings formerly appropriated to that office, but lately given by the King to Lord Aubigny. May* 31, *Whitehall.*

2. ii. *Blank draft of the warrant required.*

2. iii. *Sir Geo. Buck, Master of the Revels, to Salisbury. Solicits an allowance for rooms for the office of the revels.*

July 1. 3. Report to the Earl of Salisbury of the progress of the works at Hatfield. They are nearly completed, and the house will soon be prepared for his reception.

July 2. 4. Sir Thos. Bartlett to Salisbury. Begs employment.

July 2. Westminster. 5. The King to John Eldred and other contractors for purchase of lands in fee simple. To pass the manor of Holywell, Flintshire, to Thos. Corvin and Wm. Selby, for the use of the present tenants, according to the custom of preferring the former tenants, rather than to Sir John Egerton, who sues for the same.

July 2. Docquet of the above.

July 2. Westminster. Grant to Robt. Geathin, of Tir-y-Abbatt, co. Denbigh, of pardon for manslaughter. Latin. [*Sign Man., vol.* 1, *No.* 72.]

July 2. Docquet of the above.

July 2. Grant to Robt. Visct. Rochester, in fee simple, of the castle of Rochester, with all appurtenances, excepting knight's services. [*Docquet.*]

July 2. Grant to Theophilus Lord Howard, of Walden, on surrender of the Earl of Salisbury, of the reversion, after the Earl of Northampton, of the Keepership of the Tower of Greenwich. [*Docquet.*]

July 2. Grant to Maurice and Sarah Shipward of pension of 50*l.* per ann. during the life of the said Sarah, in consideration of 250*l.* paid to Lord Aubigny, which His Majesty was to have paid to him. [*Docquet.*]

July 2. Licence for Sir Robt. Drury, of Halsted, co. Suffolk, his wife and family, to travel for three years. [*Docquet.*]

July 2. Letter for a grant to Sir Wm. Cornwallis of the benefit of the recusancy of Margaret Browne, of Fremnoll's, co. Norfolk. [*Docquet.*]

Vol. LXV.

1611.

July 2. Letter to the Council, requiring them to inform themselves of the orders from time to time established for security of prisoners in the Tower, and to instruct the Lieutenant of the Tower accordingly. [*Docquet.*]

July 2. Letter to the Lord Chancellor to put Justices of the Peace, outlawed for nonpayment of their debts for four terms, out of the commission of the peace. [*Docquet.*]

July 2. Letter to the Bishop of Bangor and Judges of Assize, co. Carnarvon, to search out the truth of a supposed witchcraft committed on six young maids. [*Docquet.*]

July 2. Warrant to the Lord Chancellor to date the warrants of creation of Sir Geo. Saville and Sir Geo. St. Paul as baronets, on June 29 last past, notwithstanding the Stat. 18. Hen. VI. [*Docquet, July* 2 *and* 5.]

July 2. Grant to the gentlemen of the Chapel Royal of 3*l.* as a gift towards their feast. [*Docquet.*]

July 2. Warrant to the Keeper of Nonsuch Great Park to deliver two bucks to the gentlemen of the Chapel Royal. [*Docquet.*]

July 2. Similar warrant to the Keeper of Nonsuch Little Park for one buck. [*Docquet.*]

July 3. Grant to John Taylor of an almsroom in Gloucester Cathedral. [*Docquet, July* 6.]

July 3. Westminster. Grant of pardon to Robt. Pringell, of Westminster, for the manslaughter of Walter Buchanan, in the Prince's Walk. Latin. [*Sign Man., vol.* I., *No.* 73.]

July. Docquet of the above. [*Docquet, July* 6.]

July 3. London. 6. John Eldred to Salisbury. Hindrances have arisen in their contracts for leases. Craves to know the cause of his Lordship's displeasure. All he has done therein has been to serve him.

July 3. Berwick. 7. Geo. Nicholson to the Same. Satisfactory discharge of the garrison. Sir Ralph Gray and Sir Wm. Selby have not announced His Majesty's further pleasure respecting those who were to receive no more pay, but meanwhile nothing is given them. Works for the new bridge proceeding.

July 4. Letley. Thursday. 8. Earl of Hertford to the Same. Is glad the rough draft of the letter to his unfortunate grandchild pleased him. Has re-copied it, and sent it open with his seal, for the Lords to read and seal it.

Vol. LXV.

1611.

July 4. The Grange. 9. Geo. Carleton to Sir Dud. Carleton. Begs his favour for Mr. Joiner, recommended by Sir Mich. Green, who is going to Venice to practise the silk-loom stocking weaving, which is not permitted in England, for fear of ruining the knitters. Mr. Pory would have had the speculation thrown into Sir Dudley's hands, but his friends dared not accept it without consulting him. Will attend to his house at Eton. Thanks for Sir Dudley's care of his son, whose temper it is to be too easily misled. Death of Lady Norris's mother, the Countess of Lincoln.

July 4. Drury Lane. 10. Fras. Windebank to [M. de Tourval ?] Apologizes for his tardy offering of thanks, &c. for entertainment at Oxford. French.

July 4. Bishop's Auckland. 11. Wm. James, Bp. of Durham, to Salisbury. Concerning the search for one Clark, who represented himself as servant of Lady Arabella. Robt. Holtby, brother to the Jesuit, apprehended and sent to gaol for refusing the Oath of Allegiance. Requests a line of approval to Dethick and Barnes, who have intercepted his letters. *Incloses,*

11. i. *Hen. Dethick and John Barnes to the Bp. of Durham. They have committed Holtby, and intercepted letters brought to him by Collingwood, professing to be from Lady Gray. Remarks on the letters and their writers. Request general enforcement of the Oath of Allegiance. June 28, Durham. Inclose,*

11. ii. *John Taylor to Robt. Holtby. "My Lady" and his friends grieved at his trouble. My Lady and Mr. Collingwood agree well. She likes the passing the lease of Heddon. Darlington. June 26.*

11. iii. *And. Duckett to Robt. Holtby. Pities his afflictions. The Oath of Allegiance unlawful. Suggests reasons against it, to be urged by him, and that he should express willingness to take an oath of temporal allegiance. Advises him to escape by bribery. June 26.*

July 4. 12. Charges of works, &c., at sundry of His Majesty's houses in June.

July 4. Gatehouse Prison, Westminster. 13. Alex. Capell to Salisbury. Was apprehended at Canterbury, and committed to prison. Reports proceedings of the seminaries of Douay and St. Omer. Mr. Seymour, husband of Lady Arabella, is well treated by the Archduke, who will not deliver him up. Descriptions of priests and Jesuits passing into England, the disguises which they assume, and the houses they frequent. Some dangerous matter is working.

July 4. Berwick. 14. Robt. Jackson to the Same. Thanks for being appointed Commissary to the Musters of the Pensioners at Berwick. Satisfactory manner of the discharge of the garrison by Sir R. Gray and Sir W. Selby, a few old men only craving larger allowance. Those who are to be entirely dropped have not yet received their dismissal.

VOL. LXV.

1611.
July 5. 15. Thos. Woodhouse to Salisbury. Beseeches favour in his petition that he and his brother may no longer be compelled to pay the debts of Sir Hen. Gawdy.

July 5. Plymouth. 16. Sir Ferdinando Gorges, Governor of Plymouth, to the Same. Certain merchants of London are taken off Scilly, by English pirates. Increase of piracy, and necessity for its suppression. *Incloses,*

16. I. *Examination of John Collever and others who have been taken, concerning the number and strength of the pirate fleet. They have in all 40 ships and 2,000 men, and their place of rendezvous is at Marmora, in Barbary.*

July 5. Greenwich. 17. Commission to Sir Wm. Selby, Sir Wilfrid Lawson, Sir John Fenwick, Sir Wm. Hutton, Lord Cranston, Sir Gideon Murray, Sir Wm. Seaton, and Sir David Murray, constituting them Commissioners for the government of the Borders, with specified powers to preserve peace and prevent disorders and murders.

Docquet of the above. [*Docquet, June* 28.]

July 5? 18. Instructions by the Council to the Commissioners of the Borders, for the better government of those parts. [*See Oct.* 22.]

July 6. Grant to Lewis Tresham and his heirs, in fee simple, of purchase of the King's remainder in the manor of Rushton, co. Northampton. [*Docquet.*]

July 6. Grant to Pat. Maull of 600*l.* as a gift, from fines and forfeitures. [*Docquet.*]

July 6. Commission granted to Rich. Putto to find out and recover or compound for all debts, heriots, reliefs, and casualties detained from the Crown, from 30 Eliz. to 7 Jac. I., of which he is to have a fifth part, and other privileges, and also an annuity of 50*l.* [*Docquet.*]

July 6. Grant to Wm. and Robt. Angell and Justinian Povey, in fee simple, of a manor and other lands not named, at suit of Sir Baptist Hicks and others, in part of 75,000*l.* lent by them. [*Docquet.*]

July 6. Grant to Robt. Jamyson, Footman of the Prince, of an annuity of 20*l.* for life. [*Docquet.*]

July 6. Letter to the Earl of Nottingham to give warrants to the keepers of divers parks to serve Lady Elizabeth, the Lord Mayor and Aldermen of London, the Farmers of the Customs, and Tellers of the Exchequer, the Merchant Tailors' and Cloth Workers' Company, the King's Falconers, and Foreign Ambassadors, with bucks, according to the King's direction. [*Docquet.*]

July 6. Confirmation of a contract with Sir Baptist Hicks, Alderman Cockayne, and others, for the sale of the remainder of tithes, rectories, and chantry lands, of the value of 500*l.* per ann., and for converting 500*l.* per ann. of rents reserved on former sales to fee simple; and a warrant for passing the remainder of a former bargain to the value of 140*l.* per ann. of like lands. [*Docquet.*]

VOL. LXV.

1611.

July 7. Warrant dormant to the Treasurer of the Chamber to disburden the Privy Purse of divers payments of late made out of it, pursuant to a Privy Seal of Jan. 5, 1608; viz., to preachers for sermons before the King, gifts by the King for the Duke of York and Lady Elizabeth at christenings, gifts to musicians, &c. [*Docquet*].

July 7. Newgate. 19. John Moray to Salisbury. The King has spoken to his Lordship concerning his release; begs he will favour it. His long imprisonment injures his health; his estate is ruined by prosecuting a grant made him by the King for payment of his debts, for which Lord Haddington and others are sureties. Protests his innocence.

July 8. Westminster. Grant to John Moray and John Engles, of London, of pardon for the death of Richard Fell, Serjeant at the Mace in London, they being only bystanders, and not active therein. Latin. [*Sign Man., vol. I., No.* 75.]

July. Docquet of the above. [*Docquet, July* 6.]

July 8. Berwick. 20. Sir Wm. Bowyer to Salisbury. Has induced the garrison [of Berwick] patiently to receive the announcement of their discharge. Thanks for freedom from imputations of wishing them ill.

July 8. Windsor. 21. Earl of Pembroke to the Same. The King, at the request of the Earl of Shrewsbury, stays the warrant for annexing some walks in the Forest of Sherwood to the Lieutenancy of the place, till he is further informed thereon.

July 8. Westminster. Grant to Sir Wm. Wiseman of pardon for debts and forfeitures for recusancy, that he may be able to sell his lands, and pay an increased annual fine to the King. Latin. [*Sign Man., vol.* I., *No.* 74.]

July. Docquet of the above. [*Docquet, July* 6.]

July 9. Grant to Sir Geo. More of the office of Chancellor of the Order of the Garter. [*Docquet.*]

July 9. Protection from arrest for Gifford Watkin and Thos. Garway and their sureties for one year, at the suit of some of their creditors, and in consideration of their expenses towards the plantation in Ireland. [*Docquet.*]

July 9. Discharge to Rich. Hill of 400*l.* accrued to the King from an unjust judgment against him in the Exchequer. [*Docquet.*]

July 9. 22. Earl of Salisbury to the inhabitants of Fotheringay. Has referred the case of their school to Sir Ant. Mildmay and Sir Chas. Montague, but not yet received their reply. Orders them to continue Thos. Lindsell in office till further notice, having received a certificate of his good conduct. [*See July* 14.]

July 10. 23. Katherine Lady Walsh to Salisbury. Solicits his favour in her suit for relief. Her estate injured by prosecuting the King's gracious gift to her.

VOL. LXV.

1611.

July 10. Westminster. Grant of pardon to Alex. Vaughan, of Hargast, co. Hereford, Dutch Merchant, for taking a ship of Antwerp, under Letters of Marque from the States General. Latin. [*Sign Man., vol.* I., *No.* 76.]

July 10. Docquet of the above.

July 10. Grant to Robt., John, and Thos. Cotton, of purchase of the manors of Glatton and Holm, co. Huntingdon, of the Duchy of Lancaster. [*Docquet.*]

July 10. Grant to Sir Rich. Fermor, Thos. Purcill, and Adrian Kirby, of certain coppices and woodlands within the perambulation of the Forest of Chute, co. Hants. [*Docquet.*]

July 10. Warrant to pay to Thos. Visct. Haddington and Elizabeth his wife, an annuity of 1,000*l.*, and to Sir Geo. Beeston and Ellinor his wife, an annuity of 200*l.*, from the Court of Wards instead of from the Exchequer. [*Docquet.*]

July 10. Grant to Thos. Young, Footman to the Prince, of annuity of 20*l.* [*Docquet.*]

July 10. Grant to Dr. Theodore de Mayerne of pension of 200*l.* per ann., to begin from the decease of the Queen, as his present pension will then cease. [*Docquet.*]

July 10. Grant, with survivorship, to Alban Coxe and John his son, in reversion after John Pratt, of the office of Keeper of pheasants and partridges in Barnet, Hadley, South Mimms, and Totteridge, cos. Hertford and Middlesex. [*Docquet.*]

July 10. Grant to Wm. March, Groom of the Privy Chamber, on surrender of John Blagrave, of the office of Ranger in the Forest of Dean, co. Gloucester. [*Docquet.*]

July 10. Grants, with survivorship, to Alex. Harris and John Burrough, of the office of Bailiff and Collector of the King's Chantry Rents in London and Middlesex. [*Docquet.*]

July 10. Warrant to pay to Wm. Shaw 500*l.* from fines and forfeitures, as a free gift. [*Warrt. Bk.*, III., *p.* 35.]

July 10. Docquet of the above.

July 11. Warrant for certain payments to Visct. Rochester, as Keeper of the Palace of Westminster, in place of Lord Knyvet, for keeping and preserving wild beasts and fowl in St. James's Park and Garden and Spring Garden, and for gardeners there, &c. [*Warrt. Bk.*, III., *p.* 23.]

July. Docquet of the above. [*Docquet, July* 10.]

July 11. Warrant dormant for payment of wages to Edw. Ball, appointed Groom of the Privy Chamber, vice Ferdinando Heyborne. [*Docquet, July* 10.]

1611. Vol. LXV.

July 11. Warrant dormant for delivery to Edw. Ball of stuff for livery. [*Docquet, July* 10.]

July 11. Warrant for delivery of stuff to Lord Hay, Gentleman of the King's Robes, for the King's Maundy, &c. [*Docquet, July* 10.]

July 11. Licence to Sir Rowland Lytton, Geo. Smyth, Philip Lytton, Geo. Nodes, and Sam. Harvey, to travel for three years. [*Docquet, July* 10.]

July 11. Letters to the Master and Fellows of Clare Hall, Cambridge, for Rich. Thomson, Fellow there, to be chosen Proctor of the University, the election falling to that house this year. [*Docquet, July* 10.]

July 11. Warrant to pay to Robt. Treswell, Surveyor of Woods south of Trent, 73*l.*, for finishing Chapel Hainault Lodge, co. Essex, &c. [*Warrt. Bk.*, III., *p.* 23.]

July. Docquet of the above. [*Docquet, July* 10.]

July 11. Grant to Katherine Bridges, mother of the maids, of 100*l.*, as a gift. [*Warrt. Bk.*, III., *p.* 23.]

July. Docquet of the above. [*Docquet, July* 10.]

July 11. Warrant to pay 200*l.*, and other sums, to Thos. Bedingfield, Master of the Tents, Hales, and Pavilions, for repair and provision of the same. [*Warrt. Bk.*, III., *p.* 23.]

July. Docquet of the above. [*Docquet, July* 10.]

July 12. Sprowston, Norfolk. 24. John Corbet to Salisbury. Begs leave of longer absence for the recovery of his health. Is ordered to try his native air.

July 12. Hampton Court. 25. Earl of Nottingham to Sir John Norris, Comptroller, and Sir John Trevor, Surveyor of Windsor. To survey the further repairs necessary for a lodge in the Great Park, Windsor. With direction by Trevor for an estimate thereof. [*See July* 23.]

[July 12.] Friday. 26. Hen. Earl of Northampton to Visct. Rochester. Examination of [the Earl of Northumberland] on the charges of Elks, his servant. He is much changed, reserved, cautious, and timid in his answers. He confesses now that he did persuade his brother to excuse Thos. Percy's taking the Oath [of Allegiance, as Gentleman Pensioner], but denies the other accusations, and complains of Elks as a discontented rogue. Sir Walter Raleigh examined, but found as bold, proud, and passionate as ever.

July 14. 27. Duke of Lenox to Salisbury. Has left a servant to attend his direction for the money.

July 14. 28. Earl of Salisbury to Sir Ant. Mildmay and Sir Chas. Montague. On their report, is certified of the incompetency of Thos. Lindsell. Authorizes them to remove him from the situation of schoolmaster at Fotheringay, and to appoint Elam, or some other, in his place, as they think fit.

VOL. LXV.

1611.
July 14. 29. Note of payments of contributions from several towns, counties, and persons, since May 30.

July 15. Amesbury, Monday. 30. Earl of Hertford to Salisbury. Hopes his grandchild, Wm. Seymour's, reply to his letter will be fitting. Lady Hertford is rabbit hunting at Salisbury's castle warren of Old Sarum. Thanks for a present of chessmen contained in the compass of a walnut shell.

July 15. Westminster. Grant to Robt. Salby, of London, of pardon for life only, for stealing silk and satin dresses, jewels, &c., from Lord Roxburgh. Latin. [*Sign Man., vol.* I., *No.* 77.]

July 15. Docquet of the above.

July 15. Holyrood House. 31. Earl of Dunfermline to Salisbury. Solicits that the pension, &c. of Aristotle Knowsley, schoolmaster of Berwick for 40 years, be continued to his son. *Incloses,*

31. I. *Petition of Arist. Knowsley to Salisbury for reversion to his son of his pension of* 12*d. per diem.*

July 15. London. 32. Sir John Bennet to Sir Dud. Carleton. Favours granted to Sir Hen. Wotton, and his ingenious discourse. Will send his son into Italy for a year. Beseeches directions for him at Venice. The Archbishop of Canterbury is sworn of the Privy Council. Dr. King elected Bishop of London, &c. The Landgrave of Hesse has been to woo Lady Elizabeth, and the Palatine of the Rhine is coming. Lord Carew gone to Ireland about the Ulster plantation. Earl of Northumberland more closely confined, Elks, a discontented servant, having inculpated him in the powder treason. Sir Walter Raleigh more restrained than before, &c.

July 16. Westminster Abbey. 33. Tim. Elks to Thos. Lumsden. Remarks and suggestions as to obtaining evidence on four presumptive points against the Earl of Northumberland, in connexion with the gunpowder treason. His taking the house next the Parliament house. Admitting Percy to be Gentleman Pensioner without an oath. His warning to be absent from Parliament; and Percy's speech while the treason was in working. Thinks Whitelock, who was with Percy at Syon the day before, knew something, but was bribed by the Earl to secrecy. [Geo.] Whitehead to be examined.

July 16. 34. Sir Hen. Hobart to Salisbury. Sir Hum. Winch having opportunity to send for the things he has left in Ireland, wishes to know whether the King will use him there or here.

July 16. 35. Thos. Dewhurst to the Same. The house which he holds in Westminster on a lease from the Crown is claimed by the Dean of Westminster as parcel of the college.

July 16? 36. John Anthony to the Same. Relative to Jesuits in England and their correspondence abroad. Has good means of information, because the Romanists still suppose him to be one of themselves.

Vol. LXV.

1611.

July 17. Hampton Court. 37. Earl of Nottingham to Salisbury. Fears the pardon offered to pirates comes too late to do any good. Strongly opposes the idea of sending out a small force for their suppression, as it can yield only dishonour.

July 17. Windsor. 38. Sir Thos. Lake to the Same. The letters from the King of Denmark are about the loan of ships, his war with Sweden, &c. The King refuses to sign the letter to Fitzherbert, saying he will do more harm than Mole good. His Majesty has signed the book of the Great Farm [of the Customs]. He goes to-morrow to Englefield, and returns on Friday.

July 18. Berwick. 39. Geo. Nicholson to the Same. Has received moneys and paid the garrison [of Berwick]. Sends the muster book, and excuses his own non-attendance, on account of the administration of the Earl of Dunbar's effects. The bridge progressing.

July 18. Paris. 40. Lord Clifford to the Same. Rejoices at the news of his wife's health and of her visit to Lady Derby. Has drawn on him for 100*l.* for the expenses of his journey. French.

July 18. 41. Note of debts of the Crown requiring assignation.

July 18. Westminster. Grant to John Brereton, of Barrow, co. Chester, of pardon for life only, for manslaughter. Latin. [*Sign Man., vol.* I., *No.* 78.]

July. Docquet of the above. [*Docquet, July* 19.]

July 18. Grant to John Barkley of 100*l.* as a free gift. [*Warrt. Bk.*, III., *p.* 26.]

July. Docquet of the above. [*Docquet, July* 19.]

July 18. Warrant to pay to Lord Aubigny 2,000*l.*, due to him by Visct. Montague, for which he holds a recognizance from the King. [*Warrt. Bk.*, III., *p.* 25.]

July. Docquet of the above. [*Docquet, July* 19.]

July 18. Warrant to pay to the Duke of Lenox 1,422*l.* 17*s.* 3*d.*, in lieu of his diet at Court, which the King has thought fit to convert into money. [*Warrt. Bk.*, III., *p.* 26.]

July. Docquet of the above. [*Docquet, July* 19.]

July 18. Warrant for allowance to Lord Knollys of all fines levied in the Court of Common Pleas, "prolicentia concordandi," commonly called post fines, in consideration of his payment of 2,272*l.* 8*s.* per ann. [*Warrt. Bk.*, III., *p.* 26.]

July. Docquet of the above. [*Docquet, July* 19.]

July 19. Grant to Adam Newton, Secretary to the Prince, in reversion after Sir Fulk Greville, of the office of Secretary of the Principality of Wales, and Clerk of the Council there. [*Docquet.*]

Vol. LXV.

Grant to Thos. Hodgson of pension of 2s. per diem, for services at Berwick, as lieutenant of 100 footmen. [*Docquet.*]

Grant to Frances, wife of Wm. Anderton, and Ann, wife of Hen. Serborne, daughters of Fras. Dacres, of pensions of 50*l.* per ann. each, and a pension of 50*l.* per ann. to Thos. Gray, during the life of Elizabeth, another daughter of Fras. Dacres. [*Docquet.*]

Letter to the Lord Treasurer to pay an annuity of 200*l.*, formerly granted to the Earl of Oxford, to him, and not to the Countess, his mother, although he be a minor. [*Docquet.*]

42. Licence of Council for Mabel Griffith to pass beyond seas and live abroad, but not to repair to Rome.

43. Mayor, &c. of Berwick to Salisbury. Proceedings in re-building Berwick Bridge. Desire the storehouses for a grammar school, to be maintained by Sir Wm. Selby, and the stores for building the bridge. Lenient dealings with the soldiers for payment of their debts.

44. Sir Dud. Carleton to the Same. The Prince of that State promises, at the King's request, to detain Wm. Seymour, if he should come into their dominions. Has explained that the King's displeasure with Seymour was not on religious grounds, but that he should presume to marry a near relation of His Majesty without leave, and contrary to promise, and then run away from his easy restraint.

45. Robt. Bury to the Same. The late Jane Shelley, wife of Wm. Shelley, being a Papist, demised lands, &c. in Shropshire, to raise money for Jesuits' Colleges. Mr. Grobban, of the Chancery, knows how her property was left.. It was large ; she having 3,000*l.* a year, and living sparingly.

46. Petition of Rowland Yarrow, of Yarrow, in Tynedale, to Sir Jas. Altham and Sir Edw. Bromley, Justices for Northumberland, for redress of an assault committed on him at Jedburgh, in revenge for his going to Court to inform against the authors of the raid of Scotsmen into England, and murder of Lionel Robson and others, May 25, 1611. [*See May* 26.]

47. Visct. Fenton to Salisbury. Breadshaw is willing to refer his interest in the patent for gold and silver thread to Salisbury's decision.

48. Sir Edw. Seymour to the Same. Thanks for being made a baronet, and for the wardship of young Parker, his son-in-law, which has now come to him by the death of Parker's grandfather.

VOL. LXV.

1611.
July 22. Canon Row. 49. Eliz. Countess of Oxford to the Earls of Salisbury and Northampton. Intreats their interference for the punishment of John Hunt, who seduces her son into evil courses, leads him to extravagance, and prejudices him against her authority. Has spent much of her income on her son, during the eight years he has been with the Prince. *Incloses,*

49. I. *Articles by the Countess Dowager of Oxford against John Hunt, for misleading and corrupting the Earl her son, and for preying upon his estate.*

July 22. Grant to Hen. Beswick, on surrender of Lawrence Whitfield, of the office of keeper of the King's ponds in Westminster Park. [*Docquet.*]

July 22. Grant to Sir Wm. Bowyer of pension of 10*s.* per diem, on consideration of the dissolution of Berwick Garrison. [*Docquet.*]

July 22. Grant to Arnold Herbert of pension of 100*l.* per ann., which the Earl of Dunbar had formerly allowed him. [*Docquet.*]

July 22. Warrant for payment to Arnold Herbert of 50*l.*, due to the Earl of Dunbar at his death for his half-year's allowance for diet, and by him assigned to Herbert. [*Docquet.*]

July 22. Grant to Sir Wm. Irving, Gentleman of the Prince's Privy Chamber, of the manor of Ashby Ledgers, co. Northampton, and other lands in Ashby Ledgers, which came to the King by attainder of Robt. Catesby. [*Docquet.*]

July 23. Letter to the Sheriff of Yorkshire to continue to Thos. Saville the office of County Clerk during good behaviour. [*Docquet, July* 22.]

July 23. Grant to Edw. Burton of an almsroom in the Hospital of Ewelme, co. Oxford. [*Docquet, July* 22.]

July 23. 50. Sir Wm. Craven, Lord Mayor, and the Aldermen of London, to the Council. Represent the grievances sustained by the freemen of that city, by reason of artizans and traders who engross the Dutch and French trade. Necessity of enforcing the laws against foreigners.

July? 51. List of the numbers of strangers resident in London, and their different trades. Total number 686.

July 23. 52. Certificate by Sir John Norris and Sir John Trevor of the decays of a lodge in the Great Park, Windsor, and estimate of the expense of repairs, &c. [*See July* 12.]

July 24. Letter to the President and Council of the Marches of Wales to hold their Sessions for a certain period at Shrewsbury, instead of at Ludlow. [*Docquet, July* 22.]

1611. Vol. LXV.

July 24. Warrant to pay to Wm. May 45*l.* for erecting a lodge in the Great Park at Hampton Court. [*Warrt. Bk.*, *p.* 28.]

July. Docquet of the above. [*Docquet, July* 25.]

July 24. Westminster. Warrant to pay 600*l.* to Jas. Johnson for services appointed. [*Warrt. Bk.*, III., *p.* 35.]

July. Docquet of the above. [*Docquet, July* 25.]

July 24. Westminster. Grant to Theophilus Higgons, of London, a converted recusant, of pardon for former offences in matters of religion. Latin. [*Sign Man.*, *vol.* I., *No.* 79.]

July. Docquet of the above. [*Docquet, July* 25.]

[July] 24. Westminster. Grant to Sir Chris. Hatton and Fras. Needham, in part recompence for the great mansion house, manor, and park of Holdenby, of rents, &c. of manors and lands, cos. Northampton, Devon, Bedford, Stafford, and Leicester. Latin: imperfect. [*Sign Man.*, *vol.* I., *No.* 80.]

July. Docquet of the above. [*Docquet, July* 25.]

July 24. Westminster. Grant to Fras. Morrice and Fras. Phelips on nomination of Sir Ant. Cope, and other contractors, of chantry lands, &c. named, in cos. York, Lancaster, Northampton, Huntingdon Norfolk, Suffolk, Wilts, Berks, Monmouth, Essex, Leicester, Cumberland, Stafford, and Westmoreland, as part of grants to be made to the said contractors. [*Sign Man.*, *vol.* I., *No.* 81.]

July. Docquet of the above. [*Docquet, July* 25.]

July 24. Similar grant to the Same of chantry lands, tithes, &c. &c. named, in cos. Cardigan, Carmarthen, York, Cornwall, Devon, Suffolk, Derby, Lincoln, Nottingham, Gloucester, Hertford, Northumberland, Durham, Somerset, Surrey, Oxford, Monmouth, Dorset, Lancaster, Middlesex, Salop, Stafford, Gloucester, Kent, Montgomery, Hertford, Pembroke, Northampton, Leicester, Bucks, Huntingdon, Norfolk, and Glamorgan. Latin. [*Sign Man.*, *vol.* I., *No.* 82.]

July. Docquet of the above. [*Docquet, July* 25.]

July 24. Grant to Capt. Jos. May of the benefit of the recusancy of Geo. Smith, of Onenyborough. [*Docquet, July* 25.]

July 24. Letter to the Lord Treasurer to direct the officers of the ports to permit Roger Turlot, merchant stranger, to transport 400*l.* worth of his household plate to Middleburgh. [*Docquet, July* 25.]

July 24. Enlargement of the instructions, dated Feb. 7, 1610–11, for the Commissioners for sale of the King's lands, manors, and other hereditaments; made in behalf Sir Hen. Carey, who bought the manor of Minster, co. Kent. [*Docquet, July* 25.]

July 25. Grant to Fras. and Thos. Needham of license to erect and endow a free grammer school, to be called "The Free Grammar School of Fras. Needham, in Needham, Co. Suffolk;" also to erect an almshouse to be called "The Almshouse of Fras. Needham, in Needham, co. Suffolk;" with a grant of incorporation of the governors thereof. [*Docquet.*]

Vol. LXV.

1611.

July 25. Grant to Fras. Needham and John Yeomans, and the heirs of the said Francis, in fee simple, of the manors of Barking and Needham, co. Suffolk, with liberty to impark 400 acres; also the advowson of the churches of Barking-cum-Needham and Frostenden, co. Suffolk, in consideration of the same and four other advowsons being bestowed upon poor scholars to be chosen out of a free grammar school which the said Needham builds in Needham. [*Docquet.*]

July 25. Grant to Sir Roger Aston of an addition to his coat-of-arms. [*Docquet.*]

July 25. Grant to Patrick Abercromby of 40*l.* as a free gift. [*Docquet.*]

July 25. Grant to Robt., son of Sir Wm. Bowyer, of pension of 100*l.*, on surrender of the same sum, part of a pension by Lady Burgh. [*Docquet.*]

July 25. Farnham. 53. Sir Thos. Lake to Salisbury. Sends letters for the Duke of Mantua and Marquis of Brandenburg, and warrants for the rewards not exceeding 300*l.* The King's reply to the Duchess of Brunswick is that the Lady Elizabeth is partially engaged. The Queen sends to excuse her hunting with the King.

July 26. Farnham. 54. The Same to the Same. Sends letters to be delivered to the Landgrave of Hesse's son, before he leaves London. Capt. Wood to be appointed Lieutenant to Sir W. Monson in the ships that are to go to sea, and not Mr. St. John.

July 27. Warrant to pay 300*l.* in rewards to the servants of certain foreign Princes, and, in addition, 30*l.* to Sebastian la Pierre, the Duke of York's dancing master; 40*l.* to John Bewchesne, his singing master; and 40*l.* to the Keeper of the Privy Purse. [*Warrt. Bk.*, III., *p.* 27.]

July. Docquet of the above, with note that the additions were made at the express order of the Lord Treasurer. [*Docquet, July* 28.]

July 27. Westminster. Grant to Sir Robt. Basset, upon certain conditions, of pardon for life only for treasons, traitorous speeches, &c., by him committed, having been lately distracted. Latin. [*Sign Man., vol.* I., *No.* 83.]

July 28. Docquet of the above.

July 28. 55. Sir Walter Covert, Sir Thos. Eversfield, and John Middleton to the Earl of Nottingham. Arrival at Horsham of John Blackman, or Blackfan, a dangerous Papist, who has been thirty years at Rome, the Archduke's Court, &c. Describe his person.

July 28. Farnham. Warrant for setting up a pale between the Great Park and Sunning-hill Park, the expenses to be defrayed from the revenues of Windsor Castle. Also for felling trees needful for that purpose. [*Warrt. Bk.*, II., *p.* 200.]

July 28. Grant to Hen. Fleetwood and his sureties of protection from his creditors. [*Docquet.*]

VOL. LXV.

Grant to John Russell of a pension of 100*l.* per ann. in consideration of his having paid 500*l.* for the King to Lord Aubigny. [*Docquet.*]

Grant to And. Whitlaw of a pension of 30*l.* per ann. in consideration of his having paid 150*l.* for the King to Lord Aubigny. [*Docquet.*]

56. Edw. Reynoldes to Mr. Beeston. For payment of arrears of interest and of the principal [of his debt] as soon as means allow.

57. Thos. Lord Darcy to Salisbury. Excuses for not having attended him when in London.

58. Wm. Typper to the Same. On the power of the Crown to restore by patent the lands, &c. of persons attainted by Parliament. *Incloses,*

58. I. *Note of attainders and restitutions from Edw. IV. to Hen. VIII.*

58. II. *Notes of Acts of Parliament,* 11 *Hen. VII., granting to that King certain manors forfeited by attainders.*

59. Note of munition and other necessaries needful for St. Andrew's Castle.

60. Petition of John Morrison to Salisbury for payment of 400*l.*, remainder of 900*l.* due to him for an ewer of agate delivered to His Highness. [*See July* 18, 1608.]

61. Charges of the day wages and provisions for the works at Somerset House for July.

62. Charges of the works done at the Friars at Richmond, June and July 1611.

63. Sir Hen. Hobart to Sir Thos. Lake. To have inserted into the patent of the French merchants a clause prefixed, maintaining its validity against the "Act for free trade to Spain, Portugal, and France," or any other Act.

64. Sir Hen. Wotton to Salisbury. Reminds him of the business touching Mr. Mole, by Lovelace the bearer, who would go to Rome to secure some moneys due to him, and depending on Mr. Fitzherbert's return. Has been ill, but is better. [*See July* 17.]

65. Sir Julius Cæsar, Chancellor of the Exchequer, to the Same. Particulars of documents sent for signature, &c. Lord Houth's submission and release. *Incloses,*

65. I. *Note of the pensions paid since July* 18.

65. II. *Memorandum of the payments now most pressing, Aug.* 1.

Vol. LXV.

1611.

Aug. 1. 66. Robt. Bell to Salisbury. Pains taken to detect pirates in Ireland. They are encouraged by Sir John Roper, and so numerous that a merchant ship can hardly escape. Necessity of attacking them. *Incloses,*

66. I. *Humph. Curson to Robt. Bell and the merchants in London. The pirates are trimming their ships near Crookhaven in Ireland. His endeavours and anxiety to be after them. July 21, Plymouth.*

Aug. 1. Gravesend. 67. Sir Robt. Stewart to Salisbury. Note of leave-taking. Begs not to be forgotten while absent, for assistance as to his debts; leaves Geo. Trussell his solicitor.

Aug. 2. York. 68. Lord Sheffield, President of the North, to the Same. In favour of the widow of Jonas Waterhouse, His Majesty's late Attorney before the Council in the North, for payment of 187*l.* 2*s.* 5*d.* arrears of wages and reward for 2½ years service. *Annexed is,*

68. I. *Petition of Sence, widow of Jonas Waterhouse, to the Same, for payment of moneys due to her late husband, &c., and some reward for his services.*

Aug. 3. Salisbury. Proclamation for restraint of building in and about London. Printed. [*Proc. Bk., p.* 245.]

Aug. 5. Letter to the Bishop of Winchester to attend the King at Tichbourne, in a matter concerning Dr. Laud. [*Docquet. See Sept.* 23.]

Aug. 5. Grant to Claud Hamilton and Walter Allison of the benefit of the recusancy of Zachary Fryer, Fras. Lockey, and Hen. Jarrett, all of London. [*Docquet.*]

Aug. 5. Letter to the Provost and Fellows of King's College, Cambridge, to grant to the widow of Dr. Fletcher, deceased, the term of ten years in the parsonage of Kingwood, co. Hants. [*Docquet.*]

Aug. 5. Release to Earl of Clanricarde and Lady Frances his wife, sole executrix of Sir Philip Sydney, who was executor of Sir Hen. Sydney, and sole daughter and heir of Sir Fras. Walsingham, and executrix of Lady Ursula Walsingham, who was executrix of Sir Fras. Walsingham, of all sums and debts owing to the Crown by any of the above-named parties. [*Docquet.*]

Aug. 5. Warrant to the Master of the Great Wardrobe for stuff delivered for the King's use, for half a year, ending Lady-day last. [*Docquet.*]

Aug. 5. Grant to Sir Robt. Newdigate of prolongation of protection for six months from all arrest for the debts of Lord Clifton, for whom he is bound as surety. [*Docquet.*]

Aug. 5. Letter to Sir Julius Cæsar and other Commissioners to assemble for reforming errors and settling all things with the undertakers for supplying London with water. [*Docquet.*]

VOL. LXV.

1611.
Aug. 5. Letter to the Lord Treasurer for a grant to Humph. May to be employed in such despatches as shall pass between the Lord Deputy of Ireland and this country; also to be employed to draw all such bills, warrants, and letters as are to pass His Majesty's signature for the service of that Kingdom; and to have a patent in reversion of a Clerkship of the Signet, and an allowance of 200 marks per ann. [*Docquet.*]

Aug. 5. Grant to Humph. May of pension of 200 marks per ann. for official services. [*Docquet. See Irish Corresp., Aug. 5,* 1611.]

Aug 6. Salisbury. Warrant to pay to Robt. Barker, the King's Printer, 167*l.* 1*s.* for printing and binding books. [*Warrt. Bk.,* III., *p.* 30.]

Aug. Docquet of the above. [*Docquet, Aug.* 5.]

Aug. 6. 69. Tim. Elks to [Thos. Lumsden?] Whitehead sent word to the Countess of Northumberland that he would say nothing about the Earl that could hurt him.

Aug. 7. Oatlands. 70. Earl of Nottingham to Salisbury. Search to be made about Court and elsewhere for a suspicious man who is practising to shoot the King. Hopes His Majesty's favour for his son Charles. Is waiting on the Duke of York in his progress, during which they will make war on the King's deer.

Aug. 8. Licence to Wm. Goring and Edw. Dowse to travel for three years. [*Docquet.*]

Aug. 8. Grant to Ann Mattingley, of Watford, co. Herts., of pardon for stealing a woollen cloth. [*Docquet.*]

Aug. 8. Grant to Jas. Watkinson and Jos. Field, Aldermen, of Kingston-upon-Hull, of certain lands in Lound, co. York, in lieu of other lands called Trepitt in the same county, or county of Kingston-upon-Hull. [*Docquet.*]

Aug. 9. 71. Charges of the works, &c. at His Majesty's houses in July.

Aug. 10. Salisbury. Confirmation of a grant made by the Lord High Admiral, July 13, 1611, to Sir Nich. Lusher, of Shooland, co. Surrey, Sir Hugh Wirrall, of Enfield, co. Middlesex, and others, of the office of measuring coals, grain, corn, and salt, to be shipped within the Lord Admiral's jurisdiction. [*Sign Man., vol.* I., *No.* 84.]

Aug. 10. Docquet of the above.

Aug. 10. Grant in trust to the Lord Treasurer, Lord Privy Seal, and Sir Julius Cæsar, of divers lands, manors, and castles, co. Northumberland, formerly granted to the late Earl of Dunbar, since whose death divers imperfections are conceived to be in the said grant; therefore a commission is to be appointed to survey the same. [*Docquet.*]

1611. VOL. LXV.

Aug. 10. Grant to the Lord Treasurer and others in trust of the lands last named, for the purpose of enabling the King to dispose thereof, after survey taken and respect had to the former grant to the Earl of Dunbar, and agreement between him and the Earl of Suffolk. [*Docquet.*]

Aug. 10. Grant to the Earl of Montgomery, in reversion after Geo. Pollard and Sir John Danvers, of the Wardenship of the Forests of Pewsham and Blackmore, Devizes, co. Wilts. [*Docquet.*]

Aug. 10. Grant to the Same, in reversion after Sir Hen. Brown and Sir Alex. Hay, of the Keepership of Hendley Park, co. Surrey. [*Docquet.*]

Aug. 10. Grant of pension of 2*s.* 6*d.* per diem to John Simpson, appointed to attend Visct. Fenton in such services as he or his deputy shall require. [*Docquet.*]

Aug. 10. Grant to Ant. Lewis, on surrender of Edw. Altham, of the Captaincy of West Tilbury, co. Essex, and of the new fortifications, &c. there. [*Docquet.*]

Aug. 10. Grant to Thos. Marbury, of the benefit of the recusancy of Lewis Richardson and Elizabeth Waferer. [*Docquet.*]

Aug. 10. Grant to Michael Kirkham of a pension of 50*l.* per ann. on surrender of a like pension granted to George Kirkham. [*Docquet.*]

Aug. 13. Londesborough. 72. Earl of Cumberland to Salisbury. Sends the assurance of the jointure [of Salisbury's daughter, married to his son], which has been stayed by the Assize business. Thanks for favours, &c.

Aug. 13. Salisbury. 73. Edw. Lord Wotton to the Same. Requests imprest of 1,000*l.* for providing wax at a cheaper rate for the King's household.

Aug. 13. Grant to Thos. Rymer of an almsroom in Christchurch, Oxford. [*Docquet.*]

Aug. 13. Grants to Edw. Thomson and Humph. Warren of almsrooms in Durham. [*Docquet.*]

Aug. 13. Grants to John Davies and John Grave of almsrooms in Bristol. [*Docquet.*]

Aug. 13. Grant to John Thompson of an almsroom in Rochester. [*Docquet.*]

Aug. 13. Grant to Rich. Dish of an almsroom in Worcester. [*Docquet.*]

Aug. 15. Fleet. 74. Rich. Heaton to Salisbury. Has repeatedly petitioned for relief from sufferings caused by false accusations, promising if liberated not to meddle any more with recusants, finding the business so difficult and dangerous.

VOL. LXV.

1611.

Aug. 16. Pontefract. 75. Sir Hen. Savile [jun.], Sir Hen. Slingsby, and Thos. Bland to Salisbury. Certify their proceedings with the copyhold tenants of Pontefract, in persuading them to compound for uncertain fines.

Aug. 16. Warrant for the chains for certain ministers of foreign Princes, to be delivered from the jewel house, and for payment of 40*l.* each to the servants of the Duke of Mantua, Marquis of Brandenburg, and "the Barbarian." [*Warrt. Bk.*, III., *p.* 28.]

Aug. Docquet of the above. [*Docquet, Aug.* 17.]

Aug. 17. 76. John Dacombe to Salisbury. The Earl of Bedford has conveyed Covent Garden in trust for the present maintenance of the Countess, who will transfer to his Lordship the things desired by him therein.

Aug. 17. Goldsborough. 77. Earl of Cumberland to the Same. Young Braithwaite, the late lawyer's eldest son, has killed his servant in so foul a manner that it must be found wilful murder. He had a pardon two years ago for stealing plate from his father. Requests permission to redeem some land adjoining Brougham Castle, his principal house in Westmoreland, mortgaged to Braithwaite's father, and now descended to him.

Aug. 17. Grant of 228*l.* 4*s.* to John Murray, servant of the Queen, and 50*l.* to John Hume, servant of the King, as gifts. [*Docquet.*]

Aug. 17. Grant to Gilbert Raleigh, in reversion after Sir Carew Raleigh and Sir Carew Reynell, of the office of Lieutenant of the Isle and Captain of the Castle of Portland, co. Dorset. [*Docquet.*]

Aug. 17. Grant to Hen. Palmer, in reversion after Sir Hen. Palmer and Sir Guildford Slingsby, of the office of Comptroller of His Majesty's Ships. [*Docquet.*]

Aug. 18. Westminster. Warrant to pay 1,000 marks to Capt. Wm. Murray from casualties in the Exchequer. [*Warrt. Bk.*, III., *p.* 35.]

Aug. Docquet of the above. [*Docquet, Aug.* 17.]

Aug. 18. 78. Wm. Lord Knollys to Salisbury. Novel exactions by the deputies of the Duke [of Lenox] as alnagers on cloth, very prejudicial to the Yorkshire clothiers.

Aug. 19. Beaulieu. 79. Sir Thos. Lake to the Same. The King will shortly join the Queen at Oatlands. He desires the patent for the ordnance to be sent him. Arguments to be used with the Chancellor of Denmark in favour of peace with Sweden. The Poles prevail in Muscovy. The King goes on Thursday to the Isle of Wight.

Aug. 19. Elnerton. Monday. 80 Visct. Lisle to the Same. Will be careful for his Lordship's lodging at Oatlands. The Queen so much indebted to him that he should never lack a lodging in her house.

Vol. LXV.

1611.

Aug. 19. 81. Charges of works, &c. at His Majesty's houses in June and July.

Aug. 20. Offley. 82. Sir Rich. Spencer to Sir Dud. Carleton. Consents for his nephew Carleton to travel further into Italy under his Lordship's direction, and sends 100*l.* for his expenses.

Aug. 20. 83. Sir Walter Cope to the Same. English stocking weavers, after fruitless experiments here, have gone over to Venice. The embers of the powder plot raked up again by Tim. Elks, the Earl of Northumberland's servant, who seeks to prove that his master knew of the plot beforehand, and brings in Carleton's name, though the best men acquit him of all blame. *Annexes,*

83. I. *Particulars [by Sir W. Cope] of the examination of the Earl of Northumberland touching his knowledge of the hiring of Whynniard's house by Thos. Percy. The Earl thinks that Carleton and Hippesley desired him to write about it for Percy. John Rowliffe examined, remembered Percy's persuading Carleton and Hippesley to mention it to the Earl, as the house would be convenient for his disrobing after Parliament. John Hippesley denied having moved the Earl about the house, but said that on the morning of the Gunpowder Plot he told the Earl that Percy had a house at Westminster, for which he said he was sorry.*

Aug. 21. Beaulieu. 84. Sir Thos. Lake to [Salisbury]. The King would prefer Dr. Jonas [Carisius, the Danish Ambassador's] not coming to Court till he reaches Farnham or Oatlands. In the draft of the High Commission, the King dislikes that part marked with three crosses, &c., as seeming to limit his power of granting a larger commission if he chose.

Aug. 21. Grant to Geo. and Thos. Whitmore, at nomination of John Eldred and others, of certain manors, lands, &c., value 72*l.* 0*s.* 2¼*d.* per ann., and also of the hundred of Barton Regis, co. Gloucester, Winckleiff, co. Devon, and manor of Cockhamstead, co. Herts. [*Docquet.*]

Aug. 21. Grant to Thos. Goodall, of London, Barber-Surgeon, and his sureties, of protection for 12 months from arrest for debts of Sir Robt. Stewart, for which he is bound. [*Docquet.*]

Aug. 21. Licence to Sir Robt. Basset to come into the realm and remain there six months, he giving certain bonds on his arrival to remain in such places as shall be appointed. [*Docquet. See Aug.* 31.]

Aug. 25. Woodstock. 85. Sir Chas. Cornwallis to [Salisbury]. The Prince is moved by the Spanish proceedings, thinking he cannot marry honourably except in Spain or France, and begs his Lordship to "unvizard the matter in France," thanking him for his wise opinion on it. State of the repairs going on at Richmond.

VOL. LXV.

1611.

Aug. 26. Beaulieu. 86. Sir Thos. Lake to [Salisbury]. The King approves of the clause of the High Commission, with an alteration specified. Sir Robt. Basset is to be confined in some remote place, such as his own house in Cornwall, for six months, &c. Dr. Jonas [Carisius] had a private audience yesterday, &c.

Aug. 27. Tuesday. 87. Visct. Fenton to the Same. The King surprised to find from Sir John Digby that his overtures to the Spanish Ambassador for the Prince's match with the Infanta were discovered. The Ambassador is to be spoken with, and assured that the King will accept no younger daughter, as talked of. Dr. Jonas has proposed that the King of Denmark should deal for a match between the Count Palatine and the Lady Elizabeth, but as the Duke of Bouillon has proposed it, he must not be neglected.

Aug. 29. 88. Preamble and abstract of the High Commission for Ecclesiastical Causes, granted for suppression of heresy.

Aug. 29. York. 89. Lord Sheffield to Salisbury. Increase of Papists who refuse the Oath of Allegiance. Is told that the King will grant their forfeitures to his needy servants. If so, wishes for a share thereof.

Aug. 29. Grant to the Queen of the manor and park of Oatlands, co. Surrey. [*Docquet.*]

Aug. 30. Warrant dormant to deliver to Wm. Bruncard two thirds of such munition, powder, &c. as he shall discover to have been committed to divers persons, and embezzled, from 20 Eliz. to 1 Jac. I., and of all fines paid into the Exchequer therefor. [*Docquet.*]

ug. 30. 90. Chancellor Ellesmere to Salisbury. Has directed Wm. Pinches to take charge of the books and papers of the Lower House. The Queen's evidences, lately in [Ralph] Ewen's charge, should be committed to some proper officer.

ug. 31. rnham. 91. The King to the Same. Will be much offended if the States elect Vorstius, who has published a blasphemous book, as Divinity Professor at Leyden. Desires Sir Noel Caron to unite with Mr. [Sir Ralph] Winwood to prevent so great an evil, &c. Draft indorsed [by Sir Thos. Windebank], "This was the first occasion that ever gave me access to His Majesty."

ug. 31. 92. Copy of the above.

Aug.? 93. Discourse on the Treatise of Vorstius concerning God, with the apology, pointing out its fallacies, &c. Italian.

Aug.? 94. Note on, and extracts from the Treatise of Vorstius concerning God, relating to his opinion of King James. Latin.

Aug. 31. Wiston. 95. Sir Robt. Shirley to [Salisbury]. Prays the stay of seizure on his father, Sir Thomas, now lying sick, for arrears of rent of certain parsonages due by him to the Crown.

VOL. LXV.

1611.
Aug. 31. Letter to the Council directing them to confine Sir Robt. Basset, who has licence to remain in the realm for six months, to his house in Cornwall, or some friend's house of good conformity in religion, remote from London. [*Docquet.*]

Aug.? 96. Sir Hen. Savile to Sir Dud. Carleton. Arrangements about his Eton property. Surprised that the Bishop should have forgotten him, as they were once correspondents. Rumours that a storm is likely to burst upon Geneva. Hopes the Bernese will not forsake them.

VOL. LXVI. SEPTEMBER, OCTOBER, 1611.

Sept. 1. Bagshot. Sunday. 1. Visct. Fenton to Salisbury. The King approves all his Lordship's letters, except the remark that there was no haste in the matter of the Lady Elizabeth. It should not be neglected, since the King of Denmark has moved it. Understands that the motion proceeds from the Marquis of Brandenburg. Dr. Jonas should be acquainted with what has been done.

Sept. 2. 2. Description by Ralph Colphab [Thomas Cariat], of Brasennose College, Oxford, of a philosophical feast, the guests at which were Chris. Brook, John Donne, Master Cranfield, Art. Ingram, Sir Robt. Phillipps, Sir Hen. Neville, Mr. Connock, Mr. Hoskins, Rich. Martin, Sir Hen. Goodere, John West, Hugh Holland, and Inigo Jones. In Latin rhymes.

Sept. 3. King's Bench, Southwark. 3. Chas. Topcliffe to Salisbury. John Hume, Page of Honour, has died in a house opposite the prison where he is injuriously detained, having paid his debt to Jas. Steward. Has advanced money for Hume, and procured him attendance during his illness. Requests reimbursement.

Sept. 3. Augusta. 4. John Chamberlain to Sir Dud. Carleton. His journey tedious by reason of suspicion of the sickness Was obliged to proceed in bye ways through fields, and was stayed on the borders of Bavaria. Hochselius is keeper of the library at Augusta. Cannot find the books which Mr. Horne wished him to buy. Is going to Frankfort.

Sept. 4. Windsor. 5. Robt. Paddon to Salisbury. Solicits the place of Ralph Ewens, Her Majesty's Auditor, deceased, for Wm. Court, who was his deputy.

Sept. 4. Milton. 6. Sir Wm. Fitzwilliam to the Same. Begs not to be condemned unheard, for his non-attendance this summer on the Earl of Exeter.

Sept. 4. 7. Bond of Chas. and Geo. Chambers, of London, under penalty of 400*l.*, to assign to Ellis Rothwell their grant of the benefit of the recusancy of Thos. Bagshaw, of the Ridge, co. Derby.

Sept. 4. 8. Copy of the above obligation.

VOL. LXVI.

1611.

Sept. 5. Houghton. 9. Sir John Gray, Sir Thos. Beaumont, and Sir Geo. Belgrave to Salisbury. Understand the King is displeased with the county of Leicester about the composition for the provision of the household. Have offered to compound for the same. Ask advice as to whether they should address the King or Council thereon.

Sept. 7. 10. Charges of works, &c. on His Majesty's houses in August.

Sept. 8. 11. Sir Art. Capell and others to Dr. Atkins. Require him to send a horse and man, properly equipped, to the muster of train-bands for Herts, on Oct. 1. With particulars of the arms required for a light horseman.

Sept. 8. Ludlow Castle. 12. Lord Eure and Council of Wales to Salisbury. Request despatch of the pardon for Watkyn Howell and Wm. Thomas Prithorith, convicted of felony.

Sept. 8. 13. Memorandum of the distribution of 4*l.* to the servants of the Archbp. of Canterbury, on the consecration of Dr. King, Bishop of London.

Sept. 9. Grant to Rich. Blount and his sureties of protection for a year, to enable him to sell his lands in order to pay his creditors. [*Docquet.*]

Sept. 9. Grant to Geo. Chambers of the benefit of the recusancy of Thos. and Hen. Bagshaw, Chris. Rolleston, and divers other recusants, cos. Derby, Stafford, and Hereford. [*Docquet.*]

Sept. 9. Grant to Robt. Hay, Groom of the Bedchamber, of pension of 200*l.* per ann. for life. [*Docquet.*]

Sept. 9. Presentation of John Archibald to the vicarage of Bromsgrove, with the Chapel of King's Norton, dioc. Worcester. [*Docquet.*]

Sept. 9. Grant, with survivorship, to John and Wm. Lugar, of the office of Maker of Blackjacks and other necessaries of leather for the household, Tower, Navy, and Standards. [*Docquet.*]

Sept. 10. Hampton Court. Proclamation for restraint of building in and about London. Printed. [*The same as that of Aug.* 3. *Proc. Bk., p.* 247.]

Sept. 10. Grant to Christiana, widow of Dr. Martin Schoverus, late Physician to the Queen, of 150*l.*, as a free gift. [*Warrt. Bk.*, III., *p.* 28.]

Sept. Docquet of the above. [*Docquet, Sept.* 12.]

Sept. 11. 14. Sir Geo. Chaworth to Salisbury. A friend of his has found a suit, which, besides a good rent to the King, will yield near 3,000*l.* per ann. Offers, if it may be conferred on himself, to place one half at his Lordship's disposal. Pleads his seven years' service to the King.

Sept. 11. Wanstead. Wednesday. 15. Sir Roger Aston to [the Same]. Sends His Majesty's letter to the King of Denmark. The King sends a stag of his own killing for Dr. Jonas [Carisius]. The report that Lord Cranston had spoken ill of the King of Denmark is false.

1611. Vol. LXVI.

Sept. 11. Wanstead. 16. John Murray to Salisbury. Sends the bearer for the King of Denmark's letters, which His Majesty wishes for at once.

Sept. 11. Salisbury House. 17. Earl of Salisbury to Sir John Gray and others. They may, if they please, address the King directly with terms for the composition for purveyance in Leicestershire; but he will probably refer their proposal to the Council. [*See Sept.* 5.]

Sept. 12. Wanstead. 18. Earl of Pembroke to Salisbury. To forward the petition of his cousin, Capt. Jasper Herbert, that the few horse which Sir Edw. Herbert has in pay may be continued to Jasper Herbert, if he should outlive him. [*See Irish Corresp., Nov.* 3.]

Sept. 12. Writ of restitution of temporalities of the Bishopric of London for Dr. John King. [*Docquet.*]

Sept. 12. Letter to the Dean and Canons of Windsor for a lease to Geo. Marshall of certain lands in Sutton-Courtney, co. Berks, now in tenure of And. Windsor. [*Docquet.*]

Sept. 12. Grant to Wm. Hunt, in reversion after Edw. Kirkham, of the office of Yeoman of the King's vestures or apparel of masques, revels, and disguisings, and of apparel and trappers of horses for jousts and tourneys. [*Docquet.*]

Sept. 12. Grant to Hen. Smith of the Prebends of Milton Manor, co. Oxford, and Binbrooke, co. Lincoln, founded in Lincoln Cathedral, void by promotion of Dr. King as Bishop of London. [*Docquet.*]

Sept. 12. Grant to Wm. Jones of an almsroom in Peterborough. [*Docquet.*]

Sept. 12. Grant to Thos. Throwre of an almsroom in Norwich. [*Docquet.*]

Sept. 13. Venice. 19. [Sir Dud. Carleton] to Sir Walter Cope. Would be made unhappy by the suspicions of the powder plot current against him, but that he has a noble protector and patron. His innocency will protect him. Never had the conferences or correspondence with Percy, of which he is accused. Mr. Chamberlain will relate particulars of a coolness between himself and Percy, which led him to wish to change his situation. Hopes his present official position will make people tender of his reputation.

Sept. 16. Fotheringay. 20. Barth. Elam to John Ross. Requests him to obtain the warrant for his salary as schoolmaster, due at Michaelmas. The Bishop [of Peterborough] questions the Lord Treasurer's right to appoint him, and threatens to put another in his place.

Sept. 17. Amesbury. Tuesday. 21. Earl of Hertford to Salisbury. Cannot prevail on Sir John Rodney to undertake the journey to find his unfortunate grandchild, Wm. Seymour. Suggests sending John Pilling, the youth's former tutor, who could dissuade him from errors in religion. Wishes young Rodney were removed from him.

Sept. 18. London. 22. Tim. Elks to [Thos. Lumsden]. Private affairs. If he can serve the King, wishes to do it at once, for he has intelligence of mischief devising against himself.

VOL. LXVI.

1611.

Sept. 19. Theobalds. 23. Sir Roger Aston to Salisbury. The King desires to know if Dr. Jonas is gone away satisfied. The grapes were welcome. The old buck to be killed when the Prince comes. His Majesty has surveyed the ground that is to be taken into Theobald's Park.

Sept. 19. Grant to Edm. Dickinson of pardon for horse stealing. [*Docquet.*]

Sept. 19. Grant in reversion to Jos. White of a Gunner's place in the Tower. [*Docquet.*]

Sept. 19. Grant to Edw. Faulkner of the office of Clerk of the Prick and Cheque at Deptford Strond, co. Kent. [*Docquet.*]

Sept. 19. Letter to the Lord Chancellor, Lord Treasurer, and Lord Privy Seal, to acquaint Sir Wm. Killigrew with the patent granted to John Michell for the sole making of writs of "Supersedeas quia improvide" in the Court of Common Pleas, and to order him to conform thereto. [*Docquet.*]

Sept. ? Warrant whereby the King pledges himself not to grant away any other of the profits belonging to the officers of the Court of Common Pleas, beside the sole making of writs of supersedeas, lately granted to John Michell. [*Warrt. Bk.*, I., *p.* 198.]

Sept. 19. Licence to Sir Lewis Watson, of Rockingham, co. Northampton, to travel. [*Docquet.*]

Sept. 19. Grant to John Slany of the full benefit of the recusancy of Dr. John Halsey, deceased. [*Docquet.*]

Sept. 19. Grant to Thos. Knyvet, in reversion after Robt Bowyer and Fras. Crane, of the office of Clerk of the Parliament. [*Docquet.*]

Sept. 21. Letter to the Council to give order to Sir Wm. Bowyer and Hen. Yelverton to cause certain jewels in the hands of the said Bowyer, and found on the person of the Lady Arabella and her company at her intended departure, to be sold for the benefit of her creditors, &c. [*Docquet.*]

Sept. 21. Grant to Alex. Miller of the benefit of the recusancy of Grace Finch, widow. [*Docquet.*]

Sept. 21. Grant to John Wriothesley, on surrender of Edw. Monox, of the office of Assistant to the Officers of the Admiralty. [*Docquet.*]

Sept. 22. 24. Ralph Dobbinson to Salisbury. Exculpates himself from imputations against his conduct towards Widow Vincent, Sir Stephen Proctor, and the town of Westminster. False accusations of a knight not named.

Sept. 23. 25. The King to the Bp. of Winchester. Considers that the election of Dr. Laud as President of St. John's College, Oxford, was no further corrupt or partial than all elections are liable to be; therefore wishes it to stand, and clearer interpretation of the Statutes to be made for the future.

Sept. 23. Docquet of the above.

Vol. LXVI.

1611.

Sept. 25. 26. Earl of Salisbury to [Wm. Trumbull, English Ambassador in Flanders]. Approves his remonstrance made against the banishment of English cloths. [*Extract.*]

Sept. 26. Warrant to pay 40*l.* to Sir Robt. Leigh for repair of a bridge at Waltham Forest, and 10*l.* to John Norden, surveyor, for repair of the pales of Farnham Park. [*Warrt. Book,* III., *p.* 29.]

Sept. 26. Docquet of the above.

Sept. 26. Warrant to pay various sums, amounting to 52*l.* 3*s.*, to John Thorp, surveyor, for repairs of the posts, pales, and rails of Richmond Park, carried away by the flood in the last winter. [*Warrt. Bk.,* III., *p.* 28.]

Sept. 26. Docquet of the above.

Sept. 26. Presentation of Dr. Jos. Hall to the archdeaconry of Nottingham, diocese of York. [*Docquet.*]

Sept. 26. Grant to Robt. Holmes, of Oxford University, of pardon for manslaughter of John Misson. [*Docquet.*]

Sept. 26. Grant to the Yeomen of the Privy Buckhounds of 12*d.* per diem, and to the grooms and waggoner of the said hounds 6*d.* per diem, as a gift for attendance this summer quarter. [*Docquet.*]

Sept. 26. Warrant for delivery of stuff to Robt. Hay, Groom of the Bedchamber. [*Docquet.*]

Sept. 26. Grant to Sir Wm. Bowyer, Captain of the Garrison at Berwick, of annuity of 5*s.* per diem, and 5*s.* per diem to his wife and Geo. Bowyer, his son, with survivorship. [*Docquet.*]

Sept. 26. Grant to Thos. Oliver of an almsroom in Ely Cathedral. [*Docquet.*]

Sept. 26. The like to John Braderton in Chester Cathedral. [*Docquet.*]

Sept. 26. Grant to Thos. Langhorne, of London, in reversion after Peter Bland, of the office of skinner to the King. [*Docquet.*]

Sept. 26. Instalment through four years of 1,019*l.* 8*s.* 4*d.*, first fruits of the Bishopric of London, for Dr. John King. [*Docquet.*]

Sept. 26. The like of 283*l.* 16*s.* 5½*d.*, first fruits of the Bishopric of Gloucester, for Dr. Giles Thompson. [*Docquet.*]

Sept. 26. Grant to Jas. Maxwell, in reversion after John Murray, of the keepership of Guildford Park. [*Docquet.*]

Sept. 27. Amesbury. Friday. 27. Earl of Hertford to Salisbury. Wm. Seymour is now in Paris. Will do anything the King wishes concerning him.

Vol. LXVI.

1611.

Sept. 28. 28. Tim. Elks to Thos. Lumsden. The late Capt. Whitelock knew of the Earl of Northumberland's intention to be absent from Parliament on the day of the powder treason. *Incloses,*

28. I. *List of parties to whom Whitelock was likely to name it, with suggestions for their examination.*

28. II. *Notes of Capt. Whitelock's statements about the Earl, and of his intercourse with several persons named in the above list.*

28. III. *Names of parties to be examined on the several points of the above notes, and cautions to be used in the examination.*

28. IV. *Points on which each party is to be specially questioned, and generally on the favour in which Thos. Percy was held by the Earl.*

Sept. 29. 29. The Same to [the Same]. Discourse with Mr. Emerson relative to the Earl of Northumberland's intention to absent himself from Parliament on the day of the Gunpowder Plot, Percy having planned a scheme for him to go to Highgate, to meet a man who, he pretended, would make him his heir.

Sept. 29. 30. Rich. Earl of Dorset to Salisbury. Professes friendship and service.

Sept. 29. 31. Muster roll of the garrison at Sandgate Castle.

Sept. 29. 32. Names of officers and gunners admitted within Dover Castle and Mote's bulwark, and a requisition for their pay up to Michaelmas.

Sept. 29. 33. Charge of the Great Wardrobe for the last year.

Sept. 29. 34. Account book of payments made to messengers of the chamber and others, since July 23, 1610.

Sept. 29. Letter to Sir Wm. Killigrew. Not to suffer writs of supersedeas to be sealed before being allowed by John Michell. [*Docquet.*]

Sept. 29. Eton. 35. Sir Hen. Savile to Sir Dud. Carleton. The papers promised in August have not yet reached him. Lord Northumberland inculpates Carleton in the hiring of the house at Westminster by Percy. Advises him to take no notice unless directly charged.

Sept. 30. London. 36. Dr. Geo. Carleton to the Same. Sends the Bp. of Ely's last book. Intends to publish some theological treatises on the subject of his lectures at Oxford. Present degraded state of the Greeks. Begs catalogues of the succession of the ancient oriental bishoprics.

1611. VOL. LXVI.

Sept. 30. 37. Abstract of an account of the moneys expended in building andrepairing the King's houses, since his accession.

Sept. 30. Letter to the Lord Treasurer, to give order to the farmers of customs, &c. for observing certain regulations signed by the King for preventing abuses amongst merchants trading between England and Scotland. [*Docquet, Sept.* 19 *and* 30.]

Sept. 30. Letter to the Earl of Shrewsbury, to send to London certain persons who have killed deer in the King's Park of Sheriff Hutton. [*Docquet.*]

Sept. 30. Warrant for the watching liveries for the Captain and Yeomen of the Guard. [*Docquet.*]

Sept. 30. Grant to Hen. Buck of pension of 6*d*. per diem, from the death of Lawrence Weeks, who had the like pension. [*Docquet.*]

Sept. 30. Grant to Wm. Smith, sen., keeper of the deer in Cranborne Chace, of pension of 20*l*. per ann., with reversion to William, his son. [*Docquet.*]

Sept. Grant to Fras. Wilkins of an almsroom in Christ Church, Oxford. [*Docquet.*]

Sept. 38. Edw. Hayes to Salisbury. Professions of devotion. Begs leave to continue his waterworks, which are better than the Amwell waters. The city needs both Mr. [Hugh] Middleton's supply and his.

Sept. [York.] 39. Lord Sheffield to the Same. Has heard of an intention of disforesting divers forests. Hopes that of Galtres, near York, may be spared, as its loss would be very prejudicial to the place.

Sept. 40. Walter Fitzwilliam to the Same. Requests him to favour his suit. *Incloses,*

40. I. *Particular of the patent desired by Walter Fitzwilliam, to have the return of all writs for fines and recoveries in the Common Pleas. Proffers to keep a distinct calendar of them.*

[Sept.] 41. Petition of Geo. Norris to the Same. For a lease of two parts of the lands of Edw. Tarleton, recusant, which were granted to Rich. Bradshaw.

Oct. 1. Hatfield. 42. Robt. Liminge to Thos. Wilson. Reports progress in the buildings erected at Hatfield for the Earl of Salisbury.

Oct. 1. 43. List of payments due from the Crown, with marginal notes [by Salisbury] of such as are to be first paid.

Oct. 1. 44. Simon Basill, Surveyor of the Works, to Salisbury. The Lord Privy Seal wishes him to pull down and alter his house so much as will be very detrimental to his estate. Solicits direction.

VOL. LXVI.

1611.

Oct. 2. Carmarthen. 45. Sir Geo. Devereux to Salisbury. Prays protection for some poor neighbours, against a mighty man, who would lay heavy fines on them for certain Crown lands.

Oct. 3. Cambridge. 46. Justices of Cambridgeshire to the Earl of Suffolk, Lord Lieutenant of Cambridgeshire and Suffolk. Pray him to move the Lord Treasurer not to grant a lease of the Castle Yard at Cambridge to Mr. Brooke, as it is used for musters, the Sheriff's pound, &c.

Oct. 3. Warrant to pay to Roger Pilkinhorne 72*l.* for his charges in fitting out a ship for apprehending Griffin the pirate and his company, and for their capture and imprisonment at Launceston, Cornwall. [*Warrt. Bk.*, III., *p.* 29.]

Oct. 4. Salisbury House. 47. Salisbury to the Undertakers of the Copper Works in Cornwall. Approves of Mr. Marlott as surveyor of the copper works, but wishes John Milward to give occasional information on the same.

Oct. 4. 48. Proposed order of precedency of the different ranks of nobility, baronets, knights, officers of state, &c., &c., with queries upon doubtful points relating thereto.

[Oct. 4.] 49. Copy of the above.

Oct. 5. The Hague. 50. Chamberlain to Carleton. Describes his journey from Frankfort. Excursions in Holland with Sir Horace Vere and Sir John Burlacy. Sir Thos. Knollys and Lascelles arrived. Sir Calisthenes Brooke, lately dead, and Sir Robt. Rich; also rich Sutton, who bought the Charter House for his intended hospital. Court news in England. The pirates refuse pardon, and are gone to Florence to be commanded by Sir Robt. Dudley.

Oct. 5. Hampton Court. 51. Dr. Theod. de Mayerne to Salisbury. The Queen's general health good, and her local affection improving. Wishes to stay with her till she is well. French.

Oct. 6. Morlewood. 52. Sir John Stafford to the Same. Has refused to admit certain surveyors to view Bristol Castle, which it is said is about to be sold, because they had no warrant to show. Hopes the King is not driven to sell the castle of the second town in the kingdom, but if so, the citizens wish to buy it.

Oct. 6. 53. John Baylie to the Same. Great weakness of the castles and forts along the coast, for want of the proper allowance of men. Proposes that he should be made Muster Master and Surveyor of all the Castles, from Gravesend to St. Michael's Mount, Cornwall.

Oct. 6. Royston. 54. Sir Roger Aston to [the Same]. The King has amended the enclosed letter, and desires the despatch of it and others. He approves Mayerne's wish to remain with the Queen. A bark to be sent to bring over wine and fruit trees, &c.

VOL. LXVI.

1611.

Oct. 6. Berwick. 55. Mayor, &c. of Berwick to Salisbury. Progress of Berwick Bridge. Desire wood from Chopwell Forest. *Inclose,*

55. I. *Account of moneys disbursed for the building of Berwick Bridge from June* 19 *to Sept.* 28, 1611.

55. II. *Plot of the work completed for Berwick Bridge, Oct.* 6, 1611.

Oct. 6. 56. [Earl of Salisbury] to the Receiver of Northamptonshire. To detain the half year's salary due to the schoolmaster at Fotheringay till further orders, as it is claimed both by Thos. Lindsell and Barth. Elam.

Oct. 8. Powerscourt. 57. Lady Frances Cromwell to Salisbury. For licence for her son to spend three or four years in France.

Oct. ? 58. Edw. Lord Denny to the Same. Recommends John Leet, an ancient lawyer in Gray's Inn, to the fifth place void in the Exchequer.

Oct. 8. 59. Same to the Same. Recommends the bearer's petition.

Oct. 8. Fleet. 60. Rich. Heaton to the Same. Is imprisoned on false accusations. Begs favour for a petition on a certain suit in the Exchequer.

Oct. 9. Whitehall. 61. Earl of Northampton to the Same. The Council recommends granting a petition for immunity from impost on whale fins, brought in this year with great peril of the petitioners' lives. O'Bryan's suit for lands in Wexford is unseasonable; importance of conciliating the affections of the people in Ireland.

Oct. 9. 62. Earl of Shrewsbury to the Same. Requests shutters for the windows, boards before the doors, and repair of a hole in the roof of the rooms [in the Tower], where his wife is lodged.

Oct. 10. 63. The King to the Knights and Gentlemen of Hertfordshire, concerning the inclosure of Enfield Chace. Fragment.

Oct. 10. Paris. 64. Hen. Lord Clifford to Salisbury. Being now free from the unpleasing company of physicians, certifies his recovery. Mr. [Wm.] Beecher will have announced his intended return to England.

Oct. 11. Royston. 65. Sir Thos. Lake to [the Same]. The King has signed the letter for Enfield Chace. The commoners should have been assured that he will not disgrace his chace by inclosing more land. Sir Wm. Killigrew to be questioned why he refuses to seal the writs subscribed by Mr. Murray.

Oct. 12. Royston. 66. Same to [the Same]. Forwards letters and Privy Seals for Sir Robt. Shirley and for Dr. Jonas' expenses. His Majesty heard of his care for Archy's coat [the Court Fool], which is like to make sport.

Oct. 12. London. 67. Sir Thos. Lowe to the Same. Has appointed four experienced merchants of the Levant Company to wait on Sir Robt. Shirley.

1611. VOL. LXVI.

Oct. 12. Peterborough. 68. Thos. Dove, Bp. of Peterborough, to the Council. Has not been negligent in administering the Oath of Allegiance to all in his diocese above the age of 18. Peice, of Washingley, a notorious recusant, lives in Huntingdonshire, and is beyond his reach.

Oct. 13. Royston. 69. Sir Thos. Lake to [Salisbury]. The King approves the draft of the Privy Seals for the loan, and desires that they be addressed to a few of ability to lend 100*l.* or 100 marks, rather than to a multitude for smaller sums. The letters for Lorraine are sent; those for the Archduke to be written over again, because the clerk wrote the subscription, which should be in the King's hand.

Oct. 13. Royston. 70. The Same to the Same. Lord Oxford's claim to Havering Park is to be inquired into. The King will grant it if it be a right, but fears neither the Earl nor his mother would take care of the game.

Oct. 13. Royston. 71. Visct. Fenton to the Same. The King satisfied with the letter and proclamation for Scotland. He wishes some means to be devised to prevent the exportation of moneys by persons going on travel.

Oct. 13. Cambridge. 72. Dr. Valentine Carey to Visct. Rochester. Solicits the Deanery of Lincoln, according to His Majesty's promise to Sir Roger Aston.

Oct. 13. Warrant to pay 109*l.* 6*s.* for the lodging and diet of Dr. Jonas Carisius, Ambassador from the King of Denmark; 30*l.* each to two chiaus or messengers from the Turkish Court; and 100 marks to Patrick Gordon, agent for the King with the King of Poland. [*Warrt. Bk.*, III., *p.* 29.]

Oct. 14. Bristol. 73. Mayor, &c. of Bristol to Salisbury. Have deputed John Whitson, Alderman, to make composition for purchase of Bristol Castle.

Oct. 14. Queen's College, Oxford. 74. Edw. Nicholas to his father, John Nicholas. Could not obey his command, on account of the absence of the Provost. Reasons why he did not write earlier, being a tyro in academic affairs.

Oct. 15. Cambridge. 75. Thos. Brooke to Dr. Montaigne, Dean of Westminster. Desires to be allowed the herbage growing in the Castle Yard, Cambridge, but will not interfere with the citizens' use thereof.

Oct. 16. 76. Edw. Reynoldes to Fras. Mills. Particulars of correspondence on a proposed reformation in the office [of the Privy Seal]. A loan is projected. Asks if Mills will accept the charge of clerkship thereof.

Oct. 16. 77. Particulars of agreement between the King's Commissioners and the tenants in Enfield Chace, for the inclosure of 120 acres thereof.

Oct. 16. 78. Copy of the above.

Oct. 16. 79. Particulars of the patent granted to Sir John Bourchier and others, as contractors for the sole manufacture of alum.

VOL. LXVI.

1611.

Oct. 16. 80. Bond of Wm. Hoord, of Bishop's Candal, co. Dorset, to Robt. Waller, of Sidbury, co. Devon, under penalty of 1,000 marks, to hold him harmless as to a recognizance for 500*l.*, given in Hoord's behalf, in an action of trespass entered against him by John Cole.

Oct. 17. Fleet. 81. Rich Heaton to Salisbury. Is committed on suspicion only. Prays to be allowed to instruct his counsel, and to have the records searched upon his cause.

Oct. 17. 82. Charge of work, &c. at His Majesty's houses in September.

Oct. 18. 83. Lady Frances Clifford to Salisbury, her father. Respect and affection. Desires him to thank Lord and Lady Cumberland for their kindness to her.

Oct. 18. 84. Earl of Nottingham to the Same. Thanks for his annuity bestowed by the King of 1,000*l.* per ann. Was to receive 500*l.* on account from Art. Ingram.

Oct.? 85. Arguments addressed to the Lords [Commissioners for the Office of Earl Marshal] by the Serjeants-at Law, in favour of their being allowed precedency over Knights, whose creation is of later date than their own. With request for a decision of the controversy.

Oct. 20. 86. Petition of the Serjeants-at-Law to the King to be allowed precedency over Knights, the Earl Marshal's Court having failed to satisfy their wishes; with the King's reply. Indorsed is a copy of the above arguments. Imperfect.

[Oct. 20.] 87. Copy of the above petition similarly indorsed. [*Imperfect, but supplying the blanks in the preceding paper.*]

Oct. 20. 88. Petition of Wm. Warmoth, of Newcastle-on-Tyne, to Salisbury. For lease of the coal mines of Cocken, co. Durham. With reference, report, and order thereon.

Oct. 21. Royston. 89. John Murray to the Same. To hear the cause between himself and the tenants of Plumpton. Hopes Sir Wm. Killigrew will be satisfied that he [Murray] does not wish to wrong him in the wire business.

Oct. 22. Royston. 90. Sir Thos. Lake to [the Same]. The King disappointed that all the Privy Seals [for the loan] are not sent for signature. He did not require a second draft. They are to be prepared as quickly as possible.

Oct. 22. 91. Articles agreed on by the Commissioners for the government of the Borders, at their general meeting in Carlisle. Chiefly collected out of former instructions. With queries relative to the Commission of July 5.

Oct.? 92. Tim. Elks to Thos. Lumsden. Sends a friend to report his condition. Asks what hopes of the success of his business.

Oct. 25. 93. The Same to the Same. To favour his petition to the King for protection against the great man [the Earl of Northumberland], who seeks his destruction.

VOL. LXVI.

1611.

Oct.? 94. Tim. Elks to Thos. Lumsden. Has left his lodging for fear of being arrested through mischievous treachery. Is in great distress for money.

Oct. 26. 95. Dr. Matt. Gwynn to Salisbury. Has good hopes that his charge, the noble Earl, will recover from the small-pox. Particulars of his state.

Oct. 26. Milan. 96. Edw. Lord Vaux of Harrowden to the Same. Thanks for favours to himself and his mother. Sir Oliver Manners, who is ill of a fever, entreats favour for prolonging his absence beyond his licence, being unable to return from illness and the Earl of Rutland not having sent him any money.

Oct. 28. Londesborough. 97. Earl of Cumberland to the Same. Is glad to hear that his son pleases his Lordship. Has sent letters from the Border Commissioners, who have held a meeting at Carlisle, &c.

Oct. 28. 98. Dove, Bishop of Peterborough, to the Same. Barth. Elam too ignorant to be a good schoolmaster at Fotheringay, and his election informal. Wishes a worthier than he or Lindsell had been chosen. Begs help towards rebuilding the school.

Oct.? 99. Dr. Hen. Atkins to the Same. Has seen the noble Lord at Enfield, who, like Job, from the crown of his head to the sole of his foot is covered with sores. Dr. Lister and his attendant minister all things necessary to him.

Oct. 29? Enfield. Tuesday Morning. 100. Dr. Matt. Lister to the Same. Little alteration for the better in his Lordship. The pain and soreness great. Care is taken of my Lady's preservation.

Oct. 30. 101. [Edw. Reynoldes] to the Earl of Northampton, Lord Privy Seal. Recommends Mr. [Fras.] Mills as Clerk for the Loans. Mr. [Thos.] Packer, as a reversioner, might serve under him without disgrace.

Oct. 31. [Theobalds.] 102. Miles Whytakers to Salisbury. The King has been round the new ground to be inclosed in the park: 100 men are at work on the paling. Asks orders for the diet of the King's Commissioners, Sir Robt. Wroth and Sir Thos. Dacre, who will meet there.

Oct. 103. Sir Fras. Bacon to the Same. Approves his minute [of the proclamation for altering the prices of gold coin]. Sends for insertion a clause enabling the subject to refuse light gold, and two others concerning the weight of the coin, and the value to be fixed on ancient coins. [*See Nov.* 23.]

Oct. 104. Muster roll of the garrison of Deal Castle.

Oct. 105. Five similar lists, with slight alteration.

Oct. 106. Earl of Salisbury to the [Earl of Dunfermline] Chancellor of Scotland. The King resolves to establish Consuls in Spain, for support of merchants trading there; the expense to be borne by an impost on the merchandise. Thinks the Scots should pay the impost also, as they will share the advantage.

VOL. LXVII. NOVEMBER, DECEMBER, 1611.

1611.
Nov. 2. Abergwilly. 1. Ant. Rudd, Bp. of St. David's, to Salisbury. Information concerning Robt. Acton and his family, and other recusants who have removed from England and settled in his diocese.

Nov. 2. Westminster, Saturday. 2. E. Reynoldes to Fras. Mills. The Lord Privy Seal has chosen him [Mills] as Clerk for the Loans, in spite of [Thos.] Packer's efforts. He must hasten to town.

Nov. 3. Sunday. Tottenham. 3. Earl of Hertford to Salisbury. Asks directions for John Pelling, his chaplain, who is just going to Wm. Seymour at Paris. Will allow his grandchild 200*l.* per ann. at the King's pleasure. Begs that young Rodney may be removed from him.

Nov. 3. Letter to the Commissioners for Sale of the King's Lands, to allow Simeon Brograve to compound for the manor of Cockhamstead, co. Hertford, of which Dorothy, his wife, and her ancestors, have been seized for 237 years. [*Docquet.*]

Nov. 3. Grant to Edm. Woodcock of an almsroom in Ewelme Hospital, co. Oxford. [*Docquet.*]

Nov. 4. Westminster. Grant to Pet. Anthoine Bourdin, Sieur de St. Anthoine, and Julien Bourdin, Sieur de Fontenay, in France, and their heirs, of denization. Latin. [*Sign Man., vol.* I., *No.* 85.]

Nov. 4. Docquet of the above.

Nov. 4. Westminster. Grant to Jeremy Ross of pension of 40*l.* per ann. for life, upon surrender of a like pension by Robt. Browne, Gentleman of the Cellar. [*Sign Man., vol.* I., *No.* 86.]

Nov. 4. Docquet of the above.

Nov. 4. Westminster. Warrant to pay 985*l.* to John Harris, for jewels for the King's use. [*Sign Man., vol.* I., *No.* 87.]

Nov. 4. Entry of the above. [*Warrt. Bk.,* III., *p.* 30.]

Nov. 4. Docquet of the above.

Nov. 4. Westminster. Grant to Sir John Dormer and John Symonds, of the King's two thirds of the lands of Lady Curzon, recusant, being the manor of Addington, co. Bucks, at nomination of Wal. Toderick, to whom the benefit of her recusancy was granted. Latin. [*Sign Man., vol.* I., *No.* 88.]

Nov. 4. Docquet of the above.

Nov. 5. 4. Sir Robt. Oxenbridge to Salisbury. For dismissal of a second suit brought against him by Sir Edm. Lucy, touching the lease of the manor of Punsburn, bequeathed to him by Sir Hen. Cock.

Nov. 6. Whitehall. 5. Earl of Shrewsbury to Miles Whytakers. The King sends a white hind, with the woman that nurses it, to be carefully kept till his coming to Theobalds.

Vol. LXVII.

1611.

Nov. 6. Croxteth. 6. Sir Rich. Molyneux to Salisbury. The copyholders of Westerby, Lancashire, wish to have their appearance for composition of their estates postponed till Candlemas.

Nov. 6. London. 7. John Chamberlain to Sir D. Carleton. Has reached London. Intelligence of friends there. Carleton has again been in danger of implication in Lord Northumberland's affair. Particulars of his own voyage from the Hague home, &c.

Nov. 6. Westminster. Grant in reversion to Geo. Griffith of a Poor Knight's room at Windsor. [*Sign Man., vol.* I., *No.* 89.]

Nov. Docquet of the above. [*Docquet, Nov.* 8.]

Nov. 7. St. James's. 8. Sir Robt. Carey and Sir Jas. Fullerton to the Officers of the Prince's Household. The clerk of the Duke [of York's] kitchen and the master cook need a lodging in the Prince's house.

Nov. 7. 9. Certificate of the Justices of Peace and Coroners of cos. Brecon and Radnor to Chief Justice Sir Geo. Snigg, in favour of Jas. Lewis, of Llanellwith, Radnor, who had slain Richard ap John, of Llanvaier, in Builth, co. Brecon. [*See* 1612, *July* 2.]

Nov. 7. Letter to Sir Thos. Edmondes, Resident Ambassador with the French King, to recommend the cause of the Scottish Guard for the French King's person to the Council of the French King, they desiring to be restored to their original number, which of late has been diminished, and supplied with Frenchmen, or else to dispose of their places. [*Docquet, Nov.* 8.]

Nov. 7. Confirmation of Commission passed in France by the French King for levying the remainder of the dowry of Mary, Queen Dowager of France, Mother of the King. [*Docquet, Nov.* 8.]

Nov. 8. Whitehall. 10. Earl of Salisbury to the Receiver of Northamptonshire. Has confirmed the appointment of Barth. Elam, as schoolmaster at Fotheringay, and orders the annual stipend of 20*l*., with arrears, to be paid to him.

Nov. 8. 11. Sir Thos. Shirley to Salisbury. Thanks for staying Sharpeigh's Commission. His debt to the Crown of 13,572*l*., &c., being agreed to be paid by 200*l*. yearly, he begs stay of process out of the Pipe Office to extend his manor of Bugbrook, Northamptonshire, for a Crown debt.

Nov. 8. Westminster. Warrant for felling 1,800 oaks for the Royal Navy in the New Forest, Shotover, Stowe Wood, and Barnwood. [*Sign Man., vol.* I., *No.* 90.]

Nov. 8. 12. Draft of the above.

Nov. 8. Docquet of the above.

Nov. ? Whitehall. 13. [Lord Treasurer and Earl of Nottingham to the Woodwards of the above forests]. Order to deliver the above trees for the use of the Navy.

VOL. LXVII.

1611.

Nov. 8. Westminster. Warrant for felling 2,000 loads of crooked timber for the Royal Navy, in cos. Norfolk, Suffolk, Essex, Kent, Sussex, Hants, Berks, Bucks, and Oxford, besides 200 trees out of the manor of Sunning, co. Berks. [*Sign Man., vol.* I., *No.* 91.]

Nov. 8. Docquet of the above.

Nov. 8. Westminster. Warrant to pay 20*l.* per ann., and 20*l.* already due, to Jehu Webb, Master of the Tennis Plays, for instructing the Duke of York in that exercise, and providing rackets and balls for him. [*Sign Man., vol.* I., *No.* 92.]

Nov. 8. Entry of the above. [*Warrt. Bk.,* III., *p.* 31.]

Nov. 8. Docquet of the above.

Nov. 8. Westminster. Grant to John Norton, jun., of Cotherstoke, co. Northampton, of pardon for life only, for taking 10*l.* from his friend Walton Kirkham, which he immediately restored. Latin. [*Sign Man., vol.* I., *No.* 93.]

Nov. 8. Docquet of the above.

Nov. 8. Warrant dormant for delivery of stuff annually to Jas. Leigh, the King's Plasterer, and Jeronimo Talcott, his Bricklayer and Tiler, for their livery. [*Docquet.*]

Nov. 8. Grant to Hugh Lee of the office of Consul for the merchants trading to Lisbon and Portugal. [*Docquet.*]

Nov. 8. Grant to Fras. Cottington of the office of Consul for Seville, Andalusia, and Granada. [*Docquet.*]

Nov. 8 ? Blank grant of the Consulship of the Spanish ports from Seville to Carthagena and Ayamonte. [*Warrt. Bk.,* I., *p.* 182.]

Nov. 8. Grant, in reversion, to Robt. Wilson of an Ostringer's place for life. [*Docquet.*]

Nov. 8. Grant to Robt. Quarrier, in reversion after Geo. Garrett, of a Falconer's place, for life. [*Docquet.*]

Nov. 9. Letter to the Bailiffs of Shrewsbury to settle the teachers of the free school there according to the institutions and customs thereof; and, in case of difficulty, to refer to the Bishop of Coventry. [*Docquet, Nov.* 8.]

Nov. 9. 14. Katherine Lady Walsh to Salisbury. For grant of the suit which the King gave her deceased husband for his services against the powder traitors, which he did not live to enjoy, &c.

Nov. 9. Cheshunt. 15. Sir Thos. Dacre to the Same. Has consented to sell his lands [at Theobalds] to the King, and solicits present payment.

Nov. 9. Fleet. 16. John Fitzwilliam to the Same. Has been robbed in prison, and suspects the warden of complicity therein. Desires freedom for a time to prosecute the robbery, and not to be removed from his present apartment, which contains his money and papers.

Nov. 9. 17. Charges of works, &c. at the King's houses in October.

Nov. 10. 18. Earl of Exeter to Salisbury. Sir Philip Sherard is unfit to be High Sheriff for Leicestershire, having the falling sickness. Hopes the King will choose another.

VOL. LXVII.

1611.

Nov. 10. 19. Sir Wm. Waad to Salisbury. Requests the wardship of the son of Chris. Estwick, if the latter should die.

Nov. 10. Westminster. Grant to Rich. Hinson of a pension of 3*s*. 4*d*. per day, on surrender of a like pension by Wm. Stallenge. [*Sign Man., vol.* I., *No.* 94.]

Nov. 10. Docquet of the above.

Nov. 10. Westminster. Grant to Sir Hen. Thynne, and five others, &c., of the accustomed reward of 5*s*. per ton on building six ships named. [*Sign Man., vol.* I., *No.* 95.]

Nov. 10. Docquet of the above.

Nov. 10. Westminster. Grant to John Brooke, of Gatton, co. Lancaster, of pardon for manslaughter. [*Latin. Sign Man., vol.* I., *No.* 95.]

Nov. 10. Docquet of the above.

Nov. 10. Westminster. Warrant for payment of the expenses of the Ambassador from the Duke of Savoy. [*Sign Man., vol.* I., *No.* 97.]

Nov. 10. Entry of the above. [*Warrt. Bk.*, III., *p.* 31.]

Nov. 10. Docquet of the above.

[Nov. 10.] Grant to Geo. Salter and John Williams of lands, &c. in cos. Lincoln, York, Northampton, Bedford, Leicester, Sussex, Flint, Norfolk, and Essex, total value 206*l*. 18*s*. 8½*d*. per ann., in consideration of the surrender by them of other lands, value 199*l*. 2*s*. 2½*d*. per ann., in part of two contracts for lands with Wm. Garway and others. Latin. [*Sign Man., vol.* II., *Nos.* 22, 23.]

Nov. 10. Docquet of the above.

Nov. 10. Grant to Rich. Adams of an almsroom in Ewelme Hospital, the grant to be dated July 5, 1605, Adams having lost his grant of that date. [*Docquet.*]

Nov. 11. Grant to Lawrence Garnet of an almsroom in Ely. [*Docquet, Nov.* 10.]

Nov. 11. Grant to Thos. Jones of an almsroom in St. Warbott's Cathedral, West Chester. [*Docquet, Nov.* 10.]

Nov. 11. Whitehall. 20. Wm. Lord Knollys to Salisbury. Recommends Thos. Moyle to be Sheriff of Oxfordshire, instead of John Wellisborne, who is dangerously ill of the palsy.

Nov. 12. 21. Sir Philip Coningsby and Auditor Thos. Fanshaw to the Same. At Mrs. Babington's request, they have tried to compromise with Mr. Beecher concerning the award of lands granted him by the Court of Exchequer, but he refuses all offers. She thinks the lands belong to her son, and desires some other course to be thought upon.

Nov. 12. 22. Anne Lady Cooke, widow, to the Same. Recommends to him a former servant of hers as cook.

Nov. 12. 23. Sir Rich. Ogle to the Same. Concerning an ancient book of records relating to the county, in his [Ogle's] custody, which [Thos.] Browne, the surveyor, demands, as appertaining to Her Majesty's manor of Spalding.

Vol. LXVII.

1611.

Nov. ? 24. Petition of Thos. Browne, surveyor, of Suffolk, to Salisbury. Mr. Auditor denies him his fee of surveyor, unless he survey sundry decayed rents in Bury [St. Edmund's]. Prays to have his allowance and reasonable charges for the said survey, which is extremely difficult.

Nov. 12. Westminster. Confirmation of transfer of grant from Sir Jas. Spens, of Wirmestone, Scotland, to Robt. Jossy, of the moiety of 6,000*l.* old debts due to the Crown. [*Sign Man., vol. I., No.* 98.]

Nov. Docquet of the above. [*Docquet, Nov.* 10.]

Nov. 12. Grant to Sir Hen. Hobart, Thos. Plumstead, and John Gooch, of the manor of Cawston, Southawe Wood, &c., &c., and the rectory of Cawston, co. Norfolk, on nomination of John Eldred and other contractors, as part of the 50,000*l.* due to them. Latin. [*Sign Man., vol.* I., *No.* 99.]

Nov. Docquet of the above. [*Docquet, Nov.* 10.]

Nov. 13. London. 25. John Chamberlain to Sir D. Carleton. The Prince grows very like his mother. Sig. Fabricio [Sir Hen. Wotton] courts him much. Paul Pindar gone to Constantinople. Sir Robt. Shirley, as Ambassador from Persia, has had sundry audiences. The Ambassador from Savoy arrived. Sir John York and Sir Wm. Ingleby apprehended as being concerned in the powder treason. Certain Jesuits taken at the house of Lord Vaux's mother. Discontent at the number of protections [from arrest]. Money scarce at Court. Privy Seals [for a loan] feared. Rich Sutton is not dead, but Sir John Gray and Sir Allan Percy are. Sir Thos. Overbury restored to Court. Report of raising troops for Denmark. The King gone to Royston.

Nov. 14. Hadham. 26. Sir Art. Capell to Salisbury. Presents him with a brace of does. Thanks for his liberality to his son.

Nov. 14. Lease to Lord Knollys of the post fines for 31 years, on surrender of his former lease. [*Docquet, Nov.* 30. *See Dec.* 19.]

Nov. 14. Letter to Sir Lawrence Tanfield, Chief Baron of the Exchequer, requiring him to see that Jas. Maxwell, Gentleman Usher, has justice with expedition, in as much of his suit for reprisals due to the King as is proved in that court. [*Docquet, Nov.* 10.]

Nov. 15. Warrant to pay certain sums for stuffs delivered for the King's use. [*Docquet, Nov.* 17.]

Nov. 15. Letter to the Earl of Oxford, commanding him to forbear killing deer in Havering Park, whereof he has the charge, for ten years. [*Docquet, Nov.* 17.]

Nov. 16. 27. Memorandum, made in the Queen's Council Chamber at Somerset House, of gratuities agreed to be given by tenants of Her manors of Leeds, Barwick, Scole, and Ackworth, for confirmation of their fines during her life.

Nov. 17. Royston. 28. Dr. Theod. de Mayerne to Salisbury. M. de Vitry's illness is very serious, on account of his age and weakness. The issue doubtful.

VOL. LXVII.

1611.

Nov. [17]. [Royston.] 29. Lord Hay to Salisbury. M. de Vitry is comforted by his Lordship's visit, and does not wish his friends in France to be told of his condition.

Nov. 17. Newmarket. Sunday. 30. Sir Roger Aston to [the Same]. The King is anxious about M. de Vitry. Lord Hay is left at Royston to keep him company. My Lord of Canterbury is to send the act of 1562 to Sir Noel Caron. Twelve falcons are come from Denmark for the King, and six for his Lordship, of which latter the King has taken two, and hopes he will not be angry. *Incloses,*

30. I. *Dr. Theod. de Mayerne to the King. Sends, by His command, an account of the illness of M. de Vitry. Nothing unfavourable has transpired thus far. Nov. 16, Royston.*

Nov. 17. 31. Petition of Giles Hawkridge to Salisbury, for a lease of concealed lands in the parishes of Oakhampton, &c., co. Devon, and Stratton, co. Cornwall. With reference and report thereon.

Nov. 17. Westminster. Demise to Adrian Clitterbooke of the King's two parts of lands, &c. in Whiteplace and Bullocks, in Cookham, co. Berks, belonging to Sir Edw. Mansfield, recusant, at suit of Clement Edmondes, to whom the benefit of his recusancy was given. Latin. [*Sign Man., vol.* I., *No.* 100.]

Nov. 17. Docquet of the above.

Nov. 17. Grant to John Carse, Page of the Bedchamber, of the benefit of the recusancy of Isabel, widow of Sir Wm. Thorold, of Panton, co. Lincoln. [*Docquet.*]

Nov. 18. Merton College, Oxford. 32. John Morley to John Chamberlain. Has sent him a chest of books to the Saracen's Head, without Newgate. Begs his acknowledgment of them.

Nov. 18. 33. Earl of Northumberland to Salisbury. Hopes his zeal as Lord Treasurer to fill the King's coffers will not make him too eager in exacting his own fine. Thinks the King, who exhorted Elks to say only truth and add nothing from malice, is too just and noble to desire his ruin. Hopes for better times.

Nov. 18. Cambridge. 34. Dr. Barnaby Gooch to the Same. Being chosen his Lordship's deputy, as Vice Chancellor of Cambridge, will execute the duties to his best ability, and not be needlessly troublesome to him.

Nov. 18. Newmarket. 35. Humph. May to the Same. Has delivered the despatch from France, and complimented the King that two great Princes offer him their alliance for the Princess. His Majesty wishes the negociation with the Elector Palatine to proceed by the Duke of Bouillon, and he will reply to the Ambassador of Savoy after he has spoken with that of Spain. His Ambassador in Spain is to condole with that King [on his Queen's death]. M. Caron to be assured that the letters written to the States against Vorstius were not divulged by the King's direction, &c.

VOL. LXVII.

1611.
Nov. 18. Westminster. Grant to the Earl of Nottingham of the manor of Halling, and other lands, &c. in Croydon and Mitcham, co. Surrey. Latin. [*Sign Man., vol.* I., *No.* 101.]

Nov. Docquet of the above. [*Docquet, Nov.* 17.]

Nov. 19. 36. Lucy, Marchioness of Winchester, to Salisbury, her uncle. Solicits favour for the petition of Mr. Aylmer.

Nov.? 37. —— to [the Same]. Complains that the Receiver of Yorkshire levies on Lord Sheffield's lands the arrears of Mowgrave, about which a settlement was made. Requests him to induce his niece, the Marchioness of Winchester, to pay 366*l.* owed by her to Lord Sheffield's late mother, for whom the writer is executor, and bequeathed by her to her grandchildren. Also that Lord Sheffield's annuity of 500*l.* for twenty-eight years may be made payable out of the alum, rather than the Exchequer, as its sale value would then rise 300*l.* or 400*l.*

Nov. 19. Wrest. 38. Earl of Kent to the Same. Has discharged the service required [of certifying the names of parties suitable for the loan]. Has not set down [Robt.] Sandey, who has a house and land in the parish of Luton, he being a merchant of London. Could not choose fewer than seventy-six persons to raise the sum required.

Nov. 20. 39. Edw. Reynoldes to Fras. Mills. Grieved that Mills should think the employment in the service of the loans will hasten his end. Offers to take it himself if he desires to resign.

Nov. 20. 40. Sir Roger Aston to [Salisbury]. Arrival of a post from Royston from Dr. Mayerne, bringing intelligence that M. Vitry's life is despaired of. The bark to be hastened to Rouen.

Nov. 20. [Royston.] 41. Lord Hay to [the Same ?] The bearer can witness to the present state of M. Vitry. Will do what he can for him while living, and what is due after death.

Nov. 20. London. 42. Chamberlain to Carleton. The widow of Sir Wm. Cornwallis has obtained the wardship of her son. Suitors for Sir Allan Percy's widow. [Arthur] Ingram, the great undertaker, has broken for large sums. The King is hunting at Newmarket. The Queen is at Greenwich. The Ambassador from Savoy has obtained a cold answer. It is now rumoured that the King of Spain himself wants the Princess Elizabeth. Met Casaubon at the Bishop of Ely's. He was scarcely contented with his pension of 300*l.* per ann. He envies Turquet [Mayerne]'s preferment. Gave Sig. Candido's letters to the Bishop [of Ely], who complains that his foreign letters are opened before they reach him.

Nov. 20. Westminster. Grant to David John Philipp, of Landochy Pennadz, co. Glamorgan, of pardon for life only, for receiving stolen cattle. Latin. [*Sign Man., vol.* I., *No.* 102.]

Nov. Docquet of the above. [*Docquet, Nov.* 17.]

VOL. LXVII.

1611.
Nov. 21. Westminster. Grant to Dr. Rich. Milborne of the Deanery of Rochester, vacant by the death of Dr. Thos. Blague. Latin. [*Sign Man., vol.* I., *No.* 103.]

Nov. Docquet of the above. [*Docquet, Nov.* 22.]

Nov. 22. Friday. 43. Humph. May to [Salisbury]. Returns the Privy Seal and Proclamation signed, &c. The is King glad that his Lordship is now in earnest about the proclamation [for raising the price of gold] though he had been cold about it at first. The Spanish Ambassador comes to His Majesty.

Nov. 22. Newmarket. 44. Sir Roger Aston to the Same. The King pleased with the despatch of his letter to France, and with the care for the convoy of M. de Vitry's body to Westminster. Lord Hay and M. Mayerne are gone to see it embalmed. The Ambassador has had audience, and went hunting with His Majesty. The Prince remains with the King.

Nov. 22. 45. Fras. Earl of Cumberland to the Same. Had communicated his instructions to his deputies in the three counties and Newcastle. Sends lists of persons fit for the loan, with sums annexed.

Nov. 22. 46. Petition of Sir Marmaduke Darell and Sir Thos. Bludder to the Same, for payment of portion of 4,933*l.* 14*s.* 3*d.*, due to them for victualling the Navy. *Annexed is,*

46. I. *Monthly account of sums due for victualling the Navy, from April to Sept.* 1611. *Oct* 4.

Nov. 22. Westminster. Grant to Sir Fras. Prince, of Forriatt Monachorum, near Shrewsbury, of pardon for manslaughter. Latin. [*Sign Man., vol.* I., *No.* 104.]

Nov. 22. Docquet of the above.

Nov. 22. Letter to the two Chief Justices to take some speedy course for repair of the highways between London and Royston, and to receive direction therein from the Lord Treasurer, &c. [*Docquet.*]

Nov.? 47. Proposals for repairing during the winter the highways to Royston and Newmarket, five miles round London, and afterwards the roads throughout England.

Nov. 23. Newmarket. 48. Sir Thos. Lake to [Salisbury]. The Ambassador in Spain is to add to his condolence the consolation that the late Queen brought many fair children and died in childbed of a son. Returns certain Privy Seals; that for [Wm.] Stewart is filled up for 1,000 marks, &c.

Nov. 23. Strand. 49. Sir John Spilman to the Same. Entreats order for payment of the old debt of 4,781*l.* due two and a half years ago. The Queen owes him also 3,000*l.* lent to her, and his part in 9,000*l.* which Her Majesty owes to [George] Herriot, for the Prince's sword and other jewels.

Vol. LXVII.

1611.

Nov. ? 50. Notes [by Salisbury] of the proportion of alloy to be mixed with the bullion for the current coin, and of the danger of export of gold, from its value being proportionably greater than that of silver.

Nov. ? 51. Statement addressed to the King, of the loss sustained by England in exchange of coin with other countries, and proposal of remedy by raising the price of gold in proportion to silver to the same standard as in the States, and by coining English moneys of corresponding value to those of foreign nations.

Nov. ? 52. Project for meeting the increase of value laid upon the coins of the Low Countries, by issuing a copper coinage corresponding thereto, and by raising the value of English silver and gold coins, in order to prevent the losses of merchants in foreign trade, and encourage the importation of bullion.

Nov. ? 53. Statement by the Officers of the Mint that the raising of the value of English silver coins by making a pound Troy of silver worth 3*l.* 11*s.* 6*d.*, only equalizes the value of English moneys with those of foreign countries, and that to prevent the export of gold, its price must be raised in proportion.

Nov. ? 54. Table of the rates of gold and silver coins, showing how much and in what reigns their value was enhanced, from Edw. I. to 9 Jac. I.

Nov. 23. Newmarket. Proclamation concerning the alteration of the prices of gold, and fixing the value of the different pieces current. Printed. [*Proc. Bk., p.* 250.]

Nov. ? 55. Project to raise 500,000*l.* on loan to the King, by coining brass money, of the size of silver coins, to that amount, and compelling their acceptance in certain proportions by the people, to be repaid in seven years with silver, as a means of preventing the export of coin and bullion, caused by the rise in value of foreign coin.

Nov. 23. Londesborough. 56. Earl of Cumberland to Salisbury. Similar to that of Nov. 22. The estimate for Cumberland and Westmoreland is more than twice as much as in the loan of 2 Jac. I.

Nov. 24. Sunday. Hertford House, Canon Row. 57. Earl of Hertford to Salisbury. Sends for the King's approval his instructions to his chaplain, who is now ready for France. Prays that young Rodney may be removed from his grandson, Wm. Seymour.

Nov. 24. 58. Geo. Abbot, Archbp. of Canterbury, to the Bishop of Peterborough. Recommends care in not allowing the deprived ministers, Barbon, Sheffield, Dod, &c., to preach in his diocese, as the King would be much offended.

Nov. 24. Eton. 59. Sir Hen. Savile to Carleton. Money matters. Wants one more Greek book. Family news. College promotions.

Nov. 24. Letter to the Mayor, &c. of London, to punish persons who harbour thieves and receive stolen goods. [*Docquet, Nov.* 25.]

VOL. LXVII.

1611.

Nov. 25. Whitehall. 60. Earl of Salisbury to Sir Thos. Lake. Asks where the fruit-trees sent to the King by the French Queen are to be planted. The apples and pears are inferior to the English, the *Poire Chrétienne* excepted. Has received the King's letters for France, Spain, &c.

Nov. 25. Wrest. 61. Earl of Kent to Salisbury. Recommends Thos. Ansell, of Burford, as Collector for the Privy Seal Loans in that county [Bedford]. Thinks Robt. Sandey, now Sheriff, may be rated at 30*l.* or 40*l.* for the loan.

Nov. 25. 62. Thos. Wilson to [the Same]. Project of a Frenchman for supplying Hatfield with water, erecting fountains, &c. Asks instructions about fruit-trees sent for the King and his Lordship from the French Queen.

Nov. 25. 63. Plan of the waterworks to be erected [at Hatfield ?].

Nov. 25. Westminster. Warrant to pay certain sums to Robt. Treswell, Surveyor of the Woods south of Trent, &c., for repairing the fences of Woking Park, co. Surrey, and Cornbury Park, co. Oxon. [*Warrt. Bk.*, III., *p.* 31.]

Nov. 25. Docquet of the above.

Nov. 25. Westminster. Grant, with survivorship, to And. Bassano and Edw. Norgate, of the office of Tuner of His Majesty's virginals, organs, and other instruments. [*Sign Man.*, *vol.* I., *No.* 105.]

Nov. 25. Docquet of the above.

Nov. 25. Westminster. Grant, in reversion, to John Day of a Poor Knight's room in Windsor. [*Sign Man.*, *vol.* I., *No.* 106.]

Nov. 25. Docquet of the above.

Nov. 25. Westminster. Grant to Edm. Nevill of the fines due on thirty alienations of land without licence, not pardoned, to be proved and recovered by him. [*Sign Man.*, *vol.* I., *No.* 107.]

Nov. 25. 64. Abstract of the above.

Nov. 25. Docquet of the above.

Nov. 25. Westminster. Grant to Chas. Chambers, Groom of the Chamber to the Queen, and his brother George, of protection from arrests, &c. for six months. [*Sign Man.*, *vol.* I., *No.* 108.]

Nov. 25. Docquet of the above.

Nov. 25. Westminster. Grant to Robt. Meinges of 400*l.* from the King's third of forfeitures of recusants to be brought in by Ralph Beeston and Ralph Bowes. [*Sign Man.*, *vol.* I., *No.* 109.]

Nov. 25. Entry of the above. [*Warrt. Bk.*, III., *p.* 31.]

Nov. 25. Docquet of the above.

Nov. 25. Westminster. Grant to Wm. Stewart of 1,000 marks, as a gift, from forfeitures in the Exchequer. [*Sign Man.*, *vol.* I., *No.* 110.]

Nov. 25. Docquet of the above.

VOL. LXVII.

1611.

Nov. 25. Westminster. Grant to Lord Admiral Nottingham of an annuity of 1,000*l.* per ann., besides a former annuity of 1,700*l.*; also 300*l.* per ann. to Chas. Howard, his now youngest son, from the death of his father, till he attains fourteen years of age, and afterwards of 1,000 marks per ann., all inalienable. [*Sign Man., vol.* I., *No.* 111.]

Nov. 25. Docquet of the above.

Nov. 25. Grant to Isaac Waterhouse of pension of 3*s.* per diem, for service at Berwick, &c., on surrender of pensions to the same amount by himself and Thos. Barrett. [*Docquet.*]

Nov. 26. 65. Earl of Montgomery to Salisbury. His brother [the Earl of Pembroke] received his Lordship's letter, and will be there to-day.

Nov. 26. 66. Lord Sheffield to the Same. Sends up the prisoners by Rich. Outlaw, Pursuivant, whose service he commends. The poverty of the Courts of the North now prevents their paying any rewards or even fees. Was obliged to conduct the search for these prisoners at his own charge.

Nov. 26. Westminster. Grant to the Earl of Montgomery, in reversion after Sir Wm. Herbert, of the office of Keeper of Folly John Park, in Windsor Forest. [*Sign Man., vol.* I., *No.* 112.]

Nov. Docquet of the above. [*Docquet, Nov.* 27.]

Nov. 26. Westminster. Presentation of Wm. Loe to the rectory of Severnstoke, diocese of Worcester. [*Sign Man., vol.* II., *No.* 1.]

Nov. Docquet of the above. [*Docquet, Nov* 25.]

Nov. 26. Westminster. Re-grant, in reversion, to Thos. Loviband, nominated by John Eldred, and other contractors, of Shute Place, with lands in Brixton, Isle of Wight. [*Sign Man., vol.* II., *No.* 3. *See* 1611, *June* 16.]

Nov. Docquet of the above. [*Docquet, Nov* 25.]

Nov 26. Westminster. Grant to Sir Phil. Carey, Wm. Pitt, and John Williams, in fee simple, of the manor and lordship of Minster, co. Kent. [*Sign Man., vol.* II., *No.* 4.]

Nov. Docquet of the above. [*Docquet, Nov.* 25.]

Nov. 27. Westminster. Warrant to pay to Robt. Anstruther 169*l.* 2*s.*, for the expenses of Dr. Carisius, the Danish Ambassador. [*Sign Man., vol.* II., *No.* 5.]

Nov. 27. Entry of the above. [*Warrt. Bk.*, III., *p.* 31.]

Nov. 27. Westminster. Grant to Thos. Webber of a pension of 50*l.* per ann., until he shall be appointed Chief Cook of the King's kitchen. [*Sign Man., vol.* II., *No.* 6.]

Nov. 27. Docquet of the above.

Nov. 27. Westminster. Re-grant to Sir Wm. Herrick of a Teller's place in the Exchequer, in reversion after Sir Edw. Carey, Sir Wm. Bowyer, Sir Fras. Egiock, and Thos. Watson, the present Tellers. [*Sign Man., vol.* II., *No.* 7.]

Nov. 27. Docquet of the above.

VOL. LXVII.

1611
Nov. 27. Grant to Wm. Meaker, alias Meiger, of a Poor Knight's room in Windsor. [*Sign Man., vol.* II., *No.* 8.]

Nov. 27. Docquet of the above.

Nov. 27. Letter to Sir Geo. Waldegrave to preserve the King's pheasants at the manor of Hitcham, co. Suffolk. [*Docquet.*]

Nov. 27. London. 67. John Chamberlain to Sir Dud. Carleton. Lord Northumberland's last tempest has blown over, but his fine of 30,000*l.* will be called for. He [Carleton] was called in question because the Earl said he might have written a letter for Percy's lodging, but Epsley [John Hippisley] denied there being any letter written. Deaths of Brook, the lawyer, and of M. de Vitry, Sir Wm. Bowes, Harry Constable, and Fontaine, the French preacher. The Savoy Ambassador lingers; that of Spain went privately to the King at Newmarket. The Prince receives Berkhamstead from Sir Hen. Carey, as belonging to the Duchy of Cornwall.

Nov. 28. Westminster. Re-grant, in reversion, to Sir Hen. Bowyer of the office of one of the four Tellers of the Exchequer, after Sir Wm. Herrick is placed, &c. [*Sign. Man., vol.* II., *No.* 9.]

Nov. Docquet of the above. [*Docquet, Nov.* 27.]

Nov. 28. Cardiff. 68. Justices of Glamorganshire to Salisbury. Send up Chris. Hawkes, of Lincolnshire, who professes to know of certain traitors in Ireland who deal with pirates' goods, but will reveal nothing except to the King or his Lordship. *Inclose,*

68. I. *Information to the above effect given by Chris. Hawkes to the Justices of Glamorganshire. Nov.* 28.

Nov. 28. 69. Particular of the possessions of the late Monastery of Tynemouth, Northumberland.

Nov. 29. Boughton-Malherbe. 70. Edw. Lord Wotton to Salisbury. Incloses a letter and certificate received from his Deputy Lieutenants [concerning the loan], which comes short of his expectation.

Nov. 29. Newmarket, Friday. 71. Visct. Rochester to the Same. The King wishes to know what account the judges and justices of the peace give as to enforcing the Oath of Allegiance. It is a point essential to government, and necessary for the supply of the King's needy servants. [*See Dec.* 7.]

Nov. 29. 72. Sir John Roper to the Same. For the wardship of the son of Sir John Smith, of Kent, if the latter should die.

Nov.? 73. Ralph Beeston to the Same. Has solicited the King for a renewal of his protection, to gain time for the payment of his debts.

Nov. 29. Westminster. Grant to Ralph Beeston and Ralph Bowes, and their sureties, of protection from arrests, &c. for six months. [*Sign Man., vol.* II., *No.* 10.]

Nov. Docquet of the above. [*Docquet, Nov.* 30.]

Vol. LXVII.

1611. Nov. 29. Westminster. Re-grant, in reversion, to Robt. Seymer of the office of one of the four Tellers of the Exchequer, after the placing of Sir Wm. Herrick and Sir Hen. Bowyer. Latin. [*Sign Man*, *vol.* II., *No.* 11.]

Nov. 29. Letter to Geo. Chute, desiring him to enable his son, Sir Walter, to pursue his course in the King's service, by supplying him with means. [*Docquet, Nov.* 30.]

Nov. 30. Blackfriars. 74. Constance Lady Lucy to Salisbury. Thanks for accepting her orphan son to his service.

Nov. ? 75. Rich. Procter to the Same. Begs him to take his eldest son as chaplain.

Nov. 30. Brantingham. 76. Jane Jobson to the Same. For a stipend to maintain a preacher at Brantingham. Recommends Mr. Procter, the bearer.

Nov. ? 77. The Same to the Same. Complains of ill-treatment by her husband, and of his turning out a preacher who lived with them, for taking her part. Begs a small annuity.

Nov. 30. Lease to Lord Knollys of post fines, on surrender of a former lease, dated Nov. 18. [*Docquet.*]

Nov. 78. Eliz. Countess of Derby to Salisbury. Her cousin is free from the small-pox, and shall take Atkins' medicines. The suit of Sir Wm. Herbert was for Sir Rowland Stanley's lands, entailed on his brother-in-law. Requests that he may compound for them.

Nov. 79. Jane Drummond to [the Same]. Returns a bill signed by Her Majesty. Has acquainted her with what his Lordship said on her loving nobody but dead pictures. The Queen replied that she is more contented with her pictures than he with his great employments.

Nov. 80. Reasons by John Kendrick of the removal of the English merchants from Stade to Hamburg.

Nov. 81. Account of the receipts and clerks' fees of the Hanaper and Petty Bag, since Michaelmas Term.

Dec. 4. Westminster. Warrant to pay to Alex. Miller 57*l.* 13*s.* 4*d.* half yearly, being two parts of the fine of 173*l.* per ann. from the manor of Grovehurst and other lands, &c., co. Kent, of Grace Finch, recusant, with arrears, from the time of his grant, amounting to 134*l.* 11*s.* 1*d.*, he paying a yearly rental of 38*l.* 8*s.* 11½*d.* [*Warrt. Bk.*, III., *p.* 32.]

Dec. Docquet of the above. [*Docquet, Dec.* 8.]

Dec. 4. London. 82. John Chamberlain to Sir Dud. Carleton. The Dorcas has arrived. Carleton's presents are distributed. The Lord Treasurer angry with his bill of travelling charges. Causes in the Star Chamber. Shepherd and Hennings pilloried. Sir Jas. Creichton imprisoned and fined. The Earl of Southampton not going into Spain. Redress demanded of the Spanish Ambassador for wrongs to English merchants. His visit to Newmarket was to hint that the King of Spain might propose for the Lady Elizabeth. Sir Dudley Diggs busy with the discovery of the north-west passage. The Lord Treasurer has rheumatism in his right arm. Sir Wm. Herbert arrested on an execution for 5,000*l.*

Vol. LXVII.

1611.

Dec. ? 83. Opinions in reference to suitable alliances for the Prince of Wales and Princess Elizabeth. Danger of encouraging Popery by introducing a daughter of Savoy or Spain into England. The Prince of Piedmont an unequal match for the Princess, unless the King of Spain will give him the duchy of Milan on his marriage, which is not likely, as that King is said to want her for himself. She could not marry him without changing her religion, and such a marriage would be dangerous to the two that are between her and the Crown. A match with Sweden or the Prince Palatine suggested for her, and for the Prince one with the house of Saxony, Brandenburg, or Palatine.

Dec. ? 84. Opinion against a Spanish match for the Princess of England as dangerous to the life of the King; also against Italian matches, either for the Prince or Princess, arguing that she should marry into Protestant Germany, and naming the Palatine house as most suitable. Italian.

Dec. ? 85. Copy of the above.

Dec. 5. Newmarket. 86. Visct. Fenton to [Salisbury]. The King sends a note of some abuses in the Mint House, or in the merchants of bullion; is sorry to hear of his indisposition.

Dec. ? 87. Thos. Warwick to the Same. Sends a project of reform of the Mint, suggested by his cousin [Rich.] Martin, jun. The strangers engross 10,000*l.* of Spanish money; 11 chests of dollars ready for the Turkey voyage.

Dec. 6. Greenwich. 88. Lord Harrington to the Same. Begs he will give express commands for payment of moneys due for her Grace [Lady Elizabeth's] necessaries.

Dec. 6. 89. Sir Thos. Shirley to the Same. Thanks for his favour in the lease of the manor of Braybrooke, touching Lord Zouch.

Dec. 6. Westminster. Grant to Sir Patrick Hume of 200*l.* as a gift, out of fines and forfeitures. [*Warrt. Bk.*, III., *p.* 35.]

Dec. Docquet of the above. [*Docquet, Dec.* 8.]

Dec 6. Westminster. Warrant to pay to John Norden 125*l.* for reparations at Sandham Castle, Isle of Wight, and 50*l.* to Robt. Anstruther for expenses of Dr. Carisius, sent from the King of Denmark. [*Warrt. Bk.*, III., *p.* 33.]

Dec. Docquet of the above. [*Docquet, Dec.* 8.]

Dec. 7. Royston. 90. Earl of Pembroke to Salisbury. The King content that the Ambassador of Savoy should receive his answer from himself at Theobald's. He desires to have the law put in execution relative to the Oath of Allegiance, and asks what is done to the negligent justices of Northamptonshire.

Dec. 7. 91. Charges of the works, &c. at His Majesty's houses in November.

VOL. LXVII.

1611.

Dec. 7. Billiter Lane, London. 92. John Lamote, stranger, to Salisbury. Desires an audience to disclose some secrets he heard beyond the seas. Suggests restraint of impost on black and brown thread, that the English poor may be employed in its manufacture; and requests a patent to seize all thread imported from such foreign parts as have banished English cloth, and the farm of the imposition on that manufactured in England.

Dec. 8. 93. Earl of Shrewsbury to the Same. Visct. Rochester has hinted at some alteration in His Majesty towards himself. Requests explanation. Sends a bunch of liquorice, with directions for planting it.

Dec. 8. Warrant to pay 56*l.* 8*s.* 3*d.* to John, son of Sir Peter Young. [*Docquet.*]

Dec. 8. Grant to Thos. Warwick of the office of Keeper of Lincoln Castle, and the gaol and houses there, part of the Duchy of Lancaster, on restitution of a former patent for the same granted to Fras. Hustwood. [*Docquet.*]

Dec. 8. Grant to John Gray of the benefit of the recusancy of Margaret and John Gainsford, of Idbury, co. Oxford. [*Docquet.*]

Dec. 8. Grant to Chris. Mainwaring of the right of action and suit for recovery to the King's use of the advowson of the rectory of Rewe, co. Devon, and of the first and second advowson thereof for himself. [*Docquet.*]

Dec. 8. Grant to Thos. Norris of pension of 6*d.* per diem, in compensation for injuries received in apprehending depredators in the woods at Enfield. [*Docquet.*]

Dec. 8. Warrant for necessaries for the stable for the King, Queen, Prince, Duke of York, and Lady Elizabeth. [*Docquet.*]

Dec. 8. Warrant for the Officers of the Mint to take 45*s.* to the King's use on every pound troy of gold coined. [*Docquet.*]

Dec. 8. Grant to Edm. Sawyer of a sixth reversion of an auditorship of the Exchequer. [*Docquet.*]

Dec. 8. Letter to Sir Robt. Stewart signifying that the King declines to intermeddle in the differences between the Kings of Denmark and Sweden, until he understands the disposition of the King of Sweden in that matter. [*Docquet.*]

Dec. 8. Licence to Sir Thos. Wentworth, of Wentworth House, co. York, to travel. [*Docquet.*]

Dec. 10. 94. Sir Wm. Waad, Lieutenant of the Tower, to Salisbury. Concerning certain effects detailed, left by Wm. Seymour in the Tower at the time of his escape. Claims the goods as his due, and also payment for debts incurred by Seymour for physic, tapestry hangings, &c., with certificates relating to those debts.

VOL. LXVII.

1611.

Dec. 10. Westminster. Warrant to pay 262*l.* 2*s.* 5*d.* to Sence, relict of Jonas Waterhouse, for arrears of her late husband's allowance, and for fees and wages disbursed by him to divers of the Council of the North. [*Warrt. Bk.*, III., *p.* 33.]

Dec. 10. Docquet of the above.

Dec. 10. Westminster. Warrant to pay to Sir Rich. Martin, Master of the Mint, 160*l.* for sundry models, tools, and engines for improvement of the coin. [*Warrt. Bk.*, III., *p.* 34.]

Dec. 10. Docquet of the above.

Dec. 10. Westminster. Warrant to pay to Sir Carew Raleigh 82*l.* 0*s.* 10*d.* for surplusage of his account for repairs of Portland Castle and Gillingham Park. [*Warrt. Bk.*, III., *p.* 32.]

Dec. 10. Docquet of the above.

Dec. 10. Warrant to pay necessary sums to Miles Whytakers for inclosing 687 acres of land, to be added to Theobald's Park. [*Warrt. Bk.*, III., *pp.* 30 *and* 36.]

Dec. 10. Docquet of the above.

Dec. 10. Westminster. Warrant to pay 600*l.* remaining due to Wm. Ramsay of 1,200*l.* bestowed on him by His Majesty, out of forfeitures, and not yet paid. Also 100*l.* to Fras. Cottington, about to be sent into Spain; and certain sums to persons who brought fruit-trees to His Majesty from the Queen Regent of France. [*Warrt. Bk.*, III., *p.* 33.]

Dec. 10. Docquet of the above.

Dec. 10. Grant to Hen. St. George of the office of Pursuivant-at-Arms for life. [*Docquet.*]

Dec. 10. Grant to Humph. May, in reversion after Robt. Kirkham, of a Clerkship of the Signet. [*Docquet.*]

Dec. 11. Baynard's Castle. 95. Visct. Lisle to Salisbury. Prays to be remembered, as he wishes to discharge some cumbersome debts.

Dec. 11. 96. Petition of Robt. Meverell to the Same, for a lease, without the clause of "Si quis plus dure voluerit," of certain lands in Darleton, co. Nottingham. With references and report thereon.

Dec. 12. Westminster. 97. Anne Lady Bruncard to the Same. Begs to have 100*l.* advanced out of the money due to her late husband, who deserved so well of the Prince and State, &c.

Dec. 13. Royston. 98. Earl of Pembroke to the Same. The King is well and merry, and very solicitous for his Lordship's health. He approves the project for the reformation of the Navy, and wishes the Prince and Sir Robt. Cotton to be present when it is discussed in Council.

VOL. LXVII.

1611.

Dec. 13. Tavistock. 99. Wm. Earl of Bath to Salisbury. Sends his certificate of the names and rates of the men of ability for the present loan in Devonshire and Exeter. The sum rated in the county, exclusive of the city of Exeter and the clergy, is with much ado brought to 5,121*l.*

Dec. 13. Grant to John Ingram of Milborne, co. Cornwall, of pardon for piracy. [*Docquet.*]

Dec. 13. Warrant dormant to pay 6*d.* per diem to John Wilchen and Humph. Story, as wages for keeping the King's spaniels. [*Docquet.*]

Dec. 13. Demise to Wm. Ashton of the King's benefit from recusants, to the value of 62*l.* 12*s.* 10*d.* [*Docquet.*]

Dec. 13. Licence to Sir Thos. Woodhouse to travel for three years. [*Docquet.*]

Dec. 13. Warrant dormant to pay certain allowances to Rich. Berwick, Falconer, in reversion after Chris. Berwick. [*Docquet.*]

Dec. 13. Grant to Thos. Dixon of the benefit of the recusancy of Thos. Walstide, Martha Skrimsher, Mary Polewhely, Robt. Fitzherbert, of Somerset, Gerard Gifford, Fras. Chamberlain, and Edw. Lane. [*Docquet.*]

Dec. 15. Westminster. Warrant to pay 600*l.* to Patrick Maull, remainder of 1,200*l.* forfeitures bestowed on him for services as Gentleman of the Bedchamber, &c. [*Warrt. Bk.*, III., *p.* 34.]

Dec. 16. Royston. 100. Sir Thos. Lake to Salisbury. Sends warrants, &c. signed, and letters of the King's own penning, which his Ambassador [in France] is to deliver to M. du Moulin, and to say that the King deals so plainly with him because he wishes the next edition of his book to be free from exceptions.

Dec. 17. Canterbury. 101. Thos. Mills to the Same. Attended M. de Vitry's corpse to Dover, fearing the clamorousness of some of his creditors. He never came to England with money sufficient for his expenses, &c.

Dec. 17. 102. Estimate of damage sustained by fire by Edw. Bridges the Post, and others, at Canterbury, May 27, 1611, when Bridges' stables were burnt by M. de Vitry's servants.

Dec. 17. Westminster. Warrant to pay to Wm. Hogan, Keeper of the Stillhouse and Gardens at Hampton Court, 100*l.*, for planting apricots and sundry choice fruit-trees there. [*Warrt. Bk.*, III., *p.* 36.]

Dec. 17. Docquet of the above.

Dec. 17. Letter to the Lord President of the Marches of Wales requiring a return of persons within that district capable of lending money to the King. [*Docquet.*]

Dec. 17. The like to the Earl of Worcester. [*Docquet.*]

Dec. 17. Grant to Alex. Rigby, in reversion after Roger Rigby, of the office of Clerk of the Peace in Lancashire, for his own and for his son's life. [*Docquet.*]

VOL. LXVII.

1611.

Dec. 17. Presentation of Art. Price to the vicarage of Godshill, diocese of Winchester. [*Docquet.*]

Dec. 17. Letter from the King to Henry Prince of Wales, to give order for selecting 200 trees within the manor of Sunning, for the use of the Navy. [*Docquet.*]

Dec. 17. Grant to Fras. Fowler of the Guidership of the Almshouse, Radcliffe, Bristol. [*Docquet.*]

Dec. 18. Theobalds. Wednesday. 103. Sir Roger Aston to Salisbury. To take a copy of the letters the King sent for M. du Moulin, and give his opinion thereon.

Dec. 18. London. 104. Chamberlain to Carleton. Proclamation for raising the value of the gold coin. The Privy Seals begin to come abroad thick and threefold. Legal appointments. Rich Sutton dead, and left 20,000*l.* ready money for charities, beside 8,000*l.* a year to the Charterhouse, and other gifts: his poor kindred have only 400*l.* a year. Newport, Admiral of Virginia, returned. Sir Thos. Gates arrived there.

Dec. 18. 105. Sir Hen. Savile to the Same. His Eton property. Books wanted. Death of Sir Allan Percy. His widow, who was intended for Lord St. John, has married Lord Darcy's eldest son.

Dec. 19. Theobalds. 106. Visct. Haddington to Salisbury. To expedite the grant to Mr. Price of a little benefice in the Isle of Wight.

Dec. 19. Newhall. 107. Earl of Sussex to the Same. The King promises to favour him in any grant not of the ordinary course.

Dec. 19. Letter to Sir Thos. Edmondes, the King's Ambassador, resident with the French King, touching the delivery of a letter in French to M. du Moulin, Minister at Paris. [*Docquet.*]

Dec. 19. Grant to Barth. Rogers of the office of Usher of the Court of Wards and Liveries, with reversion to Rich. Ellis and Edw. Hill. [*Docquet.*]

Dec. 19. Lease to Lord Knollys of the post fines for thirty-one years, on surrender of a former lease, and certain conditions. [*Docquet.*]

Dec. 19. Lease to the Same of the benefit of the post fines as above. [*Docquet.*]

Dec. 20. St. James's. Warrant from Henry Prince of Wales to Salisbury, to pay 4,000*l.*, due to Sir Edw. Carey for erecting the house within the Prince's Park at Berkhamstead, and for other things purchased from him. [*Warrt. Bk.*, III., *p.* 34.]

Dec. 21. 108. Katherine Lady Walsh to Salisbury. Although her husband lost his life in suppressing rebels, she is in worse case than the wives even of offenders, who have tasted, in some degree, of the King's bounty. Recommends her cause to his Lordship's justice.

Dec. 21. King's Bench. 109. Sir Thos. Shirley to the Same. Thanks for his contribution of 30*l.* towards his relief. Begs its payment at once, that he may be liberated before he is eaten up with gaol taxes.

VOL. LXVII.

1611.

Dec. 21. Paris. 110. Jean de Barclay to Salisbury. Begs payment of his pension. French.

Dec. 21. Grant to John Edge of an almsroom at Ewelme, co. Oxford. [*Docquet.*]

Dec. 21. Licence to Arthur Blewett to travel for three years. [*Docquet.*]

Dec. 21. Grant to Alex. Erskine, son and heir of Visct. Fenton, of the chief stewardship and keepership of Ampthill House and parks, in reversion after the said Viscount and Lady Elizabeth, his wife. [*Docquet.*]

Dec. 21. Grant to John White of an almsroom in Winchester. [*Docquet.*]

Dec. 22. Theobalds. 111. The King to the Earl of Mar, Treasurer of Scotland, and the Commissioners of Rents there. Warrant to grant a reversion of Sir Wm. Bowyer's Scotch pension to his wife and son George, with survivorship.

Dec. 22. Westminster. Warrant to pay certain sums to Robt. Treswell and Cuthbert Ogle for repair of the fences about Bedingfield Lawn, co. Northampton, and the lodges there, and of the fences about Houghton Park, in Ampthill, co. Bedford, and in the Great Park of Nonsuch, with orders to fell trees for the said repairs. [*Warr. Bk.*, III., *p.* 36.]

Dec. Docquet of the above. [*Docquet, Dec.* 24.]

Dec. 23. Westminster. Warrant to pay rewards and expenses not exceeding 200*l.* to persons bringing up Jesuits from Northamptonshire; and 25*l.* 5*s.* 10*d.* to Sir Fras. Fortescue, Keeper of Cornbury Park, co. Oxford, for erecting stone walls for enlarging the said park. [*Warr. Bk.*, III., *p.* 36.]

Dec. 24. Docquet of the above.

Dec. 24. 112. Fras. Mills to Salisbury. Prays advance of 100*l.* by way of imprest, towards his expenses for attending the service of the general loan.

Dec. 24. 113. Memorandum of the number of Privy Seals [for loans] already despatched to certain places and counties.

Dec. 24. Presentation of Thos. Downe to the vicarage of Buckland-Brewer, diocese of Exeter. [*Docquet.*]

Dec. 25. Letley, Christmas. 114. Earl of Hertford to Salisbury. Backwardness of the service of loan in Somersetshire, which, though larger and wealthier than Wiltshire, lends 700*l.* less. Congratulates him on his recovery.

Dec. 25. Westminster. Warrant to pay certain sums to John Williams and others for plate, gifts for the new year, christenings, Ambassadors, the Queen, &c., &c., for coffers, cutlery, &c. [*Warrt. Bk.*, III., *p.* 37.]

Dec. Docquet of the above. [*Docquet, Dec.* 24.]

Dec. 27. Grant to Rich. Swinborne of an almsroom in St. Stephen's, Westminster. [*Docquet.*]

Dec. 27. Licence to Lord Cromwell to travel. [*Docquet.*]

VOL. LXVII.

1611.

Dec. 27. Warrant to discharge Sir Robt. Harley, Ranger of the Forests of Bringwood and Mochtree, co. Hereford, of certain rents from lodges there, due to the Crown under the conveyance made to His Majesty by Sir Hen. Lindley. [*Docquet.*]

Dec. 27. Grant to Peter de la Rue, stranger, of pardon for killing Hen. Nead, Fencer. [*Docquet.*]

Dec. 28. Westminster. Warrant to pay 200*l.* to Meredith Morgan for a masque to be performed at Court at Christmas. [*Warrt. Bk.*, III., *p.* 38.]

Dec. Docquet of the above. [*Docquet, Dec.* 27.]

Dec. 28. Westminster. Warrant to pay 3,024*l.* 13*s.* 10*d.* to Lord Stanhope, Treasurer of the Chamber, for surpluses of his account, &c. [*Warrt. Bk.*, III., *p.* 38.]

Dec. Docquet of the above. [*Docquet, Dec.* 30.]

Dec. 28. Westminster. Warrant to pay to Edw. Bridges, innkeeper, 150*l.* for losses by fire, occasioned by the followers of M. de Vitry, deceased. [*Warrt. Bk.*, III., *p.* 38.]

Dec. Docquet of the above. [*Docquet, Dec.* 27.]

Dec. 28. Westminster. Warrant to pay necessary sums to Fras. Mills and others, Clerks of the Privy Seal, for extra attendance in expediting the loan. [*Warrt. Bk.*, III., *p.* 38.]

Dec. Docquet of the above. [*Docquet, Dec.* 30.]

Dec. 28. Westminster. Warrant to discharge the Earl of Worcester, Master of the Horse, of 400*l.* advanced for horses, &c. provided for His Majesty's service, and to pay him 361*l.* 12*s.* 4*d.* balance of his account, and 400*l.* imprest for purchase of horses. [*Warrt. Bk.*, III., *p.* 38.]

Dec. Docquet of the above. [*Docquet, Dec.* 30.]

Dec. 30. Grant to Sir Robt. Maxwell and Robt. Morrison, his servant, of protection for a year from arrest for debts due to Wm. Watt, tailor, of London. [*Docquet.*]

Dec. 30. Commission for Edm. Marlow to be Captain and Chief Commander of two ships, the James and the Solomon, destined for the East Indies; also for John Gurney to succeed him if he should die. [*Docquet.*]

Dec. 30. Commission for Thos. Best and Thos. Aldworth to be Captains of two other ships also intended for the East Indies. [*Docquet.*]

Dec. 30. Licence for Thos. Hetley to be a common baker at Peterborough, with remission of all penalties for not having served apprenticeship to that trade. [*Docquet.*]

Dec. 30. Newington. 115. Geo. Carleton to his brother, Sir Dud. Carleton. His distress for his mother's death and his son's rash journey is increased by his wife's serious illness. Has been ill himself.

VOL. LXVII.

1611.

Dec. 30. Nuffield. 116. Dr. Geo. Carleton to his cousin, Sir. Dud. Carleton. Death of Sir Dudley's mother, and her eulogy. Wishes to know whether a Jesuit must needs be a priest.

Dec. 31 London. 117. John Chamberlain to the Same. Sir Walter Cope, in recompence of Carleton's presents, promises to see his allowance better paid. The Ambassador of Savoy is angry that the Palatine Prince is likely to be preferred to his master. The Duke of Wirtemberg at Court. A cutpurse, taken in the Chapel Royal, will be executed. The new Baronets claim precedency over the younger sons of Barons. Corbet, Clerk of the Council, old Lady Barnes, and the Countess of Lincoln dead. Cottington, Secretary to Cornwallis, made Consul at Seville.

Dec. 31. Westminster. Warrant to pay 1,200*l.* in gold to Sir Roger Aston, whereof 1,000*l.* is for the King's new year's gift to the Prince of Wales, and 200*l.* to the Duke of York. Also 103*l.* 10*s.* 2¾*d.* arrears of rent due to the Prince, and 100*l.* to the Duke for his new year's gifts. [*Warrt. Bk.*, III., *p.* 39.]

Dec. 31. Docquet of the above.

Dec. 31. Licence for the Earl of Salisbury and his heirs to convey lands or tenements, part of his manor of Hatfield, in fee simple or otherwise, to such persons as he may think fit, notwithstanding the Statute of "Quia emptores terrarum," or any other statute. [*Docquet.*]

Dec. 31. Warrant to pay 3*l.* per week to Florence McCarty, prisoner in the King's Bench. [*Docquet.*]

Dec. 31. Grant of incorporation to the Parish Clerks of London and its Liberties. Each Parish Clerk to bring to the Clerks' Hall weekly a note of all christenings and burials; and to be able to sing the Psalms of David, and to write. [*Docquet.*]

Dec. 31. Lease, in reversion, to Phil. Lord Wharton and Sir Thos. Wharton, his son and heir, for services of Sir George Wharton, His Majesty's servant, deceased, of the manor of Thormanby and appurtenances, co. York. [*Docquet.*]

Dec. ? 118. Tidings from England that the King is very thoughtful about the marriage urged by the agents of the Prince Palatine, in opposition to that of Savoy. He is unwilling to displease the greater part of his nobility by uniting his daughter to a Papist. The Earl of Salisbury argued strongly against it, pointing out the importance of caution in the present projected alliance of France and Spain, Spanish influence prevailing greatly in France since the death of that King. He pointed out the mischiefs resulting from the concourse of Catholics at the foreign Ambassadors' services. They were remonstrated against. The French Ambassador made excuses. The Spanish declared that he would not invite persons, but neither would he prevent their coming. The Venetian replied satisfactorily. Italian.

Vol. LXVII.

119. Petition to the King of the Baronets for maintenance of their dignities and privileges, and of the Viscounts and Barons that their younger sons may have precedence over the Baronets; with historical precedents, arguments, and replies on both sides. Imperfect.

120. Arguments [by a Baronet] in favour of a clearer wording of their patent of creation, by which it may appear that their rank is equivalent to that of the ancient bannerets or baronets, and comes next to that of a baron.

Undated, 1611?

? 121. Thos. Cuthbert to Salisbury. Sir Wm. Bowyer threatens to commit him, because he brought certain informations to his Lordship concerning Berwick. Begs a trial of his deserts, before which he dares not repair to Berwick.

122. Wm. Greenwell and Thos. Stiles to the Same. Have delivered into the King's store since 3d May last, cordage to the value of 8,400*l.* Request that the 4,000*l.* promised them in February may be paid earlier, to maintain their credit and enable them to continue the service.

123. Sir Thos. Eversfield to the Same. His brother being assaulted in the street by Sir Edm. Morgan and others, a man of Sir Edmund's was killed, for which his brother is prosecuted. Prays protection for him.

124. Robt. Bath to ——. Will be utterly undone if Sir Reynold Argall and Randoll have his lands, and retain the purchase money. Begs the Lord Treasurer will stay their lease of his lands.

125. John Marow to Salisbury. Suggestions of benefits to accrue to the King from taking into his hands certain ecclesiastical law proceedings, and to the poor from a special legal commission, and from an office for the prosecution of legacies left for charitable uses.

126. Sir Walter Raleigh to the Queen. Hopes His Majesty will consider the advantages he might derive from the riches of Guiana before it be too late, as his health suffers much from the rigorous confinement of eight years. Attests his innocency.

The Queen to Lord Carew, Her Vice Chamberlain and Receiver General. Blank warrant for payment of money. [*Dom. Corresp.*, *March* 3, 1612.]

127. Elizabeth Lady Reade to Salisbury. Hopes her mean present, her own labour, may find acceptance, being from a fatherless child.

128. Elizabeth, Countess of Rutland, to the Same. Begs his favour towards a suit of Mr. Tirell, who has married her near kinswoman.

129. Ann Wallwyn to the Same. Solicits the wardship of the son of Jas. Tomkins, who is likely to die.

VOL. LXVII.

1611? 130. Katherine Lady Walsh to Salisbury. Thanks for the grant of her request; since which, Sir Thos. Lake informs her that it is the King's pleasure to take away 500*l.* of the 1,500*l.* granted; if so, she must be content.

131. Sir John Wentworth to the Same. Has served the Prince a year in his Privy Chamber. Begs to be appointed his groom in ordinary.

132. [Thos. Wilson] to the [Chancellor of] Cambridge. Statement of the inconveniences resulting from the annexation of the King's gift of Terrington Parsonage to the Divinity Lectureship of Cambridge, which is changed every two years. Proposal that a new lectureship be erected thereon, to be called the "Chancellor's lectureship, and to be in the gift of the University."

Greenwich. Friday. 133. Lord Wotton to the Lord Treasurer. Recommends the issue of a certain commission, as one of the best means to prevent mischief in this dear time.

134. Petition of John Baynard to the Council. Served the late Queen against the Irish rebels. Has been seven years a prisoner in the Gate House, Westminster, at the King's expense. Prays to be released, and placed in the Charter House.

135. Petition of Abraham Campion to Salisbury, for payment of 7,277*l.* 12*s.* 3*d.*, the surplus of his accounts due from the King and Prince for the past three years.

136. Petition of John Croker and Sam. Hales to the Same, not to be charged extra fees in passing their grant of part of Sir Rich. Lee's lands, escheated to the Crown, because mention of payment of the purchase money was omitted from their patent.

137. Petition of Thos. Dudgion, Bookbearer and Underkeeper of the Records of the Court of King's Bench, to the Same. Sir John Stafford, who has married John Whynniard's widow, claims rent from him for two tenements built by himself, with permission, in Old Palace Yard, near the ground leased to him by John Whynniard. Prays that he may pay his rent to the King, lest he be charged with a double payment. *Annexed is,*

137. I. *Conditions of the grant made to John Whynniard of waste land adjoining Westminster Palace, and to the Earl of Northampton of land near Whitehall.*

138. Petition of Sir Thos. Fairfax to the King, for instalment of fines imposed on himself, father, and brother, in 32 Eliz. His brother, Sir Chas. Fairfax, was slain at the siege of Ostend, and left no estate; and he has heavy sums to pay on the death of his father. With note to the Lord Treasurer to the same effect.

Cambridge. 139. Petition of certain Fellows of Queen's College, Cambridge, to Salisbury, for an inhibition to the Vice Chancellor and others not to deprive them for their refusal to acknowledge the newly-elected Proctor, until his Lordship has confirmed the validity of his election.

VOL. LXVII.

1611 ? 140. Petition of Orlando Gibbons, Organist of the King's Chapel, to Salisbury, for a lease in reversion of 40 marks per ann. of Duchy lands, without fine, as promised him by the Queen.

141. Petition of Robt. Treswell, Surveyor of the Woods, to the Same and Sir Julius Cæsar, for licence to dig for yellow ochre in the Forests of Dean and Shotover, paying for it 6*l*. 13*s*. 4*d*. per ann.

142. Petitions of divers Merchant Strangers of London to Salisbury. Are much impeded in their trade by the citizens of London, who prevent their buying needful commodities. Pray that a free market may be erected.

143. Petition of Merchant Strangers and others, traders in the new drapery, in Norwich and Colchester, to the Same, against the citizens of London, who will allow none but those free of the city to buy or sell within its precincts. Pray for a free market outside the city.

144. Petition of the King's tenants on Tower Hill to the Same. To compel Timberley to surrender Faulder's lease, on which they may be enabled to renew leases of their tenements.

145. Petition of Wm. Worthington to the King. For confirmation of a grant of the estates of Lady Parkins and John Gibbons, found guilty of conveying the Lady's daughter beyond the seas into a nunnery.

146. Latin verses in honour of Robert Earl of Salisbury, signed D. H.

147. List of Gentlemen of the Privy Chamber sworn in, ordinary and extraordinary.

148. List of the great offices of the Crown [by the Earl of Nottingham; with additions by Salisbury].

149. Essay addressed to the King on State abuses, especially the overgrown power of the House of Suffolk, and of the Earl of Salisbury, and their oppressions of the subject.

150. Statement of the advantages to accrue from granting to private persons the collection of the King's fees for respite of homage, which are now paid into the [Remembrancer's] Office.

151. Answers to objections stated against removing the payment of fees for homage from Mr. Osborne, the Lord Treasurer's Remembrancer's Office, to assignees appointed by the King.

152. Copy of the above.

153. Grant to Patrick and Rich. Black of the office of tailors to the Duke of York.

154. Reasons to induce [Salisbury] to admit Sir John Stafford to be purchaser of Bristol Castle, he offering a much larger sum for it than do the citizens. [*See Oct.* 6, 1611.].

Vol. LXVII.

1611 ? 155. Estimate by John Norden of expenses of repairs done or to be done about castles in Hampshire and Dorsetshire.

156. Plot of Falmouth Fort and Haven, by John Norden.

157. Note of the rich saddles in the office of His Majesty's saddler.

158. Account of half-yearly payments of 23*l.* 12*s.* 8*d.* made by the churchwardens of St. Saviour's, Southwark, to the Receiver General of Surrey, as rent of the rectory there, from 4 to 9 Jac. I.

159. "My late Lord's intent and purposes," being to have Sir Geo. Trenchard put out of the stewardship of a certain manor [belonging to the Principality of Wales;] to obtain the records relating to it from Mr. Bowyer, keeper of the town records, and to procure it from the Prince, by lease or exchange.

160. Notes from records on the precedence hitherto observed among the Officers of the Navy, proving that it was not affected by the personal rank of the officer, and showing the inconveniences that will ensue if the patent of Baronets be allowed to give them precedence above their superior officers.

161. Arguments by Ralph Brooke, York Herald, against the claim of the members of the Corporation of London to be styled Baron, and as to precedence of Aldermen knighted. Imperfect.

162. Notes of the lamentable state of Northumberland, and prevalence of recusancy there since the Earl of Dunbar's death, by the evil government of Roger Wodrington and Edw. Gray, officers of Lord Howard de Walden and Lord Wm. Howard.

163. Statement of the increase of recusancy in Northumberland, on account of the influence of Lord Wm. Howard and his recusant officers in those parts.

164. Remarks [addressed by Rich. Rainsford to Salisbury], in answer to objections against his project for demanding a tribute of the tenth fish from foreigners fishing in the British seas. Is willing to renew a project undertaken three years before, for farming this tribute. [*See Nov.* 17, 1608.]

165. Writ of Habeas Corpus addressed to the Earl of Northampton, Lord Warden of the Cinque Ports, for bringing up Godfrey Hubbard, before Sir Thos. Fleming, Chief Justice of the Common Pleas. With note of objection to the above, as being contrary to the rights of the Cinque Ports.

166. Hen. Earl of Northampton to the Mayors, &c. of the Cinque Ports. To confirm to John and Chas. Young the right assigned to them by the executors of the late Sam. Thomas, in Letters Patent granted to him of the moiety of all fines for unlawful transportation of ordnance.

VOL. LXVII.

1611? 167. State of a cause between Mr. Godfrey, Clement Stepney, and others, against the executors of Mr. Maize and others, of New Romney, in reference to a tax attempted to be levied on the plaintiffs, which they resist on the ground that their lands at Promhill lie in the liberties of Lydd, and not in those of New Romney.

168. Notes relative to the jurisdiction over Ingmersh and Promhill, contested between the towns of Romney and Lydd.

169. Arguments to prove that the accounts and records of receivers, bailiffs, &c., taken before the Auditors of the Exchequer, should be given up yearly to the two Treasurers of the Remembrancer Office and Clerk of the Pipe, and not preserved by the several Auditors.

VOL. LXVIII. JANUARY—APRIL, 1612.

1612.

Jan. 1. Dresden. 1. Sir Henri de Gunderrot to Lord Hay. Presumes to request the King, Queen, and Prince of Wales to stand sponsors to his new-born son. Hopes his Lordship will second the request with his accustomed fine words, and will himself be another sponsor. French.

Jan. 3. Brussels. 2. Louis Porter de Figueroy to his brother-in-law, Edm. Porter. Acknowledges his letters. Will ask leave to visit him, and will bring him a hawk. Asks for a water dog.

Jan. 3. 3. Collection of all sums expended in building and repairing the King's residences, from his accession until Michaelmas 1611.

Jan. 4. Northampton House. 4. Earl of Northampton, Lord Warden of the Cinque Ports, to Sir Thos. Waller. Incloses a warrant from the Ambassador to the Dutch Captain to transport the other two pirates. Wishes he could with justice spare the Frenchman. Consents to the restoration of the boat run aground at Dover to the poor proprietor thereof.

Jan. 4. Buntingford, Hertfordshire. 5. Articles agreed upon by gentlemen of Hertfordshire, according to a letter from the Council, dated December 12, 1611, touching the repair of the highways between Puckeridge and Royston.

Jan. 4. Plymouth. 6. Sir Ferdinando Gorges to Salisbury. The pirates hesitate to repair to the Isle of Wight, according to his Lordship's direction, and have taken refuge in Ireland till they hear the success of their ship. They talk of going over to the Duke of Florence.

Jan. 5. Westminster. Warrant for payment of 1,500*l.* to Roger Houghton, to the use of the Earl of Salisbury, on payment of the same into the Exchequer by Sir Hen. Carey, for purchase of his Lordship's manor of Snettisham, co. Norfolk. [*Warrt. Bk.*, III., *p.* 39.]

Jan. 6. Docquet of the above.

Jan. 6. Grant to Capt. Thos. Muse of pension of 20*d.* per diem for life. [*Docquet.*]

Vol. LXVIII.

1612.

Jan. 6. Grant to Sir Geo. Douglas and George and James, his sons, born in Scotland, of denization. [*Docquet, Jan.* 6 *and Feb.* 12.]

Jan. 6. Grant to Sir Edw. Ratcliffe and his sureties of protection for a year, if his creditors' certificate prove true. [*Docquet.*]

Jan. 6. Grant to Hen. Hutchinson and his sureties of protection till Bartholomew tide ensuing. [*Docquet.*]

Jan. 6. Presentation of Dr. Fowes, Chaplain to the Prince, to the rectory of Severnestoke, and revocation of the same granted to Wm. Lee. [*Docquet.*]

Jan. 6. Grant to Robt. Tardy of an almsroom in Ewelme, co. Oxford. [*Docquet.*]

Jan. 6. Grant to Wilkes Fitchett of pension of 18*d.* per diem, on surrender of that granted to Geo. Eskott. [*Docquet.*]

Jan. 6. The usual warrant to the Master of the Great Wardrobe for stuff delivered for His Majesty's use in the last year. [*Docquet.*]

Jan. 6. Warrant to pay 100*l.* per ann. to Robt. Maull, one of the King's Pages. [*Warrt. Bk.*, III., *p.* 39.]

Jan. 6. Docquet of the above. [*Docquet, Jan.* 6 *and* 31.]

Jan. 7. Westminster. Warrant to pay 193*l.* 14*s.* 4*d.* surplus of account, and 100*l.* imprest, to Sir Geo. Buck, Master of the Revels. [*Warrt. Bk.*, III., *p.* 39.]

Jan. Docquet of the above. [*Docquet, Jan.* 6.]

Jan. 8. London. 7. Sir John Bennet to Sir Dud. Carleton. Requests him to guide the movements of his son in his Italian travels, especially should he have a "fond desire," as many "English youths have, to see Rome ere he return." Much talk about rich Sutton's bequest of 200,000*l.* for charitable uses, which is so great that the lawyers are trying their wits to find some flaw in the conveyance.

Jan. 8. 8. Wm. Pemberton to Salisbury. To move Dr. [Valentine] Carey, [Master of Christ's College, Cambridge,] to cause his brother to be elected to the fellowship which he is about to leave for employment in the Church abroad.

Jan. 10. Westminster. 9. Grant to John Griffith of the office of Assistant to the Warden of the Cinque Ports, in place of Sir Hen. Palmer, deceased. Latin.

Jan. 10. Westminster. 10. Copy of the above.

Jan. Docquet of the above. [*Docquet, Jan.* 6.]

Jan. 10. 11. Charges of works, &c. at the King's houses in December last.

Jan. 12. Eton. 12. Sir Hen. Savile to [Carleton]. Hopes he will be able to get Palladius for him. Young Lady Hoby dead. Mr. Audley, of Harrow-on-the-Hill, offers Carleton 100*l.* per ann. for Stoke parsonage.

VOL. LXVIII.

1612.

Jan. ? 13. Particulars of a commission [from Sir Hen. Savile to Carleton]. For the purchase of Palladius' Life of St. Chrysostom, printed at Venice, and other works of St. Chrysostom. Latin.

Jan. 13. 14. Thos. Russell to Salisbury. Has not heard of [John] Milward, sent down to the copper works. Sir Wm. Godolphin can speak of the produce, &c. from the mine; 300 tons of ore landed at the works. Hopes to produce copper by Easter.

Jan. 14. Londesborough. 15. Fras. Earl of Cumberland to the Same. Leaves the time of his son's return to his Lordship's disposal. Thanks for his attempt to induce the merchants to favour his matter. Is proceeding for payment of his debts, &c.

Jan. 14. 16. The King to the Earl of Northampton, Lord Privy Seal. To issue Privy Seals for payment as soon as possible of 26,526*l.* 19*s.* 4*d.*, debts of the Queen to divers artificers of London.

Jan. 15. Royston. 17. Geo. Calvert to [Salisbury]. Is writing out the discourse which the King began concerning Vorstius. His Majesty desires Sir Noel Caron to send a promised translation of the long Dutch letter, which he received from Vorstius.

Jan. 15. London. 18. Chamberlain to Carleton. Departure of the Ambassador of Savoy. Presents to him and his secretary. Wotton may probably be sent to Savoy with the answer. Losses by play at Court. Deaths of Sir Wm. Selby, Sir Leonard Holyday, and Sir John Leigh. The Baronets have had a second defeat in their claim of precedence over Barons' younger sons. Sir Ralph Winwood in trouble with the States, for opposing Vorstius' admission to Leyden. Rich Sutton's will called in question, &c.

Jan. 15. Grant to Charles Duke of York, in reversion after the present Lord Admiral, of the office of High Admiral of England for life, with exception of pirates' goods, as the King would not have the conscience of the Duke "burdened with things of so litigious a nature." [*Docquet.*]

Jan. 15. Grant to Lord Knyvet of purchase in fee simple of Northmill, in Stanwell, co. Middlesex. [*Docquet.*]

Jan. 15. Grant to Geo. Budd, of London, and his sureties, of protection for a year. [*Docquet.*]

Jan. 15. Grant, in reversion, to And. Wright, of a Yeoman Waiter's place in the Tower. [*Docquet.*]

Jan. 15. Lease to Thos. Lloyd of the amerciaments and perquisites of the Hundred Courts, County Courts, &c., to be holden by the Sheriffs in sundry counties of South and North Wales, except certain fines due to the Prince of Wales, &c. [*Docquet.*]

Jan. 15. Grant to Roger Savage of an almsroom in Canterbury Cathedral. [*Docquet.*]

VOL. LXVIII.

1612.

Jan. 18. Letter to the Lord Chamberlain, Earl of Worcester, Lord Knyvet, and Sir Julius Cæsar, directing them to view certain obsolete and broken jewels in the Tower, and consider which and how many of them may be altered into other forms, to be sent as tokens to the Duke of Savoy. [*Docquet.*]

Jan. 18. Letter to the Council to order certain priests to be conveyed to one of the ports, and carried out of the kingdom, by request of the Duke of Savoy. [*Docquet.*]

Jan. 18. Warrant to pay to the creditors of John Maria Lugaro, Groom of the Queen's Privy Chamber, licensed by the Queen to go abroad for three years, at the request of the Ambassador of the Duke of Savoy, the annuity of 100*l.* due to him. [*Docquet.*]

Jan. 18. Warrant dormant for delivery of stuff yearly to John Bateman, the King's bookbinder, for his livery. [*Docquet.*]

Jan. 18. Letter to the Master and Fellows of Magdalen College, Cambridge, to elect John Elton Fellow. [*Docquet.*]

Jan. 19. 19. List of Privy Seals despatched to counties and places enumerated.

Jan. 21. Whitehall. 20. [Earl of Salisbury?] to Sir Hen. Hobart, Attorney General. Rich. Stapleton, who claims half the possessions of Visct. Beaumont, relinquishes those now in the hands of the King, Queen, or Prince, and is willing to compound for the remainder with the present possessors. The King wishes the Attorney to treat thereon, &c.

Jan. 21. Berwick. 21. Mayor, &c. of Berwick to Salisbury. Operations at Berwick Bridge. *Inclose,*

21. I. *Account of moneys disbursed for building the stone bridge at Berwick, from June* 20 *to Dec.* 24, 1611. *Jan* 7, *Berwick.*

Jan.? 22. Petition of the Same to the Same, for grant of 1,500*l.* more, to carry on the building of the bridge.

Jan. 21. Berwick. 23. Sir Ralph Gray and the Mayor, &c. of Berwick to the Same. Concerning the survey of ordnance and munition remaining at Berwick, Wark, and Norham. *Inclose,*

23. I. *Note of ordnance at Berwick, Wark, and Norham. Jan.* 13, 14, 15.

Jan. 21. Berwick. 24. Geo. Nicholson to the Same. Has sent up his last half year's account for Berwick to Auditor Gofton. Ten of the pensioners and old Sir Wm. Selby dead.

Jan. 22. Truro. 25. John Milward to the Same. Sends a treatise on the inconvenience of the exportation of coin caused by the use of foreign goods, but proving that the reformation thereof, by restraint of the

1612. Vol. LXVIII.

trade, would produce still worse evils. Fears he can do little service at the copper works, another being placed there. [*See Jan.* 13.] *Annexed is,*

25. I. *Treatise by John Milward on the coin of the realm. The reasons of its diminution, suggestions for its preservation in the kingdom, importance of establishing an exchange, &c. Inscribed to the King.*

Jan.? 26. Note of persons guilty of transporting gold into France, buying it above the Mint price, melting down and selling coin, &c.

Jan. 23. Bishop's Auckland. 27. Bishop of Durham to Salisbury. Is going to Bath to recruit, after half a year's sickness and lameness, the relics of his attendance on Lady Arabella. Sir Geo. Selby, Sheriff, and his Chancellor, Dr. Colmore, will attend to his duties. Recommends his Lordship to try Bath. The Privy Seals for loans are double those in the second year of the King. Recommends that the loans in Norhamshire and Bedlingtonshire be paid to the collector of Durham, to which county they really belong, though claimed by Northumberland.

Jan. 23. Greenwich. 28. Robt. Visct. Lisle to the Same. Has given his message to the Queen. Anstruther is only waiting to kiss her hand before he sets out [for Denmark].

Jan. 23. 29. Note of munition necessary for Calshot Castle, taken by John Norden, Surveyor.

Jan. 24. Royston. 30. Sir Thos. Lake to Salisbury. The Earl of Abercorn is discouraged because the land fallen to him in Ireland is not fitting his degree, although he took land to please the King and encourage others. His Majesty proposes to allow him a company of twenty-five horse in compensation, and to pay them without extra charge, by reducing the pay of all the horse from English to Irish money, as already done with the foot.

Jan. 24. Bishop's Auckland. 31. Bishop of Durham to the Same. In behalf of Isaac Foxcroft, of Yorkshire, who, wishing to settle in Ireland, desires letters in his favour to the Lord Deputy.

Jan. 25. 32. Eliz. Lady Kincleven to the Same. Begs him to bestow on Thos. Lammas the vicarage of Tottington, co. Norfolk, which is in the gift of her son, but during his minority is in his Lordship's hands.

Jan. 25. Westminster. Warrant to pay 3*l.* per week to Florence McCarty from June 1, 1611, since which time he has been prisoner in the Marshalsea. [*Warrt. Bk.*, III., *p.* 40.]

Jan. Docquet of the above. [*Docquet, Jan.* 24.]

Jan. 25. Westminster. Warrant to pay to Wm. Stacey, Under-keeper of Marybone Park, 100*l.*, for his great charge in keeping deer there for His Majesty's recreation in hunting. [*Warrt. Bk.*, III., *p.* 40.]

Jan. 25. Docquet of the above.

Vol. LXVIII.

1612.

Jan. 25. Warrant to pay money, not exceeding 8,000*l.*, to Wm Haydon, servant of the Prince, for his own use, out of sums arising on compositions, &c. for defective titles. [*Docquet.*]

Jan. 25. Warrant to the Lord Chancellor, and other Commissioners for defective titles, to grant a sum of money to Wm. Haydon, from compositions for defective titles, with allowance for his charges. [*Docquet.*]

Jan. 25. Letter to the Bp. of Durham, thanking him for admitting Capt. Hodson as Muster Master of the county palatine of Durham, for the sake of the late Earl of Dunbar. [*Docquet.*]

Jan. 25. Grants of licences to sell wines in several towns and counties. [*Docquet.*]

Jan. 25. Grant to Sir Jas. Sandilands and his sureties of protection for six months. [*Docquet.*]

Jan. 25. Warrant for Privy Seals for payment of debts not exceeding 16,526*l.* 19. 4*d.*, due by the Queen to persons whose names are contained in a schedule subscribed by her officers. [*Docquet.*]

Jan. 25. Letter to Sir Robt. Carey, Sir Jas. Fullerton, and Thos. Murray, authorizing them, in the absence of the Prince and the officers of white staves of his household, to repress disorders in the house of the Duke of York. [*Docquet.*]

Jan. 25. Warrant to pay 2,029*l.* 2*s.* 9*d.* to Sir John Spilman for jewels delivered for the King's use, and 2,000*l.* to John Luce, merchant stranger, of London, surplus of a debt of 4,029*l.* 2*s.* 9*d.* [*Docquet.*]

Jan. 25. Grant to Sir Marmaduke Darell and Sir Allan Apsley, of the office of Surveyor General of Victuals for the King's Navy and Marine Affairs, on surrender of a former grant to the said Sir Marmaduke Darell and Sir Thos. Bludder. [*Docquet.*]

Jan. 25. Grant to Sampson Darell, in reversion after his father Sir Marmaduke Darell and Sir Allan Apsley, of the office of Surveyor of the Victuals of the Navy. [*Docquet.*]

Jan. 25. Warrant for delivery of the accustomed livery to Hen. St. George, Pursuivant-at-Arms. [*Docquet.*]

Jan. 27.
Langham Hall. 33. Warkin Prott to Salisbury. Sir Gamaliel Capell's report that he flatly denied to accede to the loan on Privy Seal is false. Could not pay it at the time, and solicits to be excused, or payment to be respited till Lady-day. Has never received back 40*l.* lent 39 Eliz.

Jan. 27.
Gloucester. 34. Deputy Lieutenants of Gloucestershire to the Same. Complain that, though they sent up a list of persons fit for the loan, Privy Seals are not sent to all those, but are sent to some others not in their list, and to some for greater sums than they set down.

VOL. LXVIII.

1612.

Jan. 27. Westminster. Warrant for payment of 9,045*l.* 18. 10¼*d.* to the Prince of Wales, in full satisfaction of rents reserved for a whole year ending Michaelmas last, as parcel of the assignation of 12,190*l.* 2*s.* 9*d.* allowed to him yearly for support of his state. [*Warrt. Bk.*, III., *p.* 37.]

Jan. Docquet of the above. [*Docquet, Jan.* 25.]

Jan. 29. Grant, with survivorship, to Sir Jas. and John Scudamore, of the office of Steward of the lordship of Kidwelly, Carnallen, and Iskennen, also Constable and Porter of Kidwelly Castle, in Wales, belonging to the duchy of Lancaster, on surrender of a former grant to Sir Jas. Scudamore. [*Docquet.*]

Jan. 29. Grant, with survivorship, to Sir Robt. Carey and Thos. Carey, his second son, in reversion after the Earl of Northumberland, of the custody of Tynemouth Castle, Northumberland, and the forts and holds thereto belonging. [*Docquet.*]

Jan. 29. Grant of pardon to Grace Jewett and five other women, found guilty of murders, but reprieved for especial causes, and left in confinement many years. [*Docquet.*]

Jan. 29. Grant to Wm. Gwynn of the seventh reversion of an auditorship in the Exchequer, in consideration of services performed by his late father, Rich. Gwynn, as Deputy to Auditor Hanbury. [*Docquet.*]

Jan. 29 London. 35. Chamberlain to Carleton. The Privy Seal moneys come in well. The Prince much engrossed with martial sports. Lord Cranborne in great favour with him. He is going to the King at Royston. The King has been writing in French against Vorstius. The Lord Treasurer nearly recovered. Some of the pirates have accepted pardon, others stand aloof in Ireland. Judge Fenner and Blackwell, the arch-priest, dead. Visct. Rochester and Sir John Harrington have the reversion of Sir John Roper's office. Sir Hen. Wotton is to prepare for Savoy. Pory's employment in France was to carry a treatise by the Bishop of Ely and Casaubon to Cardinal Peron, and to present to Thuanus Queen Elizabeth's life, collected by Camden Clarencieux, with the help of Sir Robt. Cotton. Sir Rich. Smith thanks Carleton for favours to his son, &c.

Jan. 30. Westminster. Warrant to pay to Meredith Morgan 80*l.*, for charges of a masque performed at Christmas. [*Warrt. Bk.*, III., *p.* 40.]

Jan. Docquet of the above. [*Docquet, Jan.* 31.]

Jan. 30. Westminster. Warrant to pay to Hen. Seckford, administrator of Sir Hen. Seckford, 85*l.* 9*s.* 6*d.* due for surplus of his account, in his late office of Master of the Tents, Pavilions, and Hales. [*Warrt. Bk.*, III., *p.* 40.]

Jan. Docquet of the above. [*Docquet, Jan.* 31.]

Vol. LXVIII.

1612

Jan. 31. Rogeston's Grange. 36. Anne Lady Herbert to Salisbury. Presumes to offer to his Lordship the first fruits of his godson's, her son Edward's, Latin. *Incloses,*

36. I. *Complimentary verses addressed to Robert Earl of Salisbury, Lord High Treasurer. Latin.*

Jan. 31. 37. Sir Gamaliel Capell to the Same. Begs that Nich. Collins' appeal against his Privy Seal be not granted. His backwardness has hindered others from advancing their money, and they wait the success of his petition. *Incloses,*

37. I. *Reasons why Nich. Collins, of Little Laver, is rated at 80l. towards the loan. Jan. 31, Essex.*

Jan. 31. Windsor. 38. Jas. Hudson to the Same. His Majesty having granted him the forfeiture of Mr. Kyfin's estate, solicits order for the prisoner's enlargement and pardon.

Jan. 31. 39. Petition of Robt. Meverell to the Same. Details the circumstances of his possession of certain lands at Darleton, co. Nottingham, which have been been in his family 300 years. Prays for a lease thereof, on payment of a reasonable increase of rent and a fine, without the proviso, "Si quis plus dare voluerit." With report thereon by Sir Jas. Altham and Sir Walter Cope. [*See Dec.* 11, 1611.]

Jan. 31. Letter to Thos. Wright, Paymaster of the Forces in the Low Countries, to remit to Sir Rich. Wigmore, one of the Captains at Flushing, cheques incurred by reason of his absence from ill health. [*Docquet.*]

Jan. 31. Grant to Rich. Rice of the benefit of the recusancy of Elizabeth Horseman, co. Oxford, and Eleanor Kemp, of Pentlow, co. Essex. [*Docquet.*]

Jan. 31. Grant to John More and John Castle, in reversion after Wm. Trumbull, and in trust for his son William, of the office of a courier or post. [*Docquet.*]

Jan. 31. Grant to Wm. Walker, in reversion after Thos. Sheffield, of the office of keeper of the new orchard and lodge, the old great garden, and the new garden, at Greenwich, for life. [*Docquet.*]

Jan. 31. Warrant to pay to Edw. Blount and Ant. Dyott, one half the sums accruing to the King from the lands of Visct. Beaumont. [*Docquet.*]

Jan. 31. Grant to Rich. Nealman of a pension of 12*d.* per diem, on surrender of a like pension by John Stone. [*Docquet.*]

Jan. 31. Grant to Rich. Southcott of a rentcharge of 20*l.* per ann., forfeit by attainder of Thos. Osbaldeston for felony and murder. [*Docquet.*]

Jan. 31. Letter to the President and Fellows of Magdalen College, Oxford, to elect Fras. White Fellow. [*Docquet.*]

VOL. LXVIII.

1612.

Jan. 31. Commission of appeal to decide a controversy for debt between two privileged persons of the University of Oxford, John Preston and Hen. Marman, which the University authorities have failed to decide. [*Docquet.*]

Jan. 31. Grant to Thos. Powell, on surrender of Rich. Reading, of the keepership of the stables at Hampton Court for life. [*Docquet.*]

Jan. 31. Warrant for payment of wages and livery to Rich. Berwick, appointed Falconer in reversion after Chris. Berwick. [*Docquet.*]

Jan. 40. Wm. Style to Salisbury. For his father to be excused the Privy Seal loan for 20*l.* He is 1,000*l.* in debt, and his Christmas hospitalities to the poor have been heavy upon him.

Jan. 41. Sir Wm. Monson to the Same. Advises measures for capture of a pirate vessel.

Jan. 42. Thos. Packer to the Same. For allowance for attending in the business of the loans, three weeks before Mr. Mills came to town, and also for attendance at the loan of 2 Jac. I.

Jan. 43. Wm. Wintle to the Same. To write in his favour to Mr. Hull, for whose daughter he is a suitor.

Jan. 44. Wm. Seymour to the Council. Is glad of an opportunity to show his obedience, which he would maintain were the performance ever so difficult. Thanks for their mild proceedings, and begs an increase of the King's benignity.

Jan. 45. Note of such sums as remain due to the Treasurer of the Navy.

Feb. 2. 46. Sir Thos. Shirley to Salisbury. To favour his petition to the King for power to sell his lands, by which means he could discharge his debt to the Crown, and free his friends, who are sureties for him, from danger, and meanwhile for protection for himself and friends from prosecutions for debt.

Feb. 2. Eton. 47. Sir Hen. Savile to Carleton. Letting of Stoke parsonage. Begs that Mr. Wake may have his first volume of Chrysostom to make a collation with a MS. in the Venice Library. With postscript from Lady Savile to Lady Carleton, her daughter, that she blesses her portrait twice a day, but has not heard from her for three weeks.

Feb. 2. Westminster. 48. Grant to the Company of Vintners of London of incorporation and licence to retail wines, with confirmation of former privileges.

Docquet of the above. [*Docquet, Jan.* 29.]

Feb. 3. Dunham. 49. Sir Geo. Bouthe to Salisbury. Has sent out the Privy Seals as collector of the loan for Cheshire, but some persons proving incompetent to pay, desires some blank Privy Seals, which may be directed by him to private money lenders. Requests permission to export yearly one hundred dozen of calfskins in his own bark.

VOL. LXVIII.

1612.

Feb. 3. 50. Certificate of rents of the manors in the Queen's jointure, and their several modes of tenure and fines.

Feb. 4. 51. Edw. Kendall to Thos. Wilson. Sends the three patents, and requests payment of the fees for them, which he will repay, if the enrolments are decided to belong to him [Wilson]. With note by Kendall's servant of receipt of the above fees.

Feb. [4 ?] 52. Thos. Thomson to the Same. The reports of the size and value of the stone which he has are malicious and exaggerated. Will resign his place as manager of the works at Hatfield, if they are credited.

Feb. 5. 53. Rich. Carmarthen to Salisbury. Some of those to whom the merchants' petitions were referred have been suspected of corruption; disclaims the imputation, &c., and begs the petitioners may be referred to the Barons of the Exchequer.

Feb. 5. Delapre. 54. Sir Wm. Tate to the Same. Has sent up the money received for the loan, with a paper of considerations thereon.

Feb. 6. Warrant to pay to Alice Woodrove, mercer, 457*l.* 12*s.* 10*d.*, for wares supplied for the Queen. [*Warrt. Bk.*, III., *p.* 41.]

Feb. 6. Warrant to pay to Thos. Williams, administrator of Jas. Freeland, embroiderer, deceased, 870*l.* 14*s.* 3*d.*, for wares supplied for the Queen. [*Ibid.*, I., *p.* 41.]

Feb. 6. Like warrant to pay to John Hull, mercer, 229*l.* 7*s.* 11*d.* [*Ibid.*, *p.* 40.]

Feb. 6. Like warrant to pay to Edw. Barnes, mercer, 598*l.* 10*s.* 3*d.* [*Ibid.*, *p.* 40.]

Feb. 6. Like warrant to pay to Abraham Speckaet 816*l.* 5*s.* 9*d.* [*Ibid.*, *p.* 41.]

Feb. 6. Like warrant to pay to Sir Baptist Hicks, mercer, 1,909*l.* 0*s.* 1*d.* [*Ibid.*, *p.* 41.]

Feb. 6. Grant to Horatio Lupo of the place of Musician on the Violin for life. [*Docquet.*]

Feb. 6. Grant to Dr. Thos. Clayton of the office of Reader of the Physic Lecture in Oxford, on surrender of Dr. Warner, to whom the reversion is granted after Dr. Clayton. [*Docquet.*]

Feb. 6. Grant to Peter Orrell of pardon for supposed manslaughter. [*Docquet.*]

Feb. 6. Grant to John Ibson, Robt. Faldington, Thos. Graver, and John Fountaunce, in fee simple, of the manor of Alne and Tollerton, co. York. [*Docquet.*]

Feb. 6. Lease to Fras. Phelips and Edw. Ferrers of divers mills, with their appurtenances; also re-grant of certain mills, co. Northampton. [*Docquet.*]

VOL. LXVIII.

1612.
Feb. 6. Grant to John Kitchin of pardon for robbery. [*Docquet.*]

Feb. 6. Grant to Peter Eston, Wm. Harvey, &c., of pardon for piracy. [*Docquet.*]

Feb. 7. Warrant to pay to the Earl of Nottingham, High Admiral, 1,628*l.* 8*s.* for 708 Flemish ells of rich hangings, at 46*s.* per ell, delivered by him for His Majesty's use. [*Warrt. Bk.*, III., *p.* 41.]

Feb. 7. Commission of Review to the Archbp. of Canterbury and others, to re-examine a sentence passed by Sir Lawrence Tanfield and others, delegates in a Chancery commission, in favour of Robt. Withers, a singing man in the cathedral of Exeter, against the Bishop of Exeter, who, for a breach of divers local statutes, deprived the said Withers of his place; Withers having obtained the sentence in his favour by falsification of records. [*Docquet.*]

Feb. 7. London. 55. Sir Thos. Lowe, Governor of the Company of Merchant Adventurers, to Salisbury. Requests a continuation of the permission to export 90 tuns of English beer for the diet of those of the company who reside at Middleburgh.

Feb. 8. 56. Charges of the works, &c. on the King's houses in January.

Feb. 8. 57. Account of payments of loan money from various court and county collectors.

Feb. 9. 58. Edm. Nevill (signed Westmoreland) to Salisbury. Finds the expenses attending his grant of fines on lands passed without licence of alienation so great, that he wishes the grant to be rather for a certain sum to be derived from alienations, than for a number of them.

Feb. 9. Whitehall. 59. [Earl of Salisbury] to the King. If learned Mayerne had blundered in his case, as reported, the King's visit would have cured him. Has received a despatch from the new Secretary [Sir Robt. Naunton]. Tenderness in dealing with heretics is full of danger.

[Feb. 9]. Royston. 60. Sir Thos. Lake [to Salisbury]. The King is determined to exercise his right of remanding by his prerogative, if it cannot be done by law. If the Ambassadors will not prevent English subjects from hearing mass in their chapels, His Majesty will appoint a guard to seize English subjects going to mass. As to the Earl of Abercorn's business [*see Jan.* 24], the captains of the horse pocket all the soldiers' pay; therefore the men can be no losers by the proposed abatement. The King has had an hour's dispute with four of the Baronets, touching their claim for precedency before the sons of Barons.

[Feb. 9.] 61. Copy of the first and last pages of the above.

Feb. 12. London. 62. Chamberlain to Carleton. Private affairs. The King's book [against Vorstius] publishing in French, Latin, and English. Books written by [Rich.] Sheldon, a converted priest, and [Wm.] Warmington, Cardinal Allen's chaplain. The Queen, Treasurer,

1612. VOL. LXVIII.

and Chamberlain going to Bath. A lottery in hand for furthering the Virginia voyage. A Bermuda company forming. Lady Shrewsbury still in the Tower for refusing to answer interrogatories. Moll Cutpurse, a notorious beggar, has done penance in St. Paul's. Sir Thos. Bodley has a grant from the Stationers' Company of a copy for his library of every book printed. Sir John Bennet has undertaken to build the schools at Oxford. Dr. Maxey is Dean of Windsor. Suicide of a son of the Bp. of Bristol, from fear of the disgrace of flogging.

Feb. 12. Warrant to pay to Visct. Rochester 12,000*l.* out of debts due from France and Holland, to enable him to purchase certain lands. [*Warrt. Bk.*, III., *p.* 42.]

Feb. 12. Grant to Sir David Murray of 2,000*l.*, parcel of the sum of 4,000*l.* payable by Visct. Montague. [*Docquet.*]

Feb. 12. Grant to Sir Robt. Douglas, Master of the Horse to the Prince, of an annuity of 1,000 marks, and 500 marks to his executors and administrators, during the life of Sir David Murray. [*Docquet.*]

Feb. 12. Grant to Martin and Wm. Freeman, in fee simple, of lands not named, value 43*l.* 0*s.* 3*d.* per ann., parcel of the lands assigned to John Eldred, Art. Ingram, and others, in lieu of the lands called Angels, conveyed by them to the Prince. [*Docquet.*]

Feb. 12. Letter for a grant to the Earl of Montgomery of the benefit of the recusancy of Sir Hen. James, of Kent; Sir John Shelley, Sir John Carill the elder, Sir John Carill the younger, Sir John Morley, Sir Thos. Carill, co. Sussex; Sir John Whitbrook, co. Salop; Rich. Cotton, co. Hants; Wm. Padage, co. Kent; Chas. Waldegrave and Geo. Gryme, co. Norfolk; John Wright, co. Essex; Alban Butter, co. Northampton; Barth. Freemond, co. Surrey; and Edw. Gage, co. Hereford. [*Docquet.*]

Feb. 12. Grant to Sir Hen. Carey, in fee simple, of the manor of Snettisham, co. Norfolk. [*Docquet.*]

Feb. 14. Lease to Fras. Drake of the manor of Walton-upon-Thames, co. Surrey. [*Docquet.*]

Feb. 14. Warrant to pay to Robt. Meinges 360*l.* 0*s.* 7*d.*, from the King's benefit of the recusants granted to Ralph Beeston and Ralph Bowes. [*Docquet.*]

Feb. 16. Bishop's Auckland. 63. Wm. James, Bishop of Durham, to Salisbury. Thanks for his honourable dealings in the purchase of Durham House, &c. If the Oath of Allegiance be not strictly enforced, it had better not have been promulged.

Feb. 17. Londesborough. 64. Fras. Earl of Cumberland to the Same. Rejoices at his son's return, and longs to see him with his intended wife, his Lordship's daughter.

Feb. 17. Warrant to pay to John Decro 18*l.* 3*s.* 6*d.*, for lands purchased for enlarging the Park at Theobald's. [*Warrt. Bk.*, III., *p.* 42.]

VOL. LXVIII.

1612.
Feb. 17. Like warrant for 70*l.* to Wm. Wilford, for lands for the like purpose. [*Warrt. Bk.*, III., *p.* 42.]

Feb. 17. Like warrant for 5,600*l.* to Sir Robt. Wroth. [*Ibid.*, *p.* 43.]

Feb. 17. Like warrant for 700*l.* to Dr. Atkins, for his interest in the tithes of lands purchased for the like purpose. [*Ibid.*, *p.* 44.]

Feb. 17. Like warrant for 600*l.* to Wm. Thomas. [*Ibid.*, *p.* 43.]

Feb. 17. Like warrant for 184*l.* to Roger and Jane Thraps. [*Ibid.*, *p.* 43.]

Feb. 17. Like warrant for 3,840*l.* to Sir Thos. Dacre, of Debden, co. Essex, for lands called the St. Giles, in the parish of Cheshunt, for the like purpose. [*Ibid.*, *p.* 43.]

Feb. 17. Like warrant for 58*l.* 10*s.* to Hum. Walcott. [*Ibid.*, *p.* 44.]

Feb. 17. Warrant to pay to Sir Wm. Herrick 40*l.*, for a tablet of gold, a seal, and repair of certain jewels. [*Ibid.*, *p.* 42.]

Feb. 17. Warrant to pay 1,000*l.* to Stephen le Gouch, merchant stranger, for a jewel of "one fair large pendant diamond, cut with fancies on all sides, and pierced at the top," delivered for the Queen. [*Ibid.*, *p.* 44.]

Feb. 17. Warrant to pay 1,500*l.* to Peter James, jun., merchant stranger, for a jewel in the form of a rose set about with four diamonds, delivered to the Queen. [*Ibid.*, *p.* 44 *bis.*]

Feb. 17. Warrant to pay to John Norden 81*l.* 6*s.* 8*d.*, for repairs speedily to be made at Calshot Castle, co. Hants; and 251*l.* for repairs of a breach made by the sea near the castle. [*Ibid.*, *p.* 42.]

Feb. 20. Grant to Julio Camillo Crema, an Italian, of 100*l.* as a free gift. [*Ibid.*, *p.* 45.]

Feb. 20. Strand. 65. Sir Hen. Savile, [jun.], to [Carleton]. Sir Dudley and Lady Carleton missed at Christmas from Eton. The sons of Sir Thos. Bland, Sir John Thornhaugh, and Serjeant Hutton travelling in Italy.

Feb. 24. Raby Castle. 66. Sir Geo. Freville to Wm. James, Bp. of Durham. Onbe half of Fras. Brackenbury, whose estate is terribly wasted by his want of forethought. *Annexes*,

66. I. *Fras. Brackenbury to Sir Geo. Freville. Laments that his ruined estate will not supply him the means of appearing before the Bishop, to answer informations exhibited against him. Feb. 24.*

Feb. 26. London. 67. Chamberlain to Carleton. His money not to be obtained on account of the Lord Treasurer's sickness. Particulars of his dangerous state and recovery. Candidates for his offices. The Judges charged by the King to look diligently on their circuits to the Oath of Allegiance. Mrs. Vaux, Lord Vaux's mother, condemned to perpetual imprisonment, for refusing to take it. [Bartholomew] Legate, sentenced to be burnt for denying the

1612. VOL. LXVIII.

divinity of Christ. Seven sail of pirates gone for the East Indies. Proclamation in Spain for better treatment of our merchants. An Ambassador arrived from Denmark to ask help in the wars. Forces proposed to be sent under certain noblemen.

Feb. 28. Warrant to pay to Rich. Batten, Ranger of Whichwood Forest, co. Oxon, 34*l.* 18*s.* 4*d.*, for extraordinary charges of John Ardes, Edw. Bowman, and Jas. Clerk, under-keepers, in ditching, paling, walling, &c., for the purpose of dividing the forest from the lands of the Bishop of Winchester. [*Warrt. Bk.*, III, *p.* 45.]

Feb. 28. Warrant to pay to John Raimond, purveyor of poultry, 500*l.*, in satisfaction of losses sustained in making provisions of poultry at set prices. [*Ibid.*, *p.* 45.]

Feb. Letter to the Governor and Company of Virginia to suffer Daniel Tucker, a personal adventurer since the first plantation, to pass by the next ship to England. [*Docquet.*]

Feb. Grant to Geo. Reding of annuity of 10*l.*, in consideration of service in the office of Clerk of the Escheats, in the Court of Common Pleas, from the death of the late Fras. Anderson. [*Docquet.*]

Feb. Grant to Wm. Ledsham of pension of 2*s.* per diem, on surrender thereof by John Hope. [*Docquet.*]

Feb. Grant to Thos. Willoughby of pardon for manslaughter. [*Docquet.*]

Feb. 68. John Killigrew to Salisbury. Will be disgraced if his suit be refused. Begs that three houses only may give entertainment to distressed mariners and passengers.

March 3. 69. Copies of blank warrants, letters, &c. from the King, Queen, and others, as follows:—For a muster-master's place; for exemption of the King's servants from serving on juries; for renewal of a lease; for compromise with creditors [*imperfect*]; for preferment of a poor scholar; licence for the Duke of York's players, Anno 9; for payment of money; for assisting the keeper of the game; for presentation to a living; for protection to the servant of a member of Parliament during its sittings; for grant of an almsroom [*imperfect*]; for protection of the King's game [*imperfect*]; for grant of the office of chief carpenter; in behalf of one that sustained loss by fire, March 3, 1612; licence to exhibit certain games in Surrey; for transport of ordnance; for a badger or carrier of corn; for grants of recusants' lands.

March 3. Drury House. 70. Wm. Lord Paget to Salisbury. Reminds him of his suit, &c.

March 4. Westminster. Grant to the city of Derby of incorporation, &c. [*Sign Man.*, *vol.* I., *No.* 2.]

March 6. Westminster. Grant to Sir Baptist Hicks, Rich. Pyatt, Edw. Barkham, Aldermen, and eleven others, of London, of tenements in Grub Street, the Old Jewry, and Queenhithe, on nomination of Sir Walter Cope and others, contractors for parsonages. [*Ibid.*, *No.* 12.]

Vol. LXVIII.

1612.

March 7. 71. Charges of works, &c. at the King's houses in February.

March 8. Kew. 72. Lord Harrington to Salisbury. Requests him to cause his suit to be referred to the King's Counsel-at-Law, from whom he may expect speedier resolution than from the judges, now on their circuits.

March 9. Westminster. Grant to Rich. Talbot, in reversion after Jas. Leigh, of the office of Master Plasterer for life. [*Sign Man.*, *vol.* II., *No.* 13.]

March 9. Westminster. Warrant to Chancellor Ellesmere to issue a writ subjoined under the Great Seal, to the Sheriff of Lichfield, for Edw. Wightman, of Burton-on-Trent, to be publicly burnt as a heretic. [*Ibid.*, *No.* 14.]

[March 9.] 73. English translation of the above writ.

March 10. Warrant to pay sums certified by the Earl of Suffolk, Lord Chamberlain, for defraying the charges of the Ambassador lately arrived from the King of Denmark. [*Warrt. Bk.*, III., *p.* 45.]

March 12. Westminster. 74. Warrant to repay to Thos. Scudamore, Receiver, of Yorkshire, 3,220*l.*, paid by him for the charges at Berwick, and to allow sums necessary therefor in future; also discharge to Sir Edw. Carey, for his allowance to Wm. Garway on his account of 400*l.*, advanced for the same purpose.

[March 12.] Entry of the above. [*Warrt. Bk.*, III., *p.* 46.]

March 13. Beaupier. Glamorganshire. 75. Sir Jas. Perrot to Salisbury. Thinks Chris. Hawkes, sent by his Lordship, has not sincerity nor skill enough to apprehend a Jesuit, as he promised. Certain Jesuits and priests keep up intelligence amongst the recusants resident in Worcestershire, Monmouthshire, Herefordshire, and South Wales. If some trusty professed Romanist would come amongst them, he might discover and reveal much of their haunts and practices.

March 13. Whitehall. 76. Order in Council to the Lord Warden of the Cinque Ports, to prevent the unlawful shipping and transporting of ordnance and other munition.

March 16. Warrant to the Lord Chancellor to issue a writ subjoined for the burning of Barth. Legate, of London, convicted "of divers horrible heresies and blasphemous opinions." [*Sign Man.*, *vol.* I., *No.* 15.]

March 17. Westminster. Grant to Sir Baptist Hicks, on nomination of Sir Wm. Ryder and others, contractors for parsonages, of purchase of the rectory of Cheltenham. [*Ibid.*, *vol.* II., *No.* 16.]

March 20. 77. Edm. Nevill (signed Westmoreland) to Salisbury. Requests permission to assign 300*l.* out of his annuity of 600*l.* to Edw. Wardour and Bevis Thelwall, who have lent him large sums of money.

March 21. London. 78. Chamberlain to Carleton. The Lord Treasurer well recovered. He was much visited by the Royal Family and others. There were many "forward to part the bear's skin." Sir Thos. Lake was gene-

Vol. LXVIII.

1612.

rally spoken of as Secretary. A Danish Ambassador has arrived to press for mariners. The Duke of Bouillon is expected on a double errand from the Palatine of the Rhine and from the Queen Regent of France. Presents taken by Sir Hen. Wotton to Savoy. Lord Vaux committed to the Fleet for refusing the Oath of Allegiance. The Prince, Visct. Rochester, &c. ran a match at the ring against the Duke of Lenox, &c. Apprentice riots; robberies. Quarrel between Ramsay and the Earl of Montgomery. Private affairs.

March 21. 79. Thos. Lord Grey to Salisbury. Inquires after his health. Exhorts him to resignation and preparation for another world. Will pray constantly for his recovery.

March 22. Grant to Fras. Morris and Fras. Phelips, at suit of sundry contractors for lands, of purchase of rectories, lands, rents, &c., in cos. Hereford, Cornwall, Brecon, Worcester, Pembroke, York, Cumberland, Northumberland, Bedford, Lincoln, Dorset, Notts, London, Warwick, Suffolk, Durham, Devon, Anglesea, Carmarthen, Berks, Gloucester, Somerset, Wilts, Essex, Leicester, Hertford, Salop, Monmouth, Carnarvon, and Surrey; total value 953*l.* 10*s.* 2¾*d.* per ann. Latin. [*Sign Man., vol.* II., *Nos.* 17—21.]

March 22. 80. Robt. Heath to Thos Phelippes. Has spoken to Mr. [Geo.] Shires about accepting his offer for Kirby Misperton. He inclines to it, but will need full assurance that the money will be forthcoming. With marginal annotations [by Phelippes].

March 23. 81. Sir Wm. Godolphin to Salisbury. Has delivered up his Spanish guest, John Dalston, alias Salkeld, with papers relative to his conversion from Popery. Has received 700*l.* on certain Privy Seals, making a total of 3,000*l.* for his county. *Incloses,*

81. I. *Note of points required to be established by those who assert the absolute supremacy of the Pope.*

March 25. Crabbet. 82. Robt. Heath to Thos. Phelippes. Never promised that Mr. Shires should accept his offer, but if he has the money ready at the time, thinks he will take it, and restore his land. Will do his utmost to induce him. Sees not how he can end Phelippes' differences with Sir James.

March 25. London. 83. Chamberlain to Carleton. The Lord Treasurer's uncertain state. Sir Edw. Cecil is gone as the Prince's proxy, to stand sponsor to Count Ernest of Nassau's child. Lord Willoughby tries to raise 4,000 men for Denmark. Ramsay sent to the Tower. [*See Mar.* 21.] Accident to Lord North whilst tilting with the Earl of Montgomery. Legate, the Arian, burnt in Smithfield for heresy. Pirates still busy. Lady Dacre lately dead, leaving the title to her son, Sir Hen. Lennard. Dr. Holland died at Oxford last week, &c., &c. The King anxious that the late Marsilio's panegyric apology for him should not be lost.

VOL. LXVIII.

1612.
March 25. Indenture between Robt. Earl of Salisbury and Thos. and Rich. Turner, of London, whereby they covenant, on consideration of 600*l.*, to provide toils, buckstalls, and carts for deer hunting during eight years. [*Case A., James I.; No. 2.*]

March 26. Barnard Castle. 84. Talbot Bowes to Salisbury. Has established Wm. Cooke as keeper of the great park of Barnard Castle, instead of Wm. Hogg; but there is a dispute about the ownership of Hogg's residence.

March 26. Grant to Art. Ingram, sen., of the office of Secretary and Keeper of the Signet in the North of England for life, with reversion to Dr. Wm. Ingram, Chris. Brooke, Rich. Martin, and Rich. Goldthorpe. [*Grant Bk., p.* 94.]

March 26. Commission to the Lord Treasurer and Chancellor of the Exchequer for the time being, to make commissions for delivery of wood yearly in the forest of Dean, co. Gloucester, for erection of iron works, &c. [*Ibid., p.* 90.]

March 27. Eton. 85. Sir Hen. Savile to Carleton. Letting of Stoke parsonage. The college has granted Mr. Wake three years' longer residence.

March 30. Tavistock. 86. Earl of Bath to Salisbury. Thanks for his forbearing to require the second certificate of persons fit for the loans, until the deputies met at the Assizes have sent it to the Council.

March 30. Grant to John Lenning of the office of Messenger or Pursuivant of the Court of Wards and Liveries for life. [*Grant Bk., p.* 95.]

March 31. London. 87. John Whitson to Salisbury. Has resigned, at his Lordship's request, some alum imported for him, to the patentees, who refused to allow him to compound, and claimed it as forfeit.

March. 88. Eliz., Countess of Derby, to [the Same]. Joy on his amendment. Defers her visit to London till the heat of the summer be past.

March? 89. Edw. Reynoldes to his cousin Raymond. Instructions how to proceed against —— Dimery, who is endeavouring to cheat him [Reynoldes] in some money transactions. [*See* 1614, *Oct.* 23.]

March? 90. Edw. Reynoldes to Sir John Rawlins. Advises caution in his investments. Sir Geo. Coppin should be applied to for advancing him money, and not allow him to run up scores at his lodgings and borrow from his poor friends. Cannot lend him more, nor pay the tailor for the dress of his servant, being so cheated himself.

March. 91. Lord Treasurer Salisbury and [Lord Admiral Nottingham] to [the Woodwards of Shotover, Stowe Wood, and Barnwood]. Warrant to deliver 800 trees for repairing three old ships, and building a new one in lieu of one decayed, for the Royal Navy. [*See Nov.* 8, 1611.]

March. 92. Account of payments made during the past year by the Farmers of Customs to the Cofferer of the Household, Master of the Wardrobe, Tellers of the Exchequer, &c. Total 109,120*l.* 19*s.* 9½*d.*

VOL. LXVIII.

1612.

April 1. Court at Whitehall. 93. Earl of Northampton to the Mayor of Folkestone and others. Appoints them Commissioners for restraint of passage at that place.

April 2. Grant to Sampson Lennard of the place and precedency of the eldest son of Lord Dacre of the South, for life, as the eldest son of a Baron. [*Grant Bk.*, *p.* 94.]

April 3. Grant to Thos. Warren of the office of Lute-player to the King. [*Ibid*, *p.* 101.]

April 5. Grant to John Howse, of the office of Master of St. John's Hospital, in Cirencester, co. Gloucester, for life. [*Ibid*, *p.* 94.]

April 5. South Lambeth. 94. Sir Noel de Caron to Salisbury. Recommends a man who has worked for him ten years in building his house at South Lambeth, &c., to the place of Clerk Surveyor at Hampton Court. French.

April 6. London. 95. Wm. Kindt to the Same. For payment of 1,000*l.* on account of the great table diamond sold by Jean de Luce. French.

April 10. Daventry. 96. Wm. Clarke, Postmaster, to Lord Stanhope [Master of the Posts]. Furnished Lewis Harris, Pursuivant, with two able post horses, to carry him to Coventry, and he refuses to pay for them, and has been violent and abusive. Begs Lord Stanhope to report his proceedings to the Lord Treasurer.

April 10. Madrid. 97. Sir John Digby to [Salisbury]. Thinks the English merchants will trade much more quietly, owing to recent concessions of the King of Spain in their behalf. Example of the effects of these regulations. [*Extract.*]

April 10. 98. Charges of works, &c. at the King's houses in March.

April 16. Ratcliffe. 99. Wm. Stallenge to Salisbury. Begs respite of certain moneys owed by him, and payment of the allowance due to him for his office of Searcher.

April 18. Madrid. 100. Sir John Digby to the Same. [The Spanish Ambassador] is to intreat His Majesty to remove the English from Virginia. Fears there will be attempts to remove them by force. [*Extract.*]

April 20. Hackness. 101. Sir Thos. Posthumus Hoby to the Same. Thinks the order sent him to proceed no further in securing to himself Whitby and Whitby-Strand, concealed lands, recovered by him for the Crown, is caused by Sir Rich. Cholmley, who boasts of having obtained a reversion of the lease, and tries to prejudice his Lordship against him.

April 21. Grant to the Masters and Wardens of the Mystery or Science of Girdling, of leave to build an hospital of the foundation of Geo. Palin, to consist of six aged men. [*Grant Bk.*, *p.* 93.]

April 23. London. 102. John King, Bishop of London, to Carleton. Has been ill all the winter. Thanks for congratulations on his preferment. The Lord Treasurer ill of scurvy and dropsy, and his life in suspense. He is going to Bath. The Duke of Bouillon's visit postponed. The Count of Hainault here, on a marriage treaty between the Princess Elizabeth and Count Palatine of the Rhine.

Vol. LXVIII.

Power to Rich. Putto to search and examine all debts and forfeitures, &c. due to the King, from 13 Eliz. to Michaelmas, 8 Jac. I., during pleasure. [*Grant Bk., p.* 96.]

Presentation of Edw. Waterhouse to the church of Kibworth, co. Leicester. [*Ibid, p.* 101.]

103. [Carleton] to Chamberlain. Commends to him two Protestant strangers, formerly friars, who have never been in England before, and do not know the language. Wishes him to introduce them secretly to the Archbishop of Canterbury.

104. Chamberlain to Carleton. The King refuses the Baronets' precedence over Barons' younger sons, but grants them the arms of Ulster in a canton, and other privileges. Sir Robt. Cotton sent out of the way when the case was heard, because he was furnished with records in their favour. The Duke of Bouillon arrived, and lodged at the Charterhouse, with a train of 200. Lord Aubigny and his wife quarrel with her father, Lord Clifton, who, in his anger, threatens to marry again. Lord Rochester made a Privy Councillor and reconciled to the Queen. The Lord Treasurer worse, but "the vigor of his mind maintaines his weake body." He has three physicians, Atkins, Poe, and Lister; and two secretaries, Finet and Sherburn. His loss would be much lamented. Sir Thos. Lake has the signet.

Statement of the dignity and privileges of a Baronet, and of the settlement of the controversy for precedence between Baronets and the younger sons of Viscounts and Barons, which is decided against the Baronets; but they are to be considered Knights, and their heirs male knighted when of age. [*Dom. Corresp.*, 1616, *Nov.* 4.]

Statement of the dignity and form of creation of a Knight Banneret. [*Ibid.*]

Statement of the rank of a Baron, and of the mode of creation, and admission by writ. [*Ibid.*]

Power granted to Sir Hen. Thynne to use martial law in his voyage to Persia. [*Grant Bk., p.* 96.]

105. Survey of tenements and lands in the forest of Wire, co. Worcester, with names of the tenants, their rentals, &c.

Lease to Fras. Burrell, Robt. Shafto, and Hen. Chapman, of Newcastle-upon-Tyne, of the third part of a tenement called Grindley, alias Greenlawe, co. Durham, and of a coal mine there, late the property of John Lyons, Receiver of Durham and Northumberland, a debtor to the Crown. Latin. [*Sign Man., vol.* II., *No.* 24.]

106. Petition of Agnes, widow of Robt. Appleby, Purveyor of the Blackjacks, Buckets, &c. to His Majesty, to Salisbury, that she may enjoy her late husband's place for life. [*See April* 3, 1609.]

VOL. LXIX. MAY, JUNE, 1612.

1612.

May 1. Horrad's Park. 1. Sir Fulk Greville to Salisbury. Thanks for the return of his instrument, which is honoured by his Lordship's use of it. Wishes him increase of health.

May 2. Grant to Hugh Middleton of licence to perform all arts to further the bringing of springs and waters into the city of London. [*Grant Bk., p.* 95.]

May 3. Grant, in reversion, to Sam. Henshaw, of the office of a Teller in the Exchequer for life. [*Ibid, p.* 93.]

May 7. Lambeth. 2. Sentence of deprivation and degradation by the Ecclesiastical Commissioners against Nath. Tattersall, Perpetual Vicar of Oswestry, co. Salop, for grave crimes. Latin.

May 10. Eton. 3. Sir Hen. Savile to Carleton. Wishes to know whether it will be well to send 50 or 100 copies of his strictures. Uncertain whether they would pass in a popish country, though they contain no heresy, unless they treat them as they did his "Anglicani Scriptores," and order the preliminary epistle to be expunged.

May 13. London. 4. John Chamberlain to the Same. Feast given at Court to the Duke of Bouillon. The young Duke of [Wirtemburg?] dangerously wounded at the tilt by Sir Thos. Somerset. The King of Denmark thought to be dead, and the Queen and her ladies mourned a week in white taffeta. The Earl of Northumberland's fine reduced from 30,000*l.* to 10,000*l.* Sir Hen. James refusing the Oath of Allegiance, the Earl of Montgomery has begged his goods and lands, worth 1,600*l.* or 1,700*l.* per ann. The Lord Treasurer still in a dangerous state. The King transacts business and writes despatches, with no help but his Secretary. Mutilated.

May 13. 5. Copy of part of the above, made before the mutilations.

May 13. Whitehall. Proclamation for the apprehension of the Lord Sanquair and of Robt. Carlisle, a Scottish borderer, for the murder of [John] Turner. Printed. [*Proc. Bk., p.* 254.]

May 13. Grant to Sir Robt. Cholmondeley, Bart., and Wm. Bourchier, Esq., of 1,200*l.* out of old debts due to the Crown. [*Grant Bk., p.* 90.]

May 13. Grant, in reversion, to Sir Edw. Howard, of the office of keeping the Privy Lodgings and Wardrobe at Hampton Court for life. [*Ibid, p.* 93.]

May? 6. Reasons of the inequality of the "exchange between England and other countries," to the prejudice of England.

May? 7. Observations, by Malines, on the detriment to English trade by the coinage remaining at a fixed price, whilst that of foreign nations rises and falls; of this merchant strangers take advantage to export money, and thus lower the price of English goods and raise that of foreign goods.

VOL. LXIX.

May ? 8. Queries relative to coinage; whether the price of silver should not be raised as that of gold is; whether merchants should not be prohibited paying a larger price for it than is paid by the Mint; with suggestions for regulating the export of coin by the East India Company, &c.

May 14. Whitehall. Proclamation concerning the bringing in of gold and silver, either in foreign coin or bullion, with list of the prices at which it will be received at the Mint, which merchants are forbidden to exceed. Printed. [*Proc. Bk., p.* 256.]

9. Statement of the disadvantages resulting from the export of coin, which is owing to the under-valuation of English money, and proposal to redress it by raising the value of the coin 1*d.* in the shilling, with arguments on the advantages thereof, and answers to objections. The King should do it quietly with the advice of a few experienced persons.

May 20. London. 10. Chamberlain to Carleton. The Duke of Bouillon departed yesterday with presents of plate, value 4,000*l.* Is uncertain whether Lady Elizabeth's business be effected. Disputes between the Scots and the English. Turner the fencer assassinated by the servants of Lord Sanquair, whose eye he had accidentally put out. Proclamation to apprehend Lord Sanquair, who has surrendered himself, and confessed his guilt. Lord Vaux condemned to perpetual imprisonment and loss of property. The Lord Treasurer's health variable; he is returning from Bath.

May 22. 11. Sir Julius Cæsar to the Clerks of the Signet. To engross a warrant prefixed, for payment of rewards to the servants of the King of Denmark for bringing red deer, and 10*l* to Rich. Lazomby for expenses of conveying them to sundry of the King's parks.

UNDATED.*

Greenwich. 12. Robt. Browne to Salisbury. Begs redress for breach of contract and other injuries from his landlord, Rich. Warner, waterman, of Greenwich.

Richmond. Sunday. 13. Salomon de Caux, [Engineer to the Prince,] to [Thos.] Wilson, Secretary to the Lord Treasurer. Asks if the Rocher has arrived in London. Wishes the drawings and shells sent to be shown to the Lord Treasurer and returned. French.

14. Thos. Coo to Salisbury. Thanks him for procuring his enlargement from the Fleet, and from the jurisdiction of the Lord Chancellor. Prays his Lordship again to entertain him in his service.

---

* To the Letters and Papers Nos. 11 to 55 it has not been practicable to assign precise dates, but as they all bear the handwriting or some mention of the Earl of Salisbury, it has been deemed advisable to place them immediately before his death, which took place May 24, 1612.

VOL. LXIX.

15. Cornelius Drebbel to Prince [Henry]. The Lord Mayor has refused him permission to hold a lottery; has no other means of subsistence. Begs the Prince's influence with Lord Treasurer Salisbury for leave to have one beyond the jurisdiction of the city. Latin. *Annexing,*

15. I. *Petition of the Same to [Salisbury] containing the proposed conditions of his lottery.*

Fountaingate. Cardigan. 16. Thos. Jones to Salisbury. His Lordship's father was descended from his great grandfather, Howell Moythey, of Fountain Court. Prays that an action brought against him in the Exchequer may be transferred to the local courts, on account of his age.

17. Sir Rich. Knightley to the Same. Thanks for composition of his fine, and favour towards his son.

18. Elizabeth Dowager Lady Russell [widow of John, son of Fras. second Earl of Bedford,] to Lord Treasurer [Salisbury], her nephew. Complains of distraint committed upon her land by Sir Sam. Sandys and Chas. Dingley. Thinks a lady of her place is "no way subject to any justice of peace's letter."

19. Sir Robt. Yaxley to the Same. Requests an appointment to the hospital at Leicester for poor soldiers, and also a loan of 100*l*., for which the Duke of York will stand security.

20. Petition of Chris. Babham to the Same, for lease of thirty acres of coppice in Cookham, co. Berks.

21. Petition of Sir Wm. Bamfield, Captain of Sandsfoot Castle, co. Dorset, to the Same, respecting the decay of the castle, of which Sir Geo. Trenchard and Sir John Williams have made a second survey, the first not being deemed minute enough.

22. Certificate of Sir Rich. Gargrave, Thos. Bland, and Geo. Shelleto, justices of the peace, to the Same, that Mr. Everingham's information as to speedy repairs required by the Court House of Barnsley is correct.

23. Petition of Ann Benbery to the Lord High Treasurer [Salisbury?]. She and her brother have been engaged in an expensive lawsuit for recovery of their estate, fraudulently detained. Prays to be admitted to conference with the King, to whom she is willing to re-deliver the land in question.

24. Petition of Chris. Bond and Thos. Worgan to Salisbury. Are prisoners in the Gatehouse for a misdemeanor in the Forest of Dean: beg a speedy hearing or release upon bail.

25. Petition of Hen. Browne, and Elizabeth his wife, daughter of Geo. Mainprise, of Thwing, on Yorkshire wold, deceased, to the Same, for a lease of certain lands there, of which Geo. Mainprise had a lease from Queen Elizabeth. With reference thereon.

VOL. LXIX.

26. Petition of Elinor, widow of John Denis, of Puckle-Church, Gloucestershire, to Salisbury, for the wardship of her son, her husband having died suddenly.

27. Petition of Capt. John Duffield to the Same, for arrears of his pension. With order for granting it.

28. Petition of Wm. Ellery, carpenter, of Greenwich, to the Same, for relief, having been unjustly deprived of a great quantity of timber by the King's Master Carpenter. With reference thereon.

29. Petition of John Flashman to the Same, to have the custody of Wm. Rogers, of Plympton, his near kinsman, an idiot, which was formerly granted to him, but afterwards to Johan Rogers, his stepmother, who has unlawfully sold away the property.

30. Petition of Wm. Gooderick, Under-Bailiff of the Queen's Manor of Farnham Royal, co. Bucks, to the Same, for holding a Court Baron at Farnham, to prove the Queen's title to some concealed lands, the rents of which are due at Michaelmas next.

31. Petition of Honoria, widow of Sir Hugh Harris, to the Same, for a gift or loan of 10*l.* to relieve her great necessities.

32. Petition of Margery, widow of Edw. Isham, to the Same, that the pension of John Sellinger, sold by him to her late husband, who bequeathed it to his daughters, be not paid to Sellinger, who unjustly claims it, till the suit thereon be decided in the Court of Exchequer.

Fleet Prison. 33. Petition of Thos. Jones, baker, of the Liberty of the Tower, to the Same. Has been wrongfully expelled from two houses near the Tower by Paramour and Jordan. The process has been obtained by the influence of the parties with Baron Altham. Prays that his cause may be heard by some other judge.

34. Petition of Hugh Miller to the Same, that having expended 14*l.* 2*s.* above the amount delivered him for repairing the lodge and fences of the little park at Eltham, he may have the above sum repaid to him. With note by Salisbury, refusing compliance.

35. Petition of Dorothy Morgan, and of Charles and Anne, her orphan son and daughter, to the Same. Her late husband, Capt. Wm. Morgan, spent many years in the late Queen's service, and obtained promise from his Lordship of a surveyor's place of Customs in Ireland, but died, before possessing it, in debt. Prays permission to sell the place for her relief. With note by Salisbury, that such promise was never made to the deceased, nor could the place be granted to any one for money.

36. Petition of the inhabitants at the New Gate, near Drury Lane, to the Same. They have petitioned the Queen to give a name to the place of their abode, and have been referred to him. Request him to give it a name on her behalf.

VOL. LXIX.

Marshalsea Prison. 37. Petition of Rich. Nichols, Constable of the Parish of St. Martin in the Fields, to the Council. Was committed for being present at serving a warrant in the Earl of Salisbury's stables, for taking up posthorses for His Majesty's service. Acknowledges his fault, and prays discharge.

38. Petition of Thos. Penkithman, of Warrington, co. Lancaster, to Salisbury. Has expended much money in building houses in Shoe Lane, London, on the ground of the Earl of Derby. They have been taken possession of by one Shute, under pretence of a prior lease of the said ground, on which the petitioner had a warrant for payment to him of 50*l.* in compensation by the Earl, of which he solicits performance.

39. Petition of Beale Sapreton to the Same. Has served in Ireland under command of Sir Rich. Morrison, Vice President of Munster. Relatives deceased have bequeathed to him two Privy Seals of 10*l.* each, of which he solicits payment.

40. Petition of Jas. Scott, of Cawson, co. Norfolk, to the Same. Has been wrongfully served with process in the Court of Exchequer, at the plea of Philips and Furrier, concerning a tenement and water-mill, &c. Can show good evidences of his title to them. Prays that his Lordship will nominate persons to examine the said cause.

41. Petition of Cuthbert Thursby to the Same. Is Keeper of Wolles Park, Bishopric of Durham. Prays that allowance may be made for repair of the lodge.

42. Petition of Dr. Rich. Trevor to the Same. Dr. Craig, Physician to the King, obtained a grant of the goods of the late Wm. Williams, outlaw, of which grant the petitioner and Sir John Egerton obtained assignment by composition. Hen. Williams, son of the deceased, has, in the meantime, obtained award of the goods, under plea of administration. Prays that their Lordships will direct the said Hen. Williams to pay him the fine decreed in the said award. With reference thereon.

43. Petition of Randolph Tweedale, sailor, to the Same. Has followed the King many miles in his progress with his petition, which, being referred to Salisbury, he begs that his suit may be granted.

44. Petition of Simon Wells to the Same. Was presented to the living of Terrington, co. Norfolk, by Lord Stanhope; but the Vice Chancellor of Cambridge claiming the right of presentation, the Bishop has made stay of his admission. Has brought proof of Lord Stanhope's right to the presentation, and prays for institution to the said living. With reference and report thereon.

45. Petition of Hen. York to the Same, for a pass to go to Bergen-op-Zoom, in Brabant, in search of his brother, Robt. York, a soldier, falsely reported to be dead, by those who withhold his property.

Vol. LXIX.

46. Petition of ——— to the Lord High Treasurer, that as his debt is installed, a lease granted on his lands for payment thereof may be revoked. Mutilated.

47. Note of ordnance now remaining on board His Majesty's ships, and of gunpowder required for them, and for other purposes.

48. Grant in fee farm to the Earl of ———, of lands, value 100*l.* per ann., in the survey of the Exchequer and the Duchy of Lancaster.

49. Warrant to the Attorney General to draw a licence [to —— Radzivill?] for the sole making and importing of bay salt for thirty-one years.

50. Petition of the Dutch Church in London, called the Austin Friars, or Jesus Temple, to the Lord Treasurer, that the tenure of the land which they have bought of the Marquis of Winchester for a churchyard may be changed into free soccage, it being now held in capite.

51. Notes on behalf of the Marquis of Winchester on a claim made by the members, &c. of the Dutch Church to a burial ground on his land, and their objections against the building of a shed near their church in Austin Friars. Referred by Salisbury to be heard by the Earl of Exeter.

52. Statement of the advantages that would be derived to common law and policy, from keeping a general registry in London of all births, marriages, and deaths.

53. Copy of the above.

54. Proposal for a grant of the general registrarship of all christenings, marriages, and burials within the realm, on condition of payment of pensions to certain captains, lieutenants, &c., who have served in the Irish wars, out of the profits thereof. Imperfect. *Annexed is,*

54. I. *Abstract of a proposal for establishing a general registry office in London.*

55. Reasons proving the benefit of certain newly-invented windmills, as requiring little wind. They would lead to the putting down of many watermills which impede the navigation of small rivers.

May 26. Tuesday. 56. Earl of Northampton to Visct. Rochester. A messenger has arrived, at whose setting out the news was not known of the death of the little man [the Earl of Salisbury], for which so many rejoice, and so few even seem to be sorry, except Pembroke, Hay, and Cope. Is near his mistress, and wishes Rochester as near his, if any one can love so ugly and deformed a fellow.

May 27. London. 57. Chamberlain to Carleton. The Lord Treasurer died at Marlboro' Parsonage, on his way from Bath, on the 24th instant. Never knew so great a man so soon and so generally censured. His will and property. His offices not yet disposed of. The Treasurer-

1612. VOL. LXIX.

ship and Mastership of the Court of Wards to be put in commission for a time. Sir Thos. Lake holds the Signet. The Earl of Northampton is likely to succeed to the Treasurership. The compromise between Hawley and Maxwell broken off, because Maxwell would not apologize on his knees.

[May.] 58. Extract from Sir Robt. Naunton's "Fragmenta Regalia," describing the character of Robt. Cecil, Earl of Salisbury.

[May.] 59. "The character of Robert late Earl of Salisbury, Lord High Treasurer of England," lauding his courtesy, ability, and disinterestedness.

May? 60. Treatise by Robert late Earl of Salisbury on the dignity and duties of a Secretary of State.

May? 61. Copy of the above, printed at London in 1642.

May? Copy of the same. [*Dom. Corresp., May* 10, 1603.]

May 28. Westminster. 62. Patent of the King decreeing precedency of the younger sons of Viscounts and Barons over Baronets, and conferring on the latter the privilege of knighthood, and an augmentation of arms. Printed.

[May 28.] 63. Notes from the above patent.

May. Lambeth. 64. Note of the distribution of 11*l.* given by Lord Sanquair to the Yeomen of his Grace [the Archbishop of Canterbury's] house.

June 1. 65. Petition of Thos. Wilson, Keeper of State Papers, to the King. Has reduced the papers to order out of extreme confusion, but receives only 30*l.* a year from the King. Had obtained a grant of certain rents and arrears, but during his illness John Hale, Cup Bearer, obtained a grant of the same, refused the compromise of 200*l.* offered him by Wilson, and gave him the lie. Requests reparation, that he may quietly proceed in his important work.

June 6. 66. Examination of Mary, wife of John Woods, of Norwich. She was sent for by Mrs. Suckling to tell her when her husband, Dr. Suckling, would die, and was offered a large reward if she would poison him, which she refused to do.

June 11. London. 67. Chamberlain to Carleton. Judge Foster buried, and also the late Lord Treasurer, at Hatfield. Small funeral, and no great stir. Sir Walter Cope, Calvert, Dackombe, and Hewten, executors. Wilson has an annuity of 40*l.* The Treasury will be put into commission, the Mastership of the Wards into meaner hands. Sir Fras. Bacon talked of. Numerous candidates for the Secretaryship, but the King says he is prettily skilled in the craft himself, and will execute it till he is weary. Two priests hung at Tyburn, for not leaving the country after being twice banished. Earl Arundel and his son, Visct. Montague, present at the execution. Hawley and Maxwell are reconciled before the Council, Maxwell apologizing. The Scots are afraid; 300 have returned to Scotland. *Incloses,*

67. I. *Epigram and anagram on the late Earl of Salisbury, and epigram on the Scots.*

VOL. LXIX.

1612.

[June 16.] 68. Notes for an [intended] speech [by Sir Geo. Carew] in the Court of Wards, on his appointment to succeed the Earl of Salisbury as Master of the Court of Wards and Liveries.

[June 16.] 69. Discourse addressed to the Court of Wards [by the Same] at his first sitting as Master of the Wards, on the objects of the Court, and the points to be attended to for its due administration. [*See for the basis of this Paper, Bacon's Works, vol.* III., *p.* 364, *fol. edit.*]

June? 70. Regulations for the Master and Council of the Court of Wards and Liveries, for increase of the King's revenue from leases of wards, lands, fines, &c.

June 17. London. 71. Chamberlain to [Carleton]. Arrival of the friars. One is lodged with the Archbp. of Canterbury, and the other will go to his Grace of York. The Bishops are not very fond of such guests, unless they be men of note, thinking they can have plenty of them, if they provide them maintenance. The King is at Eltham; he is going to visit the Master of the Rolls at Wanstead, and the Countess of Oxford at Havering. Sir Geo. Carew appointed temporary Master of the Wards, with limited salary and powers. Commissioners for the Treasury appointed. The Earl of Northampton talked of as Treasurer, but he wishes the accounts to be thoroughly looked into first. Sir Hen. Neville has failed of the Secretaryship, because of the flocking of Parliament men to him. The King says he will not have a Secretary imposed on him by Parliament. Lord Sheffield has a grant of the Papists in Yorkshire. Sir Geo. Carew answers the French letters, Levinus Munck those of the Low Countries, Mr. Calvert the Spanish and Italian, and Sir Thos. Lake the home letters. Sir Hen. Wotton is sent for home, and is most likely to be Secretary; the late Treasurer wrote in his behalf; the Queen and Prince favour him, and as Lord Rochester was lately reconciled to him, he will not oppose it. Disputes before the Council between the town of Oxford and the University. That of Cambridge is in trouble for choosing the Earl of Northampton Chancellor, when the Duke of York was a candidate. Sir Thos. Shirley, jun., being in prison for debt, took poison, but recovered. The Queen's Secretary dead.

June 17? 72. The King to the High Steward of Oxford. To proceed to hear and determine, with the Vice Chancellor and Mayor, the differences between the Town and University.

June 22. Charter House. 73. Robt. Earl of Sussex to Sir Thos. Lake. Recommends Sir John Sames and Sir Rich. Weston as Deputy Lieutenants for the county [Middlesex]. Sir John Sames has fully explained his conduct in Parliament, against which the King objected.

June 23. Commission to the Lord Chancellor, the Earl of Northampton, and others, to sell any copyhold or customary lands in the survey of the Exchequer or duchy of Lancaster. [*Grant Bk., p.* 90.]

VOL. LXIX.

1612.

June 24. Grant to Edw. Harris of the place of a Poor Knight at Windsor [*Grant Bk., p.* 93.]

June 24. Westminster. 74. Edw. Reynoldes to Sir John Rawlins. Discontent of his creditors on his departure from England. Urges him to frugality and privacy. Blames him for neglecting his debt to —— Twitty, the Chancellor's Secretary. His enemies try to procure his revocation.

June 25. London. 75. Chamberlain to Carleton. The Court stays at Greenwich till the progress next month. A Prince of Modena there. Parliament expected. The King will order the same men as before to be returned, they knowing the business. [Robt.] Carlisle and [Jas.] Irwin, who killed Turner [the fencer], executed. Lord Sanquair indicted as Robt. Creichton, and, pleading not guilty, will be arraigned no Saturday. He wanted his titles to be given him, but was refused. Some Lords begged in vain that he might only be banished. Libels every day on the late Lord [Salisbury]. In his last letter to the King, in which he recommended Sir Hen. Wotton, he vowed he was 100,000*l.* poorer than when he entered the Treasurership. Sir Walter Cope and Sir Hen. Beeston disallow his will, as savouring of a giddy head, and not like the rest of his actions. Sir Walter Cope says that one of the conditions of Wotton's promotion shall be that he shall favour him [Carleton]. The King wrote with his own hand for Sir Ralph Winwood, who has arrived, and gone to His Majesty at Wanstead.

June 25. 76. Copy of the above.

June 26. London. 77. R. Kirkham to the Same. His attendance has prevented his earlier thanks for favours. Sends inclosures.

June? 78. Account of provisions delivered and received by the Convert of Ipswich for and from certain ships, &c.

June? 79. List of certain quantities of merchandise sent on board the Mary Constant by the French nation.

VOL. LXX. JULY—SEPTEMBER, 1612.

1612.

July 2. London. 1. Chamberlain to Carleton. The two Carmelites have made a public confession of their conversion at the Italian Church. Sir Fras. Bacon was the man of most note present. Confession and execution of Lord Sanquair. The Countess of Shrewsbury still persists in refusing to answer questions, pleading the privilege of her nobility. She is remanded to the Tower. Death of Sir Peter Eure. Libels on the late Lord Treasurer. He is accused of juggling with all parties. A design of laying open some of his Hertfordshire grounds on the very day of his funeral was prevented. The King employs Sir Ralph Winwood to write letters, but says nothing to him about the Secretaryship, which is still in suspense. Winwood is most likely to have it, but it is said the King has promised the Queen not to bestow it till Sir Hen. Wotton's return.

VOL. LXX.

1612.

July 2. Westminster. Grant to Jas. Lewis, of Builth, co. Brecon, of pardon, for manslaughter of Rich. ap John. Latin. [*Sign Man., vol.* II., *No.* 25. *See Nov.* 7, 1611.]

July 3. Frankfort. 2. Wm. Lord Roos to [Sir Thos. Lake]. Thanks for furthering the honour lately imposed on him by the King. Is going to Italy.

July 3. 3. Order in Council that the citizens of London be permitted to exercise arms in the Artillery Garden or other convenient place, provided their number be not more than 250.

July 6. Grant to Edw. Morgan, co. Monmouth, of pardon for refusing the Oath of Allegiance, with promise that it shall not again be tendered to him. [*Sign Man., vol.* II., *No.* 26.]

July 6. Docquet of the above.

July [7 ?] Grant to Hen. Earl of Northampton of the manor of Clun, and other lands, co. Salop, the moiety for himself and the other moiety for the Earl of Suffolk, with confirmation of his title to certain waste grounds concealed and recovered by him within the said manors. Latin. [*Sign Man., vol.* II., *No.* 27.]

July 7. Lease to Thos. Merry of certain messuages, &c. belonging to the Ordnance Department, at suit of Sir Roger Dallison, Lieutenant of the Ordnance, to whom they were previously granted. [*Ibid., No.* 28.]

July 9. London. 4. Chamberlain to Carleton. Zuniga, the Spanish Ambassador, has had his first audience, and the King is coming from Windsor to Whitehall to give him a second. His chief errand is to acquit himself of accusations about the Gunpowder Treason, laid against him by the late Lord Treasurer, whom he would have accused of "some unwarrantable practices," had he been living. The Virginia plantation likely to come to nothing, through the idleness of the English. Ten men, sent to fish for their relief, have slipped off to England, and fill the town with ill reports about it. Elphinstone, late Secretary of Scotland, dead. Sir John Roper's office granted to Rochester and Sir John Harrington. Sir Thos. Bodley is failing. He has the dropsy and scurvy, and has been mistreated by Dr. Atkins. Sir Hen. Wotton and Sir Thos. Lake talked of for Secretaries. The latter impeded in his preferment by "his Xantippe." Sir Ralph [Winwood] returning to Holland, but with promises of remembrance from the King.

July 11. Westminster. 5. Grant to Maurice Abbot of the moiety of old debts due to the Crown to be collected by David Abercomby, John Say, Ant. Gibson, and Matthias Fowle, to the amount of 16,000*l.*, on surrender of a similar grant to Visct. Lisle.

July 11 ? 6. Bill of costs in the case of Elihu Wynn v. Clement Piggott since Michaelmas 1611.

July 12. 7. Wm. Foster to Sir John Conway. Requests him to send the hounds and other things. The bearer does not know of his being where he is.

VOL. LXX.

1612.

July 15. London. 8. Chamberlain to Carleton. Sir Ralph Winwood is returning to the Hague. It is thought he will soon be back again, and that Sir Hen. Neville or Wotton will be the other Secretary. Lord Beauchamp dead. Harry Boughton and Mrs. Fowler apprehended for coining foreign gold. Sir W. Cope has written an apology for the late Lord Treasurer, setting forth his own sufficiency. Winwood knows not who has tampered with and opened Carleton's letters, unless it be De Quester.

July 16. Grant to Thos. Creichton of all jewels, debts, and goods of Robt. Creichton, felon. [*Grant Bk., p.* 90.]

July 17. Theobalds. Proclamation prohibiting the deceitful dyeing of silk, or bringing in or selling of silk deceitfully dyed. Printed. [*Proc. Bk., p.* 259.]

July 17. Westmintser. Grant to Wm. Glover, of Westminster, and Sam. Evans, of East Greenwich, of pardon for robbery at Greenwich Palace. Latin. *Sign Man., vol.* II., *No.* 29.]

July 18. 9. List of persons in different counties who are to be called on to take the Oath of Allegiance.

July 20. 10. Sir Rice Griffin to Thos. Fensden [?] Requests him to obtain the removal of Geo. Kempson from the office of High Constable of Barlichway hundred, co. Warwick, he being guilty of many offences.

July 22. Grant to And. Lanyer of the place of a Musician on the Flute, for life. [*Grant Bk., p.* 95.]

July 22. Croydon. 11. Archbp. Abbot to the King. The lingering in England of the Spanish Ambassador, Don Pedro de Zuniga, is very suspicious. He has secretly dispersed 12,000*l.* or 13,000*l.* already in England, and tampers by night with the Lieger Ambassador from France. He was in England at the time of the powder treason, and God knows what share he had in that business.

July 23. London. 12. Chamberlain to Carleton. The Spanish Ambassador's lingering is not much liked. The King begins his progress. The Queen, Prince, Lady Elizabeth, and Duke of York were with him at Theobalds. The Prince lives chiefly at Richmond, but is going part of the progress, and then waits for the King at Woodstock. The two friars have preached at the Italian Church. Sir Ralph Winwood sailed [for Holland] on the 16th. Lord Chandos and the Countess of Worcester gone to the Spa, and the Earl of Arundel will follow. It is reported that the Signet will be taken from Sir Thos. Lake and given to Visct. Rochester, &c. Much talk and many wagers laid about the Secretaryship. The Lord Chamberlain has changed the Messengers at Court, and put two officers over them called Clerks of the Cheque.

July 23. 13. Order in Council on a dispute between the City and University of Oxford concerning the duties of the night walk, which belongs to the University; but the City is allowed to join in any search after felons, or in hue and cry.

VOL. LXX.

1612.

July 26. Bletsoe. Grant to the Company of Discoverers of the North-west Passage of Incorporation, Henry Prince of Wales being constituted Supreme Protector, with grant of certain portions of the profits to the first discoverers and adventurers therein in 1610, and to Capt. Button and his sailors, now sent out to perfect the discovery. [*Sign Man., vol.* II., *No.* 30.]

July 25. Bir. 14. Fras. Harewell to Fras. Conyers. Health of their families. Sends a new defazance, the counterpart of which is sealed to Sir Edw. Conway, and begs the return of the old one.

July 27. Downham in the Isle. 15. Lancelot Andrews, Bp. of Ely, to Sir Thos. Lake. The Bishop of Chichester, being weary of the Mastership of Pembroke Hall, purposes to make it over to —— Muriell, who is not worthy of it, and will only admit fellows who will promise him their vote. Hopes such a mischief may be averted, and that Dr. [Nich.] Felton, a most fitting person, may be chosen.

July 28. Castle Ashby. Grant to Thos. Harries and Geo. Allen, of Thornton, co. Pembroke, of pardon for coining. Latin. [*Sign Man., vol.* II., *No.* 31.]

July 29. Bishopthorpe. 16. Tobias Matthew, Archbishop of York, to the Earl of Suffolk or Sir Thos. Lake. Is willing to entertain Johannes Maria, the converted Carmelite friar, who has come to him with a letter from the Archbishop of Canterbury, which agrees with His Majesty's letter on the subject.

July 30. Eton. 17. Sir Hen. Savile to Sir Dud. Carleton. Thanks for the "variæ lectiones" sent of the oration "Ου Θεος ου Χριστος." Directions for the purchase of books. Sir Geo. Carew succeeds the late Lord Treasurer as Master of the Wards. Incloses a letter from his Grace of Canterbury.

July 30. Castle Ashby. Grant to the town of Wokingham of incorporation, with licence to hold a weekly market and yearly fair. [*Sign Man., vol.* II., *No.* 32.]

July 31. 18. Note of the lands in the entail, specifying those which remain in the King's hands, or are assigned to the Queen, Prince, and Duke of York, or have been sold.

July 31. 19. Certificate of the fines and casual profits of the Courts of the Manors, &c. now in the King's hands, during the first nine years of his reign.

July ? [York.] 20. Lord Sheffield to Visct. Rochester. There being no Foreign Secretary, requests him to acquaint the King that a packet of letters for the Venetian Ambassador was sent to him; an Italian gentleman, well accompanied, who professed to be the Venetian Ambassador, has passed through York on his way to Scotland. Thinks it strange that an Ambassador should travel like a spy. Requests instructions how to conduct himself towards him on his return.

Vol. LXX.

1612.

Aug. 1. Grant to Ellis Holcombe of the office of keeping the game from Southwark to Lambeth Marsh and elsewhere, co. Surrey, for life. [*Grant Bk., p.* 93.]

Aug. 1. Greenwich. 21. Hen. Earl of Northampton to [Visct. Rochester]. Hopes he will escape the enemy, who tried to shorten his days by strawberries and cream. The little lord [Salisbury], when at Bath, wished never to be separated from the Welsh Earl [Pembroke], who is likely to prove an alchemist. Sends an epitaph [on Salisbury], written in answer to Sir Walter Cope's apology, which, though severe, is true. Forwards letters from Sir John Digby, who is honest, discreet, and has " found out the right haunte to the trewe hart of honor."

Aug. 1. Audley End. 22. Earl of Suffolk to Sir Thos. Lake. Begs that he will not seek the benefit of the pardon of Frerch, the horse-stealer, having obtained a grant of it long before for Sir Wm. Woodhouse.

Aug. 2? Sunday. Greenwich. 23. Hen. Earl of Northampton to the King. Sends three advertisements, which remind him of the roses, violets, and gillyflowers he used to send to His Majesty from thence. The first concerns the Archduke. The second, the Muscovy company, who have prospered strangely, got within nine degrees of the pole, saw 700 whales, and brought home 17. The third, that the ships of another company have possessed the Bermudas, which the Spaniards have deserted, on account of the frequency of hurricanes. Wonders the people who thrive so well under His Majesty are not more thankful to him.

Aug. 3. Croydon. 24. Archbp. Abbot to the Same. Zuniga has removed to the house of the Lieger Ambassador, Alonzo de Velasquez, in the Barbican, that he may more freely transact his secret business. Velasquez has been more free with his masses, having a bell rung and holding several in the day. He sends scandalous reports of English affairs to Spain and Italy. The King of Spain has an advantage in England, because he can avail himself of discontented Catholics. The proffered courtesies of the Queen of France should be received with suspicion, as she is guided by Villeroy and Sillery, both under Spanish influence. The Persian and Turk have agreed on points of trade, so Sir Robt. Shirley's negociation is over, and he may go back when he pleases.

[Aug. 3.] Monday. 25. Hen. Earl of Northampton to [Rochester]. Long discussion at the Council about trade with the Archduke's country, in reference to carrying over dressed cloth, but the decision postponed till former treaties are examined, and the merchants bring in fuller information. The Solicitor General has prepared the commissions, instructions, &c. for gathering in the aid for the marriage of her Grace [Princess Elizabeth] in better form than were those for knighting the Prince. The matter of tokens [copper farthings] to be discussed on Friday. Lord Vaux's sister has presented a petition that her brother and mother may, on account of the hot season, be removed from their keeper's house in town to that in the country; but they being imprisoned for life on a præmunire, the matter rests with the King.

VOL. LXX.

1612.

[Aug. 3.] Greenwich. 26. Hen. Earl of Northampton to [Rochester]. A private Ambassador has arrived from the Count Palatine, who has gone post-haste to the King. Don Pedro removed to the Barbican, and promises to be gone in a month. The Ambassador Lieger is gone to Putney.

Aug. 6. London. 27. Edw. Palavicino to Sir Thos. Lake. Details his disappointments in the nonpayment of the debt due to him from the Crown. Sig. Lomellino has come over about it, and will deduct 5,000*l.* from the 13,000*l.* owing, on condition of prompt payment. *Annexes,*

27. I. *Statement by Edw. Palavicino of the debts due to Horatio and Fabricio Palavicino by the late Queen, for purchase of alum, and for a loan of 33,000l. on security of her own bonds obligatory, and those of the City of London. Fabricio has sent over his son-in-law, John Vincenzo Lomellino, to urge payment of his share, that of Horatio, deceased, being already paid to Sir Oliver Cromwell and Anne, his wife, presumptive executors.*

Aug. 6. Kirby Misperton. 28. Thos. Phelippes to the Same. Complains of the conduct of the Archbp. of York, to whom the King referred a dispute touching the benefice of Kirby Misperton, and who opposes the presentation thereto of a clerk of the Earl of Rutland.

Aug. 7. 29. Hen. Earl of Northampton to Visct. Rochester. Regrets that the King was not satisfied with his former letter about trade with the Archduke. Recapitulates certain points concerning it. The merchants are busy preparing their report thereon. Lord Harrington's proposal for the tokens was brought forward; he wishes their currency to be voluntary. Suggests that his Lordship be allowed to coin a limited number only, reserving the rest for the King.

Aug. 8. 30. The Same to the Same. The Council advise that the aid for marrying the Princess be levied not according to strict form, but by commission, for ease of the subject. As the King is anxious to know at once the points in question relating to trade into Flanders, has ascertained that the Archduke, on the petition of four of his provinces, has promised to grant no more of the special licences by which dressed cloths were allowed to be imported. He could easily be brought to reason, if lawns and cambrics were forbidden to be imported into England, where a greater value of them is vended than of cloth in Flanders. *Incloses,*

30. I. *Memorandum of things to be considered touching the levying of the aid for the marriage of the Lady Elizabeth. That it should be double or treble to that levied for the Prince; her marriage being conducive to religion, the law granting the King double her dowry, and many persons having avoided the aid for the Prince.*

Vol. LXX.

1612.

Aug. 9. Audley End. 31. Earl of Suffolk to Sir Thos. Lake. Forwards two letters from Sir Lewis Lewkenor relative to the warrants for certain Ambassadors, and containing news from France and Italy. Asks instructions how to treat this stranger [Prince Perretti].

Aug. 9. Clare Hall. 32. Fellows of Clare Hall to the Same. Hope the King will permit, according to their Statutes, their free election of a master of their College, and will approve the person whom they are about to elect. Latin.

Aug. 10. Croydon. 33. Archbp. Abbot to the King. His Majesty's efforts to reconcile the French Ministers and those of the Duke of Bouillon have failed, chiefly because M. du Moulin concealed from the synod the King's letters signifying his desire for a peace, and Tilenus has written another book against Moulin. Particulars of the seizure and examination of Blackman, the Jesuit, who came at night out of the Spanish Ambassador's house in the Barbican, and who was Confessor of the English Colleges at Rome and Valladolid; also of papers taken upon him or written by him. Blount and Pelham, Jesuits, are sought for. Jones their present, and Holtby their late superior are now in London. The private intercourse between Zuniga and the French Lieger was because public intercourse was forbidden, on a point of etiquette. *Annexed is,*

33. I. *Advice by James I. that the dispute respecting the nature of justification through Christ, carried on by Du Moulin and Tilenus, should be for ever buried, as being needless and injurious to religion. French.*

Aug. 10. Greenwich. 34. Earl of Northampton to the Same. Recommends Dr. Sharpe to succeed as Provost of King's College, Cambridge, if the King choose to nominate according to precedent, though contrary to the Statutes.

Aug. 10. Greenwich. 35. The Same to Sir Charles Cornwallis, Treasurer to the Prince. Has commended Dr. Sharpe to the King for the Provostship of King's College, but dares not, on his conscience, urge His Majesty to force him on the Fellows, who would die rather than have him, the Statutes giving liberty of election, which liberty he himself, as Chancellor, persuaded the King lately to allow to St. John's College. Being brought up in King's College, cannot be so ungrateful as to injure their privileges. The placing of Provosts by former Kings has been *de facto*, but not *de jure*.

Aug. 10. Greenwich. 36. Earl of Northampton to Sir Thos. Lake. The merchants' report on the trade with Flanders is not ready; has sent a merchant to inform the King thereon. Was sorely pressed by the Prince to commend Dr. Sharpe to the Provostship, but would not, in conscience, urge what is contrary to the Statutes. It is reported that Lord Zouch will be Lord Treasurer. Is glad that Lake stands well with Rochester.

VOL. LXX.

1612.
Aug. 11. Croydon. 37. Archbp. Abbot to Visct. Rochester. Sends the book of Tilenus against Moulin.; and another, printed abroad by Papists, to disgrace His Majesty's godly proceedings.

Aug. 11. London. 38. Chamberlain to Carleton. Sir Thos. Bodley's addition to the library at Oxford is a fair building. Mr. Wadham's new college would have been handsome if better placed. A new quadrangle built at Merton College. The Queen begins her progress on the morrow. Sir Hen. Wotton is gone to the King with his pictures and projects. The Count Palatine's Ambassador gave Lady Elizabeth's letters to Prince Henry, and his to her. He could not gain an audience of the Queen. Insult done to the Spanish Ambassador. Death of the Countess of Rutland. She is privately buried in St. Paul's, by her father, Sir Philip Sydney. Sir Walter Raleigh is said to have sent her pills that despatched her. Lord Lisle and the Countess of Clanricarde inherit most of her property. The Countess of Essex has bought Sir Roger Aston's house at Hounslow. Sickness in our army in Denmark. A commission out to Sir Thos. Parry and others to devise projects for raising money. They harp most on debasing the money. Prince Perretti, brother to Cardinal Montalto, is in London incog.

Aug.? 39. Proposal for coining twopenny pieces and halfpence, to be made half sterling.

Aug.? 40. Proposals that the twopennies, pence, and halfpence to be made of copper shall be half sterling, as being more acceptable to the subject; with statement of the profit that will accrue to the King therefrom. Specimens of blank coin are annexed.

Aug? 41. Proposition to remedy the under-valuation of English moneys by the coinage of small silver moneys of coarser silver, so as to raise the value of the larger money in proportion. The old standard to be observed in payments of rents—the new in ordinary bargains; with calculation of the profits that will accrue to the King therefrom.

Aug.? 42. Statement of the profit that will arise to the King from raising the 1*s.* to 13½*d.*, from coining the pound of gold into forty-four sovereigns, and from making small silver coins from coarser silver.

Aug.? 43. Proposed proclamation for the issue of copper money, to be called imprest money, and made legally payable in the proportion of 5 per cent., with other moneys, to be called in again after seven years, the object being to prevent the exportation of gold and silver, and relieve the King's present wants.

Aug.? 44. Propositions for raising money to pay the King's debts by disposing of part of his revenue, as cottages wanting repairs, decayed forests, &c.; also compounding for wardships, and changing copyholds into leaseholds; also for saving expense by throwing the cost of reparation of the King's parks and lodges on the keepers.

VOL. LXX.

1612.

Aug. 12. York House. 45. Lord Chancellor Ellesmere to Sir Thos. Lake. Death of Sir John Rodney, Sheriff of Somersetshire. Sends the names of four persons qualified to serve, from whom the King will choose a Sheriff to act for the rest of the year.

Aug. [12.] 46. Earl of Northampton to [Rochester]. Vindicates himself from the King's charge of tardiness in the business of the trade with the Archduke, time being required for examination of former treaties and the merchants' books, before a true report can be made. Will hasten it as much as possible. Hopes a project, mentioned by his Lordship, implying danger to the King, is not true. Lord Vaux and his mother owe him thanks for his intercession, though they expect little mercy where the Metropolitan [Archbp. Abbot] is mediator. Many people, noting his Lordship's skill in answering letters, and his urbanity, wish to see him Secretary. The Earl of Pembroke wishes to be reconciled to him.

Aug. 12. 47. The Same to Sir Thos. Lake. On receipt of his letter, repaired to London to quicken the merchants on the matter of the Archduke. Found all the rest of the Council abroad. The merchants not ready with their answers. Thinks the merchant whom he sends to the King [Lionel Cranfield] will tell him more than they all.

Aug. 13. Strand. 48. Sir Julius Cæsar to the Same. Will return a full answer to His Majesty, touching the business of Lord Haddington.

Aug. 13. Grant to Lewis Duke of Lenox of the manor of Cobham and other lands, co. Kent. [*Grant Bk.*, *p.* 94.]

[Aug. 14.] 49. Earl of Northampton to [Rochester]. Riots in the Forest of Dean on occasion of cutting down wood for the Earl of Pembroke, who is much disliked. Means taken to suppress them. Instructions for the aid are ready. Sends an offer for farming the Customs from a company of able persons, which is to be kept secret if not accepted.

Aug. 14. Strand. 50. Sir Julius Cæsar to Sir Thos. Lake. Is obliged to delay his answer in Lord Haddington's matter, on account of difficulties and the absence of the Judges on their circuits.

Aug. 15. Strand. 51. The Same to the King. Cannot pay the 500*l.* to Lord Haddington, because not a penny of the money from which payment was to be made is received. Lord Vaux and his mother offer 2,000*l.*, and Wm. Vavasour 700*l.*, for their pardon and release; and Wm. Middleton, of York, and Rich. Townley, of Lancashire, 500*l.* each, to be excused the Oath of Allegiance. Dares not accept the offers, as being contrary to His Majesty's resolution. They, and other recusants, will be proceeded against according to law.

Aug. 17. Croydon. 52. Archbp. Abbot to the Same. Rumours in Holland of the murder of Prince Maurice, like those which preceded the murder of the French King. Fears some great conspiracy, because a general fast and prayers are ordered in Italy, such as took place before the

VOL. LXX.

1612.

Powder Treason. Blackfan, alias Blackman, kept close prisoner in the Gatehouse. He is well known to the Archduke. Zuniga detains prisoner in his house a converted Italian priest, who came to England for refuge. If Sir John Digby were to proceed thus in Madrid, the people would rise against him. The French Queen is jealous of Zuniga's long delay, and wishes alliance with England.

Aug. 17. Croydon. 53. Archbp. Abbot to [Rochester]. Will, at the King's command, hold good correspondence with the Venetian Ambassador.

[Aug. 17.] Monday. 54. Earl of Northampton to [the Same]. Perplexities in the Irish affairs, owing to the inconsistent steps taken by the Deputy to vindicate the King's title to dispose of the lands. Details how the matter stands with the French, relative to their claim to detain English troops beyond six months. A letter from the French King, which would have thrown light on the subject, is missing, the "little Lord" [Salisbury] having "made his own cabinet the treasurie of the state's whole evidences and intelligence." The French demand delivery of their bond on the subject, which is yielded, after an authentic copy has been taken, on condition of their paying 60,000*l.*, the King's necessities being so great. Report from Oxfordshire that Lady Stoner has at length taken the Oath of Allegiance; and the late sharp proceedings have brought many to church. Banbury Castle recommended as a fit prison for recusants. The King should be cautious in going to Wanstead, as many have died there.

[Aug. 20.] 55. The Same to [the Same]. Has taken great pains on Lord Dingwall's behalf to understand the business [of the Receivership of Alienation fines]. There are three officers, who, acting as deputies to the Treasurer and Chancellor, ought to sit in person, which it is unfitting for his Lordship to do, and the profits are scarcely anything but the salary of 120*l.* per ann., because the subjects are so clamorous against those exactions; therefore his Lordship should have something better from His Majesty. Hopes a reply to the proposal of the men who offer a higher rate for the Customs, which the old farmers deceitfully profess themselves willing to relinquish. The Archbishop and Council consent to the removal of Lord Vaux and his mother to the country, if they can be still under charge of their keeper. Sends for the King a letter, showing the state of his own affairs, which have been much injured by his reluctance to press, in time of want, for the profits of a patent granted him in exchange for that of starch, which the late Lord Treasurer gave to Lord Hay. Has enough to live as the King's beads-man, though not as a Councillor, but will be content with all, part, or nothing, at His Majesty's pleasure. *Incloses*,

55. I. *The Same to the Same. Glad the King approves the course taken about the riots in Dean Forest. His Majesty's reply about the undertakers [of Customs] is very judicious. Will never press the King, when he is in want, but is eaten up by debts incurred in building his new house. Will abate 2,000l. out of the 8,000l. owing him by His Majesty, and 1,000l. out of his patent of 4,000l.*

1612. VOL. LXX.

per ann. till the starch brings in as much. If others abated in like proportion, good results would follow. Begs leases of lands left by the contractors for the remainder of his debt, Aug. 20.

55. II. *Statement of the value of grants by the King to the Earl of Northampton, viz.:—Lands fallen to the Crown by attainder of his house, 325l. per ann. Office of Warden of the Cinque Ports, 102l. per ann. Wardship of Lord Windsor, value 940l. Grant of starch, 4,500l. On its surrender, a patent for 4,000l. per ann., of which not a penny has been received. Wages and diet as Lord Privy Seal, 960l., being a deduction of 800l. per ann. from former allowances.*

Aug. 20. Dover Castle. **56. Licence by the Earl of Northampton, Lord Warden of the Cinque Ports, to David Cornée, of Dieppe, to fish on the English coast, leave for six additional barks being granted at the solicitation of M. de la Boderie, the French Ambassador, with one for himself, on condition that the French will be satisfied with this number, and raise no further disturbance on the coasts.**

Aug. 22. 57. Edw. Reynoldes to Sir John Rawlins. Hears he is again taken captive in Circe's den. He is not out of the reach of his creditors, though in France, for they threaten to obtain a Privy Seal for his revocation, which he must obey if received, or hazard the loss of all he has, and be proscribed as a rebel.

[Aug. 22.] 58. Copy of the above, with slight differences.

Aug. 25? Tuesday. 59. Earl of Northampton to Rochester. On account of the mischiefs likely to arise by the establishment, in certain inhabited places, of houses for making gunpowder, the Council have given orders for their suppression.

Aug. 27? 60. The Same to [the Same]. Sends papers relating to the aid to be granted on the marriage of the Princess Elizabeth. Thanks for delivery of his paper to the King. Is delighted that His Majesty is sensible of his disinterestedness of service, and distinguishes between him and others who only aim at their own ends, and who drink full draughts of bounty, while he thirsts and pines. Requests that the suit may not be renewed to His Majesty; it suffices for him once to be acquainted with the state of his affairs. *Incloses,*

60. I. *Abstract of that which was allowed and directed by the Lords touching the aid for the Lady Elizabeth; with extracts from the instructions to be issued to the Commissioners for compounding for the aid.*

Aug. 30. Warrant to the Lord Chancellor to make Commissions for levying the aid for the Princess Elizabeth. [*Grant Bk., p.* 101.]

Aug.? 61. Earl of Northampton to [Rochester]. [The Spanish Ambassador, complaining of delay of justice to Spanish subjects, by prohibitions issued by common law against the decisions of

VOL. LXX.

1612.

the Admiralty court, would not refer Davies' case to that court. The English have to complain of similar delays of justice in Spain. A report is preparing thereon. Is indignant that a person of his rank, one of the three Commissioners [on the Gunpowder Plot], who hunted Garnet and the rest from the bar to the gallows, should now be accused of covering their crimes, and that such an accusation should have been made before the Council [of the North] three months before, and only just revealed to himself by Lord Sheffield. Sends Lord Sheffield's letter, and the examinations of his accusers. [*See Howell's State Trials, Vol.* II., *p.* 862.]

Aug. ? 62. Statement of the loss which the King will incur by accepting the offer of the farmers of the Customs to pay 20,000*l.* fine, and 6,000*l.* per ann. increase of rent.

[Sept. 3.] Thursday. 63. Earl of Northampton to [Rochester]. The Merchant Adventurers have resolved to retire from Middleburgh, and to petition that no interlopers be allowed to trade in the dominions of the Archduke, who, when his people are unable to sell their own productions, and obliged to fetch cloth from England, will repent his bravado. Hopes the King will not be induced to believe the interested reports of those who favour the old farmers of the Customs, nor to renew their grant, if even they offer as much as the new adventurers, seeing they do it of force. They are so angry at their tricks being discovered, that they attack Sir John Swinnerton's character. La Roche offers to disclose secrets from France. Udall has informed of the haunts of dangerous persons, who are now privately searched for. The wife of Mr. Nevill, who calls himself Westmoreland, writes that her husband and his mistress are going to Spain, with a licence which he has for the Spa, which is therefore stayed.

[Sept. 3.] Whitehall. Thursday. 64. Earl of Suffolk to the Same. [Edw.] Allen, the Master of the Bears, is dead. Recommends Tom Badger to succeed him, he having the finest breed of bull-dogs in England.

Sept. 6. 65. State of the accounts between Dr. [Rich.] Butler, [Archdeacon of Northampton,] and Dr. John Lambe, proctor. *Annexing,*

65. I.—VI. *Schedules A, B, C, D, E, F, containing particulars of the above accounts, from April* 1602.

Sept. 10. 66. Will of Dr. Rich. Butler, of Sprotton, co. Northampton.

Sept. 11. Ware Park. 67. Chamberlain to Carleton. Has seen Sir Julius Cæsar, who professes much wish for Carleton's promotion. The Prince gave the King an entertainment at Woodstock. Sir Michael Hicks dead at his house in Essex. Sir Stephen Le Sieur going as Ambassador to the new Emperor. Fires at Ely, Birmingham, and Tiverton.

Sept. 12. 68. Probate of the will of Sir Geo. Wandesford, of Sleningford, co. York, declaring his brother, Wm. Wandesford, sole executor. *Annexing,*

68. I. *Will of the Same, dated* 1597, *June* 20, *made in preparation for going abroad with the Earl of Essex.*

VOL. LXX.

1612.

Sept. 15. 69. Archbp. Abbot to the King. Details the grounds on which he has apprehended a man calling himself John de Horneck, and professing to be a Hollander and a Protestant, on suspicion of his being the Jesuit, Abraham Vlaming, against whom Mr. Trumbull has written, as a desperate fellow, and founder of an order of knighthood called the Order of Martyrdom.

Sept. 18. 70. Edw. Reynoldes to Sir John Rawlins. Traces in his last letter the style of the Circe into whose hands he has again fallen, in spite of his former resolutions to discard her for treachery. Thinks him unwise in sending for his trunks, as it may give his creditors a clue where to find him.

Sept. 20. 71. Note of the distribution of 4*l.* to the servants of the Archbp. of Canterbury by Dr. Smith, Bp. of Gloucester, at his consecration.

Sept. 21. Northampton House. 72. Commission by the Earl of Northampton, Lord Warden of the Cinque Ports, constituting the Captains of Sandown, Deal, and Walmer Castles, and others, Commissioners for restraint of passage at the creeks and landing places along the coast, between Sandwich and Dover.

Sept. 21. Whitehall. Proclamation signifying the King's grant to Jos. Usher, Warner Rich, and Gŏdfrey de Vette, of Letters Patent for the sole making and erecting of certain engines devised by them for raising water to supply houses, &c., and for draining overflowed grounds. Printed. *Annexing,*

Offer of the aforesaid engineers to exhibit and explain their engines to all engineers, and to erect them at their own charges, to be paid for when tried and put in practice. [*Proc. Coll.*, No. 18 A.]

Sept. 23. 73. Names of the Prisoners in the Tower:—"The Lady Arbella [Stuart], Countess of Shrewsbury, Erle of Northumberland, Lorde Grey, Lorde Cobham, Sir Walter Raleighe, Mr. Patrick Rewthan, Sir Cormack O'Neale, brother to Tyrone, Sir Donel O'Cane, Sir Neale Garvey, Sir Thomas Bartlet, Mr. Mathews, Mr. Nectan O'Donell, sonne to Sir Neale Garvey, William Baldwin, Jesuite."

Sept. 24. Whitehall. 74. The Council to the Sheriffs, Deputy Lieutenants, and Justices of Peace of Somersetshire. The manor of Kingsbury being granted by the King to the Earl of Hertford, John Gerard, the occupier, refused to yield it, either on demand, or on decision of the law, and resisted by force three commissions issued to expel him. Require them to call out the posse comitatus, attack the house with ordnance if needful, and rather beat it to the ground than suffer him to remain in it, and to apprehend all concerned in defending it.

Sept. 24. Sir Thos. Lake to Carleton. The King is going to Royston, unless prevented by the Count Palatine's arrival. The vacant offices remain in suspense. In the secretaryship "His Majesty thinketh he is best himself." The treasurership will probably be offered to the Earl of Northampton. [*Venice Corresp., Sept.* 24.]

VOL. LXX.

1612.

Sept. 25. Weston. 75. Ralph Sheldon to Sir Thos. Lake. The King has no waste lands, woods, &c. in Malvern Chace, but has the wastes in Feckenham Forest, the woods of which were lately sold.

Sept. 27. 76. Muster roll of the garrison of Sandgate Castle.

Sept. 29. 77. Note of the distribution of 42*s.* 6*d.* given by the Duke of York, when he dined at Croydon, to the yeomen of Archbp. Abbot's house.

Sept. 29. 78. Account of the quantity of French wines brought into the realm in six years, from Michaelmas 4 to 10 Jas. I. With note of a suit to be allowed to furnish the wines which the farmers provide for the King's household, at the rates charged by them, they paying in money the deductions hitherto allowed for provision of wines.

Sept. 29. Tuesday. Greenwich. 79. Earl of Northampton to Rochester. The agent of Savoy says that an Ambassador will be sent about the match, as soon as it is understood that it will be agreeable, and any dower asked will be given. He wished to know whether the Florence match was likely to take effect. Don Pedro [de Zuniga] complains of the opening by the Custom House officers of a chest sent to him; also that no great men visit him. Has imprisoned a coachmaker who, for a small debt, stopped the coach of the Venetian Ambassador. His secretary urges that the man should be extremely tortured for this contempt.

Sept.? 80. Discourse addressed to the Prince on the dangers and inconveniences of his matching with a sister of the Duke of Florence; viz., encouragement of Popery, discontent at home, distrust caused to Protestant allies, &c.

Sept.? 81. Discourse on the advantages of the proposed match with Florence over that with Savoy, the Duke of Savoy being poor, always engaged in broils, and subservient to Spain; whereas the Florentine Grand Duke is rich, a man of honour and influence, a friend to Queen Elizabeth and the King, and his country advantageous for the Levant trade. Comparative dignity of the two Princes. Florence independent of Spain and Rome, &c.

[Sept. 31.] Thursday. Greenwich. 82. Earl of Northampton to Rochester. Forwards a report from the merchants lately sent over [to Flanders], which shows to what miserable straits those princes have reduced themselves. Foscarini complains that committal is not punishment enough for Melfell the coachman, and refuses all petitions and submissions of his wife. Has referred her to the Council, as also Don Pedro, who renews his complaint against the Custom House officers.

Sept.? 83. The Same to the Same. The Lords [Commissioners for the Treasury?] have been diligent in considering the best means for raising the King's profits. Compromise with the Persian Ambassador [Sir Robt. Shirley] about his return thither, so as to avoid sending him with English ships and sailors, who so often turn pirates in remote countries. The English merchants trading

VOL. LXX.

1612.

to France object to the 3*d.* asked from foreigners, but upon slight grounds. Lady Arundel is made happy by a permission to join her husband [at the Spa], and requests a prolongation of his licence for six months.

Sept. ? 84. List of annuities paid to servants of the late Queen in lieu of their offices, and of those paid to some servants of the present King, Queen, and Royal Family.

VOL. LXXI. OCTOBER—DECEMBER, 1612.

[Oct. 7.] 1. Earl of Northampton to Rochester. Has examined, along with the two others appointed by the King, Sir Hen. Wotton's statements relative to the Savoy match. The dower, 700,000 crowns, is less than was expected. Sir Henry urges a reply, but they refuse to give one without consulting others of the Council.

[Oct. 7.] 2. Earl of Worcester to Lake. Asks whether the King will write back to the Count of Emden, and what reward should be given to the gentleman and grooms who brought the horses.

[Oct. 8.] 3. Earl of Northampton to the King. The first patent of farming the customs was made too low, by taking a medium of seven instead of ten years, by omitting several items, and by calculating on the old, not the increased rates. The second patent had similar faults, and thus the two last Treasurers pared down the robe imperial for their own profit. For the third patent Sir John Swinnerton offered a large advance; but the late Lord Treasurer rated him soundly for it, and declared he should not have it, let his best friends in Court strain as they would. The customs were re-let at an advance of 15,000*l.*, but Scottish customs and other things thrown into the bargain, that made it just as good for the farmers and as bad for the King as before. The great custom is now to be let to the best advantage, and it is hoped that that of the wines will fall in.

Oct. ? 4. Observations on the defalcations unjustly claimed by the farmers of customs for articles which were not included in their original grant, or which are brought in from some new colony; and also on the disadvantage of their retaining the rent half a year in their hands. Drawn up for the King's benefit in demising the great farm of the customs.

[Oct. 8.] Thursday. 5. Earl of Northampton to [Rochester]. Has written to the King on the [Council's] proceedings for his profit. Hopes the patent for the wines may be dissolved by law. Urgency of the agent of Savoy to obtain despatch of his business. Has persuaded [the Countess of Arundel] to desist from her intended voyage, as most unfitting for her to take before spring, and likely to do more hurt to herself than good to her lord. "The bodey of the most worthy Quen in the world [Mary Queen of Scots] is neer the towne, and the lordes are preparinge to waite on it."

VOL. LXXI.

1612.

Oct. 8. Royston. 6. Visct. Rochester to Northampton. Exculpates himself from the charge of seeking the office of Master of the Horse to the prejudice of the Earl of Pembroke, or from compelling the Earl of Worcester to sell it for fear of the King's displeasure. Has been very careful of the rights of the English nobility. Refused Lord Montague's escheat, and Cobham Hall, on that account. Is "the courtier whose hand never tooke bribes."

Oct. 8. 7. Copy of the above.

Oct. 8. 8. Muster roll of the garrison of Mote's Bulwark.

Oct. 9. 9. Muster roll of the garrison of Sandown Castle.

Oct. 9. 10. Muster roll of the garrison of Walmer Castle.

Oct.? 11. Names of the watchmen of Dover Castle certified by Sir Thos. Waller to the sheriff of Kent, as exempted from attendance on juries, &c.

Oct. 9. London. 12. Giov. Franc. Biondi to [Carleton]. The Savoy match nearly concluded. The King demands as a condition that nothing shall be done by the Duke of Savoy against Geneva, without consulting him. The Duke only asks the private exercise of her religion for the Princess, and leaves the dower to the King's generosity. The match is rather one of necessity than choice, but all approve it except the churchmen. The Archbp. of Canterbury has opposed it in vain. The King continues him [Biondi] his pension and received him well. Is told by the Earl of Shrewsbury that the Countess of Arundel persists in going to Italy to join her husband, that he may continue his course of medicine, without wishing to return home. Italian.

Oct. 9. Lambeth. 13. Giulio Cesare Vandoni to [the Same]. Thanks for his introduction of him to the Archbp. of Canterbury, who has received him most kindly.

Oct. 9. Lambeth. 14. The Same to Isaac Wake. Dines almost daily at the Archbp. of Canterbury's table. His brother Maria equally well received by his Grace of York, who promises him a benefice. Hopes his clothes have been sent off from Venice.

Oct. 9. 15. Memorandum by John Pepys, that he has delivered that day to the Archbp. of Canterbury two bundles of the examinations of the conspirators in the Gunpowder Plot, "and the little bundele of Garnett's letters, written with orenge;" endorsed with notes by Pepys of other papers sent, and also that he has received all back, except the treatise on equivocation and the copy of the indictment. July 1, 1614.

[Oct. 10.] Saturday at 11. 16. Earl of Northampton to [Rochester]. Thanks for the King's favours. The Council have held long consultations [on the farm of the customs]. Mr. Solicitor has best pursued the mystery of iniquity. The Brandenburg Ambassadors have not yet arrived from Dover.

1612. Vol. LXXI.

Though the King's mother's body was brought late to town to avoid a concourse, yet many in the streets and windows watched her entry with honour into the place whence she had been expelled with tyranny. She is buried with honour, as dead rose-leaves are preserved, whence the liquor that makes the kingdom sweet has been distilled. Was reminded of the bedlam courses taken by the "littell one" [Cecil] and his father, in inflaming the Queen's ears, though they covered themselves by the passions of Walsingham. But when the Queen's decay threatened ruin to his [Cecil's] house, he sang "another songe by the quille," and having aided the King's ascent to the throne, was supported by him. [*See Sir Robt. Cecil's Secret Corresp. with Jas. VI.* 12*mo.* 1766.]

[Oct. 10.] Saturday at 2. 17. Earl of Northampton to Rochester. Has sent directions to Sir Thos. Waller, his lieutenant at Dover, to guard against a certain peril threatened for the King, and is satisfied of his diligent care. *Incloses,*

17. i. *The Same to Sir Thos. Waller. Charges him to keep strict watch lest any persons ill affected to His Majesty may steal over, on pretence of belonging to the train of the Count Palatine. Sept.* 6, *Greenwich.*

Oct. 11. 18. Lord Chancellor Ellesmere and Earl of Northampton to the King. Report the frauds used for eight years past in the farming of the customs, to the King's great loss. The lease is found to have expired, and the farmers might be called to account for their frauds. The patentees for French and Rhenish wines have by dunning got a renewal of their lease, but the lawyers think it might be overthrown, and as it was obtained by fraud, His Majesty may annul it with honour. The Solicitor and Serjeant Montague have been very zealous about it.

Oct. 12. Royston. 19. Visct. Rochester to Sir Thos. Lake. Sends the writs signed for the Commission. Has delivered the letter from Sir John Digby.

Oct. 13. Royston. 20. Levinus Munck to the Same. The Spanish Ambassador Lieger has complained to his Court of want of justice in the Admiralty Court here. Sir John Digby is to be informed thereon, and on any other point which he should know. The easterly wind gives hope of the arrival of the Count Palatine.

Oct. 13. Grant, in reversion, to Robt. Vernon, of the office of keeping the King's house at Newmarket, co. Somerset, for life. [*Grant Bk., p.* 96.]

Oct. 13. 21. Statement of the laxity of the four Commissioners, the Provost Marshal, and the twenty-five horsemen, on the English borders, in the apprehension of thieves and outlaws. The soldiers have but half their pay, the garrison favour thieves, and the commissioners do nothing. Those on the Scottish borders are so active and vigilant that the thieves fly to England.

VOL. LXXI.

1612.

Oct. 16. Grant to Sir Thos. Monson of the office of keeper of naval and other warlike instruments and ammunition for life. [*Grant Bk.*, *p.* 95.]

Oct. 16. Grant to Sir Pat. Hume of the office of governor of the Poor Knights at Windsor. [*Ibid.*, *p.* 93.]

Oct. 16. Grant to Otho Nicholson of the office of receiver of money for assart lands, &c. [*Ibid.*, *p.* 95.]

Oct. 17. Licence to Sir Hen. Neville to build upon a parcel of meadow ground bordering upon Tothill Fields, co. Middlesex. [*Ibid.*, *p.* 95.]

Oct. 21. Utrecht. 22. Sir Edw. Cecil to [Thos. Murray]. Has found in the hands of an officer a set of models of all engines and artillery fit for an army, which he recommends as fitting subjects of study for the Prince, as showing by demonstration rather than theory "the verie practice of everie thinge, either defensive or offensive." They are valued at 1,000*l.*

Oct. 21? 23. Memorial of what will be required for the tables of the Elector Palatine, viz., 10 covers for his own table, 18 for the table for persons of rank; the third table for the 14 pages is to be served with what is removed from the first; and the fourth for the 24 valets, coachmen, &c., with what goes away from the second. French.

Oct. 22. London. 24. Chamberlain to Carleton. Arrival and reception of the Count Palatine. His graceful bearing. The King gave him a ring worth 1,800*l.* He is lodged at Essex House, and cares not for ring nor tennis, but is always with his mistress. Some persons called to account for speaking disparagingly of the match. He is thought equal in dignity to the best prince in Italy, and not far behind in revenue. The match with Savoy cools, and will fail unless farmed by Sir Hen. Wotton, who is contriving an exchange between Baldwin, the Jesuit, and Mole, Lord Roos' tutor, so long prisoner in the Inquisition at Rome. Lord Vaux transferred to the custody of the Dean of Westminster. Sir Thos. Edmondes thought of as Secretary. Terrible storm, in which fifty vessels were cast away near Yarmouth. Visct. Fenton has sold his interest in Amtphill Park to the keepers.

Oct. 22. 25. Copy of part of the above.

Oct. 23. Stanhoe. 26. Hen. Cursson to Thos. Wilson. Is troubled to receive order for payment to the Court of Wards of certain profits on the manor of Stanhoe, for wardship of his son-in-law, Thos. Baxter. Hopes Wilson has discharged all, according to the conditions of purchase promised.

Oct. 29. Carlisle. 27. Commissioners for the Borders to the King. Vindicate themselves from the charge of the Scottish Commissioners that they have not done justice to Scotchmen. Have not failed in one particular to give them even stricter justice than the laws would afford to an Englishman.

VOL. LXXI.

1612.
Nov. 1. Grant, in reversion, to Edw. Kelk of the office of Bailiff of Sandwich for life. [*Grant Bk.*, *p.* 94.]

Nov. 2. Westminster. Grant to Sir Tim. Hutton, of Mask, co. York, of the next advowson of the rectory of Aldingham, diocese Chester, to present John Rowthe, of Strafforth, co. York. Latin. [*Sign Man.*, *vol.* II., *No.* 33.]

Nov. 2. Westminster. Grant to Miles Smith, Bishop of Gloucester, of installation of his first fruits, to be paid in four years. [*Ibid.*, *No.* 34.]

Nov. 3. Westminster. Warrant to the Treasury Commissioners for payment of 2,000*l.* to Sir Robt. Vernon, Cofferer of the Household, for defraying the charges of the Count Palatine. [*Ibid.*, *No.* 35.]

Nov. 3. Westminster. Commission of Lieutenancy for Sussex and the city of Chichester, to the Earls of Nottingham, Arundel, and Dorset, renewed for the sake of adding the Earl of Dorset to the commission, [*Ibid.*, *No.* 36.]

Nov. 3. Westminster. Warrant to the Commissioners of the Treasury to advance 500*l.* to Lord Harrington, for the expenses of the Princess Elizabeth, and further sums from time to time. [*Ibid.*, *No.* 37.]

Nov. 4. Westminster. Presentation of the Rev. Rich. Smyth to the rectory of Shire, co. Surrey. Latin. [*Ibid.*, *No.* 38.]

Nov. 4. London. 28. Chamberlain to Carleton. Conjectures about the Secretaryship. The great favourite [Rochester] causes delay by embracing too much at once. Wotton has lost his chance through the King's hearing that he wrote an epigram, describing an Ambassador as "a good man sent to lie for the sake of his country." He vainly endeavours to turn it off as a jest. The Prince having a fever was prevented dining in the city, as invited by Sir John Swinnerton, Mayor, but the Count Palatine went, behaved very courteously, going to salute the Lady Mayoress, and had a present of 1,200 ounces of plate. There were a grand show and pageants, but a storm on the water endangered many barges. Death of Judge Yelverton and Sir Edw. Drury. The King and Archbp. of Canterbury stand sponsors for Dr. [Isaac] Casaubon's child.

Nov. 5. Westminster. Re-grant to the Earl of Southampton of pension of 2,000*l.* per ann., passed again on account of a defect in the former grant, made June 11, 1611. [*Sign Man.*, vol. II., *No.* 39.]

Nov. 6. Westminster. Grant to John Endecot and Matthew Burgh of the sole licence of the art of making artificial stone resembling marble and porphyry, according to a mode by them invented. [*Ibid.*, *No.* 40.]

Nov. 7. 29. Physician's report on the post-mortem examination of Henry Prince of Wales. Latin.

Nov. 7. 30. Translation of the above.

VOL. LXXI.

1612.

Nov. 10. Charing Cross. 31. Sir Thos. Lake to Carleton. Death of the Prince of Wales in the pride of his years, on the anniversary of a memorable deliverance, and the eve of his sister's marriage. The King, apprehending the worst, and not enduring to be so near the place, removed to Theobalds, and kept his bed. The Queen is at Somerset House. They have not seen each other "for feare to refresh the sense of the wound." His body opened on account of vulgar rumours about his death, which was proved to be from the hand of God. German Ambassadors come about the inheritance of Cleves.

Nov. 12. London. 32. Chamberlain to the Same. Particulars of the last illness, death, and post-mortem examination of the late Prince. Turquet [Mayerne] much blamed for bad treatment of him. A cordial was sent him by Sir Walter Raleigh, who loses by his death his greatest hope of release. His debts are to be paid and his pensions continued. His revenue of 60,000*l.* returns to the King, till Prince Charles is older. The Duchy of Cornwall is said to revert to the Crown, as being entailed only on the King's first-born. The Prince's early death was prophesied, because he never cast his first teeth. Distress of the King and Queen, and of Lady Elizabeth, who went several times in disguise to see him, but was refused admission, for fear of contagion. He had intended to conduct her to Germany.

Nov. 14. Westminster. 33. Sir Hen. Wotton to Rochester. Death of Sir Geo. Carew. Requests the reversion of his pension of 200*l.* in addition to his own of 200*l.*, having served the King abroad twice as long as Carew.

Nov. 14? 34. Sir Fras. Bacon to the Same. Begs to be remembered, if the Mastership of the Court of Wards is to be given to a lawyer, the Mastership of the Rolls being taken from lawyers.

Nov. 14. Florence. 35. Sir Robt. Dudley (signed Warwick, &c.) to Sir David Fowlies, Cofferer to Prince Henry. Sends to the Prince a treatise important to his security and profit, and hopes he will undertake the matter. Sold his Highness his estate of Killingworth at small value, only reserving to himself the constableship of the castle. Wishes to sell Itchington and Balsall for settlement of his estates. *Incloses,*

35. I. *Discourse proving from precedent the importance of naval supremacy, and recommending the adoption of a new sort of vessel, called the Gallizabra, invented by himself, as being more efficient, less costly, and requiring fewer men than ordinary vessels. Florence, Nov.* 12, 1612. *Indorsed with note of presentation to Charles I. Jan.* 1. 1630.

[Nov.] 36. Copy of the above discourse.

Nov. 16. Exchequer. 37. Extract from Domesday Book, relating to the lands of Wm. Pevrel, in Colwick, Nottinghamshire.

1612. VOL. LXXI.

Nov. 17. Westminster. Grant to John Wright of the office of Sub-clerk of the House of Commons for life. Latin. [*Sign Man., vol.* II., *No.* 41.]

Nov. 17. Westminster. Warrant for advance of 3,000*l.* to Sir David Fowlies, Cofferer to the late Prince, and for payment of sums due to him on the Prince's account. [*Ibid., No.* 42.]

Nov. 17. Westminster. Warrant for advance of sums necessary for the charges of the funeral of Prince Henry. [*Ibid., No.* 43.]

Nov. 17. Westminster. Grant to Wm. Earl of Pembroke of the stewardship of all lands in Cornwall and Devon belonging to the Duchy of Cornwall. Latin. [*Ibid., No.* 44.]

Nov. 18. Theobalds. Grant to Luke Bryan of 100*l.*, being a concealed debt due to the Crown from the heirs of ——— Drew, because, for five years after his decease, they continued to receive an annuity of 20*l.* per ann. granted him by the late Queen. [*Ibid., No.* 45.]

Nov 18. Westminster. Grant to Sir Rich. Wigmore of licence to import cod and ling for twenty years longer, until the amount of 16,000 lasts, formerly granted to him, is made up. [*Ibid., No.* 46.]

Nov. 18. Westminster. Grant to the Same of the King's two parts of the lands, &c. of John Gainsford and Margaret Gainsford, widow, both of St. Dunstan's, London, and Katherine Denham, widow, of Piddington, co. Oxford, value 86*l.* 13*s.* 4*d.* per ann., in part of his grant of 1,000*l.* of recusants' lands. Latin. [*Ibid., No.* 47.]

Nov. 18. London. Isaac Wake to Carleton. Gave his [Carleton's] letters to Sir Thos. Overbury, who said Rochester was gone with the King to Theobalds and Royston. Went to Theobalds; found out "Rochester's lodgings by the store of company that was about it." Asked him for portraits of the King and himself for Carleton, and hopes to obtain them. Sir Geo. Carew dead, and Sir Walter Cope succeeds him as Master of the Wards. [*Venice Corresp., Nov.* 18.]

Nov. 19. London. 38. Chamberlain to the Same. The Prince's death taking away hopes of supply by his marriage, a Parliament is talked of for February; there is much canvassing for vacant offices. The King gone from Kensington to Theobalds and Royston. The Princess's marriage postponed, lest Ambassadors coming to condole for the Prince should find feasting and dancing. The Prince's debts are 9,000*l.*, but his property is worth much more; his medals and coins worth 3,000*l.* His papers show that he had many vast conceits and projects. A mad youth rushed into St. James's naked, pretending to be the ghost of the late Prince. Lewis Baily, one of his chaplains, is called to account for preaching on the decay of religion, owing to Popery in the Council. The King declares zeal for religion. Death of Sir Hen. Roe and Sir Geo. Carew, Master of the Wards. Candidates for the place of the latter.

VOL. LXXI.

1612.

Nov. ? 39. Petition of Sir Mervin Touchet, son and heir of Geo. Lord Audley, to the Commissioners for the Earl Marshalship, for answer to certain queries on precedence of the children of peers, which concern himself and his younger brothers and sisters.

Nov. ? 40. Answers to the preceding queries, by Wm. Segar, Garter.

Nov. 19. Theobalds. Warrant for payment of 2,000*l.*, out of fines and forfeitures, to Robt. Jossy, Groom of the Bedchamber; Sir John Shaw, to whom the grant was previously made, having died. [*Sign Man., vol.* II., *No.* 48]

Nov. 19. Theobalds. Grant to Sir Walter Cope of the office of Master of the Court of Wards and Liveries until May 16 next, and thenceforward during pleasure. Latin. [*Ibid., No.* 49.]

Nov. 19. Theobalds. Grant to John Manley of the Messenger's and Cryer's offices in the co. palatine of Chester, during pleasure. Latin. [*Ibid., No.* 50.]

Nov. 20. Theobalds. Grant to Chas. Chambers, Groom of the Privy Chamber to the Queen, and George, his brother, of protection from arrests for debt for twelve months. [*Ibid., No.* 51.]

Nov. 20. Theobalds. Warrant for payment to Thos. Stone of 500*l.*, which he has advanced to Sir Robt. Dudley beyond the seas, in part of 7,000*l.* which was to be paid by the late Prince for purchase of the manor and parks of Killingworth. [*Ibid., No.* 52.]

Nov. 20. Theobalds. Warrant for payment to Wm. Ryder, Gentleman Harbinger, of sums necessary for lodgings and stabling for the attendants of the Elector Palatine and Count Henry of Nassau. [*Ibid., No.* 53.]

Nov. 20. Theobalds. Warrant for payment to Alice Lady Dudley of a pension of 300*l.* per ann. from the Exchequer, as formerly granted to her from the rents of Killingworth, forfeited by Sir Robt. Dudley for contempt in not returning to England. [*Ibid., No.* 54.]

Nov. 21. Royston. Grant to Sir Edw. Peyto and Peter Peyto, his servant, both of London, of pardon for manslaughter of Thos. Pilkington in a sudden affray. Latin. [*Ibid, No.* 55.]

Nov. 21. Royston. Grant to Miles Whytakers, Keeper of the manor of Theobalds, of an annuity of 40*l.* Latin. [*Ibid., No.* 56.]

Nov. 25. London. Isaac Wake to Carleton. Sir Hen. Wotton much troubled at the death of the Prince, from whom he looked for advancement, the more so that the King is displeased with him, because Gaspar Schoppius has lately printed a treatise to prove that Protestants profess equivocation as well as Jesuits, in which he cites as an example Wotton's definition of Ambassadors. [*Venice Corresp., Nov.* 25.]

Nov. 26. London. 41. Giov. Franc. Biondi to [the Same]. The patent for his pension is made out, but not signed yet, on account of the King's absence. The death of the Prince ends all hopes of a Savoyan match, and Gabellione is returning. Italian.

VOL. LXXI.

1612.
Nov. 26. London. 42. Chamberlain to Carleton. Sir Walter Cope has taken his place in the Court of Wards. He owes his elevation solely to the King, and says he will execute his office sincerely with clean hands. The King begins to digest his late loss, and orders the young Prince to be kept within stricter compass than his late brother. Sir Thos. Lake, Sir Fras. Bacon, and Sir Fulk Greville have all been spoken of for the Secretaryship. Several persons committed for reporting a difference at the Council-table between the Archbp. of Canterbury and Lord Privy Seal. Escape of seven Seminary priests from Newgate. Chapter of the Garter held to elect the Count Palatine and the Count Maurice. Horton, the stationer, dead. Enumerates the death of many great persons during the year. Serjeants Dodderidge and Nicholls made judges.

Nov. 26. Grant to Sir Augustine Nicholls of the office of Justice of the King's Bench during pleasure. [*Grant Bk., p.* 95.]

Nov. 26. Royston. Grant to Hen. Miles and Robt. Cudworth, both of London, of lands in co. Worcester, and of the advowson of Rushton All Saints, and land, co. Northampton, in part of a grant to Lord Aubigny of concealed lands, value 1,000*l.* per ann. Latin. [*Sign Man., vol.* II., *No.* 57.]

Nov. 26. Royston. Grant of foundation of an alms-house and grammar school at Stowe-on-the-Wold, co. Gloucester, endowed by the late Rich. Shepham; the Corporation of Chipping Norton, co. Oxford, to be the Governors. Latin. [*Ibid., No.* 58.]

Nov. 26? 43. List of the pirate captains over whom Peter Eston is General.

Nov. 26. Westminster. Re-grant to Peter Eston and his men, pirates, of pardon, on condition of their restoring the ship Concord, and the goods taken by them in it, and the Bonaventure. Renewed because the former pardon never reached Eston, he being near Newfoundland. [*Sign Man., vol.* II., *No.* 59.]

Nov. 26. Royston. Grant, with survivorship, to John Norden and Alex. Nairn of the office of Surveyors of the King's castles, forts, parks, lodges, forests, and chaces, cos. Kent, Surrey, Sussex, Hants, Berks, Dorset, Wilts, Somerset, Devon, and Cornwall. [*Ibid., No.* 60.]

Nov. 26. Royston. Warrant for payment of 200*l.* to Sir Robt. Wroth and Sir John Brett, to distribute to such tenants as pretend a right in the waste lands in Enfield Chace, which have been taken in to enlarge Theobalds Park. [*Ibid., No.* 61.]

Nov. 27. Royston. Grant to the Earl of Dorset, on surrender of Sir Hen. Guildford, of the offices of Keeper of Broyle Park and Ranger of Ringmer Wood, co. Sussex. Latin. [*Ibid., No.* 62.]

Nov. 27. Royston. Grant to Peter Eston, Gilbert Roope, and others, pirates, of pardon, on conditions specified before. [*Ibid., No.* 63.]

Nov. 27. Royston. Grant to Ralph Beeston and Ralph Bowes of protection from arrests for debt for six months. [*Ibid., No.* 64.]

VOL. LXXI.

1612.

Nov. 27. Royston. Grant to Wm. Whitmore and Jonas Vernon, both of London, of lands, tenements, &c., in cos. York, Lincoln, Leicester, Norfolk, Middlesex, Essex, Worcester, Warwick, Cumberland, Sussex, Devon, Brecon, Carmarthen, Cardigan, Pembroke, Derby, Nottingham, Oxford, Hertford, Surrey, Kent, Somerset, Dorset, Wilts, Gloucester, and Hants, value 385*l.* 2*s.* 0¼*d.* per ann., to be considered as payment of 8,304*l.* 2*s.* 8¾*d.*, in part of the grant of lands, value 20,000*l.*, to Wm. Whitmore, Art. Ingram, and Geo. Whitmore, contractors. Latin. [*Sign Man., vol.* II., *No.* 65.]

Nov. 28? 44. Opinion on the lawfulness of subjecting Ambassadors and their attendants to punishment, for crimes against the laws of nations and of the land where they are resident. Indorsed "A Paper proving the Lawfulness of putting to Death the Portugals for the Murther upon the Exchange."

Nov. 29. Grant to John Wright of the office of Sub-clerk of the Parliament for life. [*Grant Bk., p.* 101.]

Nov. 29. Royston. Warrant for payment to Sir Wm. Cornwallis of 2,000*l.* as a free gift. [*Sign Man., vol.* II., *No.* 66.]

Nov. 29. Royston. Grant to Robt. Strickland of the office of Filazer of the Court of Exchequer at Chester. [*Ibid., No.* 67.]

Docquet of the above. [*Docquet, March* 31, 1613.]

Nov. 29. Royston. Grant to Jas. Douglas of pension of 200 marks per ann. for service in the affairs of Scotland. [*Sign Man., vol.* II., *No.* 68.]

Nov. 30. Royston. Grant to John French of Marton, Warwick, of pardon for highway robbery of John Pardoe; sued for by Pardoe because French preserved his life, which his accomplice, who was hung for the robbery, threatened to take. Latin. [*Ibid, No.* 69.]

Nov. 30. Royston. Grant to Sir Noel de Caron of the office of Keeper of Bagshot Park, Surrey, on surrender of Sir Wm. Harmon, to whom it was assigned by Sir Hen. Guildford. Latin. [*Ibid, No.* 70.]

Nov. 30. Royston. Lease to Hen. Sherfield and Nich. Duck of the manor of Carnanton, co. Cornwall, on surrender of a former lease by Rich. Hewett, because the rent was raised on supposition that the fines were arbitrable, whereas they prove to be certain. Latin. [*Ibid., No.* 71.]

Nov. 30. Royston. Grant to John Carse of debts due to the Crown from the recusancy of Wm. Mullins, of Tidcombe, co. Wilts, deceased. Latin. [*Ibid., No.* 72.]

Nov. 30. Westminster. Grant to Sir Lewis Tresham, Bart., of remainder of the manor of Rushton, co. Northampton, devolved on the Crown by attainder of Fras. Tresham. [*Ibid., No.* 73.]

Nov. 31. Grant to Sir Thos. Vavasour of the office of Knight Marshal of the Household for life. [*Grant Bk., p.* 96.]

VOL. LXXI.

1612.

Nov. Royston. 45. Warrant for a grant to Visct. Rochester, on payment of 20*s.*, of certain lands, co. Essex, lately belonging to Thos. Lord Darcy.

Nov. 46. Accounts of the Petty Bag and Hanaper since Michaelmas Term.

[Nov.] 47. List of 132 inferior servants of the late Prince's household and chamber, with estimate of the sum requisite to allow them two thirds of a year's wages for their relief, being 1,723*l.* 4*s.* 4*d.*

Nov. ? 48. Brief drawn up for the King by Rich. Connock, Auditor of the late Prince, of the state of his revenue, amounting to 54,315*l.* 7*s.* 10¾*d.*, and of the debts owing by and to him, which leave a balance for His Majesty of 9,471*l.* 8*s.* 1¾*d.*, besides jewels, horses, medals, and other things of great value.

Nov. ? 49. Translation from an epistle of Calvin relative to the death of Prince Henry, eulogizing his early piety and promise. Prince Charles so hopeful that "there is no great prince in Christendom that doth not wish himself such a sonne."

Nov. ? 50. Account of the receipts and issues of the Exchequer during the Treasurership of the Earl of Salisbury, averaging 600,000*l.* per ann.; the ordinary income being under 500,000*l.*, the rest was obtained by loans, sales of land, &c.

Nov. ? Statements by the Commissioners of the Revenue of probable abatements in the annual expenditure, from the following causes, viz.: Marriage of the Lady Elizabeth, 10,000*l.* Reduction in the Pension List 4,000*l.* Reductions in the King's household expenses, 6,000*l.* Allowances made to the late Prince Henry, 50,000*l.* Office of Works, if no fresh buildings be undertaken, 18,000*l.* Deduction from the allowance to Irish Commissioners, 700*l.* With several minor abatements. [*Imperfect MSS., Jas. I., No. 2. Fol.* 22.] *Annexed is,—*

Statement of certain ordinary annual receipts of the Exchequer, total 249,276*l.* [*Ibid.*]

Dec. 2. London. Isaac Wake to Carleton. Thos. Murray hopes to fulfil Carleton's wish for a portrait of Prince Charles, and Sir John Harrington, for one of Lady Elizabeth. Carleton's nephew sworn an equerry, having bought Powell's place for 600*l.* The Palatine Prince has come back to visit his mistress, and grows in the good opinion of all. Sir Rich. Coxe and others imprisoned during pleasure, for slandering the Earl of Northampton. Mr. Trumbull called home to be Clerk of the Council. Prince Charles kept as strictly as when he was Duke of York, and will not have the reins loose as early as his brother. The King will keep the Duchy of Cornwall, as belonging to the eldest son, not to the heir. To keep the Prince from Popery, "two sober divines, Dr. Hackwell and another, are placed with him, and ordered never to leave him." [*Venice Corresp., Dec.* 2.]

VOL. LXXI.

1612.

Dec. 3. London. 51. Giov. Franc. Biondi to Carleton. Much talk about the marriage of the Prince. France tries to negotiate it. Those who think of religion wish for Denmark, but the King opposes it, as he desires the marriage to bring him some new alliance. Talk of marrying one Infanta of Savoy in Denmark, the other in Spain. Parliament will not meet, as the King's necessities are relieved by the increase of 20,000*l.* per ann. on the death of the late Prince. Italian.

[Dec. 5.] Circumstantial account [by Sir Chas. Cornwallis] of the illness and death of Prince Henry, the post-mortem examination and lying in state. [*Dom. Corresp., April* 25, 1616.]

[Dec. 5.] 52. Copy of the above. Mutilated.

Dec. ? 53. Copy of the above post mortem, with note of the date of the Prince's death and funeral. Latin.

Dec. ? 54. Translation of the above.

Dec. ? 55. Queries in reference to the mourning and place of Prince [Charles] at the funeral of [Prince Henry ?].

Dec. ? 56. Draft of the intended funeral procession of Prince Henry.

Dec. 7. 57. Proceeding at the funeral of the Right High and Mighty Prince Henry, Prince of Wales, &c.

Dec. 7. 58. Copy of part of the above.

Dec. 59. Note of mourning given to the servants of the Archbp. of Canterbury, at the funerals of the Earl of Dunbar, Mr. Sutton, and Prince Henry.

Dec. 9. 60. Examination of Chris. Marshall, of Norwich, Draper. Practices of Mary, wife of John Woods, to poison her husband or be divorced from him. She professes to have a familiar spirit.

Dec. 10. 61. Testimony of Mary Lunne, of Consford. Mary Woods and her husband slept at her house, and stole some articles of dress, and a brass pot. With her bond to appear against her at the Sessions.

Dec. 10. 62. Testimony of Kath. Mason, that she received in person the before-named goods, stolen by Mary Woods.

Dec. 10 ? 63. Examination of Peter Walker's wife, relative to money obtained from her by "cunning Mary," alias Mary Woods, on pretence of saving her from death by witchcraft.

Dec. 10. London. 64. Giov. Franc. Biondi to Carleton. Scotland has very unexpectedly sent the Princess [Elizabeth] 20,000*l.* for a wedding present. Count Henry leaves for Holland. Italian.

Dec. 17. London. Isaac Wake to the Same. The vacant offices are to be filled up. Sir Ralph Winwood is gaining ground. Visct. Rochester has been in some disgrace, but his credit is much increased by his tender attentions to the King during a recent illness. Sir Thos. Lake had a commission to correspond with foreign Ambassadors, and keep them informed of all matters of consequence; this was thought a step

VOL. LXXI.

1612.

to the Secretaryship; but he assumed too much upon it, and it was taken away. Latham, a priest, hanged at Tyburn. So many Catholics were present that they spoke of attempting a rescue. The Council have had meetings to suppress recent assemblies of Catholics, who speak too boldly. Lord Darcy sent for by his friends, lest his lands be forfeited for recusancy. Sir Hen. Wotton has printed a letter to defend the King against the charge of sending Ambassadors "*ad mentiendum reipublicæ causâ.*" [*Venice Corresp., Dec.* 19.]

Dec. 17. London. 65. Chamberlain to Carleton. Sir Rich. Coxe, and five others, fined in the Star Chamber for reporting a slander against the Lord Privy Seal. Bailey, the Prince's Chaplain, being enjoined to explain his sermon, repeated his accusation, and others have preached in the same strain. Solemn obsequies performed for the Prince at Oxford, and elegies written. Death of Sir Wm. Sydney, Lord Lisle's eldest son; also of old Sir Thos. Shirley, and Sir John Harrington. The King gone from Royston to Theobalds. Sir Fras. Bacon, in his Essay on Deformity, has described to the life his little cousin [Salisbury]. Sir Hen. Wotton has printed a reply to Schoppius. A priest, named Latham or Molyneux, hanged at Tyburn, and died confidently. Mischief of allowing scaffold harangues.

Dec. 18. 66. Sir Wm. Fleetwood to the Same. The Prince's death owing, not to poison, but to the pestilential fever of the season. The King has returned from Royston to Whitehall; his grief moderated. He promises to consider the servants of the late Prince, whose death adds 50,000*l.* per ann. to his income. Mourning is soon to be laid aside, on account of the Lady Elizabeth's marriage, the dower agreement being signed. Projected changes of office. Begs, for a friend, a pound of quicksilver from the mines of Istria, which cannot be had without special licence, as it is reserved for the King of Spain's use in his goldworks in India.

Dec. 18. 67. Declaration of Fras. Conyers, of Ragley, co. Warwick, in behalf of Sir Edw. Conway, that he will deliver to Fras. Harewell, before Jan. 1 ensuing, a bond by which the late Sir Thos. Harewell and Fras. Harewell were pledged in 220*l.* to pay 110*l.* to Wm. Stannard, of London. *Annexed is,*

67. I. *Receipt by Fras. Harewell of the above bond, Dec.* 20, 1612.

Dec. 19. London. 68. Isaac Wake to Lady [Carleton]. Cannot get the Queen's picture yet. She sits in a darkened room hung with black, but speaks cheerfully. Funeral of Prince Henry; 2,000 mourners followed him from St. James's to Westminster by Charing Cross. Nine banners were carried by Earl's sons. Under the canopy a goodly image of the Prince, clothed in his richest garments, which caused many tears and sighs. Never beheld so much sorrow. Account of the mourners and of the ceremonial in the church. The Heralds, after proclaiming the late Prince's titles, wished Prince Charles longer life than his brother.

VOL. LXXI.

1612.
Dec. 20. Licence to Sir Rich. Wigmore to buy as much cod and ling as shall amount to 12,732 lasts for 21 years. [*Grant Bk.*, *p.* 101.]

Dec. 25. London. Isaac Wake to Carleton. Went to church to see the King's first appearance after the Prince's death. The people pleased with his cheerfulness. The Prince Palatine and Lady Elizabeth there. The King in bed with a sore toe, but will not have it called the gout. Chapter of the Garter at Whitehall. The young Palatine and Count Maurice made Knights. Sir John Swinnerton charged the farmers of customs before the Council with defrauding the King in his imposts. A posthumous work of Parsons, the Jesuit, attacks Sir Hen. Wotton. Saw the King, Prince, and Lady Elizabeth go to chapel. The Bishop of Ely preached. The King received the communion. [*Venice Corresp.*, *Dec.* 25.]

Dec. 25. 69. Extract from the above.

Dec. 31. London. 70. Chamberlain to Carleton. Little prospect of Carleton's advancement, but hopes he will get allowance for mourning. The six months' commission for the Treasury is renewed. Sir Thos. Lake, at the affiancing of the Lady Elizabeth, translated the service into French so badly as to excite laughter. The Scots, since the Prince's death, wished to have her married to the Marquis of Hamilton. The Lord Mayor [Sir John Swinnerton] accused the farmers of customs of defrauding the King of 70,000*l.* a year, but they were acquitted. An Ambassador, come from Lorraine to condole, is expected to offer a match for the young Prince. Death of Lady Webb.

Dec. 31. London. Isaac Wake to the Same. The King is gone to Hampton Court. Mourning allowances to be given to foreign Ambassadors. On Dec. 27, the contract was solemnized between the Prince Palatine and Lady Elizabeth. Details of the ceremony. The Queen absent, not from distaste, but a fit of the gout. Overtures from Spain and France for matching the Prince. The latter likely to be accepted. [*Venice Corresp.*, *Dec.* 31

Dec. 31. 71. Extract from the above.

Dec. 31. Licence to Jos. Usher, Warner Rich, and Godfrey de Vette, to devise and exercise the new kind of instrument or engine to be wrought by water, wind, man, or horse, for fourteen years. [*Grant Bk.*, *p.* 97. *See Sept.* 21.]

Dec. 31. 72. Edw. Reynoldes to Sir John Rawlins. Remonstrates against his demand of 500*l.* towards his intended journey to Italy. Sir Geo. Coppin, who holds his money, will not advance it beforehand. Refuses to lend him more himself. Urges his return to Rouen, and thence to England. Points out the consequences of his prodigality. Sir Peter Osborne, Mr. Christopher, and himself are equal in the trust for him.

[Dec. 31.] 73. Duplicate of the above.

VOL. LXXI.

UNDATED. 1612?

1612? 74. Susan Nicholas to her brother, Edw. Nicholas, at Oxford. Has sent him accounts, and will send socks and books. Hopes he will come home this Whitsuntide.

75. The Same to the Same, at Oxford. Could not write before, having the toothache and the mumps.

[Oxford.] 76. Wm. Bow to the Same. Thanks for his Latin letter; college news.

77—84. Latin verses and orations written by Edw. Nicholas at college; most of them in letters addressed to his father. Eight papers.

85, 86. Two similar papers from Matthew Nicholas.

Anonymous to ———. For warrants to search Sir Art. Ashin's house, called White Webbs, much frequented by recusants, where the Gunpowder Treason was hatched; also another house, a mile distant, at Holly Bush Hill, equally dangerous. [*Gunpowder Plot Bk., No.* 235.]

87. Thos. Wilson to Ambrose Randolph, his son-in-law. Sends him another mistress to wear next his heart, and prevent his doting too much on his new wife. Has not her present ready yet.

88. Articles exhibited against Gerard Prior, Vicar of Elsfield, diocese Worcester, by his parishioners, complaining of many irreverent and immoral acts.

89. Tract, addressed by Sir Walter Cope to the King, on the injuries sustained by the English from the Hollanders in trade, more especially in coinage, cloth, and fishing.

90. Rough draft of the above tract.

91. Reasons why the copyholders of Spaldwick, co. Huntingdon, refuse to purchase their copyholds; and notes on the state of the manor, addressed to some party who wishes to purchase it.

92. Memorandum of the quantities of plate given to certain foreign Ambassadors [chiefly French], from 21 Eliz. to 10 Jac. I., and of that received by Sir Geo. Carew, when Ambassador in France.

93. List of the Lords, Bishops, and Peers of England, and of the Ladies Dowager.

94. Licence to Edw. Sheldon, of Beoly, co. Worcester, to go to the Spa for recovery of his health.

95. Account of the lands and possessions of the late Monastery of Kirkstall, co. York.

96. Estimate of the benefit that His Majesty receives in household provisions bought by composition and by convention, besides the benefit of carriage at his removals.

VOL. LXXI.

1612 ? 97. "Extracts out of the records, wherein may be collected by what means the Kings of England have and may raise money, written by Sir R[obert] C[otton], Knight and Baronet."

98. Points for consideration in an intended commission for managing the King's revenue, viz., to supervise the compositions with recusants, many of whom pay nothing or much less than ordered by law; to revise debts installed, and procure their speedy payment; to examine into the sales of the King's woods, many of which are sold much below their value; to grant fee-farm leases of the Crown lands at greatly augmented rents; to take the accounts of the Receiver of the Court of Wards and Liveries, as the new orders must greatly increase its revenues; to estimate the income and expenditure of the Crown, and assign certain revenues to certain objects which are of greatest importance.

99. Arguments to prove that the revenue of the Court [of Wards], arising from rents of wards' lands, may be greatly increased; with instances from lands in Northamptonshire.

100. List of fees of officers in the Courts at Westminster, officers of the household, captains and soldiers of castles and bulwarks, keepers of houses, parks, forests, and chaces, &c.

101. The Dean, Prebendaries, and Scholars of Christ Church, Oxford, to Rochester. Complimentary. Request him to become their patron, and a member of their college, which boasts a regal foundation, and has the Duke of Lenox, Lord Aubigny, Sackvilles, Cliffords, and Sydneys, as members. Latin.

102. Orders issued by Sir John Swinnerton, Lord Mayor of London, and Conservator of the River Thames and Waters of Medway, for the preservation of the fish, especially salmon, in the Thames. Printed.

103. Notes of the title of the City of London to the conservancy of the Thames from Staines Bridge, westward, to the water of Medway, eastward.

104. Plan of Bowewood, in Chippenham Forest, co. Wilts.

105. Memorial showing the disadvantages to general trade from the Merchant Adventurers' Company exporting so large a quantity of undressed cloth, and proposing that, by way of penalty, they should pay a sum of money to His Majesty.

106. Observations by Mr. Misselden on "The occasion of the great imposition upon English Cloth in the Prince Cardinal's countries, and the cause of the continuance thereof."

Divers commissions to the Earls of Ellesmere, Salisbury, and Northampton, and others, to hear and try rebellious persons in divers counties. [*Grant Bk. p.* 90.]

Vol. LXXII. January—May, 1613.

1613.

Jan. 1. 1. Sir John Swinnerton to Rochester. Offers him 1,000*l.* per ann. to obtain for him the farming of the imposts on wines, which in the late Queen's time he had for twelve years, and raised from 6,000*l.* to 15,000*l.* Has been instrumental in raising the customs 33,700*l.* per ann. *Incloses,*

1. i. *Offer by Sir John Swinnerton and others to pay for the tonnage and imposts on French and Rhenish wines* 22,000*l. per ann., being an advance of* 8,000*l. over the former rent, and* 6,000*l. fine, to be disposed of by Visct. Rochester.*

Jan. 1? 2. Fras. Jones, Wm. Garway, John Wolstenholme, and Nich. Salter, to the King. Have proved themselves free from all fraud in their patent for French wines, and, though they know their patent is good in law, have authorized Visct. Rochester to offer on their behalf an increase in rent of 3,000*l.* per ann.

Jan. 2. London. 3. Sir Thos. Hunt, Sir Wm. Herrick, and Sir Thos. Hewitt, to Sir Robt. Cotton. Think the Aldermen of London have misinterpreted an order issued from the Commissioners of the Earl Marshalship, in claiming thereon precedence over Knights, whereas they had only petitioned for the precedence of knighted Aldermen over other Knights. Request him to represent the case to the Lord Privy Seal, who is "so noble and judiciall in respecting titles of honour."

Jan. 5. 4. Statement of the fraudulent conduct of Sir John Swinnerton, in reference to his lease of the farm of sweet wines, in shifting an unfair proportion of his rent on to the new imposts, which are now in mortgage to the City of London, and which he, being Mayor, takes care shall not be redeemed. With reference thereon.

[Jan. 5.] 5. Copy of the above, with slight addition.

Jan. 6. Court at Whitehall. Sir Thos. Lake to Carleton. The black is wearing out, and the marriage pomps preparing. The winter has been stormy and rainy. The physicians hope for much sickness in the spring, and the countrymen fear a murrain of cattle. The Countess of Oxford lately dead, and the Countess of Bedford dangerously sick. [*Venice Corresp., Jan.* 6, 1613.]

Jan. 6. Grant to Bonham Norton of the office of printer and bookseller in the Latin, Greek, and Hebrew tongues, for thirty years. [*Grant Bk., p.* 96.]

Jan. 7. London. 6. Chamberlain to Carleton. The Council have urged the King to appoint new officers, especially Secretaries. His inclination is for Sir Ralph Winwood. Rochester favours Sir Hen. Neville. The Duke of Bouillon is an earnest solicitor for Sir Thos. Edmondes. Rochester is in hand for the reversion of Lord Darcy's land. The great winds have demolished Dover pier. Messengers of condolence are come from the Duke of Guise and Prince of Conti. Sir Matthew Carew said to be cheated of 9,000*l.* in a purchase from Sir Wm. Bond.

Vol. LXXII.

1613.

Jan. 7. London. 7. Giov. Franc. Biondi to Carleton. Much talk about a Spanish Armada which is gathering; some say it is for Virginia, some for England, some for Ireland. The latter most probable, because of the intelligence of Spain with Ireland; but the Hebrides Islands might afford a counterpoise. Splendid presents of plate made by the Prince Palatine to the Princess's household; 2,000*l.* value to Lord Harrington, 700*l.* to Mrs. Dudley, and 200*l.* to each of her other ladies. The King kept in London by bad weather. The offices unfilled. Little hope of Sir Hen. Wotton's becoming Secretary, because he is negligent, and does not help himself in court, where idolatry is necessary. Italian.

Jan. [8]. 8. Petition of the Clerks of the Signet and Privy Seal to the King. Complain of the loss of their fees, by sundry grants being passed by immediate warrant to the Great Seal, contrary to ancient custom, by which cause their clerks also lose the writing of the grants.

[Jan. 8.] 9. Copy of the above.

Jan. 8. 10. Draft of the above.

Jan. 10. Whitehall. 11. The Council to the Sheriffs, Deputy Lieutenants, and Justices of Counties. Renew the order of 27 Eliz. for taking away all armour from recusants, except what is needed for defence of their houses. Notice also to be taken what horses they keep fit for service.

Jan. 14. London. 12. Giov. Franc. Biondi to [Carleton]. Death of the Duke of Mantua. Carleton may perhaps be sent to condole with the Duchess. The King gone with a small train of forty persons to Royston. The Earls of Montgomery and Salisbury, and Lord Hay, practising for the wedding masque. Has made excuses to the Venetian Ambassador that Wake, now in England, does not visit him. His [Biondi's] pension being settled, wishes his papers sent, and his books, which Carleton has in pledge. Is intimate with Giulio Muscorno, Secretary to Foscarini, the Venetian Ambassador, and wishes Carleton to speak a good word for him privately at Venice. Italian.

Jan. 14. London. 13. Chamberlain to the Same. The Venetian Ambassador, Foscarini, displeased that Mr. Wake has not visited him. Biondi has got his pension of 100*l.* per ann. Both the Italian friars complain of shabby treatment from the two Archbishops. The King is gone to Royston and Newmarket. He took up a quarrel between Edw. Sackville, son of the Earl of Dorset, and Lord Bruce of Kinloss, who intended to go abroad to fight. Garter King-at-Arms gone to deliver the order of the Garter to Prince Maurice. Sir Rich. Morrison has bought the presidency of Munster from Lord Danvers for 3,000*l.*

Jan. 16. Newmarket. Proclamation against the use, manufacture, or importation of pocket-dags, or pistols, and commanding the surrender of all such. Printed. [*Proc. Coll., No.* 19.]

Jan. 18. London. 14. Denys Rasingham to Edm. Porter. His father sent for yesterday to Beaconsfield to Porter's brother, who lies very sick. The Stratford carrier has brought letters for Mr. Porter, but not the brawn.

VOL. LXXII.

1613.

Jan. 18. Newmarket. Proclamation against transportation of corn and grain, on account of its high price and apprehended scarcity. Printed. [*Proc. Coll., No.* 20.]

Jan. 20. London. 15. Receipt by Wm. Kindt of 2,000*l.*, for a great table diamond sold to the King by Jean Luce [de Luz], at Christmas 1611. French.

Jan. 22. London. Isaac Wake to Carleton. The King abroad. Sir Thos. Glover comes to town, and holds his head as high as though there were no charge against him. The match with a daughter of France eagerly pursued. [*Venice Corresp., Feb.* 1.]

Jan. 27. 16. Tim. Elks to Thos. Lumsden, Gentleman of the Privy Chamber. Is compelled to leave England to avoid the practices of his adversaries; cannot sustain his suits against so great a man [the Earl of Northumberland] without the King's special grace. Requests the value of half the goods taken from him by the malice of his adversaries.

Jan. 27. 17. Examination of Arnold Cranche, of Canterbury, respecting Wm. Colson, who said the Oath of Supremacy would make the King a pope, railed against the English clergy, and boasted of the friends he had in London.

Jan. 27? Lord Chancellor Ellesmere to the King. Regrets his inability from old age longer to discharge the duties of his office, and assigns his reasons for wishing to resign. [*Dom. Corresp., April* 25, 1616.]

Jan. 28. Newmarket. 18. Sir Humph. May to [Sir Thos. Lake?]. The King will answer the Lord Chancellor's letter on Saturday, from London. He was satisfied with the explanations about Sir Robt. Hitcham.

Jan. 28. London. 19. Chamberlain to Carleton. Great cause before the Court of Wards between Lady Lake and Lady Cæsar. The King has a bad toe, but it must not be called the gout. The Council complain of delays in business for want of assistance; but Sir Hen. Neville's hopes will be hindered by a breach between him and Visct. Fenton about the executorship of Sir John Norris. Rumours of danger from Papists, who are to be disarmed. Sir Thos. Glover has arrived, and justifies himself from any charge. Lady Shrewsbury, who has long had the liberty of the Tower, is in closer restraint, on account of some information given against her by Lady Arabella. Judge Williams and Sir Ant. St. Leger dead. Sir Thos. Bodley at his last gasp. A Hamburgh vessel has been cast away, value 80,000*l.* The Prince [Palatine] goes to Windsor to be installed on the 7th instant. He and the Princess are to leave in April.

Jan. 31. London. Isaac Wake to the Same. Disputes between Visct. Fenton and Sir Hen. Neville about Sir John Norris's will. Sir Thos. Bodley dead, "leaving all lovers of learning sorrowful bemoners of their owne loss in his." Some Egyptians [gipsies] in Leicestershire refusing to disband when summoned, the Earl of Huntingdon sent forces against them, which led to a report that the Papists were arming. Sir Peter Buck to be examined for scandalizing the Earl of Northampton. [*Venice Corresp., Feb.* 10.]

VOL. LXXII.

1613.
Jan.
Whitehall.

20. The Council to the Lord Lieutenant of Worcestershire. The King having ordered general musters on account of the late boldness of recusants, &c., he is to view the forces of the county, fill up the trained bands, supply defects of arms or furniture, repair the beacons, and see that a store of powder is laid up. The county is to be mustered in divisions, but on the same day, if possible, lest one man lend his horse or arms to another.

Jan.?

21. Request that the King would grant the farm of the imposts on all wines to the wine merchants, with the sole licence of importation of wines, for which they offer 65,000*l.* per ann., being an advance of 20,000*l.* upon the previous rent.

Jan.?

22. List of twenty-five grants of rents, recovered by Dr. Branthwait for Gonville and Caius College, since he was chosen Master.

Feb. 4.
London.

23. John Chamberlain to Alice Carleton. Projected marriage of Sir Hen. Savile's daughter Elizabeth with the only son of Sir Wm. Sedley, of Kent, who married the Lady Abergavenny. The Countess of Salisbury has a daughter, and lies in in great state. The Prince Palatine feasted the Council, showing great attention to the Archbishop. Liberality of Count Maurice to Garter King-at-Arms and Sir Ralph Winwood, on receiving the Garter. Death of Sir Thos. Bodley. Particulars of his will. He has left legacies to great people, 7,000*l.* to his library, and 200*l.* to Merton College; but little to his brothers, his old servants, his friends, or the children of his wife, by whom he had all his wealth.

Feb. 5.

Order in Council, made by the King's special direction, to restrain the killing and eating of flesh in Lent, or on Fridays throughout the year. Printed. [*Proc. Bk., p.* 263.]

Feb. 9.

24. Assignment by Isabel, widow of Lancelot Coker, of Barking, and Thos. Green, of East Smithfield, and Katherine his wife, to Thos. Cranwell, of London, of the lease of a tenement in Chitterling Alley, in the parish of All Saints, Barking, in London, leased to Lancelot Coker by Elizabeth, widow of Sir Fras. Cherry.

Feb. 10.
York House.

25. Lord Chancellor Ellesmere to Carleton. Desires his promotion, and will do all in his power to forward it.

Feb. 11.
London.

26. Chamberlain to the Same. Return of the Court from Windsor, where the Count Palatine and Count Maurice, represented by Count Louis of Nassau, were made Knights of the Garter. The Lords displeased that Count Maurice had precedence given next to the Princes. The Queen grows more favourable to the marriage, and it is hoped will be present. Suspicion of some intended treachery. The city has raised 500 musketeers to guard the Court. General musters ordered. Troubles in Ireland feared. Details of preparations for fireworks and mock fights on the water, Sir Robt. Mansell being commander. The Princess's followers have no means to provide their equipage, but to sell knightages at 150*l.* each. All her gentleman attendants are Scots, but the women, English. A benevolence

1613. Vol. LXXII.

talked of to be kept sacred for defence of the realm. Circuits of the judges changed. Lady Bedford, the Queen, Countess of Derby, and Lord Admiral stand sponsors for the Countess of Salisbury's daughter.

Feb. 12. London. Isaac Wake to Carleton. Visct. Rochester promises Carleton the pictures. Thos. Murray, who is about the Prince, is much courted, but his honesty makes him well esteemed. The Count Palatine made Knight of the Garter, and took the oath with a salvo of the laws of the empire; Count Louis with a similar one, for the constitutions of the United Provinces. Particulars of the feast. Lady Elizabeth going into Germany. Details of her suite, who are all Scots, which displeases the English. Count Schomberg governs the Prince Palatine. Sir Thos. Glover is confident of escaping blame, and boasts his services as rescuing 300 Christians from slavery, obtaining privileges for English ships in the Levant ports, &c. Sig. Foscarini * wooing a daughter of Sir Fras. Lacon. Anxiety of the Ambassadors to be invited to the coming feast. [*Venice Corresp., Feb.* 12, 1613.]

Feb. 12. 27. Extract from the above.

[Feb.] 28. Extracts from the above two letters; also from a third, not given, naming the persons forming the suite of the Princess. Lord and Lady Harrington are going, at their own expense, to see her settled in Germany. The Queen caresses the Count Palatine as if he were her own son. Lady Arabella, though still in the Tower, has shown her joy by buying four new gowns, one of which cost 1,500*l.*

Feb. 14. 29. James [?] Hay to Sir Thos. Lake. Signifies the King's pleasure to grant to John Bird a fine of 100 marks, imposed on Hen. Wayles, of Norfolk.

Feb. 18. London. 30. John Chamberlain to Alice Carleton. Fireworks on the water. Details of the marriage ceremony of the Prince Palatine and Princess Elizabeth. Dresses of the ladies. Masque of the Lords, and of the Middle Temple and Lincoln's Inn men, described. That of the Inner Temple and Gray's Inn, which was the marriage of the Thames and the Rhine, devised by Sir Fras. Bacon, failed, the King being so weary and sleepy that he refused to see it till Saturday. No farthingales were admitted at any of these shows.

Feb. 18. 31. Extract from the above, with slight alterations.

Feb. 22. London. 32. John Finet to Carleton. The Archduke's Ambassador refused to attend Lady Elizabeth's wedding, because the Venetian Ambassador was invited to an earlier part of the festival. The King offered explanations, but they were unavailing. Pretensions of the French and Venetian Ambassadors to have chairs, &c. at the feast. The French Ambassador's lady threatened to leave, because Lady Effingham wished to take precedence of her. Details of the marriage

* Expressed in the original in cipher, thus—15. 35. 44. 8. 4. 41. 24. 32. 22.

1613. Vol. LXXII.

ceremonial, the dresses, order of procession, splendid jewellery, &c. The jewels of the King, Queen, and Prince were valued at 900,000*l*. Masque of the Lords rich and ingenious, and those of the Inns of Court much commended. The King's feast to them was paid for by certain noblemen who were vanquished at the ring. The Prince improves daily, and has thrice carried off the ring. The King gone to Royston, where the Count Palatine is to join him.

Feb. 22. 33, 34. Two extracts from the above.

Feb. 22. Strand. 35. Sir Julius Cæsar to Carleton. Thanks for favours shown to his son at Venice. Cannot write news, as he has not even time to salute his friends.

Feb. 22. London. 36. Giov. Franc. Biondi to [the Same]. Mr. Wake leaves with such good opinions of all, especially of the King, that he should be obliged to Carleton for having sent him over.

Feb. 22. Whitehall. 37. Thos. Murray to the Same. A great wound recently inflicted on England and Europe [by the death of Prince Henry], but still hopes left for the future. Will send the Prince's portrait, when finished, to Sir Hen. Savile.

Feb. 22. 38. Account of sums paid into the receipt of the Pells by Fras. Jones, collector of the new impositions, since Oct. 1611. Total 2,261*l*. 7*s*. 0½*d*. Latin.

Feb. 22. Special commission to Hen. Earl of Kent of Lieutenancy in co. Bedford. [*Grant Bk.*, *p*. 89.]

Feb. 24. Commission to the Lord Chancellor, the Earl of Northampton, and others, to sell any lands in the survey of the Exchequer, Duchy or County Palatine of Lancaster, and to pass defective titles. [*Ibid.*, *p*. 89.]

Feb. 24. Lambeth. 39. Archbp. Abbot to Carleton. The two honest men sent over by Carleton last year do very well. Has received an Italian treatise dedicated to the King, being a supplication to all Christian Princes against the Court of Rome. As all despatches are now addressed to the King, Carleton will have a good opportunity to show his industry and good parts.

Feb. 24. Lambeth. 40. The Same to the Same. Has concerted with Wake a cipher to be used in correspondence between himself and Carleton, when necessary. Wake's long delay is not for want of diligence, but because he cannot get his despatch.

Feb. 24. London. 41. Sir Thos. Overbury to the Same. Note of affection. Sir Hen. Neville and Sir Robt. Killigrew desire remembrances.

Feb. 24. London. 42. Andrews, Bishop of Ely, to the Same. Reference to a matter on which he had spoken with Mr. Chamberlain, whose late writing is not suitable to see the light. Revising the Council of Trent is a matter of great importance, but God and Christian Princes must take up this matter by other means than the pen.

VOL. LXXII.

1613.

Feb. 25. King Street. 43. Sir Hen. Wotton to Carleton. Is in Westminster with a few books about him, "more attending the study of truth than of humor;" contented with his own poor thoughts, and "vicinæ nescius urbis." Has lost two great patrons within the year.

Feb. 25. Chancery Lane. 44. Sir Matt. Carew to the Same. Has endured great misfortunes, his estates in Worcestershire, for which he paid 9,000*l.* to Sir Wm. Bond, proving to be much encumbered. His son [in law] Cromer, ill; one of his sons roving after hounds and hawks, the other studying in the Middle Temple, but doing little at law. His daughter is his only comfort.

Feb. 25. Durham House. 45. Adam Newton to [the Same]. Waited to reply to Carleton's letters in hope that the late Prince would also write, but his "incomparable loss" has precluded that hope, and also his own chance of doing Carleton service.

Feb. 25. London. 46. Sir Edw. Phelips to the Same. Festivities at the marriage of the Princess. The Masques of the Middle Temple and Lincoln's Inn were praised above all others. The King feasted the Inns of Court, sitting at the same board. No Treasurer nor Secretary yet appointed, nor likely to be. The question whether the Duchy of Cornwall now reverts to the King or to the Prince is settled in favour of the latter.

Feb. 25? London. 47. Declaration of the King confirming the title of Prince Charles, Duke of York, to the Duchy of Cornwall, to which his right is proved by legal arguments and former precedents, which are all given at length. Published by the King's command. Printed.

Feb. 25. London. 48. Chamberlain to Carleton. Was sent for by Sir Walter Cope to see Carleton's papers burnt [his letters to the late Earl of Salisbury]. The King went on Monday to Theobalds, Royston, and Newmarket. The Prince and Count Palatine will follow him. The match gives general satisfaction, and the Queen is quite reconciled to it. The masque of the Gray's Inn and Inner Templars came off very well, and the masquers were entertained by the King, but at the cost of the Prince and his followers, who laid a wager for the charges of the feast, and lost it in running at the ring. No Peers created except the Deputy of Ireland, who is made Lord Chichester. Sir Thos. Bodley, in his life written by himself, never mentions his wife nor Secretary Walsingham, nor the Earl of Leicester, who were his chief raisers. At the late wedding, Lyon King-at-Arms wore the arms of Scotland before those of England, which was much noted.

Feb. 26. 49. Examination of Rich. Grimstone, Pursuivant. Was sent by the Countess of Essex after Mary Woods, to whom she had delivered a ring set with a diamond and some money, to take charge of when she was going in haste to Court. Davison, of Norwich, says that Mary Woods professed skill in palmistry, deluding simple women and threatening if they prosecuted her, to accuse them of trying to poison their husbands.

Vol. LXXII.

1613.
Feb. 26. 50. Re-examination of Rich. Grimstone. He did not persuade Mary Woods to call herself a laundress, but if she would have returned him the goods which Lady Essex sent him to reclaim, he would have let her alone, though he knew of the Lord Chief Justice's warrant against her.

Feb. 26. 51, 52. Copies of the two preceding papers.

Feb. 26. Suffolk. 53. Examination of Mary Woods, of Stratton-Strawless, near Norwich. She received a goblet and a diamond from Mrs. Clare, and a ring from Lady Essex, with the promise of 1,000*l.* if she would procure some poison to kill the Earl of Essex, that should not act within three or four days. She repented afterwards, would not get it, and left London.

Feb. 26. 54. Examinations of Fras. Minshull and John Woods relative to the peculations of Mary Woods.

Feb. 26? 55. Relation of [Rich. Grimstone], Pursuivant, of his apprehension of Mary Woods. She refused to give up the goods, and when told she must go before the justice, said she would declare that she had them given to induce her to poison the Earl of Essex.

Feb. 26. Commission to the Lord Chancellor, Earl of Northampton, and others, to allow to Robt. Typper such recompence as they, or any five of them, shall think meet, for his service concerning the Commission for sale of lands, &c. [*Grant Bk., p.* 89.]

Feb. 26. London. 56. Wm. Lake to Carleton. Thanks him for hastening his return to England, and giving him a letter of recommendation which will avail him should Sir Thos. Lake be advanced.

Feb. 26. London. 57. Sir Hen. Savile to the Same. Sends more copies of his work; the price is 8*l.* per copy, exclusive of carriage. Death of Sir Thos. Bodley; he is to be buried by his own appointment at Merton College Church, Oxford.

Feb. 26. London. 58. Sir Hen. Neville to the Same. Sends no news, as his Secretary [Wake] will tell all. Thanks for remembrances. All wheels standing still, depending upon that at Court.

Feb. 26. Savoy. 59. Geo. Lord Carew to the Same. Will endeavour to obtain for him a portrait of the Queen, but the mourning for the Prince, the marriage of the Princess, and the Queen's own indisposition, have prevented his soliciting it hitherto.

Feb. 27. The Pall of London. 60. John King, Bishop of London, to the Same. The festivals have passed, not without caution against "some practise so much prognosticated." The King shows his people that he will not be surprised sleeping. Rome would be mistress of the church, and Spain, of nations. The University [of Oxford] prospers, for though the "great Ptolemee [Sir Thos. Bodley] is gone, he liveth in his bountifull legacy."

Vol. LXXII.

1613.

Feb. 27. Doctor's Commons, London. 61. Dr. Hen. Marten to Carleton. Thanks for remembrance. His [Marten's] old servant Nicholas is now coachman to the Lord Chief Baron of Ireland.

Feb. 27. London. 62. Sir John Bennet to the Same. Is trustee to Sir Thos. Bodley's will, making the University of Oxford his heir. Thanks him and Lady Carleton for their kindness to his son in his dangerous sickness.

Feb. 27. London. 63. Sir Thos. Lowe to the Same. Thanks for kindness to his son and to Hen. Parvis.

Feb. 28. London. 64. Matthew de Quester to the Same. Sent him packets from Mr. Wake last week. Professes zeal in his service.

[Feb.] 65. Nich. Lanyer to the Same. Love and service. Refers to Mr. Wake for news. The world so altered since the death of his good master [the Prince] that he knows not which is "the more dangerous attempt, to turne courtier or cloune."

[Feb.] 66. Anagrams on the Princess Elizabeth and Frederic Count Palatine, by Geo. Tashe, formerly page to the King's father.

March 1. 67. Sir Dud. Digges to Carleton. Has lost powerful friends, but will still be glad to serve him. Though strange changes grow in Court, all will go well.

March 1. 68. Giov. Franc. Biondi to [the Same]. A new Ambassador expected [from Venice]. Will be glad when he comes. Sends him a new engraving. Does not believe the report that the last sent was by Marta, Neapolitan Professor in Padua. The Savoyan Ambassador daily expected. Illness of the Lord Chancellor, and Earls of Northampton and Somerset. Lord Harrington, in order to pay his debts, which are 30,000*l.*, obtained leave to call in all tradesmen's tokens, and to coin a brass money, which should be generally current, but the King stopped the patent at the entreaty of the Duke of Lenox, who wanted to share the profit. This Harrington refused, and now neither he nor his wife is able to attend the Princess on her journey, on account of their debts. The King intends to choose some other lady. Italian.

March 3. Whitehall. Order in Council on a Petition referred to them by the King, from the Clothworkers and Dyers of London, that the Statutes against the export of undyed and undressed cloths should be enforced, and no licences granted therefor. The Petitioners, with the Merchant Adventurers and other parties concerned, are ordered to bring in their reasons and replies to Sir Julius Cæsar, Chancellor of the Exchequer, and the Attorney and Solicitor General, who are to report thereon. [*Dom. Corresp.*, *March* 14.]

March 3. Copy of the above. [*Ibid.*]

March ? 69. Observations on the suit of the Clothworkers and Dyers, that all cloths may be dressed and dyed before they are exported, showing

VOL. LXXII.

1613.

the benefits that would accrue, answering objections, and stating the inconveniences of the present mode of exporting cloth undressed and undyed.

March ? 70. A Merchant of the Eastland Company to Lord ——. Gives a detailed account of the state of the cloth trade in various counties of England, of the amount of exports of cloth, dressed or undressed, by the Eastland, Turkey, Spanish, Barbary, and Merchant Adventurers' Companies, and shows the difficulties of the proposed project for the Merchant Adventurers to have their cloths dyed and dressed before exportation.

March 4. Newmarket. 71. The King to the Archbp. of Canterbury. Cautions to be observed in examining Sir John York, Sir Wm. Ingleby, and others, on suspicion of being concerned in the Powder Treason.

March 5. London. 72. Giov. Franc. Biondi to [Carleton]. A gentleman called Bacon, a relation of Lord Wotton, begs to be recommended to him. The English Ambassador in Spain writes words of peace about the Spanish Armada. The Prince Palatine is at Cambridge.

March 7. London. 73. Grant by Wm. Segar Garter King-at-Arms, to Gideon Launey, the King's servant, and his brothers, sons of Dr. Wm. Launey, who died in London in 1610, of the arms of the family of Launey, of Belmesnil, in Normandy, from which they are descended.

March 11. London. 74. Chamberlain to Carleton. Lord Lisle offered his son Sir Robt. Sydney to Sir Hen. Savile's daughter, who is already engaged to Sir Wm. Sedley. The Palgrave presented Sir Hen. Savile with gold plate, value 50*l.* for his Chrysostom. The Princess's train will be but small, as all expenses are to be saved. The Count Palatine's household is dismissed, which she takes much to heart. He and the Prince went to Cambridge, where they had excellent comedies. The King escaped a great danger at Newmarket, from the sinking of the foundations of the house where he was. Many coiners apprehended. Lord Harrington, in recompence of 30,000*l.* spent on the Princess, has a licence to coin farthings. The Archduke is to have the offer of redeeming the Burgundy plate, or else it will be coined. Lady Arabella ill of convulsions, and said to be distracted. Sir Thos. Glover has cleared himself of all charges. Giov. Battista, the friar at York, wrote a Latin poem on the marriage.

March 12. London. 75. Giov. Franc. Biondi to the Same. Sends him a book which he bought at St. Paul's. The Prince Palatine will not leave till April 24. Italian.

March ? 76. Edw. Reynoldes to [Thos. Martin ?]. Has yielded to the request of his nephew to be allowed to go over to France with the Ambassador.

March 12. Grant to John Holloway of the Controllership of the Customs and Subsidies in the Port of London, for life. [*Grant Bk., p.* 94.]

Vol. LXXII.

1613.

March 13. Lambeth. 77. Examination of John Meden. Is a Scotchman, and Master Gunner of a Spanish merchant ship, and brought figs and tobacco into England, but no chests of silver. Was once at the Spanish Ambassador's, and heard mass, but knows no one there. Was at Newgate, and confessed by a priest there.

March 14. 78. Order in Council that Sir Walter Cope, Master of the Wards, the Master of the Rolls, Lord Chief Justices, and Chief Baron, be joined with the persons already named, to hear the cause relative to the dyeing and dressing of cloth for exportation. [*See March* 3.]

March 14. 79. Copy of the above.

March 16. Paris. Sir Thos. Edmondes to Sir Thos. Lake. Sir Geo. Shirley is much troubled to hear that his armour has lately been taken out of his house in Northamptonshire, on pretext of his being a recusant. He is not one, has always kept a preacher, and been diligent, as a Justice of the Peace, in administering the Oath of Allegiance. Is going to the Spa when the weather permits. [*French Corresp., March* 16, 1613.]

March 17. London. 80. Giov. Franc. Biondi to [Carleton]. His [Carleton's] conduct in Venice much praised by the Venetian Ambassador in England, who is not popular. The King favours him because he professes to be a Protestant, but the Councillors ridicule him. The King not yet returned. The nobles eagerly waiting for office. Sends a work of Giov. Maria, one of the two friars sent into England; also the Epithalamia [on the Palatine's marriage], written at Oxford. The Spanish Ambassador complains of one of them, and his adherents say they will all be burnt. Italian.

March 18. 81. List of the armour, horse furniture, and weapons of Wm. Copley, received by John Woodman, Constable of Reigate.

March 20. Whitehall. 82. The Commissioners for Defective Titles to the pretended owner of the lands in Sillesworth, co. Northampton, forfeit by the attainder of Sir Wm. Catesby, and granted by Hen. VIII. to John Halliwell. Require him to repair to Wm. Typper, before April 1, to make composition for his defective title, according to the proclamation, as otherwise the course of law against him cannot longer be stayed.

March 20. 83—89. Certificates from different parties to prove that Christian Wilhelmson brought the trade of making smalt or blue starch into England in 1603; that he erected ovens, mills, &c., at Southwark, for its manufacture, at great expense; that Abraham Baker learned the secret of the work from his people; and that the pretexts of Baker and others that they are the inventors, by which they have obtained a Patent for its sole making, are false. With certificate by the Painter Stainers' Company of London, that Wilhelmson's smalt was good, but that sold by Baker so bad that they are obliged to send for a supply from abroad. Seven papers.

Vol. LXXII.

1613.

March 20. Grant to Jas. Lord Hay of the Office of Keeper of the Great Wardrobe, for life. [*Grant Bk.*, *p.* 93.]

March 23. 90. Lease from Edw. Waringes to Thos. Fitzgerald, both of London, of a messuage in Kingston-upon-Thames, co. Surrey.

March 25. London. 91. Chamberlain to Carleton. The great funeral at Oxford is the last act of Sir Thos. Bodley's vanity, whose ambition appears in many ways. Death of Langley, the Town Clerk thrust on the city by the late Lord Treasurer. The King returned to town. Actors in the great tilting at Court. The King angry with the Cambridge men for a disputation whether elective or hereditary sovereignties are preferable. Report that the Pope is preparing forces against Ireland. All shipping stayed till Lady Elizabeth is gone, there being such decay of navigation that 2,500 mariners cannot be furnished without much ado. The Master of the Rolls withstands the proposal of the Earls of Suffolk and Salisbury to relinquish to the King their patents for currants and Venice glass and silks, because they will be grievances complained of next parliament. Count Henry of Nassau in love with the Earl of Northumberland's daughter.

March 26. Nottingham. 92. Commissioners for the Musters in Nottinghamshire to the Council. Have held the musters as required, and supplied the defects of horses, arms, powder, and beacons; but some of the clergy refused to appear, being lately surveyed by order of the Archbp. of York.

March 26. London. 93. Lord Admiral Nottingham to the Mayor, &c. of Exeter. Commissions them, according to the tenor of his patent, of April 4, 1610, which is recapitulated, to impress ships, mariners, stores, &c. for the suppression of pirates, in recompence whereof they are permitted to keep for their own use the vessels and goods of such pirates as they shall seize.

March 26. Westminster. Warrant for payment of 2,350*l.* to Thos. Stone, to be given by him to Sir Robt. Dudley to complete the sum of 7,000*l.* for Killingworth Park, bought for the late Prince. [*Sign Man.*, *vol.* III., *No.* 1.]

March 27. Knowsley. 94. Wm. Earl of Derby, Lord Lieutenant of Cheshire and Lancashire, to the Council. Has taken the musters, but will be unable to return a perfect certificate by April 1. The deficiencies being great cannot be made up in so short a time. *Incloses.*

94. I. *Certificate of the musters in Cheshire. March* 18.

March ? 95. Queries respecting provisions, &c. for the musters, in Cheshire, and the maintenance of the soldiers who are to be sent to Ireland.

March 27. Licence to Edm. Brunt to make and use in England and Wales a new kind of engine for dressing meal, for twenty-one years. [*Grant Bk.*, *p.* 102.]

March 29. Grant to Wm. Salisbury of the land called the Tervyn Maure *alias* Gwern-Vawr and Bryn y Keliog, &c., co. Denbigh, and to Hugh Middleton, of the Park of Ruthin, co. Denbigh. [*Ibid.*, *p.* 119.]

VOL. LXXII.

1613.

March 29. Gift by Wm. Jones, citizen and haberdasher of London, of the foundation of a school in the town of Monmouth, appointing the four Wardens of the Haberdashers' Company and their successors to be Governors of the same. [*Grant Bk., p.* 117.]

March 29. Bletsoe. 96. Oliver Lord St. John to the Council. Has held the musters, but had great difficulty in filling up the number of the forces in Huntingdonshire, viz., 400 foot and 46 horse, besides 48 foot and 5 horse provided by the clergy. Many of the better sort being dead or removed, he has had to join two or three yeomen together to supply a petronel.

March 29. Grant to Robt. Gorges, of Plymouth, of pardon for manslaughter of Alex. Hamon, of Exeter, in a sudden quarrel. Latin. [*Sign Man., vol.* III., *No.* 2.]

March 29. Westminster. Commission appointing the Earl of Nottingham to take the command of the squadron of six ships and pinnaces appointed to convey the Lady Elizabeth and the Elector Palatine into the Low Countries. [*Ibid., No.* 3.]

March 30. Lambeth. 97. Archbp. Abbot to [Carleton]. The King is pleased that Carleton checked the Capuchin friar who spoke scandalously about Queen Elizabeth. Knows nothing bad of Biondi, but is always suspicious of Italian convertitos. The Venetian Ambassador's Secretary complained falsely before the Recorder of London that his master was plotting his assassination.

March 30. Charter House. 98. Fras. Earl of Rutland to the Council. Details the proceedings of his Deputy Lieutenants in taking the musters, &c. in Lincolnshire. They have added 80 to the footmen, but the horse are much decayed. *Incloses.*

98. I. *Certificate of the musters in Lincolnshire.*

March 30. Confirmation of the liberties formerly granted to the Company of English Merchants for discovery of new trades in Russia and Muscovy, and prohibiting all, not of that Company, to trade in Cherry Island, Greenland, or other Islands discovered by the said Company, &c.; also granting new liberties. [*Grant Bk., pp.* 117, 128.]

March 31. Westminster. Warrant to pay to Sir Edw. Cecil 330*l.*, the balance due for armour, value 450*l.*, made for the late Prince. [*Sign Man., vol.* III., *No.* 4.]

March 31. Westminster. Warrant for payment of necessary sums to Sir Andrew Keith, Master of the Horse to the Princess Elizabeth, to defray expenses of the two coachmen and their servant who brought the rich coach presented to her by her husband. [*Ibid., No.* 5]

March. 99. Certificate of the defective and unserviceable armour in the County Palatine of Durham.

[March.] 100. Account of payments made by the Farmers of the Customs, and allowed on their account for the year 10 Jac. I.

[March.] 101. Similar account, not duplicate.

VOL. LXXII.

1613.

March ? Rye. 102. Indictment of Robt. Alexander, of Newhaven, Sussex, and other mariners, for an assault committed March 29, 1613, on the sea near Maidstone, in the Cinque Ports, on Nich. Sprage and others, and for taking their boat and nets, &c.

April 1. Lambeth. 103. Archbp. Abbot to [Carleton]. Sir Wm. Waad knows no such person as Babington alias Ducking, who is an impostor, as was another Englishman, Mapleton, who went abroad and raised money by pretending to have suffered for the Romish cause, and then ran away with another man's wife.

April 1. 104. Hen. Earl of Southampton to the Council. Has ordered the musters in Hampshire. The arms are satisfactory; the powder and beacons shall be attended to.

April 2. Charter House. 105. Robt. Earl of Sussex to the Same. Musters of the foot have been held in Essex, but those of the horse are not yet complete.

April 2. Licence to the Wardens and Company of Booksellers of London to print and sell Cato's distichs and other books for twenty-one years. [*Grant Book, p.* 128.]

April 2. Grants to Sir Jas. and Sir Robt. Carr, of Scotland, of denization. [*Docquet.*]

April 2. Grant to Wm. Moys, Second Clerk of the Avery to the King, of pension of 40*l.* per annum. [*Docquet.*]

April 2. Warrant for payment of necessary sums to Lord Hay for charges of Lady Elizabeth's journey into Germany. [*Docquet.*]

April 2. Letter to Auditor Gofton for discharge to Jeffrey Duppa and Geo. Freeman, Brewers, of an arrear of 88*l.* 4*s.*, incurred by removing beer for His Majesty, and not through their default. [*Docquet.*]

April 2. Warrant for delivery of a coat, &c. to Archibald Armstrong. [*Docquet.*]

April ? 106. Petition of Roger Bassett to the King, to be admitted Servant of the Crossbows to the Prince.

April ? 107. List of Prince Charles's servants.

April ? 108. Another list, annotated with changes expected on the establishment of his household.

April ? 109. Annotated list [by Sir Jas. Fullerton] of persons to be considered of by the King as fit to be made of the Prince's household, including all his present servants, and forty-nine of those who served the late Prince.

April ? 110. Copy of a portion of the above list.

April ? 111. Draft of a portion of the above list, with fuller annotations. The meaner servants are omitted, as fit to be decided on by a Commission rather than by the King.

Vol. LXXII.

1613.

April 2. Warrant for payment of yearly allowances to the servants of the late Prince Henry, appointed now to attend Prince Charles. [*Docquet.*]

April 2. Warrant for payment of 127*l.* 14*s.* to Mons. Schantmalt, sent to the King with hawks from Mons. Vitry. [*Docquet.*]

April 2. Warrant for delivery of stuff to the footmen, coachman, and littermen of the Queen, Prince, and Lady Elizabeth, for their liveries. [*Docquet.*]

April 2. Indenture for delivery of 1,000 tons of alum per ann. for four years to Wm. Turner and others, on their resignation of an annuity of 6,044*l.* payable to them by the King. [*Docquet.*]

April 2. Like indenture, conveying to His Majesty the alum mines, &c., with the stock, &c. [*Docquet.*]

April 3. 112. List of Commissioners of Oyer and Terminer for piracy in the Cinque Ports.

April 5. Commission to Sir Edw. Cecil to receive and pay all moneys for the journey of Lady Elizabeth and her husband, and their trains. [*Grant Bk., p.* 106.]

April 5. Canon Row. 113. Edw. Earl of Hertford to the Council. Desires a longer time for the musters of Wiltshire and Somersetshire, to supply defects concealed by former borrowing of arms. Zeal of Bristol for the King's service in the musters. *Incloses,*

113. I. *Certificate of musters for the city of Bristol. Total force* 300. *March* 21.

April 10. 114. Warrant by Wm. Ward, Mayor of Dover, Marshal of the Admiralty Court of the Cinque Ports, and Collector of the Droits, &c., appointing Peter Dibb, of Dover, to act as his deputy. Latin.

April 16. Grant to Robt. Strickland of the office of Keeper and Filer of all bills, &c. in the Court of the Exchequer of Chester, for life. [*Grant Bk., p.* 120.]

April 16. London. 115. Giov. Franc. Biondi to [Carleton]. The Princess is gone. Lord Harrington's patent for farthings is limited to 25,000*l.*, so that it is feared he may lose by it, as they will be easily imitated. The Queen tried to persuade the Venetian Ambassador that the Duke of Savoy wanted to marry one of his daughters to the King of Denmark, which is not true, the Duke having refused a sister of the King of Denmark. Italian.

April 16. Wrest. 116. Hen. Earl of Kent to the Council. Has taken the musters in Bedfordshire. All is in good condition excepting the horse. Begs a reduction in the number required, the county being so small.

Vol. LXXII.

1613.

April 20. 117. Sir Peter Freshville and Sir John Harpur, Deputy Lieutenants of Derbyshire, to the Earl of Shrewsbury, Lieutenant. Have held the musters, and found all in good condition except the horse forces, which require further time. The clergy, on an order from the Bishop, refuse to appear.

April 20. Coventry. 118. Order made at the Court Leet of Coventry that all broadcloths manufactured in the city be brought to the Cloth Hall, to be weighed and sealed, on penalty of a fine.

April 21. Whitehall. 119. The Council to the Lieutenant of the Tower. Order him to receive and keep close prisoner Sir Thos. Overbury, against whom the King is displeased for a matter of high contempt.

April 22. Westminster. Grant to Lord Vaux, of Harrowden, of his lands, &c. of Harrowden, and others, cos. Essex, Bedford, Nottingham, Lincoln, and Cambridge, which were forfeited to the King, on his conviction in a Præmunire, for refusing the Oath of Allegiance. [*Sign Man., vol.* III., *No.* 6.]

April 23. Commission to the Lord Chancellor and others to sell, for ready money, the King's remainders of entailed lands within the survey of the Exchequer and Duchy of Lancaster. Wm. Typper appointed to attend the said service, and receive one sixth of the profits. [*Docquet.*]

April 23. Re-grant to Edw. Greg of the Examinership of the Court of Exchequer of Chester, to which he was appointed by the late Prince, with reversion to his son, Robt. Greg. [*Docquet.*]

April 23. Grant to Fras. Morris and Fras. Phelips, and their heirs, of purchase of rectories, lands, &c. not named; value 110*l.* 3*s.* per ann. [*Docquet.*]

April 27. Grant to Inigo Jones, in reversion after Simon Basill, of the office of Surveyor of Works. [*Docquet.*]

April 29. London. 120. Chamberlain to Carleton. Poverty of the Exchequer, &c. The Prince Palatine and Lady Elizabeth are detained by contrary winds. She is meanly attended as to ladies, having only the Countess of Arundel and Lady Harrington. The King and Queen accompanied them to Rochester; the Prince to Canterbury. The King refused a suit of the Prince Palatine for the delivery of Lord Grey, and several other requests, which made the Prince complain that he was treated as a child rather than as a son. Lord Grey and Lady Arabella are kept more closely than before, because he sent her love messages by one of her women. The Countess of Shrewsbury more restrained, and on good cause. The King, desiring to falsify the report that Rochester ruled him, and Overbury, Rochester, determined to remove Overbury. Some foreign embassy was pressed upon him, which he positively declined, saying the King could not in law or justice compel him to leave his country; for which contempt he was sent to the Tower. The King declares this is no slight on Rochester, in whose conversation he delights more than in any man's living. The Exchequer being at

1613. Vol. LXXII.

a dead stand for want of money, Rochester gave them for the King a chest of gold of 22,000*l.* Many peers refuse to concur in a request for the dukedom of Richmond to be granted to the Duke of Lenox. Lady Essex accused by a wise woman of a design to poison her husband, wherefore her friends have dropped the idea of suing for a divorce. Some of the nobility of Muscovy having offered to put themselves under the King's protection, he is full of a scheme to send an army there, and rule that country by a deputy, and is sanguine of success. Projects for carrying on the Persian trade by way of the Caspian Sea, Volga, and Dwina, to Archangel, and thence to England. The Queen, with a noble train, gone to Bath. At Lord Knollys' house, *en route*, she was entertained with a masque, by the Lord Chamberlain's four sons and others.

April 30. Release to Lewis Duke of Lenox of sums owing for the subsidy and alnage of vendible clothes and draperies, and for the moiety of the forfeitures thereof. [*Grant Bk., p.* 127.]

April. 121. Sir Hen. Savile to Carleton. Sends him thirty-six copies [of his work on St. Chrysostom]. Begs him to present one to the Seignory [of Venice], who will perhaps give in exchange a medal worth half a zechin, with a suitable inscription. A match concluded for Bess Savile with Sir Wm. Sedley's son.

April? 122 Charge for decorations, &c. of the vessels employed to convey the Elector Palatine and Princess Elizabeth to Holland, and also for their diet during the voyage.

May 1. Tavistock. 123. Wm. Earl of Bath to the Council. Musters in Devonshire. The trained bands are 5,000 men, but not half of them know how to use their weapons. Asks an order that their sporting time, which they chiefly spend in hurling, should be given to exercising their weapons. Some able men refused to produce their horses, and require punishment.

May 1. 124. Legal opinion of Thos. Harris, Serjeant, Rich. Godfrey, and Ant. Diet, Counsellors at Law, viz., that contempts in Chancery are punishable only in Chancery, and that those committed before the general pardon are remitted thereby; that the fees of Crown offices are inalienable; and that persons accused of offences against the Crown and state may be imprisoned on suspicion, &c., &c.

May 2. Grant to Wm. Carpenter of the office of Waiter in the Port of London, for life. [*Grant Bk., p.* 104.]

May 4. 125. Justices of Buckinghamshire to Chancellor Ellesmere, Lord Lieutenant. Details of the musters, &c. Request a mitigation of the number of horsemen required. The clergy viewed according to a taxation sent by the Bishop of Lincoln.

May 4. Court. 126. Wm. Earl of Pembroke to the Council. The musters have been held in Cornwall. The county being near Spain, not the train bands merely, but the whole forces are mustered. They have always been spared raising horses, the county being unsuited for them.

Vol. LXXII.

1613.

May 9. 127. Will of Margaret Hendy, widow. Indorsed is probate thereof, dated May 14.

May 11. 128. Edw. Reynoldes to Sir John Rawlins. Advises him to return home, pay off his debts, settle his property, and live with some friend. Offers him a home on easy terms. Should his advice be rejected, will have nothing more to do with him.

May 13. London. 129. Chamberlain to Carleton. Suspicions about Burlamachi's reckonings and rate of exchange. Conditions of young Tollerby's father's will, &c. Sir Robt. Killigrew released from the Fleet. Sir Wm. Waad discharged from the lieutenancy of the Tower, on complaint of having embezzled jewels from the Lady Arabella. Sir Gervas Helwys of Lincolnshire succeeds him, &c. Quarrel between Lord Bruce of Kinloss and Sir Edw. Sackville. Libel on the late Lord Treasurer thrown into the court in a sealed box, directed to the King. Bostock and Waller fined and pilloried for reporting that some of the Council had implored the King for toleration of religion. One Scot called in question for a sermon at Court, which the Lord Privy Seal thought aimed at him, but the King said he had heard the sermon, and would have censured it had there been need. The Merchant Adventurers wished to remove to Amsterdam, but the King decides that they remain at Middleburgh, or else Zealand would become too poor to pay their share of the 40,000*l.* yearly reimbursed to him from thence. The Marquis de Villa come from Savoy to treat on the match. It is Wotton's doing, who has no other means to push himself forward.

May ? 130. "A Politique Dispute aboute the Happiest Marriage for the Most Noble Prince Charles," being a statement of the arguments for and against a match with Savoy; showing its evil consequences to England; advising delay in the Prince's marriage for the present, in order to keep all aspirants in check; and at length a marriage with France.

May 13 ? 131. Note of groceries sent to Ragley. Total value 7*l.* 5*s.* 6¼*d.*

May 13. 132. List of furniture, &c. left at London, and of such as is to be sent down [to Ragley, for Sir Edw. Conway].

May 15. 133. Examination of Isabel, wife of Wm. Peel, on the practices of Mary Woods to procure money from her and others, on pretence of giving them husbands or children. Knew nothing of an attempt of Lady Essex to get poison to kill her husband.

May 16. Commission to Geo. Archbp. of Canterbury, and others, to examine the nullity of the marriage between the Earl of Essex and Lady Frances Howard. [*Grant Bk., p.* 97.]

[May 17.] 134. Articles propounded by Lady Fras. Howard as the grounds of her suing a divorce from Robt. Earl of Essex, presented to the Court of Delegates.

VOL. LXXII.

1613.

May ? 135. Reasons to prove the necessity for making small copper coins, as done in all kingdoms of Europe, to avoid the great abuse of leaden tokens made by the city of Bristol, and by private men in England. Indorsed [by Thos. Wilson], "The necessaryness of making of brass farthings."

May ? 136. Copy of the above.

May ? 137. Descriptive list of the coins of brass current in Europe.

May ? 138. Note of the inconveniences of tradesmen's tokens, to be remedied by a coinage of brass farthings, to be issued or redeemed at 21*s.* worth the pound sterling, which will profit the King, avoid the constant loss of the very small silver coins, prevent export of bullion, and be a relief to the poor, as they will thereby receive small alms.

May ? 139. Project, by Gerard Malines, for the making, by competent persons, of farthing tokens of copper, to prevent the abuses of tradesmen's tokens; based on the grounds of the preceding paper; the King to have half the money received for the tokens, and to be at no expense.

May ? 140. Abstract of a similar project for making farthing tokens of copper.

May ? 141. Remonstrance against the project for farthing tokens, as likely to encourage coining, and to injure tradesmen, who for tokens must sell 21*s.* worth of wares, and then only receive 20*s.* for the tokens.

May ? 142. Grant to John Lord Harrington of the sole privilege, for three years, of making farthing tokens of copper, the acceptance thereof to be voluntary; and for the first year they are to be redeemable at the rate issued, viz., 20*s.* for 21*s.* worth of tokens.

May 19. Whitehall. Proclamation of the effect of Lord Harrington's patent for farthing tokens, and prohibiting the use of tradesmen's tokens. Printed. [*Proc. Coll.*, *No.* 21.]

May 19. Hertford House, in Canon Row. 143. Edw. Earl of Hertford to the Council. Report of musters in Somersetshire and Wiltshire. The foot companies are made complete, and the horse will be so before Midsummer.

May ? Tower. 144. Sir Gervase Helwys to [Rochester ?]. Will attend him with a letter from the Earl of Shrewsbury, to make good what is past, and intreat her Ladyship's stay.

May ? 145. Sir John Lidcott to [Sir Thos. Overbury]. It would not do to acquaint Sir Robt. Killigrew with the business. Overbury will be kept in prison on pretence of the King's wrath. He is cozened on all hands. His servant, Lawrence [Davies], must be had out of the way. Advises him to send Lawrence an angry message, on which he may say he cannot endure the trouble he is at, and may

VOL. LXXIV.

1613.

take his dismissal, when he shall be sent away safely, under an assumed name. Lord Rochester is to be cozened, for no honest quarter can be held with him.

May 19. 146. Sir Thos. Lake to Carleton. Thanks for his present. The Ambassador of Savoy lingers, and it is said that Gabellione, who negociated the late Prince's marriage, is returned; so something is thought to be on foot. Sir Thos. Overbury is sent to the Tower for saying he could not and would not accept a foreign employment. The King has long wanted to get rid of him at Court. Sir Robt. Killigrew committed for holding intercourse with Overbury in prison. Sir Wm. Waad removed from the lieutenancy of the Tower; his daughter imprisoned, and others examined relative to offences there. The Countess of Shrewsbury and Lord Grey made close prisoners. Lady Elizabeth well received in the Low Countries. The Queen at Bath, and the King going to Greenwich.

May 20. Westminster. Proclamation against payment of light Spanish silver coin, and calling in the defective Spanish money now in circulation. Printed. [*Procl. Coll., No.* 22.]

May 26. Madrid. 147. Sir John Digby to [Sir Thos. Lake]. The interests of merchants trading with Spain are so injured for want of a settled company, that Parliament should be as anxious to re-establish as they were to overthrow it. [*Extract.*]

May 28. Ashby. 148. Hen. Earl of Huntingdon to the Council. Report of musters in Leicestershire. Has added ten more to the number of horse.

May 31. 149. Bond of John Osborne, of Buckby Longa, co. Northampton, to Sir Owen Oglethorpe, of Chalfont St. Giles's, Bucks, and Valentine Saunders, under penalty of 200*l.*, to perform the conditions of the lease of a house, &c. in Rowell, held from the Crown, and transferred by them to Osborne.

May ? Grant to Sir Peter Saltonstall of fines, value 800*l.*, due by the Sheriffs of counties, from Mich. 1614 to Easter 1615, for non-appearances of recusants summoned. [*Warrt. Bk.*, I., *p.* 186.]

VOL. LXXIII.

"A Book of Proclamations, published since the beginning of His Majestie's most happy reigne over England, &c. untill this present moneth of Feb. 3, Anno Dom. 1609. Imprinted at London, by Robt. Barker, printer to the King's most excellent Majestie." Continued to Feb. 5, 1613. These proclamations are calendared under their respective dates.

1613. VOL. LXXIV. JUNE—OCTOBER, 1613.

June 1. Greenwich. Order in Council, founded on recommendation of the Lord Mayor and Recorder of London, that no bricklayer in London, or within two miles round, shall be permitted to do the work of a plasterer, whereby they injure the Plasterers' Company and the foreign plasterers. *Prefixing,*

> *Recapitulation of orders made March* 3, 1580, *and confirmed March* 18, 1585, *by the Mayor of London, Sir Thos. Pullyson, and others, regulating the respective trades of plasterers and bricklayers. London, April* 5, 1585. [*Dom. Corresp., Aug.* 13, *infra.*]

June 5. Grant of special licence to Adam Newton, John Southcote, and John Wood, to use the art of steeping seed to be sown, for the furtherance of tillage in England and Wales, for eleven years. [*Grant Bk., p.* 118.]

June 5. Westminster. Proclamation of the effect of Letters Patent granted to Adam Newton, John Southcote, and John Wood, for the use of their new invention of a liquor for steeping all kinds of grain for sowing. With note by the patentees of their willingness to give information, &c. upon it. Printed. [*Proc. Coll., No.* 22 *A.*]

June 10. London. 1. Chamberlain to Carleton. Sir Robt. Mansell committed to the Marshalsea for resisting a commission to reform abuses in the Navy, and Whitelock, the lawyer, for pronouncing the commission illegal, and speaking too boldly against the authority of the Marshal's court. The Irish Parliament is adjourned, because the Popish faction will not recognize the new boroughs erected by the King, and also on account of a dissention in the choice of a Speaker. The case of Sutton's hospital is arguing before all the Judges, most of whom incline towards it. The cause of the Earl of Essex's divorce in hearing at Lambeth. The Queen well entertained at Bristol and elsewhere. The Ambassador of Savoy well received; Sir Hen. Wotton is never away from him. The Aldermen have Privy Seals for loans of 200*l.* before their old money is paid. Death of Mr. Hare, of the Court of Wards, and Sir Geo. Gifford.

June 11. Westminster. Proclamation for apprehension of John Cotton, of Warblington, otherwise of Subberton, co. Hants, on suspicion of high treason. With description of his person. Printed. [*Proc. Coll., No.* 23.]

June 13. Lease to Sir Thos. Challoner of the manor of East Garston, co. Berks, and a stock of 200 sheep. [*Docquet.*]

June 13. Presentation of John Wood to the parish church of East Mersea, diocese of London. [*Docquet.*]

June 13. Whitehall. 2. Proceedings in Council in the case of Sir Robt. Mansell and James Whitelock, lawyer, on June 12, for contempt. A commission being issued for inquiry into abuses in the navy, Sir Robt. Mansell employed Whitelock to take exceptions to the said commission, who did so in a very contemptuous and disloyal manner,

VOL. LXXIV.

1613.

attacking the King's prerogative, for which he stands charged, as does Sir Robert, for seeking undutifully to oppose His Majesty's proceedings. On hearing their charges, both expressed penitence and submission, begged remission of further penalties, and restoration to favour. They were required to set down their submissions in writing, which they did, and the following day, June 13, after grave admonitions to beware of meddling with His Majesty's prerogative, they were liberated and restored to favour.

June 14. 3. Examination of Mary Woods. Gave a powder to Lady Essex to wear round her neck, because she wished to have a child.

June 14? 4. Visct. Rochester to Dr. Craig. The King wishes him to attend on Sir Thos. Overbury when he requires it, and to give him as much of his company as is needful.

June 15. Grant, in reversion, to Hen. Lord Danvers, of the office of Keeper of St. James's Palace, &c., co. Middlesex, for life. [*Grant Bk.*, *p.* 111.]

June 15. 5. Grant to Sir Robt. Wroth of purchase of the manor of Loughton, alias Luckton, co. Essex. Latin.

June? 6. Statement that if the King resume the imposts of French and Rhenish wines, there is offered for the eight years remaining of the lease 19,000*l.* per ann., being 5,000*l.* more than the present rent, a fine of 10,000*l.* and 200 tuns allowance for the King's household.

June? 7. Wm. Garway, John Wolstenholme, and Nich. Salter to the King. Though their grant of the farm of French wines is good in law, they are willing to offer for its confirmation 16,000*l.* in money, or 12,000*l.* in money and 2,000*l.* increase in rent, or 5,000*l.* increase in rent.

June 17. 8. Order in the cause of the King v. Wm. Garway, Nich. Salter, John Wolstenholme, and John Bowsar, lessees of the customs on French and Rhenish wines, that on account of certain frauds detailed in obtaining their lease, the profits be sequestered into the hands of indifferent persons, to hold them till the case is decided by law.

June 20. Palace of Westminster. 9. Warrant for payment to Sir Roger Dallison, Lieutenant of Ordnance, of 1,294*l.* 7*s.* 8*d.* for providing and transporting munitions to Ireland; indorsed with note of payment thereof by Edw. Wardour.

June 23. London. 10. Chamberlain to Carleton. Sir Thos. Bodley's executors cannot excuse him of unthankfulness to many of his relatives and friends, he being "so drunk with the applause and vanitie of his librarie, that he made no conscience to rob Peter to pay Paul." The decision on Sutton's [will] case given in its favour by ten judges against one. The divorce between the Earl and Countess of

VOL. LXXIV.

1613.

Essex is soon to be decided, and is important, as opening a gap which would not soon be stopped. It is said that Rochester is in love with her. The King and Queen at Greenwich. The King going on a progress.

June? 11. The King to the Executors of Thos. Sutton, of Cambridgeshire, and the Governors of the Charter House, Middlesex. Requires them to assign a meet allowance to Roger Sutton, son of the late Thos. Sutton, who was overlooked in his father's disposition of his large estates.

June? 12. Draft of the above.

June? 13. Case of the above Roger Sutton, in his suit for a portion out of the estate of his late father Thos. Sutton, with proofs of his filiation.

June? 14. Copy of the above.

June 23. Westminster. 15. Grant, with survivorship, to Thos. Lake and Wm. Hill, of the office of writing, expediting, and exemplifying all letters patent of the King's lands, &c. within the survey of the Exchequer. Latin.

June. Docquet of the above. [*Docquet, June* 13.]

June 25. Venice. 16. Sir Dud. Carleton to the King. Seizure, at Melamocco, of Bibles translated into Portuguese for the use of the Jews, by the Pope's Nuncio, who declared that the Bible was the cause of all heresy. The people deride, and call to mind a saying of the present Pope, "that the preaching of the gospel is the destruction of the church."

June 26. Greenwich. 17. Grant to Edw. Polton, in reversion after his father John Polton, of the place of Falconer to the King.

June? 18. Earl of Northampton to Sir Thos. Waller, to deliver up the pirates of the States, to a Dutch man-of-war sent over to fetch them away.

June? 19. Considerations on the project for alum, presented by Mr. Ingram, and [Robt.] Johnson; viz., the present state of the three years' lease of the three northern houses; Sir Wm. Clavell's contract with the Master of the Wards [Sir Walter Cope]; the necessity of fixing the limits of the King's charges, &c.

June? 20. Statement addressed to the King of the result of an investigation by Sir Walter Cope, Art. Ingram, and Robt. Johnson, on the state of the alum works, as left by the late farmers; of their arrangements to pay them 77,500*l.* worth of alum, in lieu of their expenses; with an estimate of the charge and profit of the alum works. Sir Wm. Clavell offers to contract for his alum and coal mines.

June? 21. Account of the present state of the alum business, according to the preceding arrangements, with suggestions of a modification thereof, in reference to a proposed patent for alum.

VOL. LXXIV.

1613.

June ? Re-grant to the Earl of Northampton and Sir Julius Cæsar, of the honours, lordships, and manors of Tynedale and Wark, the Castle of Wark, and other lands, &c., co. Northumberland, by them transferred to the Crown, with a view to their re-conveyance to Lady Elizabeth, wife of Lord Walden, daughter and co-heir of the late Earl of Dunbar. [*Sign Man., vol.* III., *No.* 8.]

June 28. Grant to John Okes of the office of Clerk of the Great Wardrobe, for life. [*Grant Bk., p.* 118.]

July 1. London. 22. Giov. Franc. Biondi to [Carleton]. The Ambassador Extraordinary of Savoy [Marquis de Villa] has done little towards the match. Gabellione, the resident, will treat of it. The Marquis presented to the Queen a casket of rock crystal; to the Prince a suit of Milanese armour, after the model of those made for Charles V. and Francis I.; and to the King, a tiger, and lioness, and a lynx, which died on the road. The King is going to Hampton Court. There are movements in Ireland, but not of consequence. Italian.

July 2. Grant to John Gilbert of the office of Keeper of York Castle, for life. [*Grant Bk., p.* 125.]

July 3. Oatlands. Grant to Arthur, son of Sir Art. Dakins, of Long Cowton, co. York, of pardon for manslaughter of Wm. Green, Gent., it being done in self-defence, and he very penitent. Latin. [*Sign Man., vol.* III., *No.* 9.]

July 3. Oatlands. Warrant to the Receiver, &c. of Cheshire and North Wales, to pay 500 marks to Edw. Dodd, Baron of the Exchequer of Chester, for the repair of Chester Castle. [*Ibid., No.* 10.]

July 3. Oatlands. Grant to Jas. Balfour, of London, of pardon for life only, for manslaughter of Edw. Harvy, of Enfield. Latin. [*Ibid., No.* 11.]

July 3. Oatlands. Warrant for payment to John Tonstall, Gentleman Usher of the Queen, of 220*l.* expended for her use at Bath. [*Ibid., No.* 12.]

July 3. Oatlands. Grant to Patrick Black of the office of Tailor to the Prince. [*Ibid., No.* 13.]

July 3. Oatlands. Grant to Geo. Story of the office of Forester of Coverdale, co. York. Latin. [*Ibid., No.* 14.]

July 3. Oatlands. Warrant for payment of 17*l.* 10*s.* to John Murray, Keeper of the Privy Purse, for half a year's rent of the coppices in Wanborough Wood, co. Surrey, transferred to him by Visct. Montague, who has leased them to the King. [*Ibid., No.* 15.]

July 4. Sunday. 23. Earl of Northampton to Sir Thos. Lake. The Council has sat ten or twelve hours daily, on the business laid on them by the King. Have been forced to dismiss the gold and silver business, and also that of the [fishing] busses, as involving many points in the treaties with Burgundy and Holland. All their time is spent on the care of the King's estate, in which several mysteries have been fathomed. The question of the Parliament postponed.

VOL. LXXIV.

1613.

July 4. Oatlands. Grant to Thos. Matthew, on surrender of Dan. Sheberden, of the office of Waiter in the Port of London. Latin. [*Sign Man.*, *vol.* III., *Nos.* 16.]

July 4. Oatlands. Grant to Sir Clement Higham of 200*l.* recognizance, forfeited by Thos. Buckley, of Dalham, and John Tayler, of Gaseley, both co. Suffolk, for the non-appearance of Buckley before the consistory of St. Paul's, to answer for his marriage with Margaret Notts, his late wife's sister. [*Ibid.*, *No.* 17.]

July 4. Oatlands. Grant to Sir Thos. Tyringham, in reversion after Sir Chas. Howard, of the keeping of the Great Park of Windsor. [*Ibid.*, *No.* 18.]

July 7. Dover Castle. 24. Grant by the Earl of Northampton, Lord Warden of the Cinque Ports, to Nich. Leureulx, of Dieppe, of licence to fish on the coasts of the Cinque Ports.

July 7. 25. Like licence for Chas. de la Mare, of Dieppe; with note of its enrolment by John Packenham, Registrar of the Cinque Ports, and also by the Recorder of Rye, &c.

July 8. London. 26. Chamberlain to Carleton. The King is at Whitehall, the Queen at Somerset House. The Lords busy in ordering the Prince's household. The Irish Parliament deputies have been heard and refuted by the King. The trustees under Sutton's will have been to the Charter House to take possession, &c. The divorce of the Earl of Essex is delayed. Sir Lionel Cranfield appointed to succeed Sir Thos. Waller, Lieutenant of Dover Castle, who is dead; he grows in favour with the Lord Privy Seal. The Earl of Northumberland has quarrelled with Ruthven's [the Earl of Gowrie's] brother, in the Tower Garden. The Marquis of Villa, Ambassador from Savoy, has departed with rich presents. Much surprise at such close intercourse with so weak a Prince. Sir Hen. Wotton upholds himself thereby, it being all his employment, &c.

July 8. Westminster. Warrant for payment of 10,000*l.* to Sir Oliver Williams, alias Cromwell, being part of 16,000*l.* for purchase of the Forest of Waybridge, co. Huntingdon. [*Sign Man.*, *vol.* III., *No.* 19.]

July 8. Westminster. Presentation of Tim. Revett to the vicarage of North Petherton, co. Somerset, void by promotion of John Tanner to the Bishopric of Derry. Latin. [*Ibid.*, *No.* 20]

July 8. Westminster. Re-grant to Arnold Herbert and Meredith Morgan, servants of the Earl of Suffolk, of divers manors, lands, &c., in cos. Lincoln, Salop, and Essex, formerly conveyed by the Earl to the Crown. Latin. [*Ibid.*, *No.* 21.]

July 8. Westminster. Grant to John Puckle, on surrender of John Codwell, of the office of Collector of the Customs in the port of Chichester. [*Ibid* , *No.* 22.]

VOL. LXXIV.

1613.
July 8. Grant to Wm. Wigmore, of Lucton, Hereford, and Robt. Soulley, of Soulley, Denbigh, at suit of Sir Hugh Carmichael, of lands, co. Denbigh, and all other lands, goods, and debts forfeited to the Crown by the attainder of John Edwards, of London, for refusing the Oath of Allegiance. [*Sign Man., vol.* III., *No.* 23.]

July 10. Kingston. 27. Deputy Lieutenants of Surrey to the Earl of Nottingham, Lord Lieutenant. Have held the musters and made up the deficiencies, but they fall heavy on some parties, because the King's servants, and the citizens of London, many of whom are residents in the county, claim exemption.

July 12. Whitehall. 28. Order in Council to the Master and Wardens of the Incorporated Company of Shipwrights, authorizing them to apprehend and call before the Company persons using the art and mystery of shipbuilding, contrary to their charter; and journeymen or apprentices of shipwrights, unlawfully departing from their masters.

July 12. 29. Copy of the above.

July 12. Theobalds. Warrant to advance 144*l.* 5*s.* to Nich. Gibbon, master carpenter, for the repair of Portsmouth Castle, and the Lieutenant's house there. [*Sign Man., vol.* III., *No.* 24.]

July 12. Theobalds. Grant to Owen Vaughan, of Lloydiarth, co. Montgomery, of purchase of the manor of Kenlleth Owen, and other lands, co. Denbigh, value 15*l.* 13*s.* 2*d.*, at suit of John Eldred, Art. Ingram, and others, contractors for lands. Latin. [*Ibid., No.* 25.]

July 13. Theobalds. Grant to Thos. Dirdo, of Gillingham, Dorset, of pardon for piracy, of which he stands indicted, but is not guilty. Latin. [*Ibid., No.* 26.]

July 13. Theobalds. Grant to Wm. Clarke, on surrender of John Lister, of the office of Forester, in Galtres, co. York. Latin. [*Ibid., No.* 27.]

July [13 ?] Court at Theobalds. 30. [Sir Thos. Lake ?] to Hen. Spiller. To make a return of the particulars of all lands, &c. of recusants, whether indicted or convicted or not, the value of which should have been paid in since His Majesty's accession; and also of all grants made thereof.

July ? 31. List of such recusants as have during the present reign returned to church, and of those who have received the Sacrament, and have taken the Oath of Allegiance; with statement of the value of the lands and goods restored to each, which would otherwise have been forfeited to the King, and a note of grants made by the King out of recusants' fines, &c.

July 13. 32. Proceedings in Council on a complaint by the Mayor of London, against Sir Gervase Helwys, Lieutenant of the Tower, who, on arrest of Dr. Palmer, the Chaplain, on a writ of execution, seized and imprisoned, by way of Withernam, the bodies of several citizens passing Tower Hill, to detain them till Palmer was liberated. Helwys pleaded that being new in his office, he was informed by the wardens and officers that this was the

1613. Vol. LXXIV.

customary course, and therefore adopted it. The Aldermen produced a decree of 1595, in a similar case, limiting the powers of the Lieutenants of the Tower and condemning the custom of Withernam, which the Council confirmed, and ordered a copy thereof to be sent to the Lieutenant.

July 14. Eton. 33. Sir Hen. Savile to Carleton. Likes Padre Paolo's censure. Cannot do anything for Mr. Horne during his absence so far, for the vacancies at Eton have to be filled up within a month, and cannot be held back, there being 100 applications.

July 14. 34. List of payments made by Wm. Garway since Oct. 1609, on account of the new impositions.

July 14. Theobalds. Grant to Thos. Turffett, of a Gunner's place in the Tower. Latin. [*Sign Man., vol.* III., *No.* 28.]

July 14. Theobalds. Warrant for payment to Hen. Mayson of 146*l.* 11*s.* 7*d.*, being the balance of 195*l.* 2*s.* 3*d.* required for rebuilding the Tolbooth of Barnard Castle. [*Ibid., No.* 29.]

July 14. Theobalds. Warrant to pay to Sir Chris. Hatton 80*l.* for a grey gelding, bought for the King's use. [*Ibid., No.* 30.]

July 14. Theobalds. Grant to John Drawater of a Gunner's place in the Tower. Latin. [*Ibid., No.* 31]

July 14. Grant to Wm. Whitmore and Jonas Verdon of the site of the manor of Haywood and Shutborough, and certain lands there, and in Colwich, co. Stafford, in part payment of 20,000*l.*, advanced by Whitmore and other contractors. Latin. [*Ibid., No.* 32.]

July 14. Theobalds. Grant to David Lewes, of Lincoln, of the office of Vermynter or Vermyntaker, in England, to destroy "foxes, grayes, fichenos, polcates, wisells, stotes, fares, badgers, wildecats, otters, hedgehogges, rattes, mice, mouldewarpe or waute, and other noysome vermine, destroyers of cornes;" also "crowes, choughs, or rookes, mertons, furskites, molekites, bussardes, scagges, cormorants, ringtails, irones or osprayes, woodwales, pies, jayes, ravens or kightes, kingefishers, bulfinches and other ravenous birds and noysome fowl, devowrers of corn, &c." [*Ibid., No.* 33]

July 16. Theobalds. Grant to Wm. Risbrooke of the office of Underkeeper of His Majesty's House at Richmond, as he held it under Sir Thos. Gorges deceased, agreeably to a former patent by the late Prince. [*Ibid., No.* 35.]

July ? Grant to Nich. Bird of the office of Underkeeper of the House and Palace of Richmond, co. Surrey, in reversion after Wm. Risbrooke. [*Warrant Bk.* I., *p.* 217.]

July 17. Westminster. Grant to Sir Thos. Hewett of the King's reversion of the lands in cos. Kent, Essex, Bedford, and York, fraudulently conveyed to the Crown by John and Sir Wm. Hewett, his brothers, in order to defeat the settlement thereof by Wm. Hewett, of London, their late father. [*Sign Man., vol.* III., *No.* 36.]

VOL. LXXIV.

1613.

July 17. Brussels. 35. Jas. Maitland to [Visct. Rochester]. Solicits permission to sue in the Scottish Courts for revocation of the attainder passed upon his father [Wm. Maitland, of Lethington], for services to the King's mother, in spite of the Act of 1584 against such suits. Arguments in favour thereof. Wishes the revocation to be in Parliament, the lands being elsewhere bestowed. Applies to his Lordship because their fathers were friends, and involved in the same cause and overthrow. Has lately seen, at Rheims, Mary Seaton, who served the King's mother from her infancy to the last; she is old and decrepid; and depends on the charity of Mdme. de Spier, the Duke of Guise's sister. Solicits an annuity for her. [*See Acts Parl. Scot., vol.* III., *p.* 297.]

July 19. Windsor. Warrant for payment of 10,000*l.* to the Elector Palatine, in Amsterdam, before Aug. 10, as part of the dowry of the Princess Elizabeth. [*Sign Man., vol.* III., *No.* 37.]

July 19. Windsor. Warrant for the repayment of money lent to His Majesty for eighteen months, on Privy Seals, in the ninth year of His reign. [*Ibid., No.* 38.]

July 20. Farnham. Warrant to pay 472*l.* to Sir Wm. Monson, Admiral, and 228*l.* to Capt. Geo. Wood, Vice-Admiral of the Narrow Seas, for the wages of their seamen, which are in arrears since 1608. [*Ibid., No.* 39.]

July 20. Farnham. Grant to Thos. Hobson, of Cambridge, of pension of 200*l.* per ann., during the life of Agnes Knight, of Gravesden, Cambridge, at the suit of Awdrey Lady Walsingham, on surrender of her pension of 500*l.* per ann. [*Ibid., No.* 40.]

July 20. Farnham. Grant to the Earls of Suffolk, Worcester, and Northampton, of a pension of 300*l.* per ann. during the life of Awdrey Lady Walsingham, on surrender by her of a former pension of 500*l.* per ann. [*Ibid., No.* 41.]

July 20. Farnham. Grant to Fras. Phelips and Edw. Sawyer of the Castle and Crown, and Venours Wharf, with appurtenances, St. Mary's Somerset, Queenhithe, London, in part of 15,000*l.* to be granted to Sir Walter Cope, and others, contractors for rectories. Latin. [*Ibid., No.* 42.]

July 20. Farnham. Grant to Sir Thos. Leigh, Bart., of Stoneleigh, and Sir Thos. Lucy, of Charlcote, Warwick, of an annuity of 200*l.*, for the use of Lady Alice, wife of Sir Robt. Dudley, during her life. Latin. [*Ibid., No.* 43.]

July 23. Basing. Grant to Mathias Fowle, of London, of 2,400*l.*, old debts due to the Crown. [*Ibid., No.* 44.]

[July 24.] Saturday. 36. Earl of Northampton to Rochester. Sir Lionel Cranfield has put the affair of the farmers [of customs] into good trim. They boast of their victory. Would not have allowed them to come off so well had they not shrouded themselves "under the grace of swete Rochester." Recommends Cranfield's own particular. [*Grant of the Surveyorship of Custom. See July* 26.]

VOL. LXXIV.

1613.

July ? 37. Arguments on the advantage to be derived from public proceeding at law against the farmers of French wines. It will show the deceits of the present lease, and the value of the farm; bring to light the pensions paid to those who helped to deceive His Majesty in it, and enable him to recover 80,000*l.* of their past profits. If a compromise is made with the present farmers, they will say, as did the farmers of the great customs, that they have paid money to the King for peace. By keeping the farm in his hands, from Michaelmas to Christmas, the chief wine quarter, he would gain from 15,000*l.* to 20,000*l.*

July ? 38. Names of the nightly watch, and of their deputies, in Dover Castle, in the time of Sir Thos. Waller, Lieutenant; with a memorandum of his death, July 24, 1613.

July ? 39. Names of the Gunners, and their deputies, at Dover Castle, in the time of Sir Thos. Waller, Lieutenant.

July 24. Andover. Grant to Edm. Bradshaw and Hugh Cressy, of London, of the sole privilege of making all manner of earthen vessels, after the manner used in Fayence, for twenty-one years, they having perfected this art, and brought it into the kingdom. [*Sign Man., vol.* III., *No.* 45.]

July 25. 40. Licence by Thos. Fotherley and Robt. Stapleton, Commissioners for the Earl of Northumberland's lands in Yorkshire, to Hen. Kildale, to let his tenement in Topcliffe to Geo. Rawdon, of Rawdon, for the remainder of his lease; and licence to Geo. Rawdon to let the same to any person of honest life and good behaviour, who will not be chargeable to the parish of Topcliffe.

July 26. Andover. Grant to Sir Patrick Murray, K.B., second son of John Lord Murray, Earl of Tullibardine, Gentleman of the Privy Chamber, of denization. Latin. [*Sign Man., vol.* III., *No.* 46.]

July 26. Andover. Warrant for payment of 4,000*l.* to Geo. Herriot, for a chain and hatband set with diamonds, delivered to the late Prince. [*Ibid., No.* 47.]

July 26. Andover. Grant, with survivorship, to Sir Patrick Murray, K.B., second son of the Earl of Tullibardine, and Dame Elizabeth, his wife, of an annuity of 300*l.* per ann. [*Ibid., No.* 48.]

July 26. Grant to Sir Lionel Cranfield of the office of Surveyor General of the Customs, Subsidies, and Impositions, to prevent the loss sustained by negligence and deceit. [*Ibid., No.* 49.]

July 27. Liddiard. Grant, with survivorship, to Thos. Ivatt and Sam. Jones, in place of Wm. Stallenge, of the office of Searcher in the Port of London, on surrender of former patents. [*Ibid., No.* 50.]

July 27. Liddiard. Grant to Julian Bourdin, Sieur de Fontenay, nephew of the Sieur de St. Anthoine [Peter Bourdin], of a pension of 50*l.* per ann., on surrender of a like pension by Peter de la Costa, servant to the late Prince. [*Ibid., No.* 51.]

VOL. LXXIV.

1613.

July 27. Liddiard. Warrant to pay to Edw. Pannell 32*l.* 6*s.*, for the keep of twelve Irish greyhounds. [*Sign Man.*, *vol.* III., *No.* 52.]

July 27. Liddiard. Grant to Sir Wm. Anstruther and Hen. Huntley, of the Middle Temple, of the remainder of the King's fourth part, reserved upon Sir Thos. Shirley's Patent of old Debts due to the Crown, after the payment of 4,000*l.* already granted to Sir Jas. Erskine. [*Ibid.*, *No.* 53.]

July 27. Liddiard. Warrant to advance 200*l.* to John Tonstall, Gentleman Usher to the Queen, for her expenses in going to Bath for the waters. [*Ibid.*, *No.* 54.]

July 27. Liddiard. Warrant to pay to Sir Roger Dallison, Bart., Lieutenant of the Ordnance, 2,833*l.* 6*s.* 8*d.*, in part payment of 3,873*l.* 6*s.* 8*d.*, for purchase of 362 tons of round iron shot, the allowance of 6,000*l.* per ann. for ordnance not sufficing for this expense. [*Ibid.*, *No.* 55.]

July 27. Liddiard. Warrant to pay to Salomon de Caux, Engineer, 50*l.*, for attendance on the late Prince. [*Ibid.*, *No.* 56.]

July 27. Grant to Sir Art. Ingram, Martin Freeman, Geo. Lowe, and Rich. Gouthorpe, of all customs, subsidies, &c. in Ireland, for nine years and a half. [*Grant Bk.*, *p.* 127.]

July 28. London. 41. Auditor Fras. Gofton to Rochester. Cannot fulfil the King's command to send an account of the entire revenue, until the return to town of the officers of the Exchequer, who must then have orders from Sir Julius Cæsar for their certificates. Requests further directions, and that, the business being weighty, Auditor Hutton may be joined with him in it.

July 31. Charlton. Grant to Hen. Gibb, Groom of the Bedchamber, of an annuity of 200*l.* per ann. [*Sign Man.*, *vol.* III., *No.* 58.]

July 31. Charlton. Grant to the Same of 90*l.* per ann., in lieu of diet. [*Ibid.*, *No.* 59.]

July 31. Charlton. Grant to John Jefferson, in reversion after Robt. Offley, of the office of Bowstring Maker in the Tower. [*Ibid.*, *No.* 60.]

July 31. Docquet of the above.

July 31. Charlton. Grant to Thos. David, of Cathan, co. Glamorgan, John Griffith, of Merthyr Cynog, and Howell John Howel, of Llanvigan, co. Brecon, of pardon for felony, the first having discovered himself, and the others having small evidence against them. [*Sign Man.*, *vol.* III., *No.* 61.]

July 31. Docquet of the above.

VOL. LXXIV.

1613.
July. Grant to John Cooke and Jas. Scroghan, of London, at suit of Esme Lord Aubigny, of lands in cos. Sussex, Berks, Kent, Warwick, Worcester, Lincoln, Hants, Somerset, Middlesex, Hertford, York, Surrey, and Carmarthen. Imperfect. Latin. [*Sign Man., vol.* III., *No.* 62.]

July? 42. Note of certain particulars touching the revenue of recusants, on which to question the Clerk of the Pipe. Indorsed, "Mr. Jarvis to search and certify these particulars."

July? 43. Note of the request of Wm. Davis and Rich. Browne, Messengers, for a moiety of the fines of married women, recusants, incurred by the Statute 7 Jac. I., and of those for harbouring recusants contrary to the Statute 3 Jac. I. The arrears are supposed to be 200,000*l.*

July? 44. Advice to the King to hold a Parliament, in order to remove the bad impressions caused by the discords of the last Parliament, which did not proceed from disloyalty, but from a wish for redress of certain grievances. It should be called for Michaelmas, and meanwhile the King should be gracious to the people, who flock to see him during the progress, and should redress the grievances complained of last Parliament. He should communicate with the Commons personally or by his ministers, not through the Lords, and receive their replies by members chosen by themselves, not nominated by him.

July? 45. Copy of the above. *Incloses,*

45. I. *Collection of such things as have been desired to be obtained of His Majesty for the good of his people.*

July? 46, 47. Two copies of the above collection.

July. 48. Account of the payment to Lord Hay, Gentleman of the Robes, of 1,000*l.* per quarter, for charges of His Majesty's robes and apparel of all sorts for his person, since April 25, 1608.

Aug 1. London. 49. Chamberlain to [Carleton]. Waterworks brought into Ware Park. News from Savoy, reported by Sir Hen. Wotton, whose nephew, [Albert] Morton, is going thither as the King's agent. The Queen, shooting at a deer at Theobalds, shot the King's favourite hound. He was angry at first, but afterwards sent her a diamond as a legacy from his dead dog. They were never on better terms. The King has added four more Commissioners in the cause of the divorce between the Countess of Essex and her husband., and it is now thought the marriage will be dissolved. The Aldermen are pressed to lend 2,000*l.* each to the King. The Countess of Cumberland lately dead, also old Simons, of Oxfordshire. The Earl oi Bedford has had a dangerous fall. His Countess is returned to Court after her sickness, but no longer paints, which makes her look strange amidst so much paint and powder. The King displeased

VOL. LXXIV.

1613.

with Mayerne's recommendation of Dr. Burgess. The Virginia Company, having taken captive the daughter of a King who was their greatest enemy, exact good terms for her ransom. Several gentlemen became adventurers, and are now compelled to fulfil their contract; cut-work bands are so much in fashion that 6*l.* or 7*l.* are paid for a pair of them.

Aug. 4. Croydon. 50. Archbp. Abbot to [Carleton]. The great officers still unsettled. In the Irish Parliament the Popish party took exception to the Burgesses sent from the new corporations erected by the King, and chose a speaker of their own. The dispute is referred to the King. The hasty fire kindled by the Duke of Savoy is extinct. The man who gave the advice concerning the Viceroy of Naples and the Spanish Ambassador is to be sent for into England.

Aug. 4. Grant to Wm. Curteen, merchant, of 1,567*l.*, for money delivered by him by way of loan. [*Grant Bk., p.* 104.]

Aug. 12. Commission to the Earl of Northampton to sell ruinous houses, castles, &c. [*Ibid., pp.* 98 *and* 109.]

Aug. 12. Commission to Lord Chancellor Ellesmere and others to sell the lands [entailed] contained in an indenture, May 8, 7 Jac. I., and to sell wood and timber in any forests or parks. [*Ibid., pp.* 98, 109.]

Aug. 12. Commission to Sir Thos. Lassells to compound for sale of the manor of Knaresborough, co. York. [*Ibid., p.* 109.]

Aug. 13. Whitehall. 51. Order in Council for apprehending disorderly bricklayers, who, contrary to the previous order, practise the work of the plasterers. [*See June* 1, *supra.*]

Aug. 14. Commission to the Bishops of London and of Coventry and Lichfield to hear the cause between Young and Goodwin. [*Grant Bk., p.* 102.]

Aug. 14. Commission to the Lord Chancellor to sell any [entailed] lands contained in an indenture, dated May 8, 7 Jac. I., and to execute any commissions directed to them for that purpose. [*Ibid., p.* 109.]

Aug. 15. Grant of protection to Sir John Bourchier and others, merchants royal. [*Ibid., p.* 102.]

Aug. 16. Commission to the Lord Chancellor declaring the King's resolution to sell any of the [entailed] lands contained in an indenture, dated May 8, 7 Jac. I., and requesting him to perform the same. [*Ibid., p.* 98.]

Aug. 16. Grant to Fras. Morris of the house, &c. in the old palace at Westminster, near the Upper House of Parliament, for fifty years. [*Ibid., p.* 117.]

Aug. 21. Grant to John Eldred, Wm. and Ralph Freeman, and Adrian Moore, of the pre-emption and transportation of tin for seven years and a half. [*Ibid., p.* 112.]

VOL. LXXIV.

1613.

Aug. 22. Walls. 52. Dr. Theodore de Mayerne to [Rochester]. The King is threatened with a multiplication of his fits of gravelly cholic, unless he will listen to advice, and adopt the necessary remedies. Has written him a long discourse on the subject, but fears he will throw it aside unread. Begs him to read it to His Majesty, and urge on him the necessity of attending to it. Wishes four experienced physicians to be joined with himself in the charge of the King's health. French.

Aug. 23. Bellasis. 53. Sir Wm. Waad to the Same. Has been Clerk of the Council in Ordinary for thirty years, but being now in disgrace, is willing to surrender his patent to Mr. [Fras.] Cottington, who has dealt with him for it.

Aug. 28. Grant to Robt. Harcourt, Sir Thos. Challoner, and John Rovenson, and to the heirs of the said Robert, of all that part of Guiana or continent of America between the rivers Amazon and Dollesquebe, &c. [*Grant Bk., p.* 126.]

Aug. 28. Grant to Sam. Offish of the office of Yeoman Waiter in the Tower, for life. [*Ibid., p.* 112.]

Aug. 31. Bath. 54. Dr. Theo. De Mayerne to Rochester. Is sorry for his indisposition. Hopes the King is acquainted with the letter which he [Mayerne] wrote to His Majesty upon his health, and is prepared to adopt a regime. Sends a list of the medicines and precautions required. Understands the prisoner [Sir Thos. Overbury] is ill, and vomits; can do but little for him at a distance. French.

Aug. 31. Bath. 55. The Same to the King. Sends by his command an account of the Queen's health, which is much improved, she having the faith in the baths which often leads to a cure. Entreats His Majesty's attention to the prescriptions necessary for his own health.

Sept. 1. Grant, in reversion, to Hen. Elsing and Thos. Knyvet of the office of Clerks of the Parliament, for life. [*Grant Bk., p.* 112.]

Sept. 5. Grant to Sir Baptist Hicks of payment to him from Sir Marmaduke Darell, Sir John Trevor, and Sir Thos. Bludder, of the several sums of 2,050*l.*, 2,016*l.* 13*s.* 4*d.*, and 1,833*l.* 6*s.* 4*d.*, out of the money arising from imposition on coals. [*Ibid., p.* 126.]

Sept 9. London. 56. Chamberlain to [Carleton]. Sir Ralph Winwood has returned from Holland, and had an interview with the King, but the Secretaryship was not named. He who holds it really [Rochester] will not soon give it up, and may take the title. The projectors at a loss to find schemes to get money, all the land not entailed being sold. The Ambassadors' pay is nine months in arrear. The farmers of the wines have compounded for 16,000*l.* fine and 6,000*l.* increase of rent. Quarrels or threatened duels between Lord Bruce and Sir Edw. Sackville, Lord Chandos and Lord Hay, the Earl of

VOL. LXXIV.

1613.

Rutland and Lord Danvers, and the Earl of Essex and Hen. Howard. Progress of the Divorce Bill [of the Countess of Essex]. Commissioners appointed to hear the Irish deputies, who are confined at Croydon. Sir Robt. Brett made Lieutenant of Dover Castle. Death of Lords Harrington and Russell, Sir Oliver Manners, Sir Wm. Godolphin, and Sir Rich. Weston. Marriages of Sir Art. Ingram, Sir Hen. Montague, and Sir Wm. Webb. The King come to town.

Sept. 11. Wanstead. Proclamation prohibiting the bringing in of French wines before Dec. 1. Printed. [*Proc. Coll., No.* 24.]

Sept. 13. 57. Sir John Swinnerton to Rochester. Prays him to obtain for him a prolongation of his lease of the farm of sweet wines, in compensation for his services in discovering the frauds in that of the French and Rhenish wines, the farm of which he failed to obtain, his Majesty having compounded with the former farmers. His many services have raised the revenue of the Crown 60,000*l.* a year.

Sept. 21. Whitehall. 58. Earl of Suffolk to Sir Thos. Lake. To draw up a grant to Hen. Martin of the place of Serjeant Trumpeter, void by decease of Benedict Browne.

Sept. 22. Madrid. Sir John Digby to the King. The Spanish Ambassador has sent home the following particulars of the English Court, viz. :—That the King grows too fat to be able to hunt comfortably; spends much time in reading, especially religious works, and eats and drinks so recklessly that it is thought he will not be long lived; he is obstinate in his religious opinions; his chief favourites are Scotchmen, and especially Visct. Rochester. That the Queen leads a quiet life, not meddling with business, and is on good terms with the King. That the Prince is a fine youth of sweet disposition, and, under good masters, might be easily trained to the religion his predecessors lived in. That the Council is composed of men of little knowledge, some Catholics, but most schismatics or atheists, and the King resolves on all business with Visct. Rochester alone, who is no persecutor of Catholics. That the Duke of Lenox and Lord Hay are pensioners of France. That Catholics are persecuted by the Archbp. of Canterbury and Bp. of London, and by the King, in hope to propitiate Parliament into granting subsidies, and that he may have their forfeitures to give to his servants. This persecution was increased, and a fresh Oath of Allegiance exacted, from the fright caused by the death of the late King of France. That the King has impaired his revenue by sale of his lands, &c., and yet is five millions in debt, and is profuse in his gifts. The Earl of Northampton opposed in Council the calling a Parliament for supplies, because they would censure the King's modes of raising moneys. He intends to raise three millions by sale of the Royal woods and of deer. The shipping, castles, and forts going to decay. [*Spanish Corresp., Sept.* 22.]

VOL. LXXIV.

1613.

Sept. 22. Grant to Fras. Godolphin of the office of Receiver General in cos. Devon, Cornwall, and York, for life. [*Grant Bk., p.* 125.]

Sept. 24. Grant to Fras. Cottington of the Clerkship of the Privy Council, for life. [*Ibid., p.* 110.]

Sept. 25. 59. Memorandum that the cause between Lady Fras. Howard and the Earl of Essex was begun May 17, 1613, and sentenced Sept. 25.

Sept. 26. Grant to Sir Robt. Phelips of lease of Sherborne Park, &c., co. Dorset, for ninety-nine years. [*Grant Bk., p.* 118.]

Sept. 28. Licence to Sir Lionel Cranfield to receive 3*d.* in the pound imposed upon merchant strangers, above the charges paid by natural subjects, for exportation and importation of merchandise. [*Ibid., p.* 104.]

Sept. 28. London. 60. Sir Ralph Winwood to [Carleton]. Sir Thos. Overbury found dead in bed at the Tower. Sir John Lidcott, his brother-in-law, begged his body, but was refused. The marriage between the Earl of Essex and Lady Fras. Howard pronounced null and void by the Bishops of Winchester, Lichfield, Rochester, and others; the Archbp. of Canterbury, Bishop of London, and others, dissenting. No money is to be had. The King and Queen at Hampton Court, where the advisability of a Parliament will be discussed.

Sept. 30. Reading. 61. Order by the Commissioners of Sewers for Berkshire and Oxfordshire, that Rich. Harrison keep in repair the banks of the River Loddon, adjacent to Whistley Mill, of which he is occupant.

Sept.? 62. Answer of Wm. Barker to the questions propounded by the Archbp. of Canterbury and other Commissioners, relative to his registration of the sentence pronounced in the Court of Delegates, in the cause between the Lady Fras. Howard and Robt. Earl of Essex, in which Dr. Edwardes wished him to insert, contrary to custom, the protests of several of the Commissioners, &c.

Sept.? 63. Commission by Hen. Earl of Northampton, Lord Warden, &c., appointing Sir Robt. Brett, Lieutenant of Dover Castle, the Mayor of Sandwich, and others, to be Deputies for the charge of the passage at Sandwich.

Sept.? 64. Duplicate of the above.

Sept.? 65. Declaration by Walter Devereux and Rich. Ouseley, of the falsity of a new relation of the quarrel between the Earl of Essex and Hen. Howard, since the King reconciled them, which relation differs "in some mayne points" from that which they subscribed, and which showed that they might have fought if they would. [*See Nichols' Progresses, vol.* II., *p.* 676.]

Sept. 66. Monthly account of the fees of the Clerks of the Signet.

VOL. LXXIV.

1613.
Sept. 67. Indenture of lease from the Wardens of the Company of Farriers of London to Robt. Glover, of London, their Clerk, and Elizabeth, his wife, of certain rooms in their house, commonly called the Trinity Hall, or Common Hall of the late dissolved fraternity or guild of the Holy Trinity, in the parish of St. Botolph Without, Aldersgate, London.

Oct. 1. Tenterden. 68. Certificate of the Commissions of Sewers that the salt marshes near Rye Harbour might be regained from the sea without prejudice to the haven, leaving a fifth part to be discharged by a sluice for cleansing the harbour.

Oct. 3. Grant to Robt. Thorne of the office of taking Affidavits in the Court of the Marches of Wales, for life. [*Grant Bk., p.* 119.]

Oct. 4. Grant to Rich. Kilborne alias Hunt, and Thomas Tilsley, of the benefit of all Moorefalls, in the New Forest, cos. Southampton and Wilts, for twenty-one years. [*Ibid., p.* 127.]

Oct. 4. Grant to Clement Edmondes of the office of Muster Master General, for life. [*Ibid., p.* 112.]

Oct. 6. Creation of Lewis Duke of Lenox to the rank of Baron Settrington, co. York, and Earl of Richmond. [*Ibid., p.* 127.]

Oct 6. Note of the creation of Lewis Duke of Lenox as Earl of Richmond and Baron Settrington, which was done without investiture, because he was a Duke before. [*Dom. Corresp., Nov.* 4, 1613.]

Oct. 6. 69. [Justices of Peace ?] of Cornwall to Rich. Carnsew, Treasurer of the eastern division of the county. To pay from the county stock for maimed soldiers, 40*s.* to Thos. Jones, hurt in the service in Ireland, in lieu of any future yearly payment. *Annexed are,*

69. I. *Carnsew's remonstrance against paying the above, he being already 3l. in advance. Oct.* 14, 1613.

69. II. *W. Rescarrock's reply to Carnsew, stating that if his moneys had been duly levied at Michaelmas, he would have had funds in hand. Rescarrock, Oct.* 23, 1613.

69. III. *Receipt by Thos. Jones of the above sum of* 40*s., dated May* 4, 1614.

Oct. 8. Grant to Sir Thos. Savage [in reversion after his father-in-law Lord Darcy] of the dignity of Baron Darcy, of Chiche, co. Essex. [*See Nov.* 25. *Grant Bk., p.* 120.]

Oct. 9. Walmer Castle. 70. Inventory of the store and munition of Walmer Castle in charge of Wm. Boughton, Captain, taken before Sir Robt. Brett, Lieutenant of Dover Castle.

Oct. 9. 71. Copy of the above.

VOL. LXXIV.

1613.

Oct. 9. Sandown Castle. 72. Similar inventory of the store and munition of Sandown Castle under the custody of John Haydon, Captain.

Oct 9. 73. Copy of the above.

[Oct. 9.] 74, 75. Drafts of the above two inventories.

Oct. 11. Mote's Bulwark. 76. Similar inventory of the store and munition at Mote's Bulwark, near Dover, under the custody of Thos. Fyneux, Captain. With a few memoranda relating thereto of later date.

Oct. 11. 77, 78. Two copies of the above.

[Oct. 11.] 79. Draft of the above.

Oct. 11. 80. Muster roll of the garrison of Mote's Bulwark.

Oct. 11. 81. Copy of the above.

Oct. 11. Sandgate Castle. 82. Inventory of the store and munition of Sandgate Castle, under the custody of Geo. Fenner, Captain, taken before Sir Robt. Brett.

Oct. 11. 83. Draft of the above.

Oct. 11. 84. Invento ry of Stores and Munitions of Arch-cliff Bulwark, Dover.

Oct. 12. Grant, in reversion, to Sir Chas. Howard of the office of keeping Byfleet Park, &c., co. Surrey, for life. [*Grant Bk., p.* 126.]

Oct. 14. 85. Letters of Attorney of Chris. Wivell, delegating to John Lambe and others the ecclesiastical jurisdiction in the bishopric of Lincoln, during the vacancy, which was conferred on himself by Roger Parker, Precentor and Canon Residentiary. Latin.

Oct. 14. London. 86. Chamberlain to Carleton. Sir Thos. Overbury dead, and buried in the Tower. The manner of his death is not known. The corpse was very offensive. Nobody pities him, and his own friends do not speak well of him. Dr. Abbot was likely to be made a Bishop, but his brother, the Archbp. of Canterbury, has lost some favour about the great [divorce] business. The marriage between the Earl of Essex and Lady Fras. Howard dissolved. Particulars of the settlement by the King of the quarrel between the Earl [of Essex] and Hen. Howard. Lord Coke hesitates to leave the Chief Justiceship of the Common Pleas and accept that of the King's Bench, which is urged on him by the King, who wishes to make Sir Fras. Bacon Attorney. Yelverton spoken of as Solicitor, because of his services to the King in Parliament. Death of Lord Petre and of Sir John Brograve, Attorney of the Duchy, who is succeeded by Moseley. Sir Ralph Winwood and Sir Hen. Neville despair of the Secretaryship, which is likely to fall on Sir Thos. Lake. Lord Rochester pays 20,000*l.* for lands belonging to the Dacres and Nevills in Westmoreland, and is to be made Earl of Westmoreland.

VOL. LXXIV.

1613.

Oct. 19. Grant to Thos. Fitz-Hughes and Roger Pennell of the moiety of moneys raised on composition for defective titles, for two years. [*Grant Bk., p.* 112.]

Oct. 21. London. 87. Giov. Franc. Brondi to [Carleton]. Has spent a month at St. Edmundsbury, and would much like to reside there. Sir Hen. Wotton follows the Court, by command of the King. There has been a long discussion on the embassies to France and Spain. It is expected that Wotton will be sent to one place or the other. Italian.

Oct. 21. Royston. Grant to John Sandiland, Groom of the Bedchamber to the late Prince, of a pension of 200*l.* per ann. [*Sign Man., vol.* III., *No.* 63.]

Oct. 22. Commission to Lord Chancellor Ellesmere, Hen. Earl of Northampton, and others, to allow to Robt. Typper, his executors and assignees, due reward for his services in the commission for sale of lands, with authority to draw out warrants for lands not yet granted. [*Grant Bk., p.* 103.]

Oct. 25. 88. List of the Gunners Watch of Dover Castle, and their deputies, Oct. 18–25.

Oct. 27. Grant to Sir Fras. Bacon of the office of Attorney General during good behaviour. [*Grant Bk., p.* 102.]

Oct. 27. London. 89. Chamberlain to Carleton. Sir Ralph Winwood intends to press for his despatch [to Holland], lest it be supposed that he is lingering after the Secretaryship. Sir Hen. Neville is now quite fallen, and it is thought that Sir Thos. Lake will hold the place, but without the title, under Rochester, who is made Treasurer of Scotland. Sir Edw. Coke called up to the Chief Justiceship of the King's Bench, to his own regret, and that of all the officers of Common Pleas. Sir Fras. Bacon made Attorney General; it is feared he will prove a dangerous instrument. A Spanish match talked of. Reception of an Ambassador from the new Emperor of Muscovy, whose election is likely to be questioned. The Muscovy Company resolve to defend by force the whale fishing in Greenland, which they discovered a few years ago, from the Hollanders, who have sent deputies about it. The Spaniards threaten to drive the English from the Bermudas. A piece of amber as big as a giant found there. The East India vessels returned, richly laden. Dr. Carrier, the King's Chaplain, is turned Papist, and more are likely to follow, so many priests and Jesuits arriving and passing unpunished. Sir Thos. Edmondes likely to be Secretary under Rochester. Proclamation by the King himself on the late quarrel between the Earl of Essex and Hen. Howard.

Oct. 28. Edinburgh. 90. Sir Thos. Hamilton to Rochester. The note commanding his Lordship's admission to the [Scottish] Council was readily obeyed. Discontents at Sir Gideon [Murray's] promotion. Lord Roxburgh will try to prove his complaint against his unnatural kinsman. All the

1613. VOL. LXXIV.

King's wishes not likely to be accomplished, as people do not choose to do and undo at pleasure. *Incloses,*

90. I. *Transactions of the Council of Scotland. Visct. Rochester admitted of their number, at the King's command. Geo. Graham, the Earl of Monteith's uncle, sentenced to the horn, for sending a challenge to a duel. The clan Gregor to be summoned to make their lands peaceable, and the heads of two of their offenders to be sent and set upon the west post of Edinburgh, &c., &c., Oct.* 27.

Oct. 28. London. 91. Giov. Franc. Biondi to [Carleton]. Albert Morton's going delayed. Will follow Carleton's advice in remaining in London. An Ambassador come from Muscovy to renew the trade, broken off by war. Italian.

Oct. 30. Whitehall. 92. Earl of Nottingham to the Master and Wardens of the Company of Shipwrights. Requires them to apprehend and bring before their company all persons who refuse to conform to the regulations of their charter, and to imprison them until compliance, they being chiefly poor men and unable to pay a fine.

Oct. 31. Grant to Rich. Pitt of the office of Gun-founder for life. [*Grant Bk., p.* 96.]

Oct. 93. Note of a debt of 718*l.* 12*s.* 5*d.*, due to Thos. Woodrove, mercer, for wares delivered for the Queen's use, since Midsummer 1612.

VOL. LXXV. NOVEMBER, DECEMBER, 1613.

Nov. 2. Westminster. Grant to Walter Thomas, of London, of pardon for life only, for manslaughter in a hasty quarrel. Latin. [*Sign Man., vol.* III., *No.* 64.]

Nov. 2. Westminster. Re-grant to John Levingston, Groom of the Bedchamber, of a messuage called Besse Place, with divers lands and tenements in Perrivale, alias Parva Grenford, alias Cornhill, and in Harrow, co. Middlesex, with discharge of all arrears of rent due on the former grant. Latin. [*Ibid., No.* 65.]

Nov. 2. Westminster. Grant to Robt. Young of a pension of 80*l.* per ann., for life. [*Ibid., No.* 66.]

Nov. 3. Creation of Robt. Visct. Rochester to the Barony of Brancepeth, bishopric of Durham. [*Grant Bk., p.* 120.]

Nov. 4. Bishop's Auckland. 1. Wm. James, Bp. of Durham, to the Council. Particulars of the musters in the county of 400 trained and 400 untrained men. A fresh supply of arms, horses, &c. will be needed for the service. *Incloses.*

1. I. *Names of the principal recusants in the diocese of Durham, and numbers of those of the vulgar sort. Total, men* 171, *women* 348; *with a list of such as are reclaimed.*

VOL. LXXV.

1613.

Nov. 4. 2. Ceremonial of creating Sir Robt. Carr Visct. Rochester, Earl of Somerset.

Nov. 4. Westminster. Warrant to Geo. Lord Carew, Master, and Sir Roger Dallison, Lieutenant of the Ordnance, to pay to Will. Cudner a pension of 40*l.* per ann., for service in the Ordnance. [*Sign Man., vol.* III., *No.* 67.]

Nov. 5. Whitehall. Proclamation prohibiting the raising of the prices of victuals within the verge of the Court. Printed. [*Proc. Coll., No.* 25.]

Nov. 5. Grant to John Gragge [Craig?] of the office of Physician in Ordinary to Prince Charles, for life. [*Grant Bk., p.* 109.]

Nov. 6. Grant to Edw. Grent, citizen and mercer, Robt. Moore, and two others, of the office of Surveyor in the cities of London and Westminster, and elsewhere, for punishment of vagrants. [*Ibid, p.* 125.]

Nov. 6. Westminster. Warrant to John Pymme, Receiver of Wiltshire, to pay yearly to Geo. Hungerford, 13*s.* 4*d.* per load, for eight loads of hay for the King's deer in Braydon Forest. [*Sign Man., vol.* III., *No.* 68.]

Nov. 7. Hackney. 3. Robt. Lord Rich to Sir Thos. Lake. Will send his cast of hawks to the King as required, but Sir Thos. Monson is unjust in accusing him of taking up the hawk, knowing it to be his or the King's. Bought it of a hawk keeper, and hopes it will not be taken from him to please Sir Thos. Monson.

Nov. 8. Westminster. Warrant to pay to Hen. Seckford, Master of the Pavilions, &c., 33*l.* 6*s.* 8*d.* per ann., for providing a convenient place for the office of pavilions, hales, and tents, as previously allowed to Thos. Bedingfield, deceased. [*Sign Man., vol.* III., *No.* 69.]

Nov. 8. Westminster. Grant to John Gray, the King's servant, of the keeping of the Common Gaol of Salop, for life. Latin. [*Ibid, No.* 70.]

Nov. 8. Grant to John Hutton of the office of Master of the Hospital of King James in the Charter House, for life. [*Grant Bk., p.* 126.]

Nov. 11. London. 4. Chamberlain to Carleton. The King has made six new Knights, though he has of late been sparing of the dignity, wishing to raise the price of knighthood to 500*l.* Ceremony of Visct. Rochester's creation as Earl of Somerset, Baron Brancepeth, &c. It is thought he will be made Marquis of Orkney. The marriage between him and Lady Frances is put off till Christmas, the Queen being won over, and promising her presence. Chief Justice Coke made a Privy Councillor. The Muscovy Ambassador has presented the King with rich sable and fox furs. Great damage done on the east coast by a very high tide. The loss in Kent alone is 200,000*l.* Skevington and Bray, who were engaged in a lawsuit, killed each other in a sudden encounter. The Bishop of Rochester refusing Coventry, the Dean of St. Paul's [John Overall] is likely to have it, and [Valentine] Carey, Master of Christ's College, Cambridge, will

1613. VOL. LXXV.

succeed him. Lady Jane Drummond is to marry Lord Roxburgh. [John] Dackombe is to be Master of Requests. Sir Fras. Bacon has a fit of the stone.

Nov. 11. Westminster. Warrant to the Customers of Lyme and Tapsome for entering in the custom books as Taunton cottons certain coarse cottons made at Taunton and Chard, and charging on them a duty of 16*d.* the piece, and not the impositions on baize. [*Sign Man., vol.* III., *No.* 71.]

Nov. 11. Theobalds. Grant to John Medhoppe, of London, of pardon for life only, for clipping and filing twelve pieces of gold coin, he being young and penitent. Latin. [*Ibid., No.* 72.]

Nov. 11. Westminster. Warrant for payment of 460*l.* to John Murray, Keeper of the Privy Purse. [*Ibid., No.* 73.]

Nov. 11. Westminster. Warrant to pay to Sir Jas. Fullerton, Keeper of the Privy Purse to the Prince, 1,000*l.* per ann., instead of the former allowance of 600*l.* [*Ibid., No.* 74.]

Nov. 11. Theobalds. Warrant to pay to Jas. Droane 106*l.* 12*s.*, for transportation of twenty-two tons of beer to Heidelberg, for the use of the Electress Palatine. [*Ibid., No.* 75.]

Nov. 11. Westminster. Warrant to pay to Wm. Marlott, employed to carry the pardon to Capt. Gilbert Roope and other pirates, 150*l.* for expenses, and 100*l.*, paid by him for Roope's ship, which was afterwards restored to a Frenchman, its proprietor. [*Ibid., No.* 76.]

Nov. 12. Westminster. Grant to Wm. Beesley, of Bleasdale, Lancashire, of pardon for the violent rescue of Thos. Coffin, alias Barnaby, a Seminary priest. Latin. [*Ibid., No.* 77.]

Nov. 12. Westminster. Grant to John Jones, in reversion after his father Thos. Jones, and Rich. Turner, of the office of Master of the Tents and Toils. Latin. [*Ibid., No.* 78.]

Nov. 12. Westminster. Grant to Sir Robt. Phelips, son of Sir Edw. Phelips, Master of the Rolls, of the next nomination of a Clerk to the Petty Bag, in the Court of Chancery. [*Ibid., No.* 79.]

Nov. 12. Westminster. Grant to Miles Whytakers, a keeper of Theobalds Park, of a pension of 50*l.* per ann., in lieu of pasturing twenty-two cattle, the pasturage being reserved for preservation of the deer. [*Ibid., No.* 80.]

Nov. 12. Westminster. Warrant for repayment to Matthew Chubbe of 1,000*l.* advanced by the King's desire to the town of Dorchester for rebuilding it after a fire, to be paid out of the next subsidy that shall be granted. [*Ibid., No.* 81.]

Nov. 12. Westminster. Grant to Wm. Damport, footman, of a pension of 40*l.* per ann., for life. [*Ibid., No.* 82.]

VOL. LXXV.

1613.
Nov. 13. Westminster. Grant to John Ward, of Walpole, Norfolk, of pardon for life only, for stealing seven bullocks. Latin. [*Sign Man., vol.* III., *No.* 83.]

Nov. 13. Westminster. Grant to Thos. Powell, on surrender of Wm. Vaughan, of the office of Solicitor General in the Marches of Wales. Latin. [*Ibid., No.* 84.]

Nov. 13. Westminster. Grant to Rich. Lazomby, keeper of Theobalds Park, of a pension of 50*l.* per ann., in lieu of pasturage there of twenty-one cattle. [*Ibid., No.* 85.]

Nov. 13. 5. Grant of a pension of 50*l.* per ann. to John Ferris, master cook to the late Prince Henry; with note of its enrolment in the Exchequer, Oct 3, 1661.

Nov. 13. [Whitehall.] 6. Earls of Northampton and Suffolk to the Solicitor General. Order him to draw up a grant to Visct. Fenton of the King's remainder of lands in Berkshire granted to Lord Norris and his issue male, reserving the ancient rents. With the reply thereto, dated Jan. 7, 1614, asking whether the rent is to be 10*l.* 17*s.* 5*d.*, as paid by Lord Norris, or 100*l.* 17*s.* 5*d.*, the real value of the land.

Nov. 14. 7. Earl of Suffolk to Sir Thos. Lake. Complains that the Chancellor [of the Exchequer] has passed to another a grant of the keepership of Manshall Park, Derbyshire, which the King had promised to him for Harry Howard.

Nov. 14. Westminster. Warrant to pay to Luke Whetstone, of London, and five others, the usual bounty of 5*s.* per ton on six new ships built by them, amounting to 1,330 crowns. [*Sign Man., vol.* III., *No.* 86.]

Nov. 14. Westminster. Grant to John Tindall of a Gunner's place in the Tower. Latin. [*Ibid., No.* 87.]

Nov. 14. Westminster. Presentation of Wm. Huchenson to the rectory of Kenne, diocese of Exeter. Latin. [*Ibid., No.* 88.]

Nov. 14. Westminster. Ratification of the appointment by the Lord High Admiral of Sir Fras. Howard to be Lieutenant and Admiral of the Narrow Seas for life. [*Ibid., No.* 89.]

Nov. 17. 8. Thos. Wilson to Ambrose Randolph, his son-in-law. Requests him to pay 104*l.* 3*s.* 4*d.* to Geo. Allington, to redeem a bond, the last he has in the world.

Nov. 17. Whitehall. 9. Earl of Suffolk to Sir Thos. Lake. The business of the patents of Sir Jerome Bowes and Sir Edw. Zouch, and their companies, for manufacture of glasses, has been heard, and Bowes refuses the offered compromise of 1,000*l.* per ann. Lord Coke suggests a new patent for Zouch, reserving the 1,000*l.* for the other patentees, which they would then be compelled to accept, and thus "finish this good commonwealth's work which His Majestie hath so prudentlie seene into."

VOL. LXXV.

1613.
Nov. 17. 10. Particulars of assart lands, purpresture, and other Crown lands in the Forests of Saulcey and Whittlewood, co. Northampton, according to an inquisition taken at Oundle, the ancient rents being 43*s.* 2*d.*, and present yearly value 112*l.* 12*s.* 6*d.*

Nov. 18. 11. Earl of Suffolk to Sir Thos. Lake. The death of the pretended Chancellor of Hereford will enable the King to favour Silvanus Skory, who has a just claim to the Chancellorship. Begs his Majesty's letters in his favour.

Nov. 18. 12. The Same to the Same. Urges the suit of Silvan Skory, who did good service to the King formerly, when he dared not avow it.

Nov. 18. 13. Earl of Northampton to the Same. Sends the petition of the merchants to the Council, on which the King is requested to write to the King of Denmark and Duke of Holstein. It is impossible to redress abuses in the Navy, whilst the pay is so much in arrear that the wives and children of the sailors are hardly kept from making outcries at the gate. The King has already lost 100,000*l.* by pilfering, since the commission was given for discovery of frauds in the Navy. Waits to publish the proclamation on duels till the King's proclamation thereon shall have been seen and admired by all. The Earl of Lenox and Dackombe are called up about Bromfield and Yale.

Nov. 18. 14. Earl of Nottingham to the Same. The provision of hay for the deer in Linchford Walk will cost 40*l.*, at 26*s.* the load; it cannot be had nearer than Farnham. A similar sum will be needed for Saunders Walk. The deer elsewhere can feed on the browse. Wm. Lucas is the man who is to have the warrant for preservation of partridges.

Nov. 18. Whitehall. 15. Earl of Suffolk to the Same. Desires him to forward two letters to the Earl of Rutland and Lord Willoughby of Eresby, requesting them to be of the company of masquers.

Nov. 18. Westminster. 16. Rich. Neyle, Bishop of Coventry and Lichfield, to the Same. Sends the mortmain which the King granted to St. John's College, Oxford, to be signed, and to pass the signet, &c.

Nov. 18. Westminster. 17. Commission to the Lord Chancellor and others, empowering them to treat with Knights and Gentlemen, duly qualified and willing to compound for the dignity of Baronet.

Nov. 18. Royston. Grant to the Bishop of Winchester of licence to hold a weekly market and two yearly fairs in his manor of Hambleden, co. Hants. Latin. [*Sign Man., vol.* III., *No.* 90.]

Nov. 18. Royston. Grant to Abraham Allen of the office of Surgeon to the King, in place of John Nasmyth, deceased. [*Ibid., No.* 91.]

Nov. 18. Royston. Grant to David Ramsay, Groom of the Bedchamber to the late Prince, of a pension of 200*l.* per ann. [*Ibid., No.* 92.]

VOL. LXXV.

1613.

Nov. 18. Royston. Warrant to the Earl of Northampton to exercise the office of Steward of the Manors of Lewisham, Sayscourt, East Greenwich, West Greenwich, Le Shrofold, Bankers, Deptford, and Stroud; and of Bailiff of the Manors of East Greenwich and Sayscourt, till the Stewardship, void since the death of the Earl of Salisbury, is filled. [*Sign Man., vol.* III., *No.* 93.]

Nov. 18. Royston. Grant to John Okes, in reversion after Robt. Tyas and Bevis Thelwall, of the office of Clerk of the Great Wardrobe. Latin. [*Ibid., No.* 94.]

Nov. 18. Royston. Warrant for payment of 50*l.* each, to Sir Thos. Erskine, Hen. Gibb, of the Bedchamber, and Hugh May, of the Privy Chamber, for their charges in going into the Low Countries. [*Ibid., No.* 95.]

Nov. 18. Royston. Grant to Sir Fras. Knollys and Rich. Arrowsmith, Yeoman of the Chamber, of the keeping of Bishop's Bearewood Walk and Lodge, in Windsor Forest. [*Ibid., No.* 96.]

Nov. 18. Royston. Grant to Walter Rumsay, of Gray's Inn, and Edw. Fettiplace, of Lincoln's Inn, on surrender of Rich. Delabere, of the office of Attorney General, cos. Carmathen, Cardigan, Pembroke, Radnor, and Brecknock. [*Ibid., No.* 97.]

Nov. 18. Royston. Grant to Lawrence Parke, of Whitbeck, Cumberland, at the nomination of Wm. Whitmore and Jonas Verdon, Contractors for lands, of the manor lands, &c. of Whitbeck, and others, co. Cumberland, parcel of the late Priory of Coningshead. Latin. [*Ibid., No.* 98.]

Nov. 20. Royston. Grant to St. John's College, Oxford, of licence to purchase more lands to the value of 300*l.* per ann., the number of Fellows being increased from thirty to fifty. Latin. [*Ibid., No.* 99.]

Nov. 20. Grant, in reversion, to Wm. Darwin, of the office of Yeoman in the Armoury at Greenwich, for life. [*Grant Bk., p.* 111.]

Nov. 20. Whitehall. 18. Earl of Suffolk to Lake. Sir And. Keith must give satisfaction to Lord Harrington for his unmannerly proceeding towards his father during the Embassy, and also to Bushell for the same. The Commissions for the Chamber and Household of the Prince must be expedited. Details what is already done therein. Lady Burgh is disabled by illness from going [to the Electress Palatine]; sends names, for the King's choice, of ladies suitable to supply her place. Mrs. Dudley declares she does not mean to marry Schomberg, and her friends are sending for her home. The deer given by the King to Count Maurice are shipped. The Officers of the Toils beg that the deer for Bagshot Park may be taken in three places instead of six, as less injurious to the toils. *Incloses,*

18. I. *List of four ladies, Lady Cecil, wife of Sir Edw. Cecil, Lady Warburton, Lady Howard, widow of the Lord Admiral's brother, and Mrs. Goring, with their qualifications for attending on the Electress.*

VOL. LXXV.

1613.

Nov. ? 19. Sir Geo. Chaworth to the King. Requests him to give order for drawing a grant to him of the making of 100, or at least 30 or 40, free denizens.

Nov. 20. Strand. 20. Sir Julius Cæsar to Sir Thos. Lake. The Bishop of Chester has sealed up and inventoried the books of Anderton, a recusant, deceased; but his goods cannot legally be sequestered before conviction. Sir Geo. Chaworth and Sir Walter Chute's requests have been fulfilled. Has ordered a commission for Lord Haddington's matter, touching the arrears of recusants.

Nov. 20. Westminster. 21. Thos. Watson, Teller of the Exchequer, and Receiver of First Fruits, to the Same. Became bond for Wm. Shaw, to whom the King granted 1,500*l.* bounty money, which has never been paid. Is called on by Shaw's creditors, and begs leave to deduct the 1,500*l.* from his next payment of first fruits. Has gained 14,000*l.* to the King by the escheat of Sir Hen. James, and has always favoured the Scots.

Nov. 20. 22. Thos. Sayer to the Same. Details of the proceedings in the Court of Wards, in the suit between Lady Lake and her sister, Lady Cæsar. Has seen the latter, and she is willing to come to a compromise, and join in destroying the will. *Incloses,*

22. I. *Order of the Court of Wards and Liveries relative to the division of rents between Lady Lake and her sister, Dame Susan Cæsar, widow, daughters and coheirs of Sir Wm. Ryder, deceased. Nov.* 18.

Nov. 21. Royston. Grant to Sir Edm. Sheffield, second son of Lord Sheffield, of the Pallistership and Keepership of the Park of Sheriff-Hutton, co. York, with rental of the herbage for life. Latin. [*Sign Man., vol.* III., *No.* 100.]

Nov. 21. Royston. Commission to the Lords Commissioners for the Treasury to sell the jewels and plate of the Dukes of Burgundy, which have long remained in the Treasury at Westminster. [*Ibid., No.* 101.]

Nov. 21. Royston. Warrant to pay to Sir Wm. Herrick 45*l.* 15*s.*, for jewellers' work. [*Ibid., No.* 102.]

Nov. 22. Royston. Grant to Geo. Banckes, of Edmonton, Middlesex, of pardon for life only, for horse-stealing, the evidence being weak, and his character good. Latin. [*Ibid., No.* 103.]

Nov. 23. Royston. Grant to John Hussey of the office of Musician, in place of Alfonso Lanier, deceased. [*Ibid., No.* 105.]

Nov. 23. Royston. Grant to Wm. Ramsay and Thos. Lumsden, in reversion after Sir Wm. Gascoigne and Thos. Athy, of the Stewardship of Galtres, co. York. Latin. [*Ibid., No.* 106.]

Nov. 23. 23. Earl of Northampton to Lake. Touching the pepper-corns, the merchants protest they have nothing which they have not rightly acquired by traffic with the Great Mogul. Care is needful therein lest the East India trade be injured. Has sent the King's directions

Vol. LXXV.

1613.

to the Earl of Shrewsbury by the Lieutenant [of the Tower], who was to take home the prisoner [Lady Arabella]. His Majesty's pleasure concerning Talbot, and the protection sought by Chambers, shall be delivered to the Lords. The Bishop of Durham has written to the Lords touching Border affairs.

Nov. 24. Whitehall. 24. Earl of Suffolk to Lake. Order has been taken with the Keeper of Egham Walk, for the King's six wild pigs, until they are fit to be turned out. Sir Edw. Cecil has been ordered to request his lady to attend the Electress at Heidelberg. Difficulties about the officers of the Prince's household, &c., &c.

Nov. 24. London. 25. Giov. Franc. Biondi to [Carleton]. Sir Hen. Wotton is appointed Ambassador to France, but will not go till April. Intends to go with him. Costly ballets preparing for the Earl of Somerset's marriage, which is to be on Feb. 20, after the Parliament. Barbarigo will not come for six months yet. Italian.

Nov. 24. Royston. Grant to Edm. Sawyer and Wm. Trigg, of London, at suit of Sir Art. Ingram and other contractors, of lands in cos. York, Carmarthen, Anglesea, Brecon, Lincoln, Northampton, Nottingham, Northumberland, Essex, and Norfolk, value 53*l.* 15*s.* 8*d.* per ann. Latin. [*Sign Man., vol.* III., *No.* 107.]

Nov. 25. Royston. Grant to David Ramsay, Clockmaker Extraordinary, of a pension of 50*l.* per ann. [*Ibid., No.* 108.]

Nov. 25. Royston. Grant to Thos. Tilsley of the office of a Yeoman Pricker. [*Ibid., No.* 109.]

Nov. 25. Royston. Grant to Rich. Hunt of the office of a Yeoman Pricker. [*Ibid., No.* 110.]

Nov. 25. Royston. Warrant to repay to Sir Robt. Phelips 800*l.*, which he advanced for a lease of Sherborne Park. Also to draw a grant to the Earl of Somerset of the manor of Sherborne and all manors, lands, &c., co. Dorset, whereof Sir Walter Raleigh was possessed, and the Rectory or Prebend of Sherborne, for which he has paid 20,000*l.* [*Ibid., No.* 111.]

Nov. 25. Royston. Grant to Lord Wm. Howard of purchase of the manor, lands, &c. of Irthington, and others, co. Cumberland, value 18*l.* 12*s.* 4*d.* per ann. Latin. [*Ibid., No.* 112.]

Nov. 25. Royston. Warrant to pay to the Earl of Somerset 2,000*l.*, as interest for moneys advanced by him for the purchase of the manor of Raby, and other lands in the bishopric of Durham, and for other sums disbursed by him for the King. [*Ibid., No.* 113.]

Nov.? 26. Petition of Geo. Brabant and Rich. Dighton, Keepers of the East and West Parks of Brancepeth, co. Durham, to Somerset, for permission to continue in their said places, now that the manor of Brancepeth is conveyed to his Lordship.

VOL. LXXV.

1613.

Nov. 25. Commission to Sir Wm. Selby, and others, to keep the peace, &c. in Northumberland, Westmoreland, &c., on the Borders. [*Grant Bk., p.* 97.]

Nov. 25. 27. Earl of Northampton to Somerset. The prisoner is sent back to Mr. Lieutenant, though a request for longer absence had been proposed. The place intended for the escape was under a study of Mr. Revenes [Ruthven ?]. It has been carried on with great mystery and secrecy.

Nov. 25. London. 28. Chamberlain to Carleton. The King bears the expense of the approaching marriage [of the Earl of Somerset], and the Queen that of Mrs. Drummond. Greenwich is added to the Queen's jointure by her late pacification. Discontent because a servant of Sir Fras. Bacon was found guilty of manslaughter for killing a Scot in self-defence. Prosperity of the East India trade. Some books of Suarez, the Jesuit, derogatory to princes, burnt at Paul's Cross. Mischief done by the floods in Lincolnshire, Norfolk, and the Isle of Ely. The two friars are sick; the younger is weary of being with the Archbp. of York; they gather the charity of well-wishers. Sir Thos. Savage has obtained the reversion of the title and lands of his father-in-law, Lord Darcy, which returned to the Crown for want of male heirs, by giving 24,000*l.* and half the land to the Earl of Somerset. Lady Burgh gone to reside with the Electress Palatine, with an allowance of 500*l.* per ann. Sir Stephen le Sieur is recalled from the Emperor's Court, being unacceptable.

Nov. 25. Royston. Grant to John Dackombe, of the Savoy, and Wm. Noy, of Lincoln's Inn, nominated by the Earl of Somerset and Lord Darcy, of the manor of Skighawe, and other lands in Essex, of which Lord Darcy, of Chiche, was tenant in tail; the remainder vested in His Majesty, being by him granted to the Earl of Somerset, who has agreed with Lord Darcy thereupon. Latin. [*Sign Man., vol.* III., *Nos.* 114, 115.]

Nov. 29. Newmarket. Grant to Art. Bogg, of the Privy Kitchen, of the benefit of the outlawry of Wm. Gateacre, reserving a tenth part to the King, subject to the clauses of moderation prescribed in the King's book of bounty. [*Ibid., No.* 116.]

Nov. 29. Newmarket. Grant to Geo. Sewell, servant to Prince Charles, of the keeping of Huntingdon Gaol. Latin. [*Ibid., No.* 117.]

Nov. 29. Newmarket. Grant to John and Dan. Williams, of London, of the office of Keepers of the Books of Entries of Ships coming into the port of London with foreign merchandise. [*Ibid., No.* 118.]

Nov. ? 29. Earl of Northampton to Lake. Sir Wm. Constable means to procure His Majesty's letter for a place in the Brill, which his cousin, Sir Horace Vere, Governor, long since promised to Sir Hen. Peyton. Hopes the King will allow the Governors of Flushing and Brill to give away their own places, according to their patents.

VOL. LXXV.

1613.

[Nov.] 30. Account of the Hanaper and Petty Bag since Michaelmas Term.

Dec. 2. Royston. Proclamation prohibiting the import of dressed felt hats or caps, in order to encourage the dressing of them at home. Printed. [*Proc. Coll., No.* 26.]

Dec. 2. 31. Northampton to [Lake]. The bark Pearl shall be brought from Ireland to London, as the King commands. This course is the safest both for the Ambassadors and the proprietors, but the Lord Admiral thinks that by his patent, all those matters belong to his jurisdiction. The cargo is not so valuable as was reported. Asks for an answer to the Bishop of Durham's letter, touching the disposing of the Borders, &c.

Dec. 3. 32. Earl of Suffolk to the Same. Thanks for favour to Hen. Howard concerning Manshall Park. Asks a renewal of the warrant for the sale of land. A Privy Seal to be drawn for the Gentlemen's Masque, adding 100*l.*, to be given to Sir Sigismund and Hen. Zinzan, for the running at the tilt.

Dec. 3. Whitehall. 33. Earl of Suffolk and Sir Julius Cæsar to the Same. To draw a warrant for payment to Meredith Morgan of sums needful for the Gentlemen's Masque at Christmas.

Dec. 3. Grant, in reversion, to Geo. Ravenscroft, of the office of Keeper of the Council Chamber, for life. [*Grant Bk., p.* 120.]

Dec. 5. Whitehall. 34. Duke of Lenox to Lake. [Edw.] Sackville laughs at the idea that there was an attempt on his life, as reported, only his horse was struck by some drunken fellow; but Archibald Primrose says one Bruce is resolved to kill him.

Dec. 7. London. 35. Sir Walter Cope to Somerset. Sir Rich. Cheetwood little deserves His Majesty's favour in a certain cause. Sends his own answers thereon.

Dec. 7. Strand. 36. Sir Julius Cæsar to Lake. Sends an inventory of Anderton's books, to be presented to the King from the Bishop of Chester. *Incloses,*

36. I. *List of Popish books [belonging to Anderton ?].*

Dec. 8. 37. Earl of Suffolk to the Same. Asks a warrant for the expenses of Mrs. Mercer, a skilful midwife, to be sent to Heidelberg to attend her Grace. Hopes Edw. Sackville may be allowed to run at the tilt at his cousin's marriage, in spite of Primrose's report. No haste in adding Thos. Murray to the commission for the Prince's chamber. Wishes the Lords Marshal would end the quarrel between young Cornwallis and Patrick Ramsay. A mere commandment will not be sufficient to prevent the Judges inditing young Weston. Some other course must be thought of.

VOL. LXXV.

1613.

Dec. 8 Wednesday. 38. Earl of Northampton to Lake. Mr. Marshall finds the corruptions under a certain patent have been flagrant. The complainants will speak more freely when sworn before a commission. Hopes the King will stand firm in allowing Lord Cavendish to purchase Harlington. Lady Shrewsbury is almost mad about it. Hopes the foundation of trade with the Great Mogul is well laid. Our merchants have had a bloody struggle with the Portuguese. The Spanish Ambassador's proffers about trade are to be heard. *Incloses*

38. I. *Articles concluded between the Governor of Amadevaz, on the part of the Great Mogul, and Capt. Thos. Best, on the part of the King of England and the East India Company, for settling a trade and factory at Surat and other places. Oct.* 21, 1612.

Dec. 8. 39. Sir Walter Cope to the Same. Sir Rich. Cheetwood's case is altogether misconceived. The granting his petition will be a dangerous precedent. The King will be daily importuned, and his Court disgraced, if parties are allowed to refuse compliance with decrees, without express letters from His Majesty.

Dec. 9. Whitehall. Thursday. 40. Earl of Northampton to the Same. Fears that Her Majesty will displace him from his office of Keeper of the Game in Greenwich Park, with possession of the lodge. Was brought up in the place from a child; has expended upwards of 2,000*l.* there, and desires to lay his bones there. Requests the King, in passing the grant of it to the Queen, to provide for his remaining, otherwise he will be at the mercy of a wrathful mistress, and his expulsion will be inevitable.

Dec. 9. Lease to John Gray of the King's two parts of the lands of Eliz. and Thos. Wells, recusants. [*Docquet. Dec.* 9 *and Feb.* 1614.]

Dec. ? 41. Project for raising the King's revenue by instituting an office for registering debts contracted upon usurious bonds, bills of exchange, &c.

Dec. ? 42. Project for increase of the King's revenue by his resuming into his own hands the grant of sole importation of tobacco, and regranting it to an agent, who will yield him half the profits, estimated at 15,000*l.*; with reasons why he may resume the grant.

Dec. ? 43. Proposition that one year's rent be paid in advance by His Majesty's tenants, farmers, fee-farmers, and others, to be allowed again in three years.

Dec. 9. London. 44. Chamberlain to Carleton. Sir Ralph Winwood lately at Royston. The King suffers from relaxation of the uvula. Great lack of money. Projects abound, but they all come to nothing, except the sale of lands; the value of 2,000*l.* per ann. sold since Michaelmas, and another 2,000*l.* ordered; but of the 17,000*l.* which was to come in this week, and was intended to stop some urgent claims, the King reserves 10,000*l.* for jewels for the bride, and the other 7,000*l.* for other followers. The very guard for his person, and his

VOL. LXXV.

1613.

postmen from Royston, are unpaid. Sir Hen. Neville and Sir Thos. Lake no more spoken of for Secretaries. Sir Thos. Edmondes may be the man, but he can be ill spared [from France] during the marriage treaty. The Lord Chief Justice has summoned recusants to the King's Bench, and committed many for refusing the Oath of Allegiance. All persons who go abroad to fight duels are to be censured in the Star Chamber. Death of Lord Berkeley, whose granddaughter has married Lord Coke's eldest son; and of Sir John Leveson, Sir Wm. Walgrave, father and son, and young Sir Wm. Cornwallis.

Dec. 9. Grant to Thos. Hooper, Ranger of Cranborne Chace, of a forfeited recognizance of 300*l.*, acknowledged by Edw. Downes, his brother-in-law, deceased, as surety for Jeremy Downes, which grant is intended for the relief of the children of the said Edw. Downes. [*Docquet. Dec.* 9 *and Feb.* 1614.]

Dec. 9. Presentation of David Owen to the parsonage of All Saints, St. Gregory, Northampton. [*Docquet.*]

Dec. [1]1. 45. Earl of Northampton to Lake. Thanks for the King's request to the Queen not to thrust him out of Greenwich Park. She professes that she does not intend it; but his security depends upon an express provision in the grant, without which she would have power to do it as soon as her patent is passed.

Dec. ? 46. Statement of grants of offices and lands made to Thos. Sheffield and Lord [Northampton ?] in Greenwich.

Dec. 11. Commission to the Lord Chancellor and others for the sale of lands entailed according to indenture, dated 8 May, 7 Jac. I. [*Grant Bk., p.* 109.]

Dec. 11. Whitehall. 47. Duke of Lenox to Somerset. To procure the King's direction to stay the ministers of Lord Harrington from proceeding in the matter of the farthing tokens, they opposing, for their own profit, the transfer thereof to the Duke, though he has offered terms satisfactory to Lord Harrington.

Dec. 13. Great St. Bartholomews. 48. Lord Chief Justice Hobart to Lake. The escheats incurred by Lord ———, Sheriff of Cumberland, for escapes connived at, come to 415*l.*, and should be levied at once; but it would be grievous to his Lordship, and against the King's own book [for granting or withholding of suits], and also without precedent, to grant the fines to another, rather than have them levied to the King's own use.

Dec. 14. Commission to the Lord Chancellor and others to sell reversions or remainders of lands in the survey of the Exchequer and Duchy of Lancaster, inheritable of divers persons by former entails. [*Grant Bk., p.* 103.]

VOL. LXXV.

1613.
Dec. 19. 49. —— Sanders to the King. Concerning the proceedings at law for the confiscation of the goods of the pirate, lately executed, left in the hands of an Earl in Ireland. The Lord Privy Seal, to whom it was referred, refused to have anything further to do in the matter. Thinks it a pity that so rich a prize should be lost, and proposes means to recover it by law. [*See Dec.* 2.]

Dec. 20. Confirmation to Hen. Earl of Northampton of the office of Keeper of Greenwich Park, and the herbage and pannage of the same. [*Grant Bk., p.* 117.]

Dec. 20. Commission to the Lord Chancellor, &c. to sell on lease any (entailed) lands contained in an indenture, dated 8 May, 7 Jac. I., in the survey of the Exchequer or Duchy of Lancaster, including wood and timber. [*Ibid., p.* 105.]

Dec. 20. Commission to Sir Robt. Carey, Sir Jas. Fullerton, and Sir Robt. Carr, for the rule and government of Prince Charles and all his family above the stairs. [*Ibid., p.* 105.]

Dec. 20. Commission to Sir David Fowlies, Cofferer, for the rule and government of Prince Charles and his household below stairs. [*Ibid., p.* 105.]

Dec. 23. Confirmation of the sentence annulling the marriage between Robt. Earl of Essex and Lady Fras. Howard. [*Ibid., p.* 111.]

Dec. 23. Grant to Wm. Garway, John Wolstenholme, and Nich. Salter, of the customs and subsidies on currants for seven years. [*Ibid., p.* 125.]

Dec. 23. 50. Memorandum of the delivery of a messuage and tenement called Vambers Poole by John Vaughan, under warrant of attorney from his mother, Judith Vaughan, widow, to Thos. Fitzgerald and Frances his wife, &c.

Dec. 23. London. 51. Rev. Geo. Carleton to Padre Paolo, at Venice. Disapproves the endless contentions in the church. Thinks the true church is that which serves the same God, and holds the same rule of faith, wherever it be placed. God is glorified by his delivering the English church from tyranny, and preserving the integrity of other churches through it. Their church the more to be pitied as being near the fountain of evil [Rome]. Thinks true Christian membership is not being united with one church or another, but having the communion of saints, &c. Latin.

Dec. 23. London. 52. Chamberlain to Carleton. Much whispering about offices. Sir Ralph Winwood will ask to be sent back to Holland if he be not appointed soon, having had so many promises. Sir Thos. Overbury prevented his having the place last year. He is too plain for the tender ears of the age. Lord Coke rivals the Earl of Northampton for the Treasurership. Sir Fras. Bacon prepared a costly Masque in honour of the approaching marriage, and will accept no help towards the charge. He feasts the whole University of Cambridge, and lives in splendid style, though he pretends he will take

VOL. LXXV.

no fees. The ship Advantage burnt in Scotland. Schomberg is come over to obtain leave for Mrs. Dudley to remain with the Electress Palatine. The King has spoken approvingly to [Geo.] Carleton on his new work.

Dec. 30. London. 53. John Chamberlain to Alice Carleton. Description of the marriage of the Earl and Countess of Somerset, of the Masque that night, and the running at the ring the next day. The Dean of Westminster preached in commendation of the young couple. Details of rich presents given to them by many of the nobility, Sir Thos. Lake, Sir Ralph Winwood, and others; also by the City, the Merchant Adventurers, East India Company, &c. Sir Hen. Bowyer dead.

Dec. 31. 54. Indenture between Edw. Grent, Robt. More, Martin Smyth, and Fras. Hexham, all of London, Patentees of the office of Surveyor, for giving in the names of the inmates within three miles of Westminster and London, and for enforcing the laws for maintenance of the poor, and suppressing vagrancy, whereby they agree to divide the said limits into four parts, north, south, east, and west, and each to exercise his office within one of the said divisions; also to hire a house for the business of the office, to keep registers, &c.

UNDATED. 1613?

1613? 55. Petition of David Drummond to the King for a grant, on behalf of Rich. Connock, lessee of the manor of Lylesdon, co. Somerset, of all debts due to the Crown from that manor, which was forfeited by attainder of Hen. Duke of Suffolk.

Satirical papers relating to the foundation of a Mock College for Innocents or Fools, to be called Gotam College, Oxford, as follows:—

56. Epistle to the reader, and account of the circumstances attending the foundation.

57. Licence for the above foundation from the Emperor of Morea.

58. Foundation charter of Sir Thos. a Cuniculis.

59. Foundation statutes of the college.

60. Copy of the above, with additions.

61–65. Five papers relating to the regulations, offices, and privileges of the above-named college.

66. Complimentary ode to Dr. Wm. Laud, President of St. John's College; indorsed with notes [by Laud] relative to the above-named Gotam College.

67. Notes on the course pursued upon the petition of Sir John Bourchier and [Wm.] Turner to the King, that he would redeem his pledges in making payments to their creditors for the alum business. The petitioners desire that the King would enter bonds for the payment, and that their bonds may be discharged.

VOL. LXXV.

1613?

Pig and Capon, Aldersgate Street.

68. R. Lane to ———. Details of frauds practised in the alum manufacture by Turner and his company, the late Earl of Salisbury, and Sir Art. Ingram. Offers to expose and rectify them.

69. Statement that the Patent granted 19 Eliz. to the Company of Tallow Chandlers to be searchers of soap, vinegar, and barrelled butter in London, Southwark, St. Katherine's, &c., was deputed to the late Lord Chamberlain for life, and for ten years after his death; that he sold the right to the Lord Mayor of London; that the period having now lapsed, it again devolves on the Tallow Chandlers, whose right to exercise it is questioned by the offenders.

70. Observations touching the commercial treaty with France, the necessity which compelled the establishment of a French commercial company, and the advantages that have accrued therefrom.

71. Statements respecting the title of Wm. Essex, and the heirs of Lawrence Rushbrook, to a farm belonging to the late monastery of Wallingford, Berks. Thos. Hansacker, a lawyer, who married Rushbrook's widow, combines with Essex to defraud the heirs of the land.

Grant to John Slade, of Pool, Cheshire, and Thos. Brooke, of London, on payment of 1,884*l.* 2*s.* 4*d.* by Sir Thos. Savage, of the manor and lordship of Frodsham, co. Chester, value 43*l.* 16*s.* 4*d.* per ann. Latin. [*Sign Man., vol.* III., *No.* 119.]

72. Sir Dud. Diggs to the Lord Chief Justice. Requests him not to mention the letter from Sir John Digby till he see him at York House.

73. Reasons for the petition [by some of the Justices of Northamptonshire] to the King for alternating the Quarter Sessions between Northampton and Kettering; with answers thereto.

74. Copy of the above reasons.

75. Precedents for the use of other counties, of twenty-three counties which hold their Quarter Sessions in divers towns.

76. Statement of reasons why the Quarter Sessions should be held at Northampton, and not elsewhere.

77. Petition of the Plasterers' Company to the Council. Complain of encroachment on their privileges by the Tilers and Bricklayers, who in the suburbs of London employ poor men, not of the Company of Plasterers, contrary to the terms of their charter.

78. Note that in a commission lately issued, at nomination of Hen. Howard and Hen. Gibbs, for granting patents of charter warren to those who desire them, the scale of fees to be paid is made so low that the Secretary and Clerks of the Signet are great losers thereby. Request for redress therein, or stay of the grant.

Vol. LXXV.

1613?

79. Statement of the terms of a proposition to purchase the reversions in the Crown of lands entailed, value 500*l.* per ann.; with arguments in its favour.

80. Copy of the above.

81. Project for searching out concealed lands, to the value of 10,000*l.* or 12,000*l.*, the reversion whereof is now in the Crown, the entail being spent; one third to devolve on the finder and two thirds on the grantee.

82. Statement [addressed to Hen. Earl of Northampton] of abuses in the hospitals of St. John and St. Giles, near Wilton, the funds of which are appropriated by the masters, &c., instead of going to the poor. The King having issued a commission of inquiry, the masters will reform their abuses, if they know his Lordship will take notice thereof.

Northampton House.

83. [Earl of Northampton, Lord Warden of the Cinque Ports,] to his Deputy. Commands him to examine and punish persons dredging oysters within the liberty of Brightlingsea, in the place allotted to John Wolphe.

84. Memoranda of abuses committed in the manufacture of Spanish cloth and kerseys by bad dyeing and over stretching on the tenters.

85. The Council to the Justices of Peace and Officers of Corporations. To put in force the regulations for searching and sealing cloths, in order to prevent the making of false and deceitful cloth, which is much complained of by the Merchant Adventurers, and very injurious to trade. The Deputy Alnager is to be one of the searchers.

86. Warrant to pay to Sir Alex. Hay, Secretary for Scotland, 635*l.* 1*s.* 5*d.* for levy and transport of 200 men from Scotland to Ireland, and for two months' wages for them.

87. Warrant to the Lord Chancellor to draw out a commission of lieutenancy for the county of Gloucester, for Visct. Lisle, Chamberlain to the Queen, and Lord Berkeley.

88. Copy of the above.

Vol. LXXVI. January—March, 1614.

1614.

Jan. 1. 1. [Sir Dud. Carleton] to [Geo.] Carleton. Private business. A lease of his property held from [Eton] College to be renewed.

Jan. 5. London. 2. Chamberlain to Sir Dud. Carleton. Celebration of the marriage still continues. The presents of plate are valued at 12,000*l.* The Masque is repeated, though it is ill timed, being in mimicry of the Irish, and likely to exasperate them. Tilting on new year's day described. The King ordered the Lord Mayor to feast the new

1614 Vol. LXXVI.

married couple, and would accept no excuse, so the City gave them a play, masque, and banquet, in Merchant Tailors' Hall. Sir Ralph Winwood gave the bride his four splendid horses, which she had borrowed for her procession to the City. Sir Horace Vere's grant of the company of the late Sir Wm. Constable stands good, rather than that of the King. [Wm.] Trumbull succeeds Sir Thos. Edmondes as Clerk of the Council, and [John] Dackombe is Master of Requests. Winwood is in great probability of the Secretaryship, and Carleton is spoken of to succeed him in Holland.

Jan. 6. London. 3. Sir Thos. Middleton to Somerset. Sends a copy of the letter from the Bp. of St. Asaph to the Archbp. of Canterbury about John Edwards, a dangerous recusant, whom it would be mischievous to pardon.

Jan. 12. 4. Wm. Branthwaite [Master of Gonville and Caius College, Cambridge,] to Thos. Wilson. Has two scholarships vacant, and will be glad to fill them up at his nomination, if he knows of any friend's sons who are good grammar scholars, and of that country.

Jan. 12. Grant to Lady Eliz. Howard of the castle and manor of Wark, in Tynedale, &c., in co. Northumberland and bishopric of Durham. [*Grant Bk., p.* 126.]

Jan. 20. 5. Fras. Mabbe to Thos. Mabbe, Under Sheriff [of Kent]. Sends the names of the watchmen in Dover Castle who are exempted from service.

Jan. 20. London. 6. Chamberlain to Carleton. Private news. Delivery of presents to Sir Ralph Winwood. The King at Audley End, where a creation of officers is at length hoped for, according to the proverb, "Be the day never so long, at last comes even-song." Lord Knollys spoken of as Chamberlain, but that would be a slight on the Earl of Pembroke's long services. Parliament certainly expected, and the Colonels of that Militia are mustering and showing themselves. Sir John Digby comes home, whilst the King of Spain goes towards France to complete the double marriages.

Jan. 24. Commission to the Lord Chancellor and others to pay all such sums as are appointed for the King's affairs, and to make leases of lands, &c. in the survey of the Exchequer, or in the counties of Northumberland, Westmoreland, and Cumberland, and to compound for the discharge or abatement of any debt or forfeiture for extended or custody lands. [*Grant Bk., p.* 103.]

Jan. 25. Londesborough. 7. Fras. Earl of Cumberland to Somerset. Thanks for furthering the renewal of his lease in Bewcastle. Is going to the Border counties, and desires to know if he can do His Majesty any service there, &c.

Jan. 26. Grant to John Dackombe of the annuities of 4,500*l.*, 300*l.*, and 2,205*l.*, for providing French and Gascony wines for the household, for twenty-one years. [*Grant Bk., p.* 111.]

VOL. LXXVI.

1614.

Jan. 26. 8. Sir Hen. Savile to Carleton. Has given the fellowship at Eton to one younger than Mr. Horne, but who helped him three years, day and night, at his great work of St. Chrysostom. Has discharged his daughter [Lady Carleton's] bill of exchange to save his credit. Wishes the grandees would be more careful on that point, but hopes matters are mending.

Jan. 27. Royston. 9. Sir Thos. Lake to the Same. News of the friars sent over by Carleton. His Grace of Canterbury has many such renegadoes, who abjure for wives and benefices. A Parliament talked of. Those most adverse to the Court promote it most. Great joy at the birth of Lady Elizabeth's son. *Incloses,*

9. I. *Archbp. Abbot to the Bishop of Bath. Details of two Carmelite friars, sent over by Carleton, and entertained by himself and the Archbp. of York. They publicly renounced Popery, but not being promoted as they hoped, now declare that they were always Papists at heart, and prepare to return to Rome. Details their equivocation in denying their recantation.*

Jan. 31. Commission to Sir Julius Cæsar, Chancellor and Sub-Treasurer of the Exchequer, to examine all debts of recusants, depending in the Exchequer, and to allow or disallow of discharge thereof, as they shall think fit. [*Grant Bk., p.* 110.]

Jan. ? 10. Bill in the Court of Exchequer for a subpœna against Sir Thos. Middleton, Mayor, the Sheriffs and Aldermen of London, and Wm. Clarke, Thos. Russell, Wm. Hart, and Rowland Sone, who call in question the right of the Crown to certain waste lands, highways, &c. in the city of London, and have erected buildings, &c. thereon.

Jan. ? 11. Interrogatories to be administered to witnesses relative to buildings erected near Bevis Marks, Bishopsgate Street, and Hounsditch, by Wm. Clarke, Thos. Russell, Wm. Hart, and Rowland Sone, on land supposed to be waste ground belonging to the City of London.

Jan. ? 12, 13. Copies of part of the above.

Jan ? 14. Answer of Sir Thos. Middleton, Lord Mayor of London, Sir Stephen Soame, Sir Thos. Lowe, Sir Thos. Cambell, and Sir Wm. Craven, Aldermen, Thos. Bennett and Hen. Jaye, Sheriffs, Wm. Clarke, Thos. Russell, Wm. Hart, and Rowland Sone, to the information brought against them by the Crown relative to the right of possession of the streets, walls, ramparts, ditches, and waste places in and about London, stating the grounds on which they consider them to belong to the City by the charters of Henry VI. and Henry VII., and also of His present Majesty in Sept. 24, 1608; with special answers of Clarke, Russell, Hart, and Sone, to the charge of intrusion into certain of these lands brought against them in the above information.

Jan. ? 15. Details of encroachments made upon the highways by buildings in different parts of London.

VOL. LXXVI.

1614.

Jan. Leghorn. 16. Sir Robt. Dudley to [Sir David Fowlies] .Has invented a new description of ship, of such extraordinary force and swiftness that no three of the King's ships could stand against it. Would gladly make his invention of use to his own country, if the King will accept it; if not, will employ it elsewhere, especially against the Turks. The Venetians are eager to obtain it. [*See May* 11.]

Feb. 1. Lease to John Murray, Groom of the Bedchamber, of the land called Plumpton Head and others, co. Cumberland. [*Grant Bk., p.* 117.]

Feb. 2. Hampton Court. 17. Hen. Earl of Northampton, Warden of the Cinque Ports, to Wm. Ward, his Collector General, and others. To permit Geo. Rands and Robt. Hudson to recover all lost anchors in the Cinque Ports, and to sell them for their own use, reserving one third of the value to himself. With corrections [by Edw. Nicholas] for making the same grant to Wm. Ward, of Dover, and Thos. Fulnetby, of Sandwich.

Feb. 3. London. 18. Chamberlain to Carleton. Finds no truth in the rumour that he [Carleton] is to be recalled, and Calvert to succeed him. The King has had nine petitions in five days against Sir Walter Cope, as Master of the Wards, rather for weakness of judgment than corruption. Lord Roxburgh marries Mrs. Jane Drummond at Somerset House. The King is invited to be present at the shows and devices. Sir Thos. Edmondes has returned without leave, hoping for promotion in the coming appointments. The two friars sent over by Carleton have proved notable knaves, declaring they were never other than Catholics. They are committed by the Archbp. of Canterbury to safe custody, &c. They had liberal presents from the Bishops and many others.

Feb. 4. Grant to John Bucke of the office of making all brass and iron ordnance and guns, for life. [*Grant Bk., p.* 102.]

Feb. 5. Grant to Jeronimo Ross of the office of Keeper of the Wardrobe at Hinchinbrook and Royston, for life. [*Ibid., p.* 120.]

Feb. ? Warrant for the Attorney General to prepare a Commission for Sale of Court Leets. [*Docquet, Feb.*]

Feb. 7. Commission to Sir Fras. Bacon and others, for ten years, to compound for granting Court Leets in England and Wales. [*Grant Bk., p.* 104.]

Feb. 7? Warrant for a grant of the benefit of the Leets aforesaid for Lord D'Aubigny, reserving to the King 20*s.* for each grant. [*Docquet, Feb.*]

Feb. 7? Grant to Ellen Felton of 300*l.*, for services of her late husband. [*Docquet, Feb.*]

Feb. 7? Warrant to pay 100*l.* to M. de Tournon for teaching the Prince to toss the pike. [*Docquet, Feb.*]

VOL. LXXVI.

1614.
Feb. 7. Hackwood. 19. Amerigo Salvetti to [Fras] Windebank. Wishes to know what their mutual friend at Florence, R. C., has communicated to Mr. Windebank, that he may send him his own opinion on the matter. Italian.

Feb. 10. London. 20. Chamberlain to Carleton. Their friend [Sir Ralph Winwood] has failed for the present in his hopes of advancement. His qualities described. Twelve Commissioners appointed to consider the French marriage, which must be decided on, as there is talk of marrying the second daughters and second sons of France and Spain. Mrs. Drummond's marriage cost the Queen 3,000*l.* Sam. Danyell wrote a pastoral, solemn and dull. The Lord Mayor and Aldermen were invited the day after, had rich gloves, and gave the bride a cup with 200 Jacobuses. Quarrel between the Earl of Essex and young Heydon, who is sent to the Fleet. The King has gone to Newmarket, and left the Council to decide about a Parliament.

Feb. 13. Rochester. 21. Mayor and Citizens of Rochester to Somerset. Hearing that the King intends to call a Parliament, they offer him the nomination of one of their two burgesses.

Feb. 16. 22. The Council to the King. Have debated the reasons pro and con, in reference to calling a Parliament, and culled out such points of grievances as were complained of at the last Parliament, which the King might redress without prejudice. Think that on the ground of his pressing necessities, it would be better to call one, and if so, it should be done at once, that it may begin before May 3, when the Irish Parliament meets. Mutilated.

Feb. 16. 23. Transcript of the above [supplying most of the deficiencies].

[Feb. 16.] 24. Hen. Earl of Northampton to [Somerset]. The Council have resolved upon the letter which they present to His Majesty, but if the King decides to confer with the Council before the writs go forth [for Parliament], it cannot sit before May.

Feb. 16. 25. Lease from Thos. Wilson, of Hertford, to Hen. Smyth, of London, and Rebecca his wife, of closes called Great-graies in Hertfordshire.

Feb. 16. Grant to Nich. Dawnton, with reversion to Wm. Edwards, of the office of General to the Company of Merchants trading to the East Indies. [*Grant Bk.*, *p.* 110.]

Feb. 16. Grant to the Queen of an annuity of 39*l.* 16*s.* 5½*d.* from the manor of Romsey, Hampshire, and other things in divers other counties. [*Ibid.*, *p.* 101.]

Feb. 17. Thursday. 26. The Chief Justices and Counsel-at-law to Somerset. The propositions for Parliament delivered by His Majesty are so important that they request time for further consideration, and leave to deliver their answers verbally, that they may be assisted by His Majesty's "judicious and apposite questions."

VOL. LXXVI.

1614.

Feb. 17. London. 27. Chamberlain to Carleton. Proceedings in the Star Chamber on the case of Sir Stephen Proctor, accused of trying to involve two Yorkshire knights on suspicion about the Powder Plot, and of slandering the Lord Privy Seal. Doubtful whether his sentence of 3,000*l.* fine, imprisonment, and pillory, will stand. Talbot, an Irish lawyer, fined 10,000*l.* for malapert speeches to the King, on the Oath of Allegiance and authority of the Pope. A proclamation, with a book annexed, issued against duels. Doubt whether Sir Hen. Neville or their old friend will be the person promoted, but they are not jealous of each other, both relying on their great friend. Strange that three Roberts, with the same surname, should be favourites of the King, Queen, and Prince [Earl of Somerset, Sir Robt. Carr, and Sir Robt. Carey]. The States have given Sir Hen. Savile a chain worth 40*l.* or 50*l.* for his Chrysostom. The work sells but poorly. Hopes [Alice Carleton] will not return home in discontent.

Feb. 17. 28. Extract from the above.

Feb. 17. London. 29. John Chamberlain to [Alice] Carleton. There has been little snow and not half an hour's rain these three months. Certain marriages detailed. The Queen has feasted all who gave presents to her last bride [Mrs. Drummond]. She is marrying Miss Southwell, another of her maids, to Rodney, of Somersetshire. Lord St. John has married a daughter of Lord Montague, but they disagree. The match between Lord Burleigh's eldest daughter and Lord Lisle's son broken off. Birth of a son of Sir Robt. Wroth.

Feb. 19. Grant to the Queen of the capital messuage of Greenwich House and other things, co. Kent, for a hundred years, if she should live so long. [*Grant Book, p.* 102.]

Feb. 21. Hackwood. 30. Amerigo Salvetti to [Fras.] Windebank. Sends back the letter of R. C. Expects shortly to be in London, and will consult with him thereon. Italian.

Feb. 23. York House. 31. Lord Chancellor Ellesmere to Lake. Explains the cause of his delay in putting the Great Seal to the patent for glasses. Fears that the Bill for the preservation of woods, as at present devised, will be occasion of question in this hopeful Parliament. Wishes for a consultation thereon.

Feb. 23. Bellasis. 32. Sir Wm. Waad to the Justices of Peace and Treasurers for maimed Soldiers, Cornwall. Recommends James Coade, Serjeant to Sir Thos. Rotherham, wounded in Ireland, for a pension. *Annexed is,*

32. I. *Order on the Treasurer of the Eastern Division of Cornwall to pay to the above* 4*l.* *in full discharge of all future claims, dated May* 30, 1614.

Feb. 24. Grant to Wm. Trumbull of a Clerkship in the Privy Council, for life. [*Grant Book, p.* 119.]

VOL. LXXVI.

1614.
Feb. 24. Grant to Sir Marmaduke Darell and Sir Allan Apsley of 9,600*l.* per ann., for victualling the Navy. [*Grant Bk., p.* 111.]

Feb. 24. London. 33. John Chamberlain to Alice Carleton. Marriage of Mrs. Jones's daughter to Skinner, a merchant's son of the town. Writs for the Parliament are issued. Mutilated.

Feb. 24. St. Bartholomews. 34. Sir Ralph Winwood to [Carleton]. His own movements uncertain. Carleton is mistaken in supposing he is to be superseded; he may possibly be removed to Holland. Sir Thos. Edmondes is come over in hopes of advancement, but his success is doubtful.

March 1. 35. Matthew Chubbe to Sir Thos. Lake. Concerning the purchase of land for the portion of his daughter, the wife of Levingston, which is to come to 2,000*l.* Particulars of a farm worth 3,000*l.*, which he contemplates purchasing, Levingston advancing 1,000*l.* towards it.

March 2. Hackwood. 36. Amerigo Salvetti to [Fras.] Windebank. Hears from his letter that he participates in this comedy of ladies. Has done his best to keep himself and Windebank free. Sends back Lady Symon's letter, and hopes they shall escape that tempest. Has watched Philpott well, that they may not be yet discovered. Is pleased that affairs in France are likely to be accommodated. Italian.

March 2. Hackwood. 37. The Same to the Same. The secret is out. Has just received letters from Sherborne; the mother and daughter are full of displeasure; cannot conceive how the matter has been divulged; sends a copy of his lettter in reply, that Windebank may tell the same tale. Italian.

March 2. 38. Agreement between Wm. Smith and John Dackombe, in reference to a projected marriage between Hen. Smith, son of Sir Hen. Neville *alias* Smith, and Alice, daughter of John Dackombe.

March 3. London. 39. Chamberlain to Carleton. Calvert disclaims the idea of succeeding Carleton. Sir Dud. Diggs is moving every stone to obtain employment. Neither Wotton nor Morton likely to have places. Winwood must be governed by his pilot. Much bustling for seats in Parliament. The City has chosen Sir Thos. Lowe and Mr. Fuller, and refused Sir Hen. Montague, as being the King's Serjeant. Lord Harrington dead, leaving his estate to his sisters, Lady Bedford and Lady Chichester. Sir Thos. Howard is to marry Lord Burleigh's eldest daughter, and settles on her 3,000*l.* in land. He has the reversion of the treasurership of the chamber and of the post fines. Lord Fitzwalter marries Sir Michael Stanhope's daughter, assuring her 2,000*l.* The King is at Chesterford Park, where Somerset keeps his lady, but he has taken a small house for her at Thistleworth, to be near Dr. Burgess.

March 3. Grant to Eliz. Lassells, of London, widow, of pardon for clipping and filing fourteen 20*s.* pieces. Latin. [*Sign Man., vol.* III., *No.* 120.]

VOL. LXXVI.

1614.

March 4. Grant to John Verdon and Edw. Leach of the office of assaying tin in Devon and Cornwall, for life. [*Grant Bk., p.* 119.]

March 4. Grant to Hen. Champante of the office of Clerk or Keeper of the storehouses and docks for ships in Portsmouth, for life. [*Ibid., p.* 105.]

March 5. Bishopthorpe. 40. Tobias Matthew, Archbp. of York, to Somerset. Cautions him against certain persons backward in religion, or recusants, who seek to bear office in the northern parts, and try to supplant Hen. Sanderson, Constable of Brancepeth Castle, whose long and faithful services for twenty-eight years he details, and urges support and recompence for him.

March 6. 41. Statement by Leonard Rountree of four articles to prove the superiority of the Protestant over the Romish faith, which were sent to him by Dr. Favour; of his replies thereto; and conversations upon them with Wm. Outlaw, Mr. Burton, and Mr. Harwood. Imperfect. [*Seemingly written from prison and for publication.*]

March? 42. L[eonard] R[ountree] to Matthew Kellison, President of [Douay] College. Explains, at his request, his opinions on divers points of Romish doctrine and discipline. Latin.

March 7. Westminster. Grant to Geo. Hugheson of the office of bailiff of Holford, Gretton, and Kittesgate, co. Gloucester. Latin. [*Sign Man., vol.* III., *No.* 121.]

March 7. Westminster. Licence to the Company of Haberdashers of London to erect an almshouse and free school in Monmouth, and to purchase lands, value 200*l.* per ann., for the maintenance of them and of a preacher there, at the expense of Wm. Jones, one of their company. Latin. [*Ibid., No.* 122.]

March 8. Grant to Sir Wm. Pooley of advowson of the rectory of East Dereham and Terrington, co. Norfolk, for ninety years. [*Grant Bk., p.* 118.]

March 8. Grant, in reversion, to Sir Roger Wilbraham, of the office of Constable of Chester Castle, for life. [*Ibid., p.* 119.]

March 10. Dover Castle. 43. John Packenham to the Mayors, &c. within the jurisdiction of the Cinque Ports. Requests their attention to orders from the Council for the observance of Lent. *Incloses,*

43. I. *The Council to the Earl of Northampton. Request him to send their orders for better observance of Lent to the several towns in the Cinque Ports. March* 3, 1614.

43. II. *Earl of Northampton to John Packenham. Sends the Orders of Council for the due observance of Lent. Hopes the magistrates of the Cinque Ports will set a good example to those of lower rank. Northampton House, March* 7, 1614.

March 12. Grant to Sir Edwin Sandys of the moiety of the manor of Northbourne and others, co. Kent. [*Grant Bk., p.* 120.]

Vol. LXXVI.

1614.

March 12. 44. Memorandum of payments to John Whynyard, as Keeper of the Palaces of Westminster and Hampton Court, since Nov. 21, 1610.

March 13. Chiswick. 45. Graye Conyers to his father, Fras. Conyers. Sir Edw. Conway is to marry a grocer's widow in London, worth 5,000*l.* or 6,000*l.*; she is lame and in years.

March 15. Hackwood. 46. Amerigo Salvetti to [Fras.] Windebank. Glad he approves of the letter which he has sent to Lady Symons; will let some time elapse that she may be appeased. Returns him his French verses. Italian.

March 16. 47. Account of payments to John Williams, goldsmith, for gold plate given to the Princess Palatine for the baptism of her son. Latin.

March 16. Lambeth. 48. Archbp. Abbot to [Carleton]. Particulars of two friars sent over by Carleton; of their entertainment by himself and the Archbp. of York; of their preaching in the Italian church; their visits to Oxford and Cambridge; their returning to their former faith; their apprehension and escape. They were tampered with by the Chaplain of Foscarini, the Venetian Ambassador. Julius Cæsar, one of the friars, gave 100 crowns to obtain the Pope's pardon for leaving their order. The Spanish Ambassador has meddled much in such affairs, and receives much money from the King of Spain, with which he bribes the servants of other Ambassadors, of the King, Council, &c. Foscarini, whose own secretary has played the viper to him, is made his dupe. Wishes the insolencies of Papists at home and abroad were punished. Is glad the Archbp. of Spalato continues firm. A plot was laid to seize and carry him to Rome. [Partly in cipher, deciphered.]

March 17. London. 49. Chamberlain to the Same. The King was in town during Shrove Week, and then went to Oking. He visited the Lord Chancellor and Privy Seal, who are ill. Concourse at Uxbridge for choosing Sir Julius Cæsar and Sir Thos. Lake Knights for Middlesex. A servant of Sir Fras. Darcy committed for saying that the King had forbidden his master to stand. Contested elections for Parliament; even in meaner boroughs, letters and countenance prove not so powerful as was imagined. Randall Crew designed Speaker. Sir Thos. Edmondes' project for a match with France not much liked, except by the King and a few Scots. The elder friar has escaped. The keeper of the Gatehouse, and a servant of Lord Vaux, suspected of connivance. Sir Robt. Wroth dead, leaving a young widow with 1,200*l.* jointure, a son, a month old, and his estate 23,000*l.* in debt. The Earl of Somerset has borrowed Sir Baptist Hicks's house at Kensington, and there settled his lady, &c.

March 17. Westminster. 50. Grant to Edm. Brunt, of London, of a patent for an engine for dressing and bolting meal, invented by him.

March 17. Grant to John Green of the Controllership of the Customs and subsidies of wool in King's Lynn, during pleasure. [*Grant Bk.*, *p.* 251.]

Vol. LXXVI.

1614.

[March 17.] Grant to Sir Geo. Chaworth of the Keepership of the Forests of Kingswood and Fellwood, vacant by decease of Lord Berkeley. [*Docquet, Feb.*]

March 19. Grant to Geo. Donhalt, and Leonore his wife, of a messuage in the parish of St. Mary's, Aldermanbury, London, for life. [*Grant Bk., p.* 111.]

March 22. Grant to Abraham Abercromy and Ellis Jolly of the office of Saddler to Prince Charles, for life. [*Ibid., p.* 101.]

March 23. Grant to Fras. Godolphin and John Packer of the office of Prothonotary of the Chancery, for life. [*Ibid., pp.* 113, 125.]

March 26. Grant to John Brook of the office of a Teller in the Exchequer, for life. [*Ibid., p.* 146.]

March 28. Grant to Hen. Martin of the office of Serjeant Trumpeter, for life. [*Ibid., p.* 141.]

March 28. Westminster. Grant to Wm. Elliotts and Matthias Meysey of a patent for a new method of making steel, by them invented; with proviso of revocation, if found injurious to the commonwealth. [*Sign Man., vol.* IV., *No.* 1.]

March 28. 51. " A Trew Declarcion of the Discoverie of the mayne Landes, " Ilandes, Seas, Ports, Havens, & Creekes, lyenge in the North-west, " North, and North-east partes of the World," by the Fellowship of English merchants for Discovery of New Trades (the Muscovy Company), sworn to by many of the parties before Dr. Trevor, Judge of the Admiralty; giving particulars of the voyages of Sir Hugh Willoughby in 1553; Stephen Borough, 1556; Sir Martin Frobisher, 1576–78; Art. Pett and Chas. Jackman, 1580; Sir Humph. Gilbert, 1583; John Davies, 1585–7; Wm. Hudson, 1608; Stephen Bennett, 1610–11; in proof that the English were the first discoverers in those parts, and established and long enjoyed the trade with Russia, and the whale fishery, without disturbance from the Hollanders, who, attempting to join in the trade, were, by the King's leave, prevented.

March 29. Special Commission to the Lord Chancellor and others, declaring the King's resolution to sell some of the [entailed] lands contained in an indenture of 8 May, 7 Jac. I. [*Grant Bk., p.* 137.]

March 31. Grant to Chris. Playle of the office of Purveyor for Timber in the Tower, for life. [*Ibid., p.* 141.]

March 31. London. 52. Chamberlain to Carleton. The Venetian Ambassador has attempted to murder his Secretary. An extraordinary Ambassador coming from Savoy. On Sir Robt. Wroth's death, Sir Chris. Hatton vindicated the Earl of Oxford's claim to the Keepership of Waltham Forest. Sir Art. Chichester, Lord Deputy of Ireland, has arrived. Parliament about to assemble, &c. The Archbp. of York preaches the sermon, and Dr. Abbot is Prolocutor of Convocation. Contested elections. Complaints of the tricks of Sheriffs. Sir Ralph Winwood is sworn as Principal Secretary, and Sir Thos. Lake made a Councillor without office. Sir Thos. Edmondes, who came over, has returned much disappointed.

VOL. LXXVI.

1614. [March.] 53. Sir Herbert Croft to Somerset. Addresses him as a faithful Councillor of the King and lover of the Commonwealth. Thinks, from a conversation detailed, which he had with the King at their last interview, that His Majesty is misinformed on the subject of the four English counties belonging to the Marches of Wales, and therefore, being chosen member [for Herefordshire] in the ensuing Parliament, and pledged to urge the exemption of the counties, writes a full account of the whole affair for His Majesty's information. Arguments at great length in favour of the exemption. With marginal remarks [in the King's hand], and also a concluding note, according Sir Herbert's request that the matter may be discussed in his own presence. *Incloses,*

53. I. *The Same to the Same. Gives an historical view of the question of the jurisdiction of the Council of Wales over the four English Border counties, proving that they do not lawfully belong to the Marches of Wales. With similar marginal notes by the King. [See Journals, Commons, vol. I., p. 467.]*

March? Grant to Geo. Ravenscroft, in reversion after Thos. Graves and Geo. Cockes, of the office of Keeper of the Council Chamber. [*Sign Man., vol.* IV., *No.* 2.]

VOL. LXXVII. APRIL—SEPTEMBER, 1614.

April 2. 1. Sir Wm. Fleetwood to Carleton. Having entered into partnership with Mr. Yates, who has a patent for the sole making and export of litharge, inquires what sale there will be for it in Italy and Turkey, and whether agents for it could be found. Renews a request for three or four pounds of pure mercury from the mines of Istria. *Annexed is,*

1. I. *Note of the previous sending of the above mercury, consigned to Thos. Stone, merchant.*

April 2. Hertford. 2. Thos. Wilson to Ambrose Randolph. Intended to meet the Earl of Somerset at Theobalds, but as a new Secretary is made, the matter must proceed through him. Has written letters to him and Mr. Levinus [Munck], which must be delivered at once.

April 3. Hertford. 3. The Same to the Same. Is sorry the delivery of his letter has been delayed; begs he will send it immediately.

April 3. 4. Rich. Gosson to Somerset. The Company of East India Merchants, of whom he is one, have agreed to present his Lordship with gold plate, value 600*l.* Requests to be entrusted with the making thereof having purchased the gold by order from the Company.

VOL. LXXVII.

1614.

April 3. 5. Memorandum of the distribution of 4*l.* to the servants of the Archbp. of Canterbury, at the consecration of Dr. John Overall, Bp. of Lichfield and Coventry.

April 5. Grant to Anne, Roger, and James Wright, of licence to keep a tennis court at St. Edmund's Bury, co. Suffolk, for life. [*Grant Bk., p.* 153.]

April 7. London. 6. Chamberlain to Carleton. The King and Prince rode in procession to the opening of Parliament. Particulars of the King's speech, promising to maintain religion, peace, and prosperity, and promising them easy and gracious access. Randall Crew chosen Speaker, being recommended by Secretary Winwood, in a suitable speech. Winwood's course will be difficult, so many jealous eyes being upon him. He holds office on hard conditions, and has no lodging at Court yet. Several elections won by clamour are questioned. Death of old Dr. Ovenden, of All Souls College, and Dr. Spencer, of Corpus Christi.

April 7. Grant to Sir Ralph Winwood of the office of Secretary of State, for life. [*Grant Bk., p.* 153.]

April 8. Grant to Ralph Freeman of the Clerkship of the Ordnance, for life. [*Ibid., p.* 133.]

April 8. Grant to John Milward and Gabriel Barbor of the office of Controller of the Mint in the Tower, for life. [*Ibid., p.* 136.]

April 11. Grant to John Overall, Bishop of Coventry and Lichfield, of discharge of 503*l.* 17*s.* 6*d.*, the first fruits of that bishopric. [*Docquet.*]

April 11. Grant, with survivorship, to Wm. Gateacre, and Sir Fras. Lacon, of the office of Cockmaster, for life, on surrender of a former grant to Gateacre. [*Docquet.*]

April 11. Grant to Peregrine Gastrell and Ralph Lownes of purchase of the manor of East Garston, and the site of the manor of Pougheley, co. Berks. Also grant to Hen. Edes of a tenement in Coggeshall called the Cock. [*Docquet.*]

April 11. Grant to Hen. Skynner and John Mason of purchase of the manor of Islingham, co. Kent. [*Docquet.*]

April 11. Grant to John Griffith of purchase of certain lands and tenements, cos. Anglesey and Carnarvon, value 8*l.* 14*s.* per ann. [*Docquet.*]

April 11. Grant to Edw. Fitton and John Pewtrace of purchase of the manor of Wetwang, co. York. [*Docquet.*]

April 13. Grant to Dr. Atkins of purchase of certain lands, parcel of the manor of Newport Pagnell, co. Bucks, passed by special favour, though belonging to the Queen's manor of Ampthill. [*Docquet.*]

VOL. LXXVII.

1614.

April 13. Grant to Chas. Burton, on surrender of Michael Kirkham, of the office of keeping the King's game of hares, pheasants, &c., near Richmond. [*Docquet.*]

April 13. Letter to the Dean and Canons of Christchurch, Oxford, to admit a son of Isaac Casaubon to the first scholarship void in that house, promising that their grant to him shall not be taken as a precedent for others. [*Docquet.*]

April 13. Grant to Jas. Mills of the captaincy of Calshot Castle, co. Hants, for life. [*Grant Bk.*, *p.* 136.]

April 14. Commission to the Lord Chancellor and others to sell [entailed] lands contained in the indenture of 8 May, 7 Jac. I. [*Ibid.*, *p.* 137.]

April 14. Grant to Chris. Greene of a prebend at Bristol. [*Ibid.*, *p.* 133.]

April 14. Grant to Sir —— Cooke of the stewardship of the manor of the late monastery of Bury St. Edmunds, co. Suffolk, for life. [*Ibid.*, *p.* 137,]

April 14. London. 7. Chamberlain to Carleton. The Parliament proceeds, with the usual altercations. Sir Fras. Bacon objected to as member for the University of Cambridge, on the ground of his being Attorney General, but admitted to sit "pro hac vice." Many members questioned and thrown out for holding offices, &c. Dr. [Art.] Lake, not Dr. Abbot, to be Prolocutor. The whole house is to receive the communion, not at Westminster Abbey, "for feare of copes and wafer cakes," but at St. Margaret's, when absentees are to be noted. The house is so full that late comers hardly find room. The King, in a speech to the whole assembly, in the banquetting room, intreated relief for his wants, and hoped it would be called the Parliament of love; wished nothing to be done in exchanging favours for grants, but all of free will, and offered certain favours, as abolition of old debts, redress of homage, wardships, &c. The Secretary proposed the matter of subsidies to the Commons, but it was postponed. The Secretary gone to Court; he has his 1,400*l.* for secret service. He is jealously watched, but will do, as long as he stands well with the King. The House occupied against undertakers. The Lord Privy Seal dangerously ill.

April 14. Westminster. 8. Grant to Zouch Allen, on surrender of John Skillicorne, of pension of 5*s.* a day. Latin.

April 20. Venice. 9. [Sir Dud. Carleton] to Dr. Geo. Carleton. Thanks for his book; though highly esteemed for its learning, it is criticised in three points, viz., for pronouncing the doctrines of the Church of Rome to have been unsettled till the Council of Trent, for allowing some traditions, and for confining ordination to Bishops only. Congratulates the Doctor on his degree; is sanguine of his promotion, he having two such pillars as the King, and Archbp. of Canterbury to support him.

Vol. LXXVII.

1614.

April 20. Licence to Sir Ralph Gray to hold a weekly market and yearly fair in the manor of Wark, and a weekly market and two yearly fairs in the manor of Wooler, co. Northumberland. [*Grant Bk., p.* 133.]

April 21. Commission to Capt. David Middleton, General of [a merchant ship of] the East India Company, to use martial law during the voyage. [*Ibid., p.* 137.]

April 21. 10. Petition of Julius Watson, Minister of Congerston, co. Leicester, to the Bishop of Lincoln, for redress against Robt. Rudyard, an Apparitor, who has caused him to be fined and excommunicated, on false charges of violence and slander. With reference and order thereon.

April 21. Lambeth. 11. Archbp. Abbot to [Carleton]. The Parliament has sat fifteen days, but done nothing except naturalize the Prince Palatine and his children, and declare the Lady Elizabeth and her offspring next in succession after the Prince. Sir Thos. Edmondes is over about a marriage with the second daughter of France; and Sir John Digby, an excellent minister, on his own private business. Asks whether the Earl of Tyrone intends to come nearer, as reported, and if a Roman nobleman has engaged his fortune to attend him to Ireland.

April 22. [Carleton] to Chamberlain. Begs him to remember him for [the Provostship of] Eton College when vacant, but hopes Sir Hen. Savile will long live to enjoy it. Peter Young and Mr. Newton have letters for it from the King. Reminds him of "a good morsel," which is to be given to obtain it. [*Venice Corresp., April* 22.]

April 30. Whitehall. Commissioners for the Treasury to the Officers of the Customs. To enforce the execution of Orders in Council that no beer be transported stronger than at the rates allowed, excepting for long voyages, on account of the quantity of malt and corn consumed in making strong beer. [*Dom. Corresp., March* 27, 1616.]

April? 12. Memorandum of Burgesses returned to Parliament, who were elected for more than one place.

April? 13. Draught of a speech by [Sir John Coke] in the House of Commons, on the necessity of union with the King; caution in listening to grievances; and danger of reliance upon Spain. Indorsed is an abstract of a patent to [Robt.] Treswell, in reference to the survey of woods.

April? 14. First and second answer of the King to the complaint made in Parliament against the patent [for wine licences] granted to the Lord Admiral and his son the Lord of Effingham, declaring its legality, but signifying his willingness to grant no further licences on expiration of the present patent. Indorsed [by Rochester] "License for Wynes."

May 3. Special licence to Chris. Abdy, John Lewis, John Packer, and Roger Pennell, to use the art of making indigo neale for thirty-one years. [*Grant Bk., p.* 145.]

Vol. LXXVII.

1614.

May 5. Grant to John Murray of 150*l.* as a free gift. [*Docquet.*]

May 5. Grant to the Earl of Northampton and his heirs of purchase of the King's remainder of the manor of Sedgley, and the chace or waste of Baggeridge and Whites-wood, co. Stafford. [*Docquet.*]

May 5. Grant to the merchants trading to the East Indies of safe conduct. [*Docquet.*]

May 5. Seven several letters to the Princes of those countries. [*Docquet.*]

May 9. 15. Sir Herbert Croft to Somerset. Is sorry the King is displeased with him, and refused to knight his son. If His Majesty will consult Lord Sheffield, he will assure him that the granting the wish of his countrymen [for exemption of the Border counties from the jurisdiction of the Council of Wales] will be rather advantgeous than hurtful to the Council of the North. Has now done his utmost; if he fail, his countrymen will blame him for consenting to give the King their money, when they cannot obtain their birthright to the laws of the kingdom.

May 10. Sir Ralph Winwood to [Carleton]. Troubles with the recusant Irish Parliament. Several of them were sent for to England, and, refusing to submit, sent to prison. Impositions give a rub in the English Parliament. Sir Thos. Parry disgraced and put out of Parliament, for trying to bring in Sir Walter Cope and Sir Hen. Wallop for Stockbridge, they not having been chosen. Albert Morton going for Savoy. [*Venice Corresp., May* 10.]

May ? 16. Sir Robt. Dudley [signed Warwick and Leicester] to [Somerset]. Though unknown to him, rejoices in his zeal for the King's service. Wishes to be an instrument of good to his country, and renews an offer lately made through Sir David Fowlies. Though the matter, by its great importance, may seem strange and difficult, it is of consequence to the security of England. Has had long study and practice, and can perform what he offered.

May ? 17. Minutes of a projected reply to the above letter. Thanks for Sir Robert's good opinion. If his service prove answerable to what he promises, will endeavour to procure recompence accordingly; to be directed, "To my honourable friend, Sir Robt. Dudley, Knight, &c."

May 11. 18. Specification by Sir Robt. Dudley of the advantages to be derived from his newly invented ship, and the conditions which he is willing to bind himself that it shall perform.

[May 11.] 19. Petition of Sam. Willingham, Parson of Stane, co. Lincoln, to Lord Chief Baron Tanfield, for protection against John West and others, who, having failed in a suit to deprive him of certain lands in Hotoft, co. Lincoln, persecute him in the enjoyment thereof.

May 11 ? 20. Petition of the Same to Lord Chancellor Ellesmere, to be admitted to search in formâ pauperis, for records relating to the above lands.

VOL. LXXVII.

1614.

May 11. 21. Affidavit of Sam. Willingham before the Court of Exchequer, that John West and Robt. Hastings seized and carried away his corn.

May 12. London. 22. Chamberlain to Carleton. Winwood promises to attend to Carleton's allowances. Sir Thos. Parry suspended [from the Chancellorship of the Duchy of Lancaster], and he, Sir Walter, Sir Hen. Wallop, and Sir John Chamberlain, discharged the House, as untruly elected. The House busy with elections, privileges, and impositions. Sir Walter Chute offers to undergo all the odium of undertakers, though nobody thought him worth suspecting. Winwood has won reputation by speaking against recusants and idle churchmen, but the Bishops call him a puritan for it. The King is patient with Parliament; if they stand stiff, and refuse to supply his wants, he will be driven to worse ways, to which both law and pulpit encourage him. Four Irish Knights imprisoned for a malapert petition. Sir Thos. Gates says, the Virginia colony, though wonderfully productive if cultivated, will fall if not supported. Quarrel at Flushing between Sir Mich. Everard and Sir John Throgmorton. Calvert spoken of for Holland. Albert Morton gone for Savoy. Wotton silenced by Mr. Pory's discourse.

[May 13.] 23. Reasons why the grant of the Great Covent Garden [Parish of St. Botolph without Aldgate], made to the late Queen by the Master and Fellows of Magdalen College, Cambridge, should not be confirmed by the House of Commons. With answers thereto.

May 15. 24. Will of Thos. Crompton, of the Middle Temple, Prothonotary in the Court of Common Pleas, dated Nov. 12, 1612, with a codicil, dated May 15, 1614.

May 18. Bedford House. 25. Lady Harrington to Somerset. Is reduced to great straits for want of the money so long due to her, for which she pays heavy interest; cannot allow the honour of the dead to perish, if even she have to suffer greater misery. Requests a definite answer, that she may settle her affairs accordingly.

May 19. London. 26. Chamberlain to Carleton. The Secretary is full of business at Parliament all morning, and committees in afternoons, beside his own duties. The clergy think he scandalized the church in his speech, and tell the King that he wishes to be the head of the puritans, but he has satisfied his Majesty about it. The Parliament is occupied in crying down impositions. Sir Hen. Neville has calmed them about undertakers. Dick Martin came to the House as a counsellor to plead for maintenance of the colony of Virginia, but so schooled the House, that he was called to the Bar to make submission. Serjeant Boy [Bovey], of the Cellar, committed to the Marshalsea, for seducing Sir Thos. Gardiner's daughter. Sir Thos. Lake, though a Councillor, keeps his Clerkship of the Signet, and would be Chancellor of the Duchy [of Lancaster], but Sir Thos. Parry will not resign to him. Sir John Digby boasts of his occupation as the highest in the King's service, except the Deputyship of Ireland. He is returning [to Spain].

VOL. LXXVII.

1614.

May 22. Court at Whitehall. 27. Lancelot Andrews, Bishop of Ely, to Sir John Ogle. Thanks for his sending him Utenbogardt's book. Thinks it learned, and agrees with it in the main, but as convocation is going on, has been unable to give it proper attention. Has sent it to the King, but thinks that in this busy Parliament time, his Majesty has not had leisure to read anything on that subject, though "wonderfully inclyned thereunto, yea more than any Prince else in the worlde."

May 23. Grant to Fras. Jones, Wm. Garway, and Nich. Salter, of all customs and subsidies on merchandise imported or exported, for seven years. [*Grant Bk., p.* 134.]

[May 24.] 28. Reasons against the Bill for the revocation of the Act 5 Eliz. cap. 5., prohibiting the import of cod and ling in barrels.

[May 24.] 29. Similar paper of reasons, showing the utility of the licences granted by the late Queen and the King for the bringing in of barrelled fish by certain patentees, which modify the Act, whilst its repeal would benefit only foreigners.

May 26. London. 30. Chamberlain to Carleton. Sir Hen. Wotton spoke in Parliament in favour of impositions, alleging foreign examples. Winwood and Lake seconded him. Arguments on the other side. Wentworth said the reward of Spanish impositions was the loss of the Low Countries; of French, the murder of their Kings, &c. The Lords refused to confer with the Commons thereon, the Bishop of Lincoln condemning the Lower House as a factious assembly, &c., which remarks are discussed in a Committee of the Commons. An attack made on the order of Baronets, rather to disgrace than suppress them. Winwood conducts himself well and courageously. Sir Thos. [Howard] has married Lord Burleigh's daughter, and is made Master of the Prince's House.

May 31. Grant to John Hope of a pension of 2*s.* per diem, on surrender of the like pension by Wm. Ledsham. [*Docquet.*]

May 31. Licence to Sir Fras. Lacon and his heirs to keep a weekly market and three yearly fairs in Cleobury, co. Salop. [*Docquet.*]

May 31. Grant to Jas. Bagg, jun., on surrender of Jas. Bagg, his father, of the office of Comptroller of the Customs at Plymouth and Fowey. [*Docquet.*]

May 31. Grant to John Garnett of pardon for manslaughter of his servant, by a blow given him in correction, which was resisted, Garnett being of civil and quiet carriage. [*Docquet.*]

May 31. Licence to William, son of Sir Ralph Gray, to travel for three years. [*Docquet.*]

May 31. Grant to Hen. Hastings of purchase of the contingent remainder of the manor of Piddletown, co. Dorset. [*Docquet.*]

May 31. Grant, with survivorship, to Sherrington Talbot and Edw. Leighton, of the office of Master of the Game, and Keeper and Ranger of the Forest of Feckenham, co. Worcester, on surrender of Thos. Leighton, who held the office jointly with his father, Sir Thos. Leighton, deceased. [*Docquet.*]

Vol. LXXVII.

1614.

May 31. Grant to Sam. Knightly of the goods escheated by the suicide of Hen. Walton, tenant of the manor of Marchington, co. Stafford. [*Docquet.*]

May 31. Grant to Fras. Ogle of the office of one of the King's Serjeants-at-Arms. [*Docquet.*]

May ? 31. Lewis Owen to Sir Ralph Winwood. Has lately arrived sick and poor, after spending many years abroad for his country's benefit. Is returning to Brussels, proffers his services, and will be thankful for favour.

June 1. Eton. 32. Sir Hen. Savile to Carleton. Is willing to sell Sassamine a copy of his work [St. Chrysostom] at half price, in return for some MS. sent by him. Wants to collate Epiphanius with an ancient Greek copy. Mr. Secretary can answer nothing about Carleton's removal till Parliament is over. Sorry that Carleton's wife and sister do not agree.

June 1. London. 33. Chamberlain to the Same. Great delay of the Parliament in supplying the King's wants. The Lords refuse to concur in a censure on the Bishop of Lincoln, without a trial, and also to confer with the Commons on impositions. A breach between the two Houses feared. The King was offended, and wrote to the Commons. They waited on him to defend themselves, saying that they were unfit to proceed to matters of business, till cleared of the Bishop's imputations. They do little, and quarrel amongst themselves. The Muscovy Ambassador has left, and [John] Merrick is going thither as English Ambassador.

June 2. Grant to Nedtracy Smarty and Shacherly Tracey of the office of Storekeeper of Ammunition, &c. in the Tower and elsewhere. [*Grant Bk., p.* 142.]

June 7. 34. Note by the Clerk of the Parliament of the meeting, prorogation, and dissolution of Parliaments since 5 Eliz., 1562.

June 7. 35. Transcript of the above.

June 9. London. 36. Chamberlain to Carleton. The Commons refusing satisfaction from the Bishop of Lincoln and growing insolent, the King sent them word he would dissolve them unless they attended at once to his wants. Bold speeches of several members, on which a commission was issued to dissolve the Parliament. The time was short, and discontents so great that they took no steps to mend matters, the House being more like a cockpit than a council; and on the 1st, the House was dissolved, and some members summoned to the Council, and sent thence to the Tower. Capt. Best has brought home a ship richly laden from the East Indies, but another is lost at Bantam, and Sir Hen. Middleton dead there. Sir Thos. Edmondes refuses to return without money.

June 13. Hackney, Middlesex. 37. Coroners inquest on the body of Edw. Worthington, slain by Wm. Snead, of Hackney, who is thereby found guilty of wilful murder. Latin.

VOL. LXXVII.

1614.

June 15. London. 38. Ottaviano Lotti to Giov. Florio, of the Privy Chamber. Sends him a small token of affection. His friend has gone away, contrary to the wishes of everybody. It will be thought that he is either served ill or has had very ill fortune. Italian.

June 16. St. Bartholomews. Sir Ralph Winwood to Carleton. Never saw so much faction and passion as in the late unhappy Parliament, nor so little reverence of a King or respect of the public good. The impositions were the great grievance, also a speech of the Bishop of Lincoln taxing the Commons with sedition, and the King's messages were thought to abridge the liberty of the House. The break-neck was some seditious speeches, which made the King impatient, and it was whispered to him that they would have his life and that of his favourites before they had done, on which he dissolved them. Four of their tribunes, Sir Walter Chute, Chris. Neville, Hoskins, and Wentworth, are sent to prison, and Sir Chas. Cornwallis and Dr. Lionel Sharp are to go. The clergy are supplying the King's wants by a voluntary contribution, and the Council do the same. Much money is thus expected. The Earl of Northampton dying. [*Venice Corresp., June* 16.]

June 17. Littleton. Friday. 39. Earl of Hertford to Somerset. Has spoken with the King concerning his grandson, Wm. Seymour, now in France. Thanks for the grant of the markets, which will be a great relief to his poor tenants. It is the only suit he has had since the King's accession. Sends his mite towards the present occasions, corresponding rather to his overcharged estate than to his heart.

June 17. Wingfield House. 40. Sir Rowland Lytton to Carleton. Hopes his [Lytton's] daughter Smith has brought him a young godson. Illness of Sir Ant. Cope.

June 21. Greenwich. Proclamation for continuance to Anne Lady Harrington of the patent for farthing tokens, which is questioned on the death of the two Lords Harrington. Printed. [*Proc. Coll., No.* 28.]

June 22. 41. And. Sharp to Somerset. Requests him to intercede with the King for the enlargement of his brother Dr. [Lionel] Sharp from his close confinement, or for permission that his wife and himself may visit him, he being sick.

[June 22.] [Tower.] 42. Sir Chas. Cornwallis to the King. Is distressed with his displeasure. Was prevented by accident from becoming a member in Parliament, but his intended speech there, though misrepresented by Dr. Sharp and Mr. Hoskins, was to persuade the House to supply His Majesty's wants; to entreat him to prevent the increase of Papists, which proceeds from the suppression of faithful ministers, &c.; to remonstrate against the match projected for the Prince with France; and to request that as many English as Scots may occupy places about his person, and that the future resort of the Scots be discountenanced.

VOL. LXXVII.

1614.

June ? 43. Sir Chas. Cornwallis to the King. Is sincerely penitent for his fault, and implores forgiveness, in consideration of his innocency of intention, and his long and faithful services. Ought not, as the King's servant, to have entered on such matters without his leave. *Incloses,*

43. I. *Statement that his reasons in his motion touching the Scots were not of personal jealousy, having sold his plate to help some distressed Scots in Spain, and being attached to many of that nation; but the resolution was so general to give nothing unless the Scots, who were thought the cause of the King's excessive charges, were removed, that he advised its being so far yielded to as to bring in no more; and as to impositions, that any deemed grievous should be objected to, but not the power to make them questioned.*

[June.] 44, 45. Copies of the two preceding letters.

June 22. Licence to Sir Rich. Houghton, Bart., to make alum, and to transport 500 tons yearly for twenty-four years. [*Grant Bk., p.* 134.]

June 22. Westminster. 46. Warrant to the officers of the Exchequer and Attorney General to take further orders to enforce the execution of a statute passed in Parliament against the assignation of private debts to the King, in order that the creditor may have the advantage of suing in his Majesty's name, thereby gaining an undue advantage over the debtors and over the other creditors, and causing distrust in business.

June 23. London. 47. Alex. Williams to Carleton. Goes from the Chancellor of the Exchequer to Mr. Bingley for money, but cannot get any. Sir Thos. Edmondes stays merely for want of money. Wishes there were no worse paymaster than Burlamachi.

June 24. 48. Bill of Fabian Simpson, Keeper of the Gatehouse, to the Council, for diet, &c., for the past quarter, of the prisoners Wm. Meers, Rich. Yorke, Ralph Mercer, Thos. Kightley, Robt. Knight, John Todd late Bishop of Down, and Wm. Westby, committed by them; total 84*l.* 6*s.* 2*d.*

June 24. Declaration by the King of certain points to be observed in the assignment of debts to him. [*Grant Bk., p.* 145.]

June 26. 49. G[eo. Margitts] to the Duke of Lenox. Notes in brief the modes in which the King has been defrauded of the fines, &c. of recusants. Nothing remains to be done to perfect the good work of redressing them, but to finish the commission already drawn up. *Annexing*

49. I. *Warrant to Sir Fras. Bacon, Attorney General, to draw up a commission authorizing certain persons to inquire of all debts and arrears of recusants, whereof His Majesty has been defrauded by sheriffs and inferior officers.*

49. II. *Transcript of the above, indorsed "Project of a warrant for a commission touching recusants."*

1614. Vol. LXXVII.

49. III. *[Geo. Margitts] to the Lords [of the Council]. Sends records to prove the extent of the frauds committed on His Majesty, in the affairs of recusants, by non-payment of moneys received, by arrears of rents unpaid, by lands leased at under values, by lands in charge for which nothing is paid, &c. [Hen.] Spiller's conduct complained of, and a request made that to avoid clamour, commissioners may be appointed for each county, to examine the steps to be taken by himself and others, to redress these abuses.*

June? 50. Memoranda for a special commission for recovery of the arrears due from recusants, whereof the King has been defrauded; with note from Sir Edw. Coke to the suggester of the commission, giving his opinion against its legality, as being contrary to the forms prescribed in the statute.

June 29? 51. Description of the three modes of proceeding in the Star Chamber, by ore tenus or confession, by information, and by bill and answer. The nature of the causes there judged,—as riots and unlawful assemblies; frauds, cozenage, forgeries, &c.; abuses of officers of justice, &c.; and of those that are refused to be there tried,—as capital crimes, petty causes, &c. The considerations that mitigate or aggravate punishments there, &c. With notes of certain points of jurisdiction much debated in the Court, and of the nature of suits favoured or otherwise therein.

June 29. 52. [Earl of Somerset] to Sir G. Murray. The King has signed the two papers. Campbell has offered 8,000 marks yearly and 2,000*l.* fine for Islay, but is to be brought to higher terms. His proposition for reducing and civilizing the isles is only in general terms.

June 30. London. 53. Chamberlain to Carleton. Divers members of the late Parliament called up for their speeches and imprisoned. A plot is discovered by those who opposed the meeting of Parliament, to embroil matters, by urging on points which the King would not bear, as taking away impositions, restoring silenced ministers, removing the Scots, &c. Hoskins and others were hired to forward the plot. Chris. Nevill is removed to the Fleet on making submission, and Wentworth, being thought rather simple than malicious, is detained only to satisfy the French Ambassador. The Master of the Rolls has lost favour about these matters. Sir Randall Crew knighted and made Serjeant-at-law. Death of the Lord Privy Seal Northampton. Particulars of his last illness, and will. He ordered his body to be buried in a chapel in Dover Castle, and several Popish ceremonies were observed at his funeral. He is reported to have received extreme unction. He begged that the Earl of Pembroke and Lord Lisle, his enemies, might not have any of his offices. Somerset is made Privy Seal, and will be made Warden of the Cinque Ports. The bishops, judges, and nobility, &c. are offering contributions to the King. He has sent to borrow 100,000*l.* from the city of London.

1614. Vol. LXXVI.

Sir John Merrick going Ambassador to Muscovy with [Wm.] Beecher as Secretary. Sir Thos. Edmondes, on returning [to France], can only get 400*l.* out of 1,400*l.* due to him for allowances.

June 30. London. 54. Chamberlain to Alice Carleton. The new Globe play-house is said to be the fairest in England. The Earls of Suffolk and Somerset stood sponsors to Sir Art. Ingram's child, and the King was at the christening. Ingram was chosen Sheriff, but excused himself. Peter Proby, formerly Secretary Walsingham's barber, takes the office on him, but is opposed.

June ? 55. Inhabitants of Herefordshire to the Earl of Somerset. Hearing that he favours the exemption of the Border counties from the jurisdiction of the Council of Wales, request his influence with the King, that they may at length obtain their desire.

June ? 56. Copy of the above.

July 1. Westminster College. 57. Dr. Geo. Montaigne, Dean of Westminster, to Sir Thos. Lake. Commends the learning and good conduct of Dr. Porter. Hopes his suit for preferment will succeed.

July 1. Appointment of Sir Randall Crew to be Serjeant-at-law during pleasure. [*Grant Bk., p.* 137.]

July 1. Grant to Nathan Owen of the office of Receiver in cos. Northampton and Rutland, for life. [*Ibid., p.* 141.]

July 2. Grant to John Acworth of the office of keeping all storehouses at Woolwich, co. Kent, for life. [*Ibid., p.* 145.]

July 2. Westminster. Grant to Robt. Davies, of Liverpool, of pardon for stealing a mare. Latin. [*Sign Man., vol.* IV., *No.* 6.]

July 2. Westminster. Grant to Ralph Hansby of purchase of certain sheep-pastures in the manor of Bishop's Wilton, co. York, value 16*l.* 18*s.* 4*d.* per ann. Latin. [*Ibid., No.* 7.]

July 2. Westminster. Grant to Sir Wilfrid Lawson of pardon for the escape of John Hudson, prisoner, convicted of murder, from Carlisle gaol, when Lawson was High Sheriff of Cumberland, the escape being without his privity. [*Ibid., No.* 8.]

July 2. Westminster. Letters of Privy Seal to the officers of the Exchequer and the Attorney General, prohibiting the ejection of subjects from their lands, &c. upon information of intrusion, until the case has been tried, and verdict given in the King's behalf. With exceptions for entailed lands, and expired or forfeited leases. [*Ibid., No.* 9.]

July 3. Westminster. Grant to David Holland of purchase of the manor of Dinorben Vawr, and other lands of the lordship of Denbigh, value 12*l.* 16*s.* 4*d.* per ann. Latin. [*Ibid., No.* 10.]

VOL. LXXVII.

1614.

July 4. Grant, in reversion, to Rich. Lewis of the captaincy of the Block-house of West Tilbury, co. Kent, for life. [*Grant Bk., p.* 135.]

July 4? Grant to John Throckmorton and Edw. Ramsay, in fee simple, of the manor and park of Miserden and other lands, co. Gloucester, belonging to the King, as heir of Edm. Plantagenet, Earl of Kent, granted for the benefit of Hen. Jernegan, an ancient tenant thereof, with reservation of a fine levied thereon to Throckmorton and Ramsay. Latin. [*Sign Man., vol.* IV., *No.* 11.]

July. Docquet of the above. [*Docquet, July* 24.]

July 5. Whitehall. Sir Ralph Winwood to Carleton. On the unhappy dissolution of Parliament, the clergy offered a gratuity. The Council and many of the higher classes have followed their example. On the 18th, the King goes to visit the Earl of Shrewsbury, and returns by Woodstock and Rycot. Great business about settling the King's estate, which is most necessary, his wants being very great. [*Venice Corresp., July* 5.]

July 5. Westminster. Grant to Robt. Seymer of the office of Receiver of the voluntary contributions of loving subjects, both in money and plate, for the service of Ireland, the Navy, and the Cautionary Towns in the Low Countries, which are to be employed for no other use; the money to be paid into the Exchequer, and the plate sent to the Mint for coinage. [*Sign Man., vol.* IV., *No.* 12.]

July. Docquet of the above. [*Docquet, July* 24.]

July 5. Westminster. Warrant to pay over all the voluntary contributions for Ireland, the Navy, and the Low Countries, to Robt. Seymer, appointed Receiver, and to pay allowances to him and his clerks. [*Sign Man., vol.* IV., *No.* 13.]

July 5. Westminster. Grant to Jas. Gibb of a pension of 200*l.* per ann., on surrender of a like pension by John Gibb, his father, Groom of the Bedchamber. [*Ibid., No.* 14.]

July 5. Westminster. Letters of Privy Seal to the Master, Attorney, &c., of the Court of Wards, prohibiting the vindication of His Majesty's title to lands, &c. by secret offices and inquisitions, which have proved very prejudicial to the subject. Drawn after the form of one of the bills of grace, offered by the King to the House of Commons, last Parliament. [*Ibid., No.* 4.]

July 6. Westminster. Similar letters directed to the Court of Exchequer, in the form of one of the bills of grace. [*Ibid., No.* 3.]

[July 6.] Similar letters directed to the Lord Chancellor. [*Ibid., No.* 5.]

July 6. Westminster. Grant to Stephen Langdon of a Gunner's place in the Tower. Latin. [*Ibid., No.* 15.]

July 6. Westminster. Grant to Sir John Wynn, Bart., of purchase of the lease of lands, coal mines, &c., cos. Carnarvon, Anglesea, and Flint, value 34*l.* 17. 6*d.* per ann. Latin. [*Ibid., No.* 16.]

VOL. LXXVII.

1614.

July 7. Westminster. Grant to Sir Thos. Shirley and his sureties of protection for one year from arrest for debt. [*Ibid.*, *No.* 17.]

July 7. Grant to Sir Robt. Killigrew of the office of Captain or Keeper of Pendennis Castle, co. Cornwall, for life. [*Grant Bk.*, *p.* 135.]

July 7. London. 58. Chamberlain to Carleton. It is a question whether the Parliament be dissolved or no. The naturalization of the Prince Palatine passing through both Houses, confirmed by the King, and sent away under the Broad Seal, argues an Act, and this a Session. Talk of finding an error in the dissolution. The King is granting by proclamation many of the things wished for, to prepare for a benevolence. The City refuses to lend 100,000*l.*, but offers 10,000*l.* as a gift. Many rich men give more than two subsidies, but the Bishops, who led on the contribution, do not give a quarter of their subsidy. Case argued in the Star Chamber as to its jurisdiction, and whether the husband is to pay the wife's fine incurred there. Sir John York, his wife and brothers, fined and imprisoned for a scandalous play acted in favour of Popery. Dr. Palmer, and Crompton, a gentleman usher, committed to the Tower, for some business concerning the Lady Arabella, who is "far out of frame this Midsummer moone." Lord Grey desperately sick. Death of [Isaac] Casaubon and Sir Wm. Cornwallis. Sir Edw. Swift, who married Lord Sheffield's daughter, has killed himself. Sir Rowland Lytton fast decays, &c.

July 8. Westminster. Commission of Lieutenancy for the Earl of Huntingdon, for cos. Leicester and Rutland. [*Sign Man.*, *vol.* IV., *No.* 18.]

July. Docquet of the above. [*Docquet*, *July* 14.]

July 9. London. 59. Edw. Reynoldes to Fras. Mills. Particulars of the death of Lord Privy Seal Northampton, through the injudicious opening of a tumor in his thigh. The Seal is in custody of the Earl of Somerset. Preparations are making by the clerks to avoid the payment of such large fees to the next Lord Privy Seal. Their receipts are but poor. Fears that Somerset's frequent absences in following the King will prove prejudicial to them. Necessity for accuracy and secrecy in their accounts.

July 9. Westminster. Presentation of Geo. Warburton to the rectory of Longworth, diocese of Salisbury. Latin. [*Sign Man.*, *vol.* IV., *No.* 19.]

July 9. Westminster. Grant to Wm. Dackombe and his sureties, of protection from arrests for debt for a year. [*Ibid.*, *No.* 20.]

July 9. Westminster. Warrant for payment of 81*l.* 11*s.* 6*d.* to Susan Westwood, executrix of John Taverner, late Surveyor of Woods on this side Trent, in lieu of Taverner's moiety of a fine due from Geo. Pollard, Keeper of the Game in Blakemore, co. Wilts, but pardoned by the King. [*Ibid.*, *No.* 21.]

July 9. Westminster. Lease to the Earl of Cumberland of the castle and lands of Bewcastle, co. Cumberland, formerly kept by an officer, with a fee of 20*l.* per ann. Latin. [*Ibid.*, *No.* 22.]

VOL. LXXVII.

1614.

July 9. Westminster. Grant, with survivorship, to John Coward and his son, of the Keepership of the Game of Venery and Falconry about Thetford. [*Ibid., No.* 23.]

Docquet of the above. [*Docquet, May* 31.]

July 9. Westminster. Grant to Sir Chas. Howard, jun., of the Rangership of Finchamstead, and of the walks of Bigshott, Easthampstead, aad Blackwater alias Sandhurst, in Windsor Forest, now held by Sir Chas. Howard, sen. Latin. [*Sign Man., vol.* IV., *No.* 24.]

July 9. Westminster. Grant to Wm. Bowler of the office of Bailiff of the Hundreds of Holford, Gretton, and Kittesgate, co. Gloucester; with certificate by John Pymme, Receiver General of the County, of his fitness for the place. [*Ibid., No.* 25.]

July 9. Westminster. Grant to Elizabeth Roger, of Llanerochwell, Montgomeryshire, spinster, being pregnant, of pardon for manslaughter. Latin. [*Ibid., No.* 26.]

July 10. Westminster. Warrant to pay 208*l.* 13*s.* 4*d.* to Sir John Leigh, Lieutenant of the Isle of Wight, for repair of the Castles of Sandham and Cowes. [*Ibid., No.* 27.]

July 10. 60. Warrant from Sir Robt. Brett, Deputy Warden of the Cinque Ports, on the death of the Earl of Northampton, to the Mayor and Jurats of Winchelsea, desiring them to continue the execution of their office for examining and restraining the passage across the sea, at the ancient town of Winchelsea.

July 11. 61. Sir Fras. Bacon to Sir Thos. Lake. Orders certain alterations in the warrant for Lord Walden's grant of lands forfeit by the attainder of [Ambrose] Rokewood.

July 11. London. 62. Francis [titular] Lord Dacre to the Same. Begs the renewal of his protection from arrest for three years, as the debts for which he is in danger arose from non-payment of the pension promised him by the King when in Scotland.

July 11. Warrant dormant for yearly delivery of stuff to Jas. Duncan, the Queen's tailor, for his livery, during pleasure. [*Docquet, July* 14.]

July 11. Warrant dormant to the Treasurer of the King's Chamber, signifying that all warrants directed to him, subscribed by Sir Ralph Winwood, Secretary of State, shall be sufficient for issuing the King's treasure. [*Docquet, July* 14.]

July 11. Letter to Sir Chris. Hatton and others, officers of Waltham Forest, concerning the preservation of the game there. [*Docquet, July* 14.]

July 11. Grant to Thos. Earl of Suffolk of the office of Treasurer of the Exchequer, during pleasure. [*Grant Bk., p.* 142.]

July 11. Westminster. Warrant for payment of compensation to Edw. Fitton, for his services. [*Sign Man., vol.* IV., *No.* 28.]

July. Docquet of the above. [*Docquet, July* 14.]

Vol. LXXVII.

1614.

July 11. Westminster. Warrant to pay to Wm. Pickering, Master of the Armoury at Greenwich, 200*l.*, balance of 340*l.* for armour gilt and graven for the late Prince. [*Sign Man., vol.* IV., *No.* 29.]

July. Docquet of the above. [*Docquet, July* 14.]

July 11. Westminster. Warrant for payment of 40*l.* per ann. to Phineas Pett, during the time of his service. [*Sign Man., vol.* IV., *No.* 30.]

July. Docquet of the above. [*Docquet, July* 16.]

July 12. Westminster. Grant to Visct. Haddington of 2,000*l.* out of compositions for recusants' goods, to be levied according to the commission issued Jan. 30, 1614. [*Sign Man., vol.* IV., *No.* 31.]

July. Docquet of the above. [*Docquet, July* 14.]

July 12. Westminster. Grant to Ferdinando Bickley, Edw. Bushe, Agnes Gower, Eliz. Francklin, and Thos. Morris, prisoners condemned at Dorchester, of pardon, in consideration of their help in quenching the fire at Dorchester. Latin. [*Sign Man., vol.* IV., *No.* 32.]

July 12. Grant to Rich. Kerry of the office of Gamekeeper at Windsor, for life. [*Grant Bk., p.* 135.]

July 13. Warrant to pay to Jas. Bovy 128*l.*, disbursed by him above the last year's allowance for wines. Also to advance him 120*l.* for the present year. [*Sign Man., vol.* IV., *No.* 33.]

July. Docquet of the above. [*Docquet, July* 14.]

July 13. Grant to Fras. Curtis of an almsroom in Winchester. [*Docquet, July* 14.]

July 13. Lambeth. 63. Archbp. Abbot to Carleton. The Venetian Ambassador and his Secretary are reconciled. Dr. Marta complains of the coldness of Carleton, because, though his pension has been fairly paid him by the King's desire, he is kept hungry. The Earl of Suffolk made Lord Treasurer, and Earl of Somerset Lord Chamberlain. [*Partly in cipher, deciphered.*]

July 14. London. 64. Chamberlain to [the Same]. Mr. Secretary tries to induce the King to give Carleton a place nearer home. A certain knight has offered 2,000*l.* for Carleton's place; a bad bargain when 1,200*l.* is already owing to Ambassadors. The King told the Earl of Suffolk that he made him Treasurer for his fidelity and integrity, not for his Greek and Latin, his epigrams and orations; and that he made Somerset Chamberlain because he would bestow a place so near himself on the friend whom he loved above all men living. Lord Walden made Captain and Sir Geo. Goring Lieutenant of the Gentleman Pensioners. Earl of Worcester spoken of as Lord Privy Seal, and Pembroke to succeed him as Master of the Horse. The King going on a progress to Sherwood Forest. The Lord Treasurer inducted into his office. The Chancellor made him a speech, urging him to follow the examples of his earlier predecessors rather than of the later ones, which would do harm, not good. The Deputy of Ireland is returned, not overcharged

1614. Vol. LXXVII.

with money. Lawrence Hide is Queen's Attorney instead of Sir Robt. Hitcham, who is made Serjeant with eleven others. Death of Lord Grey in the Tower, and of Sir Ant. Cope. Sir Stephen Le Sieur returned.

July 14. Westminster. Commission to the Archbp. of York, the Lord Chancellor, Lord President of the North, and others, to exercise ecclesiastical jurisdiction within the province of York. Drawn on the precedent of the recent commission to the province of Canterbury, the form of these commissions being lately altered by advice of the Council. Latin [*Sign Man., vol.* IV., *No.* 34.]

July. Docquet of the above. [*Docquet, July* 16.]

July 14. Warrant to furnish Sir Thos. Tyringham, Master of the Privy Buck Hounds, with sixteen beds and provision for thirty horses, and for the King's hounds, in all places adjacent to the Court, at such reasonable prices as are set down in the warrant, dated July 21, 1613. [*Docquet.*]

July 15. Florence. 65. Sir Robt. Dudley [signed Warwick] to Sir David Fowlies. Hopes for a reply to his proposition about the ships. Hearing that the Parliament is refractory, and obstinate against the Scottish nation, mentions a project which he learned in the school of the late Grand Duke Ferdinand, and intended for the King's service, at the very time that Sir Stephen Le Sieur, in his cups, pronounced him a rebel. His project will enable the King "to do what he please with his owne, as an absolute monarch as he is," will secure him from foreign invasion and rebellion at home, and double his revenue. Will communicate it only to some faithful Scot, Somerset or some other, commissioned by the King to treat with him. Mentions it out of pure loyalty, not from a wish to return home, having received too many discourtesies from his friends and kindred, the greatest persons in the kingdom, to desire his return.

July 15. Westminster. Warrant for payment of 939*l.* to —— Walcot, to be employed for certain secret services. [*Sign Man., vol.* IV., *No.* 36.]

July. Docquet of the above. [*Docquet, July* 16.]

July 16. Grant to Sir Robt. Gordon, in fee simple, of divers castles, lands, and fisheries in Ulster, formerly granted, under the Great Seal of Ireland, to Geo. Murray and Sir Robt. McLellan, and others. [*Docquet.*]

July 16. Westminster. Warrant for reprieve of Rich. Lonne, a lunatic, condemned for killing John Somers, and for his restoration to his father and friends. [*Sign Man., vol.* IV., *No.* 38.]

July 16. Docquet of the above.

July 16. Presentation of Geoffrey King to the rectory of Aldingham, co. Lancaster. [*Docquet.*]

July 16. Warrant dormant for delivery to Hugh Aston, Groom of the Robes, of stuff for his livery. [*Docquet.*]

VOL. LXXVII.

1614.

July 16. Grant to Chris. Buckminster, on resignation of Philip Harries, of an almsroom in Ewelme. [*Docquet.*]

July 16. The like for Thos. Croxford, on resignation of Wm. Eastman. [*Docquet.*]

July 16. Grant to John Grent and Thos. Aylesbury of the surveyorship of ships, barks, and other vessels for navigation. Recommended by the Lord Admiral, as a most assured way to know how the shipping increases or diminishes. [*Docquet.*]

July 16. Warrant to Sir John Kidderminster, Chief Steward of Langley-Marsh, co. Bucks, to find out His Majesty's right to a cottage and two crofts of lands in that manor, to seize them, and re-grant them to Geo. Child, the next heir. [*Docquet.*]

July 16. Letter to the Archbp. of Canterbury and the Lord Chancellor, for Dr. Dee to be elected Physician of the hospital to be erected for Thos. Sutton, Esq. [*Docquet.*]

July 16. Warrant dormant for delivery to Jas. Wright, huntsman, of stuff, for his livery. [*Docquet.*]

July 17. Westminster. Warrant for payment of 20,000*l.* to Philip Burlamachi, to be paid to the Elector Palatine, as second half of the 40,000*l.* dower with the Princess Elizabeth. [*Sign Man., vol.* IV., *No.* 39.]

July. Docquet of the above. [*Docquet, July* 16.]

July 17. Grant to Rich. Tratford of the office of Receiver in the principality of North Wales, for life. [*Grant Bk., p.* 142.]

July 18. Commission to the Archbp. of Canterbury concerning ecclesiastical affairs. [*Ibid., p.* 146.]

July 18. Letter to the Master, &c. of Trinity College, Cambridge, to cease from prosecution, &c. in the cause between them and Dr. Thompson, King's Chaplain and Senior Fellow there, who has referred the dispute to the King, as undoubted visitor. [*Docquet, July* 24.]

July 21. Royston. Grant, with survivorship, to John and Fras. Bonnall, of the office of keeping silkworms at Whitehall and Greenwich. [*Sign Man., vol.* IV., *No.* 40.]

July. Docquet of the above. [*Docquet, July* 24.]

July 21. Royston. Grant to Leonard Welsted of purchase of the manor of Burltford, late of the monastery of Ambresbury, &c., co. Wilts; value 47*l.* 9*s.* 10*d.* per ann. Latin. [*Sign Man., vol.* IV., *No.* 41.]

July 21. London. 66. Chamberlain to Carleton. The King gone to Theobalds and Royston. Sir Walter Cope likely to lose his place, because his want of dignity makes the Court of Wards less profitable than before. Lord Danvers will compound with Lord Sheffield for the Presidency of the North. Nine new Serjeants chosen, who pay 600*l.* each. Sir Hen. Wotton is to be sent to settle the business of Cleves.

VOL. LXXVII.

1614.

He [Carleton] cannot be promoted till a fit successor is found. He should not neglect Winwood. His despatches are thought too long. Winwood has obtained the keeping of Ditton Park, worth 150*l.* a year. Sir John Digby demands 900*l.* for his journey back to Spain, but will hardly get 600*l.*

July 22. 67. Lord Admiral Nottingham to the Master, Wardens, and Assistants of the Trinity House. Orders them to commit masters and owners of ships unlawfully taking up ballast, to the Marshalsea, without bail, until further orders.

July 22. Hawnes. Grant to Sir Hen. North and his heirs, of purchase of the site and grange of the manor of Mildenhall, co. Suffolk, late of the monastery of Bury St. Edmund's, with the free warren of conies there, and also of other lands in Suffolk, and of the manors of Methwold and Hilgay, co. Norfolk. Latin. [*Sign Man., vol.* IV., *No.* 42.]

July 22. 68. Probate of the will of Nich. Sharpe, of Frisby-upon-Wreak, Leicestershire, dated Dec. 30, 1612.

July 23. Westminster. Proclamation prohibiting the export of cloths undyed and undressed, after Nov. 2, and revoking all special licences to that effect, granted to the Merchant Adventurers and others. Printed. [*Proc. Coll., No.* 29.]

July 23. Licence for Jas. Bovy, Serjeant of the Cellar, to pass beyond seas for providing wines. [*Docquet, July* 24.]

July 23. Licence to Sir Fras. Lovell to travel for three years. [*Docquet, July* 24.]

July 23. Letter to the Paymasters of Flushing to continue payments due to Sir Robt. Sydney, Captain of 100 foot there, notwithstanding his remaining in England. [*Docquet, July* 24.]

July 23. Letter to the Company of French Merchants touching the settling of their trade and government in France, and the re-delivery of their patent. [*Docquet, July* 24.]

July 24. Grant to John Waller and Thos. Pursell of the Forest of Pamber, co. Hants, consisting of the soil only, the woods being sold away, and the deer gone. [*Docquet.*]

July 24. Letter to the Lord President of the North and Judges of Assize, requiring them at their next assembly to examine what places his Majesty's councillors and Secretary of that Presidency anciently held, and to restore them to their right. [*Docquet.*]

July 24. Westminster. Warrant to the Earl of Suffolk, Lord High Treasurer, to issue moneys upon the warrants directed to the late Commissioners of the Treasury, as though there had been no change in that office. [*Sign Man., vol.* IV., *No.* 43.]

July 24. Docquet of the above.

Vol. LXXVII.

1614.

July 25. Westminster. Grant to Hen. Gisborne, alias Mattis, of the office of Gunner and Master Smith in the Tower. [*Sign Man., vol.* IV., *No.* 44.]

July. Docquet of the above. [*Docquet, July* 24.]

July 25. Westminster. Grant to Thos. Wilson and Ambrose Randall [Randolph], on surrender of Levinus Munck and Thos. Wilson, of the office of Keepers and Registrars of Papers and Records concerning matters of state and council, with the fee of 3*s.* 4*d.* per diem. [*Sign Man., vol.* IV., *No.* 45.]

July. Docquet of the above. [*Docquet, July* 24.]

July? 69. Thos. Wilson to Ambrose Randolph, his son [in-law]. To send him 20*l.*, which shall be returned at a certain time; 20*s.* to be paid for the patent, which is enrolled in Mr. Bingley's office.

July 25. Westminster. Grant to Roger Palmer, Cupbearer to the Prince, of a pension of 100*l.* per ann., on surrender of a like pension by Sir Robt. Killigrew, appointed Keeper in reversion of Falmouth Castle, in place of the late Sir Wm. Godolphin, who had a grant of the keepership, on condition of resigning to Palmer a pension of 10*s.* per diem. [*Sign Man., vol.* IV., *No.* 46.]

July. Docquet of the above. [*Docquet, July* 24.]

July 25. Westminster. Warrant to Robt. Seymer of the Jewel House, Receiver of the Contributions for Ireland, &c., to issue moneys on warrant from the Lord Treasurer, &c., instead of the Commissioners of the Treasury. [*Sign Man., vol.* IV., *No.* 47.]

July 25. Westminster. Grant to John Sotherton, Baron of the Exchequer, of the benefit of the outlawries of David Waterhouse and Sir Edw. Waterhouse, for whom he is security, until the creditors are paid, and he freed from his bonds; the surplus to remain to the King. [*Ibid., No.* 48.]

July. Docquet of the above. [*Docquet, July* 24.]

July 26. Westminster. Warrant for payment of 5,536*l.* 3*s.* 4*d.* to Sir Lionel Cranfield, in part purchase from him and his partners of their interest in tavern licences. [*Sign Man., vol.* IV., *No.* 49.]

July 26. Westminster. Grant to Ann, wife of Robt. Bowers, of London, of pardon for life only, for clipping and filing coin. Latin. [*Ibid., No.* 50.]

July 26. Westminster. Grant, with survivorship, to Rich. and Nowell Warner, of the office of Barge Master. Latin. [*Ibid., No.* 51.]

July 26. Westminster. Grant to Sir Fras. Barington, Bart., of the King's reversion in the manor of Aston Clinton, alias Auston Clinton, co. Bucks, which he wishes to sell, on his yielding to His Majesty a like interest in the manor of Hatfield Broad-oak, alias King's Hatfield, co. Essex. Latin. [*Ibid., No.* 52.]

Vol. LXXVII.

1614.
July 26.
Westminster.
Grant to Sir Wm. Cope, Bart., on tenure of knight's service, of purchase of certain lands, cos. Oxford and Gloucester, late of the monastery of Brewerne, co. Oxford, for the sum of 1,347*l.* 6*s.* 8*d.* Latin. [*Sign Man., vol.* IV., *No.* 53.]

July 27.
Westminster.
Grant to Wm. Ramsay, of the Bedchamber, in reversion after Thos. Lord Bruce and Sir Wm. Cavendish, of the Mastership of the Game, and keeping of the House and Parks at Ampthill, co. Bedford. Latin. [*Ibid., No.* 54.]

July 27.
Westminster.
Grant to Thos. Betham, of Rowington, co. Warwick, and his heirs, of the site of the manor of Rowington, with the appurtenances, late belonging to John Duke of Northumberland, attainted. [*Ibid., No.* 55.]

July.
Docquet of the above. [*Docquet, July* 24.]

July 27.
Westminster.
Warrant to pay to Sir Hen. Carey, Keeper of Marybone Park, 25*l.* 13*s.* 6*d.*, for repairs and building six new bridges; also 10*l.* to Chris. Hammond for finishing the lodge in Chapel Hainault, Waltham Forest. [*Sign Man., vol.* IV., *No.* 56.]

July 27.
Westminster.
Grant to Anne Aston, daughter of Sir Roger Aston, deceased, of a pension of 200*l.* per ann. for seven years, from the Exchequer, Sir Roger's former pension from the customs being void, on account of the new composition with the farmers. [*Ibid., No.* 57.]

July 28.
Westminster.
Grant to Thos. Williams of a Gunner's place in the Tower. Latin. [*Ibid., No.* 58.]

July 28.
Westminster.
Grant to Sir John Vaughan and Sir John Constable of the manors of Llanymthivery, Perveth, and Henriun, co. Carmarthen; also of the office of Lieutenant of the Castle of Llanymthivery, on surrender thereof by Geo. Lord Audley and Sir Mervin Audley, his son. Latin. [*Ibid., No.* 59.]

July 28.
Westminster.
Grant to Art. Mainwaring, in reversion after Sir Hugh Beeston, of the office of Controller of Records, Fines, Amerciaments, &c., cos. Chester, Flint, and Carnarvon. Latin. [*Ibid., No.* 60.]

July 28.
Westminster.
Grant to Percival Hobson, and others, of Barnsley, in fee farm, of purchase of divers cottages, lands, &c. in Barnsley, parcel of the manor of Barnsley-cum-Dodworth, late of the Monastery of Pontefract, co. York, for the sum of 1,051*l.* 7*s.* 8*d.* Latin. [*Ibid., No.* 61.]

July.
Docquet of the above. [*Docquet, July* 24.]

July 28.
Croydon.
70. Archbp. Abbot to [Carleton]. Sudden arrival of the King of Denmark at Somerset House, the Queen's residence. The cause of his visit much wondered at, but it is only one of kindness. He leaves on Monday, the King going with him to Gravesend.

Vol. LXXVII.

1614.

July 29. Commission to the Earl of Suffolk, &c. concerning the demise of lands. [*Grant Bk., p.* 148.]

July 30. Westminster. Warrant to pay 100*l.* to Jas. Sandilands and Pat. Abercromy; also 70*l.* to Sir And. Keith, disbursed in his attendance on the Electress Palatine. [*Sign Man., vol.* IV., *No.* 62.]

July 30. Westminster. Grant to Lord Sheffield, Sir John Bourchier, and Thos. Russell, on rent of 200*l.* per ann., of the sole making of copper, by a new way of dissolving the ore in water, on failure of a former grant, dated Jan. 26, 1610, to Thos. Russell and others; with provisoes of compensation for loss to the customs from non-importation of copper, and of non-increase in its price. [*Ibid., No.* 63.]

July 31. Westminster. Grant to Geo. Marr, of Scotland, of denization. Latin. [*Ibid., No.* 64.]

July 31. Westminster. Grant to the Governors of the Free School of Jas. Pemberton, in Eccleston, co. Lancaster, of licence to purchase lands in mortmain to the value of 40*l.* per ann., for which he has left money, the former lands being only worth 30*l.* per ann. [*Ibid., No.* 65.]

July 31. Westminster. Warrant to issue moneys not exceeding 1,000*l.*, for rewards to the servants of the King of Denmark, and for his entertainment. [*Ibid., No.* 66.]

July? Warrant to the farmers of French and Rhenish wines for payment of 1,584*l.* to Jas. Bovy for fifty-five tuns of wine, to be yearly furnished for the King's use. [*Ibid., No.* 67.]

July. Whitehall. 71. Project of a warrant to the Attorney and Solicitor General to draw up a commission to Geo. Margitts, Hen. Smyth, and Thos. Oveatt, to search out the concealed fines, &c. of recusants, of which the King is deprived by fraudulent proceedings in the Exchequer, granting to them one fourth of the sums thus to be raised at their own cost.

[July.] 72. Draft of the above.

July? 73. Earl of Nottingham to Somerset. Requests that a grant for the bearer of the keeping of the hare warren at Hampton Court, which his Lordship has stayed, may pass the Privy Seal.

July? [Greenwich.] 74. Nicolas de Rebbe to Sec. Winwood. Sends his address that his passport may not be retarded. Wishes to be described therein as "Nicolas de Rebbe, Gentleman, of Flanders, Historiographer of Modern Times." Reminds him of the papers belonging to him, viz., a letter patent to write history, two letters missive, and a book of his arms. French. [*See* 1614. *Undated, No.* 93.]

Aug. 4. London. 75. Chamberlain to Carleton. He is to remove from Venice to the Low Countries. Departure of the King of Denmark. He had hunting, bear-baiting, fencing, or other amusements, daily. Whispers about the cause of his coming are, that had the Earl of Northampton lived, he would have complained of him for unreverent

VOL. LXXVII.

usage of the Queen, or that he wished the King to help Brandenburg in the attempt on Cleves. Plate value 5,500*l.* presented by His Majesty to him and his followers. The Archduke's Ambassador is earnest to have his precedence over the Venetian Ambassador declared. Sir Thos. Lake interlopes into the business of Sir Ralph Winwood; he tried to get half the diet as Latin Secretary, but failed. Sudden death of Sir Walter Cope, heart-broken at the death of his brother, and threatened loss of his place. Particulars of his will, &c.

76. Hen. Lord Danvers to Carleton. Congratulates him on his expected removal to the Low Countries. Sir Wm. Udall has done good offices to procure it.

Warrant for payment of 51*l.* to John Murray, of the Bedchamber, to be disbursed for the King's special service. [*Docquet.*]

Grant to Peter Edgecombe of a fee-farm rent of 50 marks on lands in Cornwall. [*Docquet.*]

Grant, with survivorship, to Sir Oliver Cromwell and Henry, his son, of the office of Rangers and Principal Keepers, Woodwards, Bow-bearers, and Masters of the Game, of Waybridge Forest, co. Huntingdon. [*Docquet.*]

Grant to Wm. Hall of purchase of Hadnock wood, co. Monmouth, parcel of the Duchy of Lancaster. [*Docquet.*]

Grant to Sir Robt. Carr and Thos. Reade of the sole draining of the King's drowned lands, mines, groves and coal-pits, in England and Wales, with one third of the drained lands, for a rent of 100*l.* [*Docquet.*]

Grant to Hen. Gibb, of the Bedchamber, of certain lands forfeited by the attainder of Wm. Stillington, of Yorkshire, convicted in a præmunire for refusing the Oath of Allegiance. [*Docquet.*]

Discharge for the Lord Treasurer and other Commissioners, of certain secret jewels in the Tower, delivered by the King's command to the Queen. [*Docquet.*]

77. Sir Hen. Savile to Carleton. He is to go to Holland, and Sir Hen. Wotton is to succeed him. Instructions relative to certain transcripts, &c., procured for him by Carleton. Will not wear the medal sent him till it is completed, lest ignorant people take it for a whistle or a tool.

Grant to Sir John Mallet, Thos. Henton, and Dan. White, of purchase of lands, &c., parcel of the manor of Wellington, co. Somerset. [*Docquet.*]

Grant to Jas. Prowse, Rich. Perry, and John Gibbons, of purchase of land in the manor of Wellington, co. Somerset, and of a messuage in Shafton, co. Dorset. [*Docquet.*]

Lease to Sir Noel Caron of the rents of Assize, and perquisites of the Courts Leet of the manor of Kennington, co. Surrey. [*Docquet.*]

VOL. LXXVII.

1614.

Aug. 17. Brackenborough. 78. Alex. Williams to Carleton. Has paid over some of Carleton's money to Burlamachi, who deals favourably with him, and says he shall want no service from him. Sir Hen. Savile gives hopes that he will do somewhat for Carleton's scholar.

Aug. Letter to the Lord Chancellor to stay proceedings against Robt. Wolverston till next term. [*Docquet.*]

Aug. 22. Grant to Sir Ant. Mildmay of pardon for contempt against the Court of King's Bench, and release of a fine imposed for the same. [*Docquet.*]

Aug.? 79. Reasons in behalf of a request by the Queen, for a patent empowering her to compound with strangers for the grant of licences to fish on the English coasts.

Aug. 24. 80. Archbp. Abbot and Lord Chancellor Ellesmere to Thos. Wilson. Command him to search the records in his custody relating to the King's jurisdiction and right on the seas, and of fisheries upon the coast, and to hold them ready for inspection.

Aug. 28. Letter to the Attorney General for trying the King's title to the manor of Miserden, co. Gloucester, according to course of law. [*Docquet.*]

Aug. 28. Letter to the President and Vice President of the Marches of Wales for the admission of Rowland White and Thos. Alured, as Remembrancer of the Court there. [*Docquet.*]

Aug. 30. Grant to John Jack and Abraham Abercromy of the office of Saddler, for life. [*Grant Bk., p.* 134.]

[Sept. 5.] 81. Thos. Wilson to [Edw. Lloyd]. Intends to prosecute his claim to the custody of Wythen, son of the late Enian Jones, as the King's ward, and also to obtain a fine, because Lloyd's father married the ward to his own daughter.

Sept. 8. Northampton House. Earl of Suffolk to the Officers of Customs in the Port of London. The King having directed observance of the charter granted to the Company of Merchants trading to France, no entry of goods exported to or imported from France is to be taken, except from persons free of the Company. [*Dom. Corresp., March* 27, 1616.]

Sept. 11. Wanstead. Proclamation prohibiting the bringing in of whale fins by any but the Muscovy Company, who have established the whale fishery near their newly discovered land called King James's land. Printed. [*Proc. Coll., No.* 30.]

Sept. 11. 82. Edw. Lloyd to [Thos. Wilson]. Has strong evidence that Wythen Jones is not a King's ward. His marriage took place before his father's death. Will not yield up the case uncontested.

[Sept. 12.] 83. Heads of a letter to be written from the Lord Chamberlain to Sir Robt. Dudley.

Sept. 12. Wanstead. 84. R. S. [Lord Chamberlain Somerset] to Sir Robt. Dudley. Thanks for his good opinion. Should the services proffered in his late letter prove answerable to his promises, will try to secure him contentment.

VOL. LXXVII.

1614.

Sept. 12. Letter to Mrs. Redigon Cole, recommending to her in the way of marriage Sir Edw. Southcote, Gentleman Pensioner. [*Docquet.*]

Sept. 14. 85. The Council to the Sheriffs and Justices of Peace in Wales. To make strict search lest the recusants and suspicious persons disarmed by the orders of Jan. and Feb. 1613, purchase armour again; and to send up a certificate of the armour taken, and the names of the parties from whom it has been received.

Sept. 14? Grant to the Wardens, &c. of Winchester College, Oxford of licence to purchase lands in mortmain, value 30*l.* per ann. [*Warrt. Bk.*, I., *p.* 233.]

Sept. 14. 86. Grant to the University of Oxford of licence to purchase lands in mortmain, to the value of 666*l.* 13*s.* 4*d.*, for support of learning. [*Copy taken in* 1633.]

Sept. 15. Grant to the Lord Mayor, &c., of London, of the office of coal meting. [*Grant Bk.*, *p.* 135.]

Sept. 18. London. 87. Matthew de Quester to Carleton. Requests him to supply with money, if necessary, the bearer, Michael de Coster, a post under his charge, despatched with letters on His Majesty's service.

Sept. 19. Letter to the Master of the Rolls, to confirm and grant three reversions of the office of one of the Six Clerks in Chancery. [*Docquet.*]

Sept. 19. Grant to Dixie Hickman, servant to the Lady Elizabeth, of safe conduct. [*Docquet.*]

Sept. 20. Letter to Sir Thos. Dale, Marshal of the Colony in Virginia, directing him to send home Eliezer Hopkins. [*Docquet.*]

Sept. 20. Melvill. 88. Sir Robt. Melvill to Somerset. Sends his old investment to prove his right to the barony of Brentland. Has served thirty years unrewarded.

Sept. 23. Grant to Pat. Jenkin of the toll of tin in the manor of Helstone and elsewhere, co. Cornwall, for life. [*Grant Bk.*, *p.* 134.]

Sept. 24. Grant to Wm. Ramsyer of the office of Keeper of Ampthill honour, &c., co. Bedford, for life. [*Ibid.*, *p.* 141.]

Sept. 25. Grant to Edw. Price of pardon for manslaughter of Maurice Price in a sudden quarrel. [*Docquet.*]

Sept. 25. Letter to the Archbp. of Canterbury, to remove Thos. Preston, Priest, prisoner in the Clink, for recovery of his health. [*Docquet.*]

Sept. 26. Hampton Court. Proclamation prohibiting the export of sheep wools, wool fells, and fullers' earth, as injurious to the manufacture of cloth at home. Printed. [*Proc. Coll.*, *No.* 31.]

Sept. 26. 89. Muster roll of the trained band of the town of Lydd.

Sept. 27. Grant to Thos. Barrett of the office of Gamekeeper at Nonsuch, co. Bucks, for life. [*Grant Bk.*, *p.* 146.]

Vol. LXXVII.

1614.

Sept. 28. Croydon. 90. Archbp. Abbot to the Bp. of Peterborough. The King wishes to know the truth of a report that several silenced ministers, especially Mr. Dod and Mr. Cleaver, are suffered to preach in his diocese; and also that Mr. Catelyne, of Northampton, though professing conformity when questioned, does not "use perpetuall conformity;" the refractory disposition of the people of that town cannot be borne with.

Sept. 30. Licence to Thos. Browne, Toby Steward, and Nich. Burghley, to make stone pots for twenty-one years. [*Grant Bk., p.* 146.]

Sept. 30. 91. Roll of the general musters of the town of Hastings.

Sept. Grant to Gilbert Raleigh, in reversion after Sir Carew Raleigh and Sir Carew Reynell, of the office of Lieutenant of the Isle and Captain of the Castle of Portland. [*Docquet.*]

Sept. Letter to the Dean and Chapter of Windsor to grant to Dr. Hammond, the King's Physician, a lease of Hamme Farm, Chertsey, co. Surrey. [*Docquet.*]

[Sept.] 92. Account of the rent received for Rowell and Orden, co. Northampton, for ten years past; with note of payments made to Meredith Morgan, for masques.

Vol. LXXVIII. October—December, 1614.

Oct. 1. Grant to Sir Julius Cæsar of the office of Master of the Rolls, for life. [*Grant Bk., p.* 147.]

Oct. 1. 1. Statement of the origin and progress of the pre-emption of tin from the first grant thereof, shewing the mischief that would ensue by the surrender of the present patentees, on account of a proviso in their patent that no other shall sell tin for a year afterwards, if they have a stock in hand.

Oct. 2. 2. Muster roll of the select band of footmen in Winchelsea, and of their deputies.

Oct. 2. 3. Muster roll of the garrison of Camber Castle.

Oct. 3. Grant to Marmaduke Lloyd of the office of Attorney in the principality of Wales, for life. [*Grant Bk., p.* 135.]

Oct. 3. Commission to Sir Julius Cæsar, Master of the Rolls, to hear and determine all causes pending in Chancery. [*Ibid., p.* 147.]

Oct. 3. Exeter. 4. Earl of Bath to the Council. On arrival of the orders for disarming recusants, Sir Wm. Courtney, Deputy Lieutenant and Colonel of a Regiment, confessed that his lady is a recusant, and that he never receives the communion, though he has taken the Oath of Allegiance. He tendered his resignation, which was accepted till further directions. The Earl of Pembroke should be requested to redress

1614. Vol. LXXVIII.

disorder in the Stannaries, arising from the other inhabitants being more heavily charged [for the musters] than the tinners. Complaint that the exemption of Dartmouth from taking part in the musters is a dangerous precedent.

Oct. 4. Whitehall. 5. Sir Ralph Winwood to Somerset. To know when the Ambassador just arrived from the Elector of Brandenburg may wait upon the King.

Oct. 4. 6. List of perpetuities, annuities, pensions and fees, payable out of the Exchequer.

Oct. 4. 7. Roll of the general musters of the town and port of New Romney.

Oct. 4? 8. Muster roll of the general band of the port of Hithe.

Oct. 4. Grant to Geo. Proctor of the office of Reader in Civil Law in the University of Cambridge, for life. [*Grant Bk., p.* 141.]

Oct. 6. Grant to Fras. Ogle of the office of Serjeant-at-arms, for life. [*Ibid., p.* 141.]

Oct. 6. 9. Muster roll of the town of Folkestone.

Oct. 7. 10. Muster roll of the garrison of Sandgate Castle.

Oct. 7. 11. Duplicate of the above.

Oct. 8. 12. Muster roll of the garrison of Mote's Bulwark.

Oct. 8. Edinburgh. 13. Sir G. Murray to Somerset. Sir Jas. Stewart paid 20,000 marks for the "Whitsunday term of his tax of Orkney," and will soon owe as much for the Martinmas term. Has delayed till further directions pressing him for the accounts of the preceding year, when the rebels committed so many spoils.

Oct. 9. 14. [The Council] to Lord St. John of Bletsoe. Regret his cold dealings in the meeting held in Bedfordshire for promoting the benevolence, his influence being great in that county; and also the absence of his name from the list of free givers who have already promised contributions. Advise a different course, if he wishes to preserve the King's good opinion.

Oct. 10. Mansfield. 15. Sheriff and Justices of Nottinghamshire to the Council. Have completed the musters according to order.

Oct. 10. Grant to Wm. Lord Knollys of the office of Master of Wards and Liveries, for life. [*Grant Bk., p.* 135.]

Oct. 10. Sandwich. 16. Muster roll for the town of Deal, a member of Sandwich.

Oct. 10. 17. Muster roll of the garrison of Deal Castle.

Oct. 10. Sandwich. 18. Muster roll for the towns of Ramsgate, Walmer, and Sarr, members of Sandwich.

Oct. 10. 19. Muster roll of the garrison of Walmer Castle.

Oct. 10. 20. Muster roll of the garrison of Sandown Castle.

1614. Vol. LXXVIII.

Oct. 10. 21. Note of shot and powder expended by Ant. Sandes, Lieutenant of Walmer Castle, since Oct. 9, 1613, at the funeral of the Earl of Northampton, late Lord Warden, and on other occasions.

Oct. 10. Royston. Proclamation prohibiting the import of alum. All alum brought in to be forfeited and given to Robt. Johnson, the King's Agent, for immediate export. Printed. [*Proc. Coll.*, *No.* 32.]

Oct. 11. 22. Duplicate of the above.

Oct. 11. 23. Oliver St. John to the Mayor of Marlborough. Sends the arguments on which he grounds his opinion that the mode of raising money by benevolences is against law, reason, and religion.

Oct. 11. 24. Geo. Margitts to Sir Ralph Winwood. The completion with the Attorney General of the grant to the Duke of Lenox, himself, and others, of the commission for recusants, is hindered, because the Warden of the Fleet will not allow some of the parties, who are under his custody, to appear before the Attorney General. Spiller and his party boast that they were favoured, and their opponents reproved, at the Council table.

Oct. 11. 25. Extracts from the Court Roll of Wyrardisbury, Bucks, of the admission of John Helen as tenant of the messuage called Gospits, and other lands in the said manor; and of the surrender thereof by Ralph Helperby and Wm. Greene.

Oct. 11. 26. General muster roll of the town and port of Sandwich.

Oct. 27. Draft of the above.

Oct. 11. 28. General muster roll of the select band of the town of Fordwich.

Oct. 12. London. 29. John Chamberlain to Isaac Wake. Sir Dud. Carleton's removal from Venice is countermanded. Sir Edw. Phelips, Master of the Rolls, is dead, and is succeeded by Sir Julius Cæsar, though with limited powers. Sir Fulk Greville made Chancellor and Under Treasurer of the Exchequer, in spite of his age; and Lord Knollys, Master of the Wards. Sir Walter Chute released, but loses his place, and is restrained within three miles of his father's house. Skit on him and his fellow prisoners. The free gifts will reach the value of a subsidy. The King and Prince at Royston. The Merchant Adventurers' Company dissolved. Patent for making glasses given up in favour of those who undertake to make them with Scotch coal.

Oct. 12. Whitehall. Earl of Suffolk to [the Officers of the Customs]. To permit Robt. Johnson, of London, to export alum duty free, either such as is made in England, or is seized and forfeited for being imported contrary to proclamation. [*Dom. Corresp.*, *March* 27, 1616.]

Oct. 12. Northampton House. 30. The Same to [Somerset]. The new Serjeants invite His Majesty to their feast as usual. If the King will return them thanks, they are happy men. It is not meant that he should be present, the feast being within two days.

Oct ? 31. Bill of poultry for the Serjeants' feast at the Middle Temple.

VOL. LXXVIII.

1614.

Oct. 12. Grant to Sir Fulk Greville of the Chancellorship of the Exchequer, on surrender by Sir Julius Cæsar, now Master of the Rolls. [*Docquet.*]

Oct. 12. Grant to the Same of the Under Treasurership of the Exchequer, on surrender by Sir Julius Cæsar. [*Docquet.*]

Oct. 12. Warrant to pay to Sir Julius Cæsar 500*l.*, disbursed by the King's command to Bernard Lindsay. [*Docquet.*]

Oct. 12. Warrant to pay to Peter Van Lore 2,000*l.*, for jewels delivered at Christmas last for the King's use. [*Docquet.*]

Oct. 12. Grant to Hugh Rich, of Bagborough, Somerset, of pardon for horse stealing. [*Docquet.*]

Oct. 13. Margate. 32. Muster roll of the parishes in the Isle of Thanet.

Oct. 13. Grant to Sir Thos. Glover of the office of Collector of Fines in Ecclesiastical Causes, for life. [*Grant Bk., p.* 133.]

Oct. 14. Grant to Fras. Smith of the office of Bailiff of the Hundreds of Chelmsford and Dunmow, co. Essex, for twenty-one years. [*Ibid., p.* 142.]

Oct. 14. 33. Roll of the general musters at Faversham.

Oct. 15. Strand. 34. Thos. Wilson to Ambrose Randolph. Recommends the bearer, Hugh Panton, to the service of Randolph's brother, Mr. Garratt, whom he would be glad to know, from respect for his brother the Earl.

Oct. 17. Grant to Hen. Cæsar of the deanery of Ely, for life. [*Grant Bk., p.* 147.]

Oct. 18. Cambridge. 35. Robt. Wilmot to his Brother. Religious admonition on the departure of the latter for the East Indies.

Oct. 20. Court at Royston. 36. Earl of Pembroke to the Council. Wishes to know particulars of the abuses in the Stannaries complained of by the Earl of Bath. If it be merely that the tinners are mustered apart from the rest of the county, that is their privilege by charter. They seek no exemption from the musters, but only to be kept to themselves.

Oct. 20. 37. Lease from John Atwood, of London, to Ralph Cowper, of Petworth, Sussex, of two tenements in Petworth and Kirdford, co. Sussex, late the property of Sir Thos. Shirley, deceased.

Oct. 21. Grant to Milon Gnarisborough of the office of Gamekeeper at Richmond, for life. [*Grant Bk., p.* 133.]

Oct. 23. 38. Edw. Reynoldes to John Castle. Private business. Negligence of his cousin Raymond in getting in his debts. Mr. Mills thinks the charge of processes should be borne by suitors, &c.

VOL. LXXVIII.

1614.

Oct. 24. Royston. Proclamation commanding the repair of noblemen and gentlemen to their several countries, at the end of the term, for Christmas hospitalities and relief of the poor. Printed. [*Proc. Coll., No.* 33.]

Oct. 28. Commission to Sir Lawr. Tanfield, Lord Chief Baron of the Exchequer, to compound for free warren. [*Grant Bk., p.* 138.]

Oct. 28. Northampton House. Thos. Earl of Suffolk to the Officers of the Customs at London. To desist from charging the duties of strangers on Wm. Crosse, who has proved himself to be an Englishman. [*Dom. Corresp., July* 24, 1615.]

Oct. 30. Rufford in Nottinghamshire. 39. Earl of Shrewsbury to the Council. His deputy lieutenants have held the musters in Derbyshire. *Incloses,*

39. I. *Sir Peter Freshville and Sir John Harpur, Deputy Lieutenants of Derbyshire, to the Earl of Shrewsbury. Have completed the musters, and filled up the number of horse, in spite of the decay of many ancient families. The clergy have declined the musters, till the pleasure of the Bishop be known. Oct.* 20.

Oct. 30. 40. Arguments and extracts from records, to prove the precedency of the Master of the Rolls above the Chancellor of the Exchequer. Mutilated.

Oct. 41. Observations addressed to Sec. Winwood on the ill consequences of the coinage of farthings, the metal employed being so base that they are easily imitated; with notes proving the profit of English copper coinage much to exceed that of other countries; and queries on the amount of money coined. French.

Oct.? 42. Sir John Vaughan to Somerset. Thanks for his promise to intercede with the King for the grant of a place under the Prince. Will continue his attendance if desired, or else repair to his county.

Oct. Letter mandatory to the Warden and Fellows of All Souls College, Oxford, to elect Gawin Stewart a fellow of that house; with order for sealing the above forthwith. [*Docquet.*]

Nov. 3. Court. 43. Earl of Pembroke to the Council. His deputies have attended to the musters in Cornwall, but the training was obliged to be deferred till after harvest. The foot intend to exercise regularly. They renew their suit to be excused troops of horse, the country being unfit for it.

Nov. 4. 44. Geo. Margitts to Sir Ralph Winwood. Certain records must be compared with his notes, or the cause so beneficial to the King will fall to the ground. The records are kept from his party, but are open to recusants. Spiller is so impudent that he will not be questioned by any other course.

Nov. 7. Chester. 45. W. Harrington to Capt. Faithful Fortescue. Particulars of the pretentious conduct of Edw. Scory in the voyage from Ireland, the landing at West Kirby, and going by Chester to London. Will deliver Sir Toby Caulfield's letters.

VOL. LXXVIII.

1614.

Nov. 7. Grant to Sir Lionel Cranfield of compositions for licences for selling wine in England and Wales, and also of the fines and rents for the same, for two years and a half. [*Grant Bk.*, *p.* 147.]

Nov. 8. Grant to the Same of the office of Receiver of Fines and Rents for Licences to sell Wine in England and Wales, for life. [*Ibid.*, *p.* 147.]

Nov. 9. Grant to Rich. Charcroft of the Captaincy of Sandgate [Castle], co. Kent, for life. [*Ibid.*. *p.* 147.]

Nov. 9. Theobalds. Proclamation against the export of woollen yarn, as injurious to the cloth trade. Printed. [*Proc. Coll.*, *No.* 34.]

Nov. 9. Hunsdon House. 46. Ralph Lord Eure to the Council. Has ordered the musters in Shropshire, but the bailiffs of Shrewsbury refuse to send their thirty-nine men out of the town, on plea of a Statute 4 & 5 Phil. and Mary.

Nov. 10. Lichfield. 47. Robt. Earl of Essex to the Same. Has held the musters in Staffordshire, and found great deficiency of arms and want of practice in the bands.

[Nov.] 48. Statement of the suit of the King v. Sir Thos. Whorewood and others, for intruding into the demesne of the Forest of Kinfare, co. Stafford. Indorsed " Mr. Ayliffe's brief."

[Nov.] 49. Proofs on the King's part, and answer, in the above case.

[Nov.] 50. Objections on the defendants' part in the above case, and their proofs of title.

[Nov.] 51. A similar brief of objections, &c.

[Nov.] 52. Memorandum of the contents of the manors of Stourton and Kinfare.

Nov. 12. 53. Order of Court in the cause of the King v. Sir Thos. Whorewood and others, touching assart lands, purprestures, &c., in the forest of Kinfare, co. Stafford, permitting the examination of aged persons as witnesses for the defendants, as to the boundaries of the plots, contrary to the usual custom not to admit witnesses against records.

Nov. 14. Bletsoe. 54. Lord St. John to the Council. Has held the musters in Huntingdonshire. The foot are in good condition, but the great defects in the horse, caused by removals, deaths, decay of families, &c., are too numerous to be supplied.

Nov. 15. Letley. 55. Earl of Hertford to the Same. Many defects in the musters of Somersetshire, Wiltshire, and Bristol, on account of ill weather &c. Promises to supply all.

Nov. 16. Newmarket. Warrant to the Treasurer, &c. of the Exchequer to appoint yearly four merchants, two of whom shall be Merchant Strangers, to taste all wines imported as Rhenish wines, for preventing deceit in passing off

1614. Vol. LXXVIII.

French wines as Rhenish. Also to take bond of wine merchants not to compound any wines called Rhenish within the kingdom. [*Sign Man., vol.* IV., *No.* 69.]

Nov. 17. Grant to Robt. Gray, of Newcastle-on-Tyne, a Seminary Priest, who is now converted, and has taken the oaths, of pardon for going beyond the sea, there becoming a Romanist, and returning to England. [*Ibid., No.* 70.]

Nov. 17. 56. [Earl of Somerset] to the Council. The King, at request of the French Ambassador, has exempted the French nation from payment of head money within the Cinque Ports. Will do anything in his power, as Provisional Warden, to execute the order.

Nov. 18. 57. Earl of Rutland to the Same. Has held the musters in Lincolnshire. Will try to supply the defects of the horse. Asks what is to be done with those who refuse to attend, and whether the clergy are to be called to the training.

Nov. 18. Grant to Isaac and Rich. Johnson of the office of Clerk of the Rolls, for life. [*Grant Bk., p.* 134.]

Nov. 19. Grant to Thos. Punter of the office of keeping the garden at Newmarket, for life. [*Ibid., p.* 141.]

[Nov. 20.] 58. The Council to the King. Congratulations on his escape from a dangerous accident in falling from his horse, &c.

Nov. 22. 59. Examination of John Legatt, of London, silk weaver, and Thos. Williamson, relative to their stealing cushions from the manor house, Woodstock, burning them, and selling the gold and silver of the burnt lace.

Nov. 22. Rufford. 60. Robt. Pierrepoint to Clement Edmondes, Clerk of the Council. To excuse him for non-appearance before the Council, as summoned, on account of sickness. *Annexing,*

60. i. *Gilbert Earl of Shrewsbury to the Clerk of the Council in waiting. Requests him to inform their Lordships that Pierrepoint is quite unable to take so long a journey without great danger. Rufford, Nov.* 22, 1614.

Nov. 23. Grant to Thos. Bond, sen. and jun., of the office of cleaning the King's hangings and carpets, for life. [*Grant Bk., p.* 146.]

Nov. 24. London. 61. Chamberlain to Carleton. Sir Ralph Winwood has land worth 1,000*l.* a year in Buckinghamshire. The King had a dangerous fall in hunting. The fortune of Villiers, the new favourite, seems to be at a stand. Money is to be raised by a commission to levy fines on all buildings erected within seven miles of London since 1603, contrary to proclamation. The brewers yield to an impost on beer, to avoid its being carried off for the King's household. A Jew pirate arrested, who brought three Spanish prizes into Plymouth, and was set out by the King of Morocco. Sir Thos. Roe sent, at the East India Company's expense, Ambassador to the Great Mogul.

VOL. LXXVIII.

1614.
Nov. 27. Grant to John Southaick of the office of Porter in the citadel of Carlisle, for life. [*Grant Bk., p.* 142.]

Nov. 28. Northampton House. Earl of Suffolk to the Officers of Customs at London. Directs them to suffer the Eastland merchants to re-transport their corn to foreign parts without export duties, in case of its not finding sale in England, although, by order in Council, dated Jan. 1613, they are no longer free from import duties. [*Dom. Corresp., March* 27, 1616.]

Nov. 62. The Same and Chancellor Ellesmere to the Earl of Somerset. Have considered the objections against the proposed patent for Sir Hen. Neville, for prosecuting offenders who spoil His Majesty's woods, and also Sir Henry's replies, and see no reason why the grant may not pass, the objections being unfounded or frivolous.

Nov. Wrest. 63. Earl of Kent to the Council. Has held the general musters in Bedfordshire; exercised the footbands, which are in good state; and will train the horse in better weather. The arms and ammunition are in good state, and also the beacons.

Dec. 1. Licence to Gabriel Armstrong to hold a Court Leet in the manor of Kempston, or elsewhere, co. Notts. [*Grant Bk., p.* 145.]

Dec. 1. Golden Grove, Carmarthen. 64. Sir John Vaughan to Sir Hen. Neville. Has taken great pains about the King's gifts in the county; the inhabitants, though poor, are willing to contribute, and have paid in the amount of three subsidies. They will, if requested, give the King the money laid aside for Irish service, and for building a house of correction. Has persuaded the chief gentlemen in Brecknockshire, a county that once refused its money, to contribute this time. Begs Somerset's influence, that he may be sworn into the place which he desires to occupy, on the creation of his gracious master [Charles, as Prince of Wales]. Sends 100*l.* to Somerset as a new year's gift.

Dec. 1. London. 65. Chamberlain to Carleton. Details of the settlement of Sir Walter Cope's affairs. His debts are 27,000*l.* The Bishop of St. David's is dead. Much suing for his place. In spite of poverty, a Masque is preparing, towards which the King gives 1,500*l.* The principal motive for it is said to be the gracing of young Villiers. Attempts are made to keep the Secretary away from Court, for he wins ground when he is there. Cautions Carleton against meddling with Holland affairs.

Dec. 2. Lambeth. 66. John Sanford to Sir. Thos. Edmondes, Ambassador at Paris. Condolences and advice on the death of Lady Edmondes.

Dec. 2. Newmarket. Proclamation revoking the Merchant Adventurers' Charter, its legal surrender, necessary for preventing the export of undressed cloth, not being completed. Printed. [*Proc. Coll., No.* 35.]

Dec. 4. Newhall. 67. Earl of Sussex to the Council. Has held the musters of foot in Essex, and will hold those of the horse. All defects are or shall be supplied.

Vol. LXXVIII.

1614.

Dec. 5. Northampton House. 68. Earl of Suffolk to the Auditor and Receiver of Kent. Warrant for continued payments of the wages, &c. due to the officers and garrisons of the forts and castles of the Cinque Ports, notwithstanding the vacancy of the Wardenship. *Prefixes,*

68. I. *The King to the Earl of Suffolk. Understanding that since the death of the late Lord Warden, the officers, &c. of the Cinque Ports have been unpaid, the warrant for their payment being directed to the Lord Warden only, authorizes him to give warrants for continuance of payment, with discharge of arrears. Newmarket, Nov.* 24, 1614.

Dec. 4. Tavistock. 69. Earl of Bath to the Council. Has completed the musters in Devonshire. Asks leave to wall up a postern door in Exeter Castle, by which bankrupts and rogues steal in and out, and by which thousands, in time of trouble, could enter the city without resistance.

Dec. 9. 70. Lease from Thos. Wilson, of Hertford, to Jas. Bovy, Serjeant of the Cellar, of the Sill House in the Strand, near Durham House.

Dec. 15. London. 71. Chamberlain to Carleton. The Spaniards' ill dealing with the Duke of Savoy, and their dubious course in Holland. [Clement] Edmondes going to treat with the States, about the East India trade and Greenland Fishery. Mr. Finet returned from Spain, whither he carried presents of animals, armour, &c. The Earl of Ormond dead. Dud. Norton has failed to supplant Sir Rich. Cooke in Ireland. Winwood gone to the King at Theobalds. Sir Fulk Greville reported likely to be Principal Secretary, &c., &c.

Dec. 15. Lambeth. 72. Archbp. Abbot to [the Same]. The Archbp. of Spalato is to travel to Holland with Carleton; he is not to expect great entertainment in England, but shall have a private life in a university and 200*l.* per ann. Carleton's detention at Venice has been because Sir Hen. Wotton stayed longer in Holland than was expected, but Carleton is to succeed him there in spring.

Dec. 15. 73. Certificate of musters co. Surrey, viewed by Wm. Lord Howard, of Effingham, and others, deputy lieutenants of the county.

Dec. 19. Croft. 74. Sir Herbert Croft to Somerset. The King having promised to consult his Council as to the exemption of the four English shires from the jurisdiction of the Court of Wales, urges him to remind His Majesty thereof, and to give them his influence. The Attorney General's opinion is in their favour, and the Lord Treasurer promises his furtherance. It being asked as matter of grace, the King could revoke it if he chose.

Dec.? 75. Sheriff and Justices of Worcestershire to the Same. Thanks for his endeavours to procure that county exemption from the jurisdiction of the Council of Wales, which the King has partially granted. Request him to press for their total exemption.

VOL. LXXVIII.

1614.

Dec.? 76. Inhabitants of Herefordshire to Somerset. Thanks for his favour in their efforts to free their county from the jurisdiction of the Council for Wales, which has long been very grievous and and oppressive.

Dec.? 77. List of the Gentlemen of cos. Hereford, Worcester, and Salop, who have subscribed the letters written to the Earl of Somerset.

Dec. 19. 78. Sentence of deprivation by the Archbp. of Canterbury and others, Commissioners Ecclesiastical, against Edm. Peacham, Rector of Hinton St. George, co. Somerset, for a libel against the Bishop of Bath and Wells, and other libels. Latin.

Dec. 22. London. 79. Chamberlain to Carleton. Little hope of Carleton's removal. Sir Hen. Wotton desires to remain in Holland as ordinary Ambassador. The King came to town, and thence went to Hampton Court. None of the projects for money succeed, and nobody is paid. Lord Walden is made Captain of the Pensioners. Lord Burleigh woos the Earl of Northumberland's daughter, which may bring about her father's release, but he cares little for restraint, except for the disgrace. Sir Albert Morton made Clerk of the Council. Sir Moyle Finch dead, &c.

Dec. 25. 80. Christmas Ode addressed to the King by John Sharp, petitioning for some gift which Sir Thos. Lake will explain. Latin.

Dec. 31. 81. Sir Thos. Bartlett to Sir Ralph Winwood. Requests his influence to obtain the charter for the pin-makers. Will give him, in gratitude, either 4,000*l*. of the imposts on foreign pins, or the moiety of the profits of the commerce in pins. Begs a speedy reply, as the cause will not bear delay.

Dec.? 82. Earl of Sheffield to Somerset. Bewails the woful accident of the death of his children; that of his eldest son deprives him of the means of paying his debts, his lands being entailed upon his grandson, only three years old. Begs favour in the applications he may make to the King. [*His three sons were drowned in crossing the Humber, Dec.* 1614.]

UNDATED. 1614?

1614? 83. Notes [by Edw. Nicholas] of certain rents which he holds in trust, the reversion being for Sir Robt. Carr, and of other business matters in connexion with the Earl of Somerset.

84. Particulars of the first and second loans raised by the King, showing wherein the second, which realized 116,381*l*., fell short of the first; with suggestions for issuing Privy Seals for a loan which shall equal the first. Indorsed [by Somerset] "Project upon Loanes."

85. Extracts of censurable passages from a pamphlet lately published, and presented to His Majesty, entitled "The Trades Increase," on the importance of increasing English shipping.

Vol. LXXVIII.

1614? 86. "Project for a Suit to the King," being a proposal that his Majesty shall take into his own hands, or bestow on whom he thinks proper, certain fees which in 20 Eliz. the judges of the King's Bench imposed, viz., 4*s*. for every procedendo, 3*s*. for an habeas corpus, and 8*d*. for a latitat.

Grant to Sir John Bourchier, of Grimston, co. York, Wm. Turner, Rich. Bowdler, of London, and others, farmers of the alum works, of renewal of protection for six months longer, the alum works being not yet settled. [*Sign Man., vol.* IV., *No.* 71.]

87. The King to [the Lord Mayor, &c. of London]. To stay the prosecution of Sir Baptist Hicks, on complaint by Sir Thos. Hayes, Alderman, of violence offered in a quarrel between them. Sir Baptist being a Knight, and servant of the King, the cause is to be tried elsewhere.

88. [The Lord Mayor of London] to the [Chapter of Trinity College, Cambridge]. Nominates Thos. Shirley to one of the Palin Exhibitions, in place of Peter Ashton, in accordance with a proviso of Mr. [Geo.] Palin's will, that the nomination, if neglected by the College, shall rest in the Lord Mayor of London. *Annexed is,*

88. I. *Extract of the will of* [*Geo.*] *Palin, referred to in the above, granting a legacy for founding four Scholarships in Trinity College. March* 4, 1610

Canterbury. 89. Francesco Carter to his brother, John Courthouse, servant of the Earl of Oxford. Intreats assistance, being thrown into prison by the justices of Canterbury, for being ignorantly the bearer of certain letters for London, the contents of which were so suspicious that the letters were sent up to the Council. Spanish.

90. Sir Wm. Bruncard to Somerset. Desires Rowland may be ordered to set down in writing the sums he will accept for discharge of the debt to him, and may be severely punished for the outrage he has done his [Bruncard's] reputation, &c.

91. Humph. Jobson to Edw. Anthony. To draw up a grant for a pension to a poor man for destroying vermin in Windsor Forest and elsewhere, which he will move "my Lord" to commend to the King. As to the other appeal, "my Lord" has passed the office, in reversion, under his own hand, but it is not yet granted by the King.

92. Thos. Earl of Suffolk to [his son-in-law, the Earl of Somerset]. Certain particulars remain with the King's counsel. The purchasers stay in town to despatch their bargains. Fragment.

93. Nich. de Rebbe to the King. Was sent by the King to Holland, in company of Sir Hen. Wotton, but recalled by Dr. Mayerne, his Majesty wanting him for some affairs. Prays that the pension granted him eighteen months before may be paid, as from his experimental knowledge of the science of the greatest cabinet of Europe, he can much aid the King in reducing his enemies. French.

Vol. LXXVIII.

? 94. Petition of Capt. John Balfour to the King. Is ruined by not obtaining permission to transport 500 men whom he levied for the King of Sweden. Has been a year and a half in Ireland, overseeing his brother's workmen to further the King's building there. Begs a small pension from the Exchequer of Scotland.

95. Petition of Sir Robt. Bannister to the Earl of Somerset, for satisfaction from Sir Gilbert Houghton for divers sums of money due on forfeited bonds.

96. Petition of the fourteen ordinary Grooms of the Chamber to the Same, to procure them a certain allowance in lieu of their diet, and bills for services, such as preparing the King's houses, riding journeys, waiting on Ambassadors, &c. Seven of them will serve monthly, and submit to fines in case of neglect of service.

97. Petition of John Graham, Surveyor of the King's Stables, to the Same, for leave to recover a debt of 1,000*l.* from Sir John Graham by course of law, having been himself arrested for want of the money. With note [by Somerset] that Sir John Graham promises to pay it in May next.

98. Petition of Allen Hodgkin to the Same, for leave to recover by law 100*l.* lent on bond to Sir John Lindsay and Sir Jas. Auchterlony, as Sir James is going to travel beyond seas.

99. Petition of Dr. Hen. Hook to the King, for relief to the inhabitants of Nettleton, Lincolnshire, being Crown land, the royalties, &c. of which are usurped by others, to the damage of His Majesty and the poor people.

100. Petition of Peter Kebblewhite, of Redbourn, Wilts, to the Earl of Somerset, for leave to recover a debt of 10*l.* from Ellis Mills, by course of law.

101. Petition of Robt. Lathorpe to the Same, for leave to prosecute Wm. Smith, Yeoman Pricker, who has failed in payment of his share in a joint bond for 16*l.*

102. Petition of Wm. Lawrence to the Same, for leave to recover a debt of 9*l.* from Wm. Penson, Herald-at-Arms. With order thereon.

103. Petition of Wm. Talbot, executor of Sir John Talbot deceased, to the King, for remainder of a grant of the yearly value of 100 marks, in manors, rectories, and parsonages, granted to Sir John Talbot, April 1605. *Annexed is,*

103. i. *Warrant for passing the remainder of a grant of* 100 *marks per ann., in manors, rectories, &c., made to the late Sir John Talbot, to his executor, Wm. Talbot.*

104. Petition of Bessy Walling, servant to the late Prince Henry, to the King, for grant of a lease of the manors of Shoston and Sunderland, co. Northumberland, concealed lands, in compensation for her past services, her former petition for the enrolment of apprentices in Westminster having failed.

Vol. LXXVIII.

1614 ?

105. Note by [Geo. Muncrieff ?], Falconer to the King, of the disproportion of the allowances now paid him with those which he received from the late Prince, for charge of hawks, dogs, &c.

106. Effect of a [proposed] Bill to repeal the Acts of 3 & 4 Jac. I., for bringing the New River into London; stating the objections against those Acts, and answers to the objections.

107. Note of the price of certain pictures sent by Johan Baptista Crescentio to [Sir Dud. Carleton]. Spanish.

108. Note that by mediation of Sir Robt. Brett, Deputy Warden of the Cinque Ports and Lieutenant of Dover Castle, the suit in the Court of Chancery at Dover, And. Bredgate v. Edw. Sturman, is to be settled by arbitration.

109. The King to Sir Edw. Noel, Master of the Game in the forest of Lyfield, co. Rutland. To prohibit hunting or destruction of game and deer there for three years, the deer being diminished by a disease lately come amongst them.

110. List of patents to Noblemen, Knights, and others, which are wanting.

111. Request that His Majesty would enforce the imposition of a shilling in the pound, levied on silks in the first year of his reign, and also twopence on every yard of cyprus.

112. Declaration of the proceedings between the new Company of Merchant Adventurers and the Senate of Stade, during the past two years, relative to the settlement of the Company there, or at Hamburgh.

113. Precept by Sir Robt. Brett, Lieutenant of Dover Castle, requiring the attendance of the ordinary watchmen of the said castle, "well furnished in apparel with coats, rapiers, and daggers fitting;" with list of the names of the watchmen.

114. Commission appointing the Lord Chancellor, the Lord Treasurer, and others, Justices of the Peace for Hertfordshire, to inquire into all felonies and offences there, and to proceed against the offenders according to law. Latin.

115. Memoranda relating to the conveyance of lands by Thos. Earl of Suffolk to Sir Thos. Howard, his son, for which alienation, no licence having been taken out, Sir Thomas is fined 500*l.*, and is liable to a similar fine for the re-conveyance to him of the said lands, by virtue of the commission for defective titles.

116. Particular of the lands belonging to Sir Ant. Mildmay lying in the Forest of Clive, co. Northampton, and of other lands in Wiltshire.

VOL. LXXIX.

1614?

117. Interrogatories for the examination of Katharine Eppes as to her part in procuring a contract of marriage between her brother, John Eppes, and Mrs. Anna Hayward. Annotated [by Sir Edw. Coke].

118. Interrogatories [by Sir Edw. Coke] for the examination of a certain person, on the contents of a letter touching a service tending to the glory of God, and the good of a great man, conveyed to his servant Thackray, by Rich. Arnold, Sir Robt. Dormer's man.

119. Advertisements addressed by M. Briot to the Lords Commissioners for the Coinage, on the importance of not lowering the standard of coinage by debasing it or raising its nominal value; with statement of the course adopted by England, France, and Spain, since 1537.

120. Statement of the under-value set upon English money in foreign countries, as proved by the placard of the Low Countries, in which the proportionate estimate of English and Flemish money is set down.

121. Notes on the advantage arising to the Crown from raising the value of a shilling to 13½d., and the proportion of silver to gold 12½d. or 13.

122. Memorandum of the profit arising to the King by raising the shilling to 13½d.; the gold proportionably; and coining the smaller moneys of coarser silver.

123. Suggestions as to the means of preventing foreign nations from taking advantage of the English in exchange of moneys, viz., the raising English coins in nominal value, so as to make them equivalent to the value of foreign coins.

124. Discourse on the advantage of the use of gold and silver in commerce, and of the advantage which other countries have over England, in their frequently raising the value of their gold and silver moneys; with suggestion for raising the value of English money.

VOL. LXXIX.

Book of Abstracts of Inquisitions Post-mortem, &c., chiefly from 6 to 12 Jac. I., but a few earlier; classified into counties, which follow in alphabetical sequence. With an index of the names of the persons deceased. The following Inquisitions of Nobles or Knights occur:—

County.	Name.	Date of Death.	Date of Inquisition.	Heirs.
Devon	Acland, Sir Art.	1611. Dec. 26.	1612. Sept. 18.	John, son.
Lincoln	Ayscough, Sir Edw.	1612. March 9.	1612. April 24.	Edward, cousin.
Gloucester Leicester Suffolk Sussex Somerset	Berkeley, Sir Thos.	1611. Nov. 22.	1612. Aug. 13.	George, son
York	Bethell, Sir Hugh.		1611. April 3.	
Gloucester	Biggs, Sir Thos.	1614. May 4.	1614. Oct. 6.	Thomas, son.

Vol. LXXIX.

County.	Name.	Date of Death.	Date of Inquisition.	Heirs.
Salop, Worcester	Blount, Sir Geo.		1611. Sept. 3.	Walter, son.
York, Hertford	Bruce, Ed., Lord, of Kinloss		1611. April 6.	Edward, son.
Surrey	Carew, Sir Fras.	1612. May 16.	1612. July 30.	Catherine Lady Aubigny, and 3 others.
Wigorn	Clare, Sir Fras.	1608. June 8.	1614. Oct. 6.	Ralph, son.
Middlesex	Cleere, Sir Edw.		1611. March 21.	Edward, son.
Norfolk, Kent	Colvile, Sir Thos.		1612. Nov. 21.	Richard, brother.
York, Norfolk, Suffolk	Cornwallis, Sir Wm.	1611. Nov. 13.	1612. March 17.	Frederic, son.
Westmoreland	Curwen, Lady Eliz.		1611. Aug. 30.	
York, Surrey	Darcy, Sir Edw.	1612. Oct. 28.	1613. Feb. 12.	Sir Robert, son.
Berks, Hants, Oxon, Wilts	Dunch, Sir Wm.		1611. March 5.	Edmund, son.
Lincoln	Eure, Sir Peter	1612. June 25.	1612. Aug. 11.	Ralph, son.
Leicester	Greisley, Sir Thos.		1612. March 20.	Sir George, son.
Northampton	Hatton, Sir Wm.	1597. March 12.	1612. Aug. 10.	
Derby, Kent, Lincoln, Northumberland	Home, Sir Edw.	1609. July 4.	1611. Aug. 5.	Sir Edward, son.
Gloucester, London, Notts	Hicks, Sir Mich.		1612. Oct. 7.	William, son.
Lincoln	Horseman, Sir Thos.		1611. April 8.	Thomas, nephew.
Kent, Essex, Hertford	Huddleston, Sir Edw.	1606. Dec. 14.	1607. Oct. 5.	Henry, son.
Dorset, Hants	Jefferey, Sir John		1611. July 26. 1611. June 26.	George, son.
Surrey	Leechford, Sir Rich.		1611. Oct. 17.	Richard, son.
Hants	Leigh, Sir John		1612. June 4.	Thomas, son.
Kent, Surrey	Leigh, Sir Olive	1611. March 14.	1612. July 30.	Francis, son.
Essex	Leigh, Sir Robt.		1612. July 1.	Robert, son.
Wigorn	Leighton, Sir Thos.		1611. Oct. 2.	Thomas, son.
Stafford	Littleton, Sir Edw., sen.		1611. April 1.	
Lincoln	Locton, Sir John		1611. May 16.	William, son.
Westmoreland	Lowther, Sir Rich.		1611. Sept. 27.	
Berks, Essex, Surrey, Wilts	Lucas, Sir Thos.		1611. Nov. 8.	Thomas, son.
Kent	Palmer, Sir Hen.	1611. Nov. 20.	1612. July 31.	Leven, son.
Norfolk, Suffolk	Paston, Sir Wm.		1611. Sept. 3.	
Bucks	Peckham, Sir Geo.		1608. June 21.	George, son.
Berks	Peyton, Sir Thos.		1611. April 5.	Samuel, son.
Lincoln	Regden, Sir Wm.		1611. Aug. 5.	Robert, son.
Bucks, Middlesex	Roe, Sir Hen.	1612. Nov. 12.	1613. Feb. 4.	Henry, son.
Sussex, Warwick	Rutland, Eliz. Countess of	1612. Sept. 1.	1612. Oct. 30.	Robert Visct. Lisle.
York	Scrope, Thomas, Lord		1611. April 13.	
Bucks	Scudamore, Sir John		1611. Sept. 20.	
Dorset	Somers, Sir Geo.	1611. Nov. 9.	1612. July 26.	Nicholas, cousin.
Suffolk	Tollemache, Sir Lionel, Bt.	1612. Sept. 6.	1613. Jan. 19.	Lionel, son.
Herts, London, Middlesex	Wild, Sir Humph.		1611. April 2.	

VOL. LXXX. JANUARY—JUNE, 1615.

1615.

Jan. 5. London. 1. Chamberlain to Carleton. No news at Court but dull plays. Projects still discussed: one is to make fifty Barons at 6,000*l.* each, but they could scarcely be found; another, by [Wm.] Hakewill, to grant a general pardon for 5*l.* each, which they estimate at 400,000*l.*, but it would not come to nearly so much. Oliver St. John, of Wiltshire, committed for dissuading a benevolence; and Peacham, of Somersetshire, for seditious discourses. Sir Walter Raleigh's book, which he hoped would please the King, is called in, for too free censuring of Princes. Sir Edw. Hoby has answered [Hen.] Fludd, the Papist. Earl Arundel accused of misconduct at Rome. Clement Edmondes going on merchants' business to Holland. Wotton lingers there. Le Sieur and others intrigue for his place, but Winwood wishes Carleton to have it.

Jan. 6. Commission to Wm. Keeling and Geo. Berkley to be Generals of [vessels of] the East India Company, with a special commission to use martial law during the voyage. [*Grant Bk., p.* 148.]

Jan. 7. Grant to Duncan Primrose of the office of one of the King's Physicians, for life. [*Ibid., p.* 141.]

Jan. 10. Order in Council for restraint of killing and eating flesh during Lent. Printed. [*Proc. Coll., No.* 36.]

Jan. 11. 2. Sir Thos. Bartlett to the King. Demonstrates the manner of carrying on the commerce in pins, according to hisproject. *Annexes,*

2. I. *Project by Sir Thos. Bartlett to supply the kingdom with pins, both of foreign and home manufacture.*

[Jan.] 3. Copy of the above project.

Jan. 12. London. 4. Chamberlain to Carleton. The Masque at Court on Twelfth Night. The Spanish Ambassador refused to be present, because Sir Noel Caron, the States' Ambassador, was there. The Spaniards have shown more bravado lately. The King going to Royston and Newmarket, where he will remain till Shrovetide.

Jan. 14. 5. Sir Thos. Bartlett to the King. Intreats that he may not be deprived of the benefit of his project for the manufacture of pins, by the journeymen pinners and others, who are trying to usurp the trade for themselves. Will give the King the whole profits, except 3,000*l.* per ann., reserved to compensate his losses, &c. for seven years, through the deprivation of his former patent.

Jan. 16. Grant to Fras. Curle of an Auditorship in the Court of Wards and Liveries, for life. [*Grant Bk., p.* 148.]

Jan. 17. Grant to John Wells, of the office of Clerk and Keeper of the Stores and the Storehouses at Deptford and elsewhere, co. Kent, for life. [*Ibid., p.* 142.]

Vol. LXXX.

1615.

Jan. 18. Whitehall. 6. The Council to Sec. Winwood, the Master of the Rolls, Lieutenant of the Tower, and others. Require them to examine Edm. Peacham, prisoner in the Tower, respecting his authorship of a treasonable book and if he should be obstinate in refusing to give needful information, to use the manacles.

Jan. 19. Grant to the Company of Pewterers of London, of the pre-emption of 500,000 weight of tin yearly, for five years. [*Grant Bk., p.* 135.]

Jan. 20. Grant to Nathaniel Giles of a prebend of Windsor, for life. [*Ibid., p.* 133.]

Jan. 21. Commission to the Archbp. of Canterbury and others, to reprieve from execution such persons as they shall think fit for foreign employment. [*Ibid., p.* 138.]

Jan. 21. Whitehall. 7. Sir Ralph Winwood to [Somerset]. Wesel is likely to be given up, the King's heroical declaration having struck the blow. Thinks that Sir Thos. Edmondes might encourage the Duke of Mayenne's intention to assist the Duke of Savoy, without committing the King, though His Majesty would think 15,000*l.* well spent, to establish that Duke against the Governor of Milan. The King might claim satisfaction for the disrespectful carriage of Cardinal du Peron towards himself in the [French] States, as he punished Wentworth for unseemly language against the late King of France.

Jan. 24. Bishop's Auckland. 8. The Bishop of Durham to the King. Understands the Lord Chamberlain has a Commission of Lieutenancy over that Bishopric; begs that the country may be informed that it was for no neglect on his own part, having discharged the service for six years, with great pains.

Jan. 25. Eton. 9. Sir Hen. Savile, jun., to Carleton. Thanks him for lending 20*l.* to his brother, who failed to receive remittances sent to Geneva, and requests him to have an eye to his conduct whilst he is abroad, &c.

Jan. 26. London. 10. Chamberlain to the Same. The English captains and others in Holland much want Carleton there instead of Wotton, who is not affable, always busy, but despatching little. Mr. Williams is out of heart in running from one officer of state to another, to get Carleton's money. Sir Thos. Edmondes threatens to return home if not supplied, having neither money nor credit left. Even poor De Quester, the Postmaster, who is daily employed, runs up and down for 600*l.* due to him for postage. The King of Spain promises to surrender Wesel, but meanwhile they fortify it, and make warlike preparations. The Spanish Ambassador excepts against Caron, [the States' Ambassador], which his predecessor never did. Thos. Sackville, son to the old Lord Treasurer, is restrained to Padua for some years; his practices deserved a sharper censure, but he was spared for his father's sake. Report that Sir Rich. Cooke and his family are cast away on their journey to Ireland.

VOL. LXXX.

1615.

Jan. 26. 11. Exemplification of the excommunication of John Bodell, of Breedon, in the archdeaconry of Leicester, for contumacy, Nov. 8, 1614. Latin.

Jan. 31. Clifton. 12. Chas. Bussy to Mr. Carter, at Auditor Curle's. Asks the balance due to his late brother on his last account, on behalf of his widow and children.

Jan.? 13. Reasons by the Merchants of the Staple, founded on the state of the wool growth and manufacture, in the several counties of England, why it is impossible to dispense with wool chapmen, as dealers between the wool growers and manufacturers.

Jan.? 14. Petition of the Broggers of Wool of Warwickshire to the Council. They are hindered by the wool-staplers in buying from and selling to poor persons small quantities of wool. Pray to be allowed to exercise their trade without molestation. Numerously signed.

Jan.? 15. Observations on the dangers that may ensue by the intended suppression of the broggers of wool, and statement of the great increase of profit to the poor, and also to the customs, by manufacture of wool into the new draperies, rather than into cloth.

Jan.? 16. Comparative statement of the price of workmanship, number of persons employed, and amount of custom paid for three loads of wool, as employed in the manufacture of cloth or of new drapery.

Feb. 1. London. 17. John Chamberlain to Alice Carleton. Cannot sell the glasses she has sent, because they are out of fashion. Wants six looking glasses. The weather very severe. The Thames almost closed up. The floods have done great damage, &c. The Lord Chancellor improves.

Feb. 2. London. 18. Earl of Argyle to Somerset. Asks explanations why the warrants he received from the King are refused or questioned. His servants have been negligent in paying in his rents. Will secure promptness in his future payments. Is busy prosecuting the suit granted him by the King. *Annexed is,*

18. I. *Statement by the Earl of Argyle of his proceedings in erecting a town at Kintyre, by His Majesty's request. He dealt out land, built a justice-house, prison, and school; contributed towards a church, and maintains a schoolmaster and curate. Begs a warrant for prolonging the time assigned him for building the town, having been in the King's service against the Clan Gregor, and the validity of his first warrant being questioned.*

Feb. 3. Grant to Wm. Tranter of an Attorney's place in the County Court of Hereford. [*Docquet.*]

Feb. 3. Warrant to pay to Wm. Deane 102*l.*, due to him from Thos. Grey, who is outlawed at his suit. [*Docquet.*]

Feb. 3. Grant to Robt. Trotter, Farrier to the Prince, of denization. [*Docquet.*]

VOL. LXXX.

1615.

Feb. 3. Grant to the Lord Mayor, &c. of London of eight almshouses in the parish of St. Peters. [*Grant Bk., p.* 135.]

Feb. 3. Grant to Lawr. Makepeace of the office of Registrar of the Court of Chancery, for life. [*Ibid., p.* 136.]

Feb 4. Commission to the Earl of Somerset of Lieutenancy in the Bishopric of Durham. [*Ibid., p.* 149.]

Feb. 4. Hague. 19. [Clement] Edmondes to Somerset. There is a controversy between the Greenland and East India Companies in Holland, as to whether free trade should be made general. The latter oppose it, wishing to exclude the English from the Moluccas; the former uphold it, wishing to gain the fishery of the whale.

Feb. 4. Saturday. 20. Report of Dr. Thos. Ridley and Dr. Thos. Edwardes in the case of [John] Lambe v. John Wiseman and Frances, his wife, of Strixton, co. Northampton, accused of incest, and of profanation and dilapidation of the church and chancel of Strixton. They find the former charge groundless, his wife being grand-daughter of the brother of his late wife, and not within the prohibited degrees. The other charge should be examined by the whole Court. Lambe prosecutes Wiseman in several courts, merely for the sake of molesting him. [*See March* 15.]

Feb. 6. 21. [Edw. Reynoldes] to [Fras. Mills]. Difficulties in persuading Mr. [Hugh] Allington to sign certain indentures prepared by Mills and Sir Thos. Clerk, for reformation of abuses in the office of Privy Seal; gives the arguments by which he was prevailed on. Pertinacity of [Thos.] Packer, Allington's deputy, in insisting on signing *Annexes,*

21. I. *Clerks of the Privy Seal to Hugh Allington. Remonstrate against the presumption of his deputy, Thos. Packer, who signs as though he were a clerk. Request that he may be ordered to subscribe only as a deputy, as do the sons of Sir Thos. Clerk and Fras. Mills, who are their deputies.*

Feb. 7. Paris. 22. Dr. Theo. de Mayerne to Somerset. Sorry to be detained by his affairs from the service of the King his master. Is the less uneasy because in this frost, diseases make a truce with the body, and because his Lordship is well, and has no need of him.

Feb. 8. London. 23. Earl of Shrewsbury to the Same. Begs him to grant a favourable hearing to [Hen.] Sanderson, a faithful servant to the late Queen, whose enemies are bent on injuring him.

Feb. 8. Chancellor's House. 24. The Council to the King. Ask leave to defer the proceedings against Oliver St. John till the next term, on account of the ill health of the Chancellor, and absence of many others of the Council.

Feb. 9. Commission to the Earl of Somerset to inventory the jewels remaining in the secret jewel house in the Tower. [*Grant Bk., p.* 149.]

VOL. LXXX.

1615.
Feb. 9. London. 25. Matthew de Quester to Isaac Wake. Has distributed his letters. Mr. Secretary has returned from the Court at Newmarket to his house at St. Bartholomews. The King came to Royston the day before, will be at Theobalds on the 11th, and at Whitehall on the 16th.

Feb. 9. London. 26. Chamberlain to Carleton. Proceedings of Sir Walter Cope's executors for payment of his debts. His house at Kensington, &c. offered for sale. The old Earl of Kent dead. If his brother, who succeeds him, has no heir male, the earldom descends to one Grey, a minister. Dispute between Sir Ant. Mildmay and Sir Edw. Montague. Sir Hen. Neville's suit for prosecution of spoilers of woods overthrown; he is dangerously ill. Oliver St. John's appearance in the Star Chamber for dehorting his neighbours from the benevolence is deferred. Peacham, though sixty years old, was racked, but nothing could be got from him. The King much incensed against him.

Feb. 10. Nuffield. 27. Dr. Geo. Carleton to Sir D. Carleton. Has entered the Prince's service at the request of Sir Jas. Fullerton, and is commended both by King and Prince. Shameless avidity of persons about the Court for preferment. Thinks that he begs best who makes his service speak for him. Would be silent about the Prince rather than tell an untruth, but must praise his accomplishments, his skill in riding, running at the ring, &c. He has more understanding than the late Prince at his age; is "in behaviour sober, grave, swete; in speache very advised;" without any evil inclinations; and willing to take advice.

Feb. 11. Order of the Convocation of the University of Oxford, imposing fees upon degrees, to be applied in payment of the expenses of building the new schools. [*Dom. Corresp., Nov.* 13, 1626.]

Feb. 12. Gravesend. 28. Sir Robt. Anstruther to Somerset. Being unable to satisfy his creditors, has persuaded Sir Pat. Murray and Sir Jas. Auchterlony to stand security for his debts, making over his pension to them. Beseeches that it may be increased, as he is taking this journey on the King's service.

Feb. 16. Lambeth. 29. Archbp. Abbot to [Carleton]. Thanks for the fine glasses sent him. Sir Hen. Wotton is settling differences in Holland. His remaining there uncertain. If the Archbp. of Spalato resolve to come to England, his portion will suffice him to live at one of the universities, without state, only keeping a servant or two, and sometimes attending the King in London.

Feb. 16. London. 30. John Chamberlain to Alice Carleton. Severe frost with much snow. Lady Beauchamp has a son, Lady Haddington a daughter. Lady Cheek died through a blunder of the surgeon, who punctured an artery in bleeding her. Sir Geo. Hayward, and his sister, wife of Sir Rich. Sandys, are gone mad. Bruckshaw, the brewer,

1615. VOL. LXXX.

imprisoned for refusing to serve the King on credit, 16,000*l.* being due to the King's brewer.

Feb. 17. 31. Conveyance from Edm. Duffield and John Babington, of London, to John Lambe, of Northampton, of a messuage in Lichborough, and other lands, tithes, &c., co. Northampton. Also of the rectories of St. Giles and St. Edmund near Northampton, of St. Sepulchre in Northampton, and of Cold Ashby, co. Northampton.

Feb. 17. Friday. 32. Matthew de Quester to Carleton. Receipt and transmission of letters. The King has come from Theobalds, to spend his Shrovetide at Whitehall. More snow than has been known for thirty-six years. An Ambassador from Brandenburg has arrived, to solicit aid for the Protestant Princes.

Feb. [17?] 33. Geo. Margitts to Sir Ralph Winwood. Complains of the delays of the Attorney General in his business, as injurious to His Majesty's interests. Prays him to stir him up in it. Sends a petition and letter to the King.

Feb. 18. 34. The Same to the Same. Dealings of Spiller and the Barons of the Exchequer with the Attorney General and others, to delay and thwart his proceedings by keeping Grimston and [Rich.] Heaton in durance, and postponing the drawing up of his grant. As the Attorney says he has not time to do it, begs it may be handed over to the Solicitor; the order for it to be given by an indorsement upon his petition. *Annexes,*

34. I. *Form of the indorsement required for the drawing up of his grant. Feb.*

Feb. 18. London. 35. Giov. Franc. Biondi to [Carleton]. Sir Thos. Edmondes is over on the French alliance. The Duke of Lenox and the Scots wish for it, but not the English. The French Ambassador grieves to find them so Spanish, but perhaps a Spanish Ambassador would think them French. Sir Hen. Wotton spoken of for France. Giov. Maria is fled; the other friar taken, and ready, he says, for martyrdom. Fears it will not come to that, the King being rather religious than fanatic.

Feb. 18. Northampton House. 36. Earl of Suffolk to Wm. Christmas, Woodward of the New Forest, and Nich. Gibbons, Master Carpenter of Portsmouth. Directions for felling thirty tons of timber in the forest, for the repairs of Portsmouth Castle, the tops and lops to be sold for payment of the carriage.

Feb. 20. Grant to Cornelius Artson of the office of Falconer, for life. [*Grant Bk., p.* 145.]

Feb. 22. Whitehall. 37. The Council to the Mayor, &c. of Canterbury. Recommend the project of a lottery, for the benefit of the plantation of Virginia.

Feb. 23. London. 38. Chamberlain to Carleton. Affairs of Lady Cope. Disorders multiply daily for want of money. Most of the projects vanish away like dreams, but Pope Hakewill's for pardons is going on. The Queen cannot go to Bath for want of money, and all the moneys

VOL. LXXX.

due in March are forestalled. Most of the Judges concur to find Peacham's case treason. Hoskins and his compeers are still in the Tower, though his wife, who is a poetess, has sent a petition in rhyme to the King for his release. Sir Walter Raleigh recovering from an apoplexy caused by his chemical experiments. The Lord Chancellor relapsed. The Merchant Adventurers have voluntarily resigned their charter to the King, but the new company are perplexed with complaints of the clothiers, who cannot sell their cloth. Leave is granted for its export undyed and undressed, till the workmen are provided, which is thought hard on the old company. The Spanish Ambassador gives entertainments. Great warlike preparations making in Spain. The Earl of Orkney beheaded.

Note of plans to be adopted to rectify recent abuses by the Kings-at-Arms, in granting coats of arms, viz., that a commission be given for revocation of all arms recently assumed, unless confirmed by the King's Letters Patent. [*Dom. Corresp., Aug.* 1, 1622, *p.* 51.]

Draft of a commission to the Earls of Suffolk, Nottingham, Worcester, and many other noblemen and gentlemen, to reform abuses in the office of arms. [*Ibid, p.* 49.]

Commission to the parties above named to redress abuses in the Office of Arms. [*Ibid., p.* 55.]

Commission to the Earl of Kent of lieutenancy in co. Bedford. [*Grant Bk., p.* 149.]

39. Rich. Heaton to Sir Ralph Winwood. Corrects two errors in the form of the paper sent to the Lord Chief Justice, for a commission for discovery of arrears of recusants. Is certain that, with these corrections, there can be no legal exceptions to the commission.

Grant to Sir Robt. Douglas of 1,000*l.* as a free gift. [*Docquet.*]

Grant to Wm. Thomas of pardon for manslaughter, being an abettor only; as he might have had the benefit of clergy, if he had been able to read. [*Docquet.*]

Grant to Jevan Jenkin of pardon for horse-stealing six years before, being well conducted ever since. [*Docquet.*]

Licence to Philip Rosseter and others to bring up a convenient number of children by the name of "Children of the Revels to the Queen," for exercising "the quality" of playing. [*Docquet.*]

Grant to Edw. and Simon Thelwell of the office of Recorder of Ruthin, co. Denbigh, for life. [*Grant Bk., p.* 142.]

Grant to Sir Phil. Carey of the office of keeping Marybone Park, co. Middlesex, for life. [*Ibid., p.* 148.]

40. [The Queen] to Sir John Spilman. Orders him to repair to Whitehall, to receive directions concerning a loan to be raised for her by pawning certain jewels. [*See March* 26.]

VOL. LXXX.

1615.

[Feb.] 41. Petition of Thos. Chaloner to the Council, that the farmers of the alum may be ordered to continue to him his pension of 40 marks per ann., granted for his former labours in discovering the alum mines in Yorkshire.

March 1. Grant to Sir Wm. Cope, Bart., of the office of keeping the armoury, for life. [*Grant Bk., p.* 148.]

March 2. London. 42. Chamberlain to Carleton. Wishes him success in his negociations at Turin. The King will be at Cambridge on the 7th. Peacham has been questioned on some speeches, but his trial is deferred, and will be put off altogether, like those of Sir Maurice Berkeley, and several ministers. Hakewill's scheme for pardons is dashed, but there is another project for raising money by charging 20*l.* or 30*l.* each for confirmation of armorial bearings, illegally granted by the heralds. Sir Art. Ingram sworn Cofferer of the King's household, but the Officers of the Green Cloth, and even the Black Guard, objected to the appointment, violently pleading the King's promise that places should pass in succession, and that they would rather be hung than have such a scandalous fellow over them. The King promised redress; but though the Queen and Prince took their part, the King confirmed the office to Ingram.

March 3. Grant to the Master and Assistants of the Hospital at Newark of foundation [as the Hospital] of King James. [*Grant Bk., p.* 134.]

March 3. Royston. Grant to Thos. Dixon and John Williams, Serjeants-at-Arms, of two acres of waste ground at Castleton, parish of Hope, co. Derby, to erect a corn mill on the river Ashopp. [*Sign Man., vol.* IV., *No.* 72.]

March 3. Royston. Grant to Thos. Weston, of London, of licence to alienate in mortmain to the Dean and Chapter of Gloucester a messuage and land, parcel of the manor of Hyncledon, co. Gloucester. Latin. [*Ibid., No.* 73.]

March 3. Royston. Grant to Wm. Jordan and Nich. Hooker, of London, nominees of Edw. Lord Morley, of the sole printing of a small book, entitled "God and the Kinge; or, a Dialogue shewing that our Sovereign Lord King James, being ymediate under God within his Dominions, doth rightfullie claime whatsoever is required by the Oathe of Allegiance;" with instructions for the same to be taught in Latin and English, in all schools, as a means to "season yonge mindes against the pestilent doctrines of the Jesuites." [*Ibid., No.* 74.]

March 3. Royston. Grant to Hen. Clerke, of the Middle Temple, of the next presentation to the rectory of Hathern, co. Leicester, in trust to present his brother, Sam. Clerke. Latin. [*Ibid., No.* 75.]

March 6. 43. Warrant to Sir Fras. Bacon, Attorney General, to draw up a commission to the Archbp. of Canterbury, Lord Chancellor, and others, for discovery of all debts and arrears of recusants, of which the King has been defrauded.

VOL. LXXX.

1615.

March 7. London. 44. Fras. Cottington to [Sir Ralph Winwood]. Has waited fourteen times on the Lord Chief Justice, to obtain his perusal of the order about Palache, but he defers it till his return from his circuit. Asks whether it shall be completed without him.

March 8. 45. Geo. Margitts to the Same. Spiller procures further delays, urging that the records cannot be so speedily searched. Begs the immediate grant of his lease, lest Spiller find some plea to thwart it, as he has done others. Thinks the Lord Chief Justice had better be left out of the commission, as he has been a kind of sinner that way himself.

March 8. Grant to Justinian Povey of the office of Receiver in cos. Suffolk and Huntingdon, for life. [*Grant Bk., p.* 141.]

March 10. London. 46. Geo. Carleton to Sir D. Carleton. Expenses of repairing his buildings. Wishes to get a scholarship at Merton College, for his son Dudley, now at Eton.

March 10. Friday. London. 47. Matt. de Quester to Lady Carleton. The two last packets of letters arrived together, the former being detained by the rain and snow. Many parts of England are overflowed, and the tides higher about London than were ever known. Mr. Finet is at Cambridge with the King.

March 13. Eton. 48. Sir Hen. Savile to Carleton. Thinks him unwise in not being more cordial with Sir Ralph Winwood, who is really his friend, and likely to be more powerful. The King has been at Cambridge, in all glory and pomp. Sorry the market for the Chrysostom is so down. Private affairs.

March 13. Newmarket. Grant to Sir Geo. Chaworth, in reversion after Sir John Stafford, of the office of Constable and Keeper of Bristol Castle. Latin. [*Sign Man., vol.* IV., *No.* 76.]

March 15. Church at Wellingborough. 49. Answers of John Wiseman to the articles exhibited against him by John Lambe, formerly Proctor. Lawfulness of his marriage with his present wife. Was not bound by his lease to repair the church at Strixton, but has done so several times. Never used it to put cattle in, nor to store timber, &c. Has not taken the windows, bells, &c. for his own use, nor spoken irreverently of Norbury, the minister. Was never warned during his lease to repair the church. [*See Feb.* 4.]

March 15. Newmarket. Presentation of Thos. Kaye to the rectory of Barnesbrough, diocese of York. Latin. [*Sign Man., vol.* IV., *No.* 77.]

March. Docquet of the above. [*Docquet, March* 16.]

March 15. Newmarket. Warrant to pay to And. Boyd 1,000*l.* as a free gift. [*Sign Man., vol.* IV., *No.* 78.]

March. Docquet of the above. [*Docquet, March* 16.]

Vol. LXXX.

1615.

March 15. Newmarket. Grant to Nich. Hoare of a Gunner's place in the Tower. Latin. [*Sign Man., vol.* IV., *No.* 79.]

March. Docquet of the above. [*Docquet, March* 16.]

March 15. Newmarket. Warrant to pay to Wm. Earl of Salisbury 900*l.*, for purchase from him of the almshouse next the King's stables in Cheshunt, co. Hertford, near to Theobalds, and 200*l.* for Park Grove and Hill Grove, next to Enfield Old Park, co. Middlesex. [*Sign Man., vol.* IV., *No.* 80.]

March 15. Chester. 50. The Merchants of Chester to Somerset. Request that none but those of their company may be allowed to share the benefits of the licence for exportation of tanned calf skins.

March 16. 51. Chamberlain to Carleton. The King's handsome reception at Cambridge on the 12th. The Prince was there, but the Queen was not invited, and there were no ladies but of the Howard family. The Lord Treasurer lived magnificently in St. John's College, spending twenty-six tuns of wine in five days. His lady was at Magdalen's, founded by his grandfather Audley. The King and Prince at Trinity. Comedies by the men of St. John's, Clare, and Trinity. Particulars of the plays, disputations, and orations. [Fras.] Nethersole, the University orator, was blamed for calling the Prince "Jacobissime Carole." Paul Thompson, the gold clipper, pardoned, and keeps his livings. Sir Art. Ingram keeps the name of Cofferer till Michaelmas, but Sir Marmaduke Darell discharges the business. Many courtiers made M. A., but few doctors. Winwood pleaded in vain for [Thos.] Westfield, and the King for John Donne, for whom the University is threatened with a mandate, which they will obey, but will also give him such a blow that he were better without his degree. The Bishop of Chichester, Vice Chancellor, is peremptory on those points.

March 16. London. 52. Edw. Reynoldes to [Fras. Mills]. Details at length his arguments with Thos. Packer against his claim of right to sole subscription, as deputy of [Hugh] Allington in the office of Privy Seal, former deputies having signed as such, not in their own right.

March 16. Presentation of Thos. Darley to the parsonage of Winterton. [*Docquet.*]

March 16. Warrant for the same allowance of diet to Jeremy Ross, Keeper of the King's Wardrobe at Royston, Hinchinbrook, and other places, as paid to the late Wm. Meredith. [*Docquet.*]

March 16. Newmarket. Grant to Rich. Earl of Dorset of licence to enfranchise the copyholds belonging to his manors of Chalvington and others, co. Sussex, and of Pontesbury alias Ponsbury, co. Salop. Latin. [*Sign Man., vol.* IV., *No.* 81.]

March 17 Newmarket. Warrant for payment of 2,952*l.* 1*s.* 4*d.* to Geo. Herriot, for jewels and workmanship for Prince Charles. [*Ibid., No.* 82.]

VOL. LXXX.

1615.

March 17. Newmarket. Grant to John and Hen. Salkeld, of Morland, co. Westmoreland, Seminary Priests, now converted, of pardon for going beyond seas, and being reconciled to the Church of Rome, with power to John Salkeld to retain the vicarage of Wellington, co. Somerset. Latin. [*Sign Man., vol.* IV., *No.* 83.]

March 17. St. Anthony. 53. Wm. Carnsew to Rich. Carnsew. St. John sent to the Tower for dissuading his neighbours of Marlborough from consenting to an unlawful benevolence. Also the Minister of Hindon [Edm. Peacham], who said that gold and silver he had none, but he would pray for the King. Though old, he has been racked, and his study searched. They would have been censured in the Star Chamber, but the Chancellor was ill and could not sit. His wife will take pains in building Carnsew House, if she can have the neighbouring close.

March 18. Northampton House. 54. Warrant to John Denham, farmer of the Forest of Barnwood, to allow Peter Pett and Daniel Duck, shipwrights, to take away the chips used in squaring timber assigned for the Navy, which are challenged by the keepers of the forest as their due.

March 18. Newmarket. Grant to Sir Art. Savage and Thos. Savage, in reversion after Jane Sybil Lady Grey, widow, of the keeping of the Park and Chace of Whaddon, co. Bucks. Latin. [*Sign Man., vol.* IV., *No.* 84.]

March 18. Letter to Lord Danvers, Chief Keeper of Whichwood Forest, recommending Rich. Batten to be continued under him as Ranger of Whichwood and Keeper of Shorthampton Walk. [*Docquet.*]

March 20. 55. Table of fees, fare, &c. in the Fleet-Prison, according to the different rank of the prisoners.

March 20? 56. Statement of the means of subsistence of poor prisoners, debtors, recusants, and priests, in Newgate.

March 22. Theobalds. Warrant to pay to Sir Sigismund and Hen. Alexander, Equerries to the King, 100*l.*, for defraying the charge of their runnng at the tilt on March 24 next. [*Sign Man., vol.* IV., *No.* 85.]

March 22. Theobalds. Grant to Lancelot Routledge, of Thompson's-Walls, Northumberland, of pardon for manslaughter in a sudden quarrel. Latin. [*Ibid., No.* 86.]

March 23. Whitehall. Proclamation against export of gold and silver coin, either for payment for goods imported to a greater amount than the exports, or for the profit to be derived from the higher standard value of the English coin. Printed. [*Proc. Coll., No.* 37.]

March 23. Whitehall. Proclamation against sending children to be educated in foreign seminaries, or money for payment for such education, and recalling those already sent. Printed. *Annexing,*

I. *Clauses of the Statute 3 Jac. I. prohibiting the sending abroad of English children to be educated, without licence from Council, inflicting penalties on transgressors, and depriving those thus sent of all right of inheritance in England, unless they return within six months.* [*Ibid., No.* 38.]

VOL. LXXX.

1615.

March ? 57. List of the sons and daughters of English parents who are at St. Omer, Douay, and other foreign seminaries and nunneries, and of English officials resident at the above colleges.

March 24. Commission to the Earl of Suffolk, &c. concerning dyeing cloth before it is exported. [*Grant Bk., p.* 148.]

March 25. 58. Note of all the cloths and kerseys exported from London between Dec. 25, 1613, and March 25, 1614, and the similar dates in the following year, showing a decrease of 17,211 in the latter period.

March 25. 59. Copy of the above.

March 25. Austin Friars. Sir Fulk Greville to the Officers of the Customs at the Port of London. The dispute between Ralph Freeman and Co., late farmers of the pre-emption of tin, and Thos. Dunning and Co., present farmers, having been decided, Freeman is permitted to export tin in bars, according to their agreement. [*Dom. Corresp., July* 24, 1615.]

March 25. 60. Agreement by Sir John Spilman for re-delivery of certain diamonds to the Queen or her assigns, with interest, on repayment of 3,000*l.*, which he has advanced upon them.

March 26. 61. Drawing of eleven diamonds received by Sir John Spilman from the Queen.

March 26. Whitehall. 62. Agreement [by the Queen] for repayment of interest on 3,000*l.*, lent by Sir John Spilman, and for repayment of the principal in a year.

March 26 ? 63. Note of the Queen's jewels, and the persons to whom they have been delivered by Sir John Spilman.

March 26. Letter to the Chapter of St. David's, to choose Dr. [Rich.] Milbourne as Bishop of that see. [*Docquet.*]

March 26. Grant to Wm. Beecher, in reversion after John Tooke or Fras. Curle, of the office of Auditor of the Court of Wards and Liveries. [*Docquet.*]

March 27. Westminster. Congé d'elire to the Precentor and Chapter of St. David's, to elect a Bishop. Latin. [*Sign Man., vol.* V., *No.* 1.]

March. Docquet of the above. [*Docquet, March* 26.]

March 28. Hampton Court. Grant to John Lewis, of Llangeler, co. Carmarthen, of confirmation of title to certain lands purchased by him in Carmarthenshire. Latin. [*Sign Man., vol.* V., *No.* 2.]

March 29. Docquet of the above.

March 29. Westminster. Grant to Edm. Peshall and Edw. White, of London, of the late imposition of 2*s.* per lb. on tobacco imported for ten years, paying to the King 3,500*l.* the first year and 7,000*l.* per ann. afterwards, with sole

1615. VOL. LXXX.

power to import tobacco and to name persons for selling the same. With a proviso of determination at six months' notice, if found prejudicial to the State. [*Sign Man., vol.* V., *Nos. 3 and* 4.]

March 29. Docquet of the above.

March 29. Warrant for delivery of certain parcels of stuff to John Murray, by John Cotton, Keeper of the King's Standing Wardrobe at Theobalds. [*Docquet.*]

March 29. Presentation of Humph. Vero to the parsonage of Harthurst, diocese of Norwich. [*Docquet.*]

March 29. Warrant for Sir Thos. Vavasour, Marshal of the Household, and all Justices of the Peace, to aid Sir Wm. Alexander and John Phillip to apprehend and send into Scotland all idle persons of that nation. [*Docquet.*]

March 29. Warrant for payment to Walter James of 338*l.* 9*s.*, remaining due for the Masque at Christmas last. [*Docquet.*]

March. 64. Account of payments made by the farmers of the Customs for the Household, wardrobe, for rewards, and into the Exchequer, during two years past.

March. 65. List of warrants contained in the account of the Queen's Household expenses, which are defective, owing to the bills of disbursements not being produced.

March ? 66. Draft of an intended Commission from Council for seizing the money of recusants, collected to send abroad, or to supply priests and Jesuits, contrary to the late Proclamation.

April 1. 67. Certificate [by Hen. Spiller] of the general state of the King's revenue from recusants, showing which portions of it may be increased, and which are in arrears, or entirely withheld.

April ? 68. Exceptions against the above and other certificates of the revenue from recusants' fines, &c., lately sent in [by Hen. Spiller], showing their fraud and fallacy. The writer offers to increase this revenue 40,000*l.* a year, by just and honourable means. The lists of recusants are imperfect, being sent in by churchwardens, who are afraid to accuse powerful recusants.

April ? 69. Statement addressed to the King [by Spiller] of the profits devolving on the Crown from recusants in the last year of Queen Elizabeth and in the present year; showing the cause why it is so much less now than then, on account of the conformity of many recusants, and the leases and grants made by His Majesty of the lands, fines, &c. of the recusants; with a breviate of the total loss to the Crown from these causes, being upwards of 26,000*l.* per ann.

April ? 70. Statement of the fallacies in the above account, every item of which is untrue, and which would prove that the present revenue from recusants, stated at 7,200*l.* 12*s.* 2½*d.*, amounts to hardly a fourth of the sum discharged to them since the King's accession.

VOL. LXXX.

1615.

April 4. London. 71. Chamberlain to Carleton. The Queen in danger of dropsy. The dissolved Merchant Adventurers complain that they are not allowed to bring in their goods from abroad, nor export them, unless they will join the new company, who have undertaken what they cannot perform.

April ? 72. Note of the Gunners in [Dover Castle ?], with the dates of their admission, from July 15, 1612; also dates of the deaths of several of them.

April 4. Grant to Jane Sybil Lady Grey of the manors of Bittlesden, Gifford, and others, co. Bucks. [*Grant Bk., p.* 173.]

April 6. London. 73. John Chamberlain to Alice Carleton. Lady Winwood's looking-glasses need not be bought, &c. Sir John Merrick sent Ambassador Extraordinary into Muscovy. Lady Cope has sold her house in the Strand, and is removing to a smaller one of 30*l.* a year in Drury Lane, the result of making too great a show before. Death of Sir Robt. Drury. Sir Art. Ingram removed from the Court, in spite of many efforts, the household being so bent to have him out. [Isaac] Wake is to reside at Turin in the place of [Albert] Morton.

April 6. Commission to the Lord Chancellor for issuing commissions as to provisions and carriages for the King's household. [*Grant Bk., p.* 159.]

April 6. Commission to all Justices, &c. to aid in making provision for the King's household. [*Ibid., p.* 184.]

April 7. London. 74. Chamberlain to Carleton. The King came to town for the 24th of March, which passed off with prayers, preaching, tilting, &c. He went to Hampton Court. Sir Art. Ingram delays leaving his place at Court. He is to go to Yorkshire on the alum business. His conduct much canvassed. The Earl of Thomond has bought the presidency of Munster from Lord Danvers for 3,200*l.* Mayerne has returned from France, and brought over the Minister Du Moulin. John Donne and one Cheke made Doctors at Cambridge, by the King's command. They are blamed for using such means, and Donne is envied for obtaining, over worthier men, the reversion of the deanery of Canterbury. The King talked of going privately to Cambridge, to see two of the plays again, or of sending for the players to town.

April 12. Westminster. Proclamation of Letters Patent commanding that no greater customs be taken from Scottish men or Scottish ships than from English and Irish, and that Scottish ships be not accounted strangers' bottoms, but free bottoms. Printed. [*Proc. Coll., No.* 38.]

April 15. 75. Order by Dr. Daniel Dunn, Judge of the Arches' Court, in the case of ——— and ——— Burde v. Wm. Judkin, of Everdon, all of the diocese of Peterborough, prohibiting any proceedings against the said Burdes, except in the Ecclesiastical Courts, and citing Judkin to appear in the Arches' Court. Latin.

VOL. LXXX.

1615.

April ? 76. Imperfect draft of orders for government of the priests to be sent to Wisbeach Castle; with demands by [Matthias] Taylor [Keeper of the Castle], for certain additions and further directions.

April 16. Whitehall. 77. The Council to the Bishop of Ely. Request him to supervise the priests to be sent to Wisbeach Castle, and to appoint learned divines to converse with those who wish it, for satisfying their consciences. Letters are sent to the neighbouring justices, cautioning them against any attempt at escape or rescue. *Inclose,*

77. I. *Orders for the better government, &c. of the priests to be sent to the Castle of Wisbeach, under the charge of Matthias Taylor, Keeper of the Castle. April* 16, 1615.

April 16. 78. Copy of the above orders.

April 17. 79. Names of priests, recusants, &c. confined in Newgate and the Clink prisons; with note [from the priests] that, being unable to provide themselves with bedding and other necessaries for their removal to Wisbeach, as required, they beg that orders may be taken for their providing.

April. 80. List of Popish priests imprisoned in Newgate and the Gate House, at Easter 1615.

April ? 81. Brief notes of the character, age, and temper of most of the above priests. Indorsed "Note of the Priests which are most turbulent at Newgate."

April ? 82. List of books and MSS. belonging to the above priests. Indorsed "Letters from the Priests at Wisbeach."

April ? 83. Notes relating to the above priests, naming the counties whence they came, &c.

April ? 84. Descriptions of the characters, &c. of Alex. Faircloth, Rich. Cooper, Geo. Muskett, and John Ainsworth, four of the above priests.

April 17. Whitehall. Proclamation prohibiting the bringing in of commodities from the Levant by any not free of the Company, and enforcing execution of the statutes for the restraint of import and export of goods in strangers' bottoms. Printed. [*Proc. Coll., No.* 40.]

April 17. Grant to Wm. Garway and Nich. Salter of permission to defalcate 315*l.* yearly from their accounts, in respect of 150 tuns of wine imported duty free. [*Grant Bk., p.* 173.]

April 18. Grant to Thos., Earl of Arundel and Surrey of Lieutenancy in co. Norfolk. [*Ibid., p.* 154.]

April 18. Grant to Wm. Browne of the office of Pursuivant of the Court of Wards and Liveries, for life. [*Ibid., p.* 146.]

April 18. Commission to the Feodary of Somerset and others to inquire of the lunacy of Hugh Martin. [*Ibid., p.* 182.]

April 18. Commission to the Feodary of Devon and others to inquire of the idiocy of Thos. Marshall. [*Ibid., p.* 182.]

Vol. LXXX.

1615.

April 18. Savoy. 85. Geo. Lord Carew to Sir Thos. Roe, Ambassador to the Great Mogul. Sends to his remote world "the ensuing rapsody of things past." January:—Death of the Earl of Kent, and of Sir Moyle Finch, who left the richest widow in England. Lord Beauchamp has a son. February:—John Donne made King's Chaplain, and a Doctor. Earl of Orkney in Scotland beheaded and his lands escheated. March:—Earl of Thomond made President of Munster. Sir Robt. Drury dead; his three sisters are his heirs. Commissioners sent for settlement of the East India and Greenland trade with the Hollanders; but it is likely to fall through, the Hollanders requiring a league offensive and defensive against Spain in the Eastern world, and the King resolving to adhere firmly to the peace with Spain. Lord Berkeley and Lord Fitzwalter married to daughters of Sir Michael Stanhope. Lady St. John dead, and her son-in-law, Lord Howard of Effingham, falls in for a portion of the inheritance. April:—Count Schomberg married to Ann Dudley. An expedition sent to discover the north-west passage, and another by Greenland to the north-east passage. Great talk at Court of the rising fortune of Mr. Villiers, "a gentleman of good parts."

April 22. Westminster. Proclamation restraining the usual allowances of fee-deer to the justices in eyre, lieutenants, rangers of parks, &c., great numbers of deer having been destroyed by the extraordinary frost and snow. Printed. [*Proc. Coll., No.* 41.]

April 23. Eton College. 86. Sir Hen. Savile to Thos. Horne. Instructions as to the purchase of books in Italy—Tully's works, Greek liturgies, &c.

April? 87. Account of pictures, looking glasses, and other furniture, bought for the Earl of Somerset by [Sir Dud. Carleton].

April 25. Venice. 88. Note of consignment to the Earl of Somerset of sundry pictures, painted by Tintoretto, Paul Veronese, Bassano, Titian, and Schiavone. Italian. With an addition [by Sir D. Carleton].

April 25. Grant to Wm. Cook of a Gunner's place in the Tower, for life. [*Grant Bk., p.* 181.]

April 25. Grant to Sir Jas. Fullerton of the office of registering affidavits in Chancery, for life. [*Ibid., p.* 173.]

April 26. London. 89. Edw. Blount to Carleton. Has got Carleton's bill of exchange cashed by Mr. Cuttell at the rate of 57½. Wishes it to be paid to the Guadagnis.

April 27. Grant to Robt. Christian and Thos. Motteshed of the office of Receiver of Fines on unlawful Marriages, &c. [*Grant Bk., p.* 157.]

April. [Ches]terford? 90. Sir Ralph Winwood to Lord ———. Requests him to inform the King of his purpose. Will acquaint the Ambassador of Savoy with the directions he has received for conclusion of the peace. Fragment.

VOL. LXXX.

1615.

April 27. 91. Note of receipt of contribution money from persons and places specified, since Feb. 15, with the amounts.

April 27. 92. Effect of the Pope's commission to the English Papists at the Spa, authorizing them to choose a Catholic Archbp. of Canterbury.

[April.] Seville. 93. Advices from England of the persecutions of Catholics, containing three extracts:—First, from a letter of a priest in the English college at Seville, taken prisoner Jan. 18, 1615, describing his sufferings at Newgate, the ill-treatment of Lord Vaux and many others, the renewal of the severe laws against Catholics; and ascribing to retributive justice the misfortune of Lord Sheffield, President of York, in the death of his six sons. Second, from a letter of an English Seminary Priest, dated Brussels, April 9, 1615, relating that John Ainsworth interrupted an English minister in divine service, and succeeded in preaching himself; that the Archbp. of Canterbury would not let the King permit the French Ambassador to carry away certain priests with him, unless they would promise not to return, which they refused; that the Council oppose the Spanish match, &c. Third, from a letter from London, April 17, 1615, on the refusal by the King to accept large sums of money offered by the Catholics, to secure freedom from persecution; the questioning of Muskett and Ainsworth before the Council; the projected removal of the priests to Wisbeach; the efforts of foreign Ambassadors in their favour, &c. Spanish. Printed.

April. 94. Petition of the Priests committed to Wisbeach Castle to the Council, for modification of the strictness of their orders. If debarred from intercourse with their friends, they will be unable to obtain money for their fees. Request reduction in the amount of fees. Indorsed "The Priests' First Project."

April? 95. Bishop of Chester to [Sir Thos. Lake]. Asks direction how to proceed with certain [Catholics], who refuse to be bound for revocation of their children from foreign seminaries. Imperfect. [*See Proc., March* 23, 1615.]

May 3. 96. Geo. Margitts to Sir Ralph Winwood. Requests him to examine Mr. Sanderson's project, which will bring great profit to the King, and for which four aldermen of London are willing to advance 100,000*l.*; also to take bail for certain prisoners, and to be careful lest "the foulness of the Barons" [of the Exchequer] and of Mr. Spiller lead them to wrong wording for the exceptions in the pardons.

May 4. Commission to the Lord Chancellor and Sir Fras. Bacon, Attorney General, to engross and put the Great Seal to certain Acts of a Parliament in Ireland. [*Grant Bk., p.* 159.]

May 8. 97. Commission [not signed] to the Archbp. of Canterbury, Lord Chancellor, and others, to examine and recover all arrears due to the Crown from recusants.

May 9. 98. Order specifying the number of printing presses which are to be allowed to certain printers mentioned.

Vol. LXXX.

1615.

May 9. 99. Lord Treasurer Suffolk and the Barons of the Exchequer to Sir Hen. Fanshaw. Postpone the hearing of the cause of the King v. Sir Thos. and Gerard Whorewood, till the first day of next term, June 15.

[May 10.] [The Council] to [the Justices of Peace for Westmoreland], in behalf of Wm. Walker, a maimed soldier, whose pension of 5*l.* a year has been discontinued, without reason assigned. [*Dom. Corresp., Oct.* 9, 1614.]

May 10. 100. Indenture between Sir Geo. Shirley, of Staunton-Harrold, co. Leicester, Bart., and Hen. and Thos. Shirley, his sons, and Robt. Earl of Essex, for settling a jointure on Lady Dorothy Devereux, second sister of the said Earl, on her marriage with Hen. Shirley.

May 14. Whitehall. 101. The Council to the Lord Mayor. Order him to summon all knights, gentlemen, doctors of the civil law, &c., in London, who refuse to find men and arms, or contribute in proportion to their assessments for the musters of the trained bands; the exempt liberties are also to be assessed.

May 15. Special Commission to the Archbp. of Canterbury and others, to inquire and compound with offenders for erecting new buildings, not of brick or stone, and harbouring inmates, since the feast of St. Michael, 1st Jac. 1. [*Grant Bk., p.* 157.]

May 19. Commission to Hen. Howard, Hen. Gibb, and others, to grant free warren. [*Ibid., p.* 184.]

May 20. Grant to Hen. Howard and Hen. Gibb of all sums arising upon composition for free warren. [*Ibid., p.* 174.]

May 20. London. 102. Chamberlain to Carleton. We wish for peace amongst our friends, because it is useless to show our teeth unless we can bite, and we have no means even for necessary expenses. Young Owen arraigned for traitorous speeches on the lawfulness of killing excommunicated kings, &c. Ogilvie, a Jesuit, executed at Glasgow for similar opinions. Lords Fenton and Knollys, the new Knights of the Garter, will rival each other in the splendour of their trains, in riding to Windsor. Somerset still holds the Wardenship of the Cinque Ports, though Lord Zouch and the Earl of Montgomery are talked of for it. The lawyers nettled because the King went to Cambridge to see the play "Ignoramus," which ridiculed them. Death of Dr. Neville, Dean of Canterbury, and Sir Wm. Lower.

May 20. Saturday. 103. Order of the Court of Exchequer for sequestration of certain lands of Sir Chas. Cavendish in Sherwood Forest, for neglect in not answering a bill of complaint exhibited against him at suit of Otho Nicholson. *Annexing,*

103. I. *Certificate by the Commissioners of the Exchequer, of their sequestration of certain lands in Sherwood Forest, co. Notts, belonging to Sir Chas. Cavendish. May.*

Vol. LXXX.

1615.

May 20. 104. Account of the ordnance shipped from Meechinge, Sussex, since July 26, 1614, and of its destination.

May 21. Court at Greenwich. 105. The Council to Alderman Sir Thos. Lowe, of London, and Wm. Towerson. At request of the late Company of Merchant Adventurers, the King permits them to meet once, though not as a company, to confer upon the dyeing and dressing of cloths. The result of their conference is to be reported to the Council.

May 22. 106. Thos. Wilson to [Ambrose Randolph]. Requests him to join with him in a bond for 100*l.*, which he has borrowed.

May 22. Grant to Clem., John, and Thos. Harvey, and Robt Charleton, citizens and merchants of London, of the pre-emption of all tin, in cos. Devon and Cornwall, and elsewhere, excepting that granted to the Pewterers, for five years. [*Grant Bk., p.* 174.]

May 22. Special licence to Jas. Wood and four others to sow all kinds of grain, for twenty-one years. [*Ibid., p.* 166.]

May 23. Greenwich. Proclamation for making glass with sea coal and pit coal only; prohibiting the use of wood on account of the waste of timber; also prohibiting the import of foreign glass. Printed. [*Proc. Coll., No.* 42.]

May 24. Ely House. 107. [Bp. of Ely] to [Matthias] Taylor. Answers of the Council to divers points of the requests made by the priests at Wisbeach; their breviaries may be restored, and they may see or write to friends who wish to relieve them, without the names being known, &c. Cannot allow his own house to be used for prisoners, as it was during the vacancy of the bishopric.

May 24. Grant to Wm. Hougate of licence to hold a Court Leet in the manor of Saxton, and others, co. York. [*Grant Bk., p.* 174.]

May 25. London. 108. Chamberlain to Carleton. Particulars of the procession of the new Knights of the Garter, Lord Knollys and Visct. Fenton, with 300 attendants each, to Windsor. The King stood at Somerset House to view it. The great project of dyeing and dressing cloth is at a stand. The clothiers complain that the cloth lies on their hands, and the cloth-workers that they have less work than before. The new Company quarrel, and the old Company, too rashly dissolved, are requested to resume the trade and set all straight again. Lady Chichester, only sister of the Countess of Bedford, dead. Dr. [John] Richardson made Master of Trinity College [Cambridge]. Duel between two Scots, both Ramsays, one of whom, Lord Haddington's brother, is dead of his wound.

May 27. 109. List of contributions to the benevolence from certain persons and places, since April 29, 1615.

May 31. Greenwich. Proclamation commanding due execution of the Statutes of Hen. VIII. and Edw. VI. against falsifying wool and woollen yarn, and corruptions in the mixture of wools. Printed. [*Proc. Coll., No.* 43.]

VOL. LXXX.

1615.

May 31. Grant to Sir Basil Brooke and Robt. Chaldecott of the office of Clerks or Overseers of the Ironworks in the Forest of Dean, co. Gloucester, &c., for fifteen years. [*Grant Bk.*, *p.* 154.]

May. 110. Petition of the [old Company of] Merchant Adventurers to the Council. Thanks for permission to meet; though they see no ground to change their former opinions, yet they will undertake to export to Germany and the Low Countries 1,000 cloths, dyed and dressed for sale, and if the experiment succeed, to proceed with more. Pray for restoration to their former trade.

June 1. Grant to Philip Earl of Montgomery, [Sir] Thos. Howard, [Sir] Robt. Mansell, [Sir] Edw. Zouch, and others, of all glasses forfeited [for being imported] contrary to a proclamation of this year concerning making glasses. [*Grant Bk.*, *p.* 165.]

June 3. 111. Edw. Reynoldes to [Fras.] Mills. Opposition by Mr. Gall to the setting up of a partition between the Signet and Privy Seal Offices. Dividends for the month. Decrease in fees.

June 5. Grant to the wardens and poor of Trinity Hospital, East Greenwich, founded by the Earl of Northampton, of divers liberties. [*Grant Bk.*, *p.* 176.]

June 7. 112. Answer of the new Company of Merchant Adventurers to the Council, that being bound to export 6,000 cloths, dyed and dressed, in the first year, they will export 12,000 the second, and hope to undertake 18,000 the third; and, in time, to dye and dress all the cloth which they export, according to their charter.

June 8. Grant to Sir Chas. Howard, jun., of the office of keeping Mortlake Park, &c., co. Surrey, for life. [*Grant Bk.*, *p.* 175.]

June 10. 113. Detailed account by Dr. [John] Howson [Prebend of Christ Church, Oxford], of an interview with the King and Archbp. of Canterbury, in which the latter, on the representation of his brother, Dr. Abbot, accused him of personalities in preaching at Oxford; of refusing to render up his sermons, when required; of laxity in reference to Popery; of quarrelsomeness with the deans, and other prebends. His defence, denying some of the charges; excusing himself for not preaching oftener against Popery, because of the far greater prevalence of Puritanism, &c. The King's remarks thereon, and the final decision that stop should be put to pulpit controversies in Oxford; the adverse parties reconciled, and Howson requested to preach more frequently against Popery, and to be more careful in his future conduct. [*Indorsed by Laud.*]

June 13. 114. Bond by Thos. Alport and Fras. Needham, of London, under penalty of 150*l.*, to pay to Robt. Cambell, of London, 105*l.* on Dec. 16 following.

June 15. London. 115. Chamberlain to Carleton. The project of pardons, and Silvanus Skory's device for enlarging the privileges of Baronets, and raising the price to 3,000*l.*, are dismissed. The inquiry after build-

VOL. LXXX.

1615.

ings newly erected proceeds; if prosecuted to extremity, it will yield a large sum, but cause many murmurs. Report of Peers to be created by purchase. It would be more liked if the money went to the King, but Lord Sheffield has the benefit of Sir Robt. Dormer, who pays 10,000*l.*, and Sir G. Villiers has a grant of another, probably Sir Nicholas Bacon; Dackombe has the reversion of the Chancellorship of the Duchy. Sir John Kennedy and Sir Geo. Belgrave committed to the Gate House, for falsely accusing a gentleman of scandalous speeches against the Scots. Sir Chas. Cornwallis, and Drs. Sharpe and Hoskins, released from the Tower. Du Moulin preached before the King, and is made a Prebend of Canterbury. The Bishop of Winchester likely to be made Lord Privy Seal. Mr. Camden has published his "Annales," down to 1588, written "as well and indifferently as the time will afford."

June 17. Bishop's Auckland. 116. James Bp. of Durham to Sir Ralph Winwood. Will employ Geo. Fortune as requested. Ten years before, there were 700 recusants in his diocese; by the Ecclesiastical Commission, &c. they were reduced to 400, but have increased again. Has spent three weeks in personal visitations to make a true report on them. Mr. Smaithwaite is very useful in his present position as a minister in Northumberland, and shall be protected against Roger Wodrington's practices, but is not fit for a prebend at Durham, because he has not had a university education.

June 19. Grant to Thos. Chamberlain, Serjeant-at-law, of the office of Justice in cos. Carnarvon, Merioneth, and Anglesea, during pleasure. [*Grant Bk., p.* 181.]

June 23. London. 117. Edw. Blount to [Carleton]. Money affairs. His bills drawn on the Guadagnis, in Venice, have been returned.

June 25. 118. Bond from Edw. Bright to Jacob and Robt. Cambell, of London, under penalty of 300*l.*, to pay 115*l.* to the Ironmongers' Company, and discharge the other conditions of a bond to them, for which Jacob and Robt. Cambell are his sureties.

June 25. Grant to Thos. Cowley of the Surveyorship of all Honours, Castles, &c., co. Chester, for life. [*Grant Bk., p.* 160.]

June 26. Greenwich. 119. The Council to Somerset, as Provisional Governor of the Cinque Ports. The musters there having been neglected in some places, and very defective in others, fresh musters are to be held, and great care taken to supply all defects in arms, horses, &c. No exemption to be allowed to the clergy or the King's servants.

June 26. 120. Affidavit of Edw. Proctor, of Norwell-Woodhouse, co. Notts, of having served the writ of injunction directed by the Court of Exchequer, to the tenants of Sir Chas. Cavendish in Sherwood Forest.

June 27. 121. Note of the money found in the purses of the Romish priests in Wisbeach Castle, on a search made by Order of Council. Total sum, 80*l.* 19*s.* 10*d.*

VOL. LXXX.

1615.

June 27. Grant to Robt. Hay of all arrears of rents due to the King and the late Queen from the Levant Company. [*Grant Bk., p.* 175.]

June 29. London. 122. Chamberlain to Carleton. Singular conduct of the Bp. of Winchester in aspiring, amid so many difficulties, to a place which he cannot long enjoy. A satirical bill was posted on the Exchange, offering a reward for tidings of him, as he had run away from his diocese. Lord Hay is made an English Baron. The wits say, baronies "were wont to be given by entayle, but now they go by bargain and sale." The prisoners at Newgate rose against their keepers, and tried to set the prison on fire. Difference between the Chancery and King's Bench, because the King's Bench deliver prisoners by Habeas Corpus. The Lord Chancellor has set a dangerous example, if his authority should light on one of less integrity and judgment. He is thought the ablest Chancellor that has been many a day, and any defects are now ascribed to the sourness of age. The Lord Treasurer has recovered. Death of Dr. Wilson, of Dr. Langley, his successor, Dr. White, who wrote so well against Papists, and Sir Rowland Lytton.

June 29. Creation of Jas. Lord Hay as Baron Hay, of Sawley, co. York. [*Grant Bk., p.* 175.]

June 30. Creation of Sir Robt. Dormer, Bart., as Baron Dormer, of Wing, co. Bucks. [*Ibid., p.* 173.]

June 30. Westminster. 123. Bp. of Lincoln to John Lambe. The clergy of the diocese being less forward than was hoped in the benevolence, they are no longer to enjoy exemption from providing arms for the musters. Requests him to search the old books, and give notice to them of what is required from each. Those whose livings are below 40*l.* are to be spared; those of 40*l.* and 50*l.* to be put two to a musket; of 60*l.*, two to a corslet; of 70*l.* to 100*l.*, muskets; 100*l.* to 140*l.*, corslets; 140*l.* to 200*l.*, petronels; and above 200*l.*, lances. They are to understand that the arms are for defence of religion and the country, not for foreign service. *Incloses,*

123. I. *Archbp. of Canterbury to the Bp. of Lincoln. Commends the execution of the orders contained in a letter transcribed, from the Council to the Archbishop, dated June* 26, 1615, *requesting him to have certificates sent in from all the dioceses in his province, of such clergymen as are able to pay their proportions for provisions of arms for the musters, to be rated according to the value of their livings. Lambeth, June* 29, 1615.

June. 124. —— to Lord ——. The King permits Dr. Laud's return to Oxford, having made an end of all those matters, the Archbishop himself having acknowledged the error of his brother in it, and Dr. Abbot having apologized by saying that all the University understood Dr. Laud's remarks were meant for him. Imperfect. Indorsed [by Laud], "What His Majestye sayd concerninge Dr. Abbot's sermon against me."

VOL. LXXX.

1615.

June? 125. Account of the classes of persons composing the new Merchant Adventurers' Company, and of the fallacious representations adopted by them to delude Government into the belief that they are greatly increasing the export of dyed and dressed cloths, according to the terms of their patent. Imperfect.

June. 126. "Antithesis between the Old and New Companies of Merchant Adventurers," showing the confused elements of which the new Company is composed, the separate interests which they have to consider, and the advisability of restoring the old Company of experienced merchants.

June? 127. Petition to the Council of such Members of the old Merchant Adventurers' Company as have joined the new Company. They have submitted to the new project [for dyeing and dressing cloths in England], because they would otherwise be great losers, as their capital is embarked in the trade, but their past experience gives them little hope of success in the sale of dressed cloth. Begs they may not be blamed if the project fail, and may compound with the other members to confine themselves to the sale of white cloth.

June? Remission to Philip Earl of Montgomery of his offer of 330*l.* increase of rent, for the custody of coppices, parcel of the manor of Woodstock, co. Oxford, above the rent now paid for them by Sir Hen. Lee. [*Sign Man., vol.* V., *No.* 5.]

June? 128. Bp. James to John Packer, attendant on the Lord Chamberlain [Somerset]. Claims nothing which his predecessors, the Bishops of Durham, have not enjoyed unquestioned. Has not intermeddled in his Lordship's affairs, and has treated his servants kindly, but has been maligned. Regrets that at St. George's Feast, his Lordship was attended by Sir John Claxton, Sir Wm. Blakeston, and other recusants of the diocese, who, by law, should not leave their bounds, nor come within ten miles of Court. Sends to his Lordship, as Governor of that country, a list of the recusants in his diocese.

June? 129. Petition of Roger Parker, Dean of Lincoln, and Rich. Carrier, Vicar of Wirksworth, to the Council. Carrier is one of six ministers near the Peak of Derbyshire who have a right to a tithe of lead ore, which is now called in question by Wm. Bamford. Pray for an order that the said claim may be allowed.

VOL. LXXXI. JULY—SEPTEMBER, 1615.

July 1. Special licence to Sir Hen. Williams and Nich. Goffe to make oil and pith out of vines, and soap with sea coal, for twenty-one years. [*Grant Bk., p.* 166.]

July 1. Westminster. Grant to Sir Wm. Uvedale, in reversion after Lord Stanhope, of the office of Treasurer of the Chamber. Latin. [*Sign Man., vol.* V., *No.* 6.]

July 3. Oatlands. Grant to Chas. Glemmond and John Walcott, of London, nominees of the Earl of Argyle, of certain marsh grounds left by the sea in

1615. VOL. LXXXI.

Wigtoft, Moulton, Holbeach, and Tydd-St.-Mary, co. Lincoln, to be drained at the expense of the Earl, with reservation of a fifth portion, and a rent of 50*l.*, to the King, and of certain common lands to the neighbouring townships, &c. Latin. [*Sign Man., vol.* V., *No.* 7.]

July 3. Oatlands. Grant to Wm. Shaw, one of the Queen's Chaplains, of denization. Latin. [*Ibid.*, No. 8.]

July 3. Oatlands. Grant to John Levingston, Groom of the Bedchamber, of lands, value 500*l.* per ann., forfeited to the Crown by attainder of the Gunpowder traitors, but withheld by pretended entails and fraudulent conveyances, to be discovered by him. [*Ibid.*, *No.* 9.]

July ? Demise to John Levingston of lands in Preston and Bisbrooke, co. Rutland, of Holbeach House, &c., co. Stafford, Grimoldby, &c., co. Lincoln, forfeited to the King by Sir Everard Digby, Stephen Littleton, and John Grant, the Gunpowder traitors. Latin. [*Ibid.*, *No.* 15.]

July 3. Oatlands. Grant to Wm. Bulkeley, of Lledwigan Lles, co. Anglesea, of pardon for the murder of Wm. Lloyd, it being his first offence. Latin. [*Ibid.*, *No.* 10.]

July 3. Oatlands. Presentation of Wm. Bayley to the rectory of Wappenham, co. Northampton; with note by the Bp. of Lincoln, that, although the right of presentation has rested with his predecessors 300 years, he requests the King's confirmation of Bayley's presentation for further security. Latin. [*Ibid.*, *No.* 11.]

July 3. Westminster. Release to the Earl of Huntingdon of arrears which may hereafter be claimed from the manor of Loughborough, co. Leicester, which is let for life to Catherine Countess Dowager of Huntingdon for 5*l.*, its true rent being 115*l.* [*Ibid.*, *No.* 12. *See June* 15, 1610.]

July 3. Oatlands. Grant to Sir Robt. Anstruther of a pension of 200*l.* per ann. for life, on surrender of a former pension of 160*l.* [*Ibid.*, *No.* 13.]

July 3. Oatlands. Grant to Art. Radcliffe, of Thropton Spittle, and Edw. Hall, of Fallowlees, co. Northumberland, of pardon for manslaughter of Wm. Hall. Latin. [*Ibid.*, *No.* 14.]

July 4. London. 1. Edw. Reynoldes to Fras. Mills. Explains the proceedings in the dividend of fees to the Officers of the Privy Seal.

July 4. 2. Copy of the above.

July 4. Westminster. Grant to Thos. ap Thomas, of Talgarth, co. Brecon, and Watkin Rees, and Milo Richards, of Laleston, co. Glamorgan, of pardon for small felonies. Latin. [*Sign Man., vol.* V., *No.* 16.]

July 5. Oatlands. Warrant for payment to the King's footmen of 33*l.*, for delivering into the Jewel House a silver gilt cup presented to the King by the town of Cambridge. [*Ibid.*, *No.* 17.]

Vol. LXXXI.

1615.

July 6. Dover Castle. 3. Licence by the Earl of Somerset, Provisional Governor of the Cinque Ports, for Reynold Howgatt, of Treport, to fish on the Sowe and elsewhere on the English coasts.

July 6. 4—7. Like licences for Bennett Melliot, Michel du Fresne, Jehan Saunier, and Nich. Capetrell, all of Dieppe.

July 7. Westminster. Grant to Don Diego de Sylva, a Spaniard, of denization. Latin. [*Sign Man., vol.* V., *No.* 18.]

July 7. Westminster. Grant to Edw. Harrison, Keeper of the Chace of Martindale, Westmoreland, of the moiety of Star Chamber fines of 600*l.*, mitigated to 206*l.* 13*s.* 4*d.*, to be levied at his expense on Hen. Dacres and others for riotous hunting in the above chace. [*Ibid., No.* 19.]

July 7. Westminster. Grant to Hen. Bradshaw, of Duffield, co. Derby, of pardon of a fine of 100*l.* for receiving and uttering false coin, it being done in ignorance. [*Ibid., No.* 20.]

July 7. Westminster. Grant to John Davies, of Shrewsbury, of pardon for being accessory to the robbery of the Exchequer House of Shrewsbury, he having confessed and discovered the crime. Latin. [*Ibid., No.* 21.]

July 7. Westminster. Grant to Wm. Beck of pardon for manslaughter of Rowland Greenhead at Skelsmergh, co. Westmoreland. Latin. [*Ibid., No.* 22.]

July 7. Westminster. Lease to Sir John Leigh of concealed Crown lands, to be discovered by him, value 30*l.* per ann. [*Ibid., No.* 23.]

July 7. Westminster. Grant to Hen. Smyth, of Chevening, Kent, of pardon for life only, for a small robbery committed four years before. Latin. [*Ibid., No.* 24.]

July 7. Westminster. Release to the Earl of Somerset for all sums of money, jewels, plate, &c. belonging to the King, which have passed through his hands, and pardon for all minor offences, as frauds, conspiracies, extortions, contempts, &c., but not for any other offence affecting life or limb. [*Ibid., No.* 25.]

July 8. Westminster. Presentation of Geo. Barnard to the rectory of West Hesterton, diocese of York. Latin. [*Ibid., No.* 26.]

July 8. 8. Geo. Margitts to Sir Ralph Winwood. Mr. Spiller has not cleared himself, as he pretends. He has not come to the true point. Begs that he may be examined according to certain questions. He has produced a false writ to justify himself. Mr. Jarvis will prove his disorderly conduct in the Exchequer. If these accusations are disliked, they must be respited till Parliament.

July 8. Guildhall. 9. Precept by the Lord Mayor to the Warden and Company of Weavers, to certify the grievances which they suffer by aliens and foreigners resident within the city, similar precepts being issued to all the companies, at request of the Committee for considering Grievances caused by Aliens.

Vol. LXXXI.

1615.

July 8. 10. Questions in theology proposed for discussion at the University of Oxford, July 8 and 10, with the names of the speakers. Latin. Printed.

July 9. 11. Note of the distribution of 4*l.* to Archbp. Abbot's servants at the consecration of Rich. Milbourne, Bp. of St. David's.

July 9. Westminster. Grant to the city of Winchester of licence to found an hospital for the maintenance of four aged men, four children, and two scholars at Oxford and Cambridge, pursuant to the will of Peter Symonds, mercer, of London, who conveyed for that purpose messuages, lands, &c. in cos. Hants, Essex, and Surrey. The Warden of St. Mary's College, Winchester, and six others, to be governors. Latin. [*Sign Man., vol.* V., *No.* 27.]

July 9. Westminster. Lease to Chris. Bainbridge, in reversion after Thos. Matthew, of a certain toll, mill, furnace and close, in Bowes, parcel of the lordship of Middleham in the archdeaconry of Richmond, co. York. Latin. [*Ibid., No.* 28.]

July 10. Office of Revels. 12. Sir Geo. Buck to [John] Packer, Secretary to Lord Chamberlain Somerset. The King has been pleased, at the mediation of the Queen in behalf of Sam. Danyell, to appoint a company of youths to perform comedies and tragedies at Bristol, under the name of the Youths of Her Majesty's Royal Chamber of Bristol. Has consented to it, as being without prejudice to the rights of his office. Has received no wages since Dec. 1613. Begs payment of arrears.

July ? 13. Notes relating to the King's purpose in the grant prepared for Sir Fras. Hildesley, Wm. Turner, and John Reeve, of the alum agency, that he intends to include only the agency, and to grant the carriage to other parties, on certain provisoes.

July ? 14. Particulars of the patent granted to Sir Fras. Hildesley, Wm. Turner, and John Reeve, as overseers of the King's alum works.

July 12. Grant to Sir Fras. Hildesley, Wm. Turner, and John Reeve, of the office of Agents for Surveying the Alum Works, and of the carriage and sale of the alum, they bearing all the casualties, and receiving a pension of 766*l.* 13*s.* 4*d.* per ann. [*Sign Man., vol.* V., *No.* 29.]

July 13. London. 15. Chamberlain to Carleton. His despatches must be sent to Sec. Winwood, not to Somerset. His removal to the Low Countries, probable, &c. The King begins a progress into Hampshire and Wiltshire. Sir Art. Ingram, with much difficulty, ejected from Court, and Sir Marmaduke Darell sworn Cofferer. The Bp. of Winchester lingers still, in hope of the place [of Lord Privy Seal]. The Archbp. of Canterbury sick of an ague. Sir Wm. Uvedale succeeds Sir Thos. Overbury in his reversion of the Treasurership of the Chamber. The Aldermen urged to lend the King 100,000*l.*, but, after many refusals, they agree to lend 30,000*l.* Peacham to be tried for treason in Somersetshire; if he submits, he will have no great harm. Dick Taverner, guilty of killing several persons, is apprehended, but the

VOL. LXXXI.

1615.

Queen favours him. Question concerning the right of Lord Roos to carry the sword before the King, settled by Sir Robt. Cotton, who has ever some old precedent in store. Death of Sir Hen. Neville, &c.

July 13. Westminster. Grant to Silvanus Davis of pardon for highway robbery, he being young and having saved the life of the person robbed, whom his accomplice wished to murder. Latin. [*Sign Man., vol.* V., *No.* 30.]

July 13. Westminster. Grant to Sir Lewis Tresham, Bart., of certain houses in London, lately occupied by Alderman More's widow and others. Latin. [*Ibid., No.* 31.]

July 13. Theobalds. Grant to Edw. Lord Zouch of the office of Lord Warden of the Cinque Ports and Constable of Dover Castle, for life. Latin. [*Ibid. No.* 32.]

July 14. 16. Inventory of the brass and cast iron ordnance of Dover Castle, with the names of the several platforms, &c. surveyed and delivered over by Sir John Brooks to Sir Thos. Hamon, now Lieutenant of Dover Castle, Deputy Warden of the Cinque Ports, &c.

July 15. Theobalds. Licence to Thos. Lord Wentworth to enfranchise his copyholds and grant the wastes of his manors of Stebenhuth and Hackney, co. Middlesex, reserving the ancient Crown rents. Latin. [*Sign Man., vol.* V., *No.* 33.]

July 16. Theobalds. Grant to Philip Constable, of Washam, of pardon for manslaughter of Wm. Hungate, of North Dalton, both co. York. Latin. [*Ibid., No.* 34.]

July 16. Theobalds. Proclamation absolutely prohibiting the erection of any more private houses in London, and enforcing penalties against transgressors. Printed. [*Proc. Coll., No.* 44.]

July 17. Theobalds. Presentation of Israel Edwards to the rectory of East Mersey, co. Essex, void by resignation of John Wood. Latin. [*Sign Man., vol.* V., *No.* 35.]

July 17. Theobalds. Grant to Dr. Rich. Foster, of St. Anthony's parish, London, of pardon of a fine of 146*l.* 13*s.* 4*d.* for recusancy, he having now conformed. Latin. [*Ibid., No.* 36.]

July 17. Theobalds. Grant to Sir Oliver Cromwell of so much of the benefit of a lease of messuages and land in Buckworth, co. Huntingdon, forfeited by the outlawry of Amias Clifton, as will secure him in his engagement for payment of 600*l.* to the creditors of the said Clifton. [*Ibid., No.* 37.]

July 19. Theobalds. Grant to Orlando Gibbons of two bonds forfeited by Lawrence Brewster, of Gloucester, and his sureties, for his non-appearance before the High Commission Court at Lambeth. [*Ibid., No.* 38.]

July 19. Theobalds. Grant to Sir John Temple, on surrender of Peter Temple, of the office of Keeper of Camber Castle, co. Sussex. Latin. [*Ibid., No.* 39.]

Vol. LXXXI.

1615.
July 19. Theobalds. Grant to Rich. Lord Dingwall of protection from arrest for debt for eight months. [*Sign Man., vol.* V., *No.* 40.]

July 19. Westminster. Grant to Rich. Giles, of London, of the office of seizing and burning all logwood and deceitful dyeing woods brought into the port of London; and also of keeping a register of all merchandize seized for not paying due customs, to avoid its being discharged by the under officers of customs, without due warrant. [*Ibid., No.* 42.]

July 19. Westminster. Grant to Sir Hen. Montague, Serjeant-at-law, of the reversion on an estate tail granted to Sir Jas. Wingfield, of the castle, manor, and park of Kimbolton, the manor of Swineshead, and other rights and hereditaments, co. Huntingdon, for which he has paid 560*l.* to [Wm.] Heydon, in part of his grant of 4,000*l.* out of entailed remainders. Latin. [*Ibid., No.* 43.]

July 19. Westminster. Grant to the town of Tiverton, co. Devon, of incorporation, the town having been twice consumed by fire, to the loss of 350,000*l.*, through the negligence of some of the inhabitants, for want of government. Latin. [*Ibid., No.* 44.]

July 19. Theobalds. Grant to Jas. Achmouty, Groom of the Privy Chamber, of a pension of 100*l.* per ann. [*Ibid., No.* 45.]

July 20. Westminster. Warrant to the Earl of Pembroke and Sir Walter Montague, Constable and Deputy Constable of the Forest of Dean, to preserve the woods there, and to signify His Majesty's displeasure against recent spoilers thereof. [*Ibid., No.* 46.]

July 20. London. 17. Chamberlain to Carleton. Receives much kindness from Winwood, though he is thought austere. He wins favour by his upright and sincere carriage; not like some of his rivals, who procure such pardons that the Lord Chancellor says he dares not seal them unless he have a pardon for it. The Bishop of Winchester is dismissed with good words, without the office. Gibb, of the Bedchamber, sent from Court, for carrying messages from the Lord Chamberlain to Mrs. Murray, of the Queen's Bedchamber. A new Ambassador come from France, and Chancellor Zamoiski's son from Poland. The King gone to Windsor, the Queen to Bath. The summer hot and dry. Old Garway, of the Customs, knighted for giving security for the Aldermen's last money.

July 20. 18. Petition of Martin Lumley, Alderman of London, to Somerset, for a licence to arrest Patrick Black, Tailor [to the Prince], for a debt of 400*l.*; with order thereon.

July 20. Westminster. 19. Letters Patent granting to Sir Rich. Coningsby, for a rent of 200*l.* per ann., the imposition of 5*s.* per gross on playing cards, and the office of Inspector of all playing cards imported, in recompence of 1,800*l.* due to him from the King, and of his Patent for the sole export of tin, granted by the late Queen.

July. Warrant for the above grant, dated July 19. [*Sign Man., vol.* V., *No.* 41.]

VOL. LXXXI.

1615.

July 21. Proclamation of the Patent granting to Sir Rich. Coningsby the right of searching and sealing all playing cards made in England or imported. Printed. [*Proc. Coll., No.* 44 A.]

July 21. Westminster. Grant to Geo. and John Story, of Burnfoot, Cumberland, of pardon for manslaughter of Robt. Story. Latin. [*Sign Man., vol.* V., *No.* 47.]

July 21. Westminster. Warrant to Lord Treasurer Suffolk to search what number of cloths, undressed, have been exported the last ten years, by the licence granted to the late Earl of Cumberland, that the present Earl may be compensated for any diminution caused by the King's desire to have cloths dyed and dressed within the realm. [*Ibid., No.* 48.]

July 21. Grant to Alex. Levingston of the parsonage house of Charminster, co. Dorset. [*Grant Bk., p.* 177.]

July 21. Grant to Wm. Huggins of a messuage, &c. in Mickelay, &c., co. York, for twenty-one years. [*Ibid., p.* 175.]

July 21. Grant, in reversion, to Wm. Beecher, of an Auditorship in the Court of Wards and Liveries, for life. [*Ibid., p.* 154.]

July 22. Grant to Thos. Visct. Fenton, Roger, John, and Matthew Gwyn, and Chris. Nicholls, of all forfeitures on statutes concerning wool, for thirty-one years. [*Ibid., p.* 173.]

July 23. London. 20. Edw. Reynoldes to Sir John Rawlins. Expostulates with him on his extravagant courses, especially his drinking wine mingled with the costly drugs of spice and sugar. Advises him to conceal himself from certain guests, and keep in private.

July 23. 21. Duplicate of the above.

July ? 22. E. R. [Edw. Reynoldes. The Same to the Same]. Advises him on his removal to a new lodging, to reform his expensive habits. Thinks a joint of meat per day, with some "quelque chose," sufficient. Urges moderation in the use of liquors.

July ? 23. The Same [to the Same]. Reproves him for foolish conduct in reference to his removal, being guarantee for him in his new lodgings. Urges him to steadiness and reformation, else must discontinue all correspondence with him.

July 23. Basing. Grant to Hugh May, in reversion after Sir Hen. Neville, Groom of the Privy Chamber, of the Keepership of Mote Park, in Windsor Forest. Latin. [*Sign Man., vol.* V., *No.* 49.]

July 24. Northampton House. 24. Earl of Suffolk to the Officers of the Customs at London. Directs them to permit English merchants to export and import goods in foreign bottoms till Aug. 31, notwithstanding the late proclamation.

July 25 ? 25. Note of the towns in the Cinque Ports, and memorandum of the Lord Warden's speech, when he took the Oath of Supremacy, and the oath of his office. Indorsed, "Shepway [Sheppey ?] Court att my Lord's taking his oath."

1615. Vol. LXXXI.

July 25? 26. Sir Hen. Mainwaring's instructions for the Lord Warden's droit gatherers, in reference to their seizure of the anchors, goods, &c. of wrecked vessels.

July? 27. Petition of Harry Barnacle, Blacksmith to the Castle of Dover, to Lord Zouch, for one of the places now void, which was promised him by the late Sir Thos. Waller.

July? 28. Petition of Stephen Hamon to the Same, to be re-appointed Master Carpenter of Dover Castle, having been displaced, after the death of Sir Thos. Waller, in favour of Rich. Hamon.

July? 29. Petition of Rich. Hamon to the Same, to be continued in the place of Master Carpenter of Dover Castle, which he held under Sir Robt. Brett.

July? 30. Petition of Mark Willes to the Same, to be appointed to one of the vacant offices in Dover Castle, in consideration of his services as a sworn watchman there, under Sir Robt. Brett.

July? 31. Petition of John Goodwin, sen., of Dover, to the Same. Having bought a gunner's room in the Castle for his son, from a servant of the late Lord Warden, now finds that such purchases, though allowed by the late Warden and Sir John Brooks, are unlawful; but having no other resource for his son, prays that the place may be given him.

July? 32. Petition of Thos. Charrold, of Dover, to the Same, for continuance in his office of keeping and trimming the arms at Dover Castle.

July 25. 33. Orders and Decrees made by the Brethren of the Cinque Ports at Broad Hill, July 22, and at Romney, July 25, that all burgesses chosen to represent the ports shall be freemen thereof, or officers of the ports who shall be sworn freemen; their liberties being injured by having Barons ignorant of their charters, &c.

July 26. London. 34. Edw. Reynoldes to Sir John Rawlins. Has framed a letter as if written by Sir John Rawlins, for the purpose of casting a mist before the Italian's eyes. Advises him to live very privately.

July 26. Andover. Commission to the Earl of Suffolk and Sir Fulk Greville, Treasurer and Chancellor to the Exchequer, for enfranchising or selling copyholds in the survey of the Exchequer, with reservation of the ancient rents; for compounding for commons and wastes, and for buying in the perquisites of Courts. [*Sign Man., vol.* V., *No.* 50.]

July 26. Duplicate of the above. [*Ibid., No.* 51.]

July 28. Salisbury. Warrant to Sir Thos. Parry, Chancellor, and Sir Edw. Moseley, Attorney of the Duchy of Lancaster, to grant a commission of survey of the manor of Kidwelly, co. Carmarthen, with power to compound with the tenants for enfranchisement, on their doubling the rents; and also for a grant to the Duke of Lenox of all fines paid therefor, beyond the doubled rents. [*Ibid., No.* 52.]

VOL. LXXXI.

1615.
July 28.
Lincoln.
35. Geo. Permorte to John Lambe. Devotion to his service. The sequestrations should not be issued for the old arrears without sufficient warrant. Many are willing to pay, if their acquittances were ready.

July ?
36. Aña Maria Çamudio [wife of the Archduke's Ambassador] to the Queen. Intercedes for release of ten priests, undertaking that their superiors shall not again send them to England. They cannot make promises for themselves, being under authority of others. French. *Incloses,*

36. I. *List of the names of priests at Wisbeach Castle for whose liberty, particularly ten of them, Donna Aña Maria Çamudio petitioned.*

July 29.
London.
37. The Same to the Same. Renews her request in behalf of the priests. French.

July 29.
Grant of incorporation and divers liberties to the society of London for plantation of the Summer Islands. [*Grant Bk., p.* 177.]

July 29.
Grant to Nich. Guy of the office of Musician for the Flute, in place of John Phelps, deceased. Latin. [*Sign Man., vol.* V., *No.* 53.]

July 29.
Salisbury.
Grant to Thos. Bassano of the office of Musician, in place of John Phelps, deceased. Latin. [*Ibid., No.* 54.]

July 30.
Salisbury.
Grant to John Willie, in reversion after Bonham Norton, of the office of printing grammars and grammar books. [*Ibid., No.* 55.]

July 30.
Salisbury.
Grant to Thos. Garland, on surrender of Wm. Damport, footman, of pension of 40*l.* per ann. [*Ibid., No.* 56.]

July 30.
Salisbury.
Grant to the Earl of Montgomery of 3,000*l.* for twenty-one years, on surrender of his patent for the impost on tobacco. [*Ibid., No.* 57.]

July 30.
Salisbury.
Licence to Sir Edw. Howard to erect and maintain a lighthouse at Dungeness, and to have 1*d.* per ton from all ships passing by it for fifty years, with orders to the officers of customs to collect the above duty. [*Ibid., No.* 58.]

July 31.
Salisbury.
Grant to Sir Gilbert Houghton of three fourths of the fines accrued to the King during the last ten years in the Common Pleas, which have been kept back after verdict, to be recovered by him. [*Ibid., No.* 59.]

July 31.
Salisbury.
Approbation of the Lord Treasurer's order for exporting certain quantities of herrings from Yarmouth in strangers' bottoms, and for exporting plate to Scotland and Ireland; and authorizing him to grant similar licences in future. [*Ibid., No.* 60.]

July 31.
Salisbury.
Grant to Sir Hen. Lee, Bart., deceased, and his executors, &c., of pardon for wastes and spoils in Woodstock Park. [*Ibid., No.* 61.]

VOL. LXXXI.

1615.

July 31. Salisbury. Warrant to the Lord Treasurer authorizing his former licences for exporting and importing goods in strangers' bottoms, notwithstanding the late proclamation, and permitting him to grant similar licences until Christmas Day next. [*Sign Man., vol.* V., *No.* 62.]

July 31. Salisbury. Commission to Sir Thos. Lassells, Sir Thos. Fairfax, of Denton, co. York, Sir Fras. Hildesley, and others, to compound with the freeholders and copyholders of Knaresborough Forest, co. York, for inclosing the wastes there, and disposing of the woods, with reservation of some part for the poor. [*Ibid., No.* 63.]

July 31. Salisbury. Grant to University College, Oxford, of confirmation of lands, tenements, &c., in Newcastle-upon-Tyne, and in cos. Oxford, Berks, Essex, York, and Montgomery, with liberty to purchase other lands in mortmain, to the value of 200*l.* per ann., their number of scholars being increased. Latin. [*Ibid., No.* 64.]

July 31. 38. Geo. Margitts to Sir Ralph Winwood. Asks favour in a petition to the King for release of the prisoners confined on account of the questioning of Spiller, and earnestly urges permission to bring Spiller to account, even if it be at his own charges.

July 31. Philip Lane. 39. Warrant of Lord Zouch to the Mayor of Dover, and other Commissioners of the passage, to permit Thomas de Zamoiski, a Pole, who has been in England to see the King and Court, to embark at Dover with his train; but to be careful that no English person steal over in his company.

July? 40. Information touching English recusants abroad, and the election, in June 1615, of Dr. Thos. Worthington to be Popish Archbp. of Canterbury; with a list of the English present at the Spa on that occasion. Worthington is going to Rome, and thence to England.

July? 41—43. Proceedings of John Andrew against Elizabeth Andrew, alias Goodman, his wife, of the diocese of London, in a cause for restitution of conjugal rights. Three papers. Latin. *Prefixed is,*

41—43. I. *Power of Attorney from Geo. Pormorte, notary, of Lincoln, to John Lambe, of the Court of Arches, to decide in the above cause. Latin.*

July? 44. Petition of Edw. Russell to Somerset, that Hamond Claxton, who with others has raised large sums in Norfolk and elsewhere, by Letters Patent, pretending great losses from fire, may not obtain the pardon before judgment which he solicits, knowing himself guilty, and fearing the results of the suit commenced against him for the good of the commonwealth by the petitioner, who would thus lose his costs.

Aug. 1. 45. Bond from Thos. Alport and Fras. Needham, of London, under penalty of 150*l.*, to pay to Robt. Cambell, of London, 100*l.* before Feb. 3 ensuing.

VOL. LXXXI.

1615.
Aug. 7. Grant, in reversion, to John Browne of the office of Gunstone Maker, for life. [*Grant Bk., p.* 155.]

Aug. 7. Merton College. 46. Rev. Thos. Horne to [Carleton]. Particulars of his journey from Venice to London. Saw Dr. Diodati at Geneva. Attempt to detain him (Horne) in Berne, to extort money from him. Did not go by Heidelberg, the Prince and Princess Palatine being near Bohemia. Arrived in London July 26. Found the Archbp. of Canterbury gone to Canterbury, for the first time since his election, and the Secretary gone on progress with the King. The Bp. of London gave him little hope of advancement, being crowded with letters for livings from the King and Queen, and from noblemen.

Aug. 9. Westminster. 47. Commission to Lord Zouch to appoint deputies for granting licence to Englishmen to go beyond the seas, on their taking the necessary oaths.

Aug. 9. Westminster. 48. Copy of the above, with instructions and cautions to be observed by the Commissioners for licensing the passage. None but known merchants are to sail from or land in any ports but Dover, Rye, or Sandwich.

Aug. 9. 49. Copy of the above commission, and instructions.

[Aug. 9.] 50, 51. Two copies of the above instructions.

Aug. ? 52. Blank warrant [by Lord Zouch] appointing Commissioners of the passage in the ports between Dover and Sandwich, to prevent any persons sailing or landing but in accordance with the above instructions.

Aug. ? 53. Form of one of the French fishing licences granted by Lord Warden Zouch in accordance with His Majesty's grant of six additional fishing-boats, at request of M. de la Boderie, late French Ambassador. Latin.

Aug. 9. Durham Castle. 54. Bp. James to Archbp. Abbot. Sends information given by a Polish surgeon [Chris. Newkirk], a pretended Catholic, and much courted by the priests, who wish to learn from him how to make still powder. He is to meet Winter and Digby in Doncaster. They have given him an altar, devotional books, beads, &c. Has furnished him with a horse and money for the journey. The King's life is the object aimed at.

54. I. *Informations of Chris. Newkirk. July* 16, 1615. *Met Humph. Clesby, of Morpeth, who, talking of a sermon preached against Popery at Paul's Cross, said there would soon be a redress of their oppressions, and that the burning of Wymondham, laid on the Catholics, was done by two sailors. Pretended to be a Catholic, because he wished to know more of Clesby.*

VOL. LXXXI.

1615.

54. II. *July 24, 1615. Clesby told him that in Queen Elizabeth's time a man might hear mass for 100 marks, but now it is treason; that had this persecution been suspected, the King had not come to the crown so quietly; but there would soon be an alteration, both in King and Prince. Nine priests coming over from the Pope. Sundry meetings projected at Cleveland, in Yorkshire, and elsewhere. Wm. Ogle, Sutheran, and Carter, priests, are among the conspirators. They are much afraid of admitting strangers.*

54. III. *Aug. 2, 1615. Sir Thos. Blakeston has a dispensation from the Pope to conform. Meetings of Papists are held at his house, at Sir John Claxton's of Nettleworth, Mr. Hodgson's of Heborn, Mr. Swinburn's of Capheaton Castle, Northumberland, and others.*

54. IV. *Aug. 7, 1615. Went with Clesby to his lodging, where an altar, books, and beads were given him from a chest full of them. Was present at a mass, where were six persons. Clesby said the King and Prince had not long to live, many means being wrought for their despatch. Particulars of priests and their meetings. Is to meet Digby and Winter at Doncaster on Aug. 10.*

Aug. 14. 55. Edw. Reynoldes to [Sir John Rawlins]. Reproaches him severely for his dissolute life. Must abandon him unless he reforms.

Aug. 15. 56. Certificate by the Weavers' Company, of London, of the grievances by them sustained from aliens, in response to an order thereupon of July 8. The aliens injure the trade, employ more journeymen than allowed by statute, and then conceal them when search is made; live more cheaply, and therefore sell more cheaply, than the English; import silk lace contrary to law, and engross the custom of foreigners. With suggestion that, the wars and persecutions which drove them to England being over, they should be compelled to return. Indorsed is a note for "the newe devise of a loome for many peeces at once to be prevented."

Aug. 15. Chatham. 57. Sir Guildford Slingsby, Sir Rich. Bingley, and Sir Peter Buck, to Peter Buck, Clerk of the Cheque at Chatham. To enter Hen. Goddard and John May as Assistants to the Master Shipwrights.

Aug. 16. Durham Castle. 58. Bp. James to Archbp. Abbot. Sends intelligence. The dancer named therein was offered liberty, instruction, and time to reflect on taking the Oath of Allegiance, but was resolute, and refused all. Flocking of priests, even in a walled town like Newcastle, where, a few years ago, was not one recusant. Danger from the King's lenity towards priests. Some mischief in hand; great need for caution. Has sent Newkirk to York to a meeting of priests, furnished with beads and a manual, that he may

VOL. LXXXI.

1615.

not be suspected. Thinks Moore not ill affected, though he spoke unadvisedly. He is a communicant. *Incloses,*

58. I. *Information by Chris. Newkirk of his conversation with Wm. Sutheran, a priest, who told him that the dancer imprisoned at Durham was well supported by the priests; that France, Spain, and Spinola had each 20,000 men ready; that the North of England would raise 20,000 more, for a hurly-burly, on a certain signal. Meeting of priests projected at York. Aug. 9, 1615.*

Aug. 17. Canterbury. 59. Archbp. Abbot to Sir Ralph Winwood. Sends the examination made by the Bp. of Durham of [Rich.] Moore, and advises that he may be set free on bond. Sends other papers of consequence. Young Winter is the son and brother of the Winters who died in the Powder Treason, a desperate young fellow, rooted in Popery, and brought up at Sir Wm. Ingleby's, Yorkshire. Great watchfulness required. The meetings for masses have other objects also. Sends Floyd's examination. *Incloses,*

59. I. *Examination of Rich. Moore. He heard it said abroad that the King's nativity had been cast, and that he could not live more than a year. Also, that it was wonderful the Pope did not excommunicate the King, and that the condition of English Catholics was most miserable, the Archbp. of Canterbury and the Secretary being the heads of the Puritans, and having offered to pay all the King's debts, if he would put the recusants to the Oath of Allegiance, and take the benefit of their refusal to swear. Also, that at a dispute before the King at Cambridge, between a Puritan and a Protestant, the Puritan so urged the Papists' arguments that the Protestant burst for grief. Aug. 1, 1615.*

59. II. *Examination of Griffith Floyd. Details of his past life, his entering the society of Jesuits, residences abroad, &c. Grew weary of the Jesuits, because they attended more to politics than religion, and left them. Was not at Brunsberg, in Prussia, in 1609 or 1610. Never employed the printer there, except to print philosophical theses, and an oration of St. Bernard. Never spoke to Gaspar Sicochius, nor saw Bartolus Passenius' work. Blamed the publishing in Poland of books slandering the King, and solemnly protests that he had no hand in them. Aug. 17, 1615.*

Aug. 17? 60. Statement by Archibald Ranking of his conference in prison with Floyd. He said Father Parsons sent him to England after the Powder Treason, to appease the Catholics. In 1611 he complained to the Pope of the Jesuits, and begged their recall from England, for which Parsons had him put in restraint. Promises great services, if the King will grant him life and liberty.

Aug. 17? 61. Answers given by Floyd to the questions by Ranking. His intercourse with Parsons. Remonstrated with him on his

1615. Vol. LXXXI.

writings. The Jesuits meddling in State affairs. His mode of life. The Catholics consider him as a rejected Jesuit, and a spy of the State.

Aug. 17? 62. Draft of the first page of the above.

Aug. 18? 63. Examination of Helen Pendleton alias Floder, condemned for the burning of Wymondham. Description of certain maimed soldiers, sailors, &c. whom she found on the road near Howlbruck, Derbyshire, who said they were employed by Lord Stanley [Sir William Stanley ?] beyond the seas in plots. John Bradshaw said he was hired to kill the King with pocket dags. Particulars of their journey to Wymondham. Did not carry powder or match whereby they could be suspected of such a crime.

Aug. 20. 64. Further examination of the Same. Details of wandering companies employed by Lord Stanley and others for the burning of towns, &c. in which there are any Protestants or Puritans. Their places of meeting. Mr. Townley, of Burnley, Mrs. Anderton, of Lostock, and Mr. Clifton, near Preston, Lancashire, favour them. Their captain is a conjuror named Ambler. Aug. 19 and 20.

Aug. 21. Axbridge. 65. Commission to Edw. Lord Zouch of Lieutenancy of the Cinque Ports and their members.

Aug. 23. Bishop's Auckland. 66. Bp. James to Archbp. Abbot. Transmits further informations, all extremely dangerous to the State. Hopes Newkirk deals faithfully. He has learned many strange things in a short time. Begs that the posts may be instructed to convey his letters speedily. *Incloses*,

66. I. *Chris. Newkirk to the Bp. of Durham. Met in Yorkshire with Winter, Rokewood, and John, William, and Thos. Digby, and Percy, &c. After consultation, they agreed to admit him into their confidence, and told him they were authorized by the Pope to take vengeance for the martyrdom of their friends, on pretence of complicity in the Powder Treason. Had made three engines invented by Signor Alex. Maletesto, who was commended to them by Marquis Spinola, and were going into Cardiganshire to try one of them. They boast that the Bishops, wanting money, take it of recusants; that the King dares not attack Catholics of any degree; and that the Earl of Northumberland is kept in prison, not for treason, but for fear of his influence in Northumberland; that the Council knew of the escape of the priests from Wisbeach, and that they were there only for show. They curse the Archbp. of Canterbury, who persecutes them mightily. They have vessels in almost every haven. Thinks they had better be apprehended when they get to London. Begs safe messengers for convoy of his letters, and assistance for his wife, that she may be in London and near him at his imprisonment. York, Aug.* 20, 1615.

VOL. LXXXI.

67. Chamberlain to Carleton. The progress draws to an end. The King, Queen, and Prince meet at Windsor, and Winwood is to have the Seals. Sir Thos. Lake expects to be Home Secretary. The Spanish and Archduke's Ambassadors visit the Earl of Exeter, at Burleigh and other places in Northamptonshire. Lord Zouch very diligent in his new government. The towns in Kent are full of French women and children, come over for fear of troubles there. Marquis Bonnivet, Lieutenant of Picardy, arrived. A merchant ship lost at Hamburg; two others seized in France and Spain, for exporting coin. Death of Sir Thos. Dacre, Sheriff of Hertfordshire. Peacham tried and condemned for high treason.

68. Petition of Alice, widow of George Martyn, of Dover, to Lord Zouch. Prays that a suit wrongfully commenced against her by John Swanton, for part of a debt due to him by her late husband, may be dismissed, as she is not administratrix. With reference thereon indorsed.

69. Thos. Wilson to Ambrose Randolph. Death of —— Agarde. Advises Randolph to apply for his place of Keeper of the Exchequer Records, which is in the gift of the Chamberlain. It would be dangerous to the State should Sir Robt. Cotton, who will strive for it, succeed to put in a person devoted to him. He already injures the keepers of State papers, by "having such things as he hath coningly scraped together."

Proclamation of Letters Patent granting licence to Sir Edw. Howard to erect and maintain a lighthouse at Dungeness, in Kent, and to receive 1*d.* per ton on all ships passing there, to be collected by the farmers of customs. Printed. [*Proc. Coll., No.* 45 *B.*]

70. Second examination of Griffith Floyd. Was sent into England, after the Powder Treason, to know whether Garnet was privy to it otherwise than in confession; whether he was as delicate in diet and as familiar with Mrs. Anne Vaux as reported, whereof he "found too much." Garnet's successor Holtby, Father Blount, and others, finding him to dislike the meddling of Jesuits, sent him off to Wales. Heard them say that the King and Salisbury knew of the Powder Treason, months before its breaking out. Cardinal Bellarmine said that the letter written by the King to the Pope from Scotland was lost in the dispersion of Clement VIII.'s papers. Can do service by declaring the falsehood of reported persecutions in England, and by getting the Jesuits recalled thence. Thinks M. Maillan, a Gentleman of the Pope's Chamber, who came over as a pretended agent of the Duke of Lorraine, wrote the book called Passenius.

Grant of incorporation, with divers privileges, to the new Company of Merchant Adventurers. [*Grant Bk., p.* 176.]

71. Note of the company, ordnance, munition, &c., in Deal Castle, taken by Lord Zouch; with memoranda of later date.

72. Like note for Walmer Castle.

Vol. LXXXI.

1615.

Aug. 31. 73. Examination of Edm. Peacham. Had no assistance in compiling his work. Sir John Sydenham confirmed some parts of it, but was not the author. Intended no harm, and would have taken out the venom before he published it. Declares he can confess no more, though offered his life to reveal all.

Aug. 31. Dover. 74. [Lord Zouch] Lord Lieutenant of the Cinque Ports, to Thos. Andrews. Re-appoints him Captain of the select band of soldiers in Dover, according to his commission to supply all defects since the previous musters.

Aug. 31 ? 75. Blank commission [by the Same], appointing him to the command of the Train Bands in the town of Winchelsea.

Aug ? Grant to Sir Thos. Gerard, Bart., and Patrick Malde [Maull], Groom of the Bedchamber, of His Majesty's fifth part of certain marsh grounds left by the sea, in Lincolnshire, to be recovered by Chas. Glemmond and John Malrea. [*See July* 3. *Sign Man., vol.* V., *No.* 65.]

Sept. 1. Grant to Robt. Bendbo of the office of a Messenger in the Exchequer, for life. [*Grant Bk., p.* 154.]

Sept. 2. 76. Statement of the decayed condition of Sandown Castle. The sea wall perished, the stone work and lead decayed, the bridge and stairs rotten, the glass broken, &c.

Sept. 2. 77. Inventory of ordnance, munition, &c. in Sandown Castle, under the charge of Capt. John Haydon; with notes of later date.

Sept. 3. 78. Lease from Thos. Lord Arundel, of Wardour, to John Lambe, of Northampton, of lands in Sillesworth, co. Northampton.

Sept. 4. 79. Inventory of the ordnance, munition, &c. of Sandgate Castle, under the charge of Capt. Geo. Fenner.

Sept. 6. 80. Petition of Agnes, widow of John Wenlock, of Dover, to Lord Zouch, to grant her some relief out of moneys remaining at Dover Castle, belonging to Samson Bate, of London, who killed her husband.

Sept. 8. Dover Castle. 81. Warrant by Lord Zouch to the Deputy of Margate, the Minister of St. John's Church there, and others, constituting them Commissioners for the passage, at the above port.

Sept. 9. Bath. 82. Coroner's inquest on the body of Jonathan Pigott. Verdict of manslaughter against Fras. Lord Norris, who struck him with a sword, at the Litten in Bath. Latin.

Sept. 10. 83. Memorandum by Geo. Blee and Edw. Keamish, that they saw Lord Norris thrust Lord Willoughby in the breast, before Jonathan Pigott was slain.

Sept. 10 ? Lord Norris to the King. His discoursing with Lord Willoughby in a church or churchyard proves that he was not intending to quarrel, but Lord Willoughby assaulted him treacherously and unexpectedly. His slaying Lord Willoughby's man was purely in self-defence, as the man drew upon him. Throws himself on the King's justice and compassion. [*Imperfect MSS., Jac.* 1, *No.* 2, *p.* 27.]

Vol. LXXXI.

1615.

Sept. ? 84. Account [by Sir Wm. Waad] of his dismissal from the lieutenancy of the Tower, on accusation of too great indulgence to the prisoners, especially Sir Thos. Overbury, although he had refused all access to him, even to the Earl of Somerset's servants; but seeing him ill, he had wished him to have a servant to attend him, which was refused. Sir Gervase Helwys admitted Rich. Weston to attend Overbury, on the recommendation of Sir Thos. Monson. It was commonly reported in the Tower that he was murdered. His brother-in-law was not allowed to see him when dying, nor his body to be brought out of the Tower. Somerset dissuaded Overbury from going to Russia to serve the King, as requested, promising to save him from any mischief for refusal.

Sept. ? 85. Memoranda [by Sir Edw. Coke] of questions to be put to the coroner and others who saw the body [of Sir Thos. Overbury], as to its condition, and to the Lieutenant of the Tower as to his keepers, his food, physician, &c.; also, as to what is to be done with the Lieutenant, if there be any suspicion of him, and of questions to be put to accused and accusing parties, as to why the thing was so long kept a secret, and is now revealed.

Sept. 10. 86. Sir Gervase Helwys to the King. Found that Weston was intending to poison Overbury, and so terrified him that he had him at his service to deceive those who sent the poisons, by pretending to administer them, but not doing so. At length Overbury being ill, Weston confessed that the apothecary's servant was corrupted to poison him with a glister. Knows none but Weston and Mrs. Turner who were actors in it. Interviews between her and Weston, when the cause of his death was called in question, in July last.

Sept. 10? 87. Digest of the former part of the above, with marginal queries [by Coke] to be put to Helwys thereon.

Sept. 11? 88. [Sir Ralph Winwood] to [Lord Chief Justice Coke] Directions as to the examinations of Mayerne, the French apothecary, Weston, the Lieutenant of the Tower, Mrs. Turner, and Sir Thos. Monson, on Overbury's death. Only mean persons being yet accused, their strict trial will best vindicate the great persons who may be indirectly implicated. Imperfect.

Sept. 11? 89. Memorandum [by Sir Edw. Coke] of interrogatories to be put to, and presumptions against Sir Thos. Monson, the Lieutenant of the Tower, and Weston.

Sept. 11? 90. Note [by the Same] on the advisability of proceeding in Sir Thos. Overbury's case by the ordinary course of justice, as was done in Queen Elizabeth's time, and not troubling His Majesty in it.

Sept. 11? 91. [Lord Chief Justice Coke] to Lord ———. Suggests that commissions, indictments, &c. may be prepared, as the term approaches, and the expectations of good men await justice.

1615. Vol. LXXXI.

Sept. 12. Dover Castle. 92. Petition of Thos. Morris, of Dover, mariner, to Lord Zouch, against Thos. White, to whom he had lent 40*l*., and who refuses to repay it. With order thereon.

Sept. 12. Bath. 93. Verdict of manslaughter given by the jury against Lord Norris, for having slain Jonathan Pigott, servant of Lord Willoughby, with a thrust of his rapier; Lords Willoughby and Norris having before had a quarrel, and Pigott having assaulted Lord Norris and his servant.

Sept. 12. 94. Muster roll of the garrison of Deal Castle.

Sept. 12. 95. Muster roll of the garrison of Walmer Castle.

Sept. 13. 96. Examinations of John Williamson, of Southwark, Archibald Williamson, of Queenhithe, Jas. Sutton, Solicitor for the Dutch congregation, and Borchart Broeckman, Dutchman, relative to evil words against the King, spoken in drink by Broeckman, who was formerly an intelligencer employed by Sir Robt. Cecil in Spain.

Sept. 13. Dover Castle. 97. Warrant by Lord Zouch appointing the Mayor, Minister, and others, of Folkestone, Commissioners for the passage at that port.

Sept. 14. 98. Similar warrant by the Same appointing the Mayor, Ministers, and others, of Dover, Commissioners for the passage at that port. With alterations made later.

Sept. 15. Ware Park. 99. Chamberlain to Carleton. The Court has been in progress. The King at Theobalds. The Bp. of Winchester, after much delay and contest, is sworn of the Privy Council. The Queen returned from Bath, but is worse. Lord Norris in danger, for slaying a man of Lord Willoughby's, in a quarrel renewed between them. Sir Hen. Fanshaw is taking musters. Carleton's cousin Lytton is training his company at Hitchin. The summer has been long and dry.

Sept. 15. 100. Muster roll of the garrison of Sandown Castle.

Sept. 15. 101. Copy of the above, with later memoranda.

Sept. 16. Dover Castle. 102. Warrant by Lord Zouch to the Captains of Sandown, Deal, and Walmer Castles, their Deputies and Gentleman Porters, the Ministers of those places, and others, constituting them Commissioners for the passage at the creeks and landing places between Sandwich and Dover.

Sept. 16. Theobalds. Proclamation commanding due execution of Forest Laws for the restraint of swine, &c., that the deer which suffered by the rigour of last year may have sufficient pannage. Printed. [*Proc. Coll.*, *No.* 45.]

Sept. 17. Ferrybridge. 103. Chris. Newkirk to [the Bp. of Durham]. Sickness of Alex. Maletesto, the engineer of the plotters. A foot and horse race is to be given at Hambleton by the Earl of Rutland, &c., on Sept. 30, to afford them an opportunity to assemble. All the conspirators will meet at London, on Oct. 14.

VOL. LXXXI.

1615.

Sept. 17. Dover Castle. 104. Warrant by Lord Zouch appointing the Mayor, Minister, and others, of Hythe, Commissioners for the passage there.

Sept. 17? 105. Names proposed for insertion, in place of others [*probably in some commission for passage*].

Sept. 18. London. 106. [E. Reynoldes] to his cousin [Raymond] for aid in the prosecution of two bad debts of Ford and Brinkworth. Thanks for the care of his cousin Castle at Oxford.

Sept. 18. Dover Castle. 107. Warrant by Lord Zouch to the Bailiff, Minister, and others, of Seaford, constituting them Commissioners for the passage there.

Sept. 18. 108. Licence by the Same for Jehan Saunier, of Dieppe, to fish on the English coasts.

Sept. 23. 109. Robt. Boteler to ——. Begs that the Lord Warden will attend to the repairs of Camber Castle, the moneys for it having been issued long before; and will also secure the exemption of the retainers from all other services. *Prefixed is,*

109. I. *Note by Boteler of such old stores as he found in the Keep of the Castle, on his coming there, twenty years before.*

Sept. 25. Dover. 110. [Wm.] Ward to Lord Zouch. Sends Robt. Hudson's certificates for finding lost anchors in the roads of the kingdom, a service of importance for the recovery of valuable anchors and cables, and a saving to other ships, whose cables are cut by those anchors. *Incloses,*

110. I. *Sir Wm. Monson and sixteen others, Captains, &c., to [the Same]. Recommend Robt. Hudson to be continued in his place of sweeping for lost anchors; the service, which is very important, being invented by his father, and improved by himself. They have so cleared the Downs that ships can now safely anchor there, which before they could not do, on account of the multitude of lost anchors.*

110. II. *Note of the anchors and cables of divers of the King's ships, to the value of 1,100l., which were lost in the Narrow Seas and the Downs, and found by the industry of Geo. Rands and Robt. Hudson from 1599 to 1613, both before and since they had the King's pension of 30l. per ann.*

Sept. 27. 111. Declaration by Rich. Weston that he knows no cause of the sudden death of Sir Thos. Overbury but sickness; that some potion which he took made him very ill, but that he took cold in the Tower Council Chamber, going to see a friend in Sir Walter Raleigh's garden. No one ever persuaded him to give out scandalous reports about his death.

Sept. 27. 112. Muster roll of the garrison of Mote's Bulwark.

Sept. 113, 114. Two drafts of the above, dated Sept. 17 and 24.

VOL. LXXXI.

1615.

Sept. 28. 115. Details of a consultation in Council on the plans to be adopted for paying the King's debts, and lessening his expenses. Sir Thos. Lake thinks a Parliament the only mode. Preparations to be made for it, by removing the notion that the King would lavish all that was given among his favourites; by reducing his expenses, and by redressing grievances formerly complained of, especially impositions; business important to the State, as fishing, cloth-dressing, &c., to be proposed to Parliament. The Lord Chief Justice dwelt on the necessity of abatement of expenditure. Pensions not to be paid till the King is out of debt. The customs to be increased, and grants in which the King had been deceived to be called in. Parliament is the only mode of paying the King's debt of 700,000*l*. Importance of not tampering with the elections; last Parliament recommendations sometimes ended in sending in persons most averse to the King. Imperfect.

Sept. 28. 116. Memorandum of certain items of expenditure relating to the King's service during the past year. Indorsed "Moneys recalled."

Sept. 28. Duchy House. 117. Examination of Rich. Weston. Mentioned to the Lieutenant of the Tower the purpose to poison Overbury, but, at his remonstrances, threw the poison away. Has seen Mrs. Turner lately about some private property. Has not been prompted to conceal anything.

Sept. 29. Duchy House. 118. Re-examination of the Same. Mrs. Turner told him Lady Somerset would reward him if he would give Overbury what she sent him, which he received from Franklin, of Tower Hill. Acknowledges the truth of Helwys' relation of Overbury's death.

Sept. 29. 119. Muster roll of the six Gunners of Arch-cliff Bulwark, Dover, whose wages for the last year are unpaid.

Sept. 29. Paris. 120. M. Du Moulin to the King. Points out the fallacies in M. du Tilloy's refutations of objections in the King's book to the authenticity of the Charter of the Abbey of St. Médard, of Soissons. French.

Sept. 30. London. 121. E. Reynoldes to Fras. Mills. The profits of the Privy Seal Office were much greater when the Seal was settled in London. Talk of bestowing the Seal elsewhere. The King's servants are not exempted from charge in the musters. Will furnish a musket. Advises alacrity therein.

Sept. 122. Blank leaf, indorsed "Remonstrance to Capt. Le Faye concerning Capt. Gifford's practices."

Sept.? 123. Motion of the Attorney General in the cause The King v. Sir Chas. Cavendish, in the Court of Exchequer. That as the writ of sequestration [*see May* 20] has not taken due effect, the lands being chiefly in the defendant's hands, a writ of injunction may be issued, if he do not answer the bill before Nov. 1.

VOL. LXXXII. OCTOBER, 1615.

1615.

Oct. 1. 1. Examination of Anne, widow of Geo. Turner, M.D. Denies all knowledge of poison given to Sir T. Overbury by Weston, or of money sent to Weston by the Countess of Somerset, &c.

Oct. 1. 2. Examination of Robt. Bright, Coroner of Middlesex. The body of Sir T. Overbury at the inquest was worn to skin and bone; an ulcer and blisters found on it. Has not been spoken to by any one about this matter.

Oct. 2. 3. Examinations of Rich. Weston. Was urged by the Countess of Essex to give poisoned water to Sir Thos. Overbury, but, mentioning his purpose to the Lieutenant of the Tower, was terrified by his rebukes, and threw the water away. Afterwards gave him tarts, jellies, &c. sent him by the Earl of Somerset; 20*l.* was offered to an apothecary to give him a glister, but the Lieutenant would allow no one to do it but his own apothecary. Rewards given or promised him by Lady Essex. Has received 180*l.* from her, through Mrs. Turner, &c. Oct. 1 & 2.

Oct. 2. 4. Examination of William, son of Rich. Weston. Took a glass of water from the Countess of Essex, to whom he had carried a feather, to his father in the Tower.

Oct. 2. 5. Examination of Rich. Weston. Mrs. Turner sent him last summer to sound the Lieutenant of the Tower about the rumours of Overbury's murder. Further particulars of his death.

Oct. 2. Dover Castle. 6. Nich. Knott, Marshal of Dover Castle, to Rich. Younge, Secretary to the Lord Warden. The watchmen of the castle beg exemption from the musters. Recommends certain inhabitants to supply the places of those gunners who live at a distance. *Incloses,*

6. I. *The Same to Lord Zouch. Complains that some of the gunners neglect their duty, only ten of them, who are named, residing in or near Dover, and those refusing to obey authority. Knows persons who are fit substitutes for those who do no duty. Dover Castle, Oct. 2.*

Oct. ? 7. Names of the Gunners of Dover Castle, and of their substitutes.

Oct. ? 8. Names of such Gunners in [Dover] Castle as lost their places.

Oct. ? 9. Note of money to be received for the Gunners at Dover Castle, with deductions for allowances to the King's receivers.

Oct. ? 10. Petition of Thos. Harvey, of Ilthorne, to Lord Zouch, for a Gunner's place in Dover Castle; is willing to become a resident.

Oct. ? 11. Petition of Robt. Owen, Tanner, of Dover, to the Same, to admit him as a Gunner in Dover Castle, in place of Rich. Austen, his brother, who does not live near the castle.

Oct. ? 12. Petition of John Sweeting, of Dover, to the Same, to be appointed a Gunner of Arch-cliff Fort, Dover, in place of John Jagger, of London, dismissed for non-residence.

Oct. 2. 13. E. Reynoldes to Fras. Mills. Decline of the profits of their office, from the King's long absences, the delays in sealing processes, &c.

1615. Vol. LXXXII.

Oct. 3. Sherburn House. 14. —— Blaxton to Thos. Murray, Tutor to the Prince. The displanting of Brancepeth Park and sale of the lands proceed. The deer are sent to Raby, and all is desolation at Brancepeth. Will bring up the rents at Martinmas.

Oct. ? 15. Memorandum of privileges, &c. belonging to the Prince by virtue of his charter, in the manors of Barnard Castle, Raby, and Brancepeth, co. Durham.

Oct. 3. 16. Muster roll of the garrison of Sandgate Castle.

Oct. 3. 17. Inventory of munition in Sandgate Castle.

Oct. 3. 18. Wm. Ward to Lord Zouch. Thinks the hoy is no wreck, although forsaken, the men being saved. Will make composition with the savers. News from Spain that 3,000 Spanish soldiers are at Lisbon, ready to put to sea, but sickly and ill apparelled.

Oct. 3. 19. Examination of R. Weston. Showed the Lieutenant of the Tower the glass with poisoned water, and told him it came from the Countess of Essex. He said she had sent him tarts, &c. for Overbury. They looked bad after standing a day.

Oct. 3. 20. Examination of Sir Gervase Helwys. Sir Thos. Monson requested him to place Weston with Overbury, to prevent his receiving any letters, and told him such might be sent in tarts and jellies. Thinks Monson innocent of any knowledge of the murder.

Oct. 3. 21. Examination of Mrs. Turner, confronted with Franklin and Weston. Denies sending to inquire after Overbury, or giving Weston 180*l.*

Oct. 3. 22. Examination of Paul de Lobell, Apothecary. Gave no medicine to Overbury, except by the advice of M. Mayerne; but saw that he had waters, plasters, &c., which were not bought from himself.

Oct. 3. 23. Examination of Lawrence Davies, servant to Overbury. Was never allowed to see his master,Lord Rochester pretending that that would hinder his liberty. He had no plasters from him, except two for the spleen, for which also Sir Walter Raleigh sent him plasters. Produces a letter from Overbury, written a fortnight before his death, alluding to a letter from the Earl of Suffolk to him. *Annexed are,*

23. i. *Sir Thos. Overbury to Lawrence Davies. Desires him to show a certain letter to his sister, and to send a copy of it to Lord Ro[chester], and another to his father. Is better, and hopes to be free before Michaelmas.*

23. ii. *Copy of the above.*

23. iii. *Earl of Suffolk to Sir Thos. Overbury. Promises his best assistance to procure his liberty, though the King is too much offended with him for it to be done speedily. Will claim his promised services to reconcile him with Lord Rochester. Aug. 23, 1614.*

VOL. LXXXII.

1615.

Oct.? 24. Relation of [Giles] Rawlyns [servant of Somerset]. Took Overbury a powder, which he had from Sir Robt. Killegrew, and which was sent by Rochester, on pretence that it would make him sick, and afford an excuse for requesting his freedom. Another vomit was sent by Rochester through Lawrence Davies. Weston had an interview with Rochester, after Overbury's death, having promised Overbury to return him a certain letter with a powder in it.

Oct. 3? 25. Copy of the above.

Oct. 4. 26. Examination of Giles Rawlyns. Was taxed with indifference, being cousin-german of Sir Thos. Overbury, for not inquiring into his death. Sent a petition to the King that it might be examined into by law rather than by the Council. Was not dissuaded by any one from the prosecution. Could not see Overbury at his window as usual, for a fortnight before his death.

Oct. 4. 27. Examination of Elianor Dunne. Was called to lay out Overbury's body, and found on him many yellow blisters.

Oct. 4. Newhall. 28. The Earl of Sussex to the Council. His deputy lieutenants returned him books of the musters of foot, both laity and clergy, but not of the horse; therefore sent back the books for completion.

Oct. 4. Grant to Simon Lenton and Mich. Stanhope of a coppice in Rockingham Forest, co. Northampton, for twenty-one years. [*Grant Bk., p.* 176.]

[Oct. 5.] 29. Queries [by Coke] for the examination of Sir Thos. Monson, as to his share in the appointment of Helwys as Lieutenant of the Tower, and of Weston as Keeper; his knowledge of the poisons sent, &c.

Oct. 5. 30. Examination of Sir Thos. Monson. Recommended Weston to be Overbury's keeper, at request of the Countess of Essex and Earl of Northampton. Required the Lieutenant to allow him neither visitors nor letters, and advised him to search any tarts or jellies sent, for letters. Knew nothing of Weston's saying that what was given him made him ill.

Oct. 5. 31. Examination of John Wolf Rumler, French Apothecary. Was never appointed to administer medicine to Overbury, but wrote to the Lieutenant to say that it was the King's pleasure he should do so.

Oct. 5. 32. Examination of Simon Merston, one of the King's Musicians. Carried small tarts and jelly for Overbury, from the Countess of Somerset to the Lieutenant of the Tower, to whom alone he was ordered to give them.

Oct. 5. 33. Examination of R. Weston. Was brought up a tailor, but did not follow the trade. Has served several masters. Does not know Simon [Merston], who served Sir Thos. Monson. Was once committed for coining sixpences.

Vol. LXXXII.

1615.

Oct. 6. 34. Examination of R. Weston. Conveyed letters, and was privy to secret meetings between the Countess of Essex and Lord Rochester, at Mrs. Turner's and elsewhere. Delivered letters from Rochester to Overbury, but none with any powder in them. Did not take back any powder to Rochester after Overbury's death.

[Oct. 6.] 35. Queries [by Sir Ralph Winwood] to be proposed to Alderman Jones.

[Oct. 6.] 36. Declaration of Alderman Jones, in reply to the above queries, that Mr. Whitaker had several interviews with Mrs. Turner, after she was placed in his keeping, and brought her friendly messages and presents from the Countess of Essex, who sent him a piece of plate for his kindness to her, which he refused to accept.

Oct. 6. 37. Examination of Sir T. Monson. At request of the Countess, told Weston to go to Whitehall, but did not know that he was sent for on any particular errand.

Oct. 6. Grant, in reversion, to John Kay, of the office of Master Surveyor of the Ordnance in the Tower and the stores, in England and Ireland, for life. [*Grant Bk., p.* 176.]

Oct. 7. 38. Sir Wm. Waad to Lord Chief Justice Coke. Sends Maximilian Wade to answer any question which he can.

Oct. 7. 39. Testimony of Lawrence Davies. Weston gave him a letter to take from Overbury to Lord Rochester, promising to do his endeavour to be a means of friendship between him and others, but saying that concerning the marriage, he would never advise him. Gave Weston several letters from Rochester for Overbury, out of one of which a powder fell, part of which, after his death, Weston said he would take back to Rochester.

Oct. 7. 40. Deposition by Augustine Harrys, of Stepney. Being in Spain, he asked Willoughby's page how his master dared walk out late at night, to which he replied that he was safe, being armed with a privy coat.

Oct. 9. 41. Order of the Court of Exchequer in the cause the King v. Sir Chas. Cavendish, that if Sir Charles still delay to answer the suit of Otho Nicholson, for certain lands claimed as assarted in Sherwood Forest, a writ of injunction shall be issued, banishing him and his tenants from the lands. [*See Nov.* 28.]

Oct. 9. 42. Ambrose Randolph to Thos. Wilson. Applies for the return of money lent him; with note [by Wilson] that he cannot pay it at present.

Oct. 11. Ipswich. 43. Robt. Redmayne to the Churchwardens of St. Mary Towars. Requires them to reform certain nuisances in the churchyard, and to build proper seats in the church, where the sacrament may be received in an orderly manner, kneeling, and not sitting or standing. Any who are refractory on this point are to be certified in the next consistory court at Norwich.

VOL. LXXXII.

1615.

Oct. 12. Royston. Proclamation enforcing the statute of 15 Eliz., forbidding the import of French wines in any but English vessels. Printed. [*Proc. Coll.*, *No.* 46.]

Oct. 12. Standon. 44. Lord Chief Justice Coke to Winwood. The Earl of Lincoln is gone to Court about his late father's will. Is executor to it, with the younger brother of the present Earl. The Prerogative Court will decide who shall have the present administration, charge of the funeral, &c. Hopes the King will leave it to the course of law.

Oct. 12? 45. Petition of Anne Turner to the Lord Chief Justice, begging for speedy trial or enlargement on bail, for the sake of her fatherless children. Hopes her three or four examinations have proved her innocent of the things of which she is maliciously accused.

Oct. 13. 46. Examination of Lawrence Davies. Overbury was very temperate, cheerful, and healthful; had no complaint but the spleen, caused by study, for which he had an issue, and sometimes took medicine and had plasters. Thinks Rochester persuaded him not to go on the embassy. Several of his letters to Rochester intimate that the fault of his imprisonment lay upon him.

Oct. 13. 47. Examination of Hen. Peyton, servant to Overbury. To the same purport as the above. Overheard a conversation between his master and Rochester, whom he upbraided for intercourse with that base woman, the Countess of Essex, and said he would ruin himself by it, and he would leave him and stand alone. Rochester replied he could stand alone, and they parted in anger, and were not reconciled before Overbury's commitment.

Oct. 14. Skipton Castle. 48. Fras. Earl of Cumberland to Sir Thos. Lake. Would be willing, at the King's request, to resign the keepership of Skalme Park to Thos. Potts, the King's servant, for the breeding and training of hounds; but it lies in a fenny country, and the deer are so diminished and the woods so wasted that it is quite unfit for the purpose. Has accepted the keepership from the Archbp. of York, designing to replenish and restore the park.

Oct. 16. Whitehall. 49. Earl of Somerset to John Poulter, Messenger of the Chamber. Orders him to apprehend Robt. and Thos. Southby and Peter Cotten, and bring them before him. *Annexed is*,

49. I. *Roger Thorpe to the Same. He will find him at Mr. Shellitoe's office, Gray's Inn.*

Oct. 16. Bellasis. 50. Sir Wm. Waad to Lord Chief Justice Coke. Savery lives at Middleburg, but often visits Flushing, and therefore Lord Lisle or Sir John Thockmorton could easily arrest him. Saul and his wife, who heard Savery's speeches, are in London.

Oct. 16. Lambeth. 51. Archbp. Abbot to the Same. Has examined Dr. Savery on an accusation of spreading Popish books beyond seas, but has been requested to put questions to him relating to a matter now before his Lordship, and therefore refers it to him. Savery pretends to be a doctor, but is probably a conjurer.

1615. Vol. LXXXII.

Oct. 16? 52. Interrogatories to be propounded to Savery, as to whether he knows Mrs. Turner, her maid Margaret, Rich. Weston, or Foreman, the conjuror, and their practices against the Earl of Essex; and whether he did not threaten Mrs. Turner to disclose them, unless rewarded.

Oct. 16. Nottingham. 53. Commissioners for musters, co. Nottingham, to the Council. Have held the musters of the county, supplied all defects, and given orders for the training of the bands.

Oct. 16. Northampton House. Earl of Suffolk to the Officers of Customs at London. To permit Sir Thos. Edmondes, Ambassador in France, to export salt, cheese, fish, ca ndles, and butter, forhis own use. [*Dom. Corresp.*, *March* 27, 1616.]

Oct. 16. 54. Examination of Edm. Aspenall. Bought three pictures, three years before, from Weston, to be used in making figures in wax or paste. Two were bought from him by his landlord, Mr. Simcock.

Oct. 17. Tuesday morning, 4 o'clock. 55. Lord Chief Justice Coke to the King. Has traced the pictures and other bad things from Weston to Aspenall, and from him to Simcock. Sends them for the King to see, but begs their return. Indorsed "From my Lord Coke to the King, touching the puppits and carecters."

[Oct. 17.] 56, 57. Memoranda [by Coke] relating to the proposed trial of Weston and Mrs. Turner; the counsel to be employed therein; the commitment of the Earl and Countess [of Somerset, &c.], the unlawful contempt of the Earl the preceding day, &c. [*See No.* 46.] Two papers.

Oct.? 58. Opinions of the Lord Chancellor, Duke of Lenox, Lord Zouch, and Lord Chief Justice Coke, Commissioners in Overbury's cause, that the proofs against the Earl of Somerset as accessory to Overbury's murder are pregnant, and that the Seals, &c. should be taken from him, and he be committed to the Tower. Would have sent him there before the King's return to Whitehall, if he had not held the Seals.

Oct. 17. York House. 59. [Commissioners on Overbury's cause] to [the Earl of Somerset]. Having occasion to examine him on certain points, require him to keep his chamber near the Cockpit, and see none but his own servants.

Oct. 17. York House. 60. [The Same] to [the Countess of Somerset]. Require her to keep her chamber at the Blackfriars, or at Lord Knollys' house, near the Tilt-yard, seeing none but her own servants.

Oct. 17. Philip Lane. 61. Rich. Younge to [Nich. Knott], Marshal [of Dover Castle]. Lord [Zouch] has convinced Lord Wotton [Lord Lieutenant of Kent] that all the guard, even those who have land in the county, can claim exemption from musters, but wishes the guard "to carry themselves mannerly toward the deputy lieutenants." Lord Zouch is not displeased with the honours done to Lord Wotton at the castle, but they must not be a precedent for other visitors.

VOL. LXXXII.

1615.

Oct. 18. York House. 62. Commissioners in Overbury's cause to the King. Have put the Earl and Countess in restraint. Weston and Mrs. Turner are in the close custody of the Sheriffs of London. The Earl, by his own private warrant, caused a search in the house of William, son of Rich. Weston, on pretence of seeking bonds, when a trunk, box, and bag, containing papers relating to Mrs. Turner, were seized and carried away. The Earl and Countess attempted to send a cheering message to Mrs. Turner, on which account the Earl is removed to the Dean of Westminster's, under custody of Sir Oliver St. John.

[Oct. 18.] 63, 64. Two drafts of the above. Imperfect.

Oct. 18. Wednesday. 65, 66. Declaration by John Poulter that he was sent by the Countess, with a woman and a constable, under warrant from the Lord Chamberlain [Somerset], to search for any writings concerning Mrs. Hind; knows not what was in the box; read nothing but a certain letter, which the constable wanted to keep, but got it back from him. Mrs. Hind did not know what papers were meant, till she went to the Countess. Brought the box and bag to the Lord Chamberlain. Two papers.

Oct. ? 67. Assignment of Sir Lawrence Hyde, Mr. Ware, and Mr. Sterrell to be counsel to Nich. Overbury, to give in evidence upon the trial of Rich. Weston for the death of his son, Sir Thos. Overbury.

Oct. 19. Royston. 68. Warrant to Sir Edw. Coke to examine Sir David Wood, who is supposed to be able to throw light on the matters now under investigation.

Oct. 19. Royston. 69. Visct. Fenton to the Lord Chancellor. The King hopes the Commissioners will prosecute their business. When they want directions from him, they must ask for them, otherwise his silence implies approval of their doings.

Oct. 19. 70. List of writings and records, &c., belonging to Dover Castle and other places in the Cinque Ports, assigned over to Edw. Lord Zouch, Lord Warden, by John Griffith, Secretary to the late Earl of Northampton.

Oct. 19. 71. Report of the first arraignment of Rich. Weston for the murder of Sir Thos. Overbury. [*Differing from the report printed in Howell's State Trials, vol. II., p. 911.*] *Annexed are,*

71. I., II. *Two letters from the Countess of Essex to Dr. [Foreman] and Mrs. Turner, lamenting her miserable life with her husband, and the impossibility of her being happy whilst he lives, and alluding to her love for Rochester. [Produced on Mrs. Turner's trial, and printed, with slight differences, in Howell, vol. II., p. 931.]*

Oct. 19. 9 p.m. 72. The Lord Chief Justice and Judges of the King's Bench to the King. Rich. Weston was indicted at Guildhall, but, refusing to be tried, incurred the penalty for standing mute, the torments of which were laid before him. Thinks he has been persuaded to this course in hope to save the accessories, who could not thus be pro-

1615. VOL. LXXXII.

ceeded against, save by Act of Parliament. The Commission adjourned till Monday; meanwhile preachers will be sent to him to persuade him to stand trial. The examinations were publicly read, even those accusing the Earl and Countess of Somerset; also His Majesty's directions about finding out the foul fact, and his determination to have justice done, which were much applauded by the hearers. Ask directions how to proceed with Weston.

Oct. [19]. 73. Extract from the above.

Oct. 20. Royston. 74. The King to the Chief Justice and Judges of the King's Bench. Approves their proceedings against Weston. Should he continue obstinate in his refusal to stand his trial, judgment is to be pronounced against him, and to be executed. He is to be examined as to who persuades him to such a course; and also the Earl and Countess of Somerset, as to whether it is their doing, and the evil is to be pointed out to them of ruining the man's soul, as he will be his own murderer if he persist. All lawful courses to be taken to sound this foul fact to the depth.

Oct. 20. 75. Copy of the above, with corrections.

Oct. 20. 76. Fair copy of the above.

[Oct. 20.] Friday. Whitehall. 77. Duke of Lenox to Coke. Wishes to go to the King, unless his presence is required in the business before them.

Oct. 20. 78. Lord Chancellor Ellesmere to the Same. Fruitless efforts of the Bishop of London with Weston. The Duke [Lenox] is hastening to Court. *Incloses,*

78. I. *Bishop of London to the Lord Chancellor. Has failed in his endeavours to persuade Weston to take his trial. Oct. 20.*

Oct. 20. Claxton. 79. Hen. Gardy to the Same. Begs that his son may be excused serving a second year as Reader in Clifford's Inn, it being a hindrance to his practice at the bar.

Oct. 21. Royston. 80. The King to the Commissioners on Overbury's cause. Orders them to examine the Countess of Somerset, and confront Weston with her and Mrs. Turner, and with the Earl himself, if needful, before Weston's second arraignment. Asks their opinion on a paper sent him [by Thos. Lumsden], intimating that Weston, since his arraignment, recanted his examinations, on account of which he is again to be made to acknowledge them. The judges are to prorogue their session, if the time prove too short for this. The Lieutenant and Sir Thos. Monson to be examined. With postcript by the King, urging them to get at the truth of the business by all lawful means.

Oct. 21. 81. Copy of the above.

VOL. LXXXII.

1615.
Oct. 21. Westminster College. 82. Sir Oliver St. John and Dean Montaigne to the Lords Commissioners. And. Ferguson, a servant of the Lord Chamberlain, offered a bribe to one of the Dean's men, to deliver a letter to a servant of his Lordship who attends him, and receive a reply. Ask directions.

Oct. 21. 83. Lord Chief Justice Coke to Winwood. Would gladly send the examinations to His Majesty, were it but to show him how many are in his own handwriting, but they cannot possibly be spared in examining other persons.

Oct. 21. 84. Examination of Sir David Wood. Was crossed by Rochester and Overbury, because Rochester would not procure for him a suit worth 2,200*l.*, unless he might have 1,200*l.* The Countess of Essex offered him 1,000*l.* if he would revenge himself and her on Overbury. He said he would be hangman to nobody, nor go to Tyburn at a woman's word; but if Rochester would promise him, before a witness, to protect him if he were intercepted, he would be the readier for her sake to give him knocks. She said this could not be done, but he might be killed coming late home from Sir Chas. Wilmot's.

Oct. 21. Wrest. 85. Chas. Earl of Kent to the Council. The musters in Bedfordshire have been duly held, and all the points required carefully attended to, and fulfilled. The clergy's arms also mustered.

Oct. 22. 86. Lord Chief Justice and Judges of the King's Bench to the King. Any further confronting or examining of a delinquent, after his conviction, is not according to law. The statements in [Lumsden's] paper are false and malicious. Weston was not commanded silence, but urged to plead for his innocence. His refusing trial satisfies all of his guilt, and any interference with the course of law in his case would bring scandal on His Majesty's justice.

Oct. 22. 87. Draft of the above [by Coke].

Oct. 22. Serjeants' Inn. 88. The Same to the Same. Thanks for his allowance of their services. The Bp. of London cannot persuade Weston to stand his trial. The Commissioners concur in their opinion that he should not be examined again, lest it cause a reflection on the former proceedings; therefore the Earl and Countess will not be examined till after Monday, when justice will proceed, according to His Majesty's directions.

Oct. 22. 89. Commissioners for Overbury's cause to the Same. Detail the grounds on which they concur in the opinion of the Judges that it would not be well to re-examine Weston, and confront him with the other parties accused, such a proceeding being without precedent and dangerous. If he continue obstinate, he is to receive judgment of "Payne forte et dure," for standing mute.

Oct. 22. York House. 90. Coke to Winwood. Will proceed against Weston to-morrow, as his standing mute was equal to a confession; to go to Court and do nothing would be so ridiculous that he cannot do it without express commands from His Majesty.

VOL. LXXXII.

1615.

Oct. 23. Royston, 8 p.m. 91. Winwood to the Commissioners in Overbury's cause. They are to proceed according to their best judgment with Weston, who deserves no pity. To stop scandal, he should again be made to acknowledge his examinations. The King would think it Coke's masterpiece, if he could discover who persuaded him to stand mute. His Majesty requests an answer, point by point, to the slanderous paper lately sent. [*See No.* 75.]

Oct. 23. Royston. 92. The Same to the Chief Justices and Judges of the King's Bench. Similar to the above.

Oct. 23. 93. Sir Oliver St. John to the Commissioners. His charge is safe. Will intermit no care, day or night, and be as circumspect as possible about letters or messages. *Incloses,*

93. I. *Account of the behaviour of [the Earl of Somerset], and a note of those who called on him since Oct.* 20.

Oct. 24. Royston. 94. Winwood to the Same. The King, hearing that Weston has submitted to trial and received judgment, and that the sessions are postponed till Thursday, thinks Mrs. Turner will then be arraigned. Wishes her to be examined before all the Commissioners; as also the Earl and Countess, Sir Gervase Helwys, Sir Thos. Monson, and all others connected, directly or indirectly, with the business, with all possible expedition.

Oct. 24. 95. [The Same] to the Bp. of Durham. To restrain the servants of the Earl of Somerset from felling and selling the woods and lands of Brancepeth and other parks within his diocese.

Oct. 24. Serjeants' Inn. 96. Lord Chief Justice and Judges of the King's Bench to the King. Weston, after resisting the persuasions of the Bishops of London and Ely, at last told the Sheriff that he would stand his trial, but hoped they would not make a net to catch the little fishes, and let the great go. At his trial, he confessed his examinations, and that he was leniently dealt with and patiently heard. The verdict was unanimous, and judgment was awarded; meanwhile special care is to be taken of his soul. The King's justice much commended by the multitudes present.

Oct. 24. 97. Commissioners in Overbury's cause to Winwood. Desire His Majesty's warrant to commit the provisional custody of the Tower to Sir John Keys. Send a packet, forwarded by Sir Oliver St. John, addressed to Somerset.

Oct. 24. 98. Declaration of Wm. Piers and others, that Weston declared he had revealed all he knew to Lord Coke, that all he had confessed was true, and that if he should recollect anything further before his death, he would reveal it.

Oct. 24. Lambeth. 99. Archbp. Abbot to the Bp. of Ely. Desires that Commissioners should be sent to re-examine the priests now in Wisbeach, who pre-

1615. VOL. LXXXII.

viously declined answering, and to note any explanations or alterations of those who answered undutifully. *Incloses,*

99. I. *Interrogatories administered to the priests [at their former examinations in Newgate and the Gatehouse] on the respective powers of the King and Parliament, of temporal Judges, the Pope, Council, &c., and on the legality of the Oath of Allegiance.*

99. II—XXVI. *Answers to the above interrogatories, given separately by Thos. Thomson, Rich. Cowper, Wm. Harbert, Edw. Smith, Hum. Peto, John Chamberlaine, Wm. Davies, Peter Symonds, Rich. Kellett, Rich. Davies, Rich. Dyer, Stephen Smith, Fras. Kemp, Fras. Greene, Robt. Tuke, Gervase Poole, Alex. Fairecloth, Thos. Browne, Thos. Keighley, Martin Harrington, Thos. Blunt, John Richardson, Edm. Cannon, Geo. Muskett, and John Ainsworth. March* 20—30, 1615. *Twenty-five papers.*

Oct. ? 100. List of the priests sent to Wisbeach.

[Oct. 24.] Royston. 101. Dr. A. Savery to Coke. His threats to Mrs. Turner meant, that if she would not give him the reward she promised, for trying to induce Sir Art. Mainwaring to marry her, he would betray her dealings to Sir Arthur, and accuse her before the Arches' Court for loose conduct. Begs that his wife may have access to him.

Oct. 25. Royston. 102. The King to the Commissioners in Overbury's cause. Authorizes them to commit the custody of the Tower to Sir John Keys provisionally, till some other is resolved on. Helwys, Sir T. Monson, and the Earl and Countess to be examined with all speed.

Oct. 25. York House. 103. Commissioners in Overbury's cause to Winwood. To send up as soon as possible Sir Thos. Monson and Thos. Lumsdale [Lumsden] now attending at Court.

Oct. 25. 104. The Lord Chancellor to Coke. Has just received a letter from His Majesty to the Commissioners. They must meet early to-morrow, as Mr. Secretary waits at Court for their answer.

Oct. 26. 105. Examination of Dr. Thos. Campion. Received 1,400*l.* from Alderman Helwys, on behalf of Sir Gervase Helwys, for the use of Sir Thos. Monson, the Midsummer after Sir Gervase became Lieutenant of the Tower. Knows not for what consideration it was paid.

Oct. 26. Royston. 106. Sir R. W[inwood] to the Lord Chancellor. Sir Thos. Monson is not in Court, and Lumsden is gone to London, and must be inquired after.

Oct. 26. York House. 107. Commissioners in Overbury's cause to Winwood. Have examined the Earl of Somerset, Mrs. Turner, and Sir G. Helwys, whom they have sequestered from office, and given in charge to Alderman Swinnerton. The Countess is with Sir Wm. and Lady Smithe.

VOL. LXXXII.

1615.

Oct. 26. 108. Examination of Edw. Sackville. Was present at Tyburn when Weston was executed, and asked him to confess his crime with his dying breath, since that would satisfy all.

Oct. 26. 109. Examination of Sir John Lidcott. Was present at Tyburn with Sir John Hollis, Sir John Wentworth, and many other Knights. Asked Weston whether he had poisoned Overbury. He replied that he had left his mind with the Lord Chief Justice. Asked him nothing further, though urged to do so.

Oct. ? 110. Petition of the Same to the Commissioners on Overbury's cause, for liberty. The motive of his questioning Weston was not that he had any doubt, but because he thought that by a public confession, others would be satisfied. His continuance in prison would injure his reputation.

Oct. 26. Royston. 111. The King to the Archbp. of Canterbury and others. To examine Sir Robt. Cotton on a charge of communicating secrets of State to the Spanish Ambassador; if it be true, to seize his papers and books, and cause them to be brought into the Paper Chamber at Whitehall, and to proceed against him as his offences deserve.

Oct. 26. Royston. 112. The Same to the Same. To examine into an unmannerly and seditious message sent to His Majesty by Sir Thos. Howard.

Oct. 26. 113. Commissioners of Musters for Middlesex to the Council. Have held the musters, but found the arms so bad that they ordered men of ability to provide new ones and to wear them themselves; 1,000 foot are thus supplied, but the horse are backward. The Mint men, Trinity House men, ship carpenters, and Thames watermen pretend exemption from the service. The Bishop of London has sent the certificate of the clergy.

Oct. 26. 114. Lease from Jeffry Davids to Fras. Osbaldeston, both of London, of a messuage in Smithfield, known by the sign of the Catherine Wheel.

Oct. 26. Royston. Proclamation prohibiting the sale or export of tin, on pain of confiscation, unless it be first assayed and stamped, according to the ordinances of the Stannaries. Printed. [*Proc. Coll., No.* 47.]

Oct. 26. Royston. Proclamation establishing the continuance of His Majesty's farthing tokens, and prohibiting the use of all other tokens. Printed. [*Ibid., No.* 48.]

Oct. 27. 115. The Lord Chancellor to Coke. Has received two letters from Sir W. Smithe, which cannot be answered till they meet. *Incloses,*

115. I. *Sir Wm. Smithe to the Commissioners in Overbury's cause. Has taken the Countess of Somerset in charge. The Cockpit is unfit for her, there being many doors and few keys. She intends to go to Lord Aubigny's house*

1615. Vol. LXXXII.

in Blackfriars. Desires he may first inspect the place and appoint her apartment. She wishes to diet his family. She will have six women servants and several men to attend her. Has refused Hen. Howard, who wished to see her. Cockpit, Oct. 27.

115. II. *Sir Wm. Smithe to the Commissioners in Overbury's cause. Thinks Lady Somerset's list of attendants too large: she has no means to maintain them. Walter James has gone to borrow* 10*l. of the Lord Treasurer or Lady Knollys, to buy wood, &c. for the Blackfriars, but may be arrested on account of debts for which he stands bound for the Earl. The Cockpit is so solitary that watch has to be kept all night. Has refused her Ladyship's offer to find food for his family, considering her wants. Asks whether he may grant her request to send some one to know how her lord does. Cockpit, Oct.* 27.

Oct. 27. Friday Evening. 116. The Lord Chancellor to Coke. The Countess of Somerset has removed to Blackfriars, so their meeting at Whitehall is frustrated. Desires to see him to-morrow morning, and will summon the other Commissioners.

Oct. 28. 117. Examination of Thos. Burke. Was bribed to convey a message and money from the Countess of Somerset to Mrs. Turner, and to get to know whether Mrs. Turner had been examined, and what confession she had made.

Oct. 29. 118. Examination of Dr. Fras. Anthony. He and his wife have twice sold aurum potabile to a servant of Overbury, while he was in the Tower, as an antidote for poison.

Oct. 29. Bishop's Auckland. 119. Bishop of Durham to Sir R. Winwood. The order for restraining the Earl of Somerset's followers from disparking and selling woods and lands at Brancepeth will give more delight in that country than anything since the King's accession.

Oct. 30. Theobalds. 120. Sir R. Winwood to the Commissioners in Overbury's cause. To attend His Majesty at Whitehall, at three o'clock to-morrow.

Oct. 30. Dover Castle. 121. Nich. Knott to Rich. Younge. The country watch will meet to express their thanks [for exemption from musters]. Asks whether certain pieces of ordnance are to be fired in honour of the King's holiday, Nov. 5, as has been usually done. Only seven out of the sixteen gunners are to be seen.

Oct. 31. 122. Sir Wm. Waad to Coke. The wife of Langton, a warder in the Tower, having taken some broth left by Overbury, was made very ill. Overbury had wished to have a servant of Waad to provide his diet.

Oct. 31. Warrant to pay 20*l.* per ann. to Edw. Darcy, Groom of the Privy Chamber, for wages. [*Warrt. Bk., vol.* I., *p.* 62. *This is clearly dated* 1595, *but the mention of King James shows that the date is false.*]

VOL. LXXXII.

1615.

Oct. Holborn. 123. Lord Chief Justice Coke to [Sir John Keys]. Warrant to receive Sir Thos. Monson into custody, and to allow no one to have access to him.

Oct. ? 124. Request to Lord [Coke] to question Franklin on what became of the Earl and Countess of Essex's wedding ring, and Savery on his predictions of troubles and alterations in Court. With notes [by Coke] of remarks [to be made to Franklin]. Also indorsed with queries [by the Same] relating to a banquet given at Highgate by a Papist to the late Prince, the May-day before his death.

Oct. 125. Estimate of moneys due to Sir Thos. Edmondes for diet and intelligence, as Ambassador to France, and for the Secretaryship of the French tongue. Balance still unpaid 2,226*l.* 6*s.* 8*d.*

Oct. 126. Reports made by English mariners, and repeated by the Captain of Pendennis Castle, Falmouth, of the departure from Lisbon, in September, of a Spanish war fleet of twenty-seven vessels; and report by the Mayor of Dover of the arrival of three of them in the roads, and of their hiring pilots to conduct them to Dunkirk.

Oct. ? 127. Petition of Sir Valentine Brown to Coke, to know how to secure the settlement on himself of an annuity of 200*l.* due to him from his uncle Sir Thos. Monson, who is now called in question.

Oct. ? 128. Note [by Coke] that Sir Art. Mainwa[rin]g, the Prince's carver, lay at Mrs. Turner's house when the Prince sickened.

Oct. 129. Statement of the dangerous state of decay of Deal Castle; the sea-wall is eaten away, the lantern decayed, &c. If no present remedy be applied, the charge will be much greater. With list of munition and other stores required for supply of the castle.

Oct. 130. List of reparations necessary to be done at Walmer Castle.

VOL. LXXXIII. NOVEMBER, 1615.

Nov. 1. 1. Sir R. Winwood to Coke. Has examined the bearer who was sent by the Earl of Essex, but sends him for further questioning. *Incloses,*

1. I. *Statement by Fras. Halliday, of St. Mark's, that he was told that Franklin had received* 100 *Jacobuses for compassing the marriage between the Earl and Countess of Somerset; that he says he can raise a devil, &c. Cath. Pasley was employed between Franklin and the Countess and Mrs. Turner.*

VOL. LXXXIII.

1615.

Nov. 1. Westminster. Grant to Sarah Fairfax, of Norwich, of pardon for stealing ten pairs of stockings, she being only fifteen, and this her first offence. Latin. [*Sign Man., vol.* V., *No.* 66.]

Nov 2. Grant to Jas. Barker of the captaincy of the bulwarks at Dover, for life. [*Grant Bk., p.* 154.]

Nov. 2. Dover Castle. 2. Nich. Knott to Rich. Younge. The watchmen who formerly watched in the gunners' places are entitled to part of their yearly pay, which is therefore not to be paid in full to the present gunners.

Nov. 2. 3. Examination of Edw. Norman. Was told by Jeffry Platt, waterman, that a gentleman came to him at the Blackfriars ferry, and bade him tap at a certain window of the Countess of Somerset's house, and deliver letters to her man, saying they were from the King and Council, which he did.

Nov. 2. 4. Examination of Jeffry Platt, to the same effect as the above. No money was given him for his pains.

Nov. 3. 5. Sir R. Winwood to the Commissioners in Overbury's cause. The King wishes them to consider the petition of Walter James, and to allow him to speak with the Earl of Somerset on his domestic affairs, in presence of the Lieutenant of the Tower. *Incloses,*

5. I. *Petition of Walter James, servant of the Earl of Somerset, to the King, for protection against his master's creditors, having borrowed large sums for his master in his own name. Also for leave to receive the revenues of the Earl's estate, and discharge his debts therefrom.*

Nov. ? 6. Petition of Walter James to Chief Justice Coke, to the same effect as the preceding.

Nov. 3. Grant to Sir Lionel Cranfield of the office of Surveyor of Customs and other things belonging thereto, for life. [*Grant Bk., p.* 158.]

Nov. 4. 7. Earl of Pembroke to the Council. Has completed the musters of Cornwall, including also those of the tinners, being both Lieutenant of the county and Warden of the Stannaries. The County desire, as before, to be excused the horse.

Nov. 5. Chester. 8. Earl of Derby to the Same. Returns the certificates of his Deputy Lieutenants, of the musters of Cheshire and Lancashire.

Nov. 6. 9. Examination of Sir Dud. Diggs. On expressing to Sir Hen. Neville his fear that Rochester was desirous to be rid of Overbury, both he and Sir Thos. Mansell told him, from Overbury's own mouth, that he was confident Rochester would not dare to abandon him.

Nov. 6. Streatham. 10. Talbot Bowes to the Bp. of Durham. Has sent to Mr. Nun, but he delays and hesitates about waiting on his Lordship, as directed.

VOL. LXXXIII.

1615.

Nov. 7. Bletsoe. 11. Oliver Lord St. John to the Council. Transmits a certificate of the musters in Huntingdonshire. Eight days were spent in training. The foot are complete, but the horse cannot be made so, on account of the death, removal, or decay of many of those who before provided them. The county decayed by removals and inundations of the fen lands.

Nov. 7. Order of the delegates of the University of Oxford, for building the new school and imposing certain fees upon admission; to be applied towards the expense of that building and in payment of the debt due to Sir Thos. Bodley's chest. [*Dom. Corresp., Nov.* 13, 1626.]

Nov. 9. 12. Examination of Edw. Ryder. Early in October, saw Dr. Lobell, who spoke hardly against those who tried to prove that Overbury was poisoned, declared that he died of consumption, caused by melancholy, and that the glister, prepared by his son, was made by order of Dr. Mayerne, who was the only physician in England worth anything. Saw Lobell a week later, and told him it was now manifest that he was poisoned by an apothecary's boy in Lime Street. Madame Lobell explained to her husband, "That must be William, whom you sent into France;" on which he trembled violently, and said, that as William was leaving his master, he gave him a letter of recommendation to Paris.

Nov. 9. London. 13. Edw. Reynoldes to Fras. Mills. The month is barren, owing to the imprisonment of the Seal with [the Earl of Somerset]. It is now in the King's hands, which hinders business. Course to be adopted about payments of fees to the next Lord Privy Seal. New year's gifts to be diminished, because of the lessening of the profits.

[Nov. 9.] 14. Certificate by the Chief Justice and Judges of the King's Bench and other Justices of the Peace, that Rich. Weston was arraigned for the poisoning of Sir Thos. Overbury on Oct. 29, 1615; was tried, found guilty, and condemned to execution, on the 23d. Latin. *Annexed is,*

14. I. *Writ of certiorari, addressed to the above, commanding them to make the above return. Westminster, Nov.* 9, *Latin.* [*Both these documents contain minute details of the process of poisoning, from May* 9 *to Sept.* 15, 1613, *the date of Overbury's death.*]

[Nov. 10 15. Speech of Sir Fras. Bacon in the Star Chamber, in propounding the charge against Sir John Wentworth and Sir John Hollis for questioning Weston on the scaffold as to his guilt, and intimating some doubts thereof; and against Mr. Lumsden, for sending to the King a false and perverted account of Weston's arraignment.

Nov. 10? 16. Notes [by Coke] relative to the above cases, their aggravations and the penalties to be inflicted, mentioning Sir Thos. Vavasour and Hen. Vane as implicated.

VOL. LXXXIII.

1615.

Nov. 10. Royston. 17. Jas. Lord Hay to Coke. The King desires Mrs. Turner's execution to be respited till Monday or Tuesday, and that divines may have access to her, and try to draw her to confess. Priests might be secretly admitted, if thought fit.

Nov. 10. Newhall. 18. Earl of Sussex to the Council. The musters have been held in Essex; the foot are not much amiss, but hardly two thirds of the horse appear; sends the names of those who refuse. The clergy arms have been viewed by order of the Bishop of London.

Nov. 10. 19. Memorandum of the conference between Dr. John Whiting and Mrs. Turner. After many exhortations, she confessed that she knew beforehand of the poisoning of Sir Thos. Overbury, but concealed it for the sake of the Countess of Somerset, whom she loved as her own soul. She was much afflicted, and wished Weston had poisoned her, as he did the other. The Doctor consoled her, and she consented to receive the Communion the next day, though, being a Catholic, she had never before received it after the form of the Church of England.

Nov. 10. 20. Draft or rough copy of the above [by Coke].

Nov. 11. 21. Conference between Dr. Whiting and Mrs. Turner. After taking the Communion, she thanked God for the comfort she received. Called Franklin a villain, and Sir Thos. Monson proud and odious. Wished the Lieutenant of the Tower had never come there. The Earl of Northampton possibly was in the plot, for all Somerset's letters to the Countess came in his packets. Heard that the late Prince was poisoned at Woodstock, with a bunch of grapes. Weston told her he was poisoning Overbury. The Countess intends not to be hanged, but to die in child-bed. Exclaimed against the Court, and wished the King better servants, there being nothing among them "but mallice, pride, whoredom, swearing, and reioising in the fall of others;" wonders the earth does not open to swallow up so wicked a place. Lord Knollys is the only religious man.

Nov. 11. 22. John Hall to the King. Details speeches by Sir John Leedes and his wife, that the King was unwieldy and could not unlock a door, but might leap out of a window, as his father did, when the people got hold of him and threatened to hang him. Lady Leedes said she would speak treason, because the King declared that most women were atheists or Papists.

[Nov. 11.] 23. Report by Jerome Hawley of the above conversation.

Nov. 11. 24. John Cusack to Sir Ralph Winwood. Wishes to see him, to reveal a secret of great moment to the King, the discovery of which endangers the life of the revealer. Asks aid in his suits. Sir Hum. May can make any suit or suitor, be they ever so honest, disliked by the King. Begs him to write to some stationer, to lend him such works as he requires, for finishing a treatise to be presented to the King, as the first fruits of twenty years' study in the best universities of Christendom. It defends the royal prerogative,

1615. Vol. LXXXIII.

and maintains the Oath of Allegiance, from Scripture. Wishes to show the King how to prevent corruption in inferior judges, by which Ireland is ruined.

Nov. 11. Whitehall. 25. Warrant to the Constable of Wisbeach Castle, to deliver Fras. Kemp, Gervase Poole, Edw. Smith, Thos. Blunt, and Thos. Browne, priests, to Mons. de Boischot, the Archduke's Ambassador, or his Messenger, they being liberated, at his request, to be conveyed out of England. *Annexed is,*

25. I. *Order of Ferdinand de Boischot authorizing Peter Van den Velde to receive the five priests granted him from Wisbeach Castle. London, Nov. 11. French.—With note by P. Van den Velde, that he has received the said priests. Wisbeach, Nov. 15. Latin.*

Nov. 12. 26. Hen. Sanderson to Winwood, Shameful havoc of the deer at Brancepeth Park, by Emerson's servants and others, at direction of Sir John Claxton. They have made Mr. Calverly Deputy Lieutenant of the county, to serve their turn. *Incloses,*

26. I. *Sam. Sanderson to Hen. Sanderson. Harsh proceedings of Emerson on behalf of the Earl of Somerset, in claiming and selling lands, hunting deer, &c., since his [H. Sanderson's] departure. Brancepeth Castle, Oct. 26, 1615.*

26. II. *The Same to the Same. Harsh conduct of the servants of the Earl of Somerset to the tenants at Brancepeth. On the announcement by the Bishop of Durham that the further spoil of the woods was forbidden, the joy of all was exceedingly great; bells were rung, bonfires blazed, and drummers went up and down, the people shouting God save the King and the Prince; they will do anything to be the Prince's tenants again. Brancepeth Castle, Oct. 31, 1615.*

[Nov.] [Newmarket.] 27. [Sir Ralph Winwood?] to Hen. or Sam. Sanderson. To cause the wood lying at Brancepeth Castle Gate, or elsewhere, to be brought into the castle, inventoried, and laid up till further directions, and to have special care of the woods and game; the King having forbidden the Earl of Somerset's servants to meddle any further.

Nov. 28. Copy of the above.

Nov. 13. Dover Castle. 29. Nich. Knott to Lord Zouch. Begs his interest in reclaiming a debt due to him from Robt. Hobday, Gunner, who is dead, also to be remembered in the disposal of places in the castle.

Nov. 13. 30. The Guards of [Dover] Castle to the Same. Thanks for his influence with Lord Wotton in freeing them from serving in the musters of the county.

Nov. 14. 31. Statement by Sir John Leedes of the conversation at his house. Hearing that the Earl of Somerset and Sir Thos. Monson had tried to get out of their windows, Lady Leedes said she thought

VOL. LXXXIII.

1615.

they would be served like the King of Scots, who, fearing to be blown up with gunpowder, got out of the window, and was taken and hanged on a pear-tree. Mr. Hall told him he was surprised to hear Lady Leedes speak so freely. Has remonstrated with his wife, and she promises not to be so free with her tongue. *Annexed is,*

31. I. *Note by John, son of Sir John Leedes, that, talking to his father since his coming to Court about the King's hard riding, he said he was unwieldy. Thinks he heard the remark about unlocking the door from Patrick Maull.* [*See Nov.* 11.]

Nov. 14. Tyburn. 32. Statement of Mrs. Turner's conduct at her execution. She confessed the justness of her death, bewailed her many sins, prayed for the Royal Family, &c., and also for her poor lady; commended herself to Christ, and professed that she died in the faith of the Church of England.

Nov. 14. 33. Another account of Mrs. Turner's execution. Being urged by Dr. Whiting to say something, she declared herself a Protestant, and penitent; that she had been in the hands of the Devil, but was redeemed from him. Asked if she might pray for the Countess, as she wished to do so while she had breath.

Nov. 14? 34. [Lord Chief Justice Coke] to [the King]. The report that Mrs. Turner was buried with Christian solemnities is false; but, on account of her penitent death, she was laid in St. Martin's Churchyard. The King's justice generally applauded. The discovery of the Powder Poison, as of the Powder Treason, a sign of God's favour towards His Majesty. [*Rough notes for a letter.*]

Nov. 15. 35. [Sir Ralph Winwood?] to [Isaac] Wake. Sir Thos. Overbury being poisoned in the Tower, the King's love of justice led him to have the matter searched, though it might implicate some about him. The Duke [of Lenox], Lord Chancellor, Lord Zouch, and Lord Chief Justice were made Commissioners. The Earl of Somerset and his Lady involved. He was first committed to the Dean of Westminster, but afterwards sent close prisoner to the Tower; she placed in charge of Sir Wm. Smithe in the Blackfriars. Weston, Overbury's keeper, and Mrs. Turner, the Countess's woman, are executed. Sir Gervase Helwys, Lieutenant of the Tower, displaced, and will probably die for it. Sir Thos. Monson committed, for recommending Weston to his place.

Nov. 16. Office of the Revels. 36. Sir Geo. Buck to Sir Thos. Stodder. Has not credit enough with the Lord Admiral to forward the suit of Stodder, who has injured it by sending through him papers offensive to the King. Does not wish to be reconciled to his brother, whilst he follows a wayward course and hateful to the State.

Nov. 16. 37. Suggestions by Hen. Sanderson for the good of Northumberland and the Bishopric of Durham, viz.:—Suppression of recusancy; appointment of another Lieutenant in Somerset's place, who may train the people to arms; orders for preservation of the woods

1615. Vol. LXXXIII.

for the tenants to pay no further rents for Somerset's use; and for strict accounts to be demanded from Thos. Emerson for the sums he has already received. Emerson boasts that he could give a person poison which should not kill him for two years.

[Nov. 16.] 38. Deposition of Jas. Franklin. Was employed by Mrs. Turner to buy poisons. Details the kinds used, and the modes of administering them. Sir Gervase Helwys knew it; has seen letters of his relating to it. All Overbury's food was poisoned, and Lady Somerset said her reason was that he pryed too far into matters of State, and would put her party down. Has received 120*l.*, and was to have 200*l.* per ann. The Countess thought he had induced Rochester to love her. Has had 200 letters from her about it. She was enough to bewitch any man.

[Nov. 16.] 39. Abstract of the above.

Nov. 16? 40. Notes [by Coke] on the aggravations of the Powder Poison, as committed upon a prisoner, and one therefore in the custody of the Crown. Thanks to God for its discovery, as a blessing to the King, Court, and State. Weston and Mrs. Turner both confessed themselves privy to the poisoning. [*Indorsed with notes of presumptions of the complicity of the Lieutenant of the Tower.*]

[Nov. 16.] 41. Digest of the principal points in the evidence against the Lieutenant of the Tower. With numerous annotations, &c. [by Coke].

Nov. 17. Newmarket. 42. The King to Coke. Wishes him to use all possible means that Sir Gervase Helwys may still further reveal his knowledge. His execution to be respited on this account, and to leave him time to arrange his worldly affairs. His estate, out of pity, is to be granted to his wife and many children. Wishes, if precedent permit, that he should be executed in a less infamous place than Tyburn, having been Lieutenant of the Tower.

Nov. 17. 43. Memorandum by Sir Wm. Smithe of a speech of the Countess of Somerset relative to her wish to destroy herself.

Nov. 18. Newmarket. 44. The King to Coke. Wishes him to appoint a time for hearing the great cause of "*Rege inconsulto*" calmly reasoned, lest injury arise to the prerogative by its being handled in haste.

Nov. 18. 45. Sir Geo. More to the Same. The Commissioners on Overbury's cause are to meet the next day, to hear something from the Earl of Somerset, and to write to the King thereon.

Nov. 18? 46. Thos. Packwood, merchant tailor of London, to [the Same?]. John Ferris, cook to the late Prince, and afterwards preferred by Somerset to the Queen, refused to go out with Rich. Keymer, yeoman of the counting-house to the Prince, because he was making jellies for Overbury.

Nov. 18. 47. Rich. Keymer to [the Same]. What he told Packwood was, that Ferris, Master Cook to Prince Henry, had made jellies for the Earl of Somerset.

Vol. LXXXIII.

1615.

Nov. 18. 48. Sir Gervase Helwys to [Coke]. Remembers one thing more, viz., that, after Overbury's death, Lord Northampton wrote to him to send for Sir John Lidcott to see his body, in order to "satisfy that damned crew who would be ready to speak the worst," and then to bury him shortly.

Nov. 18. 49. Relation by Coke, that on Helwys' trial he was surprised when a letter was quoted from himself to the Countess, about the difficulty of destroying the scab; he confessed afterwards to Dr. Whiting that it was agreed between himself, the Countess, the Earl of Northampton, and Sir Thos. Monson, that the scab should mean Overbury. He said he suffered justly, for allowing worldly respects to lead him to conceal the plot, and for obtaining writings, &c. from Overbury, at instigation of the Countess and Earl of Northampton. He denied his guilt at the bar, because he had never any intention to murder him himself, nor any hand in it, but only failed to reveal the plots of others. With sundry observations on his conduct before and at his trial, &c.

Nov. 18. 50. Copy of the above relation, with additions.

Nov. 20. 51. Another copy of the relation, with particulars of Helwys' execution on Tower Hill, his penitence the preceding evening, and his speech on the scaffold, regretting his denial of his guilt at his trial; he prayed for those, some of whom were in the Tower, that shared the bloody deed, and exhorted the bystanders to avoid gaming, which was one means of his ruin, and to live godly and virtuous lives.

Nov. 20. 52. List of the Officers and Gunners of Dover Castle, with their wages.

Nov. 21. Whitehall. Earl of Suffolk to Rich. Gyles, waiter for prohibited woods. To permit Marmaduke Peckett, merchant of London, to transport a ton of logwood consigned to him by mistake, and seized for the King as prohibited wood, on his bond to bring in no more false dyeing woods. [*Dom. Corresp., March* 27, 1616.]

Nov. 22. Bletsoe. 53. Oliver Lord St. John to Coke. Has heard a report that the Countess of Somerset counterfeited being with child, that she might invite the King, Queen, and Prince to the christening, and poison them.

Nov. 22. Newmarket. 54. [Sir R. Winwood] to the Lord Chancellor. The King has pricked Rich. Floyd, of Marington, as Sheriff for Montgomeryshire, in lieu of Sir John Hayward, who is unfit, from not having lands in the county.

Nov. 22. 55. Statement [by Sir Geo. More] that the Earl of Somerset twice requested an interview with Lord Knollys and Lord Hay, that he might send by them a message of consequence to His Majesty; that the Commissioners in Overbury's cause refused this, but offered to attend on him themselves, as being appointed to examine his cause, but he declined the offer. He requested payment of his rents, which are detained from him.

VOL. LXXXIII.

1615.
Nov. 23. 56. Commissioners in Overbury's cause to the King. Detail the preceding request of Somerset, and their refusal. Will have to examine him shortly, and will press him to tell what he wishes to communicate. In answer to his request for pen, ink, and paper, to write something about his private affairs, they told him the Lieutenant of the Tower should write for him, which he refused.

[Nov. 23.] 57. Draft of the above [by Coke].

Nov. 23? [Newgate.] Thursday. 58. Thos. Deane to Sir Thos. Vavasour. Desires him to send his servant Birt, to be made acquainted with an evil deed against his worship. *Annexed is,*

58. I. *Certificate by Thos Abent, who received the above letter, that these were the contents, to the best of his memory. Nov.* 23.

Nov. 24. 59. Hen. Sanderson to Winwood. Has received orders to take care of Chopwell, as well as Brancepeth Wood. Emerson's plot is not the first devised against him. *Incloses,*

59. I. *Earl of Shrewsbury to the Same. Details the faithful services of Hen. Sanderson, Constable of Brancepeth Castle, especially in preserving the woods and game there, sometimes at his own expense. He has many enemies, and would have been ruined, had Emerson's commission lasted. Would be glad for him to receive some reward. Nov.* 20.

Nov. 24. Westminster. Grant to the Bishop of Lincoln of the patronage of the rectory of Wappenham, co. Northampton, long belonging to that bishopric, but lately claimed for the King. Latin. [*Sign Man., vol.* V., *No.* 67.]

Nov. 25. 60. Statement by John Arderne, that Mrs. Saul, who keeps a confectioner's shop in Holborn, sent for him to say that she was likely to be questioned respecting the banquet which she served, on May-day before the Prince's death. With note [by Coke] of its receipt, Nov. 28.

Nov. 25. 61. [Sir Ralph Winwood] to [the Commissioners in Overbury's cause]. The King wishes Jerome, son of Jas. Hawley, now close prisoner in the Gatehouse, to be released, on condition of his not going further away than his father's house at Brentford.

Nov. 25. Hatfield. Broad Oak. 62. Sir Fras. Barington to Lord Zouch. Recommends the bearer, formerly a Deputy Gunner at Dover, to a vacant Gunner's place there.

Nov. 26. Newmarket. 63. Sir R. Winwood to Coke. The King wishes only such women to be placed about the Countess of Somerset, at her delivery, as will be answerable that she does not miscarry, either by her own wilfulness, or by the malice of any other.

Nov. 26. Newmarket. 64. [The Same] to the Commissioners on Overbury's cause. If the message which Somerset wishes to send to the King relates to the cause in hand, he is to tell it to them. If not, the King is to be

1615. Vol. LXXXIII.

acquainted therewith. The Lord Treasurer is ordered to take charge of the Earl's goods and moveables.

Nov. 26? 65. [Lord Chancellor Ellesmere and Lord Coke, two of the Commissioners for Overbury's cause,] to the King. The Earl of Somerset's answer is, that the message which he desired to send by Lords Knollys and Hay does not concern the criminal part of the business.

Nov. 26? 66. Notes [by Coke] relative to the procuring poisons, trying them on a cat, &c.; and the Earl of Somerset's knowledge thereof. [*Seemingly for Franklin's examination*].

Nov. 26? 67. Notes [by the Same] of sundry points of evidence [against Franklin?], preceded by [earlier] notes of the places, &c. of trial of the principal and accessories in the plot.

Nov. 27. Whitehall. 68. The Council to the King. Have considered the propriety of calling a Parliament to relieve his pressing necessities, but fear it will take too much time. Do not like to decide upon it except at a full meeting of the board. Request the King to appoint a day when the Councillors with him can meet those in London, to discuss the point.

Nov. [27]. Westminster. Grant to the bakers of Bristol of incorporation, with proviso of revocation, if just cause be shown by the mayor and commonalty of Bristol. [*Sign Man., vol.* V., *No.* 68.]

Nov. 27. 69. Copy of the above.

Nov. 27. 70. Substance of Franklin's arraignment. His examinations read, confessing the purchase of poisons from him by Mrs. Turner, who tried their effect on a cat. The Countess showed him a letter from Rochester, saying he wondered the business was not despatched, and he thinks it meant Overbury's murder. On Weston's apprehension, she sent for him, and urged him to confess nothing. Weston said that, the Countess's turn being served, they would both be poisoned. He was found guilty by the jury.

Nov. 27? 71. Notes [by Coke] on the office of Attorney General. Indorsed are notes relating to the design to poison Weston and Franklin, had not Weston been apprehended.

Nov. 27? 72. Notes [by the Same] on the share of Sir Thos. Monson in the Powder Poison. The three first offenders, though at first denying it obstinately at their trials, were afterwards brought to confession, but this man [Franklin] confessed freely. [*Indorsed with many notes, some containing presumptions against the Earl of Somerset.*]

Nov. 27. Serjeants' Inn. 73. Lord Chief Justice Coke to the King. Conviction of Franklin. He and others have discovered sufficient matter against the Earl of Somerset. Particulars of the poisons provided by Franklin. On Weston's arrest, the Countess sent for Franklin, and urged him not to confess, but to say he had never seen her, and only came to Mrs. Turner about physic. He confessed he had a spirit at his command.

VOL. LXXXIII.

1615.

Nov. 28. 74. Relation by Dr. Whiting of his conversation with Franklin. He said that the Lord Treasurer was in the plot; that the Countess of Somerset was the most impudent woman that ever lived; that there were greater persons in it than yet known, and more to be poisoned and murdered; that he was to have had 500*l.* to be employed to the Palgrave and Lady Elizabeth; that Somerset never loved the Prince nor Lady Elizabeth; that there lies a long tale about an outlandish apothecary placed with the late Prince; that Lady Somerset got money from the old lady [her mother], &c. [Written by Coke], with notes that Lobell should be questioned how he meant to become apothecary to Prince Charles, and Franklin whether he was ever wished to work against the Queen.

Nov. 28. 75. Copy of the above relation.

Nov. 28. 76. Testimony of Rich. Adams and Thos. Peade, Nov. 24, that Mrs. Brittain said Mrs. Callcot had offered her 5*l.* to have the providing of half the Countess of Somerset's christening banquet, and that Mrs. Saul was the woman who served the banquet when the Prince was poisoned; which speech was denied by Mrs. Brittain, Nov. 28.

Nov. 28. 77. Examination of Susan, wife of Edwin Saul, confectioner, of High Holborn. Three years before, a banquet was sent for from her shop, by Lord Arundel's man, for the Princes, on May-day 1612, when they went a-maying to Highgate. It was of dried and candied fruits. Biscuit bread was used, which was not served by her.

Nov? 78. Bill and answer, with proofs on both sides, and answers to proofs, in the cause of the Attorney General v. Sir Chas. Cavendish, as to the right contested between him and the Crown, to certain lands in Sherwood Forest, Roome Wood, Burnt Hastings, Kirkby, Tyngo, and Edenstowe assarts, &c. [*See May* 20, *and Sept., No.* 122.]

Nov.? 79. Duplicate of the above.

Nov.? 80. Plan of Sir Chas. Cavendish's estate in Nottinghamshire, comprehending the village or town of Carburton, Roome Wood, Burnt-Hastings, Hurst Field, and Welbeck Abbey.

Nov.? 81. Plan of Kirkby Plot, marking out the lands possessed therein by Sir Chas. Cavendish.

Nov.? 82. Plan of Tyngo and Edenstowe, assart lands, similarly marked.

Nov. 28. 83. Writ of ejectment, directing Sir Chas. Cavendish to deliver up certain lands in Sherwood Forest to Otho Nicholson.

Nov. 29. 84. Franklin's relation of a plot against Mrs. Chattock, devised by Mrs. Parselewe, Mrs. West, and Old Nan of Wapping, witches. Indorsed with notes concerning the commitment of Mrs. Brittain.

VOL. LXXXIII.

1615.
Nov. 29? 85. [Lord Chief Justice Coke] to the King. Thanks for his personal directions. Sir Thos. Monson's trial deferred, that he may be a witness against the Countess. Franklin is only respited to give further light. The newly-discovered villanies touch not the King nor Prince that now is, but some persons near to his Majesty.

Nov. 30. 86. Lease by Mary, widow of Wm. Ferrand, of Mitcham, Surrey, demising to Dr. Hen. Kirkman, of Northampton, and John Pope, of London, Advocates of the Court of Arches, certain chambers and rooms in the parish of St. Bennett's, Paul's Wharf.

Nov. 30? 87. Bill of charges by Hen. Halfheid, Keeper of the King's Game at Royston, with note of request for payment.

Nov. Westminster. Grant to Wm. and Edw. Hodgson of pardon for manslaughter of Fras. Lund, all of Dent, Yorkshire. Latin. [*Sign Man., vol.* V., *No.* 69.]

Nov. 88. List of records and writings concerning Dover Castle, left at Clifford's Inn by John Packenham, late clerk, and delivered to Lord Zouch by Nich. Packenham.

Nov. 89. Duplicate of the same.

VOL. LXXXIV. DECEMBER, 1615.

Dec. 1. 1. Sir Stephen Soame to Coke. Sir Thos. Monson earnestly desires an answer to the inclosed. *Incloses,*

1. I. *Petition of Sir Thos. Monson to the Commissioners, that the Bishops of Ely and Lincoln, his brothers, and his wife, may have access to him in the presence of Sir Stephen Soame.*

Dec. 1. 2. Information that the losses sustained both by the King and the farmers of customs, from the alum works in the north, proceed from want of good government there, and want of judgment and integrity in the factors and agents. With remedies proposed, and answers by Dr. Jordan to the objections which he expects to be made against him by the farmers of alum.

Dec. 1 3. Complaint of Dr. Edw. Jordan against Sir Art. Ingram and others, farmers of the King's alum works in the north, for fraudulent conduct in reference to his contract for the alum mine at Slapwash.

Dec. 2. Commission to Sir Julius Cæsar, Master of the Rolls, to hear and examine causes in Chancery. [*Grant Bk., p.* 181.]

Dec. 2 Newmarket. 4. Sir R. Winwood to Coke. The King wishes to get at the bottom of Franklin's speech about being employed to Heidelberg, as thereon may depend matters of great consequence.

Dec. 2. London. 5. Decree in the Court of the Archbp. of Canterbury, ordering payment of 24*s.* by Thos. Bird, of the diocese of Lincoln, to Hen. Palmer. Latin.

Vol. LXXXIV.

1615.

Dec. 3. 6. Note of the distribution of 4*l.* to the servants of Archbp. Abbot, at the consecration of Dr. Robt. Abbot, Bishop of Salisbury.

Dec. 4. 7. Notes [by Coke] of the evidence against Sir Thos. Monson.

Dec. 4? 8. Miscellaneous notes [by the Same] relative to the discovery of the poisoning. Mention of the Lord Treasurer, Earl of Northampton, &c.

Dec. 4. 9. [Lord Chief Justice Coke] to the King. At Sir Thos. Monson's arraignment, he was told that on account of recent discoveries, he would not yet be proceeded with, and he was sent under guard to the Tower. The people reviled him bitterly by the way. He strongly protested his innocence, but did not deny his Popery.

Dec. 4. Bellasis. 10. Sir Wm. Waad to Coke. Mrs. Horne, who served his wife six years, afterwards went to the Countess of Essex. She sent him word of the intention to displace him from the Tower, before it occurred; and when Overbury's death was talked of, said some of them would have to account for it some day, and that her Lord [Somerset] was never gladder than when he heard it.

[Dec. 5.] 11. Sir Thos. Monson to the Same. His trial being postponed, the following questions, which he then intended to ask, may be put to the Lord Treasurer, viz., whether the appointment of Sir Gervase Helwys to be Lieutenant, and not Sir Roger Dallison, was done by Northampton only. Whether Helwys was an instrument to make Overbury submissive to the Treasurer and his house, for former wrongs done them.

Dec. 5. 12. Sir Thos. Fanshaw to [the Same]. Transmits the inclosed, which he found on the stairs leading to his Lordship's room at the Temple. *Incloses,*

12. I. *Anonymous to the Same. The Bishop of Bristol's wife is a suspicious person in Overbury's affair. She is intimate with the Countess of Somerset and her mother, and given to chemistry and making extracts, powders, &c., of which "the fairest flower in this English garden hath taisted, tho' not so effectually as was intended;" dares not give his name, lest he may be undone thereby, as others have been. Dec. 4.*

Dec. 5. Dover Castle. 13. Warrant by the Lord Warden of the Cinque Ports for the apprehension of Jas. Boreman, of Deal, to answer to certain charges.

Dec. 5. Ludlow Castle. 14. President and Council of Wales to Winwood. At the King's request, have proceeded against Sir John Wynn, Bart., of Gwydder, for various flagrant acts of oppression. Have fined him 1,000 marks, and request he may be discharged from the Council of the Marches, and the Lieutenancy of the County. He refused to appear, and is gone to London. Should he be allowed trial there, the consequences would be very mischievous.

VOL. LXXXIV.

1615.
Dec. 5. 15. Petition of Ann Jacob to Lord Zouch, for compensation to her from Peter Fountayn, who has detained the profits of certain houses, &c. of her late husband, during his minority, and suffered them to go to decay. With references thereon, dated Dec. 5 and 8, and Aug. 7, 1616. *Annexed is,*

15. I. *Covenant of Peter Fountayn to Ann Jacob, to repair one of the above tenements. Dover Castle, Dec.* 11.

Dec. 8. Temple. Friday. 16. Geo. Pormorte to ——. Has pleaded for him in the suits commenced against him by his friends. Will bear his burden, and show him how to avoid their mutual adversaries.

Dec. 8. Southampton. 17. Mayor, &c. of Southampton to Sir Thos. Lake. Offer him the first burgess's place for their town, having heard that there will soon be a Parliament.

Dec. 8. Grant to Dr. John Prideaux of the office of Divinity Lecturer at Oxford. [*Grant Bk., p.* 165.]

Dec. 9. Dover Castle. 18. Examination of Jas. Boreman. Gave no money for his place of Master Porter of Sandown Castle. The Captain and Lieutenant have been absent many weeks together.

Dec. 9. 19. [Lord Coke] to the King. Penitent death of Franklin. He confessed all his examinations, and owned his guilt; said that Coke had wronged him in accusing him of the murder of his wife, which he stedfastly denied; but the woman who tended her in her last sickness, declares she died in agonies, after taking a powder by his direction. Something is still behind, which must not be trusted to writing. *Incloses,*

19. I. *Confession of Jas. Franklin, made after his judgment, that he is guilty of poisoning Overbury, but not his own wife; that he had not spoken blasphemy, nor dealt in conjuring, as accused. With a note [by Coke], that he wished this confession to be published after his death.*

[Dec. 9.] 20. Draft of the above confession. Indorsed are memoranda of accounts of Hen. Morris with his brothers, 1594.

[Dec. 9.] 21. Description of Franklin's conduct before and at his execution. He declared himself justly punished, and acknowledged the truth of his examinations. Said three great Lords were in it, who had not been named as yet, but would not say who they were.

[Dec. 9.] 22. Draft of the above [by Coke].

Dec. 9. Newmarket. Proclamation requiring noblemen, gentlemen, &c. to reside at their chief mansions in the country, for the better maintenance of hospitality. All Lieutenants and Justices of Peace, who do not spend nine months in the year in their counties, are to lose their commissions. Printed. [*Proc. Coll., No.* 49.]

Dec. 11. 23. Memorandum that John Brown and [Thos.] Raymond were sworn Gunners of Dover Castle.

VOL. LXXXIV.

1615.

Dec. 11. 24. Petition of Thos. Young, of Dover, to Lord Zouch. Having long served as a Deputy Gunner in Dover Castle, begs to be appointed Gunner in the room of [Chas.] Crimble, living in Ireland. With note of his being sworn in.

Dec. 11. 25. Petition of Alex. White, of Dover, to the Same, to be appointed Gunner of Dover Castle. With note of his being sworn in.

Dec. 12? 26. Edw. Reynoldes to Fras. Mills. Has received his dividend [of the Privy Seal fees] for him, which is larger than was expected, the profits of the Hanaper and Petty Bag being good. The lately imprisoned Seal is now in the hands of Mr. Murray of the Bedchamber. They should not be niggardly in their new year's gifts to the Masters of Requests.

Dec. 12. 27. Confession of Frances Brittain. Placed Mrs. Horne and Mrs. Shirley, Sir Thos. Shirley's daughter, with the Countess of Essex. Mrs. Thornborough [the Bishop of Bristol's wife] was very intimate with the Countess and her mother, and would see them even in bed. Never stayed in the room when Mrs. Thornborough was there. The Countess never came to prayers, which were said daily in the house.

Dec. 12. 28. Examination of Mrs. Anne Horne. Never could satisfy the Countess of Essex in her service. Informed Sir Wm. Waad that he would be discharged from the Tower, out of dutiful feeling to him and Lady Waad, whom she had served.

Dec. 12. Grant to Hen. Corbin of the office of Gamekeeper in the lordship of Burnet and elsewhere, cos. Hertford and Middlesex, for life. [*Grant Bk.*, *p.* 157.]

Dec. 14. Grant of confirmation to the East India Company of licence for exporting foreign bullion, &c. [*Ibid.*, *p.* 177.]

Dec. 16. 29. Examination of Mrs. Horne. Mrs. Thornborough obtained some lands in Yorkshire by means of the Countess of Somerset, and gave her money for them. Brought the Countess biscuits to the Cockpit. The Countess gave her [Mrs. Horne] the ring with which she was married to the Earl of Essex, which she gave to her sister, married to Dalival, an Italian, who now wears the ring.

Dec. 16. 30. Examination of Stephen Clapham. Mrs. Thornborough was very intimate with the Countesses of Suffolk and Somerset, and Lady Walsingham, but knows not what business they had together.

Dec. 20. London. 31. Edw. Reynoldes to Fras. Mills. Sends the dividend of Privy Seal fees. Endured so much under the late testy Lord [Northampton], by standing out alone against his claim to a fifth part of their fees, that he will not do it again, unless supported by his fellows. Misconduct of Mr. Clerk, and of [Edw.] Anthony.

Dec. 20. London. 32. Draft of the above letter. [A passage erased mentions that Sir Thos. Lake has dismissed Anthony from the Signet Office, for embezzlement.]

VOL. LXXXIV.

1615.
Dec. 21. Royston. 33. Sir Ralph Winwood to Coke. Requires him to meet the King at Whitehall, on Saturday night.

Dec. 21. Commission to Ben. Joseph to command [a ship] of the East India Company, and to use martial law, &c.; with reversion to Hen. Popewell. [*Grant Bk., p.* 157.]

Dec. 22. Grant to John Hunt of the office of Serjeant-at-Arms, for life. [*Ibid., p.* 175.]

Dec. 22. 34. Examination of Anne, wife of Wm. Taylor, of Southwark. Was sent for to Durham House, by a Lady who offered to introduce her to the Countess of Essex, but she refused the offer. Three Court ladies, she knows not their names, called on her, one of whom, said to be the Countess, asked her nativity, which she cast for her, and told her she was unfortunate in her marriage, and born to much trouble. Was taught astrology by her mother.

Dec. 23. London. 35. Edw. Reynoldes to Fras. Mills. A firm stand must be taken against the exactions of any future Lord Privy Seal, the profits of the office being so much decreased.

[Dec. 24.] 36. Petition of the Merchants of the Staple [to the Council] for confirmation of a permission to continue their trade of buying and selling wools, notwithstanding the informations of John Gwynne and others, who try to frustrate their trade, by revival of an ancient statute against Broggers, which is misapplied against them.

[Dec. 24.] 37. "The present case of the staplers," being the abstract of another petition to the same effect.

Dec. 24. Grant to John Smith of the office of keeping the Blockhouse, near Gravesend, for life. [*Grant Bk., p.* 166.]

Dec. 25. 38. Charge of Her Majesty's robes, wardrobe, chamber, and gifts, from Midsummer, 1612, to Christmas, 1615.

UNDATED. 1615 ?

1615 ? 39. Petition of Jas. Maxwell to the King, for relief from a literary king to a literary man. Details of his past life. Has maintained the cause of the Church of England against four celebrated writers, written two poems complimentary to His Majesty, and laboured at deducing his genealogy. Latin.

40. Petition of Sir Herbert Croft to the Lord Chief Justice, to read the statement annexed of a claim made by Joan Caswall to a copyhold tenure in Ivington, co. Hereford, which he had granted to Robt. Band, and the right to which had been decided in Band's favour by common law, and in the Queen's Court. Wishes to know whether he intends to comply with Mrs. Caswall's importunity, and re-hear the case.

VOL. LXXXIV.

41. Petition of Peter Webster to Lord Zouch, for payment of his arrears as a Gunner of Sandgate Castle.

1615? 42. Petition of Walter Neale, Captain of the Company of the Artillery Garden in London, to the King, to be appointed to the place of Muster Master of the City, as he now exercises and disciplines the principal citizens, and there is a "necessary dependency" between the two places.

Warrant for payment of 200*l.* to Walter Balconquall. [*Sign Man., vol.* V., *No.* 70.]

43. Petition of Simon Sturtevant to the King, for a patent of his inventions of "Pressware and Wood Pleits," for conveyance of water by pipes, and for jointing and folding wood.

44. "Sir Walter Raleigh's Dialogue," being a contemporary copy of his Prerogative of Parliaments; in a "dialogue between a Councillor and a Justice of Peace." With a dedication to the King.

45. John Norden to Sir Fulk Greville, Chancellor of the Exchequer. Remarks relative to the best mode of proceeding in the proposed survey of the Crown lands. Thinks descriptions of the manors better than plans, which are very expensive. Reluctance of freeholders to submit to a survey, or produce their deeds.

46. Survey of the Forest of Kingswood, co. Gloucester, and Chace of Filwood, co. Somerset, by John Norden.

47. Memorandum of certain half-yearly payments in Kent, for 13 Jac. I.

Sept. ? 48. Moneys paid since Michaelmas, 1615, upon the dormant Privy Seal, dated Nov. 6, 1608.

49. Warrant of dispensation for D—— and his wife from prosecution for recusancy; he being old and infirm, and otherwise carrying himself dutifully.

50. Note of divers Acts of Parliament, from 7 Edw. IV. to 13 Jac. I., relating especially to ecclesiastical and regal prerogative, and the title to the Irish crown.

51. Inventory of the ordnance in Camber Castle, including the new store, of which the receipt by Peter Temple, Captain, from Lord Carew, Master of the Ordnance, dated May 17, 1613, is given; and also of the portions of the old store remaining.

52. Account of the amounts received from the several farms of different branches of the customs, total 201,305*l.* 9*s.* 2*d.*, and estimate of increase of rent which might be demanded for the several farms, amounting to 46,400*l.*

Antwerp. 53. Laws of the Fellowship of the Blessed Virgin, instituted in the College of Jesuits, and approved by the Apostolic See. Printed.

5? Vol. LXXXIV.

54. Statement of the case between the residents on the lands of the Hospital of St. Thomas, Southwark, and Mr. Todd, their minister, who claims a larger allowance from them than that provided for by their charter from King Edw. VI.

Statement of the ground in Holtoft, co. Lincoln, belonging to divers abbeys and priories. [*Dom. Corresp.*, *May* 11, 1614.]

Statement by the inhabitants of Holtoft to the Assembly of Judges and Justices at Lincoln, of the persons there guilty of depopulation, and of the inconvenience resulting therefrom. [*Ibid.*]

55. Warrant for the surrender of the ship Edwin, of London, in the custody of Lord Zouch, to Geo. Bargrave and Jas. Brett, on their writ of indemnification. Imperfect.

56. Lord Danvers to [Sir Dud. Carleton]. Begs him to deliver the enclosed letter with his own hand to [Lord] Roos.

57. The King to the Fellows of Trinity Hall, Cambridge. Recommends Thos. Wilson, Keeper of State Papers, to be elected Master of that College at the next vacancy.

58. Directions for drawing up a report on the comparative advantages of Middleburgh or Dort, as the residence of the new Company of Merchant Adventurers.

59. Orders by Sir John Jolles, Lord Mayor of London, for the preservation of fish within the river Thames.

60. Note of the fees paid by the masters of passage boats and passengers of Dover, at Calais, Boulogne, Dieppe, and St. Valery, and of fees, &c. received from the masters of passage boats and passengers of those towns at Dover; with complaint of a recent edict forbidding Englishmen to sail from Calais in any but French vessels.

61. List of names of persons in Dover, the Isle of Thanet, and Folkestone. [*Probably those of persons intending to fish during the year. See a similar list, Sept.* 10, 1610.]

62. Bill of charges by Dunkin, for journeys to the Hague, and to Mr. Trumbull, at Brussels.

Vol. LXXXV. 1615.

5. Sir Walter Raleigh's "Prerogative of Parliaments" [*see No.* 44 *supra*], followed by "A short View of the Reign of Henry III., by Sir Robt. Cotton."

VOL. LXXXVI. JANUARY—APRIL, 1616.

1616.

Jan. 1? 1. Wm. Seymour to the King. Is penitent for the transgressions of his youth, and implores pardon, and leave to come home. *Annexed is,*

1. I. *The Council to Seymour, conveying the King's permission for him to return. Jan. 5, 1616.*

Jan. 1. Grant to John Potkin of the Clerkship of the Pavilions, &c., for life. [*Grant Bk., p.* 165.]

Jan 1. Grant to Sir Rich. Morrison of the lieutenancy of the ordnance, and keeping of the storehouses near Aldgate, London, and the artillery garden, for life. [*Ibid., p.* 165.]

Jan. 2. Special licence to Simon Sturtevant and Abraham Williams to use the mystery of fortage and lineage for thirty-one years. [*See undated,* 1615, *No.* 43. *Ibid., p.* 166.]

[Jan. 2.] Grant to the Earl of Worcester of the office of Lord Keeper of the Privy Seal. Latin. [*Warrt. Bk.,* I., *p.* 175.]

Jan. 4. Grant to Thos. Platt of the Clerkship of the Great Wardrobe, for life. [*Grant Bk., p.* 165.]

Jan. 4. 2. Memorandum of the wreck of the Abraham on the Godwin Sands, and the disorderly conduct of the Deal boatmen, in violating their agreement made with the captain touching the salvage, rifling the goods, &c.

Jan. 4. 3. Memorandum of the wreck of the Jonas on the Godwin Sands, and similar complaint against the Deal boatmen, for bursting open the merchants' packs, and rifling them, &c.

Jan. 5. 4. Thos. Fulnetby to Lord Zouch. Two ships ashore on the Godwin Sands. Some of the goods landed.

Jan. 5. 5. Note of sums due to victuallers of Dover, for diet and lodging of [Capt. Thos. Hill's company], lately serving at sea under Capt. Mainwaring, who were stayed by authority on Dec. 24, 1615.

Jan. 8. 6. Confession of the Countess of Somerset, that in her letter to the Lieutenant of the Tower about sending tarts, jelly, wine, &c. for Overbury, she meant that the tarts and jellies then sent, wherein were poisons, should be given to Overbury that night *Prefixed is,*

6. I. *Countess of Essex to the Lieutenant of the Tower. Forwards tarts, jellies, &c. sent to her. He is not to allow his wife to taste the tarts or jellies, for there are letters in them, but none in the wine. Sir Thos. Monson will bring news. [With marginal notes by Coke, endeavouring to prove therefrom the complicity of the Earl of Somerset.]*

VOL. LXXXVI.

1616.

Jan. 8. 7. Queries [by Coke] for examination of [Sir Wm. Monson ?] as to his connexion with foreign Princes, or favouring English Jesuits and priests, &c. in Flanders. With queries for the Countess of Somerset relative to the meaning of her letter, Franklin's mission to the Prince Palatine, the death of Prince Henry, the sickness of the Queen, &c.

Jan. 8 ? 8. Memoranda [by the Same] on searches to be made for papers belonging to Somerset, in Coppinger's or Lord Norris's custody, and precautions against their being destroyed.

Jan. 10. Special licence to Rich Dike, Matthias Fowle, and Fras. Dorrington, to make Venice gold and silver thread, &c., for twenty-one years. [*Grant Bk., p.* 160.]

Jan. 11. Philip Lane. 9. [Lord Zouch] to [Thos.] Fulnetby. Sir Noel Caron, Ambassador of the States, having solicited that the goods of two ships wrecked on Godwin Sands may be safely kept for their owners, directs him to see them placed in custody of the Mayor of Sandwich.

Jan. 15. Chester. 10. Wm. Aldersey to Sir Thos. Lake. Relates a dispute between the Ironmongers of Chester and Thos. Aldersey, whom they refuse, contrary to an Order in Council, to admit into their Company, because he is also a merchant embroiderer.

Jan. 16. Commission to Thos. Earl of Suffolk, Lord Treasurer, and others, to execute the office of Earl Marshal. [*Grant Bk., p.* 160.]

Jan. 20. Dover. 11. Peter Dibb to Rich. Younge. Has taken possession of the goods and parts of the great ship cast on Godwin Sands, which is broken in pieces; and also one anchor and cable. A portion, cast ashore at Dymchurch, in Romney Marsh, was claimed by Sir Ant. Deering. *Annexed is,*

11. I. *Note of the sums realized by the sale of the above goods and portions of the ship, Jan.* 29.

Jan. 20. Walmer Castle. 12. Capt. Wm. Boughton to Lord Zouch. The late storms have greatly injured the sea-wall near Walmer Castle. It needs speedy attention, as do also the roofs of the Castle, which admit the rain.

Jan. 21. Dover. 13. Peter Dibb to Rich. Younge. Begs for directions to the Bailiff and Jurats of Lydd not to meddle with anything that concerns the Lord Warden's jurisdiction.. *Incloses,*

13. I. *Robt. Martin and Peter Stronghill to Peter Dibb. Have taken up portions of a wreck driven on shore near Lydd, but the town claims them. Ask whether they are to give them up. Tuesday.*

[Jan. 22.] 14. Petition of Robt. Godfrey to Lord Zouch, to be appointed Porter of Dover Castle, in place of his late father, Wm. Godfrey. *Annexing,*

14. I. *Certificate in his favour by Sir Thos. Ingham, his late master, and And. Steward. Jan.* 22, 1616.

Vol. LXXXVI.

1616.

Jan. 22. Deal Castle. 15. Wm. Byng to Edw. Lord Zouch. The recent storm has carried away the beach and part of the outer wall of Deal Castle.

Jan. 24. Savoy. 16. Geo. Lord Carew to [Sir Thos. Roe]. Sends items of news since his last of the preceding April, as follows :—

April.—Young Walter Raleigh wounded Robt. Finet, the Lord Treasurer's servant, in a duel; he fled to the Low Countries, and is received by Prince Maurice. Sir Walter has the liberty of the Tower. Geo. Villiers knighted, with a pension of 1,000*l.* per ann., and is "like to prosper in the way of a favorite." Sir Julius Cæsar has married the widow Hungall, sister to young Lady Killegrew. Oliver St. John fined 5,000*l.*, with imprisonment for life, and a public confession, on account of a letter he wrote to the Mayor of Marlborough.

May.—Lady Chichester, Sir Hen. Bromley, and Lady St. John, dead. A daughter of the great Earl of Essex married to Sir Geo. Shirley. The Irish Parliament prorogued, and a subsidy granted; Sir Dud. Norton sent over as Secretary. Lord Hay made a Baron of England, also Sir Robt. Dormer, who paid 8,000*l.* to Lord Sheffield for it, "besides other driblets elsewhere." John Dackombe joined with Sir Thos. Parry, as Chancellor of the Duchy of Lancaster.

June.—Sir Chas. Cornwallis, Dr. Sharpe, and Mr. Hoskins, set free from prison, "and will no more burne there fingers with Parliment busines."

July.—Sir Hen. Neville, who aimed at the Secretaryship, dead; also Lady Grey, mother to Lord Grey, of Wilton. Baronet Portman, of Somersetshire, married to the Earl of Derby's eldest daughter.

August.—Peacham, a minister, sentenced to be hanged, drawn, and quartered, for writing a sermon against the King and Government; but execution stayed. The Bp. of Winchester sworn a Councillor, at intercession of the Earl of Somerset. Sir Brian O'Brian, the Earl of Thomond's son, married to Lady Sanquair.

September.—Lord Norris pardoned for manslaughter of a servant of Lord Willoughby, with whom he had a sudden quarrel. Lady Arabella dead in the Tower, and buried by night in her grandmother's tomb in Henry VII.'s chapel. The Dowager Countess of Dorset, the late Lord Treasurer's widow, and the Earl of Lincoln, dead.

October.—The King being informed at Bewdley that Sir Thos. Overbury was poisoned, "though the information poynted at the Erle of Somerset," ordered strict inquiry. Particulars of the poisoning. Weston hanged at Tyburn. Sir John Hollis, Sir John Wentworth, Sir John Lidcott, Edw. Sackville, and Lumsden the pensioner, fined or imprisoned for their conduct relative to the trial.

November.—The Duke of Lenox made Lord Steward of the Household. Mrs. Turner hanged; and also Sir Gervase Helwys, who implicated the Earl and Countess of Somerset, Earl of Northampton, and Sir Thos. Monson. Sir John Leedes and his wife, Monson's daughter, committed for "unreverent speeches of the Kinge, and spekinge to much of this poysoninge busines." Sir Thos. Chaloner

VOL. LXXXVI.

1616.

and old Lady Windsor dead. The Duke of Brunswick, aided by the King of Denmark, was besieging Brunswick, but raised the siege on approach of Count Henry.

DECEMBER.—Death of Sir Chas. Wilmot's wife, Lord Howard of Effingham, and Mrs. Dudley, Count Schomberg's wife. Sir Thos. Monson arraigned for Overbury's murder, but proceedings stayed. Jas. Franklin executed for it. The Countess of Somerset delivered of a daughter. Coppinger, and other servants of the Earl, imprisoned. Earl of Pembroke made Lord Chamberlain. Sir Robt. Cotton imprisoned, for reasons unknown. The Queen and Prince stood sponsors for the Countess of Argyle's twin sons.

JANUARY.—Earl of Worcester made Privy Seal instead of Master of the Horse, with a large pension. Sir Geo. Villiers made Master of the Horse. Sir Thos. Lake joined with Sir Ralph Winwood as Principal Secretary. Lady Penelope Spencer, the Earl of Southampton's daughter, dead. The Lord Deputy of Ireland removed and the Lord Chancellor and Chief Justice of Ireland appointed as substitutes. Sir Wm. Monson imprisoned; cause unknown. Cottington going to Spain. Sir John Digby to be recalled. Lord Roos to marry Sir Thos. Lake's daughter. Nothing done in reference to the north-western or north-eastern passages. The Virginia and Bermuda plantation sleeps.

Jan. 25. 17. Warrant from the Commissioners on Overbury's cause to the Marshal of the King's Bench, to bring Mrs. Thornborough before them at York House.

Jan. [25]. 18. Notes [by Coke] of interrogatories to be used to Mrs. Thornborough, as to her preparations of certain waters and powders, her procuring and delivery of poisons, the means by which she obtained a grant of lands near Knaresborough, Yorkshire, and what she had heard of an attempt against the Prince, Palsgrave, or Lady Elizabeth.

Jan. 28. Dover Castle. 19. Nich. Knott, Marshal of Dover Castle, to Rich. Younge. Denies having said that Sir Robt. Brett kept poor watch, when he was Lieutenant of the Castle. Asks where to get money to pay for Capt. Hill's Company.

Jan. 28. Whitehall. 20. Winwood to [Lake]. The inclosed shows that the Archduke does not speak such plain language as the Spanish Ambassador does for the reduction of Wesel. An Ambassador arrived from the Marquis of Brandenburg.

Jan. 30. 21. Lord [Zouch] to Thos. Fulnetby. Orders restoration of the goods wrecked on the Godwin Sands to Valentine de Best and Louis Van Hobrook, factors for the proprietors, on composition with the savers.

Jan. 22. [E. Reynoldes to Hugh Allington?], Clerk of the Privy Seal. Remonstrates against his entering into a composition with young Lane for the reversion of his office in the Privy Seal, which he had promised to his [Reynoldes's] kinsman, Castle. Offers to buy it for his kinsman.

VOL. LXXXVI.

1616.

[Jan.] 23. E. Reynoldes to Fras. Mills. The Earl of Worcester made Lord Privy Seal. The clerks should consult how to oppose his demand of one fifth of the fees, should he make it, as the last Lord Privy Seal did; will stand firm in his refusal, if supported by his colleagues. Mr. Packer seeks to trick his cousin Castle out of his reversion, in behalf of his own son.

Jan.? 24. [The Same] to John Packer. Reproaches him for breaking his promise of giving his interest in the reversion of his place to Reynoldes's cousin Castle, and using it in behalf of his own son, who is still an infant.

Jan.? 25. Notes by Sir Lionel Cranfield of articles which are not to be altered in custom or impost, in the book of rates, and of those which are to be altered; with memorandum that this alteration will ease those who make the clamour in Parliament, and that the changes are in lowering imposts on necessary things, and charging them on superfluities.

Jan.? 26. Book of debts due to officers, servants, and creditors, in the office of Ordnance, of which payment was made to Sir Roger Dallison, late Lieutenant thereof, but which he failed to discharge, and therefore they make part of the sum of 9,900*l.* in which he is indebted to the King, and for which his lands are extended.

Feb. 1. 27. List of patent offices and appointments, giving the names of the persons to whom granted, and date of grants, from 1 to 13 Jac. I.; with index of offices.

Feb. 1. 28. Certificate by Justinian Povey, the Queen's Auditor, of Her Majesty's entire income, and of the sources from which it is derived; total 25,929*l.* 7*s.* 4¾*d.* per ann.

Feb. 1? 29. Similar account [by the Same], and remarks on the fines for composition on copyhold lands and on leases. With memorandum, in another hand, "to see what good may be done, pro auro Reginæ."

Feb. 1? 30. List of the law offices that are established by prerogative, without Act of Parliament, to all of which belong fees.

Feb. 1. Licence to Wm. [Robt.?] Lord Dormer, Master of the Hawks, to take up hawks, for life. [*Grant Bk., p.* 160.]

Feb. 2. 31. Examination of John Lepton, Groom of the Privy Chamber. Wrote to Sir Wm. Monson, and told him that the King, on reading the evidences against Sir Thos. Monson, thought there was not one unanswerable; that therefore Sir Thomas's trial was deferred for want of evidence, and that he had good friends at Court, meaning thereby Sir Hum. May, Lord Haddington, and others. Heard the King's opinion from the Bp. of Bath and Wells.

Feb. 2.
Newmarket. 32. Winwood to Lake. The King wishes the French Ambassador to be treated with courtesy, the matter being trivial; and also desires to know the proceedings of the new company [of Merchant Adventurers], a speedy course being needful.

VOL. LXXXVI.

1616.

Feb. 2. Newmarket. 33. Winwood to Lake. Incloses a mandate from the King to the Council, to summon before them the Earl of Cumberland, Lords Walden and Wm. Howard, touching disorders on the Borders, &c.

Feb. ? 34. Account of the misconduct of Lord Wm. Howard in receiving all the chief recusants of the north, named; in keeping Geo. Skelton, a rebel and Papist, as his officer; in oppressing his neighbours and tenantry, &c. Also of the misconduct of Roger Wodrington, in countenancing the outlaws on the Borders. A Lord of Misrule was allowed to interrupt the Christmas service at Bampton. Wodrington and others were with Percy and others at Lord Wm. Howard's, a little before the Gunpowder Plot broke out.

Feb. 4. 35. John Lepton to Sir Hum. May. Has been obliged to confess mentioning his name in a letter to Sir Wm. Monson, which has fallen into the hands of the Lord Chief Justice. Thinks it cannot prejudice him, as it only proved his love to Sir Thos. Monson, whose innocence will, it is hoped, prove him worthy of love.

Feb. [4]. 36. The Same to the Bp. of Bath and Wells. Is very sorry to have been obliged to mention his name in his examination, as having heard from him certain things which he wrote to Sir Wm. Monson. Would have been ruined had he refused to say where he had the information.

Feb. 4. Newmarket. 37. Duke of Lenox to Sir Edw. Coke. He is to go alone, or with one other person, to speak to the Earl of Somerset on two subjects not concerning Overbury's affair.

[Feb. 4.] 38. Queries [by Coke] for the examination of the Earl of Somerset, as to his share in the committal of Overbury; the opposition made by Overbury to his marriage with the Countess of Essex; his recommending Weston as Overbury's keeper; Weston's share in the secret correspondence between himself and the Countess; his correspondence with Overbury in the Tower, and sending powders to him.

[Feb. 4.] 39. Queries [by the Same] on several of the above points; also queries for the Earl and Countess, relating to the poisoned waters, tarts, and jellies, &c.

Feb. 4. 40. Petition and declaration of the new Company of Merchant Adventurers to the Council, that they shall be utterly unable to maintain their ground, if the points in their charter, said to be illegal, are reformed. Their whole work rests on the King's prerogative, by which alone it can be supported. Beg confirmation of their charter, and freedom from prosecutions by law.

Feb. 5. Dover. 41. Wm. Ward to Lord Zouch. Requests licence to fit out an armed vessel to repress unlicensed fishing of French boats on the English coast. Asks no reward but a moiety of the boats taken.

Feb. 6. Newmarket. 42. Winwood to [Lake]. Sends the warrant for the Earl of Exeter. The French Ambassador's request is to be granted. The Attorney General justifies the patent of the new Company [of Merchant Adven-

1616. VOL. LXXXVI.

turers]. The King would rather they broke up of their own accord than on advantage taken of their patent. If the old Company be re-established, they are to perform their promises for increase of the revenue.

Feb. 6. Newmarket. 43. R. Kirkham to Lake. The King was yesterday on horseback, and bore it well. Is weary for want of employment.

Feb. 6. 44. Statement by [Auditor Povey] of the Queen's debts, total 18,948*l.* 3*s.* 5*d.*; with suggestion for investigation into the bills.

Feb. 7. 45. Statement by the Earl of Cumberland, that he cannot account for the increase of outlaws on the Borders, except that some have returned from abroad, and others are protected by friends at Court. Has sent sixteen garrison soldiers to repress them. Wishes more stability in the Commissions for Oyer and Terminer. Thinks things would go worse if the Berwick garrison were dismissed.

Feb. 7? 46. "Advertisement for His Majesty," showing that former customs levied on export of wool were much reduced upon cloth made in England, for the encouragement of the cloth trade, and proposing that the Merchant Adventurers shall pay increased duties on all cloths exported undyed and undressed, whilst those dyed and dressed in England remain at the former duties, for encouragement of home labour.

Feb. 7 47. Copy of the above.

Feb. 7. 48. Warrant of permission for the dissolved Company of Merchant Adventurers to assemble and deliberate on the best means to re-establish their former trade, if the new Company fail to perform their contract.

Feb. 8. Serjeants' Inn. 49. Lord Chief Justice Coke to the King. Has committed Lepton to the King's Bench, as not fit to continue near His Majesty, on account of his scandals. Sir Thos. Monson is made more obstinate by the King's opinion that the evidence against him is weak. Has had an interview with Somerset, who denies any knowledge of the letters in cipher addressed to him. Told him of his approaching trial, but he seemed insensible to his danger, and would not have a word of submission to His Majesty recorded. Has found thirteen fortune-tellers in London, and bound them to appear. Has just received a letter from Somerset, who now confesses the presumptions against him to be strong. Advises the King not to yield to any of his petitions. Some use may be made of certain passages in his discourse, which come near to confession.

[Feb. 8.] 50. Draft of the above.

Feb.? 51. Notes [by Coke] inculpating the Earl of Somerset as guilty of high treason, for discovering to Don Diego Sarmiento de Acunas, then Spanish Ambassador in England, the contents of certain private letters from Sir John Digby to the King; and also for revealing the contents of other Ambassadors' letters, to the great danger of the King and kingdom, and receiving a pension from the King of Spain. Indorsed "Notes for an Indictment."

VOL. LXXXVI.

1616.

Feb. ? 52. Queries [by Coke] for the Earl of Somerset, on his correspondence with the Earl of Northampton about the Countess of Essex, and with Sir Thos. Monson, as to where the letters were deposited, why some were destroyed, some fetched away, &c.; also as to his interviews with Paul de Lobell and Franklin, &c.

Feb. ? 53. [Commissioners on Overbury's cause] to the King. Have been to Somerset, and answered his requests about speaking to Sir Robt. Carr, &c. In answer to his hope that he might not be tried, told him that the course of justice required it, as he was indicted as accessory to the murder, and the proofs pregnant against him. Urged him to confession, in hope of mercy. Told him of the disposal of his offices, for which he seemed not to grieve, but said he was sorry his wife was guilty of so foul a fact. He made answer to some very material points.

Feb. 8? 54. Notes [by Coke] that the Earl of Somerset should be further examined, and explain his declaration of Feb. 7, that he assented to Overbury's imprisonment. Also notes for the regulation of his trial, and that of the Countess.

Feb. 8. 55. Order in Council to the new Company of Merchant Adventurers, forbidding the export of undressed cloth by any but merchants of the company, they having complained of trouble by interlopers, and permitting them, till June 24, to export a small quantity of white cloth, the proportions to be afterwards settled.

Feb. 9. 56. Statement by Chief Justice Coke, that the Queen authorizes the bearer to visit certain tradespeople named, and examine the bills due to them from her, and the amounts that have been paid thereon. With notes by the parties concerned, of the sums due to them.

Feb. 9. Newmarket. 57. Winwood to Coke. The Lieutenant of the Tower is to procure from the Earl of Somerset the articles from France, relating to the marriage between the Prince and the second daughter of France, and they are to be forwarded to the King forthwith.

Feb. 10. Charing Cross. 58. Lake to Winwood. Sends documents for His Majesty's signature. The Lord Chancellor does not mend; his recovery is doubtful.

Feb. 10. Newmarket. 59. Winwood to [Lake]. The King dislikes the resolution of the Council to furnish the fishermen trading to the north with two small ships to secure them from pirates, and thinks it a needless and unprecedented charge. Sir Jas. Hamilton will be sent to answer any complaints against him. Mr. [Wm.] Seymour has returned, and is to see the King to-morrow.

Feb. 12. Dover. 60. Peter Dibb to Rich. Younge. A small bark, laden with Caen stone, is cast away between Lydd and Rye, &c. Has seized his Lordship's anchor and cable therefrom. Begs that the Hythe boats may go out to fish a day or two earlier than allowed, there being but little supply of fish.

VOL. LXXXVI.

1616.

Feb 13. Ash Wednesday. Newmarket. 61. Winwood to Lake. The King will write to the Council himself on the cloth business; he persists in his opinion against the grant of two ships to protect the fishermen, notwithstanding the Council's reasons. To-morrow he dines at the Lord Gerard's. The Bishop of Bath has made a learned sermon to preach before him.

Feb 15. 62. Petition of Thos. Mullins to Sir Julius Cæsar, Master of the Rolls; being subpœnaed at the suit of Wm. White, prays for a commission to take his answer in the country, as he is fearful of a plot to arrest him if he comes to town. With order thereon.

Feb. 15. 63. Bond of Sam. de Fische, Philip Burlamachi, and others, under a penalty of 10,000*l.*, to indemnify Lord Zouch for delivering to them the portion saved of the cargoes of three Dutch vessels wrecked on the Godwin Sands, which they are authorized by the proprietors to receive, and to pay droit and salvage dues.

[Feb. 15.] 64. Draft of the above obligation. Indorsed is a draft of a similar indemnity on bond of Jas. Hugessen, for delivering to Thos. Hoyer the value of an Emden vessel, wrecked.

Feb. 16. Philip Lane. 65. [Lord Zouch to Thos.] Fulnetby. Orders to deliver to Sam. de Fische, and others, such portion of the goods of three Dutch vessels, stranded on the Goodwin Sands, as was saved by the inhabitants of the towns adjacent.

Feb. 16. Grant to Thos. Aylesbury of the Surveyorship of the Navy, for life. [*Grant Bk., p.* 154.]

Feb. 17. 66. Certificate that two letters only were taken by the Lieutenant of the Tower from the papers of the Earl of Somerset, by virtue of the warrant from the Lord Chief Justice, viz., one from Sir Hen. Wotton to him, Nov. 23, 1613, and one from him to Sir Thos. Edmondes, Nov. 25, 1613.

Feb. 18. Oxford. 67. Sir H. Savile to Carleton. His Venice money will serve to repay Sir Wm. Sedley, whom Carleton should visit, if possible. Sec. Winwood will give orders on the Leyden book business.

Feb. 19. London. 68. E. Reynoldes to Fras. Mills. Thinks the Clerks will be obliged to allow the Lord Privy Seal's claim to one fifth of the fees, on certain conditions subscribed by himself and Mr. Allington, and sent for Mills' and Sir Thos. Clerk's signature, if approved. Should his Lordship claim more, they must go to law. *Incloses,*

68. I. *Account addressed by Edw. Reynoldes to [his Fellow Clerks of the Privy Seal] of his interview with the Lord Privy Seal, who urges his claim to one fifth of the fees, as enjoyed by his predecessor. Gives reasons why they should cede to his request, rather than go to law about it. Annexing,*

68. II. *Certificate by Hugh Allington, Fras. Mills, and Edw. Reynoldes, of their opinion that it would be better to tender one fifth of the fees to the Lord Privy Seal.*

Vol. LXXXVI.

1616.

Feb. 19. Grant to John Bendbo and Rich. Daw of the office of examining all Letters Patent under the Great Seal, for life. [*Grant Bk.*, *p.* 154.]

Feb. 20. Whitehall. Earl of Suffolk to John Wolstenholme. Appoints him to keep a private register of all moneys brought in by the East India Company, in order to prove that they bring in as much money as, by licence, they export. [*Dom. Corresp.*, *March* 27, 1616.]

Feb. 23. 69. Edw. Reynoldes to Fras. Mills. Complains of the negligence of the Deputy Clerks of the Privy Seal in their accounts, and of their passing grants gratis; thus giving away fees which are not their own.

Feb 23? 70. Warrant for delivery to Augustine Vincent, Rouge-Rose Pursuivant, of a coat-of-arms of red and blue damask.

Feb. 23? Copy of the above. [*Dom. Corresp.*, *July* 8, 1606.]

Feb. 26. Grant to And. Boyd of the office of Surveyor of Coals, for life. [*Grant Bk.*, *p.* 155.]

Feb. 26. Westminster. The King to the University of Cambridge. Will not grant the petition of the town of Cambridge to be made a city, if the University fears that there would be danger of its giving them any preeminence over the University, which is the glory of the town, and under his own special protection. Latin. [*Dom. Corresp.*, *May* 8, 1616.]

Feb. 26. 71. Petition of And. and John Rand to Lord Zouch, for satisfaction from the owners of the Jonas, wrecked on the Godwin Sands, for their exertions in saving the ship.

Feb. 28. 72. Examination of Thos. Skinner, son of Sir Thos. Skinner, of Lannam Park, Suffolk. Attempted to pass the seas without permission, because his money was done and he wished to join his father in Paris. Has been abroad in Italy and France, but did not take out nor bring over letters.

Feb. 28. Blackfriars. 73. Sir Wm. Smithe to Lord Zouch. Begs him to free and send up Thos. Skinner, his wife's nephew, who, being driven out of doors by his mother, tried to cross the seas at Dover, but was detained and imprisoned; he has travelled much, and is a most accomplished youth.

Feb. 28. 74. Petition of Hen. Martin, Serjeant Trumpeter to the Queen, for a lease in reversion of certain lands in Hampton-in-Arden, co. Warwick. With reference to the Earl of Worcester and the Queen's Council; and their report in favour of the petition.

Feb. 28. 75. Petition of Edw. Bates, Gunner of Arch-cliff Bulwark, to Lord Zouch. Certain moneys being lodged in the Chancery Court at Dover, which John Goodwin was condemned to pay for wrongs offered to his son, Sampson Bates, begs that his son's bill may be taxed at once, that there may be no further delay in his receiving the money.

1616. Vol. LXXXVI.

Feb.? 76. Petition of Edw. Bates to Lord Zouch, for an order that he may receive certain money which had been paid into Court for his son Sampson Bates, on an action for debt against Mr. Lennard, of Dover.

[Feb.] 77. Arguments by the Skinners' Company against a proposed patent for the tanning of gray conyskins, showing that it would prove a monopoly, and injure home trade and that of the Eastland merchants, leading the King of Poland to drive them from their residence in his territories.

Feb.? 78. List of the Commissioners of Sewers for Kent and Sussex, and of those who are to be added to the Commission.

Feb.? 79. Note of the limits of jurisdiction of the above Commissioners.

Feb.? 80. Edw. Sherburn to Carleton. The Lord Treasurer will not consent to the re-delivery of the parcels to Carleton without a warrant from the Lords Commissioners, though the Lieutenant [of the Tower] declares that the Earl of Somerset wishes it. Has urged the necessity of money, that Carleton may set out on his new employment, and hopes to obtain it.

March 1. 81. Giov. Franc. Biondi to the Same. The Ambassador of Savoy has gone to Newmarket, but is anxious to see him [Carleton] before he embarks.

March 1. 82. Note of the plate [*provided for Sir D. Carleton on his going Ambassador to Holland ?*].

March 2. Canterbury. 83. Dr. Geo. Newman to [Lord Admiral Nottingham ?]. The claim of the men of the Cinque Ports to be free from the Lord Admiral's jurisdiction was first originated by a factious person at Romney, about 1611, and cannot be supported by ancient precedent. Great inconveniences would result from yielding to it. With an envelope transmitting the same to Lord Zouch.

March 2. Barnsley. 84. Examination of Corstovell, wife of Wm. Wilson, of Barnsley, co. York. Has frequently heard mass said in the house of Ant. Monson, at Carlton, co. Lincoln, with whom she was servant, and several of the servants and others prophesied a turn in favour of Popery, just before the Gunpowder Treason.

March 2. Newmarket. Grant to Hen. Henn of 200*l.* amerciaments, and any future similar amerciaments, imposed on the Sheriffs of the county and town of Carmarthen, for not executing processes for issues on jurors, which issues were formerly granted to Henn and others. [*Sign Man., vol.* V., *No.* 71.]

March 2. Westminster. Licence to Sir Thos. Leigh, Bart., to impark 700 acres of his own land in Stoneleigh and Fletchampstead, co. Warwick, with liberty of free warren therein. Latin. [*Ibid., No.* 72.]

March 3. Audley End. 85. Earl of Suffolk to Lake. Has received letters from Ireland about revenue and subsidy. Sends a letter directed to the Council for the King's perusal, also the subsidy book.

VOL. LXXXVI.

1616.

March 3. 86. Lord Knollys to Lake. Hears that the Clerk of the Acatry is dead; therefore it is a fit occasion for Waterer to be preferred to his place.

March 4. Newmarket. Grant, in reversion, to Michael Cole and Wm. Thomazon of the office of Bailiff Itinerant in Cheshire, with survivorship. Latin. [*Sign Man., vol.* V., *No.* 73.]

March 4. Newmarket. Licence for the instalment of the first fruits of the Bishopric of Salisbury, amounting to 1,246*l.* 14*s.* 6½*d.*, to be paid in four years. [*Ibid., No.* 74.]

March 5. Ludlow Castle. 87. Ralph Lord Eure and the Council of Wales to Sir Ralph Winwood. Sir John Wynn's servants, who are in prison, are well treated, and would be liberated if they would petition the Court. Sir John's complaint, that whilst he is attending on the Lord Chancellor for his opinion, on a reference from His Majesty, his goods are sold for his fine, &c., is entirely untrue. Are slandered by his petition to the King, and his relations to others.

March 6. Blackfriars. 88. Sir Wm. Smithe to Lord Zouch. Thanks for sending up his nephew Skinner, who is not, as was feared, a Catholic, though many attempts have been made to pervert him. Shall try to reconcile him with his parents.

March 6. 89. Petition of Robt. Butler, of Camber Castle, Sussex, to the Same. Sam. Sampson having charged him, both to his Lordship and the Mayor of Winchelsea, for embezzling the King's store or munition, desires to know whether his Lordship will hear the matter, or leave it to the Court of Winchelsea.

March 7. Westminster. Grant to Geo. Hope, on surrender of Peter Sharpe, of the office of Master of St. John's Hospital, Chester; with reversion thereof to Wm. Hope, on surrender of Thos. Corbin. Latin. [*Sign Man., vol.* V., *No.* 75.]

March 8. 90. Agreement between Capt. Hen. Mainwaring and Joachim Wardeman, of Lubeck, of purchase by the former, for 200*l.*, of a certain vessel, with ordnance, lying in the port of Dover.

March 8. Licence to the Wardens and Company of Stationers of London to print primers, almanacs, &c. [*Grant Bk., p.* 177.]

March 8. Westminster. Presentation of John Scott to the rectory of Keyston, co. Huntingdon. Latin. [*Sign Man., vol.* V., *No.* 76.]

March 8. Westminster. Grant to Geo. Wilson, of Rochester, of the first reversion of one of the six Principal Masterships of the Navy. [*Ibid., No.* 77.]

March 8. Westminster. Grant to Thos. Visct. Fenton of the King's reversion of certain lands and tenements, cos. Berks, Oxon, and Hants, granted by Henry VIII. to Hen. Norris and his heirs male, the present heir being Lord Norris. [*Ibid., No.* 78.]

1616. Vol. LXXXVI.

March 9. Westminster. Warrant to deliver to Rich. Crockford the bonds, &c. for recovery of the King's moiety of the fine to be paid by Jas. Browne, brewer, of Deptford, for unlawful brewing, which is granted to Crockford. [*Sign Man., vol.* V., *No.* 79.]

March 9. 91. Chris. Marshall, Deputy to Mr. Randoll, to Lord Zouch. A French fishing boat has been brought into Rye Harbour with a great quantity of fish on board, the nets being much finer than allowed. Sends up the boat's licence and patterns of the nets.

March 10. Rye. 92. Wm. Ward to the Same. Has been out several nights to examine the licences of French fishing boats. Found some correct, but others had only copies; has captured one of these as a lawful prize, and begs directions. Disorderly conduct of the people at Rye, who might remedy these mischiefs if they chose.

March 10. Dover Castle. 93. Lord Z[ouch] to Wm. Ward. The copy of the licence used by the French vessel is insufficient, but must leave it to the Admiralty Court to judge if she be lawful prize. The matter of the French vessel, taken by mariners of Rye fishing with unlawful nets, must also be examined.

March 10. Dover Castle. 94. The Same to the Mayor of Rye. Desires him to send two of the Frenchmen belonging to the captured boat, with some of the captors, to Dover for examination; and also the agreement made between the English and French, as to the size of the nets to be used.

March 11. Whitehall. Earl of Suffolk to the Farmers of the Customs. To deliver up their bonds for customs on divers goods sent to the new plantation in Ireland, the King permitting them to be transported free of custom, and to defalcate the amount from their accounts. [*Dom. Corresp., March* 27, 1616.]

March 13. Indenture of grant to Sir Edw. Dymock, Wm. Clarke, Thos. Whitley, and Art. Dee, of a fourth part of all fines and forfeitures on alienations, for six years or longer, if the lease of the farm of fines on alienations to the Treasurer and Chancellor of the Exchequer continue. [*Sign Man., vol.* V., *No.* 80.]

March 14. Westminster. Grant to Rich. Hutton of the Clerkship of the Manor Court and lordship of Middleham and Richmond, in the archdeaconry of Richmond. Latin. [*Ibid., No.* 81.]

March 14. London. 95. Edw. Sherburn to [Carleton]. Has removed the pictures, and marked those left with Lord Danvers. Rumour that on the death of the old Lord Chancellor, Winwood is to take his place. Sir Matthew Carew will give security for a proffered loan from Carleton. The Prince took a ring from Sir Geo. Villiers's hand, and, putting it on his own, forgot it and lost it, on which Villiers complained to the King, who chided the Prince so severely as to bring him to tears, and forbade him the presence till the ring was restored. The King's boundless affection for Villiers cannot continue, wanting a sound foundation. Sudden death of Sir Hen. Fanshaw.

VOL. LXXXVI.

1616.
March 16. Westminster. Grant to Ellis ap Edward ap Howell, of co. Carnarvon, of pardon for horse-stealing, he being young, and this his first offence. Latin. [*Sign Man., vol.* V., *No.* 82.]

March 16. Westminster. Grant to the Duke of Lenox of the mise or tallage of the tenants of Kidwelly, co. Carmarthen, and the fines for passing freehold lands in fee farm; also of authority to compound for certain wastes, on payment of 100*l.* per ann. increased rent. [*Ibid., No.* 83.]

March 16. Westminster. Warrant to Lord Carew, Master of the Ordnance, to increase the labourers' pay from 6½*d.* to 10½*d.* per diem. [*Ibid., No.* 84.]

March 17. Westminster. Grant to Sir Jerome Bowes of annuity of 600*l.* out of the new patent for glass works, in consideration of his former rents from the old glass works. [*Ibid., No.* 85.]

March 19. Westminster. Grant to Sir Chris. Hatton of the office of Remembrancer in the Exchequer, with reversion to Sir Art. Harris, at nomination of Lady Fanshaw, in trust for the children of Sir Hen. Fanshaw, the late Remembrancer. Latin. [*Ibid., No.* 86.]

March 19. Westminster. Warrant for payment to Maurice Abbot, Robt. Bell, and others, of the usual bounty of 5*s.* per ton for building six new ships. [*Ibid., No.* 87.]

March 19. Newcastle. 96. Wm. Morton to Winwood. Everybody believes Roger Wodrington guilty in the Gunpowder Treason. Points of presumption against him therein. He, in matters of religion, and his brother Sir Henry in matters of justice, are the roots of all the evil in those parts. Would have accused Roger, but the late Earl of Salisbury protected him. The Earl of Dunbar repressed the Wodringtons, and the country was brought to a quiet state, but after his death all grew worse again. Suggests that extended powers be given to Lord Sheffield, &c. *Incloses,*

96. I. *Statement by John Smaithwaite, parson, of Elsdon, of the oppressions of Roger Wodrington and his followers, his seducing many persons to Popery, admitting recusants on to juries, releasing felons through bribery, &c. He is said to be the treasurer of the Papists in the North, and was intimate with Percy, the Gunpowder traitor.*

March ? 97. Complaint of Hen. Jekin, one of the brethren of St. Thomas's Hospital, Sandwich, to Lord Zouch, against two of the Mayors of the town, for illegally sending him to prison, and for their fraudulent conduct in managing the affairs of the hospital.

March 20. 98. Wm. Elwood, Mayor of Sandwich, and John Harbert, to [the Same]. Answers the points in Jekin's petition, pointing out its mis-statements, and justifying the conduct of former mayors.

VOL. LXXXVI.

1616.

[March 20.] 99. Petition of Wm. Hugbone, of Eastry, Armourer, to Lord Zouch, for the place of Armourer at Dover Castle. *Annexing,*

99. I. *Certificate by Sir Sam. Peyton and others in favour of Wm. Hugbone, testifying his skill, &c. in his trade.* *March* 20, 1616.

March 20. Westminster. Grant to Capt. Edw. Davies of a mitigated fine of 40*l.*, imposed by the Commissioners Ecclesiastical on Thos. Dawson, stationer of London, for his contempt in printing certain books, contrary to the patent granted to Robt. Barker. [*Sign Man., vol.* V., *No.* 88.]

March 22. Westminster. Grant to John Huzie of pardon for a rape on Eliz. Newman, both of Sandwich. Latin. [*Ibid., No.* 89.]

March 22. Grant to Wm. Gibbons of the office of one of the six Chief Masters of the Navy, for life. [*Grant Bk., p.* 174.]

March 23. London. 100. Edw. Sherburn to [Carleton]. The Earl of Arundel hesitates to accept the Jupiter's head, having had so many presents from Carleton. Lady Suffolk comes to London, to be restored to the Queen's favour. The Secretary of Scotland sworn of the Privy Council. Lord Hay to be sent into France, to congratulate the marriage. Mr. Finet knighted. Sir Walter Raleigh released from the Tower, but not allowed to come to Court. He is to have seven ships for the voyage to Guiana. The Lord Chancellor is content to resign the keeping of the Seals to the Attorney General. Lady Exeter with child, &c.

March 24. Court of Admiralty, London. 101. Commission from the Lord Admiral to Nich. Leate and John Dike, merchants of London, to fit out a ship to take pirates and sea-rovers, and to reserve for themselves three fourths of the value of the ships and goods seized.

March 24. Cheshunt. 102. Rich. Percivall to his son, Rich. Percivall. Urges him to reveal any circumstances he knows that may relate to the murder of Overbury, and to deliver up certain abstracts, dismissing scruples lest he should injure his master, or any one.

March 24. 103. Orders by the Queen for her Receiver to give an account of the money in his hands, and gather in her debts, and the 2,000*l.* fines for the copyholds of Spalding and Gedney. The creditors are then to be paid by proportion; but Her Majesty's jewels first to be redeemed, &c.

March 24. 104. Analysis of the Queen's revenue and proposed expenditure, leaving 9,000*l.* a year for discharge of her debts. With copy of the preceding orders, and arguments in favour of their immediate adoption. Indorsed [by Coke], "This to be kept to Her Majesty herself."

March ? 105. Plan devised [by Sir Edw. Coke] for payment of the Queen's debts, by raising her revenues on copyholds, &c., by issuing no warrants for money but under her own hand, limiting her expenditure to 16,000*l.* a year, having her accounts regularly made up, her property inventoried, her bills gathered in, &c.; with request to know with whom he is to confer on the business.

Vol. LXXXVI.

1616.

March ? 106. Motives why their Majesties should change the fines of copyholders of estates of inheritance [within Her Majesty's jointure] from uncertain to certain.

March 25. 107. Debts incurred by the Queen since Christmas, 1615. Total amount, 1,155*l.* 18*s.* 7*d.*

March 25 ? 108. List of the Queen's household, and officers of her revenue, with the fees, wages, and annuities paid to each. Total, 4,119*l.* 14*s.* per ann.

March 25. 109. Sam. Calvert to Carleton. Regrets failing to take leave of him. Thanks him for admitting Mr. Sherburn into his service. Recommends Capt. Phillipps, who has served twenty years under Sir Horace Vere, and is returning to Holland after a short visit to England. Sir John Digby has returned, and is to be Vice Chamberlain, or Deputy of Ireland. Sir Walter Raleigh at liberty, but under a keeper. The tilting was grand, and three of the Lord Treasurer's sons were there. The French discontented with the treatment of their Ambassador in Spain, and of the ladies who went with their Princess.

March 25 ? Grant to Edw. Aldred, the King's servant, of remission of all fines and forfeitures due to His Majesty, for alienations without licence of the manor of Foulmere, co. Cambridge, which was much encumbered by Sir John Skinner, before it came into his hands. Latin. [*Sign. Man., vol.* V., *No.* 90.]

March 25. Westminster. Grant to Thos. Lord Knyvet and Robt. Lloyd, Admiral to the Queen, of 12,000*l.*, moiety of old debts due to the Crown, in lieu of a similar grant to Ralph Ewens, the Queen's late Auditor, which was frustrated by his decease. [*Ibid., vol.* VI., *No.* 1.]

March 26. 110. Petition of John Phillips, Vicar of Faversham, to Lord Zouch, to judge in his cause touching an outrageous misdemeanor against him by John Upton, of Faversham, or else to permit him to resort to the Court of Canterbury.

March 26. Westminster. Grant to Sir Hen. Baynton of the King's reversion of the entailed manors, &c. of Bromham and Clench-juxta-Wyke, co. Wilts, parcel of the lands of Battle Abbey, co. Sussex, in part of a grant to Wm. Heydon of 8,000*l.* from reversions of entailed estates. Latin. [*Sign Man., vol.* VI., *No.* 2.]

March 27. Westminster. Grant to John Harper, Wm. Pratt, and Jeremy Drury, of a patent for the sole making of a table for casting accounts by them invented, by which " any questions arithmetical may be resolved, without the use of pen or compters." [*Ibid., No.* 3.]

March 27. 111. Chamberlain to Carleton. Death of Sir Hen. Fanshaw [Remembrancer of the Exchequer]. Through the influence of Sec. Winwood, Sir Chris. Hatton and Sir Art. Harris have the office in trust for his son, who is not yet of age, and John West acts as deputy. Death of Sir Jerome Bowes and Sir Ralph Coningsby, of Peacham, the minister, in Taunton Gaol, and of three sons of Lord Abergavenny, who were drowned. Alderman Cockayne and

1616. Vol. LXXXVI.

his party, supported by the King, have defeated the old Merchant Adventurers, contrary to the opinion of most of the Council. Disputes between the Chancellor and Lord Chief Justice Coke, on *præmunires*. The Queen came to the tilting on the 25th. Lords Dingwall and Hay carried the bell. Sir Walter Raleigh is freed, and is visiting places built since his imprisonment. Many adventurers join him, and he risks 16,000*l.* of his own. Winwood was the chief means of delivering both him and the Countess of Shrewsbury. The King sent for some young Cantabrigians to Royston, to act before him a play which he had heard commended.

March 27. Whitehall. 112. Earl of Suffolk to the Officers of Customs at London. His Majesty having resolved that the new Company of Merchant Adventurers shall proceed, no imports or exports to or from the places where they trade are to be allowed, by any not of the Company, and no others are to export white cloths, &c.

March 28. 113. Statement of the past and present state of Northumberland, showing the increase of recusants and outlaws, chiefly by the misconduct of Roger Wodrington and Lord Wm. Howard.

March 28. Westminster. Grant to Chas. Green, in reversion after John Ditcher, of the office of Under-graver in the Mint. Latin. [*Sign Man., vol.* VI., *No.* 4.]

March 28. Westminster. Grant to Wm. Palden, executor of Jas. Knowles, of licence to purchase lands for the foundation of an hospital at Long Preston, co. York, pursuant to the will of Jas. Knowles, and incorporating the vicars and five of the inhabitants of Long Preston as governors. [*Ibid., No.* 5.]

March 28. Westminster. Warrant for payment to Sir John Fenwick, appointed to the custody of Tynemouth Castle, during the restraint of the Earl of Northumberland, of 100 marks per ann., out of the rents of the said Earl. [*Ibid., No.* 6.]

March 28. Westminster. Warrant for payment to the Same of the usual allowances for the Gunners, &c.. at Tynemouth Castle. [*Ibid., No.* 7.]

March 29. Westminster. Grant to Arnold Oldsworth and Lucy his wife, and her heirs, of lands in Brenchley and elsewhere, co. Kent, on condition of her keeping them from alienation by her brother. Latin. [*Ibid., No.* 8.]

March 29. Westminster. Discharge to Peter Van Lore, on inspection of his accounts by the Council, of all moneys from time to time issued to him. [*Ibid., No.* 9.]

March 29. Grant to Eligion Sutton of the office of Constable of Harlech Prison, &c., co. Merioneth, for life. [*Grant Bk., p.* 185.]

March 30. Grant to Sir Peter Saltonstall of the office of keeping the Little Park at Windsor, for life. [*Ibid., p.* 185.]

March 30. Dover. 114. Presentments by the jury of Dover, Ringwold, and Kingsdown, upon certain articles given in charge at the Admiralty Court of Dover, of divers persons, for maltreating or embezzling the persons or goods from the Dutch vessels lately wrecked on the Godwin Sands, and other misdemeanors. *Annexed is,*

114. i. *Similar presentments for the Isle of Thanet. March* 27.

VOL. LXXXVI.

1616.

March 30. London. 115. Edw. Sherburn to Carleton. Lady Somerset committed to the Tower, and Sir Robt. Cotton to Alderman Harvey. Gives Carleton a bond of 1,000*l.* as security for just dealings in his accounts, &c.

March ? 116. Recapitulation of the proceedings in the alum business. Grant of the first patent seven years before, and its surrender on composition for annuities. Grant of remainder of the term to John Bourchier and Wm. Turner, who have also surrendered it on composition. Suggestion for a commission to investigate the past and present state of the affair, and regulate it for the future.

March 30. Westminster. Commission to the Archbp. of Canterbury and others to examine the alum business, and to consider how it may be established for his Majesty's profit, with due consideration of those who may claim pensions therefrom. [*Sign Man., vol.* VI., *No.* 10.]

March ? 117. Interrogatories to be administered to the alum patentees and the merchants that first erected the works, to the makers, to the first and second farmers of the works, and their agents, &c., the object being to discover the double dealing of certain parties who induced the present patentees to rent them at a high rate, besides paying compositions agreed to by the King for 13,000*l*, per ann. more.

March ? 118. [The Council] to Lord Zouch. The King wishes him to settle the suit of Joachim Wardeman, of Lubeck, touching a ship taken from him by Capt. Mainwaring.

March 30. Westminster. Grant to Fras. Morgan, Fras. Barnard, and others of the fee-farm of the town of Kingsthorpe, co. Northampton, at suit of the tenants of Kingsthorpe, who were heretofore obliged to renew their lease every forty years, &c., on payment of increased rent. Latin. [*Sign Man., vol.* VI., *No.* 11.]

March 30. Westminster. Grant to Thos. Pudsey, of Stapleton, co. York, of a pension of 160*l.* per ann., during the life of Faith, his wife, in consideration of his father having lent 1,000*l.* to Mary Queen of Scots, which was never repaid. [*Ibid., No.* 12.]

March ? 119. Statement by Fras. Bernard [Gentleman Porter of the Tower] that an anonymous letter was brought him, desiring him to obtain a private interview for the writer with "that miserable lady" [the Countess of Somerset]; that he took it to Sir Josceline Percy, when Sir Chas. Manners said it would be an easy way to win 100*l.* by delivering a letter to Lord or Lady Somerset. *Annexed is,*

> 119. I. —— *to the Same. Urges him by their ancient friendship to allow him one half hour's interview with the Countess, pledging himself not to attempt her escape.*

March ? Parma. 120. Anonymous to the Earl [or Countess ?] of Somerset. Wishes he were out of his troubles. Hopes, though tongues dishonour him, things will soon be quieted. Advises him to keep secret his former night visits at St. James's, lest the vulgar might be suspicious, and

1616. VOL. LXXXVI.

to suffer disease with honour, rather than incur the hazard of downfall or infamy by a weak resistance. All in cipher. [*This letter is addressed to the Earl of Somerset, but it begins "Madame."*]

March? 121. Key to the cipher in which the above letter is written.

March? 122. Decipher of the above letter. Indorsed [by Coke], "Letters in cyphers unto the Erle of Som."

March. 123. Valuation of unserviceable military stores at Berwick, total value 68*l.* 1*s.* 1*d.*, given by the King to Robt. Thomson, of the Robes, April 5, 1616; with a subsequent indorsement [by Sir John Coke] relative to sale of stores at Norham Castle, 1633.

March? 124. Petition of John Graham, Surveyor of the Stables, to the King, for a letter to the Chief Justices in behalf of his daughter, widow of Wm. Cockayne, whose child is in danger of losing its inheritance, by the efforts of its uncle, Alderman Cockayne, in behalf of another nephew.

April 1. Grant to Sir Geo. Chaworth of the office of Constable and Keeper of Bristol Castle, for life. [*Grant Bk., p.* 181.]

April 1. Grant to Robt. Halfheid of the office of keeping the Hawks at Royston or elsewhere, in cos. Hertford and Cambridge, for life. [*Ibid., p.* 206.]

April 1. Newcastle. 125. Sir Hen. Anderson, Sheriff of Northumberland, to Winwood. Bad condition of the county as to recusancy. Many of the recusants were concerned in the Gunpowder Treason. Quarrel between Lord Wm. Howard and Roger Wodrington. Sir Geo. Selby and Mr. Riddell, Aldermen of Newcastle, complained of.

April 2. Westminster. 126. Letters Patent conferring on John Huyssy, Lord of Cattendick, in Zealand, the degree of a Knight. Latin.

April 4. Philip Lane. 127. Lord Zouch to the Mayor of Rye. To commit to custody certain fishermen of Barking, for using nets unlawfully small.

April 4. Whitehall. 128. Abraham Williams to [Carleton]. The Countess of Somerset is removed from Blackfriars to the Tower, and will be arraigned next week, "for His Majesty will have justice to take place without partiality." Sir John Digby made Vice Chamberlain and a Privy Councillor. Sir Oliver St. John made Deputy of Ireland. Albert Moreton going to Heidelberg, as Secretary to the Electress Palatine.

April 5. Grant to Rich. Hatton of the office of Clerk of Middleham and Richmond, &c., for life. [*Grant Bk., p.* 206.]

April 6. Grant to Geo. Wilson of the office of Chief Master of the Navy, for life. [*Ibid., p.* 227.]

April 6. London. 129. Sir Horace Vere to Carleton. Most of the Council incline to give up the Cautionary Towns [Flushing and Brill], but the Earl of Pembroke and Sir Thos. Lake wish to keep them. The King gone to Theobalds and Royston. Promotions at Court. Sir Chas. Wilmot made Governor of Connaught, and Sir Hen. Docwra Treasurer of Ireland.

VOL. LXXXVI.

1616.

April 6. London. 130. Chamberlain to Carleton. Lady Somerset committed to the Tower. She passionately entreated that she might not be put in Sir Thos. Overbury's lodgings, so Sir Walter Raleigh's were prepared for her. Lady Suffolk's coming to town hastened her commitment. The King gone to Theobalds, and thence visits the Lord Treasurer at Chesterford. Sir Art. Chichester newly arrived. The business of the Cautionary Towns handled at the Council. The decision is left with the King, but they must be given up, for there is no money to maintain them, and the soldiers are starving. Sends part of the play presented by the young Cambridge scholars before the King at Royston.

April 8. 131. Bailiff and Curates of Lydd to Lord Zouch. A portion of a ship wrecked on the Godwin Sands, and a piece of iron ordnance cast on shore there, are safely preserved for the owners.

April 9. London. 132. Edw. Sherburn to [Carleton]. Delivery of letters, &c. Sends a note of Winwood's allowances when in Holland. The Earl of Arundel, with Inigo Jones, has viewed the pictures, &c., and Arundel and Lord Danvers wish each to have half of them. Sir Oliver St. John made Lord Deputy of Ireland, by Villiers's influence, whose power is so great "as what he will shall be." The arraignment of Lord and Lady Somerset and Sir Thos. Monson is deferred. Attempt made to corrupt the keeper of the Countess in the Tower, to procure an interview with her, intending an escape. Pompous funeral of Sir John Grimes, a favourite of Sir Geo. Villiers, in Westminster Abbey. The butchers of King Street buried a dog in Tothill Fields, in ridicule of the ceremony, saying, the soul of a dog was as good as that of a Scot. Several of them are apprehended, and will be whipped. The communion cloth, two copes, and Prince Henry's robes, stolen from the Abbey Church. The King is at Newmarket, the Queen at Greenwich, and the Prince at St. James's. Sec. Winwood increases in favour.

April 9. 133. Hen. Lord Danvers to the Same. Has received the picture of the Creation, but thinks it too grave, and wishes to exchange it for "soum toyes fitt to furnish a lodge," from the best hands. Lord Hay's journey to France promises a match for the Prince. Fears necessity will enforce the surrender of the Cautionary Towns. The great prisoner to be tried the last of the month.

April 9. Oxford. 134. Inquisition post mortem of the lands, &c. of Edw. Morgan, deceased, by which it appears that Robt. Wyncott, of Kingham, co. Oxon, was indebted to the said Morgan, at his decease, in the sum of 250*l.*, but that he had no other property in the county. Latin.

April 11. Commission to Edw. Lord Wotton and others, for examining witnesses in divers causes in controversy between Walter Earl of Ormond and Rich. Lord Dingwall, and others. [*Grant Bk., p.* 200.]

Vol. LXXXVI.

1616.

April 16. Tuesday. 135. Sir Fras. Bacon to Coke. The King requires all the examinations of Sir Wm. Monson to be sent to him.

April 17. 136. Wm. Morton to Winwood. Mr. Smaithwaite is going to London, and will give further particulars of Roger and Sir Hen. Wodrington's factious proceedings. Has heard that Philip Thirlway, of Hexham, confessed on his death-bed that Roger Wodrington had a great share in the Powder Plot.

April ? 137. Petition of Wm. Dowland, Gunner of Camber Castle, to Lord Zouch. Having accepted his place of Gunner in lieu of 30*l.* bequeathed to him by his late master, the Earl of Northampton, and wishing to retire into the country, begs leave to sell the place.

April 17. 138. Petition of the Same to the Same, that he may give his place to a friend, and have some recompence for the 30*l.* which he paid for it.

April 18. Grant to Alex. and Vincent Glover of the office of Gamekeeper in Lambeth Marsh and elsewhere, co. Surrey, for life. [*Grant Bk., p.* 210.]

April 19. Grant to John Michell of the office of keeping the Seal and signing writs in the Common Pleas, during pleasure. [*Ibid., p.* 213.]

April 19. 139. Bond of Allart Garbart, of St. Omer, Artois, under penalty of 100*l.*, to deliver all passengers by his boat to the Commissioners for Passage, and not to convey away any person who has not a licence.

April 19. 140. Draft of the above.

April 20. 141. Sir Matthew Carew to Carleton. Hopes his son Thomas will deserve well in Carleton's service. Sir Charles intercepts much of the profit of his place. Wishes Carleton would take up the mortgage, which his niece, Lady Carew, has on his house.

April ? 142. List of the Knights of the Garter, anno 1616.

April 20. London. 143. Chamberlain to Carleton. The King arrived from Theobalds, for St. George's Feast, and then returns for Thetford and Newmarket. The Earl and Countess of Somerset's arraignment deferred. The Earl was examined by the Duke of Lenox and others. Coke has given up the business into the Attorney General's hands. Sir Geo. Villiers threatened with the small-pox, which would have ended his favour. Sir John Grimes, his late favourite, buried with great solemnity at Westminster. The people in mockery buried a dog in Tothill Fields. Several concerned therein whipped by Order of Council.

April 20. Whitehall. 144. Abraham Williams to the Same. The Earl of Somerset has been twice examined in the Tower. The decision about the surrender of the Cautionary Towns is referred by the King to the Council.

April 20. London. 145. Edw. Sherburn to the Same. Private affairs. Lord Arundel and Lord Danvers have agreed to take the whole parcel of pictures, &c.

Vol. LXXXVI.

1616.

[April 21.] 146. Petition of the Company of Pinmakers to the Council, for a day on which to be heard against the claim of aliens to import foreign pins.

April 22. St. James's. 147. Hen. Lord Danvers to Carleton. The Spanish marriage probable, though likely to be delayed. The King will not give up the Cautionary Towns, if he can find any other way of gaining money.

April 24. Grant to Jas. Maxwell of the office of collecting the subsidy of tollage in the port of London, for life. [*Grant Bk., p.* 221.]

[April 24.] 148. Names of the Lords appointed to try the Earl and Countess of Somerset for the murder of Sir Thos. Overbury, with the King's letter of summons, commanding their attendance at the trial, and a list of the witnesses. [*See Howell's State Trials, vol.* II., *p.* 951.]

April 25. 149. Edw. Sherburn to Carleton. Has forwarded him two tuns of 6*s.* beer, &c.

April 25. Serjeants' Inn. 150. The Judges to the King. Regret their inability to comply with his directions, as communicated by the Attorney General, to postpone a certain cause, but the order being contrary to law, they are bound by their oaths not to regard it. [*See Dom. Corresp., June* 6.]

[April 26.] 151. Petition of John Lamote, Wm. Crosse, Adam Lawrence, and John Stephens, to the King, that, as born in England, though of foreign parents, and submitting to law, church, and government taxes as subjects, they may export and import merchandize, paying only such customs as English merchants pay.

April 26. London. 152. Alex. Williams to Sir Dud. Carleton. Taverner is condemned in the King's Bench. The nobility are summoned for the arraignment [of the Earl of Somerset]. The Earl of Rutland and Sir Geo. Villiers made Knights of the Garter, and the latter Visct. Beaumont.

April 27. St. James's. 153. Hen. Lord Danvers to the Same. Lieut. Darrell begs a prolongation of leave of absence, being employed by Lord Wotton as Muster Master of Kent. Lord Hay intends to pass by the Hague, on his return from France and Heidelberg. Lord Roos pleased with his embassy to Spain. The King has given to Lord Lisle 6,000*l.*, and to Sir Horace Vere the reversion, after Lord Carew, of the Mastership of the Ordnance.

April 27. Grant to Geo. and Wm. Hope of the office of Master of St. John's Hospital in Chester, for life. [*Grant Bk., p.* 206.]

April 28. Grant to Thos. Chamberlain of the office of Justice of cos. Chester, Flint, Denbigh and Montgomery, for life. [*Ibid., p.* 197.]

April 28. London. 154. Sir Geo. Goring to Carleton. Is to go to France with Lord Hay, who expects to sail every day. The arraignments to be on May 14. Sir Robt. Carr and Mr. Gibb have been examined, and confined to their chamber, but freed again.

VOL. LXXXVI.

1616.

April 28. Newmarket. 155. Petition of Jane, widow of Nich. Darcy, to the King, for a grant of the benefit of transportation of all manner of lime, burnt and slacked, limestone, chalk, &c., by strangers, in recompence of the services of her late husband to Queen Elizabeth. With reference thereon and report, objecting to it as a monopoly.

April ? 156. Petition of the Same to Lord Zouch. Her patent for the sole transportation of limestone from Kent, Essex, and Sussex being complained against, as injurious to the town of Dover, refers the final decision thereon to his Lordship.

April 29. Westminster. Presentation of Thos. Darley to the rectory of Winterton, with the chapel of East Somerton, co. Norfolk. Latin. [*Sign Man., vol. VI., No.* 13.]

April 29. Licence to Rich. Hale to erect a grammar school in the town of Hertford, and grant of divers liberties to the elders and burgesses of the town, as governors of the said school. [*Grant Bk., p.* 206.]

April 29. Whitehall. 157. Fras. Blundell to Carleton. Will not believe the arraignments will take place till he sees them. The Cautionary Towns to be yielded for 200,000*l.*, but the King would not give them up "if money could be made any other wayes." The Lords are displeased because Sir Oliver St. John was nominated Deputy of Ireland through the private influence of Sir Geo. Villiers.

April 29. Oxford. 158. Sir Hen. Savile to the Same. Sorry for his daughter [Lady Carleton's] hoarseness. Will thank Sir Wm. Sedley for his kind entertainment of Carleton.

April 30. Whitehall. 159. The Council to Lord Zouch. The musters in the kingdom having been found generally defective, they are again to be taken. All the bands, trained or untrained, to be reviewed, the trained bands kept well disciplined under their own officers, and especially the defects in the horse to be supplied; also the clergy arms to be viewed, powder and bullets, &c. supplied.

April 30. London. 160. Chamberlain to Carleton. Resolution taken to part with the Cautionary Towns; the commanders, Lord Lisle, Sir Horace Vere, and Sir Edw. Conway, being pensioned off. Surprise that the Earl of Rutland and Sir Geo. Villiers are made Knights of the Garter, the former having a recusant wife, and the latter being so little known and poor; but the King has given him Lord Grey's lands, and will give him some of Somerset's. The Commissioners [for Overbury's cause] go often to the Tower. Sir Robt. Carr and Gibb of the Bedchamber, confined for burning letters and papers. Lord Roos appointed Ambassador Extraordinary for Spain. He and his mother called in question for slandering Winwood. Taverner condemned to death, for killing Bird five years before.

April. 161. Account of moneys paid from the Exchequer to Hugh Middleton, goldsmith of London, for charges in bringing the water from

1616. VOL. LXXXVI.

Amwell and Chadwell to London, by virtue of Letters Patent, dated May 2, 1612. Total 2,262*l.* 9*s.* 6½*d.*

April. 162. Copy of the above.

VOL. LXXXVII. MAY, JUNE, 1616.

May 1. 1. Statement of Wm. Barroway as to the residence and salary of the Porter of the Minories for forty years past; sent to an attendant of Lord Carew.

May 1. Hythe. 2. Mayor of Hythe to Lord Zouch. Has apprehended certain persons fishing with unlawful nets on the coast. The most dangerous are not yet taken. Some of them shot at the fishermen who went to seize them.

May 2. 3. Examination of Rich Copeman, of Hexham, Northumberland. His former master John Sicklemore, Seminary Priest, previous to the Powder Plot, collected large contributions from the recusants of Hexham; Roger Wodrington, being then Bailiff, knew of this collection, and directed the recusants. Was imprisoned by him for going to church, &c. Faukes is reported to have been at Dilston, by the name of Johnson, before the conspiracy.

May 3. 4. Examination of Alex. Ridley, of Whitsheeles, Northumberland. Money was said to have been gathered in Hexham towards the Powder Plot. Phil. Thirlwall, of Hexham, repented on his deathbed not having discovered some who had a hand in the plot, and charged others to do it.

May 3. 5. Examination of Thos. Fenwick, of Wallington, Northumberland. Entered Percy's service in Oct. 1605, and went with his man Tailbois to London, with two horses laden with money. Particulars of their proceedings after the plot was found out; also of his recent mode of life, intercourse with Robt. and Geo. Thirlwall, recusants, &c. Is now in the service of Sir John Fenwick.

May 3. 6. Receipt by John Diglett from Paul Bayning, Bart., of the post fine, &c. of the manors of Champneys, with appurtenances and pastures in Woodham Ferris, co. Essex, &c., which fine was advanced by Diglett to Fras. Smythe, the bailiff.

May 4. 7. Recognition by Robt. Fleming, of Dover, master and part owner of the Phœnix, wrecked upon the Godwin Sands, that his bark by "this casualty doth absolutely belong and appertain as a wreck to Lord Zouch, in right of the royalty due unto him as Lord Warden of the Cinque Ports."

May 4. Philip Lane. 8. [Lord Zouch] to Thos. Fulnetby. Desires that the Phœnix may be repaired at his own charge, and given back to Mr. Fleming, the master.

May 4. 9. Note of certain goods concealed out of the wrecked goods upon the Godwin Sands, seized by the Searcher of Dover.

VOL. LXXXVII.

1616.

May 4. London. 10. Edw. Sherburn to Carleton. Private affairs. Mr. Bingley has promised payment of Carleton's allowance, &c. at the end of the month.

May 5. Dover Castle. 11. Nich. Knott to Rich. Younge. Apologizes for having sent an unsigned letter. Requests to know whether the Mayor has received any money for him from Capt. Mainwaring's men.

May ? 12. Request by [Chas.] Buckland that Robt. Wyncott may satisfy a debt of 250*l.* due to Edw. Morgan, the arrears of whose recusancy were granted by the King to John Carse, and by him sold to Buckland. [*See April* 6, 1610.]

May 6. Monday. 13. Order in the Exchequer for a subpœna to Robt. Wyncott, of Kingham, co. Oxon, to show cause why he should not answer to His Majesty a debt of 250*l.* due by him to Edw. Morgan, recusant.

May 7. Newcastle-on-Tyne. 14. Wm. Morton to Sir Ralph Winwood. Is glad of the restraint of Roger Wodrington, whose oppressions have done great harm in Northumberland. He is confident of escape from the accusation of making a collection for Catholics. Instances of his misconduct, and that of his brother Sir Henry, whilst the Judges look on, "bite their lips, and scratch their heds, and saie in private, 'See you not to what a pass wee are comm in Northumberland?'" Hundreds would complain, but they "fere his letting loose agen, and his brother Sir Harrie's heavi hand." Has been a minister thirty-four years. Will come to town on this business, if needful.

May 7. Newcastle-upon-Tyne. 15. The Same to Archbp. Abbot. Has been prevented by long sickness from coming to town, to tell what he knows of Roger Wodrington. Details the presumptions of his complicity in the Powder Plot, &c.; his favour with the late Earl of Salisbury, and with Lord Wm. Howard, the Earls of Suffolk and Somerset, &c., who have protected him from accusation. Though he is now committed, people are so afraid of his return, and of Lord Wm. Howard, that they dare not accuse him.

May 7. 16. Petition of Wm. and Eliz. Kirkby to Sir Julius Cæsar, that, being sickly, they may be allowed to give in their answers by commissioners, in the suit brought against them by Edw. Galland. With order thereon.

May 7. Grant to Wm. Wollascot of licence to hold the court in the manor of Brixton and others, co. Berks, [*Grant Bk., p.* 227.]

May 8. 17. Lord Chancellor Ellesmere to the King. Prays, on account of great bodily and mental infirmities, to be discharged from his office.

May 8. Sandwich. 18. John Oliver, Under Droit-gatherer of Sandwich, to Lord Zouch. A claim was made by an officer of the Lord Admiral to a ship wrecked on the Godwin Sands, which has been recovered by the men of Sandwich for Lord Z ouch.

VOL. LXXXVII.

1616.

May 8. Grant to Hum. Robinson of the grange of Ridding, &c., co. York. [*Grant Bk.*, *p.* 195.]

May 8. Grant to Rich. Miller of licence to hold the court in the manors of Sturmer, Heasworth, &c., cos. Essex and Suffolk. [*Ibid.*, *p.* 221.]

May 10. Commission to Lord Ellesmere to be Steward of England for the time being. [*Ibid.*, *p.* 168.]

May 10. 19. Survey of the repairs most needful for the castles of Camber, Sandgate, Walmer, Deal, and Sandown, and for Arch-cliff Bulwark and Mote's Bulwark; taken by command of Lord Zouch.

[May 10.] Grant to Sir Horace Vere of the office of Master of the Ordnance. [*Grant Bk.*, *p.* 187.]

May 11. 20. Warrant from the Archbp. of Canterbury, commanding Jeremiah Park, of diocese Lincoln, to appear before the court of St. Paul's, in the appeal of the cause of the said Park *v.* Thos. Bullingham, and others. Latin.

May 12. Dover Castle. 21. Thos. Fulnetby to Rich. Younge. If Lord Zouch thinks he has a right to the two pieces of ordnance which are at Romney, because they came floating, some masts and other things also came floating, which shall be seized.

May 13. 22. Petition of John Mynterne, sen., and John Mynterne, jun., to Sir Julius Cæsar, for their answers to be taken by commission, in a certain suit, they living in Dorsetshire. With order thereon.

May 15. 23. List of payments made to Wm. Herrick, John Spilman, and Geo. Herriot, King's Jewellers, in part of the fee of 150*l.* a year, granted them by the patent of their office, Nov. 9, 1603. Total, 1,725*l.*

May 15. Grant to Fras. Tunstie of an annuity of 500*l.*, for life. [*Grant Bk.*, *p.* 191.]

May 15. Grant to Sir Wm. Smithe of the office of Marshal of the Marshalsea in the King's Bench. [*Ibid.*, *p.* 189.]

May 17. London. 24. Edw. Sherburn to [Carleton]. The Earl of Shrewsbury is dead, leaving only 1,500*l.* out of 16,000*l.* a year in land to his brother and successor, with whom he had some quarrel. The Lord Treasurer and his Lady gone to Audley-End, for shame at the arraignment of their daughter and son-in-law, the Earl and Countess of Somerset, but this is postponed, because the Countess is unwell, and the Earl, seeing he must be tried, which he would not believe before, promises to discover some matters which nearly concern the King and State. Letter from Thos. Walker, a crazy Captain, to the Archbp. of Canterbury, railing against Barnevelt, &c. Abraham Williams has had great difficulty in getting Carleton's bills for transportations, intelligences, secret services, &c. allowed; they were thought too high. Mrs. Vincent's barbarous murder of her children.

May 18. London. 25. Chamberlain to the Same. The trial of Somerset and his Lady put off. Great prices given for seats in Westminster Hall.

1616. VOL. LXXXVII.

Taverner is reprieved; also Anderson, condemned for murder. A woman condemned for murdering her own children, because her husband wished them to be brought up Protestants. Dr. Morton elected Bishop of Chester. Dr. Godwin has published a Latin history, from Henry VIII. to Elizabeth. Winwood is busy with the Earl of Shrewsbury's executorship. His getting the Countess out of the Tower gained her 50,000*l.* or 60,000*l.* She has 20,000*l.* jointure. Winwood is offended with a letter of advice written him by Carleton, &c.

May 20. Commission to Wm. Earl of Pembroke, Lord Chamberlain, to receive inventories, and call to account all persons known to possess wardrobe stuff. [*Grant Bk., p.* 167.]

May 21. Commission to the Archbp. of Canterbury and others to treat with Sir Noel de Caron for yielding the town of Flushing to the States General. [*Ibid., p.* 168.]

May 22. Commission to Sir Horace Vere to yield the town of Brill, &c. to the States General. [*Ibid., p.* 168.]

May 22. Commission to Robt. Visct. Lisle to yield the town of Flushing, &c. to the States General. [*Ibid., p.* 167.]

May 23. Greenwich. 26. [Thos.] Murray to Carleton. The Prince leaves the decision as to the purchase of the models [of warlike engines] to the opinions of Sir Horace Vere and Sir Edw. Cecil. If bought, the payment is to be arranged within a year, lest, by stipulating for delay, the wants of the Exchequer should appear.

May 24. 27. Report [sent by Edw. Sherburn to the Same], of the proceedings at the trial of the Earl of Somerset. [*Very different from the report in the State Trials, vol. II., p.* 966.]

May 25. London. 28. Chamberlain to the Same. Has been at the Earl of Somerset's trial since six in the morning, and paid 10*s.* for his place. The Earl denies everything; says his letters are counterfeit, but refuses to write that comparison may be made of the hand. The Countess confessed; her behaviour too confident, though she made a show of tears. It is thought she will not die. Both were very civilly treated at their trials.

May 25. London. 29. Edw. Sherburn to [the Same]. The Countess of Somerset on her trial confessed herself guilty. Her noble carriage, and yet deep penitence, commended her to all. The trial lasted not two hours. Some say she will be reprieved, but the King, at the first discovery of the plot, so protested that the law should take its course, that he can hardly spare her. The Earl's trial lasted ten hours; his carriage was undaunted, but though he was allowed to take notes, his defence was poor and idle. He had the same sentence of Guilty.

May 26. London. 30. The Same to the Same. His Majesty has conferred the honour of the Garter upon Lord Lisle, who is going to Flushing.

VOL. LXXXVII.

1616.
May 26. 31. Declaration of the Serjeants-at-Arms, that they will allow to John Williams, Serjeant, 20s. out of every 5l. of their increased fees from persons knighted, which fees have been obtained by his diligence in prosecuting their suit. *Annexed is,*

31. I. *Grant to the Serjeants-at-Arms of increase of fees from 1l. to 5l., to be received from all persons on whom the honour of knighthood shall be conferred; the fees of the Gentleman Ushers, Daily Waiters, and Kings and Heralds-at-Arms having been similarly raised.*

May 27. Canterbury. Monday. 32. Rich. Marsh to Rich. Younge. The pirate vessels were captured between Margate and Broadstairs. Process should issue in the jurisdiction where the fact was committed, and precedents from records prove that it was within the jurisdiction of the Cinque Ports.

May ? 33. Arguments in favour of granting a patent for making writs of latitat, the same as granted for other writs.

May 27. Grant to Geo. Spatchurst of the Receivership of all Fines upon actions by way of latitat or otherwise, in the King's Bench, for life. [*Grant Bk., p.* 185.]

May 29. London. 34. Edw. Palavicino to Carleton. The Friday when the Lady [Countess of Somerset] was tried, the proceedings were "the fayrest, respective, honorable, gracefullest," "for judgement, reverence, humblenesse, discretion, that ever yet presented itself." Her behaviour was noble, graceful, and modest. Her confession shortened the trial; and the Lord High Steward pronounced the sentence so gently that she knew not that she was condemned. The second day when the Earl was tried, it was ten at night before sentence was given. Thinks from the proofs that he persuaded his wife to the crime. The general wish is that the King may spare him; is surprised at it, for he was covetous, ambitious, and untrue to his word.

May 30. London. 35. Edw. Reynoldes to Fras. Mills. Sends him his dividend. Complains of Edm. Clerk, deputy to his father Sir Thomas, in the office, for not attending to it himself, but leaving to his man, H. Rolfe. Will reduce the cost of the dividend dinners.

May 30. London. 36. The Same to the Same. Suspects Thos. Packer of fraud, in pretending to excuse payment of fees in the office of the Privy Seal.

May 30. Lambeth. 37. Examination of Roger Wodrington. Was acquainted with [Thos.] Percy. Came up to London before the Powder Plot, and on his way home was taken and examined before the Council at York. Only heard by report of the collection made from recusants. His intercourse and quarrel with Philip Thirlwall. Has impanelled Romanists as jurors, but never reproached Protestants for their religion. Has caused Mr. Smaithwaite's parishioners to attend his meetings for recovery of stolen goods on Sunday, but only a few times.

May 30. 38. Informations against the Same, on which the above examination is founded.

1616. Vol. LXXXVII.

May 30. Grant to Sir Horace Vere of an annuity of 800*l*., for life. [*Grant Bk.*, *p.* 191.]

May 31. Grant to Robt. Visct. Lisle of an annuity of 1,000*l*., for life. [*Ibid.*, *p.* 219.]

May 31. Lambeth. 39. Archbp. Abbot to Winwood. The King wishes an advowson speedily drawn up for the next prebend in Canterbury, to be conferred on Dr. Alex. Chapman, Chaplain to the Princess Elizabeth. Roger Wodrington, whose guilt clearly appears, must be confined and kept out of his own district, as a warning to others.

May 31. London. 40. Edw. Sherburn to [Carleton]. The Earl of Somerset and his Lady were desired to prepare for their end, but are still respited. During the Earl's trial, the King was so extremely uneasy lest he should say something, that he could take no food till told that he had only spoken about the business. Sir Thos. Parry, Chancellor of the Duchy of Lancaster, deceased. It is thought Sir Thos. Edmondes will have the place, not Mr. Dackombe. The Venetian Ambassador and the old Countess of Cumberland dead. Sir Thos. Monson is to be brought to trial. The King boxed the Prince's ears, for turning a water-spout on Sir Geo. Villiers in jest, in the garden at Greenwich. M. Schomberg is come over, on a contest between the Palsgrave and Lady Elizabeth, because he does not wish to allow her the precedency in public assemblies, out of her own Court.

May. Greenwich. [Sir Ralph Winwood] to Sir Hen. Wotton. Surrender of Flushing and Brill. Most of the troops are taken into the State's service, under Col. Sydney, Lord Lisle's son; the rest pensioned off by the King. Lord Lisle made Knight of the Garter. Lord Hay going Ambassador to France. Trial of the Earl and Countess of Somerset. She pleaded guilty, wore a resolved and settled countenance, and after sentence, bowed three times to the Peers, before leaving the bar. The Earl was pale, showing both guilt and fear of death. The evidence was clear that he led to Sir Thos. Overbury's imprisonment, by persuading him to refuse the preferment offered him by the King, and then sent him poison. His defence poor and disjointed. [*Venice Corresp., May.*]

June 1. Lydd. 41. Bailiff and Jurats of Lydd to Rich. Younge. Refuse to deliver up a piece of ordnance recovered from the sea by certain persons of their town, without a special warrant from Lord Zouch, and until they know the owners, and can obtain a reward from them for the savers.

June 4. 42. List of contributions to the benevolence, by certain persons and places named, from Oct. 10, 1615.

June 4. Grant to John Tindall of a Gunner's place in the Tower, for life. [*Grant Bk.*, *p.* 191.]

June 4. Commission to the Archbp. of Canterbury and others to examine all who can give testimony concerning speeches touching the jurisdiction of the Court of Chancery, in case of præmunire. [*Ibid.*, *p.* 168.]

VOL. LXXXVII.

1616.
June 5. Grant to Wm. Earl of Pembroke, of the office of Constable of the prison of Radnor, &c., co. Radnor, for life. [*Grant Bk., p.* 214.]

June 6. 43. The King to Lord Treasurer Suffolk. Great abuses have crept into the Exchequer, by the accounts being kept in the hands of the auditors, and passed without due examination; by non-inrolment of records, &c., with other misdemeanors which require reformation. Enjoins him to draw out a table of Exchequer offices, to call in all the accounts of receivers, &c. from the time of Queen Mary, and all rent rolls, court rolls, &c., and have them properly deposited.

June 6.
Whitehall. 44. Proceedings in Council, to which the twelve Judges are summoned, concerning the King's right to grant letters in commendam. His Majesty's statement of his previous proceedings. The arguments of Serjeant Chibborne against the King's right to grant commendams, on which His Majesty had ordered the Judges to postpone their verdict till they had consulted with him. Their refusal to do this, as being illegal; his absolute command for delay, if his prerogative would be touched on in the argument, &c. The King censured both the substance and form of the Judges' letter, on which they all fell on their knees to beg pardon. After further arguments between Lord Chief Justice Coke, the Chancellor, the Attorney General, and the King, the Judges were asked severally if they would obey any future similar mandate sent by His Majesty, which all promised except Lord Chief Justice Coke, who said "he would do that should be fit for a Judge to do." The Judges promised that in further arguing the case, they would not only reprove any bold speeches against the prerogative, but would declare and maintain the King's right to grant commendams. His Majesty, after lecturing them on the due performance of their duties, dismissed them, and asked the opinions of the Council, which were all against the refusal of the Judges to stay proceedings at his request. *Inserting,*

44. I. *Sir Fras. Bacon to the Lord Chief Justice, commanding stay of proceedings till consultation with His Majesty. April* 25, 1616.

44. II. *The Judges to the King, in reply, refusing postponement. Serjeants' Inn, April* 27. [*See Dom. Corresp., April* 27.]

44. III. *The King to the Judges. Objects to their refusal, because though not wont to interfere with the speedy course of justice, this case intrenched upon his prerogative, which he will think wounded if even allowed to be publicly disputed, having already been too boldly dealt with in Westminster Hall. Cases being so often postponed for light causes, their pleading their oath to his prejudice is a frivolous pretence. Absolutely forbids their proceeding further, till they have communed with him on the cause.*

Vol. LXXXVII.

1616.

June 6. 45. Rough draft of part of the above proceedings, omitting the documents.

June 6. Charing Cross. 46. Sir Robt. Brett to Rich. Younge. Had permitted Chas. Crimble, Gunner of Dover Castle, to go into Ireland, before he left his charge of Dover Castle.

June 6. Lambeth. 47. Certificate of sentence of deprivation for simony, against Thos. Bold, Rector of Winwick, Lancashire.

June 7. London. 48. Alex. Williams to Carleton. The execution of the Earl of Somerset is daily looked for. A crowd assembled at Tower Hill on Monday, expecting it to take place.

June 8. 49. Bond of John Blackney, of Drogheda, and Hum. Tookey, of London, under penalty of 1,000*l.*, to indemnify Lord Zouch for restoring to Blackney certain goods recovered from a wreck, within his jurisdiction.

June 8. Philip Lane. 50. [Lord Zouch] to Thos. Fulnetby. Warrant to deliver the goods saved from the Phœnix, of Dover, lately wrecked on the Godwin Sands, to John Blackney, one of the owners.

June 8. London. 51. Chamberlain to Carleton. The Earl of Somerset stands on his innocency, and only requests that he may be beheaded, not hanged, and that his daughter may inherit some of his lands. Lady Knollys and others have visited the Countess. Sir Thos. Monson's trial deferred, and it is thought no more will be heard of it. The King very bitter against Lord Coke, about the proceedings in the commendam case. He bears up well, but there is a commission to examine him on the præmunire, and to rip up his former life. Winwood supports him. Death of Sir Owen Oglethorpe and Sir Thos. Parry. Sir John Dackombe knighted and made Chancellor of the Duchy of Lancaster, though he was opposed because he was guilty of foul dealings about the pardon of the Earl of Somerset, &c. Bacon likely to be of the Council, though his place as Attorney is an objection.

June 8. Grant to Sir Fras. Eure of the office of Justice in cos. Carnarvon, Merioneth, and Anglesea, during pleasure. [*Grant Bk., p.* 209.]

June 10. Grant to Ant. Weldon of the Prison of Rochester, &c., co. Kent. [*Ibid., p.* 227.]

June 10. Grant to Sir Rich. Wilbraham of licence to hold the Court in the manors of Tilston, Bunbury, &c., co. Chester. [*Ibid., p.* 227.]

June 10. Dover Castle. 52. Nich. Knott to Rich Younge. The Castle Guard are threatened with punishment if they do not appear at the musters, notwithstanding the agreement between Lord Zouch and Lord Wotton. Has advised them to go, but without their arms, and explain the case; begs further directions.

June 10. Oxford. 53. Sir Hen. Savile to Carleton. Commissions him to deal with J. Bell in an exchange of books; also to purchase for him four horses, the price not to exceed 100*l.*, which "is much in a beggar's purse."

VOL. LXXXVII.

1616.

June 11. Grant to Hen. Finch of the office of Serjeant-at-Law, during pleasure. [*Grant Bk., pp.* 209, 217.]

June? 54. Note of the fees, &c. of the Chancellor of the Duchy of Lancaster.

June 12. London. 55. Edw. Sherburn to [Carleton]. Mr. Dackombe, now Sir John, has, by means of the Prince, or rather Sir Geo. Villiers, succeeded as Chancellor of the Duchy of Lancaster. Sir Fras. Bacon is made a Privy Councillor, and will be Keeper of the Great Seal; the Lord Chancellor being made President of the Council and Earl of Flint. At the creation of the Prince [as Prince of Wales,] Sir Geo. Villiers will be made Earl of Leicester, and other creations will take place. Lord Coke has received great disgrace by his stout carriage in the business of the commendams, the King calling him knave; his deposition is expected. His Majesty carries things more secretly and absolutely than before. Sir Robt. Cotton, and the servants of the Earl and Countess of Somerset, are released. No money in the Exchequer; the sums paid by the States are already disposed of, except 7,000*l.* or 8,000*l.* for the King's progress.

June 13. St. Martin's Lane. 56. John More to the Same. Thinks Carleton will be permitted to go to the Spa. The instalment [of the Prince] will be at Windsor, July 9, when it is thought the Lord Chancellor and Master of the Horse will be created earls.

June 13. Grant to Sir Wm. Throgmorton, Bart., of the office of Master of the Wild Beasts in Crossland Chace, co. Gloucester, for life. [*Grant Bk., p.* 189.]

June 14. Strand. 57. G. Gerard to Carleton. Weak defence of [the Earl and Countess of Somerset] by their Counsel. The people assembled several times on the Tower Hill, expecting their execution; but it is now thought their lives will be spared. The King displeased with Lord Chief Justice Coke about the business of commendams, and his harshness in the late trial has made him enemies; his fall is spoken of. One of Sir Geo. Villiers' brothers made Groom of the Chamber to the Prince, and another is to be Knight Marshal. Lord Eure willing to resign the Presidency of Wales to Lord Chandos, but Lord Gerard tries to obtain it. The King feasted by Alderman Cockayne and the new Company of Merchant Adventurers, who gave him 1,000*l.* in a basin and ewer of gold. Dyers, cloth dressers, with their shuttles, and Hamburgians, were presented to the King, "and spake such language as Ben Jonson putt in theyre mouthes." Lord Carew sworn a Councillor, at the Queen's request. The Prince to be made Prince of Wales, without cost. The Chancellor is about to resign, and will be made, for his long services, Earl of Buckingham, and President of the Council during the Prince's minority. Sir Robt. Cotton liberated, although he assisted the Earl of Somerset to falsify the evidence brought against him. The two Monsons still in the Tower.

Vol. LXXXVII.

1616.

June 14. Grant to Hugh Cavendish of the office of keeping the Armoury at Westminster, for life. [*Grant Bk.*, *p.* 197.]

June 14. Grant to Thos. Leeds of licence to hold the Court of Crenston, co. Kent. [*Ibid.*, *p.* 220.]

June 14. Grant to Sir Geo. Villiers of the office of keeping the Honour ot Hampton Court, &c., cos. Middlesex and Surrey, for life. [*Ibid.*, *p.* 187.]

June 15. London. 58. Edw. Sherburn to Carleton. The King stood godfather to Lord Salisbury's son and heir. Lord Cobham's release is expected; also Sir Walter Raleigh's pardon, for the gentlemen will not hazard going with him unless he obtain it.

June 17. 59. Petition of Edw. Barkley to Sir Julius Cæsar, for a power to answer by commissioners in the country, in the suit against him by Stephen Miller. With order thereon.

June 17. Dover Castle. 60. Nich. Knott to Rich. Younge. Ingratitude of the County Guard, who fail to give the 20*l.* or 30*l.* which they promised, if they might obtain exemption from the musters.

June 18. London. 61. Daniel More to Sir Thos. Riddel. [And.] Boyd has succeeded in getting his seals of office made, though his answers to the objections of their party against his patent [of the Surveyorship of Coals] are very unsatisfactory, but he has many friends in Council.

June 18. 62. Thos. Wilson to Ambrose Randolph. Is engaged in a suit about Sir Roger Wilbraham's place at Court. Sends Mrs. Wilson to take care of him and Mrs. Randolph in their sickness.

June 19. Proclamation against serving warrants for fee deer in the King's forests. [*Grant Bk.*, *p.* 213.]

June 19. 63. Means devised for raising 100,000*l.* for the King, viz., further sale of mills, chantry lands, ruined castles, &c., extension of the terms of leases, for a present fine and increased rents. If it is to be done by borrowing, 1,000 persons should be asked for 100*l.* each, on security of land, especially those who have received favours from His Majesty. Lord Fenton's project of respite of homage to be reconsidered.

June 19. 64. Similar brief memoranda of means proposed for raising 100,000*l.*

June 20. Ragley. 65. Fras. Conyers to Sir Edw. Conway, his nephew. Asks directions in the management of Conway's stables and farm. Thos. Comes has cited the inhabitants of Loddington to appear and answer his claim to some tithes belonging to his late uncle John Comes. Has dismissed Mr. Wright, curate of Loddington; after notice was given him, he ceased to pray for Conway and his family, as he was wont to do.

VOL. LXXXVII.

1616.
June 21. London. 66. Daniel More to Sir Thos. Riddel. Thinks it advisable to postpone till next term their further opposition against Mr. Boyd's patent for surveying coals at Newcastle, the King having ordered his prerogative not to be argued upon, without his foreknowledge, and the expected promotions of law officers creating great uncertainty. *Annexed are,*

66. I. *Reasons offered by the Mayor, &c. of Newcastle-upon-Tyne, against the patent granted to Mr. Boyd for surveying coals, as being unnecessary, unprofitable, and illegal.*

June 21. Licence to John Norborn to hold the Court in the manor of Goteacre and elsewhere, co. Wilts. [*Grant Bk., p.* 214.]

June 21. Licence to Sir Wm. Webbe to hold the Court in the manor of Dipdon, co. Hants. [*Ibid., p.* 225.]

June 21. Licence to Jos. Winston to hold the Court in the manor of Stoke-Lacy, &c., co. Hereford. [*Ibid., p.* 225.]

June 21. Licence to Hen. Samborne to hold the Court Leet in the manor of Moulsford and elsewhere, co. Berkshire. [*Ibid., p.* 185.]

June 21. Licence to Ralph Rudcliffe to hold the Court in the manor of Maydencroft and elsewhere, co. Hertford. [*Ibid., p.* 195.]

June 22. London. 67. Chamberlain to [Carleton]. The King dined at Alderman Cockayne's, and had a present of 1,000*l.*, and the Prince of 500*l.* The Alderman was knighted. Sir Fras. Bacon sworn of the Council, and was to have been Lord Keeper, but the Lord Chancellor is unwilling to part with the Seals. Various changes talked of, to make place for him. Peerages proposed. The progress to Rufford is to begin on July 19. Lord Gerard has bought the Presidency of Wales from Lord Eure. Sir Robt. Cotton is enlarged, and the two Monsons will soon follow. The Lord Treasurer restored to favour. Lord Coke has had much ado to beat off the storm. His Lady has solicited much for him, and refuses to sever her interests from his, as is desired. If he escape, it will be because the King is told that if he falls, he will be honoured as the martyr of the commonwealth. Sir Thos. Dale has brought from Virginia Pocahuntas, the daughter of Powatan the King, who is married to Rolfe, an Englishman. The country promises well, but no present profit is expected.

June 22. London. 68. Edw. Sherburn to [the Same]. The Bp. of Winchester dead of apoplexy. The Bp. of Bath and Wells to succeed him. The King's speech in the Star Chamber on the præmunire is to be printed, to show the falseness of the report that he is ill affected to the law of England. Lord Arundel will take all the pictures, but delays payment.

June 23. Greenwich. 69. Petition of Fras. Needham and others, creditors of Thos. Alport, the King's servant, to the King, for means to be taken with

1616. Vol. LXXXVII.

a few obstinate creditors of Alport, who will not accept of instalments to be paid in four years, as the rest have done. With reference to the Lord Mayor of London.

June 24. Grant to Hen. Thornton of the office of Heater of the Wax in Chancery, for life. [*Ibid.*, *p.* 189.]

June 24. Grant to Robt. Erskine and Patricius Maccalla of the office of Tailors to the King, for life. [*Ibid.*, *p.* 209.]

June 26. Philip Lane. 70. [Lord Zouch] to [Matt.] Hadde, Steward of the Court of [Dover]. He is to postpone the cause of Duffield v. Ward, till Ward can appear in person; has no objection to the transfer of this cause to Westminster, if the parties wish it, and it can be without prejudice to his jurisdiction.

June 26. Whitehall. 71. [The Council] to the King. The charges against Sir Edw. Coke were declared, viz.:—1st, that he bound over Sir Chris. Hatton, under penalty of 6,000*l.*, not to pay a debt of 12,000*l.* due to the Crown by the late Chancellor Hatton; 2nd, that he uttered contemptuous speeches in his seat of justice, especially in the case of Glanvile v. Allen, threatening the jury, and declaring the common law of England would be overthrown; 3rd, that he behaved disrespectfully to the King, in being the only judge that refused to submit in the matter of the commendams. His answers to these points detailed. His behaviour was submissive.

[June 26.] 72. Copy of the above.

[June.] 73. [Sir Edw. Coke] to the Queen. Begs that she and the blessed Prince will again intercede for him. Has to show cause why he should not part with 1,500*l.* per ann. for five years, at the petition of Sir Robt. Rich.

June 29. London. 74. Edw. Sherburn to Carleton. Sir Robt. Naunton is sworn Master of Requests, and Sir Thos. Lake's son, Clerk of the Council. Lord Coke has answered poorly to the accusation of defrauding the King, by persuading Sir Chris. Hatton not to redeem his land by paying the King's debt, the lease of the land meanwhile belonging to Coke, by his marriage with Lady Hatton. His Majesty has accepted Sir Robt. Rich's offer to pay off the debt and redeem the lease, which Coke will lose, and possibly his place also. The King has ordered all his own works and speeches to be printed in one volume. Sends papers on Timmerman's business. The reason why his suit is so much opposed is, that he has a large stock of strangers' money in his hands; and if permitted to erect refining houses, would soon engross all the trade. If the Queen, whose servant he is, would interfere, it might be accomplished. *Incloses,*

74. I. *Order in Council for staying the erection of a house for refining sugar, by Paul Timmerman, a foreigner, made denizen; the said erection being objected to by the Mayor, &c. of London, as injurious to the sugar merchants and refiners. Whitehall, Oct.* 8, 1615.

Vol. LXXXVII.

1616.

74. ii. *Certificate of the Grocers' Company in favour of the erection of sugar-houses in London, by Paul Timmerman, or any others, the sugar refiners combining together to buy up and raise the price of sugar, and refining badly. Grocers' Hall, Oct.* 27, 1615.

74. iii. *Reasons why Paul Timmerman, being a denizen and Her Majesty's servant, should be permitted to use the trade of sugar-baking in London. It will injure none, few English using the trade; and is agreeable to the Grocers' Company, &c.*

74. iv. *Objections of the sugar merchants and refiners of London to the erection of a sugar house in the city by Paul Timmerman, as being illegal, against the city liberties, dangerous as an example, and inconvenient to the State, as injuring the home trade.*

74. v. *Answers of Paul Timmerman to the above objections.*

June 29. Licence to Sir Hen. Savile, Bart., to hold the Court in the manor of Waterfrist and others, co. York. [*Grant Bk., p.* 185.]

June 30. Warrant to Sir Geo. More to deliver Sir Walter Raleigh from the Tower. [*Ibid., p.* 220.]

June 30. Whitehall. 75. The Council to Lord Treasurer Suffolk, Lord Knollys, Master of the Wards, Sir Fulk. Greville, Chancellor of the Exchequer, Sir Julius Cæsar, Master of the Rolls, and Sir Fras. Bacon, Attorney General. Require them, with the assistance of some officers of the Exchequer and Court of Wards, to consider a project inclosed, for raising money and easing the subject by composition for respite of homage, or to devise some other project for it. *Annexing,*

75. i. *Propositions for the increase of the King's revenue by composition for homage, and by disforesting distant forests, chaces, &c.*

75. ii., iii. *Rates of fines levied for respite of homage, and of fees paid thereon to the Remembrancer of the Exchequer and the attorneys; with lists of the number of briefs sent to the several towns and counties from the Treasurer's Remembrancer's office. Two copies. Latin.*

June 30. Greenwich. 76. The Council to Lord Zouch. For Sir Art. Ingram and others, contractors for the alum works, to have permission to burn and carry away the ashes of kelp or sea oare, anywhere within the Cinque Ports.

June? 77. Petition of John Thurloe, of Margate, to the Same, that whereas his Lordship has prohibited the sale of a certain weed called kelkes (kelp), he may have licence to dispose of some which he has on hand, under certificate from the clothiers that it is good for dyeing cloth.

June 30. Greenwich. 78. Order by the King, that the strangers belonging to the Dutch and French churches be not molested in the exercise of their

1616. Vol. LXXXVII.

trades, because they are not free of the city of London, nor have served apprenticeship.

June 30. 79. Copy of the above.

June? 80. Arguments in favour of erecting the office of registrar of all stores brought into or delivered from the ordnance; with request to forward the desire of the writer to be placed in the office, by writing in his behalf to Lord Carew.

June? 81. Draft of the above. Indorsed "Papers about the Minnories."

June 30. 82. Account of the debts owing by His Majesty in the Office of Ordnance, for stores purchased since April 1, 1614, total 13,500*l.*; and for allowances due for the same period to the officers and servants, 2,408*l.* 3*s.* 9*d.*

June? 83. Petition of Thos. Carrolle, cutler, of Dover, to Lord Zouch, to be paid his charges for cleaning certain arms belonging to the castle of Dover.

June? 84. The King to Archbp. Abbot. Signifies his presentation of Rich. Cole to the rectory of Michel-Marsh, diocese of Winchester, that see being vacant.

Vol. LXXXVIII July—October, 1616.

July 1. Grant to Bernard Paises of a Gunner's place in the Tower, for life. [*Grant Bk., p.* 215.]

July 1. Grant to Sir Rich. and Rich. Weston of the office of collecting the little customs in the port of London, for life. [*Ibid., No.* 227.]

July 1. 1. [Lord Zouch] to Dr. Cocks, Physician at Poictiers. Thanks for his letters; will be happy to see him at Dover Castle, where he holds from the King the government of the Cinque Ports. Will be glad to receive and train one of his sons, as he understands the education of youth. French.

July 2. Gildenston. 2. Eliz. Williams to Carleton. Describes their newly purchased residence of Gildenston as abundant in grain, fruits, and flowers. Seven men are to be hanged for a robbery of 700*l.* in the house of Lord Hunsdon, who is building a monument in Hunsdon Church for himself and family.

July 3. 3. Alex. Williams to the Same. Glad he has leave to go to the Spa. Lord Coke is forbidden his circuit and the Council table.

July 3. Grant to Robt. Maxwell of the office of a Serjeant-at-Arms, for life. [*Grant Bk., p.* 213.]

July 4. 4. E. Reynoldes to Fras. Mills. The dividend of fees is larger than usual. Their letter has not yet been delivered to the Lord Privy Seal.

July 4? Westminster. Warrant to pay to Barnaby Rich, the eldest Captain of the Kingdom, 100*l.* as a free gift. [*Sign Man., vol.* VI., *No.* 15.]

VOL. LXXXVIII.

1616.
July 4. Westminster. Grant to Rich. Edwards, in reversion after Griffin Jones, of the Portership of Ludlow Castle. Latin. [*Sign Man., vol.* VI., *No.* 16.]

July 4. Westminster. Warrant to pay to Thos. Dallam, of London, 300*l.*, for a large double organ, to be set up in the Chapel Royal at Edinburgh. [*Ibid.*, *No.* 17.]

July 4. Westminster. Warrant to pay to Edm. Lord Sheffield 1,000*l.*, towards the repair of the King's House at York. [*Ibid.*, *No.* 18.]

July 4. Westminster. Grant to Meredith Morgan and Robt. Vaughan, in reversion after Hugh Hanley and Rich. Bull, of the office of Examiner before the Council of the Marches of Wales. Latin. [*Ibid.*, *No.* 19.]

July 4. Westminster. Grant to Sir Thos. Brereton, of Hadley, Rich. Brereton, of Malpas, Thos. Bressy, of Buckley, and Thos. Bulkeley, of Bickerton, all co. Chester, of remission of certain fines imposed on them by the Court of Star Chamber. [*Ibid.*, *No.* 20.]

[July 4.] Entry of the above. [*Warrt. Bk.*, I., *p.* 255.]

July 5. Westminster. Declaration explaining that the statute ordering the garbling of spices was not meant to extend to such spices as are exported again unopened, and releasing the East India Company from all suits on informations for non garbling of whole chests or packs. Also that the licence to that company to export 30,000*l.* coin or bullion for each voyage shall be restrained to 60,000*l.* per ann., whatever number of voyages are made within the year. [*Sign Man.*, *vol.* VI., *No.* 21.]

[July 5.] Grant to the Queen of the Honor of Pontefract, co. York, with the members thereof, parts of the Duchy of Lancaster. Latin. [*Ibid.*, *No.* 14.]

July 5. Ragley. 5. Fras. Conyers to Sir Edw. Conway. Repairs needed at Loddington. Thos. Comes refuses proposals of mediation, and will go to law about the tithes. Details of Conway's property and affairs.

July 6. London. 6. Chamberlain to Carleton. The King at Windsor. The Earl of Somerset still wears the Garter and George. Lord Hay in hope of the Garter. He had twenty suits of apparel made for so many days, and then heard the French had changed their fashion. Haddington's skit upon him and his company. The King dined with the Earl of Exeter, at Wimbledon. Coke is dismissed the Council and his circuit, and ordered to revise his reports. He makes matters worse by trying to defend himself, and not submitting to the King. Some say he dived too deeply into secrets in the late business. His wife has lost the Queen's favour, for uncivil words to Lady Compton, Sir Geo. Villiers' mother. Church promotions. Sir Robt. Naunton made Master of Requests. A ship arrived from the East Indies, value 140,000*l.*

July 7. 7. Note of the distribution of 4*l.* to the Archbp. of Canterbury's servants, at the consecration of Dr. Morton, Bp. of Chester.

Vol. LXXXVIII.

1616.

July 8. Windsor. Warrant to pay to —— Wyat 50*l.*, in part of his allowance as a Commissioner, employed to compound with Sir Robt. Dudley, in Florence, for purhase of the castle and manor of Killingworth. [*Sign Man., vol.* VI., *No.* 22.]

July 8. Windsor. Warrant to pay to John Tindall, Master Gunner, 231*l.* 14*s.* 8*d.* for land service in the north parts of Scotland, with his company, &c. [*Ibid., No.* 23.]

July 10. Westminster. Warrant for payment of certain sums to John Williams for plate for the King's use; also for presents of plate to Lady Jane Drummond, on her marriage; to John Murray of the Bedchamber; to His Majesty's Valentine, Lady Walsingham, and to attendants on Ambassadors; also for sundry payments to the coffer makers, and to silversmiths for cases, &c. for jewels; and to the beadles of the Goldsmiths' Company for searching among the goldsmiths for plate stolen from the King. Total warrant, 6,733*l.* 6*s.* 11*d.* [*Ibid., No.* 24.]

July 10. Canterbury. 8. Thos. Fulnetby to Rich. Younge. The Lord Admiral has captured a rich ship of Dunkirk, in the Downs, within his Lordship's jurisdiction, and sent it to Portsmouth; a thing which it belongs not to him to do.

July 10. Grant to Sir Rich. Edwards of the office of Keeper of Ludlow Castle and others in Shropshire, for life. [*Grant Bk., p.* 209.]

July 11. London. 9. Edw. Sherburn to [Carleton]. Difficulties about the security for a loan offered by Sir Matthew Carew. The Earl of Arundel has directed Inigo Jones to pay 200*l.* for the pictures. The Earl of Rutland, Sir Geo. Villiers, and Lord Lisle, made Knights of the Garter. Sir John Roper created Lord Thynney [Teynham] on condition of giving his office to Villiers' brother; and Sir John Hollis made Lord Houghton, for 10,000*l.* to defray Lord Hay's expenses to France. Lady Hatton is banished Court for some speeches about Lady Compton, Sir Geo. Villiers' mother. *Incloses,*

9. I., II. *Accusations and articles of capital injustice, præmunire, and high treason, against Sir Edw. Coke, for the judgment given by him in the King's Bench,* 13 *Jac. I., to the diminution of the King's prerogative, classing His Majesty with his own subjects, supporting his conclusions by forged seditious reports, and, by his judgment, disabling the King from giving or receiving grants. If his offences be examined, they will be found greater than Cardinal Wolsey's. Signed Nich. Geffer. Two copies.*

July ? 10. Statement of damage done to the King by Sir Edw. Coke's mode of including Admiralty jurisdiction in grants of lands on the sea coast; with suggestions for its remedy, by a commission of inquiry.

July 11. Philip Lane. 11. Lord Zouch to Lord Roper [of Teynham]. Will yield to his request in behalf of his servant Jennings; but Jennings must appear before him at Dover.

VOL. LXXXVIII.

1616.
July 11. Philip Lane. 12. [Lord Zouch] to Lord Roper. Of similar tenor. Jennings' supposed offence is so insufferable that he must not fail personally to appear in the Chancery Court at Dover, where justice will be done. [*Copy by Rich. Younge, signed with his name.*]

July 11. Westminster. Grant to the Earl of Southampton of pardon of a bond of 1,000 marks, forfeited for non-fulfilment of his pledge to have a survey of, and to pay for, certain woods belonging to manors, &c., in cos. Somerset, Essex, Suffolk, and Wilts; with permission to dispose at pleasure of the aforesaid woods. [*Sign Man., vol.* VI., *No.* 25.]

July 11. Westminster. Release to the Mayor and Burgesses of Berwick of 132*l.* 3*s.* 4*d.*, arrears of the rent for the fishing in the Tweed, the fishing there being much decayed. [*Ibid., No.* 26.]

July 11. Westminster. Grant to Hen. Gibb, of the Bedchamber, for the benefit of his father, John Gibb, of lands called Brading, Isle of Wight, which have been much overflowed by the sea, and are to be inclosed at his expense. [*Ibid., No.* 28.]

July 11. Westminster. Grant to Sir Eustace Hart, of Southampton, of pardon for adulteries and fornications. Latin. [*Ibid., No.* 29.]

July 11. Westminster. Grant to Visct. Haddington of the lands and goods of Giles Carter, late of Netherswell, co. Gloucester, forfeited by attainder and outlawry for murder. [*Ibid., No.* 30.]

July 11. Westminster. Grant to Sir Geo. Goring, of Dauny, Sussex, of pension of 200*l.* per ann., on surrender of a former similar pension. [*Ibid., No.* 31.]

July 13. Whitehall. 13. R. W. [Sir Ralph Winwood] to Carleton. Grounds of proceeding against Coke. A year ago the King remonstrated with him and the Lord Chancellor, about the disgraceful disputes on the limits of their jurisdictions, and bade them be moderate and refer any difficult cases to himself; yet after that, many suitors in the Chancery were indicted of præmunire in the King's Bench. Conduct of Coke in the commendam case, and relative to Chancellor Hatton's debt. His sentence. Mr. Trumbull is to request the Archduke that Surley McDonnell and his comrades may be sent over, to receive the punishment of pirates.

July 13. London. 14. Wm. Beecher to the Same. The King has gone as far as Wanstead on his progress. He has decided that the Earl of Somerset's arms may stand, as the Statutes of the Garter only prescribe their being taken down for high treason. Lord Coke has been censured, and conducted himself very humbly. Sir John Hollis and Sir John Roper made Barons, for money, &c.; it is said others will be made on the same terms, like Cardinals at Rome. Proposal to unite the English and Dutch East India Companies.

July 13. 15. Edw. Sherburn to [the Same]. Sends the first impression of the King's speech, but it must be kept secret, lest the corrections intended should render the second impression disconsonant. Lady Somerset has this day had her pardon sealed, and the Earl's

1616. Vol. LXXXVIII.

is expected. Lord Roos has spoiled the sale of Carleton's statues, by giving all those collected in his travels to the Earl of Arundel, &c.

[July 13.] 16. Grant to the Countess of Somerset of pardon, as accessory before the fact to the murder of Sir Thos. Overbury, she having confessed her guilt, and pleaded for mercy. Latin.

[July 13.] Entry of the above. [*Warrt. Bk.*, I., *p.* 206.]

July 13. Westminster. Grant to John Zouch, in reversion after Audley Ladd, of a lease of the manor of Terrington, and certain marsh lands in Terrington, co. Norfolk. Latin. [*Sign. Man.*, *vol.* VI., *No.* 33.]

July 14. Theobalds. Grant to Sir Geo. Keire of the materials of the King's house at Grafton, co. Northampton, reserving wood for repair of the lodge. Likewise of a lease of the site of the said house, gardens and orchards. Latin. [*Ibid.*, *No.* 34.]

July 14. Theobalds. Warrant for payment of 50*l.* to Lord Stanhope, for sending packets to and fro during the King's progress into the northern parts, where there is no ordinary and common stage-way laid. [*Ibid.*, *No.* 36.]

July 14. Theobalds. Grant to Hen. Mynours, Master of the Otter-hounds, of licence to take hounds, beagles, spaniels, and mongrels for His Majesty's disport. Also to seize such hounds &c. as may be offensive to the King's game. [*Ibid.*, *No.* 37.]

[July 14.] Entry of the above. [*Warrt. Bk.*, I., *p.* 212.]

July 14. Westminster. Grant to Jeremy Heron, in reversion after Thos. Cardell, of a pension of 140*l.* per ann. [*Sign Man.*, *vol.* VI., *No.* 38.]

July 14. Theobalds. Warrant for payment of 60*l.* to Robt. Treswell, Surveyor General of Woods, for a survey to be made of the manor of Barking, co. Essex. [*Ibid.*, *No.* 39.]

July 15. Theobalds. Grant to Robt. Stacy of 20*l.* per ann. for keeping the King's deer in St. John's Wood, co. Middlesex. [*Ibid.*, *No.* 41.]

July 15. Theobalds. Licence to the Fishmongers' Company of London to found Jesus Hospital, in Bray, Berkshire, pursuant to the will of Wm. Goddard, Fishmonger of London, who gave for the foundation certain lands, messuages, &c. in London and Berkshire. Also, grant to the Wardens and Assistants of the Fishmongers' Company, of incorporation, as Governors thereof. [*Ibid.*, *No.* 42.]

July 16. Theobalds. Grant to Sir Robt. Cotton of pardon for all offences, according to the tenor of a coronation pardon, with exception of treason, but no remission of duties or payments. Latin. [*With interlineations by command of the King. Ibid.*, *No.* 43.]

July 16. 17. Lease from Hen. Philippes, of Orpington, Kent, to Thos. Hartley, of London, of a house, land, &c. at Orpington, rent 28*l.* per ann.

VOL. LXXXVIII.

1616.
July 16. Theobalds. Warrant to pay to Sir Thos. Smythe and the East India Company, the usual bounty for building three large ships. [*Sign Man., vol.* VI., *No.* 45.]

July 16. Theobalds. Writ of restitution of the temporalities of bishopric of Chester to Thos. Morton, elected Bishop. Latin. [*Ibid., No.* 46.]

July 16. Theobalds. Grant to Thos. Duckworth, Groom of the Bedchamber to the Lady Elizabeth, Electress Palatine, of livery and wages, for life; a former patent during pleasure having ceased. [*Ibid., No.* 47.]

July 17. Theobalds. Grant to Sir Geo. Villiers, Master of the Horse, of the manors of Whaddon and Nash, and the Park and Chace of Whaddon, co Bucks. Latin. [*Ibid., No.* 48.]

July 17. Theobalds. Warrant to Sir Rich. Molyneux, Receiver-General of the Duchy of Lancaster, to pay yearly 2,400*l.* to Lord Stanhope, Treasurer of the Chamber, instead of 3,000*l.*, his receipts being diminished by sale of lands and increase of the Queen's jointure. [*Ibid., No.* 49.]

July 17. Theobalds. Warrant for payment of 906*l.* 19*s.* 6*d.* to Sir Rich. Morrison, Lieutenant General of Ordnance, for stores for Ireland. [*Ibid., No.* 50.]

July 17. Commission and instructions to Lord Sheffield, President of the Council in the North, concerning determining causes in those parts. [*Grant Bk., p.* 200.]

July 17. 18. Anna Lady Carleton to Sir Dud. Carleton. Has supped with the Lord Treasurer. Will do all she can to get him his money, by which she will do him knight's service.

July 18. Theobalds. 19. Thos. Murray to the Same. Thanks him on the Prince's behalf for his attention in the business of the models. The money shall be paid as appointed.

July 18. Theobalds. 20. Petition of Sir Wm. Slingsby to the King. Understands His Majesty is displeased about the direction of a way which has been altered by him in Long Acre; proffers entire submission, and will cause the way to be altered as His Majesty may direct. With order thereon, that the King wishes the way at Long Acre and over against it to be made fit for his passage, as speedily as possible.

July 18. Dover. 21. Proceedings at a sessions of Oyer and Terminer at Dover, for the trial of certain pirates. With lists of the juries. *Prefixed are,*

21. I. *Presentment by the jury of four of the prisoners for execution, and exoneration of one.*

21. II. *Writ by Lord Zouch to the Mayor, &c. of Dover, summoning thirty-six men to sit on the above causes. Dover, July* 4, 1616.

VOL. LXXXVIII.

1616.
July 18. Confirmation of the practice of the Chancery Court for relief in equity. [*Grant Bk., p.* 197.]

July 18. Commission to Sir Fras. Bacon and others to certify their perusal of precedents concerning complaints relievable in equity in Chancery, and of statutes of præmunire, and other things concerning the same. [*Ibid., pp.* 193, 198.]

July 18. Theobalds. Discharge to the Treasurer of the Exchequer for remissions by him granted of goods and merchandises forfeited to the King for offences against the laws concerning customs, committed by ignorance or mistake; with licence to exercise similar power in future, provided the customs exceed not the sum of 5*l.* [*Sign Man., vol.* VI., *No.* 53.]

[July 18.] Entries of the above. [*Warrt. Bk.,* I., *pp.* 190, 223.]

July 18. Theobalds. Grant to Sir Geo. Selby, Sir John Fenwick, and John Dudley, of the barony of Langley, castle and borough of Mitforth, lordships of Tuggel, Preston, and Swinhoe, co. Northumberland, and manor of Beamish, Bishopric of Durham, lands of Thos. late Earl of Northumberland; with proviso in case of the recovery of the lands by the late Earl's daughter. Latin. [*Sign Man., vol.* VI., *Nos.* 54, 55.]

July 19. Leadenhall. 22. Robt. Bell to Winwood. The chief points to be complained of against the French are, that they will not appoint conservators to settle disputes in trade, as agreed by treaty in 1606; that they continue to require the English to fire at the castle of Blois, contrary to the treaty of 1610; that during the late troubles between the King and princes, the taxes on Bourdeaux wines were raised; that an East Indian vessel wrecked on the shores of Bretagne was plundered to the amount of 70,000*l.*, and no restitution can be obtained; and that the import of paper fit for playing cards is forbidden.

July 20. 23. Note by Robt. Bendbo of his account with Mr. Crowe for receipts of fees for certain patents, &c.

July 20. Arundel House. 24. Thos. Earl of Arundel to Carleton. Thanks for his present of a "greate anticke head." Hopes his and Lady Carleton's visit to the Spa is rather for recreation than on account of ill health.

July 20. London. 25. Chamberlain to the Same. The Earl of Rutland, Sir Geo. Villiers, and Lord Lisle installed Knights of the Garter. A chapter held about taking down the Earl of Somerset's arms, but the King decided against their removal. Lord Hay was frequently going and coming between the King and the Earl, who now has the liberty of the Tower. Terms of Lady Somerset's pardon. The people enraged against her; they attacked a coach in which the Queen and other ladies had come privately to town, thinking it was Lady Somerset. Sir John Hollis made a baron, and paid 10,000*l.*

1616.

to Lord Hay, for his French journey. Sir John Roper also made a baron, but 5,000*l.* only of his 10,000*l.* went to Winwood, to whom it was promised, necessity not permitting more. The Earl of Arundel sworn of the Privy Council, and the Queen has obtained that honour for Lord Carew, &c.

July 20. London. 26. Edw. Sherburn to [Carleton]. Thos. Murray has given a Privy Seal for 250*l.* as first payment for the models. Somerset has the liberty of the Tower, &c.

July 20. Westminster. Grant to Sir Hen. Crook and Ant. Rous, on surrender of Sir Art. and Geo. Mainwaring, of the office of Clerk of the Pipe. Latin. [*Sign Man., vol.* VI., *No.* 56.]

[July 20.] Entry of the above. [*Warrt. Bk.*, I., *p.* 218.]

July 20. Westminster. Grant to Hen. Fleetwood and his sureties, of protection from arrest by his creditors till Oct. 9. [*Sign Man., vol.* VI., *No.* 57.]

July 20. Westminster. Warrant to the Wardens of the Mint to coin, at cost price, the large sums in Flemish ryders to be paid to the King's use, by Phil. Burlamachi and Giles Van de Pute, for the United Provinces, his Majesty being willing to relinquish his profit in the coinage. [*Ibid., No.* 58.]

[July 20.] Entry of the above. [*Warrt. Bk.* I., *p.* 208.]

July 20. Westminster. Grant to Hen. Mynours of the office of Otter-hunter, from the death of John Parry. Latin. [*Sign Man., vol.* VI., *No.* 59.]

[July 20.] Entry of the above. [*Warrt Bk.*, I., *p.* 212.]

July 20. Westminster. Grant to John Harris and Affrodose Younge of a fourth part of all such rents as they shall discover to be reserved to the King on Letters Patent, and through neglect not put in charge. [*Sign Man., vol.* VI., *No.* 60.]

July 20. Westminster. Grant to Sir Geo. Douglas and Geo. Douglas, his son, of the moiety of fines for offences upon the statute of 5 Edw. VI., against hot pressing of cloths, to be prosecuted at their charge, with certain powers reserved to the Court of Exchequer. [*Ibid., No.* 61.]

July 20. Westminster. Warrant for inquiry into and payment of the debts of the late Earl of Somerset and his wife, attainted; and power to Sir Geo. More, Sir Hen. Yelverton and Clement Edmondes, to pay the said debts, which power had before been given only to the Treasurer and Under-Treasurer of the Exchequer. [*Ibid., No.* 62.]

[July 20.] Entry of the above. [*Warrt. Bk., p.* 205.]

July 20. Westminster. Grant to Nich. Bird, in reversion after Wm. Risbrooke, of the office of Under-keeper of Richmond Palace. [*Sign Man., vol.* VI., *No.* 63.]

[July 20.] Entry of the above. [*Warrt. Bk.*, I., *p.* 217.]

July 20. Westminster. Warrant for a survey of certain old stone walls and decayed towers within the precincts of Bristol Castle, intended as a free gift to Sir Geo. Chaworth, the Keeper. [*Sign Man., vol.* VI., *No.* 64.]

VOL. LXXXVIII.

1616.

July ? Grant to Sir Geo. Chaworth, Keeper of the Castle of Bristol, of certain decayed stone walls therein. [*Warrt. Bk.*, I., *p.* 187.]

July 20. Westminster. Grant to Hen. Mole, in reversion after Wm. Nevill and John Mole, of the office of Examiner of Witnesses before the Council of the North, on surrender of a like patent to Geo. Wetherhead. [*Sign Man.*, *vol.* VI., *No.* 65.]

[July 20.] Entry of the above. [*Warrt. Bk.*, I., *p.* 215.]

July 20. Westminster. Warrant to pay to Robt. Treswell, Surveyor General of Woods South of Trent, 277*l.* towards the reparations of Guildford Park. [*Sign Man.*, *vol.* VI., *No.* 66.]

July 20. Westminster. Warrant for payment of 1,000*l.* to Arch. Napper and Sir Wm. Bruncard, in part of their Privy Seal of 4,000*l.* King's bounty money, out of which money the payments due to Sir Fras. Stewart and Sir Jas. Auchterlony are next to be made, and then the remaining 3,000*l.* to Napper and Bruncard to be discharged. [*Ibid.*, *No.* 67.]

July 20. Westminster. Grant to Nath. Rich and Robt. Hatton, on payment of 9,000*l.*, of the yearly rent of 1,500*l.* reserved to the Crown on a lease by the late Queen, to Wm. and Fras. Tate, of lands enumerated of Sir Chris. Hatton, Lord Chancellor, in cos. Northampton, Rutland, Leicester, Dorset, and Chester, and of Hatton House, St. Andrew's, Holborn, which were extended for debts due to the late Queen. The grant is made for the security of Sir Robt. Rich and Sir Chris. Hatton, who have compounded with the King for the debt. Latin. [*Ibid.*, *No.* 68.]

July 20. Westminster. Grant to Sir John Rous and Robt. Shute, on payment of 1,000*l.*, of all the King's benefit in the extent upon the lands of the late Chancellor Hatton, in case of failure in performance of the condition of a former grant to the Archbp. of Canterbury, Earl of Exeter, and Lord Chief Justice Coke, of the remainder of the King's interest in the above lands, extended for debt, after the payment of the reserved rent of 1,800*l.* to the Crown, with proviso that, if the said rent were not duly paid, the grant should be void. Also made for security of Sir Robt. Rich and Sir Chris. Hatton. [*Ibid.*, *No.* 69.]

July 21. Westminster. Confirmation to Geo. Lord Berkeley, of royalties, liberties, &c. within the lordship and hundred of Berkeley, &c. and Portbury, cos. Somerset and Gloucester, as held by other lords, notwithstanding their not being fully expressed in his charters. Latin. [*Ibid.*, *No.* 70.]

July 22. Westminster. Re-grant to Thos. Visct. Fenton, of the King's reversion of the manors of Flamborough and Holme, &c., co. York, late belonging to Sir Robt. Constable, attainted; a former grant thereof being defective. Latin. [*Ibid.*, *Nos.* 72, 73.]

July 22. Westminster. 27. Letters Patent declaring that for settlement of the claims of Fras. Earl of Rutland, heir male of Edw. late Earl of Rutland, and of Wm. Cecil, son of Lord Burleigh and grandson of the Earl of

Vol. LXXXVIII.

1616.

Exeter, heir general of the said Earl, to the barony of Roos, the latter shall have the ancient title of Lord Roos, with a seat in Parliament, and the former the title of Lord Roos of Hamlake.

July 22. Westminster. 28. Commission to the Archbp. of Canterbury, Lord Admiral, Sir Wm. Sedley, and others, authorizing them, by virtue of the Statute of 43 Eliz. for redress of misemployment of moneys &c. bequeathed for charitable uses, to inquire what lands, moneys, &c. have been so bequeathed in the county of Kent, and into any misemployment thereof, and to give orders for their true employment in future. The inquisitions to be returned into Chancery.

July 23. St. James's. 29. Hen. Lord Danvers to Carleton. Wishes the exchange of his picture of the Creation for some curious glass. Lady Hatton's estate involved in the blow given to her husband.

July 23. Bletsoe. Grant to Sir Geo. Villiers, Master of the Horse, of the office of Chief Justice in Eyre, north of the Trent. Latin. [*Sign Man., vol.* VI., *No.* 74.]

[July 23.] Entry of the above. [*Warrt. Bk.*, I., *p.* 220.]

July 24. Bletsoe. Warrant dormant for payment of 600*l.* every six months to Lord Knyvet, for reparations at Oatlands and other residences of the Queen. [*Sign Man., vol.* VI., *No.* 75.]

July 24. Bletsoe. Warrant for payment to Sir Hen. Mynne, Paymaster of the Gentlemen Pensioners, of sums not exceeding 6,000*l.* per ann., for increase of wages of the Captain, Lieutenant, Standard-Bearer, Clerk of the Cheque, Gentleman Pensioners, Gentlemen-at-Arms, and Harbinger. [*Ibid., No.* 76.]

July 24. Bletsoe. Discharge to Lord Treasurer Suffolk of 20,000*l.*, which by His Majesty's private direction he disbursed to Lord Hay. [*Ibid., No.* 77.]

July 24. Bletsoe. Grant to Pat. Ruthven, prisoner in the Tower, of 200*l.* per ann., for apparel, books, physic, &c. [*Ibid., No.* 78.]

July 24. Edmonton. [Sir John Dackombe, Chancellor of the Duchy of Lancaster] to Gilbert Gerard, Clerk of the Duchy. Warrant for a lease to S. O. of the mines, quarries, and coal-pits in Kidwelly. [*Dom. Corresp., Dec.* 11, 1618, *Note Bk., p.* 11.]

July 25. London. 30. Edw. Sherburn to [Carleton]. Private affairs. The King, Queen, and Prince in progress. The Earl and Countess of Somerset together in the Tower.

July 25. Bletsoe. Grant to Edw. Woodward and Thos. Garrett, goldsmiths of London, at nomination of the Duke of Lenox and Countess of Bedford, of patent for coining farthing tokens of copper; all other tokens to be suppressed, the patent being similar to that of Lord Harrington, except in the rectifying of certain inconveniences. [*Sign Man., vol.* VI., *No.* 79.]

July 28. Castle Ashby. Commission to Sir Walter Raleigh to command an expedition to South America, for promotion of trade and conversion of the heathen,

1616. VOL. LXXXVIII.

with power to elect captains, and to use martial law, &c.; the fifth part of all gold, silver, and jewels to be reserved to the King. With promise that he shall quietly enjoy what he obtains. [*Sign Man., vol.* VI., *No.* 80.]

[July 28.] Entry of the above. [*Warrt. Bk.*, I., *p.* 209.]

July 29. Mannington. 31. Sir Chris. Heydon to his son, Capt. John Heydon. To ask leave of absence from Lord Zouch, and to come and see him.

July 30. 32. Certificate of the Commissioners of Sewers of Rye, that Rother or Appledore channel, Tellingham channel, and Winchelsea creek may be united, and that the best place for a haven between Rye and Winchelsea would be Dimsdale Creek.

July 30. Kirby. Warrant to pay to Sir Jas. Sandilands 150*l.* as a free gift. [*Sign Man., vol.* VI., *No.* 82.]

July 30. Kirby. Grant to John Frende, Serjeant-at-Arms, of the benefit of a bond of 250*l.* forfeited by Stephen Aynscombe, of Mayfield, and Wm. Gulder, of Mechin, both co. Sussex, for failing to bring in a certificate that the ordnance shipped in the Sea Flower has not been unlawfully transported. [*Ibid., No.* 83.]

July 30. Kirby. Grant to John Allen of a rent of 13*l.* 6*s.* 8*d.*, payable to His Majesty by the Corporation of Evesham and Bengworth, co. Worcester, from the fines of the manor courts, together with the arrears thereof, unpaid for thirteen years. [*Ibid., No.* 84.]

July 30. Kirby. Warrant to the Lord Treasurer, &c. to give credit to Lord Admiral Nottingham for certain brass ordnance, in part discharge of his debts to His Majesty. [*Ibid., No.* 85.]

July 31. Apthorpe. Grant to Sam. and John Jones, of London, of small parcels of concealed lands in cos. Essex, Suffolk, Norfolk, Hertford, Sussex, Bucks, Warwick, Worcester, Leicester, Gloucester, Northumberland, Lincoln, and York, total value 17*l.* 14*s.* 3*d.* per ann., in part of the grant to John Gray, the King's servant, of concealed lands, value 66*l.* 13*s.* 4*d.* per ann. Latin. [*Ibid., Nos.* 86, 87.]

July. Westminster. Grant to Sir Thos. Howard of the fines assessed upon trespassers in the Forest of Braydon, co. Wilts; with arrears thereof, in consideration of his repairing all the lodges in the forest. [*Ibid., No.* 88.]

[July.] Entry of the above. [*Warrt. Bk.*, I., *p.* 226.]

July. 33. Thos. Hunckes to Sir Edw. Conway. Much regrets his son Fulk's resolution to be a soldier; would rather he used a flail or spade; but, failing to persuade him, and being unable to provide for him, has consented to his return. Is too poor to pay his expenses.

[July.] 34. Observations by Edm. Sawyer on the Great Roll of the Pipe, its inadequacy to the present state of the office, and the undue powers which it gives to certain officers of the Pipe.

[July.] 35. Copy of the above.

July ? 36. Memorandum of the manner of proceedings touching recusants, in the Pipe and Treasurer's Remembrancer's offices, &c.

VOL. LXXXVIII.

1616.

[July.] 37. Project concerning the levying of His Majesty's debts, and reformation of abuses in the Pipe relating to them.

July. 38. Petition of John Greenfield, purveyor of fish, to Lord Zouch, to be appointed Gunner in Camber Castle.

July. 39. Petition of Robt. Cochrane to the Same, to hear a case between him and Nich. Lobdell, of Hastings, long pending in the Court of Chancery at Dover.

Aug. ? 40. Petition of Toby Chapman and Wm. Warner, for themselves and others, clothiers of Gloucester, to the Council, to take order that the Merchant Adventurers and others, who formerly bought their cloths weekly, but have lately ceased, may continue so to do, as the loss of their trade is the ruin of thousands.

Aug. 2. 41. The Council to the Justices of Peace, co. Gloucester. Thanks for their forwarding the complaint of the weavers, fullers, and spinsters of the county, touching the decay of their clothing trade. The Merchant Adventurers say that the deceitful making of Gloucestershire cloth is much complained of, and prevents their purchasing so much of it. Recommend redress of deceits, and have ordered the Merchant Adventurers to buy the cloth.

Aug. 3. 42. Mons. de Tourval to Fras. Windebank. Sorry he cannot visit him, being obliged to go to Bedfordshire. Compliments. Spanish.

Aug. 5. Burley. 43. The King to Lord St. John, Lord Mordaunt, and other Knights and Gentlemen of Bedfordshire. Requests them to remedy the decay of game in those parts, on penalty of his heavy displeasure, and of his withholding his presence from those parts, which he has usually visited every second year, for sporting.

Aug. 5. Newcastle. 44. Sir Hen. Anderson to Winwood. Has summoned the gentlemen of the county, according to command, to consider the means for suppressing theft and disorder in Northumberland, and they have appointed the Earl of Shrewsbury, Sir Ralph Gray, and many others, to attend His Majesty at Rufford, and report thereon.

Aug. 6. Burley. 45. The Council with the King to the Council at London. His Majesty thanks them for their attention to the Gloucestershire clothiers' petition. They are to summon Sir Wm. Cockayne, Governor of the new Company [of Merchant Adventurers], remonstrate seriously with him on the failure of their promises to buy up the cloth, in spite of the King's private warnings not to undertake more than they could accomplish, and order him to send His Majesty daily accounts of their progress. Such of the Company as fail in buying the quantities which they severally undertook are to be threatened with punishment for their cozenage.

Aug. 6. 46. [The Council] to the Justices of the Peace, cos. Northampton, Lincoln, and Cambridge. Recommend the granting, if possible, of two enclosed petitions relating to the fens. They are not to be discouraged in that business, but to send two of their number to report their grievances.

VOL. LXXXVIII.

1616.

Aug. 7. Hatton House. 47. Hen Lord Danvers to Carleton. Wishes to have, instead of Rubens' Creation, some work of his fit for a small room, such as his Lordship's Daniel in the Lion's Den. The King wishes to increase his amity with Scotland by a visit there, with many of his Court. The Spaniards angry with the bonfires made on the conclusion of the treaty [with Holland] about the East India trade.

Aug. 9. Obligation of Wm. Graves, of East Barnet, Kent, under penalty of 20*l.*, to be true and faithful in the keeping of the King's game and venery in His Majesty's chace of Enfield, co. Middlesex. [*Dom. Corresp., Dec.* 11, 1618. *Note Bk., p.* 13.]

Aug. 10. Licence to Wm. Elliotts and Matthias Meysey to convert iron into steel, for twenty-one years. [*Grant Bk., p.* 209.]

Aug. 10. 48. T[hos.] W[ilson] to Sir Geo. Villiers. Sends him a catalogue of the heads of principal matters in the State Paper Office; will make particular collections on any subject he may choose. Solicits furtherance of his suit to be appointed Master Extraordinary of Requests. *Annexes,*

48. I. *Thos. Wilson to the King. Has been twenty-six years in the service of the State, ten of which have been spent in arranging the State Papers, which were in extreme confusion. Begs a Mastership of Requests, whereby he would have access to His Majesty, and could oftentimes present to him such matter out of his papers as would be not unworthy of consideration, there not being so much use made of them "as the treasure therein hidden" deserves. If not thought fit for that place, requests diet at Court, in addition to his salary of* 30*l. per ann.*

Aug. 13. London. 49. Biallnante Suatedi [?] to Giov. Florio, of the Queen's Privy Chamber. Will be at Oatlands to receive Her Majesty's commands. Italian.

Aug. ? 50. "Remedies for the stand of cloth," i.e. decay in the trade, by compelling certain companies and classes of people to purchase proportionate quantities of cloth weekly, &c.

Aug. 13. Whitehall. 51. The Council in London to the Council with the King. According to orders, have remonstrated with Sir Wm. Cockayne and the other merchants who, failing in their promises, have reduced the clothing trade from a flourishing state to decay; and have ordered them immediately to buy up the Gloucestershire cloth now in London, and such as shall be weekly brought in.

Aug. 15. London. 52. Edw. Sherburn to [Carleton]. Death of Sir Roger Wilbraham, Master of Requests, who is succeeded by Sir Robt. Naunton, &c.

Aug. 15. 53. Thos. Cousant to Lord Zouch. Sends Leonard Rountree, a priest, from Louvaine, who has recanted once, but returned to Popery, and was banished the realm; he is now in want, and offers to recant again. *Annexes,*

53. I. *Examination of Leonard Rountree; particulars of his past life, changing his faith, and banishment. Dover Castle, Aug.* 15.

VOL. LXXXVIII.

1616.

Aug. 16. Dover Castle. 54. Petition of Thos. Partridge to Lord Zouch, against the increase by the Mayor of Dover of impositions on malt and wheat carried through the town to be shipped. With reference thereon.

Aug. 17. London. 55. Edw. Reynoldes to Fras. Mills. The Lord Privy Seal says they must petition the King if they wish for diet, which will be a very troublesome course. Saddler, his Secretary, is a dangerous fellow, and must be satisfied with the present he wishes for: 300 marks said to have been offered for the Lord Privy Seal's fifth of the fees, the farm of which would subject the office to injurious siftings. The month has yielded a great harvest of fees, &c.

Aug. 19. London. 56. Giov. Franc Biondi to [Carleton]. Signor Colantino still intends to leave Italy. The intended Ambassador [of Savoy?] will not come if the war continue. Italian.

Aug. 20. London. 57. Edw. Sherburn to [the Same]. The King intends to create Sir Geo. Villiers, the man by whom all things must pass, Visct. Beaumont. Advises him to try for the reversion of the Mastership of Requests.

Aug. 21. Strand. 58. M. de Tourval to [Fras. Windebank]. Has to go to France. Death of Lord Dacre, of Sussex, and of Judge Nicholls. Sir Geo. Sandys and others, hanged for highway robberies at Kensington, of twelve or thirteen persons in an evening. Magnificent reception of Lord Hay in France; but some apprentices, who had been waiting all day for his reception, which was not till night, grew angry, and threw stones. His friends have published an elaborate description of his entry into Paris. Revolt in Picardy against the Mareschal d'Ancre. French.

Aug.? 59. F[ras.] W[indebank] to Tourval. Regrets that Tourval is going to France. It is said at Court that the Prince of Condé is taken prisoner in France, and the Duke of Bouillon escaped. The King displeased with the disgrace he has incurred in the person of his Ambassador. Italian.

Aug. 24. London. 60. Chamberlain to Carleton. The Earl of Somerset and his Lady allowed to be together. The Earl of Northumberland much in their Company. The Duke of Lenox returned from Scotland, whither he attended the Marquis of Huntley, who was excommunicated by the Scots' Kirk, but absolved at Lambeth by the Archbp. of Canterbury. A new ague has appeared. Lord Dacre, Sir Roger Wilbraham, Sir Clement Scudamore, Sir Goddard Pemberton, Judge Nicholls, and others, dead of it, yet the season is good, and the harvest plentiful.

Aug. 27. Creation of Sir Geo. Villiers as Baron of Whaddon and Visct. Villiers. [*Grant Bk.*, *p.* 191.]

Aug. 28. Grant to Rich. Jones, on surrender of Rich. Ward, of the office of Serjeant-at-Arms, to attend the Lord President for the Marches of Wales. [*Sign Man.*, *vol.* VI., *No.* 89.]

Aug. 29. Oxford. 61. Thos. Wilson to the Lord Chancellor. Proceedings at Court:— On Saturday the King hunted at Woodstock, and dined with Lord Danvers at Thornton Park. Sunday.—The Vice Chancellor and doctors of Oxford came with an oration and petition. Monday.—The

1616. VOL. LXXXVIII.

King killed two or three great stags in the forest; the Queen, Prince, and whole Court present. Tuesday.—Dr. Laud preached, with great applause, from Miriam's leprosy, as a warning to detractors against government. Villiers was made a Viscount; description of the ceremony; the King's part performed with great alacrity. The French Ambassador had an audience. The King is going from Rycot to Bisham, Lord Norris's, and thence to Easthampstead, Bagshot, Aldershot, and Windsor.

Aug. 31. London. 62. Edw. Sherburn to Carleton. Private affairs. Will send him a cook.

Aug. 63. Petition of Wm. Johnson, carpenter, of Lambeth, to Lord Zouch, to cite before his Lordship certain arbitrators who hold money in trust for his step-daughters, brought up by him, but refuse him the interest for their support. They being in his Lordship's jurisdiction, he cannot seek redress by common law.

Aug. 64. List of the English who were at the Spa in July and August 1616; with notes of their residences, and of such as are Papists.

Sept. 1. Chertsey. 65. Sir Matthew Carew to Carleton. Regrets the precipitate return of his son Thomas; he would have had better chance of rising with his Lordship than with Lord Carew, who has already two secretaries. Report that Lord Coke is to be made a Baron, and to transfer his Chief Justiceship to Recorder Montague.

Sept. 1. Newington. 66. Geo. Carleton to Edw. Sherburn. Offers securities for money to be advanced to him by his brother, Sir Dud. Carleton.

Sept. 2 London. 67. Thos. Carew to Carleton. Lord Carew refuses to accept him, thinking the position too ignoble for his birth. Hopes the Earl of Arundel may take him as Secretary, &c.; if not, will gladly return to Carleton.

Sept. 3. London. 68. Chamberlain to the Same. New troubles have arisen in France. The King is hunting about Windsor. He will go to Havering, Waltham Forest, and Theobalds, and then christen the Earl of Montgomery's son at Enfield. Sir Geo. Villiers created Baron Whaddon and Visct. Villiers; the Queen and Prince present. Rumour that the Earl of Somerset will have leave to traverse his indictment. The Greenland ships have returned, and killed 130 whales. A ship has newly arrived from the Bermudas or Summer Islands, &c.

Sept. 3. Oxford. 69. Sir Hen. Savile to the Same. Is going to Eton, after spending fourteen months at Oxford, whither the King came from Woodstock, had an oration and a sermon, and gave his hand to be kissed. The Prince dined at Christchurch, at his [Carleton's] cousin's house.

Sept. 3. Cambridge. 70. Dud. Carleton to his father [Geo. Carleton]. Has chosen a new tutor, a kinsman of Sir Wm. Green, of Milton. Sends to his brother John his verses on the Gunpowder Plot.

Sept. 4. Gildenston. 71. Eliz. Williams to her brother, Sir Dud. Carleton. Recommends to his service the bearer, —— Hudson, who desires to spend some time in the Low Countries.

Vol. LXXXVIII.

1616.

Sept. 4. Grant to Jas. Partridge of the office of Keeper of the Council Chamber, for life. [*Grant Bk., p.* 215.]

Sept. 4. Grant to Thos. Edwards, sen., of the office of Sealer in Chancery, for life. [*Ibid., pp.* 209, 217.]

Sept. 5. Grant to Sir Chas. Howard, jun., of the Stewardship of the manor belonging to the honor of Windsor, &c., for life. [*Ibid., p.* 206.]

Sept. 5. Schonhoven. 72. Thos. Michell to Lord Zouch. Hopes he will not stop the payment of the rents of his lime-kilns at Dover till his debt to Allen is paid off, as he would be reduced to turn pirate or robber if he received no money from England.

Sept. 6. 73. ——— to [Tobie Matthew]. Has interceded with the Earl of Arundel, Lady Ruthven, and Sec. Winwood, to prevail upon the King to permit his [Matthew's] return; and hopes that by their help, and that of Lord Roos, Lord Villiers, and Sir Fras. Bacon, it may be accomplished.

Sept.? 74. Statement [by Tobie Matthew] of reasons which may facilitate his retnrn to England after nine years' absence; his error was only such as is committed by many of his religion; pleads his loyal and exemplary conduct whilst abroad.

Sept. 7. Grant to Edw. and Nath. Thorold of the office of Marshal of the Marshalsea of the Exchequer, for life. [*Grant Bk., p.* 191.]

Sept. 7. Grant to Wm. Holland of a Falconer's place, for life. [*Ibid., p.* 206.]

Sept. 7. Grant to Thos. Leech of a Yeoman Waiter's place in the Tower, for life. [*Ibid., p.* 220.]

Sept. 8. London. 75. Edw. Sherburn to Carleton. Private money affairs. Will tell none of his Lordship's concerns to Thos. Carew.

Sept. 11. 76. Statement by the new Company of Merchant Adventurers, that the Hollanders thwart their trade, by prohibiting the use of cloth dyed and dressed in England, both by public edict and private confederation. They petition for removal of the edict. The Hollanders also promote their own cloth manufacture, which must be met by prohibiting export of wools out of Scotland as well as England, and by stopping broggers of wool who raise the price. They request sundry privileges to enable them to carry on their trade. Are willing to grant free admission to the old Merchant Adventurers, or any who wish to join them.

Sept. 11. London. 77. Thos. Carew to [Carleton]. Though Lord Carew will not employ him, he promises to favour and help him. Lord Roos has taken leave of the King, and has provided himself with a splendid suite in costly liveries, who pace the streets everywhere. He has a present of 5,000*l.* from the King, 5,000*l.* for extraordinaries, and 16*l.* per day. Lord Dingwall has returned from Venice. Albert Morton is going to Heidelberg. Sir Edw. Cecil arrived. A breach has taken place between Visct. Villiers and Sec. Winwood, which will throw business into Lake's hands.

1616. Vol. LXXXVIII.

Sept. 11 ? 78. Edw. Sherburn to [Carleton]. [Thos.] Carew has been with Lord Carew, who has no employment for him, but will recommend him to the Earl of Arundel.

Sept. 11 ? 79. Memoranda by Sir John Dackombe relative to the business of the Duchy Court [of Lancaster], and his own affairs.

Sept. 11 ? Tutbury. 80. [Sir John Dackombe] to ———. Orders him to deliver to Thos. Trevor all the records belonging to the Duchy Court of Lancaster, late in custody of Wm. Pourven, deceased.

Sept. 12. Grant to Matt. Brooke of the Clerkship of the Prick and Cheque of the Navy in Portsmouth, &c., for life. [*Grant Bk., p.* 167.]

Sept. 13. 81. Commission from Lord Zouch to the Mayor of Dover and others, to hold a Court of Lode Manage, for appointing able men to be masters or pilots of ships, and for punishing any misdemeanor amongst them.

Sept. 14. Dover. 82. Fras. Raworth to [Lord Zouch]. Has surveyed the house mentioned in Ann Jacob's petition, and finds it very old, but in as good condition as when Peter Fountayn first came to it. Cannot persuade him to a compromise with Mrs. Jacob.

Sept. 14. 83. Account of the quantities of cloth remaining in store in cos. Gloucester, Worcester, and Wilts. [*See Sept.* 11.]

Sept. 16. Havering. 84. Visct. Villiers to Sir Thos. Lake. To inquire into a patent granted to the late Mr. Havers, for collecting threepence in the pound, increased customs payable by strangers, on which a yearly rent was reserved to the King, and some benefit to himself [Villiers].

Sept. 17. Grant to Sir Fras. Steward of the office of keeping the walks in Cranborne Chace, &c., Berkshire, for life. [*Grant Bk., p.* 189.]

Sept. 19. 85. Alex. Williams to Carleton. Hopes he was benefited at the Spa, &c. Begs a cast of falcons for his son.

Sept. 19. Thistleworth. 86. Sir Horace Vere to the Same. Landed at Gravesend, and visited Secretary Winwood. Lady Winwood ill. The King is at Theobalds, and was prevented by a pain in his side from attending the christening of Lord Montgomery's son, &c.

Sept. 20. Tunstall. 87. Thos. Carew to the Same. Lord Arundel promises to take him, if he can shake off two other competitors. Lord Roos's stay being prolonged by fresh business, he has taken a second leave of the King, &c.

Sept. 20. Tattershall Castle. 88. Earl of Lincoln to the King. Sir Hen. Fiennes, refusing the King's order that they should appoint mediators in their dispute about the possession of a deer-park, daily kills the deer, ill treats the keepers, &c. Craves redress.

VOL. LXXXVIII.

1616.

Sept. 21. Saturday. 89. Edw. Sherburn to [Carleton]. Has carried the models to St. James's, where the Prince will give directions to the Dutchmen for setting them up. The King has had a fall from his horse, which, with his old disease, the gout, compels him to be carried to his coach. To morrow he will stand godfather to Lord Montgomery's son. Sir John Egerton has a son, after his many daughters, which will add a year to the old Lord Chancellor's life. Complaints of the clothiers against the new Company of Merchant Adventurers. The King sees he has been much abused, but, to uphold the company, promises to "venture 40,000*l.* himself (sed ubi est?)," and retaliates the Dutch edict, by giving the Company leave to remove into Flanders or Germany.

Sept. ? 90. Remarks on the places where the new Merchant Adventurers' Company and the Eastland Merchants should sell dyed or undyed cloths.

Sept. 21. Grant to Art. Squibb of a Tellership in the Exchequer, for life. [*Grant Bk., p.* 189.]

Sept. 23. Faversham. 91. Thos. Kennett to Rich. Younge. Encloses a note of the boat owners, victuallers, and hackney men of Faversham.

Sept. 23. 92. Muster roll of the garrison of Walmer Castle.

Sept. 24. 93. Muster roll of the garrison of Mote's Bulwark.

Sept. 24. Durham. 94. Zeth Beridge [alias Wm. Morton] to Winwood. Details of the condition of the people, government, and religion, and of the state of the town of Newcastle-on-Tyne. Popery flourishes, and the river is in danger of being blocked up. Names and characters of the principal men. Throughout the bishopric of Durham, Popery prevails, so that at the ports, Hartlepool, Sunderland, Tynemouth, &c., the recusants can import and export as they will. Gives the names and character of the principal ladies amongst them, also of the prebendaries of Durham. Many of the clergy very base. The chief reason why law is badly administered is the covetousness of the Bishop and his bad officers. Thinks the royalties should be taken from the Bishop, who is thus a king in the country; several bishops, formerly good men, have been spoiled by too much power. The same government should be introduced there as has been in Northumberland.

Sept. 24. 95. Memorandum of the powder spent this year at Sandown Castle.

Sept. 25. 96. Muster roll of the garrison of Dover Castle.

Sept. 25. Commission to the Earls of Suffolk, Worcester, Nottingham, Pembroke, and Arundel, and the Duke of Lenox, to exercise the office of Earl Marshal. [*Dom. Corresp., Aug.* 1, 1622.]

Sept. 25? 97. Request of the Merchant Adventurers for authority to depute a merchant authorized by the Council, to visit the clothing counties, and enforce the execution of the statutes for true making of cloth.

VOL. LXXXVIII.

1616.

Sept. 26. Hampton Court. 98. Order in Council confirming the Orders of the 8th and 15th Oct., 1615, forbidding Paul Timmerman, stranger denizen, to erect a sugar-house in or near London; the Attorney General, on full hearing of the case, having decided that the erection of sugar-houses by aliens will prejudice the refiners of the city of London. [*See June* 29, 1616.]

Sept. [28]. 99. M. de Tourval to [Fras.] Windebank. Confesses himself beaten by the excellent scholarship and dainty conceits of his French letter. Wishes to be his scholar in English. Has returned from a racing journey to Cambridge and Colchester.

Sept. ? 100. The Same to the Same. In behalf of a young man who fears that he shall not be capable of entering Windebank's service. French.

Sept. 28. Grant to Arch. Hay of the office of Surgeon to the King, for life. [*Grant Bk., p.* 206.]

Sept. 29. 101. Account of the King's receipts and expenditure for the past year, showing an excess, in ordinary expenditure above the income, of 86,906*l.*, reduced by extraordinaries to 8,690*l.*

Sept. 29. 102. Muster roll of the garrison of Deal Castle.

Sept. 30. 103. Muster roll of the garrison of Sandown Castle; with notes of later date.

Sept. 104. Proposals by the officers of the Mint to prevent the exportation of gold, by cutting a pound of sterling silver into 3*l.* 10*s.* 6*d.*, instead of 3*l.* 2*s.*, so as to make it equal to foreign coins; and to make a corresponding change in gold coins.

Sept. 105. Statement of the inconveniences arising from making the new gold lighter. It causes inequality in the present currency; the old coins are exported; clippers are encouraged to lessen their weight, and pass them for the new coins; foreign mints will lower their moneys, &c.

Sept. 106. F. Rives to [the Archbp. of Canterbury ?]. His opinion is against the power of the King to translate Bishops to other sees, without the consent of the parties. Arguments to support it. Ill consequences that would result from a contrary course.

Sept. ? 107. Names of men of Deal that are masters or part owners of boats.

Sept. ? 108. List of mariners at Deal from whom bonds are to be taken.

Sept. ? 109. Similar list of mariners at Rye.

Sept. 110. Book of sums owing for stores and work, and for allowances for the Office of Ordnance, during the past quarter.

Oct. 1. Grant to Albert Morton of a pension of 200*l.* during his office of Secretary to the Lady Elizabeth, Electress Palatine. [*Grant Bk., p.* 213.]

Oct. 2. Grant to Philip Earl of Montgomery of the office of keeping the palace called York Place, &c., in the city of Westminster, for life. [*Ibid., p.* 213.]

VOL. LXXXVIII.

1616.

Oct. 2. Whitehall. 111. Order in Council, on request of Sir Hen. Montague, Recorder of London, for redress of inconveniences to the city from concourse of aliens, that the Council shall consider the complaint; meanwhile His Majesty removes the restraints of his letter of June last, permits the citizens to maintain their privileges by law, and promises them all lawful assistance therein.

Oct. ? 112. Statement of the steps taken in former times and in the present reign against aliens, in spite of which they multiply so fast as to enhance the price of provisions, lodging, &c., and by their ingenious machines, &c. usurp the trade from the English. Suggestion that the benefit of the laws be taken against them.

Oct. ? 113. Alphabetical list of 121 trades exercised by strangers [in London ?], and of the numbers in each trade; total, 1,343. [*With reference to the folios of some book in which the names were probably entered.*]

Oct. 4. Thistleworth. 114. Sir Horace Vere to [Carleton]. The Prince has not yet had time to view the models. Hopes he will pay the Dutchman who brought them and set them up. The King is gone to Royston; the Queen is at Oatlands. Lord Arundel is anxious to serve his Lordship in a certain affair.

Oct. 4. London. 115. Giov. Franc. Biondi to [the Same]. Is sorry his letters were lost. Does not write, because, not going to Court, he hears little news. Tidings from Italy; the Duke of Savoy defeated by the Spaniards. French fraud more busy than ever, &c. Begs letters for Colentino to Heidelberg, whither he means to go. Italian.

Oct. 4. Whitehall. 116. Abraham Williams to [the Same]. Godfrey Bodt is an idle fellow, and his projects unconstitutional in England. The Prince is to be created Prince of Wales on Nov. 4, and the Lord Chancellor and Lord Villiers to be made Earls. Lord Hay's arrival and Lord Roos's departure expected. Albert Morton going to Heidelberg, with 200*l.* a year pension, and 50*l.* allowance.

Oct. 5. 117. Edw. Sherburn to [the Same]. [Sir Matthew Carew] is very angry with his son [Thomas], for the offence complained of by Carleton, and orders him to write a letter of submission. Lord Coke has given in a corrected copy of his reports to the Council. His removal is expected, and that Serjeant Montague, who will give most, will take his place. Sir Robt. Naunton spoken of as Ambassador to France. Sudden death of Hen. Howard, the Lord Treasurer's third son. Preparations making for the Prince's creation. The gentlemen of the Temple are erecting a new artillery garden, and the Prince is to be their General.

Oct. 7. St. James's. 118. Hen. Lord Danvers to the Same. The Prince pleased with the curious models. The King discontented with Lord Hay's ill success in France. Sir Randall Crew likely to succeed Coke.

VOL. LXXXVIII.

1616.

Oct. 10. St. James's. 119. Thos. Murray to Carleton. The Prince will detain the Fleming to acquaint him with the use of each of the models. Regrets that Burlamachi's absence has caused any delay in the payment for them.

Oct. 11. 120. Alice Carleton to the Same. Family news. Lord Hunsdon makes much of their nephew, Anthony Williams, and wishes to make a Justice of Peace of his father, who puts it off for fear of the cost.

Oct. 12. London. 121. Chamberlain to [the Same]. Death of Lady Dacre, Hen. Howard, Sir John Watts, and Sir John Scott. Lord Hay returned from France. Preparations for the Prince's creation. The Chancellor to be made a Viscount, but now he has a young grandson, he wants an earldom. Winwood has bargained with Sir Phil. Stanhope to pay 10,000*l.* to be made a Baron, Sir Wm. Cope having dallied too long about it. Somerset's lands in the north are given to the Prince. Villiers had Sherborne, but resigned it for 80,000*l.* to Sir John Digby. Sir Rich. Boyle, Sir Garrett Moore, and Sir Edw. Brabazon made Barons of Ireland. Sir John Denham succeeds Justice Nicholls as Judge of the Common Pleas. Coke allowed to perform his chamber offices, but forbidden to sit at Westminster. Justice Warburton is in disgrace for hanging a Scotch falconer of the King, contrary to his express command; and Justice Winch and Serjeant Crew, for hanging supposed witches at Leicester, when the King, whilst there, found out the imposture of the boy said to be bewitched. Sir Thos. Monson discharged on bail for a year. Lord Roos gone for Spain. Costly apparel of his retinue. He courts the Earl of Arundel, and has given him all his Italian statues. The Bp. of Ely sworn of the Council.

Oct. 12. London. 122. Edw. Sherburn to the Same. The Prince has paid the carriage of the models and diet of the Dutchman, whom he keeps for a month. The King has bestowed upon Mr. Vice Chamberlain [Sir John Digby] the manor of Sherborne, which was Sir Walter Raleigh's, and then the Earl of Somerset's, and will dispose of the rest of the Earl's lands.

Oct. ? 123. Statement of the descent of the manor of Sherborne, co. Dorset, from the time of the Conquest. On Sir Walter Raleigh's attainder it was given to Prince Henry, then to the Earl of Somerset, and now to Sir John Digby.

Oct. ? 124, 125. Two copies of the above.

Oct. ? Warrant to Sir Fras. Bacon, Attorney General, and the Court of King's Bench, requiring them to refrain, until the King's further pleasure, from urging processes against Sir Thos. Monson, of London, imprisoned for hiring Rich. Weston, of London, to poison Sir Thos. Overbury, but released on bail. [*Warrt. Bk.*, I., *p.* 198.]

Oct. 13. Eton. 126. Sir Hen. Savile to Carleton. The horses not to be bought, if they will travel no further than between Eton and London. His wife longs for the hangings, but the price is too high. Money matters.

Oct. 17. Dover. 127. Mayor, &c. of Dover to Lord Zouch. Have chosen, according to his directions, 200 men to serve in the selected band.

VOL. LXXXVIII.

1616.

Oct. 18. Elsdon in Riddesdale. 128. John Smaithwaite to Winwood. Meetings of the Popish faction, and money collecting to bribe some great man to procure the liberty of Roger Wodrington and Fras. Ratcliffe. Tyrannical conduct of Roger Wodrington. Outlaws scour the country in bands of thirty to fifty, to rob. They hope the King will make Sir Hen. Wodrington an officer, and then they need fear no punishment. The late Earl of Dunbar banished Roger, and imprisoned Sir Hen. Wodrington, and others. Nothing can clear the country but a governor who would adopt similar courses.

Oct. 21. Dover Castle. 129. Rich. Marsh to Rich. Younge. Particulars of wrecked goods. Many of them were bought by —— Hull. *Incloses*,

129. I. *List of goods wrecked in the hands of divers persons who are ordered to restore them to the Serjeant of the Admiralty, or some other person deputed by the Lord Warden. Admiralty Court, Sept. 9, 1616.*

129. II. *List of persons presented as buyers of the above goods.*

Oct. 22. Declaration concerning fees to be paid to the Serjeants-at-Arms upon knighthood. [*Grant Bk., p.* 194.]

Oct. 22. Thistleworth. 130. Sir Horace Vere to [Carleton]. The Prince delighted with the models.

Oct. 22. London. 131. Alex. Williams to the Same. Understood he had promised to lend him 500*l.* at 9 per cent., but Mr. Sherburn thinks it was only 100*l.* Begs to know the truth.

Oct. 23. 132. The Same to the Same. Thanks for his share in obtaining his son William a situation with Mr. Missenden, of Middleburgh.

Oct. 23. St. James's. 133. Hen. Lord Danvers to the Same. Thanks for the glass sent him. Sir Thos. Edmondes is to be sent for [from France], and made Comptroller, and Beecher is to succeed him there, instead of Sir Thomas's Secretary.

Oct. 23. [Lambeth.] 134. Notes from the memorials of Ch[ristopher] N[ewkirk] from Sept. 17 to Oct. 22. Proceedings of the conspirators, their ships, and agreements for purchase of gunpowder from Dunkirk and Antwerp. The Digbys are bringing in 20,000*l.* from Spain. Attends mass at the Spanish Ambassador's. Is ordered to repair to Saxton to carry on the plot, Alex. Maletesto being very ill, &c. With note [from the Bishop of Durham] that he gave Newkirk money to ride post to London.

Oct. 24. Chancery Lane. 135. Sir Matthew Carew to Carleton. Misfortunes come upon him like waves of the sea. Lost 12,000*l.* through one whom he trusted and who deceived him; the Master of the Rolls has taken away what was left; and his son Thomas, discarded from Carleton's service, is wandering idly without employment.

Oct. 24. Prince's Court. 136. Dr. Geo. Carleton to the Same. The Prince would have obtained him the Bishopric of Carlisle, but the King was so importuned that he otherwise disposed of it. Is ashamed to tell the

VOL. LXXXVIII.

1616.

manner in which bishoprics are got. Is weary of Court. Arminius, a divine and reader at Leyden, having written things that trouble the University youths, has penned a brief examination of them.

Oct. 24. Lambeth. 137. Sentence of deprivation against Robt. Pilkington, Rector of Fennotterey and Vicar of Harpford, co. Devon, for drunkenness, keeping bad company, &c. Latin.

Oct. 26. 138. Order by the Archbp. of Canterbury, on reference to him of the complaint made to the Council by Lucy Lady Molyneux, against her husband, Sir John Molyneux; viz., that Sir John shall give security to allow her 120*l.* per ann. for maintenance, she retaining her daughter Bridget, and he providing for the other children.

Oct. 26. 139. Indenture between Chris. Wandesford, of Kirklington, co. York, and Wm. Wandesford, of London, indemnifying the said William from all demands relating to the executorship of the late Sir Geo. Wandesford.

Oct. 26. London. 140. Chamberlain to Carleton. Lord Coke was called before the Lord Chancellor to answer objections to his reports. He has to be questioned by lawyers of little reputation, and is not asked to sit down. He answers so well that the objections are reduced from 28 to 5. His restoration hoped for, as the King says he means to correct but not destroy him. His Majesty expected from Theobalds. Dr. Carleton is not made Bishop of Carlisle as expected, but one Snowden, an obscure fellow. Dr. Baily is Bishop of Bangor, and Sir Robt. Naunton Master of Requests and Surveyor of the Court of Wards. Sir Hen. Guildford's house at Taplowe burnt to the ground. Sir Wm. Dormer, Lord Dormer's eldest son, dead. Reported duel between Sir Hen. Rich and Sir Ralph Shelton, &c.

Oct.? 141. Extracts from Coke's Institutes concerning the rights and duties of sheriffs.

Oct.? 142. Copy of the above.

Oct. 26. London. 143. Edw. Sherburn to [Carleton]. Sir Art. Ingram has moved the Lord Treasurer for Carleton's allowances, which are promised. Lady Cromer about to be married to Sir Edw. Hales, Bart., of Kent, whose estate is worth 3,000*l.* per ann. The Earl of Arundel refuses Thos. Carew, on hearing what Carleton has against him. Sir Hen. Rich and Sir Fras. Steward have gone over to Calais to fight a duel, but a messenger is despatched by Council to arrest them. The Prince has been indisposed.

Oct. 28. 144. Sir John Dackombe to Edw. Nicholas. Sorry for his illness; will take no one in his stead, but wait his recovery.

Oct. 28. Dover. 145. John Gray to Lord Zouch. Assertion of Brown, an impudent Papist, prisoner at Mr. Alley's for refusing the Oath of Allegiance, that St. Gregory did not declare the worship of images to be idolatry. *Incloses,*

145. I. *Note of Gregory the Great's opinions disallowing image worship, and of arguments founded thereon, used in the discussion with Brown.*

VOL. LXXXVIII.

1616.

Oct. 28. London. 146. Edw. Sherburn to Carleton. Sends back all the statues, carefully packed in twenty-four chests; also the two coach frames, and two boxes of sweetmeats from Lady Savile, &c.

Oct. 28. Grant to Edw. Orfeur of a Gunner's place at Carlisle, for life. [*Grant Bk., p.* 214.]

Oct. 28. Grant to Sir Robt. Naunton of the Surveyorship of the Court of Wards, for life. [*Ibid., p.* 214.]

Oct. 29. Dover. 147. Mayor of Dover to Lord Zouch. Asks whether he shall return to the prisoners, Smith and Brown, the balance of 5*l.* left from the 12*l.* found on them when apprehended.

[Oct.] 148. Edw. Reynoldes to the Earl of Worcester. Is prevented by illness from serving his month. Begs that his kinsman may supply his place. Desires his assistance in a renewed petition of the Privy Seal Clerks to the King, for allowance of diet.

VOL. LXXXIX. NOVEMBER, DECEMBER, 1616.

Nov. 1. London. 1. Edw. Sherburn to [Carleton]. The Earl of Arundel made Earl Marshal for the Prince's creation. The King has given him all the Earl of Somerset's pictures, &c. *Incloses,*

1. I. *Names of the persons to be made Knights of the Bath, on the creation of Prince Charles as Prince of Wales; among them is "Mr. Seymour that married the Lady Arabella."*

Nov. 1. Grant, in commendam, to Lewis Baily, Bp. of Bangor, of the Treasurership of St. Paul's, London, &c. [*Grant Bk., p.* 167.]

Nov. 2. 2. Petition of Sir Barantyne Molyns and Thos. Lever to Sir Julius Cæsar, for their answer to be taken in the country, to a bill of complaint against them by Rich. Bidford, Sir Barantyne having almost lost his sight in the service of the late Queen beyond seas. With order thereon.

Nov. 2. Rome. 3. Note of the decree of the Cardinals deputed for expurgation of books, condemning certain works, and including them in the Index Expurgatorius; amongst them are the writings of Marco Antonio de Dominis, Archbp. of Spalato.

Nov. 3. London. 4. Matthew de Quester to Carleton. Despatch of packets. Sends His Majesty's proclamation for suppressing all posts excepting those authorized by the postmasters. Complains of letters being brought from abroad by private agents, contrary to ancient custom, &c.

[Nov. 4.] 5. Bill of Mr. Black, the King's tailor, for robes for Lord Berkeley [made Knight of the Bath at the creation of the Prince].

Nov. 4. 6. Description of the ceremonial of creating the Knights of the Bath at the creation of Prince Charles; their proceeding to Henry VII.'s Chapel, Saturday, Nov. 2; taking the bath, receiving

1616. Vol. LXXXIX.

the oath, knightage by the King, offerings in the chapel, and attendance on the Prince, Nov. 4.

Nov. 4. 7. Copy of the above.

Nov. 4. Monday. Order of the creation of Prince Charles as Prince of Wales, as it was celebrated at Whitehall, and of the dinner given afterwards. [*Dom. Corresp., June* 4, 1610.]

[Nov. 4.] 8. Preamble of the patent creating Prince Charles Prince of Wales.

Nov. 4. Westminster. Grant to Thos. Snawsell, of London, of pardon for killing John Forrest. Latin. [*Sign Man., vol.* VI., *No.* 90.]

Nov. 4. Westminster. Grant to the Gardeners' Company, of London, of renewal of their charter, with additions for their better governance. [*Ibid., No.* 91.]

Nov. 4. Westminster. Warrant for erection of a prison for the High Commission Court, and appointment of Brian Wilton, Rich. Wilton, and John Thurgood successively as Wardens of it. [*Ibid., No.* 92.]

Nov. 5. Baron Sotherton's House, Whitefriars. Sir John Throgmorton to Carleton. No one knows what will become of the cloth affair. The King seems determined to carry it forward. Wishes he might see the error of changing ancient and well-known friends for new ones. Creation of the Prince. Sec. Winwood read the Patent on his knee, the Prince kneeling also. Lord Coke hopes to return to favour, by marrying a daughter of his wife to a brother of Visct. Villiers. [*Holl. Corresp., Nov.* 5.]

Nov. 6. Creation of Thos. Lord Ellesmere as Visct. Brackley. [*Grant Bk., p.* 209.]

Nov. 6. Special warrant to Geo. Reynall to deliver Rich. Taverner from the King's Bench Prison. [*Ibid., p.* 194.]

Nov. 7. 9. Edw. Sherburn to Carleton. Recommends the bearer, Wm. Harding, as a groom, &c.

Nov. 7. 10. Sir Matt. Carew to the Same. Can scarcely believe that his son would write aspersions of Sir Dudley and Lady Carleton, as he always spoke well of them. Provided for him while there was hope of the Earl [of Arundel's] taking him, or of his returning to Carleton, but now gives him over for lost. His daughter about to marry a worthy baronet, Sir Edw. Hales.

Nov. 7. 11. Mayor of Dover to Lord Zouch. Envelope. *Transmits,*

11. I. *Note of certain books unlawfully brought into the realm, and presented to the Mayor of Dover by John Prettyman, officer of the Customs. Nov.* 6.

11. II. *Examination of John Prettyman, of Dover. The above books were shown to him by Geo. Christopher, a sailor, who had brought them from Calais. Nov.* 7.

11. III. *Examination of Geo. Christopher, of Dover, sailor. Brought over a box and bundle, at request of Louis Dandine, the Calais post, not knowing that they were books; Dandine promised to call for them, &c. Nov.* 7.

VOL. LXXXIX.

12. Mayor of Dover to Rich. Younge. Smith and Brown want more money; refuses it till Lord Zouch's pleasure is known. The vessel that brought over the books was his Lordship's pinnace, which was sent for the Countess of Pembroke. *Incloses,*

12. I. *Bill of expenses of Rich. Smith and John Brown. Nov.* 7.

13. Mayor of Sandwich to Lord Zouch. Has arrested Peter Lamote alias Michael Lambert, who was detected from the description of him sent by his Lordship, and was trying to go abroad. Has also committed Simon Gerling and Thos. Preston, for serving a latitat on Joel Solley in his Lordship's jurisdiction. *Incloses,*

13. I. *Examination of Mich. Lambert. Has lived two and a half years in London, teaching French, Taught Mr. Trevor of the Inner Temple. The money found on him was not stolen from Mr. Trevor, but was partly his own earnings and partly a gift from his father. Sandwich, Nov* 7.

The Council to the Commissioners of Sewers for cos. Northampton, Huntingdon, Lincoln, and Cambridge. Sir Fras. Fane will acquaint them with the course taken with those disobedient persons who resisted their decrees. Request them to proceed as usual, without dread of law, or of the opposition of common and mean persons. [*Dom. Corresp., Dec.* 13.] *Incloses,*

14. *Order in Council, founded on a report of the Attorney General upon complaints of certain persons in cos. Northampton, Huntingdon, Cambridge, and Lincoln, against the Commissioners of Sewers, confirming the powers of the Commission to make new banks or sluices, to assess the inhabitants near to pay for them, and to imprison refractory persons; also exempting the Commissioners from suits at common law for discharge of their office. The persons committed for contempt shall not be released, till they discharge all actions and suits against the Commissioners. Nov.* 8.

15. Wm. Beecher to Carleton. The Prince's creation has passed over, with no solemnity except "a combat of barriers performed by the Inns of Court." The Courtiers did nothing, because the Prince was loth either to be left out or to take a part. It is whispered, that he is of "a weake and crasie disposition." The King has created the Lord Chancellor Visct. Brackley, for standing very stoutly for the maintenance of the prerogative. Lord Roos set out from Portsmouth, and Sir John Digby is to be sent after him. It is Lord Coke's critical day, and an evil issue is foreboded. The King deliberates about sending an Ambassador to the Duke of Savoy, who wishes to join the Princes of the Union. Quarrel between Sir Wm. Howard and Lord Monteagle's son.

16. Extract from the above.

Vol. LXXXIX.

1616.

Nov. 9. London. 17. Chamberlain to Carleton. The creation of the Prince performed at Whitehall within doors, the sharp weather and his ill health not permitting a public show. Twenty-four sons of the noblest houses made Knights of the Bath. The King was at Whitehall, to see the Prince come by water from Richmond, but the Queen would not be present, lest she should renew her grief for the late Prince, for whom the Bp. of Ely prayed by mistake, at a Court sermon. The King detained by the clothing business; he will compel the old Merchant Adventurers to enter this new company, but clothing decays apace. Lord Coke's affair in suspense; the Queen and Prince are for him, but he is not submissive enough; he has an ague. Creations of peers. Sir Robt. Naunton excuses himself from going to Flanders to demand justice against Puteanus, the author of "Corona Regia." The Earl of Salisbury's son dead.

Nov. 9. Whitehall. 18. Fras. Blundell to the Same. Thanks for favours to his brother.

Nov. 9. London. 19. Edw. Sherburn to [the Same]. The Prince is more cheerful, and Commissioners are sent to Spain about his marriage. Sir Phil. Stanhope made Baron Shelford, His Majesty bestowing the benefit, which is 10,000*l.*, on Winwood. Sir T. Edmondes sent for over to be made a Privy Councillor, Comptroller of the Household, &c. Sir Hen. Yelverton is to succeed Montague as Recorder of the city, though the city opposes it.

Nov. 10? 20. Geo. Calvert to the Lord Chief Justice. Is commanded by Sec. Winwood to signify the King's pleasure that he should repair to the Court before His Majesty's departure.

Nov. 11. Grant to Chas. Lord Effingham and Chas. Howard, his brother, successively of pension of 300*l.* during their lives, in consideration of surrendering the keeping of Windsor Great Park. [*Sign Man., vol.* VI., *No.* 93.]

Nov. 14. Westminster. Grant to John Sayer, of Worshall, co. York, recusant, of licence to travel between his houses of Worshall, Colborne, and Marrick, and from thence to any place within five miles, and to go beyond the five miles, if, in hunting or hawking, his game leads him beyond the compass. [*Ibid., No.* 94.]

Nov. 14. Order to the Lord Chancellor and others to surrender the manors of Burton, Fleming, &c., cos. York, Derby, and Suffolk. [*Grant Bk., p.* 193.]

Nov. 14. London. 21. Chamberlain to Carleton. The King gone to Theobalds. The Queen at Somerset House. Orders given for a supersedeas against Sir Edw. Coke. Four P.'s, Pride, Prohibition, Præmunire, and Prerogative, have overthrown him. Knights of the Bath entertained at Drapers' Hall by the Lord Mayor. Their rude

1616. VOL. LXXXIX.

deportment towards the citizens' wives. Earl of Dorset and Lord Clifford ordered to settle their quarrels by law. Lady Compton advised by her son, Lord Villiers, to stay away from Court, and not to intermeddle with business. Visct. Wallingford is to have 2,000*l.* a year from the Court of Wards, or the choice of the best ward that falls every year, except noblemen. Pricking of sheriffs. Bertram, a grave gentleman of nearly eighty, shot Sir John Tyndall, Master in Chancery, for deciding a case wrongly against him, and showed no remorse, saying he had done his country good. The exorbitant powers of Chancery more confirmed by Coke's weak opposition.

Nov. 14. London. 22. Edw. Sherburn to [Carleton]. Particulars of the murder of Sir John Tyndall, Master in Chancery, by Bertram, who shot him in the back with a pistol in revenge for his having decided against him in a suit on which his whole fortune depended.

Nov. 15. London. 23. Sir Horace Vere to the Same. Sends him four venison pasties half baked.

Nov. 16. Dover. 24. Examination of Thos. Cargell, of Aberdeen, before the Commissioners for Passage. Is a musician; has been two years and a half in France, and there became a Papist. The beads, Popish books, &c. which he brings over are for his own use. Is willing to take the Oath of Allegiance, and conform to the Church of England.

Nov. 17. 25. Defeasance upon a bond for 2,000*l.*, made to the Earl of Salisbury by Sir John Dackombe, under the statute for recovery of debts, on condition of payment of 1,500*l.* before May 20, 1619.

[Nov. 17.] Discharge to Sir John Digby of 10,000*l.* paid by him for the lordship, castle, and manor of Sherborne, heretofore belonging to Sir Walter Raleigh, attainted, and forfeit by the attainder of Robt. Earl of Somerset. [*Warrt. Bk.*, I., *p.* 196.]

Nov. 17? Grant to Geo. Visct. Villiers, for better support of his dignities, of the manors of Hartington, co. Derby, and ten others, cos. York, Gloucester, Warwick, Suffolk, and Lincoln, instead of the manor of Sherborne, intended for him, notwithstanding their being annexed to the Crown by the Act of Entail. [*Ibid.*, *p.* 200.]

Nov. 18. 26. Report of the Lord Chancellor's speech to Sir Hen. Montague, appointed Lord Chief Justice of the King's Bench on the deprivation of Lord Coke, warning him against aiming at popularity, against severity in repressing argument, &c., setting before him the example of Lord Chief Justice Edw. Montague, his grandfather, who never questioned the King's prerogative writs, nor proceeded "rege inconsulto," nor made void statutes, because contrary to sense or reason.

[Nov. 18.] 27. Another report of the above speech, more full than the preceding.

Vol. LXXXIX.

1616.

[Nov. 18.] 28. Reply of Sir Hen. Montague to the above speech. His motto is, Deo, regi, legi. Knows not what moved the King to choose him, but will follow his grandfather's steps. Having a private fortune, will despise bribery. Hopes assistance from his learned friends.

Nov. 18. Dover. 29. Commissioners of the Passage at Dover to Lord Zouch. Send up Smith and Brown, and also the unlawful books, &c. brought over from Dieppe by Thos. Cargell.

Nov. 18. Lambeth. 30. Examination of Thos. Fenwick, of Dilston, Northumberland. Was engaged as Percy's servant just before the Powder Plot; his journey with Tailbois, another of Percy's servants, to London, in charge of 500*l.* or 600*l.* On Percy's being proclaimed traitor, they carried the money back to Yorkshire, and left it with Fras. Ratcliffe, of Dilston. Much money was subscribed by recusants, about the time of the Powder Treason.

Nov. 18. Lambeth. 31. Examination of Fras. Ratcliffe, of Dilston, Northumberland. Was acquainted with Percy. Was at London with Roger Wodrington and Randall Fenwick, at the time of the Powder Plot, to make composition for his recusancy. Does not know Tailbois, and never received any of Percy's money, nor employed it in building a bridge and chapel, &c.

Nov. 18. 32. Notes from the examination of ——— Rod and Geo. Pierson, relative to their complicity in the escape of the priests from Wisbeach Castle.

Nov. 18. London. 33. Edw. Sherburn to Carleton. Sir Lionel Cranfield, a mere merchant, is sworn Master of Requests,—a base fellow, but the times allow anything to be done for money. Lady Harrington is going to end her days with the Lady Elizabeth; the King has given her 5,000*l.*, and 10,000*l.* to Sir Robt. Mansell, who has married Mrs. Roper, the Queen's woman. Lady Hatton has left her husband in his disgrace, taking much of his plate and jewels. Preparation for a masque, &c., which will increase the King's debt 2,000*l.*

Nov. 19. Stoneacre. 34. Capt. Geo. Fenner to Rich. Younge. Confesses his fault, in having, from necessity, taken up some of his moneys in advance, but hopes the Lord Warden will not therefore stop the whole garrison's allowance for a year, as he threatens.

Nov. 19. Golden Anchor, Bow Lane. 35. Nath. Brent to [Carleton]. The Secretary has given the place he [Brent] wished for to Sir Fras. Onslow. The Archbp. of Canterbury condemned Grotius as a busybody, for his ambition, indiscretion, &c. The King is annoyed that his letter, which Sir Noel de Caron got from him, has been printed at the Hague, as it was procured by wrong information. His Majesty told Alderman Cockayne, that if he had abused him by false information, relative to disturbances in the cloth trade with Holland, his quarters should pay for it. The King intended to examine the murderer of Sir John Tyndall, being desirous to sift the abuses of the Court of Chancery,

VOL. LXXXIX.

1616.

but the murderer hung himself. The Prince troubled with the green sickness. Sir Fras. Bacon made a Privy Councillor, and Dr. [Robt.] Snowden, by Lord Villiers' influence, Bishop of Carlisle.

Nov. 19. Grant to John Smith of pension of 12*d.* per diem, for life. [*Grant Bk., p.* 217.]

Nov. 19. Grant to Dr. John Young and his heirs of free denization. [*Ibid., p.* 227.]

Nov. 19 ? Lord Zouch to the Mayors, &c. of the Cinque Ports. To suffer John and Benj. Huett, who are licensed to go abroad anywhere but to Rome, to embark from any place in the Cinque Ports. [*Dom. Corresp., Dec.* 11, 1618. *Note Bk, p.* 30.]

[Nov. 19.] Indenture between the King and Sir John Roper, Lord Teynham, covenanting that his Lordship, having resigned his office of Chief Clerk of the Common Pleas in behalf of Robt. Heath and Robt. Shute, in trust for himself, with a reversion to Visct. Villiers, shall have the power of appointing their successors, should they die before him. [*Grant Bk., p.* 195. *See Feb.* 11, 1617.]

Nov. 20. 36. Bond of Jas. Campbell, under penalty of 500*l.*, to indemnify Lord Zouch from all claims upon the goods saved from a French bark wrecked on Margate Sands, which goods are given up to Campbell, who claims them as owner, on payment of droit rights, and composition to the savers.

[Nov. 20.] 37. Draft of the above.

Nov. 21. Licence to Innocent Lanier to weigh hay and straw brought to London and Westminster, for twenty-one years. [*Grant Bk., p.* 220.]

Nov. 22. Grant to Rich. Gyles and John Wilson of the office of Waiter, to search out and seize logwood, &c., for life. [*Ibid., p.* 210.]

Nov. 22. St. James's. 38. Hen. Lord Danvers to Carleton. Lord Knollys, on his promotion [to the Mastership of the Wards], resigns the Treasurership of the Household to Lord Wotton, who yields the Comptrollership to Sir Thos. Edmondes.

Nov. 23. London. 39. Chamberlain to the Same. Sir Hen. Montague sworn into Lord Coke's place, and went in great pomp to the Hall, accompanied by fifty earls, lords, &c. The Lord Chancellor gave him the oath, exhorting him to avoid the errors of his predecessor, especially love of popularity. He made a modest reply. Coke retires with general applause. The King said he was uncorrupt and a good justicer. His wife's friends grieved with her, for leaving him and carrying off plate, &c. He refused to sell his collar of S. S. to his successor, saying he would leave it to his posterity, that they might know they had a Chief Justice for their ancestor. He bears his misfortune well, and has gone down to his daughter Saddler's in Hertfordshire. The King displeased with the Solicitor for refusing the Recordership, the city having hastily chosen one Coventry, no favourite at Court, before his Majesty could nominate another.

1616. Vol. LXXXIX.

Bertram, who killed Sir John Tyndall, hung himself, for fear of torture. Lord Dormer dead. The old Merchant Adventurers know not how to content the King. They will not join the new company, who are trying to sell their cloths at Antwerp or Bruges. Sir Lionel Cranfield made Master of Requests, and would have been Under Treasurer, but the Lord Treasurer said he would resign, rather than be yoked to a London 'prentice. Sir Thos. Edmondes and Paul Pindar recalled. Sir Edw. Cecil is to marry Diana Drury, who, since her brother's death, is worth 12,000*l.*

Nov. 23. 40. Edw. Sherburn to Carleton. Will ship for him candles and other articles, as desired.

Nov. 23. Dover. 41. Commissioners of the Passage at Dover to Lord Zouch. Have stayed, according to his order, John and Benj. Huett, who, with their servant, Wm. Hind, had the Council's licence to go abroad.

Nov. 24. Commission to Sir Hen. Montague to receive and report on Sir Edw. Coke's Reports. [*Grant Bk., p.* 198.]

Nov. 25. Order to the Lord Chancellor and others to surrender the manor of Goxhill, co. Lincoln. [*Ibid., p.* 193.]

Nov. 25. Removal of Sir Edw. Coke from the office of Chief Justiceship. [*Ibid., p.* 197.]

Nov. 25. Dover. 42. Note of the arrival at Dover of Thomas, son of Sir Edw. Bellingham, and of Mr. Ayliff, alias Brice Christmas, who wished to go over seas, but, being challenged with an intention to fight a duel, went privately to Gravesend. A warrant was afterwards sent to Dover to stay them.

Nov. 25. Dover. 43. Mayor of Dover to Lord Zouch. Forwards a letter from Thos. Fulnetby. *Incloses,*

43. i. *Thos. Fulnetby to the Same. A French vessel, wrecked in the Downs, is seized by Sir Fras. Howard for the Lord Admiral, who claims all wrecks in the seas. Annexed are,*

43. ii. *Proofs that the Downs, Godwin Sands, and other places on that coast are within the Lord Warden's Admiralty jurisdiction.*

43. iii. *Affirmation by Wm. Young, of Milton, Kent, that the Vice Admiral of that county has always received all manner of wrecks of sea and other casualties, happening in the King's Channel, within the hundred of Faversham. Nov.* 14.

43. iv. *Collection by Mr. Fane of proofs that the Cinque Ports are exempted from the Lord Admiral's jurisdiction. Latin.*

VOL. LXXXIX.

1616.

Nov.? 44. Order of the Lord Warden of the Cinque Ports, touching the right of appropriation of wrecks of the sea.

Nov. 25. Westminster. 45. Grant to Sir Hugh Carmichael of extension of the Registrarship of Brokers, &c., in London, granted him by the City, to Westminster and two miles round London, in order to avoid robberies, which are encouraged by brokers and hucksters, &c. receiving stolen goods.

Nov. 26. 46. Edw. Sherburn to Carleton. Has shipped certain things for him in the Fortune of Dort.

Nov. 26. 47. The Council to the Lord Treasurer. On consideration of the controversy between the Thames fishermen and the Master of the King's barge, relative to the transportation of lampreys, it is ordered, that, until Christmas, 1617, the officers of customs allow the fishermen to transport their lampreys, paying the customs thereon, and 1s. per 1,000, to Rich. Warner, Master of His Majesty's barge.

Nov. [26?] Whitehall. 48. [The Same] to the Officers of Customs. They are to permit the Thames watermen to export lampreys on the above condition.

Nov. 26? 49. Petition of the Lampreymen of Kingston-upon-Hull to the Council, to remit the payment of 20s. per 1,000 customs on lampreys taken by them, on their payment of double the ancient custom, similar relief having been granted to the Thames lampreymen.

Nov. 27. Newmarket. 50. The King to Lord Zouch. The Duchess of Guise requests renewal of permission, for her people of Eu and Treport, to fish with four boats on the coasts of the Cinque Ports. Asks the reason of the discontinuance of her former permission, and if any mischief would result from its renewal.

Nov. 28. 51. [Lord Zouch] to the King, in answer to the above. The licences granted to the French have been, nine for the servants of the French King, three for the Duchess of Guise, and one for Mons. De la Boderie, late French Ambassador; they are for a year, renewable on surrender of the old licences; those of the Duchess are not renewed this year, because the old licences are not brought in. The French do great mischief, fishing with unlawful nets, at unlawful times, and when a boat is filled, its licence is sold to another.

Nov. 28. Dover. 52. Commissioners of the Passage to Lord Zouch. Have bound over John Huett the elder to appear before his Lordship, with his servant, who is Hen. Blackbeard, not Wm. Hind, as named in the pass. The younger Huett now says that his name is John, not Benjamin; that he is under nineteen, and the ward of his mother. Have sent him up in custody. *Inclose,*

52. I. *Licence by the Council to John and Benj. Huett, to travel beyond seas for three years, with Wm. Hind, their servant, but not to go to Rome. Whitehall, Nov. 15.*

Nov. 28. 53. Memorandum of receipts [of contribution to the benevolence?] from Lincolnshire and Anglesea.

VOL. LXXXIX.

1616.

Nov.? 54. Remonstrance of the Farmers of Customs against the intended proclamation for wearing English cloth, as calculated to injure trade so much that they should be obliged to give up their patent.

Nov. 29. Golden Anchor, Bow Lane. 55. Nath. Brent to [Carleton]. Sir Hen. Savile sends his resolution concerning the books. Geo. Carleton will accept Sir Dudley's offer of receiving his son, if it will not interfere with his place at King's College. Great distress in the cloth trade. The Hollanders and Alderman Cockayne blamed. The King purposes to make sumptuary laws for moderating excess in apparel. A proclamation is expected ordering the wearing of cloth, which causes great deadness in trade. The Great Turk begins to use our English merchants ill. Sir Thos. Edmondes sent for to take possession of his Comptrollership. Lord Dormer and his eldest son dead. The grandchild, "an infinite great ward," will be given to the Earl of Montgomery or Lord Knollys. Roberts, a usurer, has given the King 12,000*l.* to free himself from some imaginary forfeitures. The King is at Newmarket, the Queen going to Greenwich, the Prince at St. James's, &c. *Incloses,*

55. I. *Sir Hen. Savile to the Same. Private business. Carleton is not to accept the bookseller's offer for exchange of books, but to tell him peremptorily to pay for the books sold, and return the remaining copies. Eton, Nov.* 23, 1616.

[Nov.] 56. Note of moneys received by Wm. Bruncard and Chris. Aubrey upon the grant for issues of jurors, from April 1608 to Dec. 1613.

Nov.? Grant to Sir John Dackombe of 450*l.*, the half-year's rent arising from the lease of the provision of French and Rhenish wines for the Royal household, granted to him in trust for the Earl of Somerset, and forfeited by his attainder, in part payment of 833*l.* 6*s.* 8*d.*, disbursed by him for the King's service. Also grant of the next half-year's rent to the Duke of Lenox. [*Sign Man., vol.* VI., *No.* 95.]

[Nov.] 57. Account of rents paid for Gateshead toll, from the year 1605.

Nov. 58. List of the Commissioners for Dover Passage.

Nov.? The King to the Bp. of Winchester. Recommends Sir Peter Young, Almoner of Scotland, to the Hospital of the Holy Cross, near Winchester, void by promotion of Art. Lake to the Bishopric of Bath and Wells. Latin. [*Warrt. Bk.*, I., *p.* 194.]

Nov.? Confirmation to Robt. Heath, of the Inner Temple, and Robt. Shute, of Gray's Inn, of the Clerkship of the Court of Common Pleas, granted them by Sir Hen. Montague, Chief Justice. [*Warrt. Bk.*, I., *p.* 194.]

VOL. LXXXIX.

1616.

Dec. 1. Licence to Sir John St. John, Bart., to hold the court in the manor of Liddiard and elsewhere, co. Wilts. [*Grant Bk., p.* 195.]

Dec. 2. Grant to John Vernon and John Mallett of the office of Secretary in the principality of Wales. [*Ibid., p.* 191.]

Dec. 3. Bow Lane. 59. Nath. Brent to Carleton. Report says that Lord Coke spent two hours with the King, and was graciously received. His wife has left him, put her jewels into the hands of friends, and complains that she is undone by his weakness. Discontent between Lord and Lady Roos. He has taken her jewels, and allowed his father-in-law to pay 6,000*l.* for him.

Dec. 3. Newmarket. 60. Digest of the directions given by the King to Dr. [John] Hill, Vice Chancellor of Cambridge, and others, heads of colleges, for promotion of uniformity of religion, morality, and learning amongst the students; a yearly report to be presented to His Majesty.

Dec. 3 ? 61. Declaration by the King of his pleasure that the Chancellor, Vice Chancellor and heads of colleges, observe certain regulations subjoined, for due observance of religious worship, receiving the communion, &c. No woman to frequent the college chapels, unless when a bell is rung for an English sermon to the people. Popery and puritanism to be suppressed.

Dec. 4. Newmarket. 62. Winwood to Lord Zouch. The King has given the Duchess of Guise leave to have four French boats to fish, but if the French use that pretext for others to fish, or employ improper nets, the licences are to be forfeited.

Dec. 4. Licence to Sir Hen. Wallop to hold the court in the manor of Farleigh-Wallop, and others, co. Hants. [*Grant Bk., p.* 227.]

Dec. 6. Grant to Sir Robt. Vernon of the office of Housekeeper at Newmarket, co. Cambridge, for life. [*Ibid., p.* 191.]

Dec. 6. Grant to the Same of the office of keeping the new warren called Wilbraham Bushes, for life. [*Ibid., p.* 191.]

Dec. 6. Grant to Geo. Willmer of the office of Collector of a third in the pound imposed upon merchant strangers, for life. [*Ibid., p.* 225.]

Dec. 6. 63. Petition of John Arundel, of Trerice, Cornwall, to Sir Julius Cæsar, for a commission to take his answer in the country touching the suit of Chris. Strong. With order thereon.

Dec. 6. Westminster. 64. Grant to Dr. Wm. Laud of the office of Dean of Gloucester.

Dec. 7. 65. Sir Fras. Bacon and Sir Hen. Yelverton to the King. Think that as there is not sufficient evidence against Sir Thos. Monson, and yet it is unfitting to pass over the affair altogether, it would be best to grant him a pardon.

Vol. LXXXIX.

1616.

Dec. 7. Charing Cross. 66. Sir Thos. Lake to Lord Zouch. The King wishes him to satisfy a poor merchant of Conquet, in Brittany, whose bark was run on shore within the Cinque Ports. *Incloses,*

66. I. *Memorial to Sir Thos. Lake, by the Master of the Joan, of Conquet, for return of his boat, run on shore at Lydd.*

Dec. 7. Grant to Wm. Earl of Salisbury of Cranborne Chace, &c., cos. Dorset, Wilts, and Hants. [*Grant Bk., p.* 185.]

Dec. 7. London. 67. Chamberlain to Carleton. The Lord Treasurer has gone to Audley End to avoid importunate claims for money. Lord Coke has had access to the King, and kissed his hand. Certain processes against him are stayed, and it is hoped he will be restored to the Council board. His lady relents, but does not return to him. Earl of Montgomery has 3,000*l.* a year for twenty years, towards his debts, and the wardship of young Lord Dormer. Sir John Dormer busy with the executorship of the late Lord, and of Sir Michael Dormer's lady. The Scotch journey still talked of, and Inigo Jones has the charge of chapel pictures and furniture, but money is wanted. Roberts, of Cornwall, compelled to lend 12,000*l.*, without interest, by threat of all his property being seized for usury. Lady Cromer married to Sir Edw. Hales, Bart., and old Lady Killigrew to [Dr. Geo.] Downham, who is going to be an Irish Bishop. The Countesses of Exeter and Somerset with child.

Dec. 7. London. 68. Edw. Sherburn to [the Same]. Has obtained only 400*l.* of the money due to Carleton, all efforts being needed to obtain money for the King's journey to Scotland. Miserable cries of poor men and others, whose wages and pensions have not been paid for three years or more. Sir Lionel Cranfield is to be Under Treasurer of the Exchequer. Villiers declines in the King's favour, and Lord Mordaunt, who has better natural parts, is likely to ascend. The King promises to give Sir Edw. Coke some service, though thinking him unfit for the Chief Justiceship: many persons would be glad to see him restored to honour. Sends a justification of Sir John Tyndall against the accusations of Bertram, who murdered him, &c.

Dec. 7. 69. Writ to Wm. Ellwood, Mayor of Sandwich, to deliver up all the money in his possession received from Mich. Lambert, of London, who was convicted of stealing the same from John Bridges, of St. Dunstan's parish, London.

Dec. 8. London. 70. Matthew de Quester to Carleton. Hopes his former packet arrived safely, &c.

Dec. 8. Utrecht. 71. Capt. John Pigott to the Same. Requests him to speak to his Excellency [the Prince of Orange] to allow Sir Walter Raleigh forty or fifty men from the Low Countries.

Dec. 9. London. 72. Licence from Lord Zouch for Jacob le Ver, of Treport, to fish on the coasts of the Cinque Ports, at the nomination of Mdme. de Guise. With certificate that his nets are lawful. Latin.

1616. Vol. LXXXIX.

Dec. 9. London. 73—75. Similar licences for Jas. Brian, Rich. de Rice, and Thos. Brian, all of Treport. Indorsed "Cancelled Licenses."

Dec. 10. Dover. 76. Wm. Ward to Lord Zouch. Begs to know for what price his Lordship will sell his Burton bark. Thinks 50*l.* enough, as the purchasers will have to compound with the owners in France.

Dec. 12? 77. Sir Thos. Wynn to Rich. Younge. The people of Faversham demand no less than 5*l.* for taking up his trunk, which is more than it is worth. Desires that Lord Zouch will send expressly to order its delivery; will abide his award for the payment. *Annexes,*

77. I. *Inventory of Sir Thos. Wynn's goods wrecked at Faversham. Dec.* 12.

Dec. 13. 78. The Council to the Commissioners of Sewers, cos. Northampton, Cambridge, and Lincoln. Have received complaints from the inhabitants of the Isle of Ely, and of Holland, Lincolnshire, of a tax for Clowse Cross drain, which, from its imperfect construction, is rather prejudicial than useful. Summon a deputation of the Commissioners and inhabitants to appear at the Board, and meanwhile the tax to be suspended.

Dec. 14. Grant to Duncan Primrose of the office of Chief Surgeon to the King, for life. [*Grant Bk., p.* 215.]

Dec. 14. Dover. 79. Sir Peter Manwood to Lord Zouch. Lady Harrington detained at Dover by contrary winds. The King's ship not able to get out of the Downs for her, &c. All his Lordship's officers treat her most courteously. She has taken a severe cold, but bears it very patiently.

Dec. 14. London. 80. Edw. Sherburn to [Carleton]. The Archbp. [of Spalato] has not arrived in London, but is at Dover. The King is returning to London, to stay till he goes to Scotland. Sir Edw. Coke is likely to be made a Baron; the Queen and Prince, or his money, do much for him.

Dec. 15. Deal. 81. Thos. Cousant to his nephew, Hen. Eveseed. Desires him to seek out Edm. Sparrow and his companion in Townsend Lane, Thames Street, having given them a pass for London, and finding afterwards that they were pirates; if he should find them, he is to acquaint the Lord Warden therewith, &c.

Dec. 15. 82. Note by Dr. John Lambe, of moneys sent by the Bishop of Lincoln towards the building of St. Neot's Bridge, or paid to him by Lambe, in part of a tally of 500*l.*, struck by his Lordship in discharge of the tenths of Lincoln diocese.

Vol. LXXXIX.

1616.

Dec. 15. Newmarket. 83. The King to the Council of Scotland. Hopes he will not be coldly received in Scotland, from false prejudices as to the motives of his visit, which are, a desire to revisit his native kingdom, to hear complaints, and reform abuses. Has no intention to disturb the civil or ecclesiastical government of the kingdom, without the people's concurrence, nor to urge things, good in themselves, but generally disliked by them.

Dec. 16. Deal Castle. 84. Thos. Fulnetby to Rich. Younge. Thinks Dr. Newman's letter is nothing to the point, as to the Lord Warden's right to a certain vessel which lay seven or eight tides with no one in her. *Incloses,*

84. I. *Sir Geo. Newman to Thos. Fulnetby. The goods taken from the wreck should be inventoried; such as will spoil, sold, and the price kept; the rest stored till the owners claim and prove them as their own, to whom they are to be delivered, on payment of recompence to the savers, and of the Lord Warden's rights. Canterbury, Dec.* 15.

Dec. 18. St. James's. 85. Thos. Murray to Carleton. The Prince is pleased with the medals sent him by Carleton, and wishes for the book which explains their use. The messengers who brought them are paid. His Highness wishes Carleton's help, if needful, to procure the Chief Captain's place in the company of Sir Thos. Erskine, his Groom of the Privy Chamber, who is now sick, for Erskine's brother.

Dec. 18. Grant to John Taylor of Shipling Park, and others, co. Suffolk, for twenty-one years. [*Grant Bk., p.* 189.]

Dec. 19. Grant to John Wilson of a Prebend of St. Peter's, Westminster, for life. [*Ibid., p.* 225.]

Dec. 20. Grant to Wm. Ramsay of the office of Keeper and Captain of Holy and Ferne Islands, co. Durham, for life. [*Ibid., p.* 194.]

Dec, 20. London. 86. Matthew de Quester to Carleton. Forwards a packet of Venetian letters for his Lordship, and another from General Cecil to Lady Carleton. Geo. Martin, coming from Margate by sea, with the baggage of the Archbp. [of Spalato], was taken in a storm, and all the trunks and letters had to be thrown overboard.

Dec. 21. London. 87. Chamberlain to the Same. The Archbp. of Spalato is lodged at Lambeth, but the Archbp. of Canterbury desires to remove him to the Dean of Westminster's. The Bishop of London's eldest son made a Prebendary of St. Paul's. Sir John Swinnerton dead. Lord Rich marries Lady St. Paul, a widow of Lincolnshire. Chris. Nevill, son to the Lord Abergavenny, was bastinadoed by Sir Humph. Tufton for making love to his wife. Lord Coke graciously received at Court; it is rumoured he will be made a Baron; but some say this kindness is only to obtain his daughter for Lord Villiers' brother. Report

VOL. LXXXIX.

1616.

that Somerset will have his pardon, his jewels restored, and a pension of 4,000*l.* per ann. Lord Roxburgh made an Earl, but is discontented at not obtaining the place of Chamberlain to the Prince. His Lady leaves the Queen, and is out of favour. Sir Thos. Lake has got leave to go with the King to Scotland. Sir Thos. Edmondes has arrived in London with his Frenchman, Beaulieu.

Dec. 21. 88. Edw. Sherburn to Carleton. Sends him a paper containing the advice of a concealed friend to Sir Edw. Coke, the truth and plainness of which he thinks Carleton will like. *Incloses,*

88. I. ——— *to Sir Edw. Coke. Points out his past errors, viz., too much speaking in Court, becoming rather to a lawyer than a judge; severity towards the condemned; jesting without respect of persons; twisting the law to his own purposes; covetousness and hard dealing with the poor. Accuses him of mismanagement in the late great trial, by delaying so long, and being so anxious to accumulate evidence, that the delinquents escaped. Hopes his standing so stoutly for the commonwealth proceeded from a love of justice, not from a disposition to oppose greatness; advises him, by parting with some of his ill-gotten wealth, to save himself for future service. Exhorts him, if he escape this time, to be cautious, to remember others in misfortune, and not to delay justice; to be strict with Papists who are at the bottom of his troubles; not to be puffed up with prosperity, nor dejected in adversity.*

Dec. ? 89. Copy of the above letter to Coke.

Dec 21. Grant to Geo. Wardegar of the Clerkship of the Prick and Cheque of the Navy at Chatham, for life. [*Grant Bk., p.* 225.]

Dec. 21. Grant to Thos. Hughes of the office of Prothonotary and Clerk of the Crown, in cos. Glamorgan, Monmouth, Brecknock, and Radnor, for life. [*Ibid., p.* 205.]

Dec. 23. Grant to Peregrin Guillun of the office of Gamekeeper, near Wandsworth and elsewhere, co. Surrey, for life. [*Ibid., p.* 210.]

Dec. 23. Grant to Hen. and Edw. Fetherstone successively, of the office of Porter in the Court of King's Bench, for life. [*Ibid., p.* 218.]

Dec. 23. Grant to Wm. Dawes of the office of Writing all Licences for Collections of Relief upon casual mishaps, for life. [*Ibid., p.* 200.]

Dec. 23. Grant to Edw. Stephens of the office of Gamekeeper at the manor of Woking, co. Surrey, for life. [*Ibid., p.* 185.]

Dec. ? 90. Indictment of Thos. Bland, Wm. Whitehead, and others, for going off in a boat called the Bark, and piratically robbing a Flemish pink and other vessels off Beachey, on Sept. 8, 1616. Latin.

1616. VOL. LXXXIX.

Dec. 23. Dover. 91. Verdict of acquittal for Wm. Whitehead, Rich. Lobsey, Thos. Short, and Roland le Pennecke, on their trial for the above offences. Latin. *Annexed are,*

91. I. *Writ to the Mayor and Jurats of Dover for a jury of thirty-six, to attend at the Mount, on Dec. 23, to try certain prisoners for piracy. Dover Castle, Dec. 11. Latin.*

91. II. *Roll of the Jurymen thus summoned.*

91. III. *Writ from Lord Zouch to the Mayor and Jurats of Rye, to bring before his Lieutenant, at the Mount in Dover, Wm. Whitehead, and any other prisoners in the gaol. Dover Castle, Dec. 14. Latin.*

91. IV. *Writ from the Same to the Marshal and Gaoler of Dover Castle, to bring up Whitehead, Lobsey, Shorte, and le Pennecke, for trial, on the 23d. Dover Castle, Dec. 19. Latin.*

[Dec. 24.] Grant to Wm. Visct. Wallingford, Master of the Court of Wards and Liveries, and Treasurer of the Household, of one Wardship for every year, such as he shall choose. [*Warrt. Bk.*, I., *p.* 195.]

Dec. 24. Grant to Rich. Christmas of the office of Keeper and Captain of St. Andrew's Castle, at Hamul, co. Hants, for life. [*Grant Bk.*, *p.* 198.]

Dec. 25. 92. Bill of the assignees of Roland Love, Marshal Farrier, for marshalry in the King's courser stables, from Christmas 1615.

Dec. 26. Grant to Rich. Frampton of the office of registering affidavits in Chancery, for life. [*Grant Bk.*, *p.* 210.]

Dec. 27. Grant to Sir Geo. Hay of the yearly revenue of 240*l*, to be reserved and paid for making smalt, for divers years. [*Ibid.*]

Dec. 27. Grant to John Gelfe of a Gunner's place in the Tower, for life. [*Ibid.*, *p.* 218.]

Dec. 27. 93. Lord Zouch to the Jurats of Faversham. Requests them to join in the defence of the suits commenced in the Chancery Court of Dover against Mr. Philpot, their Mayor, the cause concerning them all alike.

Dec. 27. 94. [The Same] to Mr. Hadde. Orders stay of all proceedings against Mr. Philpot, Mayor of Faversham, till the difference between him and Mr. Kenett is determined.

Dec. 28. London. 95. Fras. Blundell to Carleton. Thanks for kindness to his brothers. Sir Hen. Wotton thinks Carleton's sending the Archbp. of Spalato to England one of his masterpieces. The Queen is unwell at Somerset House.

Dec. 28. 96. Sir Matt. Carew to the Same. Lord Arundel has no employment for his son, who is leading a vagrant and debauched life. Is unhappy in both his sons, but his "kind loving daughter" is married

VOL. LXXXIX.

1616. to "a fyne and lerned gentleman, of an exceeding good carriage;" a Baronet, who has 4,000*l.* per ann., and lives at Woodchurch in Kent, but will remove with her to Tunstall.

Dec. 30. Dover. 97. Wm. Ward to Rich. Younge. Lady Harrington conveyed to Calais in Lord Zouch's pinnace. Has kept the passage money for his Lordship, if he will receive it, because, if this company be carried over free, others will expect it, though his Lordship is at the expense of keeping up the boat.

Dec. 30. London. 98. Sir John Bennet to Carleton. Seeing Sir R. Winwood Secretary, Sir John Digby Vice Chamberlain, and Sir Thos. Edmondes sitting at Court with a white staff, he thinks Carleton's staff stands next the door. The King pays Ambassadors slackly, but makes it up when they come home.

Dec. 30. Whitehall. 99. Thos. Murray to the Same. The Prince is grateful for the two books sent him by Carleton, and will favour his advancement.

Dec. 31. Lambeth. 100. Marco Antonio de Dominis, Archbp. of Spalato, to the Same. Greatly pleased with the favours he receives from the King and all the Court; finds, like the Queen of Sheba, the greatness of Solomon more than ever it was ever reported. His manifesto is to be printed in English. The King also wishes his work on an ecclesiastical republic to be printed. The Nuncio of the Inquisition has searched his library at Venice for Protestant books, but found none, only his breviary, with all Pontifical errors marked out, which was sent to Rome. Italian.

Dec. 31? 101. Petition of Edw. Knight, of Birchington, Isle of Thanet, to Lord Zouch. Complains that, though he has to provide arms as a resident in the Cinque Ports, he is also charged with arms at the shire musters, and summoned to Council for non-appearance at the musters; prays for relief therein.

Dec. 31. 102. Book of the moneys owing for stores, allowances, &c. for the office of Ordnance, during the past quarter.

Dec. 31. Grant to Thos. Norton of the office of Guide and Surveyor of Ways, for life. [*Grant Bk., p.* 214.]

Dec. 103. Note of moneys received by Sir Thos. Howard, Master of the Prince's Horse, since Sept. 1614.

UNDATED. 1616?

1616? Warrant to the Lord Treasurer and Lord Carew, Master of the Ordnance, to permit 200 pieces of iron ordnance to be transported to the United Provinces, at the solicitation of Sir Noel Caron, Ambassador from the States. [*Warrt. Bk.*, I., *p.* 63.]

1616? Vol. LXXXIX.

Grant to Sir Fras. Stewart of purchase of lands, value 200*l.* per ann., the refuse left by the several contractors whose contracts are now all fulfilled. [*Warrt. Bk., p.* 188.]

104. Demise to Edw. Bee, of divers messuages, lands, &c., in Waltham Forest, Lainston, Moulton, Whaplode, and elsewhere, cos. Essex, Suffolk, Lincoln, Hants, Surrey, Kent, Bedford, York, and Northumberland. Latin.

Grant to Thos. Elmes, Christiana, his wife, and Anthony, their son, of lease of pastures in the parishes of Norton, Cold-Higham, and Blakesley, co. Northampton; and a rabbit warren, in Potecote. Latin. [*Sign Man., vol.* VI., *No.* 96.]

Warrant to the Officers of the Exchequer, and of the Court of Wards and Liveries, ordering the former to levy the arrears of all alienations which are recorded from 10 Eliz. to the present time, but at more favourable rates; and the latter to do the same of those from 30 Eliz.; also grant of the third of the profits to Lord Wotton, Treasurer of the Household, by whose means the detention of the duties was made known to His Majesty. [*Ibid., No.* 97.]

Grant to Hen. Raynsford, of Orpington, Kent, of the next advowson of the rectory and parish church of Blechby, co. Bucks, devolving on the Crown by attainder of Thos. Lord Grey. Latin. [*Ibid., No.* 98.]

Warrant to pay to John Murray, Keeper of the Privy Purse, 110*l.*, disbursed by him to a Frenchman. [*Ibid., No.* 99.]

Grant to the Earl of Worcester, Keeper of the Privy Seal, of a pension of 1,500*l.* per ann., to be levied from the subsidies on silks, &c. [*Ibid., No.* 100.]

Grant to the Same, of commission for making saltpetre and gunpowder in England and Ireland, with some differences from his former commission. [*Ibid., No.* 101.]

Grant to John Verney and John Mallett, in reversion after Sir Fulk Greville and Adam Newton, of the office of Secretary and Clerk of the Council and Signet before the Council of Wales. Latin. [*Ibid., Nos.* 102. 103.]

Licence to Sir Nich. Salter, Olive Kiddermister, Hugh Mascall, and others, to keep a market weekly at Enfield, co. Middlesex. Latin. [*Ibid., No.* 104.]

Discharge to Meredith Morgan and his heirs of sundry sums paid to him at sundry times, for the debts of the late Earl of Dunbar, for the expenses of masques, and for hawks, horses, cows, and dogs, sent to the King of Spain. [*Ibid., vol.* IV., *No.* 68.]

Warrant to advance 8,000*l.* to Lord Stanhope, Treasurer of the Chamber, on account of his office. [*Ibid., vol.* VII., *No.* 69.]

Vol. LXXXIX.

? Warrant to pay to David Ramsay, clockmaker, 234*l.* 10*s.*, due to him for purchase and repair of clocks and watches for the King. [*Sign Man.*, *vol.* VII., *No.* 70.]

105. Field, the Player, to —— Sutton, Preacher at St. Mary Overy's. Remonstrates against his condemnations from the pulpit of all players. Though, like other trades, that of actors has many corruptions, it is not condemned in Scripture, and, being patronized by the King, it is disloyal to preach against it.

106. [Lord Zouch] to Wm. Ward and Wm. Hart. To examine certain parties, on a complaint by the farmers of customs, of resistance made to Cottle, their searcher, in the execution of his office, on board a ship sailing from Dover.

107. Petition of Alex. Bardolle to Lord Zouch, for the place of Porter of Dover Castle, now void. Has long served Sir Wm. Tate, his Lordship's son-in-law.

108. Petition of Rich. Browne, a poor maimed soldier, to the Same, for letters to Sir Wm. Tate for his relief, according to the Statute for maimed soldiers.

109. Petition of Capt. Thos. Allen to the Council, reciting his services, and desiring the command of a fort, or a muster-master's place, being deprived, by the resignation of the Cautionary Towns, of a promised company under Sir Horace Vere.

110. Petition of Lucas Jacobs to the Council, on behalf of Jurien Heune, Wolfert Willens, and the Dantzic merchants, for permission to land a cargo of goods, which Sir Wm. Cockayne, Governor of the Eastland Company, forbids to come in, although an exception has been made, in behalf of the subjects of Denmark, against the late proclamation prohibiting importation of goods in strangers' ships.

111. Petition of Geo. Margitts to the King, for a grant, on rental of 150*l.* per ann., of the fines on originals in the Chancery Court, which belong to the Crown, but are now usurped by the Cursitors of the Court.

112. Petition of Geo. Gryme, farmer of the manor of Gimingham, Norfolk, to Sir John Dackombe, for leave to purchase timber trees to repair his house.

113. [Sir John Dackombe] to Gilbert Gerard, Clerk of the Duchy Court of Lancaster. Orders him to make commissions of inquisition into concealed lands, under certain conditions.

114. Minute of complaints [made to Sir John Dackombe] by the tenants of the manor of Soham, co. Cambridge, against John Tyler and John Ward, for enclosing to their own use ten acres of common land, and of their petition that the ground may be laid open again.

Vol. LXXXIX.

1616?

115. Sir Fras. Bacon's opinion, in reply to a case proposed, that a bishop cannot make a grant of the office of registrar for a longer time than his own life, unless confirmed by the dean and chapter; that he cannot lawfully make a grant with survivorship to two persons, and that a grant in reversion will not bind his successor.

116. Passages from a sermon by Dr. Gifford, chiefly in favour of the absolute power of kings; and from a prayer, in which he entreats deliverance from Jesuits and puritans.

117. Present state of the receipts and payments of the Treasurer of the Chamber.

118. Orders issued by the High Commission Court; recusants are not to be attacked by pursuivants acting under general warrants, &c.; regulations for the execution of commissions from the Court, the taking of bonds, gathering in of fines, &c. Mutilated.

119. Propositions for regulations to be observed in the High Commission Court for causes ecclesiastical.

120. "Orders for the High Commission Court" as to the fees, registration of the acts, and proceedings in trials.

121. Similar code of orders for the High Commission Court. Latin. [*Partial translation from the above.*]

122. Statement by Dr. Gooch, Master of Magdalen College, Cambridge, of the sentence desired in the case of the church of St. Catherine, viz., either revocation of the decision by the Dean of the Arches that it shall be considered a parish church, and have license for baptisms, marriages, &c., or, if it be so pronounced, that the Master and Fellows of Magdalen College, as proprietors, may be authorized to receive the tithes, &c., according to Lord Audley's grant.

123. Note by Otho Nicholson, of commissions issued to inquire into trespasses on the Royal forests, assart lands, concealed rents, &c. 1–14 Jac. I.

124. Reasons against the suit of the card-makers, who remonstrate against the exercise of Sir Rich. Coningsby's patent for importation of playing cards.

125. Petition of Capt. Hen. Deane to the King. Has been a soldier forty years; and his wife, Eliz. Deane, was servant to Elizabeth, Electress Palatine. Has been frustrated of a grant of 2,000 acres of land in Ireland. Having recently detected abuses in purloining wax from the King's chandlery, begs a grant of the wax stolen, and half the fines of the delinquents.

Vol. LXXXIX.

1616? 126. Statement of the fraudulent dealing of the King's chandlery-men, in purloining his wax, and selling it for their own profit.

127. Statement of a plot devised by Mr. Hall and——Perce, lessees of the two manors of which the town of Colby consists, for inclosing some of the waste lands belonging to the commoners of the town.

128. Statement of reasons why such great debts are depending before the auditors of the Exchequer.

129. Statement of the cause of the continuance and yearly increase of arrears [of the King's payments], with suggestions for clearing them off.

130. Reasons why many debts brought into the Lord Treasurer's Remembrancer's Office are desperate, and suggestions of remedy therefor.

131. Notes for perfecting the coats-of-arms of the nobility, gentry, &c. in England, Scotland, and Ireland, mentioned by Camden.

132. Memoranda from records of Ric. II. up to 14 Jac. I., showing that the Lord Wardens of the Cinque Ports have been Admirals of the Cinque Ports, and that their right of Admiralty extended to the main sea.

133. Information by Dan. Wyborne, Wm. Woolters, Robt. Robinson, and John Stock, old men of Sandwich, that in their recollection, the wrecks from Beachey Head, Sussex, to the Shoe Beacon, Essex, appertained to the Lord Warden of the Cinque Ports, and not to the Admiral of the Narrow Seas; but that the Mayor of any of the said ports could punish offenders in ships off the ports, provided the ships could be reached on horseback at low water.

134. Bill and answer in the cause the Attorney General v. Sir Hen. Neville, Sir Fras. Moore, Sir Hen. Savile, Sir Wm. Burlacy, Sir Robt. Killigrew, and Hum. Newbry, respecting the right to Ashridge and other lands in Windsor Forest. [*See Sept.* 17, 1618.]

135. Note [by Sir Dud. Carleton] of payments of rents, due in 1616.

Vol. XC. January—March, 1617.

1617.
Jan. 1.
Whitefriars.

Sir John Throgmorton to [Carleton]. The King has restored to the old Merchant Adventurers their charter, &c., with promise to grant them any reasonable privileges. The Spanish treaty is not so forward as reported, but they prevail more here with golden bullets than they would with bullets of iron, and the Spanish tongue, dress, &c., are all in fashion. It is hoped that the King is dissimulating

1617. Vol. XC.

in his favour towards them, in order to subvert some of their projects. Villiers made Earl of Buckingham, and it is said the Lord Chancellor will be Earl of Cambridge. Sir Thos. Edmondes is returning to France, to make peace between the Queen Mother and the Princes. [*Holl. Corresp., Jan.* 1.]

Jan. 2. 1. Edw. Sherburn to Carleton. The Archbp. of Canterbury desires to keep the portrait of the Archbp. of Spalato, &c.

Jan. 2. 2. [Edw. Reynoldes] to Fras. Mills. The Lord Privy Seal gives no answer about their diet. They must try to obtain it through Lord Villiers. Sir Robt. Naunton has sent back their present, because the suit did not succeed. The usual new year's gift is given to the Lord Privy Seal.

Jan. 2. Dover Castle. 3. Lord Zouch to the Sheriffs, &c. of Kent. Sends a list of the retinue and garrison of Dover Castle, in order that they may be exempt from serving on juries, &c.

Jan. 2? 4. Reasons by Mr. Thurbane why Ports-men [Cinque Ports] should not be made officers within the county, and request for certain names to be put out of the bill for jurors.

Jan. 2? 5. Allegations of the Gunners of Dover Castle and the bulwarks against the demands made upon them by the Mayor, for services as freemen of Dover, which services they affirm to be contrary to their oath taken to the Lord Warden.

Jan. 2? 6. Order to the Sheriff of Kent, to repay to Boatswain Dyer the moneys levied on his goods, for not appearing as a juror.

Jan. 2. Rye. 7. Rich. Gibbridge to Rich. Younge. Wishes Mr. Randoll to direct him where his charge is to begin, in the office of Collector of Droits for the Lord Warden, which they hold in conjunction, &c.

Jan. 4. London. 8. Chamberlain to Carleton. The Queen has been sick of the gout. She is said to aim at the regency if the King goes to Scotland. The Earl of Arundel received the communion on Christmas-day. His house at Greenwich, left him by the Earl of Northampton, is burned, which the Papists will think just retribution. Dr. Thornborough made Bp. of Worcester, and the Archbp. of Spalato may be Dean of Windsor, being well esteemed at Court. Villiers' kinsman, [Hen.] Beaumont, was to have been Bp. of Worcester, but failed, from the dislike felt of Snowdon and Baily, very unworthy men, who are made Bps. of Carlisle and Bangor.

Jan. 4. 9. Edw. Sherburn to the Same. The Ambassadors are to be paid out of 120,000*l.* to be borrowed of the City. The Queen somewhat recovered of the swelling in her leg, and is removed to Whitehall. The new Company of Merchant Adventurers is dissolved,

VOL. XC.

1617.

and the old Company restored, to the great content of the kingdom. It is thought that Alderman Cockayne will escape better than could be wished.

Jan. 4. Grant to Sir Robt. Hitcham of the office of Serjeant-at-Law, during pleasure. [*Grant Bk., pp.* 210, 221.]

Jan. 4. Licence to the Mayor and Burgesses of Gloucester to be Master and Governor of King James's Hospital, near Gloucester. [*Ibid., p.* 210.]

Jan. 5. Creation of Geo. Visct. Villiers as Earl of Buckingham. [*Ibid., p.* 191.]

Jan.? 10. Pedigree of the family of Villiers, co. Leicester, up to the creation of Geo. Villiers as Earl of Buckingham.

Jan. 5. Special licence to John Harrison to import to London pikes, carp, and other fresh fish, for twenty-one years. [*Grant Bk., p.* 205]

Jan. 8. London. 11. Sir Horace Vere to [Carleton]. The reverend man [Archbp. of Spalato] is well received by the King, and has precedence of all English Bishops. Some things about church government in his book are to be amended, before it is translated into English. If he please the King therein, he is to be made Dean of Windsor. The Earl of Arundel has received the sacrament with His Majesty, and talks sharply against Papists. The King gone to Theobalds.

Jan.? 12. Petition of Matthew Poker to Lord Zouch, for release, being committed to prison for words rashly spoken in a quarrel with Hale, one of the garrison of Dover Castle. Wishes to see an aged and sick grandmother.

Jan. 10. St. Stephen's. 13. Sir Peter Manwood to the Same. Begs that Matthew Poker, who was imprisoned for quarrelling with one of the garrison, and is now set free by Lord Zouch's command, but suspended from his office, may be restored, on promise of amendment.

Jan. 10. Grant, in reversion, to John Castell, of the office of Warden and Keeper of the Prison for the High Commission Court, for thirty-one years. [*Grant Bk., p.* 198.]

Jan. 10. 14. Bond of Michael Burnley and Jacob Braems, of Dover, under penalty of 500*l.*, to indemnify Lord Zouch for delivery to them, on behalf of the owner, of the cargo of the bark Johanne, belonging to Mondey Beauvois, a French merchant, wrecked upon the Godwin Sands.

[Jan 10.] 15. Draft of the above.

Jan. 11. London. 16. Edw. Sherburn to Carleton. Burlamachi refuses to deal further with Carleton unless some money is paid to him. Lord Villiers created Earl of Buckingham. The Lord Chancellor disappointed at not receiving the like honour; but the King wished to do special honour to Buckingham by creating him alone.

Vol. XC.

1617.

Jan. 13. Gieldenston. 17. Eliz. Williams to Carleton. Thanks for presents. Family affairs. Sir Thos. Edmondes is of the Privy Council; trusts Carleton will be the next, &c.

Jan. 13. Dover Castle. 18. Rich. Marsh to Rich. Younge. The costs of a suit in the Admiralty Court between Benj. Martin, and —— Carpenter were left unawarded. —— Dovor must be imprisoned or give bail for the 80*l.*

Jan. 13. 19. Archbp. of Spalato's request for recommendation to the Venetian Ambassador, that his clothes, and especially his books, may be permitted to be put on board an English ship, and sent to England. Italian.

Jan. 13. Grant to Thos. and Edw. Coxe of the office of Yeoman of the Wardrobe, &c., in the principality of Wales, for life. [*Grant Bk., p.* 199.]

Jan. 14. Grant to Thos. Peryent of the office of making licences and pardons of alienations, for life. [*Ibid., p.* 215.]

Jan. 14. 20. Nath. Brent to [Carleton]. The King is so set on his journey to Scotland that he calls those traitors who oppose it. His object is to establish the English hierarchy in Scotland, which the Scots dislike. An organ builder sent there declares he would have been better used amongst the Turks. The King says he will take Coventry in his return, and make the puritans there receive the communion on their knees. His Majesty was pleased at the arrival of the Archbp. of Spalato, who is well received at Lambeth, and the Bishops allow him 600*l.* a year. The King is displeased that the Archduke proceeds not more earnestly in the cause *de corona regia*, &c. Sir Walter Raleigh has made great preparation for his Indian voyage, &c.

Jan. 15. Fenwick Hall. 21. Rich. Kay to Geo. Fortun. Will not impart Swinburne's treachery to any but one of the Council, it being a mystery unfit for private persons. Will tell him the villanous speeches that were uttered.

Jan. 15. 22. Account of assignments upon the different branches of the Crown revenue, total 273,144*l.*

Jan 17. 23. Observation of a discrepancy in the returns of the King's revenue, that for 1615 being given as 469,096*l.*, and that for the present year 497,420*l.*, showing an improvement only of 28,224*l.*; whereas the increase, according to certain items set down, is 69,228*l.*

Jan. 18. Savoy. 24. Geo. Lord Carew to Sir Thos. Roe. Thanks for his description of the Mogul empire, in which all cosmographers are much mistaken; will be glad of any novelties from that country, especially books and coins. Asks how the Jesuits come on there. Sends news since the despatch of his last, as follows:—

Vol. XC.

1617.

January (1616).—Death of Sir Fras. Berkeley in Ireland, and Sir Fras. Verney at the galleys in Sicily.

February.—Lord Roos married to Sir Thos. Lake's daughter.

March.—Three grown-up sons of Lord Abergavenny drowned in a wherry near Gravesend. A private marriage discovered, which took place a year before, between Sir Robt. Sydney, Visct. Lisle's son, and the Earl of Northumberland's eldest daughter. Death of Sir Hen. Townshend, Lady Roxburgh's son, Sir Edw. Cecil's wife, and Sir Jerome Bowes. Sir Chas. Wilmot made President of Connaught. Sir Walter Raleigh freed from the Tower on the 19th, and is to go to Guiana, but not to be pardoned till his return. The Earl of Thomond resigns the governorship of Thomond, and his son Lord Brian succeeds him. Sir Dud. Carleton gone Ambassador to the Low Countries, and Sir Hen. Wotton Lieger to Venice.

April.—Sir John Digby made Vice Chamberlain and a Councillor. Lord Chichester visited England. Sir Oliver St. John appointed Deputy of Ireland. The King surrenders Flushing and Brill to the States for 200,000*l.* All the lands of Lord Grey of Wilton attainted, are given to Sir Geo. Villiers.

May.—Earl of Shrewsbury dead. Sec. Winwood and Sir Wm. Cavendish are executors. He left no land to Edw. Talbot, now Earl, but many tenants return to him, so that a great suit at law between him and the Countess Dowager is likely. Countess Dowager of Cumberland dead. Lord Lisle made Knight of the Garter. Sir Wm. Slingsby married to the daughter of Sir Stephen Broad, of Sussex. The Earl of Salisbury has a son. The reversion of Sir John Roper's place granted to Sir Geo. Villiers, and the Earl of Montgomery made Keeper of Whitehall. Brill restored to the States by its governor, Sir Horace Vere, who has in exchange 1,000*l.* per ann. pension, and the reversion of the Mastership of the Ordnance.

June.—Flushing surrendered by Lord Lisle, who is to have 1,200*l.* per ann., and his son, Sir Robt. Sydney, a regiment in the States' service. Sir Edw. Conway has 500*l.* per ann., and every captain and officer is provided for. Old Lord Admiral Nottingham has another daughter. Sir Robt. Cotton set free without trial, but has procured his pardon, "ad majorem cautelam." The sea captain Mainwaring pardoned. Sir Thos. Ridgeway discharged from his offices; Sir Hen. Docwra succeeds him as Treasurer of Wars in Ireland, and Sir Art. Savage as Vice Treasurer. And. Ramsay, Visct. Haddington's brother, slain in Fenchurch Street by the watch, whom he resisted when they stayed him. The King sat in person in the Star Chamber on the 20th, and "made a large speeche, to the admiration of the hearers, speaking more like an angel than a man." Sir Thos. Dale returned from Virginia, with several natives, including a daughter of that barbarous Prince, who married one of his men. The worst is past there, the men now living by their own industry. At the Bermudas, the rats destroy all that is planted. Barclay, a Frenchman born, the son

1617. VOL. XC.

of a Scot, and a scholar, long in the King's service, has gone to Rome, and is supposed to be the author of a scandalous book against His Majesty, which could only have been written by one intimate with him. John Villiers knighted, and made of the Prince's bedchamber.

JULY.—Sumptuous embassy of Lord Hay to France. Sir Hen. Rich, Sir Gilb. Houghton, and others, went with him. Countess of Somerset pardoned, but remains in Sir Walter Raleigh's lodging in the Tower. Earl Arundel sworn of the Privy Council, and made one of the Commissioners for the Earl Marshal's office. Sir Wm. Monson liberated; the cause of his committal unknown. He himself [Lord Carew] sworn Privy Councillor on the 20th. Lord Chichester returned to Ireland as Lord Treasurer. Bishops of Bangor, Hereford, and Chester, dead. Earl Montgomery has a son and heir. Sir Edw. Brabazon and Sir Edw. Moore made Barons of Ireland, as Sir Thos. Ridgeway will be, if he can pass his accounts.

AUGUST.—Sir Roger Wilbraham dead, and left three daughters, heirs to 4,000*l.* a year. Sir Oliver St. John gone to Ireland. M. Schomberg, the Earl of Tyrone, Justice Nicholls, and Sir Hen. Poole, of Gloucestershire, dead. The old Earl of Exeter has a daughter, and Lord Russell a son, who is likely to be Earl of Bedford. The Earl of Shrewsbury buried at Sheffield, with the greatest pomp ever seen in the kingdom. Sir Thos. Somerset married to the Countess of Ormond, in Ireland. Sir Geo. Villiers made Visct. Villiers, and Lieutenant of Buckinghamshire. The Earl of Somerset is in Sir Walter Raleigh's ancient lodgings in the Bloody Tower, the Countess in his new buildings, with the doors open between them. Sir Thos. Monson has the liberty of the Tower, and is always protesting his innocence.

SEPTEMBER.—Lady Frances Egerton, after having nine daughters, has a son, to the great rejoicing of the old Lord Chancellor. Lord Roos has taken his leave for Spain; his equipage, like that of Lord Hay, sumptuous beyond precedent. Creations of Scotch and Irish peerages. Sir Edw. Villiers knighted. Bp. of Ely sworn a Councillor. The Duke of Mantua's younger brother, the Cardinal of Mantua, secretly married in Rome.

OCTOBER.—The King, Lord Chancellor, and old Marchioness of Northampton, were sponsors to Sir John Egerton's son. Lord Hay has returned, having been feasted beyond belief. Sir Thos. Monson set free, after being confined almost a year on Overbury's affair, and twice brought to trial. Sherborne Manor, once Sir Walter Raleigh's, then Prince Henry's, then the Earl of Somerset's, then the King's, is now granted to Sir John Digby. Earl of Salisbury's son dead. Five men set sail from Bermuda in a small boat, little bigger than a double wherry, and reached England in safety. The plantation likely to fail. Sir Wm. Dormer, Lord Dormer's son, dead. Lord Cavendish inherits 4,000*l.* per ann., from the death of his brother Henry. Seven English fishing ships were intercepted between Newfoundland and Italy, by thirty Turkish frigates, and taken or sunk; Sir Rich. Hawkins, of Plymouth, thought to be in them. The Mary Anne, of London,

Vol. XC.

1617.

taken by Turkish pirates, near Malaga. A Turkish pirate vessel taken in the Thames. Countess Dowager of Pembroke returned from two years' sojourn at the Spa. The Commentaries of Matteo Riccio, a Jesuit, printed, amongst which are reports of the travels of Benedictus Goesius in the Mogul's country, China, &c., in 1603. Particulars of this work, and of a pamphlet of Corint's journeys into the same regions. Exploration of the Portuguese n Peru, where they found much gold. The North-west Passage discoverers have failed.

November.—Particulars of the ceremonial of Prince Charles's creation as Prince of Wales. Creations of peerages. Singular death of Mr. Havers, a London merchant, who professed to be struck by a watery planet. Sir Robt. Naunton and Sir Lionel Cranfield made Masters of Requests. Richard Roberts, a rich Cornishman, who covets knighthood, has lent the King 12,000*l.* without interest; more such Robertses wanted. Increase of Turkish shipping; their pirates in Algiers do great damage to the English Levant merchants; necessity of Christian Princes uniting for their extirpation; particulars of their misdeeds. Segar, Garter King-at-Arms, and St. George Norroy, knighted, but Camden Clarencieux, "inferior to neither of them in abilitie or learning, hathe not put out his topsayles." Geographical queries relating to a more ready transit of goods from the East.

December.—The breaking of two houses at Elbing and Hamburg, which held 80,000*l.* of English goods, has caused great loss to the Eastland merchants, especially Alderman Cockayne. Lady Cheeke dead, nearly 100 years old. Consecration of the new Bishops of Bangor and Bath and Wells. Lady Harrington gone to Heidelberg, at the Electress's intreaty; she had 5,000*l.* for travelling expenses. Three Englishmen quarrelling, went to Calais to fight, and were all slain. Lord Rich married to Lady St. Paul, of Lincolnshire, Chief Justice [Sir Chris.] Wray's daughter. Sir John Swinnerton, late Mayor of London, dead; also Dr. Parry, Bishop of Worcester, "a good, godly, and learned prelate." The Archbishop of Spalato, "a man of great estimation, detesting the Romish tradition, quitted his prelacy for conscience' sake," and came to London. The Levant Merchants petitioned the Council to move the King to write to the Grand Seignior against the oppressions of the Vizier Bassa, who imposes new taxes on them, and against robberies and piracies, which threaten the overthrow of their trade. The Turks complain of injuries from England in the East Indies. The Lord Deputy of Ireland is proceeding roundly against recusants, and imprisoning those who refuse the Oath of Allegiance; but the prisons will soon be too little, for no magistrates can be found that will take the Oath, so that their charters are threatened to be forfeited. Gives an idle prophecy, sent from France, about the state of the world 1620–1630. France and Spain both sue for a match with the Prince. The King deliberates, but conceals his intention. Sir Fras. Onslow joined with Sir Dud. Norton as Secretary of Ireland. Dr. Burgess, the silent minister, allowed to preach again. Warm disputes between the Hollanders and English Merchant Adventurers,

1617. VOL. XC.

because the latter now carry their cloths over dyed and dressed, and 600,000 poor in Holland are thus thrown out of work. The Hollanders prohibit the entry of the cloths, and the English threaten to remove their station from Middleburgh to the Archduke's country; agents coming over for its settlement. Sir Walter Raleigh has built a ship, the Destiny, of 500 tons, and sets sail in February for his gold mine; the Spaniards will lie in wait for him, but he will have a good fleet of 500 men, and fears nothing. York Herald played a trick on Garter King-at-Arms, by sending him a coat-of-arms drawn up for Gregory Brandon, said to be a merchant of London, and well descended, which Garter subscribed, and then found that Brandon was the hangman; Garter and York are both imprisoned, one for foolery, the other for knavery.

JANUARY.—The Earl of Northampton's house at Greenwich burnt down, in which the Earl of Arundel had household stuffs of great value. His [Roe's] proposal of opening a trade to Persia is well received by the Council; as there is a madness in England after silk rather than cloth, it would be commodious, but there are objections; as that the Grand Seignior might in anger confiscate the goods of English merchants, and that as the Persians only trade for money, it would draw 600,000*l.* a year out of the realm. Sends the Archbp. of Spalato's manifesto of the reasons of his withdrawal from Rome.

Jan. 18. London. 25. Chamberlain to Carleton. At a masque on Twelfth Night, the new-made Earl [Buckingham] and the Earl of Montgomery danced with the Queen. The Middle Templars gave Buckingham a supper. The King gone from Theobalds to Hampton Court. Difficulties in raising a loan of 100,000*l.* from the Aldermen upon security of the royal jewels, and the like sum from the farmers of the customs, without which the Scottish journey cannot proceed. Bingley and Sir Lionel Cranfield accused of peccadillos in managing the King's moneys. The Treasurer boasts that he has reduced His Majesty's expenditure 1,000*l.* below his income, but the Chancellor says he is out in his reckoning. Sir Geo. More is about to sell his place, as Lieutenant of the Tower, to Sir Allan Apsley for 2,400*l.* The Virginian woman, Pocahuntas, has been with the King; she is returning home, sore against her will. The Italian preacher, Ascanio, has run away.

Jan. 19. 26. Fras. Neale to Mr. Nichols. Begs his assistance in procuring a presentation to an hospital, and the loan of 50*l.*, which he can repay, having sent him a plan of suing out licences for alienations by which he can bring 5,000*l.* to the Prince's coffers before Michaelmas.

Jan. 20. 27, 28. Court rolls admitting Wm. Hellen, nephew and heir of John Hellen, customary tenant of a messuage and certain lands in the manor of Wyrardisbury, co. Bucks. Two papers. Latin.

VOL. XC.

1617.

Jan. 20. 29, 30. Court rolls admitting Cicely Hellen, widow, as customary tenant of seventeen acres of land in the said manor, with licence to let the same. Two papers. Latin.

Jan. 20. 31, 32. Court roll admitting the Same customary tenant of two acres of land at Fox Hill, within the said manor, relinquished by Wm. Hellen, with licence to let the same. Two papers. Latin.

Jan. 20. London. 33. Matthew de Quester to Carleton. Having had no answer to his many letters, fears they may not have been acceptable. Sends a letter from Mr. Bell, and recommends his suit.

Jan. 20. Lambeth. 34. Archbp. Abbot to Sir Thos. Roe. Importance of keeping up general intelligence from abroad. The Powers of Europe are interested in the affairs of the East, &c. Doubtful effect of a recent peace between Persia and Portugal. Sir Robt. Shirley's children all venture on great things, and come to beggary: Sir Thomas, the eldest, is in the Fleet for debt; Sir Anthony has his pension seized for debt; Sir Robert obtained Papal indulgences, &c., at Rome, and distributed them in England, and when called in question for it, laid the fault on his wife.

Jan. 20. Eton. 35. Sir Hen. Savile to Carleton. Private affairs. Commissions him to buy hangings for him, of some Scripture story, with the money to be received for the Chrysostoms.

Jan. 21. London. 36. Edw. Sherburn to [the Same]. His Majesty's journey for Scotland will be deferred if he will listen to the Lords' advice, on account of the present great wants. He has called for the Lord Treasurer's accounts, and Mr. Bingley is in such fear of detection, that he has begged leave, with tears, to resign. The King will himself take charge of Ambassadors' supplies. Lord Worcester and Lady Vere desperately ill.

Jan. 21. King's Bench. 37. Bernardino Pippi to Lord ———. Solicits his Lordship to forward his supplication to his Excellence for recovery of his lost liberty; would rather die than be banished from England, and have to return home with dishonour and loss. Italian.

Jan. 22. 38. Abstract of the patent granted to Sir Thos. and Hen. Cornwallis of the office of Groom Porter. They are to license thirty-one bowling alleys, fourteen tennis courts, and forty gaming houses in London and Westminster and their suburbs, and a bowling alley in every village within two miles of London; each to be kept by a trusty deputy, no cheating allowed, and to be closed on Sabbath days. With note of a similar patent by Queen Elizabeth.

Jan. 22. Grant to Sir Thos. and Hen. Cornwallis of the office of Groom Porters, and the licensing of bowling alleys, &c., for life. [*Grant Bk.*, *p.* 169.]

Vol. XC.

1617.

Jan. 22. Grant to Sir Pat. Hume, Master of the Hawks, of 30*l.* per month, and 10*s.* per day, for life. [*Grant Bk., p.* 205.]

Jan. 24. Grant to Sir Chris. and Sir Thos. Hatton of the office of Seneschal of the manor of Berk, co. Essex, for life. [*Ibid., p.* 205.]

Jan. 24. Dover. 39. Mayor of Dover to Lord Zouch. Mons. La Tour, the French Ambassador, has landed at Deal, with a suite of thirty attendants.

Jan. 27. 40. Petition of Margery Bredgate, grandmother, and Elizabeth Poker, mother of Matthew Poker, to the Same, that he may be restored to his place as a Gunner in Dover Castle.

Jan. 27. 41. Sir Fras. Bacon to [the Council]. The patent of Clement Dawbeney for slitting iron bars into rods, which has been called in on complaint, is found very useful to nailers and blacksmiths, and was only opposed by one Burrell, who had set up a similar engine himself.

Jan. 27. Dover Castle. 42. Nich. Knott to Rich. Younge. Understands his absence from the Castle has been complained of; it has only been on urgent occasions. Will be punctual in fulfilment of his duties.

Jan 28. 43. Order of reference to the Lord Treasurer, the Earl of Exeter, and the Bp. of Ely, on the points touching the drain of Clowse Cross, and the decay of the outfalls of the rivers Nen and Welland; a sluice to be made below Wisbeach for keeping out the silt, &c. They are to determine on whom the expense should fall, by mutual consent of the parties, if possible.

Jan. 30. Grant to Sir Thos. Compton of the office of Master of the Privy Harriers, for life. [*Grant Bk., p.* 197.]

Jan. 31. 44. Notes agreed upon relative to revenue; that the expenses be kept within a prescribed compass; the officers of the navy and wardrobe be spoken with; all assignations beforehand on the revenue be treated as debts, &c.

Jan. 31. 45. Account of the appropriation of 100,000*l.*, borrowed from the City of London; with a note of the excess of the payments proposed thereon above that sum.

Feb. 1. London. 46. Alex. Williams to Carleton. An Ambassador is come from France. The King expected from Theobalds. He has not been at Royston since Christmas. It is hoped he will stay more in London.

Feb. 2. Dover. 47. Mayor and Commissioners of the Passage at Dover to Lord Zouch. John Eason and Wm. Salisbury, alias Jenman, were seized at Broadstairs, because they landed privately from Dunkirk, and refused the Oath of Allegiance. On their way to Dover, Salisbury escaped, by negligence or connivance of Geo. Witherden, Under Deputy of

VOL. XC.

1617.

Broadstairs. Salisbury is suspected to be one Jenman, who went abroad with a pass under the name of Salisbury. [*See March* 10.] *Inclose,*

47. I. *Examination of John Eason, of Wellingborough, co. Northampton. Has been a servant in Portugal many years. Spent some time in Flanders, and being taken in a storm in crossing from Dunkirk, was obliged to land at a private place. Feb.* 2, 1617. *Dover.*

47. II. *Pass for Wm. Salisbury to go to his master, Rich. Cotton, of Warblington, co. Hants, at the Spa, Nov.* 13, 1616. *With note that the party therein named sailed for France Jan.* 17, 1617.

Feb. 2. Sandwich. 48. Commissioners for the Passage at Sandwich to the Same. Have committed Hen. Snell, of Yorkshire, and his servant Hum. Clesby, who went abroad by licence of Council in 1610, but now, on their return, refuse to take the Oath of Allegiance.

Feb. 2. 49. Thos. Lord Gerard to the Same. In favour of Jas. Linaker, whose bark was cast away in the Downs; many of his goods are cast up at Dover, and seized by his Lordship's officers.

Feb. 2. Grant to Geo. Nicholson and Hen. Shashaw, of the office of Paymaster of Pensions at Berwick, during pleasure. [*Grant Bk., p.* 214.]

Feb. 3. Grant to Wm. Robinson and Fulk Allen, of the office of registering affidavits in Chancery, for life. [*Ibid., p.* 194.]

Feb. 3. Sandwich. 50. Edw. Kelk to Rich. Younge. Snell, a Yorkshire gentleman, who landed privately at Dunkirk, professed to have a letter from Mr. Trumbull in Flanders to Mr. Tucker, of Gravesend. Six persons landed, of whom four are now taken.

Feb. 4. Special licence to John Speed for the sole printing of the book of the genealogies of the Scripture and other things, for seven years. [*Grant Bk., p.* 185.]

Feb. 6. Grant to John Ferriers of the office of Justice in cos. Carnarvon, Merioneth, and Anglesea, during pleasure. [*Ibid., p.* 207.]

Feb. 6. Grant to And. Powell of the office of Justice in cos. Glamorgan, Brecknock, and Radnor, during pleasure. [*Ibid., p.* 215.]

Feb. 7. Dunkirk. 51. [Edm.] "Neville, of Westmoreland," to the King. Recounts his services in behalf of the King's title during the life of the late Queen, and His Majesty's promises, made by his Ambassadors, the Earl of Mar and Lord Kinloss, to restore him to his ancestral estates. Has now one foot in the grave, and begs he may not die in a strange land, but, reaching the happy land of promise, in the King's favour, may sing his "Nunc dimittis."

Vol. XC.

1617.

Feb. 8. 52. Receipt by the Bp. of Lincoln of 160*l.* from Dr. Lambe, in part of the tenths of the clergy, co. Leicester.

Feb. 8. Grant to Sam. Hales of the office of keeping York Prison, for sixty years. [*Grant Bk.*, *p.* 205.]

Feb. 8. Grant to Wal. Pye of the office of Justice in cos. Glamorgan, Brecknock, and Radnor, during pleasure. [*Ibid.*, *p.* 215.]

Feb. 8. London. 53. Chamberlain to Carleton. Report that the Bishops will provide the Archbp. of Spalato with a parsonage of 600*l.* per ann. till the King does something for him. Some of his books in the press stayed by authority, on account of their tenets on jurisdiction. The King's works are published in one volume, edited by the Bp. of Winchester. Buckingham's brother Christopher made of the Bedchamber. Skit on him and his brothers. Hoskins, the lawyer, is called in question for a rhyming libel. Lord Roos is returning through France, having visited all the monasteries in Lisbon. Divers citizens are sent for to lend 3,000*l.* each for the Scottish journey. The East India Company flourishes; 1,400,000*l.* adventured for the next four years.

Feb.? 54. Estimate of the money which the King, by exercising his prerogative, might raise from the East India Company, by forced loans without interest, adventuring money in the trade, threatening the withdrawal of their patent, &c.

Feb. 8. London. 55. Nath. Brent to [Carleton]. The French Ambassador Extraordinary, Mons. de la Tour, arrived, after a narrow escape from shipwreck. The King is angry that he is not so great a man as others sent out of France. His Majesty sends sometimes to Lord Coke on private matters, and the lawyers hope he will be next Lord Chancellor. The Chancellor of the Exchequer talks of resigning, but is constant in inconstancy. All dislike the Scotch journey; but the King was so angry with Buckingham for proposing a delay that he was glad to get out of the way. Disturbance in the trade to Turkey. The Viceroy of Sicily has taken seventy Turkish gallies. Sir Edw. Hoby likely to die.

Feb. 8. London. 56. Edw. Sherburn to [the Same]. Burlamachi will continue the monthly payments, &c., now he has received some moneys. The Baron de Tour is lodged in part of Lord Salisbury's house. Buckingham is sworn Privy Councillor. The King goes to Scotland on March 15. The Lord Chancellor has surrendered the Chancellorship of Oxford to the Earl of Pembroke, the Lieutenancy of Buckinghamshire to the Earl of Buckingham, and the Stewardship of St. Alban's to the Attorney General.

Feb. 9. Dover. 57. Commissioners of the Passage at Dover to Lord Zouch. Have committed John Richardson, who refused to take the Oath of Allegiance. Would have sent him across the seas again, as a person

1617. Vol. XC.

of no moment, but he professes to belong to the Spanish Ambassador's son. *Inclose,*

57. I. *Examination of John Richardson, of Malpas, Cheshire. Left his father on becoming a Catholic. Went to London, and was commended to the service of Don Pedro, the Spanish Ambassador's son. Went with his master to Flanders, and is now returning on his business. Dover, Feb.* 8.

Feb. 9. Philip Lane. 58. [Lord Zouch] to the Mayor of Hythe. Permits the fishermen of Hythe to fish on the coasts, the French having begun to fish there; and the King having ordered strict observance of Lent, which falls early this year. The permission is not to be pleaded as a precedent.

Feb. 11. 59. Indenture quadripartite between the Earl of Buckingham, John Lord Roper, of Teynham, Chief Justice Montague, and Robt. Heath, and Robt. Shute, certifying the legal appointment of the two latter to the office of Chief Clerk of Inrolments of the Court of King's Bench, on surrender of Lord Teynham, who is to have the profits for life, after which they are to be at the disposal of Buckingham.

Feb. 11. 60. Certificate that Mondey Beauvois, French merchant, has received from the officers of the Cinque Ports his bark, the Johanne of Bourdeaux, cast away near the Downs, and a portion of the cargo, having paid 6*l.* to Lord Zouch as composition for the best cable and anchor, which belong to him as a royalty.

Feb. 11. Licence to John Ketchett to make watermills, &c., for twenty-one years. [*Grant Bk., p.* 219.]

Feb. 12. Neufchatel. 61. Capt. Wm. Turner to Rich. Younge. Thanks for his care of him. Has made a composition with Capt. Baron de Veine, to whom his goods must be delivered, except his two best armouries, which he begs him to accept.

Feb. 12. 62. Statement of the case of Sir Thos. Monson, that he was arraigned as accessory to the murder of Sir Thos. Overbury, but his trial stayed, and he sent to the Tower, where he remained nearly a year; was then released on bail, and petitioned the King to have the case investigated, and his indictment discharged. The case was referred to the Attorney and Solicitor General, who reported on it [*see Dec.* 7, 1616], on which a pardon was drawn up, grounded on the doubtful evidence of the crime. Speech of Sir Thomas at the bar of the King's Bench, pleading his pardon, and begging it to be understood, not as an evidence of guilt, but a declaration of innocence. Reply of the Lord Chief Justice accepting it as such, and rejoinder of thanks from Monson.

Feb. 12. 63. Copy of the above.

VOL. XC.

1617.

Feb. 12. Sandwich. 64. Mayor and Jurats of Sandwich to Lord Zouch. Have received a writ of restitution from the Mayor, Recorder, and others, of London, for delivery of money found on Michael Lambert, but think it invalid, because the Mayor's name is wrongly given, and because Lambert having changed the silver stolen from Mr. Trevor into gold, it is no longer the same money, but belongs to their town.

Feb. 12. Whitefriars. Sir John Throgmorton to Carleton. The business of the French Ambassador is to justify the conduct of the Queen Mother against the Princes, and to represent the French King's party as powerful enough to crush them easily, in order to daunt the King, and prevent his assisting them. It is hoped that His Majesty will consent to a plan of uniting the French Princes, the United States, and the Protestant Princes of Germany, in a league of which he shall be the head, by which they may make peace with the French King, and which would support the declining honour of England. If the Princes be left to destruction, the Queen Mother will exterminate all the Protestants in France. The King goes to the Star Chamber, to settle the government during his absence in Scotland. Yesterday Buckingham sat for the first time in the Council. [*Holl. Corresp., Feb.* 12.]

Feb. [13]. 65. Proceedings in the Star Chamber. Abstract of the King's speech. He considers himself the father and shepherd of his people, and as such determines to be *Rex pacificus*. Is come to give sentence against duels, on which he before published a sharp edict; and now desires the prisoners to stand forth. They are Mr. Christmas of Essex, and Mr. Bellingham of Sussex, two very young gentlemen. Their confessions were read, and the Solicitor General made a speech [*not given*].

Feb. 14. Grant to Sir Fras. Fane, Sir Edw. Barrett, and Wal. Barrett, of the grange of Sewall, cos. Stafford and Shropshire, so long as it remains in the King's hands, by reason of the debt of Sir Rich. Leveson, deceased. [*Grant Bk., p.* 218.]

Feb. 14. Licence to Art. Mainwaring and Nich. Archbald to execute laws, &c. concerning bankrupts, for life. [*Ibid., p.* 221.]

Feb. 14. Licence to Sir Stephen Soame to hold the Court in the manor of Great Wraton and elsewhere, co. Suffolk. [*Ibid., p.* 189.]

Feb. 14. 66. Certificate by Ant. Napleton, that on a conversation in the house of Thos. Napleton, of Faversham, about a play in which a huntsman, who was intended to represent the King, said he had rather hear a dog bark than a cannon roar, Napleton said it was a pity the King ever came to the crown of England, for he loved his dogs better than his subjects.

Feb. 15. 67. Petition of John Clavell to Sir Julius Cæsar, that he may answer by commission in a certain suit, he living 100 miles off, and the waters being too dangerous for him to come to London. With order thereon.

Vol. XC.

1617.

Feb. 17. Dover. 68. Wm. Jones to Rich. Younge. One Matthews landed from Dunkirk, who has letters directed to the French Ambassador, Mons. De la Tour, from his sons, whom he served. Thinks Eason, formerly taken, is not what he seems, but probably a priest, and that he had better be sent to the Archbp. of Canterbury, before his money is done. *Annexed is,*

68. I. *Examination of Edw. Matthews, of Walton, Norfolk. Particulars of his service in divers Catholic families. Has been abroad some years, and last served the sons of Mons. De la Tour, Ambassador in England. Refuses to take the Oath of Allegiance. Dover, Feb.* 15.

Feb. 17. London. 69. Appointment by the Archbp. of Canterbury of Matthew Isham, of Hillmorton, co. Warwick, to be Apparitor of the Prerogative Court of Canterbury. Latin. *Prefixed are,*

69. I. *Regulations concerning the duties and fees of Apparitors.*

Feb. 18. Commission to Geo. Lord Carew, of Clopton, and others, to make stay of a judgment of renunciation concerning accounts between merchants and others. [*Grant Bk., p.* 199.]

Feb. 20. 70. Memoranda of things to be finished for the settling of His Majesty's revenue; viz., the pension list to be completed; the debts to be fully stated; the King to decide whether he will have more money raised from recusants and from the petty customs; the Council to consider whether expenses cannot be lessened and revenues increased in Ireland, &c.

Feb. 20? 71. "Sum of the King's business touching the repaire of his estate," viz., regulations for his debts, ordinary and extraordinary expenses, improvements of revenue by raising certain branches of revenue, by fresh projects, and by borrowing.

Feb. ? 72. Statement of the annual allowances payable by the Crown.

Feb. 20. 73. Articles of agreement between the executors of Thos. Whetenhall and Rich. Cooke, Minister of St. Swithin's, and the inhabitants of the parish. The inhabitants promise to assist in the maintenance of a weekly lectureship there, founded by Whetenhall. Rich. Cooke, or some sufficient deputy, to be lecturer. Signed by the executors.

Feb. 20. 74. Copy of the above, signed by Rich. Cooke and many parishioners.

Feb. 21. Gloucester. 75. Hen. Aisgill and Elias Wrench to Dr. Laud, Dean of Gloucester. A libel was found in the pulpit of St. Michael's, blaming the removal of the communion table in the cathedral, as savouring of Popery; saying that obeisance was made to it, and wondering that no Elias came forward to reform such things. Think Commissioners from the High Commission Court should be appointed to inquire into and suppress the libel, care being taken that none of them "favour that scismaticall faction of the Puritanes." A preacher lately declared that he

VOL. XC.

1617.

had nothing to fear from any Herod or cruel magistrates, whilst the people favoured him, nor they anything whilst they had the preacher to pray for them.

Feb. 22. Whitehall. 76. Lord Zouch to Sec. Winwood. As to the complaint of the French Ambassador, the head money taken from the French was ordered by him to be discontinued, on the King's command, and he has heard no complaints since. Has sold the Burton boat to other parties, it being left to the pirates by its owner, and another taken in exchange.

Feb. 22. 77. Extract from the above.

Feb. 22. London. 78. Sir Horace Vere to [Carleton]. Thanks for obtaining his payments. The Countess Dowager of Dorset has given the Earl of Montgomery 100*s*., on condition of his giving her 200*l*. if the King of Spain turn Protestant. The King still intends to go to Scotland, though those about him would be glad if he would change his mind.

Feb. 22. London. 79. Chamberlain to the Same. Whales come thick on the eastern coast. Sir Thos. Monson has got his pardon; he pleaded innocence, and reflected on Coke's conduct towards him. The King made a speech in the Star Chamber about duels, wherein he bestowed many good words on the Spanish nation, and galled the French. Christmas and Bellingham imprisoned and fined 1,000*l*. each, for duelling. Little preparation making for the King's journey into Scotland. The Scots wish it deferred till grass has grown for the cattle. Entertainments given to the French Ambassador, by the King, Lord Mayor, Duke of Lenox, and Lord Hay, who makes love to the Earl of Northumberland's younger daughter. Excessive cost at banquets. The Queen's musicians made her a masque. The Vice Chancellor of Oxford, with fifty Bishops, Doctors, and Graduates, went to Baynard's Castle, to invest the Earl of Pembroke with the Chancellorship. Sir Wm. Seymour, who married the Lady Arabella, is likely to marry the Earl of Essex's sister.

Feb. 23. Eton. 80. Sir Hen. Savile to the Same. The money received for books is to be spent in horses or hangings, &c. Has dined with the Archbp. of Spalato at Lambeth, and likes him well. Will take him to Oxford.

Feb. 23. London. 81. Edw. Sherburn to [the Same]. Has a promise that his [Carleton's] allowances shall be paid. The King went to the Star Chamber, to give sentence himself—the first time that he has ever done so—against Christmas and Bellingham, for fighting a duel contrary to the proclamation. The Prince and many Lords were there, and the Earl of Buckingham made a speech, by the King's command, being the first time he had spoken in so large an assembly. The Lord Chancellor is ill, from disappointment that his earldom stays so long, and that his son is not made President of Wales, Lord Gerard having compounded for it with Lord Eure. Doubts whether

1617. Vol. XC.

Sir Fras. Bacon, the Bp. of Winchester, or Chief Justice Hobart is to be Chancellor. The Bp. of Durham disappointed by death from entertaining the King on his way to Scotland. Sir Ralph Winwood had only the same allowance as Carleton has, when Ambassador; the 4*l.* per diem was when he was Commissioner. Private affairs. The Archbp. of Spalato's works printed.

Feb. 23. Gloucester. 82. Thos. Prior to Dr. Wm. Laud, Dean of Gloucester. Ejection of Vernon and Farley from the singing men's houses. Has taken pains to suppress a libel found in St. Michael's pulpit. Asks directions on it. Birth of a child with two heads and four legs. *Incloses,*

82. I. *John Smithe to ——. Is told the Gloucester communion table is removed by the new Dean to where the high altar stood, contrary to law, and that obeisances are made to it, as though the Christ were on it. Laments the faint-heartedness of the Prebends, that none would speak a word on God's behalf. Winchcombe, Feb.* 12, 1616. *Indorsed [by Laud], "A Copye of the Libell against the removinge of the Communion Table in the Church of Glocester."*

Feb. 24. Rye. 83. Rich. Gibbridge to Rich. Younge. Requests Lord Zouch's warrant for receiving his Lordship's droits.

Feb. 24. Sandwich. 84. John Oliver to the Same. Thinks that a skiff, driven on shore in Sandwich Bay, which is claimed for Lord Wotton, is a royalty appertaining to the Lord Warden. Asks directions thereon.

Feb. 24. 85. [Lord Zouch] to the King. Requests a hearing on a wrong done to his jurisdiction by the Lord Admiral of England. Wishes fresh orders for the government of the castles and forts. Is thought too strict in enforcing those of Henry VIII., which order personal attendance of the watch, a point much neglected. Begs that some castles may be repaired which greatly need it, and order taken for restoration of the harbours, so choked by diversion of waters for private purposes, that the rivers have not force to drive back the sand.

Feb.? 86. Note of various grants for the repair of Dover Haven, viz., a tax of 3*d.* per ton on all vessels loading or unloading there, licence to export beer, corn, &c.

Feb.? 87. Note relative to the officers to be appointed for Dover Harbour, the reparations necessary, and the reformation of abuses there.

Feb.? 88. State of the revenue of Dover Harbour.

Feb.? 89. Estimate of the charges for making a mole at Dover Harbour.

Feb.? 90. Plan for Dover Haven.

Feb. 24. St. James's. 91. Thos. Murray to Carleton. The Prince begs his assistance to procure the return of Jas. Bovey, son of Serjeant Bovey, of the Wine Cellar, a boy of spirit, a good rider, lutanist, dancer, &c., who has run away to the Hague.

Vol. XC.

1617.

[Feb. 24.] 92. Mrs. A. H. to John Eason, prisoner at Dover. Condoles with him on his imprisonment, and will let his friends know where he is. Hopes for his escape. [*Intercepted. See Feb.* 2.]

Feb. 24. 93. Schedule of the liberties granted, by charter, to the Prince of Wales in his own lands, being casualties and royalties usually devolving on the Crown.

Feb. 27. Grant to John Perry of an especial pardon for usury and perjury. [*Grant Bk., p.* 215.]

Feb. 27. London. 94. Colonel R. Henderson to Carleton. Baron de Tour, the French Ambassador, was entertained by the Mayor of London and Lord Hay, and has taken leave, &c. The King will set out March 15, and be at Edinburgh May 15. Neither dreams nor predictions alter his resolution.

Feb. 27. St. John's, [Oxford]. 95. Wm. Laud, Dean of Gloucester, to the Bishop of Gloucester. His Majesty bade him reform the disorders in the cathedral, which was ill governed; he therefore caused some repairs to be made, and, with consent of the Chapter, the communion table was removed to the upper end, as is usual in cathedrals, which action is greatly traduced. Wishes the King to be made acquainted with it, and desires the Bishop's support. With marginal note, that the remark about the position of the tables in cathedrals is a gross untruth.

Feb. 28. St. James's. 96. Thos. Murray to Carleton. The Prince renews his request for preferment in the States' service, for Jas. Erskine, brother to Sir Thos. Erskine, lately deceased, in whose favour the King has waived a request for another gentleman.

Feb. 28. 97. Edw. Sherburn to the Same. Sends him three tuns of beer at 6*s*., and two tuns at 8*s*. The King's train for Scotland not yet completed.

Feb. 28. Order to the Lord Chancellor and others to surrender the manor of Fleet, co. Lincoln, into the King's hands. [*Grant Bk., p.* 194.]

Feb. 98. Order established by Lord Admiral Nottingham, for the respective duties to be performed by the Comptroller, Surveyor, and Clerk of the Navy, that each may be answerable for any neglect of duty.

Feb.? 99. Arguments in favour of the suit of J. E. [John Elphinstone?] for the licensing of pedlars and chapmen. With replies thereto, showing its illegality and inconvenience. [*Granted March* 19, 1617.]

Feb.? 100. Inventory of Ordnance at St. Michael's Mount, with note that Capt. Art. Harris holds the Mount for life, on condition of maintaining a gunner, porter, and three soldiers; and note of the reparations needed.

VOL. XC.

1617.

March [1 ?] 101. List of the Lent preachers appointed for Whitehall, the Spittal, and Paul's Cross.

March 3. Commission and instructions to Sir Giles Mompesson and others concerning the sale of woods. [*Grant Bk.*, *p.* 200.]

March 3. St. John's. Oxford. 102. Dr. Laud to the Bp. of Lincoln. Relates his proceedings in reformations in Gloucester Cathedral, and the libel passed upon him therefor. Begs assistance that he may not be brought into contempt at his first attempts at improvement, and especially that the King may be duly informed thereof. Fears the Puritans will think the monster lately born in Gloucester [*see Feb.* 23] a judgment for his changing the communion table into a high altar.

March 5. Sandwich. 103. Mayor of Sandwich to Lord Zouch. Hen. Snell and Hum. Clesby have escaped from the gaol. They previously sent a letter with bills of exchange to Dawson, a woollen-draper, in London. Hue and cry is sent after them.

March 5. Westminster. Grant to Michael Van Elderhuys, a stranger, of patent for new engines, invented by him, for raising water and draining surrounded grounds, with proviso of the allowance of commissioners of sewers, in each county where they shall be erected. [*Sign Man.*, *vol.* VI., *No.* 105.]

March 5 ? Confirmation to Jas. Morley, Robt. Morley, of the Inner Temple, and Wm. Foster, of Normanby, East Cotham, and other lands; also to Wm. Pitches, of the rectory of Reede, co. Suffolk, and certain tithes out of the manor of Alciston, co. Sussex, all on composition for defective titles. Latin. [*Ibid.*, *No.* 106].

March 5 ? Grant to the Queen of confirmation and explanation of her former charters, and of addition of some few things to make her former possessions more entire, together with certain liberties and immunities. Latin. [*Ibid.*, *Nos.* 107, 108.]

March 5 ? Grant to Sir Giles Mompesson, of Bathampton, and Thos. Mompesson, of Pewsey, co. Wilts, of the fifth part of fines and rents answerable to the King for licensing inns, in consideration of the labour of Sir Giles, appointed Surveyor and Licenser of Inns. [*Ibid.*, *No.* 109.]

March 6. Whitehall. Sir Thos. Edmondes to [Carleton]. The state of the revenue has been examined by the Lords, for moderating of expenses, but supplies are found difficult without a Parliament. [*Holl. Corresp.*, *March* 6.]

March 7. Gloucester. 104. Thos. Prior, Sub-dean, to Dr. Wm. Laud, Dean of Gloucester. Opposition of some of the prebendaries to granting Mr. Loe's lease; there is an attempt made to palm the libel upon himself or his friends. Protests his innocence.

Vol. XC.

1617.
March 7. Grant to Chris. Villiers of an annuity of 200*l.*, for life. [*Grant Bk.*, *p.* 191.]

March 7. Grant to Sir Hen. Yelverton of the office of Attorney General, during pleasure. [*Grant Bk.*, *p.* 227.]

March 7. Declaration to the Archbp. of Canterbury and others, of the King's resolution to grant the manor of Fleet, co. Lincoln, in fee farm, to Geo. Earl of Buckingham. [*Ibid.*, *p.* 193.]

March 7. Westminster. Grant to Wm. Earwood of the office of Gentleman Gaoler in the Tower. [*Sign Man.*, *vol.* VI., *No.* 110.]

March 7. Westminster Grant to William, son and heir of Walter Creswell, of special livery, and of pardon for intrusion, and a release of the rates of wardship to which the King is entitled. Latin. [*Ibid.*, *No.* 111.]

March 7. Westminster. Warrant to discharge Thos. Watson, Teller of the Exchequer, for 2,000*l.* paid by him to Sir Baptist Hicks without special warrant; also to pay to the said Hicks 126*l.* 8*s.*, in full of his account for certain cloth of tissue and gold, satins, &c., purchased five years before for the King. [*Ibid.*, *vol.* VII., *No.* 1.]

March 7. Westminster. Warrant for payment to Sir Carew Raleigh of 100*l.* as a free gift. [*Ibid.*, *No.* 2.]

March 7. Westminster. Commission to Lord Gerard, President of Wales, of Lieutenancy of North and South Wales, the Marches, and cos. Worcester, Hereford, and Salop; cos. Glamorgan and Monmouth only excepted. [*Ibid.*, *No.* 3.]

March 7. Westminster. Grant to Sir Fras. Steward of pension of 400*l.* per ann., for life, on surrender of a similar grant during pleasure. [*Ibid.*, *No.* 4.]

March 7. Westminster. Grant, with survivorship, to Ralph Smith and John Sharpe, Yeomen of the Chamber, on surrender of Ralph Smith, of the keeping of the game about Westminster Palace, and in the suburbs of London. [*Ibid.*, *No.* 5.]

March 7. Westminster. Grant to John Packer of a pension of 115*l.* per ann. from the Court of Wards, on surrender of a like pension from the Exchequer and Treasury of the Chamber. [*Ibid.*, *No.* 6.]

March 7. Westminster. Grant to Nich. Townley, of Royle, co. Lancaster, of the benefit of the recusancy of Anne Middleton, of Thurnetoft, co. York, widow. [*Ibid.*, *No.* 7.]

March 7. Westminster. Warrant for payment to Rich. Connock of 1,000 marks as a free gift. [*Ibid.*, *No.* 8.]

March 7. Westminster. Lease to Lawrence Trotter and Edw. Empson of the manor of Hooke, &c., marsh land in Sheriff Hutton, co. York, without fine, on condition of their preserving the land from inundation. Latin. [*Ibid.*, *No.* 9.]

VOL. XC.

1617.
March 7. Westminster. Grant to Wm. Shawe, of London, Chris. Frisby, of Hull, and others, of the usual bounty of 5*s.* per ton, on five ships built by them. [*Sign Man., vol.* VII., *No.* 10.]

March 7. Westminster. Grant to And. Treswell, in reversion after Robt. Treswell, his father, of the office of Surveyor of Woods on this side Trent. [*Ibid., No.* 11.]

March 8. Westminster. Warrant to pay to Jas. Maxwell 150*l.*, towards the charge of his journey into Scotland on the King's affairs. [*Ibid., vol.* VI., *No.* 12.]

March 8. Westminster. Warrant to pay to Sir Rich. Morrison 73*l.* 19*s.* 2*d.*, for eleven additional carts for the King's journey into Scotland, the fifty carts, for which 469*l.* 12*s.* 8*d.* was formerly paid, proving insufficient. [*Ibid., No.* 13.]

March 8. Westminster. Warrant to advance 50*l.* to Lord Stanhope, for sending packets during the King's progress to Scotland. [*Ibid., No.* 14.]

March 8. Westminster. Warrant to pay to the Same, as Treasurer of the Chamber, 4,000*l.*, and other sums due to him upon his accounts for 1615 and 1616, the allowance assigned him for the King's expenses being insufficient. [*Ibid., No.* 15.]

March 8. Westminster. Warrant for payment of 200*l.* over and above 880*l.* already delivered, to Thos. Wye and Ralph Cheyney for repairing St. Neot's Bridges, cos. Bedford and Huntingdon. [*Ibid., No.* 16.]

March 8. Westminster. Grant to Rich. Kerry, on surrender of Geo. Ryman, of the keeping of the Hare Warren and game of all sorts at Hampton Court. [*Ibid., No.* 17.]

March 8, Westminster. Warrant for adding the Earl of Buckingham to the Commission for executing the office of Earl Marshal. [*Ibid., No.* 18.]

March 8. London. 105. Chamberlain to Carleton. Baron Altham and Sir Edw. Hoby dead. The Frenchmen have left, after their great entertainments. That given by Lord Hay cost more than 2,200*l.*, but Lady Lucy Percy, the most desired guest, was absent; her father kept her with him in the Tower, saying he was a Percy, and he would not have her dancing Scotch jigs. Sir Allan Apsley, brother-in-law of Sir Edw. Villiers, has purchased the Lieutenancy of the Tower from Sir Geo. More for 2,500*l.* The Prince's household settled; names of the officers. Sir David Fowlies has sold his place as Cofferer to Sir Hen. Vane. Proposed changes at Court. Sir Hen. Rich offers Visct. Fenton 5,000*l.* for the Captaincy of the Guard. The Earl of Salisbury would give 6,000*l.* for it, though it is an office usually held only by Knights. The latter, being favoured by Buckingham, is likely to prevail. The old Chancellor had vowed not to seal the patent for sale of woods nor the one for inns, but the King visiting him, sealed the first in his presence, and then sending for the Great Seal, after sealing the other patents for Giles Mompesson, an ally of Buckingham, delivered it to Sir

1617. VOL. XC.

Fras. Bacon, as Lord Keeper. Riots on Shrove Tuesday; Drury Lane Playhouse attacked; Finsbury Prison broken open; houses at Wapping pulled down and injured. The King dines with the Queen at Somerset House, now to be called Denmark House.

March 8. London. 106. Edw. Sherburn to [Carleton]. The loan from the Londoners comes in so slowly that Carleton's allowance is not yet paid. Rising of the apprentices, who pulled down four houses at Wapping, and attacked Drury Lane Theatre, which they would have destroyed had they not been prevented. The King has commanded such as were taken to be executed, for example's sake.

March 10. 107. Minute of proceedings of the Commissioners for the office of Earl Marshal. Wm. Penson, Lancaster Herald, constituted Registrar. Augmentation of the Heralds' fees proposed. Complaints against Hen. St. George, Richmond Herald.

March 10. Commission to Sir Fras. Bacon, Lord Keeper, to pass grants and subscribe injunctions, decrees, and dismissions, received and given by the late Lord Chancellor. [*Grant Bk., p.* 200.]

March 10. London. 108. Sir Horace Vere to Carleton. Recommends the bearer, Widow Orrell. Her late husband distinguished himself in the sea-fight in which Admiral Heamskerk was slain.

March 10? 109. Projected stages of His Majesty's journey to, and return from Scotland, from March 15 to Sept. 10, 1617. [*Corresponding generally, but not entirely, with the stages actually made.*]

March 10. Dover. 110. Commissioners for the passage at Dover to Lord Zouch. Recapture of Wm. Salisbury, alias Wm. Jenman [*see Feb.* 2], who gave the address in London of Edw. Cotton, son of his master, Rich. Cotton, who is abroad, and of Wm. Salisbury. The French Ambassador has sailed, and with him Edw. Matthews, late prisoner.

March 10. 111. Examination of Posthumus Napleton, of Faversham. Heard Ant. Napleton threaten, that if his uncle, Thos. Napleton, bound him to his good behaviour, he would make him spend all that he had, and lose his life in the end.

March 10. Westminster. Warrant to pay to Sir Jas. Auchterlony 700*l.*, part of a grant of 2,400*l.* to Sir Fras. Steward, which is surrendered on composition. [*Sign Man., vol.* VII., *No.* 19.]

March 10. Westminster. Letters Patent declaratory of the dignity of baronet, as a mean rank between barons and knights, declaring their precedency, and that of their wives, sons, and daughters, over knights, and promising knighthood to the heir of any baronet on attaining his majority. [*Ibid., No.* 20.]

March 10. Westminster. Grant to Emanuel and Jeremy Alley, Water Bailiffs of Dover, of the Keepership of the Prison there, built by the said Emanuel, for their lives, and sixty years after. Latin. [*Ibid., No.* 21.]

VOL. XC.

1617.
March 10. Westminster. Grant to Hen. Knollys of a pension of 8*s.* per day, on surrender by Sir Rich. Musgrave of the office of Master and Surveyor of Ordnance, at Berwick, Newcastle, Carlisle, &c., and a similar pension. Latin. [*Sign Man., vol.* VII., *No.* 22.]

March 10. Westminster. Covenant from the King to Thos. Arundel, son and heir of Thos. Lord Arundel, of Wardour, that no grant of the King's reversion in any of his father's lands shall pass to his disinheritance, and forbidding any person to sue for the same. [*Ibid., No.* 23.]

March 11. Westminster. Grant to Art. Mainwaring, in reversion after Sir Rich. Bulkeley, of the office of Constable of the Castle, and Captain of the Town of Beaumaris. Latin. [*Ibid., No.* 24.]

March 11. Westminster. Grant to John Alcock of nine tenths of the goods, &c. of Robt. Newton, outlaw, subject to the satisfaction of his creditors. [*Ibid., No.* 25.]

March ? 112. Queries relative to the nature of a grant to Lord Denney of certain reliefs and heriots, and the nature and extent of a proposed commission for letting the casualties of the Crown, &c.

March 11. Westminster. Grant to Lord Denney of lease of all heriots and reliefs falling to the King, excepting those on copyhold or fee-farm lands, those payable by peers, and such as belong to lands granted to the Queen and Prince; paying for the latter 100*l.*, and for the former 139*l.* 5*s.* 9*d.* per ann. [*Sign Man., vol.* VII., *No.* 27.]

March 11. Westminster. Grant to the town of Oswestry, co. Salop, of confirmation of charter, with additional privileges. [*Ibid., No.* 28.]

March 11. London. 113. Sir Wm. Lovelace to Carleton. The Lord Chamberlain, Buckingham, Southampton, Montgomery, Sec. Lake, two Bishops, &c. going to Scotland with the King. If the Lord Chancellor recover, more bills will be preferred in the Star Chamber against him than have been against Sir Edw. Coke, who is still in great disfavour with His Majesty. A print is published in the Low Countries, of the King in his doublet and hose, with his pockets drawn out and hanging loose, and the inscription, "Have you any more townes to sell?" The Bp. of Spalato has presented several sheets of his work to the King, who thinks it learned; but has not given him any living for it. Sir Thos. Moore, Sir Robt. Vaughan, Sir Hen. Vane, and Sir Jas. Fullerton, sworn officers of the Prince's household. The French King's forces defeated by the Princes, and the Duke of Guise hurt. Rumours on the destination of the Spanish fleet, which is gathering. Sir Walter Raleigh is ready to sail.

March 12. 114. W. Easdall to Dr. Lambe, Chancellor of Peterborough. Notice of old books in his possession. His Lord [the Bp. of Peterborough?] is absent at the christening of Lord Haddington's child.

1617. VOL. XC.

March 12. London. 115. Sir Thos. Smythe to the Council. Has assembled the Companies, as required, to consult them about a fund towards defraying the expenses of a fleet against the Turkish pirates. They think 20,000*l*. a year for two years might be raised from merchants, but leave the directions to the Council.

March 12? 116. List of names [*of merchants; those with whom Sir Thos. Smythe conferred?*].

March 12. Westminster. Grant to Sir Fulk Greville of purchase of lands, &c. in the town of Warwick, value 1,000*l*. Latin. [*Sign Man., vol.* VII., *No.* 29.]

March 12. Westminster. Grant to Jas. Elliott, servant to the Prince, on surrender of Hen. Larkyn, of Westminster, of 50*l*. per ann. [*Ibid., No.* 30.]

March 12. Westminster. Warrant for payment to Sir Patrick Murray, appointed Keeper of Theobalds Parks, in the room of Miles Whytakers, deceased, and to And. Bussey, Keeper of Cheshunt Park, co. Middlesex, of sums necessary for repairing the parks, and for providing food for the deer. [*Ibid., No.* 31.]

March 12. Westminster. Grant to Sir Robt. Carr, Gentleman of the Bedchamber to the Prince, of a pension of 300*l*. [*Ibid., No.* 32.]

March 12. Westminster. Grant to Jas. Maxwell, in reversion after Sir Rich. Coningsby, of the office of Gentleman Usher and Black Rod Bearer at St. George's Feast. Latin. [*Ibid., No.* 33.]

March 12. Westminster. Grant to Fergus Graham alias Plumpe, of Saerke alias Sirke, co. Cumberland, of pardon for life only, for manslaughter of John Maxwell, late Provost of Dumfries, committed thirty years since, during which time he has been abroad. Latin. [*Ibid., No.* 34.]

March 12. Westminster. Grant to Lord Aubigny and Roger Wood, in consideration of a bond for 2,500*l*. to be paid by the former of 40,693*l*. 4*s*. 8½*d*. decreed to be paid by Geo. Leicester and Anne his wife, late wife and executrix of Urian Babington, of London, and others, for moneys paid to Babington for provision of soldiers' apparel in Ireland, of which he defrauded the Crown. [*Ibid., No.* 35.]

March 12. Westminster. Re-grant to the Earl of Buckingham of the manors of Beamont, Oakley, and others, co. Essex, escheated to the Crown by Somerset's attainder, which Lord Darcy, of Chiche, holds for life; also of the manor of Fleet and other lands, co. Lincoln, as part of the value for Sherborne, and in lieu of the manor of Taynton Magna, co. Gloucester, which is found to be granted to another. [*Ibid., No.* 36.]

March 13. Westminster. Warrant to the Lord Treasurer and others to renew the duties of 16*d*. per cloth, and 2*s*. per pound on Northern cloth, which were discontinued by the late Queen during pleasure, and have not been renewed since the King's accession; with pardon of the arrears; Sir Robt. Lloyd, Admiral to the Queen, and Thos. Murray, Secretary to the Prince, appointed Collectors of the said Customs, for twenty one years, with one third of the profits. [*Ibid., No.* 37.]

VOL. XC.

1617.

March 13. Westminster. Grant to Lord Aubigny of 5,000*l.* as a free gift. [*Sign Man., vol.* VII., *No.* 38.]

March 13. Westminster. Grant to Abraham Williams of the next reversion of a Clerkship of the Signet, after the placing of Sir Hum. May and John More. [*Ibid., No.* 39.]

March 13. Westminster. Grant to Sir Rowland Egerton of the dignity of a Baronet. Drawn after His Majesty's second declaration. Latin. [*Ibid., No.* 40.]

March 13. Westminster. Grant to Mary Lady Helwys, widow of Sir Gervase Helwys, for her jointure, of the manor house and part of the manor of Worlaby, co. Lincoln, with remainder to Sir Wm. Helwys. Also grant to Sir Wm. Helwys of the said manor of Worlaby, co. Lincoln, Saunby, co. Notts, and all other lands and goods which came to the King by the attainder of Sir Gervase Helwys, saving the fifth part of the marsh lands lately granted to him. Latin. [*Ibid., No.* 41.]

March 13. Westminster. Grant to Robt. Pye of all moneys above 3,000*l.* yearly, arising by the imposition of 3*d.* in the pound on Merchant Strangers' goods, on the expiration of a former grant of the same to Sir Lionel Cranfield. [*Ibid., No.* 42.]

March 13. Westminster. Grant to Sir John Spilman, Jeweller, of patent for making a new and more pleasant kind of playing cards, with proviso of revocation if found prejudicial. [*Ibid., No.* 43.]

March 13. Westminster. Discharge to the Treasurer and Chancellor of the Exchequer, for delivering an imperfect warrant for timber trees out of Chopwell Wood, to repair the bridge at Berwick; and warrant to continue such delivery as long as necessary. [*Ibid., No.* 44.]

March 13. Westminster. Warrant to pay to John Williams and others 6,815*l.* 6*s.* 8½*d.* for gold and silver plate for new year's gifts, presents to Ambassadors, and for the King's use; also for payments for carriage of the same, for cutlery, &c. [*Ibid., No.* 45.]

March 13. 117. Edw. Palavicino to Carleton. Begs to serve him in place of Mr. Sherburn, who is admitted Secretary to Lord Keeper Bacon. Will give security for faithful service. The King stands godfather to the child of Lady Fielding, sister to Buckingham. Sir Edw. Conway is appointed to review the island of Jersey, for redress of abuses in religion, &c.

March 13? 118. List of noblemen, &c. appointed to attend the King on his progress to Scotland.

March 13? 119. Thos. Wilson to the King. Prays for the next Mastership of Requests. It was promised to him the last year, but Sir Lionel Cranfield has been admitted instead. Could do better service than being always buried amongst the papers.

1617. VOL. XC.

March 14. Westminster. 120. Commission to the Archbp. of Canterbury, Lord Keeper Bacon, and others, for the creation of Baronets. The number in all not to exceed two hundred. The commission to expire in the February next ensuing.

March 14. 121. Account of the receipt of the Low Country money, 166,628*l.*, and of the issues made therefrom.

March 14. Westminster. Warrant to pay to Robt. Hay, Groom of the Bedchamber, 450*l.* in lieu of the stipends of his office, amounting to 150*l.* per ann. [*Sign Man., vol.* VII., *No.* 47.]

March 14. Westminster. Warrant to pay to Jas. Chambers, one of the King's physicians, 250*l.* as a free gift. [*Ibid., No.* 48.]

March 14. Westminster. Warrant to pay to Lady Jane Roxburgh, Lady of the Bedchamber to the Queen, 3,000*l*, as a free gift for long and faithful service. [*Ibid., No.* 49.]

March 14. Westminster. Warrant to pay to Philip Earl of Montgomery 4,000*l.*, as the King's gift, from the Court of Wards and Liveries [*Ibid., No.* 50.]

March 14. Commission to the Treasurer, &c. of the Exchequer, for levying funds due upon alienations of lands in Wales and elsewhere, with limitations. [*Grant Bk., p.* 198.]

March 14. Grant to Edw. Wotton of the third part of the profit upon fines for alienation of lands in Wales and elsewhere. [*Ibid., p.* 225.]

March 14. Grant to Thos. Coventry of the office of Solicitor General, during pleasure. [*Ibid., p.* 197.]

March 14. Award between the Earl of Cumberland, and the Earl and Countess of Dorset, and Hen. Lord Clifford, concerning the estating of divers lands, &c., cos. York and Westmoreland, and payment of money. [*Ibid., p.* 194.]

March 14. Grant to Sir John Villiers of the reversion of the barony of Whaddon. [*Ibid., p.* 187.]

[March 15]. Grant to Margaret Countess of Nottingham of an annuity of 600*l.*, to Chas. Howard, jun., of 500*l.*, and to Anne Howard of 250*l.* out of the new impositions on merchandise, all inalienable, and to commence from the death of Lord Admiral Nottingham, who has two pensions, amounting to 27,000*l.*, from the said impositions. [*Sign Man., vol.* VIII., *No.* 85.]

March 15. London. 122. Chamberlain to Carleton. The new Lord Keeper keeps great state. Sir Robt. Mansell married at Denmark House to Mrs. Roper, one of the Queen's Maids of Honour. Sir John Smith knighted; also three of the Farmers of the Customs, and the Lord Mayor; the King thanked them for their forwardness in the loan of 100,000*l.*, which he borrowed of the City, though it is not

VOL. XC.

1617.

yet raised. Sir Noel Caron offers 20,000*l.* from Dutch merchant strangers; 60,000*l.* worth of jewels are pledged, and the Farmers [of Customs] promise 50,000*l.* The journey to Scotland disliked by both nations, and very costly. Complaints against St. Sauveur, by Sir John Peyton, Governor of Jersey. Sir Edw. Conway and Dr. [Wm.] Bird gone to investigate. The Spanish Ambassador had well nigh overthrown Raleigh's voyage. The Spanish match said to be half made. Sir John Digby complained of, as speaking too much Spanish. Had Lord Coke consented to marry his daughter with Sir John Villiers, he might have been Chancellor, but he stuck at 10,000*l.*, and 1,000*l.* a year, saying he would not buy the King's favour too dear.

March 15. Philip Lane. 123. Examination of Edw. Dawson, of the Angel, Gracious Street, London. Delivered three letters to the Recorder's servant. Does not know Clement Richardson nor Hen. Snell, mentioned in the letters. *Annexed are,*

123. I. *Hen. Snell to his cousin, Mr. Dawson, of the Angel, Gracious Street. Begs him to keep the enclosed writing till sent for. Sandwich, Monday.*

123. II. *Geo. Conyers to Fras. Tregean, in the Fleet. Requests him to pay* 17*l.* 12*s.*, *which he owes him, to the bearer, Lawrence Richardson. Jan.* 22, 1617 [1618?].

123. III. *Clement Richardson, alias Hen. Snell, to his cousin. He and Clesby were arrested at Sandwich, for refusing the Oath of Allegiance, and have been in prison thirteen days. Begs him to effect their delivery through some servant of Lord Zouch. They would give* 10*l. for it.*

March 15. Westminster. Grant to the Earl of Suffolk of liberty to have a small pipe for conveying water to Suffolk House, inserted into the main pipe from Hyde Park to Westminster Palace. [*Sign Man., vol.* VII., *No.* 51.]

March 15. Warrant dormant to the Council to reprieve such convicted felons as, for strength of body, shall be thought fit to be employed in foreign discoveries, or other service beyond seas. [*Ibid., No.* 52.]

March 16. Theobalds. Grant to Sir Ralph Winwood and his son Richard, of the Keepership of the House and Park of Ditton, co. Bucks, with reversion to the heirs male of Sir Ralph. [*Ibid., No.* 53.]

March 16. Whitehall. 124. Petition of Hen. Gibb to the King, for the forfeiture of the recognizance by which Sir Thos. Henly pledged himself that the lands of his father were truly stated, he being then the King's ward, although he had fraudulently conspired with Sir Thos. Roberts and Robt. Sheppard to conceal and withhold from His Majesty the profits of the manor of Cheyne Court, co. Kent, which his father held. With reference thereon.

VOL. XC.

1617.

March 16. London. 125. Matthew de Quester to Carleton. Arrangements relative to the transmission of letters; begs for a line stating their receipt, and for the carriage of his Lordship's private packets. The Prince gone with the King to Huntingdon.

March 17. 126. Edw. Sherburn to [the Same]. The King gone to Theobalds; the Queen and Prince have taken their leave of him; but the Council who are to remain in England attend his Majesty, till his visiting is over. Death of the Lord Chancellor; an hour before, the King sent the Lord Keeper to promise him forthwith an Earldom, the Presidency of the Council, and a pension of 3,000*l.* a year. He said it was too late for himself, but he should be grateful if the King would confer any of them on his son. Chief Justice Montague ill. Mr. Ben made Recorder. Sir And. Noel made a Baron, and Col. Packenham knighted.

March 17. Royston. Warrant to pay 198*l.* 13*s.* 4*d.* to the Earl of Buckingham, Master of the Horse, arrears due to him on his last account, and to advance to him 400*l.* for provision of horses. [*Sign Man., vol.* VII., *No.* 54.]

March 17. Royston. Grant to Sir Lionel Cranfield of annuity of 100*l.* for his office of Master of Requests, and other services. [*Ibid., No.* 55.]

March ? 127, 128. Form of Oath to be administered to a Master of Requests. Two copies.

March 17. Westminster. Royal assent for Dr. Nich. Felton, elected Bishop of Bristol. Latin. [*Sign Man., vol.* VII., *No.* 56.]

March ? 129. The Council to the King. Certify that the petition of Sir Art. Ingram for lands in the manor of Bromley, in exchange for others surrendered, and for money, is fitting, as he offers the full value of the lands.

March 17. Royston. Grant to Wm. Ferrers and others, for the benefit of Sir Art. Ingram, of certain messuages and lands in Bromley and Hackney, co. Middlesex, in lieu of certain tithes in Humbleton, co. York, which had been granted away before. Latin. [*Sign Man., vol.* VII., *No.* 58.]

March 17. Westminster. Commission, to continue till His Majesty's return out of Scotland, to the Archbp. of Canterbury, the Lord Keeper Bacon, and others, authorizing them to make commissions for the office of Provost Marshal; commissions for effecting business in Ireland; to perfect the Ecclesiastical Commission; to pass securities for loans to the King, and issue proclamations, if necessary. [*Ibid., No.* 59.]

March. 130. Copy of the above, dated Westminster, March 21.

Vol. XC.

1617.

March 18. London. 131. Nath. Brent to Carleton. Presumes he is provided with a Secretary, and wishes now to remain in England. The Lord Chancellor died ten days after he resigned the Seals. The Lord Admiral dangerously ill. Sir John Digby goes at his own expense to Spain, as was agreed when he had Sherborne made over to him.

March 18. Dover. 132. Peter Dibb to Rich. Younge. Great damage is done to the fishery by four or five trailers in the Bay of Hythe; requests orders for their repulse.

March 18. Royston. Grant to Fras. Merlin, of Ypres, Flanders, of denization. Latin. [*Sign Man., vol.* VII., *No.* 60.]

March 19. Grant to Wm. Earwood of the office of Gentleman Gaoler in the Tower, for life. [*Grant Bk., p.* 209.]

March 19. London. 133. Matthew de Quester to Carleton. Recommends the bearer, Geo. Martyn.

March 20. Sandwich. 134. Commissioners of the Passage at Sandwich to Lord Zouch. Have stayed John Atteo, and also Martin Clark, who was hiring sailors to go to the North Cape with his brother John Clark, of Dunkirk, a warrant having been sent to stay any persons connected with John Clark.

March 20. Strand. 135. Geo. Gerrard to Carleton. Appointments in the Prince's household. Sir Allan Apsley made Lieutenant of the Tower by favour of Buckingham, he having married the sister-in-law of Sir Edw. Villiers. Old Lady Dorset ventures 2,000*l.*, on condition of receiving twenty for one when the King converts the King of Spain from Popery. Riots of the apprentices on Shrove Tuesday. The King was much moved, and has ordered the city trained bands to be drawn up every May-day and Shrove Tuesday. Most of the rich merchants have concurred to furnish His Majesty with money for his progress into Scotland; those who held back being ordered to attend the Council at Lincoln, yielded, lest they should be carried into Scotland. The Earl of Northumberland keeps his daughter, Lady Lucy Percy, in the Tower, to secure her from the addresses of Lord Hay. Chancellor [Ellesmere] having received the 8,000*l.* for surrender of his place, petitioned the King daily for eight or ten days to allow him to resign, and at last refused to seal patents sent; on which the King visited him, found him weakened in mind and body, and sent for the Seal. His Majesty sealed with it a patent for licensing inns and victualling houses, and one for raising 100,000*l.* in a year from the King's woods, and then gave the Seal to Sir Fras. Bacon, who got it cheaply, Sir John Bennet having offered 30,000*l.* for it. Legal promotions. Mr. Ben succeeds [Sir Thos.] Coventry as Recorder of London. The King has restored to the Earl of Somerset lands of his own, value 1,000*l.* per ann., and a rent-charge of 3,000*l.* out of those in his Majesty's hands. The King is constantly showing favour to Buckingham and his family. Lord Audley dead. Lord Hay made a Councillor. Sir Walter Raleigh goes, after much opposition.

Vol. XC.

1617.

[March 20.] 136. [The King to the Council]. Having ruled his own kingdom in peace, and restored tranquillity to neighbouring nations, thinks it fitting to attempt the suppression of pirates, against whose ravages his merchants sadly complain. They are to consult thereon. If a fleet is sent, the Earl of Southampton is to be its Admiral, in consideration of the age and illness of the Earl of Nottingham.

March 20. Westminster. Warrants to the Sheriffs of London and Middlesex to enlarge Isaac Williams, condemned for coining, on condition of his perpetual banishment. [*Sign Man., vol.* VII., *No.* 61.]

March 20. Westminster. Warrant to pay to Sir Rich. Morrison 325*l.* 7*s.* 3*d.*, for providing ordnance stores for furnishing the Fort of Plymouth and the Island of St. Nicholas. [*Ibid., No.* 62.]

March 20. Westminster. Warrant to discharge Thos. Bellingham and Brice Christmas, convicted before the King in the Star Chamber of duelling, from their fines of 1,000*l.* and their imprisonment, His Majesty wishing to signalize his entry into his Court of Judicature by an act of mercy. The prohibition to wear arms or approach the Court, and the injunction to make a public submission, are still to remain in force, for the sake of others. [*Ibid., No.* 63.]

March 20. Westminster. Warrant for increasing the monthly allowance to the Treasurer of the Navy for cordage, from 700*l.* to 900*l.* [*Ibid., No.* 64.]

March 20. Westminster. Warrant granted at the suit of Count Scarnaffi, Ambassador of Savoy, to liberate Wm. Danvers, Roger Walter, Nich. Johnson, and John Armstrong, prisoners in the Gate House for refusing the Oath of Allegiance, on condition of their immediate banishment. [*Ibid., No.* 65.]

March 22. London. 137. Edw. Palavicino to Carleton. Professions of service. Rumoured death of Lord Chief Justice Montague, at Exeter, in his Western Circuit.

[March 23.] 138. Account of payments made by the Farmers of the Customs to the Cofferer of the Household, Master of the Wardrobe, the Exchequer, and for annuities, in 14 Jac. I.

March 23. Grant to Sir Robt., Sir Wm., and Sir Edw. Howard of all fines on original writs in the King's Bench, for life. [*Grant Bk., p.* 205.]

March 24. 139. Examination of Chris. Saker. Wm. Tomlyn told him he was called up as a witness against Napleton; that he had often reproved him for ill speaking; that he did not remember the particular words reported, and that being so long ago, if he had remembered them, he should keep it to himself.

Vol. XC.

1617.

March 24. 140. Examination of Wm. Saffery. Has heard Wm. Tomlyn call Thos. Napleton a traitor.

March 25. 141. Examination of Dorothy Saffery. Thos. Wood said that he heard Thos. Napleton say the King loved hunting and hawking so well that all would be nought one day.

March. 25. 142. Examination of Wm. Dovers. Heard Thos. Wood make the above report of Napleton's speeches.

March 25. Burley. Grant to Sir Chas. Howard, in reversion after Fras. and Wm. Reston, of the office of Keeper of New Lodge Walk, in Cranborne, Woodward of Cookham and Bray, co. Berks, and Riding Forester of Battells Bailiwick, Windsor Forest. Latin. [*Sign Man., vol.* VII., *No.* 68.]

March 25. Westminster. Warrant to erect an office for licensing pedlars and petty-chapmen, on producing certificates of good behaviour and putting in good security; and appointing Abraham Williams, Fras. Blundell, Rowland Wynn, and others, as licensers, reserving a rent to the King of 1,000 marks after the first year. [*Ibid., vol.* VIII., *No.* 1.]

March 26. Westminster. Warrant to pay to Sir Wm. Segar, Principal King-at-Arms, 30*l.*, for limning the patent of Prince Charles, and setting up his arms and style in a copper plate, gilt and engraven, at Windsor [as Knight of the Garter]. [*Ibid., No.* 2.]

March 26. Westminster. Grant to Wm. Glover, jun., of Oldbury, co. Warwick, of pardon, for felony. Latin. [*Ibid., No.* 3.]

March 26. Westminster. Warrant to pay to Rich. Watford, shipwright, 214*l.* 18*s.* 2*d.* for three new barges; to Clement Chapman, 37*l.* 12*s.* 2*d.* for work; and to Maximilian Coult, carver, 13*l.* 14*s.* 4*d.* for carving. [*Ibid., No.* 4.]

March 26. Westminster. Warrant to pay to Randolf Bull, Keeper of the Great Clock in the Palace of Westminster, 56*l.* 13*s.* 4*d.*, for necessary repairs. [*Ibid., No.* 5.]

March 26. Westminster. Grant to Sir Mervin Touchet Lord Audley, on payment of 400*l.* to Wm. Heydon, of the King's reversion of the manor of Stowey and Stowey Parks, alias the Red Deer Park and the Fallow Deer Park, co. Somerset; the manor of Stalbridge, parcel of the late monastery of Sherborne, and the advowson of Stalbridge, co. Dorset; in part of the grant to Wm. Heydon, of 8,000*l.* entailed remainders. Latin. [*Ibid., No.* 6.]

March 26. Westminster. Warrant to Sir Rich. Molyneux, Receiver General of the Duchy of Lancaster, to pay 400*l.* to Lord Stanhope, Treasurer of the Chamber, the residue of 2,400*l.* per ann.; and signification that he shall pay to him only 1,500*l.* per ann., in future, the revenue of the Duchy being much diminished. [*Ibid., No.* 7.]

March 26. Westminster. Grant to John Sharpe, Minister, born in Scotland, of denization. Latin. [*Ibid., No.* 8.]

1617. VOL. XC.

March 26. Westminster. Re-grant to Wm. Earl of Salisbury, of Cranborne Chace, cos. Dorset, Wilts, and Hants, on account of informality in the former grant. Latin. [*Sign Man., vol.* VIII., *No.* 9.]

March 26. Westminster. Grant, in reversion, to John Chapman, of a Clerkship of the Privy Seal, and of the Court of Requests, in reversion after Hugh Allington, Sir Thos. Clerk, Fras. Mills, and Edw. Reynoldes, the present Clerks, and after the placing of Edw. Anthony, Edw. Clerke, John Packer, Thos. Packer, and Jas. Mills, previous Reversioners. Latin. [*Ibid., No.* 10.]

March 26. Westminster. Warrant for payment of 15*l.* per ann. to Garter King-at-Arms, and to the youngest Herald for the time being, viz., 5*l.* for the maintenance of a register, and 10*l.* for repairs at the Office of Arms. [*Ibid., No.* 11.]

March 26. Westminster. Warrant for payment to Sir Fras. Bacon of fees as Lord Keeper of the Great Seal. [*Ibid., No.* 12.]

March 26. Westminster. Grant to the Merchants of the Staple, of confirmation of the Charter granted to them, 3 Eliz., with transfer of the staple for wools, assigned by the late Queen to Middleburgh, Bruges, and Bergen-op-Zoom, into divers cities and principal towns in England. Latin. [*Ibid., No.* 13.]

March 26. Westminster. Grant to the Mayor, Bailiffs, &c. of Thoxted, Essex, of enlargement of charter, and confirmation of former liberties. Latin. [*Ibid., No.* 14.]

March 26. Westminster. Grant to Sir Paul Banning, Sir Baptist Hicks, and Sir Wm. Herrick, of the fines for alienations, and the profits of the Hanaper, until the 7,500*l.* which they lent to the King be repaid with interest; 8,000*l.* to Sir Noel Caron, Robt. de la Bar, and Philip Jacobson, to be first paid out of the said fines. [*Ibid., No.* 15.]

March 26. Westminster. Re-grant to Thos. Emerson, at suit of Visct. Haddington, of the manors of New Langport and Sevans, and other lands in Kent, forfeited by Sir Hen. James for refusing the Oath of Allegiance; with addition to the former grant of a condition, that, if he be disturbed therein by Martin James, son of Sir Henry, a grant to the said Martin of the other lands of Sir Henry shall be void, and Emerson compensated therefrom. [*Ibid., Nos.* 16, 17.]

March 26. Westminster. Grant to Hector Johnston, for service to the Electress Palatine, of lease of the waste ground called Hay Hill, near Hyde Park, also of another small portion near Hyde Park Corner, with power to build thereon. Latin. [*Ibid., No.* 18.]

March 26. Westminster. Grant to Sir Wm. Segar, Garter, of 10*l.* per ann. increase of fees, above other commodities anciently belonging to that place. Latin. [*Ibid., No.* 19.]

VOL. XC.

1617.

March 26. Westminster. Like grant to Sir Rich. St. George, Norroy, of 20*l.* per ann. increase. [*Sign Man., vol.* VIII., *No.* 20.]

March 26. Westminster. Like grants to Ralph Brook, York Herald, Thos. Knight, Chester Herald, Hen. St. George, Richmond Herald, Sam. Thompson, Windsor Herald, and Wm. Benson, Lancaster Herald, of 13*l.* 6*s.* 8*d.* each per ann. increase. [*Ibid., Nos.* 21–25.]

March 26. Westminster. Like grants to Sampson Lennard, Bluemantle Pursuivant, Wm. Smith, Rouge Dragon, John Gwillim, Rouge Croix, and Philip Holland, Portcullis, of 10*l.* each per ann. increase. [*Ibid., Nos.* 26–29.]

March 27. Whitehall. 143. Winwood to Lake. The apprentices have been tried and punished, as far as law permits. A proclamation ordering retirement into the country is needless, for the Londoners already say "magna civitas, magna solitudo." The Treasurer and Chancellor of the Exchequer have given in an account of how the borrowed moneys are employed in extraordinaries.

March 27. Grant of divers privileges to the Bailiffs and Burgesses of Bishop's Castle, co. Salop. [*Grant Bk., p.* 231.]

March 28. Grant to John Smith of a Gunner's place in the Tower, for life. [*Ibid., No.* 231.]

March 28. Durham. 144. Warrant by the Bishop and Magistrates of Durham, for levying the fee of Capt. Hodson, Muster-master of the County Palatine of Durham, by an assessment of 2*d.* in the pound.

March 28. Westminster. Grant to Hugh May, on surrender of Sir Posthumus Hoby, of certain rents, tithes, &c., formerly appertaining to the Dean and Chapter of Rochester, and now payable to the King. [*Sign Man., vol.* VIII., *No.* 30.]

March 28. Westminster. Presentation of John Michaelson to the rectory of Chelmsford, co. Essex. Latin. [*Ibid., No.* 31.]

March 29. 145. Edw. Sherburn to [Carleton]. Private money affairs. Has got his warrant signed for the February allowance. The Earl of Arundel's pictures to be delivered to Inigo Jones. Sir John Bennet gone to Flanders.

March 29. London. 146. Chamberlain to the Same. Death of the late Lord Chancellor on the 10th. His son solicits the earldom of Bridgewater, but the 20,000*l.* he offers for it is not enough. His father left 12,000*l.* per ann., with the character of being severe, implacable, an enemy to Parliaments, and a maintainer of exorbitant powers for the Chancery Court. He desired to be privately interred, and so has been taken to Cheshire. All his property left to his son. Sir Edw. Noel made a Baron by patent. The King now at Lincoln. Digby has taken

1617. VOL. XC.

leave for Spain. Lord Roos has returned, and gone to the King. The King of Spain gave him a jewel worth 5,000*l.* A commission of persons well affected to the Spanish business is appointed. The Virginian woman died at Gravesend on her return. Sir W. Raleigh has set out, and makes speed for fear of a countermand; it is a mere seeking his fortune; the Prince is no friend to the journey. A sermon preached before the Archbp. of Canterbury and certain other great Lords, at St. Paul's Cross, by Dr. Donne, who, in the discourse, did Queen Elizabeth "great right."

March 29. Whitehall. 147. Winwood to [Lake]. The Merchant Adventurers will either pay 50,000*l.* to the King, or perform the contract treated with Lord Fenton, but this has dangerous exceptions. The cloth-workers and dyers threaten to cut the throats of the old Company, especially Sir Lionel Cranfield. The Lords are negociating with the old company to set them on work.

March? 148. Petition of the handicraft cloth-workers and dyers in or about London to the King, that he would direct the Merchant Adventurers to employ them, for relief of their great distress.

March 29. Lincoln. 149. Lake to Winwood. The King is very angry with Lord Carew, because the carts made in the Tower for his luggage prove defective. Reminds Lake of the proclamation for persons of quality to repair into the country, and for the establishing of Provost Marshals in the neighbourhood of London. His Majesty has made his entry into Lincoln, with a good show.

March 29. Westminster. Grant to Edm. Lisle of the Captaincy of Walmer Castle, in place of Wm. Boughton, deceased. Latin. [*Sign Man., vol.* VIII, *No.* 32.]

March 29. Westminster. Warrant to pay to John Bill, Bookseller, in St. Paul's Churchyard, 469*l.* 11*s.*, for books. [*Ibid., No.* 33.]

March 29. Westminster. Discharge for Sir Hen. Hobart, Chief Justice of Common Pleas, dispensing with that part of his oath of office which forbids him to give advice to, or take fees from, any but the King, so as to enable him to hold the office of Chancellor and Keeper of the Great Seal to the Prince of Wales, together with his former place. Latin. [*Ibid., No.* 34.]

March 29. Westminster. Warrant for allowance of 208*l.* 19*s.* 7½*d.* to the Farmers of the Customs out of their rent, on account of certain wares transported custom-free. [*Ibid., No.* 35.]

March 29. Westminster. Indenture of covenant between the King and the Lord Privy Seal, concerning the making and delivery of saltpetre at the Tower, according to former rates, &c., with some differences from the former indentures. [*Ibid., No.* 36.]

VOL. XC.

1617.

March 29. Westminster. Grant to Robt. Treswell, Somerset Herald, of 13*l.* 6*s.* 8*d.* per ann., increase of salary. Latin. [*Sign Man., vol.* VIII., *No.* 37.]

March 29. Westminster. Like grant to Wm. Camden, Clarencieux, of 20*l.* per ann. increase. [*Ibid., No.* 38.]

March 29. Westminster. Revocation of Letters Patent granted to Sir Hen. Hobart, Bart., appointing him Chief Justice of the Court of Common Pleas. Latin. [*Ibid., No.* 39.]

March 29. Westminster. Grant to Sir Wm. Anstruther of the benefit of a bond of 5,000*l.*, given to the King by Esme Stuart, Lord Aubigny, and Roger Wood, for their payment of 2,500*l.* before March 25, 1618, in case the bond be forfeited. [*Ibid., No.* 40.]

March 30. Lincoln. Grant, in perpetuity, to Barth. Rogers and his heirs, on surrender of a joint patent to Barth. Rogers, Edw. Hill, and Rich. Ellis, of the office of Usher of the Court of Wards and Liveries. Latin. [*Ibid., No.* 41.]

March 30? 150. Lake to Winwood. The King is much displeased at the staying of the proclamation for removal from London, which had been so solemnly resolved on in Council; no reason could allay his passion. He insists that it proceed forthwith. He has signed a Privy Seal for 100*l.* to be given to the French violins.

March 31. Westminster. 151. Thos. Watson to Lake. Has advised Mr. Long to surrender his patent, and throw himself on Lake's courtesy, but he will not consent. Fears he [Watson] may be blamed, because a greyhound which he seized for catching a hare proves to be the Queen's.

March 31. 152. Account book of sums owing for stores, wages, &c. in the office of Ordnance for the past quarter.

March 31? 153. Allowance for a herald's coat, as it stands upon account in the wardrobe.

March 31. Westminster. 154. The King to the Officers of the Exchequer. Warrant to pay the increase in the yearly fees granted to the heralds, and the allowance for reparation of their house.

March? 155. Account of goods taken by pirates, near Portugal, from the Seraphine of Exmouth, Oct. 9, 1616, and of the damage sustained thereby; total 866*l.* 4*s.*

March? 156. Information of Rich. Foster to Sir Ralph Winwood, that having repented of his former evil courses, he will reveal the names of the many thieves who have infested the North since the death of the Earl of Dunbar, and of their Popish supporters; on condition of protection from his former friends, who seek the lives of all whom they suspect of betraying them.

VOL. XC.

1617.

March? 157. List by the Same of twenty-seven thieves and unruly persons in Northumberland, all of whom are dependents or servants of Sir Hen. Wodrington and Roger Wodrington. Were all such persons banished, the country would be as peaceable as ever.

[March.] 158. Petition of Gerard Malines and his sons to Lord Zouch, for his influence at the Council in their relief, in a dispute with the Countess of Bedford, who has coined new farthing tokens, whereby they are in danger of losing 2,000*l.* spent in the former tokens, and 500*l.* worth of copper prepared, and are also unjustly excluded from the work. [*See Feb.* 18, 1619.]

March. Grant to Wm. Earl of Pembroke, for the use of the Earl of Montgomery, of a yearly rent of 900*l.*, arising out of lands of the late Lord Dormer, which are in the King's hands during the minority of the present Lord Dormer. [*Sign Man., vol.* VIII., *No.* 42.]

VOL. XCI. APRIL, 1617.

April [1]. 1. Counter-bond from the King to the Archbp. of Canterbury, the Lord Keeper, Lord Treasurer, Lord Privy Seal, and others, to repay to Sir Noel Caron his loan of 20,000*l.* and 2,000*l.* interest by the day appointed, for security for which loan they are bound, under penalty of 30,000*l.*

April 1. Whitehall. 2. Winwood to [Lake]. The proclamation is preparing for the King's signature, although most nobles have left, and will not return unless they have lawsuits at the term, in which case they are permitted so to do.

April 1. St. James's. 3. Thos. Murray to the Same. Recommends Sir David Murray, the most trusty servant of the late Prince, and almost the only one neglected.

April 2. Hythe. 4. Mayor and Jurats of Hythe to Lord Zouch. Send up John Farsby, apprehended for using trail nets. Do not think his warrant from the King's fishmonger sufficient, not being sanctioned by his lordship. *Inclose,*

4. I. *Certificate by Wm. Angel, the King's fishmonger, that John Farsby, of Barking, is licensed to trail for plaice and soles on the coast of Kent, on condition of bringing them weekly to London, wind and weather permitting. March* 15, 1617.

April 2. 5. Indenture of conveyance of the great stone house, square court, and great garden [of the Minories] from Ant. Lowe to Sir Rich. Morrison. Fragment.

VOL. XCI.

1617.

April 2. Westminster. 6. Privy Seal grant to Edm. Lisle of the Captaincy of Walmer Castle. Latin. [*See the Sign Manual, March* 29.]

April 2. 7. Sir Rich. Sandys and Sir Geo. Newman to Lord Zouch. Have long known Thos. Napleton, of Faversham, as an honest man and good subject. The accusation against him is malicious; beg that his punishment may be light.

April 3. 8. Certificate of Dr. E. Spencer and Dr. Edw. Lapworth, that Thos. Napleton's health is very weak, and that the bath is expedient for him.

April 3. Sandwich. 9. Mayor and Jurats of Sandwich to Lord Zouch. Request that the inhabitants and pilots of Deal, a member of Sandwich, may not be joined to the Trinity House at Dover; but that each member may be governed by its own head port.

April 3. Lincoln. 10. Lake to [Winwood]. The King says that he is King of England, and will be obeyed about the proclamation; he is much moved at the excuses and delays about it. The Lord Deputy has written to the Lords concerning the small forts in Ireland. The King is much displeased with the Merchant Adventurers, who have now run off the 50,000*l.* they offered.

April [3?] 11. Geo. Lowe to Rich. Younge. Request for Thos. Lawrence to be allowed to burn kelp in Kent, for His Majesty's alum works, &c.

April 4. 12. Arguments urged by the Fishermen of Hastings against the late decision of the Admiralty, prohibiting the use of trailing nets for fishing, and praying its reversion.

April? 13. Arguments against the use of trailing nets.

April 5. Court at Greenwich. 14. Lord Carew and Sir Ralph Winwood to Lake. The defects in the carts provided for His Majesty's journey are attributed to the short notice given for them. The master wheelwright is with the carts, and can be called in question, if desired. *Inclose,*

14. I. *Sir John Keyes, Surveyor of Ordnance, to Lord Carew and Sir Ralph Winwood. The order for the carts was not given till within fifteen days before the King's departure. They could not all be made in London in the time, and therefore some had to be ordered in the country, and there was no time to survey them. The harness, being ordered only two days beforehand, had to be taken from the old stores. The money has been paid to the wheelwright, so that the deductions which the King requires for repairs cannot be made.*

April 5. Court at Greenwich. 15. Lord Carew to the Same. Regrets the King's just displeasure about the carts. The wheelwright is the only person to blame. Vindicates himself from any charge of negligence. Has served out

1617. VOL. XCI.

stores for land and sea armies, for thirty years, without reproof. Thinks the King's stores need replenishing. Will have them inventoried, and show what additions are needed, to prevent the recurrence of such a cause of displeasure.

April 5. Suffolk House. 16. Lord Treasurer and Chancellor of the Exchequer to Lake. Ask the King's pleasure whether the Star Chamber Board may not be adjourned until his return from Scotland.

April 5. St. Bartholomew's. 17. Winwood to Lord Zouch. To stay the delivery of the arms to Capt. Turner, who is an idle base fellow.

April 5. London. 18. Chamberlain to Carleton. Auditor Stanley dead. Sir John Bennet set out for Flanders. The Council have had leisure to feast each other since the King's departure. His Majesty is going to Newark. Lord Hay stays to find two barons, whose making the King bestows on him. Abercromby, a Scottish dancing-master, has the making of two Irish barons. Egerton, of Cheshire, and Townsend, of Norfolk, made Baronets. Lord Compton likely to be Earl of Northampton. The old Countess of Pembroke said to be married to Dr. Lister, who was with her at the Spa. The Lord Keeper about to remove to Dorset House, &c.

April 5. Dover Castle. 19. Lord Zouch to the Commissioners for restraint of Passage in the Cinque Ports. To stay Sam. Harlow, who wishes to go abroad without his parents' leave. *Incloses,*

19. I. *Description of Sam. Harlow; with note that his father, Robt. Harlow, of Finsbury, London, will gladly receive him home. March 29.*

April 5. 20. Deposition of Art. Saul, prisoner in Newgate. Has been employed by Sec. Winwood and the Archbp. of Canterbury, to report what English were at Douay College. Particulars of priests who have returned to England, of their meeting places, and conveyance of letters. One of them aided four recusants to escape from Newgate. Some priests in the Clink are allowed to go abroad.

April 5. Chapter[house?] Lincoln. 21. Patent from Roger Parker, Dean, and the Chapter of Lincoln, appointing Dr. John Lambe their Commissary in their peculiar jurisdictions, in cos. Northampton, Rutland, Huntingdon, and Leicester.

April 6. London. 22. Edw. Sherburn to [Carleton]. Private affairs. Hopes his having accepted a post under the Lord Keeper will not lead Carleton to think him less able to attend to his affairs. Lord Eure dead, and Lord Hunsdon cannot recover. The Earl of Rutland made Privy Councillor. Lord Roos has succeeded ill in his negociation in Spain, another argument of his great weakness. Difficulty in obtaining money for Carleton, though 10,000*l.* was laid aside for Ambassadors.

VOL. XCI.

1617.

April 7. Reading. 23. Geo. Carleton to Sir Dud. Carleton. Not having heard from him, thinks the bargain for Imworth is given up. Has told his son Dudley of Sir Dudley's good intentions towards him; he is a promising scholar, and will try to fit himself for his service. Thinks of going to the Spa, having heard wonderful accounts of cures there.

April 7. Chertsey. 24. Edw. Carleton to [Geo. Carleton]. Details his proceedings with Lady Hill, in bargaining for her lease of the manor of Imworth for Sir Dud. Carleton. Wishes his final decision.

April ? 25. Particulars of the lease of the manor of Imworth, in Thames Ditton, and its value. Indorsed [by Sir Dud. Carleton], "Particulars of the purchase commended to me by my cousin Ed. Carleton."

April ? 26. Petition of Jacob Braems to Lord Zouch, for re-delivery of certain cloths seized by the officers of customs, on his entering into a bond for his appearance when summoned; with note in favour of the petition, the goods being perishable from their wetness.

April 7. 27. Bond of the Same, with two securities, in 1,000 marks for his appearance on summons, before the Lord Warden or his deputies, at Dover Castle.

April ? 28. Petition of the Same to Lord Zouch, for discharge of Edw. West, Stephen Askew, and Robt. Anderson, committed to prison at Dover Castle for stealing his goods, as he will have to pay 42*d.* per week for their maintenance in prison, besides relieving their families.

April 7. 29. Clement Edmondes to Lake. The bearers, Fortune and Foster, have entered into a bond to appear before him, concerning outrages on the Borders, on Sir John Denham's return from the King. The Lords will settle the plantation of Wexford. They are busy trying to help the cloth-workers.

April 8. Worksop. Proclamation for all noblemen and others to depart from London within twenty days, and to return to the country, and there continue till the end of the summer vacation, unless prevented by urgent business. Printed. [*Proc. Coll., No.* 50.]

[April 12.] 30. Proclamation by the High Sheriff of Yorkshire, purporting to be by the King's pleasure, that all Popish recusants in the county should either attend service at some church or chapel within twenty days, or surrender themselves prisoners; otherwise their houses are to be pulled down, and themselves submitted to the rigour of the laws. [*See May* 18 *and* 29.]

April 13. St. John's, Thanet. 31. Inhabitants of St. John's to Lord Zouch. They consent that the burning of sea oare into kelp be continued among their poor neighbours, and beg permission for them to sell the same, without

1617. Vol. XCI.

limitation of price, and without the intermeddling of strangers. [*Signed by many of the inhabitants.*]

April 15. Westminster. 32. Thos. Watson to Lake. Has advanced 800*l.* to Sir Wm. Anstruther, to enable him to set off an informality in his grant of 2,500*l.* preventing him from making a composition in ready money for it. The Queen is not offended at his taking her greyhound, but the Lord Admiral is bitter because two of his were taken. Provost Marshals chosen for Surrey and Middlesex, and also competent watches and wards, especially near London. Lord Dorset ordered the Justices of Peace to pass their time in the country and repress disorders, &c., diligently in the King's absence. A Provost Marshal to be established in Sussex, because the iron-works on the borders of Kent and Sussex draw a multitude of rogues and beggars, &c.

April 15. Court at York. 33. Rich. Beaumont to Carleton. Proffers of service. The bearer, Mr. Fairfax, will relate the occurrences of the Court, now at York.

April 15. Mansfield, Notts. 34. Inquisition of the lands of Sir Chas. Cavendish, deceased, viz., Hardwick, Kirkby, &c., &c., co. Nottingham; valuation 137*l.* 10*s.* per ann. Imperfect. Latin.

April 15. Topcliffe. 35. Lake to [Winwood]. Particulars of the receipt and despatch of letters. The King, being desirous to preserve all the rights and ceremonies of the English Church during Easter, wishes Dr. Andrews to be sent to preach before him, and some other chaplain that may school the ministers, if needful. Some ministers from London have been to the King, to inveigh against the ecclesiastical government.

April 16. St. Bartholomew's. 36. Winwood to Lake. The Lords will attend Her Majesty this Easter at Greenwich, but on Easter Monday will go to the Spittal sermon, and dine with the Lord Mayor.

April 16. 37. Note of muster rolls and inventories of munition in the Cinque Ports, delivered to Rich. Marsh.

April 17. Gildenston. 38. Mary Williams to her uncle, Sir D. Carleton. Thanks for his kindness in granting her suit.

April 18. Gildenston. 39. Eliz. Williams to the Same. His little godson, Dudley Williams, is a goodly boy. Begs for pictures of Carleton and his Lady.

April 18. 40. Note of the charges of maintenance of Mr. Eason, John Richardson, Mr. Skinner, and Mr. Smith, prisoners in Dover Castle.

April 19. London. 41. Chamberlain to Carleton. The King is at Durham. He was so in love with the country about Lincoln, that he intends to spend part of his winters there. The chief Scots linger in town, for

1617. VOL. XCI.

want of money. In spite of the late flush, daily gifts and warrants disorder all regular payments. John Murray, of the Privy Purse, is ill or dead. Lord Hunsdon and Lord Audley, Earl of Castlehaven, dead. Drope, of Magdalen College, called in question for saying, in a sermon at St. Paul's Cross, that kings might steal by borrowing and not paying, and by unjust impositions. Sir Rich. Farmer's lady has shot one Onely, of the Temple, with a pocket-pistol, &c.

April 19. Reading. 42. Geo. Carleton to Sir D. Carleton. Private affairs. Purchase of Lady Hill's lease. Has been a Commissioner in a dispute between the city of Oxford and Christ's Church College, as to the limits of the castle, which belongs to the latter.

April 20. 43. Sir Fulk Greville to the King. Understands that he blames him for overmuch caution in proceeding with the new enclosure at Theobalds. His motive is, care to unite his Sovereign's honour and pleasure.

April 20. 44. The Same to the Same. Several freeholders who held back now consent to yield their lands, &c., for enclosure at Theobalds. Sir Thos. Dacre will treat with the commoners for their general consent, before the money given by the King is received.

April 21. London. 45. Sir Horace Vere to Carleton. The Marquis d'Ancre was slain by a Captain of the Guard of the French King, who, looking on, said, "Now am I King of France." He bade the Queen Mother keep her rooms; and sent a comfortable message to the Prince of Condé.

April 22. Whitehall. 46. Sir Fulk Greville to Lake. Regrets the King's displeasure. Was not to blame about the non-payment of wages to the King's surgeon and apothecary,—a duty which belongs to the Treasurer of the Chamber's office,—and had heard no complaints about it. Would have travelled to Scotland to justify himself, had he been young. Begs Lake's good word with His Majesty.

April 23. Suffolk House. 47. Earl of Suffolk to the Same. Finds the King was displeased that the apothecary and surgeon should be stayed for want of their money. That is only a pretence; they were paid, and might have been with His Majesty, but for their private affairs. The city does not yield quite 80,000*l.*, but the Council will try to obtain the 100,000*l.*

April 25. Brussels. Sir John Bennet to Carleton. The Queen wishes to have a standing-cloth made by an Anabaptist at the Hague, as soon as possible. The Countess of Roxburgh has written about it. [*Fland. Corresp., April* 25, 1617.]

April 25. St. James's. 48. Lord Danvers to the Same. The "increasing towardliness" of the Prince may well make Spain more labour for the alliance. Sir John Digby expects to be despatched for Spain; but French hopes are reviving.

Vol. XCI.

1617.

April 27. 49. Sir Chris. Heydon to Lord Zouch. Begs that the bearer may be allowed to sell his place, to enable him to rebuild his houses which are burnt down. Thanks for favour to his son John.

April 28. Whitehall. 50. Sir Fulk Greville to Lake. Mr. [Rich.] Hale refuses His Majesty's offer of buying his house and land for more than its value; but he is old, and will soon be out of the way. The inhabitants of Waltham Forest began to mutiny, being jealous of some intention of enclosing the commons. Has therefore requested Lord Darcy not to proceed in marking out the bounds of Waltham, till the business is completed at Theobalds. Treswell had much abuse there, in completing the surveys of the farms. He is going to arrange with other parties for their land. The business will take more time than the King expects.

April 30. St. Bartholomew's. 51. Winwood to the Same. Sends the Council's answer about Ireland and the plantation of Wexford. A commotion of the vagrant populace in London is feared. All due measures will be taken to prevent or suppress it.

April 30. Whitehall. 52. Commissioners for Spanish business in London to those with the King. Will go on till they can give Mr. Vice Chamberlain his instructions for Spain. Course proposed for suppressing pirates, by a continued force upon them for some years. *Inclose,*

52. i. *The Same to the Same. Have received the King's instructions to devise means for suppressing pirates, in order that Sir John Digby may make a fitting overture to the Spanish King for assistance. The merchants think that London would contribute 40,000l. in two years; they will not be backward, if the thing may be seriously undertaken. The pirates flock to Algiers, but the surprizing of that place is impossible. Experienced captains think the only mode would be to treat with foreign Princes, to join in maintaining forces for their gradual suppression. The assistance of Spain especially necessary, because its ports being nearest to Algiers are most convenient for re-victualling. Whitehall, April 30.*

April? 53. List of Butchers and Poulterers killing and selling flesh in Lent, without licence.

Vol. XCII. May—July, 1617.

May 1. 1. Orders taken by Sir Wm. Sedley and others, Commissioners for redress of Misemployment of Moneys bequeathed for Charitable Uses, [*see July* 22, 1616], directing the return, by Sir Peter Bush and numerous other persons, of moneys detained in their hands, which, according to an agreement with the Lord Admiral in 1590, were to

VOL. XCII.

1617.

be deducted from the pay of the mariners, for the relief of disabled seamen. *Annexed is,*

1. I. *Inquisition on which the above order is founded. April* 11, 1617.

May 1. 2. Memorandum of Rich. Hale's consent to the survey of his copyhold land, parcel of Cheshunt Manor, near Theobalds, in order to ascertain the price at which it should be sold to the King.

May 1. Bridgenorth, Shropshire. 3. Inquisition certifying the value of the lands held by Fras. Woolridge, Randall Grosvenor, Wm. Percy, Sir Fras. Lacon, Sir Thos. Jarvis, and many others, in Morffe Forest and elsewhere, Shropshire. Latin.

May 2. St. Bartholomew's. 4. Winwood to Lake. The Governor of the Muscovy Company requests His Majesty's signature to the letter forwarded. Sends letters from Lord Roos. May-day has passed in perfect quiet.

May 2. Serjeants' Inn. 5. Sir Ranulph Crew to Rich. Younge. Desires a licence for Rich. Griffin to travel into the Low Countries.

[May 2.] 6. Speech of Lord Keeper Bacon, on the appointment of Sir John Denham to succeed Baron Altham as Baron of the Exchequer. His chief duty is to maintain the King's prerogative, which is not separate from the law, but the principal part of it; to study the ancient records of the revenue; and to manage the revenue with most profit to the King, and least vexation to the subject.

[May 3.] 7. Speech of the Same to Serjeant Hutton, on his appointment to a Justiceship of the Common Pleas. Describes the office of that Court. The twelve judges should be as Solomon's twelve lions supporting the throne. Advises consultation of books, independence, impartiality, gravity, uncorruptness, &c.

May 3. Dover Castle. 8. Rich. Marsh to Lord Zouch. A Dutch ship, richly laden with bullion, specie, &c., ran on shore at Burling-gate, parish of East Dean, beyond Beachey Head; it is claimed by Payne, who holds the manor on lease. Though lately the liberty of the Cinque Ports relative to wrecks has been limited by Beachey Head, it is said to have anciently extended beyond Seaford to Rednoore, near Newhaven.

May 3. Plymouth. 9. Orders [drawn up by Sir Walter Raleigh], to be observed by the Commanders of the Fleet and Land Companies under him, bound for South America, as to the religious and orderly governance of the sailors, signals and modes of defence, in case of attack, cautions necessary on landing amongst the Indians, &c.

May 5. Newcastle. 10. Lake to Winwood. The Lords with the King agree with those in London as to the affairs of Ireland, but his Majesty insists on having the nomination of the eleven patentees. He has conferred with the Commissioners of the Borders and gentlemen of the

1617. Vol. XCII.

counties about the Borders, Lord Walden and Lord Wm. Howard being present, and has drawn up articles, to which replies are to be sent to him at Edinburgh, where he will consult the Scottish Commissioners, and settle all at a general meeting at Carlisle. A petition of the tenants of Gillesland against Lord Wm. Howard is rejected as vexatious, and some of them committed.

May 6. Bothall Castle. 11. Commissioners [for the Spanish business] with the King to the Commissioners in London. Have only just received their letters of April 30. The posts are to be reproved for tardiness. The King approves their opinions on suppression of the pirates, and an instruction for Sir John Digby is to be grounded thereon, requesting the free use of Spanish ports, and a contribution rather in money than in forces. The King asks their opinions on the time and mode of treating with France, Holland, Spain, Venice, and Savoy, for assistance. He wishes the merchants to be told that he approves their submissive carriage, and is seriously in earnest in the business.

May 6. Edinburgh. Lake to Carleton. The King anxious for conformity between the Scottish church and the English; also to obtain a better maintenance for the Scottish ministry; but success is doubtful, so many great men being interested in the tithes. The Court is magnificently entertained, but will return after the Parliament. Tobie Matthew allowed to return home, by the Duke of Buckingham's influence, and may stay if he will take the Oath of Allegiance. Sir Herbert Croft gone to France, to avoid his creditors. [*Holl. Corresp., May* 6, 1617.]

May 6. London. 12. Sir Hen. Savile to the Same. In the present want of money, it is strange to see it so wasted; out of 100,000*l.* lent so willingly, 70,000*l.* has been given away.

May 7. 13. Speech of Sir Fras. Bacon, Lord Keeper of the Great Seal, at taking his place in the Chancery Court, on the first day of term.

May 8. St. Bartholomew's. 14. Winwood to Lake. The French Ambassador has complained of the prohibition to import French wines in French bottoms, of the head money levied in the Cinque Ports, which Lord Zouch certified him was taken away, and of a tax on strangers' goods levied on a vessel from Brest. The Lord Keeper was with great pomp conveyed to Westminster Hall.

May 9. London. 15. Geo. Gerrard to Carleton. The Earldom of Buckingham entailed upon the heirs male of George, John, and Chris. Villiers. The Council are in great harmony, and feasting each other. The wife of Sir Rich. Farmer, of Oxfordshire, is in prison, for shooting a gentleman with a pistol. Lord Sheffield's wife has miscarried, and an accident has happened to Sir John Sheffield's son, the heir of that house. The Queen stays at Greenwich, and never missed one Lent sermon. The Prince and Council came to them also. The Countess of Roxburgh, her chief

VOL. XCII.

1617.

lady, is to return into Scotland, and to be succeeded by Lady Ruthven. 60,000*l.* of the last loan has been given to Scots. Quantities of plate, hangings, &c. sent to Scotland, and it was reported that the German tapestry-makers were intreated to make hangings that should look old, in order that Scotland might be thought to have had such things long ago. The Lord Keeper exceeds all his predecessors in splendour and number of servants; on his entry into office, all the Council, and all knights and gentlemen that could get horses and footcloths, attended him. Mr. Beecher is to go after Sir Thos. Edmondes [to France]. The widowed Countess of Shrewsbury is almost out of her mind, with a dread of being poisoned; her two Court sons, the Lord Chamberlain and Earl of Arundel, beg the protection of her estate, and will enjoy the fruits of it, if she do not mind.

May 9. Whitehall. 16. Order in Council on the matters at variance among the Commissioners of Sewers, viz., the drain of Clowse Cross and the outfalls of the rivers Nen and Welland; also that a new survey be made of certain lands needing draining, and Commissioners of Sewers appointed.

May 9. 17. [W. Morton] to [Winwood]. Observations on the condition of Northumberland. Ill state of the clergy; not more than twelve preaching ministers in the county. The people generally follow their masters, who are Papists or atheists. The great thieves of the county are supported by Lord Howard, of Walden, and under him by Sir Henry and Roger Wodrington and Sir John Fenwick. Entire want of justice, because these men support each other. Proposes some powerful nobleman to be appointed to overrule all, but he must be a man who will reside in the county, and keep them in with a strong hand; suggests Lord Sheffield, if he were made Lieutenant of the county. Lord Wm. Howard has so much power that he would have more partizans than the King himself.

May 10. London. 18. Chamberlain to Carleton. The new Lord Keeper went in state to Westminster, attended by more than 200 horse, the Queen and Prince sending all their followers; he made a speech in Chancery on reform in that Court, praising the earlier course of his predecessor, but excepting against his later acts; he gave his train a dinner, which cost 700*l.* On Easter Monday, the Council attended the Spittal sermon, and dined with the Mayor; but Dr. Page, the preacher, was taken up for speaking against the Spanish match. The apprentices threatened to rise on May-day, but were prevented by the measures taken to repress them. Sir Maurice Berkeley, Sir John Poultney, and Sir Drew Drury are dead. The King is at Berwick. The Archbp. of York's wife has procured the return of her son, Tobie Matthew.

May 11. Memorandum of receipt, by Thos. Hutton from Sir John Dackombe, of the survey book of the manor of Soham, co. Cambridge. [*Dom. Corresp., Dec.* 11, 1618. *Note Book, p.* 17.]

Vol. XCII.

1617.

May 12. Nuffield. 19. Dr. Geo. Carleton to Sir D. Carleton. Sends a copy of verses which he addressed to the Prince. Conversed with the Bp. of Spalato, who came to salute his Highness. He is a man well learned, but not thoroughly acquainted with the points of religion. His book is now printing, and will be in two large volumes. Bierlinck, a Dutch Papist, has answered his "Consilium Profectionis," but without casting any slight upon him.

[May 12.] [Berwick.] 20. Lake to Winwood. The Court will enter Scotland on the morrow. Certain great officers and Bishops of Scotland have been with the King, and had conference with the Bishops of Winchester and Lincoln on church matters. The English officers of state will surrender their authority this evening. Rumour that the King of Denmark, who is at sea, will visit His Majesty in Scotland.

May 14. Duchy House. 21. Memorandum by Sir John Dackombe, authorizing certain persons to be Bailiffs within the duchy of Lancaster only, for the purpose of arresting Thos. Taylor.

May 14. London. 22. Visct. Wallingford to Lake. Acknowledges two letters, one in behalf of Sir Edw. Howard, touching the Wardship of —— Rolles; the other touching Sir Geo. Hume, in the cause Baxter v. Sutton. Particulars of that cause. Prays that His Majesty will not grant any Wardship against the instructions of the Court of Wards, otherwise its revenue will decay, &c.

May 15. Suffolk House. 23. Earl of Suffolk and Sir Fulk Greville to the Same. Were much opposed by the people, in taking in ground for the enlargement of Theobalds Park; but on Lord Denney's assurance that he was inclosing nothing for himself, and that they should lose nothing, but have grounds given in exchange, they were content, and all goes on rapidly.

May 15. Suffolk House. 24. Earl of Suffolk to the Same. Lord Stafford's son, whose estate was so well preserved by the King's order, after making excuses to remain with his mother rather than come to Cambridge, proves to be a wilful Papist, and has married the daughter of an obstinate recusant. Wishes directions from the King to inquire into the case, and will meanwhile keep his hold on the estate. Sir Thos. Edmondes lately gone to France, &c.

May 15. Thursday. 25. Sir John Digby to Lord Zouch. Requests that Sir Lewis Tresham and Sir John Herbert, who with their brothers are gone to fight a duel, may be stayed if they attempt to sail from the Cinque Ports.

May 16. 26. Edw. Sherburn to [Carleton]. Private affairs. Sends a copy of the Lord Keeper's speech at the beginning of the term; he is ill with the gout, though he will not have it so called. *Incloses*,

26. I. *Purport of the Lord Keeper [Sir F. Bacon's] speech, on taking his place in the Court of Chancery. May 7.*

VOL. XCII.

1617.

May 18, Greenwich. 27. Winwood to Lake. Wishes Lady Hatton and Sir Edw. Coke would settle their differences by mediation. The bail in the cause of the Governor of Dieppe, will fall heavy upon Sir Edw. Coke. Sheriff Warton, of Yorkshire, to be called to account, relative to a proclamation against recusants [*see April* 12].

May [19]. Edinburgh. 28. Lake to Winwood. Certain towns, viz., Leicester, Leeds, Chipping Campden, and Tetbury, have prayed to be admitted as staple towns. The Attorney General having given his opinion that they may be made so at the King's pleasure, asks the Council's advice on the expediency thereof. *Incloses*,

28. I. *Sir Hen. Yelverton to Lake. His Majesty has power lawfully to erect staple towns by Letters Patent, or to change those already erected. It would save expense if several towns were included in one patent. Sir Baptist Hicks has just become a suitor for Chipping Campden. May* 13. *Annexes*,

28. II. *Petition of the Bailiff and Burgesses of Chipping Campden, co. Gloucester, to the King, for the said town to be made a staple town, the prohibition in the late proclamation of the sale of wools, except in staple towns, being very injurious to it.*

May 19. 29. [Sir John Dackombe] to Gilbert Gerard, Clerk of the Duchy [of Lancaster]. Orders him to renew Wm. Colman's lease of lands in Buckley, co. Northampton, on surrender of his former lease of the same.

May [19]. 30. Copy of the above, with variations.

May 19? 31. [The Same] to the Same. To pass a lease to Wm. Earl of Pembroke of the hundred of Apultree, parcel of the honor of Tutbury, on the cancelling of his former lease.

May 19. Duchy House. The Same to the Same. To make out a presentation of Rich. Wise to the parsonage of Defford, co. Leicester. [*Dom. Corresp., Dec.* 11, 1618. *Note Book, p.* 114.]

May 19? 32. The Same to ——. Requests him to allow the inhabitants of Glenfield to have a lease of the cow pasture there, which he threatens to take away from them.

May 19. Durham. 33. Robt. Cooper to Lake. Prays, as Steward of the Helmote Courts and Keeper of the Manor of Stockton, that his Majesty will allow him to hold the courts and preserve the manor, notwithstanding the death of the Bishop of Durham. There were riots in Durham after the Bishop was interred, but they are quieted by a report that his successor will be the Bishop of Lincoln, to whom he begs commendation.

May 20. King Street, Westminster. 34. Wm. Bp. of Exeter to the Same. The Lord Keeper refuses to dismiss the cause between Roger Bates and his [the Bishop's] son, without a public hearing.

1617. Vol. XCII.

May 20. 35. Sir David Murray to Lake. For a re-grant to himself and Mr. Russell of the sole making of brimstone and Danish copperas. Was cozened in the former grant, but the parties who persuaded him to it promise to perform their pledges, if he can get it renewed.

May 21. Duchy House. [Sir John Dackombe] to Gilbert Gerard, for renewal of a certain lease to Wm. and Elizabeth Coo, on surrender of their former lease, and payment of a fine. [*Dom. Corresp., Dec.* 11, 1618. *Note Book, p.* 18.]

May 22. Greenwich. 36. Winwood to [Lake]. The Spanish Ambassador requested in Council that the goods from a ship of Amsterdam, laden with Indian merchandise, might be sequestered, under three keys, one of which should be delivered to him. The Lord Admiral said the ship was restored to its supposed owners, under bond of 40,000*l.* to indemnify other just claimants. The Sheriff of Yorkshire was before the Lords about the proclamation against recusants [*see April* 12]. The Court of Star Chamber was held by the Lord Treasurer, on account of the illness of the Lord Keeper. Sends letters to the Grand Duke of Muscovy and King of Sweden for signature. John Merrick has well acquitted himself, in making peace between those Princes.

May 22. Doncaster. 37. Sir Thos. Cornwallis to the Same. Has undertaken a long and wearisome journey to see his gracious master, but, being taken ill by the way, cannot deliver in person the letters of the Spanish Ambassador to the King and Buckingham.

May 22. 38. Sentence of the Commissioners for Ecclesiastical Causes, depriving Meredith Mady of the rectory of Blagdon, diocese of Bath and Wells, for grave crimes and excesses. Latin.

May 22. 39. Bond of And. Cornellison Bestever, of Medenblick, Holland, and others, under penalty of 800*l.*, to indemnify Lord Zouch for restoration to Bestever, the professed owner, of the goods of a Dutch ship laden with deals, wrecked on the Godwin Sands, on payment of Lord Warden's droits, and on composition with the savers.

May 23. Suffolk House. 40. Earl of Suffolk to Lake. Many persons remain unpaid, 20,000*l.* of the City loan being yet wanting. The Council are taking a sharper course to obtain it. The great difficulty is to get money. The expenses of the Scottish journey are ill spared out of empty chests. Begs the King to sign a recommendation for a fellowship in Magdalen College, Cambridge.

May 24. 41. Bond of John Calandrini and Philip Burlamachi, under penalty of 400*l.*, to deliver to Robt. Cambell 900 Spanish ryals of Zante, for which he has paid 225*l.*

May 24. Duchy House. [Sir John Dackombe] to Gilbert Gerard. Orders him to draw out a Privy Seal for payment of twenty marks, by Sir Rich. Molyneux, Bart., Receiver General of the Duchy of Lancaster, to John Darnell, of Edmonton, for lands taken into the park at Enfield. [*Dom. Corresp., Dec.* 11, 1618. *Note Book, p.* 15.]

VOL. XCII.

1617.

May 24. London. 42. Chamberlain to Carleton. The Council remain chiefly with the Queen. The Lord Keeper has the gout; he jokes, and says he is the first beggar that has had it; he is thought too delicate to bear the burden of his place. Sir John Denham succeeds Baron Altham in the [Exchequer, and Serjeant Hutton Judge Nicholls in the Common Pleas. Sir Herbert Croft has run away to France, on account of his poverty. Lord Coke and his Lady have great wars at the Council table; she declaimed so bitterly against him that it was said Burbage could not have acted better. The Earl of Northumberland cannot divert his daughter, Lady Lucy, from Lord Hay. He allowed her to visit the Countess of Somerset, in order to have easier access to the Countess himself; she encouraged the match, and therefore he has sent his daughter away from the Tower. Lord Hay left her 2,000*l.* for her maintenance during his absence in Scotland. The old Bp. of Durham deceased. The Burghers of Edinburgh received the King in scarlet gowns, 100 of them in velvet coats and gold chains, and 300 musketeers in white satin doublets and velvet hose, and they gave him 10,000*l.* in gold. He has ordered his fruit to be sent from the Low Countries, as being nearer.

May 25? 43. Edw. Sherburn to the Same. Will do his best about the business of Eton [Provostship]; but, as nothing can be done without money, wishes to know how much he must offer for it. Sends the speeches of Judge Hutton, Serjeant Jones, and Sir John Denham. Buckingham made a Privy Councillor of Scotland. Sir Edw. Coke and his Lady reconciled by Lord Zouch and Sir Fulk Greville, although before the Council they accused one another in a grievous manner.

May 25. Kinnaird. 44. Lake to Winwood. The King has not yet chosen his eleven patentees for the plantation in Wexford. He waits to know whether the land in his gift is one fourth of the whole, or only 16,500 acres. The Court have now arrived at the farthest of their journey, as planned, but His Majesty wishes to go on to Aberdeen, thirty miles farther. The Lords would gladly spare their horses the journey.

May 25. Sunday. Dover. 45. Commissioners for the Passage at Dover to Lord Zouch. Have apprehended Jacob Coupman and Philip Palmer, as ordered. They had a pass under false names, and had taken the Oath of Allegiance, but were prevented sailing by contrary winds.

May 26. 46. Levinus Munck to Lake. To favour the bearer's suit, in which he has a collateral interest, as executor of Matthew Stilt, late of London, for whom Pat. Conley undertook a debt of 500*l.*, payable out of his suit for chantry lands.

May 26. Edinburgh. 47. News-letter describing the King's entry into Edinburgh, May 16; the procession to Holyrood House; hospitalities there; service on Sunday the 18th. On the 19th, he left for Falkland.

Vol. XCII.

1617.

May 27. Creation of John Visct. Brackley to the rank of Earl of Bridgewater. [*Grant Bk., p.* 231.]

May 27. Greenwich. 48. Winwood to Lake. The Council have deputed Lord Carew and the Chancellor of the Exchequer to report on the cause of Sir Edw. Coke and his Lady. The Londoners have not brought in the full amount of the loan. To-morrow the Barons of the Exchequer are to be examined on the true state of the recusants. On Friday Sir Edw. Coke will be brought before the Lords about the Governor of Dieppe's cause.

May 28. Hurst. 49. Rich. Harrison to Carleton. Lady Hill is inconstant about the bargain for her lease. Will do his best to forward Carleton's secret wish for the Provostship of Eton, if the old man [Sir Hen. Savile] should fall ill; but hopes he may live to see an end of the Scotchmen who are waiting for his fall.

May 28. Lambeth. 50. Archbp. of Spalato to the Same. Having left all his friends, hopes to live to see Carleton's return, that he may no longer be a stranger among strangers. Hopes to acquire friends, and learn the language, and to salute him in English at his return. His first volume is nearly through the press. Thinks the engraving of himself sent by Carleton is good. Regrets the absence of His Majesty. Italian.

May 29. Kinnaird. 51. Lake to Winwood. The King knew nothing of the proclamation made by the Sheriff of Yorkshire against recusants. The Sheriff asked His Majesty what was to be done when recusants were summoned and refused to come, to which he replied that the Judges' opinion was that, on contempt of process, they might be fetched from their houses by the Sheriff. The King has ended a quarrel between Lords Montgomery and Walden. To-morrow he makes his solemn entry into Dundee, &c. The Scottish Lords are jealous of what he may do in their Parliament.

May 31. Suffolk House. 52. Earl of Suffolk and Sir Fulk Greville to Lake. A new warrant is sent, requiring themselves and the King's learned counsel to devise means for increasing the Queen's jointure to 20,000*l.* per ann., after the life of the King. The Lords who had the warrant do not understand the business, which is very difficult, so little of the revenue remaining unassigned.

May 31. Duchy House. 53. Sir John Dackombe to Sir Nich. Salter, Woodward of Enfield Chace. To deliver three trees with tops and bushes for repairs in Enfield Chace.

May ? 54. Earl of Bridgewater to the King. To be allowed to add 240 acres of his own inclosed grounds to his park at Ashridge.

May ? 55. Petition of Jas. Douglas to the Same, for satisfaction to be made to his tenants of Maudlenfield and Castle Hill, for losses sustained by the quarries made in their fields for the fortification of Berwick.

VOL. XCII.

1617.

June ? [Sir Fras. Bacon] to Sir Robt. Floyd [Lloyd]. To move the Queen to favour a petition from the tenants of Gillingham, which is referred to the Attorney and Solicitor General. [*French Corresp., Nov.* 1616]

June 1. Whitehall. 56. Licence from the Council to Ann, wife of John Rootes, co. Hants, to go the Spa. With note that she sailed June 16, 1617.

June 2. Greenwich. 57. Winwood to [Lake]. The differences between Sir Edw. Coke and his Lady are accommodated. Sir Edw. Coke offers compensation to the French Ambassador for the error he made about the bail, but the Ambassador's demands are beyond all moderation, though the English receive many wrongs in France.

June 2. Suffolk House. 58. Earl of Suffolk and Sir Fulk Greville to the Same. Treswell has surveyed Pewsham, and thinks it would make a fine park, at little charge. The tenants are willing to compound, and the enclosure is begun. Proceedings at Hatfield Chace must be delayed, until a like survey is made, and the rights of the Crown ascertained, so as not to disturb the deer, nor stir up the people's humours too soon.

June 2. Gray's Inn. 59. Sir Hen. Yelverton to the Earl of Suffolk. Thinks Lord Zouch should have a new patent from the King for the manor of Odiham, heretofore granted to the Earl of Mar, and purchased from him by Lord Zouch.

June 3. Faversham. 60. Jo. Philpot to Lord Zouch. Requests him to stand sponsor for his son, personally or by proxy.

June 4. London. 61. Chamberlain to Carleton. Thanks for the Archbp. of Spalato's picture. The English much caressed in Scotland. So many Knights are made, that there is scarce a Yorkshire esquire left to uphold the race, and the order has descended even to the Earl of Montgomery's barber, and the husband of the Queen's laundress. Skits on Coney, a youth who is likely to be a favourite with the King. His Majesty talks of returning by the route he went, the roads in Cumberland, Lancashire, and Cheshire being impassable for coaches. The new Visct. Brackley made Earl of Bridgewater by patent. Sir Edw. Coke and his Lady reconciled; he has had to pay 4,000*l.* to the French Ambassador, for bailing a pirate. Dispute between Lord and Lady Somerset in the Tower; also between Lord Roos and his mother-in-law, Lady Lake.

June 4. Strand. 62. Geo. Gerrard to the Same. Lady Hatton accused her husband in Council of contempt against the King, for threatening her jointure, if she subscribed the articles commanded by His Majesty relative to the Hatton estates. He accuses her of taking away the plate, hangings, &c. from three of his houses, and calling him a false, treacherous villain. Lord Carew and Sir Fulk Greville, to whom the case was referred, have settled the differences. Sir Roger Owen was seized with frenzy on hearing Lord Chief Justice Hobart argue

1617. Vol. XCII.

the case of commendams, and died in a week. Our organs and church service much applauded in Scotland. Ben Jonson is going on foot to Edinburgh and back, for his profit. The Lord Keeper has only granted 400 marks to Sir Gervase Hollis, for 300*l.* detained from him twenty-five years, by an unkind brother, Lord Houghton. Lord Roos will indict his wife's family for a riot, because they tried to take her from him by force in the streets. He has settled 800*l.* a year on her, that she may conceal from his grandfather some former misconduct of his.

June 6. Grant to Sir Hen. Brown of the office of Cockmaster, for life. [*Grant Bk., p.* 231.]

June 9. 63. Lake to [Winwood]. As to Wexford, the King wishes to know whether it is one fourth or 16,000 acres that are measured out for plantation; if the latter, there will remain nothing for the church, and some of the patentees must want. A copy of Sir John Bennet's report is to be given to the Spanish Ambassador, and another to be sent to Spain, to show that the reason why the King breaks with the Archduke, and ceases commerce, is his unworthy usage of His Majesty. [*See Fland. Corresp., June* 6.]

June 9. Edinburgh. 64. Col. R. Henderson to Carleton. Content of the King and nobles with their entertainment in Scotland. His Majesty will keep his birthday, the 19th, in Edinburgh Castle. The people like the doctrines of the English Bishops and Deans, but not their ceremonies.

June 10. 65. Winwood to Lake. The Lords have adjourned for Whitsuntide. The 100,000*l.* not yet received from the Lord Mayor, &c. Knows not how it is to be repaid; the reckoning for the woods was made without the host. Will leave for Scotland July 7, but thinks Lake should return as, without a Secretary, the Lords will not like to assemble. The Lord Keeper grows weak.

June 10. London. 66. E. Reynoldes to Fras. Mills. The Lord Privy Seal displeased with the small fees allowed to his two secretaries by the clerks; advises that they have 20*l.* per ann.

June 14? 67. Lake to [Winwood]. The King has written to the Lords respecting complaints made by the Commissioners for Woods. He should know what will be the issue of that service.

June 16. Eton. 68. Sir Hen. Savile to Carleton. Sends a letter from Dr. Goodwin. Private affairs.

June 19. Edinburgh. 69. Lake to Winwood. The King is anxious to bring about the business of the Woods. He thinks it unfitting to have them cut, unless the sum intended can be furnished in four years. The Parliament in Scotland has begun, not without some heat. The Scottish Bishops are much misliked, more for their persons than their calling.

VOL. XCII.

1617.

June 21. London. 70. Chamberlain to Carleton. The French Ambassador is gone; he was little liked. Sir John Digby sets out for Spain, and takes with him a troop of notorious Catholics. Sir John Bennet has returned with small content. The University of Edinburgh has set forth good verses on the King's return thither. Exceptions taken by the Scotch at Dr. Laud, for putting on a surplice at a funeral, and at the Dean of Paul's [Valentine Carey], for commending the soul of the deceased to God, which he was forced to retract. They are so averse to English customs, that a Scottish Bishop, Dean of the King's Chapel, refused to receive the sacrament with His Majesty, kneeling. The Bp. of Rochester is Clerk of the Closet. The Countess of Arundel feasted the Lord Keeper and Judges at Highgate, after the Italian manner. The Queen is building at Greenwich, after a plan of Inigo Jones; he has a design for a new Star Chamber, which the King would fain have built, if there were money, &c.

June 24. 71. Winwood to Lake. The bearer is to acquaint His Majesty with Sir John Bennet's negociation. Sir Giles Mompesson has cleared himself before the Lords, of Mr. Treswell's accusations, &c. The moneys from the city not yet all come in. A fresh charge will have to be laid upon the Aldermen.

June 27. 72. Attorney General Yelverton to the Council. Advises that, for redress of disorder in the Spanish trade, the charter of the company being annulled in Parliament, a new charter be granted, incorporating all London merchants, not shopkeepers or retailers, who choose to enter it, and leaving the out-ports free, so as to avoid monopoly.

June 27. London. 73. Thos. Murray to Carleton. The Prince is grateful to him for sending the models, doing Capt. Erskine's business, finding out his page, and sending designs of the army and camp.

June [27?] 74. ——— to the [Same]. Proceedings of the King in Scotland. His reception at Edinburgh, and hunting at Falkland and Kinnaird. His speech in Parliament, confirming the statements of his former letter to the Council [*see Dec.* 15, 1616] as to the motives of his visit, and wishing the Scots would imitate England in worthy things, as they do in "tobacco takin, and the glorie of apparell." Questions of church government postponed to an assembly at St. Andrews. Great union between the Scotch and English. Sends theses disputed before His Majesty at Edinburgh University.

June 28. Edinburgh. 75. ——— to [Sir Fras. Bacon]. The King's speech at the opening of Parliament. He is present at the sittings daily. There are eight Bishops, eight Lords, eight Knights of Shires, and eight lay Burgesses, who all sit in one room; His Majesty removed some of the latter, as averse to his views, and appointed others. He tried, with some success, to conform church matters to those of England; also to reduce the overgrown power of the sheriffs, who are hereditary and independent; his speech at the close of Parliament. The Scots give daily feasts, to vindicate the honour of their country.

1617. Vol. XCII.

The Provost of Edinburgh entertained His Majesty. Many new Knights made, but no Peers. *Annexed is,*

75. I. *The King's speech at the opening of the Scottish Parliament. June 17. Imperfect.*

[June 29.] 76. Lake to Winwood. To-morrow the Court removes to Stirling. Lords Arundel, Pembroke, Zouch, and himself [Lake] sworn of the Scottish Council. The Parliament ended yesterday, with good content to the King. He desires to know, in the matter of Sir Giles Mompesson, whether the 25,000*l.* per ann. may be raised without spoil of his woods and forests. The Secretary of Venice has arrived, and had audience.

June 30. Edinburgh. 77. The Same to the Same. The Secretary of Venice, being lame and unable to go to Stirling, is to commit his desires to writing, and forward them.

June 30? 78. Verses addressed to the King, [by Jas. Wiseman, Schoolmaster of Linlithgow,] in the character of a lion, in a pageant prepared to receive His Majesty at the gate of that town.

June 30. Antwerp. 79. Andreas Schottus to Carleton. At request of Sir Hen. Savile, sends to Carleton letters and books for him, as he lately did a copy of the "Dialogues of Antonius Augustinus," with Gaspar Gevartius' plates. Has ordered fifty Brabantine florins to be paid to him for Savile's Chrysostom, and requests a receipt thereof. Latin.

June. 80. Walter Strickland to Lake. Requests his favour that Roger Shovin, a Frenchman, the King's crossbow maker, may have his servant, Edw. Maisters, a very able man, joined with him in his patent, instead of the reversion of it being granted to some other, as proposed.

June 30. 81. Account book of the Office of Ordnance for the past quarter.

July 3. Stirling. 82. The King to the Archbp. of Spalato. Thinks that he who has left all for Christ should be warmly received by the anointed of God, and the more the Pope fulminates against him, the more honour shall he receive. Praises the profoundness and lucidness of his work. Approves the request that the copies dispersed in his own dominions shall have the dedication to himself inserted, but not the other copies. Wishes him long life, to see the end of his excellent work. Latin.

July 3. 83. Copy of the above.

July 5. 84. Mr. Penney's accounts of money disbursed for hewing, splitting, and sawing timber, grubbing, and making saw-pits in the newly inclosed ground, carriage of timber out of the chace into the park, &c. [for the inclosure of Theobalds Park].

July 5. 85. The Attorney and Solicitor General to the Council. Their order that gentlemen residing in Essex should join with the bailiffs of

VOL. XCII.

1617.

Colchester, in deciding the controversy between the inhabitants and the Dutch congregation, is contrary to the charter of the town, which forbids others to intermeddle in their causes. Advise enforcement of the Order in Council of Dec. 15, 1616, that those of the Dutch who were anciently weavers, as well as bay and say makers, should continue so, but not the Dutch generally.

July 5. 86. Edw. Sherburn to [Carleton]. Private affairs. The Archbp. of Spalato made a Doctor at Cambridge. Carleton is on his list for a copy of his work when out. He is still well treated by the Archbp. of Canterbury. The Parliament of Scotland consents to most of the King's wishes. Several English Peers made. The Lord Keeper rises in favour.

July 5. Lambeth. 87. Archbp. of Spalato to the Same. Recommends Paul de la Ravoire, whose dealings with the Venetian resident have had no bad end, and who is well confirmed in the true religion. Has supplied him with money. Will send by him some sheets of his book. The King is to be the first to see it entire. Is going to the Universities. Italian.

July 5. London. 88. Chamberlain to the Same. Winwood's Scottish journey in suspense; the weather extremely wet, and great floods. The King has left Edinburgh, to go by the west coast of Scotland to Carlisle, whither most of the English nobles have retired. Lord Hay will try to procure the Earl of Northumberland's good will with his daughter, and the 20,000*l.* he promised her, if she would be ruled by him. The Earl is incensed with her, and with Lady Somerset, for forwarding that match. Quarrel between the Earl of Montgomery and Lord Walden, and between Winwood and the Lord Keeper. The merchants backward in the loan. Sir Walter Raleigh's fleet scattered by a storm. The Earl of Oxford wishes to raise men for Venice. Dr. Burgess preached at St. Paul's Cross. Quarrel between Sir John and Lady Packington.

July 7. Grant to Thos. Braddell of a Gunner's place in the Tower, for life. [*Grant Bk., p.* 231].

July 12. Exeter. 89. Mayor and Governor of Exeter to the Council. The merchants of Exeter have but little trade to the southern parts, but some reasonable sum will be collected, towards suppressing the pirates of Algiers and Tunis.

July 14. Suffolk House. 90. Earl of Suffolk and Sir Fulk Greville to Lake. Books are preparing for the future allowance to the Queen. Wonder that the King should expect speedy answers to things that require so much time. Have paid the huntsmen their due, but cannot pay in advance; their quarter's wages shall meet them at Carlisle. Have almost concluded everything for [the inclosure of] Theobalds Park; all is paid for, and the King will find that he pays like a King for his pleasure. Pewsham Park is in hand and will be ready by Michaelmas. Hatfield Chace will follow the year after. The Commissioners for the Woods fall short this year by one half of the 25,000*l.* undertaken, so that it is difficult to find supplies.

Vol. XCII.

1617.

July 15. St. Bartholomew's. 91. Winwood to Lake. Will relieve him at Carlisle. Begs him to deliver to the King the Archbp. of Spalato's dedication. Sir Edw. Coke and his Lady have given the Council much trouble.

July 16. Plymouth. 92. Sir Ferdinando Gorges to the Council. The merchants of Plymouth think that a small fleet will effect little against the pirates of Algiers and Tunis. Their trade is much injured by them, and still more by encroachments of the Londoners, whose proportion of 40,000*l.* towards the expedition against pirates is very inadequate, considering that they engross the commerce of the world. Sir Wm. Garway has just forbidden cotton wools, yarns, &c. to be imported by any but the Levant Company, greatly to the detriment of the town. They suggest that the best way of destroying pirates would be to make war, both by sea and land, against the Turks.

July 18. 93. Margaret Langley to Hen. Mansfield. Begs regular payment of a rent-charge of 20*l.* per ann. due to her from the lordship of Burnhall, Bishopric of Durham, which he has purchased from Sir Ralph Lawson.

July 19. Stirling. Warrant to pay to Thos. Dallam 50*l.*, in addition to the 300*l.* agreed upon, for expenses in setting up an organ in the Chapel Royal at Edinburgh. [*Sign Man.*; *vol.* VIII., *No.* 43.]

July 19. St. Barthomew's. 94. Winwood to [Lake]. Is ready for his journey, but the Council have written to request the King to allow him to remain awhile longer. Notwithstanding, if time and place be assigned him, he will go.

July 19? 95. Sir Hen. Savile to Carleton. Cannot recommend him a suitable secretary. Mr. Casaubon took the work of the Thesaurus out of his hands, two years before his death. Carleton is to reserve the 50*l.* paid him by Schottus [for the Chrysostom] for hangings, horses, &c. [*See June* 30.]

July 19. London. 96. Chamberlain to the Same. Thinks Mr. Pory a fit person for Carleton's secretary. Tobie Matthew has returned, but if he will not take the Oath of Allegiance, the King is not likely long to permit him to remain. Winwood decides, by advice of the Council, not to join His Majesty in Scotland. Lady Coke has stolen away her daughter, after Sir Edward had agreed to give her, with 20,000*l.* portion and 2,000 marks a year, to Sir John Villiers; which had he done earlier, he would have been in better plight. He took his daughter by force from a house of Lord Argyle, and gave her to Lady Compton; but she is now restored to Hatton House, on condition that Sir John Villiers has constant access to her. Coke is called in question, for breaking open the doors in search of her. Winwood defends himself in Council from a charge of faction and ambition. Old Secretary Herbert dead.

VOL. XCII.

1617.

July 20. London. 97. Alex. Williams to Carleton. The Lord Treasurer gone to Audley End, and the Chancellor to Cambridge, and thence to Warwick Castle, where he will entertain the King.

July 20. Croydon. 98. Archbp. of Spalato to Paul de la Ravoire. Greatly regrets the tumults on account of religion [in Holland]. Wishes controversial subjects were banished, under a severe penalty, from the popular preachings, and confined to the schools; both parties should establish the people on the fundamental points in which they agree, and exercise charity in those on which they differ. Has been cordially received by both Universities. Sir Hen. Savile was with him at Oxford. Italian.

July 21. 99. [Carleton] to the Archbp. of Spalato. Hopes to hear that he is as much pleased with the Universities as with the Court, which together are the compendium of all England. The specimens of his book sent are admired by all the learned. Will do his best for Paul de la Ravoire, at his recommendation. Italian.

July 22. Stirling. 100. Lake to [Winwood]. In a packet received last night were two libels against Buckingham and Lady Compton. They were delivered at Ware. That postmaster is to be examined, and reproved for daring to send a packet without a councillor's hand to it. The King will revive the custom that none send packets but the Secretaries.

July 22. Hatfield. 101. Geo. Gerrard to Carleton. Mr. Bingley, of the Exchequer, has married Sir John Grey's widow, mother of Lord Grey. A little pique has arisen between Sec. Winwood and Lord Keeper Bacon. The King is at Edinburgh, concluding his Parliament, where nothing was done but confirming stipends on preaching ministers, and establishing Justices of Peace. Half the gentleman pensioners were knighted and sent home. Lord Hay has returned from Scotland, and lives in a little house in Richmond Park, to be near Syon, where his fair mistress stays. The Earl of Oxford wants to raise 6,000 men for the States of Venice. Sir John Digby lives handsomely at his Castle of Sherborne. Sir Edw. Coke has paid 3,500*l.* as composition, for taking bail of some accused of piracy, and fears more such blows. He agrees to match his younger daughter Frances with Sir John Villiers; the match is opposed by his Lady; extraordinary proceedings in that affair; no doubt it will end in a match, and Coke be restored to the Council. Tobie Matthew returned, and lodged with the Lord Keeper.

July 22. Whitehall. 102. Edw. Sherburn to Chamberlain. Sends an account of my Lord Ambassador [Carleton's] affairs. Cannot wait upon him, being appointed to go with the Lord Keeper into the country.

July 24. 103. The Same to [Carleton]. Mr. Woodward has presented to the Queen the clock sent her by Carleton. Recommends him an efficient secretary. Difference between Sir Edw. Coke and Lady Hatton as to the bestowal of their youngest daughter; Sir Edward wishes to marry her to Sir John Villiers, whose suit is favoured by the King

July 15. St. Bartholomew's. 91. Winwood to Lake. Will relieve him at Carlisle. Begs him to deliver to the King the Archbp. of Spalato's dedication. Sir Edw. Coke and his Lady have given the Council much trouble.

July 16. Plymouth. 92. Sir Ferdinando Gorges to the Council. The merchants of Plymouth think that a small fleet will effect little against the pirates of Algiers and Tunis. Their trade is much injured by them, and still more by encroachments of the Londoners, whose proportion of 40,000*l.* towards the expedition against pirates is very inadequate, considering that they engross the commerce of the world. Sir Wm. Garway has just forbidden cotton wools, yarns, &c. to be imported by any but the Levant Company, greatly to the detriment of the town. They suggest that the best way of destroying pirates would be to make war, both by sea and land, against the Turks.

July 18. 93. Margaret Langley to Hen. Mansfield. Begs regular payment of a rent-charge of 20*l.* per ann. due to her from the lordship of Burnhall, Bishopric of Durham, which he has purchased from Sir Ralph Lawson.

July 19. Stirling. Warrant to pay to Thos. Dallam 50*l.*, in addition to the 300*l.* agreed upon, for expenses in setting up an organ in the Chapel Royal at Edinburgh. [*Sign Man., vol.* VIII., *No.* 43.]

July 19. St. Bartholomew's. 94. Winwood to [Lake]. Is ready for his journey, but the Council have written to request the King to allow him to remain awhile longer. Notwithstanding, if time and place be assigned him, he will go.

July 19? 95. Sir Hen. Savile to Carleton. Cannot recommend him a suitable secretary. Mr. Casaubon took the work of the Thesaurus out of his hands, two years before his death. Carleton is to reserve the 50*l.* paid him by Schottus [for the Chrysostom] for hangings, horses, &c. [*See June* 30.]

July 19. London. 96. Chamberlain to the Same. Thinks Mr. Pory a fit person for Carleton's secretary. Tobie Matthew has returned, but if he will not take the Oath of Allegiance, the King is not likely long to permit him to remain. Winwood decides, by advice of the Council, not to join His Majesty in Scotland. Lady Coke has stolen away her daug[hter] after Sir Edward had agreed to give her, with 20,000*l.* portio[n] ... marks a year, to Sir John Villiers; which had he ... would have been in better plight. He took his dau[ghter] ... from a house of Lord Argyle, and gave her to Lad[y] ... she is now restored to Hatton House ... Villiers has constant ... breaking open the ... in Council ... Herbert dead.

1617.

July 20. London. 97. Alex. W[illegible] Audley End an[illegible] Warwick Castle [illegible]

July 20. Croydon. 98. [illegible] the [illegible] versal [illegible] popular [illegible] s[illegible] they a[illegible] been [illegible] will [illegible]

July 21. 99. [illegible] is [illegible] [illegible] [illegible] Pa[illegible]

July 22. Stirling. 100. [illegible] two [illegible] delivered a[illegible] for [illegible] King will [illegible] Secretaries.

July 22. Hatfield. 101. Geo. Gerrard [illegible] married Sir John [illegible] has arisen between Sec. Winwood [illegible] is at Edinburgh concluding [illegible] but confirming stipend of [illegible] Justices of Peace. [illegible] and sent home. Lord [illegible] a little house in Edmonton [illegible] mistress stays. The Ear[illegible] States of Venice. Sir John [illegible] Sherborne. Sir Edw[illegible] taking bail of some [illegible] He agrees to match his [illegible] Villiers; the match [illegible] ings in that affair [illegible] restor[illegible] the [illegible] [illegible] er, [illegible] Mint, [illegible] on con- [illegible] Worker. [illegible] late Sir Rich. [illegible] as given to one [illegible] mission for the [illegible] se those of Martin [illegible] ulty in choosing the [illegible] shes to be built. Asks [illegible] n the Queen and Lady [illegible] will bring him a token

July 22. Whitehall. L[illegible] be[illegible]

July 24. [illegible] f Dr. John Griffith. Left [illegible] since at Malines, and was [illegible] crucifix, books, &c. are for [illegible] nor take the Oath of Alle-

1617. Vol. XCII.

and Buckingham, and offers with her 10,000*l.* and 1,000*l.* a year. The Lord Keeper is going to the King at Woodstock. No allowances to Ambassadors can be paid before Michaelmas. *Incloses,*

103. I. *Copy of the letter to Lord Keeper Bacon, calendared under June* 28.

July 24. London. 104. Sir John Finet to Carleton. General joy that the Electress Palatine is with child; never Princess more deserved good wishes. Projected marriage of Sir Edw. Coke's daughter with Sir John Villiers, who will have 2,000*l.* a year from Buckingham, and be left heir of his lands, as he is already of his earldom, failing his male issue. Sir Edward went cheerily to visit the Queen; the common people say he will die Lord Treasurer.

July 24. London. 105. Soames Woodward to the Same. Has waited on the Prince at Richmond, and delivered to the Queen the clock sent her by his Lordship. Dispute about it between himself and Mr. Sherburn. Hopes Carleton will not hear his enemies against him, without also hearing his vindication.

July 24. Hurst. 106. Rich. Harrison to the Same. Has spoken to Sir Hen. Savile, as of his own accord, about Carleton's succeeding him at Eton College; he is well affected towards it, and the college would favour it; advises him to get the King's promise. The Bp. of Spalato has been much pleased with the Universities.

July ? 107. Mons. de Tourval to [Fras. Windebank]. Cannot understand the letter of his man, nor devise in what language it is written. Dr. Dun's wife and infant dead. Hopes the servant whom he last recommended will suit. Is going to see the Lord Keeper, and then to Sussex with Lord Dacre. French.

July 26. 108. [Fras. Windebank] to Mons. de Tourval. Regrets that a servant provided for him by Tourval has left him hastily, on pretence that he is not competent for the service. French.

July 30. Whitehall. 109. The Council to Lord Zouch. Request his commission for restitution of bullion and goods, saved from a ship of Amsterdam, wrecked on the coast of Sussex.

July. 110. Fras. Windebank to Mr. Windsor. Reproaches him for flying from his bargain for the purchase of Clewer.

[July.] 111. Petition of Thos. Hutchins, Postmaster of Lichfield, in behalf of the posts of England, to Lord Zouch, that their arrears of pay of a year and a half may be discharged, having petitioned the King for it at Lincoln, and Lord Stanhope having promised payment in Easter week last.

July ? 112. [Sir John Dackombe] to his Brother. Has been likely to die this summer. Prays the completion of his son-in-law's estate, and his daughter's jointure, as he wishes to see his child established.

Vol. XCII.

1617. July? 113. [Sir John Dackombe] to ——. Begs that his cousin Springe may be his Under-Sheriff this year.

Vol. XCIII. August—October, 1617.

Aug. 2. St. Stephen's. 1. Sir Peter Manwood to Carleton. Sends a buck in four pasties, &c., the best venison in his power.

Aug. 4. Croydon. 2. Archbp. Abbot to Lake. Hears the King has received the title and some leaves of the Archbp. of Spalato's book. He has visited Oxford and Cambridge, and wishes to know whether His Majesty will receive him at Windsor or Woodstock.

Aug. 7. Brougham. 3. Lake to Winwood. For a warrant to be signed for the usual payments to Serjeant Bovey, who is going to France for provisions [of wine] for the King. The Lords have been busied about one Carr, of the Scotch guard, who, in his drink, threatened to kill Buckingham, as the cause of Somerset's fall.

Aug. 7? 4. Sir Robt. Aylesbury [and the Officers of the Mint] to [the Council?]. Refer to their former paper on the place of Master Worker of the Mint. The King has hitherto been deprived by him of 1,000*l.* per ann., or more, of the profits of the Mint. The specious offers now made for the place are in hopes of realizing this profit.

Aug. 7? 5. Reasons against merging the office of Master Worker of the Mint into the hands of other officers. Statement of the several duties of Master Worker, Warden, Assay Master, Auditor, and Comptroller, and of the qualifications required in a Master Worker.

Aug. 7? 6. Note of a reply to be made to the Officers of the Mint, declining their offer of saving the King 1,500*l.* per ann., on condition of his resigning into their hands the office of Master Worker. Importance of preventing fraud by continuing that office.

Aug. 8. St. Bartholomew's. 7. Winwood to [Lake]. The reversion of the late Sir Rich. Martin's office [of Master Worker] in the Mint was given to one Reynolds, with certain conditions. Sends the commission for the King to sign, but with reduced allowances, because those of Martin were in consideration of other services.

Aug. 8. London. 8. Soames Woodward to Carleton. Difficulty in choosing the kind of coach which he thinks Carleton wishes to be built. Asks further directions. Sends him letters from the Queen and Lady Roxburgh. Is coming to the Hague, and will bring him a token from the Queen.

Aug. 8. Dover. 9. Examination of Mabella, widow of Dr. John Griffith. Left England by licence in 1611; has lived since at Malines, and was coming to Bath for her health. Her crucifix, books, &c. are for her own use. Will not go to church, nor take the Oath of Allegiance.

VOL. XCIII.

1617.

[Aug. 8.] 10. Examination of Dorothy, wife of Robt. Forman, of Cheyne, Surrey. Has lived several years with her husband at Malines; but he returned to England, and sent for her. Took the Oath of Allegiance at Margate, but hesitates to take it again.

[Aug. 8.] 11. Examination of Ann, wife of Jas. Rootes, of Fairleigh, Sussex. Has been away six or seven weeks, intending to go to the Spa, but returned on account of sickness. Refuses the Oath.

[Aug. 8.] 12. Examination of Mary Greene, of Kingston, Surrey, attendant on Mrs. Rootes. Particulars of past service. Refuses the Oath.

[Aug. 8.] 13. Examination of Rich. Milles, of Marlborough, Wiltshire, servant of Mrs. Rootes. Has always been a Protestant, and will take the Oath of Allegiance.

[Aug. 9.] 14. Mayor of Faversham to Lord Zouch, Lord Warden of the Cinque Ports. Sends an examination relating to [Thos.] Bixe, who is most unworthy of favour. Complains of the minister of Faversham for associating with Bixe and other like characters. *Incloses,*

14. I. *Examination of Jas. and Alice Lambert and Oath. Dane. Heard threatening speeches used by Thos. Bixe, of Faversham, against John Philpot, Mayor of Faversham, who had imprisoned him. Aug. 9.*

Aug. 9. London. 15. Chamberlain to Carleton. Lady Winwood has made great improvements at Ditton. The King came to Carlisle on the 4th. The Earl of Arundel returned from Ireland, where he was much feasted, and made one of the Council there. The Lord Keeper is at Gorhambury. Complaints arise against him for encroachments. Lord Roos has suddenly gone away, writing that he is driven to it by Lady Lake's dealings. Sir John Digby is instructed not to hasten his return to Spain, as there is intelligence that they are treating for the marriage of the Princess with the King of Bohemia's son. The Neapolitan fleet has captured two rich Venetian gallies. Lord Hay longs for the King's return to complete his marriage; he spends all his time with his lady, giving expensive feasts; his common table in Scotland cost 300*l.* a week.

Aug. 11. 16. Lake to [Winwood]. Returns the commission for the Mint. The Guards have received 400*l.*, but are not contented, &c. Geo. Carr, who threatened Buckingham, is to be sent prisoner to London, and is to be put where he may be kept with least noise. Buckingham wishes the post at Ware to be examined, as to the man who brought the letters [libels]. The King will receive the Archbp. of Spalato at Windsor.

Aug. 12. Ashton. 17. The King to Thos. Lord Gerard, Lord President of Wales. Appoints Lord Keeper Bacon, the Earl of Buckingham, and other Knights and Gentlemen, to fill the vacancies in the Council of Wales, and orders the customary oaths to be administered to them.

VOL. XCIII.

1617.

Aug. 12. Thistleworth. 18. Sir Horace Vere to Carleton. Lady Hatton still opposes the match between her daughter and Sir Geo. Villiers, and pleads a pre-contract of the lady. The Chancellor of the Exchequer likely to marry a young widow, Lady Anderson, niece to the Earl of Buckingham, &c.

Aug. 12. Mosco Lodge. 19. John Levingston to the Same. Hopes he has persuaded his [Levingston's] mother to speak no more treason; never came in danger of the law but by her persuasion.

Aug. 12. Mosco Lodge. 20. Sir Hen. Levingston to the Same. Buckingham still continues his greatness, and is beloved of all. A Venetian Ambassador has come to complain of the King of Spain's ingratitude; his answer is deferred. The Marquis of Hamilton attended the King homeward as far as Hornby Castle, where His Majesty stayed two nights, and was royally feasted by the Earl of Cumberland. The Earl of Arundel has visited Ireland, and likes the country. Lord Gerard has feasted the King at Ashton Castle.

Aug. 12. Canterbury. 21. Sir Geo. Newman to Rich. Younge. Burling-gate, where the ship of Amsterdam was wrecked, is within the jurisdiction of the Cinque Ports. Will advise Lord Zouch to offer to hold a court for restitution of the goods. Jas. Sutton, the Dutch factor, was wrong in applying to the Admiralty Court at London, which was forward to receive the suit for recovery of the cargo.

Aug. ? 22. Petition of Joan, widow of Jeremy Garret, late Mayor of Dover, to the Commissioners for Dover Harbour, to direct Mr. Broome, executor to the late Thos. Elwood, to allow her something towards the maintenance of herself and children, from certain lime-kilns, &c., on the pier, erected by her late husband, which are in his hands, because she cannot redeem Elwood's mortgage thereon.

Aug. 12. 23. Sir Thos. Harfleet to [Lord Zouch]. Reports the result of his examination of the above petition, which is based on false premises.

Aug. 12. Ashton. Proclamation for restoring the ancient Merchant Adventurers to their former trade and privileges. Printed. [*Proc. Coll., No.* 50 *A.*]

Aug. 14. St. Bartholomew's. 24. Winwood to [Lake]. Sir Noel Caron has been with the Council. Lord Roos has suddenly left England; it is reported that he is gone to fight with Sir Art. Lake.

Aug. 16. Houghton Tower. 25. Lake to [Winwood]. The King is taking his rest after a long day's hunting. Robinson, sent thither for refusing to lend money, is as obstinate as he was in London. Has written twice or thrice to the Lord Treasurer and Chancellor of the Exchequer for money, but received no answer, at which His Majesty is much moved. The household and the huntsmen are in want, &c. Fears Lord Roos has some more desperate design than a duel afloat; his grandfather refuse him entrance to his gates; some say he has returned to town, on a letter from his wife, to settle all quarrels; parted from him on good terms at Lincoln, and has not heard from him since.

Vol. XCIII.

1617.

Aug. 17. Deal. 26. Thos. Cousant to Lord Zouch. Sends Art. Hawksworth, just landed, who has taken the Oath of Allegiance, but declares he will die a Catholic, and is a suspicious person.

Aug. 17. Croydon 27. Archbp. of Spalato to Carleton. Is greatly astonished with the Universities, which surpass all his expectations. Has been loaded with so many honours and courtesies that their very number has unfitted him to receive them properly. His opinions upon the colleges, and the neighbouring country. Has seen Minuccio's history, which is chiefly made up of what he himself has said or written to him. Sends copies of his work for Carleton, Prince Maurice, and the States. Has received a most gracious letter from the King. Italian.

Aug. 18. Enfield. 28. Geo. Gerrard to the Same. All the English Council in Scotland are made of the Scottish Council. The Earl of Arundel has gone to Ireland to buy land for his second son. Quarrel of Lord Walden with Lord Montgomery about an ape's tail. The King was royally entertained by the Earl of Cumberland, and is now at Latham, the Earl of Derby's. Lord Roos has sold his house in Charterhouse Yard, pawned his plate and jewels, and gone off secretly, with his Spanish servant Don Diego. Lady Hatton has published a contract for her daughter Frances with the Earl of Oxford, now in Venice. He sends word he will come over and see what he must do, but it is doubtful whether her fair face and the large fortune offered will induce him to risk losing the favour of the King, who urges her match with Sir John Villiers. *Incloses,*

28. I. *Obligation and oath of Frances, younger daughter of Sir Edw. Coke, to become the wife of Hen. Vere, Earl of Oxford; witnessed by her mother, Lady Hatton, July* 10.

Aug. 18. Oxford. 29. Dr. Wm. Goodwin to the Same. Details particulars of the Archbp. of Spalato's visit to the University, and his degree taking. Is preparing to preach before the King at Woodstock.

Aug. 18. 30. Will of Rich. Warde, of London, Yeoman.

Aug. 20. St. Bartholomews. 31. Winwood to [Lake]. The Lord Treasurer often said he would send 3,000*l.* to Carlisle. If the wants on the journey be so great, what will they be on the return? Has heard from Lord Roos at Calais, promising to write him the true cause of his departure.

Aug. 20. 32. Receipt by Robt. Morecroft, Alderman, of Lincoln, of part payment of the sum agreed to be given by Sir Wm. Ellis, for scouring the Foss Dike.

Aug. 21. St. Bartholomews. 33. Winwood to [Lake]. Sends a commission for His Majesty's wards in Ireland for his signature.

Aug. 22. London. Sir Art. Tyringham to Carleton. Marquis Hamilton is made an English Privy Councillor. Report that Sir Edw. Coke will be made

1617. Vol. XCIII.

Chancellor of the Exchequer; but Lady Hatton has produced a contract between the Earl of Oxford and her daughter, which will spoil her husband's game. [*Holl. Corresp., Aug.* 22.]

Aug. 22. 34. Bond by Joan Adye, of Faversham, Victualler, under penalty of 20*l.*, not to lodge nor victual persons about to cross the seas, or coming from foreign parts, without bringing them to the Commissioners of Passage.

Aug. 22. 35—54. Similar bonds by Susan Henly, Robt. Moyle, David Packer, Rich. Bayley, Rich. Cubit, John Cullyver, Wm. Gill, Adam Harbert, Rich. Quick, Ralph Payne, Abraham Neve, Thos. Michell, Lewis Michell, Stephen Harwood, Robt. Rye, John Rye, Rich. Swanton, John Trowte, Mark Trowte, and Wm. Virgo, all victuallers of Faversham. Twenty documents.

Aug. 23. 55. Similar bond by Thos. Ascue, Victualler, of Faversham.

Aug. 23. London. 56. Winwood to Lake. Sends the pardon for the poor priest. Has heard nothing of Carr, the prisoner. Lord Roos shall be sent for, when they learn what has become of him.

Aug. 23. Holyrood House. 57. Earl of Mar to the Same. This cold country affords no news, the fountain being away, of whose welfare he longs to hear.

Aug. 24. 58. Alex. Williams to Carleton. Requests him to procure for his nephew Benjamin, who wishes to travel, a place in the household of [Sir Hen. Wotton], Ambassador at Venice. Thanks for kindness to his son William at the Hague.

Aug. 26. 59. Note of the proportions to be paid by the different towns of the Cinque Ports, towards the fee of 50*l.* per ann. for Ant. Hill, Muster-master.

Aug. 26. 60, 61. Bonds by Mark Baldwin and John Daniell, of Faversham, Victuallers, similar to those of Aug. 22. Two documents.

Aug. 26. Dover Castle. 62. Licence by Lord Zouch for David Caurne, of Dieppe, to fish on the coasts of the Cinque Ports. Latin.

Aug. 26. Dover Castle. 63—67. Similar licences to Jacques Gaulett, Benest Melliot, Michael du Fresne, and to Chas. de la Mare, all of Dieppe; also a blank licence. Latin. Five papers.

Aug. 27. Ware Park. 68. Chamberlain to Carleton. Retrenchments are intended in all foreign agencies, but Beecher is to be agent in France, by favour of Buckingham. The King is in Lancashire; Lord Coke will meet him at Coventry. Carr, a Scottish gentleman, brought prisoner to London, for conspiring to kill Buckingham. Lord Walden in disgrace for quarrelling with Earl Montgomery and Lord Compton, and also for sewing dissensions between Buckingham and Marquis Hamilton, who is held the gallantest gentleman of both nations.

Vol. XCIII.

1617.

Aug. 28. Tixall. 69. Lake to [Winwood]. The King desires him to remind Sir Thos. Gardiner, of Southwark, to send some musk melons. He is much displeased that neither money nor excuse for it has yet arrived. Sir Edw. Coke has been with His Majesty, and was well received.

Aug. 28. Wells. 70. Art. Lake, Bishop of Bath and Wells, to his brother Sir Thos. Lake. Recommends Dr. Gee, the King's Chaplain, for the next residentiary at Exeter.

Aug. 28. 71, 72. Bonds by Barth. Becke and Robt. Sutton, of Faversham, Victuallers, similar to those of Aug. 22. Two documents.

Aug. 30. London. 73. Winwood to Lake. The Chancellor of the Exchequer has taken such order as he could for supply of money, and is gone forward to Court.

Aug. 31. Eton. 74. Sir Hen. Savile to Carleton. Would prefer Carleton to any one else as his successor, but the King has promised the place to Thos. Murray. Sir Hen. Wotton asked for it, but was denied. Advises Carleton how to proceed therein. Private affairs.

Sept. 1. 75. Bond of Wm. Tight, of Faversham, Sailor, similar to those of Aug. 22.

Sept. 2. London. 76. Sir Gerard Herbert to Carleton. The King is in good health, and coming to Woodstock, and thence to Windsor, for St. George's Feast. Death of old Sir John Herbert at Cardiff, and of young Lord Herbert, only son of the Earl of Montgomery. Sir Harry Portman has broken his neck. Lady Roxburgh has gone to Scotland, and Lady Ruthven succeeds her.

Sept. 3. Court at Coventry. 77. Injunction by the Attorney General against printing or selling a book compiled by the King's orders on the Oath of Allegiance, by any except Edw. Lord Morley, and his deputies, to whom the sole licence is granted therefor.

Sept. 4. 78. Bond by Hen. Danon, of Faversham, Ship Master, similar to those of Aug. 22.

Sept. 5. 79, 80. Similar bonds by Mark Pearse and Jeremy Pett, of Faversham, Shipowners. Two papers.

Sept. 7. 81. Similar bond by Geo. Southowse, of Faversham, Victualler.

Sept. 12. 82. Muster roll of the Garrison of Deal Castle.

Sept. 13. 83—85. Muster roll of the Garrison of Sandown Castle. Three copies.

Sept. 14. Windsor. 86. Winwood to Lord Stanhope, Treasurer of the Chamber. Warrant for payment of 10*l*. to Wm. Diston, for carrying letters to Brussels.

VOL. XCIII.

1617.

Sept. 15. Dover. 87. Examination of Robt. Jeneson, of Neston, near Liverpool. Went to the Spa for his health; is, and always was, a Catholic, but is not a priest. Refuses the Oath of Allegiance.

Sept. 15. Dover. 88. Examination of Fras. Edwards, Servant to the above. Particulars of his past services, and of his engagement with Mr. Jeneson, with whom he went abroad. Refuses to go to church, or take the Oath of Allegiance.

Sept. 15. 89. Note of fall of the wall at Sandgate Castle, with plan of the breach and platform.

Sept. 15. Dover. 90. Wm. Ward to Rich. Younge. Has received the old licences from Dieppe, and expects those from Treport.

Sept. 16. Eton. 91. Sir Hen. Savile to Carleton. Wishes to know the price of the hangings before they are bought. The King came back from Scotland to Windsor, and is now gone to London.

Sept. 17. Dacey. 92. Pass by the Archbp. of St. Andrews, for Edm. Canna, an Irish Franciscan, who has been prisoner in Edinburgh Castle, to go into France or Flanders, on condition of his not returning into the King's dominions without licence.

Sept. 17. 93—95. Muster rolls of the garrison of Sandgate Castle. Three copies.

Sept. 17. 96. Muster roll of the garrison of Mote's Bulwark.

Sept. 17. Croydon. 97. Archbp. Abbot to Lord Zouch. Thinks Rich. Stephenson is not the same with Thos. Stephenson, the Jesuit, who used to be with Catesby, and that, as he is willing to take the Oath of Allegiance, he should be dismissed, with a caution on his behaviour.

Sept. 19. St. Bartholomew's. [Winwood] to Sir Hen. Wotton. The Jesuit sent over by Wotton refused to confess anything, except under promise of remaining a pensioner in England, if needful for his safety; his relation when given was "so senseless and sleeveless a tale" that all were surprised at a man of learning travelling so far to tell it; he declared he had nothing further to tell, and was therefore dismissed, with 100*l.* for his journey. [*Venice Corresp., Sept.* 19.]

Sept. 25. London. 98. Sir Art. Tyringham to Carleton. Desires directions as to the greyhounds. Sir Edw. Coke recalled to the Council table. The King returned to Hampton Court.

[Sept. 27.] 99. [The Council] to the King. His revenue was proved nearly equal to his ordinary expenditure, and assignments were made on it accordingly, but his great extraordinaries have interrupted all. The 100,000*l.* to be borrowed of the Farmers of Customs, by 25,000*l.* a year, for payment of his debts, fails, because the sale of woods, from which the farmers were to be repaid, proves so injurious that they dare not pursue it. The 120,000*l.* borrowed from the City and merchant strangers, which was to have gone towards the debts, will almost all be swallowed up in extraordinaries since Christmas; viz., gifts on his departure, provision for the journey, enlarging of

1617. Vol. XCIII.

Theobalds Park, charges of Ambassadors, and the accounts from Christmas to Lady Day. The total debt is now 726,000*l.*; 114,000*l.* is provided for by sale of forests; for the rest, the ways are left to His Majesty's best judgment.

[Sept. 27.] 100. Draft of part of the above.

Sept. 29. 101. Account of certain rents from Pinchbeck, Saythorpe, Orby, &c., "which my lady hath sent unto the executores."

Sept. 29. 102. Note of abuses formerly committed in the office of Clerk of the Pipe, and now in course of reformation by Sir Hen. Crooke and Ant. Rous. [*See* 1617, *undated No.* 97.]

Sept. 30. Hampton Court. 103. Winwood to Lord Stanhope. Warrant for payment of 10*l.* to Wm. Diston. [*Same as Sept.* 14.]

Sept. 30. 104. Account Book for the Office of Ordnance for the past quarter.

Sept. 105. Account of the ordinary receipts of the Crown to Michaelmas, total 464,296*l.*, of the issues 495,844*l*, showing a deficit of 31,548*l.*, which, added to 105,481*l.* spent in extraordinaries, makes the total deficit for the year 137,029*l.* Indorsed with a comparison of the totals with those of 1616. Damaged.

Sept. 106. Rich. Clarke to the King. Having served him and the late Queen thirty years, begs for a poor Knight's place at Windsor, and payment of allowance for his place in the Star Chamber.

Sept. 107. Memorandum of butter bought above the composition, since Oct. 3, 1616; viz., for the King, 2,704lbs. at 7*d.* per lb., and for the household 9,257lbs. at 4*d.* and 5*d.*

Sept.? 108. List [by Winwood] of English scholars in foreign colleges and monasteries; with note of Fludd's writing against the proclamation.

Sept. 109. List of sums paid by the several Farmers of Customs during the past year, for the new impositions; total 16,323*l.* 10*s.* 1*d.*

Sept.? 110. The King to the Lord Mayor and Aldermen of London. To excuse Thos. Plummer from serving the office of Sheriff, on account of his deafness, the times requiring a younger and more active man.

Oct. 4. London. 111. Rich. Chamberlain to Carleton. Sends him a present of two hogsheads of English beer.

Oct. 4. 112. Sir Matt. Carew to the Same. Hopes that for the sake of their relationship and ancient friendship, he will pardon the misconduct of his son Thomas. Sir Geo. Carew's daughter Anne married against her mother's will to Rawlings, a servant of the King.

Oct. 5. Royston. 113. Petition of Sir Rich. Beaumont to the King, for a grant of Hall Lathes, part of the manor of Sandall, co. York, to be impaled with his small park adjacent. With order thereon granting the petition.

Vol. XCIII.

1617.

Oct. 6. London. 114. Sir Gerard Herbert to Carleton. Particulars of the marriage of Sir John Villiers to Frances Coke. The King, Queen, and Prince present. Lord Coke had a merry countenance. Lady Hatton was sent for, but not present, pleading sickness. She is still Alderman Bennet's prisoner. All Buckingham's and Coke's connexions were there, but not one Cecil. Sir John Digby is landed in Spain. Consolatory visit paid by the King to Lady Montgomery on the loss of her son. Sir Bernard Dewhurst dead.

Oct. 7. 115. Receipt by Thos. and Owen Manchell of certain furniture restored to them by Lady Melior Dackombe.

Oct. 8. 116. Order of Rich. Neyle, Bp. of Lincoln, releasing Chris. Wivell, his Chancellor, from his promise to refrain from concurrent jurisdiction with the Commissaries in the several archdeaconries, unless they refrain from interfering with his entire jurisdiction, during the four months of the Bishop's triennial visitation.

Oct. 8. Guildhall. 117. Act of Common Council, repealing the Act of Aug. 1, relating to the precedence of such as have been chosen Sheriff, but have fined instead of serving, as detrimental to concord amongst the City companies.

Oct. 8? 118. Note of such Citizens of the Mercers', Grocers', Drapers', Fishmongers', Haberdashers', Salters', Vintners', and Clothworkers' Companies as, being elected Sheriffs of London, have fined instead of serving; and of the precedence granted them in consequence, from 1553–1617.

Oct. 9. Westminster. 119. Patent establishing an office of General Remembrancer or Matters of Record, to avoid the expense and trouble of searches in records for charges or incumbrances on property, which impede and endanger its conveyance, where shall be kept indexes of all such records and judgments, with certain exceptions, and where abstracts of all transfers of property, wills, &c. are to be sent for entry; also appointing John Ferrour John Friend and Hen. Myles to execute the office, with certain fees. [*See Ayloffe's Introduction to Charters, p.* xxxi.]

Oct. 9. 120. List of Tenants of the Cathedral Church of Gloucester, with date and term of their leases, and amount of rental. [Indorsed by Laud.]

Oct. 9. Durham. 121. Mayor of Durham to Sir Thos. Lake. Wishes to know when the cause can be heard, concerning the vindication of the City liberties from the encroachments of the late Lord Bishop.

Oct. 9. Dover. 122. Wm. Ward to Lord Zouch. The Lode-manage Court of Dover was attempted to be held, but remonstrance was made by some men of Sandwich against their being called to the Trinity House of Dover, as they never were in former times, and are at some distance from the sea. The men of Deal also object, but they were anciently of the house.

Vol. XCIII.

1617.

Oct. 11. London. 123. Nath. Brent to Carleton. Sir John Bennet well received by the King. The Archduke's agent accuses Bennet of saying that Flanders is the receptacle of all bad humours from England; and also of saying, at the trial of an Italian mountebank for poisoning a patient, that if he had lived in the Archduke's country, he would certainly poison Englishmen. His Majesty supports him in the first, and the second is disproved. The King is angry with the Archduke, but will not show resentment, nor recall Trumbull, till he sees if the treaty for the Spanish marriage will hold. Lord Roos has run away 20,000*l.* in debt, leaving a challenge for [Sir Art.] Lake, which the King will take up when he returns. Sir Herbert Croft, ruined by his wife's excess, is travelling under the name of Nichols. The Archbp. of Spalato has printed one volume, but will take breath before another; he is disappointed that the King did not give him the vacant deanery of Westminster. An Italian Jesuit, sent over by Sir Hen. Wotton, could not obtain an audience of the King, was dissatisfied with the secretaries, and knows not what to do with himself. The Spanish Ambassador angry that Sir Hen. Marten succeeds Sir Dan. Dun as Judge of the Admiralty, Marten having ever been against him.

Oct. 11. London. 124. Chamberlain to the Same. Death of Sir Thos. Haynes, Lord Gerard President of Wales, Lord Willoughby of Parham, Sir Wm. Wray, Sir Ant. Mildmay, the Earl of Montgomery's son, and Lady Abergavenny. Sir Dan. Dun succeeded in the Arches by Sir Geo. Newman. Crowds of people went to welcome the King on his return from Scotland. Lady Coke's animosity against her husband, &c. has caused her to be accused before the Council, but she would ruin herself to overthrow him. Marquis Hamilton and the Bishop of Winchester sworn of the Council. Lord Rich is in perplexity because his wife has settled her property from him. Many new Knights made. The Lord Keeper told the Queen that his difference with the Secretary was because both are proud. The King has composed it, and declared that Winwood had never spoken to him to any man's prejudice, &c.

Oct. 12. Royston. 125. Thos. Wilson to the Constables of Sandon, Kelshall, and other towns in Hertfordshire. The King's express command is that they give notice to occupants of arable land not to plough their lands in narrow ridges, nor to suffer swine to go abroad unringed and root holes, &c., to the endangering of His Majesty and the Prince in hawking and hunting; they are also to take down the high bounds between lands, which hinder His Majesty's ready passage.

Oct. 13. 126, 127. Paul Isaacson's Bill of Painters' Work done at Shawford and Gorambury. Two papers.

Oct. 16. London. 128. Archbp. of Spalato to [Carleton]. Thanks for his presentation of his books. Went to see the King at Windsor; the Archbp. of Canterbury took him to [Eton] College, where Sir Hen. and Lady

1617. VOL. XCIII.

Savile loaded him with caresses. Still remains at Lambeth, well treated, but without power over his own movements. The King and Archbishop promise to gratify him as soon as possible.

Oct. 18. London. 129. Chamberlain to Carleton. Tobie Matthew pays night visits to the Spanish Ambassador. Sir John Digby handsomely received in Spain, and in great hopes of success. Captain Baylie, who stole away from Raleigh, gives out that he has turned pirate. The Queen is ill; she is generally wished well. Lady Killegrew, wife of the Bishop of Derry, ill. Mrs. Bridges, alias Lady Kennedy, dead. Sir Wm. Bird made Dean of the Arches, the reversioner, Sir Geo. Newman, being made Judge of the Court of Audience. Sir Edw. Villiers succeeds Sir Rich. Martin as Master of the Mint. Sir Fras. Vere has chosen Palavacino for his son's tutor, &c. Sir Herbert Croft turned-Papist.

Oct. 18. 130. Sir John Dackombe to ———. In favour of David Bourgh, servant to the Earl of Salisbury.

Oct. [20]. 131. Thos. Wilson to the King. States his services both abroad and at home, and his qualifications for the place of Master of Requests, to which he has been three times named, and the place promised. Solicits now to succeed Sir Dan. Dun.

Oct. 20? 132. The Same to Buckingham. To the same purport.

Oct. 20. Thistleworth. 133. Sir Horace Vere to Carleton. Sir Edw. Coke is to be made Baron Stoke. The Lord Keeper was in great danger of disgrace, but has made his peace with his opposers.

Oct. 20. Hinchinbrook. 134. Thos. Murray to the Same. The Prince promises to sit for his portrait for Carleton. No certainty of a Parliament. No course yet taken for paying the King's debts and settling his estate.

Oct. 21. Madrid. Fras. Cottington to [Winwood]. Sir Walter Raleigh landed by night at Lanzarote, and the people, thinking them Turks, killed fifteen, but in the morning, finding they were English, gave them leave to have water. [*Extract, Dom. Corresp., Dec.* 18, 1618,]

Oct. 22. Nuffeld. 135. Dr. Geo. Carleton to Sir Dud. Carleton. Lord Coke is tossed up and down like a tennis-ball. Lord Keeper Bacon is in slippery places, and self-interest prevails. The poor church in no better condition; preferments sold to the unworthy, and studious men scouted. Has written a treatise in refutation of Arminius, which is approved. Asks the truth of a report that, as Arminius was writing a book, his right hand rotted, and so he died. Wishes to be acquainted with Hugo Grotius, a civilian and poet of name in those parts. Talks of altering his poems, and dedicating them to the Prince.

Oct. 22? 136. Paper indorsed [by Laud], "Questions given to be disputed at Exeter College, Oxford, by Dr. Prideaux, Rector, at that time appointed to answer Barclay's Parenesis," upon points in the Arminian controversy.

1617. Vol. XCIII.

Oct. 22. Eton. 137. Sir Hen. Savile to Carleton. Will try to be excused giving Thos. Murray a certain place [the reversion of the Provostship]; will perform Carleton's request as well as he can; and thinks the Earl of Arundel a good man to be employed therein. Private affairs.

Oct. 23. 138. Sir John Dackombe to Sir Wm. Garway, Sir John Wolstenholme, and Sir Nich. Salter. Requests them to employ his wife's brother in the customs.

Oct. 23. Charing Cross. 139. Sec. [Lake ?] to the Vice Chancellor of Oxford. The King wishes the Prebend of Shipton and the Mastership of Ewelme to be annexed to the Professorships of Law and Physic, for their better maintenance.

Oct. 24. Grant, in reversion, to Thos. Brinley, of an Auditorship in the Exchequer, for life. [*Grant Bk., p.* 229.]

Oct. 25. London. 140. Chamberlain to Carleton. The King is at Hinchinbrook. The Queen still indisposed; her physicians fear an ill habit of body. Sec. Winwood has a low fever, and is much vexed with the perpetual visits of great folks. Dr. Wilkinson, the King's Chaplain, and author of several sermons, dead. Sir Wm. Cavendish has a son, which will be 100,000*l.* in his way, if his father keep his word.

Oct. 27. Dover. 141. Fras. Raworth to Rich. Younge. Has received the Lord Warden's orders for stay of Sir Peter Temple and Mr. Harris. The Archbp. of Canterbury has given Mr. Gray the parsonage of Deal, by means whereof St. Mary's parish, Dover, will be void of a preacher; recommends Mr. Reading for it.

Oct. 27. 142. Sir Edwin Sandys, Sir Roger Nevinson, Dr. Fras. Rogers, and Robt. Broome, Commissioners, to Lord Zouch. Find no sufficient ground for the petty custom or scavage in the port of Dover of 2*d.* in the pound upon strangers' goods, claimed by Emanuel Alley, the Water Bailiff.

Oct. 27. Dover. 143. The Same [Robt. Broome omitted] to the Same. To the same effect.

Oct. 27. Thistleworth. 144. Sir Horace Vere to Carleton. Sec. Winwood dangerously ill of a burning ague. The President of Wales is dead, and Lord Compton is to succeed him. Sir Edw. Villiers made Mint-master.

Oct. 27. 145. Notes of moneys received out of Cornwall for the use of the Prince [by Edw. Nicholas ?].

[Oct. 27.] 146. Digest of the above.

Oct. 28. York House. 147. Edw. Sherburn to Carleton. Sir Horace Vere has written and spoken to the Earl of Arundel, who promises his influence to obtain the Secretaryship for Carleton. Asks what steps he shall take upon it.

Oct. 28. London. 148. Nat. Darell to the Same. Sec. Winwood has been ill a week, and much visited by the nobility; he is speechless, and seemingly dying.

Oct. 28. Hanworth. 149. Sir Ben. Rudyard to the Same. Death of Sec. Winwood. The Lord Chamberlain sent post to Royston, to beg the King would

VOL. XCIII.

1617.

not hastily dispose of the place, thinking Carleton the fittest man for it. Hopes, as he is favoured by the Chamberlain, who is on good terms with Buckingham, he may succeed, if he can make his own way with the favourite.

Oct. 28. Lambeth. 150. Archbp. of Spalato to Carleton. A Milanese pretended to discover a conspiracy between France and Spain, to murder the King and Prince, and take possession of England. He is dismissed, with leave to return home, but he dares not return, after having slandered two such Princes.

Oct. 28. Plymouth. 151. Mayor of Plymouth to Lake. •Capt. Baylie refuses to pay for Ant. Wilkins and Rich. Brestwood to come up to London by horse. Will hasten both him and them to town, to give information. No other ship has come from Sir Walter Raleigh. News that Turkish pirates have taken Porto Santo and carried away the people.

Oct. 29. London. 152. Rich. Harrison to Carleton. The business of Eton College stopped by the death of Sec. Winwood. Hopes the King will appoint him [Carleton] to succeed him.

Oct. 29. Eton. 153. Sir Hen. Savile to the Same. Hopes to be the first to send tidings of Sec. Winwood's death. Thinks Carleton a fit man to succeed him, and the Earl of Arundel a suitable instrument to work for his promotion. Hopes the States would favour it.

Oct. 30. London. 154. Sir Peter Manwood to the Same. Sends him such a doe as the season affords.

Oct. 30. London. 155. Nath. Brent to [the Same]. Death of Sec. Winwood after a fever of nine days. He is much lamented. Particulars of his will. The Archbp. of Canterbury is Carleton's friend, and would have him take Winwood's place.

Oct. 30. 156. Note of moneys paid to the Treasurer of the Navy without orders, since July 1613.

Oct. 30. Receipt by John Banks, of the Strand, coachmaker, from Sir John Dackombe, of 40*l.*, in discharge of all debts. [*Dom. Corresp., Dec.* 11, 1618. *Note Book, p.* 17.]

Oct. 31. London. 157. Matthew de Quester to Carleton. Transmits a packet from Sec. Lake. The King, Queen, and Prince came to Theobalds on the 30th.

Oct. 31. London. 158. Chamberlain to the Same. Particulars of the disease, death, post mortem, and will of Sec. Winwood. Mayerne generally unfortunate with his patients. The King and Buckingham both wrote Winwood kind letters, begging him to take rest. He has fallen when in high favour. He was privately buried. The King has granted his Lady the wardship of her eldest son. Candidates for his place. Wishes Lady Hatton would recommend Carleton. His Majesty and Buckingham court her much, that she may give her daughter a large portion. The Bp. of Ely denies having written in favour of the Arminians. Sir John Hungerford's son fined and imprisoned for challenging Sir Geo. Marshall.

VOL. XCIII.

1617.

Oct. 31. Whitehall. 159. Abraham Williams to Carleton. Death of Sec. Winwood from fever; it is attributed to Dr. Mayerne's letting him blood too soon. Sir Hen. Wotton, Sir Thos. Edmondes, Sir Robt. Naunton, Carleton, and Sir Thos. Lake spoken of as successors.

Oct. 31. Whitehall. 160. Sir Fras. Blundell to the Same. Death of Sec. Winwood, after a week's illess, owing to the bad treatment of Dr. Mayerne.

Oct. 31. London. Sir Edw. Cecil to the Same. The death of the Secretary has staggered his sister Hatton's hopes of winning her cause, Lord Coke being proud of the favourite's support. Edmondes, Fulk Greville, May, and Naunton, &c. spoken of to succeed him; but Naunton most likely, being Buckingham's creature. [*Holl. Corresp., Oct.* 31.]

Oct. ? 161. The King to the Dean and Chapter of Gloucester. To suspend their statute for keeping their audit and choosing their officers on the last day of November, during the time Dr. Laud remains their Dean; his attendance on the King, and his presidency of [St. John's] College, Oxford, rendering the precise time inconvenient to him.

VOL. XCIV. NOVEMBER, DECEMBER, 1617.

Nov. 1. 1. Bond by Dumanick Mounsee, Shipowner, of Faversham, similar to those of Aug. 22.

Nov. 2. St. James's. 2. Thos. Murray to Carleton. Wishes he might succeed Winwood. Advises him not to neglect Buckingham, who will much influence the business. Recommends Lieut. David Pitcairn, who is a favourite with the Prince.

Nov. 3. Hague. 3. Carleton to Chamberlain. Several friends wish him to have the place of Sec. Winwood. The Lord Chamberlain and Earl of Arundel favour him. Has written to Buckingham about it. Would be glad not to end his few days in perpetual pilgrimage.

Nov. 3. Dover. 4. Wm. Ward to Rich. Younge. Requests that one of the [fishing] passes for Mdme. de Guise may be made in Wm. Perry's name, and that the passes may all be sent to himself, to detain till he can obtain repayment of moneys lent to the parties.

Nov. 3. Westminster. Grant to Ralph Read, of Tarporley, co. Chester, of pardon for buying a stolen coat. Latin. [*Sign Man., vol.* VIII., *No.* 44.]

Nov. 4. 5. [The King] to Sir Wm. Craven. Thanks for his care of Lady Eliz. Coke, whilst in his charge.

Nov. 4. Wellingore. 6. Alice Bate to [Dr. Lambe ?]. Sends the rent of Colby Parsonage, due by her late husband, Chris. Bate. Solicits protection against his partner, Lawrence Codinton's attempts to wrong her in the lease.

VOL. XCIV.

1617.
Nov. 4.
Madrid.
Sir Fras. Cottington to [Winwood]. The great complaint against Sir Walter Raleigh seems only to be for taking some victuals from a few Frenchmen. [*Extract, Dom. Corresp., Dec.* 18, 1618.]

Nov. 4.
London.
Sir Gerard Herbert to Carleton. The news of Sec. Winwood's death brought to the King to Huntingdon, for he could hardly believe it. Audience given to the Venetian Ambassador. Buckingham and others went to Sir Wm. Craven's, to release Lady Hatton, and left her at Exeter House with her father. She promises compliance. Lord Hay is to marry his fair mistress at the Wardrobe. The King going to Theobalds and Royston, the Queen to Denmark House. [*Holl. Corresp., Nov.* 4.]

Nov. 4.
Westminster.
Royal assent for Dr. Geo. Montaigne, elected Bp. of Lincoln. Latin. [*Sign Man., vol.* VIII., *No.* 45.]

Nov. 4?
7. Remembrance that the grant of the Keepership of Whittlewood Forest, co. Northampton, is assigned to Lord Compton by Lord Gerard.

Nov. 4.
Westminster.
Grant to Lord Compton and Sir Spencer Compton, his son, in reversion after Lord Gerard, of the office of Master Forester, &c. of Whittlewood Forest, co. Northampton; a former grant of the surrender thereof by Lord Gerard to Lord Compton being stayed as illegal. Latin. [*Sign Man., vol.* VIII., *No.* 46.]

Nov. 4.
Westminster.
Grant to Ralph Smith of a Yeoman Warder's place in the Tower. [*Ibid., No.* 47.]

Nov. 4.
Westminster.
Warrant to pay to Geo. Digby 550*l.*, for race-horses for the King. [*Ibid., No.* 48.]

Nov. 4.
Westminster.
Congé d'elire for the Dean and Chapter of Hereford. Latin. [*Ibid., No.* 49.]

Nov. 5.
Westminster.
Warrant to appoint Thos. Boorne and Hugh Richardson Searchers of all baltery and brass works imported. [*Ibid., No.* 50.]

Nov. [5].
Westminster.
8. Particulars of a patent granted to the Same, for examining all baltery, bashrones, kettles, and other manufactures of brass imported: those made of good metal to be stamped; those of bad, slit at the edge.

Nov. 5.
9. Bond of Hum. Clerk, of London; Sir Simon Clerk, of Salford, Warwick; Barth. and John Osborne, of London, under penalty of 1,000 marks, to indemnify Lord Zouch for delivering up a ship which Hum. Clerk, the owner, caused to be arrested in Dover Harbour, because of the loose conduct of Hen. Gayney, the captain.

Nov. 5.
Westminster.
Licence to Geo. Evelyn to grant to the Vicar of Caterham, co. Surrey, and his successors, for their better maintenance, his moiety

Vol. XCIV.

1617.

of the tithe corn in the said parish, notwithstanding the Statute of Mortmain. Latin. [*Sign Man., vol.* VIII., *No.* 51.]

Nov. 6. Westminster. Privy Seal Warrant for payments not exceeding 1,400*l.* per ann. to Sir Thos. Lake, for secret services. [*Ibid., No.* 52.]

Nov. 7. Doctor's Commons. 10. Sir Hen. Marten, Judge of the Admiralty, to Lake. A process was issued out of the Admiralty Court, touching the Cerf Volant, brought out of Brittany by Sir John Ferne, but is not executed.

Nov. 7. York House. 11. Edw. Sherburn to [Carleton]. Many candidates for the Secretaryship, but Sir Robt. Naunton most spoken of, as favoured by Buckingham, though Lord Houghton has offered 10,000*l.* for it, and neither honour nor place is to be achieved but by means of the Lady *Pecunia.* Sec. Lake holds the staff at both ends, having the double allowances, and will keep it as long as he can. Has distributed the pictures and other presents according to order. Fears Carleton's request for licence to export [beer], in compensation for the tardy payment of his allowance, cannot be granted. Sir Edw. Coke does not advance, nor will without his wife's influence, which she will not use for his honour. The King, Prince, Buckingham, and many others present at the marriage feast of Lord Hay and the Earl of Northumberland's daughter.

Nov. 8. London. 12. Chamberlain to the Same. Lady Hatton might have prevailed on Carleton's behalf, had she set her whole strength to it; but the King says he never was so well served as when he was his own secretary, and has delivered Winwood's Seals to Buckingham. Sir Thos. Lake has the lodging at Court, and the diet. Buckingham and others, in twelve coaches, went to fetch Lady Hatton from Sir Wm. Craven's, and brought her to her father's, at Cecil House, Strand. She has been to Court, and the King reconciled her to the Queen, to Lady Compton, and to her daughter, and will do, it is hoped, to her husband, who is restored to the Council table. Young [Hen.] King, the Bp. of London's eldest son, preached his first sermon at St. Paul's Cross; he is not so eloquent as his father. Sir John Merrick returned from Muscovy. An Ambassador from thence has come with him, who has brought the King presents of white hawks, live sables, &c.

Nov. 8. London. 13. Sir Gerard Herbert to the Same. The Bp. of Winchester feasted the nobles at Winchester House. Account of Lord Hay's marriage feast. The bride knelt whilst the King drank her health, and she drank his. The banquet cost 1,000*l.* The King gave 10,000*l.* to Lord Hay for his wedding charges. He has dined at Hatton House, and gone on to Theobalds. Sir Hen. Rich made Captain of the Guard.

Nov. 8. Duchy House. 14. Sir John Dackombe to Wm. Earl of Derby. Gives him notice to appear in the Duchy Court to answer a bill preferred against him by Peter L'Hermite.

VOL. XCIV.

1617.
Nov. 8. London. 15. John Pory to Carleton. Details of the great feast given by Lady Eliz. Hatton to the King and Prince. Lord Coke alone was absent. Lady Hatton with her daughter, Lady Villiers, stood behind the King at dinner. He knighted four of her friends, gave her half-a-dozen kisses on leaving, and was very merry.

Nov. 9. Hague. 16. Carleton to Chamberlain. General regret on Winwood's death; no loss lately has been more felt. Enumerates the parties who favour his own promotion, but has little hope, because he is a stranger to the King. News from Italy.

Nov. [10?] 17. Sir Matthew Carew to Carleton. Hopes Carleton may succeed according to his friends' expectation. Begs him not to be wanting to himself.

Nov. 10. Lambeth. 18. Archbp. Abbot to Lord Zouch. To order Mabella Griffith and other women, imprisoned at Dover for refusing the Oath of Allegiance, to be brought up to London at their own charges, for their more ready maintenance.

Nov. 10. Hinton. 19. Sir [?] John Pawlett to [Carleton]. Thanks for his presents. Is tied to this dull dirty place by the Sheriffwick.

Nov. 10. London. 20. Sir Art. Tyringham to the Same. The King gone to Theobalds. Sir Thos. Edmondes has refused the Secretaryship. Much talk of Sir Edw. Coke's Lady preventing his being made a Baron.

Nov. 10. Oxford. 21. Matthew Nicholas to Edw. Nicholas. Asks money for the payment of debts due by the former to Oriel College, for rent, &c.

Nov. 10. Dover. 22. Mayor and Jurats of Dover to Lord Zouch. The precedents of the Water Bailiffs of Rye, on which Mr. Alley supports his claim to certain customs on strangers in the port of Dover, are unfounded, and the documents he produces surreptitious. His claim would be very injurious to the interests of the town and harbour, by hindering the trading of strangers. *Inclose,*

22. I. *Note of the duties which the Water Bailiff of Dover takes to his own use, without account.*

[Nov. ?] 23. Sir John Peyton to [Carleton]. Sentence in the Star Chamber on Mr. Hungerford, for challenging Sir Geo. Marshall. Lady Hatton has entertained the King, and at his request settled 2,500*l.* per ann. on Lady Villiers, but she refused to be reconciled to Sir Edw. Coke, saying if he came in at one door she would go out at another. Capt. Baylie still affirms his report of Sir W. Raleigh, but his own men dispute it, and no other complaint is made; he is committed to the Gatehouse. The Muscovite Ambassador solemnly received at Court; he brings white furs, falcons, &c., worth 10,000*l.* Sir Thos. Edmondes has returned, but Buckingham has the Seals, and

VOL. XCIV.

1617.

opens the foreign packets. The King is resolved to reduce his expenses of housekeeping from 72,000*l.* to 50,000*l.* The Duke of Lenox has obtained a grant of a new enrolment, worth 10,000*l.* a year. No tidings of Lord Oxford's return, &c.

[Nov.] London. 24. Sir Horace Vere to Carleton. Sec. Lake has the allowance of Winwood's table, and moneys for intelligence. Sir Robt. Naunton spoken of as his successor, but it is said that Buckingham will hold the place as Somerset did. Lady Hatton feasted the King and Queen at Exeter House. Sir Edw. Coke could not be admitted a guest, though the King desired it, &c.

Nov. 12. Charing Cross. 25. [Sir Thos. Lake] to the Treasurer and Chancellor of the Exchequer. They are to join himself, the Lord Keeper, and Lord Wallingford, in considering a plan for the respite of homage for the King's benefit.

Nov. ? 26. Geo. Lord Carew, Master, and the Officers of Ordnance, to the King. Present an account of the Ordnance stores in the Tower, showing their deficient state. Pray the appointment of certain of the Council, to direct supply thereof. *Annexing,*

26. I. *Inventory of ordnance, arms, carriages, &c., in the Ordnance stores in the Tower.*

26. II. *Names of members of the Council appointed Commissioners for the Ordnance. Nov.* 12, 1617.

Nov. 12. Receipt by Dr. Geo. Montaigne, Master of the Savoy, from Sir John Dackombe, of all rents and payments due for the houses, lodgings, &c. which he holds in the Savoy. [*Dom. Corresp., Dec.* 11, 1618 ; *Note Bk., p.* 21.]

Nov. 13. 27. Wm. Harbyn to Edw. Nicholas. Requests him to send 37*l.* 10*s.* of his money remaining in Nicholas' hands; with note of receipt of the same by Hen. Butt.

Nov. 13. Westminster. Warrant to pay to persons appointed by the Queen, 250*l.* for the repairs ordered by her at the Lodge and Park of Byfleet, co. Surrey. [*Sign Man., vol.* VIII., *No.* 54.]

Nov. 13. Westminster. Grant to Wm. and Rich. Dawe, in reversion after Simeon Steward, of the office of engrossing licences and protections to gather alms for casual misfortunes. [*Ibid., No.* 55.]

Nov. 13. Westminster. Grant to John Wood, of Tintagell, Cornwall, of assignment of the bond of John Langford, of Axworth, Devon, for 400*l.*, Wood having secured the payment to His Majesty. [*Ibid., No.* 56.]

Nov. 14. Westminster. Warrant to pay 50*l.* to Dr. Art. Duck, for his charges into Scotland, and 100*l.* to Rich. Seymer, as a free gift. [*Ibid., No.* 56 A.]

Vol. XCIV.

1617.

Nov. 14. Westminster. Licence to Sir Wm. Barnes and Hugh Lydyard, to keep a weekly market and two yearly fairs at Woolwich, at the request and for the benefit of the inhabitants. Latin. [*Sign Man., vol.* VIII., *No.* 57.]

Nov. 14. Westminster. Grant to Hugh May, Groom of the Chamber, and Adrian May, his nephew, on surrender of Sir Hen. Neville, of the Keepership of Mote Park, in Windsor Forest. Latin. [*Ibid., No.* 58.]

Nov. 14. Westminster. Commission of Lieutenancy to Rich. Neyle, Bishop of Durham, of the bishopric and county of Durham. [*Ibid., No.* 59.]

Nov. 14. London. 28. Sir Gerard Herbert to Carleton. Audience of the Russian Ambassadors, their rich attire, strange demeanour, presents, &c. The King is most pleased with the hawks. They have come to renew the trade. The King is gone to Theobalds, the Queen is at Denmark House, &c.

Nov. 14. London. 29. Nath. Brent to [the Same]. Lady Hatton, who is in great favour, wishes Sir Thos. Edmondes to be Secretary, that Sir Gilbert Houghton may have his White Staff. Dares not write what Lake and his friends have offered, for him to have the sole Secretaryship. Sir John Digby's Secretary has brought despatches, and the King speaks of the Spanish match as likely to succeed. Sir Edw. Coke has redeemed the land he gave his daughter for 30,000*l.*, and now all the court is made to Lady Hatton, who has 3,000*l.* a year in land to bestow. Buckingham visited her eight times in ten days. Coke lives in the Temple, and sends for his diet to goodman Gibbes, a slovenly cook. The Bp. of Hereford deceased; the Bp. of Llandaff promoted to that see, and Dr. Carleton to Llandaff.

Nov. 15. London. 30. Chamberlain to the Same. During Winwood's last illness, had a conversation with him about Carleton. He took ill Carleton's letter of advice to him, to be more patient and mild with applicants. Lady Hatton tries to gain the Secretaryship for Lord Houghton or Hollis, whom her husband cannot endure. Reception of the Muscovy Ambassadors; their presents to the King, of furs, worth 6,000*l.*, rich dresses, weapons, &c., were carried in public. Lady Compton and her children much noticed by His Majesty; she courts Lady Hatton, who is unwilling to give as freely as expected. Talk of Buckingham's resigning the Mastership of the Horse to Marquis Hamilton, &c.

Nov. 15. Westminster. Presentation of John Hildyard to the rectory of St. Mary-by-Southampton, diocese of Winchester, in place of Dr. Robt. Reynolds, deceased. Latin. [*Sign Man., vol.* VIII., *No.* 60.]

Nov. 15. Westminster. Presentation of Simon Jucks, King's Chaplain, to the rectory of St. Olave, co. Surrey, Latin. [*Ibid., No.* 61.]

Nov. 16. Westminster. Warrant to pay 700 crowns to Sir Walter Raleigh, as a bounty for new building the good ship called the Destiny of London, of the

1617. VOL. XCIV.

burthen of 700 tons. [*There is an erasure before the name, sufficient for the words "our welbeloved subject," usual in grants of like nature.*] [*Sign Man., vol.* VIII., *No.* 62.]

Nov. 16. Westminster. Commission of Lieutenancy to Lord Compton, Lord President of Wales, for South Wales, North Wales—Glamorgan and Monmouth only excepted— also for the Marches, and the counties of Worcester, Hereford, and Salop, being the counties where the Presidents have usually been Lieutenants. [*Ibid., No.* 63.]

Nov. 17. 31. Cancelled bond from Sir John Dackombe to Wm. Earl of Salisbury, for repayment to him of 2,000*l.* Latin.

Nov. 17, Westminster. Warrant to pay to John Griffin, of Orford, Suffolk, Thos. Silvester, of Ipswich, and others, 2,022 crowns, the usual bounty on seven new built ships. [*Sign Man., vol.* VIII., *No.* 64.]

Nov. 18. Westminster. Grant of pardon to John Smith, of Burnley, Lancashire, for burglary, and to Wm. Brook, of Colne, Lancashire, for horse-stealing, being their first offences. Latin. [*Ibid., No.* 65.]

Nov. 18. Westminster. Congé d'elire to the Archdeacon and Chapter of Landaff. Latin. [*Ibid., No.* 66.]

Nov. 18. Westminster. Grant to Emma Reyney, of Coppull, and Elizabeth Ramsbothom, of Holcombe, Lancashire, of pardon for petty larcenies. [*Ibid., No.* 67.]

Nov. 18. Westminster. Grant to Geo. Hayward, of Sutton, Lancashire, of pardon for housebreaking and murder, the evidence being defective. Latin. [*Ibid., No.* 68.]

Nov. 19. Westminster. Warrant to pay to Geo. Chambers 1,000*l.*, for the like sum disbursed by him for the Lord of Lindores, deceased. [*Ibid., No.* 69.]

Nov. 19. Westminster. Warrant to Sam. Atkinson to dig for treasure-trove in the grounds of Widow Cock, in St. Hippolitus, near Hitchin, co. Herts; the treasure to come to the King's use. [*Ibid., No.* 70.]

Nov. 19. Westminster. Warrant for the erection of an office of Auditor, for casting up accounts between suitors in the Court of Chancery; and grant thereof for life to Ralph Handson and Wm. Richardson. Latin. [*Ibid., No.* 71.]

Nov. 19. Westminster. Re-grant to Sir Chas. Howard of powers for the preservation and better ordering of the deer and game in Windsor Forest, whereof he is Verderer. Latin. [*Ibid., No.* 72.]

Nov. 19. 32. Bond of Sir John Dackombe and Peter Van Lore, under penalty of 8,000*l.*, to pay 4,000*l.* to Wm. Earl of Salisbury on May 20.

Nov. 20. Thistleworth. 33. Sir Horace Vere to Carleton. Aspirants to the Secretary's place, Sir Thos. Edmondes, Sir John Bennet, Sir Hum. May, &c.

VOL. XCIV.

1617.

Nov. 20. Westminster. Warrant for payment of certain sums to Geo. Digby, to repair into Italy, to make provision of great horses for the King's service. [*Sign Man., vol.* VIII., *No.* 72 *A*.]

Nov. 20. Westminster. Re-grant to Jas. Lord Hay, Baron of Sawley, of concealed or encroached lands, value 200*l.* per ann. [*Ibid., No.* 73.]

Nov. 20. Grant to Fras. Beaumont of the Mastership of Sutton Hospital, for life. [*Grant Bk., p.* 231.]

Nov. 21. Licence to Thos. Anlaby to hold the Court in the manors of Etton, Cotgarth, and others, co. York. [*Ibid., p.* 229.]

Nov. 21. Westminster. Royal assent for Fras. Godwin, late Bp. of Llandaff, elected to the Bishopric of Hereford. Latin. [*Sign Man., vol.* VIII., *No.* 74.]

Nov. 22? 34. Aquila Wykes [Keeper of the Gatehouse] to Rich. Younge. Has received the prisoners, Mabella Griffith, Dorothy Forman, Ann Rootes, and Mary Greene. [*See Nov.* 10.]

Nov. 22. 35. Decree on a cause in the Court of the Duchy of Lancaster, between the Warden and Fellows of Manchester College and Sir Edw. Trafford, in reference to the Stewardship of the College and its fees. It is granted in favour of the plaintiffs, but with a proviso that they submit to the direction of the Court, in such stewards' leases as are already made.

Nov. 22. Cornbury Park. 36. Hen. Lord Danvers to [Carleton]. Begs that one of his servants may buy him two special felt hats of the moderate height.

Nov. 24. Westminster. Re-grant to Thos. Boorne, Robt. Lewis, and Hugh Richardson, of the office of Searchers of all Kettles and manufactures of brass imported, the former warrant being defective. [*See Nov* 5. *Sign Man., vol.* VIII., *No.* 75.]

Nov. 27. Westminster. Warrant to pay 3,000*l.* to Sir Thos. Dickenson, appointed to repair into the Low Countries about some special service. [*Ibid., No.* 76.]

Nov. 27. Westminster. Revocation of the Charter granted to the new Company of Merchant Adventurers, according to a proviso therein for its repeal. [*Ibid., No.* 77.]

Nov. [27]. Westminster. Grant to the Governor and Company of Merchant Adventurers, confirmation and restitution of all such liberties, &c. as they have heretofore enjoyed by Royal charters, the charter granted to the new company being revoked; also grant of additional privileges. [*Ibid., Nos.* 80—84.]

Nov. 27. 37. Note of receipt of 6*l.* from John Penny, through Edw. Nicholas.

Nov. 28. London. 38. Dr. Geo. Carleton to Sir D. Carleton. Sends a copy of what he has written against Arminius. Thanks for his verses. The

VOL. XCIV.

1617.

Archbp. of Spalato was much pleased with their elegance. Sec. Winwood generally regretted. Is appointed by the King and Prince to the see of Llandaff, where he can do little good, from ignorance of the language, and opposition of some great ones, who hate the truth; it is a poor bishopric, but the favours of Princes are not to be rejected.

Nov. 28. Westminster. Grant to Simon Jucks of dispensation to hold, with the rectory of Staunton, diocese of York, the parsonage of St. Olave's, lately bestowed upon him, as his predecessor, Robt. Wilkinson, did. Latin. [*Sign Man., vol.* VIII., *No.* 78.]

Nov. 28. Westminster. Grant to the Company of Merchant Adventurers of confirmation of licence to export 30,000 pieces of white undressed broad cloth per ann. [*Ibid., No.* 79.]

Nov. 29. London. 39. Chamberlain to Carleton. Sir John Villiers in ill health. The Swedish Ambassador and the Prince of Anhalt's son have arrived. Sir Thos. Lake and his Lady have preferred bills against Lord Roos, but the Earl of Exeter takes his part. The Mastership of the Savoy will be given to the Archbp. of Spalato; he is to preach to-morrow at the Mercers' Chapel.

[Nov. 30.] [Sir John Dackombe] to Gilbert Gerard. For a commission to Sir Thos. Savage, Bart., High Steward of Haughton, cos. Chester and Lancaster, to inquire into the tenures by which the tenants hold their lands from the Crown, and to collect reliefs and arrears, &c., due therefrom; also to inquire into the evidences of the tenures, and into any alienations without licence. [*Dom. Corresp., Dec.* 11, 1618. *Note Bk., p.* 24.]

Nov. 30. 40. Draft of the above.

[Nov. 30.] [The Same] to the Attorney General. To make out a grant of certain lands near Enfield to Sir Rich. Beaumont, as the King's free gift, which are to be impaled into his adjoining park. [*Dom. Corresp., Dec.* 11, 1618. *Note Bk., p.* 22.]

[Nov. 30.] 41. Draft of the above, addressed to Gilbert Gerard.

Nov.? 42. Comparison of Zealand with Holland, for conveniency of trade [for the Merchant Adventurers]; in favour of Middleburgh.

Nov.? 43. The conveniences of Middleburgh and inconveniences of Holland contrasted.

Nov.? 44. Analysis [presented to Council] of the inconveniences that would ensue from a sudden removal [of the Merchant Adventurers] from Middleburgh. [*See Oct.* 20, 1620.]

Nov.? 45. [Agent for Middleburgh] to the Council. Arguments against the removal of the Merchant Adventurers from Middleburgh.

Vol. XCIV.

1617.

Nov. 46. Account of moneys paid into the Exchequer since December, 1613, upon composition for defective titles, in cos. Kent, Sussex, and Essex.

[Nov.] 47. Report of the Lord Chief Justice and Judges of the Common Pleas to the Council, in the case between John Gill and Thos. White and others, as to a customary tithe of lead ore within the parish of Bakewell, which the Dean and Chapter of Lichfield have usually had. The miners wish for another trial; being misinformed that written depositions would do instead of the witnesses, they were at disadvantage in the last.

Nov.? 48. Petition of Wm. Shepard to Lord Zouch, for a writ of Mandatum to certain inhabitants of the Cinque Ports to appear before the High Court of Chancery, to answer his complaint of wrong as to a title to land without the ports.

Nov.? 49. Petition of the Same to the Same, on the same subject.

Dec. 4. Eton. 50. Sir Hen. Savile to Carleton. Recommends to him Sir Thos. Dale, a friend of the Earl of Southampton, who has done good service in the plantation of Virginia.

Dec. 5. London. 51. Sir Edw. Harwood to the Same. Lady Bedford greatly indebted to Lady Carleton for her present. Next term the Earl of Suffolk and Sec. Lake are to receive their doom; their successors are not known. Lady Buckingham still in the country, and it is thought her late honour was a preparative to retire. The Queen is better.

Dec. 6. London. 52. Sir Gerard Herbert to the Same. The King is said to have got the Palsgrave's consent for her Highness to come to England next spring. Pensions are to be given instead of diet, or the diet allowances reduced. A great masque in preparation against Christmas; the Prince and Buckingham are to be performers. The Bishop of Spalato preached at the Italian church, with earnestness and approbation. Art. Wingfield slain in a duel. Carleton's speech to the States, about calling a Synod, much commended.

Dec. 7. Dover. 53. Commissioners for the Passage at Dover to Rich. Younge. Have stayed an Irishman, Hen. Browne, on suspicion of his being Garret, whose stay is ordered by Sir Thos. Lake. Brown has 260*l.* in gold. Detain him till further order.

Dec. 7. Dover. 54. Same to Lord Zouch, on the same subject. Garret was footman to the Countess of Bedford. *Inclose,*

54. I. *Examination of Hen. Browne. Is a merchant of Galway. Received the money found on him for selling raw hides at St. Malo's. Asks time to consider about taking the Oath of Allegiance. Dover, Dec. 7.*

Dec. 7. 55. List of the Officers and Servants of the King and Queen's household who now receive diet, with the number of dishes allowed to each, and the alterations proposed, in order to reduce the household expenses to 50,000*l.*

Dec. 7. 56. Copy of the above.

Vol. XCIV.

1617.

Dec. 7. 57. Officers of the King's Household to the Board [of Commissioners for the Revenue]. Give a project for future expenses, showing what charges must still continue, and where abatements may be made.

Dec. 7. 58, 59. Two copies of the above.

Dec. 10? 60. Note that Jas. Andrews, of St. Botolph's parish, and Melchizedec Bennett and Abel Browne, of St. Sepulchre's, are bound to appear before the Council on Dec. 12, for using leaden tokens.

Dec. 11. Whitehall. 61. Benj. Rudyard to Carleton. The King called an assembly in Scotland, to bring their church government to the form of ours. The chief temporal Commissioner, the Earl of Montrose, was absent on pretended indisposition. The only concessions made by the ministers are, that they will administer the communion with their own hands to the people, instead of having it set on a table, and will, in case of extremity, give it to sick persons at home. The King is much troubled, though he conceals it from the English; he threatens to proceed rigorously, to deprive dissentient ministers of their portions, and to forbid any to relieve them; if he do so, what the result will be is doubtful.

Dec. 13. Northampton. 62. Sir Thos. Tyringham to the Same. Sends him a huntsman's token, two [venison] pasties. His [Carleton's] friends are earnest in favouring his interests. Knows not how he stands with the great Lord of the time.

Dec. 13. Sir John Dackombe to Thos. Pickering, Keeper of the Records at Knaresborough. To permit Jas. Button, or any other deputed by the Bp. of Worcester, to search and copy such records as relate to the Nab, near Swindon, co. York. [*Dom. Corresp., Dec.* 11, 1618. *Note Bk., p.* 23.]

Dec. 14. 63. Note of the distribution of 8*l*., given to Archbp. Abbot's servants at the consecration of Dr. Felton, Bp. of Bristol, and Dr. Montaigne, Bp. of Lincoln.

Dec. 17. Duchy House, Strand. 64. Licence from Sir John Dackombe for John Adams, butcher of St. Clement Danes, in the liberties of the Duchy, to kill flesh during Lent. With confirmation thereof by Sir Edw. Moseley [Attorney of the Duchy], Feb. 24, 1618.

Dec. 18. Rye. 65. Mayor and Jurats of Rye to Lord Zouch. Ask directions on the disposal of certain prisoners, taken up for clipping coin; the crime being committed beyond the limits of the Cinque Ports, they are to be tried at Sussex assizes. *Inclose*,

65. I. *Examination of John Robins, of Beckley, Sussex. Received 5s. of clipped money from John Breeden, &c. Dec.* 13.

65. II. *Examination of John Breeden, of Peasmarsh, Sussex. Received the money from John Cooper of Rye; did not know it to be clipped. Dec.* 13.

VOL. XCIV.

1617.

65. III. *Examination of William, son of John Breeden. Had the charge of the money to be paid to John Robins, and clipped some of it without his father's knowledge. Dec. 15.*

Dec. 19. 66. Bond of Robt. Hudson, Hum. Ambler, and Roger Dye, haberdashers, of London, in 200*l.*, to indemnify Lord Zouch for the delivery to their owners of certain goods saved from the John of Southampton, wrecked near Hythe.

Dec. 19. London. Sir Horace Vere to Carleton. The King at Theobalds. On his return to Whitehall, the issue of the consultation for lessening the household will be known. It is said that pensions are to be diminished by one third. [*Holl. Corresp., Dec.* 19.]

Dec. 20. 67. Geo. Carleton to John Chamberlain. Will spend Christmas with Sir Michael Dormer, who is as frolic as a lame man can be. Has not heard lately from Sir Dudley; fears it is because he did not send over his son Dudley as requested; but the rules of his college, where he is chosen fellow, would not admit it.

Dec. 20. London. 68. Soames Woodward to Carleton. Mr. Sherburn displeased that Sir Wm. Zouch is employed to Mr. Bingley about Carleton's money. The Archbp. of Spalato has preached at Mercers' Chapel. The East India Company are sending Sir Thos. Dale as their Admiral. Part of the money soon to be paid into the Exchequer is allotted to the Ambassadors, posts, &c.

Dec. 20. London. 69. Sir Edw. Harwood to the Same. The King just returned from Theobalds. Mr. Secretary thinks a synod a bad way to end religious dissensions, but says the King will countenance it; so say the Archbp. of Canterbury and Lord Chamberlain.

Dec. 20. 70. Petition of the Merchant Adventurers for discovery of new trades [Muscovy Company] to [the Council ?]. Their trade in Russia being hindered by the wars there, they sent out voyages of discovery into Tartary and to Norway and Greenland, which latter place they discovered, and set up the whale fishing. Were much disturbed by foreigners, but having put them down, many English, especially from Kingston-on-Hull, endeavour to interlope into their trade, and undersell them, they having all the charge of repressing foreigners, and maintaining the embassy in Russia.

Dec. ? 71. Reasons why the inhabitants of Kingston-upon-Hull should prosecute the whale fishery in the northern seas, notwithstanding the opposition of the Muscovy Company.

Dec. ? 72. Copy of the above.

Dec. 20. London. 73. Sir Gerard Herbert to Carleton. The Spanish match spoken of again. The King and Prince expected from Theobalds. Sir Thos. Gates ill of the gout. Lady Montgomery with child, &c.

1617. Vol. XCIV.

Dec. 20. 74. Chamberlain to Carleton. The King grows very froward, either from discontent or illness, but the sight of Buckingham can always quiet him. He ordered Simpson, of Trinity College, who preached before him a sermon on universal grace, to be called to account, and ordered to retract, the subject being discussed in his own presence. The Archbp. of Spalato assisted the Archbp. of Canterbury and other Bishops in laying hands on the new Bishops of Bristol and Lincoln, Drs. Felton and Montaigne. Balconquall made Master of the Savoy, and Dr. Tolson Dean of Westminster. The Swedish Ambassador asks leave to levy troops in England against Poland, and wishes the King to join the Princes of the German union in defence of religion. Young Mountjoy Blount parts with Wanstead to the King or Buckingham, in order to be made a Baron. Buckingham is joined with Nottingham in a new patent [for the Admiralty]. Young Lord Cromwell, who has not a foot of land in England, marries Lady Lower, and Sir Edw. Moseley, Lady Bowyer. The Lord Keeper reflected upon for casting slurs upon the late Sec. Winwood.

[Dec. 21.] 75. Petition of Sir Thos. Smythe, and the merchants trading to France, to the Council, to renew their order to the Lord Chief Justice of the King's Bench, to stay a suit commenced against them by Radnor, an informer, for importing playing cards, and to permit the importation of the same, on payment of the usual duties.

Dec. 22. Monday. London. 76. Sir Edw. Harwood to Carleton. Sounded Sec. Lake and Buckingham upon Carleton's advancement, but both are cool about it. Delivered his letter to the King, who spoke much on the importance of unity in religion, and declared he would believe nothing the Arminians said, except what came direct from Carleton; that he did not, like many Princes, do his business through others, but opened all his packets himself, and none dared reply to them but by his dictation; that he approved of his Excellency [the Prince of Orange's] using all legal means to put down the Arminians, especially his calling a national synod, and would advise him to do as he himself had done, call dissentients before him to maintain their opinions in his presence. His Majesty spoke favourably of him [Carleton]. Buckingham disapproves of his wish to come over, if he come in hopes of a place; he intends to have his own kinsman, Sir Robt. Naunton, made Secretary.

Dec. 23. Whitehall. 77. Thos. Murray to the Same. Change of Court officers expected. Sir Thos. Edmondes is to succeed Lord Wotton as Treasurer of the Household, and Sir Hen. Carey, Master of the Jewel House, is to be Comptroller.

Dec. 23. Westminster. Proclamation for the better and more peaceable government of the Borders. With instructions to be observed thereon. Printed. [*Proc. Coll., No.* 51.]

Dec. 24. London. 78. Edw. Reynoldes to Fras. Mills. Sir Thos. Clerk being dead, fears [Edmund] Clerk, his successor, will not prove so good a colleague.

VOL. XCIV.

1617.

Precautions for fair dealing of Mr. [Edw.] Anthony, who is to share Thos. Packer's fees.

Dec. 26. Bury [St. Edmunds]. 79. Sir John Higham to [two Justices of the Peace for Suffolk]. Sends a letter and arguments, aiming at a liberal contribution for the King, in order to prevent the marriage with Spain, which they are to communicate to the other justices, and test the disposition of the principal gentlemen; hopes that a Parliament may be summoned, and foreign attempts brought to nothing. *Incloses,*

79. I. *Dr. Willett to Sir John Higham. The King would not need foreign support, if his subjects would supply him. Requests him to submit the following considerations to the justices of peace, from amongst whom members for Parliament would be likely to be chosen. Annexes,*

79. II. *Arguments in favour of a Parliamentary grant of six subsidies and six double fifteenths, founded on the King's wants, his character and deserts, the dangers of the Spanish match, &c. With objections and answers to objections.*

[Dec.] 80. Copy of the above arguments.

Dec. 26. London. 81. Nath. Brent to [Carleton]. 5,000*l.* prevailed on Lord Wotton to retire [from the office of Treasurer of the Household]; Mr. Comptroller is to succeed him. Sir Hen. Carey to become Comptroller, and to be succeeded by Sir Ant. Mildmay [in the Jewel House].

Dec. 27. London. 82. Sir Edw. Harwood to the Same. The King asked whether it was true that a prayer, printed at Haarlem by the Dutch, called the King of Spain their sovereign. Naunton is to be Secretary, on condition that, as he has no children, he will make Chris. Villiers his heir. Sir Hen. Carey has offered 5,000*l.* for the Comptrollership of the Household, but the Lord Steward opposes him. An agent of the Arminian party is going about seeking partizans, and has seen several Bishops, but could not obtain audience of the King. Those who favour that party oppose the synod. The secret of his [Harwood's] bringing letters from Count Maurice to the King has got abroad.

Dec. 30. London. 83. Sir Gerard Herbert to the Same. Lord Clifton is sent to the Tower for saying he would kill the Lord Keeper. Ladies' masque at Lord Hay's deferred; performers in it enumerated, &c.

Dec. 31. 84. Note of periods of service and allowances of Sir Fras. Howard, Admiral of the Narrow Seas, Capt. Geo. Wood, Vice Admiral, appointed to attend the King to Scotland, and John Hogg, who conveyed the buckhounds from Harwich to Scotland.

Dec. 31. 85. Account Book for the Office of Ordnance for the past quarter.

VOL. XCIV.

1617.

Dec. 86. Account of payments made by the Farmers of the Customs for the past year.

Dec. 87—91. Account of receipts from special liveries, the Hanaper, petty bag, and assart lands, during the past year. Five papers.

1617? UNDATED. 1617?

Warrant for a grant to Sir John Dackombe and Sir Robt. Carr, Gentlemen of the Bedchamber to the Prince, of a third part of the manor of Shenston, co. Stafford, escheated to the Crown by attainder of Robt. late Earl of Somerset. [*Dom. Corresp., Dec.* 11, 1618. *Note Bk., p.* 12.]

[Sir John Dackombe] to Auditor Wm. Purvey. To send particulars of the lands of Buckby, co. Northampton, and Kerckper, co. Derby, preparatory to grants of them. [*Ibid., p.* 19.]

List of advowsons belonging to the duchy of Cornwall, with their value, and the names of the patrons. [*Ibid., p.* 112.]

List of advowsons belonging to the duchy [of Lancaster], with their value, and some particulars of leases, &c., and notes of fees to be paid on presentation. [*Ibid., p.* 120.]

[Sir John Dackombe] to Gilbert Gerard. For a commission of sewers, under the Duchy Seal, to Lord Treasurer Suffolk, Lords Windsor and Wentworth, and others, within a certain hundred, as already passed under the Great Seal, Feb. 15, 1617. [*Ibid., p.* 25.]

Grant to Thos. Ashall, Prebendary in the Cathedral of Chester, of dispensation for non-residence. Latin. [*Warrt. Bk.*, I., *p.* 230.]

Grant to Dr. John Hanmer, in trust for Edw. Basset, of the benefit of a recognizance of 1,000*l.*, forfeited by Edm. Molyneux, of Carleton Barron, co. Notts., deceased, to John Basset, of Fledborough, co. Notts., now outlawed, father of Edw. Basset. [*Ibid., No.* 86.]

Grant to the city of Chichester of confirmation of the ancient charter, with additional privileges. Latin. Imperfect. [*Ibid., No.* 87.]

Grant to the Corporation of Dorchester of the advowson of the Church of Allhallows, Dorchester, on condition of their endowing it with competent maintenance for a preacher. Latin. [*Ibid., No.* 88.]

Demise to Sir Oliver Williams, alias Cromwell, of certain pasture and meadow grounds in Waybridge Forest, co. Huntingdon, forfeited by attainder of the Earl of Somerset. Latin. [*Sign Man., vol.* VIII., *No.* 89.]

VOL. XCIV.

1617?

Commission to the Treasurer and Under Treasurer of the Exchequer, the Attorney General, and all the Judges, to compound for fines and forfeitures of goods, for non-payment of customs through negligence or ignorance. [*Sign Man., vol.* VIII., *No.* 90.]

92. Lease, in reversion, from Fras. Russell Baron Thornhaugh and his wife Catherine, to Wm. Beecher, of Fotheringay, co. Northampton, and Thos. Anstell, of Barford, co. Bedford, of the rectory, church, and appurtenances of Croydon, co. Cambridge, in reversion after Thos. Cockayne, who is to marry Dorothy Anstell.

93. The King to Sir Hen. Yelverton, Attorney General. Orders him to prepare a bill confirming certain privileges to Hen. Earl of Southampton, in his lands in Hampshire, Middlesex, and Lincolnshire, and to extend the liberties of Southampton House, from Holborn Bars to the Rolls in Chancery Lane.

94. The Same to the Mayor, &c. of London. Having recently granted a charter to the Apothecaries to become a company, for the sake of avoiding the abuses of unskilful persons, he understands that they refuse to enrol the charter. Orders their immediate conformity, and the establishment of the company "in the free practice of government."

95. Notes relative to losses sustained by the Company of Grocers, on account of the separation of Apothecaries from them, the expenses of the Irish plantation, &c.

96. Sir Robt. Mansell to the King. Requests the insertion in some grant, of the taking charge of the timber and plank in Woolwich Dockyard, &c.

97. Statement of the motives of Sir Hen. Crook and Ant. Rous, Clerks of the Pipe, in preferring to the King and Council complaints against the clerks or attorneys in the said office; it is done to conceal their own extortions upon the attorneys, and also upon the subjects, and to suppress the complaints made against them by the attorneys; with an account of the wrongs resulting to the Crown from their misconduct.

98. Notes of the particular heads and branches of the King's revenue paid into the Pipe Office, and of the nature of the business transacted in that office.

99. Statement of the case of certain petitioners for licence to export Welsh butter, when the price does not exceed 3*d.* per lb. in the summer, and 4*d.* in the winter. They paid 500*l.* fine, and engaged to pay 300*l.* a year for their licence, but it is prevented passing the Privy Seal and Great Seal, by certain parties interested in opposing it. They urge its speedy completion.

1617? Vol. XCIV.

100. Names of the principal tenants of the manor of Havering, co. Essex, together with the number of acres they severally hold, according to survey taken 15 Jac. 1.

101. Bill, answer, proofs, and notes on the cause the King v. the tenants of Havering, touching the proprietorship of the freehold of the manor.

102. Thos. Wilson, Keeper of State Papers, to the King. Suggests the creation of an office in which the chartularies of the dissolved abbeys and monasteries shall be transcribed and kept for searches, in order to prevent their alienation from the Crown, or needless litigations about them, for want of access to the title deeds.

103. The Officers of the Court of Wards to the Same. Request him to support their decree against Sir Rich. Cheetwood, who, on a false pretence, seized the child of the late Sir Thos. Bedell, of Huntingdonshire, and detained him from his grandfather and guardian, Sir Art. Capell.

104. Master and Fellows of [Pembroke Hall] Cambridge, to the Earl of Suffolk, their Chancellor. Objections against Mr. Bowd, recommended by the King, as ineligible according to their statutes. Explain certain points relating to the position of their college.

105. The Same to the King. Have received his request to elect Bowd, of Christ's College, but have no vacancy excepting one for which he is ineligible. Hope His Majesty will not be offended.

106. Wm. Parker, Lord Monteagle, to Sir Thos. Lake. Is content to abide his decision, in a cause between his cousin, Sir Thos. Penruddock, and himself.

107. Edw. Reynoldes to [Sir Hen. Savile]. Recommends his nephew for election to a vacancy in Merton College.

108. [The Same to the Same.] Thanks for his promise to promote the preferment of his nephew, Edw. Reynoldes, at the next election. Was prevented by illness from visiting him at Eton last holidays. [*See July* 29, 1618.]

109. Petition of Sir Robt. Cooke to the Council. As the Court of Exchequer has accepted bonds from his father, now in prison, for payment to the King of certain profits of the manors of Stoke and Chippenham, if they are adjudged to be due to the Crown, prays for the warrant for unsealing the doors of the manor house, and removing restraints as to the sale of wood, &c.

110. Petition of the Mariners of the ship Hopewell to [Lord Zouch?], for aid in obtaining payment of their wages, which are fourteen months in arrear, their master having hired out the ship to another. Imperfect.

Vol. XCIV.

1617 ?

111. Petition of Thos. Bromhead to the King, to be admitted to sue in formâ pauperis for restoration of his lands, unjustly detained by his uncles, to whom they were left in trust for him. With order thereon.

112. Similar petition to Sir John Dackombe, Chancellor of the Duchy of Lancaster. *Annexing,*

112. I. *Certificate by Thos. Cummocke and others of the truth of the above statement of Thos. Bromhead.*

113. Petition of Lawrence Coxe and Ann his wife, as executrix of Nich. Jacob, to Lord Zouch, on behalf of her orphan son, Rich. Jacob, for redress against Peter Fountayn, who, as guardian of Rich. Jacob, suffered two of his houses in Dover to fall to decay, during his minority. [*See Dom. Corresp., Dec.* 5, 1615.]

114. Petition of Thos. Hodson, Guide over the Kent Sands, Lancashire, to Sir John Dackombe, for continuance in his office, of which he is in danger of being deprived, through false representations that his negligence has caused the loss of several lives.

115. Petition of Sir John Killigrew to the Council, to explain whether their former letter intended that he should appoint the keepers of the four victualling houses for relief of seafaring men, erected on his lands at Smethick, near Falmouth, co. Cornwall, on his engaging himself for their good behaviour.

116. Petition of the Spanish and Eastland Merchants to the Same, for remedy against the practices of certain felt makers and haberdashers, who make felts and hats of English wool, instead of the foreign wools imported by them, which are alone fit for that purpose.

117. Petition of John Oliver to the Same, for renewal of his pension from the county of Hereford, of 3*l.* per ann. as a maimed soldier, which, through stress of poverty, he had sold five years before, for 6*l.*

118. Petition of Thos. Harvey, Gunner of Dover Castle, to Lord Zouch, for a certain lodging in the Castle, which he will repair at his own cost, and share with another, if required.

119. Petition of Wm. Hales, Gunner of Dover Castle, to the Same, to be permitted to share a lodging in the Castle granted to Harvey, another Gunner.

120. Request by [Visct. Haddington] to the King, to permit his brother, Patrick Ramsay, to sell for 140*l.* the escheat of the lands of Wassall Webling, deceased, which was granted him by the King.

121. Note of abuses resulting from the conduct of Sir Chas. Cornwallis, Collector of the Privy Seals in Norfolk and Norwich, levied in 1611, in detaining the money five years in his own hands,

1617? VOL. XCIV.

not accounting for a portion of what was levied, and otherwise oppressing the parties who are petitioners in the Star Chamber against him.

122. Statement of changes in the Courts of Chancery, Common Pleas, and King's Bench, by the grants of special offices for making writs of subpœna, capias, supersedeas, latitat, &c.

123. Note that Michael Silvester, Page to the Queen, is a suitor to the King for 30*l.*, moiety of a debt of 60*l.* due by Dr. Thos. Bonham, for practising physic for a year, without licence from the College of Physicians. With statement of the case, and of the judgment against Bonham.

124. Names of mourners at the funeral of [Susan] Countess of Kent.

125. List of persons whose pensions are appointed by the Lords [Commissioners for Revenue?] to be suspended, and of others whose pensions are to be reduced.

VOL. XCV. JANUARY, 1618.

1618.

Jan. 1. Creation of Geo. Earl of Buckingham to the rank of Marquis of Buckingham. [*Grant Bk., p.* 231.]

Jan. 2. Dover. 1. Examination of Wm. Johnson, of Hatley, Cambridgeshire. Went abroad for his health, but returns because he is not better; is a Catholic, but not a priest; his crucifix, books, &c. are for his own use; will not say how he became a Catholic, nor take the Oath of Allegiance; knows not what will become of the King, unless he reconcile himself to the Church of Rome.

Jan. 2. Lambeth. 2. Archbp. of Spalato to Carleton. Has received letters and money from the States, and a letter from Grotius, and has shown the latter to the King. Sends a copy of an oration which he made at the Italian church before many of the Court, and to the great satisfaction of the King. Has not heard lately from Paul de la Ravoire, and knows not whether he be alive or dead. Has many good words, but, as to promotion, is like the sick man in the porch, who had none to throw him into the waters. Savoy [Hospital] was promised him, but Jacob supplanted Esau. Italian.

Jan. 2. London. 3. Nathaniel Brent to the Same. Gen. Cecil tries hard for the Comptrollership, and has got the Duke's favour. Sir Hen. Mildmay said to be too young and of too mean estate to be trusted with the King's jewels. Buckingham made a Marquis without any ceremony, or even a trumpet sounding. The happy news of the King's new grandchild has caused bonfires in London, and cured the King, who has been very melancholy this Christmas. The merchants of Middleburgh and the East Indies have offered the King 50,000*l.*; 12,000*l.* is assigned for Ireland; 8,000*l.* for artillery, 4,000*l.* for the

VOL. XCV.

1618.

Prince's masque, and 17,000*l.* for Lords Hamilton, Aubigny, Hay, and Haddington. Nothing is yet known of the Spanish match. Sir Walter Raleigh arrived at Guiana; Capt. Baylie, who accused him, has fled and hidden himself. Sir Edw. Coke continues at the Temple. The Bp. of Salisbury has written a learned book on the points of religion controverted in the Low Countries.

Jan. 3. Saturday. Whitehall. 4. Earl of Arundel to Sir Edw. Conway. The King wishes Conway and Dr. Bird to deliver a verbal report of the state of certain matters [affairs in Jersey], and the ways of redress, and also to leave the report with him in writing.

Jan. 3. 5. Chamberlain to Carleton. Lord Roos is at Rome in great privacy; he left all his valuables with the Spanish Ambassador. Sir Hen. Carey has sold the Mastership of the Jewel House to Sir Hen. Mildmay, an inexperienced young man, for 2,000*l.* or 3,000*l.* Sir Ralph Freeman, who married a relation of Buckingham, has Naunton's Mastership of Requests. The Duke of Lenox, as Lord Steward of the Household, opposes Lord Wotton's resigning the Treasurership to Sir Thos. Edmondes, as being done without his consent. Offices and even Councillorships sold. Masque of Ladies led by Lady Hay, but neither the King nor Queen liked it. Lady Hatton is at Waltham with her sister. The Archbp. of Spalato has got the Mastership of the Savoy, and Balconquall, who was in possession, is made Clerk of the Closet. Lord Clifton, having been fined and imprisoned, was called to the Council, and committed to the Tower for contumacious behaviour. Sir John Finet married a lame sister of Lord Wentworth.

Jan. 4. York House. 6. Edw. Sherburn to [the Same]. Private money affairs and delivery of letters. Is quite unable to obtain Carleton's allowance from the Exchequer, nor can Sir Wm. Zouch do better, though authorized to offer a large bribe to Mr. Bingley for regular payments. Sir Robt. Naunton chosen Secretary before another, who offered 10,000*l.*; this was by favour of Buckingham, who is created Marquis, and gave a feast to the King, Prince, and nobility, when the King thus drunk to the company:—"My Lords, I drink to you all; I know we are all welcome to my George, and he that doth not pledge with all his heart, I would the devil had him for my part." Changes of office made and projected. Sir Edw. Coke and Sir Fulk Greville to be made Barons.

Jan. 4. 7. Bond of Sir Fras. Jones, Alderman, of London, to Sir Nich. Salter, and Sir John Wolstenholme, in 1,000*l.*, to redeem their joint bond of 800*l.* for payment of 525*l.* to Sam. Hare, of London.

Jan. 7. London. 8. Sir Edw. Harwood to Carleton. Buckingham has been privately created Marquis, in reward for declining the High Admiralship, on the ground of inexperience. Masque and anti-masque at Court. Little hope of the Spanish match; our Ambassador there ill treated, the priests opposing it. The King is going to Theobalds. Duel between Sir Robt. Killigrew and Capt. Burton.

Vol. XCV.

1618.

Jan. 7. London. 9. Geo. and Edw. Carleton to Sir Dud. Carleton. Terms agreed on with Lady Hill for her lease.

Jan. 9. London. 10. Matt. de Quester to the Same. Sends a packet from Sec. Lake. Begs sometimes to have the carriage of a packet, to counterpoise his charges, &c.

Jan. 9. Lord Zouch to Rich. Marsh. Forbids, by Order of Council, the future exaction of head money from French subjects landing in the Cinque Ports. [*Minute Diary, Dom. Corresp., Oct.* 20, 1618.]

Jan. 10. London. 11. Chamberlain to [Carleton]. The King and Prince were at a great supper given by the Marquis of Buckingham, which cost 600*l.* Sir Thos. Edmondes managed it after the French fashion. The Muscovy Ambassadors have dined with the King. The Lord Keeper made Lord Chancellor, and will be made a Baron. He has the benefit of making another, to pay his debts, and offered the honour to his eldest brother, who refused it. The Prince's masque proved dull. The Earl of Exeter complains of the Spanish Ambassador, that he will not get Mole liberated out of the inquisition at Rome, as promised, and now has seduced Lord Roos to go there. The King made Naunton Secretary suddenly, declaring it was of his own free will, and giving him many good lessons. He has had a masque at Theobalds, of Tom Bedlam the Tinker. Sir Hen. Carey has not yet got the White Staff. The Queen in a languishing condition. The Lady Elizabeth wishes to come over to England, &c.

Jan. 10. London. 12. Nath. Brent to the Same. Lord Wotton keeps his place, because his successor is not agreed on. Sir. Edw. Cecil, Sir Hen. Carew, and Lord Knollys are rivals for the Comptrollership. The King's project of cutting off every third dish from the tables for diet has failed through opposition. The Masque of Twelfth Night was so dull that people say the poet [Ben Jonson] should return to his old trade of brickmaking. The Prince, Buckingham, Hamilton, and others, actors. The Queen has kept at home all Christmas. Grotius has written to the Archbp. of Spalato and Bishops of Ely and Coventry, complaining that, instead of the King's healing religious dissensions, his Ambassador there [Carleton] aggravates them.

[Jan. 12.] 13. Sir Edw. Harwood to the Same. Lady Roos accused Lady Exeter of a conspiracy to poison her; the accusation proved so weak that she would let it die out, but the defendant will prove her innocence. Sir Thos. Lake would have been made a Baron, but those peers over whom, as Secretary, he would have had precedence, objected, and the King says, if he wishes to be a Baron, he must leave the Secretaryship.

Jan. 12. London. 14. Sir Gerard Herbert to the Same. On Twelfth Night was the Prince's Masque; he acted well. As the Queen could not see it, it will be repeated for her on Shrove Sunday. Marquis Hamilton won 400*l.*, and the Earl of Dorset 500*l.*, at play, in the King's chamber. Description of a Masque of Gentlemen at Lord Montgomery's at Enfield. Mrs. Middlemore, the Queen's Maid of Honour, dead. The Masque of Ladies at Lord Hay's given up, from some remark of the King or Queen, &c.

VOL. XCV.

1618.

Jan. 13. Salisbury House, Strand. 15. G. Gerrard to Carleton. Sir Wm. Uvedale made Treasurer of the Chamber. Lord Wotton will not resign the Treasurership of the Household, because, besides the 5,000*l.* offered, he wishes to be made a Viscount, which the King opposes. *Incloses,*

15. I. *List of occurrences at Court from Jan.* 1.

Jan. 13. Tuesday. 16. Depositions of John Weddel, alias Duke, of Lymehost, mariner, and Wm. Heley, of London, draper, taken before Sir Hen. Marten, Judge of the Court of Admiralty, on behalf of the Muscovy Company, concerning their voyage to Greenland, in the ship Dragon, May to July, 1617, and their attempts to compel the Hollanders to desist from whale-fishing there.

Jan. 13. Rye. 17. Examinations of Christian, wife of Thos. Lebrand, Thos. Mellow, John Grenfield, and Hen. Dann, all of Rye, relative to abusive words spoken by John Sharp against the Mayor of Rye, on Oct. 3 and 8, 1617.

Jan. 14. Lord Zouch to the Mayor of Dover. Orders him, at request of Sir Hugh Beeston, to refrain from offering the Oath of Allegiance to Rich. Jennison, at the next sessions, in hope of his conformity. [*Minute, Diary, Dom. Corresp., Oct.* 20, 1618.]

Jan. 14. London. 18. Sir Art. Tyringham to Carleton. The King gone to Newmarket. Recent preferments at Court. The Christmas very dull, chiefly owing to the Queen's absence, &c.

Jan. 15. Wodrington. 19. Sir Hen. Wodrington to Lord Treasurer Suffolk. Details his efforts to redress the country, disordered by thieves and outlaws, &c. Has unroofed the houses of several who refused to conform to the laws, and many have submitted in consequence. Has imprisoned or taken bonds of many others, so that all Tynedale and Riddesdale is tranquil. The task has been heavy for one man. Is much maligned, but looks to His Majesty's approbation for reward.

Jan. 15. Grant to Sir Fras. Bacon of all fees belonging to his office of Chancellor, and warrant for payment thereof. [*Grant Bk., p.* 229.]

Jan. 17. London. 20. Nath. Brent to Carleton. The Queen is ill with swelling in the legs. Committal of Capt. Baylie, who accused Sir W. Raleigh of piracy; the Spanish Ambassador took his part. The Countess of Exeter has cleared herself nobly of the scandal of wishing to poison Lady Lake and her daughter, laid on her by a letter purporting to be from a man of mean quality, who utterly denies knowing anything of it. Eight Barons to be made. Sir Robt. Rich has the benefit of one, for procuring Lord Hay's marriage, and the Lord Chancellor of another. Sir Nich. Bacon refuses a peerage.

Jan. 17. London. 21. Chamberlain to the Same. Sir John Bingley knighted. The King displeased with a coarse song, sung by Sir John Finet in a

VOL. XCV.

1618.

play at Court. The Merchant Adventurers have given His Majesty 50,000*l.* for protection from interlopers, which it is difficult to enforce, others claiming right of free trade, though several are imprisoned for it. There are now four Masters of Requests in Ordinary, Sir Chris. Perkins, Sir Sidney Montague, Sir Lionel Cranfield, and Sir Ralph Freeman. Sir Hum. May made Surveyor of the Court of Wards. The Archbp. of Spalato is not Master of the Savoy, but, on petitioning the King, has places worth 140*l.* per ann. Sir Thos. Lake is refused a Barony unless he resigns the Secretaryship, as otherwise his place would give him precedence of all Barons.

Jan. 18. Savoy. 22. Geo. Lord Carew to Sir Thos. Roe. Sends another gazette as follows :—

JANUARY, 1617.—Lord Roxburgh, only son and heir of the Duke of Roxburgh, dead in France. Four merchant ships taken in the straits, by Turkish pirates. Some English in the service of the Duke of Florence have committed piracies on Turkish ships, for which the Turks require restitution, though they give none for their own piracies.

FEBRUARY.—Lady Lumley dead, and left most of her estate to her niece, Lady Darcy's daughter, Sir Thos. Savage's wife. Chris. Villiers sworn of the King's Bedchamber, in place of Robin Hay, who succeeds Lord Hay as Master of the King's Robes. Christmas and Bellingham, two gentlemen of the Inns of Court, who wished to fight a duel, are fined, imprisoned, and forbidden to wear weapons. Sir Geo. Carey, Lord Deputy of Ireland, dead. Sir Edw. Cecil married to Diana Drury, Lady Burleigh's sister.

MARCH.—Sir Edw. Hoby died at Bisham, Berkshire. The Queen feasted the King on Shrove Tuesday at Somerset House, now Denmark House. Mr. Ben, of the Middle Temple, made Recorder of London. A Scotch ship taken by Turkish pirates, and Sir Wm. Carr, a Scotchman, slain. Hen. Bertie, Lord Willoughby's brother, is in the Inquisition at Rome. List of the King's intended train for Scotland. Disturbances in Scotland, from a feud between the Marquis of Huntley and Earl of Errol, which it is hoped the King's presence will pacify. The Lord Chancellor died on the 15th, at York House, leaving a large estate; his son, Visct. Brackley, created Earl of Bridegwater. Sir Edw. Noel made a Baron of Parliament, and Lord Hay a Councillor. On the 28th, Sir Walter Raleigh's ship left the river; he is gone to join his little fleet at Plymouth, and sails for the Orinoco gold mine. Five Englishmen returned from the Amazons, richly laden with gold and tobacco.

APRIL.—The book against the King was written not by Barclay, but by Puteanus, a lecturer in the University of Louvaine. Sir John Bennet ordered to request the Archduke to make an example of him, for scandalizing anointed kings. Death of Lord Eure, Lord Hunsdon, and Sir Chas. Cavendish. Sir Wm. Seymour, Lady

Vol. XCV.

1618.

Arabella's husband, married to a daughter of the Earl of Essex; his grandfather, the Earl of Hertford, settles 3,000*l.* a year on him.

May.—Mr. Hakewill, the lawyer, is married to a sister of Lady Killigrew, and niece of the Lord Keeper, and made Queen's Solicitor. Sir John Dutton made Baron of the Exchequer, and Sir Wm. Jones takes his place as Lord Chief Justice of Ireland. The Bishop of Durham died, a few days after he had fêted the King in his Palace. The Countess of Salisbury has a daughter. Sir Walter Raleigh hindered sailing, because all his companions have not arrived. Two ships have returned safe from the East Indies.

June.—Lady Farmer, Sir Wm. Cornwallis's daughter, tried for murder, for accidentally killing Mr. Onley with a pistol; she answered like a distracted person, and judgment is respited. The Earl of Abercorn's eldest son made Baron [Hamilton of] Arabane, in Ireland. The Turkish pirates do great harm to our ships in the Mediterranean; if they are not destroyed, the Levant trade will be at an end; they also damage the coast of Spain much. On the 7th Sir Walter Raleigh sailed from Plymouth with "7 good ships of war, and 3 pinnaces, exceedingly well manned, munitioned, and victualled," and 600 or 700 men.

July.—All the English Councillors who attended the King to Scotland are sworn Councillors of that realm. Sir John Herbert, the old Secretary, dead.

August.—Marquis Hamilton, of Scotland, sworn Councillor of England, at Glasgow, when the King was there. Raleigh forced back by stress of weather, first into Falmouth and then to Cork Harbour, with the loss of one pinnace. Lady Bowes, sister to Sir Wm. Wray, married to Lord Darcy of the North, and her sister to Lord Rich. The Hollanders have discovered an open sea southward of the Straits of Magellan, and free passage to the South Sea. The Countess of Roxburgh gone to live in Scotland; Lady Eliz. Grey takes her place in the Queen's Court.

September.—Sept. 6, the King returned to Woodstock, and was met by the Queen and Prince. St. George's Feast was held at Windsor on the 13th. Particulars of the dispute between Sir Edw. Coke and his wife. Raleigh set sail from Ireland on Aug. 19th, with thirteen sail and 1,000 men, and was heard of on the 23d at the North Cape, in Spain The Turkey Company's merchants so misused at Constantinople that they are doubtful whether to relinquish their trade. Lord [Cobham] was permitted by the King to go to Bath with his keeper for his health, but when cured, and returning, was seized with palsy, and conveyed to Sir Edw. More's house at Odiham, where he still lingers. The Earl of Tyrone's younger son Brian, at Brussels, found hanged, with his hands tied behind him, but the murderer unknown; the eldest son, Shane, is Colonel of the Irish regiment with the Archduke. Sir Dan. Dun, Dean of the Arches and Judge of the Admiralty, dead, and succeeded by Sir

1618. Vol. XCV.

Bernard Dewhurst. Has received one of Roe's letters; that sent by Mr. Pory miscarried. Advises him to draw a map of the Mogul's country, and to accept a MS. history of the country offered him by the Governor of Scinde, and have it translated. Wonders at his accounts of the richness and baseness of that prince. Lord Willoughby of Parham dead.

October.—Turkish pirates have been on the coasts of England and Ireland, but done no harm, paying for some fish they took; they came to view the coast; they took three Spanish ships, value 60,000*l.* Death of Mrs. Eliz. Bridges, or Lady Kennedy, Lord Chandos's daughter; of Lord Gerard, President of Wales, who is succeeded by Lord Compton; and of Sir John Parker, Captain of Falmouth, succeeded by Sir Robt. Killigrew. On Sept. 8th, Raleigh was at the Canaries, where Capt. Baylie stole from him with one vessel, professing a fear that he would turn a pirate, which many maliciously affirm him to be. Sir John Digby well received in Spain. Sir Robt. Shirley is at Lisbon, but ordered not to go to the Court; he is to negociate with the Viceroy of Portugal; his brother, Sir Anthony, is poor at Madrid, because, out of his 3,000 ducats pension, 2,000 are embargoed for his debts.

November.—The Hollanders have again attempted to discover the North-west Passage by Davies' Sea, and "it is reported that all the difficulties are past in this discovery." They found a nation of pigmies, and took two of them in a small canoe; but they, one day, seeing the ship's cook dressing a piece of pork, and thinking it was man's flesh, and that they should be devoured, leaped into the sea, and were drowned. Lady Markham, wife of Sir Griffin, did penance in a white sheet at Paul's Cross, for marrying one of her servants, her husband being still alive; she will have to do the same elsewhere, and was fined 1,000*l.*; the wonder is that either of them escaped death, to which they were liable by a recent statute.

December.—Art. Wingfield, cousin to the Countess of Bedford, slain in a duel by Ayliffe of Wiltshire, who is taken, and will, it is thought, be executed, the King being a great enemy to duels. Sir Edw. Villiers has Sir Rich. Martin's place in the Mint, worth 1,500*l.* or 2,000*l.* a year. Capt. Harvey, who was with Harcourt at Guiana, has returned thither with seventy men, to try his fortunes again. Reekes, a shipmaster, who was at Lanzarote, in the Canaries, all the time that Raleigh was there, relates that Raleigh requested the governor to allow him to enter and take in provisions; the governor promised to do so, but delayed till he had sent all the goods and women and children to the mountains, and then refused, telling Raleigh he was a pirate, and should have nothing but what he could get by his sword. Raleigh would not revenge himself, but retired; only two of his men were killed in a private skirmish. He went to the Grand Canary, where also he was ill treated, and forced to fire a shot, which killed one Spaniard, but at Gomera he was well supplied, and

VOL. XCV.

1618.

left there Sept. 20th. Sir Geo. Snigg, Baron of the Exchequer, dead. On the 29th, the King had intelligence that the Electress had another son born. Lord Clifton sent to the Tower for uttering threatening speeches against the Lord Keeper.

JANUARY, 1618.—Capt. John Baylie, who ran away from Sir Walter Raleigh, sent prisoner to the Gatehouse, Westminster. Wishes Sir Thos. Roe safe in England. Begs him to burn his gazette letters before leaving, or to return them to him.

Jan. 19. Grant to Edw. Ball of the office of Surveyor of the New River, brought from Ware to London, for life. [*Grant Bk.*, *p.* 229.]

Jan. 19. Grant to John Boreman of the office of keeping the Ponds in Westminster Park, for life. [*Ibid.*, *p.* 229.]

Jan. 20. Warrant to Sir Fras. Bacon, Chancellor, to cause depositions, &c., to be exemplified, at the request of John Murray. [*Ibid.*, *p.* 229.]

Jan. 22. Edinburgh. The King to the Sheriffs, &c. Authorizes Proclamations for the observation through Scotland of certain Christian festivals, viz., Christmas Day, Good Friday, Easter Sunday, and Ascension Day, by Act of Privy Council. [*Dom. Corresp. Nov.* 15, 1618.]

Jan. 23. Newmarket. 23. Sir Robt. Naunton to Thos. Wilson. Will forward his advancement, if anything offers; but thinks he will not be removed easily from the Sparta he has so adorned, unless Mr. Randolph apply diligently to that service. Desires the loan of a book published on the Titles of the Princes and Lords of Christendom. Indorsed [by Wilson], with notes of his reply, &c.

Jan. 24. Silverton. 24. Wm. Cotton, Bp. of Exeter, to Lake. John Lugge, organist, retains none of his Popish tendencies, though his religion is as the market goes. Has very few Papists in his diocese, but an infinity of sectaries and atheists. *Incloses,*

24. I. *Examination of John Lugge, organist, of Exeter. Has taken the Oath of Allegiance and Supremacy. Never promised his brother to become a Romanist; has had nothing to do with him for seven years; with protestation that he does and ever will detest the Pope's practices, &c. Jan.* 24.

24. II. *Certificate by Thos. Irish and others, Vicars of Exeter Cathedral, that John Lugge has received the communion, and attends church daily as other vicars choral do. Jan.* 18.

24. III. *Peter Lugge to John Lugge. Private affairs. The Spanish match thwarted by the Hollanders; they stopped the marriage of Prince Henry with the elder Infanta, and now they offer bribes,* 20,000*l. to Buckingham, &c., to hinder this match. The Spanish Ambassador mentioned*

1618. Vol. XCV.

this to the King, who declared that he should always be a good friend to his brother of Spain. London, Dec. **10**, 1617.

Jan. 28. 25. Abstract of the Charter of the Merchant Adventurers, with digests of the inspeximuses of the several charters of former Kings, from Henry IV., therein contained.

Jan. 29. Confimation to Walter Balconquall of the office of Master of the Savoy Hospital, co. Middlesex, for life. [*Grant Bk., p.* 229.]

Jan. 30. 26. Account of the dates of instalments paid from the Exchequer to the executors of Sir Roger Aston, in discharge of a debt of 10,392*l.* 14*s.* 9¾*d.*, due to him on surplus of his account as Master of the Wardrobe.

Jan. 31. London. 27. Chamberlain to Carleton. The King still at Newmarket. Sir John Dackombe dead; many competitors for his place, by favour or purchase. Lord Cavendish has lost his eldest son. Changes of Court offices. The Recorder put out of commons at the Temple, for a contempt towards the Lord Chief Justice. Sir Thos. Edmondes farms the Exchequer Seal or Green Wax with the Duke of Lenox, and the Lord Chancellor, the Great Seal or Subpœnas. The Earl of Exeter asks leave to prosecute his wife's slanderers in the Star Chamber. Recorder Ben was debarred from pleading, for disrespect to the Lord Chief Justice, but is restored by the King. The East Indian Fleet of nine strong vessels setting out. Sir Jas. Cottingham has a patent to found a Scottish East India Company, with large privileges, which crosses those already granted, but few enter it. Lord Delawarr returning to Virginia. The Venetian Ambassador is hiring ships for the Seignory, at which the Spanish Ambassador is angry.

Jan. 31. London. 28. Nath. Brent to [the Same]. The King indisposed, but will not allow that he has the gout. The Prince is at Newmarket with him. Buckingham has met with a fall. There are forty-three suitors for the late Sir John Dackombe's Chancellorship of the Duchy [of Lancaster]. Sir Lionel Cranfield is many thousands strong, but Sir Hum. May is likely to get it. The Duke of Lenox is to be made an English Duke, and also the Earls of Arundel, and Buckingham. The Venetians purpose to have an Italian General for the eight men-of-war.

Jan.? 29. Petition of Lord Compton to the King, for grant of the rent-charge on the manor of Woolford, co. Warwick, which he wishes to purchase.

Jan.? 30. List by Sir John Dackombe of muniments and papers in his possession. Indorsed, "My boxes in my presses."

[Jan.] 31—52. Accounts [by Edw. Nicholas] of receipts and expenditure in behalf of Sir John Dackombe, from April 30, 1617, when he entered on his service; with hatters' and tailors' bills, for Sir John Dackombe; and sundry memoranda. Twenty-two papers.

VOL. XCV.

1618. [Jan.] 53–59. Accounts [by Edw. Nicholas] relative to the estate of the late Sir John Dackombe; the legacies and annuities left by his will; the revenue whence they are to be discharged, and the debts owing to him. Seven papers.

Jan.? 60. Inventory [by the Same] of the household furniture of a person deceased [Sir John Dackombe], and list of debts uncancelled, &c. Imperfect.

Jan.? 61. Apology by John Everard to the Lord Mayor and Aldermen of London, for uttering, in his sermon at Paul's Cross, on Jan. 11, reproaches against the Court of Orphans, which were too lightly entertained, and, if true, unfitting to repeat before a popular assembly, and for which he has already been censured by the Bishop of London.

Jan.? 62. Petition of John Folkingham, Preacher at Burton-upon-Trent, to the King, for the living of Tatenhill, co. Stafford, belonging to the Duchy of Lancaster, the Chancellorship of which is now vacant.

Jan.? 63. Petition of Dr. John Lambe, of Northampton, to the King, for a Privy Seal, summoning Visct. Mountgarret, of Ireland, and his wife, Sir Wm. Andrews, and others, to appear before the Court of Requests, to answer in a case relating to Mousehole Close, Northampton, of which he holds a lease, which is questioned by Sir Wm. Andrews, father of Lady Mountgarret, formerly Lady Freeman, to whom it was left by her former husband, Sir Fras. Freeman.

Jan. 64. Cheque roll of the servants of the Lord Chancellor, Sir Fras. Bacon, about 160 in number. Imperfect.

VOL. XCVI. FEBRUARY, MARCH, 1618.

Feb. [1]. York House. 1. Edw. Sherburn to Carleton. Lord Wotton has surrendered his Staff of Treasurer of the Household to [Sir Thos. Edmondes], Comptroller, who is succeeded by Sir Hen. Carey. Sir Thos. Lake, Sec. Naunton, Sir Lionel Cranfield, and others, are suitors to succeed Sir John Dackombe, &c.

Feb. 1. 2. Sir John Rawlins to Sir Peter Osborne, his cousin. Requests him to pay him his money due, at Mr. Reynoldes' lodging, if possible.

Feb. 4. Newmarket. 3. Sir Thos. Lake to Visct. Wallingford, Master of the Court of Wards and Liveries. The King wishes him, Sir Jas. Ley, Attorney of that Court, and Lord Chief Justice Hobart, to consider a statute mentioned by Sir Stephen le Sieur, that there should always be two Clerks to the Court of Wards and Liveries, and to report why there is now only one, and if there be any reason,

1618. Vol. XCVI.

why the King should not grant Le Sieur's request for the second clerkship. *Incloses,*

3. I. *Petition of Sir Stephen le Sieur to the King, that in recompence for his thirty years' services as Ambassador, he may be appointed Clerk of the Court of Wards along with Nich. Hare, who, contrary to the Act of 32 Hen. VIII., c. 46., is now the sole Clerk.*

3. II. *Extract from the above Act, authorizing the appointment of two Clerks of the Court of Wards and Liveries.*

Feb. ? 4. Visct. Wallingford, Chief Justice Hobart, and Sir Jas. Ley, to the King. The Statute does not enjoin that there shall be always two Clerks in the Court, when the grant is made with survivorship. Sir Stephen Le Sieur could not lawfully be joined to the present Clerk, Nich. Hare, and he has withdrawn his request.

Feb. 4. 5. Copies of the principal portion of the two preceding letters, petition, and extract from Act.

Feb. 6. Westminster. 6. Grant to Robt. Hassard, in reversion after Peter Proby, of the office of Post of Chester.

Feb. 7. London. 7. Sir Edw. Harwood to Carleton. So many of the Duchy lands are sold that the Council advise the King to throw the residue into the Exchequer, and thus save 3,000*l.* a year, which is the expense of the Duchy officers; but some say this can only be done by Act of Parliament. Commissioners coming from Spain to renew the marriage treaty, but it is only a sham. Laky Roos's scandals against Lady Exeter are a shame to hear, but none believe them. Earl of Shrewsbury dying.

Feb. 7. London. 8. Chamberlain to the Same. The Chancellorship of the Duchy is in commission. The Exchequer officers oppose the suppression of the Duchy of Lancaster. The Earl of Exeter forbidden to prosecute in the Star Chamber for the imputation against his Lady; the King will give him satisfaction another way. Capt. Alley arrived from Sir W. Raleigh with letters; 100 of Raleigh's company dead of calenture. Death of Sir John Poyntz of Essex, and Butler of Cambridge, who left 300*l.* for a gold communion cup, and all his books and pictures to Clare Hall, but the King has sent to stay the pictures for himself. Simon Digby returned from Spain. The Papists hold up their heads and expect toleration.

Feb. 7. London. 9. Nath. Brent to [the Same]. Likes not the report that his Excellency [Count Maurice] was poisoned, although it be not true. The King has returned from Newmarket, and is pleased with Simon Digby's packet. The Spanish Ambassador says the marriage proceeds, though it is concealed. The Queen has returned from Denmark House to Whitehall, and is well again, and the King

VOL. XCVI.

1618. better. The Earl of Shrewsbury is dead; His Majesty permits the heir, who is of the house of Talbot of Grafton, to inherit, though he has taken [priest's] orders beyond seas. Lord Roos summoned home. Sir Walter Raleigh writes to his wife, that he has arrived at Guiana, but not in the midst of the mines, that the people of the country, on his first arrival, wished to make him king, &c.

Feb. 10. London. 10. Sir Wm. Lovelace to Carleton. The King stays a week longer at Newmarket. Sir Edw. Cecil has failed in his hope of the Chancellorship of the Duchy of Lancaster. If the Spanish match fails, a Parliament will have to be called for supplies. Capt. Peter Alley arrived from Guiana; he left Sir Walter Raleigh anchored in his wished-for haven, but the Spaniards were planted all along the river. The Bishop of Spalato is promised the Mastership of the Savoy and Deanery of Windsor. Death of the Earl of Cumberland [?], Sir John Poyntz, and Dr. Butler, of Cambridge.

Feb. 12. St. Leonard's, Shoreditch. 11. Certificate of the Vicar and Inhabitants of St. Leonard's, Shoreditch, of the honesty of John Brackston, butcher; with request that he may be allowed to kill and sell flesh privately, during Lent, to sick persons who bring testimonials from their ministers.

Feb. 13. London. 12. Capt. Sir Gerard Herbert to Carleton. Sir Harry Peyton is to command the ships [for Venice]. The Earl of Shrewsbury left 10,000*l.* to the Lord Treasurer, no one knows why. Capt. Peter Alley brings news that Sir Walter Raleigh and his troops are in the desired place in America, and that he was well received by the Indians; some are now kings whom he formerly put to school in England; he has sailed up the river as far as he could, and is now making boats to proceed higher; he was very ill during the voyage; Capt. Piggott, Mr. Hastings, the Earl of Huntingdon's brother, and other gentlemen with him, are dead. Lady Elizabeth is not coming over till next spring.

Feb. 14. London. 13. Geo. Carleton to the Same. Terms of the agreement with Lady Hill for her lease. Is glad Sir Dudley still wishes for his son Dudley.

Feb. 14. Saturday. London. 14. Matthew de Quester to the Same. Delay in the arrival of certain letters, on account of the frosts in Zealand. The King and Prince are come this day to Whitehall.

Feb. 14. London. 15. Chamberlain to the Same. Went to Ely House to show the Bishop the Pope's determination between the Franciscans and the Jacobins. Mr. Pory is returned, and speaks much of Wake's handsome living, and favour with the Duke [of Savoy]. The Earl of Shrewsbury dead; his land returns to his brother's daughters, as heirs-general. Dr. [Ant.] Blincow, of Oxford, dead, leaving most of his property to Oriel College. The Lord Chancellor has obtained the Provostship for his Chaplain Mr. Lewis, contrary to the wishes of many Bishops, he being only twenty-six. The Knights aggrieved because Serjeants-at-law are to have precedence of them. Thrasco, a Puritan, turning a Jewish Christian, is imprisoned, with some of

1618. VOL. XCVI.

his followers. Dr. [And.] Willett put in custody for dispersing a treatise against the Spanish match, which is said to be progressing.

Feb. 14. London. 16. Nath. Brent to Carleton. Much talk about the Spanish match; Sir John Digby has spent 12,000*l.* upon it. A discourse by Willett against the marriage was presented to the King; but Willett incurred his high displeasure for persuading persons to offer contributions, in order to hinder the match. The Queen justly implacable against Sir Robt. Floyd, who got from her a lease of the royalties of all her lands; those about her feed her anger, for Floyd had slandered them all to her, when he was highest in her favour; he rose from a serving man to an estate of 800*l.* a year, and is likely to fall as suddenly. The Bishop of London and others have given a second monition at St. Paul's to a certain heretic Spaniard; if, after a third, he persist in his heresies, he will be burnt to death. [*See Dec.* 26, 1616.]

Feb. 16. 17. Pell receipt of 71*l.* 4*s.* 11*d.* for arrears of the tenths of divers benefices, diocese of Lincoln, paid by Rich. Neyle, late Bishop.

Feb. 18. Chelsea. Earl of Nottingham to Capt. Lowe. Orders him to take command of the Dreadnought and Seven Stars, and to go to St. Andreas, or elsewhere, to fetch Sir John Digby from Spain; Sir Wm. St. John, who was appointed to go, being ill. [*Dom. Corresp., May* 12, 1622.]

Feb. 19. Philip Lane. 18. Pass [from Lord Zouch] for Capt. Bing, Captain of Deal Castle, who is going into the Low Countries.

Feb. 19. 19. Bond of John St. George, of Hatley, co. Cambridge, in 200*l.* to Lord Zouch, for the appearance of Wm. St. George, alias Johnson, prisoner in Dover Castle, either before Lord Zouch or the Archbp. of Canterbury, on Feb. 28.

Feb. 19. 20. Draft of the above.

Feb. 21. 21. Bond of Sir Hugh Beeston, of Beeston, and Wm. Whitmore, of Leighton, Cheshire, in 1,000*l.*, for the personal appearance of Rich. Whitmore, who is permitted to visit his friends for four months.

Feb. 21. L. 22. Matthew de Quester to Carleton. Receipt and despatch of letters.

Feb. 21. London. 23. Chamberlain to the Same. There are many young gentlemen at Court, which argues a turning tide. The apprentices rose on Shrove Tuesday, attacked New Bridewell, and pulled down some houses, but a strong watch prevented their doing much harm. A Cistercian monk, long a beggar about St. Paul's, is to be executed for blasphemy.

Feb. 21. London. 24. Nath. Brent to the Same. Two handsome young gentlemen frequent the Court, hoping to attract the King's notice; one is the son of Sir Wm. Monson, the other is named Bell; their folly is much

1618. Vol. XCVI.

laughed at. Trumbull has had no long audience yet; he wants to return if he can get money. Talk of removing Wake from Piedmont to France. The French Ambassador is pettish, because he thinks Spain is preferred. The Prince's masque exhibited again, with the addition of goats and Welch speeches; that of Gray's Inn pleased well. The Duke of Lenox has a grant, which the lawyers pronounce illegal, to compound with all offenders against the statute of tillage.

Feb. 21. 25. Sir Edw. Conway to Carleton. Apologizes for long. silence. Showed his [Carleton's] letter sent by Sir Wm. Zouch to the Chancellor of the Exchequer, who will favour him if he has opportunity.

Feb. 21. 26. Release by Hen. Smith, of Cressing-Temple, Essex, to Wm. and Nich. Dackombe, on payment of 400*l.*, of an annuity of 100*l.* per ann. on leases of the post fines and silk farm, bequeathed to him by the late Sir John Dackombe.

Feb. 22. London. 27. Sir Gerard Herbert to Carleton. Describes the Prince's masque, in which the Prince performed and danced very well; also the Gray's Inn masque. Details of a great feast and concert given by Lord Hay to the two Marquises [Hamilton and Buckingham].

Feb. 23. 28. The Same to the Same. Lady Roos is committed for her slanders against Lady Exeter; the Earl of Exeter and Lord Chandos, her brother, knelt to the King for justice.

Feb. 23. 29. Assignment by John Langley to Rich. Brigham, both of Lambeth, of the keepership of the Archbp. of Canterbury's mansion-house, grounds, and pasture land, called Lambeth Park.

Feb. 23. York House. 30. Edw. Sherburn to Carleton. Knows no way to secure the payment of allowances, so often promised and deferred, but for Carleton to write to tell the King how much his credit abroad suffers, from the want thereof. Lady Roos committed to the custody of the Bishop of London, and her maid to that of Mr. Doubleday. The matter is so foul that an open lawproceeding will be needed.

Feb. 23? 31. Sir Edw. Harwood to [the Same]. Wishes an extension of leave of absence. Lady Roos in custody for refusing to answer interrogatories before the Council. Sec. Lake has been on his knees before the King to plead for the honour of his house. His Majesty was displeased with him a little while ago, for sending a petition through Archy the Fool, in favour of a recusant.

Feb. 23. London. 32. Ant. Aucher to the Same. Sends him a relation from Guiana by a worthy friend; sends a brawn to Lady Carleton.

Feb. 23. Westminster. Proclamation of "Commission with instructions and directions granted by His Majestie to the Master and Counsaile of the Court of Wards and Liveries, for compounding for wards, ideots, and lunaticks." Printed. [*Proc. Coll., No.* 52.]

Vol. XCVI.

1618.

Feb. 24. 33. Examinations of Chas. Cricket and others, Fullers and Packers of Sandwich, at the instance of the farmers of the customs, respecting the stay by Geo. Moore, their Deputy Waiter, of certain packages of baize belonging to Jacob de Master and Isaac Rickasies, &c. *Prefixed is,*

33. I. *Interrogatories on which the above examinations were founded.*

Feb. 24. Court of Wards. 34. Grant to Sir John Gwyn, Bart., of Gwyddyr, co. Carnarvon; Sir Wm. Jones, Lord Chief Justice of Ireland, and Sydney Gwyn, of Bangor, widow, on payment of 100 marks, of the wardship and marriage of Richard, son of the late Richard Gwyn. *Annexing,*

34. I. *Extent of all the manors, lands, &c. of Rich. Gwyn, deceased, total value 15l. 7s. per ann., of which a third reverts to the King, during the minority of the heir, who is two years old. Penyvet, co. Carnarvon. Jan. 14.*

Feb. 24. Whitefriars, London. Sir John Throgmorton to Carleton. The King has heard the suit between the Countess of Exeter and Sir Thos. Lake in person. People fear to speak out, because Lake is powerful. Sir John Digby expected out of Spain. It is hoped that nothing will come of that negociation. The King is going to Theobalds, but returns on Saturday. [*Holl. Corresp., Feb.* 24.]

Feb. 25. 35. Prices at which different kinds of fish are sold: cod, 1*s.* 6*d.* per couple; herrings, 2*s.* per hundred, &c.

Feb. 28. Whitehall. 36. John Levingston to Carleton. The King is well. Buckingham holds his greatness. Lady Lake accuses the Countess of Exeter of attempting to poison Lady Roos and Sec. Lake; also that on the death of Sir Jas. Smith, her first husband, she was contracted to Sir Fras. Crane, and gave him 4,000*l.* for breach of contract, when the Earl of Exeter became a suitor to her.

Feb. 28. London. 37. Chamberlain to the Same. The Court gallants have vanished like mushrooms. The King ordered young Monson, who presented himself continually about him, to be reproved and dismissed. Sir Thos. Lake is in a labyrinth, not knowing how to make good his wife's imputations, and the Earl of Exeter demanding justice against such foul accusations. The Spaniard's execution is postponed.

Feb. 28. London. 38. Nath. Brent to [the Same]. The King came from Theobalds to Whitehall, and will spend his Sundays in town, for the convenience of Buckingham, who practises running at the tilt, against St. George's Feast. His Majesty makes merry with the opinions of a new sect called Thrascists; their leader, Thrasco, is in prison; and the Ecclesiastical Commission has them in chase. Sir Oliver Lambert died before his patent as Baron Lambert of Cavan reached him. Foot companies and vessels of war are preparing for Venice; the Venetian Ambassador appoints the general and captains.

VOL. XCVI.

1618.

[Feb.] 39. Statement of the difficulties in opposition to the project for establishing the manufacture of the new draperies in Hertfordshire.

Feb.? 40. Proposition submitted to [the Council] by Walter Morrall, for the encouragement of new drapery and perpetuanies, by issuing charters for their manufacture in Devonshire and other counties, according to the charter granted to Hertfordshire, for execution of which a commission and proclamation are required.

March 1. 41. Sir Hen. Savile to Carleton. Surprise at not having heard from him for so long; thinks it is because his agent [Sherburn] is so much employed by the Lord Chancellor. With note from Margaret Lady Savile, that she is almost dead with grief at not hearing from him or her daughter since Christmas.

March? Dover Castle. 42. Lord Zouch to Edw. West and —— Woodriff, waggoners, and —— Harris, fisherman. Orders them to repair to the Castle, to answer charges against them.

March 3. 43. Licence by Sir Geo. Bowles, Lord Mayor of London, for John Earle, of Southwark, butcher, to kill and sell flesh during Lent, poultry wares excepted.

March 3. 44. Order in Council for an estimate to be made of the cost of the King and Queen's diets, and those of the Royal household at the several boards.

March 3. London. 45. Alex. Williams to Carleton. Bingley listens to Carleton's offer about the payment of his allowance. Money affairs.

March 4. London. 46. Matt. de Quester to the Same. Forwards a packet from Sec. Lake. Hen. Herman has arrived, and gone to Eton.

March 5. 47. Bond of Rich. Oake and Hen. Dann, both of Rye, co. Sussex, in 100*l.*, to Lord Zouch, for the appearance at the Admiralty Court at Rye of John Pottle and Denis Damerseau, of Dieppe, taken fishing with unlawful nets.

March 5. Westminster. Grant to John Hunt, in reversion after Edw. Grimeston, of the office of Serjeant-at-Arms, to wait upon the Speaker at the time of Parliament. [*Sign Man., vol.* VIII., *No.* 91.]

March 6. Salisbury House. 48. Geo. Gerrard to Carleton. The Countess of Exeter is scarcely questioned, all believing her clear. Luke Hatton proves that he was in Somersetshire at the time Lady Roos says he discovered to her the Countess's desire of poisoning her; and the King pronounces the letter, said to be from the Countess, begging pardon for the design, a counterfeit. Sir Hum. May made Duchy Chancellor; but Buckingham is offended with him for promising the reversion of his surveyorship both to Benj. Rudyard and Mr. Packer, to secure their interest. Dr. Willett still in prison, for sounding people in Norfolk and Suffolk as to what they would give in Parliament, to prevent the Spanish match. A Spanish monk delivered over to the Sheriffs, and likely to be burnt.

Vol. XCVI.

1618.

March 6. 49. Note of payments to Sir Roger Dallison, late Lieutenant of Ordnance, on the assignment of 6,000*l.* per ann., from April 1614 to June 1615; and to Sir Rich. Morrison, now Lieutenant, for the year ending June 30, 1616.

March 7. Westminster. Grant to Jacob Blakewey of pardon for adultery with Katherine, wife of Sam. Moore, of Larden, co. Salop, for which he is indicted before the Ecclesiastical Commissioners, and the Court of the Marches of Wales. Latin. [*Sign Man., vol.* VIII., *No.* 92.]

March 7. London. 50. Chamberlain to Carleton. Loens was treasurer of Exeter Church, and wrote against the Puritans' too strict observance of the Sabbath. The Spaniard has been anathematized for blasphemy, and delivered over to the secular power. The Bishop of Salisbury dead, leaving a book half written against the Arminians. The Lord Treasurer busy learning Spanish. Lady Roos fetched home by her father and friends, to their great triumph; the case is to be referred to the Star Chamber.

March 7. London. 51. Nath. Brent to [the Same]. The King confined to bed with the gout. The Queen stays at Denmark House; she sent a present to the French King of horses and hounds. The French Ambassador is returning because he was not invited to the Prince's Masque, as was the Spanish. Court ladies begin to adopt the Catholic religion, in expectation of the Spanish match. Lady Digby delivered of a boy. The Archbp. of Canterbury much grieved with the death of the Bishop of Salisbury, his brother. The Archbp. of Spalato made Master of the Savoy; he is printing a book more strongly against Rome than ever. Lord Roos, at Rome, laughs at his wife's quarrels. The blasphemous Spaniard condemned to be burned, &c.

March 8. London. 52. Matthew de Quester to the Same. Sends a packet from Sec. Lake by Sampson Bates, who, he hopes, may bring back one from him.

March 9. 53. Reasons why the Fellowship of Merchant Adventurers desire to remove their residence from Middleburgh; with answers thereto by the Secretary of Middleburgh.

March 9. 54. List of names of Merchant Adventurers summoned to attend the Council, and bring all correspondence about the removal of the company.

March 9? 55. Reasons why Middleburgh is not inferior to Holland as a residence for the Merchant Adventurers, as regards restraint of interlopers, the exacting tare on cloth, and providing commodities for exchange.

March 9? 56. Petition of the Company of Merchant Adventurers to the King, for approbation of their resolution to remove from Middleburgh, and for their deputy to be heard against what shall be alleged by the agent

VOL. XCVI.

1618.

from Middleburgh, in opposition to their removal, for which they have already obtained His Majesty's permission.

March 10. 57. Another list of Merchant Adventurers summoned for the 12th instant, to attend the Committee appointed to consider the removal.

March 10. London. 58. Sir Gerard Herbert to Carleton. Sir Geo. Sandys hanged at Wapping for taking purses on the highway, having been formerly pardoned for like offences; his lady and son in prison as accomplices. The King suspends the execution of the Portugal heretic, wishing much for his conversion; he calls Moses a conjurer, Christ a deceiver, &c.; he has lived an austere beggar's life, and speaks Latin well. The Earl of Bridgewater likely to lose his estate, through the claims of a niece.

March 13. London. 59. Edw. Sherburn to [the Same]. Has urged to Sir Thos. Lake the necessity of Carleton's allowance as Ambassador being paid, and the honour of His Majesty's Ministers preserved by their not losing their credit. He owned all this to be true, lamented the state of affairs, but knew not how to rectify it.

March 13. 60. Sir John Bingley to Sir Thos. Lake. No money has been paid into the Exchequer upon the judgment against John Clayton and Thos. Rawson, though the informer has received his moiety.

March 14. Cumbernauld. 61. Lord Erskine to the Same. Asks what he shall do about his pension, and whether he might obtain any of the Irish lands which are to be distributed. Would civilize them, or do any other duty required.

March 15. Lambeth. 62. Archbp. of Spalato to Carleton. Has put together a little book to be sent to Venice for the instruction of the Italians; sends presentation copies. The King has given him the Mastership of the Savoy, a prebend of Canterbury, and the Deanery of Windsor.

March 16. London. 63. Chamberlain to the Same. The King is better, and going to Theobalds; the Queen has visited him several times. Dr. Fotherby, Prebend of Canterbury, made Bishop of Salisbury. Sir Hum. May got the Chancellorship of the Duchy, &c., but Lady Compton has a lease of the Duchy House. Sir Lionel Cranfield expostulated with the King on this choice, but he is much disliked for his insolence about the projected reforms of the household, which are likely to come to nothing. The Merchant Adventurers forbidden to leave Middleburgh. Lord Delawarr gone to Virginia. The Venetian Ambassador making musters.

March 16. Westminster. Proclamation renewing former prohibitions against the importation of alum, under penalty of forfeiture. Printed. [*Proc. Coll.*, *No.* 52.]

March 17. 64. Thos. Tailor to Lake. Acknowledges his letter. As concerning his most sacred Majesty, is willing to discharge all duties fitting a loyal subject.

Vol. XCVI.

1618.

March 17. Exeter. 65. Mayor of Exeter to the Council. Complains that John Prowse, one of the Justices of that city, and his son, Richard, used contemptuous and menacing language against him, whilst in his public office; thinks such courses lead to contempt of authority.

March 19. Dover Castle. 66. [Lord Zouch] to the Mayors, &c. of the Cinque Ports. Claims protection for Thos. Michell, while attending him on special service, up to March 31.

March 19. Dover Castle. 67. Commission by the Same, appointing the captains, lieutenants, and gentlemen porters of castles, the ministers of towns, and others, Commissioners of Passage, to give passports and keep a register of such persons as come in and go out of the realm, within the jurisdiction of the Cinque Ports. John Clerk appointed Clerk of the Passage.

March 19. Grant to Sir Wm. Button of the office of Overseer of the Little Customs in the Port of London, for life. [*Grant Bk., p.* 231.]

March 20. London. 68. Sir Gerard Herbert to Carleton. Lady Montgomery is safely delivered of a young Lord Herbert. The condemned heretic will be banished, not burned. The King has the gout in his leg, &c.

March 20. Hatton House. 69. Elizabeth Lady Hatton to the Same. Respect for her having been the cause of the difference between him and his wife, hopes that her thankful acknowledgment will reconcile them; finds he thinks women capable of little but compliments, &c.

March 20? Grant to Sam. Robinson, of Hovingham, and John Dent, of Marrick, both co. York, of pardon for horse-stealing. Latin. [*Sign Man., vol.* VIII., *No.* 93.]

March 21. St. Christopher's, one of the Antilles. 70. Sir Walter Raleigh to [Sir Ralph Winwood]. Detailed account of his expedition to Guiana; death of his son in a conflict with the Spaniards, who were informed, through the Spanish Ambassador in England, when and where to expect them. Capt. Keymish, who commanded the squadron up the Orinoco, finding the way to the mines well defended, failed to force a passage; reproached him on his return for having ruined him, on which he shot himself. Will return to Europe, but knows not what will become of him. *Mutilated.*

March 21. 71. Perfect copy of the above.

March 21. Westminster. Demise to Lady Elizabeth, wife of John Lord Stewart, Baron of Kincleven, and to Margaret Stewart, their daughter, of a messuage in Westminster, in reversion after the Earl of Montgomery. Latin. [*Sign Man., vol.* VIII., *No.* 94.]

March 22. Westminster. Grant to Fras. Bassett, of London, of pardon for clipping gold. [*Ibid., No.* 95].

March 22? 72. Statement of the advantages which the King may derive from purchasing and working out the invention of a foreigner, who has discovered a mode of mixing alloy with silver used for the manu-

1618. Vol. XCVI.

facture of silver thread, and has exercised it in the United Provinces, till the too great proportion of alloy practised by his partners induced the revocation of his grant.

March 22. Whitehall. Proclamation prohibiting the making of gold and silver thread &c. by any persons unlicensed by the King, or the importing it from abroad, the manufacture being now taken into His Majesty's hands. Printed. [*Proc. Coll., No.* 53.]

March 23. London. 73. Paul de la Ravoire to Carleton. Promised promotion of the Archbp. of Spalato. Sends thirty-six copies of his sermons, and of a small compendium of his other works, entitled "Scogli del naufragio Christiano."

March 24. London. 74. Sir Edw. Harwood to the Same. The King approves Carleton's proceedings. Buckingham tries to oblige people by his courtesies. The tilting a poor one; Lord Hay substituted for himself a French rider of the Prince, who carried the day. The Lord Treasurer is to be questioned, some say turned out. The officers of the Ordnance complain that the too great favour formerly shown to Sir Roger Dallison prevents their having necessary allowances, which are withheld till Dallison's debt is secured.

March 24. 75. Sir Matthew Carew to Lady Carleton, his niece. Hopes the misconduct of his son will not diminish their natural affection; would have turned him off had he not been repentant. Is glad to hear of her arrival in England.

March 24. Licence to Rich. Bannister to make cloths and beaver, &c., for twenty-one years. [*Grant Bk., p.* 241.]

March 24. Madrid. Fras. Cottington to [Lake]. The Spanish Council of War have ordered Sir Walter Raleigh's late commission to be translated into Spanish. Knows not how they will take it. [*Extract, Dom. Corresp., Dec.* 18, 1618.]

March 24. Melding, Suffolk. 76. Jas. Alington to the Same. Is not so rich as has been supposed, but is ready to perform all the duties of a loyal subject.

March 24. 77. Draft of the above.

March 24. Sandwich. 78. John Jacob and Art. Ruck to Lord Zouch. Report on a cause between Leving and Broughton, relative to the division of the estate of the late John Ballard.

March 25. Court at Whitehall. 79. Sir Hen. Carey to Carleton. Thanks for congratulations on his preferment. Is not accustomed to ceremonies, but in "upright plainness" will be glad to serve him.

March 25. Sudbury. 80. Wm. Alston to Sir Thos. Lake. Has related to Mr. Scott the particulars of his estate; is willing to discharge the duties of a good and loyal subject.

March 25. 81. Memorandum of payments made to Sir Edw. Bushell on his pension, since Michaelmas, 1615.

March 25. Westminster. Grant to Marco Ant. de Dominis, Archbp. of Spalato, of the Mastership of the Savoy, vacant by resignation of Walter Balconquall. Latin. [*Sign Man., vol.* IX., *No.* 1.]

[March 25.] Entry of the above. [*Warrt. Bk.*, I., *p.* 236.]

1618. Vol. XCVI.

March 26. Westminster. Grant to Thos. Gwillim of pardon for a riot, &c., for which he was sentenced to fine and imprisonment in the Star Chamber. [*Sign Man., vol.* IX., *No.* 2.]

March 26. 82. Gentleman Ushers and Daily Waiters to the Lord Chamberlain. The Serjeants-at-Arms contracted to allow Mr. Williams 20*s.* out of every 5*l.* accruing to them from his procuring a patent to raise Knights' fees from 20*s.* to 5*l.*, but although 120 Knights were made during the Scotch journey, Williams cannot obtain his full dues, some of the serjeants trying to evade them, and refusing to make a composition with him.

March 26. London. Thursday. 83. Sir G. Herbert to Carleton. Reception of the two Russian Ambassadors; the King's pleasant speeches to them; they would not come into the presence till fetched by the Council, that being the custom of their country; they wish to make a league with England, and to borrow 60,000*l.*, which the merchants will furnish; they went to see the tilting on the 24th, and were much pleased with it, and with the crowds that flocked about them, to and from their lodgings at Crosby Hall. Particulars of the tilt, and the devices. Capt. Harry Mainwaring knighted.

March 26. London. 84. Edw. Sherburn to the Same. Safe arrival of Lady Carleton; has provided a convenient lodging for her in Fleet Street, Lady Dale's lodging in the Blackfriars not being commodious. The Lords are in treaty with Burlamachi to pay the Ambassadors every six months. Business matters, &c.

March 26? Walden. 85. Thos. Turner to Lake. Has reported his estate to Mr. Scott; will attend him next term.

March 26? 86. John Martiall to [the Same]. Is not a moneyed man as reported, nor has expressed a wish to compound for his peace with the King, being conscious of no offence.

March 27. London. 87. Chamberlain to Carleton. Young [Monson] still pushes forward, and is well supported, but should have secured some ordinary place as attendant, before his drift was perceived. The Archbp. of Spalato has the Savoy at last, and also the prebend at Canterbury of Dr. Fotherby, now Bp. of Salisbury. Lady Coke prosecutes her husband in the Star Chamber; he is ill supported, for she will pay nothing unless she may have her will. The Venetian troops are going, commanded by Mainwaring, the late pirate. Tobie Matthew is to be in confinement at his father's. Tilting on the King's day, March 24; the Queen could not be persuaded to attend; the King visited her before going to Theobalds. Lord Roos is at Tivoli, and begs leave to stay abroad to digest his wrongs.

March 27. London. 88. Geo. Carleton to the Same. Proceedings with Lady Hill before the Attorney General, on the purchase of her lease; his son Dudley is anxious to come over to see him [Sir Dudley], but must stay over September to take his fellowship at Cambridge.

March 28. London. 89. Matthew de Quester to the Same. Packets delayed in Zealand for want of shipping, delivery of letters, &c.

Vol. XCVI.

1618.

March 28. Whitehall. 90. Benj. Rudyard to Carleton. The King's consent to Carleton's coming over must depend on the state of affairs there. Buckingham's help should be sought. Thinks his allowances would be better paid if he came to solicit for himself. Lord Chandos more improved by the waters of Newenham Mills, in Warwickshire, than by the Spa.

March 28. St. James's. 91. Thos. Murray to the Same. The King much busied in the reformation of the household, hoping to save 30,000*l.* per ann. Abuses in the Exchequer, the Navy, and Ireland, are to be examined into, if private interests do not hinder the public good, &c.

March 28. 92. [Abel Barnard] to the Same. Details of personal and family sickness. Begs a copy of his book on uniformity, &c.

March 28. Westminster. Warrant to pay to Geo. Baker, goldsmith, 683*l.* 7*s.* 2*d.*, for spangles for the coats of the guard, footmen, and messengers. [*Sign Man., vol.* IX., *No.* 3.]

March 28. Westminster. Warrant for certain payments to Robt. Cooke, Clerk of the Cheque of the Guard, for red cloth for summer liveries of the servants of the King, Queen, and Prince. [*Ibid., No.* 4.]

March 29. 93. Sir Edw. Conway to [Carleton]. The Chancellor of the Exchequer says that neither he nor the Treasurer is to blame for the tardy payments to Ambassadors, and that he will do his best for Carleton. Thanks for favours to his cousin Willoughby. The King is making reformations in the Exchequer. The quarrel between Lady Exeter and Sir Thos. Lake is a strange riddle, and will have a shameful issue on one side.

March 30. Westminster. Grant to Fras. Ayliffe, of Westminster, of pardon for manslaughter of Art. Wingfield, at the mediation of Lady Elizabeth. Latin. [*Ibid., No.* 5.]

March 30. London. 94. Nath. Brent to Carleton. Sir Benj. Rudyard is Surveyor of the Court of Wards, with promise from the King of further preferment. Dares not write of the factions among the greatest at Court. Though the two would-be favourites are dismissed, Monson's return is hoped for. Lady Roos submits her cause to the King. Lady Hatton has driven her husband into a numbness of the side, the forerunner of palsy. The King desires the continuance of the City loan another year. The Venetian Ambassador prepares eight ships; he will have a Venetian Admiral, but the real command will rest between Sir Hen. Peyton and Sir Hen. Mainwaring. The Dean of Paul's fails to succeed the Bp. of Norwich, because he was so open in offering his 2,500 thanks, that the Court lacqueys talk of it.

March ? 95. Sir Edw. Conway to [the Same]. Professions of service. Sir Walter Raleigh's son was slain at the river of Orinoco, and [Lawrence] Keymish shot himself, in despair of finding the gold mine. Raleigh's letters come charged with misfortunes and tears, and his wife is in great affliction. Sir John Digby is returning much honoured. Imperfect.

March. 96. Thos. Wilson to the King. Sends particulars of letters from Japan, describing the greatness of its Princes, who have a Court of 100,000 men, palaces that lodge 200,000, &c.; they have banished

1618. VOL. XCVI.

Jesuits, and, for fear of their stealing in disguised, will not even admit merchants. Indorsed [by Wilson], "An abstract of letters lately arryved from the East Indies, from Japan, from Mr. Cox, written to myself in Jan. 1616-7, and arived her in March 1617-8, which His Majesty read and discoursed with me about them, but cold not be induced to believe that the things written are true, but desyred to speake with the writer when he comes home, who, I told him, is very shortly to return; he is the chiefe factor for the Est Indian Company, and hath bene in those parts almost seven yeares last past."

March. 97. Commission by Lord Zouch to the Mayors of Dover, Sandwich, and others, for holding a Court of Lode-manage, for inquiry into cases relating to conducting ships to harbour, and offences of seafaring men, &c.

March. 98. Note of persons of Wiltshire and Somersetshire to be summoned before the Council for neglect at the musters.

[March.] Grant to the Pinmakers' Company of London of confirmation of their charter, and of the Orders in Council in their favour; also grant to them of the sole pre-emption of pins; with a schedule of the prices to be charged for pins. [*Sign Man., vol.* IX., *No.* 6.]

March. [Tower.] 99. —— Gaultier to Lord [Suffolk?]. Throws himself on his liberality and compassion, being in prison on an unfounded accusation, in which he also is involved. French.

March? 100. Statement of receipts by the Farmers of the Customs, during the past seven years, as compared with the rent paid to the King. Average receipts, 159,045*l.* 17*s.* 10½*d.* a year.

[March.] 101. Petition of Thos. Napleton, of Faversham, to Lord Zouch, that in consideration of the malice of his enemy, his certificate of former good conduct, his advanced age and dangerous sickness, he may be discharged on good security, and go to Bath for recovery of his health.

VOL. XCVII. APRIL—JUNE, 1618.

April 1. 1. Lord Chief Justice Montague to the Council. Has heard Hen. Corney and the petitioners against him for denying them right of common and fuel in King's Buckwood, co. Bedford, and has put them in the way to settle the matter by law. They are stirred up by others, as were the levellers in Northamptonshire.

April 1. London. 2. Chamberlain to Carleton. Lord Roos has sent letters complaining of his father and mother-in-law, but excusing his wife as misled by them; he wishes to sell lands to pay his debts. The East India Company helps the Muscovy Company with the loan to the Emperor of Russia, on condition of sharing their profits for eight years. The Scottish [East India] Company's patent revoked. Dr. [Ant.] Maxey, Dean of Windsor, offers most for the bishopric of Norwich, though the Dean of St. Paul's offered 2,500 thanks,

VOL. XCVII.

1618. Mr. Bell, the merchant, made Gentleman of the Privy Chamber. Mr. Brent is going on some small employment into France, &c.

April 1. Dover Castle. 3. Lord Zouch to Wm. Elfick, of Seaford. Appoints him Captain of the Train Bands of that town.

April 2. 4. Bp. of Exeter and Justices of Peace of Devonshire to the Council. Have examined into the ground of the Earl of Bath's complaint; find that his sealing up Mrs. Henson's closets, in order to secure his own writings and private papers, was very necessary; but though he offered to allow her to open them at any time to take out her own papers, she broke them open, by advice of a lawyer, Alex. Maynard, who has been insolent to the Earl of Bath's friends.

April 2. Thursday. London. 5. Matt. de Quester to Carleton. Sends despatches from Sec. Lake. Wm. Murray and others have gone over, without giving him notice of their journey.

April 3? 6. Sir Edw. Harwood to the Same. Advice as to Carleton's movements; the propriety of his returning home for a visit, &c. Suggests that the Lord Chamberlain should intercede with Buckingham about it. The Commission to examine into the Treasurer's Office is stayed. There are mutterings of a Parliament.

April 3. Goldsborough. 7. Sir Rich. Hutton to Lake. Has not had time fully to examine the bearer's cause referred to him, but thinks the sequestration of his habitation by the Lord President not warranted.

April 5. 8. Ambrose Randolph to [Thos. Wilson]. In favour of a match suggested between Sir Geo. Buck and Wilson's daughter, Elizabeth.

April 6. London. 9. Sir Wm. Lovelace to Carleton. Sir. Dud. Diggs is gone to the Emperor of Muscovy, to satisfy the Duke's request for 100,000 dollars, part of which sum is imposed by the King on the East India Company, the Muscovy Company being too poor to pay it alone. Sir Thos. Dale is gone, and the Venetians are embarking.

April 7. Grant to Sir Rich. Young and Robt. Pye of the office of Clerk of the Letters Patent in Chancery, for life. [*Grant Bk., p.* 252.]

April 8. Commission to the Archbp. of Canterbury and others, concerning payment of tithes in London. [*Ibid., p.* 233.]

April 8. Lake to [Carleton]. News arrived from Spain that some Englishmen have found a gold mine 250 leagues south of Florida. Sir Walter Raleigh's friends hope he may have been the discoverer. [*Holl. Corresp., April* 8, 1617.]

April 9. London. 10. Sir Gerard Herbert to the Same. Great preparations were making for the christening of the infant Lord Herbert, when he died; Lady Montgomery takes the loss very heavily, &c. Particulars of a foot-race between a man of the Duke of Buckingham and one of Sir Thos. Howard; bets of the nobility on both sides; they ran the first ten miles within the hour; Buckingham's man won, and the King has taken him into his service, as the Prince has done the other runner.

April 9. London. 11. Matt. de Quester to the Same. Sends a letter from Sec. Lake.

Vol. XCVII.

1618.

April 10. London. 12. Soames Woodward to Carleton. His reason for returning home was that his ignorance of foreign languages made him unfit to do any service abroad, beyond waiting at table. Has offered his service to Lady Carleton in England, but without effect.

April 10. London. 13. Chamberlain to the Same. The King, courtiers, and large crowds went to see a foot-race from St. Albans to London. The Earl of Somerset lives plentifully in the Tower.

April 10. 14. Affidavit of Edm. Davison, of Norwich, that he heard that all the timber in Horning Park, Norfolk, belonging to the Bishopric of Norwich, was sold, which would leave little wood for succeeding bishops.

April 10. Commission to the Lord Treasurer concerning demising parcels of the forests of Chippenham and Blackmore, co. Wilts. [*Grant Bk.*, *p.* 260.]

April 11. London. 15. Sir Edw. Harwood to Carleton. Sec. Naunton has got half of the intelligence money. The forwarders of the intended favourite have much ado to defend themselves. Suffolk is found to have only 10,000*l.* in his hands, so is likely to escape.

April 11. London. 16. Wm. Dackombe to Edw. Nicholas, his cousin. Private affairs. He is to bring up a copy of Dackombe's brother's will. His cousin Dorothy dead; her disposal of Colby parsonage, and her other property.

April 13. Confirmation and grant of fees to the Masters of Chancery, with power to the Lord Chancellor concerning the same. [*Grant Bk.*, *p.* 260.]

April 14. 17. Sheriff and Justices of Peace of Devonshire to the Council. Have failed as yet to apprehend John Prowse, as directed, but have taken bonds from Jonas Pynson and others for their appearance when required.

April 14. Westminster. 18. Commission to the Earl of Suffolk and others to discover concealed lands, encroachments, &c.; and to compound with all who receive pensions or annuities from the Crown to surrender the same, in exchange for a certain portion of these lands.

[April 14.] Entry of the above. [*Warrt. Bk.*, I., *p.* 234.]

April 14. Westminster. 19. Commission to the Chancellor of the Exchequer, the Master of the Rolls, and others, to examine all suits and petitions preferred to the King by his subjects, and to report thereon to the Council. His Majesty has caused a schedule to be drawn of such suits as he is willing to admit, or will refuse.

[April.] 20. Declaration of His Majesty's pleasure as to what suits shall be granted and what refused, in consideration of the poverty of the Exchequer, and appointing Commissioners, without whose approbation no suit is to be preferred. With a schedule annexed, containing a memorial of those things which are forbidden and of those things which are permitted to be sued for.

21. Copy of the above. Printed 1619.

1618. Vol. XCVII.

22. Another copy. Imperfect.

[April.] 23. Draft of the clause p. 18 of the above.

[April.] 24. Draft of the concluding clause of the above.

[April.] 25. Copy of the latter part of the above memorial.

[April.] 26. Copy of part of the above.

April 16. London. 27. Matthew de Quester to Carleton. Sends packets from Sec. Lake. Sir John Digby has left Madrid, and gone to the sea-coast, and will come back through France, unless he finds the King's ships, which cannot yet have arrived, waiting for him.

April 16. 28. Fras. Gofton to Sir Clement Edmondes. Sir Rich. Sutton and himself have received the accounts of Sir Robt. Mansell for the last five years, and will make them up as soon as possible.

April 16. Chelmsford. 29. Justices of Essex to the Council. Have appointed a Provost Marshal for Essex, as required, choosing Sir Nich. Coote. Have levied a rate for his entertainment on the county, but Colchester alone refuses to pay its proportion of 10*l.* Request directions thereon.

April 16. Grant to John Hepborn of the office of keeping the Block House in Kent, for life. [*Grant Bk., p.* 265.]

April 17. Grant to Sir Benj. Rudyard of the Surveyorship of the Court of Wards and Liveries, for life. [*Ibid., p.* 251.]

April 17. Grant to Pat. Murray and Thos. Potts, of the office of collecting forfeitures on the laws concerning sewers, for twenty-one years. [*Ibid., p.* 269.]

April 17. Grant to Abraham and John Jacob of the office of collecting impositions on tobacco, for life. [*Ibid., p.* 267.]

April 19. 30. Note of the distribution of 4*l.* to the servants of Archbp. Abbot, on the consecration of Martin Fotherby, Bp. of Salisbury.

[April 19.] 31. Means proposed to the Committee of Council by the Merchant Adventurers, for reformation of abuses in cloth-making; also for preventing interlopers in their trade. With marginal notes of the resolutions taken thereon.

April 20. 32. Debenture for payment to Rich. Nash, Clerk of the Armoury at Greenwich, of 36*s.* 10*d.* per month, as his wages, from April 22, 1617, the time of the death of his predecessor, John Binnion.

April 20. London. 33. Chamberlain to Carleton. Hopes he will use his permit to come over to England. The Archbp. of Spalato preached at the Mercers' Chapel, but indifferently, dwelling chiefly on the differences about keeping Easter. The Chancellor was there, in as great pomp as he went a while ago to Sir Baptist Hicks' and Barnes' shops, to cheapen and buy silks and velvets. Dr. Fotherby, when consecrated Bp. of Salisbury, protested loudly that he had given nothing

1618. Vol. XCVII.

for his promotion, and disclaimed any promises that others might have made for him. Death of Dr. Donne. The King going to Thetford.

April 21. Peterborough. 34. Commissioners of Sewers, &c., of Cambridgeshire and Huntingdonshire to the Council. Find the statements in Wm. Hetley's petition false; he refuses to obey their mandate to pay 20*l.* to the gaoler of Peterborough, John Davy, whom he has aggrieved.

April 22. New College, Oxford. 35. Matt. Nicholas to [Edw. Nicholas]. Hopes his London journey will be successful. Mr. [Dan.] Ingoll is Senior Proctor, and Mr. [John] Drope, of Magdalen, Junior.

April 22? [London.] 36. [Edw. Nicholas] to ——. [Proceedings with Mr. Dean and Mr. Auditor, relative to paying the rent of the hundred of Appletree. Is going into Somersetshire, on business for his deceased master.

April 22. Commission to the Lord Chancellor and others, to inquire about the importation of gold and silver thread. [*Grant Bk.*, *p.* 233.]

April 24. Commission to Lord Sheffield, President of the Council of the North, &c., for establishing peace in the north, and punishing offenders. [*Ibid.*, *p.* 260.]

April 24. Newcastle-upon-Tyne. 37. Commissioners for Survey of the Border Counties to the Council. Thanks for the King's care in repressing disorders by means of the active labours of the Lord President. Beg that he may continue his charge until "the reign of impiety and iniquity be suppressed" in those parts, because any failure in execution would encourage malefactors, as it has hitherto done.

April 25. 38. Thos. Turner to Lake. Is willing to advance His Majesty 10*l.*, which is as much as his estate will bear.

April 26. Whitehall. Proclamation commanding all apothecaries to compound their medicines after the directions of the Pharmacopeia Londinensis, lately compiled by the College of Physicians of London. Printed. [*Proc. Coll.*, *No.* 54.]

April 26? Licence to John Marriott of the sole printing and sale of the Pharmacopeia Londinensis, lately compiled by the College of Physicians. [*Warrt. Bk.* I., *p.* 238.]

April 27. Grant to Thos. and Kenrick Eyton of the office of Clerk and Receiver of fines and forfeitures in Wales, for life. [*Grant Bk.*, *p.* 265.]

April 29. Grant to Sir Edw. Zouch of the office of Marshal [of the Household], for life. [*Ibid.*, *p.* 253.]

April 29. 39. Sir [?] Thos. Hels, High Sheriff of Devonshire, to the Council. John Prowse is now apprehended, and sent up in charge of the Under Sheriff.

Vol. XCVII.

1618.

April 29. London. 40. Chamberlain to Carleton. The Queen removed to Greenwich, and the King going there from Theobalds. Buckingham's splendid train on St. George's Day. Wraynham, of Norfolk, censured for accusing the Chancellor of an unjust decree. Sir Dud. Diggs gone Ambassador to Muscovy.

April 29. Carlisle Castle. 41. Lord Clifford, Lord Lieutenant of Cumberland, to the Commissioners for the Survey of Malefactors, Cumberland. Urges the fulfilment of the articles in the King's proclamation for a survey of malefactors, and of the offences committed by them, and the preparation of the certificates required.

April 30. Riby. 42. Thos. Tailor to Lake. Acknowledges his letters by Pat. Scott, who assisted him in drawing up the reply. Has never been a usurer.

April. 43. Petition of the Wardens, &c. of the Trinity House to the Council. Complain of the heavy tax laid on coal vessels by Sir Wm. Erskine and Mr. Meldrum, the new patentees for keeping a lighthouse at Winterton Ness, amounting to 2,000*l.* per ann., whereas the lighthouse only costs 80*l.* or 100*l.* Have long maintained a light at Winterton Ness, which the patentees order them to discontinue.

April. 44. Names of Commissioners of Survey, and of Oyer and Terminer and Gaol Delivery, for the Border Counties.

April. Whitehall. 45. The Council to [the Lord Lieutenant of Bedfordshire]. The certificates of musters of that county being very unsatisfactory, special pains are to be taken to muster the bands afresh, to supply defects, especially in the horse, and to have them well trained. Commend Capt. John Blundell, the Muster-master, as deserving some reward for his pains.

April? 46. ——— to Mr. Hanby. To search the books for the sums issued to Sir Robt. Mansell, Treasurer of the Navy, in the Easter terms of 1617, 1618.

April. 47. Petition of Dorothy Gerveis, sister of Lord Stafford, to the Council, that Rich. Ockold may be compelled to pay her a proportion of a balance remaining in his hands, from the sale of certain lands of her late husband, during whose imprisonment Ockold took advantage of his distress, and drew him to acknowledge debts, for the sake of a supply for his present necessities.

April? 48. Petition of Robt. Jones to Sir Hen. Hobart and others, Commissioners of the Revenue, to be appointed Bailiff of the Manor of East Brent, co. Somerset.

April. 49. Petition of the poor Workmen in the King's works to the Council, that their wages, which are in arrears for twelve months, may be paid them. They have pawned their tools and furniture for food, and have nothing left.

April. 50. Report of the trial of [John] Wraynham in the Star Chamber, for slandering Lord Chancellor Bacon.

Vol. XCVII.

1618. April? 51. List of Knights and Gentlemen [Justices of the Peace?] for Yorkshire, Lancashire, and the Cinque Ports. Indorsed are notes [by Nicholas] on the trial of Wraynham.

May 2. 52. Sir Robt. Pierrepoint to Lake. Patrick Scott has offered him composition for having put money out to usury; disclaims the charge. A third of the benevolence raised in Nottinghamshire was due to his exertions.

May 3. 53. Petition of the Inhabitants of Wisbeach to the Council, against the entire charge of ditching Wisbeach river, which is usually done at the general expense, being thrown upon the inhabitants of Wisbeach hundred. The enlargement of the river from forty to sixty feet in width is very necessary to be continued.

May 3. Madrid. Sir Fras. Cottington to [Lake]. Tidings of Sir Walter Raleigh's landing have come, but the Spaniards are confident he will find neither gold nor silver in those parts. [*Extract, Dom. Corresp., Dec.* 18, 1618.]

May 4. 54. Sir Robt. Mansell to Sir Geo. Calvert, Clerk of the Council. Requests that Paul Vinion and Peter Comley, glass makers, against whom he complained for making glass with wood, contrary to the King's proclamation, may be released, on bond not to repeat the offence.

May 4. Whitehall. 55. Sir Robt. Napier, Sir Marmaduke Darell, and Sir Allan Apsley to the Duke of Lenox and others. Have taken a view of the provisions, &c. made by Sir Jas. Cunningham for Greenland, and estimated the loss which he and his associates will incur by the stay of their voyage. *Inclose,*

55. I.—III. *Estimates of the losses which the new Company may sustain by their provisions for the Greenland voyage. Three copies.*

May 4. 56. Bond of John Bargrave, of Patrick's-bourne, Kent, and Jas. Brett, of London, in 100*l*., to indemnify Lord Zouch for delivering up to them the ship Edwin, from Virginia, with her cargo, of which Bargrave is owner, and Brett master.

May 4. 57. Draft of the above.

May 5. London. 58. Chamberlain to Carleton. Sec. Lake has so many feathers pulled from him that he moves every stone to keep off competitors, and, in order to curry favour, has made Read, a Scot, Latin Secretary. Naunton is never seen nor heard of. Wraynham's hard sentence is, a fine of 1,000*l*. imprisonment, and loss of his ears. Sir Wm. Russell, the Muscovy merchant, has bought the Treasurership of the Navy from Sir Robt. Mansell, who is to be Vice Admiral. Dr. Maxey, Dean of Windsor, dead. Dr. Bridgeman, or Balconquall, to succeed him. Buckingham's favour is not at all declining.

VOL. XCVII.

1618.

May 6. 59. Earl of Exeter to the Council. Asks permission to grant a request made to him by the inhabitants of Northampton, that they may exercise and train 150 soldiers, as Coventry and other towns have done.

May 6. Grant to Edw. and Hen. Johnson of the office of Clerks of the Ordnance in the Tower and elsewhere, for life. [*Grant Bk., p.* 266.]

May 6. Grant to Edw. Hawkins and Chris. Colby, successively, of the office of Examiner and Registrar to the Commissioners for Bankruptcy in London, for life. [*Ibid., p.* 267.]

May 8. Grant to Giles Norgate of the office of Clerk of the Signet, for life. [*Ibid., p.* 249.]

May 8. Commission to the Lord Treasurer to order the collection of duty on slate stone. [*Ibid., p.* 238.]

May 8. 60. [Commissioners of Survey for the Borders] to the Council. Have made a diligent search for idle and disorderly persons in Cumberland. *Inclose,*

60. I. *Lord Wm. Howard and other Commissioners to the Same. Send a survey, and certificate prefixed, of the residences, names of offenders, nature and proof of offences of idle and disorderly persons in Cumberland, taken by virtue of the King's commission of Jan.* 10, 1618. *Also notes of such Northumberland thieves as infest the waters of Tynedale. General remarks on the district. Their certificate would have been better, could they have obtained a copy of the commission. Carlisle, April* 30, 1618.

May ? 61. Names of the lewd, idle, and misbehaved persons in Bewcastle, Arthuret, and Liddleside parishes. Signed by Sir Edw. Musgrave and Sir Wm. Hutton, two of the Commissioners for Survey of misbehaved persons.

May ? 62. Note of the Grahams transplanted who have returned from Ireland, Brill, and Flushing. Presented by the Curate of Arthuret, and signed as the preceding.

May ? 63. Names of such notorious, idle, or wicked persons as dwell within the parish of Kirklington, Cumberland. Presented by the Parson and parish officers, and similarly signed.

May ? 64. Similar list for the parish of Stapleton, Cumberland. Imperfect.

May 8. York. 65. Lord Sheffield to the Council. Has held a gaol delivery at Newcastle; the country is very disorderly, but the gentlemen are forward to assist in settling it. Will report the cause of the mischief, and the best means of reformation.

Vol. XCVII.

1618.

May 9. London. 66. Sir Edw. Harwood to Carleton. Mr. Vice Chamberlain [Digby] has arrived from Spain. The match is likely to take place; but the King has first to tell his mind to the Spanish Ambassador, who then goes to Spain, and then comes the match-maker. Lady Suffolk was reported to be forbidden coming to town, but she has arrived. Sir Lionel Cranfield has the reversion of the Mastership of the Rolls.

May 9. Grant to Art. Low of the messuage called the Westhouse, co. Suffolk, for thirty-one years. [*Grant Bk., p.* 268.]

May 10. Grant to Sir Wm. Russell of the Treasurership of Marine Causes, for life. [*Ibid., p.* 251.]

May 10. 67. Petition of Leonard Trevellyan to the Council. Has long waited the trial of John Prowse, committed at his complaint for riding on horseback into church, offering to have his horse christened, hanging up his dead grandmother's hair in the market place, as that of an old witch, &c. Begs leave to depart, and to have the forfeitures of Edw. Pomery, and John Lake, two of Prowse's coadjutors, to compensate his losses in the suit.

May 10. Lord Zouch to the Mayor, &c. of Dover. Requires them to punish all who have offended against the Order in Council, by taking head-money from the French. [*Minute, Diary, Dom. Corresp., Oct.* 20, 1618.]

May 11. Tothill. 68. Petition of Rich. Wilson and his sisters, legatees of their late uncle John Chatterton, of Market Harborough, co. Leicester, to Lord Chancellor Bacon, for a writ of subpœna against Hen. Bolt, who, by deceitful practices, persuaded the widow of the said John Chatterton to give all the goods and chattels of the deceased to him, and threatened to defraud the complainants of a legacy of 20*l.* due to them on decease of the widow.

May 11. Westminster. 69. Warrant for allowance of diet of three dishes of meat to Sir Wm. Uvedale, Treasurer of the Chamber.

May 12. High Holborn. 70. Sir Ant. Ashley to Lake. Has taken measures to ascertain Keymish's abode, and will apprehend him if possible.

May 12. London. 71. Giov. Franc. Biondi to [Carleton]. Apologizes for his long silence, and hopes it will not be attributed to ingratitude. Italian.

May 12. Alnwick. 72. Commissioners for Survey of the Borders to the Council. Have not been remiss in executing the proclamation for reformation of the country, as they never received the commission till April 20; since which time they have bestowed their best endeavours therein. None of them have countenanced malefactors, nor admitted to bail any committed for felony, as reported.

May 14. 73. Examination of Jo. Treneale. Knew that divers warrants from the Commissioners for Ecclesiastical Causes were issued against John Prowse, of Brixham, Devonshire, for profaning the church.

VOL. XCVII.

1618.

Desired Prowse not to come to his house, but did not try to hinder his apprehension. Advised him to go to London, and submit to the Archbishop.

May 14. 74. Examination of Jonas Pincent, Attorney. Was engaged by. Prowse as his attorney in divers suits, but served him no other way Obtained a prohibition for him, on the ground that his offences, being committed before the general pardon, were included therein. Gave no notice thereof to the proctor on the other side, not knowing that it was needed.

May 14. 75. Examination of Gilbert Luscombe. Is the owner of the horse on which Prowse rode into Brixham church, but it was taken without his privity. Has done nothing to secure Prowse from apprehension.

May 14. 76. Examination of Hen. Dugdale. Never concealed nor conveyed away his brother-in-law, John Prowse. Advised him to submit and make his peace. Holds none of his goods.

May 14. Serjeants' Inn. 77. Justices Warburton and Croke to the Council. Have considered the petition of the maimed soldiers of Shropshire against the town of Much Wenlock, for refusing their share of the tax for relief of maimed soldiers, on the ground that it should be levied by their own justices of peace. Think that opinion is right, but that they ought to make a common fund with the county, or the taxation would be unequal, and also to pay their arrears.

May 14. Westminster. 78. Grant to Sir Robt. Mansell of the Lieutenancy of the Admiralty of England, void by decease of Sir Rich. Leveson. With a legal opinion that he cannot be deprived of that office for any misdemeanors but such as belong to the execution of it.

May 15. Whitehall. 79. The Duke of Lenox and others, to Sir Chris. Perkins and Sir Sydney Montague. Enjoins them to see that the brewers of London make a true account, for a composition to be entered into with the King, which they are endeavouring to evade, hoping to ruin the undertaker thereof.

May 16. 80. Note of stationery furnished [to the Exchequer Office] in Easter term, 1618.

May 16. Cawood Castle. 81. Tobias Matthew, Archbp. of York, to the Council. Has written to the bishops of his province to further the service of the musters, and send in their commissions to the lieutenants. Hopes the clergy will be found willing to contribute according to their ability.

May 16. Westminster. 82. Warrant to pay 20*l.* per ann. wages to Giles Dauncer, appointed Master of the Queen's Barges, in place of Rich. Hale, deceased.

May 19. 83. The Council to the Commissioners of Sewers for cos. Northampton, Huntingdon, Lincoln, Cambridge, and Isle of Ely. Order that a sluice be made from Wisbeach river, and the river ditched, and made sixty feet wide, at the general charge of the county, and not of the hundred of Wisbeach only.

Vol. XCVII.

1618.

May 21. Grant to Nath. Bacon of the office of engrossing licences and pardons for alienations, for life. [*Grant Bk., p.* 242.]

May 22. Gray's Inn. 84. The Attorney General to Sir Geo. Calvert. Thinks the complaint against Mr. Eastman was a plot to disgrace him, and cool benevolence, as he has conducted his business advisedly. *Incloses,*

84. I. *Examination of Edw. Eastman. Has collected* 82*l.* 3*s.* 8*d. by virtue of the King's patent, for the redeeming of Englishmen taken captives by the Turks, but found the expenses of collecting so great that he followed Justice Dodderidge's advice, and sent out briefs for it by the clerks of the assize on their summer circuits. May* 22.

May 23. Special pardon to Jas. Isaack for not being an apprentice. [*Grant Bk., p.* 266.]

May 25. 85. Justices of Peace [of Devonshire] to the Council. In consequence of an order by the Farmers of the Customs, to tax over length on kerseys more than twelve yards long, they cannot obtain sale for their cloths, whereby the clothiers, weavers, spinners, and fullers are much distressed.

May 29. Grant to Sir Lionel Cranfield of part of certain moneys reserved upon the grant of subsidies for Ireland, for three years. [*Grant Bk., p.* 242.]

May 29. Grant to Wm. Holle of the office of Head Sculptor of the Iron for money in the Tower and elsewhere, for life. [*Ibid., p.* 265.]

May 30. Wisbeach. 86. Ordinances of the Commissioners of Sewers that a drain shall be made through Wivelingham and Cottenham to the Ouse, and an old drain called Meargoes, running through Haddenham and Wilberton, to carry off the overflowings of the Ouse, be repaired.

May. 87. Sir Geo. Bowles, Mayor, and the Aldermen of London, to the Council. An Exchequer commission is issued to inquire into intrusions on waste ground in the City. The inconveniences of a grant thereof previously made by the King induced the Council, in June 1614, to stay the grant, and allow the City to enjoy their own waste ground as heretofore. Beg a similar stay to the present commission.

May. 88. Account of payments made by the Tellers of the Exchequer for the purchase of cordage for the Navy, from April 1612 to May 1618.

June 1. Licence to Hen. Lloyd to keep a market in Ewell, co. Surrey. [*Grant Bk., p.* 266.]

June 1. 89. Wm. Lord Roos to the King. Fears Sir Thos. Lake has suppressed his previous letter, in hopes of cloaking over the wicked conduct of himself, his wife, and daughter, and so misrepresenting his proceedings as to procure his recall, knowing that he wished to remain abroad till freed from their injuries, and hoping that he might disobey, and thus incur the danger of the law. Lake preferred a bill to have administration of his estates in his absence,

Vol. XCVII.

1618.

intending to beg them of the King, and cheat the creditors. His diabolical devices to ruin Roos' credit, and force him to pawn his land to him, in order to raise money for his Spanish journey, and on his return, to prevent its redemption. Lady Roos, Lake's daughter, complained of her mother, and begged Roos to fetch her away. On his doing so, he was attacked, according to a plot concerted beforehand, and two of his servants wounded. He wished a trial in the Star Chamber, but Lady Lake threatened any lawyer who appeared for him [Roos] with her husband's great influence with the King. He then wished to revenge himself on Art. Lake with the sword, as brave men, driven to desperation, do. Hopes His Majesty will pardon his leaving England unlicensed, and going to Rome, he being driven thereto by despair; and will permit him to remain abroad to digest his injuries, and allow his estates to be managed by his grandfather [the Earl of Exeter], not by Sir Thos. Lake. Also that he will not allow Lady Roos' title to save her from any severity, she being a base creature, a dishonour to his grandfather's house, and not worthy to wipe the shoes of the Countess of Exeter, whom she has wronged.

June 2. Philip Lane. 90. Warrant from Lord Zouch to the Mayors, &c. of Rye, Hythe, and Hastings, to assist Abraham Baker, sole patentee for manufacture of smalt, to search and seize all smalt not stamped and sealed by himself, within their several liberties.

June 2. Philip Lane. 91, 92. Similar warrants to the Mayors, &c. of Dover and of Sandwich. Two papers.

June 3. Trinity House, Ratcliffe. 93. Master, Wardens, &c. of Trinity House to the Council. Have considered the petition of the Merchant Adventurers of Newcastle, for leave to freight in strangers' bottoms. Do not know the state of their trade, but think they might lade in small shipping of their own.

June 3. 94. List of the arms, &c. agreed upon by the Lord Bishop to be provided by the clergy of Leicester archdeaconry; specifying the names of the clergy of the several parishes, &c.

June 5. 95. List of the Priests confined in various prisons in England, all of whom the King has consented to deliver to the Spanish Ambassador, Condé de Gondomar, to go abroad. Total number seventy-four.

June 6. Bristol. 96. Mayor, &c. of Bristol to the Same. Request release and protection for five years, for Giles Penn and Wm. Penn, merchants of Bristol, who are reduced to poverty by great losses, that they may gather in their debts, for the sake of their creditors, and obtain employment.

June 9. Wells. 97. Justices of Peace of Somersetshire to the Council. Request that Mr. Towerson, and the old Company [of Merchant Adventurers], may be compelled to fulfil their promise made on their restoration, of buying up coloured cloth; great distress being occasioned in that county for want of the sale of the blue cloth there manufactured.

VOL. XCVII.

1618.

June 9. Special warrant to Thos. Earl of Suffolk and Sir Fulk Greville, to give discharge to the creditors of the late Earl of Somerset and his Lady, upon their delivery of jewels and other things pawned by them. [*Grant Bk., p.* 251.]

June [9]. Greenwich. 98. Proclamation declaring that the reported attack by Sir Walter Raleigh and his company, on the Spanish town of St. Thomas, is disliked by the King, and contrary to his instructions to preserve amity, and commanding all persons who can give information thereon to repair to the Council.

June 9. Copy of the above. Printed. [*Proc. Coll., No.* 55.]

June 10. 99. Wm. and John Hobson, and other gentlemen of Cambridgeshire, to Lake. Patrick Scott did not propose to them to pay money as composition for violating the Statute against usury, of which they have never been guilty; but asked them for a voluntary gift to supply the King's wants. Being already His Majesty's creditors, they beg not to be further charged.

June 10? 100. Information against Thos. Angel, fisherman, of Folkestone, for a disturbance committed by him in the Court House, and for abuse of the Mayor.

June 10. Rokeby. 101. Wm. Hanby to his brother, R. Hanby. Requests him to attend to some legal business for him, &c.

June 11. Lord Zouch to Capt Ward. Intends to adventure his pinnace with Mr. Bargrave to Virginia. Desires him to prepare the bargain, and advise the best course to be taken therein. [*Minute, Diary, Dom. Corresp., Oct.* 20, 1618.]

June 11. Greenwich. 102. Sir Robt. Naunton to Thos. Wilson. The King wishes the suit of the Artizan Skinners to pass for the use of Chris. Villiers, if it can be done without prejudice, as giving 300*l.* per ann. to His Majesty, and maintaining manufactures. Begs it may be compassed, if possible.

June 12. Norwich. 103. Commissioners of Sewers for Norfolk, &c. to the Council. Are opposed in their efforts to repair the dangerous sea breaches on the coast by Robt. Stannach, of Aldby, who obstinately withstood payment of his assessment, and would not be bound over to appear before their Lordships. His opposition encourages others to withhold payments, and stops the works.

June 12. General pardon to divers persons for not being apprentices. [*Grant Bk., p.* 251.]

June 13. London. 104. Earl of Southampton to [the Council]. Has held the musters in Hampshire, but many are backward, many obstinately refuse to do their share, and their example has an ill effect. Some refuse the tax for an allowance to the Muster-master.

[June 13.] 105. [The Lord Warden of the Cinque Ports] to Mons. de Villers Houdan, Governor of Dieppe. Will abstain, at his request, from

1618. VOL. XCVII.

licensing any more French fishermen. The Frenchman bound to appear at the Court at Rye must so appear, to satisfy the people, but shall be favoured in reference to his fine. French. *Prefixed is,*

105. I. *Minute of the above in English.*

June 13. 106. Certificate from Sir Rich. Wigmore and other Justices of Middlesex, that Ambrose Smith, convicted of a felony on the goods of the Earl of Arundel, is of able body for employment in Virginia or the East Indies.

June 15. Commission to Lord Treasurer Suffolk to pay 5,400*l.* to Sir Wm. Cockayne, out of the issues upon licences for wine. [*Grant Bk., p.* 243.]

June 15. Tavistock. 107. Earl of Bath to the Council. The enclosed charges have been proved against Laomedon Lippincott, whose temper is so turbulent that any punishment he could inflict would only add fuel to his clamour. *Incloses,*

107. I. *Statement of violent conduct and threatening language used by Laomedon Lippincott of Workleigh, co. Devon, against the officers of the musters. He refuses the summons to be one of the trained band, and will not pay the martial rate. June* 10.

June 15. Philip Lane. 108. Lord Zouch to all Mayors, Bailiffs, &c. of the Cinque Ports. Requests them to assist Sir Wm. Erskine and John Meldrum in collecting the penny duty on shipping, granted them by patent, for erection of the lighthouses at Winterton.

June 17. Greenwich. 109. Earl of Pembroke to the Council. To give warrant to Lord Stanhope to erect the post stage between Newmarket and Cambridge, and to appoint John Cotterill Postmaster at Newmarket.

June 17. 110. Sir Robt. Napier and Art. Crawley to the Same. The town of Luton, in Bedfordshire, is much injured by pulling down fair dwelling houses, with malting houses, and erecting in their place cottages for the poor, for the profit of certain private persons. *Inclose,*

110. I. *Statement by Lord Chief Justice Montague, that he wrote to stay the pulling down of houses* [*at Luton*], *unless with a special certificate of reasons; if this be not sufficient, an Order of State must be issued, as it concerns the commonwealth that a town should not be depopulated. May* 30.

110. II. *List of persons who have pulled down and destroyed fair houses within the town of Luton, co. Bedford. May* 28.

June 19. Grant to Wm. Adams of the office of one of the six Chief Masters of the Navy, for life. [*Grant Bk., p.* 241.]

June 19. Grant to John Murray of the mean profits of lands given for the maintenance of masses and other superstitious uses, due to the King by an Act of Parliament, 1 Edw. VI. [*Ibid., p.* 269. *See Dom. Corresp., Jan.* 14 *and* 15, *and vol.* CVI., *Feb.,* 1619.]

VOL. XCVII.

1618.

June 19. 111. Petition by the Commissioners of Sewers, of cos. Cambridge, Northampton, Huntingdon, Lincoln, Norfolk, and the Isle of Ely, to the Council. Their work is impeded because, though all agree that their main objects are to provide sufficient outfalls for the Nen, Welland, and Ouse, to take care of Lynn, Wisbeach, and other parts of Holland, there is much difference of opinion upon the mode of effecting the work. Request that a Clerk of the Council may be sent to their next sessions as umpire, and all parties will abide by a constant and resolute course, to be taken upon his opinion.

June 19. Whitehall. 112. Order in Council, in response to the above petition, for Sir Clement Edmondes, Clerk of the Council, to repair to Huntingdon on Aug. 12, to be present at the meeting of the Commissioners of Sewers, in order that, after viewing the outfalls of the waters, attended by Commissioners from each county, he may either reconcile the differences of opinion amongst them, or report thereon to the Council, that some certain course may be taken.

June 19. 113. Declaration of Alex. Fairecloth, prisoner in the King's Bench, of his willingness to go abroad with the Earl of Gondomar, so that he may not stand worse with the King thereby than he now does.

June 20. 114. Declaration of Lawrence Worthington and John Bartlett, prisoners in the Marshalsea for the Roman Catholic faith, that they willingly accept the King's favour, granted at instance of the Earl of Gondomar.

June 20. 115. Memorandum by Sir Fulk Greville of an agreement made before him between the Wardens and Company of Greenwich Hospital and Sir Nich. Stoddart, that Sir Nicholas will impale again the hospital lands, as they formerly were, and pay up the arrears of the rents due.

June 20. 116. Copy of the above.

June 20. 117. Sir Hen. Yelverton to Sir Clement Edmondes. Sends the Commission for Survey of the Navy, and some papers, which should be delivered as instructions to the Commissioners.

June [21 ?] 118. Petition of Ellen, wife of John Hupper, to the Council, that their shed in Long Acre, built by her husband, now sick, may not be pulled down, as they must then lie on the parish.

June 21 ? 119. Petition of John Gosnoll and Rich. Batten to the King, for a grant of the office of making returns of writs of entry, seisin, and covenant, which writs were formerly returned by the under sheriffs, but now usurped by attorneys. They will keep a record thereof, reduce the fee from 2*s.* to 20*d.*, and pay 20 marks per ann. to His Majesty.

June 21 ? 120. Statement of precedents of the erection of similar offices as that desired in the above petition. If the King refer the request to others, no success is to be expected. With marginal notes of objections to the precedents cited.

VOL. XCVII.

1618.

June 21? 121. Objections and answers to objections concerning the erection of an office for the return of writs of entry, seisin, and covenant.

June 23. Commission to Sir Thos. Smythe concerning the Navy. [*Grant Bk., p.* 243.]

June 23. Commission to the Archbp. of Canterbury and others, to deliver Jesuits out of prison, and banish them. [*Ibid., p.* 237.]

June 25. Madrid. Sir Fras. Cottington to [Lake]. The King of Spain is much touched with what Sir Walter Raleigh has done in the Indies. His Secretary aggravated Raleigh's misdeeds; said the King had promised to punish him as a pirate if he committed any outrage, and that the King of Spain was waiting to see what would be done. This passed before they heard of Raleigh's ill success and return; they are now better satisfied, but still refrain from doing justice to the English who appear at their tribunals, or from paying moneys due to them from the King, and look awry on himself. [*Extract, Dom. Corresp., Dec.* 18, 1618.]

June 25. Greenwich. 122. The King to the Farmers of the Customs. Some detention having lately occurred in collecting the moneys levied for Dungeness light, and granted to Wm. Lamplugh, Clerk of the Kitchen, they are to see that the same be paid as formerly, and to grant no discharge to any vessel that has not paid them.

June 25. 123. Certificate by Sir Edm. Bowyer and Sir Geo. Paul, on a petition of Thos. Mills, prisoner for debt in the King's Bench, that his creditors, seeing his poverty, consent to his release, except John Watts, who would accept the payment of his debt by instalments, but Mills is unable to find the surety which he requires.

June 25. Lambeth. 124. Archbp. Abbot to the Bishop of Gloucester. Urges him to advance the good work of contribution for those who gave relief to the persecuted English in Queen Mary's time, and are now constrained to seek relief from others. *Annexes,*

124. I. *The King to Archbp. Abbot. The inhabitants of Wesel, who formerly relieved afflicted English exiles, are now in great distress, owing to the surprise of their town by Marquis Spinola, and the oppression of the garrison; so that they are unable to support their ministry, school, or poor, and have sent over to beg assistance. Requires him to write to the bishops of his province to order collections to be made in the several dioceses for their relief. Greenwich, June* 7, 1618. *Printed.*

June 25. Lambeth. Duplicate of the above, addressed to the Bishop of London. With note from the Bishop, commending the collection to the care of the clergy of his diocese. Printed. [*Proc. Coll., No.* 55 A.]

June 26. Caen. 125. Mons. de Baal to Edw. Nicholas. Thanks for a fine Latin book sent to him, and for the care he has taken of his father. French.

Vol. XCVII.

1618.

June 26. Friday. 126. Report of proceedings, speeches, &c., in the Court of Star Chamber, on pronouncing sentence against the Countess of Shrewsbury, for contempt in not answering about Lady Arabella [Seymour's] pretended child, the sentence being 20,000*l.* fine, and imprisonment for life. She pleaded a vow as her excuse for not replying, but declared her disbelief of any child.

June 27. Greenwich. 127. Petition of the Cloth Merchants and Clothmakers of Totness to the Council, complaining that the Farmers of Customs exact more than the authorized duty on Devonshire kerseys, to the great injury of their trade; pray that the customs may be exacted as formerly. With references thereon.

[June 28.] 128. Petition of the Handy-trade Clothworkers to the Same. State that the Order in Council relative to the visiting and dressing of cloths, made for their relief, has not been complied with, although complaint has been made to the Merchant Adventurers.

June 29. New Prison. 129. Consent of John Owen, alias Collins, of the King's Bench, and Everard, alias Fras. Kemp, of the New Prison, to go abroad with the Spanish Ambassador, Gondomar.

June 29. Christ Church, Oxford. 130. Dr. Wm. Goodwin to Carleton. Congratulates him on his arrival in England. Recommends the bearer, Mr. Metkirk.

June 30. Grant of divers privileges to the Company of Brewers of London. [*Grant Bk., p.* 268.]

June 30. Grant to Sir Rich. Young, Wm. Hatcher, and Thos. Mewtas, of all fees for sealing subpœnas for opening writs, for thirty years. [*Ibid., p.* 252.]

June 30. Commission to Thos. Earl of Suffolk, Lord Treasurer, to sell or demise parcels of the forest of Hatfield, co. York. [*Ibid., p.* 233.]

June? 131. Frances Fuller to Carleton. Thanks for his favour to a distressed creature; begs him to have her petition presented to the Archbp. of Canterbury, having no garments befitting her birth and degree, nor liberty from her servitude to go out and present it herself.

June. 132. Earl of Lincoln to Sir Clement Edmondes. Requests him to procure the delivery to Sir John Danvers, of the writings relating to the lands called Moorhouse, in Chelsea, which he has sold to him.

June. 133. [Merchant Adventurers to the Council.] Send at their order the names of such obstinate interlopers as will not enter bonds, nor take oath to refrain from their practices.

June. 134. Certificate of inhabitants of St. Mary Cray, co. Kent, to the good conduct of Widow Kingsland, twenty years an inhabitant there.

VOL. XCVII.

1618.

[June.] 135. Names of those [Catholic] prisoners in the Gatehouse who are willing to go beyond the seas with the Spanish Ambassador.

[June.] 136. Similar list of Roman Catholics in the New Prison, willing to go abroad.

[June.] 137. Wm. Howes and Wm. St. George, prisoners in the Clink, to the Archbp. of Canterbury. Are willing to accept His Majesty's grant for their liberty, if it may be without offence.

June? 138. Petition of Sir Rich. Smith, Sir Wm. Russell, and Wm. Cater to the Council. The difference between them and the Muscovy Company being referred to law, and meanwhile they ordered to pay the sums taxed on them, on security given of repayment if the decision be made in their favour, they pray not to be compelled to receive as security the seal of the Company, which they think insufficient.

June. 139. Petition of Thos. Colbert, mariner, to the Same, for restoration of certain logwood imported by him, when ignorant of the prohibition, and seized by the patentees; promises to transport and sell it abroad.

June. 140. Mayor of Exeter to Lake. Has stopped certain players who came to the city desiring leave to play, because their patent was only for children and youths, whereas most of them are men. Hears they are appealing to the Council; is content they should play, if such be their Lordships' pleasure, although those who spend their money on plays are ordinarily very poor people. *Incloses,*

140. I. *Licence to John Daniel and his assigns to bring up a company of children and youths, under the title of Children of Her Majesty's Royal Chamber of Bristol, to play comedies, histories, interludes, &c., in Bristol or other towns, subject to the authority of the Master of the Revels. Westminster, July* 17, 1615.

140. II. *Letter of Assistance from the Council for Martin Slatier, John Edmondes, and Nath. Clay, to act interludes and stage plays in Bristol or any city, &c., under the power of the patent to John Daniel, they staying only fourteen days in a place, and not playing during church hours. Whitehall, April,* 1618.

June? 141. Verses addressed by Sam. Danyell to Jas. Montague, Bp. of Winchester, Dean of the Chapel, &c., consoling him in sickness.

June? 142. Note of sums paid the Exchequer for alienations and the Hanaper, from Michaelmas, 1611.

June? Grant to Thos. Lumsden, Gentleman of the Privy Chamber, of the ruinous castle of Sheriff Hutton, and the castle garth and three or four acres of ground adjoining, with benefit of wastes and spoils, since 30 Eliz. [*Sign Man., vol.* IX., *No.* 7.]

Vol. XCVIII. July, August, 1618.

1618.

July 1. Westminster. Warrant for the Bp. of Durham to compound for instalment of his first fruits, 1,638*l.* 19*s.* 3½*d.*, to be paid in four years. [*Sign Man., vol.* IX., *No.* 8.]

July 1. Westminster. Demise to Hugh Floyd and Thos. Wyse of parcel of the manor of Coldham Hall, and tenements and lands in Stanningfield, Halsted, and Lawshall, co. Suffolk, which ought to come to His Majesty by the attainder of Ambrose Rokewood, with certain reservations, as part of John Levingston's grant of concealed lands of the Gunpowder traitors, value 500*l.* per ann. Latin. [*Ibid., No.* 9.]

July 1. Creation of Mary Lady Compton to the rank of Countess of Buckingham, for life. [*Grant Bk., p.* 258.]

July 2. 1. The Farmers of the Customs to the Council. In reply to the complaint of the western clothiers, send calculations to prove that Devonshire kerseys are taxed less in proportion than other cloths.

July 2. King's Bench. 2. Sir Nich. Poyntz to the Same. Is unjustly detained in prison by Sir Geo. Reynell [Marshal of the King's Bench], on a suit for a fine for rioting, respited many years before, but for which his lands are now extended. Sir George refuses to obey the Lord Chief Justice's order to admit him to bail, and has spoken disrespectfully of the Queen, whose servant he is.

July 3. Westminster. Commission to Sir Lawrence Tanfield, Chief Baron of the Exchequer, and others, to compound with cities and towns corporate for pardons and discharges for tolls and customs by them usurped, and for obtaining new charters for the same. [*Sign Man., vol.* IX., *No.* 10.]

July 4. Westminster. Grant to Sir Thos. Somerset of one third, and to John Steward of two thirds, of the benefits arising to His Majesty from the above compositions with cities and towns, for tolls, &c. [*Ibid., No.* 12.]

July 4. Westminster. Grant to the Company of Clothiers and Clothworkers, Baize and Say makers, &c., of the borough of Colchester, co. Essex, of incorporation, for better reformation of deceits and abuses practised in the said arts. [*Ibid., No.* 11.]

July 4. Windsor. 3. Warrant for Sir Allan Apsley to be absent from his charge of Lieutenant of the Tower for forty days in each year, and authorizing Sir John Keys to act in his absence.

July? 4. Petition of Paul Bassano and John Vaudry to the Council, to confirm the annexed certificate of the Attorney General, and thus strengthen their patent against the vexatious petition preferred against them by two fishmongers, and falsely said to be in the name of the whole body of fishmongers. *Inclose,*

4. I. *Sir Hen. Yelverton to the Same. The petition of certain fishmongers against Paul Bassano and John Vaudry's patent for their invention of importing fresh salmon*

1618. Vol. XCVIII.

and lobsters, is frivolous and unfounded. Their patent is approved by the generality of the Fishmongers' Company. July 4.

July 5. 5. Recognizance of Fras. Hautaige in 50*l.* for the appearance of John Tolwin, both of Mutford, co. Suffolk, before the Council, to answer charges objected by Thos. Knight, parson of Great Worlingham, Suffolk.

July 5. Creation of Jas. Lord Hay to the rank of Visct. Doncaster. [*Grant Bk., p.* 244.]

July 5. Westminster. Warrant for payment of 100*l.* in advance, and other sums when needful, to Thos. Norris, for expenses of the commission for survey of the Navy. [*Sign Man., vol.* IX., *No.* 13.]

July 6. Westminster. Grant, in reversion, to Edw. Pitt, of the office of a Teller of the Exchequer, after the placing of Robt. Seymer, Sam. Henshaw, John Brook, and Art. Squib, who have previous reversions. Latin. [*Ibid., No.* 14.]

July 6. Westminster. Warrant to the Court of Wards to allow to Visct. Wallingford the benefit of the marriage and lands of one of the King's wards every year; and for the first year that of Edmund, son of Sir Fras. Anderson. [*Ibid., No.* 15.]

July 6. Windsor. 6. Proclamation inhibiting all persons, after Bartholomew-tide next, to use the trade of a pedlar or petty chapman, unless licensed according to the patent of March 29, 1617.

July 6. Copy of the above. Printed. [*Proc. Coll., No.* 56.]

July 7. 7. Thos. Wilson to Sir Carew Reynell. Has altered or rather re-written the draft of his proposed letter to the King; thinks it should be such as would give his Majesty an edge to the business, rather than a combat with objections. *Prefixed is,*

7. I. [*Sir Carew Reynell*] *to the King. Has formerly represented the monstrous evils caused by usury, but will produce again his reasons to show that the King may take great advantage by the venom of this serpent.*

July 7. 8. Justices of Middleton to the Council. Have examined the state of the large house lately erected in Drury Lane, assigned by Wm. Short, of Gray's Inn, to Edw. Smith, and find it is erected on the foundation of two former tenements.

July 7. Westminster. Grant to Thos. Saunderson, of Islington, Middlesex, of pardon for all usuries against the laws and statutes of England. [*Sign Man., vol.* IX., *No.* 16.]

July 7. Westmintser. Grant to John Buck, a native of France, of denization. Latin. [*Ibid., No.* 17.]

1618. VOL. XCVIII.

July 7. Westminster. Commission to the Lord Treasurer and others to make a new inventory of the jewels remaining in the Jewel House in the Tower, and of the jewels received by Lord Hay, Master of the Great Wardrobe, which have since been disposed of by His Majesty, that Lord Hay may be discharged thereof. [*Sign Man., vol.* IX., *No.* 18.]

July 7. Westminster. Licence to Sam. Atkinson and Simon Morgan, to dig for treasure-trove in abbeys, monasteries, churches, and all other places in England and Wales, first compounding with the owners thereof. A moiety of the profits to be for the King, and the remainder for themselves. [*Ibid., No.* 19.]

July 7. Westminster. Warrant to discharge Thos. Saunderson, of Islington, Gent., of 500*l.*, parcel of the 1,500*l.* adjudged against him on an information exhibited by Robt. Beddo, of London, upon the Statute of Usury, the King having consented to receive 1,000*l.* as full payment. [*Ibid., No.* 20.]

July 8. Westminster. Grant to the Bailiffs and Burgesses of Berkhampstead, co. Hertford, of incorporation. Latin. [*Ibid., No.* 21.]

July 8. Court at Windsor. 9. Petition of Lucy, wife of Sir John Molyneux, to the King. Her husband deals hardly with her, and has sold his estate, worth 30,000*l.*, to Mr. Holt, of Gray's Inn, and John Halsey, merchant of London, by their persuasion, much under its value. Prays that order may be taken with them for relief of herself and her six children. With order thereon.

July 9. Hatfield. 10. Wm. Earl of Salisbury to Carleton. Begs his influence for the pardon of Mr. Kenithorpe. Asks if he will wait on the King at Theobalds.

July? 11. Petition of the inhabitants of Ely, and other towns in the Isle of Ely, to the Council, to direct the Commissioners of Sewers to forbear from levying lawful penalties for not opening the drain called Sutton Lode, by the appointed time, because 100,000 acres of land will be overflowed, if it be opened before the main drain, the West water, is completed, and its outfalls at Wisbeach, at present stopped by their command, are perfected.

July 10. 12. The Council to the Commissioners of Sewers for cos. Northampton, Huntingdon, Lincoln, Cambridge, and Isle of Ely. To forbear putting in execution the law and penalty against the inhabitants of Ely and other towns in the Isle of Ely, for not opening Sutton Lode, until the West water and its outfalls at Wisbeach are perfected.

July 10. Commission to Wm. Earl of Pembroke, &c., to discover and punish offenders in the disbursement of the Treasury. [*Grant Bk., p.* 237.]

July 10. Westminster. Grant to Rich. Montague, the King's Chaplain, now made a Prebend in Windsor, of dispensation to retain a fellowship in Eton College, notwithstanding the statutes of the same. [*Sign Man., vol.* IX., *No.* 22.]

Vol. XCVIII.

1618.
July 10. Westminster. Grant to Lord Danvers and his heirs, on petition of Anne, wife of Sir Herbert Croft, of the Priory of Carmarthen, and divers other manors and lands expectant upon an estate entailed on Lady Conway, which reversion was conveyed to the Crown by the said Sir Herbert Croft, but is now redeemed. Latin. [*Sign Man., vol.* IX., *No.* 23.]

July 10. Westminster. Warrant for payment of 30*l.* per ann. to Philip Squire, commissioned to teach Lewis Evans, a child of great dexterity in music, to play on the Irish harp, and other instruments. [*Ibid., No.* 24.]

July 10. Westminster. Grant to the Mayor, &c. of Kidwelly, co. Carmarthen, of confirmation of their ancient franchises, with alteration in some particulars. Latin. [*Ibid., Nos.* 25, 26.]

July 11. Westminster. Grant to Dr. Jas. Chambers, for the relief of Thos. and Mary Green, of fines of 500*l.* and of 200 marks, set upon the Earl of Lincoln by the Lord Chancellor, for contempt of court in nonfulfilment of a decree to restore the jointure of Mary Green, wrongfully detained by him. With provisoes of mitigation of the fine, on the Earl's submission. [*Ibid., No.* 28.]

July 11. Creation of Sir Fras. Bacon to the rank of Lord Verulam, co. Herts. [*Grant Bk., p.* 241.]

July 11. 13. Questions in theology, civil law, medicine, and philosophy, to be discussed at the University of Oxford, July 11 and 13. Printed. Latin.

July 11. 14. Memorandum of moneys advanced on interest to the King, by the several Receivers of the Customs.

July 11. 15. Certificate of Sir Edm. Bowyer, Sir Geo. Paul, and Sir Thos. Grimes, to the Council, that they have been unable to make a composition for Geo. Burnham, prisoner in the King's Bench, with his creditors, because four of them failed to appear.

July 12. 16. Note of the distribution of 4*l.* to the servants of Archbp. Abbot, on the consecration of Geo. Carleton, Bp. of Llandaff.

July 12. Westminster. Grant to Thos. Trafford, of Bridge Trafford, Cheshire, of pardon for adulteries, &c. Latin. [*Sign Man., vol.* IX., *No.* 29.]

July 12. Westminster. Grant to Hen. Chitting, on surrender of Hen. Knight, of the office of Chester Herald, for life, with the augmented fees. Latin. [*Ibid., No.* 30.]

July 12. Westminster. Warrant to pay to the East India Company 2,061 crowns, the usual bounty for building two ships, the Palsgrave and the Elizabeth of London. [*Ibid., No.* 31.]

July [13]. 17. Petition of Thos. Powell, cutler, and other inhabitants of Blackhorse Alley, Fleet Street, to the Council, that Chris. Allanson, who is erecting there certain houses of timber on new foundations, contrary to proclamation, and to the great prejudice of the petitioners, may be compelled to pull them down, according to previous orders from the Lord Mayor and Attorney General.

1618. Vol. XCVIII.

July [14]. 18. Sir Geo. Bowles, Lord Mayor of London, to the Council. Describes the circumstances of the tumult at the Spanish Ambassador's house in the Barbican, in consequence of one of his gentlemen having knocked down a child in riding. The persons most suspected of it are taken up.

July 14. 19. Muster roll of the garrison of Camber Castle.

July 14. Gray's Inn. 20. Sir Hen. Yelverton and Sir Thos. Coventry to Sir Fulk Greville. The subject of the inclosed papers is too important to be decided by their opinion, and must be left to the Council. [*See July* 7.] *Inclose,*

20. I. *Account of the different sorts of usury practised in England, and proposal of a suit to erect an office for recording loans, exacting* 20*s. in every* 100*l. lent on usury.*

20. II. *Objections to the above proposal, and answers to objections.*

20. III. *Another paper of objections against the granting of this suit, and answers thereto; with a discourse against usury, and statement of the nature of the suit, the modes of effecting it, and reasons why His Majesty should grant it.*

July 15. Westminster. Grant to Robt. Bacon, on surrender of Peter Temple, of the office of Keeper and Captain of Camber Castle, &c. Latin. [*Sign Man., vol.* IX., *No.* 32.]

July 15. Westminster. Warrant to the Chancellor, &c. of the Duchy of Lancaster, to advance to Robt. Wilson, Keeper of Pontefract Castle, 3,000*l.*, and to allow him 100 loads of timber, and service, for the repairs of the castle. [*Ibid., No.* 33.]

July 15. Westminster. Warrant for payment of sums in advance, not exceeding 200*l.* per ann., to Sir Pat. Murray or Rich. Lazomby, for providing hay and oats for the deer in Theobalds Park. [*Ibid., No.* 34.]

July 15. Westminster. Warrant for restitution of temporalties to Geo. Carleton, Bp. of Llandaff. Latin. [*Ibid., No.* 35.]

July 15. Westminster. Warrant to pay to Lord Stanhope 50*l.*, for extraordinary posts during the King's progress in the western parts this summer, the standing posts having been discharged by His Majesty's orders. [*Ibid., No.* 36.]

July [15]. 21. Petition of the Clothmakers of Totness to the Council, to refer the hearing of the differences between them and the Farmers of the Customs to fitting persons, and meanwhile to order the farmers to charge the kerseys as before. *Annexing,*

21. I. *Answers of the petitioners to the objections of the Farmers of the Customs.* [*See July* 2.]

July 16. London. 22. Edw. Reynoldes to Fras. Mills. Has paid for him 8*l.* 10*s.* 11*d.*, his share of the dividend of Privy Seal fees, &c. Sir Clement Edmondes was uncivil to his cousin Castle, who pleaded before Council the case of their diet. Has removed to a house towards the field in Holborn.

VOL. XCVIII.

1618.

July 16. Grant to Dav. Watkins of the Controllership of the Works at Windsor Castle and other places, for life. [*Grant Bk., p.* 252.]

July 16. Grant to Gabriel Marsh of the office of Particular Surveyor of the Lands in North Wales, during pleasure. [*Ibid., p.* 260.]

July 16. Licence to John Gilbert to make an engine called a water plough, for twenty-one years. [*Ibid., p.* 265.]

July 17. Grant to Rowland White and Thos. Alured of the office of Remembrancer in Wales, for life. [*Ibid., p.* 252.]

July 17. Westminster. Warrant for payment of 20*l.*, in addition to 40*l.* already paid, and also for allowance of timber, to Sir Oliver Cromwell, to finish the works and repairs at Waybridge Park, co. Huntingdon, and for payment of any further sums that may be necessary. [*Sign Man., vol.* IX., *No.* 37.]

July 17. Westminster. Warrant to advance 400*l.* to Jas. Bovey, Serjeant of the Cellar, for provision of wines, fruits, and grapes out of France. [*Ibid., No.* 38.]

July 17. Westminster. Warrant to discharge the Dean and Prebendaries of Winchester of 160*l.* 11*s.* 7*d.*, due from them for tenths and composition for first fruits, on their payment of the same to Dr. Young, King's Chaplain and Dean of Winchester, sent on His Majesty's service into Scotland. [*Ibid., No.* 39.]

July 17. Westminster. Commission to Sir Thos. Brudnell, Sir John Tracy, Sir Wm. Cooke, and others, to survey and examine into the wastes made in the Forest of Dean by Sir Basil Brooke and others, farmers of the iron works there, proceeding on interrogatories prepared by Sir Wm. Throgmorton, Bart. [*Ibid., No.* 40.]

July 18. Westminster. Licence to Edw. Allen, of Dulwich, Surrey, to found and incorporate a college and hospital there, and to give lands to the value of 800*l.* a year. [*Ibid., No.* 41.]

July 18. 23. Justices of Middlesex to the Council. The new building erected by Mr. Smith in Drury Lane is contrary to the proclamation, as going beyond the old foundations, and converting a stable into a dwelling house.

July [18?] 24. Petition of Edw. Smith to the Same, for stay of their order to pull down certain buildings which he has erected in Drury Lane, till the old foundations can be measured, when it will be found that he has not infringed the Proclamation relative to buildings.

July [18?] 25. Request of Rich. Lecavill, Groom of the Chamber, for payment of his expenses, &c., whilst travelling about with the King's silkworms the past three months, whithersoever His Majesty went.

Vol. XCVIII.

1618.

[July.] 26. Report by Robt. le Gris, that being at Lady Drury's house when her husband was dying, Lady Markham urged Lady Drury to allow Mr. Jones to sit up with her husband; that he [Le Gris] objected to it, because Mr. Jones was a busy Catholic, and would unsettle the mind of Sir Drew, who had received the communion; that an angry altercation ensued thereon, in which he reminded Lady Markham of the villainy of the Powder Treason; that she said it was a pity it did not succeed, on which he replied that had she been a man, he had slain her on the spot, &c.

July 18. Lambeth. 27. Examination of Winifred Lady Markham, wife of Sir Robt. Markham, co. Notts. Was at the house of Sir Drew Drury, then at the point of death, but did not urge that Mr. Jones should visit him; heard no mention of the Powder Treason, nor said she wished it had taken effect.

July 19. 28. Petition of Bridget Gray to the Council, that her grandson, John Throckmorton, prisoner in Newgate for felony, may be discharged, it being his first offence, and Sir Thos. Smythe being ready to convey him beyond seas. With order thereon, that on certificate by the Lord Mayor and Recorder, that John Throckmorton was not convicted for murder, burglary, highway robbery, rape, or witchcraft, a warrant be made for his banishment. Also certificate of the Mayor and Recorder that his crime was aiding in stealing a hat worth 6s., for which his accomplice, Robt. Whisson, an old thief, was hanged, July 21 and 22, 1618. *Annexes,*

28. i. *Petition of the Same to Sir Thos. Smythe, that her grandchild, John Throckmorton, convicted of felony, may escape an infamous death, and be sent beyond sea. With order by Sir T. Smythe that he will send him abroad, if delivered to him by warrant of Council. July* 11, 1618.

July 19. Westminster. Licence to Wm. Alley, at nomination of Thos. Middleton, of the sole printing and publishing of a book by Middleton called "The Peacemaker, or Great Britain's blessing." [*Sign Man., vol.* IX., *No.* 42.]

July 19. Westminster. Warrant to Sir Hum. May, Chancellor of the Duchy of Lancaster, to pay 300*l.* to Jas. Levingston, out of fines or profits of copyhold lands of the Duchy; a former warrant to the same effect being void by death of the late Chancellor. [*Ibid., No.* 43.]

July 20. 29. The King to the Officers of Customs at Newcastle-upon-Tyne, Sunderland, and Blyth. Objections having been raised to a patent granted to And. Boyd to survey coals and prevent their being deceitfully mingled, the case has been tried in the Star Chamber, the abuse proved, and offenders fined; orders them henceforth to restrain ships laden with coals, unless they can produce a certificate from the Surveyor, of the nature and quality of the coal, &c.

VOL. XCVIII.

1618.

July 20. Chelmsford. 30. Justices of Essex to the Council. Refusal of Colchester to contribute towards the rate for payment of Sir Nic. Coote, the Provost Marshal, on pretence of their being a corporation, though the other corporations have all paid. Request that they may be ordered to show cause of refusal before their Lordships.

July 20. 31. Sir Hen. Yelverton, Attorney General, to the Chancellor of the Duchy of Lancaster. Sir Rich. Molyneux, Receiver General of the Duchy, having lent the King 1,000*l.*, a warrant is to be drawn up for it to be deducted upon his next account. With note by Sir Edw. Moseley, Attorney of the Duchy, that this is a fit warrant.

July 20. Westminster. Proclamation for removing all licences heretofore granted for erecting new buildings within the City of London, or two miles distance, prohibiting the erection of such buildings, and giving directions for re-erections, on old foundations; the walls to be of brick or stone, the rooms ten feet in height, &c. Printed. [*Proc. Coll., No.* 57.]

July 21. Westminster. Grant to Ant. Barlatier, born in Languedoc, in France, of denization, with licence to plant and sell mulberry trees and other trees and herbs. [*Sign Man., vol.* IX., *No.* 44.]

July 21. Commission to the Archbp. of Canterbury to take surrenders and demise lands in the survey of the Exchequer, for years or lives. [*Grant Bk., p.* 237.]

July 22? 32. Memoranda [by Sir Thos. Wilson, one of the Commissioners for Suits] of the proceedings of the Commission, the suits brought before them, and their decisions thereon.

July 22. Whitehall. 33. Order of Council—on a request from the Admiralty of North Holland and West Friesland, for leave to transport ordnance, their store being exhausted by furnishing ships against pirates, assisting Venice, &c.—that though at present no ordnance can be spared, yet the request shall be granted, as soon as the stores are replenished.

July 22. Basing. Proclamation granting to the Company of Pinmakers the pre-emption of pins imported, which are to be landed only in the port of London. Printed. [*Proc. Coll., No.* 58.]

July? 34. Petition of the Company of Pinmakers to the Council. Desire letters of assistance to prevent the importation of foreign pins by John Killingworth, the sole pre-emption having been granted to them.

July 23. Proclamation against the use of waggons that destroy the highways Printed. [*Grant Bk., p.* 249.]

July 24. Licence to Philip Foote to sell clay for making tobacco pipes, for twenty-one years. [*Ibid., p.* 265.]

July 24. Westminster. 35. Examination of Anne Lady Drury, widow of Sir Drew Drury. Mr. Jones is a friend of theirs, and saw her husband when near

1618. Vol. XCVIII.

death, and past consciousness. Does not think he is a priest; he was not brought by Lady Markham, nor urged by her to see Sir Drew. Nothing was said of the Powder Plot. Does not think Lady Markham is a recusant, having heard her speak against Papists.

July 24. Lambeth. 36. Examination of John Chard. Lady Markham did not urge Mr. Jones to go up to see Sir Drew Drury; did not say to her in reference to the Powder Plot, that Catholics condemn such attempts if they fail, and commend them if they prosper; never heard her say she wished it had succeeded, nor Mr. Grise [Le Gris] say she would have to answer for that speech.

July 24. Westminster. 37. Grant to Barth. Jewkes and Wm. Berker, in reversion after Sir Hugh Carmichael, of the office of Registrar of Goods laid in pawn.

July. Sign Manual of the above, dated July 10. [*Sign Man., vol.* IX., *No.* 27.]

July [24]. 38. Petition of Wm. Greenwell and Thos. Stiles, Merchants, to the Council. By the terms of their agreement for supplying cordage for the navy, they were to receive 900*l.* per month, and the surplus quarterly, and have a year's notice before surrender of the contract. Being suddenly ordered to break it off, they pray that the allowance may be continued till 1,700*l.* arrears are paid off, and that their store of hemp and tar, provided in advance, value 9,000*l.*, may be bought from them.

July 24. Westminster. Grant, at the request of the Spanish Ambassador, to John Owen, of London, attainted of treason, of pardon, on condition of quitting the realm within twenty days, and not returning without licence. Latin. [*Sign Man., vol.* IX., *No.* 45.]

July 24. Westminster. Warrant to pay 2*s.* per diem to each of the fourteen Grooms of the Chamber, in order to lessen charges, their allowances heretofore having come to a larger sum. [*Ibid., No.* 46.]

July 24. Westminster. Warrant to Sir Miles Fleetwood, Receiver of the Court of Wards, to pay 2,000*l.*, lent by him to the King, to Sir Hen. Docwra, Treasurer at War in Ireland, to be allowed on his next account. [*Ibid., No.* 47.]

July 24. Westminster. Grant to Lord Arundel of Wardour, in trust for Lady St. John, wife of Wm. Lord St. John, of Basing, of a fine of 500*l.*, set upon Sir Fras. Englefield by the Lord Chancellor, for contempt in not performing the order of Court relating to her portion; with a proviso for its mitigation, on Sir Francis' submission. Mutilated. [*Ibid., No.* 48.]

[July 25.] Warrant for conferring on Thos. Littleton, of Frankley, co. Worcester, the dignity of a Baronet. Latin. [*Ibid., No.* 49].

July 25. Commission to the Lord Chancellor, &c. to compound with offenders in new buildings. [*Grant Bk., p.* 237.]

Vol. XCVIII.

1618.
July 25.
Tottenham.
39. John Packer to Sir Thos. Lake. The King has signed the papers and bills, except one that was not subscribed. The letters to the states of Zealand require the subscription inserting.

July 25.
40. Examination of Wm. Jones. Was at Sir Drew Drury's, a little before his death, with Lady Markham, but she never urged him or any other to persuade Sir Drew to change his religion, nor was there any talk of religion, or of the Powder Treason, nor did Capt. le Gris bid him remember her words; she and Capt. le Gris had an angry argument about divorces.

July 26.
41. Sir Geo. Bowles, Lord Mayor of London, to the Council. On the complaint of Thos. Powell and others, of Blackhorse Alley, has examined the buildings there of Chris. Allanson, and finds that they are on former sites, and, being larger and more airy, will greatly improve the alley, which is very close and crowded; has ordered him to pull down the part which encroaches twelve feet upon ground formerly void.

July 26.
42. Statement [by Sir John Coke] of the condition of the Royal Navy in the times of Edw. III., 37 Hen. VIII., 2 Edw. VI., and 30 & 44 Eliz., as compared with its condition in 1618, when, out of 43 vessels, 14 are unserviceable, and 3 need repairs; so that the navy is now weaker than in the last year of Elizabeth by six good ships.

July 26.
Grant to Wm. Skolfield, on surrender of Sir Fras. Blundell, of the Stewardship of His Majesty's possessions, late belonging to the monastery of St. Edmund's Bury. Latin. [*Sign Man., vol.* IX., *No.* 50.]

July 26.
Westminster.
Congé d'elire to the Dean and Chapter of Oxford to choose a new Bishop. Latin. [*Ibid., No.* 51.]

July 27.
Westminster.
Grant, in reversion, to John Savile, of the office of Teller of the Exchequer, after the placing of all previous reversioners. Latin. [*Ibid., No.* 52.]

July 28.
Westminster.
Warrant to the Sheriff of Middlesex to pay 100*l.* per ann. to the Commissioners for redress of annoyances in Westminster, in lieu of their former allowances for diet and expenses, when on service. [*Ibid., No.* 53.]

July 28.
Westminster.
Grant to Philip Squire of a musician's place, vice Cormock M'Dermot, deceased. Latin. [*Ibid., No.* 54.]

July 28.
Westminster.
Commission to John Allen, Surveyor of the King's Gardens, Orchard, &c., at Greenwich, to take up artificers and labourers for the said gardens, &c. [*Ibid., No.* 55.]

July 28.
Westminster.
Congé d'elire to the Dean and Chapter of Ely to choose a Bishop. Latin. [*Ibid., No.* 56.]

Vol. XCVIII.

1618.

July 28. Westminster. Congé d'elire to the Dean and Chapter of Winchester to choose a Bishop. Latin. [*Sign Man., vol.* IX., *No.* 57.]

July 29. Westminster. Warrant to pay to Sir Calthorp Parker and others, the sum of 2,178 crowns, as the usual bounty on the tonnage of seven new-built ships. [*Ibid., No.* 58.]

July 29. Westminster. Warrant to pay 225*l.* to Geo. Herriot, for two diamond rings, given to the Swedish Ambassador, and to Vandenbrocke, a messenger from the Electress Palatine. [*Ibid., No.* 59.]

July 29. Westminster. Warrant for payment of 2,200*l.* to Adam Newton, for the use of Prince Charles, out of such moneys as shall be first paid of the fine of 20,000*l.* imposed on the Countess Dowager of Shrewsbury, in the Star Chamber. [*Ibid., No.* 60.]

July 29. Westminster. Grant to Hector Johnston, the King's servant, of the King's moiety of three several sums of 60*l.*, adjudged against Thurstan Tildesley, of St. Andrew's, Holborn, for not receiving the sacrament. [*Ibid., No.* 61.]

July 29. London. 43. Edw. Reynoldes to Sir Hen. Savile. Understanding there will be an election shortly in Merton College, again recommends his nephew to his favour.

July 30. King James's Newland. 44. Statement by Capt. Thos. Edge, of the wrongs inflicted upon him and other English by the Flemings, who came to fish for the whale, May to July, 1618.

July 30. Westminster. Warrant authorizing the Archbp. of Canterbury, Lord Chancellor Verulam, the Bp. of Ely, Sir Robt. Naunton, Sir Fulk Greville, Sir Julius Cæsar, and Sir Edw. Coke, Commissioners of the Treasury, to issue treasure on warrants already issued, to whomsoever directed; commanding all future warrants to be signed by the Under Treasurer of the Exchequer, and one or more of the other Commissioners, and that they shall also supply the place of the Treasurer, in drawing out sums on warrants dormant, signing fresh warrants, &c. [*Sign Man., vol.* IX., *No.* 62.]

[July 30.] 45. Abstract of the above orders to the Lords Commissioners of the Treasury.

July 30. Westminster. Warrant to pay 1,000*l.* to Philip Jacobson, for a diamond ring. [*Sign Man., vol.* IX., *No.* 63.]

July 30. Westminster. Warrant to pay to John Sostmon, agent from the Duke of Lunenburg, 140*l.*, in consideration of his attending in England by the King's command, longer than appointed by the said Duke. [*Ibid., No.* 64.]

July 31. Westminster. Warrant to pay to Sir Robt. Mansell, late Treasurer of the Navy, sums due to him, notwithstanding the surrender of his office. [*Ibid., No.* 65.]

VOL. XCVIII.

1618.

July 31. Westminster. Warrant to pay to Sir Robt. Mansell, late Treasurer, and Sir Wm. Russell, present Treasurer of the Navy, the sums respectively due to them, in discharge of 28,121*l.*, formerly assigned for building the Elizabeth, Triumph, Rainbow, and Antelope. [*Sign Man., vol.* IX., *No.* 66.]

July 31? 46. Petition of Hen. Bland, prisoner in the King's Bench, to the King. Complains that four of his creditors, after consenting to the order of Sir Edm. Bowyer, Sir Thos. Grimes, and others, for his liberation till Michaelmas, and instalment of his debts, have again imprisoned him. Prays that they may be compelled to perform their agreement.

July 31. 47. Certificate of Sir Edm. Bowyer, Sir Geo. Paule, and —— Bowyer, of the conduct of Hen. Bland's creditors, coinciding with the statements of the above petition.

July? 48. Relation, by Sir Walter Raleigh, of his voyage to Guiana. Imperfect; the first sheet wanting.

July? 49. Copy of the above. Two sheets wanting.

July. Westminster. Grant to Wm. Meades, of Over Catesby, co. Northampton, of pardon for robberies committed six years before, for which he was not indicted, but which he has voluntarily confessed. [*Sign Man., vol.* IX., *No.* 67.]

July. 50. Petition of Hen. Brooke, late Lord Cobham, to the Council, that they will move the King to allow him liberty to take the air for his health. Mr. Frederick, the King's Surgeon, will certify his weak state.

July? 51. Petition of Edm. Chamberlain, prisoner in the Fleet, to the Same, to be protected from the ill usage of the present Warden of the Fleet, where he has been confined for five years, who, though he is a gentlemen born, and in prison by being surety for his brother, Sir John Chamberlain, has lately, on some quarrel, taken away his bedding, &c., and put him into the common felons' gaol.

July? 52. Petition of the Clothiers of Reading to [the Same], that a certain stock [of cloth?] left by will to the town, may be invested in land, and the revenues applied partly to the support of trade, and partly to the relief of the poor.

July. 53. Petition of Nath. Barnard and the Clothiers of Somerset to the Same, that until the Merchant Adventurers are able to take their blue cloth off their hands, they may be allowed to export unwrought cloth.

July? 54. Petition of the Clothworkers of Southampton and Winchester to the Same, that the late unusual exportation of wool may be prohibited, the dearth of wool in England occasioning a decay of the cloth trade, and reducing 3,000 of their poor to great distress.

VOL. XCVIII.

1618.

July. 55. Petition of Sir Roger Dallison to the Earls of Pembroke and Arundel, and others, Commissioners for examining his cause, to be enlarged from the custody of a Messenger of the King's Chamber, that he may sell his lands and call in his debts, so as to be able to pay His Majesty.

July. 56. Petition of Edw. Fort, the King's Servant, to the Council, to direct the Sheriff to forbear the further pulling down of two fair houses built by him in Drury Lane, begun during Mr. Ittery's patent for building Drury Lane. Has paved the street before his doors, according to command, for three years past.

July. 57. Petition of the Grooms of the King's Chamber to the Lords Commissioners of the Treasury, for payment of their allowances, which are three years in arrear, of their expenses on the King's journey to Scotland, &c.

July. 58. Petition of Thos. Hutchins, postmaster of Lichfield, in behalf of the posts of England, to the Council. They are in great distress, their pay being three years in arrears. The King has now assigned it to be paid from the customs. Asks directions how they are to receive it, most of them living at a distance.

July. 59. Petition of Ant. Lucas, a poor maimed soldier, to the Same, for payment of his share of 60*l.*, part of a contribution raised by Westmoreland for maintenance of six soldiers, whereof two only survive. Has served three years in Ireland.

July. 60. Petition of Thos. Mills, prisoner in the King's Bench, to the Same, that John Watts, the only one of his creditors who refuses to join in a composition made for his debts, may be compelled to do so, and that he may be released from prison. [*See June* 25.]

July. 61. Petition of Wm. Noyse to the Same. Is sorry he has given offence, having always found the proportion of men and arms for which he was assessed; being eighty years old, ill, and in debt, prays to be discharged further attendance, and for his cause to be referred to the Earl of Southampton, Lieutenant of Hampshire.

July. 62. Petition of John Penington to the Same. Has lost 2,500*l.*, his whole property except his ship, on the voyage with Sir Walter Raleigh; his ship was seized at Kinsale, by the Lord Deputy of Ireland, and on his repairing to London, he was given in charge. Prays restoration of his ship, and release; not having been at St. Thomas's, he can give no information thereon.

July. 63. Petition of Robt. Stammage, of Whiteacre, All Saints, Norfolk, to the Same. Was unjustly charged with refusing to contribute his proportion towards repairing the sea bank, and was sent for to London, and committed to the custody of a messenger. Prays discharge, and that his answer may be taken in the country.

VOL. XCVIII.

1618.

July. 64. Petition of Robt. Stammage to the Council. Is justly punished for his offence against the Commissioners of Sewers of Norfolk, although it was ignorantly committed. Prays release from further punishment, or at least leave of absence from the Fleet Prison for twenty-four days, that he may attend to his lawsuits, in Norfolk, which are coming to a trial.

July. 65. Petition of the Same to the Same, to the same effect.

July. 66. Petition of Matthew and Margery Skillicorn to the Same. Was lamed by a fall in the King's works. The Lord Mayor and Aldermen of London, by their Lordships' direction, have made him a freeman of the City, but he cannot be admitted into the Horners' Company without paying the costs, which he is unable to do; begs assistance therein.

July. 67. Petition of Ann Twist to the Same, for regular payment of a pension of 50*l.* per ann., granted her in consideration of having been for thirty years laundress to Queen Elizabeth, which is now a year and a half in arrears.

July? 68. Statement of the inconveniences that will result from a recent Privy Seal Order, that all inquisitions relating to the King's revenue, as suppressed tenures, concealed lands, gathering in of debts, &c., be prosecuted by the officers in the several counties, and fourteen days' notice given before execution of process. The officers will be at heavy charges, and opportunity will be afforded for concealing goods. Proposal that the Privy Seal be called in, and grievances removed, by a speedy redress afforded to all complainants of unjust inquisitions; or, if the King be determined to continue it, that at least the gathering in of his debts be excepted therefrom.

July? 69. Account of moneys from various heads of revenue, appropriated beforehand.

July? 70. Remembrances for the Lords Commissioners for His Majesty's special service, showing that the late Lord Treasurer had suppressed a book drawn up to show the great abuses in the Exchequer, and had neglected a Privy Seal and a letter from the King, dated June, 1616, for reformation thereof. Particulars of the above Privy Seal, and of the good that would result from its being put into execution; details of sundry frauds in the late Lord Treasurer and officers of the Exchequer; with note of the good effects likely to follow from the present commission.

Aug. 2. Creation of Wm. Lord Compton to the rank of Earl of Northampton. [*Grant Bk., p.* 258.]

Aug. 2. Creation of Robt. Visct. Lisle to the rank of Earl of Leicester. [*Ibid., p.* 268.]

Aug. 4. Grant of privileges to the Company of Pinmakers of London. [*Ibid., p.* 268.]

Aug. 4. 71. Sir Thos. Watson to Sir Geo. Calvert. The small house built by Thos. Hamon in Sturton Meadow, Westminster, and ordered to be pulled down, is not affected by the proclamation, being built by

1618. Vol. XCVIII.

virtue of the licence granted to Sir Hen. Neville. Prays stay of proceedings thereon.

Aug. 4. 72. Certificate by the Justices of Peace, co. Surrey, showing what new buildings have been erected in that county, within two miles of London, since Michaelmas, 1615; with the names and quality of the builders.

Aug 4. 73. Note of certain chantry lands in London belonging to the Carpenters' Company, the rents of which are due to the King [as being granted for superstitious uses], with exoneration of the arrears thereof, for sixty-eight years, amounting to 456*l*. 13*s*. 4*d*. Latin. [*See Jan.* 14, 15, 1619.]

Aug. 5. Bagshot. 74. Sir Robt. Carey to Lord Chancellor Verulam. The Prince desires a passport for Geo. Vincent, servant of the Prince of Poland, to return, with his family, and five musicians, and certain articles purchased for the Royal Family of Poland, viz., perfume bags, beaver hats, waistcoats, gloves, and musical instruments.

Aug. 6. 75. Certificate by Sir Ant. Ben, Recorder of London, and other Commissioners for Buildings, of the new buildings erected contrary to proclamation since Michaelmas, 1615, within the liberties of the City of London.

Aug. 6. Creation of Robt. Lord Rich to the rank of Earl of Warwick. [*Grant Bk., p.* 251.]

Aug. 7. Commission to John Allen to take up workmen, flowers, &c., for the gardens and great orchard at Greenwich. [*Ibid., p.* 243.]

Aug. 7. Licence to Wm. Alley of the sole printing of the book called "The Peace Maker, or Britain's Blessing," for seven years. [*Ibid., p.* 241.]

Aug. 7. Grant to Jas. Woodward of the office of Doorkeeper of the Minories in London, for life. [*Ibid., p.* 252.]

[Aug. 7.] Creation of Wm. Baron Cavendish, of Hardwick, and his heirs male, to the rank of Earl of Devon. Latin. [*Sign Man., vol.* IX., *No.* 68.]

Aug. 8. London. 76. Paul de la Ravoire to [Carleton]. The Archbp. of Spalato can only send four copies of his book now, it being Sunday, and the printer's shop shut up, but more shall follow.

Aug. 8. London. 77. Chamberlain to the Same. Lady Compton is made Countess of Buckingham, though her husband remains a mere knight. Sir Walter Raleigh is at Salisbury, but has had no audience because of his sickness; it is thought to be leprosy, or that he has taken poison. Sir Lionel Cranfield succeeds Lord Hay as Master of the Wardrobe. A commission is to sit on the riot at the Spanish Ambassador's.

Aug. 9. Strand. 78. Abraham Williams to the Same. Lady Compton's patent as Countess of Buckingham is to be antedated, so as to give her precedence over the wives of the four new Earls. Lord Rich is to be

VOL. XCVIII.

1618.

Earl of Warwick, not of Clare. Sir W. Raleigh is in town, and committed to custody, while his lodgings in the Tower are prepared. The Spaniards and Hollanders have combined and defeated twenty-four sail of pirates in Algiers.

Aug. 10. 79. Inventory of ores, plans, MSS., jewels, &c. found on the body of Sir Walter Raleigh, with note of their disposition, as delivered to the Lieutenant of the Tower, Sir Lewis Stukeley, or Sir Geo. Calvert, or restored to himself; signed by Sir Robt. Naunton and Sir Allan Apsley.

Aug. 11. 80. Sir Hen. Savile to Carleton. Recommends Dr. Prideaux, of Exeter College, as a learned man and well read in controversies, to assist Carleton in his theological business.

Aug. 14. 81. Gentlemen of Wiltshire to [the Council?]. Certify the good conduct and skill in woollen drapery of Benedict Webb. Beg speedy ending to the suit brought against him by Geo. Mynne, of London, lest many poor persons employed by him be thrown out of work.

Aug. 14. Croydon. 82. Archbp. of Canterbury to Sir Thos. Lake. A meeting of the Council cannot be assembled before Monday. Thinks that the Lord Privy Seal and Lord Carew should be summoned from Oatlands, and that Sir Lewis Stukeley, Sir Wm. St. John, and the rest, should be ordered to appear.

Aug. 15. Chester. 83. Mayor, &c. of Chester to the Council. Thos. Burchley has obtained permission from their Lordships to keep a retail shop in Chester, on the pretext that he is a merchant, which is false. He married the widow of an embroiderer, and was allowed to enter that company and continue that trade; but he sells merceries and iron-mongery also, contrary to the law of the city, that none shall enter any trade but those who belong to the particular company.

Aug. 15. Beaulieu. Sir Robt. Naunton to Carleton. The King has had the colic, but is better, and has been on horseback these two mornings by sunrise. Sir Walter Raleigh feigned sickness in order to get leave to take medicine at his own house, and then embarked to try to reach a ship which he had in waiting at Gravesend, but was intercepted at Greenwich by Sir Lewis Stukeley, Vice Admiral of Devon, to whom he vainly offered 10,000*l.* if he would fly with him. [*Holl. Corresp., Aug.* 15, 1618.]

Aug. 15. London. 84. Chamberlain to the Same. Nine persons were indicted for the riot at the Spanish Ambassador's. Brownists fined and imprisoned. Capt. Bubbe pilloried for telling fortunes. Lady Shrewsbury, refusing the Oath of Allegiance, has incurred a præmunire, and may lose all she has. Splendid funeral of Sir Wm. Craven. Loud complaints of injuries from the Hollanders, in the East Indies and Greenland.

Vol. XCVIII.

1618.

Aug. 18. 85. Sir Thos. Coventry, Solicitor General, and Sir Ant. Ben, Recorder of London, to [the Council]. Mr. Holt and Mr. Halsey have proved that, in the sale and purchase of certain manors in Lancashire, they were losers by their transactions with Sir John Molyneux. Lady Molyneux was unable to disprove most of their allegations.

Aug. 19. 86. Appointment at a general meeting of the Commissioners of Sewers, held at Huntingdon, Aug. 12, of three Commissioners from each of the cos. Northampton, Huntingdon, Cambridge, Norfolk, Lincoln, and Isle of Ely, to accompany Sir Clement Edmondes, sent down by the Council to survey the drains and outfalls, &c., in order to settle the differences of the Commissioners; with reports of the results of their surveys, Aug. 13 to 19.

Aug.? 87. Petition of the Inhabitants of Sutton and Mepal, Isle of Ely, to the Council. The not opening Sutton Lode is highly prejudicial to them, because, though a branch of Westwater, it has a separate outfall, and is now the only good outfall for the Ouse, up to Lynn haven.

[Aug.] 88. Sir Walter Raleigh's apology, showing that he concealed from His Majesty that the Spaniard had any footing in Guiana, but thought his own previously taking possession of it for England, and the consent of the inhabitants thereto, authorized him to drive away the Spaniards. Defends his conduct on the ground of necessity, and the inimical proceedings of the Spaniards, and urges the impolicy of acknowledging that he acted wrongly, as the King's claim to Guiana would thereby be forfeited. Has lost his all, and leaves the remainder of his miserable life to the King's mercy.

Aug. 20. London. 89. Chamberlain to Carleton. Sir W. Raleigh counterfeited madness, and produced boils and blotches on his body; he has made a long apology for himself, and his friends do their best for him. Sir Lewis Stukeley is generally decried. Sir Geo. Calvert gone to Court; his Lady kept under guard. The King indisposed; his physician Mayerne has lately come from France. The man who discovered Lord and Lady Suffolk's courses is murdered. Sir John Bingley may get through. Lord Coke spoken of as Treasurer, also the Earl of Pembroke, Marquis Hamilton, and Visct. Doncaster. Much ado in suppressing buildings. Patents granted for a tax on sea coals, a tonnage on shipping for lighthouses, as is pretended; also for licensing pedlars; and Archy has one for the making of tobacco pipes.

Aug. 21? 90. Interrogatories to be administered to divers witnesses, touching the waste and ruin committed in the King's house, gardens, and lands of Maison Dieu, at Dover, by Wm. Hanington.

Aug. 21? 91. Copy of the above.

Aug. 21. Dover. 92. Depositions of numerous witnesses founded on the above interrogatories, relative to the trespasses committed by Wm. Hanington and Monings Hanington, his brother, at Maison Dieu, Dover. Aug. 21 to Sept. 4.

Aug. 21. 93. Copy of the above.

Vol. XCVIII.

1618.

Aug. 22. Sir Edw. Cecil to Carleton. It is reported from Naples that Sir Thos. Lake and Lady Roos have combined to poison Lord Roos there, by the means of certain Irishmen. [*Holl. Corresp., Aug.* 22, 1618.]

Aug. 24? 94. List [by Edw. Nicholas] of the King's [intended] journeys, from Aug. 25 to Sept. 5.

Aug. 24. 95. Bond of Jas. Hugessen, jun., of Dover, in 300*l.*, to indemnify Lord Zouch for delivering up a ship of Emden called the Golden Wagon, wrecked near Dover, to Thos. Hoyes, part owner thereof, on payment of royalties, &c.

Aug. 25. 96. Petition of Passwater Saxbey, prisoner in Bridewell, to the Council, that his whipping and imprisonment for ten weeks may be considered sufficient punishment for having thrown his hat in the King's face, in a drunken fit; deserves much more, but throws himself on His Majesty's mercy for release.

Aug. 26. London. 97. Dr. Mayerne to Carleton. Medical opinion on the state of his health, and prescription of remedies. French.

Aug. 29. London. Sir Art. Tyringham to the Same. Some secret affair makes Sir Thos. Lake's case worse than ever. It is said that death will conclude Sir Walter Raleigh's troubles. The Queen's intercession will rather defer than prevent his punishment. [*Holl. Corresp., Aug.* 29.]

Aug. 30. Sunday. Margate. 98. John Pory to the Same. Has inquired at Margate for his crossbow, &c.; sorry he did not attend his Lordship to the Hague, to witness the overthrow of those sons of Belial who hated him.

Aug. Dover Castle. 99. Warrant by [Lord Zouch], appointing ——— to be Captain of the Train Bands within the port of Hythe.

Aug. 100. Assignment by Robt. Weeks, of Siston, co. Gloucester, to the King, of bonds for performance of the conditions on which John Sturges, of Wolverton, co. Somerset, sold him a mansion-house at Wolverton and a mill in North Bradley, co. Wilts; done in order to its re-assignment to Wm. Wise, of Lincoln's Inn, to whom the lands are now conveyed.

Aug.? Notice that the King has granted to Edw. Hawkins the office of Examiner and Registrar to the Commission for Bankrupts, in order to avoid the confusion caused by the papers and deeds being deposited in many different hands, and that the office is kept in Ivy Lane, St. Paul's. Printed. [*Proc. Coll., No.* 61 A.]

Aug.? 101. Proceedings in the Chancery Court of the Cinque Ports, in the case of Lord Roper, of Teynham, and others, v. Thos. Norton, Mayor of Fordwich, and others, for carrying away fishing nets which Lord

1618. VOL. XCVIII.

Teynham, by permission, placed in the river at Fordwich, for fishing. The Mayor and four other dependants are acquitted; the others fined from 6*l*. to 3*l*. each.

VOL. XCIX. SEPTEMBER, 1618.

Sept. 1. Penshurst. 1. Robt. Visct. Lisle to Carleton. Was sorry not to see him before he left. Sends him a stag, the best he can get, as his annual tribute, &c.

Sept. 5. Drury Lane. 2. Sir Wm. Smithe to the Same. Thanks for acceptance of his son. Begs he will employ him as he thinks fit.

Sept. 5. London. 3. John Pory to the Same. Reasons why he left Carleton before his arrival at the Hague. The King is coming to Windsor. The Queen is at Oatlands, indisposed. Yesterday was the third day of Sir W. Raleigh's examination by their Lordships in the Tower, on articles sent by the King of Spain.

Sept. 7. Windsor. 4. Sir Robt. Naunton to Sir Thos. Wilson. Particulars of a Frenchman, named Cavane or Heern, who forced his way to the very table end, to see the King at dinner at Windsor, and is a very suspicious character; he is to seize him and his papers, examine him as to his business, &c., and whether he is in intelligence with Sir Walter or Lady Raleigh; if faulty, he is to be committed; if not, as little noise to be made about it as possible. With indorsement [by Wilson], that he spent three days and two nights in the service, with three men, a coach, and six horses.

Sept. 8. London. 5. Sir Edw. Harwood to Carleton. The Court is coming to town, and thence to Wanstead and Theobalds. The reports of Sir Walter Raleigh's execution are false, but he has been examined on a suspected intelligence with France, and on an attempt to escape. *Incloses*,

5. I. *Sir Walter Raleigh's apology.* [*See August, No.* 88.]

Sept. 8. London. 6. Matt. de Quester to the Same. Sends despatches from Sec. Naunton.

Sept. 9. Grant to John Browne of a Waiter's place in the port of London, for life. [*Grant Bk., p.* 242.]

Sept. 10. 7. The Council to Sir Thos. Wilson. Commission him to go to the Tower, and take charge of Sir Walter Raleigh, to remain constantly in his company, and keep him safe and close prisoner, to suffer no person whatever to have access to him, or to speak to him, except in his own hearing, and that only in case of necessity, and to communicate to them anything that occurs worth notice.

VOL. XCIX.

1618.

Sept. 10. Whitehall. Proclamation of the pardon, granted at the instance of the agent of the King of Spain, to the offenders who assaulted the late Spanish Ambassador's house in the Barbican. With strict injunctions to the apprentices not to seek redress of their wrongs by tumult, but by course of justice; and to the authorities to repress seditious tumults. Printed. [*Proc. Coll., No.* 59.]

Sept. 11. London. 8. M. de Tourval to Fras. Windebank. Thanks for his courteous letter. Cannot come this summer to visit him, and gather nosegays and eat plums. Thinks he is discontented with the Spanish marriage, because he does not write the language, and will lose it like himself, who cannot now speak it like Don Quixote, though he can write it better than Sancho Panza. Is going to eat a hot venison pie with an old friend. Spanish.

Sept. 12. 9. Sir Thos. Wilson to Sec. Naunton. The Lieutenant [of the Tower] refuses him the keys of Sir Walter Raleigh's lodging at night. Requested to have apartments where Sir Walter might sleep in a room within his. Went over the Tower in search of such, but the Earl of Northumberland and Countess of Shrewsbury have all the best rooms, and the Earl refuses to give up a brick tower, which is Lord Carew's lodging, as Master of the Ordnance, because his son lodges there when he comes to see him, though that is but rarely. Dares not take charge of Sir Walter, unless he may be removed thither, or else placed in a room above his, where he would hear any movement at night; but thither Sir Walter refuses to go except by force, and therefore fears he has some contrivances connected with the double windows in his present room. *Incloses,*

9. I. *The Same to the Same. Found Sir Walter Raleigh in bed, in a room with two windows, from either of which letters might be thrown. Asks whether to replace the man who dresses his sores by one of his own men, and whether the apothecary and surgeon, who are appointed by the King's physician, may be admitted whenever he wishes for them. Raleigh says the King may do as he pleases with him, no man being more willing to die. Asks better rooms than one bad prison chamber for his men and himself. Tower, Sept.* 11.

Sept. 14. 10. [The Same to the Same.] Has little of importance to relate, it being early days. *Incloses,*

10. I. *Notes by [the Same] of conversations with Sir W. Raleigh. Exhorted him to discover to the King any offer he had for employment in France, or anything else of consequence. He said he should have no chance of pardon if he told all he could tell; then seemed as though he would write, and at last said he knew nothing worth revealing. He related the particulars of his past history, the circumstances of the plot by Northampton and Suffolk to get rid of him and Lord Cobham at the King's accession, his after misfortunes, his attempt to*

1618. Vol. XCIX.

escape, knowing that he would be received anywhere but in England or Spain. He praised the bravery of the Romans, in ending life by suicide rather than meeting any base death. In answer to the remark that they were heathens, and knew not the peril to their souls, he said he thought there were cases in which a Christian might do it. Does not think he has courage left to try. The Lieutenant wished to remove all his drugs, but he said, if he chose to kill himself, he had only to run his head against a post. He told Sir Lewis Stukeley and La Chesnay also that the French Ambassador had a boat to help his escape if his own failed, but it was not true; he said it to encourage them. He often tries to gain information by talking on matters which may lead to it. Sept. 12, 13, 14.

Sept. 14. 11. Sir Robt. Naunton to Sir Thos. Wilson. Has read his letters to the King, who is pleased with his service, and longs for the ripening and mellowing of his observations. Hopes he will gain ground of the hypocrite, the best comfort being that he will not long be troubled with him. The keeping of the keys is to be arranged according to custom. *Incloses,*

11. I. *The Same to the Lieutenant of the Tower. Sir W. Raleigh, with Sir T. Wilson, is to remove to the brick tower; Raleigh's old servant to be replaced by one of Wilson's, and the surgeons only to see him in presence of Wilson or his servant. Sept.* 14.

Sept. 14. Grant to Sir Lionel Cranfield of the office of Keeper of the Great Wardrobe, for life. [*Grant Bk., p.* 235.]

Sept. 15. 12. [Sir Thos. Wilson] to Sir Robt. Naunton. Raleigh professes that he will send a letter to the King by Wilson, giving him a sealed copy of it, to read when the King has got his. He wishes to send Wilson's man Edward to his wife. *Incloses,*

12. I. *Relation of conferences with Raleigh. He complains grievously of illness, but his physician says he is not so ill as he pretends, and that some applications made by himself are the chief causes of his ailments. When diverted by conversation, he talks like a strong, sound man. Exhorted him to confess his dealings with the French agent and Ambassador, pretending they were already confessed by others. He declared nothing could truly be confessed to touch his fidelity; that he knew not the agent nor the Ambassador, except that the latter came, as did other Ambassadors, to see his ship before his starting. His hope was, when in France, to serve against the Spaniards. He sprinkled himself with aqua fortis that he might seem diseased and not be sent for to Court, and thus gain time. His flight was only to save his life, being warned by his friends that it was in danger, &c.*

1618. Vol. XCIX.

Thinks he is afraid of speaking out, because, if the Spanish match hold, the Spaniards will pursue him to death; if it fail, there will be a match with France, and then he would "have marred his market, by betraying the trust which perhaps they have put in him."

Sept. 15. 13. Certificate of the Commissioners of Buildings for London, of the principal buildings erected within the city, contrary to proclamations since Michaelmas, 1615.

Sept. 15? 14. Similar certificate by the Commissioners for Middlesex.

Sept. 15. Dover Castle. 15. Warrant by Lord Zouch for apprehension of Rich. Wyer, of River, who is to be brought before him at Dover.

Sept. 15. 16. Examination of Monings Hanington. Accounts of the gunpowder, lead, &c. which he had in his possession.

Sept. 15. 17. Abstract of the above. *Annexed is,*

17. I. *Note of gunpowder, lead, weapons, &c. found in the lodging of Monings Hanington at the Maison Dieu, Dover, Sept. 12, 1618.*

Sept. 15. 18. Merchant Adventurers to the Council. Send, as directed, a statement of the value of their stock of cloth at Middleburgh, which is 20,000*l.*; their debts in the United Provinces are 80,000*l.*, exclusive of those of their company in the north and west of England. Beg that if the inquiry be prompted by any impending danger, they may have timely notice.

Sept. 16. 19. Certificate by twelve masters of vessels of Dover to Lord Zouch, that all passengers from Dieppe to England are obliged to receive a pass from the Clerk of the Passage at that place, for which they pay 6*d.*

Sept. 16. Margate. 20. Thos. Busher to Carleton. Will inquire for his crossbow, which Mr. Pory says was left there. The French book is not his own, and the owner will neither lend nor sell it.

Sept. 16. Whitehall. 21. Sir Robt. Naunton to Sir Thos. Wilson. The King consents that his wife should join him, to attend in his absence. He also gives permission to Raleigh to write to him, if he will do it with a sincere desire to satisfy only His Majesty, without respect to other parties, and not play with him as he did with the Lords. Sir Allan Apsley reports well of Wilson's care and discretion.

Sept. 16. 22. Return, by the Constables, &c. of Newington, Bermondsey, of the strangers resident in the parish, with their trades, countries, &c.

Sept. 16. 23. Similar return from the parish of St. Saviour's, Southwark.

Sept. 17. 24. Similar return from the parish of St. Thomas', Southwark, with a list of all the landlords in the parish whose houses are divided, being six in number, and of their lodgers.

VOL. XCIX.

1618.

Sept. 17. 25. [Sir Thos. Wilson] to Sir Robt. Naunton. Has been busy in removing Raleigh to a safer lodging. Sends an inventory of his goods. He has chemical stuffs of all sorts. Has wormed out of him that the French agent was brought to his house by La Chesnay. The Lieutenant told him he might write to the King, if he would write no trivial nor delusory matter, telling him he had so lost his reputation for truth, that no one believed a word he said, and threatening him with death if he were not true this time, which he promised to be.

Sept. 17. 26. Licence by Lord Zouch to Benet Melliot, of Dieppe, at nomination of the Governor of Dieppe, to fish on the English coasts; with certificate of its enrolment in the records of Dover Castle, and in the Hundred Book of Rye, and also of survey of the nets.

Sept. 17. 27—34. Similar licences to Nich. Drovaulx, David Caume, Nic. de Brest, Jean Potet, Chas. de la Mare, Fras. Gournoise, Robt. Calemont, and Jean Sauvier. Indorsed is a note that these licences be delivered up to [Lord Zouch] to be cancelled, Oct. 7, 1619, after the expiration of the year. Eight papers.

Sept. 17. Wokingham. 35. Inquisition of the assart lands, purprestures, incroachments, &c. in the parishes of Hurst, Wokingham, Cookham, Sunningbill, &c., in the Forest of Windsor, now occupied by Sir Hen. Neville and others.

Sept. 17. Madrid. Sir Fras. Cottington to [Naunton]. Has received his letters of Aug. 9 and 11, informing him of the business of Bohemia, and of Sir Walter Raleigh's intended escape. [*Extract, Dom. Corresp., Dec.* 18, 1618.]

Sept. ? 36. Declaration by the Muscovy Company to the King, of the wrongs and abuses done them by the Hollanders and Zealanders in Greenland, in driving them away from their fishing, under commission from Count Maurice, the States having given Greenland to the Zealanders, and Hudson's touches and the Islands adjoining, to the Hollanders, for fishing.

Sept. ? 37. Note of the goods and provisions taken from the English by the Zealanders and others at King James' Newland, alias Greenland, in July 1618; total loss 66,436*l.* 15*s.*, besides the killing of men and spoiling of ships.

Sept. ? 38. Declaration of the injuries sustained by the Russian Company from the Dutch in Greenland, who combined, by authority of the States, to usurp their trade and drive them away from it.

Sept. 17? 39. Brief of the state of the Muscovy Company, showing their right to Greenland, with abstracts of depositions on the damages sustained by them from the Hollanders and Flemings, and estimate of their total loss thereby.

Sept. 17. 40. Depositions, taken Sept. 5–17, of Wm. Heely, of London, Robt. Salmon, of Deptford, Stephen Smith, of Gravesend, Thos. Wilkinson, of Ipswich, John Headland, and Thos. Edge, of London, and John Johnson, of Limehouse, and others, relative to the wrongs inflicted on the vessels of the Muscovy Company by the Hollanders.

VOL. XCIX.

1618.

Sept. ? 41. Petition of Robt. Salmon to the Council, for redress of damage sustained from the Hollanders, who attacked his ship when at the whale fishery at Greenland, and did damage to the amount of 900*l.*

Sept. 18. 42. Return, by the Constables and others of St. George's parish, Southwark, of the strangers therein resident, their state, condition, and country.

Sept. 18? 43. Similar return from the parish of St. Olave's.

Sept. 18? 44. Return of a search made by warrant, as to the strangers resident within the liberty of the Clink.

Sept. 18? 45. Note of the residence, &c. of Vincentius Sayos, of Bruges, within the liberty of Parish-garden, and also of Mr. Syon, a Dutchman.

Sept. 18. 46. Return of the names, &c. of strangers resident in the parish of St. Mary Magdalen, Bermondsey.

Sept. 18? 47. Similar return for the parish of Lambeth.

Sept. 18. Sir Walter Raleigh to Lady Raleigh. Is in perpetual pain with a swollen side. His keeper, Edw. Wilson, takes much pains with him. Extract [by Sir Thos. Wilson]. *Annexed is,*

Note [by Wilson] that though the Secretary said Raleigh might send the box of spirits and cordials to [Lady Raleigh], the care required being in what came from her, he [Wilson] kept it till he had talked with the apothecary. [*Dom. Corresp., Sept., No.* 9. I.]

Sept. [18?] Lady Raleigh to Sir Walter Raleigh. Is sorry for his illness, and that he has no servant of his own, but rejoices that he has so good a keeper, whose servants attend him. [*Ibid.*]

Sept. 18. 48. [Sir Thos. Wilson] to the King. Has done his best to work out what he could from this arch-hypocrite [Raleigh]. Transmits Sir Walter's letter to His Majesty, in which he has laid open all the secrets of his heart.

[Sept. 19.] Account by [Sir Thos. Wilson] of an interview with Lady Carew, who said she did not think the French agent had any commission from France to deal with Raleigh, but was induced to it by some in England connected with the Queen; that Her Majesty said she would rather have the match with Mdme. Chretienne than the Spanish lady with all her gold, and that the agent told her Raleigh would be welcomed and well treated, if he went to France. *Prefixed is,*

[*Sir Thos. Wilson to Sec. Naunton.*] *Complaints of the insolent conduct of Graves, the Doorkeeper of the Council, who refused to go in with a message from him when the Council was sitting, Sept.* 18; *marked "Not sent."* [*Dom. Corresp., Sept.* 21.]

Sept. 19. Minley, Hants. 49. Earl of Sussex to the Council. Mrs. Fras. Shutt, summoned to appear for misdemeanor, is too weak to attend at present; will attend with her the latter end of the month.

Vol. XCIX.

1618.

Sept. 19. Grant to Hugh Hennearing of the goods of John Cope, outlaw. [*Grant Bk., p.* 267.]

Sept. 19. Dover Castle. 50. Warrant [from Lord Zouch] to the Droit-gatherer of Hastings, to help to deliver eight pieces of ordnance and two murderers to Stephen Roffe, of Rye, or Robt. Wright, of Hastings.

[Sept. 20.] 51. Petition of the inhabitants of the Isle of Ely to Sir Clement Edmondes, appointed by Council to survey the drainage, for the re-opening and cleansing of the old water-courses which drain the country, and against all propositions for new rivers or drains.

Sept. 20. 52. Sir Clement Edmondes to the Council. Gives a detailed report of the survey by himself and the Commissioners of Sewers, of the state of drainage in cos. Northampton, Cambridge, and the Isle of Ely.

[Sept. 20.] 53. Draft of the above.

Sept.? 54. List of the rivers, drains, and sewers, for draining the fens, from the River Glenn to Kine Ea, anciently maintained by the country.

Sept.? 55. Estimate of the expense of works to be done in draining, &c about Skirth, Brigg, Horbling, &c.

Sept. 20. 56. List, by Wm. Holliday and Robt. Johnson, of houses demolished in and about London in 1618, by warrant from Council.

Sept. 20? 57. Petition of Stephen Gybbs, Lieutenant of Sandgate Castle, to Lord Zouch, to be maintained in possession of a seat in Folkestone Church, the right to which is challenged by John Read.

Sept. 21. Lord Zouch to Sir Geo. Newman. Begs him to favour Mr. Gybbs in his suit with John Read about a seat in church, and not to allow him to be removed without sentence. [*Minute, Diary, Dom. Corresp., Oct.* 20, 1618.]

Sept. 21. Commission to the Archbp. of Canterbury, &c. to disforest Chippenham and Blackmore Forests, co. Wilts. [*Grant Bk., p.* 235.]

Sept. 21. 58. [Sir Thos. Wilson] to the King. Has not been so indiscreet as to promise Raleigh any favour, as on authority from His Majesty; but has merely used the hope of mercy as a bait, being the only one that could draw him on to confess anything. He says the French agent told him he should find friends in France. He still denies having a commission from France, though he pretended to his fleet that he had one, when, after the disaster at St. Thomas's, they were disposed to disperse or turn pirates. He urged them to seize the Mexico fleet, with part of the spoil to satisfy France, and with the remainder make their peace with England. *Annexed is,*

58. I. *Note of a message sent to [Sir Thos. Wilson] by Sec. Naunton, that Raleigh wrote to the King that Wilson had assured him of His Majesty's mercy, to which*

VOL. XCIX.

1618.

Naunton replied that he thought Wilson would only hold out hopes to him, as was usual in examining prisoners.

Sept. 21. 59. [Sir Thos. Wilson] to Sec. Naunton. Never gave Raleigh any hopes of mercy as coming from the King, but only as from himself. Will explain all when he sees His Majesty. The Lieutenant, who is jealous of him, will try to raise prejudices against him. *Annexing,*

59. I. *Note of a conversation with Raleigh, in which he said, that in going to France, he hoped either to obtain licence to renew the expedition to Guiana, which failed through his sickness, or that the Spaniards, fearing the harm he might do them, would persuade the King to recall and pardon him.*

Sept. 22. Memoranda [by Wilson] of conversations with Raleigh, &c., since Sept. 19. He mentioned that Christopher, servant of the Governor of Guiana, who came home with him, knew of seven or eight gold mines, and wishes he might be kept in view. The physician says no one can know what all his chemical things are, unless they had seen their extraction, but thinks they should be taken from him. Raleigh said he combed his hair an hour daily before he came to the Tower, but would not take the same pains now, till he knew whether the hangman should have his head. He told Wilson some of the contents of his letter to the King. [*Dom. Corresp., Sept.* 18.]

Sept. 22? 60. Memorandum [by the Same], to ask the Lords whether [Raleigh] shall retain his chemical stuffs; also to speak of Christopher the Indian, &c.

Sept. 22. Westminster? 61. Warrant to the Commissioners of the Treasury for Count Gondomar to transport two pieces of brass ordnance to his own house at Bayonne, in Galicia.

Sept. 23. Hampton Court. 62. Sec. Naunton to Sir Thos. Wilson. He is to require Raleigh first to relate, and then to write down, the names of those of his servants or friends who saw the coming and going to him of the French agent, or La Chesnay, and whatever he knows touching the commission he sought from France. *Annexed are,*

62. I. *Notes [by Wilson] of Raleigh's answers that no one saw the French agent come; that several persons were in the parlour when La Chesnay passed through, but knows not whether any one noticed him.*

Sept. 23. Hatfield. 63. Wm. Earl of Salisbury to Carleton. Begs his continued influence with Count Maurice and the Marquis of Buckingham for Mr. Kenithorpe. Wishes to pull him out of his misery, but has not sufficient power at Court.

Sept. 23. London. 64. Sir Edw. Harwood to the Same. Projected changes of Court officers. Sec. [Lake's] case is desperate, and Lady Roos' looking worse and worse. The Lord Treasurer cannot make his peace, even by his offer of Audley End and Northampton House; but must come to a trial in the Star Chamber. Raleigh struggles hard for

1618. Vol. XCIX.

life, and, as the King is now with the Queen, it is believed he may live. The Secretary of the late French Ambassador is in custody, for favouring his escape to France.

Sept. 23. Dover. 65. Examination of Jason West, of Allhallows, London. Being told on the exchange that a certain Dutch merchant intended to carry over much gold, followed him from London to Dover to detain it, but having no warrant, could not search himself; and, through the connivance of the searcher, the Dutchman carried off the money.

Sept. 23. Dover. 66. Examination of John Sharp, of Romney. Saw six horses going to the shore, laden with wool, and a vessel ready to carry it away. The wools belonged to Geo. Lubdey [Lopdale].

Sept. 23. Copy of the above. [*Dom. Corresp., Sept.* 29.]

Sept. 24. Boston. 67. Earl of Rutland, Bp. of Lincoln, Robt. Lord Willoughby [of Eresby , and others, to the Council. The bridge [at Boston] needs repairs, but it is doubtful what parties are liable to do them; taxes have been previously rated on the inhabitants of Lindsey, Kesteven, and Holland, but no execution thereof performed.

Sept. 24. Strand. 68. Abm. Williams to Carleton. Sends a paper, termed by its author, Overall, Bp. of Norwich, the Opinion of the English Church, but which is rather his own. Buckingham has visited Sec. Lake. Commissioners arrived from Holland to settle the West Indian and Greenland disputes. The coming over of the Electress Palatine is uncertain, on account of the troubles in Germany, and the want of 100,000*l.* for the King's share of her charges.

Sept. 24. Lord Zouch to the Governor of Dieppe. Requests him to give the same entertainment to the shippers of Dover as is given here to his men, and to lay no greater tax upon them than is here imposed on the men of Dieppe. [*Minute, Diary, Dom. Corresp., Oct.* 20, 1618.]

Sept. 24. 69. [Sir Thos. Wilson] to the King. Sends a letter from Raleigh to His Majesty. Told Raleigh that the King knew he could say more than he had done in his last. Raleigh protested he had told all. Reminded him that he had not mentioned his pretended French commission. He said, if the King wished to inquire into former things, he could tell much more, and asked for paper and ink, though he said the more he confessed the sooner he should be hanged, yet he would discharge his conscience. *Incloses,*

69. I. *Sir Walter Raleigh to the Same. Spared to revenge his murdered men; discharged Spanish barks unspoiled, and forbore all parts of the Spanish Indies; therefore thinks the Spanish Ambassador has no right to complain, the Spaniards having murdered twenty-six unarmed English. Has spent his estate, lost his son, resisted his companions who wished to spoil, and returned home to fulfil his trust, though he might have sold his ships and goods, and enriched himself abroad. Throws himself on His Majesty's wisdom and goodness.*

Sept. 24? 70. Copy of the above letter of Raleigh.

VOL. XCIX.

1618.

Sept. 24. 71. Interrogatories for Raleigh relative to the persons who witnessed the coming to him of the French agent, or La Chesnay; his reported French commission, &c.; with his answers. Knows not any servants or friends that saw them, but Stukeley, who saw La Chesnay at Brentford. Did not know beforehand of the French agent's coming. Never had a French commission.

Sept. 25. Hampton Court. 72. Naunton to Wilson. The King is not satisfied with Raleigh's last examination; desires him to examine Lady Raleigh, and the rest of the servants about them in Broad Street. Raleigh's confessions are worth more than his roaring tedious letter.

Sept. 25. 73. [Wilson to Naunton.] Fears there was but mountebank's stuff in Raleigh's letter to the King. Gives his answers to the questions about the French agent, &c. Imperfect. With note [by Wilson], that he had also set down the examinations of Lady Raleigh and her servant, and what he had further gathered from Sir Walter. Indorsed, with a memorandum, that therewith was sent a copy of the confessions of Mr. Dawser, a clerk.

Sept. 26. St. Lawrence. 74. The King of Spain to Julian Sanches de Ulloa. The English King assured Gondomar, that he would either punish Raleigh and his associates, for the mischief they had done in the Indies, or send them to Spain for punishment, and would have satisfaction done therefor. He is to urge His Majesty to immediate public and exemplary punishment, the offence being notorious, and, if the goods of Raleigh and his associates do not suffice, those of his sureties are to be seized.

Sept. 27. The Grange. 75. Geo. Carleton to Sir D. Carleton. His son Dudley is elected to his Fellowship, and has leave to travel. Has provided him for his journey, and hopes Sir Dudley and Lady Carleton will excuse his rawness at first. Private news, &c.

Sept. 27. London. 76. Archbp. of Spalato to the Same. Recommends the business of the bearer, Paul de la Ravoire, and begs that he may be protected from the malice of France.

Sept. 28. 77. Notes by [Sir T. Wilson], of his conversations with Raleigh, Sept. 26, 27, and 28. He would have taken the Plate fleet if he could, and when told that it would be piracy, he said none were called pirates for millions, but only for small things, and he could have given 10,000 here and 20,000 there, and yet have 600,000 for the King. He said his death was impolitic if the Spanish match held, because he had so many friends and allies that it would make Spain very unpopular. Spoke against self murder, and said he would die in the light, and make some people known, meaning Sir Lewis Stukeley, whom he detests. He blames himself for confessing what passed with the French agent, whose friends he will thereby lose. Would not say what friends he meant, but doubtless it was the great Lady who must not be mentioned [the Queen]. Report in London that the Queen has begged his life, and that the late Bishop

1618. Vol. XCIX.

of Winchester, when visited by the King a little before his death, told him he should never see him again, and would therefore beg one thing of him, viz., the life of an old gentleman, a great offender, who yet was dearly respected by the late Queen, viz., Sir Walter Raleigh.

Sept. 28. Egham. 78. John Pymme to the Lords of the Treasury. Impossibility of raising at once 2,000*l.* by the sale of His Majesty's rent, iron, and fines on leases of the disforested grounds, Blackmore and Pewsham. Can get no sale for the iron at the price required, 12*l.* 10*s.* per ton, and has no offers, save for part of one forest.

Sept. 28. Chester. 79. Earl of Derby and Mayor of Chester to the Council. Proceedings on the petition of John Wakefield. Hen. Latham was too weak to appear before them, but they think Wakefield has been wrongfully molested. *Incloses,*

79. I. *Certificate by Hen. Latham. The Bishop's Messengers came to summon him to Court, and on his being unable to attend, insisted on his giving a bond for appearance next Court, and accepted, as surety, John Wakefield, the tutor of his children; they then accused Wakefield of being a priest, and made him go with them. Understands that though he sent to Court to depose that he was too ill to appear, his bond is now held forfeit, and that another John Wakefield is sued as his surety, being of the same name with the man who really was so.*

79. II. *Note of the charges of John Wakefield, of Wigan, in defending himself against the claim for the above bond,* 18*l.* 10*s.* 6*d.*, *and his loss of time,* 50*l.*

Sept. 29. 80. Abstract of casualties entered upon the Green Wax books since Michaelmas, 1612, for contempts, non-presenting of recusants, trespasses, recognizances, and non-appearances.

Sept. 29. 81. Sir Thos. Lake to [Naunton ?]. Sends news letters from France for the King to see. The newly chosen President of the Council there is a Jesuit. Hopes remission of his fault, and some token of His Majesty's favour.

Sept. 29. Hague. 82. D. C. [Sir Dud. Carleton] to Thos. Locke. Is troubled to find his service abroad encountered with difficulties at home. Hopes Sec. Naunton will not refuse to sign the warrants for his allowance, and that the Chancellor of the Exchequer will secure him better payment, having to take up his money in advance, at interest. Money must be borrowed to pay Lady Hill, &c.

Sept. 29. 83. Examination of John Thomas, of Harrison. Met horses carrying wool to the sea, which horses belonged to Lopdale, of Romney.

Sept. 29. 84. Another account of the above examination.

Vol. XCIX.

1618.

Sept. 29. Dover Castle. 85. Warrant, by Lord Zouch, for apprehension of John Lubdey [Lopdale], of Hastings, and Geo. Lubdey, of Romney, to be brought before him.

Sept. 29. 86. Receipts and Privy Purse expenses of Lord Chancellor Bacon, since June 24, 1618; total receipts, 4,160*l.* 12*s.*; total expenses, 3,711*l.* 9*s.* 2*d.*

Sept. 29. 87. Account of moneys paid to Sir Robt. Mansell, [late] Treasurer of the Navy, for ships in harbour, from Oct. 1611 to Feb. 9, 1617–8.

[Sept. 29.] 88. Account of moneys paid to the Same, for ships in the Narrow Seas, from April 30, 1612, to Sept. 1618.

Sept.? 89. Memoranda of payments to [the Same], for the Narrow Seas, cordage, building of ships, transporting the Lady Elizabeth and Bishop of Orkney, fetching in pirates, &c., 1613–7.

Sept.? 90. Copy of part of the above.

Sept. 29. 91, 92. Account of moneys paid to the Same, from May 5, 1617, to Sept. 9, 1618. Two papers.

[Sept. 30.] 93. Roll of the quit rents of the manor of Havering, co. Essex, due at Michaelmas, for one year. Total 66*l.* 19*s.* 3*d.*

[Sept. 30.] 94. Muster roll of the garrison of Walmer Castle.

Sept. 30. 95. Copy of the above [by Edw. Nicholas].

Sept. 30. 96. [Sir Thos. Wilson] to the King. Some have thought him indiscreet in his dealings with the arch impostor. Sets down the points confessed by him [Raleigh] in his discourses, which he always denied to the Commissioners:—First, his regret that, by confronting the French agent, he should lose the agent's friends; second, his resolution to have taken the Spanish Plate fleet, if he could; third, his contradictions in talking of the Spanish match; fourth, his sometimes desiring to die, and sometimes urging that he could do the King better service than in his grave. *Annexing,*

96. i. *Observations on contradictions in the discourses of Raleigh. Indorsed by* [*Wilson*], "*Delivered to His Majesty in his Concel Chamber, at Whytehal, which the Lords told me he redd unto them the next day, and apprehended.*"

96. ii. *Note of a conversation with Raleigh. He boasted of the wonderful things he had done, and that he had invented copper furnaces for distilling salt water into fresh, and said the saltness was caused by great mountains of salt, and that all greenness on the earth was caused by vitriol, which is the salt of the earth. Sept.* 29.

Sept. 97. [Fras. Windebank] to Mons. de Tourval. Despairs of winning the fair Castilian. Has been to Hampshire to reconcile differences between his father and brothers. Hopes to see him this Autumn. French.

VOL. XCIX.

1618. Sept. 98. Bill exhibited by the Attorney General in the Exchequer, at request of John Levingston, Groom of the Bedchamber, against Sir Thos. Leigh, Bart., of Stavely, co. Warwick, Dame Anne Catesby, Robt. Catesby, and Dr. Lambe, to make answer for fraudulently detaining from His Majesty the manor of Sillesworth and Watford, &c., co. Northampton, lands of Robt. Catesby, attainted for the Powder Plot, on pretext of their being settled on Anne Catesby, and for destroying, defacing, or ante-dating the evidences relating thereto.

Sept.? 99. Assignment by Dr. Wm. Branthwait, Master of Gonvile and Caius College, to Sir Thos. Wilson, of the next presentation of the parish church of Abinger, co. Surrey, which had been granted to Rich. Branthwait, deceased, by Sir Edw. Eldrington, of Willesden, co. Middlesex.

VOL. C. [SEPTEMBER], 1618.

[Sept.] 1. Report of a survey of the rigging and cordage of all His Majesty's ships, taken July 1618.

[Sept.] 2. Report, addressed by the Commissioners for Survey of the Navy to [the Council], of the present state of the ships, the sums that will be necessary for their repairs, the present average expenditure of the Navy, and the reasons why, notwithstanding the heavy charge, the ships are in so bad a condition.

VOL. CI. [SEPTEMBER], 1618.

[Sept. 1. Copy of the preceding Report of the Commissioners for Survey of the Navy.

[Sept.] 2. "Propositions for Bettering the State and Lessening the Charge of the Ships that now remayne."

[Sept.] 3. "Proposition for a Newe Establishment of the Navy Roiall by Addycion of more Shippes."

[Sept.] 4. "An Abstracte of the Propositions and Meanes for the Ease and Lesseninge of the Charge of the Navy"

[Sept.] 5. Copy of the Report, No. 1, in this volume.

[Sept.] 6. Copy of the Propositions, No. 2.

[Sept.] 7. Copy [by Edw. Nicholas] of the Report, No. 1, in this volume.

[Sept.] 8. Copy [by the Same] of the "Propositions," No. 2.

[Sept.] 9. Copy [by the Same] of the first three pages of "Proposition," No. 3.

1618. VOL. CII. SEPTEMBER? 1618.

Sept.? Certificate of the names of strangers dwelling in London and its liberties, with the place of their birth, and under what sovereignty they depend, &c., taken by Order of Council, Sept. 6, 1618. Classified in alphabetical arrangement of the wards.

VOL. CIII. OCTOBER, NOVEMBER, 1618.

Oct. 1. Whitehall. 1. Thos. Murray to Carleton. The King commends Carleton. Lake has little hope of returning to favour, and Naunton is oppressed with business, owing to reformations at home, and important occurrences in various European States, with almost all of which the King holds correspondence. His Majesty has read the report on the abuses of the Navy, and the officers are to be examined thereon. No nobleman is willing to be Treasurer. Sir Fulk Greville or Sir Edw. Coke is spoken of, the commission proving inconvenient.

Oct. 1. Rolls. 2. Sir Julius Cæsar to Sir Thos. Wilson. Will confer with him at the Rolls the next day, on Mons. Boislorè's suit referred to them by the King.

Oct. 1. 3. Indenture of sale from Sir Thos. Wilson, of Hertford, now residing in St. Martin's-in-the-Fields, London, of a dwelling-house, garden, &c. in St. Martin's-in-the-Fields, between Durham House, Britain's Burse, York House, and the river, to Wm. Roo, of London, for 374*l.*

Oct. 1. 4. Bond of Jason West, of London, and Wm. Hurt, of Dover, in 200*l.*, to Lord Zouch, for the appearance of the said West, now imprisoned for searching passengers without licence, but to be released for his necessary affairs.

Oct. 2. 5. Examination of John Mace, of Dover. Set sail Sept. 23; knows not the names of his passengers; would not allow Jason West to search them, because he had no commission. Received no money to get the passengers away, and knows of no gold exported. The searcher searched all, none refusing to submit thereto.

Oct. 2. 6. Examination of Edm. Jerningham, late servant of Sir Drew Drury. Mr. Le Gris has importuned him several times to say whether he did not hear Lady Markham speak about the Gunpowder Treason, or his lady and her friends refer to such speeches by her; but he remembers no such thing.

Oct. 2. Norwich. 7. Commissioners for repairing the sea breaches in Norfolk, to the Council. Have almost completed their task. Request them to send some able gentlemen to view the works, take account of the moneys expended, and examine defaulters who have failed in payment of the tax imposed therefor, on which account they have had to borrow 200*l.* on their own credit.

VOL. CIII.

1618.

Oct. 2. Licence to John Harrison to import sturgeon, for thirty-one years. [*Grant Bk., p.* 267.]

Oct. 2. Grant to Edw. Grimston of the arrears of rents from lands in Hamilton and elsewhere, co. Northumberland. [*Ibid., p.* 265.]

Oct. 2. Licence to the Wardens of the Fishmongers' Company to found an hospital called St. Peter's in St. George's parish, Surrey, with divers privileges to them and their successors. [*Ibid., p.* 267.]

Oct. 2. Grant to Hector Johnson of the moiety of the forfeitures of Thurston Tildesley, recusant. [*Ibid., p.* 266.]

Oct. 2? 8. Garrison of Deal Castle to Lord Zouch. Presentment of defaulters. Every man has watched according to appointment, but none save the watch remain in the castle at night. None of the King's provisions have been stolen from the castle.

Oct 2? 9. Similar presentment of Sandown Castle. The captain and lieutenant are guilty of non-residence, and all the rest of not doing their duties according to orders.

Oct. 2? 10. Similar presentment of Sandgate Castle. The officers and whole garrison have been deficient in their duty.

Oct. 2. Lord Zouch to Sir Robt. Naunton. Requests him to cause Sir Nich. Salter and Mr. Jacob to send up some persons that knew the Frenchmen who murdered one of the King's officers, and the circumstances of the murder, he having detained a Frenchman prisoner. [*Minute, Diary, Dom. Corresp., Oct.* 20, 1618.]

Oct. 3. The Same to the Same. An Ambassador has landed from the Great Turk; wishes to know if he should have entertainment of any kind. [*Ibid.*]

Oct. 3. 11, 12. Muster roll of the garrison of Sandgate Castle. Two copies.

Oct. 3. 13. Muster roll of the garrison of Arch-cliff Bulwark.

Oct. 3. London. 14. Sir Edw. Harwood to Carleton. The King much inclined to hang Raleigh, but it cannot handsomely be done, so he is likely to live out his days. The French agent forbidden the Court, for denying his practising with Raleigh. The Commissioners for Survey of the Navy have brought in their report, and Buckingham is joined in commission with the late Admiral. The confessor of the Spanish Ambassador has returned as agent, and is received. The King has written twice in behalf of Lady Roos, for her to have letters of administration for her late husband, though the Earl of Exeter pretends that Lord Roos made a will, &c.

Oct. 4. Eton. 15. Sir Hen. Savile to the Same. Private affairs. The Archbp. of Spalato refuses a certain lease to Sir John Kidderminster. Hopes His Majesty will not apply for it.

VOL. CIII.

1618.

Oct. 4. Tower. 16. Sir. Thos. Wilson to the King. Raleigh, having failed by bribes or flattery to bring him over to his designs, is now reserved with him. Has tried to induce him to confess that, before his late enterprise, he was in confederation with the French, to do some mischief to the Spaniards, and thereby cause a rupture between His Majesty and the King of Spain; but he explained away his divers negociations with Frenchmen, only admitting that the Prince of Rohan would have given him French ships to attack the Indian fleet, but His Majesty refused to let him go. Solicits release from his attendance; can employ his time better for the King's service, in arranging the State Papers of the last six or seven years, just received from Sir Thos. Lake, than in being with this "arch impostor."

Oct. 4. 17. Copy of the above.

Oct. 4. Whitehall. 18. Naunton to Wilson. Returns Lady Raleigh's letter to Sir Walter. Desires him to make what he can out of Raleigh's answer, and certify the same.

Oct. 4. Tower. 19. Wilson to Naunton. Sends Raleigh's answer to his wife's letter; desires it to be returned, that he may go to Lady Raleigh, and get the writings mentioned in it.

Oct. 4. Whitehall. 20. Naunton to Wilson. Returns Raleigh's letter; has not given Wilson's long letter to the King, for he would neither read that nor Lady Raleigh's letter, being glutted with business before he left.

Oct. ? 21. Sir Walter Raleigh to Lady Raleigh. Mr. Herbert advanced 1,100*l.* towards the ship [Destiny]; requests her to send him certain books and powders, and some britony.

[Oct. ?] 22. The Same to the Same. The cost of the ship [Destiny] was about 7,000*l.*, 1,100*l.* of which was adventured by Mr. [Miles] Herbert, who is to have a proportionate share in its sale; his demand for 1,200*l.* may be right. Mentions where certain writings and inventories belonging to it are; Capt. Pennington's writing, for the fourth of his ship, is to be delivered to Sir Chas. Snell.

Oct. ? 23. Abstract of Lady Raleigh's reply to the above. The only writing she has left is the agreement of the proportions of profit to be paid to Capt. Pennington, Sir John Ferne, and Sir Wm. Sellinger, for their share in furnishing the ships; all the rest were delivered to Sec. Calvert.

Oct. 4. 24. Examination of Geo. Lopdale. Helped to carry wool to the shore, which he believes was exported by John Lubdey [Lopdale]. Knows of no other wool exported lately, nor of any leather.

Oct. 5. 25. Muster roll of the garrison of Mote's Bulwark.

Oct. 26. Duplicate of the above, dated Oct. 7.

Vol. CIII.

1618.

Oct. 6. Newgate. 27. Thos. Coo to Sir Julius Cæsar and Sir Fulk Greville. His loyal service in preserving the life of his Sovereign, by discovering the London insurrection, being rewarded with famine and a dungeon, he is resolved to live no longer, leaving his son to conceal his mystical designs. *Annexed is,*

27. I. *The Same to Jas. Holly, glazier. Being basely abused by him, will cross whatever he does, and destroy him in the struggle. "Saturday, your Sabothe."*

Oct. 9 28. Presentation at a Court of Frankpledge of certain persons, with the amount of fines imposed on each, and of composition accepted. *Prefixing,*

28. I. *Articles of Misdemeanor committed by divers persons within the Manor of Ledbury Forren, co. Hereford, presented by Jas. Bond, the Prince's Bailiff. Ledbury, Oct.* 8, 1618.

Oct. 9. Whitehall. 29. Lords of the Treasury to Rich. Dodsall, of York. Command him to repair to Whitehall to take order for discharge of a great debt due by him to the King, who needs money, being about to employ large sums for repairs of the Navy and payment of his debts.

Oct. 9. Whitehall. 30. Duplicate of the above, addressed to Roger Fooke, of Staffordshire.

Oct. 10. 31. Constance Lady Lucy to Sir Thos. Lake. Received his letter, with a process; is ill, but will attend him as soon as she can; would gladly not be questioned on a matter she understands not. Lady Lake heard as much as she did.

Oct. 10. 32. List, by Robt. Johnson, of tenements on new foundations, which the Sheriff of London is directed to demolish.

Oct. 12. Lord Zouch to the Mayor of Dover. To stay all men or packets from passing, unless authorized by Sec. Naunton, and if any come in about affairs, they are to be sent to Naunton or himself. [*Minute, Diary, Dom. Corresp., Oct.* 20, 1618.]

Oct. 12. Commission to Wm. Earl of Pembroke and others, to inquire of castles and lands designed for defence of the realm, and what revenues have been withheld from the Crown. [*Grant Bk., p.* 234.]

Oct. 14. London. 33. [Chamberlain to Carleton.] Great plenty of corn, &c., more than ever known before. The Earl of Arundel, with Inigo Jones, the Surveyor, paid a visit to Ware Park, and were so pleased with the grapes and peaches that the King has sent for them twice a week ever since. Dr. Carleton and his associates preparing for the Synod, though with very poor allowances. Death of Lords St. John of Bletsoe, Roper of Teynham, Dowager Lady Dorset, and Sir Ant. Ben, Recorder; also of Lord Clifton, who killed himself for ennui, though the suits with his daughter were ended; and of Lord Delawarr, who died on his way from Virginia: the city is shipping thither 100 boys and girls who were starving in the streets. Illness of the Queen. The French agent to be removed for arrogance, and tampering with Raleigh, who begs his life basely. Quarrel between the Earl of

1618. VOL. CIII.

Somerset and his wife. Great fire in Cornhill. Pory is a sad drunkard, but would gladly return to Carleton's service. Lady Winwood will lend Carleton any of her late husband's books and papers that he wishes. Beecher is recalled from France, the King being displeased with the cashiering of the Scotch guard. Sir Dud. Diggs has returned, the Poles being within seventy miles of Moscow; he has left 60,000*l.* of the loan, in money and cloth, in good hands.

Oct. 14. London. 34. Sir Art. Tyringham to Carleton. Cannot say anything of the success of his business, but that Sir Thos. Lake's proffers of atonement are rejected, and his offer of his daughter to the Marquis's brother and friend, Sir Hen. Mildmay, utterly refused. The French King has discharged the English agent.

Oct. 14. 35. Abel Barnard to the Same. Thinks he must fasten his money, for fear of his brother at Dunkirk; his misfortunes are owing to his loving trust in his other brother.

Oct. 15. Whitehall. 36. Sir Robt. Naunton to Sir Thos. Wilson. The King releases him from the charge of Raleigh, who is to be delivered over to the Lieutenant of the Tower. Lady Raleigh is to be liberated.

Oct. 15? 37. Memoranda of Raleigh's wishes on business matters, disputed leases, &c. Desires his wife, if she can, to relieve Chris. Hanson's wife, and especially John Talbot's mother, who, having lost her son, will otherwise perish. Sir Lewis Stukeley to be called to account for the value of some tobacco which he sold at Plymouth. Indorsed [by Wilson], "A copy of the note written by Sir Wal. Rawley, in his owne hand, which hee gave me for discharging of his conscience."

Oct. 15. Custom House. 38. Sir John Wolstenholme and Sir Nich. Salter to Sir Fulk Greville. Gentlemen of Scotland have always been allowed to ship home apparel, household stuff already used, and a moderate quantity of new pewter, duty free; but a large quantity of pewter and new hangings or furniture, has paid duty. Their plate has been shipped by warrant from the Lord Treasurer.

Oct. 16. 39. Sir Hen. Carey to Carleton. All of the religion are anxious about the result of the Synod. The Prince has granted his interest in the Admiralty to Buckingham, who is to be joined with the Lord Admiral. Lord Clifton has killed himself with two knives.

Oct. 17. Langley. 40. Capt. Robt. Morton to the Same. Has got a brave boy, and wishes Carleton the same. His brother, Albert Morton, has returned ill, and is under the care of an Italian physician.

Oct. 18. Bedford House. 41. Countess of Bedford to the Same. Though Lady Exeter's business is coming to a sentence, it is quite uncertain who will be Secretary in place of Lake; she and Carleton's other friends will do their best for him.

Oct. 18. Commission to the Archbp. of Canterbury and others, to sell or demise lands which they conceive to be insufficiently conveyed. [*Grant Bk., p.* 234.]

1618. VOL. CIII.

Oct. 19. Commission to Fras. Lord Verulam, Chancellor, and others, to pass a grant of certain [concealed Crown] lands to one Pointer and others, by whom they were discovered. [*Grant Bk., p.* 235.]

Oct. 19. Netherham. 42. Sir Edw. Hext, Justice of Peace of Somersetshire, to the Council. Owen Evans, Messenger of the Chamber, pretended a commission to press maidens for the Bermudas and Virginia, and raised money thereby. He frightened away forty from one parish, who have fled to such obscure places that their parents cannot find them. *Incloses*

42. I. *Acknowledgment by Owen Evans of the receipt from Wm. Michell, of Ottery, of* 10*s., for exempting the parish of Ottery from his commission for pressing maidens. Oct.* 17.

Oct. 19. Tavistock. 43. Earl of Bath to the Council. Sends a petition of the merchants of Devon, against wrongs offered them in their fishing at Newfoundland, by those of the late plantation there.

Oct. 20. Lord Zouch to the Mayor of Dover. To re-open the passage, and suffer men and ships to sail as usual. [*Minute, Diary, Dom. Corresp., Oct.* 20.]

Oct. 20. Licence from Lord Zouch, at request of the Countess of Exeter, for Mrs. Frances de Sylva, with her children, and Gerard Heard, to pass beyond seas. [*Ibid.*]

Oct. 20. 44. Diary of official transactions, minutes of letters, &c. of the Lord Warden of the Cinque Ports, from Dec. 17, 1617, to Oct. 20, 1618. [*The more important letters are calendared under their respective dates.*]

Oct. 22. Holyrood House. The King to the Sheriffs, &c. of Scotland. Authorizes a proclamation for ministers to enforce the observance of certain acts decreed in the General Assembly at Perth, concerning the festivals of the birth, passion, resurrection, and ascension of Christ, and the descent of the Holy Spirit; also concerning the baptism, catechizing, and confirmation of children, and administration of the sacrament. By Act of Privy Council. [*Dom. Corresp., Nov.* 15, 1618.]

Oct. 24. London. 45. Chamberlain to Carleton. The King is at Royston. Buckingham, the new Admiral, compounded with the old Admiral for a round sum of ready money, &c., 3,000*l.* yearly pension to himself, 1,000*l.* to his Lady, and 500*l.* to their eldest son. Sir Thos. Vavasour has sold the Knight Marshalship to Sir Edw. Zouch for 3,000*l.*, but the King is to pay half. Raleigh has a chance of redeeming himself, if he can speak to the purpose about conveyance of jewels, abuses in the sale of lands, &c., at the King's first coming, which will reflect much upon Suffolk, Salisbury, and others. The Navy commission offers to reduce the expenses of the Navy from 56,000*l.* to 30,000*l.* per ann., and yet to build two new ships a year. Sir Dud. Diggs has been before the Council, and has leave to visit his family. By

VOL. CIII.

1618.

the death of Lord Beauchamp, Sir Wm. Seymour is now heir of the house of Hertford. The Queen improves; she has many good wishers. The Bp. of Winchester asks tidings from the Synod.

Oct. 25. Saturday. London. 46. John Pory to Carleton. Lord Rich seized a ship, worth 100,000*l.*, belonging to the mother of the Great Mogul, which Capt. Prin, General of the East India fleet, rescued and restored to its owner. The East India Company are to convey their goods by the Persian Gulf, Sir Dud. Diggs having failed to procure a transit through Muscovy. Handsome reception given to a travel-worn Turkish Ambassador, come to announce the accession of the Sultan, and to request an Ambassador in Pindar's place. Beecher returned from France, and the French agent sent off in disgrace. Capt. Yardley chosen Governor of Virginia, which is in a flourishing state. Capt. Brocket gone to Senega, to procure for the Guinea Company a better trade than that of the East Indies. Raleigh is removed from the keepership of Sir Thos. Wilson, and has a new relapse of danger.

Oct. 26. Dover. 47. Wm. Ward, Mayor of Dover, to Lord Zouch. Morgan Philipp, servant of [Matthew] Giles, Customer of Aberdawe, in Glamorganshire, who was murdered, has identified one of the Frenchmen confined in the castle as the murderer, and they confess it. Hopes provision may be made for the prisoners from their forfeited ship and goods, which are of great value.

Oct. ? 48. Fleming to [the Council]. The French prisoners [at Dover] accuse the searcher [Phil. Williams], and another, of allowing them for a bribe to export their prohibited goods, and inciting them to shoot at the Customer. The searcher and his brother have conveyed away the prisoners' goods, and sold them for 300*l.*

Oct. 27. Whitehall. 49. Licence to Lady Brett, of White-stanton, co. Somerset, recusant, to repair to London and other counties, to carry on her law business, for six months.

Oct. 28. 50. Warrant from Sir Geo. Selby and Sir John Calverly to John Hall, High Constable of Chesterward, to collect in his division, 2*d.* in the pound, and arrears of the last year, for payment of Capt. Hodson's fee as Muster-master.

Oct. 28. Commission to the Lord Chancellor to direct writs for beheading Sir Walter Raleigh. [*Grant Bk., p.* 237.]

Oct. 28. Whitehall. Naunton to Carleton. The warrant for Raleigh's execution is drawn out, and sent to the King for signature. It had better not be talked about, as it is "de futuro contingente." [*Holl. Corresp., Oct.* 28, 1618.]

[Oct. 29.] 51. "Accusations against Raleigh, cleared by him at his death;" viz., that he did not try to implicate Lord Carew and Lord Hay in his escape, nor tell Stukeley that he should have 10,000*l.*, but only promised to pay his debts. He never had a commission from the French King. His intent to find a gold mine in Guiana was not feigned; the mine is there, within three miles of St. Thomas. He never slandered the King, and need not have suffered death if he had not trusted him too much. *Indorsed are,*

51. I. *Verses written by Raleigh on the morning of his death, and given to the Dean of Westminster.*

1618. VOL. CIII.

51. II. *Copy of the preceding verses.* [*Dom. Corresp., March* 21, 1618.]

51. III. *Copy* [*by Fras. Nethersole*] *of the preceding accusations.*

Oct. 29. 52. Sir Walter Raleigh's last speech, and account of his behaviour at his execution in Westminster Palace Yard.

[Oct. 29.] 53. Another account of the proceedings at the execution of Sir Walter Raleigh, his speech and justification [much longer than the preceding].

Oct. 30. 54. Buckingham to [Naunton]. Beecher is to take leave of the French King before his departure, if possible, and to say that His Majesty attributes the unfriendly conduct not to him, but to ill counsellors. The French ministers having discredited the practices of their agent with Raleigh, Beecher is to circulate amongst them that part of Raleigh's last speech which mentions the subject.

Oct. 30. 55. Sir Edw. Harwood to Carleton. The town full of the worthy end of Sir Walter Raleigh. His christian and truthful manner made all believe that he was neither guilty of former treasons nor late practices, nor of unjustly injuring the King of Spain. No speech of a new Secretary, though the present one is loaded with business. Sir Hum. Tufton is fined 2,000*l.* to the King, and 500*l.* to Mr. Nevill.

Oct. 30. 56. Extracts by John Bradshaw, Deputy Chamberlain of the Exchequer, from the Black Book "De necessariis Scaccarii Observantiis," concerning Doomsday Book.

Oct. 30. 57. Copy of the above.

Oct. 31. London. 58. Chamberlain to Carleton. Execution of Sir Walter Raleigh. At the bar of King's Bench, he pleaded that he could not be condemned on the former sentence at Winchester, having since received a commission from the King, but this plea was overruled. Particulars of his behaviour before and at his execution, his last speech, &c. The Queen pleaded earnestly for his life, his recipes having done her so much good. A Spanish Dominican is said to have laboured for his life, because of the ill feeling towards Spain which his death would excite. Heavy fines on Sir Hum. Tufton for bastinadoeing Chris. Nevill.

Oct. 31. 59, 60. Two extracts from the above.

Oct. 31. London. 61. John Pory to Carleton. On Oct. 24, Raleigh was sent for by the Lords to Whitehall, and told that the King ordered his death on the old sentence; he begged to be beheaded, not hanged. On the 28th he was brought to the King's Bench, on a writ of scire facias, and pleaded in vain against the execution of a sentence so long passed by; he was then taken to the Gatehouse, and the next morning, to the place of his beheading, Palace Yard; his last speech and conduct; the Sheriff offered to let him come down and warm himself, but he refused, because his ague would soon be on him, and then it would be thought he quaked with fear; all who saw his end said it was impossible to show more decorum, courage, and

1618. VOL. CIII.

piety; his death will do more harm to the faction that procured it than ever he did in his life. The Queen is better. Rich. Martin, the new Recorder, dying. The East India Company have arranged with the King of Persia to bring their silks by the Persian Gulf, which will ruin the Turks and much enrich England.

Oct. 31. Grant to Sir Robt. Killigrew of the office of Prothonotary of Chancery, &c., for life. [*Grant Bk., p.* 266.]

Oct. ? 62. Petition of Cuthbert Bewick, Merchant of Newcastle-on-Tyne, to the Council, for their letters to the Mayor, &c. of Newcastle, to grant him an annuity, in consideration of his pains in preservation of the river Tyne.

Oct. 63. Average amount, for seven years, of the impost on currants in London and the outports, imported by English and strangers.

Nov. 1. Westminster. Warrant for a grant to John Gray, of concealed lands, to be discovered by him, value 38*l.* 4*s.* 10*d.* per ann., to complete a former grant of 100 marks per ann., the officers to whom it was directed being dead or displaced. [*Sign Man., vol.* IX., *No.* 69.]

Nov. 2. Westminster. Grant to Sir Thos. Watson, Teller of the Exchequer, in trust for Jas. Hudson, of the goods of Maurice Kiffin, of London, attainted for refusing the Oath of Allegiance. Latin. [*Ibid., No.* 70.]

Nov. 2. Westminster. Grant to Maurice Kiffin, of London, recusant, at suit of Jas. Hudson, of pardon of all offences of præmunire, of which he stands convicted. [*Ibid., No.* 71.]

Nov. 2. Grant to Robt. Norton of the Controllership of the Customs in Gloucester, during pleasure. [*Grant Bk., p.* 249.]

Nov. 2. 64. Estimate of the abridgments that may be made from the expenditure of the King's household as it was anno 14, the expenses then being 22,244*l.* 15*s.*, of which 1,392*l.* 4*s.* 3*d.* is already abated and 3,265*l.* 14*s.* 8½*d.* may be further abridged; also other sums, if the cast-off fish, bottles, and jugs, &c. are well disposed of, and ready money can be paid for spices and poultry.

Nov. ? 65. Statement that the chief cause of the large sums due to sundry officers of the Household is, that provisions are left in the hands of those officers, in lieu of their arrears, the value of which is never afterwards accounted for. Suggestions for a remedy of this abuse.

Nov. 2. Plymouth. 66. Mayor of Plymouth, Sir Ferdinando Gorges, and Thos. Hardwen, Deputy Vice Admiral, to the Council. Have assisted Captains Geer and Moore, according to order, in receiving and inventorying the Destiny, and her furniture, the goods of Sir Walter Raleigh. Have great difficulty in taking up seafaring men, they being much decayed for want of employment, and very loth to enter the service, for fear of long detention, and no pay at the last.

Nov. 2. 67. Sir Thos. Wilson to the King. Suggests that a large MS. of Sir Walter Raleigh, containing an account of all the seaports in the world, and also his sea charts, and his MS. treatise on the art

1618. VOL. CIII.

of war, which were taken from his house by Sir Geo. Calvert, or Sir Wm. Cockayne, should be sent to the State Paper Office; also that both his library, containing 300 or 400 books on history, divinity, and mathematics, and the library of Lord Cobham, taken by the Lieutenant of the Tower, and containing "1,000 good bookes of all learning and languages," be transferred to the King's own library.

Nov. 3. Newcastle. 68. Commissioners for Northumberland for survey of misbehaved persons to the Council. Have done their best in execution of their commission, but have only discovered the more notorious offenders. *Inclose,*

68. I. *Calendar of the notorious fugitives in Northumberland, with statement of their offences. Oct. 20.*

Nov. 3. Westminster. Warrant for a grant to Wm. Carmichael of the benefit of the denization of twenty-five foreigners, not merchants,. [*Sign Man., vol.* IX., *No.* 72.]

Nov. 3. London. 69. Matt. de Quester to Carleton. Forwards a packet by Michael Clarke, whom he has been obliged to supply with money.

Nov. 4. Clewer, near Windsor. 70. Abel Barnard to the Same. Is full of vexation and grief, brought on by his own foolish kindness; hopes to hear from him.

Nov. 4. Grant to Edm. Nicholson and Thos. Morgan of all [pretermitted ?] customs on woollen cloths and new draperies, for thirty-one years. [*Grant Bk., p.* 269.]

Nov. 4. Commission to Sir Hen. Montague and others, to assize prices for horse meal. [*Ibid., p.* 235.]

Nov. 4. Commission to the Archbp. of Canterbury, &c., to allow lands to be passed to Robt. Typper, for his services in discovering and compounding for land concealed or defective in title. [*Ibid., p.* 234.]

Nov. 4. Whitehall. 71. Warrant to Sir Thos. Wilson to seize all the books, globes, and mathematical instruments belonging to the late Sir Walter Raleigh, "which could be of small use to his surviving wife;" the books to be left where they are, but all the globes and instruments delivered to the King.

Nov. 4. 72. Commissioners of the Navy to the Council. Request that the 900*l.* per month formerly paid for cordage, and also the arrears of Sir Robt. Mansell's last account, may be applied to pay discharged workmen, to further the two new ships now in the dock at Deptford, to lay in provisions for the next year, and to begin preparations for the new docks at Chatham, &c.

Nov. 6. Westminster. Grant to Ralph Forster, of Fleetham, Northumberland, of pardon for murder. Latin. [*Sign Man., vol.* IX., *No.* 73.]

Nov. 7. Licence to Edw. Duncombe, Rich. Bowle, Hen. Lucas, and Simon Chamber, to recover all moneys, &c. unjustly detained and concealed, for seven years. [*Grant Bk., p.* 245.]

VOL. CIII.

1618.

Nov. 7. London. 73. Chamberlain to Carleton. Sends a letter written by Raleigh to the King, before he came to Salisbury, the verses he made the night before his death, and his last remembrance for his wife; particulars of his deportment the night before his execution; he was buried at St. Margaret's, Westminster. Martin, the Recorder, dead; great suit made for his place; the City plead their charter to choose his successor; the King promised them free election, but suggested [Robt.] Heath, who is likely to carry it. The Venetian and Turkish Ambassadors have had audiences. The Bp. of Winchester preached on Nov. 5. Lady Finch likely to be made a Countess; she is reconciled to her son Theophilus.

Nov. 7. London. 74. John Pory to the Same. Great suit for the Recorder's place, vacant by the death of Rich. Martin; Shute, of Gray's Inn, had the King's recommendation, and that of others, but could not succeed, having been outlawed seventeen times; Mr. Heath, the Marquis of Buckingham's lawyer, is likely to obtain it. Additional particulars of Raleigh's conduct before his death. When his barber wished to dress his hair, he asked if he had a plaster to set on a man's head when it is off. The morning of his death, his cousin, Charles Thynne, reproved him for merry discourses; he said it was the last merriment he should have, but he would look on the sad part like a man. Sir Lewis Stukeley protested to the King the truth of his accusations against Raleigh. The King is reported to have replied, "I have done amiss; his blood be upon thy head." Sir T. Wilson has seized his mathematical and sea instruments for the Lord Admiral, and catalogued his library, by the King's command. A great Lord in the Tower, who knew Raleigh well, said, if the Spanish match goes on, the Spaniards had better have given 100,000*l.* than have him killed; if not, the English had better have paid 100,000*l.* than kill him. The Venetian Ambassador Donato and the Turkish Envoy have had audience. Speech of the latter, whose son the King has touched for a swelling of the throat, &c.

Nov. 7. Eton. 75. Sir Hen. Savile to the Same. Money matters. Advises him to write to the Archbp. of Spalato, or he may lose a good bargain, the Chancellor soliciting much for Sir John Kidderminster, &c.

Nov. 7. Whitehall. Proclamation for better execution of the Statutes against the false making of broad cloths, appointing searchers to examine them, and threatening offenders with prosecution in the Star Chamber. Printed. [*Proc. Coll., No.* 60.]

Nov. 7. Westminster. Grant to Sir Hen. Reve, Gentleman Pensioner, of the arrears of certain rents long detained from the Crown, but by him brought into charge in the Exchequer. [*Sign Man., vol.* IX., *No.* 74.]

Nov. 7. Westminster. Grant to Rich. Percival, Clerk and Registrar of the Commission concerning Wards in Ireland, now employed by the Council, of licence to remain in England, and to act by deputy. Latin. [*Ibid., No.* 75.]

Nov. 8. Westminster. Licence to Capt. Gilbert Lee to transport 200,000 sheepskins and lambskins, for thirty-one years, in reversion after a former grant to

1618. Vol. CIII.

him, and on payment of the usual customs, and 20*l.* to the King, for every 100 exported. [*Sign Man., vol.* IX., *No.* 76.]

Nov. 8. Westminster. Re-grant to Sir Geo. Douglas, and George his son, of a moiety of the forfeitures to be by them levied for pressing cloth with the hot-press, the other moiety being reserved to the King; the former grant being defective. [*Ibid., No.* 77.]

Nov. 8. Westminster. Warrant to pay to Dr. Young, Dean of Winchester, 160*l.* 11*s.* 7*d.*, for expenses of his journey to Scotland last summer; a former warrant in July, for payment from the tithes of Winchester, being void, because they were granted to the Queen. [*Ibid., No.* 78.]

Nov. 8. Westminster. Warrant to pay to Munton Jennings, Keeper of the Garden at Theobalds, 50*l.*, for making a place for the silkworms, and for providing mulberry leaves. [*Ibid., No.* 79.]

Nov. 8. Westminster. Grant to Rich. Powell and his family, of remission of imprisonment, and of fines, amounting to 215*l.*, imposed on them in the Star Chamber, for a riot six years before, they being too poor to pay them. [*Ibid., No.* 80.]

Nov. 8? 76. Elizabeth Lady Raleigh to Lady Carew. Begs her influence with Sir Thos. Wilson to cease the pursuit of her husband's library, instruments, &c., which were all he had to leave to his poor child, in hope that he would apply to learning, to be fit for them; they are not rare books, but such as may be bought. The instruments are already seized, one of which cost 100*l.*, and not restored, though promised to be so.

Nov. 8. Camberwell. 77. Hen. Harper to Rich. Hanby. Asks what is due to Phineas Pett on his Privy Seal of 40*l.* per ann., and on his Patent.

Nov. 8. 78. Rich. Hanby to Mr. Owen. Asks the time from which Phineas Pett's Privy Seal for 40*l.* per ann., dated July 11, 1614, commences. *Annexed is,*

78. I *Reply that it begins from its date; with date of the payments already made upon it.*

Nov. 9. Dover. 79. Wm. Ward to Lord Zouch. Hen. Hanington, Minister of Hougham, near Dover, spoke abusively of Mr. Reading, Minister of St. Mary's, Dover, and Lord Zouch's Chaplain, and disrespectfully of his Lordship. Requests an order for removal of the two Frenchmen, their keep being chargeable.

Nov. 9. 80. John Carleton to his uncle, Sir Dud. Carleton. Buckingham often speaks well of Carleton, Marquis Hamilton lauds him much, and the King often talks of him and the affairs of Holland. Three of his best friends advise that 3,000*l.* should be offered for a post for him, especially as Sec. Naunton is likely to be Master of the Wards. Sec. Lake's cause is dying and reviving as before, and postponed till next term.

Vol. CIII.

1618.

Nov. 9. Westminster. Warrant to pay 140*l.* to Godfrey Bodt, employed on the King's special affairs beyond seas. [*Sign Man., vol.* IX., *No.* 81.]

Nov. 9. Westminster. Warrant to the Commissioners of the Treasury to limit the several allowances to the nobility for French and Rhenish wines to be imported for their private use, without impost, the total not to exceed 1,200 tuns per ann. [*Ibid., No.* 82.]

Nov. 9. Westminster. Licence to the Condé de Gondomar, in behalf of the King of Spain, to export 100 pieces of iron and two pieces of brass ordnance, free of duty. [*Ibid., No.* 83.]

Nov. ? 81. Order by the Commissioners for the office of Earl Marshal, that no persons presume to provide heraldic achievements for funerals, without authority from the Officers of Arms.

Nov. 10. Whitehall. 82—84. Proclamation by the Same, ordering that on every death of a nobleman, or gentleman, a certificate of his marriage, children, and date of death be given in to the officers of arms, and duly registered, on payment of fees set down; to extend to all except those whose estates are worth less than 1,000 marks; also prohibiting all heraldic devices not approved by the King-at-Arms. Printed. Three copies.

Nov. 10. Whitehall. Proclamation that "all vagabonds and masterless folk, boys and girls, and other idle persons," depart the Court within twenty-four hours, and that none be allowed to frequent it, either as workpeople or servants of those who have lodgings in Court, except such as are registered by the Knight Marshal. Printed. [*Proc. Coll., No.* 61.]

Nov. 10. Westminster. Warrant for a grant of patents of denization to thirty foreigners, to be named by John Bownhall; to take effect after a similar grant to John Hall. [*Sign Man., vol.* IX., *No.* 84.]

Nov. 10. Westminster. Warrant for John Moreton to transport 200 pieces of cast-iron ordnance to Scotland, for defence against damages by pirates. [*Ibid., No.* 85.]

Nov. [10]. 85. Draft of the above.

Nov. 10. Westminster. Grant to Susanna Robertson, widow and stranger, of 28*l.* 12*s.*, being the King's moiety of gold coin forfeited by her for attempting to export it, granted because she wished to send it away to pay her debts in Flanders. [*Sign Man., vol.* IX., *No.* 86.]

Nov. 11. Grant to Kenrick Edgebury of the office of Assistant to the Admiralty, for life. [*Grant Bk., p.* 265.]

Nov. 11. Licence to Zouch Allen to substitute a deputy for collecting customs in the port of Southampton. [*Ibid., p.* 241.]

Nov. 11. Commission to the Lord Chief Justice, &c. to compound for debts between prisoners in the King's Bench and Fleet, and their creditors. [*Ibid., p.* 234.]

VOL. CIII.

1618.

Nov. 11. Grant to Ralph Smith and John Sharpe of the office of Gamekeeper, &c. in the Palace of Westminster, and elsewhere, for life. [*Grant Bk., p.* 252.]

Nov. 12. London. 86. Sir Edw. Harwood to Carleton. Lord Exeter's cause cannot be heard this term, being so long that it would leave time for nothing else. Lake must go out, though he has offered carte blanche to make his peace. Suffolk talks of publishing the reasons of his being put out of the Treasurership. Lady Bedford has obtained her suit for concealed debts.

Nov. 13. Netherham. 87. Sir Edw. Hext to the Council. Sends up Owen Evans; would gladly have sent him at first, had he known it was proper, but, though imprisoned, he was treated with all the consideration due to a servant of the King. [*See Oct.* 19.] *Incloses,*

87. I. *Examination of Fras. Prewe, of Ottery, Constable of Whitleigh, co. Somerset. Owen Evans ordered him to impress some maidens for the Bermudas and Virginia. Asked for his commission, on which he showed his pursuivant's badge, and threatened him for non-compliance. Oct.* 16.

87 II. *Examination of Thos. Crocker, of Beer. Owen Evans threatened to hang him unless he would press some maidens for him. Oct.* 16.

87. III. *Examination of Wm. Michael, of Ottery. Finding that the maidens fled away through fear, offered Evans* 10*s. to free the parish of Ottery from press, which he accepted. Oct.* 16.

87. IV. *Examination of John Watts, of Weston. Evans gave him* 4*s., and required him in the King's name to press four maidens, and gave* 1*s. to Jacob Cryfe to press him his daughter. Oct.* 16.

Nov. 13. Fleet Street. 88. The Council of the Prince of Wales to the Tenants of Raby and Brancepeth. Thos. Emerson being appointed steward of those lordships, no courts are to be kept by any other.

Nov. 13. Westminster. Commission to the Lord Chancellor and others to take the accounts of Sir Hen. Carey, for the time that he and his late father, Sir Edward, had the office of Master of the Jewels, and to deliver the charge of the jewels and plate to Sir Hen. Mildmay, now Master. [*Sign Man., vol.* IX., *No.* 87.]

Nov. 13. Grant to John Philpott of the office of Pursuivant, for life. [*Grant Bk., p.* 250.]

Nov. 13. London. 89. Rich. Harrison to Carleton. Information about his garden, with which Mr. Bell finds great fault. Private affairs.

Nov. 13. London. 90. Geo. Carleton to Sir Dud. Carleton. Hopes his son Dudley gives him satisfaction. Money affairs. The King has gone to Royston, without removing Visct. Wallingford from the Court of Wards, as was expected. Begs him to thank the Provost of King's College, Cambridge, for giving Dudley leave of absence.

VOL. CIII.

1618.

Nov. 14. 91. Thos. Locke to Carleton. Has laid his petition before the Lords Commissioners. The Turkish Ambassador has taken leave. Sir Thomas and Lady Lake and Lady Roos had a conference with Buckingham.

Nov. 14. London. 92. Robt. Bell to the Same. Fears the East Indian fleets will have sailed, and that revenges will be taken before the Holland Commissioners come over to compose the wrongs. Mismanagement of Carleton's garden at Ditton.

Nov. 14. London. 93. Chamberlain to the Same. Mr. Heath is made Recorder, at the King's recommendation. Sir Lionel Cranfield, who paid 1,500*l.* for Mr. Martin's appointment, seeks satisfaction. Visct. Wallingford called to account for mal-administration in the Court of Wards, and his deposition probable. Robinson, a clerk, hung for exacting money by counterfeit Letters Patent. The pleadings on the Earl of Exeter's side in his cause fill 9,000 sheets of paper. The Archbp. of Spalato preached at the Italian Church, on a fast held for the prosperity of the reformed churches; he has sunk in estimation, by intruding into a parsonage in the gift of the Dean and Chapter of Windsor. Match proposed between Marquis Hamilton's son and Lady Chichester's daughter.

Nov. 14. London. 94. John Pory to the Same. The great cause between Lord Ormond and Lord Dingwall, who married the late Earl's daughter and heir, was decided by the King as umpire; Ormond remonstrated against the justice of the division of land, but was silenced, it being the King's doing, and under the Broad Seal. The Hollanders accused of exporting English coin, meddling with the Greenland fisheries, and undermining trades. The Turkish Chiaus has taken leave, and thanked the King for curing his son of the evil. The Queen is to receive 8,000*l.* per ann., and the King 3,000*l.*, out of the rent of the Earl of Somerset's forfeited allowance on cloths. Rich. Martin, the Recorder, had insured 1,700*l.*, the sum paid for his place, in the House of Insurance on the Exchange, and has it returned to his executors.

Nov. 15. 95. Certificate presented to the Council by the Commissioners for the preservation of the river Tyne, of their proceedings from March to Michaelmas 1618, for maintaining the navigation of the river, by preventing ballast being thrown into it, &c.

Nov. 15. Edinburgh. 96. The King to the Sheriffs, &c. of Scotland. Orders a proclamation revoking the licence granted to the Earl of Argyle to go to the Spa, because whilst abroad, he has renounced the Protestant religion, and associated with the King's rebels, and commanding his immediate return.

Nov. ? 97. Memorandum for a pass for Capt. James Colvile to go over to the Earl of Argyle, and to procure a safe conduct from the Prince of Orange for an English ship to fetch the Earl from Dunkirk.

VOL. CIII.

1618.

Nov. 15. Westminster. Grant to Sir John Stanhope, on surrender by Lord Knyvet, of the stewardship of the manors of Northfrothing, Cottingham, &c., co. York. Latin. [*Sign Man., vol.* IX., *No.* 88.]

Nov. 15. Westminster. Grant, with survivorship, to Bevis Thelwall, Euble Thelwall, and John Lloyd, on surrender of Sir Rich. Coningsby and Ralph Scrope, of the Keepership of the Park of East Hampstead, and of lands called Cunworth and Queen's Meadow, co. Berks. Latin. [*Ibid., No.* 89.]

Nov. 15. Westminster. Grant to Rich. Batten of the benefit of fines of 155*l.* imposed on Geo. Barlow, late High Sheriff of Pembroke, for neglect of service. [*Ibid., No.* 90.]

Nov. 16. Commission to the Lord Chancellor, &c., to reduce Lincoln's Inn Fields into walks. [*Grant Bk., p.* 235.]

Nov. 16. Grant of divers privileges to the Company of Adventurers of London, trading into Africa. [*Ibid., p.* 268.]

Nov. 17. 98. Thos. Locke to Carleton. Particulars of laying out the grounds at Imworth, &c.

Nov. 18. London. 99. Sir Edw. Harwood to the Same. Report says that Visct. Wallingford, being called in question, will sell his place [as Master of the Wards] to Mr. Comptroller; others say that he will not fare so well as that. The Earl of Suffolk to be called in question next term. Diego, Lord Roos' man, is returning to prove himself honest, but Lady Roos would rather he remained where he was. The Lord Chamberlain, Lord Zouch, and the Chancellor of the Exchequer spoken of for the Treasurership. English Catholics report that Barnevelt is putting himself under the protection of the King of France.

Nov. 18. Grant to Esme Lord Aubigny of the goods and chattels of Gervase Lord Clifton, felon. [*Grant Bk., p.* 241.]

Nov. 18. Westminster. Grant to Rich. Crane and Chris. Langdon of the benefit of recognizances, amounting to 400*l.*, forfeited by John Slaughter, of Slaughter, Humfrey Coles, of Swell, and Ant. Hodges, of Broadwell, co. Gloucester, for non-appearance at the assizes. With proviso of abiding by the order of Exchequer, in case of complaint against them. [*Sign Man., vol.* IX., *No.* 91.]

Nov. 18. Westminster. Warrant to the Receiver of Wiltshire for payment of fees, &c. to Rich. Grime, yeoman, of Cowsfield and West Park, Malmsbury, co. Wilts; also of necessary sums for husbandry and repairs in the said park, and of 26*s.* 8*d.* for every colt brought up by him for the King. [*Ibid., No.* 92.]

Nov. 18. Westminster. Grant to Rich. Beeke and Collubery Mayne of release of the mean profits of the manor of Haddenham, co. Bucks, taken out for their protection, because their lease is supposed to be defective. Latin. [*Ibid., No.* 93.]

VOL. CIII.

1618.

Nov. 19. Grant to Lady Elizabeth Berkeley, widow, of Cranford, Middlesex, and her heirs, at suit of the co-heirs of Sir Roger Aston, deceased, of the manor of Cranford St. John and other lands and tenements in Cranford and Harlington, co. Middlesex, late of the monastery of Thame, co. Oxon, which she purchased from them, but the former grant thereof to Sir Roger Aston was found defective. Latin. [*Sign Man., vol.* IX., *No.* 94.]

Nov. 20. 100. Note by Sir Lionel Cranfield that the King promises not to license more than four retailers of wines in the town of Greenwich.

Nov. 21. Whitehall. 101. Lords of the Treasury to Robt. Bassey of the Middle Temple. Order him to pay his debts due to the King.

Nov. 21. London. 102. Chamberlain to Carleton. The town is full of Sir Walter Raleigh; some ballads are suppressed; a declaration is preparing, contradicting many of his last assertions, but it will not be believed, unless well proved; some verses on him are ascribed to the King and Sec. Naunton. Beecher has returned, and it will now be difficult to renew intelligence with France. The comet much talked of. Lady Winwood cannot find her late husband's papers on his Holland negotiations.

Nov. 21. London. 103. Matthew Carleton to Sir D. Carleton. Has lost his father [Edw. Carleton], but sends over his brother Bostock as requested. Particulars of Carleton's Imworth property.

Nov. 21. 104. Commissioners of the Navy to the Council. Sir Robt. Mansell, instead of delivering up his ledger book and his vouchers, as he promised, has merely sent in an abstract, uncertified, of his payments, 1613–1618, and no account of his receipts.

Nov. 21. Westminster. Grant to John Levingston, Groom of the Bedchamber, for life, and for twenty-one years after his decease, of the herbage and custody of Higham Ferrers Park, co. Northampton, on determination of a previous grant to Wm. Purvey, Auditor of the Duchy of Lancaster, deceased. Latin. [*Sign. Man., vol.* IX., *No.* 95.]

Nov. 22. Westminster. Grant to Chas. Tyrrel, in trust for his sister, Mary Good, daughter of Sir Edw. Tyrrel, and her children, of the profits of the house and manor of Hardwick and other lands, her jointure, and of goods possessed before her marriage, which are forfeited by the outlawry of her husband, Thos. Good, of Hardwick, co. Gloucester. [*Ibid., No.* 96.]

Nov. 25. Westminster. Grant to Geo. Utley, of Cheshire, of pardon for horsestealing, it being his first offence. Latin. [*Ibid., No.* 97.]

Nov. 25. Westminster. Presentation of Hum. Rone to the rectory of Walsoken, co. Norfolk, void by death of Fras. Snell. Indorsed, "A presentation for trial of the King's right." Latin. [*Ibid., No.* 98.]

Nov. 25. Creation of Sir John Digby to the rank of Baron Digby of Sherborne. [*Grant Bk., p.* 244.]

VOL. CIII.

1618.

Nov. 26. Westminster. Grant, with survivorship, to Sir Nich. Salter and Nich. Salter, his kinsman, both of London, on surrender of Sir Nich. Salter, of the Collectorship of the Customs at the Ports of Chichester, Southampton, Pool, Exeter, Dartmouth, Plymouth and Fowey, Bristol, Bridegwater, Chester, Cardiff, and Milford. [*Sign Man.*, *vol.* IX., *No.* 99.]

Nov. 26. Westminster. Grant to David Ramsay of the office of Chief Clockmaker to the King, with fees and allowances for workmanship. [*Ibid.*, *No.* 100.]

Nov. 26. 105. Survey of Byfleet Park, Surrey; with note of the profit derived by Sir Edw. Howard, Keeper of the said Park, from pasturing cattle there, about which the King is to determine for the future.

Nov.? 106, 107. Note of reduction made by the King in the above allowance to Sir Edw. Howard. Two copies.

Nov. 26. London. 108. Geo. Haughfen to Carleton. Thanks for favours to his graceless kinsman, who has made no good use of them. Sir John Digby is to be made a Baron, and perhaps an Earl. Lady Ruthven reports that the Queen is better.

Nov. 26. London. 109. Archbp. of Spalato to the Same. Has been importuned by the Chancellor and others to give the place to Sir John Kidderminster, but has quieted them with stating his promise of it to Carleton, and unless the King renew the assault, will be able to keep it, in spite of the clamours of his canons, who are partisans of Kidderminster. Preached in the Italian Church, and prayed for the success of the Synod, for which prayers were also offered in the French and Dutch churches. Italian.

Nov. 28. London. 110. Chamberlain to the Same. The States' Commissioners have arrived; people begin to flout them, saying, *Brawn* is likely to be cheap, as so many *Boors* are come to town. The Court at Newmarket very merry; a feast was held at a farmhouse near, to which the King and each present brought a dish. Sir Hen. Carey is to be made Master of the Court of Wards; and Sir Edw. Villiers, Comptroller. Visct. Doncaster has a son. The Lord Chamberlain and others forwarded the marriage of Sir Thos. Smythe's son, of eighteen, to Lady Isabella Rich, without knowledge of his father, who, at their entreaty, has consented to receive her. Capt. Yardley, a mean fellow, knighted, and going as Governor to Virginia. Sends Stukeley's apology, and an authentic relation, by the Lord Chancellor, the Attorney, or Naunton, of Raleigh's affair.

Nov. 28. London. 111. John Pory to the Same. Lady Rich wishes Carleton had applied [about the Secretaryship] to Lady Bedford, who is powerful with both the Marquisses and the Lord Chamberlain, rather than to Lady Elizabeth Hatton, who has fallen out with Buckingham. Is offered the Secretaryship for Virginia, by means of Sir Geo. Yardley, the newly-elected Governor, but will not accept it without outfit as well as allowance.

VOL. CIII.

1618.
Nov. 29. Westminster. Grant to Visct. Haddington, during the lives of Elizabeth, his wife, and Bridget, their daughter, of a pension of 500*l.* per ann. Latin. [*Sign Man., vol.* IX., *No.* 101.]

Nov. 29. Westminster. Grant to Sir Mat. Boynton, of Barmston, co. York, of discharge for 1,100*l.* by him paid for the Baronetcy conferred on him. [*Ibid., No.* 102.]

Nov. 30. Westminster. Grant to Ralph Smith, Yeoman of the Bedchamber, of the office of Gaoler, co. Berks, vice Edw. Staunton, deceased. [*Ibid., No.* 103.]

Nov. 30. Whitehall. 112. Sir Benj. Rudyard to Carleton. No Treasurer will be chosen till the King has declared the reason of his depriving Suffolk of the staff. Sec. Lake's business is to come on next term, and then will be Carleton's time.

Nov.? 113. Warrant [from Lord Zouch] to [Thos.] Fulnetby, to deliver the goods saved from the Dutch bark, the Blind Fortune, lately wrecked on the Godwin Sands, to Josias Ente and Wm. Horne, on payment of customary dues.

VOL. CIV. DECEMBER, 1618.

Dec. 1. 1. Earl of Pembroke and Lord Carew to [the Council]. Have examined John Paulet's complaint against Lady Lambert, and find that the Council of Ireland ordered Sir Oliver Lambert to pay to John and Sarah Paulet 30*l.* per ann. whilst he held the wardship of Geo. Malby, as interest on 300*l.* due by the late Hen. Malby to John Paulet; think means should be taken for discharge of that and any other debt similarly due to Paulet.

Dec. 1. Newmarket. 2. Buckingham to Naunton. The King desires renewal of Lord Dingwall's protection, as he wishes to go over to Ireland, to settle the lands awarded him by His Majesty.

Dec. 2. 3. Sir Hen. Yelverton and Sir Thos. Coventry to [the Council]. The refusal of the people of Tewksbury to be mustered before the Deputy Lieutenants of the county is warranted by their charter, which authorizes the bailiffs of their town to muster them.

Dec. 2. Drury Lane. 4. Sir Wm. Smithe to Carleton. Begs he will employ his son. Information in the Star Chamber against 160 Dutchmen, for exporting 7 millions of gold, and a Ne exeat regnum granted, lest they should escape. The suit was begun by Sir Thos. Vavasour, and followed by Sir Hen. Britain, who is to have the advantage of the fines of ten of them; the rest go to the King, who is at Newmarket. The cause between Lady Exeter and Sir Thos. Lake fills 17,000 sheets of paper. The late Spanish Ambassador most honourably received in Spain.

VOL. CIV.

1618.

Dec. 3. Westminster. 5. Abraham Williams to Carleton. Sends the declaration of Raleigh's proceedings. The King going to Theobalds to give audience to the States' Commissioners. The physicians advise the Queen not to remove from Hampton Court. Safe delivery of the Electress Palatine.

Dec. 3. London. 6. Chamberlain to the Same. The Bp. of Winchester is much interested about the Synod, and has a marvellous memory. The Lord Chancellor sick. The severe frost checks the small-pox, which was in every third house. Most of the eighteen priests and Jesuits whom the Spanish Ambassador carried over are returned, and four are taken; the King says they shall truss for it.

Dec. 4. London. 7. The Same to the Same. Begs his help in [Abel] Barnard's business, who will be ruined if Carleton cannot seize certain goods on his behalf. Sir Lewis Stukeley's pamphlet was penned by Dr. Sharpe; he is commonly called Sir Judas Stukeley.

Dec. 4. London. 8. Sir Horace Vere to the Same. Nothing done in Lady Exeter's business, and Sir Thos. Lake comes not to Court. Sir John Digby returning to Spain. The Queen better, and will spend Christmas at Denmark House.

Dec. ? 9. Statement addressed to the Council, relative to the claim of Lord Zouch to Odiham Park, with the deer therein, which Sir Edw. More has held by lease from the Crown for sixty years. Lord Zouch has caused More's underkeeper to be imprisoned, for killing a buck in that park.

Dec. 4. 10. Examination of Wm. Jacob, servant to Edw. Seager, Keeper of Odiham Park. The deer killed there are usually killed by warrant from Lord Zouch, sent to Sir Edw. More, and by him to Seager; has killed one buck this season for his own friends, as he usually does yearly.

Dec. 5. 11. Memorandum by Clement Cotterell of money disbursed by his Lordship's [Buckingham's ?] appointment since Oct. 3.

Dec. 7. 12. Fras. Willisford, Thos. Philpot, and Thos. Andrew, Commissioners for Lord Zouch, to [Wm.] Hanington. Require him forthwith to restore such things as he has taken away from the Maison Dieu, and to repair all dilapidations.

Dec. 7. 13. Receipts of the Marshal, Gunners, and other officers of Dover Castle, for one year's pay.

Dec. 7. London. 14. Sir Art. Tyringham to Carleton. Thinks Carleton's promotion cannot be delayed longer than the ending of Lake's business, as he has powerful friends. Expected changes of office. The Treasurership rather offered than sued for. The Queen better, and returning to London.

Dec. 9. 15. Sir Thos. Wynn to the Same. Pains taken to prejudice the King against the Hollanders, by reporting that they have drawn his picture with his pockets hanging out, empty of money. Great care

VOL. CIV.

1618.

to get money for the King; a commission granted to survey and claim for him all lands gained from the sea in Kent, which, if extended through the kingdom, will yield 20,000*l.* or 30,000*l.* All Star Chamber fines in the late Queen's time called in, in spite of the general pardon. Lord Houghton fined 500*l.* for going to Tyburn. Diego, Lord Roos' man, was returning on summons, when he was ordered back to Spain on pain of death. Death of Lady Haddington, of small-pox. Lord Cromwell said to be drowned in returning from Ireland. Mr. Wymark seized, for wishing Raleigh's head was on Sec. Naunton's shoulders.

Dec. ? 16. Observations by Mr. Hasdonck on the value of the marsh lands in England left by the sea, which are the lawful property of the Crown. Some doubts having been lately expressed in the Exchequer as to the right thereto, he suggests the reference of the matter to some Lord of the Council, who shall receive a third of the fines for his pains.

Dec. 9. 17. Rhyming letter from Dr. Corbett to Mr. Alesbury, at Syon, ridiculing the general excitement caused by the appearance of the Court.

Dec. 10. 18. Sir Thos. Coventry to [the Council]. Sir Michael Green says he cannot pay his lady's arrears or settle her property, till he can treat with his creditors, who are out of London.

Dec. 10. Westminster. 19. Commission to the Bp. of London and others, Judges, Aldermen of London, Physicians, &c., to examine into a complaint by Dr. Hilkiah Crooke against Thos. Jenner, Governor of Bethlehem Hospital for Lunatics, as being not qualified for his office, and unskilful in medical art; also to inquire into the state of the hospital lands, and its internal government and arrangements; Dr. Crooke to have some allowance from the hospital revenues during the investigation. Latin.

Dec. 10. 20. Order from John Lord Stanhope, Master of the Posts, to the Justices of the Peace and others, to aid John King, Postmaster of Southwark, in delivery of letters within six miles round; the Constables of Kent and Surrey to keep twenty horses always ready at their own charges, the ordinary provision for posts not sufficing for present wants.

[Dec. 10.] 21. Petition of Sir Robt. Mansell to the Council, for a grant of letters of assistance, for pulling down all glass furnaces set up, and for apprehending all persons infringing his patent for the sole making of glass. He will otherwise be unable to pay the 1,000*l.* rent to the King, and 1,800*l.* to the other patentees who have resigned.

Dec. 11. Commission to the Archbp. of Canterbury to redeem and confirm mortgaged lands. [*Grant Bk., p.* 233.]

Dec. 11. Commission to Wm. Lord Knollys [Visct. Wallingford], Master of the Wards and Liveries, with directions concerning disposing of wards. [*Ibid., p.* 258.]

VOL. CIV.

1618.

Dec. 11. Licence to Clement Daubigny to make a new kind of engine to be driven by water, for cutting iron into small bars, for twenty-one years. [*Grant Bk.*, *p.* 244.]

Dec. 11. Philip Lane. [Lord Zouch] to all Mayors, Searchers, &c. To assist Wm. Hamond to search for and seize any goods attempted to be exported, contrary to the charter of the Merchant Adventurers. [*Note Bk.*, *p.* 28.]

Dec. 11? The Same to the Commissioners for restraint of passage. Orders them to detain and prevent from sailing S. H., a young gentleman wishing to travel without his parents' consent. [*Ibid.*, *p.* 29.]

Dec. 11. 22. Note book [by Edw. Nicholas], containing extracts from Scripture, notes and extracts of sermons, &c.; also numerous memoranda and drafts of letters connected with his offices as secretary to Sir John Dackombe, and afterwards to Lord Zouch, from July 24, 1616, which are calendared under their respective dates.

Dec. 11. Hurst. 23. Rich. Harrison to Carleton. The death of Carleton's cousin, Edw. Carleton, has obliged him to look after his property at Imworth; particulars of it. Private business.

Dec. 12. Beaumaris. 24. Sir Rich. Bulkeley to the Council. Denies that the person claiming to be his son is such. Was intending to repudiate his mother, but she died. Has alienated all his land from this person, but at their Lordships' earnest request, consents to allow him 40*l.* a year.

Dec. 12. London. 25. Chamberlain to Carleton. The States' Commissioners gone to an audience at Newmarket in seven coaches, and are lodged at Cambridge. All who have built new houses contrary to proclamation must be censured for contempt, and have them pulled down, unless they ransom them. Don Diego, Lord Roos' servant, was sent over, but Gondomar induced him to go to Spain first. Lord Digby has made a great supper at Whitehall. Death of Sir Thos. Garton of Sussex, Sir Hen. Butler, and Sir Thos. Cornwallis. Sir Thos. Smythe has agreed to allow his new daughter-in-law 800*l.* a year jointure, and 800*l.* a year to his son and her for maintenance.

Dec. 13. 26. David Calderwood to John Douglas, Minister of Col. Ogle's Regiment. The assembly at Perth was held at twenty days' notice, too short for several dioceses to send representatives. The pretended primate insisted on acting as moderator, and he chose from his own party the members of the privy conference, in which those who defended the established order were severely reproved. The King's letter was read, and they were assured that His Majesty would be more glad of their assent to the five articles than of all the gold of India, and would deprive them if they refused it. The votes for kneeling were taken in the privy conference, not before the whole church. Unfair proceedings in not permitting the ministers to argue the points of the five articles. When it was put to the vote, they were asked whether they would consent to the articles or disobey

1618. VOL. CIV.

the King, and those called to vote first who were known to be favourable. By unfair means in collecting the votes, the five points, viz., kneeling at the sacrament, private communion, private baptism, episcopal confirmation, and keeping of five holidays, were passed. Fears lest it may be supposed that they were passed fairly, and that the Kirk will be brought to consent to English discipline.

Dec. 13. 27. Thos. Hilton to [Sir Thos. Lake]. Withdraws his offer to suppress the scandalous book [De Corona Regia], unless he may be permitted release on good security to go and visit his father.

Dec. 14. 28. Sir Edw. Herbert to Carleton. Astrologers must determine how far the blazing star concurs with Lady Haddington's death. There will be a masque this Christmas.

Dec. 16. 29. Questions [proposed to Merchants by the Council] as to the best mode of obtaining a more plentiful import of silver, with their replies; also, appointment of a committee of officers of the Mint and merchants, to consider on the advisability of an office of exchange.

[Dec. 16.] 30. Another report of the above queries and replies, differing from the preceding, with a list of considerations [apparently to be submitted to the above-named committee] on the relative value of gold and silver.

Dec. 16? 31. Note of the charges in France for mintage of gold and silver, and of the relative fineness and value of English and foreign coins.

Dec. 17. Strand. 32. Earl of Exeter to the Council. Sir Geo. Shirley, of Northamptonshire, had all his armour and weapons taken away, during his absence at the Spa for recovery of his health, under plea that his servants were recusants, and is therefore unable to do service at the musters. As he has always been loyal and forward in service, and declares himself no recusant, hopes his case may be considered.

Dec. 18. Madrid. 33. Sir Fras. Cottington to [Buckingham]. Has told the King of Spain of the justice done on Sir Walter Raleigh. He was much pleased, and it was resolved at the Council table that he should write and thank the King for it. Extract.

Dec. 19. London. 34. Chamberlain to Carleton. Lord Doncaster has buried his young son. Night funerals are in fashion. Lady Haddington will be buried at Newhall; many noble ladies, with 100 coaches and torches, conveyed her out of town. The Countess of Salisbury had a feast and play, though her house are in trouble about a libel that condemns all their faction. The author is not found out; but Lady Wallingford was the first heard to sing it. A counter libel talked of. Wake has returned; and on his way through Paris, was much courted by the ministers there, who lay the blame of the rupture on their own agent.

Dec. 19. 35. Alice Carleton to the Same. Sends the petition of a poor couple who have suffered many crosses by sickness, death of children, &c.

VOL. CIV.

1618.

Dec. 20. London. 36. Sir Edw. Harwood to Carleton. The King dissatisfied with his interview with the States' Commissioners. He is come to town. Lady Exeter's cause will soon be heard, and then Lake's fate will be decided. She is favoured by the King. Lord Suffolk's friends give out that he will make his peace. Lord Wallingford says he will stand to the law and his patent. The King offended with two libels against the present faction; he will not let his son marry a daughter of Spain without the Pope's dispensation, for fear of future contests.

Dec. 22. Grant to John Man of the office of one of the six Chief Masters of the Navy, for life. [*Grant Bk.*, *p.* 268.]

Dec. 23. Grant to Wm. Lanke of the Clerkship of the Privy Seal, for life. [*Ibid.*, *p.* 266.]

Dec. 24? 37. Relation of an affront committed by the Deputy Sheriff and Bailiffs of Middlesex, and 200 or 300 apprentices, by rushing into the Prince's house at St. James's in search of Thos. Geare, a debtor, who fled there for refuge. They demanded him from Sir John Vaughan, the Comptroller, and, not obtaining their wish, attacked the Comptroller when he was going out in his coach, and threatened violence, and have since abused two of the Prince's servants.

Dec. 24. Gray's Inn. 38. Sir Hen. Yelverton and Sir Thos. Coventry to the Council. Have only had time to examine And. Brown respecting the riot at St. James's. *Inclose*,

38. I. *Examination of And. Brown, Under Sheriff of Middlesex. His Bailiff, Brook, endeavouring to arrest Thos. Geare, of Acton, for a debt to the King, followed him to the Prince's house. Went thither to recover his bailiff, and apologize for his indiscretion in going into a privileged place, and asked Sir John Vaughan to restore him safe. The multitude had used brickbats and hammers against his bailiff, who was much bruised and beaten by them; persuaded them not to pump him and toss him in a blanket, as they threatened. Did not excite the multitude to violence, nor use any threats to obtain the fugitive. Knows of no brawling nor challenging. Signed an arrest for Sir Rich. Price, who came to Gray's Inn in Sir John Vaughan's coach, but was not present at its execution. Dec.* 24.

Dec. 24. 39. [Abel Barnard] to Carleton. Shall not know how to thank him if he brings the difficult business to pass. Would have come over before, only he would have had to raise a subsidy towards his expenses, and it is not good thrift to shear lambs.

Dec. 28. London. 40. Paul de la Ravoire to the Same. Sec. Naunton, the Archbps. of Canterbury and Spalato are surprised that his [Ravoire's] affairs, in France, go so ill. Is with Spalato, but of no use to him, he having got another maitre d'hôtel in his absence. French.

VOL. CIV.

1618.

Dec. 28. Grant to Wm. Carmichael, of the denizations of twenty-five persons, with power to the Lord Chancellor to make the Letters Patent of Denization. [*Grant Bk.*, *p.* 258.]

Dec. 30. Grant to Endymion Porter and Rich. Peate of all fines for non-payment of subsidy, and for importation and exportation of prohibited goods, for seven years. [*Ibid.*, *p.* 250.]

Dec. 31. York House. 41. Proceedings in Council on the Coinage Question. The silver not to be raised in value at present, and uniformity in weight of coin to be observed. Making of gold foliate, and melting of coin for plate, to be forbidden. Further regulations postponed till the Committee for exchange bring their report.

Dec. 31. 42. Account of bills made to Peter [Phineas?] Pett, Shipwright, for purveyance of pine timber, from the King's woods, for repairing and building ships; allowed by Sir Wm. Russell, Treasurer of the Navy.

Dec. 31. Shepherdswell. 43. Thos. Philpot to Lord Zouch. He and the other Commissioners, on his Lordship's direction that Wm. Hanington should restore and repair all the mischief he had done [at Maison Dieu], sent him a mandate to that effect, which was given to his servant, as he refuses all letters and messages. Sends his reply, appealing to his Lordship.

Dec.? 44. Petition of John Darell to the Same, for final hearing of his suit against William and Monings Hanington, who leave unrepaired the spoil and waste committed by them at the King's house of Maison Dieu, which is leased to Sir Marmaduke Darell.

Dec. 31. 45. Amount of the office of Ordnance, for the four quarters ending Dec. 31, 1618.

Dec.? 46. Petition of Nich. Stott, Messenger of the Chamber, to Sir Robt. Naunton, to be paid for the board of Wm Atkinson, kept by him in custody thirty-five days, by order of the Council.

[Dec.] 47. Petition of Robt. Heath to Lord Chancellor Verulam. Thos. Phelippes detains from him and his partner, Geo. Shires, 200*l.*, rents from Kirby Misperton; and 200*l.* more is in the tenants' hands. Requests leave to take the property into their own hands, paying over to Phelippes any surplus remaining after discharge of their just dues. [*See May* 22, 1620.]

Dec.? 48. Petition of the Merchant Adventurers to the King, against the proposed introduction of base or copper money, which has proved injurious in Spain and Germany, and would do so in England, by disturbing public credit, and driving away merchant strangers, &c.

UNDATED. 1618?

1618? Grant, with survivorship, to Rich. Carmarthen and Joseph de Quester, of the office of Surveyor of Customs and Subsidies in the Port of London. Latin. [*Warrt. Bk.*, I., *p.* 183.]

1618? Vol. CIV.

Grant to Wm. Connock, of the office of one of the Yeomen Prickers of the Privy Buckhounds, in place of Thos. Morrall, deceased. [*Warrt. Bk.*, I., *p.* 185.]

Grant to Rich. Eveleigh of confirmation of the parsonage of Bratton-Clovelly, co. Devon. Latin. [*Ibid.*, *p.* 197.]

Grant to John Harrington of the Constableship of Carnarvon Castle, void by the death of Sir Geo. Blague. Latin. [*Ibid.*, *p.* 150.]

Grant, with survivorship, to Sir Thos. Monson and John, his son, of the Stewardship of the Honour of the Duchy of Lancaster, co. York, on revocation of the same from Edw. Supledick. Latin. [*Ibid.*, *p.* 151.]

Grant to Geo. Proctor, King's Chaplain, of dispensation to hold the rectory of Holme, Spalding-upon-Moor, with the rectory of Barwick-in-Elmett, both co. York. Latin. [*Sign Man.*, *vol.* IX., *No.* 104.]

Grant to Wm. Foote, of London, of the sole privilege of selling tobacco pipe clay, the former patentee being dead, and bad clay sold by others. [*Ibid.*, *p.* 105.]

Grant to Patrick Murray, servant to the Prince, of two parts of the forfeitures of bonds to the late Queen, entered into by John Lee, and others as sureties for him, for the due execution of the office of Keeper of the Stores for the Ordnance in the Tower. [*Sign Man.*, *vol.* IX., *No.* 106.]

49. Petition of Sir Hen. Ashley to the King, for a patent to him and his assigns to be Surveyors of all vendible beer, it being much adulterated, contrary to law.

50. Petition of Thos. Dalmahoy to the Council. Has long observed their injunction to forbear attendance at the King, Queen, or Prince's Court; prays that he may now return to his former service.

51. Petition of Geo. Fortune, prisoner in the Fleet, to Lord Chancellor Verulam and the rest of the Council. Has received corporal punishment, and been imprisoned by the Court of Star Chamber. Is sorry for his great offence, and prays for release, to keep his family from starving.

52. Petition of Hen. Gibb, Groom of the Bedchamber, to the King, for delivery to him of a bond of 3,000*l.*, assigned to His Majesty by Michael Haydon, for a debt, and granted to Gibb, but for which the parties on whom it is drawn wish to compound.

53. Petition of Wm. Hasell, Mayor of Sudbury, and others, makers of the new drapery called Says, to the Council, to be heard before their Lordships, or before Commissioners appointed by them, to answer a complaint of Sylvia Harber, that they have injured the spinsters and weavers of Sudbury.

VOL. CIV.

1618?

54. Petition of Agnes, widow of Jerome Haydon, to the Same, for balance due to her late husband, Jerome Haydon, for gilt halberts and javelins, delivered into the Tower by him, in 1613 and 1615.

55. Petition of Dorothy, wife of Arthur Hill, to the Lords Commissioners of the Treasury. Is daughter and sole heir of Edm. Nevill, Lord Latimer, late reputed Earl of Westmoreland, whose estates escheated to the Crown; prays that her annuity of 100*l.* per ann., which is in arrear, may be paid her.

56. Petition of Wm. Hilles, Free Mason, to the Council, for freedom and mitigation of his fine, having been committed to the Fleet for erecting a tenement for Robt. More, late Coachmaker to Queen Elizabeth.

57. Petition of Simon Hudson and Ralph Akherst, prisoners in the Fleet, to Lord Chancellor Verulam. Have been long imprisoned for being concerned in transporting ordnance without licence; are sorry, and pray to be released, as they are neither officers of the King, nor of the Farmers [of the Customs].

58. Petition of Wm. Jones, servant of Lord Zouch, to the Archbp. of Canterbury, for payment of his charges for bringing up Wm. St. George, a recusant, and Pierce Govey, a Frenchman.

59. Petition of the Merchant Adventurers to the Council, that the grievances sustained by their Company, especially in the taring of cloth, may be amended in the treaty on foot with the Commissioners of the States General, now in England.

60. Notes [by Carleton] of the demands of the English relative to the taring of cloth, and the objections of the Dutch thereto.

61. Petition of the East India Company to the King, for power to erect forts to defend their trade.

62. Declaration of the Same to the Same, on the wrongs lately offered to them by the Hollanders in the East Indies.

63. Petition of the Inhabitants of Swanwhich, Isle of Purbeck, co. Dorset, to the Council, for the Block House at Peverell Point to be repaired, and furnished with ordnance, for protection of Swanwhich Bay against dangerous pirates, especially the Turks.

64. Statement of depredations of Turkish pirates on a seaport borough not named, and of the decay occasioned to the town thereby, and by the expense of building a fort for defence, a bridge over the haven, a jetty, new church, &c.

65. Statement of the proceeds of sale of five serviceable ships, lately sold in the Thames for want of employment. With note of the loss which will ensue to navigation, if ships cannot find employment.

Vol. CIV.

1618?

66. Petition of John Reynolds to the Council, that John Davies, of Egerley, Shropshire, and Ant. Withering, be restrained from a malicious prosecution against him before the Commissioners for Ecclesiastical Causes, their object being to escape fulfilment of an order, either to pay for or yield possession of a house bought by him from Davies.

67. Examination of Mr. Man. A message was given him by Sir Guildford Slingsby, to tell Mr. Coke, that if he did not do him justice he would shoot him.

68. Note by Sir Guildford Slingsby as to the above message.

69. Mr. Howell's reasons for raising the coin in England; viz., that as the French King has raised the value of his coin 20*d.* in every 20*l.*, English merchants trading to France will be serious losers unless English coin be similarly raised.

70. "The reason why so little gold or silver is brought into England, and so much is transported thence;" viz., the bad making of English coin, which encourages coiners; and its deficiency in weight, which makes it less valuable in coin than in the bar. Printed.

71. Notes of coinage of gold and silver, from 1593 to 1600, and from 1611 to 1618, with the profits to the Crown derived therefrom.

72. Notes of the tenures by which certain copyhold lands of the Crown are held. Indorsed, "Copyholds and manors, the likeliest to be first dealt withal."

73. Statement of difficulties in enfranchising His Majesty's copyholders of inheritance, and suggestions on the best mode of proceeding therein.

74. Arguments to show the impracticability of raising any large sums by enfranchising copyholders. The tenants think, from former failures in such attempts, that they cannot have good security for their enfranchisement. Cautions to be adopted if the attempt be made.

75. Notes of grants of arms, decisions in heraldry, Earl Marshal's commissions, &c., from 10 Edw. II. to 1618. With list of fees to be paid by Knights of the Bath.

76. Memoranda from the council books, that all treasure of which the true owner cannot be found belongs to the King.

77. Deposition of Everard Chambers, and others, that Mr. Turnell, Vicar of Horninghold, quoted passages of Scripture, in opposition to the King's Book of Recreations on the Lord's Day.

78. Deposition of Thos. Hughes, Rich. Jarvis, and others above named, relative to words spoken by Mr. Turnell, Vicar of Horninghold, denouncing those that deposed on the King's behalf.

VOL. CIV.

1618?

79. Deposition of Thos. Swan and Rich. Jarvis, that Mr. Turnell compared from the pulpit two persons that deposed on the King's behalf, to Demas, and Alexander the coppersmith.

80. Deposition of Robt. Johnson and others above named, that if, being dulled by Mr. Turnell's long sermons, they left the church before the blessing, Mr. Turnell cursed them from the pulpit.

81. Deposition of Rich. Jarvis and others above named, that Mr. Turnell said that all those who spoke even the truth, to the hurt of their neighbour, broke the ninth commandment, meaning those who deposed against him; and that he compared John Pretiman to the devouring lion, and himself to innocent David.

82. Names of the nobility, bishops, law officers, and other principal persons, who have allowance of impost on some article not mentioned.

83. Minute of fresh privileges granted to the town of Northampton, in their new charter.

84. Note addressed by an Officer of the Exchequer to Lord ——, of the several leases made by the Queen of the imposts on sugars granted to her, proving that she is no loser by the mode in which a payment relating thereto is entered in the Exchequer accounts.

85. Case and suit of Hen. Jernegan, jun., for assurance made to him of the Manor of Musarden, whereof the title has been found defective, but as it belongs to the King as private property, not as Crown land, the Commissioners cannot grant him a composition.

86. Bill of parcels of cloth delivered for the Queen by Thos. and John Harrison, drapers. Indorsed by Sir Edw. Coke, "My signification of the Quene's debt."

87. Certificate of the persons to whom the lands belonging to Hoddesdonbury, co. Herts, have been let, since it came into possession of Sir Thos. Wilson.

88. Particulars of the manor of Hoddesdonbury, what lands are to be let, and which are already let.

89. Petition of Sir Thos. Wilson to the King, that to prevent frequent disputes about precedency among knights and their wives, his Majesty should establish an office of "The Register of Honour," to be exercised by himself and successors, the Keepers of the State Papers, the salary of which latter office is only 30*l.* per ann.

90. Sir Thos. Wilson to [Buckingham]. Forwards a collection of papers, copies of which have been sent to the Ambassador in Flanders, proving that the Archduke's towns owe the King 100,000*l.* Hopes he will remember his suit.

91. The Same to the Same. Begs him to prefer to the King his papers about his suit, which is not only for his own benefit, but that of his office, of which his Lordship is the patron.

Vol. CIV.

1618?

92. Sir Thos. Wilson to the King. Has been long in service without reward. The Clerkship of the Imposts, and a salary of 40*l.* a year for transcribing State Papers, &c., granted him by Lord Treasurer Salisbury, were taken away by the late Lord Treasurer Suffolk. Prays that they may be restored, or that an office for registering knighthood may be erected, and conferred on him.

93. Draft of the above letter, with an additional clause that the office of record of honour is sued for in opposition, by the Pages of the Bedchamber, who already receive 3*l.* 10*s.* from each person knighted, and now want 5*l.* more. Also reasons for erecting the above-named office, and annexing it to that of State Papers.

94. Copy of the reasons for erecting the office of Register of Honour.

95. Form of the proposed warrant for establishing the office for registering knighthood, and for granting it to Sir Thos. Wilson, with a fee of 5*l.* for the record of each Knight.

96. Copy of the above.

97. The Worsted Weavers of Norwich and Norfolk, and the Baize and Says Makers of Essex and Suffolk, to the Council. Request ease of their grievances, through the falsifying of yarn, and intrusion of unauthorized persons into their trade, and suggest regulations thereon. The Orders in Council for their relief, of May 26, 1617, failed of effect, for want of a proclamation.

98. Precedents in support of the right of the Lord Presidents of Wales to recommend fit persons to be appointed Judges and Bishops, within their jurisdiction.

99. Names of persons recommended to be of the Council for the Marches of Wales.

100. Note of Lord Sheffield's proceedings with certain recusants in the county of York, whose estates rest in goods only.

101. Note of the names of Jesuits and Benedictines.

102. Directions [by Sir Thos. Wilson] for the use of an equinoctial dial, which the King commanded him to have made. Imperfect.

103. Description of the several parts of an equinoctial dial, and of its uses.

104. Forsecar's five propositions, viz., to show an instrument to take the meridian altitude; to know the variations of the needle; to sail by the longitude of the equinoctial; to show the causes of the various courses of the sea in all parts of the world; to show the true quantity of time the year hath, &c.

VOL. CIV.

1618?

Dover Castle. 105. [The Lord Warden of the Cinque Ports] to Sir Edw. Bromley, Baron of the Exchequer, and Sir Hen. Yelverton. Remonstrates against the bill of Jacob Braems, of Sandwich, exhibited in Chancery, complaining of hindrance by a suit against him in the Chancery Court of Dover. Begs that no proceedings may be allowed derogatory to the dignity and privileges of that ancient court, by which the portsmen, the defenders of the realm, are saved from absence from home, through suits in London.

106. Notes of the privileges of the Cinque Ports, that no freeman or inhabitant may be compelled to appear in the courts at Westminster, without the consent of the Lord Warden; with extracts from patents proving the above privilege.

107 Petition of John Philpot, of Gray's Inn, to Lord Zouch, for renewal of an injunction, granted and afterwards revoked, forbidding Ant. Tassell to proceed against him by common law, and ordering him to abide the decision of the Chancery Court at Dover.

108. Thos. Adson, of Dover, to the Same. Prays for a place in Dover Castle.

109. Petition of Nich. Archer to the Same, to be restored to the office of providing fish for the King and the Lord Warden.

110. Petition of Fras. Bannier to the Same, for restoration of his bark, taken by English pirates, and run ashore at Lydd.

111. Petition of Wm. Byng, prisoner in Dover Castle, to the Same, for re-hearing of the sentence against him in the Chancery Court there, sentencing him to pay 220*l.* for the debts of John and Michael Cooley, whereas he has paid 800*l.* more for them than he has received from their lands and goods. *Annexed is,*

111. I. *Note requiring that the accounts of the petitioner with the Cooleys be submitted to Lord Zouch.*

111. II. *The above-mentioned accounts of Byng's receipts and disbursements.*

112. Petition of Robt. Blechenden, a poor gentleman, to the Same. Being much reduced in circumstances, though of good demeanour and reputation, begs the place of Lieutenant at Sandown Castle, or some other suitable office.

113. Petition of Thos. Butler to the Same. Was formerly his servant, but offended him by a secret marriage; is now settled in London as a silk-weaver, but is disturbed because he is not a freeman; begs his Lordship's letters to the Lord Mayor and Aldermen, that he may be made free of the City.

114. Petition of Clement Church, of Rye, to the Same. Having served twenty-five years in Ireland, the Low Countries, and Sweden, and being driven home by the cessation of war, prays for a Gunner's place in Camber Castle.

Vol. CIV.

1618?

115. Petition of Jas. Cooke, of Dover, mariner, to Lord Zouch, for a Gunner's place in Dover Castle, or the bulwarks.

116. Petition of the Same to the Same, to similar effect.

117. Thos. Copper, of Dover, to [the Same]. Requests a Gunner's place in Dover Castle, being well experienced in the service.

118. Petition of John Crumpe, of Dover, Gunner of Dover Castle, and Wm. Hogbeane, of Folkestone, Gunner of Arch-cliff Bulwark, Dover, to the Same, to be allowed to change their places, in order to conform to his orders for Gunners to reside at their posts.

119. Petition of Vincent Denn, of Deal, to the Same, for a Gunner's place in Deal Castle.

120. Petition of the Retinue and Gunners of Dover to the Same, to be supported in their privilege of exemption from watch and ward, in the town of Dover.

121. Petition of Robt. Flemyng to the Same, for permission to take out and dry certain merchandise which was consigned to him at Middleburg, for Ireland, and saved from his ship lately wrecked on the Godwin Sands.

122. Petition of Phil. Gibbon, of West-cliffe, co. Kent, and Elizabeth, his wife, daughter and co-heir of Thos. Philpot, deceased, to the Same, to be allowed to prefer a bill in the Star Chamber Court against Robert and Margaret Broome and Thos. Sampson, and Alice his wife, another daughter of Thos. Philpot, for practising on him to will most of his property away from the petitioners, and for retaining the title deeds of such lands as were bequeathed to them by Philpot.

123. Petition of Edw. Graunt, of Dover, to the Same, for a Gunner's place in Dover Castle.

124. Petition of Robt. Hales to the Same, to similar effect.

125. Petition of Wm. Harris, of Dover, to the Same, to similar effect.

126. Petition of Wm. Heblethwayt, Jurat of New Romney, to the Same, for protection against the malice of enemies. Quotes "Cicero, that worthy orator and senator of Rome," and Cyprian.

127. Petition of Rich. Heneker, prisoner in Dover Castle, to the Same, that his brother, Thos. Heneker, may be made to account for money which he gave him to discharge a bond, and for which, not being fully paid up, he is now arrested.

VOL. CIV.

1618?

128. Petition of Edw. Kempe, prisoner in Dover Castle, to Lord Zouch, to be called before him to answer any charge, or to be released.

129. Petition of Wilfrid Kettlewell, soldier of Camber Castle, Sussex, to the Same, for permission to appoint an efficient substitute, being unable personally to attend the place, as required by his Lordship.

130. Petition of Joan, widow of Abraham Marleton, of Dover, to the Same. Her land is much injured by conies, which come from the Castle grounds; prays that they may be destroyed, and she compensated for her loss.

131. Petition of Abraham Momery to the Same, for a Gunner's place in Deal Castle.

132. Petition of Ant. Napleton, of Faversham, to the Same. From inexperience in affairs of state, and respect to his late father, he concealed what should have been disclosed. Prays for pardon and release, and for his Lordship's influence to reconcile him with his uncle.

133. Petition of John Parham to the Same, for a Gunner's place at Dover Castle.

134. Petition of Randolph Partridge, Gunner of Dover Castle, to the Same, to be allowed the same rate of wages as paid to David Fidge, whom he succeeded.

135. Petition of Thos. Percivall, prisoner in the New Prison, to the Same, for release, and mitigation of the fine laid on him by the Commissioners for Causes Ecclesiastical, for scandalous speeches against the late Sir Wm. Tate.

136. Petition of Hildebrand Prusen, Rich. Ball, and others, Merchants of London, to the Same. Shows that they fitted out two ships for discovering an island in the West Indies; that the officers unlawfully committed depredations on the Spaniards, for which most of the ships' goods were seized; yet the Lord Admiral prosecutes the petitioners for the forfeitures of the ships, and the Spanish Ambassador for restoration of spoiled goods. Prays his assistance at the Council, especially as Prusen has important service to do for the King.

137. Petition of Hen. Smith to the Same, for release from prison, to which he was committed for a rescue; acknowledges his fault.

138. Petition of Peter Smith, of Dover, to the Same, for a Gunner's place at Dover Castle, or the bulwarks.

139. Petition of Robt. Taylor, Warrener of Dover Castle, to the Same, for a Gunner's place in Dover Castle.

140. Petition of Isaac Turpin, of Dover, to the Same, for a Gunner's place in Dover Castle.

Vol. CIV.

1618?

141. Petition of the Inhabitants of Walmer to Lord Zouch, to be released from the fine imposed upon them for non-appearance before his Lordship, having been delayed by the illness of Wm. Adye, one of their number.

142. Petition of Roger White, of Dover, to the Same, to be paid out of the wages due to —— Godfrey, late Porter of Dover Castle, for some cloth delivered to him.

143. Petition of Timothy Winter, Parish Clerk of Deal, to the Same, for redress against Wm. Byng, Captain of Deal Castle, who refuses the usual payments by the Captains and Gentlemen Porters of Deal and Sandown Castles, to the parish clerks of Deal, to which church the captains and garrisons usually resort.

144. Petition of Wm. Wiseman, of Hythe, to the Same, to appoint him a Gunner in Sandgate Castle, in the room of his deceased father, Fras. Wiseman.

145. Estimate of the charge for four ships of the Navy, and eight of the merchants, to be employed for suppressing pirates, and guarding the coasts. With note, that this force, aided by Holland and Zealand, will be sufficient, if well commanded, but otherwise the expense had better be spared.

GENERAL INDEX.

A.

Abbeys and monasteries, 432, 486, 507, 552.
Abbot, Geo., Bp. of London, 12; Archbp. of Canterbury, 12, 22, 31, 59, 89, 127, 135, 144, 151, 154, 158, 167, 169, 199, 200, 202, 220–222, 231, 263, 285, 288, 294, 301, 304, 367, 386, 391, 400, 406, 414, 422, 435, 440, 454, 456, 458, 475, 488, 489, 491, 503, 504, 522, 526, 541, 548, 604, 607.
........., ..., commissions to, 38, 119, 183, 246, 270, 276, 285, 286, 359, 368, 370, 387, 446, 448, 533, 547, 557, 560, 574, 585, 590, 601.
........., ..., letters of, 26, 92, 221, 252, 254, 290, 303, 315, 320, 370, 479, 485, 495, 547, 565.
........., ..., ..., to Carleton, 171, 178, 179, 197, 227, 232, 244, 249, 262, 273.
........., ..., ..., to Jas. I., 138, 140, 142, 144, 148.
........., ..., ..., to Roe, 429.
........., ..., ..., to Somerset, 143, 145.
........., ..., letters to, 175, 246, 253, 301, 302, 304, 322, 366, 378, 396, 547, 549.
........., ..., residence of, *see* Lambeth.
........., ..., servants of, 44, 73, 134, 148, 149, 161, 294, 336, 379, 502, 535, 553.
........., Maurice, 137, 355.
Abbott, Dr. Robt., 202, 228, 230, 231, 288, 290; Bp. of Salisbury, 336, 526.
Abdick, hundred, 47.
Abdy, Chris., 232.
Abent, Thos., 332.
Abercorn, Earl of, *see* Hamilton, Jas.
Abercromby, Dav., 137.
........., Pat., 64, 250.
........., Mr. 458.
Abercromy, Abm., 228, 252.
Aberdawe, 587.
Aberdeen, 405, 469.
Aberfraw, 4.
Abergavenny, Lord and Lady, *see* Nevill.
Abergwilly, 84.
Abinger, 580.
Abington, Thos., 45.
Acatry, clerk of, 353.
Achmouty, Jas., 296.
Ackworth, 88.
Acland, Sir Art., 267.
........., John, 267.
Acton, 604.
Acton, Robt., 84.
Acunas, Don Diego Sarmiento de, Spanish Ambassador, 348; Condé de Gondomar, 543, 546, 548, 549, 575, 577, 593, 602.
Acworth, John, 240.
Adams, John, 502.
........., Rich., 87, 335.
........., Wm., 545.
Addington, 84.
Admiral, Lord High, *see* Howard, Chas., Earl of Nottingham.
Admiralty, 380, 421.
.... Court, 147, 152, 180, 354, 356, 399, 424, 457, 481, 494, 525, 557.
........., judges of, *see* Dunn, Sir Dan.; Martin, Sir Hen.
........., officers of, 12, 22, 75, 228, 399, 488, 494, 504, 513, 515, 540, 593.
Adson, Thos., 611.
Adye, Joan, 483.
........., Wm., 614.
Africa, 596.
Agarde, Mr., 305.
A. H., Mrs., 438.
Ahmed I., Sultan of Turkey, Grand Seignior, 140, 427, 428.
Ainsworth, John, 283, 285, 321.
Aisgill, Hen., 435.
Akherst, Ralph, 607.
Albert, Archduke, Regent of Low Countries, 28, 54, 64, 81, 140, 141, 144, 145, 147, 165, 175, 345, 381, 424, 472, 488, 514, 515, 609.
........., Ambassadors of, 170, 251, 299, 305; *see also* Boischot.
........., Ambassadors to, 76, 609; *see also* Bennet, Sir John; Trumbull, Wm.
Alciston, 439.
Alcock, John, 443.
Aldby, 544.
Aldersey, Thos., 343.
........., Wm., 343.
Aldersgate Street, *see* London, Streets of.
Aldershot, 392.
Aldingham, 154, 245.
Aldred, Edw., 357.
Aldworth, Thos., 103.
Ale and Beer, 119, 232, 260, 437, 494, 606.
Alesbury, Mr., 601.
Alexander, Hen., 279.
........., Robt., 179.

Alexander, Sir Sigismund, 279.
........., Sir Wm., 281.
Algiers, 427, 462, 475, 476, 565.
Alienations, *see* Crown lands, alienations of.
Aliens, foreigners and strangers, 1, 46, 62. 97, 108, 150, 235, 252, 258, 302, 363, 364, 376, 377, 394, 396, 439, 460, 490, 495, 503, 528, 571, 573, 589, 590, 593.
........., resident in London, 62, 293, 397, 581.
........., ships of, 282, 283, 297, 299, 300, 419, 464, 543.
Alington, Jas., 529.
Allanson (or Allinson), Chris., 553, 559.
Allegiance, Oath of, 37, 51, 58, 81, 95, 97, 120, 121, 138, 144, 176, 199, 224, 276, 303, 321, 328, 464, 476, 484, 501, 513.
........., ..., consent to take, 71, 145, 191, 254, 405, 469, 480, 482, 485.
........., ..., refusal to take, 18, 28, 54, 71, 121, 124, 128, 137, 181, 191, 215, 251, 302, 400, 427, 430–432, 435, 447, 450, 452, 479, 480, 485, 495, 510, 565, 589.
Allen, Abm., 208.
........., Cardinal, 119.
........., Edw. (bear master), 17, 147.
........., Edw., 555.
........., Fulk, 431.
........., Geo., 139.
........., John, 388, 559, 564.
........., Capt. Thos., 419.
........., Zouch, 231, 593.
........., Mr., 393.
Alley, Eman., 400, 442, 490, 495.
........., Jeremy, 442.
........., Capt. Pet., 520, 521.
........., Wm., 556, 564.
Allhallows Church, Dorchester, 506.
........., parish, London, 576.
Allington, Geo., 207.
........., Hugh, 44, 272, 278, 345, 350, 452.
Allison, Wal., 66.
All Saints' parish, Parking, 169.
...., Norfolk, 562.
...., Northampton, 215.
Alne, 118.
Alnwick, 540.
Alport, Thos., 288, 300, 375, 376.
Alps, the, 4.
Altham, Edw., 68.
........., Sir James, Baron of the Exchequer, 45, 61, 116, 131, 441, 463, 469.
Alston, Wm., 529.
Alum, 81, 90, 125, 141, 180, 188, 217, 218, 238, 256, 282, 527.
........., farmers of, 264, 276, 359.
........., mines, 180, 276.
........., works, 294, 335, 359, 377, 457.
Alured, Thos., 252, 555.
Amadevaz, 214.
Amazon, river, 198, 514.
Ambassadors, 157, 159, 213, 348, 431, 486, 520.
........., payments made or due to, 198, 244, 417, 422, 429, 458, 478, 503, 530.
........., foreign, 21, 55, 104, 119, 155, 161, 163, 164, 170, 227, 285, 582.
........., ..., presents to, 102, 380, 445.
Amber, 203.
Ambler, Hum., 503.
........., Mr., 304.
Ambresbury monastery, 246.
........., *see* Amesbury.
America, 198, 521.
........., South, 387, 463.
Amesbury, 58, 74, 76.
Ampthill, 102.
........., house and park, 102, 153, 230, 249, 253.
Amsterdam, 183, 193, 468, 478, 481.
Amwell waters, 78, 365.
Ancre, Marquis or Maréschal d', 391, 461.
Andalusia, 86.
Anderson, Edm., 551.
........., Fras., 122.
........., Sir Fras., 551.
........., Sir Hen., 360, 389.
........., Robt., 459.
.... (murderer), 368.
........., Lady, 481.
Anderton, Frances, 61.
........., Wm., 61.
.... (recusant), 210, 213.
........., Mrs., 304.
Andover, 194, 298.
Andrew, or Goodman, Eliz., 300.
........., John, 300.
........., Thos., 600.
Andrews, Jas., 502.
........., Lancelot, Bp. of Ely, Bp. almoner, 10, 38, 90, 163, 335, 398, 404, 426, 430, 460, 491, 512, 521, 560; Bp. of Winchester, 587, 591, 600.
........., ..., letters of, 136, 171, 235, 287.
........., ..., letters to, 283, 320.
........., ..., works of, 77, 115.
........., Thos., 306.
........., Sir Wm., 519.
Angel, Thos. 544.
........., Wm., 456.
Angell, Robt., 55.
........., Wm., 55.
Anglesey, 409.
........., grants of lands in, 124, 211, 230, 241.
........., offices in, 289, 372, 431.
........., residents in, 292.
Anhalt, John George I., Count of, 23, 126, 500.
Anlaby, Thos., 499.
Annally, 33.

Anne of Denmark, Queen of James I., 12, 17, 24, 48, 57, 64, 69, 79, 96, 98, 107, 109, 113, 122, 128, 131, 136, 155, 180, 199, 251, 252, 278, 294, 301, 331, 334, 376, 384, 390, 404, 442, 448, 455, 461, 465, 469, 475, 478, 479, 501, 511–515, 520, 522, 526, 527, 530, 550, 567, 573, 576, 577, 587, 588, 592, 595, 598, 609.
........., Admiral to, *see* Lloyd, Robt.
........., apparel, &c. of, 19, 31, 118, 204, 339, 609.
........., Chamberlain to, *see* Sydney, Visct. Lisle.
........., conduct of on the Palatine marriage, 163, 169, 170, 172.
........., court and council of, 46, 88, 339, 351, 606.
........., debts of, 91, 111, 114, 348, 349, 356, 357, 609.
........., favour or disfavour of, 127, 135, 205, 214, 215, 276, 295, 356, 373, 379, 385, 413, 460, 471, 494.
........., gifts and grants to, 189, 223, 224, 370, 439, 472, 478; *see* James I., gifts of.
........., household of, 237, 281, 357, 390, 501, 525.
........., illness of, 173, 198, 282, 308, 343, 416, 422, 489, 490, 512, 513, 584.
........., jewels, &c. of, 30, 121, 171, 251, 275, 280, 356.
........., jointure, &c. of, 3, 118, 212, 346, 356, 357, 383, 470, 475.
........., journeys and sojourns of, 90, 119, 138, 143, 155, 181, 182, 185, 186, 188, 190, 195, 196, 200, 274, 296, 305, 308, 361, 387, 404, 410, 460, 464, 490, 493, 497, 526, 568.
........., ladies of, 58, 128, 167, 212, 224, 296, 406, 415, 446, 465, 484, 512, 515.
........., lands of, 11, 46, 71, 112, 131, 139, 230, 439, 443, 522.
........., letters of, 105, 275.
........., letters to, 105, 299, 376.
........., musicians and players of, 275, 294, 351, 436, 549.
........., officers of, 45, 72, 73, 114, 135, 189, 195, 245, 292, 346, 357, 541.
........., portrait of, 162, 173.
........., presence of at festivals, &c., 345, 358, 392, 428, 487, 496.
........., residences of, 249, 387, 473.
........., servants, &c. of, 26, 29, 30, 42, 69, 93, 112, 150, 157, 180, 243, 330, 377, 471, 510, 531.
........., Solicitor of, *see* Hakewill, Wm.
........., Vice-Chamberlain of, *see* Carew, George, Lord.
Anonymous letters, 359.
Ansell, Thos., 93.
Anstell, Thos., 507.
........., Dorothy, 507.
Anstruther, Robt., 9, 94, 97, 113; Sir Robt., 273, 292.
........., Sir Wm., 195, 455, 460.
Anthony, Chas., 21.
........., Edw., 21, 264, 338, 452, 505.
Anthony, Dr. Fras., 323.
........., John, 59.
Antwerp, 57, 340, 399, 408, 474.
Ap Howell, Ellis Ap Edw., 355.
Ap John, Rich., 85, 137.
Ap Thomas, Thos. 292.
Apothecaries, 536; *see also* London, Companies of.
Apparel, 410, 585.
Appeal, commissions of, 24.
Appleby, Robt., 127.
........., Agnes, 127.
Appledore channel, 388.
Apprentices, 544, 569.
........., riots of, 124, 442, 449, 453, 465, 522, 604
Apsley, Sir Allan, 114, 225, 428; Lieutenant of the Tower, 441, 449, 538, 550, 565, 569, 570–572, 575, 585, 590.
Apthorpe, 388.
Apultree, 467, 536.
Arabella, Lady, *see* Seymour.
Archangel, 182.
Archbald, Nich., 434.
Arch-cliff, Dover, 28, 202, 310, 311, 351, 367, 582, 612.
Archduke, *see* Albert.
Archer, Nich., 611.
Arches, Court of, 282, 300, 321, 335.
........., ..., Deans of, 420, 488, 489, 515; *see also* Dunn; Dewhurst; Newman; Bird.
Archibald, John, 73.
Archy, *see* Armstrong.
Arderne, John, 332.
Ardes, John, 122.
Argall, Sir Reynold, 105.
Argyle, Earl and Countess of, *see* Campbell.
Arithmetic, 357.
Arminian Controversy, 489, 491, 504, 505, 526.
Arminius, Jas., 400, 489, 499.
Armstrong, Archibald or Archy (Court Fool), 31, 46, 80, 179, 523, 566.
........., Gabriel, 261.
........., John, 450.
Armstrongs, the, 36, 38.
Arms, coats of, 31, 40, 64, 127, 134, 172, 175, 275, 421, 428, 593, 608.
........., office of, 452, 593.
Armour, 178, 189.
Armoury, Master of, *see* Monson, Sir Thos.
........., the, 276; *see* Greenwich, Tower, Westminster, Woolwich.
Arnold, Rich., 267.
Arrowsmith, Rich., 209.
Arthuret, 539.
Artillery Garden, *see* London.
Artois, 362.
Artson, Cornelius, 274.
Arundel House, 384.
Arundel, Earl of, *see* Howard, Thos.
........., John, 411.

B.

Bagborough, 257.
Bagg, Jas., 3, 235.
........., Jas., junr., 235.
Baggeridge, 233.
Bagshaw, Hen., 73.
........., Thos., 72, 73.
Bagshot Park, 72, 159, 209, 392, 564.
Baily, Dr. Lewis, 156, 162; Bp. of Bangor, 400, 401, 422, 427.
Bainbridge, Christ., 294.
Baize, *see* Wools.
Baker, Abm., 176, 543.
........., Geo., 26, 531.
Bakewell, 501.
Balconquall, Wal., 340, 504, 511, 518, 529.
Baldwin, Mark, 483.
........., Wm. (priest), 3, 148, 153
Balfour, Sir Hen., 9.
........., Jas., 189.
........., Capt. John, 265.
........., Mich., Lord Burly, 7, 9.
Ball, Edw., 57, 58, 517.
......, Rich., 613.
Ballard, John, 529.
Balsall, 155.
Baltery and brass works, 16, 493.
Bamburgh, Sir Wm., 40.
Bamfield, Sir Wm., 130.
Bamford, Wm., 291.
Bampton, 347.
Banbury Castle, 145.
Banckes, Geo., 210.
Band, Robt., 339.
Bangor, 524.
........., Bp. of, *see* Rowlands, Hen.; Baily, Dr.
Bankers, manor of, 209.
Bankruptcy, Commissioners for, 539, 567.
Banks, John, 491.
Bannier, Fras., 611.
Banning, *see* Bayning.
Bannister, Rich., 29, 529.
........., Sir Robt., 265.
........., Winnifred, 29.
Bantam, 236.
Bar, Robt. de la, 452.
Barbarian, the, 69.
Barbarigo, Georgio, Ambassador of Venice, 211.
Barbary, 55, 175.
Barbican, the, 140–142, 554, 569.
Barbon (minister), 92.
Barbor, Gabriel, 230.
Barclay, Jean de, 22, 102, 425, 514.
........., ..., Parenesis by, 489.
Bardney, 39.
Bardolle, Alex., 419.
Barford, 507.
Bargrave, Geo., 341.
........., John, 538, 544.
Barington, Sir Fras., 248, 332.
Barker, Jas., 325.
........., Robt. (King's printer), 67, 185, 356.
........., Wm., 200.
Barkham, Edw., 27, 122.
Barking, Essex, 46, 127, 382.
........., London, 169, 456.
........., Suffolk, 64.
Barkley, Edw., 374.
........., John, 60.
Barlatier, Ant., 557.
Barlichway Hundred, 138.
Barlow, Geo., 596.
........., Wm., Bp. of Lincoln, 39, 182.
Barmston, 599.
Barnacle, Harry, 298.
Barnard, Abel, 531, 585, 590, 600, 604.
........., Fras., 359.
........., Geo., 293.
........., Nath., 561.
Barnard Castle, 125, 192, 312.
Barnes, Edw., 118, 535.
........., John, 54.
........., Wm., 6, 9, 24.
........., Sir Wm., 497.
........., Lady, 104.
Barnesbrough, 277.
Barnet, 17, 20, 24, 57.
Barnett, Edw., 47.
Barnevelt, Jean d'Olden, 367, 596.
Barnsley, 130, 249, 352.
Barnsley-cum-Dodworth, 249.
Barnstaple, 47.
Barnwood Forest, 28, 85, 125, 279.
Baronets, 27, 41, 42, 43, 48, 49, 50, 53, 61, 208, 235, 288, 446.
........., precedence of, 27, 79, 104, 105, 108, 111, 119, 127, 134, 442.
Barons, 104, 105, 108, 111, 119, 126, 127, 134, 269, 298, 442, 513.
Barre, M. de la, 36.
Barrett, Sir Edw., 434.
........., Thos., 94, 253.
........., Wal., 434.
Barrow, 60.
Barroway, Wm., 365.
Bartlett, John, 546.
........., Sir Thos., 13, 27, 52, 148, 263, 269.
Barton-Bendish, 4.
.... Regis, *see* King's Barton.
Barwick, 88.
Barwick-in-Elmett, 606.
Basill, Simon, 78, 181.
Basing, 193, 297, 557, 558.
Bassa, Vizier, 427.
Bassano, And., 93.
........., Jacobo, 284.
........., Paul, 550.
........., Thos., 299.
Basset, Edw., 506.

Basset, John, 506.
........., Sir Robt., 5, 64, 70, 71, 72.
Bassett, Fras., 528.
........., John, 37.
........., Roger, 179.
Bassey, Robt., 597.
Basswell Park, 32.
Bate, Chris., 492.
........., Alice, 492.
........., Samson, 306, 526.
........., Wm., 29.
Bateman, John, 112.
Bates, Edw., 351, 352.
........., Rogers, 467.
........., Sampson, 351, 352.
Bath, 113, 120, 126, 129, 133, 140, 182, 185, 189, 195, 198, 274, 296, 306, 308, 479, 515, 532.
........., Earl of, *see* Bourchier, Wm.
.... and Wells, Bp. of, *see* Montague, Jas.; Lake, Art.
........., ..., diocese of, 468.
Bath, Knights of the order of, 27, 401, 404, 606.
Bath, Robt., 105.
Bathampton, 439.
Battells Bailiwick, 451.
Batten, Rich., 122, 279, 546, 596.
Battista, Giov., *see* Maria.
Battle Abbey, 357.
Bavaria, 72.
Baxter, Robt. 15.
........., Thos., 153, 466.
Bayley, Rich., 483.
........., Wm., 292.
Baylie, John, 79.
........., Capt., 489, 491, 495, 511, 513, 516. 517.
Baynard, John, 106.
Baynard's Castle, 99, 436.
Bayning, or Banning, Sir Paul, Bart., 365, 452.
Baynton, Sir Hen., 357.
Bayonne, 575.
Beachey Head, 415, 421, 463.
Beaconsfield, 167.
Beamish, 384.
Beamont, 44, 444.
Beamont, Fras., 499.
Beauchamp, Lord and Lady, *see* Seymour.
........., Mr., *see* Seymour, Wm.
Beaulieu, 69, 70, 71, 565.
Beaulieu, M. de, 415.
Beaumaris, 443, 602.
.... Castle, 443.
Beaumont, Hen., 422.
........., Rich., 460.
........., Sir Rich., 486, 500.
........., Sir Thos., 73.
........., Wm. Visct., 112, 116.
Beaupier, 123.
Beauvois Monday, 423, 433.
Beaver, 529.
Beck, Wm., 293.
Becke, Barth., 484.
Beckley, 502.
Bedell, Sir Thos., 508.
Bedford, Earl and Countess of, *see* Russell.
.... Hospital, 34.
.... House, 234, 585.
Bedfordshire, 93, 180, 255, 261, 319, 389, 441.
........., grants of land in, 63, 87, 124, 181, 192, 418.
........., lands and places in, 102, 249, 253, 532, 545.
........., offices in, 171, 275, 537.
........., residents in, 389, 507.
Beddo, Robt., 552.
Bedingfield lawn, 102.
Bedingfield, Thos., Master of Tents, 49, 58, 205.
Bedlington, 113.
Bee, Edw., 418.
Beecher, Wm. (agent in France), 20, 80, 87, 240, 280, 297, 381, 399, 403, 465, 483, 585, 587, 588, 597.
.........., Wm. (of Fotheringay), 507.
Beeke, Rich., 596.
Beer (Somersetshire), 594.
Beer, *see* Ale.
Beesley, Wm., 206.
Beeston, 522.
Beeston, Ellinor, 57.
........., Sir Geo., 57.
........., Sir Hen., 136.
........., Sir Hugh, 249, 513, 522.
........., Rich., 93, 95, 120, 158.
........., Mr., 65.
Belgrave, Sir Geo., 73, 289.
Bell, Robt., 66, 355, 384, 429, 533, 594, 595.
........., Mr., 522.
........., J., 372.
Bellarmine, Robt., Cardinal, 305.
Bellasis, 198, 224, 315, 336.
Bellingham, 36.
Bellingham, Sir Edw., 408.
........., Thos., 408, 434, 436, 450, 514.
Bellott, Thos., 36.
Belmesnil, 175.
Ben, Ant., Recorder of London, 448, 449, 514; Sir Ant., 518, 564, 566, 584.
Benbery, Ann, 130.
Bendbo, John, 24, 351.
........., Robt., 306, 384.
Bendloss, And., junr., 23.
Benedictines, the, 610.
Benevolence, *see* James I., benevolence granted to.
Bengworth, 388.
Benhold Wood, 37.
Bennet, Sir John, 120, 449, 488, 498.

Bennet, Sir John, letters of, to Carleton, 18, 59, 110, 174, 417, 461.
........., ..., mission of, to Flanders, 453, 458, 472, 473, 488, 514.
........., Robt., Bp. of Hereford, 426, 497.
Bennett, Melchis., 502.
........., Steph., 228.
........., Sir Thos., Alderman, 221, 487.
Beoly, 164.
Bergen-op-Zoom, 132, 452.
Beridge Zeth, *see* Morton, Wm.
Berk Manor, 430.
Berkeley, 386.
Berkeley, Lady Eliz., 597.
........., Sir Fras., 425.
........., Geo., 267.
........., Geo. Lord, 386.
........., Hen. Lord, 215, 219, 228, 284, 401.
........., Sir Maurice, 276, 465.
........., Theophila, 215.
........., Sir Thos., 267.
Berker, Wm., 558.
Berkhamstead, 39, 95, 101, 552.
Berkley, Geo., 269.
Berkshire, 86, 200, 268, 599.
........., grants of lands in, 63, 74, 89, 124, 186, 196, 207, 230, 300, 353.
........., lands and places in, 86, 130, 158, 218, 366, 375, 382, 394, 451, 514, 596.
........., recusants in, 45.
Bermondsey, 32, 571.
Bermuda Company, 120, 345.
Bermudas, the, or Summer Islands, 140, 203, 299, 392, 425, 426, 586, 594.
Bernard, Fras., 359.
Berne, 301.
Bernese, the, 72.
Bertie, Hen. Lord Willoughby, 514.
Bertram, Chris., 100, 117.
........., Rich., 100, 117.
........., Mr., 405, 408, 412.
Berwick-upon-Tweed, 8, 22, 32, 59, 94, 105, 465, 470,
........., Bridge, 4, 7, 14, 15, 19, 24, 33, 53, 60, 61, 80, 112.
........., Captain of, *see* Bowyer, Sir W.
........., garrison of, 4, 6, 17, 19, 21, 23, 25, 26, 34, 36–38, 40, 42, 46, 48, 53, 54, 56, 60–62, 76, 112, 123, 348, 431.
........., letters from, 4, 6, 7, 9, 14, 15, 17, 23, 24–26, 34, 36, 38, 40, 42, 53, 54, 56, 60, 61, 80, 112, 466.
........., lieutenant of, *see* Hodgson.
........., mayor, &c. of, 7, 15, 24, 33, 36, 42, 61, 80, 112, 381.
........., ordnance at, 112, 360, 443.
........., palace, 37.
Best, Capt. Thos., 103, 214, 236.
........., Valentine de, 345.
Bestever, A. C., 468.
Beswick, Hen., 62.
Beswick, Sam., 37.
........., Mrs. 37.
Bethell, Sir Hugh, 267.
Bethlehem Hospital, 601.
Bewcastle, 220, 242, 539.
Bewchemé, John, 64.
Bewdley, 344.
Bewfront, 45.
Bewick, Cuthbert, 589.
Bible, the, 188, 419, 429, 431, 602, 608.
Bickerton, 379.
Bickley, Ferdinando, 244.
Bidford, Rich., 401.
Bierlinck, ——, 466.
Biggs, Sir Thos., 267.
........., Thos., 267.
Bigshot, 243.
Bill, John, 454.
Bilson, Thos., Bp. of Winchester, 122, 200, 208, 289, 290, 294, 296, 308, 344, 375.
........., ..., letters of, 26, 43.
........., ..., letters to, 33, 43, 66, 75.
Binbrooke, 74.
Bindon, 1.
........., Visct., *see* Howard, Thos.
Bing, Capt., *see* Byng.
Bingley, Rich., 30; Sir Rich., 302.
........., John, Remembrancer of the Exchequer, 238, 248, 366, 428, 429, 477, 503, 511, 513; Sir John, 525, 527, 566.
Binnion, John, 535.
Biondi, G. F., 178.
........., ..., letters of, to Carleton, 151, 157, 161, 167, 171, 174, 175, 176, 180, 189, 203, 204, 211, 274, 352, 391, 397, 540.
Bir., 139.
Birchington, 417.
Bird, John, 170.
........., Nich., 385.
........., Thos., 335.
........., Dr. or Sir Wm., 447; Dean of the Arches, 489, 511
........., Mr., 364.
Birmingham, 147.
Birt, Mr., 332.
Bisbrooke, 292.
Bisham, 392, 514.
Bishop, Dr. Wm., 28.
Bishop Almoner, *see* Andrews, Lancelot.
Bishoprics, 77, 400.
Bishops, 22, 135, 164, 222, 231, 234, 239, 242, 304, 396, 420, 423, 424, 432, 443.
Bishop's Auckland, letters dated from, 34, 54, 113, 120, 204, 270, 289, 304, 323.
Bishop's Bearewood walk, 209.
Bishop's Candal, 82.
Bishop's Castle, 453.
Bishop's Wilton, 240.
Bishopthorpe. 139, 226.
Bittlesden, 282.
Bixe, Thos., 480.

Black, Pat., 107, 189, 296, 401.
........., Rich., 107.
Blackbeard, see Hind.
Blackfriars' ferry, 325; see London, Streets of.
Blackhorse Alley, see London, Streets of.
Blackman, John, 64, 142, 145.
Blackmore Forest, 68, 242, 534, 574, 578.
Blackney, John, 372.
Blackwall, 39.
Blackwater, see Sandhurst.
Blackwell, Eliz., 32.
........., Mr., 28, 115.
Blagdon, 41, 468.
Blagrave, John, 57.
Blague, Sir Geo., 606.
........., Thos., 91.
Blair, Alex., 35, 48.
Blakesley, 418.
Blakeston, Sir Thos., 302.
........., Sir Wm., 291.
Blakewey, Jacob, 526.
Bland, Hen., 561.
........., Pet., 76.
........., Thos., 415.
........., Sir Thos. 69, 121, 130.
Blaxton, Mr., 312.
Bleasdale, 206.
Blechby, 418.
Blechenden, Robt., 611.
Bleck Hall, 10.
Blee, Geo., 306.
Blencarne, Edw., 18.
Bletsoe, letters dated from, 139, 178, 259, 326, 331, 387.
Blewett, Art., 102.
Blincow, Dr. Ant., 521.
Blisworth, 14.
Blockhouse, Gravesend, 339.
............., Kent, 535.
............., Peverell Point, 607.
Blois Castle, 384.
Blondell, Geo., 31.
Blount, Edw., 116, 284, 289.
........., Sir Geo., 268.
........., John, 33.
........., Mountjoy, 504.
........., Rich., 73.
........., Rich. (Jesuit), 142, 305.
........., Walter, 268.
Bludder, Sir Thos., 91, 114, 198.
Blundell, Fras., 364, 404, 416, 451; Sir Fras., 492, 559.
........., Capt. John, 537.
Blunt, Thos., 321, 328.
Blyth, 556.
Boats and barks, see Ships.
Bodell, John, 271.
Boderie, M. de la, French Ambassador, 146, 301, 409.
........., Mdme de la, 6.
Bodley, Sir Thos., 28, 120, 137, 143, 168, 169, 172, 173, 174, 177, 187, 326.
........., Lady, 48.
Bodt, Godfrey, 397, 593.
Boetzler, Marg. Elburgh de, see Mayerne.
Bogg, Art., 212.
Bohemia, 301, 572.
........., King of, see Ferdinand II.
Boischot, M. Ferd. de, Archduke's Ambassador, 328.
Boisloré, M., 581.
Bold, Thos., 372.
Bolt, Hen., 540.
Bond, Chris., 130.
........., Jas. 584.
........., Thos., sen., 260.
........., Thos., jun., 260.
........., Sir Wm. 166, 172.
Bonds, 33, 82, 145, 207, 214, 217, 405, 455.
Bonham, Dr. Thos., 510.
Bonnall, John, 246.
........., Fras., 246.
Bonnivet, Marquis, 305.
Books, 22, 71, 72, 77, 89, 100, 101, 119, 128, 142, 143, 175, 231, 235, 289, 290, 368, 402, 403, 406, 417, 427, 474, 479, 484, 489, 511, 517, 526, 547, 590.
........., licences for, 10, 179, 276, 556, 564.
........., payments for, for the King, 21, 67, 454.
........., Popish, 12, 26, 210, 212, 213, 315, 405.
........., treasonable or seditious, 269, 270, 303, 305, 306, 404, 410, 424, 603.
........., see also Savile, Sir Hen.; Spalato, Archbp.
Boorne, Thos., 493, 499.
Booth, Robt., 22.
Boothe, Mr., 37.
Borderers, 36.
Borders, the, 20, 220, 229, 233, 240.
........., commissioners for, 21, 22, 24, 55, 82, 83, 152, 153, 212, 463, 464, 536, 537, 539, 540, 590.
........., disturbances on, 36, 61, 128, 347, 348, 459.
........., Government of, 8, 211, 213, 504.
Boreman, Jas., 336, 337.
........., John, 517.
Borlase, Sir John, see Burlacy.
Borough, Steph., 228.
Bostock, Mr., 183.
Boston, 22, 576.
Boteler, Robt., 309.
........., Thos., 11.
Bothall Castle, 464.
Boughton, Malherbe, 95.
Broughton, Edw., 6, 9, 24.
........., Harry, 138.
........., Capt. Wm., 201, 343, 454.
Bouillon, Henri de la Tour d'Auvergne, Duke of, 71, 89, 124, 126–129, 142, 166, 391.
Boulogne, 341.

Bourchier, Sir John, 16, 40, 44, 81, 197, 217, 250, 264, 359.
........., Wm., 128.
........., Wm., Earl of Bath, 5, 100, 125, 182, 254, 257, 262, 533, 545, 586.
Bourdeaux, 384.
Bourdin, Julien, sieur de Fontenay, 84, 194.
........., Pet. Ant., sieur de St. Anthoine, 84, 194.
Bourgh, Dav., 489.
Bouthe, Sir Geo., 117.
Bovey, Jas., 47, 234, 244, 247, 250, 262, 437, 479, 555.
........., Jas., junr., 437.
Bow, Wm., 163.
Bowd, Mr., 508.
Bowdler, Rich., 264.
Bowers, Robt., 248.
........., Ann, 248.
Bowes, 294.
Bowes, Sir Jerome, 207, 355, 357, 425.
........., Ra., 93, 95, 120, 158.
........., Talbot, 125, 325.
........., Sir Wm., 95.
........., Lady, 515.
Bowewood, 165.
Bowle, Rich., 590.
Bowler, Wm., 243.
Bowman, Edw., 122.
Bownhall, John, 593.
Bowsar, John, 187.
Bowyer, Sir Edm., 547, 553, 561.
........., Geo., 76, 102.
........., Sir Hen., 95, 96, 217.
........., Robt., 64, 75.
........., Sir Wm., Captain of Berwick, 4, 26, 34, 40, 42, 46, 48, 62, 64, 75, 76, 94, 102, 105.
........., ..., letters of, 4, 7, 9, 14, 15, 19, 20, 36, 42, 56.
........., Lady, 76, 102, 504.
........., Mr., 108, 561.
Boyd, And., 277, 351, 374, 375, 556.
Boyle, Sir Rich., 398,
Boynton, Sir Matt., 599.
Boys, Wm., 13.
Brabant, 132, 474.
Brabant, Geo. 211.
Brabazon, Sir Edw., 398, 426.
Brackenborough, 252.
Brackenbury, Fras., 121.
Brackley, Visct., *see* Egerton.
Brackston, John, 521.
Bradbury, Cordwall, 49.
Braddell, Thos., 475.
Braden Forest, Wilts, *see* Braydon.
Braderton, John, 76.
Bradfield, 37.
Brading, 381.
Bradshaw, Edm., 194.
........., Hen., 293.
Bradshaw, John, 304.
........., John (of the Exchequer), 588.
........., Rich., 78.
........., Robt., 33.
Braems, Jacob, 423, 459, 611.
Brailes, 28.
Braithwaite, Mr., 69.
........., Mr., sen., 69.
Brancepeth Manor and Parks, 211, 312, 320, 323, 328, 332, 594.
.... Castle, 226.
Brandenburg, Ambassadors of, 151, 255, 274, 345.
........., House of, 97.
........., John Sigismund, Marquis of, 22, 64, 69, 72, 251, 345.
Brandon, Greg., 428.
Branthwait, Rich., 580.
........., Dr. Wm., 169, 220, 580.
Brantingham, 96.
Brass, 493, 499, *see also* Baltery and brass works.
Bratie, Rich., 26.
Bratton-Clovelly, 606.
Bray, 382, 451.
Bray, Mr., 205.
Braybrooke, 97.
Braydon or Braden Forest, Wilts, 48, 205, 388.
Breadshaw, Mr., 61.
Brecknockshire, grants of lands in, 124, 159, 211.
........., offices in, 85, 209, 415, 431, 432.
........., residents in, 85, 137, 195, 261, 292.
Bredgate, And., 266.
........., Margery, 430.
Breeden, John, 502, 503.
........., Wm., 503.
Breedon, 271.
Brenchley, 358.
Brent, Nath., 583.
........., ..., letters of, to Carleton, 406, 410, 411, 424, 432, 449, 488, 491, 497, 505, 510, 512, 513, 518, 520, 522, 524, 526, 531.
Brentford, 332, 577.
Brentland, 253.
Brereton, John, 60.
........., Rich., 379.
........., Sir Thos. 379
Bressy, Thos., 379.
Brest, 464.
Brest, Nich. de, 572.
Brestwood, Rich., 491.
Bretagne, *see* Brittany.
Brett, Jas., 341, 538.
........., Sir John, 158.
........., Sir Robt., Lieutenant of Dover Castle, 199–202, 243, 266, 298, 345, 372.
.... Lady, 587.
Brewerne Monastery, 249.
Brewers and brewery, 179, 260, 354.
Brewster, Lawr., 295.

Bridewell, 567.
Bridge Trafford, 553.
Bridgenorth, 463.
Bridges, Edw., 100, 103.
........., Eliz., *see* Kennedy, Lady.
........., Hen., 15.
........., John, 412.
........., Kath., 58.
........., Robt., 30.
........., Thos., 5.
Bridgewater, 598.
Bridgewater, Earl of, *see* Egerton.
Brigg, 574.
Briggs, Hen., 34.
Brigham, Rich., 523.
Bright, Edw., 289.
........., John, 42.
........., Robt., 311.
Brightlingsea, 219.
Brill, the, 212, 368, 370, 425, 539, *see also* Holland, Cautionary towns of.
Brimstone, 468.
Bringwood Forest, 103.
Brinkworth, Mr., 309.
Brinley, Thos., 490.
Briot, M., 267.
Briscoe, Robt., 10.
Briskett, Lodowick, 37.
Bristol, 47, 180, 184, 186, 259, 294, 333, 549, 598.
........., alms-rooms in, 68.
.... Castle, 79, 81, 107, 277, 360, 385, 386.
........., mayor, &c. of, 81, 333, 543.
........., merchants of, 543.
........., Bp. of, *see* Thornborough, John; Felton, Dr. Nich.
........., prebends at, 231.
Britain, Sir Hen., 599.
Britain's Burse, 6, 17, 581.
Brittain, Fras., 334, 338.
Brittany, or Bretagne, 384, 412, 494.
Brixham, 540, 541.
Brixton, Berks, 366.
........., Isle of Wight, 44, 94.
Broad Hill, 298.
Broad, Sir Steph., 425.
Broadcloth, *see* Cloth.
Broadstairs, 369, 430, 431.
Broadwell, 596.
Brocket, Capt., 587.
Broderick, Wm., 26.
Broeckman, Borchart, 308.
Brograve, Sir John, Attorney of the Duchy of Lancaster, 202.
........., Simeon, 84.
........., Dorothy, 84.
Bromfield, 208.
Bromham, 357.
Bromhead, Thos., 509.
Bromley, 448.
Bromley, Sir Edw., Baron of the Exchequer, 61, 611.
........., Sir Hen., 344.
Bromsgrove, 73.
Brook, Chas., 38.
........., Chris., 72, 125.
........., John, 228, 551.
........., Sir John, 22, 33.
........., Wm., 498.
.... (bailiff), 604.
.... (lawyer), 95.
Brooke, or Brook, Sir Basil, 288, 555.
........., Sir Calisthenes, 79.
........., Hen. Lord Cobham, 48, 148, 374, 515, 561, 569, 590.
........., John, 87.
........., Matt. 394.
........., Ralph, York Herald, 108, 428, 453.
.... Thos., (of Cambridge), 79, 81.
........., Thos. (of London), 218.
Brooks, Sir John, Lieutenant of Dover Castle, 295, 298.
Broome, Robt., 612.
........., Marg., 481, 490, 612.
Brougham, 479.
.... Castle, 69.
Broughton, Mr., 529.
Brounker, *see* Bruneard.
Brown, Abel, 502.
........., And., 604.
........., Ant. Visct. Montague, 32, 51, 60, 120, 134, 151, 189, 224.
........., Hen. (papist), 501.
........., Sir Hen., 68, 472.
........., John, 337, 401, 403, 406.
........., Rich. (soldier), 419.
Browne, Benedict, 199.
........., Eliz., 130.
........., Hen. 30.
........., Hen. (of Yorkshire), 130.
........., Jas., 354.
........., John, 301, 568.
........., Margt., 52.
........., Rich. (messenger), 196.
........., Robt. 84, 129.
........., Thos., 254.
........., Thos. (surveyor), 87, 88.
........., Thos. (priest), 321, 328, 400.
........., Wm., 283.
Brownists, 565.
Broyle Park, 158.
Bruce, Edw., Lord Kinloss, 7, 11, 22, 167, 183, 198, 268, 431.
........., Edw., 268.
........., Sir Geo., 22.
........., Thos., Lord, 249.
........., Mr., 213.
Bruckshaw, Mr., 273.
Brudnell, Sir Thos., 555.
Bruges, 408, 452, 573.

Bruges, Grey, Lord Chandos, 47, 138, 198, 373, 516, 523, 531.
Brugg, Thos., 33.
........., Wymond, 33.
Bruncard, Anne Lady, 99.
........., Wm., 10, 13, 71, 386, 410.
........., Sir Wm. 264.
Brunker, *see* Bruncard.
Brunsberg, 303.
Brunswick, 345.
........., Duke of, 345.
........., Duchess of, 64.
Brunt, Edm., 177, 227.
Brussels, 236, 341, 484, 515.
........., letters from, 18, 24, 28, 109, 193, 285, 461.
Bryan, Luke, 156.
Bryn y, Keliog, 177.
Bubbe, Capt., 565.
Buchanan, Wal., 30, 53.
Buck, Sir Geo., Master of the Revels, 52, 110, 294, 329, 553, 549.
........., John, 551.
........., Pet., 302.
........., Sir Peter, 168, 302.
Buckby Longa, 185, 506.
Bucke, E., 37.
........., Hen., 78.
........., John, 222.
Buckeridge, Dr. John, Bp. of Rochester, 44, 47, 205, 473.
Buckhounds, *see* James I., buckhounds of.
Buckingham, Earl of, *see* Villiers.
........., Countess of, *see* Compton, Mary, Lady.
Buckinghamshire, 86, 185, 268.
........., grants of lands in, 63, 84, 230, 248, 282, 383, 388.
........., lands and places in, 12, 28, 131, 246, 253, 256, 260, 279, 290, 418, 428, 447, 596.
........., offices &c. in, 182, 426, 432.
Buckland, Chas., 366.
Buckland-Brewer, 102.
Bucklebury, 45.
Buckley, 379, 467.
Buckley, John, 11.
........., Thos., 190.
Buckminster, Chris., 246.
Buckworth, 295.
Budd, Geo., 111.
Bugbrook, 85.
Bugden, 39.
Buildings, *see* London, buildings in.
Builth, 85, 137.
Bulkeley, Sir Rich., 443, 602.
........., Thos., 379.
........., Wm., 292.
Bull, Randolph, 451.
........., Rich., 379.
Bullingham, Thos., 367.
Bullion, 92, 97, 129, 184, 338, 379; *see also* Mint and Coinage.
Bullocks, 89.
Bulstone Hundred, 47.
Bunbury, 372.
Buntingford, 109.
Burbage, Richard (actor), 469.
Burchley, Thos., 565.
Burde, ——, 282.
Burford, 93.
Burges, Fras., 40.
Burgess, Dr., 197, 225, 427, 475.
Burgh, Lady, 64, 209, 212.
........., Matt., 154.
........., Rich. de, Earl of Clanricade, 66.
........., Frances, Countess of Clanricade, 66, 143.
Burghley, Nich., 254.
Burgundy, 189.
.... plate, 175, 210.
Burke, Thos., 323.
Burlacy, Sir John, 22, 79.
........., Sir Wm., 421.
........., Lady, 33, 34.
Burlamachi, Phil., 183, 238, 246, 252, 350, 385, 398, 423, 432, 468, 530.
Burleigh, 305.
Burleigh, Lord and Lady, *see* Cecil.
Burley, 389, 451.
Burling-Gate, 463, 481.
Burltford, 246.
Burly, Lord, *see* Balfour.
Burnet, 338.
Burnfoot, 297.
Burnhall, 476.
Burnham, Geo., 553.
Burnley, 304, 498.
Burnley, Mich., 423.
Burnt Hastings, 334.
Burnthall, 23.
Burrell, Fras., 127.
........., Mr., 15, 430.
Burrough, John, 57.
Burton, Chas., 231.
........., Edw., 62.
........., Capt., 511.
........., Mr., 226.
Burton, 404.
.... Park, 413.
Burton-on-Trent, 123, 519.
Bury, Robt., 61.
Bury St. Edmund's, 88, 203, 230, 505.
.... Monastery, 231, 247, 559.
Bush, Sir Pet., 462.
Bushe, Edw., 244.
Bushell, Edw., 209; Sir Edw., 529.
Busher, Thos., 571.
Bussey, And., 444.
Bussy, Chris., 271.
Butler, Alban, 120.
........., Sir Hen., 602.

C.

Canterbury, 14, 34, 36, 54, 100, 168, 181, 301.
………, alms-rooms in, 111.
………, letters from, 100, 264, 303, 352, 369, 380, 414, 481.
………, mayor, &c. of, 34, 36, 264, 274.
………, Archbp. of, *see* Abbot, Geo.
………, Archbishopric of, 31.
………, Catholic Archbp. of, 285, 300.
………, deanery of, 282, 286.
………, prebends of, 289, 370, 527, 530.
………, Prerogative Court of, 315, 335, 357, 435.
………, province of, 245, 290.
Capell, Alex., 54.
………, Sir Art., 49, 73, 88, 508.
………, Sir Gamaliel, 114, 116.
Capetrell, Nich., 293.
Capheaton Castle, 302.
Capuchin friar, 178.
Carburton, 334.
Cardell, Thos., 382.
Cardiff, 95, 484, 598.
Cardiganshire, 209, 304.
………, grants of lands in, 63, 159.
Cards and card makers, 297, 384, 420, 445, 504.
Cards, customs on, 296, 504.
Carew, Anne, 486.
………, Fras., 14.
………, Sir Fras., 268.
………, Sir Geo., 14, 135, 139, 155, 156, 164, 486.
………, Geo., Lord Carew of Clopton, Master of Ordnance, and Vice-Chamberlain to the Queen, 218, 340, 363, 365, 373, 378, 385, 392, 393, 394, 454, 457, 470, 471, 565, 569, 587.
………, ……, journey of to Ireland, 41, 48, 59.
………, ……, letters of, 24, 47, 173, 457, 496, 599.
………, ……, ……, to Roe, 284, 344, 345, 424–428, 514–517.
………, ……, warrants, &c. to, 36, 37, 45, 105, 205, 355, 417, 435.
………, Lady, 573, 592.
………, Sir Hen., 39, 512.
………, Sir Matt., 166, 354, 380, 397.
………, ……, letters of, 172, 362, 392, 399, 402, 416, 486, 495, 529.
………, Lady, 362.
………, Thos., 392–4, 397, 399, 400, 402, 486, 529.
Carey, Sir Edw., Master of Jewels, 94, 101, 123, 594.
………, Sir Geo., Lord Deputy of Ireland, 514, 562.
………, Sir Hen., Master of Jewels, 63, 95, 109, 120, 249, 504, 505, 511, 512, 519; Comptroller of the Household, 529, 585, 594, 596, 598.
………, Sir Phil., 94, 275.
………, Sir Robt., 11, 18, 21, 85, 114, 115, 216, 224, 564.
Carey, Elizabeth, Lady, 11, 21.
………, Thos., 115.
………, Dr. Valentine, 81, 110, 205, 473.
………, John, Lord Hunsdon, 378, 398, 458, 461, 514.
Cargell, Thos., 405, 406.
Carill, Sir John, 120.
………, Sir John, jun., 120.
………, Sir Thos., 120.
Carisius, or Charisius, Jonas, Danish Ambassador, 70–3, 75, 80, 81, 94, 97.
Carleton, 15.
Carleton Barron, 506.
Carleton, Alice, letters to, 236, 398, 603; *see* Chamberlain.
……… Bostock, 597.
………, Dudley, 392, 459, 503, 521, 530, 577, 594.
………, Sir Dudley, 70, 256, 266, 284, 352, 392, 421, 425, 477, 501, 503, 607.
………, ……, letters of, 61, 74, 188, 219, 231, 477 578.
………, ……, letters of, to Chamberlain, 127, 232, 492, 495.
………, ……, letters to, 4, 9, 18, 24, 30, 48, 54, 59, 70, 77, 103, 104, 110, 121, 126, 151, 162, 169–74, 221, 229, 237, 270, 273, 277, 289, 301, 357, 362–4, 368, 369, 373, 381, 383, 384, 392–4, 398, 399, 402–4, 412, 414, 416, 417, 421, 434, 437–9, 443, 445, 449, 450, 459–61, 464, 466, 470–5, 477–9, 481, 482, 485, 486, 488, 490–2, 495, 499, 502–4, 510, 512, 513, 521, 523–5, 527, 529, 531, 533, 534, 548, 552, 564, 565, 567, 568, 571, 575, 577, 581, 585, 587, 588, 590–2, 594, 595–600, 602–4; *see also* Abbot, Biondi, Brent, Chamberlain, Danvers, Harwood, Herbert, Savile, Sherburn, Quester, Vere, Wake, Williams, Winwood.
………, Anna, Lady, 117, 121, 162, 174, 221, 236, 277, 364, 383, 384, 402, 460, 501, 528, 529, 530, 534, 577.
………, Edw., 459, 512, 597, 602.
………, Geo., 219, 410, 577.
………, ……, letters of, 54, 103, 277, 392, 459, 461, 503, 512, 521, 530, 594.
………, Dr. Geo., 217, 231, 400, 497, 500; Bp. of Llandaff, 553, 554, 584.
………, ……, letters of, 77, 104, 216, 273, 399, 466, 489, 499.
………, John, 160, 592.
………, Matt., 597.
………, Mr., 70.
Carlisle, 1, 82, 83, 443, 464, 475, 476, 480, 482.
………, citadel, 20, 261, 401.
………, gaol, 240.
………, letters from, 120, 153, 537, 539.
………, Bp. of, *see* Snowden.
………, diocese of, 399, 400.
Carlisle, Robt., 128, 136.
Carlton, 352.
Carlton, Thos., 47.

Carmarthen, Rich., 118, 605.
Carmarthen, 79.
.... Priory, 553.
Carmarthenshire, 280.
........., grants of lands in, 63, 124, 159, 196, 211, 241, 249, 280, 284.
........., offices in, 16, 209, 352.
........., towns, &c. in, 25, 298, 355, 553.
Carmelite friars, 135, 136, 138, 167, 176, 212, 221, 222, 227, 274; *see* Vandoni, Giulio Cesare, and Maria, Giovanni Battista.
Carmichael, Sir Hugh, 191, 409, 558.
........., Wm., 590, 605.
Carnallen, 115.
Carnanton, 159.
Carnarvon Castle, 606.
Carnarvonshire, grants of lands in, 124, 230.
........., offices in, 53, 249, 289, 372, 431.
........., residents in, 355, 524.
Carnsew House, 279.
Carnsew, Rich., 201, 279.
........., Wm., 279.
Caron, Sir Noel de, Holland Ambassador, 13, 21, 71, 89, 109, 111, 126, 269, 270, 343, 368, 406, 417, 447, 452, 456, 481.
........., ..., grants to, 50, 159, 251.
Carpenter, Wm., 182.
........., Mr., 424.
Carr, Sir Robt., 10; Visct. Rochester, 18, 37, 41, 98, 124, 127, 135, 138, 142, 154, 156, 161, 166, 170, 174, 181, 182, 185, 188, 199, 202; Treasurer of Scotland, Baron Brancepeth, Earl of Somerset, 204, 205, 212, 224, 225, 227, 232; Provisional Governor of Cinque Ports, and Keeper of Privy Seal, 240, 242; Lord Chamberlain, 245, 261, 263, 270, 272, 284, 286, 291, 293, 294, 296, 305, 323, 328, 329, 330, 344, 352, 366, 379, 479, 496.
........., ..., Arms and Garter of, 27, 31, 40, 381, 384.
........., ..., connection of with Overbury's murder, 307, 311–21, 324–34, 336, 342–4, 347–50, 359–64, 367–70, 372, 373, 381, 384, 385, 387, 392, 415.
........., ..., debts of, 323, 385, 544.
........., ..., grants of lands, &c. to, 52, 160, 211, 212.
........., ..., promotions of to office, 43, 115, 137, 203, 239, 244, 270.
........., ..., imprisonment of, 387, 391, 426, 471, 534, 585.
........., ..., lands, &c. of, 398, 401, 405, 410, 426, 444, 449, 506, 595.
........., ..., letters of, 95, 151, 152, 187, 239, 252, 260, 315.
........., ..., letters to, 81, 139, 143, 144, 147, 155, 165, 166, 193, 195, 198, 199, 203, 213, 215, 220, 223, 226, 228, 229, 233, 234, 237, 240, 250, 253, 255, 258, 261–4, 271–3, 278, 289, 316; *see also* Abbot, Winwood, Northampton, &c.
Carr, Sir Robt., marriage of, 205, 211, 212, 217, 219, 347.
........., ..., payments to, 48, 57, 120, 211.
........., ..., petitions to, 211, 265, 296, 300.
........., ..., secretary to, *see* Packer, John.
........., ..., servants to, 307, 313, 316, 319, 320, 325, 328, 345, 373.
........., Frances, Countess of Essex and Somerset, 217, 220, 225, 227, 332, 345, 385, 412, 469, 475; *see also* Devereux, Frances, Countess of Essex.
........., ..., connection of with Overbury's murder, 310–25, 327, 329–36, 338, 339, 342–4, 347, 349, 359–63, 367–70, 372, 373, 381, 382, 384, 387.
........., ..., imprisonment of, 387, 391, 426, 471, 585.
........., Lady Anne, 372.
........., Geo., 479, 480, 483.
........., Sir Jas., 179.
........., Sir Robt., 179, 216, 224, 250, 263, 349, 363, 364, 444, 506.
........., Sir Wm., 514.
Carre, Jean, 13.
Carrier, Dr., 203.
........., Rich., 291.
Carrolle, Thos., 378.
Carse, John, 89, 159, 366.
Carter, Fras., 17.
........., Francesco, 264.
........., Giles, 381.
........., Mr., 271.
........., (priest), 302.
Carthagena, 86.
Casaubon, Dr. Isaac, 22, 90, 115, 154, 231, 242, 476.
Caspian Sea, 182.
Castell, John, 423.
Castle Ashby, 139, 387.
.... Cornet, Guernsey, 45.
.... Hill, 470.
Castle, John, 116, 257, 309, 345, 346, 554.
Castleton, 276.
Caswall, Joan, 339.
Catelyne (preacher), 254.
Cater, Wm., 549.
Caterham, 493.
Catesby, Robt., 62, 485, 580.
........., Anne, 580.
........., Sir Wm., 176.
Cathan, 195.
Catholics, Roman, 16, 59, 104, 143, 227, 290, 399, 405, 422, 423, 473, 549, 556, 558.
........., conspiracies, &c. of, 5, 23.
........., English, 1, 61, 162, 168, 301–4, 324, 327, 353, 366, 415, 466, 520, 596.
........., ..., abroad, 64, 392.
........., examinations of, 482, 485, 510, 517.
........., increase of, 71, 237.
........., Irish, 186, 197.
........., names of, 269, 301, 347, 400.
........., northern, 135, 369, 455, 465.

Catholics, proceedings against, 26, 199, 285, 302, 303.
Cato, Marcus Porcius, 179.
Cattendick, 360.
Caulfield, Sir Toby, 258.
Caurne, or Cornée, David, 146, 483, 572.
Cautionary Towns (Flushing and Brill), *see* Holland, Cautionary Towns of.
Caux, Salomon de, 129, 195.
Cavane, Mons., 568.
Cavendish, Sir Chas., 286, 289, 310, 314, 334, 460, 514.
........., Hen., 426.
........., Hugh, 374.
........., Sir Wm., 249, 425, 490.
........., Wm. Lord, 35, 214, 426, 518; Earl of Devon, 564.
Cawood Castle, 541.
Cawson, 132.
Cawston, 88.
Cayton, 18.
Cecil, Sir Edw., General, 44, 124, 178, 180, 209, 211, 368, 393, 408, 414, 425, 510, 512, 514, 521.
........., ..., letters of, 153, 492, 567.
........., Theodosia, Lady (wife of Sir Edward), 209, 425.
........., Robt., first Earl of Salisbury, Secretary of State, Master of Wards, Lord Treasurer, Chancellor of Cambridge, &c., 3, 4, 11, 12, 51, 96, 104, 119, 130, 132, 134–138, 140, 145, 150, 152, 172, 177, 209, 218, 305, 308, 355, 366, 563.
........., ..., commissions to, 7, 18, 38, 125, 165.
........., ..., grants to, 38, 67, 68.
........., ..., lands, buildings, &c. of, 4, 52, 78.
........., ..., letters of, 13, 56, 58, 74, 76, 79, 80, 83, 85, 93, 112, 119, 125.
........., ..., letters to, 1–44, 46–49, 51–56, 58–102, 105, 106, 109–114, 116–20, 122–26, 128–30.
........., ..., notes by, 2, 26, 77, 92, 107, 131.
........., ..., official transactions of, 13, 44, 50, 64, 74, 79, 91, 105, 125, 160, 610.
........., ..., papers addressed to, 19, 42, 107, 108.
........., ..., payments to, 65, 109.
........., ..., petitions to, 25, 26, 37, 45, 50, 59, 66, 89, 91, 106, 107, 116, 127, 130, 131–3.
........., ..., secretary of, 127, 129.
........., ..., warrants to, 21, 34, 40, 43, 101.
........., ..., illnesses and death of, 39, 96, 115, 121, 123, 124, 126–129, 133.
........., ..., burial of, 134.
........., ..., epigrams, &c. on, 107, 134, 136, 140, 162, 183.
........., ..., daughter of, *see* Clifford, Frances.
........., Wm., Visct. Cranborne, 2, 4, 9, 13, 30, 115; second Earl of Salisbury, 167, 177, 278, 374, 404, 405, 412, 432, 441, 452, 458, 489, 498, 586.
........., ..., letters of, 552, 575.
........., ..., son of, 425, 426.
Cecil, Cath., Countess of Salisbury, 169, 170, 517, 603.
Cecil, Thos., Earl of Exeter, 72, 86, 133, 305, 347, 379, 386, 387, 426, 430, 481, 493, 494, 500, 539, 543, 582, 603.
........., ..., cause of, against Sir T. Lake, &c., 512, 518, 520, 523, 524, 594, 595, 600.
........., Frances, Countess of Exeter, 356, 412, 543, 586.
........., ..., cause of, against Lake, &c., 512, 513, 518, 520, 523–5, 531, 543, 585, 599, 604.
........., Lady Eliz., 235.
........., Lady Anne, 426.
........., Wm. Lord Burleigh, 35, 263, 386.
........., Eliz. Lady Burleigh, 514.
........., Wm. Lord Roos, 153, 295, 341, 382, 386, 387, 463, 582, 596, 601, 602.
........., ..., letters of, 13, 16, 18, 28, 137, 542.
........., ..., marriage of, 345, 425.
........., ..., embassy of to Spain, 363, 364, 393, 394, 397, 398, 403, 426, 432, 454.
........., ..., quarrels of with Lake family, 411, 471, 472, 480, 481, 500, 532, 542, 543, 567.
........., ..., departure of from England, 480–3, 488.
........., ..., residence of abroad, 511, 512, 526, 530.
........., Anna, Lady Roos, marriage of, 411, 425, 524, 531.
........., ..., quarrels of with Lord Roos, 472, 481, 532, 543, 567, 582.
........., ..., cause of against the Countess of Exeter, 512, 513, 520, 523, 525, 526, 575.
Cecil House, Strand, 494.
Chadwell, 16, 365.
Chaldecott, Robt., 288.
Chalfont St. Giles', 185.
Chalk, 364.
Challoner (or Chaloner), Sir Thos., 186, 198, 344.
Chaloner, Thos., 276.
Chalvington, 278.
Chamber, Simon, 590.
Chamber, Treasurer of, *see* Stanhope, John, Lord; Uvedale, Sir Wm.
Chamberlain, Lord, *see* Howard, Earl of Suffolk; Carr, Earl of Somerset; Herbert, Earl of Pembroke.
Chamberlain, Edm., 561.
........., Fras., 100.
........., John, 74, 171.
........., ..., letters of, 256.
........., ..., ..., to Carleton,
(1611):—72, 79, 85, 88, 90, 95, 96, 101, 104.
(1612):—111, 115, 119, 121, 123, 124, 127–9, 133–8, 143, 147, 153–6, 158, 162, 163.
(1613):—166–9, 172, 175, 177, 181, 183, 186, 187, 190, 196, 198, 202, 203, 205, 212, 214, 216.

Chamberlain, John, letters of, to Carleton—*continued.*
(1614):—219, 220, 222–5, 227, 228, 230, 231, 234–6, 239, 242, 244, 246, 250, 260–3.
(1615):—269, 270, 273, 274, 276, 278, 282, 286–8, 290, 294, 296, 305, 308.
(1616):—357, 361, 362, 364, 367, 368, 372, 375, 379, 384, 391, 392, 398, 400, 404, 407, 412, 414.
(1617):—422, 428, 432, 436, 441, 446, 453, 458, 460, 465, 469, 471, 473, 475, 476, 480, 483, 488–91, 494, 497, 500, 504.
(1618):—511–13, 518, 520–2, 524, 526, 527, 530, 532, 534, 535, 537, 538, 564–6, 584, 586, 588, 591, 595, 597, 598, 600, 602, 603.
........., ..., ..., to Alice Carleton, 169, 170, 217, 224, 225, 240, 271, 273, 282.
........., ..., letters to, 89, 477, 503.
........., Sir John, 234, 561.
........., Rich., 486.
........., Thos., 289, 363.
Chamberlaine, John (priest), 321.
Chambers, Chas., 30, 43, 72, 93, 157, 211.
........., Everard, 608.
........., Geo., 30, 72, 73, 93, 157, 498.
........., Dr. Jas., 446, 553.
Champante, Hen., 226.
Champneys, 365.
Chancellor, Lord High, *see* Egerton, Earl Ellesmere, and Bacon, Sir Fras.
Chancellor's house, 272.
Chancery, Court of, 119, 206, 272, 284, 290, 370, 381, 384, 406, 419, 453, 464–6, 510.
........., appeals or causes in, 3, 24, 182, 254, 266, 335, 387, 405, 501, 611.
........., clerks and protonotaries in, 24, 228, 253, 533, 589.
........., officers of, 14, 61, 393, 405, 416, 431, 498, 534.
........., wax in, 376.
Chandos, Lord, *see* Bruges, Grey.
Chapel Hainault, *see* Hainault.
.... Royal, *see* Edinburgh; James I.
Chapman, Dr. Alex., 370.
........., Clem., 451.
........., Hen., 38, 127.
........., John, 452.
........., Toby, 389.
Charcoal, 32.
Charcroft, Rich., 259.
Chard, 206.
Chard, John, 558.
Charing Cross, 24, 155, 162, 349, 372, 412, 490, 496.
Charities, money bequeathed to, 387, 462.
Charlcote, 193.
Charles, Prince, Duke of York, 67, 111, 130, 135, 149, 155, 160–3, 230, 232, 258; Prince of Wales, 273, 276, 302, 328, 334, 354, 370, 373, 376, 395, 397, 404, 413, 436–8, 454, 464–6, 478–9, 492, 533, 560, 564, 585.
........., amusements of, 171, 488, 511, 512, 523, 526.
........., Court of, 399, 606.
........., creation of, as Prince of Wales, 261, 373, 397, 398, 401–4, 427.
........., designs against, 331, 335, 345, 491.
........., expenses of, 18, 50.
........., gifts to, 189, 375, 414, 417, *see* Jas I., gifts of.
........., house of, *see* St. James's.
........., household of, 18, 114, 122, 162, 179, 190, 205, 209, 211, 213, 216, 373, 441, 443, 444, 449.
........., installation of as Knight of the Garter, 27, 48, 451.
........., jewels of, 171, 278.
........., journeys and sojourns of, 138, 172, 175, 181, 256, 277, 305, 361, 387, 392, 410, 448, 464, 491, 503, 515, 518, 521.
........., lands of, 3, 11, 28, 49, 139, 312, 398, 438, 443.
........., marriage negotiations for, 161, 163, 183, 237, 349, 361, 404, 427, 461, 511.
........., masters, &c. of, 21, 64, 86, 222, 312.
........., officers, &c. of, 28, 206, 235, 248, 373, 415, 417, 426, 454, 506, 529, 584, 594.
........., personal notices of, 158, 160, 199, 407.
........., portraits of, 160, 171, 489.
........., presence of at entertainments, &c., 345, 392, 487, 494, 495, 501, 511, 512.
........., purchase of models for, 368, 383, 395, 397–9.
........., revenues of, 428, 490, 560.
........., secretary of, *see* Murray, Thos.
........., servants of, 6, 29, 41, 42, 85, 179, 180, 212, 271, 414, 444, 531, 604, 606.
........., stables and horses of, 41, 48, 98.
........., title of to Duchy of Cornwall, 172.
........., tradespeople of, 107, 189, 228, 296.
Charles I., 155.
Charles V., 189.
Charleton, Robt., 287.
Charlton, 195.
Charminster, 297.
Charrold, Thos., 298.
Charter House, or Sutton's Hospital, 45, 79, 101, 106, 127, 135, 178, 179, 186, 188, 190, 205, 246, 499.
.... Yard, 482.
Chatham, 302, 415, 590.
Chatterton, John, 540.
Chattock, Mrs., 334.
Chawford, 5.
Chaworth, Sir Geo., 12, 73, 210, 228, 277, 360, 385, 386.

Chaworth, Lady, 42.
Cheek, Lady, 273, 427.
Cheetwood, Sir Rich., 213, 214, 508.
Cheins, 13.
Cheke, Dr., 282.
Chelmsford, 257, 453, 535, 557.
Chelsea, 522, 548.
Cheltenham, 123.
Cheque, clerks of, 26, 138, 302, 387, 531; *see also* Prick and Cheque.
Cherry Island, 178.
Cherry, Sir Fras., 169.
........., Eliz., 169.
Chertsey, 254, 392, 459.
Cheshire, 117, 325, 453, 471.
........., lands and places in, 218, 386, 372, 500.
........., offices in, 177, 189, 249, 289, 353, 363.
........., residents in, 60, 218, 379, 433, 458, 492, 522, 553, 597.
Cheshunt House and Park, 12, 86, 278, 444, 463.
.... Parish, 121, 356.
Chester, 45, 159, 258, 325, 343, 520, 565, 598.
........., alms rooms in, 76.
.... Castle, 189, 226.
........., Court of Exchequer at, 180, 181, 189.
........., Earldom and co. Palatine of, 45, 46.
........., mayor, &c. of, 565, 578.
........., merchants, &c. of, 278, 343.
........., Bp. of, *see* Lloyd, Geo.; Morton, Thos.
.... diocese of, 154, 383.
.... prebends of, 506.
Chester Herald, *see* Knight, Thos.; Chitting, Hen.
Chesterfield Park, 225.
Chesterford, 284, 361.
Chesterward, 587.
Chevening, 293.
Cheyne, 480.
Cheyne Court, 447.
Cheyney, Ra., 441.
Chibborne, Charles (serjeant), 371.
Chiche, 201, 212.
Chichester, 19, 154, 190, 506, 598.
........., Bp. of, *see* Harsnet, Sam.
Chichester, Sir Art., Lord Deputy of Ireland, 22, 23, 67, 113, 145; Lord Chichester, 172, 228, 244, 345, 361, 425, 426.
........., Frances, Lady, 225, 287, 344, 595.
Chief Barons, *see* Exchequer.
.... Justices, *see* King's Bench and Common Pleas.
.... in Eyre, *see* Talbot, Earl of Shrewsbury, and Villiers, Sir George, North; Howard, Earl of Nottingham, South.
Child, Geo., 246.
China, 427.
Chipley, 35.
Chippenham, 508.
Chippenham Forest, 165, 534, 574.
Chipping Campden, 467.
.... Norton, 158.
Chiswick, 227.
Chitting, Hen., Chester Herald, 553.
Cholmley, Sir Rich., 126.
Cholmondeley, Sir Robt., 128.
Chopwell Forest, 80, 332, 445.
Chowne, Sir Geo., 29.
Chretienne, Mdme., Princess of France, 573.
Christendom, 327, 517.
Christian, Robt., 284.
Christian IV., King of Denmark, 9, 10, 11, 28, 60, 71–74, 97, 98, 128, 129, 180, 208, 249, 250.
Christmas, Brice, *alias* Ayliff, 408, 434, 436, 450, 514.
........., Rich., 416.
........., Wm., 41, 274.
Christopher, Geo., 402.
........., Mr. 163.
Chubbe, Matt., 206, 225.
Church, Clem., 611.
Church affairs, 216, 234, 379; *see also* Religion.
Church of England, 216, 329, 339, 405, 460, 489, 576.
Church of Rome, 221, 231, 279, 428, 510, 526; *see also* Rome.
Churches reformed, 595.
Churchill, Mr. 44.
Chute Forest, 45, 57.
Chute, Geo., 96.
........., Sir Wal., 7, 96, 210, 234, 237, 256.
Cicero, Marcus Tullius, 613.
Cinque Ports, 36, 180, 260, 377, 417, 458, 460, 464, 465, 501, 502, 512.
........., Admiralty Court of, 180.
........., Marshal of, *see* Ward, Wm.
........., Chancery Court, 567.
........., coasts of, 190, 222, 409, 412, 483.
........., Lord Wardens of, 421; *see also* Howard, Hen., Earl of Northampton, Zouch, Edw. Lord.
........., mayors, &c. of, 108, 110, 226, 407, 421, 528, 545.
........., officers, &c. of, 190, 222, 226, 243, 262, 266, 297, 298, 421, 422, 433, 538.
........., places in, 179, 226, 297, 317.
........., provisional governor of, *see* Carr, Earl of Somerset.
........., rights and jurisdiction of, 108, 352, 369, 408, 409, 463, 481, 611.
Cistercian monk, *see* Spanish monk.
Clanricarde, Earl and Countess of, *see* Burgh.
Clapham, Steph., 338.
Clare, Sir Fras., 268.
........., John, 528.
........., Ralph, 268.
........., Mrs., 173.
Clarencieux, *see* Camden, Wm.
Clark, John, 449.

Clark, Martin, 449.
........., ——, 37, 54.
Clarke, Mich., 590.
........., Rich., 486.
........., Wm. (postmaster), 126.
........., Wm. (forester), 191.
........., Wm. (of London), 221, 354.
Clavell, John, 434.
........., Sir Wm., 188.
Claxton, 318.
Claxton, Hamond, 300.
........., Sir John, 291, 302, 328.
Clay, Nath., 549.
Clayton, John, 527.
........., Dr., Thos., 118.
Cleaver, Robt., 254.
Cleere, Sir Edw., 268.
........., Edw., 268.
Clement VIII., Pope, 305.
Clench-juxta-Wyke, 357.
Cleobury, 235.
Clergy, 168, 234, 237, 241, 395, 432, 465.
........., musters, &c. of, 177, 178, 181, 182, 258, 260, 289, 290, 313, 319, 322, 327, 364, 541, 543.
Clerk, Edm., 338, 369, 452, 504.
........., Hum., 493.
........., Jas., 122.
........., Sir Simon, 493.
........., Sir Thos., 44, 272, 350, 369, 452, 504.
Clerke, Hen., 276.
........., Sam., 276.
Clesby, Humph., 301, 302, 431, 439, 447.
Cleveland, 302.
Cleves, 22, 155, 246, 251.
Clewer, 478, 590.
Clifford, Geo., 3rd Earl of Cumberland, 297.
........., Margt., Countess Dowager of Cumberland, 38, 370, 425.
........., Fras., 4th Earl of Cumberland, 21, 49, 51, 82, 242, 347, 348, 446, 481, 482, 521.
........., ..., letters of, 220, 315.
........., ..., letters of, to Salisbury, 2, 8, 20, 24, 27, 35, 36, 38, 68, 69, 83, 91, 92, 111, 120.
........., ..., letters to, 1, 36.
........., Grissel, Countess of Cumberland, 82, 196.
........., Hen., Lord, 20, 27, 68, 83, 111, 120, 405, 446.
........., ..., letters of, 1, 2, 4, 12, 16, 25, 43, 51, 60, 80, 537.
........., Lady Frances, 1, 68, 82.
Cliffords, the, 165.
Clifford's Inn, 318, 335.
Clifton, 271.
Clifton, Amias, 295.
........., Gervase, Lord, 42, 66, 127, 505, 511, 517, 584, 585, 596.
........., ..., daughter of, *see* Stuart, Cath.
........., Mr., 304.
Clink, prisoners in, 253, 283, 458, 549.
........., liberties of, 573.
Clinton, Edw., 11th Earl of Lincoln, 315.
........., Hen., 12th Earl of Lincoln, 315, 344.
........., Eliz., Countess of Lincoln, 54, 104.
........., Thos., 13th Earl of Lincoln, 394, 548, 553.
Clitheroe, 43.
Clitterbooke, Adrian, 89.
Clive Forest, 266.
Cloth (broadcloth, baize, &c.), 20, 69, 76, 98, 350, 394, 402, 404, 428, 459, 526, 550, 561, 571, 595, 607.
........., customs on, 165, 348, 444, 548, 550.
........., deceits in, and searches of, 181, 219, 389, 395, 535, 591.
........., manufacture of, 253, 271, 393, 529.
........., trade in, sale, or purchase of, 164, 259, 389, 390, 406, 408, 410, 542, 543, 561.
........., dyed and dressed, 287, 291, 297, 310, 377, 385, 428, 548, 592.
........., ..., export and import of, 140, 141, 147, 174–6, 280, 288, 291, 348, 393, 428.
........., undyed and undressed, export and import of, 165, 174, 175, 247, 261, 275, 297, 348, 349, 358, 500, 561.
Clothiers and cloth makers, 19, 69, 275, 287, 377, 389, 395, 454, 459, 542, 548, 550, 554, 561; *see also* London, Companies of.
Clowse Cross, 413, 430, 465.
Clun, manor of, 137.
Coade, Jas., 224.
Coal, 13, 287, 291.
........., customs on, 198, 566.
Coal mines, 188, 241, 387.
........., Scotch, 256.
Coal, surveyors of, 351, 374, 375, 556.
.... meters, 67, 253.
Cobham, 144.
.... Hall, 151.
Cobham, Lord, *see* Brooke, Henry.
Cochrane, Robt., 389.
Cock, Sir Hen., 84.
........., widow, 498.
Cockayne, Thos., 2, 507.
........., Wm. Alderman, 55, 360; Sir Wm., 375, 419, 427, 545, 590.
........., ..., connection of with New Merchant Adventurers, 357, 373, 389, 390, 406, 410, 423.
........., Wm., 360.
.... (widow), 360.
Cocken, 82.
Cockes, Geo., 229.
Cockhamstead, 70, 84.
Cockpit, the, 316, 322, 323, 338.
Cocks, Dr., 378.
Codinton, Lawr., 492.
Codwell, John, 190.
Cofferer of the Household, *see* Vernon, Sir Robt.; Ingram, Sir Arthur; Darell, Sir Marmaduke.

Coffin, Thos., 206.
Coggeshall, 230.
Coin and coinage, 47, 83, 91, 92, 101, 113, 128, 129, 143, 164, 241, 267, 396, 603, 605, 608.
Coin, clipping of, 206, 225, 248, 278, 396, 502, 503, 528.
........., export and import of, 32, 81, 112, 113, 129, 279, 305, 379, 396, 593, 595.
Coinage, foreign, 92, 396, 424, 474, 603.
.... warrants for, 23, 98, 99, 385.
.... of farthings, 140, 141, 174, 175, 180, 184, 215, 237, 258, 322, 387, 456.
Coiners, 175.
Coining, crime of, 15, 138, 139, 293, 313, 450.
Coke, Sir Edw., Lord Chief Justice of Common Pleas, 11, 13, 176; Lord Chief Justice of King's Bench, 207, 215, 216, 310, 349, 358, 371, 379, 386, 412, 415, 432, 436, 447, 467, 470, 471, 476, 477, 483-5, 487, 489, 492, 494, 496, 497, 511.
........., ..., contests of with his wife, 469-471, 488, 495, 515, 530.
........., ..., disgrace of, 372, 373, 375, 376, 378-81, 387, 397, 398, 400, 402-8, 411, 443.
........., ..., institutes of, 400.
........., ..., letters of, 223, 307, 315, 319, 324, 376.
........., ..., ..., to Jas. I., 316, 317, 319, 320, 329, 333, 335-7, 348.
........., ..., letters to, 91, 307, 314, 315, 318, 320-3, 327, 330, 331, 335, 336, 347, 362, 371, 415.
........., ..., notes and endorsements by, 267, 332, 356, 360, 609.
...., official transactions of, 176, 239, 275, 277, 360.
........., ..., petitions to, 315, 324, 325, 339.
........., ..., proceedings of, on trials for Overbury's murder, 307, 313, 316, 319, 320, 322, 324, 326, 330-4, 336, 337, 342, 343, 345, 347-50, 362.
........., ..., promotions, &c. of, 202, 203, 205, 392, 413, 414, 432, 482, 511, 566, 581.
........., ..., warrants to, 317, 560.
........., Lady Eliz., 375, 376, 379, 380, 387, 406, 407, 411, 412, 467, 469-71, 476, 477, 481-3, 487, 488, 491-7, 511, 515, 528, 530, 531, 598.
........., ..., father of, see Cecil Thos., Earl of Exeter.
........., Frances, 414, 477, 478, 481-3, 487, 491, 497.
........., Sir John, 232, 360, 559.
........., Sir Rob., 215.
........., Mr., 608.
Coker, Isabel, 169.
........., Lancelot, 169.
Colantino, Signor, 391, 397.
Colbert, Thos., 549.
Colborne, 404.
Colby, 421, 492, 534.
Colby, Chris., 539.
Colchester, 107, 396, 475, 535, 550, 557.
........., Dutch congregation at, 475.
Cold Ashby, 274.
Cold-Higham, 418.
Coldham Hall, 550.
Cole, John, 82.
........., Mich., 353.
........., Rich., 378.
........., Mrs. Redigon, 253.
Coles, Humph., 596.
Colleges, foreign, see Seminaries.
Collever, John, 55.
Collingwood, Alice, 14.
........., Mr., 14, 54.
Collins, John, 548.
........., Nich., 116.
Colman, Morgan, 13, 22, 23.
........., Wm., 467.
Colmore, Dr., 113.
Colne, 498.
Cologne, 3.
Colphab, Ra., see Coryat, Thos.
Colson, Wm., 168.
Colvile, Capt. Jas., 595.
........., Rich., 268.
........., Sir Thos., 268.
Colwich, 192.
Colwick, 155.
Comedy, see Drama.
Comes, John, 374.
........., Thos., 374, 379.
Comet, the, 597, 601.
Comley, Pet., 538.
Commerce, see Trade.
Common Pleas, court of, 37, 60, 75, 78, 122, 299, 463, 510.
........., ..., chief justices of, see Coke, Sir Edw.; Hobart, Sir Hen.
........., ..., judges of, 501.
........., ..., clerks of, 407, 410.
........., ..., offices in, 203, 234, 362, 398, 463, 469.
Commons, House of, 23, 27, 71, 80, 156, 196, 231, 232, 234, 235, 236, 237, 241.
Companies, see London Companies.
Compton, 6, 24.
Compton, Sir Spencer, 493.
........., Sir Thos., 430.
........., Mary, Lady, 379, 380, 405, 476, 477, 494, 497, 527; Countess of Buckingham, 550, 564.
........., Wm. Lord, 458, 483, 490; President of Wales, 493, 498, 516, 518; Earl of Northampton, 563.
Comptroller of the Household, see Wotton, Edw., Lord; Edmondes, Sir Thos.; Carey, Sir Hen.
Concealed lands, see Crown lands, concealed.
Condé, Henri de Bourbon, Prince of, 391, 461.
Coney, Mr., 471.
Conformity, 72, 254, 295.

Congerston, 232.
Coningsby, Sir Phil., 87.
........., Sir Ralph, 357.
........., Sir Rich., 296, 297, 420, 444, 596.
Coningshead Priory, 209.
Conley, Pat., 469.
Connaught, Governor of, *see* Wilmot, Sir Charles.
Connock, Rich., 72, 160, 217, 440.
........., Wm., 606.
Conquet, 412.
Consford, 161.
Constable, Harry, 95.
........., Sir John, 249.
........., Phil., 295.
........., Sir Robt., 386.
........., Sir Wm., 212, 220.
Constantinople, 88, 515.
Conti, François de Bourbon, Prince of, 166.
Contribution, *see* James I., Benevolence to.
Conway, Sir Edw., 139, 162, 183, 227, 364, 388, 425, 445, 447.
........., ..., letters of and to, 374, 379, 511, 523, 531.
........., Jas., 11.
........., Sir John, 137.
........., Lady, 553.
Conyer, Mr., 19, 20.
Conyers, Fras., 139, 162, 227, 374, 379.
........., Geo., 447.
........., Graye, 227.
Coo, Thos., 129, 584.
........., Wm., 468.
........., Eliz., 468.
Cook, Wm., 284.
Cooke, Anne, Lady, 87.
........., Sir Edw., 16.
........., Jas., 612.
........., John, 196.
........., Rich., 435.
........., Sir Rich., 262, 270.
........., Robt., 531.
........., Sir Robt., 508.
........., Wm., 125.
........., Sir Wm., 25, 27, 555.
........., Sir ——, 231.
Cookham, 89, 130, 451, 572.
Cooley, John, 611.
........., Mich., 611.
Cooper, John, 502.
........., (or Cowper), Rich., 283, 321.
........., Robt., 467.
Coote, Sir Nich., 535, 557.
Cope, Sir Ant., 63, 237, 245.
........., John, 574.
........., Sir Wal. 39, 104, 116, 133, 134, 136; Master of the Wards, 156, 158, 172, 176, 188, 222, 233, 234, 246, 251, 261, 273.
........., ..., as contractor for lands, 122, 193.
........., ..., grants to, 14, 157.
........., ..., letters of, 4, 70.
Cope, Sir Wal., letters to, 74, 241.
........., ..., writings of, 138, 140, 164.
........., Dorothy, Lady, 48, 274, 282.
........., Sir Wm., 249, 276, 398.
Copeman, Rich., 365.
Copley, Wm., 24, 31, 176.
Copper, Thos., 612.
Copper works, 79, 111, 113, 250.
Copperas, Danish, 468.
Coppin, Sir Geo., 125, 163.
Coppinger, Mr., 343, 345.
Coppull, 498.
Copyhold lands, *see* Crown lands, Copyhold.
Corbet, John, 58, 104.
Corbett, Dr. Rich., 601.
Corbin, Hen., 338.
........., Thos., 353.
Corint (traveller), 427.
Cork, 515.
Corn and grain, 67, 122, 186, 232, 287.
........., customs on, 261, 391.
........., export of, 168, 261, 437.
Cornbury Park, 93, 102, 499.
Cornée, Dav., *see* Caurne.
Corney, Hen., 532.
Cornhill, *see* London, Streets of.
Cornwall, 182, 258, 325, 490.
........., grants of lands in, 63, 124, 159.
........., lands and places in, 10, 43, 79, 89, 156, 158, 242, 251, 509.
........., offices in, 200, 201, 224.
........., residents in, 71, 72, 100, 411, 412, 427, 496.
........., copper works in, 79.
........., tin in, 226, 253, 287.
........., Duchy of, 46, 95, 155, 156, 160, 172, 506.
Cornwallis, Sir Chas., Treasurer of Prince Henry, 76, 104, 161, 237, 238, 289, 344, 509.
........., Fred., 268.
........., Hen., 429.
........., Sir Thos., 429, 468, 602.
........., Sir Wm., 24, 43, 52, 90.
........., Lady, 90.
........., Sir Wm., jun., 159, 215, 242, 268, 515.
........., Mr., 213.
Corvin, Thos., 52.
Coryat, Thos., 72.
Costa, Peter de la, 194.
Coster, Mich. de, 253.
Cotgarth, 499.
Cotherstoke, 86.
Cotten, Pet., 315.
Cottenham, 542.
Cotterell, Clem., 600.
Cotterill, John, 545.
Cottingham, 596.
Cottingham, Sir Jas., 518.

Cottington, Fras., 86, 99, 104, 198, 200, 277; Agent to Spain, 345.
........., ..., letters of, 277, 489, 493, 529, 538, 547, 572, 603.
Cottle (customs' searcher), 419.
Cotton or calico, 206.
Cotton, Edw., 442.
........., Hen., Bp. of Salisbury, 7.
........., John, 57, 281.
........., John, 186.
........., Rich., 120, 431, 442.
........., Robt., 57.
........., Sir Robt., 99, 115, 127, 165, 166, 295, 305, 322, 341, 345, 359, 373, 375, 382, 425.
........., Thos., 57.
........., Wm., Bp. of Exeter, 119, 467, 517, 533.
Coult, Max., 451.
Council, the, see Privy Council and North, Council of.
Counties, Lieutenants, &c., of, 167, 185.
........., four English, see Gloucestershire, Herefordshire, Shropshire, Worcestershire.
Coupman, Jacob, 469.
Court, the, 67, 88, 169, 173, 183, 205, 214, 221, 230, 245, 284, 324, 327, 330, 360, 374, 390, 400, 407, 464, 477, 510, 513, 531.
........., amusements of, 103, 111, 177, 269, 392, 511, 514.
........., changes at, 174, 324, 441, 575.
........., diet at, 60, 390, 494, 501, 512, 525.
........., favour at, 414, 417, 422.
........., influence at, 150, 167, 346, 348.
........., ladies of, 339, 526.
........., letters from, 182, 285.
........., masques at, see Drama.
........., messengers at, 138.
........., news of, 79, 199, 391, 513, 460.
........., officers of, 504, 518, 575.
........., persons repairing to, 13, 18, 61, 172, 196, 203, 231, 273, 315, 318, 321, 329, 404, 484, 494.
........., progresses of, 308, 466, 469, 474, 568.
........., sermons at, see Sermons.
........., visitors to, 104, 128, 300, 495, 522, 524, 566.
Court, Wm., 9, 72.
Courthouse, John, 264.
Courtney, Sir Wm., 254.
Cousant, Thos., 390, 413, 482.
Covent Garden, 69.
Coventry, 126, 181, 424, 483, 484, 539.
.... and Lichfield, Bp. of, see Neyle, Rich.; Overall, John.
........., ..., diocese of, 30.
Coventry, Thos., Recorder of London, 407; Sir Thos., Solicitor-General, 446, 449, 471, 554, 566, 599, 601, 604.
Coverdale Forest, 189.
Covert, Sir Wal., 64.
Coward, John, 243.
Cowdry, 32.
Cowell, Dr. John, 36.
Cowes Castle, 243.
Cowley, Thos. 289.
Cowper, Ralph, 257.
Cowsfield, 596.
Cox, Mr., 532.
Coxe, Alban, 57.
........., Ann, 509.
........., Edw., 424.
........., John, 57.
........., Lawr., 509.
........., Sir Rich., 160, 162.
........., Thos., 424.
Crabbet, 124.
Crabes Cattle, 45.
Crafford, Thos., 28.
Craig, Dr. John, 132, 187, 205.
Cranborne chace, 78, 215, 394, 412, 451, 452.
........., Visct., see Cecil, Wm.
Cranche, Arnold, 168.
Crane, Fras., 75; Sir Fras., 524.
........., Rich., 596.
Cranfield, Lionel, 72, 144; Sir Lionel, 193, 346; Master of Requests, 427, 445, 454, 518, 519, 527; Master of the Wardrobe, 595, 597.
........., ..., grants, warrants, &c. to 194, 200, 248, 259, 325, 448, 542, 570.
........., ... promotions of, 190, 406, 408, 412, 428, 514, 540, 564.
Cranford, 597.
.... St. John, 597.
Cranston, Sir Wm., 1; Lord, 55, 73.
Cranwell, Thos., 169.
Crashaw, W. 12.
Craven, Sir Wm., 221, 492–4, 565; see also London, Lord Mayors of.
Crawley, Ant., 545.
Creichton, Sir Jas., 5, 33, 96.
........., Robt., Lord Sanquair, 128, 129, 134, 136, 138.
........., Mary, Lady Sanquair, 344.
........., Thos., 138.
Crema, Julio Camillo, 121.
Crenston, 374.
Crescentio, Johan Baptista, 266.
Cresswell, Jos. (priest), 3.
Cressy, Hugh, 194.
Creswell, Wal., 440.
........., Wm., 440.
Crew, Serjeant Randall or Ranulph, 227, 230; Sir Randall, 239, 240, 397, 398, 463.
Cricket, Chas., 524.
Crimble, Chas., 338, 372.
Crocker, Thos., 594.
Crockford, Rich., 354.
Croft, 262.

Croft, Sir Herbert, 229, 233, 262, 339, 464, 469, 488, 489, 553.
........., Anne, Lady, 488, 553.
........., Sir Jas., 17, 19, 20, 24, 43.
Croke, Sir John, Justice of King's Bench, 540.
Croker, John, 106.
Cromer, Sir Jas., 13, 172.
........., Lady, 400, 412.
Crompton, John, 2.
........., Thos., 234.
Cromwell, Dowager Lady Frances, 80.
........., Hen., 251.
........., Thos., Lord, 102, 504, 601.
........., *alias* Williams, Sir Oliver, 141, 190, 251, 295, 506, 555.
........., Anne, Lady, 141.
Crook, Sir Hen., 385, 486, 507.
Crooke, Dr. Hilkiah, 601.
Crookhaven, 66.
Crosby Hall, 530.
Cross, Sir Robt., 9.
Crosse, Wm., 258, 363.
Crossing-Temple, 523.
Crossland chace, 373.
Crowe, Mr., 384.
Crowland, 20.
Crown, debts of, 11, 27, 46, 60, 78, 106, 141, 143, 145, 296, 303, 310, 378, 421, 435, 489, 563.
........., debts to, 43, 44, 46, 71, 85, 103, 117, 127, 238, 285, 290, 346, 376, 386, 388, 389, 584, 597, 604, 609.
........., debts, grants of, 38, 66, 156, 159, 217.
........., debts, old, grants of, &c., 43, 55, 88, 128, 137, 193, 195, 357.
.... jewels, 428, 447.
.... lands, &c., 3, 11, 13, 14, 59, 65, 67, 68, 79, 112, 139, 165, 185, 188, 189, 208, 212, 241, 246, 251, 252, 265, 426, 471, 500, 559, 600, 601.
...., assart, 149, 153, 221, 259, 314, 334, 420, 506, 572.
...., chantry, &c., 10, 29, 39, 49, 55, 57, 63, 71, 122, 123, 181, 193, 265, 332, 374, 418, 564.
...., concealed, 126, 131, 137, 219, 293, 388, 419, 420, 499, 534, 563, 586, 589, 590.
...., copyhold, 7, 15, 43, 135, 143, 164, 278, 295, 298, 356, 357, 556, 608.
...., encroached, 499, 534, 572.
...., entailed, 17, 139, 181, 197, 215, 216, 219, 228, 231, 240, 296, 357, 405.
...., escheated, 23, 106, 444, 506, 607.
...., commissioners for sale or lease of, 7, 63, 81, 83, 84, 135, 173, 197, 203, 215, 216, 228, 231, 585.
...., alienations of, 8, 9, 119, 145, 354, 357, 418, 424, 428, 446, 452, 500, 542, 549.
Crown lands, grants of, 29, 32, 33, 41, 49, 62, 146, 148, 156, 189, 190, 192, 207, 241, 248, 265, 292, 293, 306, 353, 386, 445, 586.
...., sales and surveys of, 15, 43, 158, 340.
.... revenues, 3, 25, 27, 116, 135, 143, 155, 160, 165, 184, 195, 199, 214, 245, 267, 281, 295, 359, 377, 385, 396, 419, 424, 428, 430, 435, 439, 463, 479, 485, 507, 563, 584, 591, 608.
...., commissioners for, 502, 510, 537.
Croxford, Thos., 246.
Croxteth, 85.
Croydon, 90, 149, 199.
........., letters dated from, 138, 140, 142–145, 197, 249, 254, 477, 479, 482, 485, 565.
........., Cambridge, 507.
Crumpe, John, 612.
Cryfe, Jacob, 594.
Cubit, Rich., 483.
Cudner, Wm., 205.
Cudworth, Robt., 158.
Cullyver, John, 483.
Culverdon Grove, 35.
Cumberland, 92, 471, 539.
........., Earl and Countess of, *see* Clifford.
........., grants of land in, 63, 124, 159, 209, 211, 222, 242.
........., lands in, 10, 220.
........., offices in, 49, 215, 240, 537.
........., residents in, 209, 297, 444.
Cumbernauld, 527.
Cumming, Pat., 51.
Cummocke, Thos., 509.
Cunningham, Sir Jas. 538.
Cunworth, 596.
Curle, Fras., 269, 271, 280.
Currants, 177.
........., customs on, 216, 589.
Curson, Humph., 66.
Cursson, Hen., 153.
Curteen, Wm., 197.
Curtis, Fras., 244.
Curwen, Lady Eliz., 268.
Curzon, Lady, 84.
Cusack, John, 327.
Custom House, 585.
Customs, 16, 19, 49, 145, 192, 233—238, 250, 282, 310, 346, 384, 394, 435, 507, 562. *See also* Cards, Cloth, Currants, Leather, Merchandise, Pewter, Silk, Sugar, Tobacco, Wine, Wool, Customs on.
........., collectors and receivers of, 190, 411, 444, 553, 593, 598.
........., exemption from, 80, 239, 354, 585.
........., farmers of, 55, 78, 125, 144, 145, 147, 150—152, 163, 178, 193, 194, 249, 281, 335, 340, 354, 410, 419, 428, 446, 447, 450, 454, 485, 486, 506, 524, 532, 542, 547, 548, 550, 554.

Customs, grants of, 216, 235, 280, 445, 590, 609.
........., officers of, 149, 194, 227, 232, 235, 256, 296, 299, 305, 325, 402, 409, 459, 556, 589, 607, 610.
Cuthbert, Thos., 105.
Cutpurse Moll, 120.
Cuttell, Mr., 284.
Cyprian, T. C., 612.

D.

Dackombe, or Dacombe, John, 134, 208; Master of Requests, 225, 370; Sir John, Chancellor of the Duchy of Lancaster, 372, 394, 419, 466, 518, 519, 523, 534, 556, 602.
........., ..., grants to, 212, 220, 410, 506.
........., ..., letters of, 32, 69, 387, 394, 400, 419, 467, 468, 470, 478, 479, 489, 490, 494, 500, 502, 506.
........., ..., petitions to, 419, 509.
........., ..., private money affairs of, 405, 465, 491, 496, 498.
........., ..., private papers of, 518, 519.
........., ..., promotions of, 206, 289, 344, 372, 373.
........., ..., secretary to, *see* Nicholas, Edw.
........., Lady Melior, 487.
........., Alice, 225.
........., Nich., 523.
........., Wm., 242, 523, 534.
Dacre, 10.
Dacre, Lord and Lady of the South, *see* Lennard.
........., or Dacres, Fras., 61, 243.
........., ..., Eliz., 61.
........., Hen., 293.
........., Sir Thos. (of Essex), 83, 86, 121, 461.
........., ... (of Hertfordshire), 305.
Dacres, the, 202.
Daesy, 485.
Dakins, Art., 189.
........., Sir Art., 189.
Dade, John, 33.
Dale, Sir Thos., 253, 375, 425, 501, 503, 533.
........., Lady, 530.
Dalham, 190.
Dalival, M., 338.
Dalham, Thos., 379, 476.
Dallison, Sir Roger, Lieutenant of Ordance, 137, 187, 195, 205, 336, 346, 526, 529, 562.
Dalmahoy, Thos., 606.
Dalston, John, *see* Salkeld.
Damerseau, Denis, 525.
Damme, Christiana, 10.
Damport, Wm., 206, 299.
Dandine, Louis, 402.
Dane, Cath., 480.
Daniel, John, 549.
Daniell, John, 483.
Dann, Hen., 513, 525.
Danon, Hen., 484.
Dantzic merchants, 419.
Danvers, Hen., Lord, 167, 187, 199, 246, 279, 282, 354, 361, 362, 391, 553.
........., ..., letters of, to Carleton, 251, 341, 361, 363, 387, 390, 397, 399, 407, 461, 499.
........., Sir John, 68, 548.
........., Wm., 450.
Danyell, Sam., 223, 294, 549.
Darcy, Edw., 323.
........., Sir Edw., 268.
........., Sir Fras, 227.
........., Jane, 364.
........., Nich., 364.
........., Sir Robt., 268.
........., Thos., Lord (of Chiche), 40, 65, 101, 160, 162, 166, 201, 212, 444, 462.
........., Mary, Lady (of Chiche), 514.
........., John, Lord (of the North), 515.
Darell, John, 605.
........., Sir Marmaduke, 91, 114, 198; Cofferer of the Household, 225, 278, 294, 450, 538, 605.
........., Nath., 490.
........., Sampson, 114.
........., Lieut., 363.
Darleton, 99, 116.
Darley, Thos, 278, 364.
Darlington, 54.
Darnell, John, 468.
Darnley, Hen., King of Scots, 174, 329.
Darrent, Wm., 47.
Dartmouth, 29, 255, 598.
Darwin, Wm., 209.
Daubigny, or Dawbeney, Clem., 430, 602.
Dauncer, Giles, 541.
Danny, 381.
Daventry, 126.
David, Thos., 195.
Davids, Jeffrey, 322.
........., Robt., 240.
Davies, Capt. Edw., 356.
........., John, 68, 228, 293.
........., John (of Shropshire), 68, 293, 608
........., John, (traveller), 228.
........., Lawr., 184, 312, 315.
........., Rich. (priest), 321.
........., Wm. (priest), 321.
........., Mr., 147.
Davies' Sea, 516.
Davis, Silvanus, 295.
........., Wm., 196.
Davison, Edm., 172, 534.
Davy, John, 536.

Daw, Rich., 351.
Dawbeney, Clem., *see* Daubigny.
Dawes, Rich. 496.
........., Wm., 415, 496.
Dawnton, Nich., 223.
Dawser, Mr., 577.
Dawson, Edw., 447.
........., Thos., 356.
........., Mr., 439.
Day, John, 93.
Deal, 255, 336, 342, 396, 413, 430, 457, 482, 487. 490, 612, 614.
.... Castle, 305, 324, 414, 612, 613.
...., decay and repairs of, 324, 344, 367.
...., captain and garrison of, 148, 522, 582, 614.
...., muster rolls of, 83, 255, 308, 396, 484.
Dean, Forest of, 29, 32, 40, 46, 57, 107, 125, 130, 144, 145, 288, 296, 555.
Dean, Mr., 536.
Deane, Eliz., 420.
........., Capt. Hen., 420.
........., Thos., 331.
........., Wm., 271.
Debden, 121.
Deckham, *see* Dackombe.
Decro, John, 120.
Dee, Art., 354.
......, Dr., 246.
Deer, 31, 209, 308, 374; *see also* James I., Deer of.
Deering, Sir Ant., 343.
Defford, 467.
Delabere, Rich., 209.
Delapre, 118.
Delawarr, Lord, *see* West.
Delegates, Court of, 183, 200.
Denbighshire, 52, 191, 363.
........., lands in, 177, 191, 240, 275.
Denham, John, 279.
........., Sir John, Judge of Common Pleas, 398, 459; Baron of Exchequer, 463, 469.
........., Kath., 156.
Denis, Elinor, 131.
........., John, 131.
........., or Denys, Sir Thos., 18.
Denizens and denization, 376, 377, 396, 590, 605.
Denization, grants of, 84, 110, 179, 194, 210, 250, 271, 292, 293, 407, 449, 451, 551, 557, 593.
Denmark, 51, 88, 89, 113, 124, 143, 161, 419.
........., Ambassador of, 122–4, *see* Carisius.
........., Chancellor of, 51, 69.
........., King of, *see* Christian IV.
Denmark House, 442, 446, 493, 497, 514, 520, 526, 600.
Denn, Vincent, 612.
Denney, Edw., Lord, 11, 80, 443, 466.
Dent, 335.
Denton, co. Northumberland, 9, 14.
........., co. York, 300.
Deptford, 269, 354, 572, 590.
.... Strond, 75, 209.
Derby, 43, 47, 122.
........., Earl and Countess of, *see* Stanley.
Derbyshire, 258, 268, 293.
........., grants of lands in, 63, 159, 276, 405.
........., lands and places in, 207, 304, 404, 506.
........., lieutenants in, 181, 258.
........., recusants in, 43, 72, 73.
........., peak of, 291.
Derry, Bp. of, *see* Downham, Geo.
........., bishopric of, 190.
Destiny, the (ship), 428, 497, 583, 589.
Dethick, Hen., 54.
Devereux, Lady Dorothy, 286.
........., Lady Frances, 436.
........., Sir Geo., 79.
........., Robt., 2nd Earl of Essex, 344.
........., Robt., 3rd Earl of Essex, 147, 199, 200, 203, 223, 259, 286, 324, 338, 515.
........., ..., designs against, 173, 182, 183, 316.
........., ..., divorce of, 183, 186, 187, 190, 196, 199, 200, 202, 216.
........., Frances, Countess of Essex, 143, 172, 173, 182, 183, 187, 205, 213, 216; *see* Carr, Frances.
........., ..., divorce of, *see* Devereux, Robt.
........., Wal., 200.
Devizes, 68.
Devon, Earl of, *see* Cavendish, Wm.
Devonshire, 100, 182, 262, 267, 525, 548, 550.
........., grants of lands in, 63, 70, 124, 159, 606.
........., lands and places in, 89, 98, 156, 158, 296, 400.
........., offices in, 200, 283, 533, 534, 536, 565.
........., receivers in, 200.
........., residents in, 82, 496, 540, 545, 586.
........., tin in, 226, 287.
Dewhurst, Sir Bernard, Dean of the Arches, 487, 516.
........., Thos., 10, 12, 59.
Dial, equinoctial, 610.
Dibb, Pet., 180, 343, 349, 449.
Dickenson, Sir Thos., 499.
Dickinson, Edm., 75.
Diego, Don, 482, 596, 601, 602.
Dieppe, 341, 406, 525, 571, 576.
........., governor of, 267, 470, 544, 572, 576.
........., licences to fishermen of, 146, 190, 293, 309, 483, 485, 572.
Diet, Ant., 182.
Digby, Sir Everard, 292.
........., Geo., 493, 499.
........., John, 304.

Digby, Sir John, 218, 232; Vice-Chamberlain, 398, 405, 477; Lord Digby, 602.
........., ..., letters of, 126, 185, 199, 466.
........., ..., missions of, to Spain, 22, 71, 140, 145, 152, 220, 234, 247, 345, 348, 357, 403, 426, 447, 449, 453, 454, 461, 462, 464, 473, 480, 487, 489, 497, 516, 522, 535, 540.
........., ..., promotions of, 360, 417, 425, 597, 598.
........., Beatrix, Lady, 526.
........., Simon, 520.
........., Thos., 301, 302, 304.
........., Wm., 304.
Digbys, the, 399.
Diggs, Sir Dudley, 96, 174, 218, 225, 325, 533; Ambassador to Muscovy, 537, 585–7.
Dighton, Rich., 211.
Diglett, John, 365.
Dike, John, 356.
........., Rich., 33, 343.
Dilston, 365, 406.
Dimery, Mr., 125.
Dimsdale Creek, 388.
Dingley, Chas., 130.
Dingwall, Rich., Lord, 145, 296, 358, 361, 393, 595, 599.
Dinorben Vawr, 240.
Diodati, Dr. Giovanni, 301.
Dipdon, 375.
Dirdo, Thos., 191.
Dish, Rich., 68.
Diston, Wm., 484, 486.
Ditcher, John, 358.
Ditton House and Park, 21, 247, 447, 480, 595.
Dixon, Thos., 100, 276.
Dobbinson, Ra., 75.
Doctors' Commons, London, 174, 494.
Docwra, Sir Hen., Treasurer of Wars in Ireland, 360, 425, 558.
Dod, John, 92, 254.
Dodd, Edw., 189.
Dodderidge, Sir John, Judge of King's Bench, 158, 542.
Dodsall, Rich., 584.
Dollesquebe River, 198.
Domesday Book, 155, 588.
Donato, Ant., Venetian Ambassador, 591.
Doncaster, 301, 302, 468.
........., Visct., *see* Hay, James, Lord.
Donhalt, Geo., 228.
........., Leonore, 228.
Donne, John, 72, 278; Dr. John, 282, 284, 454.
Dorchester, 206, 244, 506.
Dormer, Sir John, 84, 412.
........., Sir Mich., 412, 503.
........., Sir Robt., 12, 267, 289; 1st Lord Dormer of Wing, 290, 344, 346, 408, 410, 412, 456.
........., Robert, 2nd Lord, 410, 412, 456.
Dormer, Sir Wm., 400, 410, 426.
Dorrington, Fras., 343.
Dorset, Earl of, *see* Sackville.
.... House, 18, 458.
Dorsetshire, 268.
........., grants of lands in, 63, 124, 159, 200, 211, 235, 251, 297, 386, 412, 451, 452.
........., lands and places in, 69, 108, 130, 158, 398.
........., residents in, 82, 191, 367, 607.
Dort, 341, 409.
.... Synod at, 584, 585, 587, 598.
Douay College, 54, 226, 280, 458.
Doubleday, Edw., Warden of the Mint, 20, 23, 385, 523.
Douglas, Geo., 110, 385, 592.
........., Sir Geo., 110, 385, 592.
........., Jas., 110, 159, 470.
........., John, 602.
........., Sir Robt., 120, 275.
Dove, Thos., Bp. of Peterborough, 74, 81, 83, 92, 254, 443.
........., Dr., 536.
Dover, 100, 109, 151, 202, 300, 306, 351, 354, 358, 364, 372, 393, 408, 413, 419, 509, 567, 571, 576, 592, 612.
.... Admiralty Court at, 358.
........., Chancery Court at, 266, 351, 380, 381, 389, 416, 611.
........., commissioners for passage at, 148, 308, 408, 430, 442, 469.
........., letters from, 306, 309, 343, 347, 349, 358, 383, 394, 398, 400, 401, 403, 406, 408, 409, 413, 416, 417, 430–3, 435, 442, 449, 469, 479, 485, 487, 490, 492, 495, 501, 566, 576, 587, 592.
........., mayor, &c. of, 180, 300, 308, 324, 366, 383, 391, 394, 398, 401–3, 408, 416, 422, 430, 481, 495, 513, 532, 540, 543, 584, 586, 587.
........., Mount, 416.
........., port and pier of, 28, 166, 301, 306, 308, 353, 437, 481, 490, 493, 495.
........., residents at, 180, 222, 298, 305, 306, 308, 311, 338, 341, 342, 352, 365, 378, 402, 423, 567, 581, 611–14.
........., sessions at, 383.
........., Trinity House at, 457, 487.
........., Castle, 36, 239, 295, 306, 317, 335, 378, 416, 422, 423, 459, 460, 525, 572, 613.
...., captains and gunners, &c. at, 36, 77, 151, 194, 203, 220, 282, 298, 306, 308, 311, 323, 325, 328, 331, 332, 337, 338, 343, 356, 372, 378, 395, 419, 422, 430, 509, 600, 612–14.
...., constable of, 295.
...., lieutenants of, 152, 190, 199, 200, 201, 266, 295, 345; *see also* Waller, Sir Thos.; Brett, Sir Rob.; Brooks, Sir John; Hamon, Sir Thos.
...., marshal of, 416, 600; *see also* Knott, Nich.

Dover Castle, letters, &c. from, 146, 190, 226, 293, 306, 308, 309, 311, 323, 325, 328, 336, 337, 345, 354, 366, 367, 372, 374, 391, 399, 416, 422, 424, 430, 458, 483, 525, 528, 533, 567, 571, 574, 579, 611.
...., prisoners at, 438, 442, 495, 522, 587, 611, 612.
Dovor, ——, 424.
Dowland, Wm., 362.
Dowles Forest, 45.
Downe, Thos., 102.
Downes, Edw., 215.
........., Jer., 215.
Downham in the Isle, 139.
Downham, Dr. George, 412; Bp. of Derry, 489.
Downs, the, 38, 309, 380, 408, 413, 431, 433.
Dowse, Edw., 67.
Drake, Fras., 120.
Drama, the, 175, 242, 278, 282, 286, 294, 358, 361, 419, 434, 549.
........., masques and masquers, 182, 208, 216, 220, 505, 512.
........., at court, 167, 170-2, 217, 219, 269, 406, 428, 501, 511, 512, 523, 603.
........., ..., payments for, 103, 115, 213, 254, 261, 281, 418.
Drapers' Hall, 404.
Drawater, John, 192.
Draycot, John, 44.
Drebbel, Cornelius, 130.
Dresden, 109.
Drew, Mr., 156.
Droane, Jas., 206.
Drogheda, 372.
Drope, John, 461, 536.
Drovaulx, Nich., 272.
Drummond, Dav., 217.
........., Jane, Lady, 96, 206, 212, 222-4, 380.
Drury, Diana, 408, 514.
........., Sir Drew, 465, 556-9, 581.
........., Anne Lady, 556, 557.
........., Sir Edw., 154.
........., Jeremy, 357.
........., Sir Robt., 52, 282, 284.
Drury House, 122.
Drury-lane, *see* London, Streets of.
.... Theatre, 442.
Dublin, port of, 49.
Duchy, the, *see* Lancaster, duchy of.
.... House, Strand, letters dated from, 310, 466-468, 470, 494, 502, 527.
Duck, Dr. Art., 496.
........., Dan., 279.
........., Nich., 159.
........., Wm., sen., 34.
........., Wm., jun., 34.
Duckett, And., 54.
Duckworth, Thos., 35, 383.
Dudgion, John, 106.
Dudley, Ann, 167, 209, 217, 284, 345.
Dudley, Douglas, Countess of Leicester, 90.
........., John, 384.
........., John, Duke of Northumberland, 249.
........., Robt., Earl of Leicester, 172.
........., Sir Robt., 6, 24, 79, 155, 157, 177, 193, 222, 233, 245, 252, 380.
........., Alice, Lady, 6, 157, 193.
Dudstone, 25, 27.
Duels, 208, 215, 224, 400, 408, 434, 436, 450, 466, 481, 501, 511, 514, 516.
Duffield, 293.
Duffield, Edm., 274.
........., Capt. John, 131.
.... *v.* Ward, 376.
Dugdale, Hen., 541.
Duke, John, *alias* Weddel, 513.
Dulwich, 555.
Dumfries, provost of, 444.
Dun, or Dunn, Dr., or Sir Dan., Dean of the Arches, Judge of the Admiralty Court, 282, 478, 488, 489, 515.
Dunbar, Earl of, *see* Hume, Geo.
Duncan, Jas. 243.
Dunch, Edm.. 268.
.... Sir Wm., 268.
Duncombe, Edw., 590.
Duncote, 35.
Dundee, 470.
Dunfermline, Earl of, *see* Seaton, Alex.
Dungeness lighthouse, 299, 305, 547.
Dunham, 117.
Dunkin (messenger), 341.
Dunkirk, 324, 399, 430, 431, 435,449, 585, 595.
........., ships of, 380.
Dunmow, 257.
Dunne, Elianor, 313.
Dunning, Thos., 280.
Duppa, Jeffrey, 179.
Durham, city, 24, 54, 453, 460 467, 487.
........., alms rooms at, 68.
.... Castle, 301—303.
........., mayor of, 487.
........., county Palatine of, 114, 178, 453.
........., Bp. of, *see* James, Wm.; Neyle, Rich.
........., diocese of, 34, 132, 204, 211, 220, 270, 272, 289, 291, 329, 384, 395, 476, 497.
.... prebends at, 289, 395.
.... House, Strand, 120, 172, 262, 339, 581.
........., county of, 113.
........., ..., grants of lands in, 63, 124, 127.
........., ..., lands and places in, 211, 312, 41[illegible].
........., ..., mines in, 14, 82, 127.
........., ..., offices, &c. in, 127, 497.
........., ..., recusants in, 204, 289, 291.
Dutch, 4, 109, 308, 395, 397, 398, 466, 475, 505, 572, 573, 607.
.... church in London, *see* London, Dutch church in.
.... merchants, 57, 447, 576, 599.

Dutch ships, 188, 350, 358, 463, 468, 478, 481, 599.
Dutton, Sir John, 515.
........., Sir Thos., 44.
Duty, see Customs.
Dwina river, 182.
Dye, Roger, 503.
Dyeing woods, 296, 331.
Dyers, 454.
Dyer, Rich., 321.
.... (boatswain), 422.
Dyley Woods, 18.
Dymchurch, 343.
Dymock, Sir Edw., 354.
Dyott, Ant., 116.

E.

Earl Marshal, see Marshal.
Earle, John, 525.
Earwood, Wm., 440, 449.
Easdell, W., 443.
Eason, John, 430, 431, 435, 438, 460.
East Barnet, 19, 20, 390.
.... Brent, 587.
.... Cotham, 439.
.... Dean, 463.
.... Dereham, 226.
.... Garston, 186, 230.
.... Greenwich, 138, 209.
...., Trinity Hospital at, 288.
.... Grinstead, 5.
.... Ham, 33.
.... Mersea, 186, 295.
.... Smithfield, 45, 169.
.... Somerton, 364.
East India Company, 129, 214, 217, 229, 233, 260, 338, 351, 379, 381, 432, 503, 510, 532, 533, 589.
...., Dutch, 272, 381.
...., Scottish, 518, 532.
.... India Trade, 210, 212, 223, 262, 284, 390, 587, 607.
.... India vessels, 203, 236, 379, 383, 384, 515, 518, 553, 587, 595.
...., governors of, 103, 223, 232, 269, 339.
.... Indies, 122, 233, 257, 427, 532, 545, 565, 587, 607.
Easthampstead, 243, 392, 596.
Eastland Company, 175, 261, 352, 395, 419, 427, 509.
Eastman, Edw., 542.
........., Wm., 246.
Eastry, 356.
Ecclesiastical causes, 22, 71, 257, 420.
...., commissions for, 26, 128, 246, 263, 289, 356, 448, 468, 524, 526, 540, 608, 613.
.... courts, 282.
Eccleston, 250.
Edenstowe, 334.
Edes, Hen., 230.
Edge, John, 102.
........., Capt. Thos., 560, 572.
Edgebury, Kenrick, 593.
Edgecombe, Pet., 251.
Edgmond, 30.
Edinburgh, 204, 438, 464, 469, 472, 473, 477.
........, letters from, 7, 8, 203, 255, 464, 467, 469, 472–4, 517, 595.
.... Castle, 472, 485.
........., Chapel Royal at, 379, 476.
.... University of, 473.
........., provost of, 474.
Edmondes, Clem., 89, 201, 260, 262, 269, 272, 385, 459; Sir Clem., 535, 546, 548, 554, 566, 574.
........., John, 549.
........., Sir Thos., French Secretary, 220, 222, 225, 228, 236, 238, 240, 324, 350; Comptroller of the Household, 512, 518; Treasurer of the Household, 519.
........., ..., letters of, 176, 439.
........., ..., letters to, 85, 101, 261.
........., ..., missions of in France, 215, 227 232, 270, 274, 316, 408, 415, 422, 465 466.
........., ..., promotions of, granted or proposed, 153, 166, 203, 370, 399, 404, 407, 410, 417, 424, 492, 497, 498, 504, 505, 511.
........., Lady, 261.
Edmonton, 210, 387, 468.
Edward VI., 341.
Edwardes, Dr. Thos., 200, 272.
Edwards, Fras., 485.
........., Israel, 295.
........., John, 191, 220.
........., Rich., 379.
........., Sir Rich., 380.
........., Thos., sen., 393.
........., Wm. 223.
Effingham, Lord and Lady, see Howard.
Egerley, 608.
Egerton, Sir Rowl., 445, 458.
........., Thos., Lord Ellesmere, Lord Chancellor, 129, 136, 145, 233, 271, 290, 373, 395, 397, 398; Visct. Brackley, 402, 403, 405, 422, 423, 426, 443.
........., ..., letters of, 71, 144, 152, 168, 169, 224, 252, 261, 318, 321–3, 333, 366.
........., ..., letters to, 53, 75, 182, 241, 246, 252, 317, 318, 321, 331, 391.
........., ..., official transactions of, 244, 296, 353, 356, 358, 371, 375, 381, 400, 407, 428, 432, 441, 442.

Egerton, Thos., Lord Ellesmere, &c—*continued.*
........., ..., orders and commissions to, 7, 125, 135, 165, 171, 173, 181, 197, 203, 208, 215, 216, 220, 228, 231, 245, 266, 276, 282, 285, 367, 404, 408, 438.
........., ..., proceedings of, on Overbury's cause, 316, 329, 369.
........., ..., warrants to, 53, 114, 123, 146, 219.
........., ..., illnesses of, 174, 227, 272, 275, 279, 349, 354, 436.
........., ..., death of, 448, 449, 453, 514.
........., Sir John, 52, 132, 395, 426; Visct. Brackley, 453; 1st Earl of Bridgewater, 470, 471, 514, 527.
........., Lady Frances, 426.
Egham, 578.
.... Walk, 211.
Egiock, Sir Fras., 94.
Egyptians (gipsies), 168.
Elam, Barth., 37, 58, 74, 80, 83, 85.
Elbing, 427.
Eldred, John, 5, 18, 21, 44, 47, 52, 53, 70, 88, 94, 120, 191, 197.
........., Thos., 41.
Eldrington, Sir Edw., 580.
Elections, *see* Parliament, elections for.
Elector Palatine, *see* Frederic V.
Electress Palatine, *see* Elizabeth.
Elfick, Wm., 533.
Elizabeth, Queen, 28, 41, 106, 149, 152, 178, 234, 281, 454, 578, 601, 606.
........., ..., debts of and to, 12, 38, 141, 290, 386.
........., ..., events in reign of, 10, 166, 302, 307, 431, 444.
........., ..., grants by, 26, 130, 156, 235, 296, 429, 452.
........., ..., life of, 115.
........., ..., servants of, 150, 272, 563, 607.
........., ..., service to, 9, 131, 364, 401, 486.
Elizabeth, Princess, 14, 17, 55, 138, 143, 153–155, 161, 163; Electress Palatine, 174, 185, 206, 209, 232, 301, 334, 345, 370, 427, 452, 478, 531.
........., ..., aid for marriage of, 140, 141, 144, 146.
........., ..., marriage of, 50, 59, 64, 71, 72, 89, 90, 96, 97, 104, 126, 129, 155, 156, 160, 162, 163, 169, 170, 172, 173, 175.
........., ..., dower of, 193, 246.
........., ..., gifts to, 161, *see* James I., gifts of.
........., ..., jewels, &c. of, 42.
........., ..., portrait of, 160.
........., ..., horses and stables of, 48, 98.
........., ..., household, &c. of, 167, 178, 370.
........., ..., ladies and attendants of, 169, 107, 174, 175, 209, 211–213, 217, 250, 383, 406.
........., ..., servants, &c. of, 29, 35, 41, 42, 180, 253, 420, 560.
........., ..., secretary of, *see* Morton, Albert.
........., ..., departure and journey of, 168, 170, 174, 177–182.
Elizabeth, Princess, children of, 221, 227, 510, 517, 600.
........., ..., projected visits of, to England, 501, 512, 521, 576.
Elks, Tim., 58, 59, 67, 70, 74, 77, 82, 83, 89, 168.
Ellery, Wm., 131.
Ellesmere, Lord, *see* Egerton.
Elliot, Thos., 49.
Elliott, Jas., 444.
Elliotts, Wm., 228, 390.
Elliotts, the, 36, 38.
Ellis, Rich., 101, 455.
........., Sir Wm., 482.
Elmes, Ant., 418.
........., Christiana, 418.
........., Thos., 418.
Elnerton, 69.
Elphinstone, Jas., Lord Balmerinoch, 137.
........., John, 438.
Elsdon, 355, 399.
Elsfield, 164.
Elsing, Hen., 198.
Elston, Thos., 26.
Eltham, 49.
.... house and park, 131, 135.
Elton, John, 112.
Elwood, Thos., 481.
.... (or Ellwood), Wm. 355, 412.
Ely, 147, 552.
......, almsrooms in, 76, 87.
......, Bp. of, *see* Andrews, Lancelot.
...... Cathedral, 28.
......, Deans and Chapter of, 257, 559.
...... diocese, 287.
Ely house, 287, 521.
Ely, Isle of, 212, 413, 541, 546, 552, 566, 574.
Emden, 350.
........., Count, 10, 150.
Emerson, Thos., 77, 328, 330, 332, 452, 594.
Emperor, *see* Matthias.
Empson, Edw., 440.
Endecot, John, 154.
Enfield, 67, 83, 98, 189, 392, 418, 482, 500, 512.
.... chace, 80, 81, 158, 390, 470.
.... park, 278, 468.
Engines, 368, 555, 602.
England, 27, 32, 54, 61, 79, 97, 104, 108, 140, 152, 171, 176, 183, 184, 192, 197, 233, 240, 251, 256, 262, 273, 279, 302, 303, 314, 363, 397, 424, 427, 429, 434, 448, 452, 473, 477, 485, 488, 491, 512, 517, 521, 530, 534, 535, 543, 544, 560, 566, 570, 571, 574, 589, 601.
........., Agents and Ambassadors of, *see* Albert, France, Holland, Muscovy, Savoy, Spain, Turkey, and Venice, Ambassadors to.
........., arms of, 172.

England, Clergy and Church of, *see* Church and Clergy.
........., coasts of, 79, 146, 205, 252, 293, 347, 436, 516, 572.
England, courts leet in, 222, 251, 261, 287.
........., defences of, 437, 584, 614.
........., floods in, 277, 475.
........., laws of, 375, 376.
........., manufactures of, 98, 176, 256, 271, 418.
........., merchants of, 96, 126, 149, 178, 297, 363, 428, 509, 530, 608.
........., money of, *see* Coin.
........., nobility of, 151, 164, 301, 421, 475, 609.
........., licences exercised in, 177, 259, 552.
........., ports of, 19, 63, 112, 298, 301; *see also* Cinque Ports.
........., priests and Jesuits in, 3, 59, 145, 299, 328, 458, 543.
........., residence in, absence from, or return to, 2, 5, 13, 22, 28, 80, 84, 100, 122, 136, 137, 157, 163, 167, 168, 173, 247, 260, 305, 326, 393, 416, 426, 449, 479–481, 529, 548, 560, 591, 607.
........., ships of, *see* Ships and Navy.
........., trade in, 78, 141, 164, 175, 182, 261, 348, 393, 428, 571, 607, 561.
........., treaty of with France, 1, 145, 218, 384.
........., troops of, 145, 504; *see* Soldiers.
........., visitors to, 127, 138, 145, 300, 357, 425.
Englefield, 60, 61.
Englefield, Sir Fras., 558.
Engles, John, 56.
English, 9, 36, 55, 119, 129, 147, 153, 169, 170, 237, 258, 301, 354, 375, 377, 471, 488, 502, 503, 589, 591.
........., abroad, 126, 137, 179, 203, 228, 279, 280, 300, 341, 392, 427, 458, 489, 514, 533, 542, 547, 572, 576.
Entailed lands, *see* Crown Lands entailed.
Ente, Josias, 599.
Epiphanius, 236.
Eppes, John, 267.
........., Kath., 267.
Epsley, *see* Hippesley.
Errington, John, 45.
Errol, Earl of, *see* Hay.
Erskine, Alex., 102.
........., Capt. Jas. 438, 473.
........., Sir Jas., 195.
........., John, Lord, 527.
........., Robt., 376.
.... Sir Thos., 209, 414, 438.
........., Thos., Visct. Fenton, 5, 48, 61, 68, 102, 153, 168, 207, 286, 287, 353, 374, 441, 454.
........., ..., grants to, 297, 386.
........., ..., letters of, 28, 39, 41, 48, 71, 72, 81, 97, 317.
........., Eliz., Visctss. Fenton, 102.
Erskine, Sir Wm., 537, 545.
Eskott, Geo., 110.
Essex, 86, 179, 261, 268, 327, 364, 501, 610.
........., grants of land in, 29, 46, 63, 87, 124, 159, 160, 181, 187, 190, 192, 211, 212, 248, 300, 388, 418, 444.
........., offices in, 535, 557.
........., recusants in, 116, 120.
........., residents in, 23, 32, 121, 147, 434, 474, 520, 523, 550.
.... towns, &c. in, 11, 16, 33, 37, 58, 68, 201, 257, 294, 295, 365, 367, 381, 421, 430, 452, 453, 508, 579.
.... House, 153.
Essex, Earl and Countess of, *see* Devereux.
........., Wm., 218.
Eston, Pet., 119, 158.
Estwick, Chris., 87.
Eton, 54, 72, 101, 121, 398, 508.
........., letters from, 2, 50, 77, 92, 110, 117, 125, 128, 139, 192, 236, 251, 270, 277, 284, 398, 429, 436, 472, 484, 485, 490, 491, 501, 525, 582, 591.
.... College, 2, 92, 192, 219, 221, 277, 392, 488, 552.
...., provosts of, 232, 469, 470, 478, 484, 490, 491, *see also* Savile, Sir Hen.
Etton Manor, 499.
Eu (France), 409.
Eure, Sir Fras., 372.
........., Sir Pet., 136, 268.
........., Ralph, 268.
........., Ralph, Lord, President of Wales, 4, 16, 373, 436, 458, 514.
......, ..., letters of, 16, 25, 73, 259, 353.
........., Sir Wm., 4.
Europe, 171, 184, 264, 429, 528.
Evans, Lewis, 553.
........., Owen, 586, 594.
........., Sam., 138.
Eveleigh, Rich., 606.
Evelyn, Geo., 493.
Everard, John, 519.
........., Sir Mich., 234.
Everdon, 282.
Everingham, Mr., 130.
Eversfield, Sir Thos., 64, 105.
Eveseed, 413.
Evesham, 388.
Ewell, 542.
Ewelme Hospital, 30, 62, 84, 87, 102, 110, 246, 490.
Ewens, Ralph, 71, 72, 357.
Exchange, the, 290, 595.
........., *see* Coinage.
Exchequer, Court of, 8, 13, 56, 87, 88, 155, 159, 207, 221, 234, 241, 250, 293, 310, 371, 385, 440, 508, 511, 531, 541, 542, 563, 591, 601.
........., auditors of, 98, 109, 115, 371, 421, 490.

Exchequer, Court of, Barons of, 118, 248, 274, 285, 286, 470, 515; see also Altham, Sir Jas.; Bromley, Sir Edw.; Denham, Sir John; Snigg, Sir Geo.; Sotherton, John.
........., Chief Barons of, see Tanfield, Sir Lawr.
........., Chancellor and Under Treasurer of, 258, see Cæsar, Sir J.; Greville, Sir Fulk.
........., tellers of, 55, 94–96, 125, 128, 210, 228, 395, 440, 542, 551, 559, 589; see also Watson, Thos.
........., Treasurer of, see Cecil, Earl of Salisbury; Howard, Earl of Suffolk.
........., officers, &c. of, 45, 49, 80, 195, 238, 240, 286, 306, 377, 418, 455, 520, 563, 588, 609.
........., bills and suits in, 20, 80, 130–132, 221.
........., lands in survey of, 133, 135, 171, 181, 188, 215, 216, 220, 298, 520, 557.
........., Marshalsea of, 393.
........., orders in, 43, 286, 289, 314, 366, 596.
........., payments from, 21, 25, 31, 34, 50, 57, 69, 90, 93, 157, 160, 255, 364, 518.
........., ... into, 35, 71, 109, 160, 241, 281, 450, 501, 503, 549.
........., poverty of, 181, 182, 368, 373, 534.
........., records in, 305, 371.
........., Remembrancer office in, 109, 388, 421.
........., Remembrancers, 109; see also Bingley, John; Fanshaw, Sir Hen.; Hatton, Sir Chris.; Osborne, John.
Exeter, 61, 100, 178, 254, 450, 528, 598.
........., mayor, &c. of, 177, 475, 528, 549.
........., merchants of, 475.
.... Castle, 262.
.... House, 493, 496.
........., Earl and Countess of, see Cecil.
........., Bishop of, see Cotton, Wm.
.... Cathedral of, 119, 517, 526.
........., diocese of, 102, 207, 517.
Exmouth, 455.
Eyres, Sir John, 18.
Eyton, Kenrick, 536.
........., Thos., 536.

F.

Fabricio, Signor, see Wotton, Sir Hen.
Faircloth, Alex. (priest), 283, 321, 546.
Fairfax, Sir Chas., 106.
........., Sarah, 325.
........., Sir Thos., 106, 300.
........., Mr., 460.
Fairs, see Markets.
Faldington, Robt., 118.
Falkland, 469, 473.
Fallowfield, 45.
Fallowlees, 292.
Falmouth, 509, 515.
.... Fort, 108, 248, 324, 516.
Falstolfes, 46.
Fane, Sir Fras., 403, 434.
........., Mr., 408.
Fanshaw, Sir Hen., Remembrancer of the Exchequer, 12, 13, 286, 308, 354, 355, 357.
........., Lady, 355.
........., Thos., 87, 88; Sir Thos. 336, 357.
Farleigh-Wallop, 411.
Farley, Mr., 437.
Farmer, Sir Rich., 461.
........., Lady, 461, 464, 515.
Farnham, 64, 70, 71, 76, 131, 193, 208.
Farsby, John, 456.
Farthings, see Coinage.
Faukes, Guy, 365.
Faulder, Mr., 107.
Faulkner, Edw., 75.
Faversham, 257, 395, 408, 413, 471.
........., mayor, &c. of, 416, 480.
.... residents at, 357, 434, 442, 457, 483, 484, 492, 532, 613.
Favour, Dr., 226.
Fayence, 194.
Feckenham Forest, 149, 235.
Fees, lists of, 19, 165, 255.
Fell, Rich., 56.
Fellwood Forest, 228, 340.
Felons, 30, 73, 116, 138, 195, 355, 447, 451, 596.
Felt, 213, 509.
Felton, Ellen, 222.
........., Dr. Nich., 139; Bp. of Bristol, 448, 502, 504.
........., Thos., 41.
Fenner, Sir Edw., Judge of King's Bench, 115.
........., Capt. Geo., 202, 306, 406.
Fennotterey, 400.
Fens, 389, 574.
Fensden, Thos., 138.
Fenton, Visct., see Erskine, Thos.
Fenwick, Sir John, 45, 55. 358, 365, 384, 465.
........., Randall, 406.
........., Thos., 365, 406.
........., Sir Wm., 36.
Fenwick Hall, 424.
Ferdinand II., King of Bohemia, 480.
Ferguson, And., 319.
Ferne, Sir John, 494, 583.
Ferne Island, 414.
Fermor, Sir Rich., 57.
Ferrand, Wm., 335.
.... Mary, 335.
Ferrers, Edw., 118.
........., Wal., 43.
........., Wm., 448.
Ferriers, John, 431.
Ferris, John, 207, 330.

Ferrour, John, 487.
Ferrybridge, 308.
Fetherston, Hen., 20.
Fetherstone, Hen., 415.
........., Wm., 415.
Fettiplace, Edw., 209.
Fidge, Dav., 613.
Field, Jos., 67.
........., Nath. (player), 419.
Fielding, Lady, 445.
Fiennes, Sir Hen., 394.
Fifteenths, *see* Tithes.
Figueroy, Louis Porter de, 109.
Filwood, *see* Fellwood.
Finch, Grace, 75, 96.
........., Hen., 373.
........., Sir Moyle, 263, 284.
........., Theo., 591.
........., Lady, 591.
Finchamstead, 243.
Finchingfield, 37.
Finchley Walk, 45.
Fines and forfeitures, 25, 27, 35, 78, 88, 106, 111, 126, 132, 159, 196, 198, 215, 238, 257, 260, 420, 507, 535, 584.
........., composition for, 69, 130, 220.
........., grants of, 19, 27, 55, 57, 71, 93, 97, 99, 100, 108, 119, 157, 185, 297–299, 354, 355, 385, 388, 439, 592, 596, 599, 605, 606.
........., receivers of, 284, 536.
........., remission of, 51, 56, 182, 293, 295, 357, 384, 592.
Finet, John, 127, 170, 262, 277 ; Sir John, 356, 478, 511, 513.
........., Robt., 344.
Finsbury, *see* London Streets.
.... Prison, 442.
Fire-arms, 167, *see* Arms.
First-fruits, 154. 210, 230, 555.
........., instalments of, 31, 76, 353, 550.
Fische, Sam. de, 350.
Fish and fishing, 21, 146, 156, 163, 164, 165, 189, 310, 341, 349, 354, 381, 389, 449, 456, 524, 567, 586.
Fish, customs on, 29, 108, 409.
........., export and import of, 235, 299, 316, 409, 423, 550, 582.
Fishing, licence for, 190, 252, 293, 301, 309, 347, 354, 409, 411–413, 433, 483, 492, 572.
.... nets (unlawful), 365, 409, 411, 412, 456, 457, 525.
Fishermen, 349, 350, 457.
Fishmongers, 550, 582, *see* London Companies.
Fitchett, Wilkes, 110.
Fitton, Edw., 230, 243.
Fitzgerald, Frances, 216.
........., Thos., 177, 216.
Fitzherbert, Robt., 100.
........., Mr., 60, 65.
Fitzhughes, Eliz., 38.
........., Thos., 203.
Fitzwalter, Lord, *see* Ratcliffe.
Fitzwilliam, John, 86.
........., Wal., 78.
........., Sir Wm., 72.
Flamborough, 386.
Flanders and Low Countries, 149, 250, 267, 343, 395, 404, 415, 431, 433, 449, 453, 458, 485, 488, 593.
........., ambassadors of and to, *see* Albert.
........., trade with, 141, 142, 144, 147, 165, 428.
Flashman, John, 131.
Fledborough, 506.
Fleet, Lincoln, 438, 440, 444.
Fleet Prison, 131.
........., prisoners in, 41, 43, 68, 80, 82, 86, 124, 129, 183, 223, 239, 279, 447, 561, 563, 593, 606, 607.
........., warden of, 256, 561.
Fleetham, 590.
Fleetwood, Hen., 64, 385.
........., Sir Miles, 558.
........., Sir Wm., 162, 229.
Fleming Manor, 404.
Fleming, Robt., 365, 587.
........., Sir Thos., Chief Justice of King's Bench, 91, 108, 173, 176, 218.
Flemings, the, 398, 560, 572.
Flemyng, Robt., 612.
Fletchampstead, 352.
Fletcher, Chris., 41.
........., Dr., 66.
........., Mrs., 66.
Flintshire, 52.
........., grants of lands in, 87, 241.
........., offices in, 249, 363.
Florence, 79, 149, 155, 223, 245, 380.
........., Duke of, *see* Tuscany, Grand Duke of.
Florida, 533.
Florio, Giov., 237, 390.
........., Hugh, 550.
Floyd, Griffith, 303, 305.
........., Rich., 331.
........., *see* Lloyd.
Fludd, Hen., 269, 486.
........., *see* Floyd and Lloyd.
Flushing, 116, 212, 234, 247, 315, 368, 370, 425, 539; *see also* Holland, Cautionary towns of.
Folkestone, 255, 341, 544, 574, 612.
........., mayor, &c. of, 126, 308, 544.
Folkingham, John, 519.
Folly John Park, Windsor, 94.
Fontaine, Mr., 95.
Fooke, Roger, 584.
Foote, Phil., 557.
........., Wm., 606.
Ford, 305.
Ford, Mr., 309.

Fordwich, 256, 567, 568.
Foreigners, *see* Aliens.
Foreman, Dr., 316, 317.
Forests, *see* Woods.
Forman, Robt., 480.
........., Dorothy, 480, 499.
Forrest, John, 402.
Forriatt Monachorum, 91.
Forsecar, Mr., 610.
Forsett, Edw., 40.
Forster, Ra., 590.
Fortage and lineage, 342.
Fortescue, Sir Fras., 102.
........., Capt. Faithful, 258.
........., Thos., 8.
Fortho, John, 23.
Fortune, Geo., 289, 424, 459, 606.
Fortune tellers, 348.
Foscarini, Giov. Battista, Venetian ambassador, 149, 167, 170, 227.
........., ..., Secretary of, *see* Muscorno.
Foster, Rich., 455, 459.
........., Dr. Rich., 295.
........., Sir Thos., Judge of Common Pleas, 134.
........., Wm., 137, 439.
Fotherby, Dr., Bp. of Salisbury, 527, 530, 535.
Fotheringay, 37, 56, 58, 74, 80, 83, 85, 507.
Fotherley, Thos., 194.
Foulmere, 357.
Fountaingate, Cardigan, 130.
Fountaunce, John, 118.
Fountayn, Pet., 337, 394, 509.
Fowes, Dr., 110.
Fowey, 235, 598.
Fowle, or Fowler, Matthias, 33, 137, 198.
Fowler, Fras., 101.
........., Mrs., 138.
Fowlies, Sir Dav., 4, 18, 155, 156, 216 222, 233, 245, 441.
Fox Hill, 429.
Foxcroft, Isaac, 113.
Frampton, Rich., 416.
France, 80, 84, 89, 92, 104, 115, 120, 147, 199, 203, 225, 303, 305, 391, 392, 397, 405, 413, 427, 432, 434, 464, 471, 485, 491, 514, 535, 574, 577, 597, 604.
........., agents and ambassadors of, 39, 138, 140–142, 164, 239, 260, 274, 285, 296, 346, 347, 357, 392, 434, 436, 441, 442, 464, 471, 473, 523, 526, 570, 576; *see also* Boderie, De la Tour, Verdine.
........., ..., connection of with Raleigh, 568–577, 579, 582, 583, 584, 587, 588.
........., agents and ambassadors to, 22, 100, 164, 211, 465; *see* Beecher, Wm.; Hay, Lord; Edmondes, Sir Thos.
........., coinage in, 267, 603, 608.
........., council and ministers of, 85, 142, 578, 588, 603.
........., departures to and from, 45, 282, 43 533, 566, 587.
France, despatches and letters to, 39, 89, 91, 93, 142, 578.
........., fugitives to, 39, 146, 464, 469, 576.
........., King of, *see* Francis I., Louis XIII.
........., marriage negociations with, 70, 161, 163, 168, 183, 215, 220, 223, 227, 232, 237, 274, 349, 361, 427, 461, 571.
........., merchants of, 65, 247, 423, 433.
........., natives of, 551, 557.
........., parliament of, 270.
........., Princes of, 422, 434, 443.
........., Princess of, 357, *see also* Chretienne.
........., Queen Regent of, *see* Mary de Medicis.
........., Scotch guard in, 85, 479, 585.
........., ships of, 39, 42, 341, 347, 354, 407, 408, 583.
........., treaties with, *see* England.
........., trade of and with, 51, 62, 65, 150, 235, 247, 252, 384, 504.
........., visitors to, 28, 80, 175, 237, 351.
........., wines of, *see* Wines.
Francis I. of France, 189.
Franciscans, 485, 521.
Francklin, Eliz., 244.
Frankfort, 72, 79, 137.
Frankley, 558.
Franklin, Jas., 310, 312, 324, 327, 330, 333–335, 337, 343, 345, 349.
Frederic V., Count Palatine of the Rhine, 59, 154, 157, 160, 163, 169, 170, 171, 172, 174, 175, 181, 193, 232, 242, 246, 334, 343, 345, 370, 501.
........., ambassador from, 141, 143.
........., arrival of in England, 148, 152, 153.
........., made Knight of the Garter, 158, 163, 168, 169, 170.
........., marriage proposals of, 71, 89, 97, 104, 124, 126.
........., marriage of, *see* Elizabeth, marriage of.
........., gifts of, 107, 175, 178.
........., household of, 175.
........., naturalization of, 232, 242.
........., departure and journey of, 175, 178, 181, 182, 301.
........., anagram, &c. on, 174, 176.
Frederic, Mr., 561.
Freeland, Jas., 118.
Freeman, Sir Fras., 519.
........., Lady, 519.
........., Geo., 179.
........., Martin, 120, 195.
........., Ralph, 197, 280; Sir Ralph, 511; Master of Requests, 514.
........., Thos., 35.
........., Wm., 120, 197.
Freemond, Barth., 120.
French, 136, 145, 146, 206, 313, 354, 379, 418, 425, 436, 441, 455, 493.
........., in England, 109, 305, 415, 474, 568, 582, 587, 592, 607.
........., fishing licences for, 409, 411, 433, 483, 545.

French, head money on, 260, 436, 464, 512, 540.
French church in London, 377, 598.
French, John, 159.
Fremnolls, 52.
Frende, John, 388.
Frerch, —— 140.
Freshville, Sir Pet., 181, 258.
Fresne, Michel du, 293, 483.
Freville, Sir Geo., 121.
Friend, John, 487.
Frisby-upon-Wreak, 247.
Frisby, Chris., 441.
Frobisher, Sir Martin, 228.
Frodsham, 218.
Frostenden, 64.
Fryer, Zachary, 66.
Fryerning, 11.
Fuller, Frances, 548.
........., Mr., 225.
Fullerton, Sir Jas., 28, 49, 50, 85, 114, 179, 206, 216, 273, 284, 443.
Fulnetby, Thos., 222, 599.
........., letters of and to, 342, 343, 345, 350, 365, 367, 372, 380, 408, 414.
Fulwer, Nathan, 7.
Funerals, 18, 603.
Furrier, Mr., 132.
Fyneux, Thos., 202.

G.

Gabellione, ambassador lieger of Savoy, 157, 185, 189.
Gage, Edw., 120.
Gainsford, John, 98, 156.
........., Margt., 98, 156.
Galbraith, Fras., 15.
Galicia, 575.
Gall, Mr., 288.
Galland, Edw., 366.
Galtres Forest, 78, 191, 210.
Galway, 501.
Garbart, Allart, 362.
Gardiner, Sir Thos., 234, 484.
Gardy, Hen., 318.
Gargrave, Sir Rich., 130.
Garland, Thos., 43, 299.
Garnet, Hen., 147, 151, 305.
........., Lawr., 87.
Garnett, John, 235.
Garret, Joan, 481.
........., Jer., 481.
.... (footman), 501.
Garratt, Mr., 257.
Garrett, Geo., 86.
Garrett, Thos., 387.
Garter, order of, chancellor of, 56.
........., chapter of, 158, 163.
........., King-at-arms, *see* Segar, Wm.
........., knights and companions of the, 27, 31, 48, 169, 286, 287, 362-364, 368, 379, 380, 384, 425.
........., statutes, 381.
Garton, Sir Thos., 602.
Garway, Thos., 56.
........., Wm., 87, 123, 166, 187, 192, 216, 235, 283, 296; Sir Wm., 476, 490.
Garvey, Sir Neale, 148.
Gascoigne, Sir Wm., 210.
Gascony wines, 220.
Gaseley, 190.
Gastrell, Peregrine, 230.
Gatcomb, 44.
Gate Farm, 45.
Gateacre, Wm., 212, 230.
Gatehouse, Westminster, 227, 321, 495, 588.
........., ..., letters from, 11.
........., ..., officers of, 11, 238, 499.
........., ..., prisoners in, 11, 48, 54, 106, 130, 145, 238, 283, 289, 332, 450, 499, 517, 549.
Gates, Sir Thos., 101, 234, 503.
Gateshead toll, 410.
Gatton, 31, 87.
Gaulett, Jacques, 483.
Gawdy, Sir Hen., 55.
Gayney, Hen., 493.
Geare, Thos., 604.
Geathin, Robt., 52.
Gedney, 356.
Gee, Dr., 484.
........., Sir Wm., 35.
Geer, Capt., 589.
Geffer, Nich., 380.
Gelfe, John, 416.
Geneva, 72, 151, 270, 301.
Gentleman pensioners, 33, 58, 59, 244, 253, 263, 387, 477, 591.
Gentlemen-at-arms, 387.
Gerard (or Gerrard), Geo., letters of, 51, 373, 449, 464, 471, 477, 482, 513, 525.
........., Gilbert, Clerk of the Duchy of Lancaster, 387, 419, 467, 468, 500, 506.
........., John, 148.
........., Mary, 49.
........., Sir Thos., 306.
........., Thos., Lord, 350, 373; President of Wales, 375, 391, 431, 436, 440, 480, 481, 488, 490, 493, 516.
Gerling, Simon, 403.
Germany, 1, 97, 155, 170, 179, 288, 395, 576, 605.
........., Princes of, *see* Union.
German tapestry, 465.
Gervels, Dorothy, 537.
Gevartius, Gaspar, 474.

Gibb (or Gibbs), Hen., 195, 209, 218, 251, 296, 363, 364, 381, 447, 606.
........., Jas., 241.
........., John, 241, 381.
........., Eliz., 612.
Gibbes (cook), 497.
Gibbon, Nich., 191, 274.
........., Phil., 612.
Gibbons, John, 107, 251.
........., Orlando, 107, 295.
........., Wm., 356.
Gibbridge, Rich., 422, 437.
Gibson, Ant., 137.
Gifford Manor, 282.
Gifford, Sir Geo., 16, 186.
........., Gerard, 100.
........., Capt., 310.
........., Dr., 420.
Gilbert, Sir Humph., 228.
........., John, 189.
........., John (engine maker), 555.
Gildenston, 378, 392, 424, 460.
Giles, Matt., 587.
........., Nath., 270.
.... (or Gyles), Rich., 296, 331, 407.
Gill, John, 501.
........., Wm., 483.
Gillesland, 464.
Gillingham, 191, 471.
.... Park, 99.
Gimingham, 419.
Girdling, science of, 126.
Gisborne, Hen., 248.
Glamorganshire, 63, 123, 440, 498, 587.
........., offices in, 95, 415, 431, 432.
........., residents in, 90, 195, 292.
Glanvile *v.* Allen, 376.
Glasgow, 286, 515.
Glass, 13, 207, 224, 256, 287, 288, 538.
.... works, 355, 601.
Glatton, 57.
Glemmond, Chas., 291, 306.
Glenfield, 467.
Glenn River, 574.
Glossoms Farm, 45.
Gloucester, 25, 114, 295, 589.
........., letters from, 435, 437, 439.
........., mayor, &c. of, 25, 27, 423.
........., Bp. of, *see* Thompson, Giles; Smith, Miles.
.... Cathedral, 53, 435, 437–439, 487.
........., dean and chapter of, 276, 411, 437, 438, 492.
.... diocese of, 76.
........., prebends of, 437, 439.
Gloucestershire, 229, 262, 267, 268.
........., cloth and clothiers in, &c. 389, 390, 394.
........., grants of lands in, 32, 63, 70, 124, 159, 241, 249, 276, 388, 405.
Gloucestershire, lands and places in, 29, 46, 57, 125, 126, 158, 226, 243, 252, 288, 340, 373, 386, 444, 467.
........., offices in, 114, 219, 243, 389.
........., recusants in, 32, 45.
........., residents in, 15, 35, 131, 381, 426, 567, 596, 597.
Glover, Alex., 362.
........., Eliz., 201.
........., Robt., 201.
........., Sir Thos., 168, 170, 175, 257.
........., Vincent, 362.
........., Wm. (surveyor), 4.
........., Wm. (robber), 138.
........., Wm., jun., 451.
Gnarisborough, Milon, 257.
Goddard, Hen., 302.
........., Wm., 382.
Godfrey, Rich., 182.
........., Robt., 343.
........., Wm., 343, 614.
........., Mr., 109.
Godolphin, Fras., 200, 228.
........., Sir Wm., 45, 111, 124, 199, 248.
Godourus, Wm., 17.
Godshill, 101.
Godwin, Dr. Fras., 368; Bp. of Llandaff, 497; Bp. of Hereford, 499.
Godwin, Sands, 342, 343, 345, 350, 351, 358, 361, 365, 366, 372, 408, 423, 468, 599, 612.
Goesius, Bened., 427.
Goffe, Nich., 291.
Gofton, Fras. (auditor), 112, 179, 195, 535.
Gold, 189, 427, 514, 538, 603, 605.
........., export and import of, 92, 129, 143, 396, 581, 599.
.... mine, 428, 587.
Golden Anchor, 406, 410.
.... Grove, Carmarthen, 261.
Goldsborough, 69, 533.
Goldthorpe, Rich., 125.
Gomera, 516.
Gondomar, Condé de, *see* Acunas.
Gooch, Dr. Barnaby, 89, 420.
........., John, 88.
Good, Mary, 597.
........., Thos., 597.
Goodall, Thos., 70.
Goodere, Sir Hen., 72.
Gooderick, Wm., 131.
Goodman, Eliz., *see* Andrew.
Goodridge, Thos., 30.
Goods, *see* Merchandise.
Goodwin, Dr. Wm., 46, 472, 482, 548.
........., Mr., 197.
........., John, sen., 298, 351.
Gordon, Geo. 1st Marquis of Huntley, 391, 514.
........., Pat., 81.

Gordon, Sir Robt., 245.
Gorges, Sir Art., 17.
........., Lady Helen, Marchioness of Northampton, 18, 426.
........., Sir Ferd., 55, 109, 476, 589.
........., Robt., 178.
........., Sir Thos., 192.
Gorhambury, 480, 488.
Goring, Sir Geo., 244, 363, 381.
........., Wm., 67.
........., Mrs., 209.
Gosnold, Robt., 30, 41.
Gosnoll, John, 546.
........., Thos. 41.
Gospits, 256.
Gospoole, John, 4.
Gosson, Rich., 229.
Goteacre, 375.
Gouch, Steph. le, 121.
Gould, Fras., 29.
Gournoise, Fras., 572.
Gouthorpe, Rich., 195.
Govey, Pierce, 607.
Gower, Agnes, 244.
Gowrie, Earl of, *see* Ruthven.
Goxhill, 408.
Grafton, King's house at, 382.
.... Park, 8.
.... Regis, 26.
Graham, Fergus, *see* Plumpe.
........., Geo., 204.
........., Jas., 5th Earl of Montrose, 502.
........., John, 265, 360.
........., Sir John, 50, 265.
........., Wm., 7th Earl of Monteith, 204.
Grahams, the, 38, 539.
Grain, *see* Corn.
Grammar Schools, 63, 64, 86, 364.
Granada, 86.
Grand Seignior, *see* Ahmed I.
Grange, the, 54, 577.
Grant, John, 292.
Graunt, Edw., 612.
Grave, John, 68.
Graver, Thos., 118.
Graves, Thos., 229, 573.
........., Wm., 390.
Gravesden, 193.
Gravesend, 29, 79, 249, 394, 408, 425, 431, 454, 565, 572.
........., letters from, 66, 273.
Gray, Bridget, 556.
........., Edw., 108.
........., John (King's servant), 98, 205, 214, 388, 589.
........., John (of Dover), 400.
........., Sir John, 73, 74, 88.
........., Sir Ra., 40, 46, 48, 53, 54, 112, 232, 235, 389.
........., Robt., 260.
Gray, Thos., 61.
........., Wm., 235.
........., Mr. (minister), 490.
........., Lady, 54.
Gray's Inn, residents at, 80, 209, 315, 410, 551, 552, 591, 611.
........., letters dated from, 471, 542, 554, 604.
........., masques of, 170, 172, 523.
Grayne, Robt., 37.
Great Covent Garden, 234.
.... graies, 223.
.... Missenden, 12.
.... St. Bartholomews, 215.
.... Worlingham, 551.
.... Wraton, 434.
Greeks, the, 77.
Green, Chas., 358.
........., John, 227.
........., Kath., 169.
........., Mary, 553.
........., Sir Mich., 54, 601.
........., Lady, 601.
........., Thos., 169, 553.
........., Wm., 189.
........., Sir Wm., 392.
Green Cloth, Board of, 276.
.... wax, 518, 578.
Greene, Chris., 231.
........., Fras. (priest), 321.
........., Mary, 480, 499.
........., Wm., 256.
Greenfield (or Grenfield), John, 389, 513.
Greenhead, Rowl., 293.
Greenland, 178, 203, 252, 284, 503, 513, 538, 560, 565, 572, 576.
........., Dutch Company, 272.
.... fishery, 262, 392, 503, 572, 573, 595.
Greenwell, Wm., 12, 105, 558.
Greenwich, 44, 129, 131, 215, 410, 422, 428, 565, 597.
........., armoury at, 15, 51, 209, 244, 534.
........., court at, 30, 136, 287, 457.
.... Hospital, 546.
.... letters dated from, 28, 30–32, 34, 38, 39, 41, 51, 55, 97, 106, 113, 129, 140–142, 149, 151, 186, 188, 237, 287, 289, 368, 370, 375, 377, 467, 468, 470, 471, 544, 545, 547, 548.
.... Palace and Gardens, 90, 116, 138, 185, 188, 212, 224, 246, 361, 370, 460, 464, 473, 537, 559, 564.
.... Park, 214–216.
........., tower at, 52.
Greg, Edw., 181.
........., Robt., 181.
Gregor clan, 204, 271.
Gregory the Great, 400.
Greisley, Sir Geo., 268.
........., Sir Thos., 268.

Grent, Edw., 205.
........., John, 23, 246.
Gresley, Walsingham, 15.
Gretton, 226, 243.
Greville, Sir Edw., 45.
........., Sir Fulk, 60, 158; Chancellor and Under Treasurer of the Exchequer, 256, 257, 262, 354, 385, 418, 444, 445, 453, 469, 470, 492, 511, 546, 578, 581.
........., ..., commissions to, 298, 507.
........., ..., letters of, 24, 128, 280, 458, 461, 462, 466, 470, 471, 475, 477, 481, 484.
........., ..., letters to, 340, 377, 496, 531, 554, 584, 585, 596.
........., ..., warrants to, 544, 560.
........., Thomasine, 45.
Grey, Hen., Duke of Suffolk, 217.
........., Hen., 6th Earl of Kent, 90, 93, 171, 180, 261, 273, 284.
........., Chas., 7th Earl of Kent, 273, 275, 319.
........., Susan, Countess of Kent, 510.
........., Lady Eliz., 515.
........., Hen., Lord of Groby, 477.
........., Sir John, 477.
........., Lady, 477.
........., Jane Sibylla, Lady, 279, 282, 344.
........., Thos., Lord of Wilton, 48, 124, 148, 181, 185, 242, 245, 344, 364, 418, 425.
........., Thos., 271.
.... (minister), 273.
Griffin, John, 498.
........., Sir Riee, 138.
........., Rich., 463.
.... (pirate), 79.
Griffith, Geo., 85.
........., John, 110, 230, 317.
........., John (felon), 195.
........., Dr. John, 479.
........., Mabella, 61, 479, 495, 499.
........., Mr., 24.
Grigson, Hugh, 15.
Grime, Rich., 596.
Grimes, Sir John, 361, 362.
........., Sir Thos., 553, 561.
Grimeston, Edw., 525.
Grimoldby, 292.
Grimsditch, Geo., 49.
Grimston, 264.
Grimston, Edw., 582.
........., —— 274.
Grimstone, Rich., 172, 173.
Grindley, *alias* Greenlawe, 127.
Grobban, Mr., 61.
Grosvenor, Randall, 463.
Grotius, Hugo, 406, 489, 510, 512.
Grovehurst, 96.
Gryme, Geo., 120, 419.
Guadagnis (of Venice), 284, 289.
Gualtier, M., 532.
Guard, captain and yeomen of, 26, 78, 316, 441, 480, 494, 531.
........., Black, 276.
Guiana, 105, 198, 356, 425, 511, 516, 521, 523, 528, 561, 566, 575, 587.
Guildford, Sir Hen., 158, 159, 400.
Guildford Park, 17, 76, 386.
Guildhall, 2, 293, 317, 487.
Guillin, Peregrine, 415.
Guinea Company, 587.
Guise, Charles of Lorraine, Duke of, 166, 193, 443.
........., Catherine of Cleves, Duchess of, 409, 411, 412, 492.
Gulder, Wm., 388.
Gunderrot, Sir Henri de, 11, 109.
Gunpowder, 133, 146, 169, 179, 301, 395, 418.
.... Plot, 86, 145, 147, 164, 304, 329, 347, 352, 365, 392, 406, 556, 558, 559, 581.
...., conspirators in, 74, 88, 137, 138, 175, 224, 292, 303, 355, 360, 362, 366, 369, 550, 580.
...., evidence upon, 3, 59, 70, 77, 151, 305.
Gun-stone, 301.
Gurney, John, 103.
Gustavus Adolphus, King of Sweden, 51, 98, 265, 468.
Guy, Nich., 299.
Gwern-Vawr, 177.
Gwillim, John, Rouge croix Pursuivant, 453.
........., Thos., 530.
Gwydder, 336, 524.
Gwyn, Sir John, 524.
........., Rich., 524.
........., Sydney, 524.
Gwynn, John, 297, 339.
........., Matt., 297.
........., Dr. Matt., 83.
........., Rich., 115.
........., Roger, 297.
........., Wm., 115.
Gwynn, *see* Wynn.
Gybbs, Steph., 574.

H.

Haarlem, 505.
Hackness, 126.
Hackney, 24, 205, 236, 295, 448.
Hackwell, Dr., 160.
Hackwood, 223–225, 227.
Hadde, Matt., 376, 416.
Haddenham, 542, 596.
Haddington, Visct., *see* Ramsay, Jas.
Hadham, 49, 88.

Hadley, 57, 379.
Hadnock Wood, 251.
Hague, the, 85, 138, 341, 363, 406, 437, 461, 479, 483, 567, 568.
........., letters dated from, 79, 272, 492, 495, 578.
Hainault Lodge, 58, 249.
Hakewill, Wm., 269, 274, 276; Queen's solicitor, 515.
Hale, John, 134.
........., Rich., 364, 462, 463, 541.
Hales, Sir Chas., 35.
........., Sir Edw., 400, 402, 412.
........., Robt., 612.
........., Samuel, 106, 432.
........., or Hale, Wm., 423, 509.
Halfheid, Hen., 335.
........., Robt., 360.
Hall, Edw., 292.
........., John, 327, 329.
........., John (constable), 587, 593.
........., Dr. Jos., 76.
........., Wm., 251, 292.
........., Mr., 421.
Hall Lathes, 486.
Halliday, Fras., 324.
Halling Manor, 90.
Halliwell, John, 176.
Halsey, John, 552, 566.
........., Dr. John, 75.
Halsted, 52, 550.
Halswell, Nich., 16, 51.
Hambleden, 208.
Hambleton, 308.
Hamburg, 96, 168, 266, 305, 427.
Hamburgians, 373.
Hamilton, 582.
Hamilton, Claud, 66.
........., Jas., Earl of Abercorn, 113, 119, 515.
........., Jas., 2nd Marquis Hamilton, 163, 481–483, 488, 497, 511, 512, 515, 523, 566, 592, 595, 598.
........., Sir Jas., 349; Baron of Arabane, 515.
........., Thos., 40.
........., Sir Thos. 203.
Hamme Farm, 254.
Hammond, Chris., 249.
........., Dr., 254.
Hamon, Alex., 178.
........., Rich., 298.
........., Steph., 298.
........., Thos., 563.
........., Sir Thos., 295.
Hamond, Wm., 602.
Hampshire, 86, 179, 268, 294, 544, 562, 579.
........., grants of lands in, 57, 159, 196, 247, 353, 412, 418, 452.
.... lands and places in, 30, 45, 66, 108, 121, 158, 201, 208, 223, 231, 294, 375, 411, 507, 573.
........., recusants in, 120.
Hampshire, residents in, 186, 431, 471.
Hampton Court Palace and Parks, 63, 100, 117, 126, 128, 227, 374, 600.
...., game at, 34, 250, 441.
........., King at, 37, 163, 189, 200, 263, 282, 428, 485.
........., letters dated from, 58, 60, 73, 79, 222, 253, 280, 396, 486, 575, 577.
Hampton-in-Arden, 351.
Hamul, 416.
Hanaper and Petty Bag, 51, 96, 160, 206, 213, 338, 452, 506, 549.
Hanbury, Thos., 115.
Hanby, Rich., 537, 544, 592.
........., Wm., 544.
Handson, Ralph, 498.
Haning, Robt., 49.
Hanington, Hen., 592.
........., Monings, 566, 571, 605.
........., Wm., 566, 600, 605.
Hanley, Hugh, 379.
Hanmer, Dr. John, 506.
Hansacker, Thos., 218.
Hansby, Ra., 240.
Hanson, Chris., 585.
Hanworth, 490.
Harber, Sylvia, 606.
Harbert, Adam, 483.
........., John, 355.
........., Wm. (priest), 321.
Harbyn, Wm., 496.
Harcourt, Robt., 198, 516.
Harderet, Jacob, 42.
Harding, Wm., 402.
Hardwen, Thos., 589.
Hardwick, 460, 597.
Hare, John, 186.
........., Nich., 520.
Harewell, Fras., 139, 162.
........., Sir Thos., 162.
Harfleet, Sir Thos., 481.
Hargast, 57.
Harlech Prison, 358.
Harley, Sir Robt., 103.
Harlington, 214, 597.
Harlow, Robt., 458.
........., Sam., 458.
Harman, Mr., 51.
Harmon, Sir Wm., 159.
Harper, Hen., 592.
........., John, 357.
Harpford, 400.
Harpur, Sir John, 181, 258.
Harriers, *see* James I., harriers of.
Harries, Phil., 246.
........., Thos., 139.
Harrington, John, 606.
........., Sir John, 14, 115, 137, 160, 162.
........., John, 1st Lord, 1, 141, 154, 167, 170, 174, 175, 180, 184, 199, 209, 215, 225, 387.

Harrington, John, 1st Lord, letters of, 14, 97, 123.
.........., ..., patent to, for coinage of farthings, 174, 175, 180, 184.
.........., Anne, Lady, 170, 174, 181, 234, 237, 406, 418, 417, 427.
.........., John, 2nd Lord, 209, 237.
.........., Martin (priest), 321.
.........., W., 258.
Harris, Alex., 57.
.........., Capt. Art., 438.
.........., Sir Art., 355, 357.
.........., Edw., 136.
.........., Sir Hugh, 131.
.........., Honoria, 131.
.........., John, 84, 385.
.........., Lewis, 126.
.........., Thos., 182.
.........., Wm., 612.
.... (fisherman), 525.
Harrison, 578.
Harrison, Edw., 293.
.........., John, 423, 582, 609.
.........., Rich., 200, 470, 478, 491, 594, 602.
.........., Thos., 609.
Harrow-on-the-Hill, 110, 204.
Harrowden, 181.
Harrys, Augustine, 314.
Harsnet, Sam., Bp. of Chichester, 139, 278.
Hart, Sir Eustace, 381.
.........., Wm., 221, 419.
Hartfield, 5.
Harthurst, 281.
Hartington, 405.
Hartlepool, 395.
Hartley, Thos., 382.
Harvey, Clem., 287.
.........., Sir Gerard, 31.
.........., John, 287.
.........., Sam., 58.
.........., Sebastian (Alderman), 359.
.........., Simon, 31.
.........., Thos., 287.
.........., Thos. (gunner), 311, 509.
.........., Wm., 119.
.........., Capt., 516.
Harvy, Edw., 189.
Harward, Hen., 47.
Harwich, 505.
Harwood, Sir Edw., letters of to Carleton, 501, 503-505, 511, 512, 520, 523, 529, 533, 534, 540, 568, 575, 582, 588, 594, 596, 604.
.........., Steph., 488.
.........., Mr., 226.
Hasdonck, Mr., 601.
Hasell, Wm., 606.
Hassard, Robt., 33, 520.
Hastings, 254, 389, 457, 543, 574.
Hastings, Capt. Edw., 521.
.........., Hen., 235.
Hastings, Hen., Earl of Huntingdon, 168, 185, 242, 292, 521.
.........., Cath., Countess Dowager of Huntingdon, 292.
.........., Robt., 234.
Hatcher, Wm., 548.
Hatfield, 134, 332, 477, 552, 575.
.... chace, 471, 475.
.... House, Gardens, &c., 32, 104.
...., works at, 5, 32, 52, 78, 93, 118.
.... (Yorkshire), 32, 548.
Hathern, 276.
Hatley, 510, 522.
Hatton House, 386, 390, 476, 494, 528.
.... estates, 471.
Hatton, Sir Chris. (late Chancellor), 376, 381, 386.
.........., ..., 63, 192, 228, 243, 355, 357, 376, 386, 430.
.........., Lady, see Coke.
.........., Luke, 525.
.........., Rich., 360.
.........., Robt., 386.
.........., Sir Thos., 430.
.........., Sir Wm., 268.
Haughfen, Geo., 598.
Haughton, 500.
Hautaige, Fras., 551.
Havering House and Park, 81, 88, 135, 392, 394, 579.
.... Manor, 508.
Havers, Mr., 394, 427.
Hawkes, Chris., 95, 123.
Hawkins, Edw., 539, 567.
.........., Sir Rich., 426.
Hawkridge, Giles, 89.
Hawks, see James I., falconry of.
Hawksworth, Art., 482.
.........., Giles, 34.
Hawley, Jas., 134, 332.
.........., Jerome, 327, 332.
Hawnes, 247.
Haworth, Edm., 34.
Hay, Sir Alex., Secretary of Scotland, 34, 68, 219, 356.
.........., Arch., 396.
.........., Fras., 8th Earl of Errol, 514.
.........., Sir Geo., 416.
.........., Jas., 170.
.........., Jas., Lord, Gentleman of the Robes, 91, 133, 145, 167; Master of the Wardrobe, 177, 198, 199; Baron Hay of Sawley, 331, 333, 358, 379, 384, 458, 477, 511, 514, 529; Visct. Doncaster, 551, 552, 587, 598, 603.
.........., ..., courtship and marriage of, 449, 469, 475, 477, 480, 493, 494, 513.
.........., ..., entertainments by, 436, 438, 441, 505, 512, 523.
.........., ..., grants and warrants to, 33, 58, 66, 110, 177, 499.

Hay, Jas., Lord, letters of and to, 32, 89, 90, 109, 327.
........., ..., mission of to France, 356, 361, 363, 370, 380, 385, 391, 397, 398, 426.
........., ..., payments to, 5, 179, 196, 387.
...., promotions of, real or proposed, 290, 344, 551, 566.
........., Lady Lucy, 511.
........., Robt., 73, 76, 290, 446, 514.
Hay and straw, 407.
Hay Hill, 452.
Haydon, Agnes, 607.
.... Jerome, 607.
........., Capt. John, 202, 306, 388.
........., Michael, 606.
........., Wm., 114, 296, 357, 451.
Hayes, Edw., 78.
........., Sir Thos., 264.
Haynes, Sir Thos., 488.
Hayward, Anna, 267.
........., Geo., 498.
........., Sir Geo., 273.
........., Sir John, 331.
Haywood, 192.
Headland, John, 572.
Heamskerk, Admiral, 442.
Heard, Gerard, 586.
Heasworth manor, 367.
Heath, Robt., 124, 407, 410, 433, 591; Recorder of London, 595, 605.
Heaton, Rich., 43, 68, 80, 82, 274, 275.
Heblethwayt, Wm., 612.
Heborn, 302.
Hebrides, the, 167.
Heddon, 54.
Healy, Wm., 572.
Heidelberg, 206, 211, 213, 301, 335, 360, 363, 393, 397, 427.
Helen (or Hellen), John, 256, 428.
........., Wm., 428, 429.
........., Cicely, 429.
Heley, Wm., 513.
Helmote Courts, 467.
Helperby, Ra., 256.
Hels, Sir Thos., 536.
Helstone, 253.
Helwys, Sir Gervase, Lieutenant of the Tower, 183, 184, 191, 211, 212, 270, 307, 310–313, 327, 445.
........., ..., connection of with Overbury's murder, 307, 310–313, 318, 320, 321, 325, 327, 329, 330, 331, 336, 342, 344.
........., ..., letters of, 307, 331.
........., Mary, Lady, 445.
........., Alderman Sir Wm., 321, 445.
Henderson, Col. R., 438, 472.
Hendley, John, 46.
Hendley Park, 68.
Hendy, Marg., 183.
Heneker, Rich., 612.
........., Thos., 612.
Henllan, 2.
Henly, Susan, 483.
........., Sir Thos., 447.
Henn, Hen., 352.
Hennearing Hugh, 574.
Hennings, ——, 96.
Henrion Manor, 249.
Henry III., 341.
.... IV., 518.
.... VI., 221.
.... VII., 221.
.... VII.'s Chapel, 344, 401.
.... VIII., 176, 353, 437.
.... IV. of France, 104, 144, 199, 270.
........., Prince of Wales, 4, 8, 39, 62, 75, 88, 108, 109, 111, 114, 124, 135, 138–143, 147, 153, 172, 192, 195, 266, 361.
........., ..., debts of and to, 155, 156, 160, 178.
........., ..., expenses for and of, 17, 26, 91, 98, 101, 106, 156, 244.
........., ..., jewels, &c. of, 65, 91, 194.
........., ..., letters to, 101, 130.
........., ..., marriage negociations for, 70, 71, 97, 149, 151, 185, 517.
........., ..., portrait of, 171.
........., ..., sports of, 115, 124.
........., ..., lands of, 3, 11, 21, 45, 95, 112, 120, 139, 155, 157, 177, 398, 426.
........., ..., revenue of, 8, 25, 111, 115, 160.
........., ..., chaplain to, 110, 156, 162.
........., ..., household of, 3, 85, 114, 160.
........., ..., officers of, 60, 62, 120, 155, 156, 324, 456.
........., ..., servants of, 6, 19, 26, 55, 57, 106, 114, 129, 162, 179, 180, 194, 203, 207, 208, 330.
........., ..., treasurer of, *see* Cornwallis, Sir Chas.
........., ..., illness and death of, 154–157, 160–163, 171, 172, 174.
........., ..., suspicion of poisoning of, 324, 327, 332, 334, 343.
........., ..., funeral of and mourning for, 156, 161, 162, 173, 404.
Henshaw, Sam., 128, 551.
Henslow, Phil., 17.
Henson, Mrs., 533.
Henton, Thos., 251.
Hepborn, John, 535.
Heraldry, 608.
Heralds, 162, 265, 276, 369, 442, 452, 455; *see also* Brooke, Ralph; Knight, Thos.; Penson, Wm.; St. George, Hen.; Thompson, Sam.; Treswell, Robt.
Herbert, Anne, Lady, 116.
........., Arnold, 62, 190.
........., Sir Edw., 74, 603.
........., Capt. Sir Gerard, letters of to Carleton, 484, 487, 493, 494, 497, 501, 503, 505, 512, 521, 523, 527, 528, 533.
........., Capt. Jasper, 74.

Herbert, Sir John, 466, 476, 484, 515.
........., Miles, 583.
........., Sir Wm., 94, 96.
........., Mr., 8.
........., Phil., Earl of Montgomery, 124, 128, 167, 286, 291, 428, 436, 443, 470, 471, 475, 482, 483, 512, 528.
........., ..., grants to, 68, 94, 120, 288, 299, 396, 425.
........., ..., letter of, 94.
........., ..., payments to, 5, 446.
........., ..., son of, 392, 394, 395, 426, 484, 488, 528, 533.
........., ..., wardship given to, 410, 412, 456.
........., Susan, Countess of Montgomery, 487, 503, 528, 533.
........., Wm., Earl of Pembroke, 94, 133, 140, 144, 151, 220, 239, 244, 254; Lord Chamberlain, 345, 360, 432, 436, 443, 465, 474, 490–492, 503, 533, 566, 596, 598.
........., ..., commissions and warrants to, 296, 368, 395, 552, 584.
........., ..., grants to, 40, 156, 371, 456, 467.
........., ..., letters of, 56, 74, 97, 99, 182, 257, 258, 325, 545, 599.
........., ..., letters to, 530, 562.
........., ..., payment to, 29.
........., Mary, Countess Dowager of Pembroke, 403, 427, 458.
Hereford, Chancellor of, 208.
........., Bp. of, see Bennet, Robt.; Godwin, Fras.
........., Dean and Chapter of, 493.
Hereford, Edw., 74.
Herefordshire, 229, 262, 509.
........., grants of lands in, 124, 196.
........., lands in, 103, 339, 375, 584.
........., offices in, 37, 271, 440, 498.
........., recusants in, 30, 73, 120, 123.
........., residents in, 56, 191, 240, 263.
Heretics, 119, 123, 124.
Herman, Hen., 525.
Heron, Jer., 382.
Herrick, Sir Wm., 1, 94–96, 121, 166, 210, 367, 452.
Herrings, see Fish.
Herriot, Geo., 91, 194, 278, 367, 560.
Hertford, 223, 229, 364.
........., Earl and Countess of, see Seymour.
Hertford House, 92, 184.
Hertfordshire, 57, 73, 136, 268, 360, 407, 525.
........., grants of lands in, 63, 70, 124, 159, 223, 388.
........., lands and places in, 84, 278, 338, 375, 488, 498, 552, 609.
........., offices in, 20, 266, 305.
........., residents in, 67, 80, 109.
Hesse, Maurice, Landgrave of, 59, 64.
Heton, Alice, 38.
........., Martin, late Bp. of Ely, 38.
Hethropp, 38.
Hetley, Thos., 103.
Hetley, Wm., 536.
Heune, Jurien, 419.
Hewett, John, 192.
........., Rich., 159.
........., Wm., 192.
Hewitt, Sir Thos., 166, 192.
........., Sir Wm., 192.
Hewten, Mr., 134.
Hexham, 362, 365.
Hexham, Fras., 217.
Hext, Sir Edw., 586, 594.
Heyborne, Ferd., 47, 57.
Heydon, see Haydon.
........., Sir Chris., 388, 462.
........., John, 462.
Hickman, Dixie, 253.
Hicks, Sir Baptist, 55, 118, 122, 123, 198, 227, 264, 440, 452, 467, 535.
........., Sir Mich., 147, 268.
Hicks, Wm., 268.
Hide, Lawr., see Hyde.
Higgons, Theo., 63.
High Commission, 70, 71.
.... Court, 295, 402, 420, 423, 435.
High Holborn, see London, Streets of.
Higham, Sir Clem., 190.
........., Sir John, 505.
Higham Ferrers, 597.
Highgate, 16, 17, 77, 324, 334, 473.
Highways, 221, 417, 557.
........., repair of, 10, 91, 109.
Hildesley, Sir Fras., 294, 300.
Hildyard, Sir Chris., 33.
.... Sir Chris., senr., 33.
........., John, 497.
Hilgay, 247.
Hill, Ant., 483.
........., Art., 607.
........., Dorothy, 607.
........., Edw., 101, 455.
........., Dr. John, 411.
........., Lady, 459, 461, 470, 512, 521, 530, 578.
........., Rich., 56.
........., Capt. Thos., 342, 345.
........., Wm., 188.
Hilles, Wm., 607.
Hillmorton, 435.
Hilton, Thos., 603.
Hinchinbrook, 489, 490.
........., wardrobe at, 222, 278.
Hind, Mrs., 317.
........., Wm., or Blackbeard, Hen., 408, 409.
Hinson, Rich., 87.
Hinton, 495.
Hinton St. George, 263, 279.
Hippesley, John, 70, 95.
History, see Books.
Hitcham, 95.
Hitcham, Sir Robt., 245, 423.

Hitchin, 308, 498.
Hithe, *see* Hythe.
Hoare, Nich., 278.
Hobart, Sir Hen., Attorney-General, 3, 8, 20, 27, 59, 65, 88, 112, 133, 174, 176; Chief Justice of Common Pleas, 215, 223, 360, 437, 454, 455, 471, 501, 519.
........., letters of and to, 520, 537.
Hobday, Robt., 328.
Hoby, Sir Edw., 269, 432, 441, 514.
........., Lady, 110.
........., Sir Thos. P., 126, 453.
Hobson, Edw., 34.
........., John, 544.
........., Percival, 249.
........., Thos., 193.
........., Wm., 544.
Hochselius (librarian), 72.
Hoddesdonbury, 609.
Hodges, Ant., 596.
Hodgkin, Allen, 265.
Hodgson, Edw., 335.
........., Thos., lieutenant of Berwick, 39, 61.
........., Wm., 335.
........., Mr., 302.
Hodson, Capt., 114, 453, 587.
........., Thos., 509.
Hogan, Wm., 100.
Hogbeane, Wm., 612.
Hogg, John, 505.
........., Wm., 125.
Holbeach, 292.
.... House, 292.
Holborn, *see* London, Streets of.
Holcombe, 498.
Holcombe, Ellis, 140.
Holdenby House and Park, 5, 28, 63.
Holderness, 35.
Holford, 226, 243.
Holland, David, 240.
........., Hugh, 72.
........., Phil., Portcullis Pursuivant, 453.
........., Tim., 49.
........., Wm., 393.
........., Dr., 124.
Holland, Lincolnshire, 413, 546, 576.
Holland, 44, 57, 71, 111, 120, 144, 170, 182, 188, 198, 224, 261, 262, 270, 272, 370, 417, 434, 438, 468, 482, 491, 501, 510, 529, 572, 592, 597, 614.
........., ambassador of, *see* Caron, Noel.
........., ambassadors to, 220, 234, 251; *see* Winwood, Sir Ra.; Carleton, Sir D.
........., cautionary towns, cession of, and payments for, 360–364, 368, 373, 385, 419, 425; *see also* Flushing and Brill.
........., commissioners from, 576, 595, 598, 600, 602, 604, 607.
........., departures for and visitors to, 9, 89, 161, 264, 269, 357.
........., religion in, 477.
........., ships of, 21, 57.
Holland, trade with, 62, 406, 428, 500, 526, 571.
........., treaty with, 1, 189, 390, 464.
Hollanders, 5, 148, 164, 203, 228, 284, 393, 410, 427, 513, 515–517, 565, 572, 573, 595, 600, 607.
Holle, Wm., 542.
Holliday, Wm., 574.
Hollis, Sir Gervase, 472.
........., Sir John, 322, 326, 344; Lord Houghton, 380, 381, 384, 472, 494, 497, 601.
Holloway, John, 175.
Holly, Jas., 583.
Holly Bush Hill, 164.
Holm Manor, 57.
Holme, 386, 606.
Holmes, Robt., 76.
Holstein, John Adolphus, Duke of, 208.
Holt, Mr., 552, 566.
Holtby, Rich. (Jesuit), 142, 305.
........., Robt., 54.
Holtoft, 341.
Holy Cross Hospital, Winchester, 410.
Holy Island, 6, 414.
Holyday, Sir Leon, 111.
Holyrood House, 44, 59, 469, 483, 586.
Holywell, 52.
Homage, fees for, 107, 374, 377, 496.
Home, Alex., Earl, 19.
........., Sir Edw., 268.
........., ..., jun., 268.
Honour, register of, 609, 610.
Hook, Dr. Hen., 265.
Hooke Manor, 440.
Hooker, Nich., 276.
Hooper, Thos., 215.
Hoord, Wm., 82.
Hope, Geo., 353, 363.
........., John, 122, 235.
Hope parish, 276.
Hopkins, Eliezer, 253.
Hopton, Robt., 6.
Horbling, 574.
Hornby Castle, 481.
Horne, Rev. Thos., 72, 192, 221, 284, 301.
........., Mrs. Anne, 336, 338.
........., Wm., 599.
Horneck, John de, 148.
Horning Park, 534.
Horninghold, 608.
Horrad's Park, 128.
Horse, Master of, *see* Somerset, Edw., Earl of Worcester; Villiers, Sir Geo.
Horseman, Eliz., 116.
........., Thos., 268.
........., Sir Thos., 268.
Horsham, 64.
Horton, Mr., 158.
Hoskins, Mr., 72, 237, 239, 275, 289, 344, 432.
Hotoft, 233.
Houdan, M. de Villers, 544.

Hougate, Wm., 287.
Hougham, 592.
Houghton, Sir Gilbert, 265, 299, 426, 497.
........., Sir Rich., 238.
........., Roger, 109.
........., Simon, 10.
........., Wm., 353, 363.
........., Lord, see Hollis.
Houghton Park, 73, 102.
.... Tower, 481.
Hounslow, 143.
.... Heath, 9, 34.
House, the, see Commons, House of.
Household, see Jas. I., Household of.
Houth, Lord, see St. Lawrence, Christopher.
Hovingham, 528.
Howard, Thos., Earl of Arundel, 134, 334, 385, 392–394, 397, 400–402, 416, 422, 423, 428, 465, 490–492, 545, 562.
........., ..., connection of with objects of art, 356, 361, 362, 375, 380, 382, 398, 453.
...., grants and commissions to, 154, 283, 395.
........., ..., letters of, 39, 384, 562.
........., ..., promotions of granted and proposed, 27, 31, 385, 401, 426, 474, 518.
........., ..., travels of, 138, 150, 151, 269, 480–482, 584.
........., Aletheia, Countess of Arundel, 150, 151, 181, 473.
Howard, Thos., Earl of Suffolk, Lord Chamberlain, 32, 68, 177, 190, 240; Lord High Treasurer, 244, 266, 278, 290; Chancellor of Cambridge, 312, 361, 366, 367, 375, 383, 412, 477, 521, 526, 569.
........., ..., commissions to, 250, 266, 275, 280, 343, 387, 395, 446, 506, 507, 534, 539, 545, 548, 552.
........., ..., discharges to, 251, 384, 387, 445.
........., ..., grants to, 50, 137, 193, 243, 331, 351, 354, 358.
........., ..., letters of, 147, 207, 252, 256, 258, 261, 262, 264, 274, 286, 297, 312, 316, 447, 458.
........., ..., ..., to Lake, 140, 142, 199, 207–209, 211, 213, 352, 461, 466, 468, 470, 471, 475.
........., ..., letters to, 79, 112, 139, 262, 371, 377, 409, 471, 496, 508, 513, 532.
........., ..., official transactions of, 123, 138, 262, 299, 333, 352, 354, 385, 400, 408, 428–430, 453, 456, 468, 481, 482, 585, 586, 610.
........., ..., warrants to, 247, 259, 297, 300, 388, 417, 444, 544.
........., ..., connection of with Overbury's murder, 334, 336.
........., ..., trial, &c. of, 501, 529, 531, 534, 566, 575, 594, 596, 599, 604.
........., Cath., Countess of Suffolk, 278, 334, 338, 356, 361, 367, 540, 566.
........., Lord Theoph. of Walden (eldest son of Thomas), 52, 108, 189, 243, 244, 263, 347, 464, 465, 470, 475, 482, 483.
Howard, Lady Eliz. of Walden, 189, 220.
........., Sir Thos. (2nd son of Thomas), 225, 235, 266, 288, 322, 388, 417, 533.
........., Hen. (3rd son of Thomas), 199, 200, 202, 203, 207, 213, 218, 286, 323, 397, 398.
........., Lady Frances (daughter of Thomas), see Devereux and Carr.
........., Lord Wm. (brother of Thomas), 7, 9, 21, 108, 211, 347, 358, 360, 366, 464, 465, 539.
Howard, Chas., Earl of Nottingham, Lord Admiral, Chief Justice in Eyre, South, 111, 170, 329, 408, 425, 446, 460, 504, 582, 585, 586, 591.
........., ..., commissions to, 18, 154, 178, 275, 395.
........., ..., grants, &c. to, 90, 94, 119, 232.
........., ..., letters of, 22, 38, 58, 60, 67, 82, 85, 125, 177, 204, 208, 247, 250, 522.
........., ..., letters to, 55, 64, 191, 352.
........., ..., official transactions of, 12, 50, 67, 107, 207, 213, 246, 366, 380, 388, 437, 438, 462, 468, 613.
........., ..., illness of, 449, 450.
........., Marg., Countess of Nottingham, 446, 586.
Howard, Wm., Lord of Effingham (eldest son of Charles), 232, 262, 284, 345.
........., Sir Chas. (2nd son of Charles), 190, 202, 243; Lord of Effingham, 404, 586.
........., Lady Effingham, 170.
........., Chas., (3rd son of Charles), 67, 94; Sir Charles, jun., 243, 288, 393, 404, 446, 451, 498.
........., Anne (daughter of Charles), 446.
........., Sir Wm. (brother of Charles), 209.
........., Frances, Lady, 209.
Howard, Hen., Earl of Northampton, Lord Privy Seal, Lord Warden of the Cinque Ports, 52, 78; Chancellor of Cambridge, 134, 135, 158, 183, 216, 250, 288, 298, 313, 317, 422, 428, 569.
........., ..., licences and commissions by, 146, 148, 190, 200.
........., ..., grants to, 44, 67, 106, 137, 146, 189, 193, 215, 216, 233.
...., letters of, 80, 108, 109, 126, 144, 188, 207, 215, 219, 222, 226.
........., ..., ..., to James I., 41, 140, 142, 150, 152.
........., ..., ..., to Lake, 142, 189, 208, 210, 212–215.
........., ..., ..., to Somerset, 58, 133, 140, 141, 145–147, 149–152, 193, 212, 223.
...., letters to, 5, 62, 75, 83, 111, 151, 226.
........., ..., official transactions of, 84, 110, 166, 199, 219, 338, 346, 362.
........., ..., orders and commissions to, 108, 123, 135, 165, 171, 173, 197, 203, 209, 298.
........., ..., slanders against, 160, 162, 168, 224.
........., ..., implication of in Overbury's murder, 327, 331, 336, 344, 349.

Howard, Hen., Earl of Northampton, illness and death of, 174, 227, 231, 237, 239, 242, 243.
........., ..., funeral of, 256.
........., Sir Edw., 128, 299, 305, 450, 466, 511, 598.
........., Sir Fras., 207, 408, 505.
........., Sir, Wm., 403, 450.
........., Sir Robt. 450.
........., Thos., Visct. Bindon, 1.
........., family, 278.
Howell, John, 195.
........., Watkyn, 73.
........., Mr., 608.
Howell's State Trials, 317.
Howes, Wm., 549.
Howgatt, Reynold, 293.
Howlbruck, 304.
Howse, John, 126.
Howson, Dr. John, 288.
Hoyer, Thos., 350, 567.
Hubbard, Godfrey, 108.
Huchenson, Wm., 207.
Huett, Benj., 407–409.
........., John, 407–409.
Huddleston, Sir Edw., 268.
........., Hen., 268.
Hudson, Jas., 116, 589.
........., John, 240.
........., Robt., 222, 309, 503.
........., Simon, 607.
........., Wm., 228.
........., Mr. 392.
Hudson's land, 572.
Hugbone, Wm., 356.
Hugessen, Jas., 350, 567.
Huggins, Wm., 297.
Hughes, Thos., 415, 608.
Hugheson, Geo., 226.
Hull, John, 118.
........., Mr., 117, 399.
Hull, *see* Kingston-upon-Hull.
Humber River, 263.
Humbleton, 448.
Hume, Sir Geo., 466.
........., Geo., Earl of Dunbar, Keeper of the Privy Purse, 1, 3–5, 12, 17, 18, 23, 25, 38, 39, 62, 114, 161, 189, 355, 399, 418, 455.
........., ..., death of, 6–9, 15, 19–21, 108.
........., ..., lands and goods of, 7–9, 60, 67, 68.
........., John, 69, 72.
........., Sir John, 31.
........., Sir Pat., 97, 153, 430.
Hunckes, Thos., 388.
Hundon Manor, 35.
Hungall (widow), 344.
Hungate, Wm., 295.
Hungerford, Geo., 205.
........., Sir John, 491, 495.
Hunsdon, John, 339, 525.
........., Lord, *see* Carey.
Hunsdon House, 259.
.... church, 378.
Hunt, John, 62.
........., Rich., 211.
........., Sir Thos., 166.
........., Wm., 74.
Huntingdon, 448, 493, 546, 566.
.... gaol, 212.
........., Earl of, *see* Hastings.
Huntingdonshire, 178, 259, 326, 441, 458, 536, 541.
........., grants of lands in, 57, 63, 295, 296.
........., lands and places in, 164, 190, 251, 353, 506, 555.
........., offices in, 277, 403, 546, 552, 566.
........., recusants in, 81.
........., residents in, 403, 508.
Huntley, Geo., 32.
........., Hen., 195.
........., Marquis of, *see* Gordon.
Huntly, Thos., 28.
Hupper, John, 546.
........., Ellen, 546.
Hurst, 470, 478, 572, 602.
.... Castle, 45.
.... Field, 334.
Hurt, Wm., 581.
Hussey, John, 210.
........., Sir Rich., 46.
Hustwood, Fras., 98.
Hutchins, Thos., 478, 562.
Hutchinson, Hen., 110.
Hutton, John, 205.
........., Rich. (serjeant), 121, 463, 469; Sir Rich., 533.
........., Rich. (auditor), 195, 354.
........., Thos., 465.
........., Sir Tim., 154.
........., Sir Wm., 20, 55, 539.
Huyssy, John, 360.
Huzie, John, 356.
Hyde Park, 447, 452.
Hyde, Lawr., 245, 317.
Hyncledon, 276.
Hythe, 255, 349, 365, 433, 449, 456, 503, 567, 614.
........., mayor, &c. of, 309, 365, 433, 456, 543.

I.

Ibson, John, 118.
Idbury, 98.
Ilthorne, 311.
Images, worship of, 400.
Impositions, *see* Customs.

Imworth, 459, 596, 597, 602.
Index expurgatorius, 401.
India, 162.
Indian fleet, *see* Spanish ships.
Indians (South American), 463, 521, 575.
Indigo neale, 232.
Indulgences, 429.
Infanta, *see* Isabella.
Ingham, Sir Thos., 343.
Ingleby, Sir Wm., 88, 175, 303.
Ingmersh, 109.
Ingoll, Dan., 536.
Ingram, Art., 72, 82, 90, 125; Sir Art., 195, 199, 240; Cofferer of the Household, 276, 278, 282, 294, 400.
........., ..., as contractor for lands, 120, 159, 191, 211, 448.
........., ..., as undertaker of alum works, 188, 218, 335, 377.
........., John, 100.
........., Dr. Wm., 125.
Inquisition, nuncio of, 417; *see also* Rome.
Inquisitions, 267.
Inns of Court, 514.
Inns and taverns, licences for, 248, 439, 441, 449.
Ipswich, 42, 136, 314, 498, 572.
Ireland, 25, 67, 80, 106, 167, 213, 241, 245, 248, 299, 328, 352, 418, 425, 426, 435, 448, 510, 516, 542, 591, 612.
........., affairs in, 47, 145, 160, 169, 189, 265, 462, 463, 531.
........., council of, 480, 599.
........., crown of, 340.
.... customs in, 131, 195.
........., Lord Deputy of, *see* Chichester, Art.; St. John, Sir Oliver; Carey, Sir Geo.
........., Lord Chief Justice of, *see* Jones, Sir Wm.
........., Lord Chief Baron of, *see* Methwold, Sir Wm.
........., military service in, 3, 132, 133, 201, 224, 261, 562, 611.
........., ordnance in, 187, 314, 383.
........., Parliament of, 186, 190, 197, 199, 223, 233, 285, 344.
........., plantations in, 507; *see* Ulster, Wexford.
........., pirates in, 66, 95, 109, 115, 216.
........., residents in, 33, 338.
........., officers in, 23, 234, 262, 427.
........., lands and towns, &c. in, 25, 113, 420, 457, 527, 599.
........., knights, barons, and nobility of, 234, 398, 421, 426, 458, 515, 519.
........., soldiers in and for, 50, 177, 219, 444.
........., Treasurer of wars in, *see* Docwra.
........., travellers to and from, 23, 37, 41, 48, 59, 113, 232, 258, 270, 372, 426, 480–482, 515, 539, 601.
Irish, 219, 224, 485, 501, 567.
.... bishops, 412.
Irish harp, 553.
.... money, 113.
.... soldiers, 29, 515.
Irish, Thos., 517.
Iron and ironworks, 32, 125, 288, 555, 578, 601.
Irthington, 211.
Irving, Sir Wm., 62.
Irwin, Jas., 136.
Isaac, Jas., 542.
Isaacson, Paul, 488.
Isabella Clara Eugenia, Infanta of Spain, joint regent of Flanders, 28.
Isham, Edw., 131.
........., Margery, 131.
........., Matt., 435.
Iskennen, 115.
Islay, 239.
Isles, the, 239.
........., Bishop of, *see* Knox, Thos.
Isle of Purbeck, 607.
Isle of Thanet, 257, 341, 358, 417.
Isle of Wight, 69, 97, 109, 243.
..............., grants of lands in, 5, 44, 191, 381.
Islingham, 230.
Islington, 551, 552.
Istria, 162, 229.
Italian church, *see* London, Italian church in.
.... friars, *see* Carmelite friars.
.... preachers, 428.
.... statues, 398.
.... treatise, 171.
Italians, 121, 139, 145, 178, 298, 488, 518, 527, 585.
Italy, 40, 97, 140, 142, 144, 153, 229, 284, 397, 426, 495.
........., travellers to and from, 59, 70, 110, 121, 137, 151, 163, 351, 391, 499.
Itchington, 155.
Ittery, Mr., 562.
Ivatt, Thos., 194.
Ivington, 339.

J

J. E., 184.
Jack, John, 252.
Jackman, Chas., 228.
........., Geo., 44.
........., Wm., 44.
Jackson, Robt., 54.
........., Wm., 14.
Jacob, Abm., 47, 535.
........., Ann, 337, 394.
........., John, 529, 535.
........., Nich., 509.

Jacob, Rich., 509.
........., Sir Robt., 47.
........., Wm., 600.
........., Mr., 582.
Jacobins, 521.
Jacobs, Lucas, 419.
Jacobson, Phil., 452, 560.
Jagger, John, 311.
James I., King of England :—
........., general mentions of, *passim*.
........., parents of, *see* Mary, Queen of Scots, and Darnley, Hen.
........., prerogative of, 119, 187, 327, 347, 371, 375, 380, 396, 403, 405, 432, 463.
........., designs against, 5, 23, 67, 152, 301–303, 308, 331, 426, 491.
........., entertainments to, 512, 514, 515.
........., satires, &c. against, 443, 514, 600.
........., ode, &c. to, 263, 339, 340, 473, 474.
........., opinions and proceedings of, in matters of religion, 156, 176, 183, 199, 274, 285, 288, 290, 302, 460, 464, 473, 502, 504, 527, 602.
........., messages and declarations of, 2, 172, 237, 238, 411.
........., speeches of, 230–232, 375, 381, 434, 436, 473, 474.
........., orders and instructions of, 1, 122, 377.
........., writings of, 111, 115, 119, 142, 215, 229, 310, 318, 432, 608.
........., illnesses of, 161, 168, 198, 214, 260, 395, 518, 526, 565, 566.
........., portrait of, 156.
........., apparel, &c. of, 88, 110, 119, 196, 380, 440, 445.
........., jewels, &c. of, 35, 84, 114, 168, 171, 257, 293, 510, 560.
........., personal notices of, 28, 71, 98, 99, 104, 128, 134, 146, 148, 155, 158, 162, 163, 167, 170, 175, 178, 196, 199, 217, 222, 230, 233, 235, 237, 249, 256, 273, 287, 312, 318, 320, 327, 329, 331, 348, 370, 372–375, 391, 395, 398, 406, 407, 419, 421, 423–427, 442, 445, 449, 450, 454, 455, 457, 461, 464, 470, 472, 475, 482, 484, 487, 488, 491, 494, 495, 504, 510, 511, 513, 520, 522–525, 530.
........., progresses and sojourns of, 9, 28, 37, 66, 69, 70, 84, 88, 95, 115, 132, 135, 137, 138, 145, 147, 148, 156, 162, 163, 167, 168, 172, 177, 181, 185, 188–190, 196, 199, 200, 220, 223, 225, 227, 241, 244, 249, 256, 262, 263, 269, 273, 274, 276–278, 282, 286, 296, 301, 303, 305, 308, 316, 360–362, 373, 375, 379, 381, 382, 387, 389, 392, 394, 397, 400, 404, 410, 412–415, 422–424, 428–430, 432, 434, 436–438, 441–443, 445, 448, 453, 454, 457, 458, 460, 465, 466, 469–478, 480–485, 488, 490, 491, 493, 495–497, 503, 511, 513, 515, 518, 520, 521, 524, 527, 554, 562, 567, 568, 586, 594, 599, 600, 604.

James I.—*continued*.
........., letters of, 71, 75, 101, 102, 111, 135, 175, 188, 264, 318, 321, 322, 330, 351, 371, 378, 389, 409, 410, 414, 450, 455, 474, 480, 486, 492, 507, 517, 547, 556, 586, 595.
........., letters to, 144, 152, 153, 166, 168, 187, 188, 210, 216, 223, 237, 238, 260, 269, 270, 272, 306, 307, 310, 317, 319, 327, 332, 333, 342, 349, 366, 376, 394, 409, 411, 431, 437, 448, 461, 470, 485, 486, 496, 507, 508, 520, 542, 551, 576; *see also* Abbot, Geo.; Coke, Sir Edw.; Howard, Hen., Earl Northampton; Wilson, Thos.
........., petitions to, 12, 82, 105–107, 134, 167, 179, 217, 218, 265, 325, 339, 340, 360, 363, 364, 375, 383, 419, 420, 447, 454, 467, 470, 486, 509, 518–520, 526, 546, 552, 561, 605–607, 609.
........., debts of and to, *see* Crown debts.
........., gifts of, 5, 18, 23, 32, 44, 102, 121, 153, 209, 251, 261, 275, 277, 380, 393, 398, 406, 446, 500.
........., ..., to the Queen, 46,
........., ..., to the Prince of Wales, 104.
........., ..., to the Duke of York, 56, 104.
........., ..., to the Princess Elizabeth, 1, 56.
........., gifts to, 93, 99, 180, 189, 205, 292, 373, 375, 494, 497.
........., benevolence for, 255, 256, 273, 279, 285, 287, 290, 370, 409, 538.
........., loans to, *see* London and Loans.
........., supplies for, 234, 236, 237, 333, 374, 505.
........., houses of, 8, 37, 78, 83, 86, 109, 152.
........., lands of, *see* Crown lands.
........., revenue of, *see* Crown revenue.
........., printers of, *see* Norton, John; Barker, Robt.
........., chaplains of, 203, 284, 484, 490, 497, 555, 606.
........., chapel of, 53, 104, 107, 412, 473, 549.
........., counsel-at-law of, 123.
........., surgeons and physician to, 17, 132, 208, 269, 396, 413, 446, 461, 561, 569.
........., favourites of, 154, 199, 224, 237, 260, 310, 354, 412, 471, 492.
........., goldsmiths and jewellers of, 367.
........., horses and stables of, 74, 98, 103, 132, 192, 265, 278, 416, 493, 499.
........., tradespeople of, 76, 86, 108, 112, 123, 127, 131, 211, 252, 274, 376, 401, 419, 456, 598.
........., deer of, 205, 382.
........., game and gamekeepers of, 2, 4, 9, 17, 19, 29, 34, 95, 122, 140, 214, 231, 235, 243, 244, 249, 251, 253, 257, 266, 335, 338, 362, 382, 389, 390, 415, 440, 498, 594.
........., parks and park-keepers of, 34, 113, 129, 143.
........., hunting and huntsmen of, 18, 64, 90, 91, 113, 385, 391, 392, 473, 481, 488.

James I.—*continued.*
........., hounds and buckhounds of, 76, 245, 382, 606.
........., harriers and yeomen prickers of, 47, 211, 265, 430.
........., falconers and falconry of, 55, 86, 89, 100, 117, 188, 205, 243, 266, 274, 346, 360, 393, 398, 430.
........., cockmaster to, 230, 472.
........., bargemaster to, 248, 409.
........., masters and yeomen of revels to, 17, 74.
........., masters and yeomen of tennis to, 86.
........., musicians of, 93, 118, 126, 138, 199, 210, 228, 299, 313, 559.
........., dogs and dog-keepers of, 100, 195, 196, 315.
........., gentleman of the robes to, *see* Hay, Jas., Lord.
........., groom of, 245, 360.
........., chandlery of, 420, 421.
........., equerries of, 279.
........., keeper of privy purse to, *see* Hume, Earl of Dunbar; Murray, John.
........., household of, 13, 22, 23, 26, 41, 160, 260, 262, 282, 437, 481, 525, 555.
........., ..., officers of, 3, 11, 31, 107, 125, 154 159, 165, 276, 278, 281, 294, 344, 404, 501, 502, 504, 505, 510, 536, 589.
........., ..., reforms of, 22, 23, 496, 503, 527, 531, 589.
........., ..., supplies for, 47, 68, 73, 149, 164, 187, 220, 244, 247, 250, 260, 281, 282, 410, 486.
........., servants of, 15, 26, 42, 43, 69, 72, 84, 94, 104, 122, 150, 175, 191, 205, 206, 212, 227, 289, 310, 357, 375, 388, 486, 531, 547, 560, 562.
........., footmen and pages of, 110, 292, 299.
........., privy chamber grooms, &c. of, 49, 50, 57, 77, 107, 194, 265, 296, 297, 323, 346, 440, 533, 549, 555, 558, 562.
........., bedchamber, grooms and pages of, 5, 26, 33, 73, 76, 100, 157, 195, 204, 209, 222, 241, 251, 306, 338, 364, 381, 432, 446, 497, 514, 599, 610.
........., messengers of, 315, 562, 586, 605.
........., porters and ushers, &c. of, 429, 444, 471, 511, 530.
James, Sir Hen., 120, 128, 210, 452.
........., Martin, 452.
........., Pet., jun., 121.
........., Wal., 281, 325.
........., Wm., Bp. of Durham, 211, 213, 303, 328, 395, 399, 437, 453, 467, 469, 487, 515.
........., ..., letters of, 16, 17, 34, 54, 113, 120, 204, 270, 289, 291, 301, 302, 304, 323.
........., ..., letters to, 114, 121, 304, 308, 320, 325.
Jamyson, Robt., 55.
Japan, 531, 532.
Jarrett, Hen., 66.
Jarvis, Rich., 608, 609.
Jarvis, Sir Thos., 463.
........., Mr., 293.
Jaye, Hen., 221.
Jedburgh, 61.
Jefferey, Geo., 268.
........., Sir John, 268.
Jefferson, John, 195.
Jegon, John Bp. of Norwich, 132, 531.
Jekin, Hen., 355.
Jeneson, Robt., 485.
Jenkin, Jevan, 275.
........., Pat., 253.
Jenman, Wm., *alias* Salisbury, 430, 431, 442.
Jenner, Thos., 601.
Jennings, Munton, 592.
.... (servant), 380, 381.
Jennison, Rich., 513.
Jernegan, Hen., 241.
........., Hen., jun., 609.
Jerningham, Edw., 581.
Jesuits, 3, 54, 104, 148, 157, 203, 276, 281, 303–305, 420, 424, 427, 435, 438, 578, 610.
........., colleges of, 61, 340.
........., proceedings against, 26, 28, 88, 102, 123, 142, 212, 286, 532, 547, 600.
........., English, 343.
Jersey, Isle of, 445, 447, 511.
Jewel House, 69, 248, 292.
..............., officers of, 504, 505, 511, 594.
Jewett, Grace, 115.
Jewkes, Barth., 558.
Jews, the, 188, 260.
Jobson, Humph., 264.
........., Jane, 96.
Johnson, Chas., 28.
........., Edw., 539.
........., Hen., 539.
........., Isaac, 260.
........., Jas., 63.
........., John, 572.
........., Nath., 47.
........., Nich., 450.
........., Rich., 260.
........., Robt., 256, 574, 584, 609.
........., Sir Robt., 3, 188.
........., Wm. (of Lambeth), 392.
........., Wm. (Cambridgeshire), 510.
Johnston, or Johnson, Hector, 452, 560, 582.
Jolly, Ellis, 228.
Jonas, Dr., *see* Carisius, Jonas.
Jones, Enian, 252.
........., Griffin, 379.
........., Fras., Alderman, 19, 166, 171, 235; Sir Fras., 314, 511.
........., Inigo, 32, 72, 181, 361, 380, 412, 453, 473, 584.
........., John, 206, 388.
........., Rich, 391.
........., Robt. (Jesuit), 142.
........., Robt., 537.

Jones, Sam., 194, 388.
........., Thos. (of Cornwall), 201.
........., Thos. (of Cardigan), 130.
........., Thos. (of London), 131.
........., Thos. (master of toils), 25, 49, 206.
........., Thos. (pauper), 87.
........., Wm. (haberdasher), 178, 226.
........., Wm. (pauper), 74.
........., Wm. (Catholic), 556–559.
........., Wm. (of Dover), 435, 607.
........., Wm. (serjeant), 469.
........., Sir Wm., Lord Chief Justice of Ireland, 515, 524.
........., Wythen, 252.
Jonson, Ben., 373, 472, 512.
Jordan, Dr. Edw., 335.
........., Wm., 276.
........., Mr., 131.
Joseph, Ben., 339.
Josey, Wm., 7.
Jossy, Robt., 12, 88, 157.
Jucks, Simon, 497, 500.
Judges in Eyre, Oyer, and Terminer, 284; *see also* Howard, Earl of Northampton; Talbot, Earl of Shrewsbury; and Villiers, Earl of Buckingham.
Judges and Justices of Assize, 10, 47, 95, 121. 123, 144, 170, 186, 213, 239, 247, 275, 318, 321, 326, 363, 371, 470, 473, 507, 601; *see also* King's Bench and Common Pleas, Judges of, and Exchequer, Barons of.
Judkin, Wm., 282.
Juett, Thos., 43.
Juries and jurors, 122, 151, 308, 355, 410, 416, 422.
Justice, Lord Chief of Common Pleas, *see* Coke, Sir Edw.; Hobart, Sir Hen.
Justice, Lord Chief, of King's Bench, *see* Fleming Thos.; Coke, Sir Edw.; Montague, Sir Hen.
Justices of Peace, 53, 95, 130, 176, 219, 281, 326, 337, 477.

K.

Kars, *see* Carse.
Kay, John, 314.
........., Rich, 424.
........., Robt., 19.
Kaye, Thos., 277.
Keamish, Edw., 306.
Kebblewhite, Pet., 265.
Keeling, Wm., 269.
Keeper of the Great Seal, *see* Bacon.
Keighley, Thos. (priest), 321.
Keire, Sir Geo., 382.
Keith, Sir And., 178, 209, 250.
Kelk, Edw., 154, 431.
Kellett, Rich. (priest), 321.
Kellison, Matt., 226.
Kelp (sea weed), 377, 457, 459.
Kelshall, 488.
Kemp, Eleanor, 116.
........., Fras. (priest), 321, 328, 548.
Kempe, Edw., 613.
Kempson, Geo., 138.
Kempston, 261.
Kendall, Edw., 118.
Kendrick, John, 96.
Kenilworth, *see* Killingworth.
Kenithorpe, Mr., 552, 575.
Kenlleth, Owen, 191.
Kenne rectory, 207.
Kennedy, Sir John, 289.
........., Eliz., Lady, 489, 516.
Kennett, or Kenett, Thos., 395, 416.
Kennington, 251.
Kensington, 156, 227, 273, 391.
Kent, 86, 205, 268, 340, 352, 364, 387, 456, 457, 460, 501, 535.
........., grants of lands in, 29, 63, 94, 144, 159, 192, 196, 224, 226, 230, 358, 418, 452.
........., officers in, 13, 151, 220, 262, 316, 363, 408, 422, 601.
........., residents in, 5, 29, 95, 169, 293, 382, 390, 400, 408, 417, 418, 538, 612.
........., towns, &c. in, 17, 63, 75, 96, 158, 240, 241, 259, 269, 305, 372, 374, 447, 548, 601.
........., recusants in, 49, 120.
.... Sands, 509.
........., Earl and Countess of, *see* Grey.
Ker, Robt., Baron Roxburgh, 59, 203, 206, 222; Earl Roxburgh, 415, 425, 514.
........., Jane, Countess of Roxburgh, 415, 446, 461, 464, 479, 484, 515; *see also* Drummond, Jane.
Ker, Wm., Baron Roxburgh, 514.
Kerckper, 506.
Kerry, Rich., 244, 441.
Kerseys, *see* Cloth.
Kesteven, 576.
Ketchett, John, 433.
Kettering, 218.
Kettlewell, Wilfrid, 613.
Kew, letters from, 14, 17, 123.
Keymer, Rich., 330.
Keymish, Capt. Lawr., 528, 531, 540.
Keys, Sir John, 320, 321, 324, 457, 550.
Keyston, 353.
Kibworth, 127.
Kidderminster, Sir John, 246, 582, 591, 598.
........., Olive, 418.
Kidland, 8.
Kidwelly, 115, 298, 355, 387, 553.
.... Castle, 115.

Knollys, Eliz., Lady, 372; Visctss. Wallingford, 603.
Knott, Nich., Marshal of Dover Castle, letters of and to, 311, 316, 323, 325, 328, 345, 366, 372, 374, 430.
Knowles, Jas., 358.
Knowsley, 177.
Knowsley, Aristotle, 59.
Knox, And., Bp. of Raphoe, 22.
........., Thos., Bp. of the Isles, 22.
Knyvet, Thos., 75, 198.
........., Thos., Lord, Warden of the Mint, 57, 112, 357, 596.
........., ..., grants to, 44, 111.
........., ..., warrants and payments to, 20, 23, 25, 385, 387.
Kyfin, see Kiffin.

L.

La Chesnay, M., 570, 572, 575, 577.
Lacon, Sir Fras., 170, 230, 235, 463.
Ladd, Audley, 382.
Lainston, 418.
Lake, Dr. Art., 231; Bp. of Bath and Wells 410, 427, 484.
........., Sir Art., 481, 488, 543.
........., John, 540.
........., Thos., 188, 376.
........., Sir Thos., Under Secretary, 31, 39, 106, 135, 138, 163, 215, 217, 235, 263, 310, 338; Secretary of State, 360, 393, 415, 443, 491, 494, 496, 501, 504, 512, 525, 527, 533, 576, 581, 583, 592.
........., ..., connection of with the Countess of Exeter v. Lady Roos, 500, 523, 524, 526, 531, 542, 567, 575, 585, 594, 595, 599, 600, 604.
........., ..., letters of, 191, 412, 490, 496, 519, 533, 578.
........., ..., letters of to Carleton, 148, 155, 166, 185, 221, 464.
........., ..., letters of to Salisbury, 10–13, 21–23, 60, 64, 69, 70, 71, 80–82, 91, 100, 113, 119.
Lake, Sir Thos., letters of to Winwood, 349, 454, 455, 457, 460, 463, 466, 467, 469, 470, 472, 474, 477, 479, 480, 481, 484.
........., ..., letters to, 65, 93, 135, 137, 139, 141, 142, 144, 149, 150, 152, 168, 170, 176, 185, 205, 208, 210, 213–215, 224, 225, 240, 243, 285, 315, 337, 343, 348, 455–462, 466–471, 474, 475, 479, 484, 487, 491, 494, 508, 517, 527, 529, 530, 533, 536, 538, 540, 544, 547, 549, 559, 565, 584, 603.
........., ..., papers by, 15, 25.
Lake, Sir Thos., promotions of granted and proposed, 123, 127, 134, 137, 158, 161, 173, 202, 203, 227, 228, 234, 251, 305, 345, 492, 497, 514, 519.
........., ..., daughter of, see Cecil, Anna, Lady Roos.
........., Mary, Lady, 137, 168, 210, 471, 480, 500, 513, 524, 542, 543, 584, 595.
........., Wm., 173.
Laleston, 292.
Lambe, Dr. John, Chancellor of Peterborough, 147, 202, 272, 274, 277, 300, 306, 413, 432, 458, 519, 580.
........., ..., letters of and to, 290, 299, 443.
Lambert, Alice, 480.
........., Jas., 480.
........., Mich., alias Lamote, Peter, 403, 412, 434.
........., Sir Oliver, 23, 524, 599.
........., Lady, 599.
Lambeth, 16, 186, 295, 391, 392, 414, 424, 436, 489, 523, 573.
........., letters, &c. from, 26, 128, 151, 171, 176, 178, 179, 227, 232, 244, 261, 262, 273, 315, 320, 369, 370, 372, 399, 400, 406, 417, 429, 470, 475, 491, 495, 510, 527, 547, 556, 558.
.... Marsh, 140, 362.
.... Park, 523.
........., South, 126.
Lammas, Thos., 113.
Lamote, John, 98, 363.
........., Pet., see Lambert, Mich.
Lamplugh, Wm., 547.
Lampreys, see Fish.
Lancaster, 173.
........., Duchy of, 7, 98, 289, 394, 451, 466, 502, 506, 519, 520.
........., ..., Attorneys of, see Brograve, Sir John; Moseley, Sir Edw.
........., ..., Chancellor of, see Parry, Sir Thos.; Dackombe, Sir John; May, Sir Hum.
........., ..., Chancellorship of, commission for, 520.
........., ..., Receiver-General of, see Molyneux, Sir Rich.
........., ..., officers of, 2, 21, 597; see also Gerard Gilbert.
........., ..., lands in, 9, 57, 85, 107, 115, 133, 135, 171, 181, 215, 216, 251, 379, 606.
........., ..., court, 494, 499.
........., ..., records of, 394.
........., County Palatine, 38, 171.
.... Herald, see Penson, Wm.
Lancashire, 325, 471, 483.
........., grants of lands in, 34, 63.
........., lands and places in, 43, 245, 250, 372, 500, 566.
........., offices in, 100, 177, 538.
.... residents in, 7, 87, 132, 144, 206, 440, 498.
Landochy Pennadz, 90.

Lane, Edw., 100.
........., R., 218.
........., Sir Wm., 24, 31.
Langdon, Chris., 596.
........., Steph., 241.
Langford, 43.
Langford, John, 496.
........., Margt., 43.
Langham Hall, 114.
Langhorne, Thos., 76.
Langley, 585.
........., Barony of, 384.
.... Marsh, 246.
Langley, John, 523.
........., Margt., 476.
........., Dr., 290.
.... (town clerk), 177.
Langton, Dr. Wm., 13, 16.
........., Mr., 323.
Languedoc, 557.
Lanivet, 43.
Lanier, Alphonso, 210.
........., Innocent, 407.
Lanke, Wm., 604.
Lannam Park, 351.
Lanyer, And., 138.
........., Nich., 174.
Lanzarote, 489, 516.
Lapthorne, Ant., 29.
Lapworth, Dr. Edw., 457.
La Roche, M., 147.
Larden, 526.
Larkyn, Hen., 444.
Lascelles, Mr., 79.
Lassels, Eliz., 225.
........., Sir Thos. 197, 300.
Latham, 482.
Latham, Hen., 578.
.... (priest), 162.
Lathorpe, Robt., 265.
Laud, Dr. Wm., 33, 43, 66, 75, 217, 290, 392; Dean of Gloucester, 411, 473, 492.
........., ..., letters of and to, 435, 437-439.
........., ..., endorsements by, 288, 489.
Launceston, 79.
Launey, Gideon, 175.
........., Dr. Wm., 175.
Law officers, 346, 375.
Lawns, 141.
Lawrence, Adam, 363.
........., Thos., 457.
........., Wm., 265.
Lawson, Sir Ralph, 476.
........., Sir Wilfrid, 1, 21, 55, 240.
Lawshall, 550.
Lazomby, Rich., 129, 207, 554.
Leach, Edw., 226.
Lead, 12, 34, 45, 291, 501.
Leadenhall, 384.
Leaplish, 36.
Leate, Nich., 356.
Leather, 501.
........., export of, 117, 278, 583, 591.
Leaver, 2.
Lebrand, Thos., 513.
........., Christian, 513.
Lecavill, Rich., 555.
Ledbury Forren, 584..
Ledsham, Wm., 122, 235.
Lee, 39, 42.
Lee, Capt. Gilb., 591.
........., Sir Hen., 40, 51, 291, 299.
........., Hugh, 15, 86.
........., John, 606.
........., Sir Rich., 106.
........., Wm., 110.
Leech, Thos., 393.
Leechford, Sir Rich., 268.
........., Rich., 268.
Leedes, John, 329.
........., Sir John, 327-329, 344.
........., Lady, 327-329, 344.
Leeds, 467.
........., manor of, 88.
Leeds, Thos., 374.
Leet, John, 80.
Le Faye, Capt., 310.
Legate, Barth., 121, 123, 124.
Legatt, John, 260.
Le Gris, Capt. Robt., 556, 558, 559, 581.
Leghorn, 222.
L'Hermite, Pet., 494.
Leicester, 398, 467.
........., Archdeaconry of, 271, 543.
........., hospital at, 130.
........., Earl of, *see* Dudley, Robt.; Sydney, Robt.
........., Countess of, *see* Dudley, Douglas.
Leicester, Geo., 444.
........., Anne, 444.
Leicestershire, 73, 74, 168, 185, 267, 268, 432, 458.
........., grants of lands in, 63, 87, 124, 159, 386, 388.
.... lands in, 17, 127, 232, 276, 292, 467.
........., offices in, &c., 86, 242.
........., residents in, 33, 247, 286, 423, 540.
Leigh, Fras., 268.
........., Jas., 86, 123.
........., Sir John, 111, 243, 268, 293.
........., Sir Olive, 268.
........., Robt., 268.
........., Sir Robt., 76, 268.
........., Thos., 268.
........., Sir Thos., 6, 193, 352, 580.
Leighton, 522.
Leighton, Edw., 235.
........., Thos., 235, 268.
........., Sir Thos., 235, 268.
Lenham, 29.
Lennard, Sampson, 126, 453.

Lennnard, Marg., 10th Baroness Dacre, 124.
........., Sir Hen., 11th Baron Dacre of the South, 124, 126, 391.
........., Chrysogona, Lady, 398.
........., Rich., 12th Lord Dacre, 478.
........., Mr., 352.
Lenning, John, 125.
Lenox, Duke of, *see* Stuart.
........., Countess of, *see* Stuart.
Lent, abstinence or non-abstinence in, 169, 226, 269, 433, 462, 502, 521, 525.
........., preachers and sermons in, 439, 464,
Lenton, Simon, 313.
Le Pennecke, Roland, 416.
Lepton, John, 346–348.
Le Shrofold Manor, 209.
Le Sieur, Sir Steph., 22, 147, 212, 245, 269, 519, 520.
Lesley, Sir Pat., Lord of Lindores, 498.
Lethington, 193.
Letley, 53, 102, 259.
Leureulx, Nich., 190.
Levant Company, 80, 283, 290, 427, 476, 515.
........., ports, 170.
........., trade, 149, 515.
Le Ver, Jacob, 412.
Lever, Thos., 401.
Leveson, Sir John, 215.
........., Sir, Rich., 434, 541.
Leving, Mr., 529.
Levingston, Alex., 297.
........., Sir Hen., 481.
........., Jas., 556.
........., John, 204, 225, 292, 550, 580, 597.
........., ..., letters of, 481, 524.
........., Mrs., 225.
Lewes, Dav., 192.
........., John, 232, 280.
........., Rich., 241.
Lewis, Ant., 68.
........., Godfrey, 46.
........., Jas., 85, 137.
........., Robt., 499.
........., Mr. (chaplain), 521.
.... (schoolmaster), 14.
Lewisham, 209.
Lewkenor, Sir Lewis, 142.
........., Sir Rich., 4, 25, 45.
Ley, Sir Jas., Attorney of Wards and Liveries, 50, 519, 520.
Leyden, 350.
.... University, 71, 111, 400.
Lichborough, 274.
Lichfield, 259, 478, 562.
........., Sheriff of, 123.
........., Dean and Chapter of, 501.
Lidcott, Sir John, 184, 200, 322, 331, 344.
Liddiard, 194, 195, 411.
Liddleside, 539.
Lide, Hen., 46.
Lime, 364.
Limehouse, 572.
Liminge, Robt., 78.
Linaker, Jas., 431.
Linchford Walk, 208.
Lincoln, 192, 299, 300, 449, 453, 454, 457, 460, 478, 481, 432.
.... Castle, gaol, &c., 98.
.... Hospital, 42.
........., Foss Dike at, 482.
........., Bp. of, *see* Barlow, Wm., Neyle, Rich., Montaigne, Geo.
.... Cathedral, 74.
........., Chapter House at, 458.
........., Dean and Chapter of, 81, 291, 458.
........., diocese of, 202, 290, 332, 335, 367, 413, 522.
........., Earl and Countess of, *see* Clinton.
Lincoln's Inn, 170, 172, 209, 212, 567.
.... Fields, 596.
Lincolnshire, 178, 212, 260, 267, 268, 409, 541.
........., grants of lands in, 63, 87, 124, 159, 181, 190, 196, 211, 292, 306, 388, 405, 418, 444, 445.
........., offices in, 17, 341, 389, 403, 413, 546, 552, 566.
........., recusants in, 49, 89.
........., residents in, 95, 183, 265, 352, 403, 414, 427.
........., towns, &c. in, 17, 20, 39, 74, 233, 341, 408, 438, 440, 507.
Lindley, Sir Hen., 103.
Lindores, Lord of, *see* Leslie, Pat.
Lindsay, Bernard, 257.
........., Sir John, 265.
Lindsell, Thos., 37, 56, 58, 80, 83.
Lindsey, 576.
Linlithgow, 474.
Lippincott, Laomedon, 545.
Lisbon, 314, 324, 432, 516.
........., Consul at, 15, 86.
Lisle, Edm., 454, 457.
........., Visct., *see* Sydney.
Lister, John, 191.
........., Dr. Matt., 83, 127, 458.
Litharge, 229.
Little Laver, 116.
Littleton, 48, 237.
Littleton, Sir Edw., sen., 268.
........., Steph., 292.
........., Sir Thos., Bart., 558.
Liverpool, 240, 485.
Llandaff, Bp. of, *see* Godwin, Fras., Carleton, Dr.
........., bishopric of, 500.
........., Dean and Chapter of, 498.
Llanellwith, 85.
Llanerochwell, 243.
Llangeler, 280.
Llanvaier, 85.

Llanvigan, 195.
Llanymthivery, 249.
Llanywllyn, 2.
Lledwigan Lles, 292.
Lloyd, Edw., 252.
………, Geo., Bp. of Chester, 210, 213, 285, 426.
………, Hen., 542.
………, John, 596.
………, Marmaduke, 254.
………, Robt., 46, Admiral to the Queen, 357; Sir Robt., 444, 471, 522.
………, Mrs., 46.
………, Thos., 46, 111.
………, Wm., 292.
Lloydiarth, 191.
Loane, Rich., 245.
Loans to the King, 27, 90, 91, 92, 95, 100, 102, 118, 119, 125, 193, 448, 475.
………, clerks for, 81, 83, 84, 90, 103.
………, collectors of, 93, 117, 119.
………, privy seals for, 81, 82, 88, 113–117, 263.
Lobday, *see* Lopdale.
Lobdell, Nich., 389.
Lobsey, Rich., 416.
Lobell, Paul de, 312, 326, 334, 349.
………, Mdme., 326.
Locke, Thos., letters to and from Carleton, 578, 595, 596.
Lockey, Fras., 5, 66.
Locton, Sir John, 268.
………, Wm., 268.
Loddington, 374, 379.
Loddon river, 200.
Lode Manage, Court of, 394, 487, 532.
Loe, Wm., 94, 439.
Loens, —— 526.
Logwood, 296, 331, 407, 549.
Lomellino, J. V., 141.
Londesborough, letters dated from, 2, 8, 20, 24, 27, 35, 36, 38, 68, 83, 92, 111, 120, 220.
London, 2, 13, 47, 65, 72, 78, 91, 125, 141–143, 154, 165, 166, 168, 175, 183, 185, 213, 217, 220, 225, 264, 277, 304, 310, 315, 390, 398, 406, 407, 413, 429, 434, 456, 457, 460, 462, 463, 481, 510, 533, 534, 536, 539, 577, 584.
………, aldermen of, 55, 62, 108, 122, 166, 186, 196, 221, 223, 264, 285, 287, 294, 296, 428, 473, 486, 511, 519, 542, 563, 601, 611.
………, artillery garden in, 137, 340, 342.
………, births and deaths in, 133.
………, buildings in and near, 66, 73, 221, 260, 286–288, 295, 551, 553, 555, 557, 558, 564, 571, 574, 584, 602.
………, citizens of, 107, 137, 178, 191, 287, 340.
London—*continued*.
………, City companies of, 444:—
Adventurers, *see* Guinea Company.
Apothecaries, 507.
Booksellers, 179.
Bricklayers, 186, 197, 218.
Brewers, 541, 548.
Carpenters, 564.
Clothworkers, 55, 174, 487.
Drapers, 487.
Dyers, 174.
Farriers, 201.
Fishmongers, 382, 487.
Goldsmiths, 380, 387.
Grocers, 377, 487, 507.
Gardeners, 402.
Horners, 563.
Haberdashers, 178, 226, 487.
Ironmongers, 289.
Merchant Tailors, 55, 220.
Mercers, 487.
Paperstainers, 176.
Parish clerks, 104.
Pewterers, 270, 287.
Pinmakers, 263, 363, 532, 557, 563.
Plasterers, 186, 197, 218.
Plumbers, 19.
Salters, 487.
Shipwrights, 191, 204.
Skinners, 352.
Stationers, 120, 353.
Sugar Merchants, 377, 396.
Tallowchandlers, 218.
Vintners, 40, 117, 487.
Weavers, 293, 302.
Wireworkers, 29.
………, clerk of, 177.
………, recorder of, 178, 186, 434, 447, 556; *see also* Montague, Sir Hen.; Coventry, Sir Thos.; Ben, Ant.; Martin, Rich.; Heath, Robt.
………, common council, &c., of, 2, 108, 487.
………, conspirators in, 308, 399.
………, freedom of, 62, 378, 563, 611.
………, King at, 167, 273, 413, 430, 485.
………, lands and rents in, 57, 124, 193, 382.
………, letters dated from, *passim*.
………, loans of to the King, 186, 239, 242, 294, 422, 428, 430, 442, 446, 461, 462, 468, 470, 473, 485, 531.
………, Lord Mayors of, 130, 218, 264, 486, 507, 611.
(1610-11): Craven, Sir Wm., 2, 55, 62.
(1612-13): Swinnerton, Sir John, 154, 163, 165, 166, 186, 191.
(1613-14): Middleton, Sir Thos., 219-221, 223, 253.
(1614-15): Hayes, Sir John, 272 286, 293.
(1615-16): Jolles, Sir John, 341, 376.

London, Lord Mayors of—*continued.*
(1616-17): Leman, Sir John, 434, 436, 438, 446, 460, 465, 472.
(1617-18): Bowles, Sir Geo., 519, 525, 542, 553, 554, 556, 559, 563.
........., merchants of, 11, 55, 66, 90, 114, 287, 331, 356, 427, 428, 473, 552, 613.
........., parishes of, 18, 19, 29, 49, 108, 132, 156, 169, 201, 228, 234, 272, 295, 335, 412, 502, 521, 571, 576, 581.
........., port of, 175, 182, 190, 194, 212, 296, 557, 568, 605.
........., custom officers of, 175, 363, 378, 528, 605.
........., ..., ..., letters to, 252, 258, 261, 280, 297, 316, 358.
........., recusants in, 66, 589.
........., registrar of brokers in, 409.
........., residents in, 18, 19, 23, 56, 59, 62, 63, 70, 72, 76, 103, 107, 111, 122, 123, 125, 157–159, 162, 169, 177, 189, 191–194, 196, 201, 204, 206, 207, 211, 212, 217, 218, 223, 225, 227, 248, 257, 260, 264, 268, 274, 276, 280, 286, 288, 289, 291, 296, 300, 306, 311, 322, 335, 372, 379, 382, 581.
........., removals from, 454–456, 459.
........., sheriffs, &c. of, 221, 317, 450, 487, 584.
........., ships of, 129, 341, 426, 497.
........., Streets of:—
Aldersgate-street, 5, 201, 218.
Aldgate, 234, 342.
Austin Friars, 50, 133, 280.
Billiter-lane, 98.
Bishopsgate-street, 221.
Blackfriars, 96, 316, 323, 329, 351, 353, 360, 530.
Blackhorse-alley, 553, 559.
Bow-lane, 406, 410, 411.
Broad-street, 577.
Candlewick-street, 33.
Canon-row, 62, 92, 180, 184.
Chancery-lane, 172, 399, 507.
Cornhill, 204, 585.
Drury lane, 54, 131, 282, 551, 555, 562, 568, 599.
Eastcheap, 33.
Fleet-street, 530, 553, 594.
Fenchurch-street, 425.
Finsbury, 458.
Gracious-street, 447.
Grub-street, 122.
Holborn, 65, 324, 332, 334, 540, 554.
Holborn Bars, 507.
Houndsditch, 221.
Ivy-lane, St. Paul's, 567.
King-street, 361.
Long Acre, 383, 546.
Philip-lane, letters dated from, 300, 316, 343, 350, 360, 365, 372, 376, 380, 381, 433, 447, 522, 543, 545, 602.
Old Jewry, 122.
Queenhithe, 122.
London, Streets of—*continued.*
St. Martin's-lane, 373.
Shoe-lane, 132.
Strand, 262, 282, 491.
........., letters dated from, 65, 91, 121, 144, 171, 210, 213, 257, 373, 449, 471, 564, 576, 603.
Thames-street, 413.
Townsend-lane, 413.
........., subsidies in, 14, 605.
........., suburbs of, 218, 429, 440.
........., surveyor of, 205, 217.
........., tradespeople in, 111, 294, 330, 334, 356, 364, 439, 454, 503, 513, 611.
........., travellers to and from, 1, 4, 19, 21, 64, 85, 173, 224, 258, 301, 321, 336, 356, 365, 369, 427, 433, 480, 483, 491, 495, 541, 562, 587, 600.
........., waterworks in, 66, 78, 128, 266, 364, 365, 517.
........., bishops of, *see* Abbot, Geo.; King, Dr. John.
........., diocese of, 74, 76, 186, 300, 388, 398, 402, 403, 412, 441, 444, 453, 458, 469, 476, 482, 493, 528, 538, 547, 552, 558, 565, 572, 581, 598, 606.
.... Dutch church in, 50, 133, 308, 377, 598.
........., French church in, 377, 598.
........., Italian church in, 136, 138, 227, 501, 510, 595, 598.
........., Mercers' Chapel in, 500, 503, 535.
Long, Mr., 455.
Long Cowton, 189.
.... Preston, 358.
Longe, Wm., 24.
Longworth, 242.
Lopdale, Geo., 576, 578, 579, 583.
........., John, 579, 583.
Lords, House of, 53, 190, 196, 211, 235, 236, 454, 457, 459, 470, 472, 473.
........., the, 169–171, 571, 575, 588; *see also* Privy Council.
Lorraine, 81.
........., Ambassador of, 163.
........., Henri II., Duke of, 305.
Lostock, 304.
Lotteries, 120, 130, 274.
Lotti, Ottaviano, 237.
Loughborough, 292.
Loughton Manor, 187.
Louis XIII., King of France, 16, 85, 145, 409, 434, 443, 461, 526, 587, 588, 596, 608.
Lound, 67.
Louvaine University, 514.
Love, Roland, 416.
Lovelace, Sir Wm., 443, 521, 533.
........., Mr., 65.
Lovell, Sir Fras., 247.
Loviband, Thos., 44, 94.
Low, Art., 540.
Low Countries, 92, 116, 135, 235, 241, 267, 288, 412, 443, 446, 469, 511, 611; *see also* Flanders and Holland.

Low Countries, travellers to or from, 13, 178, 209, 250, 251, 294, 344, 392, 463, 499, 522.
Lowe, Ant., 456.
........., Geo., 195, 457.
........., Sir Thos., 80, 119, 174, 221, 225, 287.
........., Capt., 522.
Lower, Sir Wm., 286.
........., Lady, 504.
Lownes, Ralph, 230.
Lowther, Sir Rich., 268.
Lubdale, or Lubdey, *see* Lopdale.
Lubeck, 353, 359.
Lucas, Ant., 562.
........., Hen., 590.
........., Thos., 268.
........., Sir Thos.. 268.
........., Wm., 208.
Luce, Jean de, 114, 126, 168.
Lucton, 191.
Lucy, Constance, Lady, 96, 584.
........., Sir Edm., 84.
........., Sir Thos., 193.
Ludlow, 61, 62.
.... Castle, 379, 380.
...., letters dated from, 4, 16, 25, 73, 336, 353.
Lugar, John, 73.
........., Wm., 73.
Lugaro, John Maria, 112.
Lugge, John, 517.
........., Pet., 517.
Lumley, Lady Eliz., 40, 514.
........., Martin, 296.
Lumsden, Thos., 210, 318, 319, 321, 326, 344, 549.
........., ..., letters to, 59, 67, 74, 77, 82, 83, 168.
Lunatics, 601.
Lund, Fras., 335.
Lunenburg, Christian, Duke of, 560.
Lunne, Mary, 161.
Lupo, Horatio, 118.
Lupton, 42.
Luscombe, Gilb., 541.
Lusher, Sir Nich., 67.
Luton, 90, 545.
Lydd, 109, 253, 343, 349, 361, 370, 412, 611.
Lydyard, Hugh, 497.
Lyfield Forest, 44, 266.
Lylesdon, 217.
Lyme, 206.
Lymehost, 518.
Lyngen, Edw., 30.
Lynn, 22, 42, 546. 566.
Lyons, John, 127.
Lytton, Phil., 58, 308.
........., Sir Rowld., 9, 58, 237, 242, 290.

M.

Mabbe, Fras., 220.
........., Thos., 220.
McCarty, Florence 104, 113.
McDermot, Cormock, 559.
McDonnell, Surley, 381.
McLellan, Sir Robt., 245.
Maccalla, Patricius, 376.
Mace, John, 581.
Macklock, Lewis, 33.
Madrid, 145, 516, 535, 538, 572.
........., letters from, 16, 126, 185, 199, 489, 493, 529, 547, 603.
Mady, Meredith, 468.
Magellan, Straits of, 515.
Maidstone, 179.
Maillan, M., 305.
Mainprise, Geo., 130.
Mainwaring, Sir Art., 24, 44, 321, 324, 385.
........., Art., 249, 434, 443.
........., Chris., 98.
........., Geo., 385.
........., Capt. Hen., 41, 298, 342, 353, 359, 366, 425; Sir Hen., 530.
Maison Dieu, Dover, 566, 571, 600, 605.
Maisters, Edw., 474.
Maitland, Jas., 193.
........., Wm., 193.
Maize, Mr., 109.
Makepeace, Lawr. 272.
Malby, Geo., 599.
........., Hen., 599.
Maletesto, Alex., 304, 308, 399.
Malines, 479, 480.
Malines, Gerard, 128, 184, 456.
Mallet, Sir John, 251.
Mallett, John, 411, 418.
Malmsbury, 596.
Malpas, 379, 433.
Malrea, John, 306.
Malton, 4.
Malvern Chace, 149.
Man, John, 604.
........., Mr., 608.
Manchell, Owen, 487.
........., Thos., 487.
Manchester College, 499.
Manley, John, 157.
Manners, Sir Chas., 359.
........., Edw., 3rd Earl of Rutland, 387.
........., Eliz., Countess of Rutland, wife of Roger, 5th Earl, 105, 143, 266.
........., Fras., 6th Earl of Rutland, 83, 141, 199, 208, 308, 363, 364, 380, 384; Lord Roos of Hamlake, 386, 387, 458.
........., ..., letters of, 178, 260, 576.
........., Sir Oliver, 83, 199.
Mannington, 388.

Mansell, Sir Robt., 169, 186, 187; Treasurer of the Navy, 406, 446, 535, 537, 538; Vice-Admiral, 590, 597, 601.
........., ..., grants and payments to, 288, 541, 560, 561, 579.
........., ..., letters of, 507, 538.
........., Sir Thos., 325.
Mansfield, 255, 460.
Mansfield, Sir Edw., 89.
........., Hen., 476.
Manshall Park, 207, 213.
Mantua, Vincent I., Duke of 64, 69.
........., Fras. III., Duke of, 167.
........., Margaret, Duchess of, 167.
........., Ferdinand, Duke of, 426.
........., Vincent, Cardinal of, 426.
Manwood, Sir Pet., 413, 423, 479, 491.
Manzer, Peter, 47.
Mapleton, Mr., 179.
Mar, Earl of, *see* Stewart.
Marbury, Thos., 68.
March, Wm., 57.
Marchington, 236.
Mare, Chas. de la, 190, 483, 572.
Margaret of Austria, Queen of Spain, 89.
Margate, 38, 257, 306, 369, 377, 407, 414, 480, 567, 571.
Margitts, Geo., 250, 419.
........., ..., letters of, 238, 239, 256, 258, 274, 277, 285, 293, 300.
Maria, Johannes, or Giovanni Battista, 139, 151, 175, 176, 212, 274; *see also* Carmelite friars.
Marine causes, *see* Admiralty.
Mariners, 122, 124, 177, 179, 308, 324, 396, 463, 508, 509, 513, 532, 589.
Marington, 331.
Market Harborough, 540.
Markets and fairs, 35, 107, 139, 208, 232, 235, 237, 418, 497, 542.
Markham, Sir Griffin, 516.
........., Anne, Lady, 516.
........., Sir Robt., 556.
........., Winifred, Lady, 556, 558, 559, 581.
Marlborough, 133, 256, 279, 480.
........., mayor of, 344.
Marleton, Abm., 613.
........., Joan, 613.
Marlott, Wm., 206.
........., Mr., 79.
Marlow, Edm. 103.
Marman, Hen., 114.
Marmora, 55.
Marow, John, 105.
Marque letters of, 57.
Marr, Geo., 250.
Marrick, 404, 528.
Marriott, John, 536.
Marsh, Gabriel, 555.
........., Rich., 369, 399, 424, 460, 463, 512,
Marshal, Earl, commissioners for the office of, 82, 157, 166, 213, 343, 395, 401, 426, 441, 442, 593, 608.
Marshall, Chris., 161, 354.
........., Geo., 40, 74; Sir Geo., 491, 495.
........., Thos., 283.
........., Mr., 214.
Marshalsea Prison, 113, 132, 186, 234, 247, 546.
Marsilio, Signor, 124.
Marston, Pet., 47.
Marta, Dr., 174, 244.
Marten, Dr., or Sir Hen., 174; Judge of the Admiralty, 494, 513.
Martial law, 127, 339, 388.
Martiall, Benj., 424.
........., Geo., 414.
........., John, 530.
........., Robt., 343.
Martin, Hen., 199, 228, 351.
........., Hugh, 283.
........., Rich., 72, 125, 234; Recorder of London, 589, 591, 595.
........., ..., jun., 97.
........., Sir Rich., 99, 479, 489, 516.
........., Thos., 175.
Martindale Chace, 293.
Marton, 159.
Martyn, Geo., 449.
........., Geo. (of Dover), 305.
........., Alice, 305.
Martyrdom, order of, 148.
Mary I., Queen, 371.
Mary, Queen of Scots, 41, 150, 152, 193, 359.
.... de Medicis, Queen Dowager of France, 85, 93, 99, 124, 140, 145, 422, 434, 461.
Marybone Park, 113, 249, 275.
Mascall, Hugh, 418.
Mask, 154.
Mason, Kath., 161.
........., John, 230.
Masque, *see* Drama.
Mass, service of, 5, 11, 12, 21, 119, 140, 176, 302, 352, 399, 545.
Master, Jacob de, 524.
Masters, Edm., 29.
Mathews, Mr., 148.
Matthew, Thos., 190, 294.
........., Tobias, Archbp. of York, 48, 135, 141, 151, 167, 177, 212, 221, 227, 228, 245, 315, 465.
........., ..., letters of, 139, 226, 541.
........., Tobie, 24, 393, 464, 465, 476, 477, 489, 530.
Matthews, Edw., 435, 442.
Matthias, Emperor of Germany, 147, 212.
Mattingley, Ann, 67.
* Maudlenfield, 470.
Maull, Pat., 55, 100, 306, 329.
........., Robt., 110.
Maurice, Prince, *see* Nassau.

Mawe, Leonard, 41.
Maxey, Dr. Ant., Dean of Windsor, 120, 532, 538.
Maxwell, Jas., 76, 88, 134, 363, 441, 444.
........., Jas. (poet), 339.
........., John, 444.
........., Robt., 378.
........., Sir Robt., 103.
May, Adrian, 497.
........., John, 302.
........., Capt. Jos., 63.
........., Hugh, 209, 297, 453, 497.
........., Sir Hum., 327, 346, 445, 492, 498, 514, 518; Chancellor of Duchy of Lancaster, 525, 527.
........., ..., grants and warrants to, 33, 67, 99, 554, 556.
........., ..., letters of and to, 89, 91, 168, 347, 557.
........., Jane, 33.
........., Wm., 63.
Maydencroft, 375.
Mayenne, Henri, Duke of, 270.
Mayerne Turquet, Dr. Theodore de, 39, 90, 91, 119, 155, 197, 264, 272, 282, 307, 312, 326, 491, 492, 566.
........., ..., grants, &c. to, 44, 45, 57.
........., ..., letters of, 39, 79, 86, 89, 198, 567.
........., Margaret Elburgh de Boetzler, 44.
Mayfield, 388.
Maynard, Alex., 533.
Mayne, Collubery, 596.
Mayson, Hen., 192.
Meades, Wm., 561.
Meaker, Wm., 95.
Meal, 227.
Mechin, or Meechinge, 287, 388.
Meden, John, 176.
Medenblick, 468.
Medhoppe, John, 206.
Mediterranean Sea, 515.
Medway River, 165.
Meers, Wm., 238.
Meinges, Robt., 93, 120.
Melamocco, 188.
Melding, 529.
Meldrum, John, 537, 545.
Melfell (coachman), 149.
Melliott, Bennett, 293, 483, 572.
Mellow, Thos., 513.
Melsham, Wm., 25.
........., Emma, 25.
Melvill, 253.
Melvill, Sir Robt., 253.
Melvin, or Melville, And., 21-23.
Mepal, 566.
Mercer, Ralph, 238.
........., Mrs., 213.
Merchandise, 32, 136, 212, 283, 354, 612.
........., customs on, 83, 200, 235, 296, 446, 454, 490.
Merchandise, export and import of, 297, 300, 363, 605.
........., Indian, 468.
Merchant adventurers, Company of, 119, 217, 219, 287, 291, 348, 358, 393, 395, 404, 408. 421, 427, 454, 514, 518, 535, 543, 548, 561, 602.
........., ..., export of undressed cloth by 165, 175, 247, 500.
........., ..., letters and petitions of, 288, 571, 605, 607.
.... places of residence abroad of, 20, 147, 183, 500, 526, 527.
...., dissolution of, 256, 261, 275.
...., restoration of, 423, 481, 499.
...., New company of, 275, 288, 291, 305, 346-349, 358, 373, 389, 390, 393, 395, 404, 454, 457.
...., ..., places of residence abroad of, 266, 341.
...., ..., dissolution of, 422, 499.
...., for new trades, see Muscovy Company.
.... strangers, 63, 107, 114, 121, 128, 200, 259, 411, 445, 447, 485, 605.
Merchants, 78, 92, 111, 118, 129, 169, 208, 228, 259, 301, 359, 410, 435, 444, 449, 450, 462, 464, 475, 603.
........., names of, 197, 501, 558, 589.
........., ships of, 66, 305, 514.
........., trading to Flanders, 140-142, 144, 149.
.... France, 51, 252, 504.
...., Spain, 83, 122, 185.
...., East Indies, 210, 214, 229.
........., royal, 197.
Mercury, 229.
Meredith, Wm., 278.
Merionethshire, 358.
........., offices in, 289, 372, 431.
Meriton Dr., 45.
Merlin, Fras., 449.
Merrick, John, Ambassador to Muscovy, 236; Sir John, 240, 282, 468, 494.
Merry, Thos., 137.
Merston, Simon, 313.
Merthyr Cynog, 195.
Metcalfe, Sir Thos., 23.
Methwold, 247.
Methwold, Sir Wm., Lord Chief Baron of Ireland, 174.
Metkirk, Mr., 548.
Meverell, Robt., 99, 116.
Mewtas, Sir Thos., 13, 548.
Mexico Fleet, 574.
Meysey, Matthias, 228, 390.
Michael Feodorowitz, Emperor of Russia, 203, 532, 533.
Michaelson, John, 453.
Michel-Marsh, 378.
Michell, John, 75, 77, 362.
........., Lewis, 483.
........., Thos., 393, 483, 528.
........., Wm., 586, 594.

Mickelay, 297.
Mickleton, 35.
Middleburgh, 63, 119, 147, 183, 315, 341, 399, 428, 452, 500, 612.
........, merchants at, 510, 526, 527, 571.
Middleham, 23, 294, 354, 360.
Middleham, Adam, 23.
Middlemore, Mrs., 512.
Middlesex, 57, 227, 268, 322, 571.
........., grants of lands in, 40, 63, 111, 159, 196, 204, 295, 597.
........., lands and places in, 153, 187, 188, 236, 275, 278, 338, 374, 382, 390, 418, 444, 448, 507, 518.
........., offices in, 6, 135, 311, 450, 460, 545, 551, 555, 559, 604.
........., residents in, 67, 210, 551, 580, 597.
Middleton, Anne, 440.
........., Capt. Dav., 232.
........., Sir Hen., 236.
........., Hugh, 78, 128, 364.
........., John, 64.
........., Robt., 17.
........., Thos., 556.
........., Sir Thos., *see* London, Lord Mayors of.
........., Wm., 144.
Milan, 83.
........., Duchy of, 97.
........., Governor of, 270.
Milanese, 491.
Milborne, 100.
Milbourne, Dr. Rich., Dean of Rochester, 91; Bp. of St. David's, 280, 294.
Mildenhall, 247.
Mildmay, Sir Ant., 56, 58, 252, 266, 273, 488, 505.
........., Sir Hen., 510, 511, 585, 594.
........., Thos., 32.
Miles, Hen., 158.
Milford, 598.
Miller, Alex., 75, 96.
........., Ellis, 265.
........., Hugh, 131.
........., Jas., 231.
........., Rich., 367.
........., Steph., 374.
Milles, Rich., 480.
Mills, Art., 49.
........., Fras., Privy Seal Clerk, 83, 102, 103, 117, 257, 272, 350, 452.
........., Jas., 452.
........., John, 37.
........., Thos., 100,
........., Thos. (prisoner), 547, 562.
Milton, 63, 72, 392, 408.
.... Manor, 74.
Milward, John, 79, 111-113, 230.
Minchinhampton, 29.
Mines, 521, 528, 531, 533, 587.
Ministers, 13, 285, 291, 308, 366, 427, 460, 465, 477, 521.
........., deprived, 92, 237, 239, 254.
........., names of, 233, 279, 289, 341, 344, 427, 435, 451, 592.
Ministry, 2, 464.
Minories, the, 365, 378, 456, 564.
Minley, 573.
Minshon, John, 10.
Minshull, Fras., 173.
Minster, 63, 94.
Mint, affairs of, 20, 25, 28, 98, 113, 129, 241, 479, 480.
........., officers of, 98, 99, 230, 322, 358, 396, 479, 489, 490, 516, 603.
........., Wardens of, *see* Knyvet, Lord, and Doubleday, Edm.
.... House, 97.
Minuccio, Minucci, 482.
Misbehaved persons, 358, 389, 456, 465, 590; *see* Borders.
Miserden, 241, 252.
Misselden, Hen., 165, 399.
Misson, John, 76.
Mitcham, 90, 335.
Mitforth, 384.
.... Castle, 384.
Mocktree Forest, 103.
Modena, Cæsar d'Este, Prince of, 137.
Mogul empire, 424, 427, 516.
........., the Great, Sultan Selim, 210, 214, 260, 284, 587.
Mole, Hen., 386.
........., John, 386.
........., Mr., 60, 65, 153, 512.
Moluccas, the, 272.
Molyneux, Edm., 506.
........., Sir John, 400, 552, 566.
........., Lucy, Lady, 400, 552, 566.
........., Bridget, 400.
........., Sir Rich., Receiver of Duchy of Lancaster, 38, 43, 85, 383, 451, 468, 557.
Molyns, Sir Barantyne, 401.
Momery, Abm., 613.
Mompesson, Sir Giles, 439, 441, 473, 474.
........., Thos., 439.
Monday, Edm., 49.
Monmouth, 178, 226.
Monmouthshire, 128, 137, 415, 440, 498.
........., grants of lands in, 63, 124, 251.
Monox, Edw., 75.
Monson, John, 606.
........., Sir Thos., Master of the Armoury, 15, 40, 51, 153, 205, 606.
........., ..., connection of, with Overbury's murder, 307, 313, 314, 318, 320, 321, 324, 327-329, 331, 333, 335, 336, 342, 344-349, 361, 370, 372, 373, 375, 398, 411, 426, 433, 436.
........., Sir Wm., 38, 64, 117, 193, 309, 343, 345-347, 362, 373, 426, 522.

Monson (young), 524, 530, 531.
Montague, Sir Chas., 56, 58.
........., Sir Edw., late Chief Justice, 405, 406.
.... Sir Edw., 273.
........., Sir Hen., Serjeant-at-Law, Recorder of London, 152, 199, 225; Master of Requests, 392, 397; Lord Chief Justice of King's Bench, 405–407, 410, 433, 448, 450, 473, 504, 518, 545, 550.
........., ..., commissions to, 408, 590, 593.
........., ..., grants to, 296.
........., ..., letters of and to, 5, 404, 53
........., Jas., Bp. of Bath and Wells, 263, 346, 350, 375; Bp. of Winchester, 432, 437, 466, 488, 494, 549, 578.
........., ..., letters to, 221, 347, 410.
........., Rich., King's chaplain, 552.
........., Sir Sidney, Master of Requests, 514, 541.
........., Sir Wal., 296.
.... Visct., *see* Brown, Ant.
Montaigne, Dr. Geo., Dean of Westminster, 81, 240, 319; Bp. of Lincoln, 493, 496, 502, 504, 543, 576.
Montalto, Cardinal, 143.
Monteagle, Lord, *see* Parker.
Monteith, Lord, *see* Graham.
Montgomery, Earl of, *see* Herbert, Phil.
Montgomeryshire, grants of lands in, 46, 63, 300.
........., offices in, 331, 363.
........., residents in, 191, 243.
Montrose, Earl of, *see* Graham.
Moore, Adrian, 197.
.... (or More), Sir Edw., 426, 515, 600.
........., Sir Fras., 421.
........., Sir Garrett, 398.
........., Rich., 303.
........., Robt., 205, 217.
........., Sam., 526.
........., Kath., 526.
........., Sir Thos., 443.
........., Capt., 589.
Moorhouse, 548.
Moray, John, 56.
Mordaunt, John, Lord, 389, 412.
More, Dan., 374, 375.
........., Geo., 524.
........., Sir Geo., 56; Lieutenant of the Tower, 330–332, 349, 350, 352, 377, 385, 428, 441.
........., John, 116, 373, 445.
........., Rich., 49.
........., Robt., 607.
........., Alderman, 295.
Morea, Emperor of, 217.
Morecroft, Robt., 482.
More Hall, 11.
Moreton, John, 593.
Morffe Forest, 463.
Morgan, Sir Edm., 105.
Morgan, Edw., 137, 361, 366.
........., Fras., 359.
........., Meredith, 103, 115, 190, 213, 254, 379, 418.
........., Simon, 552.
........., Thos., 590.
........., Capt. Wm., 131.
........., Dorothy, 131.
........., Chas., 131.
........., Anne, 131.
Morland, 279.
Morlewood, 79.
Morley, Jas., 439.
........., John, 89.
........., Sir John, 120.
........., Robt., 439.
........., Lord, *see* Parker, Edw.
Morocco, King of, *see* Muley, Sidan.
Morpeth, 301.
Morrall, Thos., 606.
........., Wal., 525.
Morrice, or Morris, Fras., 63, 124, 181, 197.
Morris, Hen., 337.
........., Thos., 244.
........., Thos. (mariner), 308.
Morris dancers, 50.
Morrison, John, 65.
........., Sir Rich., 132, 167; Lieutenant of Ordnance, 342, 383, 441, 450, 456, 526.
........., Robt., 103.
........., Thos., 36.
Mortlake Park, 288.
Mortmain, statute of, 494.
Morton, Albert, 225; Sir Albert, 263; Secretary to the Electress Palatine, 396, 585.
........., ..., mission of to Heidelberg, 360, 393, 397, 585.
........., ..., mission of to Savoy, 196, 204, 233, 234, 282.
........., Sir Geo., 6.
........., Capt. Robt., 585.
........., Dr. Thos., Bp. of Chester, 368, 379, 383, 578.
........., Wm., *alias* Beridge, Zeth, 355, 362, 366, 395, 465.
Mosco Lodge, 481.
Moscow, 585.
Moseley, Sir Edw., Attorney of the Duchy of Lancaster, 202, 298, 502, 504, 557.
Mote Park, 297, 497.
Mote's Bulwark, 77, 202, 367.
...., muster rolls of, 151, 202, 255, 309, 395, 485, 583.
Motteshed, Thos., 284.
Moulin, Peter du, 100, 101, 142, 143, 282, 289, 310.
Moulsford, 375.
Moulsham, 32.
Moulton, 292, 418.
Mounsee Dumanick, 492.
Mountgarret, Viscount and Viscountess, *see* Butler.

Mousdale, Roger, 25.
Mousehole Close, 519.
Mowgrave, 90.
Moyle, Robt., 483.
........., Thos., 87.
Moys, Wm., 179.
Moythey, Howell, 130.
Much Wenlock, 541.
Mulberry trees, 29.
Muley, Sidan, King of Morocco, 260.
Mullins, Thos., 350.
........., Wm., 159.
Munck, Levinus, 50, 135, 152, 229, 248, 469
Muncrieff, Geo., 266.
Munition, *see* Ordnance.
Munster, 132.
........., presidency of, 167, 282, 284.
Muriell, Mr., 139.
Murray, Sir David, 55, 120, 456, 468.
........., Geo., 245.
........., Sir Gideon, 55, 203, 239, 255.
........., Sir Jas., 22.
........., John, Lord, Earl of Tullibardine, 194.
........., John, Groom of the Bedchamber and Keeper of Privy Purse, 17, 74, 80, 82, 233, 338, 380, 418, 461.
........., ..., grants, warrants, &c. to, 36, 76, 189, 206, 222, 251, 281, 545.
........., ..., letters of, 74, 82.
........., John, Queen's servant, 69.
........., Pat., 535, 606.
........., Sir Pat., 194, 273, 444, 554.
........., Eliz., Lady, 194.
........., Thos., 114, 160, 170, 213, 385; Secretary to Prince Charles, 444, 484, 490.
........., ..., letters of, 171, 368, 383, 398, 414, 417, 437, 438, 456, 473, 489, 492, 504, 531, 581.
........., ..., letters to, 153, 312.
........., Wm., 533.
........., Wm. (rector), 43.
........., Capt. Wm., 69.
........., Mrs., 296.
Musarden, 609.
Muscorno, Giulio, Secretary of the Venetian Ambassador, 167, 178, 227, 228, 244.
Muscovy, 69, 178, 182, 494, 538, 587; *see also* Russia.
........., Ambassadors of, 203-205, 236, 494, 495, 497, 512, 530.
........., ..., to, *see* Merrick, John; Diggs, Sir D.
.... Company, or Merchant Adventurers for New Trades, 140, 203, 228, 252, 463, 503, 513, 532, 533, 549, 572.
........., Emperor of, *see* Michael, Feodorowitz.
........., Grand Duke of, 468.
Muse, Capt. Thos., 109.
Musgrave, Sir Rich., 443.
........., Sir Edw., 539.
Muskett, Geo., 283, 285, 321.
Muster-masters and commissioners, 34, 37, 54, 79, 114, 122, 177, 201, 322, 340, 363, 419, 453, 483, 537, 544, 545, 587.
Musters, 40, 60, 73, 79, 177, 290, 306, 311, 323, 328, 372, 374, 417, 527, 532, 544, 599, 603.
........., orders for holding, 169, 286, 289, 290, 364, 537, 541.
.... reports of county, 177, 178-182, 184, 185, 191, 204, 258-262, 313, 316, 319, 322, 325-327, 544.
.... rolls of, 77, 83, 149, 151, 202, 253-257, 308-310, 312, 395, 396, 460, 484, 485, 554, 579, 582, 583.
Mutford, 551.
Myles, Hen., 487.
Mynne, Geo., 565.
........., Sir Hen., 387.
Mynours, Hen., 382, 385.
Mynterne, John, 367.
........., John, jun., 367.

N.

Nab, the, 502.
Nairn, Alex., 158.
Nan, Old (witch), 334.
Napier, Sir Robt., 538, 545.
Naples, 567.
........., fleet of, 480.
........., viceroy of, 197.
Napleton, Ant., 434, 442, 613.
........., Posthumus, 442.
........., Thos., 434, 442, 450, 451, 457, 532, 613.
Napper, Arch., 386.
Narrow Seas, 20, 193, 207, 309, 421, 505, 579.
Nash Manor, 383.
Nash, Rich., 535.
Nasmyth, John, 208.
Nassau, Ernest, Count of, 124.
........., Henry, Count of, 157, 177, 161, 344.
........., Louis, Count of, 169, 170.
........., Maurice, Prince of, 144, 209, 344, 482, 504, 505, 520, 572, 575.
........., ..., made Knight of the Garter, 158, 163, 167, 169.
Naunton, Sir Robt., Under-Secretary of State, 119, 134; Master of Requests, Surveyor of Court of Wards, 404, 422; Secretary of State, 519, 534, 538, 560, 565, 574, 575, 578, 581, 584, 597, 598, 601, 604, 605.
........., ..., letters of, 565, 570, 587.
........., ..., letters of, to Wilson, 517, 544, 568, 570, 571, 575, 577, 583, 585.
........., ..., letters to, 578, 582, 583, 588, 599, *see* Wilson.

Naunton, Sir Robt., promotions of, real or rumoured 376, 379, 390, 397, 400, 401, 427, 492, 494, 496, 504, 505, 511, 512, 592.
Navy, the, 99, 241, 559, 584, 614.
........., ..., abuses in, 186, 208, 531, 580, 581.
........., ..., commission for survey of, 546, 547, 551, 580, 582, 586, 590, 597.
........., ..., officers of, 23, 30, 50, 64, 69, 108, 114, 117, 226, 246, 350, 353, 356, 360, 394, 430, 438, 450, 491, 545, 581, 604.
........., ..., supplies for, 12, 20, 73, 85, 86, 91, 101, 105, 125, 133, 225, 279, 450, 542, 558, 579, 590.
........., ..., Treasurer of, *see* Mansell, Sir Robt.; Russell, Sir Wm.
Nead, Hen., 103.
Neale, Fras., 428.
........., Wal., 340.
Nealman, Rich., 116.
Necton, Jas., 6.
Needham, 63, 64.
Needham, Fras., 63, 64, 288, 300, 375.
........., Thos., 63.
Nen River, 430, 465, 546.
Neston, 485.
Nether Darwen, 34.
Netherham, 586, 594.
Nethersole, Fras., 278, 588.
Netherswell, 381.
Nettleton, 265.
Nettleworth, 302.
Neufchatel, 433.
Neve, Abm., 483.
Nevill, Chris., 414, 588.
........., Edm., of Latimer, titular Earl of Westmoreland, 93, 119, 123, 147, 431, 607.
........., Edw., Lord Abergavenny, 357, 414, 425.
........., Rachel, Lady Abergavenny, 169, 488.
........., Wm., 386.
Neville, Chris., 237, 239.
........., Sir Hen., 72, 153, 166, 168, 171, 225, 234, 261, 273, 297, 325, 564,
........., ..., letters of and to, 173, 261.
........., ..., promotions or failures of, 135, 138, 202, 203, 215, 224.
........., ..., death of, 295, 344.
........., Sir Hen., 421, 497, 572.
........., Dr. Thos., Dean of Canterbury, 286.
........., Mrs., 147.
Nevills, the, 202.
Nevinson, Sir Rog., 490.
New Bridewell, 522.
.... Forest, 85, 201, 274.
.... Langport, 452.
.... Lodge, 451.
.... Prison, 548, 549, 613.
.... River, 266, 517.
New Romney, *see* Romney.
.... Sarum, *see* Salisbury.
New drapery, 107, 271, 525, 590, 606.
Newark, 458.
........., King James's Hospital at, 276.
Newbury, Hum., 421.
Newcastle-upon-Tyne, 34, 82, 91, 300, 302, 375, 395, 443, 539, 543, 556, 589.
........., letters from, 8, 14, 175, 355, 360, 366, 389, 463, 536, 590.
........., mayor, &c. of, 14, 360, 375, 589.
........., residents in, 127, 260.
Newdigate, Sir Robt., 66.
Newenham Mills, 531.
Newfoundland, 158, 426, 586.
Newgate, 89, 176, 321, 332.
........., keeper of, 10, 11.
........., prisoners in, 10, 56, 158, 279, 283, 285, 290, 458, 556, 584.
Newhall, 101, 261, 313, 327, 603.
Newhaven, 179, 463.
Newington, 103, 393, 571.
Newkirk, Chris., 301–304, 308, 399.
Newman, Eliz., 356.
Newman, Dr. or Sir Geo., 352, 414, 457, 481; Dean of the Arches, 488, 489, 574.
Newmarket, 91, 152, 260, 411, 545.
........., King and court at, 90, 95, 96, 167, 172, 175, 223, 269, 273, 352, 361, 362, 410, 513, 518, 520, 521, 598, 599, 602.
........., letters from, 10–13, 89, 91, 92, 95, 97, 167, 168, 212, 259, 261, 262, 277–279, 328, 330–332, 335, 337, 346–350, 352, 353, 364, 409, 411, 414, 517, 519, 599.
Newport (Admiral), 101.
Newport Pagnell, 230.
Newton, Adam, 39, 60, 172, 186, 418, 560.
........., Dr. Fogg, 2.
........., Robt., 443.
........., Thos., 11.
........., Mr., 232.
Neyle, Rich., Bp. of Coventry and Lichfield, 86, 200; Bp. of Lincoln, 232, 292, 335, 413, 432, 466, 467, 487; Bp. of Durham, 522.
........., ..., conduct of in Parliament, 235–237.
........., ..., grants, commissions, &c. to, 197, 332, 497, 550.
........., ..., letters of and to, 208, 290, 439.
Nicholas, Edw., Secretary to Sir John Dackombe and to Lord Zouch, 499, 518, 519, 580.
........., ..., letters of, 81, 536.
........., ..., letters to, 164, 400, 495, 496, 534, 536, 547.
........., ..., notes, papers, corrections, &c. by, 164, 222, 263, 490, 538, 567, 579, 602.
........., John, 81.
........., Matt., 164, 495, 536.
........., Susan, 164.

Nicholls, Sir Augustine, Justice of Common Pleas, 158, 391, 398, 426, 469.
........., Chris., 297.
Nichols, Rich., 132.
........., Mr., 428.
Nicholson, Edm., 590.
........., Geo., 42, 46, 48, 431.
........., ..., letters of, 4, 6, 7, 15, 17, 23, 26, 34, 38, 40, 53, 60, 112.
........., Otho, 153, 286, 314, 334, 420.
Nodes, Geo., 58.
Noel, Sir And., 448.
........., Sir Edw., 266, 453, 514.
Nonsuch Park, 53, 102, 253.
Norborn, John, 376.
Norbury (minister), 277.
Norden, John, 45, 48, 76, 97, 108, 113, 121, 158, 340.
Norfolk, 86, 212, 268, 300, 544, 563, 581, 610.
........., grants of lands in, 32, 45, 63, 87, 88, 120, 159, 211, 247, 382, 388.
........., lands and places in, 2, 46, 58, 109, 113, 132, 226, 364, 419, 534, 597.
........., offices in, 283, 509, 546, 563, 566.
........., recusants in, 49, 52, 120.
........., residents in, 32, 132, 170, 207, 435, 458, 525, 537.
Norgate, Edw., 93.
........., Giles, 539.
Norham, 6, 112.
.... Castle, 360.
Norhamshire, 113.
Norman, Edw., 325.
Normanby, 439.
Normandy, 175.
Norris, Fras., Lord, 54, 207, 306, 308, 343, 344, 353, 392.
........., Geo., 78.
........., Hen., 353.
........., Sir John, 58, 62, 168.
........., Thos., 98, 551.
Norroy, King-at-arms, see St. George, Rich.
North, the, 31, 125, 303, 382, 455, 536.
........., Catholics and recusants in, 347, 355.
.... Council of, 1, 94, 99, 147, 233, 247, 369, 386.
...., attorney of, 66.
...., president of, see Sheffield, Lord.
North Bradley, 567.
.... Cape, 449, 515.
.... Dalton, 295.
.... East passage, 228, 284, 345.
.... West passage, 96, 139, 228, 345. 427, 516.
.... Holland, 557.
.... Petherton, 190.
North Dudley, Lord, 124.
........., Sir Hen., 247.
Northampton, 218, 254, 306, 502, 519, 539, 609.
Northampton, Archdeacon of, 147.
........., Earl of, see Howard, Hen.; Compton, Wm., Lord.
........., Marchioness of, see Gorges, Lady Ellen.
.... House, 575.
...., letters dated from, 109, 148, 219, 226, 252, 256, 258, 261, 262, 274, 279, 297, 316.
Northamptonshire, 102, 268, 305, 458, 532, 541, 574.
........., grants of lands in, 55, 62, 63, 87, 158, 159, 211, 274, 306, 313, 359, 386, 418, 467.
........., lands and places in, 8, 10, 18, 85, 102, 118, 165, 176, 207, 215, 254, 266, 292, 332, 382, 493, 506, 580, 597.
........., offices in, 28, 97, 218, 389, 403, 413, 546, 552, 566.
........., receivers of, 80, 85, 240.
........., recusants in, 120, 176.
........., residents in, 26, 37, 75, 86, 147, 185, 272, 274, 335, 403, 431, 507, 561, 603.
Northbourne, 226.
Northfrothing, 596.
Northmill, 111.
Northumberland, Duke of, see Dudley, John.
........., Earl and Countess of, see Percy.
Northumberland, 108, 113, 212, 268, 289, 304, 329, 358, 366, 389, 395, 456, 465, 539, 590.
........., grants of lands in, 63, 67, 124, 189 211, 220, 384, 388, 418.
........., lands and places in, 95, 115, 220, 232, 302, 582.
........., mines in, 9, 14, 45.
........., offices in, 49, 61, 360, 590.
........., receivers of, 127.
........., recusants in, 108, 329, 358, 360, 365.
........., residents in, 38, 45, 279, 292, 365, 406, 590.
Norton, 418.
Norton, Bonham, 166, 299.
........., Dud., 3, 52, 262; Sir Dud., 344, 427.
........., John (King's printer), 21.
........., John, jun., 86.
........., Robt., 589.
........., Thos. (surveyor), 417.
........., Thos., mayor of Fordwich, 567, 568.
Norway, 503.
Norwell-Woodhouse, 289.
Norwich, 107, 134, 161, 172, 173, 325, 509, 534, 544, 581, 610.
........., alms-rooms in, 74.
........., Bp. of, see Jegon, John; Overall, John.
........., Consistory Court at, 314.
........., diocese of, 281, 532, 534.
Nottingham, 177, 316.
........., archdeaconry of, 76.

Nottingham, Earl of, *see* Howard, Chas.
Nottinghamshire, 177, 255, 316, 538.
........., grants of lands in, 63, 99, 124, 159, 181, 211, 445.
........., lands and places in, 17, 116, 155, 258, 261, 286, 334, 460.
........., residents in, 289, 506, 556.
Notts, Marg., 190.
Noy, Wm., 212.
Noyse, Wm., 562.
Nuffield, 104, 273, 466, 489.
Nun, Mr., 325.

O.

Oake, Rich., 525.
Oakhampton, 89.
Oakley, 444.
Oatlands, 29, 69–71, 387, 390, 397, 565, 568.
........., letters dated from, 67, 189, 190, 291, 292.
O'Brian, Sir Brian, 344.
O'Bryan, Donatus, Earl of Thomond, 282, 284, 425.
........., Henry, Lord, 425.
........., Mr., 80.
O'Cane, Sir Donel, 148.
Ockold, Rich., 537.
Odiham, 471, 515, 600.
O'Donell, Nectan, 148.
O'Ferrols, the, 83.
Offish, Sam., 198.
Offley, 70.
Offley, Robt., 195.
Ogilvie (Jesuit), 286.
Ogle, Cuthbert, 102.
........., Fras., 236, 255.
........., Colonel Sir John, 235, 602.
........., Sir Rich., 87.
........., Wm., 302.
Oglethorpe, Sir Owen, 185, 372.
Okes, John, 189, 209.
Oking, 227.
Old Sarum, 59.
Oldbury, 451.
Oldsworth, Arnold, 358.
........., Lucy, 358.
........., Mich., 51.
Olive, John de, 11.
Oliver, John, 366, 437, 509.
........., Thos., 76.
O'Neale, or O'Neil, Brian, 515.
........., Sir Cormack, 148.
........., Hugh, Earl of Tyrone, 232, 426, 515.
........., Shane, 515.
Onely, Mr., 461, 515.
Onenyborough. 63.
Onslow, Sir Fras., 406, 427.
Orange, Maurice, Prince of, 595; *see also* Nassau.
Orby, 486.
Orden, 254.
Ordnance, 29, 36, 40, 69, 71, 112, 137, 222, 353, 367, 370, 388, 574.
........., export of, 19, 108, 122, 123, 388, 417, 557, 593, 607.
........., Lieutenants of, *see* Dallison, Sir Roger; Morrison, Sir Rich.
........., Master of, *see* Carew, Geo.
........., notes, inventories, &c. of, 65, 133, 201, 202, 287, 295, 305, 306, 312, 324, 340, 438, 460.
........., officers of, 40, 137, 153, 205, 230, 314, 342, 346, 367, 378, 443, 457, 496, 529, 539.
........., payments for, 195, 450.
.... house, 48.
.... office, 378, 396, 417, 455, 474, 486, 505, 605.
Ore, *see* Lead, Silver.
Orfeur, Edw., 401.
Orford, 498.
Orinoco River, 514, 528, 531.
Orkney, 255.
Orkney, Earl of, *see* Stewart, Patrick.
Orleans, 47.
Ormond, Earl and Countess of, *see* Butler.
Orphans, court of, 519.
Orpington, 382, 418.
Orrell, Pet., 118.
.... (widow), 442.
Osbaldeston, Fras., 322.
........., Thos., 116.
Osborne, Barth., 493.
........., John (of Northamptonshire), 185.
........., John, Remembrancer of the Exchequer, 12, 107, 377, 493.
........., Sir Pet., 163, 519.
Osgodby, 18.
Osman I., Sultan of Turkey, 582, 587.
Ostend, 106.
Oswestry, 128, 443.
Ottery, 586, 594.
Oundle, 208.
Ouse River, 542, 546, 566.
Ouseley, Rich., 200.
Outlaw, Rich., 94.
........., Wm., 226.
Outlaws, 212, 248, 399, 597.
Oveatt, Thos., 250.
Ovenden, Dr., 230.
Over Catesby, 561.
Overall, Dr. John, Dean of St. Paul's, 205; Bp. of Coventry and Lichfield, 230, 512; Bp. of Norwich, 576.
Overbury, Nich., 317.
........., Sir Thos., 88, 156, 181, 187, 216, 294.

Overbury, Sir Thos., letters of, 171, 312.
........., ..., letters to, 184, 312.
........., ..., imprisonment of, 181, 184, 185, 198, 307, 347, 361, 370.
........., ..., poisoning and death of, 200, 202, 307, 309–317, 319, 323, 325–327, 329–331, 333, 336, 337, 342, 344, 345, 347, 349, 363, 370, 382, 398, 426, 433.
........., ..., servants to, 184, 312, 315, 323.
........., ..., commissioners in the cause of, 316-323, 329–331, 335, 345, 352, 364.
........., ..., ..., letters of, 316, 317, 319–321, 332, 333, 349.
........., ..., ..., letters to, 318, 320–323; *see* Winwood.
Owen, Dav., 215.
........., John, 548, 558.
........., Lewis, 236.
........., Nathan, 240.
.... Robt., 311.
........., Sir Roger, 471.
........., Wm., 4.
........., Mr., 286, 592.
Oxenbridge, Sir Robt., 84.
Oxenhoath, 29.
Oxford, 28, 54, 120, 124, 135, 138, 177, 227, 309, 392, 461, 521.
.... Castle, 461.
........., Dean and Chapter, 559.
........., mayor of, 135.
........., letters from, 350, 361, 364, 372, 391, 392, 482, 495.
........., Earl and Countess of, *see* Vere.
.... University, 77, 117, 162, 173, 174, 176, 253, 273, 288, 290, 294, 326, 478, 482, 553.
........., ..., disputes of, with the Town, 135, 138.
........., ..., visitors to or residents at, 76, 117, 164, 392, 475, 477, 479.
........., ..., Chancellors of (Egerton, Earl Ellesmere), 432; (Herbert, Earl Pembroke), 436.
........., ..., Vice-Chancellors of, 135, 391, 436, 490.
........., ..., High Steward of, 135.
........., ..., lectures at, 118, 337, 490.
........., ..., library at, 28, 143, 187.
........., ..., colleges in, viz.:—
All Souls, 230, 258.
Brasen nose, 72.
Christchurch, 46, 68, 78, 165, 231, 288, 392, 461, 548.
Corpus Christi, 230.
Exeter, 489, 565.
Gotam (mock college), 217.
Magdalen, 13, 16, 49, 51, 116, 461, 536.
Merton, 89, 143, 169, 173, 277, 301, 508, 560.
Oxford University, Colleges in—*continued.*
New, 536.
Oriel, 495, 521.
Queen's, 81.
St. John's, 33, 43, 75, 208, 209, 217, 438, 439, 492.
University, 300.
Wadham, 143.
Winchester, 253.
Oxfordshire, 86, 145, 200, 268.
........., grants of lands in, 63, 159, 249, 300, 353.
........., lands and places in, 17, 20, 28, 30, 62, 74, 84, 93, 102, 110, 122, 158, 291, 597
........., recusants in, 98, 116.
........., residents in, 156, 196, 361, 366, 464.
........., sheriffs of, 87.

P.

Packenham, John, 190, 226, 335.
........., Nich., 335.
........., Col. Phil., 448.
Packer, David, 483.
........., John, 228, 232, 291, 294, 346, 440, 452, 559.
........., Thos., 83, 84, 117, 272, 278, 369, 452, 505, 525.
Packington, Sir John, 475.
........., Lady, 475.
Packwood, Thos., 330.
Padage, Wm., 120.
Paddon, Robt., 72.
Padua, 279.
........., Neapolitan professor in, 174.
Page, Edm., *alias* Wheller, 35.
........., Dr., 465.
Paget, Chas., 21.
........., Lord Wm., 122.
Paintings, *see* Pictures.
Paises, Bernard, 378.
Palache, ——, 277.
Palatine House, 97.
........., Prince, *see* Frederick.
Palavicino, Edw., 141, 369, 445, 450, 489.
........., Fabricio, 141.
........., Horatio, 141.
Palden, Wm., 358.
Palin, Geo., 126, 264.
Pall, the, of London, 173.
Palladius, works of, 50, 110.
Palmer, Hen., 69, 335.
........., Sir Hen, 69, 110, 268.
........., Leven, 268.
........., Phil., 469.
........., Roger, 248.

Palmer, Dr., 191, 242.
Palmistry, *see* Witchcraft.
Pamber Forest, 247.
Pamphlets, *see* Treatises and Books.
Pannell, Edw., 195.
Panton, 89.
Panton, Hugh, 257.
Paolo, Padre, 192, 216.
Papists, *see* Catholics, Roman.
Paramour, Mr., 131.
Pardoe, John, 159.
Parham, John, 613.
Paris, 1, 25, 76, 84, 101, 261, 326, 351, 391, 603.
........., letters from, 1, 2, 4, 12, 13, 16, 25, 43, 51, 60, 80, 102, 176, 272, 310.
.... garden, 17.
Park, Jerem., 367.
Parke, Lawr., 209.
Parker, Sir Calthorp, 560.
........., Edw., Lord Morley, 276, 484.
........., Sir John, 10, 516.
........., Roger, 202, 291, 458.
........., Wm., Lord Monteagle, 403, 508.
........., Mr., 42, 61.
Parkins, Lady, 107.
Parliament, 70, 135, 185, 193, 202, 211, 223, 224, 230, 233–235, 245, 293, 321, 344, 346, 439, 464, 473, 525.
........., absence from, 5, 59, 77.
........., acts of, 7, 65, 238, 242, 318, 340, 520, 545.
........., anticipations of and proposals for, 136, 156, 161, 189, 199, 200, 220, 221, 228, 310, 333, 489, 505, 521, 533.
........., clerks of, 75, 159, 198, 236.
........., dissolution of, 2, 4, 9, 18, 236, 237, 241, 242.
........., elections for and seats in, 225, 227, 229, 230, 232, 234, 310, 337, 505.
........., members or barons of, 122, 232, 236, 237, 239, 514.
........., orders and proceedings in, 38, 196, 231, 232, 234–237.
........., speeches in, 232, 235, 236.
.... house, 59, 197.
Parma, 359.
Parry, Hen., Bp. of Worcester, 427.
........., John, 385.
........., Rich., Bp. of St. Asaph, 2, 220.
........., Sir Thos., Chancellor of the Duchy of Lancaster, 4, 17, 143, 233, 234, 298, 344, 370, 372.
Parselewe, Mrs., 334.
Parsons, *see* Ministers.
Parsons, Robt. (Jesuit) 163, 303.
Partridge, Jas., 393.
........., Randolph, 613.
........., Thos., 391.
Parvis, Hen., 174.
Pasley, Cath., 324.
Passage of seas, 61, 243, 581, 586.
........., commissioners for, 126, 148, 200, 300, 301, 306, 308, 309, 362, 405, 406, 408–410, 430–432, 442, 449, 458, 469, 483, 501, 528, 571, 602.
Passenius, Bartolus, 303, 305.
Paston, Sir Wm., 268.
Patents, 13, 17, 19, 20, 61, 69, 145, 146, 150, 176, 177, 207, 214, 224, 232, 351, 384.
........., lists of, 266, 346.
Patrick's-bourne, 538.
Paul, Sir Geo., 547, 553, 561.
Paul V., Pope, 177, 188, 224, 227, 285, 302–305, 474, 517, 521, 604.
Pauler's Pury, 8.
Paulet, John, 599.
........., Sarah, 599.
........., Wm., Lord St. John, 558.
........., Lady St. John, 558.
........., Lucy, Marchioness of Winchester, 90.
Paul's Cross, *see* St. Paul's.
Paul's Wharf, 335.
Pauncil Walk, 28.
Pawlett, Sir John, 495.
Payne, Ra., 463, 483.
Peace, Justices of, *see* Justices.
Peacham, Edm. (minister), 263, 269, 270, 273, 275, 276, 279, 294, 305, 306, 344, 357.
Peade, Thos., 334.
Peate, Rich., 605.
Pearse, Mark, 484.
Peasemarsh, 502.
Peckett, Marmaduke, 331.
Peckham, Geo., 268.
........., Sir Geo., 268.
Pedlars, 438, 451, 551, 566.
Pedro, Don, *see* Zuniga.
Peel, Wm., 183.
........., Isabel, 183.
Peers, creations of, 289, 404, 426, 427, 475.
Peice, Mr., 81.
Pelham (Jesuit), 142.
Pelling, *see* Pilling, John.
Pell office, 171.
Pemberton, Sir Goddard, 391.
........., Jas., 250.
........., Wm., 110.
Pemble, Thos., 33.
Pembroke, Earl of, *see* Herbert, Wm.
Pembrokeshire, 139.
........., grants of land in, 63, 124, 159.
........., offices in, 209, 596.
Pendennis Castle, 10, 242, 324.
Pendleton, Helen, 304.
Penington, John, 562.
Penkithman, Thos., 132.
Penn, Giles, 543.
........., Wm., 543.
Pennell, Roger, 203, 232.

Penney, Mr., 474.
Pennington, Jos., 20.
........., Capt., 583.
Penny, John, 499.
Penruddock, Sir Thos., 508.
Penshurst, 568.
Penson, Wm., Lancaster Herald, 265, 442, 453.
Pentlow, 116.
Penyvet, 524.
Pepys, John, 151.
Perce, Mr., 421.
Percival, Rich., 591.
Percivall, Rich., sen., 356.
........., Rich., jun., 356.
........., Thos., 613.
Percy, Sir Allan, 88. 101.
........., Mary, Lady, 90, 101.
........., Sir Josceline, 359.
........., Thos., 58, 70, 74, 77, 95, 304, 347, 355, 365, 369, 406.
.... Thos., 7th Earl of Northumberland, 384.
........., Hen., 9th Earl of Northumberland, 82, 115, 128, 168, 194, 358, 449, 475, 569.
........., ..., conduct of in the Tower, 48, 148, 190, 263, 304, 391, 441, 469, 569.
........., ..., implication of in the Gunpowder Plot, 58, 59, 67, 70, 77, 85, 95.
........., ..., letters of, 8, 10, 29, 89.
........., Dorothy, Countess of Northumberland, 67.
........., Lady Dorothy, 425.
........., Lacy Lucy, 177, 263, 436, 441, 449, 469, 475, 480, 493; *see* Hay, Lady Lucy.
........., Wm., 463.
Perkins, Sir Chris., Master of Requests, 514, 541.
Peron, James Davy, Cardinal du, 115, 270.
Perretti, Prince, 142, 143.
Perrot, Sir Jas., 123.
Perry, John, 438.
........., Rich., 251.
........., Wm., 492.
Persall, John, 44.
Persia, 127, 182, 428, 429.
........., King of, *see* Shah, Abbas,
........., Ambassador to, 88, 149.
Persian, the, *see* Shah, Abbas.
.... Gulf, 587, 589.
Perth, 586, 602.
Peru, 427.
Perveth Manor, 249.
Peryent, Thos., 424.
Peshall, Edm., 280.
Peterborough, 103, 536.
........., alms-rooms at, 74.
........., Bp. of, *see* Dove, Thos.
........., diocese of, 81, 92, 282.
........., Chancellor of, 443.
Peterly, 12.
Peto, Humph., 321.
Petre, John, 1st Lord, 202.
Pett, Art., 228.
........., Jeremy, 484.
........., Phineas or Peter, 244, 279, 592, 605.
Petty Bag, *see* Hanaper.
Petworth, 257.
Peverell Point, 607.
Pevrel, Wm., 155.
Pewsey, 489.
Pewsham Forest and Park, 68, 471, 475, 578.
Pewter, custom on, 585.
Pewtrace, John, 230.
Peyto, Sir Edw., 157.
........., Pet., 157.
Peyton, Hen., 315.
........., Sir Hen., 212, 521, 531.
........., Sir John, 447, 495.
........., Sam., 268.
........., Sir Sam., 356.
........., Sir Thos., 268.
Pharmacopeia Londinensis, 536.
Phelippes, Thos., 124, 605.
........., ..., letters of, 5, 41, 141.
........., Sir Edw., Master of the Rolls, 3, 135, 172, 176, 177, 206, 239, 253, 256.
........., Fras., 49, 63, 118, 124, 181, 193.
Phelips, Sir Robt., 72, 200, 206, 211.
Phelps, John, 299.
Philip III., King of Spain, 89, 90, 96, 97, 126, 162, 220, 227, 348, 418, 436, 449, 454, 462, 481, 505, 577, 593.
........., ..., intercourse of, with England, 140, 270, 518, 569, 583.
........., ..., displeasure, &c. of, against Raleigh, 547, 568, 588, 603.
Philipp, D. J., 90.
........., Morgan, 587.
Philippes, Hen., 382.
Philips, Mr., 132.
Phillip, John, 281.
Phillipps, Capt., 357.
........., John, 357,
Philpot, John, mayor of Faversham, 416, 471, 480.
Philpott, John (of Gray's Inn), 611.
........., John, Rouge-dragon Pursuivant, 594.
........., Thos., 600, 605, 612.
........., Mr., 225.
Phipps, Fras., 6.
........., Hum., 33.
Physicians, College of, 510, 536.
Picardy, 391.
........., Lieutenant of, 305.
Pickenham, 49.
Pickering, Thos., 502.
........., Wm., 244.
........., Mr., 22.
Pictures, 4, 96, 170, 284, 316, 354, 361, 362, 375, 387, 390, 401, 412, 453, 494, 520,

Piddington, 156.
Piddletown, 235.
Pidgeon, Mr., 48.
Piedmont, 523.
........., Victor Amadeus, Prince of, 97.
Pierrepoint, Robt., 260; Sir Robt., 538.
Piers, Wm., 320.
Pierson, Geo., 406.
Piggott, Clem., 137.
Pigott, Jonathan, 306, 308.
........., or Piggott, Capt. John, 412, 521.
Pilkinhorne, Roger, 79.
Pilkington, Robt., 400.
........., Thos., 157.
Pilling, or Pelling, John, 74, 84, 92.
Pincent, Jonas, 541.
Pinchbeck, 486.
Pinches, Wm., 24, 71.
Pindar, Paul, Ambassador to Turkey, 88, 408, 587.
Pins and pinmakers, 263, 269, 363, 532, 557.
Pipe office, 85, 388, 389, 507.
........., ..., clerks of, 44, 109, 196, 385, 486, 507.
Pippi, Bernardino, 429.
Piracies, 55, 180, 416, 427, 477, 513, 577.
Pirates, 55, 111, 122, 124, 149, 158, 216, 381, 436, 455, 471, 489, 516, 530, 611.
........., capture of, 79, 117, 188, 260, 356, 369, 427.
........., contributions for suppression of, 464, 475, 476, 579.
.... pardons for, 15, 60, 100, 115, 119, 158, 191, 206.
........., proceedings against, 22, 109, 177, 383, 413, 415, 450, 462, 464, 557, 565, 574, 614.
........., protection against, 349, 593, 607.
Pirehill, 2.
Pitcairn, Lieut. Dav., 492.
Pitches, Wm., 439.
Pitt, Edw., 551.
........., Rich, 204.
........., Wm., 94.
Plague, the, 72.
Plantagenet, Edm., Earl of Kent, 241.
Plate, gold and silver, 19, 299.
Platt, Jeffry, 325.
........., Thos., 342.
Play and players, *see* Drama.
Playden, 49.
Playdon Manor, 49.
Playle, Chris., 228.
Plummer, Thos., 486.
Plumpe, *alias* Graham, Fergus, 444.
Plumpton, 82, 222.
Plumstead, Thos., 88.
Plymouth, 55, 66, 109, 178, 235, 260, 426, 463, 514, 515, 585, 589, 598.
.... Fort, 450.
........., governor of, 55.
Plymouth, mayor of, 491, 589.
........., merchants of, 476.
Plympton, 131.
Pocahuntas, Indian Princess, 375, 425, 428 454.
Poe, Dr., 127.
Poetry, 72, 263, 601.
Poictiers, 378.
Pointer, Mr., 586.
Poker, Matt., 423, 430.
........., Eliz., 430.
Poland, 296, 303, 504.
........., King of, *see* Sigismund III.
........., Prince of, *see* Uladislas.
........., royal family of, 564.
Poles, the 69, 300, 301, 585.
Polewhely, Mary, 100.
Pollard, Geo., 68, 242.
Polton, Edw., 188.
........., John, 188.
Pomery, Edw., 540.
Ponsbury, 278.
Pontefract, 69, 249.
.... Castle, 554.
........., honor of, 379.
Pool, 218, 598.
Poole, 47.
Poole, Gervase (priest), 321, 328,
.... Hen., 32.
........., Sir Hen., 426.
Pooley, Sir Wm., 226.
Pope, John, 335.
........., Sir Wm., 20.
Pope, the, 22, 124, 321; *see also* Clemen. VIII., Paul V.
........., nuncio of, 118.
Popery, 97, 156, 160, 226, 303, 336, 355, 395, 546.
........., conversions from, 124, 221, 279, 355, 427, 428, 449.
........., conversions to, 203, 433, 489, 526.
........., encouragement or favour of, 149, 242, 352, 435.
........., opposition to, 288, 301, 411.
Popewell, Hen., 339.
Popish See, 340; *see also* Rome.
Pormorte, Geo., 299, 300, 337.
Portbury, 386.
Portcullis, *see* Holland, Phil.
Porter, Edm., 35, 109, 167.
........., Endymion, 605.
........., Dr., 240.
Portland Isle, 69, 254.
.... Castle, 69, 99, 254.
Portman, Sir Henry, Bart., 344, 484.
Porto Santo, 491.
Ports, *see* England, ports of, and Cinque ports.
Portsmouth, 29, 226, 380, 394, 403.
.... Castle, 191, 274.
Portugal, 429, 431, 455.
.... trade with, 65, 86.

Portugal, Viceroy of, 615.
Portuguese, 214, 427, 527.
Pory, John, 33, 48, 54, 115, 234, 476, 516, 521, 571, 585.
........., ..., letters of to Carleton, 495, 567, 568, 587, 588, 591, 595, 598.
Post fines, 60, 88, 96, 101, 225, 365, 523.
Postmasters and postmen, 17, 23, 36, 44, 100, 126, 215, 304, 401, 402, 464, 477, 478, 480, 545, 562, 601; *see also* Quester.
Posts and packets, 17, 44, 90, 116, 277, 448, 491, 496, 504, 512, 520, 530, 535, 545.
Posts, payments for, 382, 441, 503, 554.
........., Master of, *see* Stanhope, Lord.
Potecote, 418.
Potet, Jean, 572.
Potkin, John, 342.
Pottle, John, 525.
Potts, Thos., 315, 535.
Pougheley Manor, 280.
Poulter, John, 315, 317.
Poultney, Sir John, 465.
Poulton, Fras., 34.
Pourven, Wm., 394.
Povey, Justinian, 55, 277, 346, 348.
Powatan, Indian chief, 375.
Powell, And., 431.
........., Rich., 592.
........., Thos., (equerry), 117, 160.
........., Thos., (solicitor), 207.
........., Thos., (cutler), 553, 559
Powerscourt, 80.
Poyntz, Sir John, 520, 521.
........., Sir Nich., 550.
Pratt, John, 57.
........., Wm., 357.
Preachers, 56, 96, 176, 226, 318, 435, 465, 490, 506.
Precedence, 134, 157, 169, 514, 521, 609; *see also* Baronets, precedence of.
Prerogative Court, *see* Canterbury.
........., ecclesiastical, 340.
........., regal, 340; *see also* James I, prerogative of.
Prest, auditors of, 52.
Preston, Lancashire, 304.
........., Northumberland, 384.
........., Rutland, 292.
Preston, John, 117.
........., Sam., 14.
........., Thos., (priest), 253.
........., Thos. (of Sandwich), 403.
Pretiman, John, 609.
Prettyman, John, 402.
Prewe, Fras., 594.
Price, Art., 101.
........., Edw., 253.
........., Maurice, 253.
........., Sir Rich., 604.
Prick and cheque, clerks of, 75, 394, 415.
Prideaux, Dr. John, 337, 489, 565.
Priests, Romish, 3, 10, 11, 54, 104, 119, 123, 134, 145, 176, 203, 281, 287, 289, 301–304, 327, 435, 511, 600.
........., prisoners, 253, 279, 283, 285, 299, 320, 321, 406, 458, 483, 543.
........., ..., liberation and banishment of, 112, 328, 543.
........., English, abroad, 3, 28, 285, 343.
Primrose, Arch., 213.
........., Duncan, 269, 413.
........., Jas., 11.
Prin, Capt., 587.
Prince Cardinal, *see* Albert.
........., the, *see* Henry and Charles, Princes.
Prince, Sir Fras., 91.
Prince's Walk, 53.
Princes, Christian, 171, 427.
........., foreign, 24, 41, 64, 69, 343, 462.
........., of Union, *see* Union.
........., Protestant, 274.
Pringle, Robt., 30, 53.
Printers, 166, 285, 299, 303.
Printing, fines for, 356.
........., licence for, 10, 353, 431, 484, 536.
Prior, Gerard, 164.
........., Thos., 437, 439.
Prisoners, 2, 11, 30, 94, 116, 285, 383, 483.
Prithorith, Wm. Thos., 73.
Privy Council, the, 9, 73, 74, 99, 125, 144, 156, 166, 168, 236, 260, 262, 304, 313, 321, 325, 347, 350, 352, 358, 374, 395, 400, 429, 439, 448, 449, 456, 460, 463, 464, 465, 468, 469, 473, 479, 481, 482, 502, 523, 530, 551, 565, 566, 573, 574, 586, 591, 613.
...., advices and decisions of, 109, 145, 223, 455, 462, 520, 603.
...., banishment from, 378, 379.
.... books, 608.
........., ..., chamber, keepers, &c. of, 213, 229, 393, 573.
...., clerks of, 50, 104, 160, 198, 200 220, 224, 260, 263, 376, 538, 546.
...., entertainments of, and to, 169 458.
...., letters of, 148, 167, 181, 219, 223, 226, 253, 255, 260, 270, 272, 274, 283, 286, 287, 289, 333, 342, 359, 364, 376, 377, 389, 409, 413, 448, 478, 485, 537, 541, 552, 568.
...., letters to, 16, 17, 20, 24, 53, 62, 72, 75, 81, 112, 117, 177–180, 182, 184, 185, 204, 238, 239, 254, 257–262, 313, 316, 319, 322, 325–327, 389, 390, 430, 450, 473–476, 479, 500, 528, 532–536, 539–545, 548, 550, 551, 554, 555, 557, 559, 565, 566, 571, 573, 574, 576, 578, 586, 587, 589, 590, 594, 597, 599, 601, 603, 604. 610.
...., licences by, 61, 279, 409, 431, 471.
...., members of, 59, 127, 176, 183, 199, 205, 227, 228, 234, 272, 308, 344, 356, 360, 372, 373, 375, 385, 398, 404, 407, 424–426, 432, 434, 449, 458, 482, 488, 496, 514, 515, 601.

Privy Council, orders in, 55, 123, 137, 138, 174, 176, 186, 191, 197, 226, 232, 261, 269, 289, 290, 310, 343, 349, 362, 376, 396, 397, 403, 465, 475, 512, 517, 525, 532, 540, 546, 548, 557, 581, 586, 610.
...., petitions to, 19, 20, 106, 132, 218, 271, 276, 285, 288, 291, 339, 347, 363, 389, 409, 419, 444, 503, 504, 508, 509, 537, 538, 540, 546, 548–550, 552–558, 561-563, 566, 567, 573, 589, 601, 606–608.
...., proceedings in, 13, 15, 48, 80, 134, 135, 140, 146, 150, 151, 158, 162, 163, 189, 199, 237, 241, 245, 256, 281, 285, 310, 360, 361, 371, 428, 461, 468, 469, 470, 471, 476, 488, 579, 605.
...., references and reports to, 149, 208, 264, 287, 397, 427, 435, 467, 500, 507, 534, 535, 549, 554, 595, 600.
...., restoration to, 477, 485, 494.
...., summons to, 260, 417, 511, 526, 532, 544.
...., warrants to and from, 51, 447, 556, 574.
Privy Purse, Keeper of, *see* Hume, Earl Dunbar, Murray, John.
Privy Seal, Lord, 289, 326, *see also* Howard, Hen., Earl of Northampton; Carr, Robt., Earl of Somerset; Somerset, Edw., Earl of Worcester.
........., ..., clerks, &c. of, 5, 103, 167, 242, 272, 345, 346, 350, 351, 401, 452, 472, 509, 604; *see also* Reynoldes, Edw.; Mills, Fras.
........., ... office and officers, 5, 44, 81, 272, 278, 288, 292, 310, 311, 338, 339, 369, 391.
Proby, Pet., 240, 520.
Proclamations,—
(1611): 23, 32, 37, 38, 66, 73, 92.
(1612): 128, 129, 138, 148.
(1613): 167, 168, 184, 185, 186, 199, 205, 213.
(1614): 237, 247, 252, 253, 256, 258, 259, 261.
(1615): 279, 282–284, 287, 295, 297, 305, 308, 315, 322, 337.
(1616): 374.
(1617): 459, 481, 504.
(1618): 523, 527, 529, 536, 544, 551, 557, 569, 591, 593.
Proclamations, book of, 185.
Procter, Rich., 96.
........., Mr., 96.
Proctor, Edw., 289.
........., Geo., (King's chaplain), 606.
........., Geo., 255.
........., John, 9.
......, Sir Steph., 75, 224.
Prombill, 109.
Protestants and Protestantism, 127, 148, 149, 157, 176, 226, 303, 304, 329, 368, 369, 434, 436, 480, 595.
Prott, Warkin, 114.
Provost Marshals, 448, 454, 460.
Prowse, Jas., 251.
Prowse, John, 528, 534, 536, 540, 541.
........., Rich., 528.
Prusen, Hildebrand, 613.
Prussia, 303.
Puckeridge, 109.
Puckering, Mr., 43.
Puckle, John, 190.
Puckle-Church, 131.
Pudsey, Thos., 359.
........., Faith, 359.
Pulham Manor, 46.
Pullyson, Sir Thos., 186.
Pulter, Art., 49.
Punsburn Manor, 84.
Punter, Thos., 260.
Purcill, Thos., 57, 247.
Purefey, Gam., 47.
Pursell, *see* Purcill.
Puritans and Puritanism, 234, 288, 303, 304, 411, 420, 424, 435, 439, 521, 526.
Pursuivants, 34, 94, 126, 172, 351, 420, 594.
Pursuivants-at-arms, *see* Gwillim, John; Holland, Phil.; Leonard, Sampson; Philpot, John; St. George, Hen.; Smith, Wm.
Purvey, Wm., 12, 506, 597.
Purveyance and purveyors, 20, 73, 74, 389.
Puteanus, Erycius, 404, 514.
Putney, 141.
Putto, Rich., 55, 127.
Pyatt, Rich., 122.
Pye, Robt., 445, 533.
........., Wal., 432.
Pymme, John, 205, 243, 578.
Pynson, Jonas, 534.

Q.

Quarrier, Robt., 86.
Queen, *see* Anne of Denmark.
........., late, *see* Elizabeth.
Queenhithe, 308.
Queen's meadow, 596.
Quendon, 29.
Quester, Joseph de, 605.
........., Matt. de, Postmaster, 138, 270, 273, 274, 277, 401.
........., ..., letters of to Carleton, 174, 253, 274, 412, 414, 429, 448, 449, 491, 512, 521, 522, 525, 530, 533, 535, 568, 590.
Quick, Rich., 483.
Quicksilver, 162.

R.

Raby Castle, 121.
........., manor, 211, 311, 594.
Radcliffe Church, Bristol, 101.
Radcliffe, Art., 292.
Radnor (informer), 504.
Radnor prison, 371.
Radnorshire, 85, 371.
........., offices in, 85, 209, 415, 431, 432.
Radzivill, ——, 133.
Ragley, 162, 183, 374, 379.
Raimond, John, 122.
Rainsford, Rich., 108.
Raleigh, Sir Carew, 69, 99, 254, 440.
........., Gilb., 69, 254.
........., Sir Wal., 105, 275, 374, 387, 412, 491, 497, 517, 529, 578, 597, 598, 600, 601, 603.
........., ..., lands and goods of, 211, 398, 405, 426, 589, 590–592.
........., ..., in prison, 48, 58, 59, 148, 344.
........., ..., lodgings, &c. of in Tower, 309, 361, 426.
........., ..., medicines, &c. prepared by, 143, 155, 312.
........., ..., letters of, 105, 528, 573, 576, 583.
........., ..., letters to, 573.
........., ..., release of, 356–358, 377, 425.
........., ..., voyages of, 424, 425, 428, 443, 447, 449, 454, 463, 475, 489, 511, 514–516, 520, 521, 528, 533, 538, 544, 547, 562, 566.
........., ..., complaints against, 489, 493, 495, 513.
........., ..., illness of, 564–567, 569, 570.
........., ..., re-imprisonment of in Tower, 565, 568–579, 582, 583, 585, 586.
........., ..., execution of, 587, 588, 591.
........., ..., works of, 269, 340, 341, 561.
........., Eliz., Lady, 521, 531, 568, 573, 577, 583, 585, 590–592.
........., Wal., jun., 344, 528, 576.
........., Carew, 531.
Ramsay, And., 425.
........., Dav. (groom) 208.
........., Dav., (clockmaker) 211, 419, 598.
........., Edw., 241.
........., Jas., Visct. Haddington, 23, 56, 144, 210, 244, 346, 379, 443, 452, 509.
........., ..., grants and payments to, 5, 57, 381, 511, 599.
........., ..., letters of, 39, 101.
........., Eliz., Visctss. Haddington, 57, 273, 599, 601, 603.
........., Bridget, 599.
........., Pat., 23, 213, 509.
........., Wm., 35, 99, 210, 249, 414.
........., Mr., 124, 287.
Ramsbothom, Eliz., 498.
Ramsgate, 255.
Ramsyer, Wm., 253.
Rand, And., 351.
........., John, 351.
Randoll, Mr., 105, 354, 422.
Randolph, Amb., 248, 314, 517, 533.
........., ..., letters to, *see* Wilson.
........., Mrs., 374.
Rands, Geo., 222, 309.
Ranking, Arch., 303.
Raphoe, Bp. of, *see* Knox, Andrew.
Rasingham, Denys, 167.
Ratcliffe, 126.
........., Trinity House, *see* Trinity House, London.
Ratcliffe, Sir Edw., 110.
........., Fras., 399, 406.
........., Hen., Visct. Fitzwalter, 225, 284.
........., Robt., Earl of Sussex, 101, 135, 179, 261, 313, 327, 573.
Ravenscroft, Geo., 213, 229.
Ravoire, Paul de la, 475, 477, 510, 529, 564, 577, 604.
Rawdon, 194.
Rawdon, Geo., 194.
Rawlings (servant), 486.
Rawlins, Sir John, 519; letters to, *see* Reynoldes, Edw.
Rawlyns, Giles, 313.
Raworth, Fras., 394, 490.
Rawson, Thos., 527.
Raymond, Thos., 337.
........., Mr., 125, 309.
Raynsford, Hen., 418.
Read, John, 574.
........., Ralph, 492.
........., Thos., Latin secretary, 538.
Reade, Eliz., Lady, 105.
........., Kath., 32.
........., Thos., 251.
........., Wm., 34.
Reading, 200, 459, 461, 561.
Reading, Rich., 117.
........., (minister), 490, 592.
Rebbe, Nich. de, 250, 264.
Recusancy, 51, 56, 162, 295, 329, 340, 406.
Recusants, 12, 41, 43, 63, 68, 169, 185, 196, 210, 220, 226, 258, 300, 302–304, 355, 364, 369, 388, 395, 420, 435, 459, 466, 470, 523, 603.
........., arrears of fines of, 221, 238, 239, 250, 275, 276, 281, 285, 366.
........., composition with, 165, 244.
........., grants of lands of, 10, 23, 24, 29–33, 38, 43–45, 49, 52. 63, 66, 68, 72, 73, 75, 78, 84, 89, 93, 96, 98, 100, 116, 120, 122, 156, 159, 191, 214, 366, 440, 582, 589.
........., imprisonment of, 11, 145, 279, 283, 458.

Recusants, proceedings against, 144, 164, 167, 233, 234, 253, 254, 427, 470.
Redbourn, 265.
Redich, Alex., 28.
Reding, Geo., 122.
Redmayne, Robt., 314.
Rednoore, 463.
Reede rectory, 439.
Reekes (shipmaster), 516.
Rees, Watkin, 292.
Reeve, John, 294.
Reeves, Mr., 42.
Regden, Robt., 268.
........., Sir Wm., 268.
Reigate, 176.
Relief, collections for, 415, 496.
Religion, 63, 74, 141, 142, 156, 303, 393, 411, 475, 503, 504, 511, 517; *see also* Church, Protestantism, Puritanism, Popery, Rome.
Renell, *see* Reynell.
Requests, Court of, 519.
........., clerks of, 452.
........., Masters of, 206, 220, 338, 376, 379, 390, 391, 445, 448, 489, 511, 514.
Rescarrock, W., 201.
Reston, Fras., 451.
........., Wm., 451.
Reve, Sir Hen., 591.
Revels, Master of, *see* Buck, Sir Geo.; Tilney, Edm.
........., office of, 294, 329.
Revenue, *see* Crown Revenue.
Revett, Tim., 190.
Rewe rectory, 98.
Rewthan, *see* Ruthven.
Reynall, Sir Geo., 402, 550.
Reynell, Sir Carew, 69, 254, 551.
Reyney, Emma, 498.
Reynoldes, Abm., 10.
........., Edw., jun., 508.
........., Edw., Privy Seal Clerk, 37, 350, 452, 519.
........., ..., letters of, 3, 65, 83, 125, 175, 257, 309, 345, 401, 508, 560.
........., ..., ..., to Fras. Mills, 5, 44, 81, 84, 90, 242, 272, 278, 288, 292, 310, 311, 326, 338, 339, 346, 350, 351, 369, 378, 391, 422, 472, 504, 554.
........., Edw., letters of, Sir John Rawlins, 125, 136, 146, 148, 163, 183, 297, 298, 302.
........., Cath., 37.
........., Hen., 48.
Reynolds, John, 608.
........., Dr. Robt., 497.
........., Mr., 479.
Rheims, 193.
Rhine, the, 170.
........., Palatine of, *see* Frederic.
Riby, 537.
Riccio, Matteo, 427.
Rice, Rich., 38, 116.
Rich, Capt. Barnaby, 378.
........., Sir Hen., 400, 426, 441, 494.
.... Hugh, 257.
........., Nath., 386.
........., Sir Robt., 4, 79, 376, 386, 513.
........., Robt., Lord, 205, 414, 427, 488, 515; Earl of Warwick, 564, 587.
........., Frances, Lady, 488.
........., Lady Isabella, 598; *see* Smythe.
........., Warner, 148, 163.
Richards, Milo, 292.
Richardson, Clem., *see* Snell.
........., Hugh, 493, 499.
........., John, 432, 433, 468.
........., John, (priest), 321.
........., Dr. John, 287.
........., Lawr., 447.
........., Lewis, 68.
.... Wm., 498.
Richmond, dukedom of, 182.
........., lordship of, 354, 360.
........., letters from, 39, 48, 129.
........., the Friars at, 50, 65.
.... Palace and Park, 26, 32, 50, 70, 76, 138, 231, 257, 385, 404, 477.
........., Yorkshire, 23.
........., ..., archdeaconry of, 294, 354.
Richmond Herald, *see* St. George, Hen.
Rickasies, Isaac, 524.
Rickling Manor, 29.
Riddell, Thos., 360; Sir Thos., 374, 375.
Riddesdale, 8, 399, 513.
Ridding Grange, 367.
Ridge, the, Derby, 72.
Ridgeway, Sir Thos., 425, 426.
Ridley, Alex., 365.
........., Dr. Thos., 272.
Rigby, Alex., 100.
........., Rog., 100.
Ringmer Wood, 158.
Ringwold, 358.
Ripton, 24.
Risbrooke, Wm., 385.
River, 571.
Rivers, Sir Geo., 5.
Rives, F., 396.
Roberts, Rich., 410, 412, 427.
........., Sir Thos., 447.
.... (priest), 10.
Robertson, Susanna, 593.
Robins, John, 502, 503.
Robinson, Humph., 367.
........., Robt., 421.
........., Sam., 528.
........., Wm., 431, 595.
........., Mr., 481.
Robson, Lionel, 36, 61.
Rocher, the (ship), 129.

Rochester, 181, 353.
........., alms-rooms in, 68.
.... Castle, 52.
........., mayor, &c. of, 223.
.... prison at, 372.
........., Visct., *see* Carr, Robt.
........., Bp. of, *see* Buckeridge, John.
........., Dean and Chapter, 91, 453.
Rock manor, 44.
Rockingham, 75.
.... Forest., 313.
Rod, ——, 406.
Rodney, Sir John, 74, 144.
........., Mr., 224.
.... (young), 39, 74, 84, 92.
Roe, Hen., 268.
........., Sir Hen., 156, 268.
........., Sir Thos., 260.
........., ..., letters to, *see* Abbot, Geo.; Carew, Lord.
Roffe, Steph., 574.
Roger, Eliz., 243.
Rogers, Barth., 101, 455.
........., Dr. Fras., 490.
........., Joan, 131.
........., Wm., 47.
........., Wm. (idiot), 131.
Rogeston's Grange, 116.
Rohan, Hen., Prince of, 583.
Rokeby, 544.
Rokewood, Amb., 243, 304, 550.
Rolfe, H., 369.
Rolfe, Mr., 375.
Rolles (ward), 466.
Rolleston, Chris., 73.
Rolls House, 507, 581.
........., clerks of, 260.
........., Master of, 155, 258, *see* Phelips, Sir Edw.; Cæsar, Sir Julius.
Rome, 3, 61, 149, 173, 216, 227, 381, 407, 409, 417, 426, 428, 511, 526, 542.
........., Church of, *see* Church.
........., Court of, 171.
........., English college in, 28, 142.
........., Inquisition at, 153, 512, 514
........., letters from, 5, 401.
........., nobleman of, 232.
........., visitors to, 28, 64, 65 110, 300.
Romney, 298, 352, 367, 576, 578, 579.
Romney Marsh, 343.
........., New, 109, 255, 612.
Romsey, 223.
Rone, Humph., 597.
Roo, Wm., 581.
Roome Wood, 334.
Roope, Capt. Gilb., 158, 206.
Rooper, Ant., 49.
Roos, Lord and Lady, *see* Cecil.
........., Lord of Hamlake, *see* Manners, Fras., Earl of Rutland.
Rootes, John, 471.
........., Ann (of Hampshire), 471, 499.
........., Jas., 480.
........., Ann (of Sussex), 480.
Roper, Sir John, 66, 95, 115, 137; Lord, Teynham, 380, 381, 385, 407, 425 433, 567, 584.
........., ..., letters to, 380, 381.
........., Mrs., 406, 446.
Ross Manor, 35.
Ross, Jeremy or Jeronimo, 84, 222, 278.
........., John, 74.
Rosseter, Phil., 275.
Rother, *see* Appledore.
Rotherford, Jas., 35.
Rotherham, Sir Thos., 224.
Rothwell, Ellis, 5, 72.
Rouen, 90, 163.
Rouge Croix, *see* Gwillim, John.
Rouge Dragon, *see* Smith, Wm.
Rountree, Leon, 226.
Rous, Ant., 385, 486, 507.
........., Sir John, 386.
Routledge, Lancelot, 279.
Rovenson, John, 198.
Rowdon, John, 33.
Rowell, 185, 254.
Rowell, John, 41.
Rowington, 249.
Rowland, Mr., 264.
Rowlands, Hen., Bp. of Bangor, 53, 426.
Rowliffe, John, 70.
Rowthe, John, 154.
Roxburgh, Lord and Lady, *see* Ker.
Royal Family, 123, 150, 329; *see also* Jas. I.; Anne, Queen; Henry and Charles, Princes; Eliz., Princess.
Royle, 440.
Royston, 90, 91, 109, 215.
........., game, &c. at, 2, 335, 360.
........., house and garden at, 8, 37, 89, 214, 430.
........., King at, 88, 148, 156, 162, 167, 171 172, 246, 256, 269, 273, 358, 360, 361, 397, 490, 493, 586, 594.
........., letters from, 10, 21, 23, 79, 82, 88, 89, 90, 97, 99, 100, 111, 113, 119, 151, 152, 157, 160, 203, 208–213, 221, 246, 256, 258, 276, 315, 317, 318, 320–322, 327, 339, 448, 449, 486, 488.
........., wardrobe at, 222, 278.
Rubens, Peter Paul, 390.
Ruck, Art., 529.
Rudcliffe, Ra., 375.
Rudd, Ant., Bp. St. David's, 84, 261.
Rudyard, Sir Benj., 490, 502, 525, 531, 535, 599.
........., Robt., 232.
Rue, Pet. de la, 103.
Rufford, 258, 260, 375, 389.
Rumler, J. W., 313.

Rumsay, Wal., 209.
Rushbrook, Lawr., 218.
........., Mrs., 218.
Rushton, 55, 159.
........., All Saints, 158.
Russell, Fras., 2nd Earl of Bedford, 130.
........., Sir John (son of Francis), 130.
........., Eliz., Lady (wife of John), 130.
........., Edw., 3rd Earl of Bedford, 69, 196.
........., Lucy, Countess of Bedford, 69, 166, 170, 196, 225, 287, 387, 456, 501, 516, 585, 594, 598.
........., Wm., 1st Lord Russell, of Thornhaugh, 199.
........., Eliz., Lady (wife of William), 48.
........., Fras., 2nd Lord Russell, of Thornhaugh, 426, 507.
........., Cath., Lady (wife of Francis), 507.
........., Wm., (son of Francis), 426.
........., John, 65.
........., Edw., 300.
........., Sir Wm., Treasurer of the Navy, 538, 540, 549, 561, 605.
........., Thos., 111, 221, 250, 468.
Russia, 178, 307, *see also* Muscovy.
........., Ambassadors of and to, *see* Muscovy.
........., Emperor of, *see* Michael Feodorowitz.
.... Company, *see* Muscovy Company.
........., trade with, 228, 497, 503.
Ruthin, 275.
.... Park, 177.
Ruthven, Alex., Earl of Gowrie, 190.
........., Barbara, Lady, 393, 465, 484, 598.
........., Pat., 148, 212, 387.
........., Wm., 190.
Rutland, Earl of, *see* Manners.
Rutlandshire, 240, 242, 266, 458.
........., grants of lands in, 292, 386.
Ruytnick, Simeon, 50.
Rycot, 241, 392.
Ryder, Edw., 326.
........., Wm., 157.
........., Sir Wm., 123, 210.
Rye, 49, 190, 201, 301, 349, 388, 396, 437, 495, 513, 525, 545, 572, 574, 611.
........., letters dated from, 179, 354, 502, 513.
........., mayor, &c. of, 354, 360, 416, 502, 513, 543.
Rye, John, 483.
........., Robt., 483.
Ryman, Geo., 441.
Rymer, Thos., 68.

S.

S. H., 602.
S. O., 387.
Sabbath, the, 429, 526, 564, 584.
Sackville, Thos., 1st Earl of Dorset, 344.
........., Cecilia, Countess of Dorset (wife of Thomas), 344.
........., Robt., 2nd Earl of Dorset, 270.
........., Anne, Countess of Dorset, (wife of Robt.), 436, 449, 584.
........., Rich., 3d Earl of Dorset, 5, 77, 154, 167, 405, 446, 460, 512.
........., ..., grants to, 18, 158, 278.
........., Anne, Countess of Dorset (wife of Richard), 446.
........., Edw., 322, 344.
........., Sir Edw., 167, 183, 198, 213.
........., Thos., 270.
Sackville Place, 18.
Sackvilles, the, 165.
Saddler (secretary), 391.
........., Mrs., 407.
Saffery, Wm., 451.
........., Dorothy, 451.
St. Albans, 432, 534.
St. Andreas, 522.
St. Andrew's, Holborn, 386, 560.
.... Castle, Hants, 30, 41, 45, 65, 416.
........., Scotland, 473.
........., Archbp. of, *see* Spottiswood, John.
St. Anthony (Cornwall), 279.
St. Anthony's parish, London, 295.
St. Asaph, diocese of, 2.
........., Bp. of, *see* Parry, Rich.
St. Bartholomew's (London), 273.
........., letters dated from, 225, 237, 458, 460, 462–464, 476, 479, 481, 482, 485.
.... Hospital, Sussex, 49.
St. Bennett's parish, London, 335.
St. Bernard, 303.
St. Botolph's parish, London, 201, 234, 502.
St. Briavell's Castle, &c., 40.
St. Bride's parish, London, 18.
St. Catherine's Church, Cambridge, 420.
St. Christopher's (Antilles), 528.
St. Chrysostom, Life, &c. of, 110, 111, 117, 175, 182, 221, 224, 236, 277, 429, 476.
St. Clement Danes' parish, Middlesex, 49, 502.
St. David's, Bp. of, *see* Rudd, Ant.; Milbourne, Rich.
........., Dean and Chapter of, 280.
........., diocese of, 84.
St. Dunstan's parish, London, 18, 156, 412.
St. Edmund's rectory, Northampton, 274.
St. Edmundsbury, *see* Bury St. Edmunds.
St. George, Hen., Bluemantle Pursuivant, 99, 114; Richmond Herald, 442, 453.

St. George, John, 522.
........., Rich., Norroy King-at-arms, 31, 427, 453.
........., Wm., 522, 549, 607.
St. George's Feast, 291, 362, 444, 484, 515, 524.
.... parish, Southwark, 573.
...., Surrey, 582.
St. Giles' Hospital, Wilton, 219.
.... rectory, Northampton, 274.
St. Gregory, *see* Gregory.
St. Hippolitus, 498.
St. James's Palace and Park, 19, 26, 57, 156, 162, 187, 359, 361, 395, 410, 604.
........., letters dated from, 85, 101, 363, 387, 397–399, 407, 414, 437, 438, 456, 461, 492, 531.
St. John, Sir John, 411.
........., Oliver, 256, 269, 272, 273, 279, 344.
........., Sir Oliver, 317, 319, 320; Lord Deputy of Ireland, 360, 361, 364, 425, 426, 427, 457.
........., Oliver, Lord of Bletsoe, 101, 224, 255, 317, 584.
........., ..., letters of and to, 24, 178, 326, 331, 389.
........., Dorothy, Lady, 284, 344.
........., Rowl., 24.
........., Sir Wm., 64, 522, 565.
........., Lord and Lady, *see* Paulet.
St. John's, 2.
........., Isle of Thanet, 459.
.... Church, Margate, 306.
.... Hospital, Chester, 353, 363.
...., Cirencester, 126.
...., Wilton, 219.
.... Wood, 382.
St. Katherine's, London, 218.
St. Lawrence, Chris., Lord Houth, 65.
St. Lawrence, 577.
St. Leger, Sir Ant., 50, 168.
St. Leonard's parish, Shoreditch, 521.
St. Malo, 501.
St. Margaret's Church, Westminster, 231, 591.
St. Mark's, 324.
St. Martin's-in-the-Fields parish, London, 132, 581.
St. Martin's churchyard, 329.
St. Martin's-lane, *see* London, Streets of.
St. Mary-by-Southampton, 497.
.... Cray, Kent, 548.
.... Magdalen's Hospital, Newcastle-on-Tyne, 40.
.... Magdalen's parish, Bermondsey, 573.
.... Overy, 419.
.... Towars, Ipswich, 314.
St. Mary's Aldermanbury, London, 228.
St. Mary's-at-hill parish, London, 49.
St. Mary's College, Winchester, 294.
.... Hospital, Newcastle, 30.
St. Mary's parish, Dover, 490, 592.
...., Guildford, 17.
St. Medard's Abbey, Soissons, 310.
St. Michael's Church, Gloucester, 435, 487.
.... Mount, Cornwall, 79, 438.
.... feast, 286.
St. Neot's bridge, 413, 441.
St. Nicholas' island, 450.
St. Olave's rectory and parish, 497, 500, 573.
St. Omer, 54, 280, 362.
St. Paul, Sir Geo., 53.
........., Lady, 414, 427.
St. Paul's, 175, 522.
.... Cathedral, London, 120, 143, 522.
.... Churchyard, 454.
.... consistory, court of, 190, 367.
........., Dean of (Valentine Carey), 473, 531, 532.
........., prebends of, 414.
........., treasurer of, 401.
.... Cross, 212, 301, 439, 454, 461, 475, 494, 516, 519.
St. Peter's parish, Tower, 19, 272.
........., Westminster, 414.
.... Hospital, 582.
St. Sauveur, M., 447.
St. Saviour's parish, Southwark, 108, 571.
St. Sepulchre's parish, London, 29, 502.
.... rectory, Northampton, 274.
St. Stephen's, 423, 479.
........., Westminster, 37, 102.
St. Swithin's Church, 435.
St. Thomas's Hospital, Southwark, 341.
........., ..., ..., Sandwich, 355.
.... parish, Southwark, 571.
.... town (South America), 544, 562, 574, 587.
St. Valery, 341.
St. Warbott's Cathedral, Chester, 87.
Saker, Chris., 450.
Salby, Rob., 59.
Salford, 493.
Salisbury, 7, 564, 591.
Salisbury, Wm., 177 ; *see* Jenman.
Salisbury, Bp. of, *see* Cotton, Hen.; Abbot, Rob. ; Fotherley, Martin.
........., Cathedral, 7.
.... diocese of, 242, 353.
........., Earl and Countess of, *see* Cecil.
.... court, 18.
........., letters from, 7, 66–68, 298–300.
........., mayor of, 50.
........., Tailors' Company at, 50.
Salisbury House, Strand, 18, 74, 79, 513, 525.
Salkeld, Hen., 279.
........., John, 124, 279.
Salmon, Rob., 572, 573.
Salop, *see* Shropshire.
Salt, 22, 67, 133, 316.
Salter, Geo., 87.

Salter, Nich., 19, 166, 187, 216, 235, 283; Sir Nich., 418, 470, 490, 511, 582, 585, 598.
........., Nich., 598.
........., Wal., 26.
Saltonstall, Sir Pet., 185, 358.
........., Sir Sam., 41.
Saltpetre, 418, 454.
Salvetti, Amerigo, 223, 224, 225, 227.
Samborne, Hen., 375.
Sames, Sir John, 135.
Sampson, Sam., 353.
........., Thos., 612.
........., Alice, 612.
Sandall Hall, 32.
Sandall Manor, 486.
Sanders, Wm., 37.
........., Mr., 216.
Sanderson, Hen., 226, 272, 285, 328, 329, 332.
........., Mich., 15.
.... Sam., 328.
Sandes, Ant., 256.
Sandey, Robt., 90, 93.
Sandgate Castle, 77, 149, 202, 259, 306, 312, 340, 367, 574, 582, 614.
........., ..., muster rolls of, 255, 485.
Sandham Castle, 97, 243.
Sandhurst, *alias* Blackwater, 243.
Sandiland, John, 203.
Sandilands, Sir Jas., 114, 388.
........., Jas., 250.
Sandon, 488.
Sandown Castle, 148, 202, 255, 306, 337, 367, 395, 582, 611, 614.
...., muster rolls of, 151, 308, 396, 484.
Sandsfoot Castle, 130.
Sandwich, 255, 256, 437, 447, 529.
........., mayor, &c. of, 154, 200, 343, 355, 366, 403, 412, 434, 439, 457, 524, 532, 543.
.... residents in, 222, 421, 487, 611.
.... passage at, 148, 200, 301, 308, 431, 449.
Sandys, Sir Edwin, 226, 490.
........., Sir Geo., 391, 527.
........., Sir Rich., 273, 457.
........., Lady, 273.
........., Sir Sam., 130.
Sanford, John, 261.
Sanquair, Lord and Lady, *see* Crichton.
Sapreton, Beale, 132.
Sarr, 255.
Sarum, *see* Salisbury.
Sassamine, ——, 236.
Saul, Arthur, 458.
........., Edwin, 315.
........., Susan, 315, 332, 334.
Saulcey Forest, 208.
Saunby, 445.
Saunders, Edw., 14.
........., Valentine, 185.
Saunders Walk, 208.
Saunderson, Thos., 551, 552.
Saunier, Jehan, 293, 309.
Sauvier, Jean, 572.
Savage, Sir Art., 279, 425.
........., Rog., 111.
.... Thos., 279.
.... Sir Thos., 201, 212, 218, 500, 514.
........., Eliz. Lady, 514.
Savery, Dr. A., 315, 316, 321, 324.
Savile, Sir Hen., Provost of Eton, 111, 171, 232, 252, 377, 410, 421, 470, 474, 477, 478, 488.
........., ..., letters of, 30, 284.
........., ..., letters of, to Carleton, 2, 50, 72, 77, 92, 101, 110, 117, 125, 128, 139, 173, 182, 192, 221, 224, 236, 251, 277, 350, 372, 392, 398, 410, 429, 436, 464, 472, 476, 484, 485, 490, 491, 501, 525, 565, 582, 591.
........., ..., letters to, 508, 560.
........., ..., purchase of books for, 50, 110, 111, 139, 284, 372.
...., works of, 128, 175, 474.
........., Marg., Lady, 117, 401, 488, 525.
........., Sir Hen. jun., 69, 121, 270, 364.
........., Eliz., 169, 175, 182.
........., John, 559.
Saville, Sir Geo., 53.
........., Thos. 62.
Savoy, 196, 233, 234, 464.
........., Chas. Emanuel, Duke of, 104, 112, 149, 151, 180, 197, 262, 270, 397, 403, 521.
........., ..., agents, &c. to, *see* Wotton, Sir Hen.; Morton, Albert; Wake, Isaac.
........., Ambassador of, 50, 87–90, 95, 97, 104, 111, 112, 149, 150, 174, 185, 186, 228, 284, 352, 391; *see* Gabellione; Scarnaffi; Villa.
........., marriage negociations with, 97, 111, 115, 124, 150, 153, 157, 183.
........., Princesses of, 151, 161.
Savoy, the (Strand), 212, 510.
........., ..., letters dated from, 47, 173, 284, 344, 424, 514.
.... Hospital, master of, 496, 500, 504, 511, 514, 518, 521, 526, 527, 529, 530.
Sawyer, Edm., or Edw. 98, 193, 211, 388.
Saxbey, Passwater, 567.
Saxony, Christian II., Duke of, 11.
........., House of, 97.
Saxton Manor, 287, 399.
Say, John, 137.
Sayer, John, 404.
.... Thos., 210.
Sayos, Vincentius, 573.
Sayscourt, 209.
Saythorpe, 486.
Scarborough, Castle, 50.
Scarnaffi, Antonio, Count de, Ambassador of Savoy, 450.

Schantmalt, Mons., 180.
Schiavone, André Medula, 284.
Schomberg, Count Meinhard de, 170, 209, 217, 284, 370, 426.
........., ... (wife of), *see* Dudley, Ann.
Schonhoven, 393.
Schoppius, Gaspar, 157, 162, 303.
Schottus, Andreas, 474, 476.
Schoverus, Dr. Martin, 73.
........., Christiana, 73.
Scilly Isles, 55.
Scinde, Governor of, 516.
Scole Manor, 88.
Scory, Edw., 258.
Scotch Guard, *see* France.
.... prisoner, *see* Blair, Alex.
Scotland, 7, 18, 21, 22, 32, 44, 51, 78, 81, 150, 161, 172, 217, 219, 265, 281, 299, 380, 461, 465, 471, 475, 480, 502, 514, 593.
........., affairs in, 8, 21, 159, 284.
........., Almoner of, 410.
........., Chancellor of, *see* Seaton, Earl Dunfermline.
........., Courts and Council of, 21, 23, 193, 203, 204, 414, 469, 474, 482, 515.
........., King's visits to, 243, 390, 412–415, 424, 428, 429, 432, 434, 436–438, 441–443, 445, 447–449, 458, 466, 468, 469, 472–477, 485, 488, 505, 512, 515, 530, 562.
........., Lords of, 18, 22, 421, 470.
........., natives of, 110, 179, 250, 451.
........., Parliament of, 464, 470, 472, 473–5, 477.
........., Secretary for, *see* Hay, Sir Alex.
........., sheriffs, &c. of, 586, 595.
........., ships of, 282, 514.
........., travellers to and from, 38, 134, 391, 469, 477, 484, 496, 555, 592.
........., Treasurer of, *see* Stewart, Earl of Mar; Carr, Earl of Somerset.
... ., visitors to or residents in, 88, 139, 515, 585.
........., Bishops of, 466, 472, 473.
........., English Church service in, 424, 464, 472, 473, 517, 586, 603.
........., kirk and ministers of, 391, 502, 586, 602.
Scots, 2, 30, 83, 129, 134, 153, 163, 169 170, 176, 199, 210, 212, 227, 237–239, 245, 274, 281, 287, 398, 458, 460, 470, 473, 483, 514 538.
.... on Borders, *see* Border disturbances.
........., King of, *see* Darnley, Hen.
........., Queen of, *see* Mary.
Scott, Jas., 132.
........., John, 183, 353.
........., Sir John, 398.
........., Patrick, 529, 530, 537, 538, 544.
Scripture, *see* Bible.
Scroghan, Jas., 196.
Scrope, Ralph, 596.
Scrope, Thos., Lord, 268.
Scudamore, Sir Clem., 391.
........., Sir Jas., 115.
........., John, 115.
........., Sir John, 115, 268.
........., Thos., 17, 123.
Sea ore, *see* Kelp.
Seafaring men, *see* Mariners.
Seaford, 5, 309, 463, 533.
Seagar, Edw., 600.
Seal, Keeper of Great, *see* Bacon, Sir Fras.
Seaton, Alex., Earl of Dunfermline, Chancellor of Scotland, 7, 9, 22, 33, 34, 36, 83.
........., ..., letters of, 8, 44, 59.
........., Mary, 193.
........., Sir Wm., 1, 55.
Seckford, Hen., Master of Pavilions, 14, 115, 205.
........., Sir Hen., Master of Toils, 14, 115.
Secretary of State, *see* Cecil, Robt., Earl of Salisbury; Winwood, Sir Ra.; Lake, Sir Thos.; Naunton, Sir Robt.
........., French, *see* Edmondes, Sir Thos.
........., Latin, *see* Read, Thos.
Sedgley, 233.
Sedley, Sir Wm., 169, 175, 182, 350, 364, 387, 462.
Segar, Wm., Garter King-at-arms, 157, 167, 169, 175; Sir Wm., 427, 428, 451, 452.
Selby, Sir Geo., 8, 113, 360, 384, 587.
........., Sir Wm., 10, 21, 40, 46, 48, 53–55, 61, 111, 112, 212.
........., Wm., 52.
Sellinger, John, 131.
........., Sir Wm., 583.
Selme, Dr. Dan., 34.
Seminaries or Colleges, foreign, 279, 280, 285, 486.
Seminary priests, 3, 26, 51, 158, 206, 260, 279, 285, 365.
Sempill, Sir Jas., 33.
Sempringham Hed House, 29.
Senega, 587.
Serborne, Hen., 61.
........., Ann, 61.
Serjeants' Inn, letters dated from, 25, 319, 320, 333, 348, 363, 371, 463, 541.
Serjeants-at-arms, 35, 236, 255, 276, 339, 369, 378, 388, 391, 399, 525, 530.
Serjeants-at-law, 82, 239, 240, 246, 256, 289, 296, 373, 423, 521.
Sermons, 162, 288, 290, 301, 344, 411, 420, 460, 465, 490, 504, 602, 609.
.... at Court, 183, 350, 392, 404, 504.
.... at St. Paul's Cross, 454, 461, 494, 519.
Sevans Manor, 452.
Severnstoke, 94, 110.
Seville, 3, 86, 285.
........., Consul at, 86, 104.
........., English college at, 285.
Sewall, 434.
Sewell, Geo., 212.

Sewell, John, 26.
Sewers, Commissioners of, 352, 439, 465, 506, 546, 552, 563, 566, 574.
........., ..., letters of and to, 403, 413, 536, 541, 544, 552.
........., ..., orders and certificates by, 200, 201, 388, 542.
........., ..., laws for, 535.
Seymer, Rich., 496.
........., Robt., 96, 241, 248, 551.
Seymour, Sir Edw., Bart., 42, 61.
........., Edw., Earl of Hertford, 30, 39, 148, 515.
........., ..., letters of, 48, 53, 59, 74, 76, 84, 92, 102, 180, 184, 237, 259.
........., Frances, Countess of Hertford, 39, 59.
........., Edward, Lord Beauchamp, 30, 138, 284, 587.
........., Honor Lady Beauchamp, 273.
........., Wm., 48, 53, 59, 61, 74, 98, 342, 349, 401; Sir Wm., 436, 514, 587.
........., ..., escape and residence of abroad, 38, 42, 54, 76, 84, 92, 237.
........., ..., letters of, 117, 342.
........., Lady Arabella, 54, 75, 113, 168, 183, 242, 401, 436, 548
........., ..., charges of, 4, 16, 34.
........., ..., escapes of, 38, 39, 41–44, 212.
........., ..., illnesses of, 16, 17, 19, 20, 175.
........., ..., imprisonment of, 148, 170, 181, 183, 211.
........., ..., journeys of, 16, 17, 20, 24.
........., ..., letters of and to, 14, 16.
........., ..., recapture of, 44, 48, 51.
........., Fras., 39.
Shafto, Rob., 127.
Shafton, 251.
Shah Abbas the Great, Sultan of Persia, 140, 589.
Shalford, 37.
Sharp, And., 237.
........., John (poet), 263.
........., John (of Romney), 513, 576.
Sharpe, John (yeoman), 440, 594.
........., John (minister), 451.
........., Dr. Lionel, 142, 237, 289, 344, 600.
........., Nich., 247.
........., Pet., 353.
Sharpeigh, Mr., 85.
Shashaw, Hen., 431.
Shaw, Sir John, 157.
........., Wm., 57, 210.
........., Wm. (chaplain), 292.
Shawe, Wm. (ship-builder), 441.
Shawford, 488.
Sheberden, Dan., 190.
Sheffield, 426.
Sheffield, Edm., Lord, President of the Council in the North, 40, 90, 135, 147, 210, 233, 242, 245–247, 285, 289, 344, 355, 465, 533, 610.
........., ..., commissioners and instructions to, 245, 383, 536.
Sheffield, Edm., Lord, grants and payments to, 36, 250, 379.
........., ..., letters of, 66, 71, 78, 94, 139, 263, 539.
........., Lady (mother of Lord), *see* Dudley, Douglas.
........., Mariana, Lady (wife of Lord), 464.
........., Sir John (eldest son of Lord), 464.
........., Sir Edm. (2nd son of Lord), 210.
........., Elizabeth (daughter of Lord), 242.
........., Thos., 116, 215.
.... (minister), 92.
Sheldon, Edw., 164.
........., Ralph, 149.
........., Rich. (priest), 119.
Shelleto, Geo., 130, 315.
Shelley, Sir John, 120.
........., Wm., 61.
........., Jane, 61.
Shelton, Sir Ra., 400.
Shenston Manor, 506.
Shepard, Wm., 501.
Shepham, Rich., 158.
Shepherd, Mr., 96.
Shepherdswell, 605.
Sheppard, Robt., 447.
Sherborne Castle, 477.
.... Manor and Park, 200, 211, 225, 398, 405, 426, 444, 449.
.... Monastery, 451.
Sherard, Sir Phil., 86.
Sherburn, Edw., 127, 357, 392, 399, 445, 477, 478, 503, 525.
........., ..., letters of to Carleton, 352, 354, 356, 361–363, 366–368, 370, 373–376, 380, 381, 385, 387, 390–395, 397, 398, 400–402, 404–406, 408, 409, 412, 413, 415, 422, 423, 429, 432, 436, 438, 442, 448, 453, 458, 466, 469, 475, 477, 490, 494, 511, 519, 523, 527, 530.
Sherburn House, 312.
Sherfield, Hen., 159.
Sheriff Hutton Castle and Park, 78, 210, 440, 549.
Sheriffs, 400, 405, 517, 525.
Sherwood Forest, 56, 244, 286, 289, 314, 334.
Ship-building, 125, 191, 428, 586, 605.
........., rewards for, 87, 207, 355, 383, 441, 497, 498, 553, 560, 561.
Ships and shipping, 19, 31, 60, 109, 199, 212, 246, 263, 315, 349, 359, 359, 419, 424, 426, 437, 508, 515, 530, 532, 538, 595, 607, 613.
Ships, capture of, 380, 426, 493, 562.
........., cargoes of, 136, 556, 576.
........., fees and customs on, 282, 299, 305, 341, 437, 545, 566, 576.
........., invention of new, 155, 222, 223, 245.
........., masters of, 247, 394, 571.
........., sent against pirates, 177, 356.
........., to and from East Indies, 103, 236, 379.

Ships, wreck of, 298, 309, 342, 343, 345, 349–351, 358, 361, 365, 366, 372, 384, 399, 407–409, 414, 421, 423, 433, 463, 468, 478, 481, 503, 567, 599, 612.
Shipling Park, 414.
Shipton prebend, 490.
Shipward, Maurice, 52.
........., Sarah, 52.
Shire Rectory, 154.
Shires, Geo., 124, 605.
Shirley, Sir Ant., 429, 516.
........., Sir Geo., 176, 286, 344, 603.
........., Hen., 286.
........., Sir Robt., 71, 80, 88, 140, 149, 429, 516.
........., Sir Robt., jun., 429.
........., Thos., 264, 286.
........., Sir Thos., sen., 162, 195, 242, 257, 338.
........., ..., letters of, 12, 13, 43, 71, 85, 97, 101, 117.
........., Sir Thos., jun., 135, 429.
........., Mrs., 338.
Shoe Beacon, 421.
Shooland, 67.
Short, Thos., 416.
........., Wm., 551.
Shorthampton Walk, 279.
Shortis, Wm., 35.
Shotover Forest, 27, 85, 107, 125.
Shovin, Roger, 474.
Shrewsbury, 62, 91, 259, 293.
........., bailiffs of, 86.
........., exchequer house of, 293.
........., Earl and Countess of, *see* Talbot.
Shropshire, 205, 229, 259, 262, 268, 541.
........., grants of lands in, 61, 63, 124, 137, 190, 434.
........., lands and places in, 235, 278, 380, 443, 453, 463.
........., offices in, 440, 498.
........., recusants in, 120.
........., residents in, 128, 263, 526, 608.
Shutborough Manor, 192.
Shute Grange, 44.
.... Place, 94.
Shute, Robt., 132, 386, 407, 410, 433, 591.
Shutt, Frances, 573.
Sibson, Thos., 35.
Sicily, 425.
........., Viceroy of, 432.
Sicklemore, John, 365.
Sickness, the, *see* Plague.
Sidbury, 82.
Sigismund III., King of Poland, 81, 351, 466.
Signet, office of, 288, 338.
........., keeper of, 125, 127, 134, 138.
........., secretary and clerks of, 37, 67, 99, 129, 167, 200, 218, 234, 418, 445, 539.
Silk, 29, 428, 523.
........., customs on, 18, 266, 418.
Silk, dyeing of, 138.
.... weavers, 260, 611.
Silkworms, 29, 246, 555, 592.
Sillery, Nicolas Brulart de, 140.
Sillesworth, 176, 306, 580.
Silver, 34, 44, 189, 396, 538, 605.
........., export and import of, 92, 129, 143, 176, 603.
Silverton, 517.
Silvester, Mich., 510.
.... Thos., 498.
Simcock, Mr., 316.
Simons, Mr., 196.
Simony, 372.
Simpson, Fabian, 238.
........., John, 68.
.... (servant), 23.
.... (preacher), 504.
Sirke, 444.
Siston, 567.
Skalme Park, 315.
Skelsmergh, 293.
Skelton, Geo., 347.
Skevington, Mr., 205.
Skighawe, 212.
Skillicorn, Matt., 563.
........., Marg., 563.
Skillicorne, John, 231.
Skinner, Sir John, 357.
........., Thos., 351, 353.
........., Sir Thos., 351.
........., Sir Vincent, 17.
........., Mr. (merchant), 225.
........., Mr. (prisoner) 460.
Skinners' Company, *see* London, Companies of.
Skinners, 544.
Skins, *see* Leather.
Skipton Castle, 315.
Skirth, 574.
Skolfield, Wm., 559.
Skory, Silvanus, 208, 288.
Skrimsher, Martha, 100.
Skynner, Hen., 230.
Slade, John, 218.
Slaidburn, 9.
Slany, John, 75.
Slapwash, 335.
Slate stone, 539.
Slatier, Martin, 549.
Slaughter, 596.
Slaughter, John, 596.
Sleningford, 147.
Slingsby, Sir Guildford, 69, 302, 608.
........., Sir Hen., 69.
........., Sir Wm., 13, 383, 425.
Smaithwaite, John, 289, 355, 362, 369, 399.
Smalt, 176, 416, 543.
Smarty, Nedtracy, 236.
Smethick, 509.
Smithfield, 124, 322.

Smith, Amb., 545.
........., Edw. (of London), 551, 555.
........., Edw. (priest), 321, 328.
........., Fras., 257.
........., Geo., 63.
........., Hen. (of Essex), 225, 523.
........., Hen. (prebendary), 74.
........., Hen. (prisoner), 613.
........., Sir Jas., 524.
........., John, (keeper of blockhouse), 339, 407.
........., John (burglar), 498.
........., John, (gunner), 453.
........., Sir John, 95, 446.
........., Dr. Miles, Bp. of Gloucester, 148, 154, 438, 547.
........., Pet., 613.
.... Ralph, 440, 493, 594, 599.
........., Rich., 401, 403, 406, 460.
........., Dr. Rich., 42.
........., Sir Rich., 115, 549.
........., Steph. (of Gravesend), 572.
........., Steph. (priest), 321.
........., Wm., Rouge-dragon Pursuivant, 453.
........., Wm., sen., 78, 265.
........., Wm., jun., 18, 225.
........., Lady, 237.
Smithe, John (of Winchcombe), 437.
........., Sir Wm., 321–323, 329, 330, 351, 353, 367, 568, 599.
........., Lady, 321.
Smyth, Geo., 58.
........., Hen. (robber), 293.
........., Hen., 223, 250.
........., Rebecca, 223.
.... Martin, 217.
........., Rev. Rich., 154.
Smythe, Fras., 365.
........., Sir Thos., 383, 444, 504, 547, 556, 598, 602.
........., Lady Isab., 602.
Snawsell, Thos., 402.
Snead, Wm., 236.
Snell, Sir Chas., 583.
........., Fras., 597.
........., Hen., *alias* Richardson, 431, 439, 447.
Snelling, Wm., 33, 46.
........., Eliz., 46.
Snettisham, 4, 109, 120.
Snigg, Sir Geo., Baron of the Exchequer, 85, 517.
Snowden, Dr. Rob., Bp. of Carlisle, 400, 407, 422.
Soame, Sir Steph., 221, 335, 434.
Soap, 291.
Soham, 419, 465.
Soldiers, 50, 119, 130, 132, 152, 177, 224, 304, 509, 539, 541, 562.
........., levy of, 219.
Solicitor-General, *see* Bacon, Sir Fras.; Yelverton, Sir Hen.; Coventry, Sir Thos.
Solly, Joel, 403.
Somers, Sir Geo., 268.
........., John, 245.
........., Nich., 268.
Somerset, Earl of, *see* Carr, Robt.
........., Edw., Earl of Worcester, Master of the Horse, 48, 151, 244; Lord Privy Seal, 345, 346, 350, 351, 378, 391, 422, 429, 454, 456, 472, 565.
........., ..., commissions and warrants to, 41, 103, 275, 395.
........., ..., grants to, 193, 342, 418.
........., ..., letters of and to, 100, 112, 150, 401.
........., Elizabeth, Countess of Worcester, 138.
........., Hen., Lord Herbert, 32.
........., Sir Thos., 128, 426, 550.
Somerset Herald, *see* Treswell, Robt.
.... House, 46, 88, 155, 190, 222, 249, 287, 404, 416, 442; *see also* Denmark House.
...., works at, 16, 17, 51, 65.
Somersetshire, 102, 180, 184, 259, 267, 294, 525, 536.
........., grants of lands in, 41, 47, 63, 124, 159, 196, 251, 451.
........., lands and places in, 152, 158, 190, 217, 263, 279, 340, 381, 386, 537, 594.
........., offices, &c. in, 144, 148, 283, 543, 586.
........., recusants in, 100, 587.
........., residents in, 224, 257, 269, 344, 532, 567.
Sone, Rowland, 221.
Sostmon, John, 560.
Sotherton, John, Baron of the Exchequer, 248, 402.
Soulley, 191.
Soulley, Robt., 191.
South Lambeth, 13.
South Mimms, 57.
South Sea, 515.
Southaick, John, 261.
Southampton, 47, 381, 503, 561, 593, 598.
........., mayor, &c. of, 337.
........., county of, *see* Hampshire.
........., Earl of, *see* Wriothesley.
.... House, 507.
Southawe Wood, 88.
Southby, Robt., 315.
........., Thos., 315.
Southcote, Sir Edw., 253.
........., John, 186.
Southcott, Rich., 116.
Southsea, 45.
Southowse, Geo., 484.
Southwark, 46, 72, 140, 176, 218, 308, 339, 484, 525, 601.
Southwell, Eliz., Lady, 37.
........., Miss, 224.

Sowe River, 293.
Spa, the, 459, 480.
........., licences to visit, 147, 150, 164, 373, 378, 431, 471, 595.
........., visitors to, 138, 150, 176, 285, 300, 384, 392, 394, 427, 458, 485, 531, 603.
Spain, 11, 93, 96, 140, 149, 167, 173, 182, 203, 219, 232, 284, 303, 305, 308, 314, 421, 436, 472, 491, 515, 523, 533, 570, 577, 588, 599.
........., aid of, against pirates, 462, 464.
........., Ambassadors of, 10—12, 22, 39, 71, 89, 91, 95, 96, 104, 126, 146, 176, 197, 199, 214, 227, 269, 270, 274, 275, 305, 322, 345, 399, 433, 447, 468, 472, 488, 489, 511, 513, 517, 518, 520, 526, 528, 540, 554, 558, 564, 565, 569, 576, 582, 599, 600, 613; *see* Zuniga; Acunas, Count Goudomar.
........., Ambassador lieger of, 141, 152; *see also* Velasquez.
........., Ambassadors, &c. to, 89, 91, 175, 357, 511; *see* Digby, Sir John; Cecil, Lord Roos; Cottington, Fras.
........., council of war of, 529.
........., English and Scotch in, 122, 147, 238.
........., Infanta of, 71, 480, 517.
........., King of, *see* Philip III.
........., Queen of, *see* Margaret of Austria.
........., marriage negotiations with, 70, 97, 161, 163, 203, 223, 285, 363, 404, 427, 447, 461, 465, 480, 488, 497, 501, 505, 511, 517, 520–522, 524–526, 540, 569, 573, 577, 579, 591, 604.
........., money of, 97, 185, 267, 605.
........., ports of, 86, 464.
........., ships of, 176, 260, 324, 443, 516, 577, 579, 583.
........., trade with, 65, 83, 185, 235, 473, 509.
........., travellers to and from, 29, 99, 262, 345, 520, 540, 601, 602.
........., war preparations in, 275, 312.
Spalato, M. Antonio de Dominis, Archbp. of, 227, 262, 273, 471, 500, 504, 512, 582, 591, 604.
........., ..., conversion of from Popery, 417, 427, 428, 474.
........., ..., letters of, 417, 470, 482, 488, 491, 510, 527, 577, 598.
........., ..., letters to, 474, 477.
........., ..., preaching of, 500, 501, 503, 535, 595.
........., ..., promotions of, granted and proposed, 422, 423, 432, 475, 500, 511, 514, 521, 526, 529, 530.
........., ..., visit of to England, 413, 414, 416, 424, 427, 436, 466, 478, 480, 482, 488, 489.
........., ..., works of, 401, 417, 423, 432, 437, 443, 466, 470, 474–477, 479, 482, 488, 526, 529, 564.
Spalding, 87, 356.
Spalding-upon-Moor, 606.
Spaldwick, 164.
Spaniards, 10, 12, 104, 124, 140, 146, 203, 269, 293, 390, 397, 428, 482, 516, 521, 522, 524, 526, 528, 538, 565, 566, 570, 571, 575, 576, 583, 591, 613.
Spanish Armada, 167, 175.
.... Indies, 576, 577.
.... monks, 522, 523, 525–527, 588.
Sparrow, Edm., 413.
Spatchurst, Geo., 369.
Speckaet, Abm., 118.
Speed, John, 431.
Speke, Sir Geo., 47.
Spencer, Sir Rich., 70.
........., Lady Penelope, 345.
........., Dr., 230.
........., Dr. E., 457.
Spens, Sir Jas., 88.
Spices, garbling of, 379.
Spier, Mdme. de, 193.
Spiller, Hen., 41, 191, 239, 256, 258, 274, 277, 281, 285, 293, 300.
Spilman, Sir John, 1, 35, 46, 91, 114, 275, 280, 367, 445.
Spinola, Ambrose, Marquis, 303, 304, 547.
Spinsters, 606.
Spittal, the, 439, 460, 465.
Spottiswood, John, Archbp. of St. Andrew's, 485.
Spracklin, Jeremy, 19.
Sprage, Nich., 179.
Spring Garden, 57.
Springe, Mr., 479.
Sprotton, 147.
Sprowston, 58.
Squibb, Art., 395, 551.
Squire, Phil., 553, 559.
Stacey, Wm., 113.
Stacy, Robt., 382.
Stade, 96, 266.
Stafford, Edw., 466.
........., Edw. Lord, 466, 537.
........., Sir John, 33, 79, 106, 107, 277.
Staffordshire, 259, 268.
.... grants of lands in, 63, 192, 233, 292, 434, 506.
........., lands and places in, 2, 236, 259, 519.
........., recusants in, 44, 73.
........., residents in, 584.
Staines Bridge, 165.
Stalbridge, 451.
Stallenge, Wm., 29, 87, 126, 194.
Stammage, Robt., 562, 563.
Standon, 315.
Stane, 233.
Stanhoe, 153.
Stanhope, John, Lord, 132, 486.
........., ..., as Treasurer of the Chamber, 8, 56, 103, 243, 291, 383, 418, 420, 451, 461, 484.

Stanhope, John, Lord, as Master of the Posts, 126, 382, 441, 478, 545, 554, 601.
........., Sir John, 596.
........., Mich., 313.
........., Sir Mich., 225, 284.
........., Sir Phil., 43, 398; Lord Stanhope of Shelford, 404.
Stanley, 6.
Stanley, Sir Rowland, 96.
........., Wm., Earl of Derby, 41, 132, 177, 325, 482, 494, 578.
........., Eliz., Countess of Derby, 41, 60, 96 125, 170.
........., Lady Anne, 344.
........., Lord or Sir Wm., 304.
........., (auditor), 458.
Stannach, Robt., 544.
Stannard, Wm., 162.
Stannaries, the, 255, 257, 322.
........., wardens of, 325.
Stanningfield, 550.
Stanson, Eric, 6.
Stanwell, 111.
Staple, merchants of the, 271, 339, 452; *see also* Wool.
.... towns, 467.
Stapleton, 359, 539.
Stapleton, Rich., 112.
........., Robt. 194.
Starch, 145, 146, 176.
Star-chamber, 33, 215, 273, 279, 326, 375, 425, 434, 436, 443, 450, 458, 468, 473, 486, 591, 606.
........., causes in, 5, 19, 96, 162, 224, 239, 242, 495, 510, 518, 520, 526, 530, 537, 543, 548, 556, 575, 599, 612.
........., fines in, 293, 379, 530, 560, 592, 601.
State, the, 5, 99, 303–305, 329, 367, 377.
.... abuses in, 107.
.... affairs of, 330.
.... officers of, 466.
State paper office, 390, 590.
.... papers, 134, 248, 252, 305, 445, 583, 609.
..................., keeper of, *see* Wilson, Thos.
States, the, *see* Holland.
Staunton, Edw., 599.
Staunton-Harrold, 286.
.... rectory, 500.
Stavely, 580.
Stebenhuth, 295.
Steel, 228, 390.
Stephens, Edw., 415.
........., John, 363.
Stephenson, Rich., 485.
........., Thos., 485.
Stepney, 314.
Stepney, Clem., 109.
Sterrell, Mr., 317.
Steward of the Household, *see* Stuart, Duke of Lenox.
Steward, Lord High (for Overbury's trial), *see* Egerton.
Steward, And., 343.
........., or Stewart, Sir Fras., 386, 394, 400, 418, 440, 442.
........., Jas., 72.
........., John, 550.
........., Simeon, 496.
........., Toby, 254.
Stewart, Gawin, 258.
........., Sir Jas., 255.
........., John Earl of Mar, Treasurer of Scotland, 7, 35, 102, 431, 471, 483.
........., John, Lord Kincleven, 528.
........., Eliz., Lady Kincleven, 113, 528.
........., Marg., 528.
........., Pat., Earl of Orkney, 275, 284.
........., Sir Robt., 11, 12, 30, 34, 40, 51, 66, 70, 98.
........., Wm., 91, 93.
Steynton, Robt., 43.
Stiles, Thos., 12, 105, 558.
Stillington, Wm., 251.
Stilt, Matt., 469.
Stirling, 474, 476, 477.
Stirrop, Thos., 39.
Stock, John, 421.
Stockbridge, 233.
Stocking weaving and weavers, 54, 70.
Stockton, 467.
Stoddart, Sir Nich., 546.
Stodder, Sir Thos., 329.
Stoke, 110, 117, 125, 508.
Stoke-Lacy, 375.
Stone, artificial, 154.
Stone, John, 116.
........., Thos., 157, 177, 229.
Stoneacre, 406.
Stoneleigh, 193, 352.
Stoner, Lady, 145.
Story, Geo., 189, 297.
........., Hum., 100.
........., John, 297.
........., Robt., 297.
Stott, Nich., 605.
Stourton, 259.
Stowe-on-the-Wold, 158.
Stowe Wood, 28, 85, 125.
Stowey Manor and Parks, 451.
Strafforth, 154.
Strand, *see* London, Streets of.
Strangers, *see* Aliens.
Stratford, 167.
Stratton, 89.
Stratton-Strawless, 173.
Streatham, 325.
Strickland, Rob., 159, 180.
........., Wal., 474.
Strixton, 272, 277.
Strong, Chris., 411.

Stronghill, Pet., 343.
Stuart, Esme, Lord Aubigny, 42, 46, 52, 60, 65, 127, 165, 196, 222, 322, 455, 511, 596.
........., Cath., Lady Aubigny, 42, 127, 268.
........., Lady Arabella, *see* Seymour.
........., Lewis, Duke of Lenox, 42, 60, 69, 124, 165, 174, 182, 199; Baron Settrington and Earl of Richmond, 208, 256, 274, 318; Steward of the Household, 387, 391, 395, 436, 505, 511, 523.
........., Lewis, Duke of Lenox, grants to, 144, 298, 355, 410, 444, 445, 496.
........., ..., letters of, 58, 213, 215, 318, 347, 541.
........., ..., letters to, 238, 538.
........., ..., promotions of, 201, 344, 518.
........., ..., as commissioner on Overbury's cause, 316, 318, 329, 362.
........., Marg., Countess of Lenox, 344.
Stubb, Edw., 32.
Stukeley, Sir Lewis, 565, 566, 570, 577, 585, 587, 591, 598, 600.
Sturges, John, 567.
Sturman, Edw., 266.
Sturmer Manor, 367.
Sturtevant, Simon, 340, 342.
Sturton Meadow, 563.
Style, Wm., 117.
Suarez, Fras. (Jesuit), 212.
Suatedi, Biallnante, 390.
Subberton, 186.
Subsidies, 1, 10, 11, 38, 49, 182, 194, 199, 206, 231, 242, 261, 352, 505, 542, 605; *see also* London, Subsidies in.
Suckling, John, 9.
........., Dr., 134.
........., Mrs., 134.
Sudbury, 529, 606.
Suffolk, Duke of, *see* Grey, Hen.
........., Earl of, *see* Howard, Thos.
........., house of, 107.
Suffolk House, 447.
................, letters dated from, 458, 461, 466, 468, 470, 471, 475.
Suffolk, 86, 173, 267, 268, 434, 610.
........., grants of lands in, 35, 63, 124, 247, 388, 405, 414, 418, 439, 550.
........., lands and places in, 2, 35, 63, 64, 95, 230, 231, 367, 381, 404, 529, 540.
........., offices in, 505.
........., receivers in, 277.
........., residents in, 52, 88, 190, 351, 498, 525, 551.
Sugar, custom on, 609.
Sugar and sugar houses, 376, 377, 396.
Suits, commissioners for, 22, 534, 557.
Sultan, the, *see* Osman I.
Summer Islands, *see* Bermudas.
Sunderland, 395, 556.
Sunning Hill Manor and Park, 64, 86, 101, 572.
Supledick, Edw., 606.
Supremacy, Oath of, 168, 297, 517.
Surat, 214.
Surley, Case, 32.
Surrey, 122, 262, 268.
........., grants of land in, 63, 71, 90, 124, 159, 177, 196, 254, 418.
........., lands and places in, 17, 68, 93, 140, 154, 158, 159, 189, 202, 251, 288, 294, 362, 374, 415, 496, 497, 542, 580, 598.
........., offices in, 191, 262, 460, 564, 601.
........., receivers in, 108.
........., recusants in, 31, 120.
........., residents in, 67, 335, 480, 555.
Sussex, 13, 86, 267, 268, 352, 364, 391, 460, 478, 501.
........., assizes in, 502.
........., grants of lands in, &c., 45, 87, 120, 159, 196, 257, 388, 439.
........., lands and places in, 5, 17, 158, 278, 287, 295, 357, 421, 613.
........., lieutenants for, 154.
........., recusants in, 120.
........., residents in, 38, 179, 353, 381, 388, 425, 434, 480, 493, 502, 525, 602.
........., Earl of, *see* Ratcliffe, Robt.
Sutheran, Wm., 302, 303.
Sutton, Eligion, 358.
........., Jas., 308, 481.
........., Sir Rich., 535.
........., Rob., 484.
........., Roger, 188.
........., Thos., 45, 79, 88, 101, 110, 111, 161, 186–188, 190, 246.
.... (preacher), 419.
........., Mr., 466.
Sutton Hospital, see Charter House.
........., Hereford, 30.
........., Isle of Ely, 566.
........., Lancashire, 498.
Sutton Lode, 552, 566.
Sutton-Courtney, 74.
Swan, Thos., 609.
Swanton, John, 305.
........., Rich., 483.
Swanwhich, 607.
Sweden, 60, 69, 97, 611.
........., King of, see Gustavus.
........., Ambassador of, 500, 504, 560.
Swedes, 10, 11.
Sweeting, John, 311.
Swell, 596.
Swift, Sir Edw., 242.
Swinborne, Rich., 102.
Swinburn, Mr., 302.
Swinburne, Mr., 424.
Swindon, 502.
Swineshead, 296.
Swinglehurst, Robt., 9.

T.

Theobalds, House and Park at, 75, 84, 86, 158, 196, 229, 274, 278, 362, 400, 428, 463, 554.
........., keepers of, 157, 206, 207, 444, 524, 592.
........., King's visits to, 83, 138, 155, 156, 158, 162, 172, 191, 246, 262, 273, 308, 360, 361, 392, 394, 404, 430, 448, 491, 493, 495, 497, 503, 511, 512, 527, 530, 537, 552, 568, 600.
........., letters, &c. from, 75, 83, 101, 102, 138, 156, 157, 191, 192, 206, 259, 279, 295, 296, 308, 323, 382–384, 447.
........., repairs at, 99, 120, 121, 444, 461, 462, 466, 474, 475, 486.
........., wardrobe at, 281.
Theology, 294.
Thetford, 362, 536.
........., gamekeepers at, 2, 243.
Thirlwall, Geo., 365.
........., Phil., 362, 365, 369.
........., Robt., 365.
Thistleworth, 225.
........., letters dated from, 394, 397, 399, 481, 489, 490, 498.
Thomas, John, 578.
........., Sam., 19, 108.
........., Wal., 204.
........., Wm., 121, 275.
Thomazon, Wm., 353.
Thomond, 425.
........., Earl of, *see* O'Brynn.
Thompson, Dr. Giles, Bp. of Gloucester, 44, 47, 76.
........., John, 68.
........., Paul, 278.
........., Sam., Windsor Herald, 453.
........., Dr., 246.
Thomson, Edw., 68.
.... Rich., 58.
........., Robt., 360.
........., Thos., 118.
........., Thos., (priest), 321.
Thompson's Walls, 279.
Thormanby, 104.
Thornborough, John, Bp. of Bristol, 120; Bp. of Worcester, 422.
........., Mrs., 336, 338, 345.
........., Sir John, 50.
Thorne, Robt., 201.
Thornhaugh, Sir John, 121.
Thorold, Edw., 393.
........., Nath., 393.
........., Sir Wm., 89.
........., Lady Isabel, 49, 89.
Thornton, Hen., 376.
Thornton, 139.
.... Park, 391.
Thorp, John, 76.
Thorpe, Roger, 315.
Thoxted, 452.
Thraps, Roger, 121.
........., Jane, 121.
Thrascists, 524.
Thrasco, ——, 521, 524.
Thread, 98.
........., gold and silver, 33, 61, 343, 529, 536.
Throckmorton, John, 241, 556.
Throgmorton, Sir Art., 8.
........., Geo., 38.
........., Sir John, 234, 315, 402, 421, 434, 524.
.... Sir Wm., 373, 555.
Thropton Spittle, 292.
Throwre, Thos., 74.
Thuanus (De Thou), Jas. Augustus, 115.
Thurbane, Mr., 422.
Thurgood, John, 402.
Thurloe, John, 377.
Thurnetoft, 440.
Thursby, Cuthbert, 132.
Thwing, 130.
Thynne, Chas., 591.
........., Sir Hen., 87, 127.
Thynney, or Teynham, Lord, *see* Roper, Sir John.
Tichborne, 66.
Tidcombe, 159.
Tight, Wm., 484.
Tildesley, Thurstan, 560, 582.
Tilenus, Daniel, 142, 143.
Tilloy, M. du, 310.
Tilney, Edm., Master of the Revels, 17.
........., Thos., 17.
Tilsley, Thos., 201, 211.
Tilston Manor, 372.
Tiltyard, the, 15, 316.
Timber and trees, 28, 43, 125, 216, 228, 279, 287, 419, 445, 470, 605.
.................., felling of, 12, 64, 85, 86, 274, 474.
Timberley, Mr., 107.
Timmerman, Paul, 376, 377, 396.
Tin, export or sale of, 296, 322.
........., preemption of, 197, 254, 270, 280, 287.
Tinners, 255, 257, 325.
Tindall, John, 207, 370, 380.
Tintagell, 496.
Tintern, 29.
Tintoretto, Giacomo Robusti, 284.
Tir-y-Abbatt, 52.
Tirell, Mr., 105.
Tithes and fifteenths, 11, 31, 38, 39, 121, 413, 432, 439, 448, 453, 505, 522, 533, 555, 592.
Titian, Vecelli, 284.
Titles (to lands), defective, 18, 114, 171, 203, 439, 501, 590.
...., ..., commissioners for, 176, 266, 609.
Tiverton, 147, 296.
Tivoli, 530.
Tixall, 484.
Tobacco, 514, 585.

Tobacco, custom on, 280, 299, 535.
........., import of, 176, 214, 280, 281.
.... pipes, 557, 566.
...., clay, 606.
Todd, John, Bp. of Down, 238.
........., Mr., 341.
Toderick, Wal., 84.
Tokens, 184, 502; *see* Coinage of farthings.
Tollemache, Sir Lionel, 268.
........., Lionel, 268.
Tollerby, Mr., 183.
Tollerton, 118.
Tolwin, John, 551.
Tomkins, Jas., 105.
Tomlyn, Wm., 450, 451.
Tonstall, John, 189, 195.
Tooke, John, 280.
Tookey, Humph., 372.
Topcliffe, 194, 460.
Topcliffe, Chas., 72.
Tothill, 540.
.... Fields, 153, 361, 362.
Totness, 548, 554.
Tottenham, 84, 559.
Totteridge, 57.
Tottington, 113.
Touchet, Geo., Lord Audley, 157, 249, 420; Earl of Castlehaven, 449, 461.
........., Sir Mervin, 137, 249; Lord Audley, 451.
Tounson, Dr., Robt., Dean of Westminster, 504.
Tour, Baron de la, French Ambassador, 430, 435, 438.
Tournon, M. de, 222, 432.
Tourval, John l'Oiseau-de, 54, 66, 389, 391, 396, 478, 569, 579.
Tower, the, 73, 131, 195, 202, 228, 309, 311, 316, 320, 321, 338, 344, 364, 454, 591.
........., armoury in, 40, 51, 607.
.... gunners' places in, 43, 75, 192, 207, 241, 248, 249, 278, 284, 370, 378, 416, 453, 475.
........., gentleman gaolers, and porters in, 359, 440, 449.
........., jewels in, 18, 30, 112, 251, 272, 552.
........., letters from, 27, 48, 184, 237, 532, 569, 583.
........., Lieutenants of, *see* Waad, Sir Wm.; Helwys, Sir Gervase; More, Sir Geo.; Apsley, Sir Allan.
........., mint in, 230, 542; *see also* Mint.
........., ordnance in, 236, 314, 496, 539, 606.
........., prisoners in, 48, 53, 80, 98, 120, 124, 136, 148, 168, 170, 181, 185, 200, 211, 212, 236, 242, 245, 270, 275, 307, 323, 329, 331, 336, 344, 347, 356, 359–362, 368, 373, 384, 385, 387, 425, 426, 433, 441, 449, 469, 471, 505, 511, 517, 532, 534, 565, 568, 575.
........., release from, 289, 373, 377, 426, 433.
........., yeoman waiters or warders in, 111, 198, 323, 393, 493.
Tower Hill, 107, 191, 310, 331, 372, 373.
.... Garden, 190.
Towerson, Wm., 287, 543.
Townley, Nich., 440.
........., Rich., 144.
........., Mr., 304.
Townsend, Sir Rich., 458.
Townshend, Sir Hen., 45, 425.
Tracy, Sir John, 555.
........., Shacherly, 236.
........., Sir Thos., 32.
Trade, 14, 17, 20, 92, 107, 126, 128, 140, 141, 178, 204, 214, 219, 302, 377, 387, 503, 561, 595.
........., free, 272, 514.
Trafford, Sir Edw., 499,
........., Thos. (receiver), 25.
........., Thos. (of Cheshire), 553.
Tranter, Wm., 271.
Tratford, Rich., 246.
Treasurer, Lord High, 507; see Cecil, Earl of Salisbury; Howard, Earl of Suffolk.
.... of the Household, *see* Knollys, Lord; Wotton, Lord; Edmondes, Sir Thos.
Treasury, Commissioners for, 134, 135, 149, 163, 210, 247, 248, 563, 595.
........., ..., letters of and to, 232, 578, 584, 597.
........., ..., petitions to, 562, 607.
........., ..., warrants to, 154, 560, 575, 593.
Treatises, 71, 77, 115, 134, 155, 157, 171, 327; *see also* Books.
Tredway, Edw., 30.
Trees, *see* Timber.
Trenchard, Sir Geo., 108, 130.
Treneale, Jo., 540.
Trent, Council of, 171, 231.
.... River, lands north of, 31, 49, 387.
...., ... south of, 46, 58, 93, 242, 386, 441.
Trepitt, 67.
Treport, 293, 409, 412, 485.
Trerice, 411.
Tresham, Fras., 159.
........., Lewis, 55; Sir Lewis, 159, 295, 466.
........., Sir Thos., 26.
Trestean, Rich., 35.
Treswell, And., 441.
........., Robt. (surveyor), 21, 28, 46, 58, 93, 102, 107, 232, 382, 386, 441, 462, 471, 473.
........., Robt. (Somerset Herald), 455.
Trevellyan, Leon., 540.
Trevor, Sir John, 30, 58, 62, 198.
........., Dr. Rich., 132, 228.
........., Thos., 394, 403, 434.
Trigg, Wm., 211.
Trinity House, London, 247, 322, 536, 543.
Trotter, Lawr., 440.
........., Robt., 271.

Trowte, John, 483.
........., Mark, 483.
Trumbull, Wm., agent to Archduke Albert, 76, 116, 148, 160, 220, 224, 341, 381, 431, 488, 523.
........., Wm., jun., 116.
Truro, 112.
Trussell, Geo., 66.
Tucker, Dan., 122.
........., Mr., 431.
Tuckey, Wm., 9.
Tufton, Humph., 29; Sir Humph., 414, 588.
........., Sir John, 49.
Tuggel, Lordship of, 384.
Tuilleries, the, 25.
Tuke, Rob., 321.
Tullibardine, Earl of, *see* Murray, John.
Tunis, 475, 476.
Tunstall, 394, 417.
Tunstall, Fras., 23.
Tunstie, Fras., 367.
Turffet, Thos., 192.
Turin, 276, 282.
Turk, the, or Great Turk, see Ahmed I.; Osman I.
Turkey, 175, 229.
........., Ambassador of, 587, 591, 595.
........., Ambassador to, see Pindar, Paul.
........., Company, see Levant Company.
........., Court of, 81.
........., ships of, 426, 427, 432, 514.
........., trade with, 27, 432.
Turks, 222, 424, 427, 476, 542, 589.
........., (pirates), 427, 444, 491, 514, 515, 607; *see also* Pirates.
Turlot, Roger, 63.
Turnell, Mr., 608.
Turner, Anne, 307, 310-312, 315-318, 320, 321, 323, 324, 327, 329, 330, 333, 334.
........., Dr. Geo., 311.
........., John, 128, 129, 136.
........., Rich., Master of Tents and Toils, 125, 206.
........., Thos. (of London), 125.
........., Thos. (of Walden), 530, 536.
........., Wm., 180, 218, 264, 294, 359.
........., Capt. Wm., 433, 458.
Turquet, *see* Mayerne.
Turpin, Isaac, 613.
Tuscany, Ferd., Duke of, 40, 109, 149, 245, 514.
Tutbury, 394, 467.
Tweed River, 14, 24, 381.
Tweedale, Randolph, 132.
Twist, Robt., 5.
........., Ann, 563.
Twitty, Mr., 136.
Tyas, Robt., 209.
Tyburn, 40, 134, 162, 319, 322, 329, 330, 344, 601.
Tydd-St.-Mary, 292.
Tyler, John, 419.
Tyndall, Dr., 45.
........., Sir John, 405, 406, 408, 412.
Tyne River, 589, 595.
Tynedale, 61, 189, 220, 513, 539.
Tynemouth Castle, 115, 358.
.... Monastery, 95, 395.
Tynemouthshire, 29.
Tyngo, 334.
Typper, Robt., 173, 203, 590.
........., Wm., 65, 176, 181.
Tyringham, Sir Art., letters of to Carleton, 482, 485, 495, 513, 567, 585, 600.
........., Sir Thos., 190, 245, 502.
Tyrone, Earl of, *see* O'Neil.
Tyrrel, Chas., 597.
........., Sir Edw., 597.

U.

Udall, Sir Wm., 251.
........., Mr., 147.
Uladislas, Prince of Poland, 564.
Ulloa, Julian Sanches de, 577.
Ulster, 23, 56, 59, 127, 245, 354.
Union, Princes of, 403, 434, 504.
United Provinces, *see* Holland.
Unton, Mr., 2.
Upton, John, 357.
Usher, Jos., 148, 163.
Usury, statute of, 551, 552, 554.
Utenbogardt, —— 235.
Utley, Geo., 597.
Utrecht, 153, 412.
Uvedale, Sir Wm., Treasurer of the Chamber, 291, 294, 513, 540.
Uxbridge, 227.

V.

Vachell, John, 26.
Vagrants, 205, 217.
Valladolid, 142.
Vambers Poole, 216.
Van de Pute, Giles, 385.
Van den Velde, Pet., 328.
Van Elderhuys, Mich., 439.
Van Hobrook, Louis, 345.
Van Lore, Pet., 11, 257, 358, 498.
Vandenbrocke, —— 560.
Vandoni, G. C., 151, 227; *see also* Carmelite Friars.

Vane, Hen., 326.
........., Sir Hen., 441, 443.
Vaudry, John, 550.
Vaughan, Alex., 57.
........., John, 216.
........., Judith, 216.
........., Sir John, 249, 258, 261, 604.
........., Owen, 191.
........., Robt., 379.
........., Sir Robt.. 443.
Vaux, Edw., Lord of Harrowden, 83, 121, 124, 181, 227, 285.
........., ..., imprisonment of, 129, 140, 144, 145, 153.
........., Mrs. Anne, 88, 121, 140, 144, 145, 305.
Vavasour, Sir Thos., Knight Marshal, 159, 281, 326, 332, 586, 599.
........., Wm., 144.
Veine, Capt. Baron de, 433.
Velasquez, Alonso de, 140, 141.
Venetians, 222, 518, 533.
Venice, 2, 111, 117, 151, 167, 176, 216, 289, 350, 417, 464, 475, 477, 521, 524, 527, 557.
........., Ambassadors of, 104, 139, 145, 149, 170, 174, 176, 180, 228, 244, 251, 370, 475, 481, 493, 518, 524, 531, 591, *see also* Foscarini, Barbarigo, Donato.
........., Ambassadors of, Secretary to, *see* Muscorno.
........., Ambassadors to, 424; *see* Carleton, Sir D.; Wotton, Sir Hen.
........., glass, 177.
........., gold, 50; *see also* Thread, gold and silver.
........., letters from, 61, 74, 127, 188, 231, 284, 414.
........., prince of, 61.
........., secretary of, 474.
........., seignory of, 182, 518.
........., ships of and for, 480, 518, 521, 531.
........., silk, 177.
........., travellers to and from, 24, 54, 59, 70, 171, 301, 393, 482.
........., troops, 527, 530.
Verdine, de la, Marshal, French Ambassador, 3, 9.
Verdon, John, 226.
........., Jonas, 159, 192, 209.
Vere, Sir Fras., 489.
........., Hen. de, Earl of Oxford, 61, 62, 81, 88, 228, 264, 475, 477, 482, 496.
........., Eliz. de, Countess of Oxford, 61, 62, 81, 135, 166.
........., Sir Horatio, 79, 212, 220, 357, 363, 364, 367, 368, 370, 419, 425.
........., ... letters of to Carleton, 360, 394, 397, 399, 405, 423, 436, 442, 461, 481, 489, 490, 496, 498, 503, 600.
........., Mary, Lady, 429.
Verney, Sir Fras., 425.
........., John, 418.
........., Sir Rich., 6, 9, 24.
Vernon, John, 411.
........., Robt., 152; Sir Robt., 411.
........., Sir Robt., Cofferer of the Household, 31, 154.
........., Mr., 437.
Vero, Humph., 281.
Veronese, Paul, 284.
Verulam, Lord, *see* Bacon, Fras.
Vessels, *see* Ships.
Vette, Godfrey de, 148, 163.
Vice-Admiral, *see* Mansell, Sir Robt.
Vice-Chamberlain, *see* Digby, Sir John.
Villa, Marquis de, Ambassador of Savoy, 183, 189, 190.
Villeroy, Charles de Neufville, Marquis de, 140.
Villiers, Chris., 432, 440, 464, 505, 514, 544.
........., Sir Edw., 426, 441, 449, 489, 490, 516, 598.
........., Sir Geo., Master of the Horse, 362; Visct. Beaumont, 364; Baron Whaddon and Visct. Villiers, Chief Justice in Eyre North, 393, 405; Earl of Buckingham, 422, 432–434, 436, 443, 448, 464, 468, 478, 480, 483, 487, 495–497, 504; Marquis of Buckingham, 517, 525, 529, 531, 533, 537, 575, 576, 586, 591, 592, 595, 598, 600.
........., ..., favour, &c. of, with the King, 260, 261, 284, 344, 354, 361, 370, 407, 412, 449, 481, 504, 511, 538.
........., ..., grants to, 289, 374, 383, 387, 405, 425, 444.
........., ..., promotions, &c. of, 345, 363, 373, 380, 384, 391, 392, 397, 422, 423, 426, 428, 441, 469, 496, 510, 511, 582, 585.
........., ..., lands of, 398, 425, 440.
........., ..., letters of, 394, 588, 599.
........., ..., letters to, 390, 489, 603, 609.
........., ..., presence of at fêtes, masques, tiltings, &c., 494, 501, 512, 523, 524.
........., ..., designs, &c. against, 477, 479, 480, 483.
........., ..., mother of, *see* Compton, Lady.
........., ..., brothers of, *see* Villiers, Sir John, Sir Edw., and Christopher.
........., ..., relations of, 361, 445, 481.
........., Sir John, 426, 446, 500.
........., ..., marriage, &c. of, 414, 447, 464, 476–478, 481, 482, 487.
........., Frances Lady, 495; *see also* Coke, Frances.
........., family, 423.
Vincent, Augustine, 351.
........., Geo., 564.
........., Mrs., 367.
........., widow, 75.
Vinion, Paul, 538.
Vintners, 51.
Virginia, 120, 122, 167, 538, 544, 545, 586, 594.

Virginia, English colony in, 126, 137, 234, 253, 274, 345, 587, 598.
........., governor and company of, 122, 197.
........., natives of, 375, 425, 428; *see* Pocahuntas, Powatan.
........., passengers to and from, 48, 101, 425, 518, 527, 584.
Virgo, Wm., 483.
Viscounts, 127, 134.
Vitry, M. de, 32, 34, 36, 88–91, 95, 100, 103, 180.
Vlaming, Abm., 148.
Volga, River, 182.
Vorstius, Conrad, 71, 89, 111, 115, 119.

W.

Waad, Sir Wm., Lieutenant of the Tower, 53, 179, 183, 185, 307, 338.
........., ..., letters of, 39, 42, 87, 98, 198, 224, 314, 315, 323, 336.
........., ..., letters to, 181.
........., Lady, 338.
Wadham, Nich., 11.
Wade, Max., 314.
Waferer, Eliz., 68.
Wake, Isaac, 117, 125, 151, 167, 171, 173, 174, 282; Agent to Savoy, 521, 523, 603.
........., ..., letters of, 162.
........., ..., ..., to Carleton, 156, 157, 160, 161, 163, 168, 170.
........., ..., letters to, 256, 273, 329.
Wakefield, 7.
Wakefield, John, 578.
Wakelyn, Geo., 43.
Walcall, 38.
Walcot, Mr., 245.
Walcott, Hum., 121.
........., John, 291.
Waldegrave, Chas., 120.
........., Sir Geo., 95.
Walden, 530.
........., Lord and Lady, *see* Howard.
Wales, 46, 108, 177, 251, 259, 305.
........., Courts in, 111, 222.
........., justices of, 25, 31.
........., lands and places in, 115, 446, 552.
........., offices in, 60, 253, 254, 336, 440, 498, 536, 555.
........., Princes of, *see* Henry and Charles.
........., receivers for, 25, 31, 189, 246.
........., recusants in, 84, 123.
........., wardrobe in, 424.
........., Marches of, 440, 498.
Wales, Marches of, Court of, 201, 353, 536.
........., ..., President and Council of, 25, 31, 60, 379, 480.
........., ..., jurisdiction of, 229, 233, 240, 262, 263, 610.
........., ..., letters of and to, 62, 73, 100, 252, 336, 353.
........., ..., Secretary of, 411, 418.
........., ..., Solicitor-General in, 207.
........., President of, *see* Eure, Lord; Gerard, Lord; Compton, Lord.
Walgrave, Sir Wm., 215.
Walker, Pet., 161.
........., Mrs., 161.
........., Thos. 367.
........., Wm. 19, 116, 286.
........., Wm. (soldier), 286.
Waller, John, 247.
.... Robt., 82.
........., Sir Thos., Lieutenant of Dover Castle, 36, 46, 109, 151, 152, 188, 190, 194, 298.
........., Ann, Lady, 46.
........., Mr., 183.
Wallingford Monastery, 218.
........., Visct., *see* Knollys.
Wallington, 365.
Wallop, Sir Hen., 233, 234, 411.
Walls, 198.
Wallwyn, Ann, 105.
Walmer, 255, 614.
Walmer Castle, 148, 201, 256, 305, 324, 343, 367, 454, 457.
...., muster rolls of, 151, 255, 308 395, 579.
Walmsley, Sir Thos., Justice of Common Pleas, 32.
Walpole, 207.
Walsh, Kath., Lady, letters of to Salisbury, 56, 86, 101, 106.
Walsingham, Sir Fras., 66, 152, 172, 240.
........., Awdrey, Lady, 193, 338, 380.
........., Lady Ursula, 66.
Walsoken Rectory, 597.
Walstide, Thos., 100.
Waltham, 11.
.... Forest, 10, 45, 76, 228, 243, 249, 392, 418, 462, 511.
Walter, Roger, 450.
Walton, Hen., 236.
Walton, Norfolk, 435.
Walton-upon-Thames, 120.
Wanborough Wood, 189.
Wandesford, Chris., 400.
........., Sir Geo., 147, 400.
........., Wm., 147, 400.
Wandsworth, 415.
Wanstead, 135, 136, 145, 381, 504, 568.
........., letters dated from, 73, 74, 199, 252.
Wappenham, 292, 332.
Wapping, 334, 442, 527.
Warblington, 186, 431.

Warburton, Geo., 242.
........., Sir Pet., Judge of Common Pleas, 3, 398, 541.
........., Lady, 209.
Ward, John, 207, 419.
........., Rich., 391.
........., Wm., Marshal of the Admiralty Court of the Cinque Ports, 180, 419.
........., ..., letters of and to, 222, 309, 312, 347, 354, 413, 417, 485, 487, 492, 587, 592.
........., Mr., 376.
........., Capt., 544.
Warde, Rich., 482.
Wardegar, Geo., 415.
Wardeman, Joachim, 353, 359.
Wardour, Edw., 123, 187.
Wardrobe, the, 455, 493; *see also* Hinchinbrook; Royston; Theobalds; Wales.
........., book of, 13.
........., charges of, 19, 77.
........., clerks of, 189, 209, 342.
.... officers of, 430.
........., Master of, *see* Aston, Sir Roger; Hay, Jas., Lord; Cranfield, Sir Lionel.
Wards and Liveries, court of, 135, 165, 168, 210, 246, 524, 551.
........., ..., commissions, instructions, &c. to, 1, 7, 135, 466, 523.
........., ..., Masters of, *see* Cecil, Earl of Salisbury; Carew, Sir Geo.; Cope, Sir Wal.; Knollys, Lord.
........., ..., payments to or from, 31, 57, 153, 405, 440, 446.
Wards and Liveries, Court of, attorney of, 241, 519; *see also* Ley, Sir James.
...., auditors of, 269, 280, 297.
........., ..., clerks and messengers of, 125, 519, 520.
...., officers of, 101, 186, 283, 377, 400, 401, 418, 455, 508, 514, 531, 535, 594, 598.
........., ... receivers of, 165, 558.
Wards and wardships, 30, 143, 146, 153, 231, 281, 405, 440, 447, 466, 482, 551, 599, 601.
........., suits for grants of, 6, 42, 49, 61, 90, 95, 105, 131, 252, 416, 491, 524.
Ware, 477, 480, 517.
...... Park, 147, 196, 308, 483, 584.
Ware, Mr., 317.
Wares, *see* Merchandise.
Waringes, Edw., 177.
Wark, 112, 189, 220, 232.
.... Castle, 189, 220.
Warmington, Wm., 119.
Warmoth, Wm., 82.
Warner, Nowell, 248.
........., Rich., 129, 248, 409.
........., Wm., 389.
........., Dr., 118.
Warr, Lord de la, *see* West, Thos.
Warren, Humph., 68.
........., Thos., 126.
Warrington, 132.
Wartòn, Sir Michael, Sheriff of Yorkshire, 467.
Warwick, Thos., 97, 98.
Warwick, 9, 444.
........., Castle, 477.
Warwick, Earl, *see* Rich.
Warwickshire, 268.
........., grants of lands in, 124, 159, 196, 388, 405.
........., lands and places in, 138, 351, 352, 518, 531.
........., residents in, 28, 159, 162, 193, 249, 271, 435, 451, 493, 580.
Washam, 295.
Washingley, 80.
Waterer, Mr., 353.
Waterfrist, 377.
Waterhouse, Edw., 127.
........., Sir Edw., 248.
........., David, 248.
........., Isaac, 94.
........., Jonas, 66, 99.
........., Sence, 66, 99.
Watermills, 433.
Waterworks, 78, 93, 148, 163, 196, 340, 364, 439.
Watford, 67, 580.
Watford, Rich., 451.
Watkin, Gifford, 56.
Watkins, Dav., 555.
Watkinson, Jas., 67.
Watson, Julius, 232.
........., Sir Lewis, 75.
........., Thos., Teller of the Exchequer, 94, 210, 440, 455, 460; Sir Thos., 563, 589.
Watt, Wm., 103.
Watts, Sir John, 398.
........., John, 547, 562.
........., John, (of Weston), 594.
Waybridge Forest, 190, 251, 506, 555.
Wayles, Hen., 170.
Ways, *see* Highways.
Weavers, 475, 542, 606, 610.
Webb, Benedict, 565.
........., Jehu, 86.
........., Sir Wm., 199, 375.
........., Lady, 163.
Webber, Thos., 94.
Webling, Nich., 46.
........., Wessell, 46, 509.
Webster, Pet., 340.
Weddell, John, *see* Duke.
Week, 30.
Weeks, Lawr., 78.
........., Robt., 567.
Welbeck Abbey, 334.
Weldon Ant., 372.

Welford, John, 30.
Welland River, 430, 465, 546.
Wellingborough, 277, 431.
Wellingore, 492.
Wellington, 251, 279.
Wellisborne, John, 87.
Wells, 484, 543.
Wells, John, 269.
........., Simon, 132.
........., Thos., 214.
........., Eliz., 214.
Welsted, Leon., 246.
Wenlock, John, 306.
........., Agnes, 306.
Wentworth, Sir John, 106, 322, 326, 344.
........., Thos., Lord, 295, 506, 511.
........., Sir Thos., 98.
........., Mr., 235, 237, 239, 270.
Wentworth House, 98.
Wesel, 270, 345, 547.
West, Edw., 459, 525.
........., Jason, 576, 581.
........., John, 72, 357.
........., John (of Lincolnshire), 233, 234.
........., Thos., Lord De la Warr, 48, 518, 527, 584.
........., Mrs., 334.
West Chester, 87.
.... Friesland, 557.
.... Greenwich, 209.
.... Ham, 33.
.... Hesterton, 293.
.... Indies, 48, 576, 613.
.... Kirby, 258.
.... Park, 596.
.... Tilbury, 68, 241.
.... Water, 552, 566.
West-cliffe, 612.
Westby, Wm., 238.
Westerby, 85.
Westfield, Thos., 278.
Westhouse, 540.
Westminster, 6, 18, 25, 75, 91, 162, 172, 376, 396, 407, 409, 429, 559.
........., armoury at, 374.
.... College, 59, 240, 319.
........., Courts at, 165, 611.
.... Hall, 367, 371, 398, 407, 464, 465.
.... houses in, 59, 70, 77, 528, 563.
........., letters, &c. dated from, *passim.*
.... Palace and Park, 33, 43, 57, 62, 106, 187, 197, 227, 440, 447, 451, 517, 588, 594.
...., residents in, 5, 53, 138, 444.
........., surveyor of, 205, 217.
........., treasury at, 210.
.... Abbey, 59, 231, 361, 362.
........., Dean of, 59, 153, 217, 317, 329, 414, 504, 587; *see also* Montaigne, Dr. Geo.; Tounson, Dr. Robt.
Westminster, deanery of, 488.
Westmoreland, 69, 92, 212, 268, 562.
........., grants of lands in, 63.
........., lands in, 202, 220, 293, 446.
........., offices in, 49, 286.
........., residents in, 279.
Weston, 149, 594.
Weston, Rich. (murderer of Overbury), 307, 309–314, 316–320, 322, 326, 327, 329, 330, 333, 344, 347, 398.
........., Rich., 378.
........., Sir Rich., 135, 199, 378.
........., Sir Simon, 2.
........., Thos., 276.
.... (young), 213.
........., Wm., 311, 317.
Westwood, Susan, 242.
Wetherhead, Geo., 386.
Wetwang, 230.
Wexford, 80.
........., plantation of, 459, 462, 469, 472.
Whaddon Manor and Park, 279, 383, 446.
Whales, 80, 140, 203, 228, 252, 272, 436, 503, 513, 560.
Whaplode, 418.
Wharton, Sir Geo., 104.
........., Phil., Lord, 104.
........., Sir Thos., 104.
Wheat, *see* Corn.
Wheller, *see* Page, Edm.
Whetenhall, Thos., 435.
Whetstone, Luke, 207.
Whichwood Forest, 20, 122, 279.
Whinfield, 38.
Whisson, Robt., 556.
Whistley Mill, 200.
Whitacre, *see* Whytakers.
Whitaker, Mr., 314.
Whitbeck, 209.
Whitbrook, 29.
Whitbrook, Sir John, 120.
Whitby, 126.
.... Strand, 126.
White, Alex., 338.
........., Dan., 251.
........., Dorothy, 45.
........., Edw., 280.
........., Fras., 116.
........., John, 102.
........., Joseph, 75.
........., Margery, 10.
........., Sir Rich., 45.
........., Roger, 614.
........., Rowld., 252, 555.
........., Thos., 308, 501.
........., Wm., 350.
........., Dr., 290.
Whiteacre, 562.
White-stanton, 587.
Whitefriars, 402, 421, 434, 524.

Whitehall, 14, 44, 106, 163, 246, 275, 314, 323, 402, 404, 422, 425, 439, 520, 584, 588, 602.
........., King's visits to, 28, 126, 137, 162, 166, 190, 235, 273, 274, 316, 323, 339, 404, 503, 521, 524, 529, 579.
........., letters dated from, *passim*.
........., Paper chamber at, 322.
Whitehead, Geo., 59, 67.
........., Wm., 415, 416.
Whitelock, Jas., 186.
Whitelock, Capt., 59, 77.
Whiteplace, 89.
Whiteswood, 233.
Whitewebbs, 164.
Whitfield, Lawr., 62.
Whiting, Dr. John, 327, 329, 331, 334.
........., Wm., 14.
Whitland, 16.
Whitlaw, And., 65.
Whitleigh, 594.
Whitley, Thos., 354.
Whitmore, Geo., 70, 159.
........., Rich., 522.
........., Thos., 70.
........., Wm., 5, 41, 44, 159, 192, 209, 522.
Whitsheeles, 365.
Whitson, John, 81, 125.
Whittlewood Forest, 28, 208, 493.
Whorewood, Gerard, 286.
........., Sir Thos., 259, 286.
Whynniard, John, 70, 106.
Whynyard, John, 227.
Whytakers, Miles, 83, 84, 99, 157, 206, 444.
Wich, Wm., 4, 20.
Wicklift, 49.
Wicklift, Merill, 49.
Widmer, Rich., 35.
Wigan, 578.
Wightman, Edw., 123.
Wigmore, Sir Rich., 12, 116, 156, 163, 545.
........., Wm., 191.
Wigtoft, 292.
Wilberton, 542.
Wilbraham, Sir Rich., 372.
........., Sir Rog., Master of Requests, 50, 226, 374, 390, 391, 426.
Wilbraham Bushes, 411.
Wilcben, John, 100.
Wilhelmson, Christian, 176.
Wild, Sir Humph., 268.
Wildgoose, Reade, 18.
Wilford, Jas., 29.
........., Thos., 29.
........., Wm., 121.
Wilkins, Ant., 491.
........., Fras., 78.
Wilkinson, Robt., 500.
........., Thos., 572.
........., Dr., 490.
Willens, Wolfert, 419.
Willes, Mark, 298.
Willesden, 580.
Willett, Dr. And., 505, 522, 525.
Williams, Abm., 342, 367, 445, 451.
........., ..., letters of, to Carleton, 360, 362, 397, 492, 564, 576, 600.
........., Alex., 270.
........., ..., letters of, to Carleton, 238, 252, 363, 372, 378, 394, 399, 430, 477, 483, 525.
........., Ant., 398.
........., Sir David, 3, 168.
........., Dan., 212.
........., Dudley, 460.
........., Eliz., letters of, to Carleton, 378, 392, 424, 460.
........., Hen., 132.
........., Sir Hen., 291.
........., Isaac, 450.
........., John, 87, 94, 212.
........., John (jeweller), 19, 102, 227, 380, 445
........., John, (serjeant), 276, 369, 530.
........., Sir John, 130.
........., Mary, 460.
........., Sir Oliver, *see* Cromwell.
........., Phil., 587.
........., Thos., 118, 249.
........., Wm. (late), 132.
........., Wm., 399, 483.
Williamson, Arch., 308.
........., John, 308.
........., Thos., 260.
Willie, John, 299.
Willingham, Sam., 233, 234.
Willisford, Fras., 600.
Willmer, Geo., 411.
Willoughby, Sir Hugh, 228.
........., Robt., Lord of Eresby, 124, 208 306, 308, 314, 344, 576.
........., Thos., 122.
........., Wm., Lord of Parham, 488, 516.
........., Mr., 531.
Wilmot, Sir Chas., 319; President of Connaught, 360, 425.
........., Rob., 257.
........., Lady, 345.
Wilson, Edw., 573.
........., Eliz., 533.
........., Geo., 353, 360.
........., John, 407.
........., John (prebendary), 414.
........., Rich., 540.
........., Robt., 554.
........., Robt., (othringer), 86.
........., Thos., Keeper of State Papers, 5, 134, 184, 248, 341, 557, 580, 609, 610.
........., ..., letters of, 6, 93, 106, 252, 390, 391, 551, 609.
........., ..., ..., to Amb. Randolph, 164, 207, 229, 248, 257, 287, 305, 374.

Wilson, Thos., letters of to Jas. I., 390, 445, 489, 508, 531, 573, 574, 576, 579, 583, 589, 610.
........., ..., ..., to Naunton, 569, 570, 572, 573, 575, 577, 583.
........., ..., letters to, 78, 118, 129, 153, 220, 252, 314, 533, 568, 581; *see* Naunton.
........., ..., as Keeper of Sir Walter Raleigh, 570, 573–575, 577, 585, 587, 590–592.
........., ..., leases, &c. from, 223, 262, 581.
........., Mrs., 374.
........., Wm., 352.
........., Corstovell, 352.
........., Dr., 290.
Wilton, 219.
Wilton, Brian, 402.
........., Rich., 402.
Wiltshire, 102, 180, 184, 259, 268, 294, 394.
........., grants of lands in, 5, 63, 124, 159, 246, 357, 412, 452.
........., lands in, 68, 158, 165, 201, 242, 266, 375, 381, 388, 411, 534, 567, 574, 596.
........., residents in, 265, 269, 439, 480, 516, 532, 565.
........., recusants in, 159.
........., receivers of, 205, 596.
Wimbledon, 379.
Winch, Sir Humph., Justice of Common Pleas, 59, 398.
Winchelsea, 254, 306, 388.
........., creek 388.
........., mayor, &c. of, 242, 353.
Winchcombe, 437.
Winchester, 294, 561, 588, 592.
........., alms-rooms in, 102, 244.
........., Marquis and Marchioness of, *see* Paulet.
........., Bp. of, *see* Bilson, Thos.; Montague, Jas.
........., Dean and Chapter of, 555, 560.
........., diocese of, 101, 378, 497.
........., Prebends of, 555.
Winchester House, 494.
Winckleiff, 70.
Windebank, Fras., 54, 71, 579.
........., ..., letters to and of, 39, 223–225, 227, 389, 391, 396, 478, 569.
Windsor, 27, 137, 168, 286, 287, 392, 451, 515, 552, 590.
.... Castle and Park, 58, 62, 64, 169, 190, 296, 358, 373, 379, 404, 479, 480, 484, 485, 488, 555, 568.
.... Forest, 209, 243, 264, 297, 421, 451, 497, 498, 572.
........., house of, 393.
........., letters from, 56, 72, 116, 193, 380, 484, 550, 568.
........., poor knights of, 18, 30, 85, 93, 95, 136, 153, 486.
Windsor, Dean, &c., of, 74, 120, 254, 422, 423, 521, 527, 531, 538, 595; *see also* Spalato, Archbp. of.
........., prebends at, 270, 552.
Windsor Herald, *see* Thompson, Sam.
Windsor, And., 74, 478.
........., Thos. Lord, 29, 146, 506.
........., Lady, 345.
Windmills, 133.
Wines, 46.
........., custom on, 30, 150, 166, 169, 187, 199, 220, 283, 384.
........., licence to sell, 114, 117, 232, 259, 545, 597.
........., Rhenish, 152, 187, 199, 250, 260, 410, 593; *see also* France and Gascony, wines of.
........., Spanish, 30.
........., sweet, 30, 47, 199.
Winestead, 33.
Wingfield, Art., 501, 516, 531.
........., Sir Jas., 296.
........., Sir Rich., 23.
Wingfield House, 9, 237.
Winston, Jos., 375.
Winter, Robt., 3, 301–304.
........., Tim., 614.
Winterton, 278, 364.
.... lighthouse, 545.
........., Ness, 537.
Wintle, Wm., 117.
Winwick, 372.
Winwood, Sir Ralph, Master of Requests, 169, 217, 220, 225, 234; Secretary of State, 247, 251, 260, 277, 296, 305, 345, 354, 361, 385, 393, 394, 404, 417, 425, 475, 476, 496.
........., ..., as Ambassador in Holland, 22, 71, 111, 137, 138, 198, 203, 220, 361, 437.
........., ..., elevation of to the secretaryship, 135, 136, 161, 166, 202, 216, 220, 223, 228, 230, 231.
........., ..., grants to, 447
........., ..., letters of, 284, 320, 321, 328, 329, 331, 370, 391, 411, 458, 484–486.
........., ..., ..., to Carleton, 200, 225, 233, 237, 241.
........., ..., ..., to Somerset, 255, 270.
........., ..., to commissioners on Overbury's cause, 320, 323, 325, 332.
........., ..., ..., to Coke, 307, 320, 324, 332, 335, 339, 349.
........., ..., ..., to Lake, 345–347, 349, 350, 453, 454, 456, 457, 460, 462–464, 467, 468, 470–473, 476, 479, 481–484.
........., ..., letters to, 236, 250, 256, 258, 263, 270, 274, 275, 277, 285, 289, 293, 300, 303, 320, 321, 323, 327, 328, 332, 336, 353, 355, 360, 362, 366, 370, 384, 389, 395, 399, 436, 457, 465, 489, 493, 528.

Winwood, Sir Ralph, official proceedings of, 243, 244, 258, 269, 278, 294, 314, 321, 350, 357, 358, 368, 372, 393, 398, 402, 406, 455, 458, 486.
........., ..., visits of to the King, 214, 262, 273, 301.
........., ..., slanders, &c. against, 261, 364, 476.
........., ..., quarrels of, with Lord Bacon, 475, 477, 488, 504.
........., ..., illness and death of, 490-495, 97, 500.
........., ..., books and papers of, 585, 597.
........., Lady, 282, 394, 480, 491, 585, 597.
........., Rich., 447.
Wire, forest of, 127.
Wirksworth, 291.
Wirmestone, 88.
Wirrall, Sir Hugh, 67.
Wirtemberg, John Fred., Duke of, 104, 128.
Wisbeach, 430, 538, 541, 542, 546, 552.
.... Castle, priests confined at, 283, 285, 287, 289, 299, 304, 320, 321, 328, 406.
.... River, 538, 541.
Wise, Rich., 467.
........., Wm., 567.
Wiseman, Frances, 272, 277.
........., Francisco, 614.
........., Jas., 474.
........., John, 272, 277.
........., Wm., 614.
........., Sir Wm., 56.
Wiston, 71.
Witchcombe, Frances, 45.
Witches and witchcraft, 29, 53, 161, 172, 398, 540.
Witherden, Geo., 430.
Withering, Ant., 608.
Witherington, *see* Wodrington.
Withernam, custom of, 191.
Withers, Rich., 45.
........., Robt., 119.
Wivelingham, 542.
Wivell (or Wyvell), Chris., 36, 202, 487.
Wodrington, 513.
........., Sir Hen., 21, 355, 362, 366, 399, 456, 465, 513.
........., Roger, 289, 360, 369, 370.
........., ..., misconduct of, &c., 108, 347, 355, 358, 365, 866, 399, 456, 465.
........., ..., complicity of, in gunpowder treason, 362, 365, 406.
Woking Manor and Park, 93, 415.
Wokingham, 139, 572.
Wolles Park, 132.
Wolphe, John, 219.
Wolsey, Cardinal, 380.
Wolstenholme, John, 166, 187, 216, 351; Sir John, 490, 511, 585.
Wolverton, 567.
Wolverston, Robt., 252.
Woollascot, Wm., 366.
Wood, Sir Dav., 317, 319.
........., Capt. Geo., 22, 64, 193, 505.
........., Jas., 287.
........., John (minister), 186, 295.
........., John, 21, 186.
........., John (of Cornwall), 498.
........., Owen, 4.
........., Roger, 444, 455.
........., Thos., 451.
Woodchurch, 417.
Woodcock, Edm., 84.
Woodham Ferris, 365.
Woodhouse, Thos., 55.
........., Sir Thos., 100.
........., Sir Wm., 140.
Woodman, John, 176.
Woodriff, Mr., 525.
Woodrove, Alice, 118.
........., Thos., 204.
Woods, John, 134, 161, 173.
........., Mary, 134, 161, 172, 173, 183, 187.
Woods and forests, 12, 224, 261, 273, 300, 308, 374, 377, 420, 449, 474, 605.
........., commissioners for, 472, 475.
........., officers of, 28, 85, 242, 251, 296, 470.
........., overseers and surveyors of, 46, 381, 382, 386, 440.
........., sale and survey of, 29, 165, 199, 216, 232, 247, 439, 441, 485, 486, 534.
Woodstock, 70, 260, 327, 391, 515.
........., King's visits to, 138, 147, 241, 391, 392, 479, 482, 484.
.... Park, 299.
Woodward, Edw., 387.
........., Jas., 564.
........., Soames, 477-479, 503, 534.
........., Thos., 31.
Wooler, 232.
Woolford, 518.
Woolridge, Fras., 463.
Wools, 271, 287, 297, 339, 452, 467, 509, 524, 565, 610.
........., custom on, 206, 227, 271, 590.
........., export of, 253, 259, 348, 393, 561, 583.
Woolters, Wm., 421.
Woolwich, 240, 497, 507.
........., armoury at, 51.
Worcester, alms-rooms in, 68.
........., Bp. of, *see* Parry, Hen.; Thornborough, John.
........., diocese, 73, 94, 164.
........., Earl of, *see* Somerset, Edw.
Worcestershire, 229, 262, 268, 394.
........., grants of lands in, 124, 158, 159, 196, 388.

Worcestershire, lands and places in, 127, 172, 235, 388.
........., officers in, 169, 262, 440, 498.
........., recusants in, 123.
........., residents in, 35, 164, 263, 558.
Worgan, Thos., 130.
Workleigh, 545.
Works, office of, 160.
........., ..., workmen of, 537, 563.
........., ..., charges of, 8, 14, 21, 29, 39, 54, 67, 70, 73, 82, 86, 97, 110, 119, 123.
........., officers of, 78, 181, 555.
Worksop, 459.
Worlaby, 445.
Worshall, 404.
Worthington, Edw., 236.
........., Lawr., 536.
........., Dr. Thos., 300.
........., Wm., 107.
Wotton, Edw., Lord, Comptroller of the Household, 175, 361, 407; Treasurer of the Household, 418, 437, 504, 505, 511-513, 519.
........., ..., letters of, 68, 95, 106.
........., ..., as Lieutenant of Kent, 316, 328, 363, 372.
........., Edw., 446.
........., Sir Hen., 17, 59, 88, 136–138, 143, 153, 154, 157, 162, 163, 167, 203, 211, 225, 234, 235, 246, 274, 350, 416, 484, 485, 492.
........., ..., letters of and to, 65, 172, 370, 485.
........., ..., mission of to Holland, 262–264, 269, 270, 273.
........., ..., ... to Venice, 251, 425, 483.
........., ..., negotiations of with Savoy, 111, 115, 124, 150, 183, 186, 190, 196.
Wray, Sir Chris., 427.
........., Sir Wm., 488, 515.
Wraynham, John, 537, 538.
Wrench, Elias, 435.
Wrest, 93, 180, 261, 319.
Wrexham, 25.
Wright, And., 111.
........., Jas. (of St. Edmundsbury), 230.
........., Jas., (huntsman), 246.
........., John (Sub-clerk of Parliament), 156, 159.
........., John (recusant), 120.
........., Lionel, 2.
........., Rich., 2.
........., Robt., 574.
........., Roger, 230.
........., Anne, 230.
........., Thos., 116.
........., Mr. (curate), 374.
Wriothesley, Hen., Earl of Southampton, 40, 96, 154, 345, 381, 443, 450, 501, 507, 562.
........., ..., letters of, 179, 544.
Wriothesley, John, 75.
Wroth, Sir Robt., 37, 83, 121, 158, 187, 224, 227, 228.
Wyat, Mr., 380.
Wyborne, Dan., 421.
Wye, Thos., 441.
Wyer, Rich., 571.
Wykes, Aquila, 499.
Wymark, Mr., 601.
Wymondham, 301, 304.
Wyncott, Robt., 361, 366.
Wyndham, Hen., 19.
Wynn, Elihu, 137.
........., Sir John, 241, 336, 353.
........., Rowl., 451.
........., Sir Thos., 413, 600.
Wyrardisbury, 256, 428, 429.
Wyse, Thos., 550.
Wyvell, Roger, 18.
Wyvill, Chris., *see* Wivell.

Y.

Yale, 208.
Yardley, Capt., 587; Sir Geo., 598.
Yarmouth, 153, 299.
Yarrow, 61.
Yarrow, Rowl., 61.
Yates, Mr., 229.
Yaxley, Sir Robt., 130.
Yelverton, Sir Chris., Justice of King's Bench, 3, 154.
........., Hen., 75; Sir Hen., Solicitor-General, 202, 274, 385, 404, 407, 433, 434; Attorney-General, 440, 467, 471, 484, 530, 550, 553, 580, 598.
........., ..., commissions, warrants, &c., to, 250, 507.
........., ..., letters of, 411, 467, 471, 473, 474, 542, 546, 550, 557, 599, 604.
........., ..., letters to, 207, 500, 507, 611.
........., Capt., 3.
Yeomans, John, 64.
York, 19, 40, 139, 144, 175, 302, 303, 369, 584.
.... Castle, 189, 432.
........., Duke of, *see* Charles, Prince.
.... Herald, *see* Brooke, Ralph.
........., King's house at, 379.
........., letters from, 35, 66, 71, 78, 139, 304, 539.
........., Lord Mayor of, 38.
........., President of, *see* Sheffield, Edm. Lord.
........., Archbp. of, *see* Matthew, Tobias.
.... diocese of, 76, 277, 293, 500, 541.
.... province of, 245.

York House, 218, 345, 514.
...., letters from, 144, 169, 224, 316, 317, 319, 321, 490, 494, 511, 519, 523, 581, 605.
.... Place Palace, 396.
York, Hen., 132.
........., Sir John, 88, 175, 242.
........., Robt., 132.
Yorke, Rich., 238.
Yorkshire, 135, 267, 268, 275, 282, 304, 406, 486.
.... clothiers of, 19, 69.
........., grants of lands in, 5, 18, 63, 67, 87, 104, 118, 124, 159, 192, 196, 211, 230, 240, 249, 297, 300, 345, 367, 379, 386, 388, 405, 418, 440.
........., lands and places in, 9, 17, 78, 98, 164, 194, 197, 210, 287, 290, 294, 300, 302, 338, 358, 377, 404, 446, 448, 499, 502, 548, 596, 606.
........., offices in, 189, 191, 538.
........., receivers of, 21, 90, 123, 200.
........., recusants in, 49, 251, 404, 440, 467, 468, 470, 610.
........., residents in, 15, 113, 147, 154, 189, 224, 264, 295, 335, 352, 359, 400, 431, 467, 471, 528, 599.
.... sheriffs of, 33, 62, 459, 467, 468, 470.
.... Wold, 130.
Young, Chas., 19, 108.
........., John (searcher), 19, 108.
........., John, 98.
........., Dr. John, Dean of Winchester, 407, 555, 592.
........., Pet., 232.
........., Sir Pet., 98, 410.
........., Sir Rich., 533, 548.
........., Robt., 204.
........., Thos. (footman), 57.
........., Thos. (gunner), 338.
........., Wm., 408.
........., Mr., 197.
Younge, Affrodose, 385.
........., Rich., secretary to Lord Zouch, letter of, 316.
........., ..., letters to, 311, 323, 325, 343, 345, 349, 366, 367, 369, 370, 372, 374, 380, 395, 399, 403, 406, 413, 414, 417, 422, 424, 430, 431, 433, 435, 437, 449, 457, 463, 481, 485, 490, 492, 499, 501.
Ypres, 449.

Z.

Zamoiski, Thos. de, Chancellor of Poland, 296.
Zante, 468.
Zealand, 183, 360, 500, 521, 530, 559, 614.
Zealanders, 572.
Zeasencott, 45.
Zinzan, And., 28.
........., Hen., 18, 213.
........., Sir Sigismund, 18, 213.
Zouch, Sir Edw., 13, 207, 288, 536; Knight Marshal, 586, 593.
........., Edw., Lord, 97, 142, 286, 295; Lord Warden of the Cinque Ports, 316, 329, 388, 417, 421, 469, 471, 474, 600.
........., ..., certificates and bonds to, 350, 372, 407, 423, 433, 459, 493, 503, 522, 525, 538, 567, 571, 581.
........., ..., commissions to, 301, 304.
........., ..., commissions by, 394, 528, 532.
........., ..., diary of transactions of, 586.
........., ..., letters of, 306, 343, 345, 350, 354, 360, 363, 372, 376, 378, 380, 381, 407, 409, 416, 419, 422, 433, 436, 437, 458, 512, 513, 525, 528, 533, 540, 544, 545, 574, 576, 582, 584, 586, 602, 611.
........., ..., letters to, 309, 311, 312, 328, 332, 342, 343, 344, 347, 351, 353–355, 359, 361, 364–366, 377, 390, 393, 394, 398, 400–403, 406, 408, 409, 413, 430–432, 434, 439, 442, 449, 456, 457, 459, 462, 463, 466, 469, 471, 478, 480–482, 485, 487, 490, 495, 501, 502, 529, 582, 587, 605.
........., ..., official transactions of as Lord Warden of the Cinque Ports, 305, 309, 316, 317, 335, 341, 343, 352, 365, 367, 370, 372, 399, 403, 406, 408, 409, 414, 422, 437, 464, 481, 596, 600, 611.
........., ..., petitions to, 298, 305, 306, 308, 311, 337, 338, 340, 343, 351, 352, 353, 356, 357, 362, 364, 377, 378, 389, 391, 392, 417, 419, 423, 456, 459, 478, 501, 508, 509, 532, 574, 605, 611–614.
........., ..., writs, warrants, and licences by, 300, 301, 306, 308, 309, 336, 383, 412, 413, 416, 483, 543, 567, 571, 572, 574, 579, 586, 599.
........., ..., Secretary to, *see* Younge, Rich.; Nicholas, Edw.
........., ..., servants of, 447, 607.
........., John, 382.
........., Sir Wm., 503, 511, 523.
Zuniga, Don Pedro, Spanish Ambassador, 137, 138, 140–143, 145, 149, 433.

ERRATA.

*** *Readers are particularly requested to correct the errata in their respective copies, as the Index answers only to copies thus corrected.*

Page 4, No. 27, *for* the Same, *read* Salisbury.
" 17, Entry 5, *for* Gudourons, *read* Godourus.
" 32, No. 87, *to* Will Whor. *add* Knight.
" 39, No. 10, *for* the King, *read* the Prince.
" 39, No. 12, and 71, No. 91, *for* Sir Thos. Windebank, *read* Francis.
" 39, No. 13, *for* the Same, *read* Salisbury.
" 48, No. 54, *for* Bishop of York, *read* Archbishop.
" 54, No. 9, *for* Lady Norris, *read* Lord Norris.
" 64, No. 54, *for* Mr. St. John, *read* Sir Wm. St. John.
" 69, No. 75, and 130, No. 22, *for* Thos. Bland, *read* Sir Thos.
" 72, No. 2, *for* Cariat, *read* Coryat.
" 108, No. 165, *for* Common Pleas, *read* King's Bench.
" 115, Entry 3, *before* Sir Jas. Scudamore *put* Sir John.
" 120, No. 6, *for* Alban Butter, *read* Alban Butler.
" 125, Entry 1, *for* Thos. and Rich. Turner, *read* Thos. Jones and Rich. Turner.
" 126, No. 102, *for* Hainault, *read* Anhalt.
" 132, No. 40, *for* Cawson, *read* Cawston.
" 134, No. 67, *before* Visct. Montague *put* and.
" 135, No, 71, *for* Sir Hen. Wotton, *read* Sir Ralph Winwood.
" 159, Entry 1, *for* Vernon, *read* Verdon.
" 174, No. 68, *for* Somerset, *read* Rochester.
" 192, July? Entry 10, *dele the whole Entry.*
" 209, Entry 1, *for* Deptford and Stroud, *read* Deptford Strond.
" 217, No. 54, *for* More, *read* Moore.
" 232, No. 14, *for* Rochester, *read* Somerset.
" 234, No. 22, *for* Sir Walter, *read* Sir Walter Cope.
" 235, No. 30, *for* Prince's house, *read* Prince's horse.
" 242, Entry 9, *for* Blakemore, *read* Blackmore.
" 265, No. 104, *dele the whole Entry.*
" 279, No. 53, *for* Hindon, *read* Hinton.
" 299, No. 35, *for* Permorte, *read* Pormorte.
" 303, No. 59 II. *for* Sicochius, *read* Schoppius.
" 334, No. 77, *for* Lord Arundel, *read* Earl of Arundel.
" 344, Oct., *for* Bewdley, *read* Beaulieu.
" 360, No. 128, *for* Albert Moreton, *read* Sir Albert Morton.
" 361, No. 131, *for* curates, *read* jurats.
" 362, No. 136, *for* Thirlway, *read* Thirlwall.
" 363, No. 150, date, *for* April 25, *read* April [27].
" 367, No. 23, *for* Wm. Herrick, *read* Sir Wm. ; *for* John Spilman, *read* Sir John.
" 370, Entry 5, *for* State's, *read* States'.
" 399, No. 132, *for* Missenden, *read* Misselden.
" 407, No. 38, *dele* Mastership of Wards.
" 421, No. 134, *for* Newbry, *read* Newbury.
" 412, No. 71, and 504, No. 76, *for* Prince of Orange, *read* Count Maurice, of Nassau.

ERRATA.

Page 424, Entry 17, *for* Gieldenston, *read* Gildenston.
" 452, No. 7, *for* Banning, *read* Bayning.
" 452, No. 2, *for* Edw. Clerk, *read* Edm.
" 453, No. 2, *for* Benson, *read* Penson.
" 481, No. 18, *for* Sir Geo. Villiers, *read* Sir John.
" 493, Entry 1; 538, Entry 4; 547, Entry 4; 572, Entry 5; 693, Entry 33, *for* Sir Fras. Cottington, *read* Fras.
" 501, No. 51, transfer the Entry to Dec. 5, 1618.
" 504, No. 74, *for* Tolson, *read* Tounson.
" 514, No. 22, *for* Duke Roxburgh, *read* Earl.
" 516, Line 11, *for* Lord Chandos' daughter, *read* cousin-german.
" 536, Line 2, *for* Dr. Donne, *read* Dr. Dove.
" 551, No. 8, *for* Middleton, *read* Middlesex.
" 553, Entry 11, *for* Hen. Knight, *read* Thos.
" 567, No. 95, *for* Hoyes, *read* Hoyer.
" 572, No. 27, *for* Caume, *read* Caurne.
" 582, No. 14, *for* late Admiral, *read* Lord Admiral.
" 583, No. 23, *for* Sec. Calvert, *read* Sir G.
" 594, No. 87 III. *for* Michael, *read* Michell.
" 601, No. 17, *for* Court, *read* Comet.

LONDON:
Printed by George E. Eyre and William Spottiswoode,
Printers to the Queen's most Excellent Majesty.
For Her Majesty's Stationery Office.